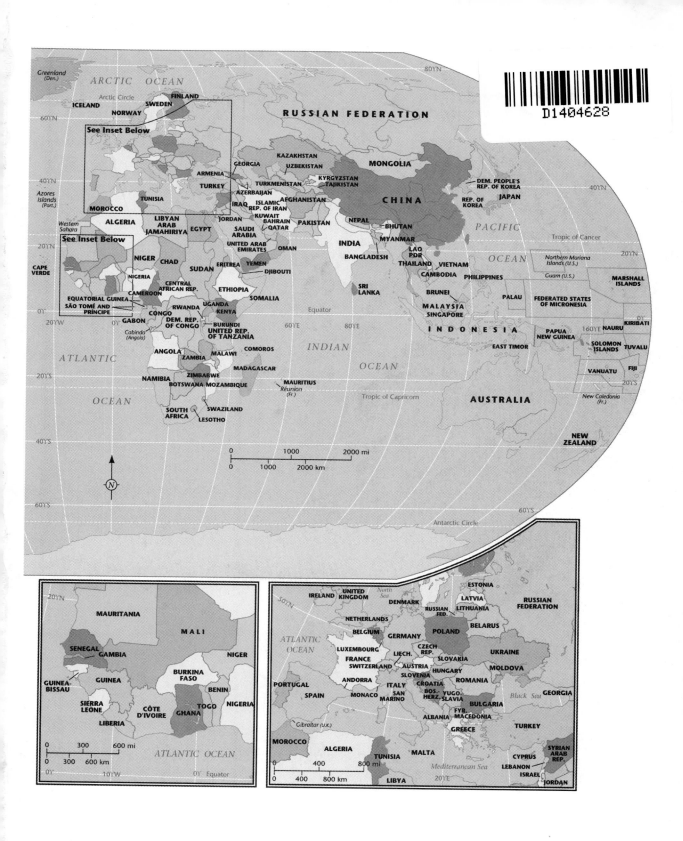

❖

American Foreign Policy

Pattern and Process

American Foreign Policy
Pattern and Process

Sixth Edition

Eugene R. Wittkopf
Louisiana State University

Charles W. Kegley, Jr.
University of South Carolina

James M. Scott
University of Nebraska at Kearney

Australia • Canada • Mexico • Singapore • Spain
United Kingdom • United States

THOMSON

WADSWORTH

Political Science Editor: David Tatom
Senior Developmental Editor: Sharon Adams Poore
Assistant Editor: Heather Hogan
Editorial Assistant: Dianna Long
Technology Project Manager: Mindy Newfarmer
Marketing Manager: Janise Fry
Marketing Assistance: Mary Ho
Advertising Project Manager: Brian Chaffee
Project Manager, Editorial Production: Dianne Toop
Print/Media Buyer: Rebecca Cross

Permissions Editor: Stephanie Keough-Hedges
Production Service: Peggy Francomb/Shepherd, Inc.
Copy Editor: Terri Winsor
Illustrator: Steve Werner
Cover Designer: Cassandra Chu Design
Cover Images: © Jay Coneyl/Getty Images/Stone
Cover Printer: Banta/Harrisonburg
Compositor: Shepherd, Inc.
Printer: Banta/Harrisonburg

Printed in the United States of America
1 2 3 4 5 6 7 06 05 04 03 02

For more information about our products, contact us at:
Thomson Learning Academic Resource Center
1-800-423-0563
For permission to use material from this text,
contact us by:
Phone: 1-800-730-2214 **Fax:** 1-800-730-2215
Web: http://www.thomsonrights.com

Library of Congress Cataloging-in-Publication Data

Wittkopf, Eugene R., 1943-
   American foreign policy : pattern and process / Eugene R.
Wittkopf, Charles W. Kegley, Jr., James M. Scott.—6th ed.
   p. cm.
   Kegley's name appears first on the previous ed.
   Includes bibliographical references and index.
   ISBN 0-534-60048-4
   1. United States—Foreign relations. I. Kegley, Charles W.
II. Scott, James M., 1964- III. Title
JZ1480 .W58 2002
327.73—dc21

                                        2001056907

Wadsworth/Thomson Learning
10 Davis Drive
Belmont, CA 94002-3098
USA

Asia
Thomson Learning
5 Shelton Way #01–01
UIC Building
Singapore 068808

Australia
Nelson Thomson Learning
102 Dodds Street
South Melbourne, Victoria 3205
Australia

Canada
Nelson Thomson Learning
1120 Birchmount Road
Toronto, Ontario M1K 5G4
Canada

UK/Europe/Middle East/Africa
Thomson Learning
High Holborn House
50151 Bedford Row
London WC1R 4LR
United Kingdom

Latin America
Thomson Learning
Seneca, 53
Colonia Polanco
11560 Mexico D.F.
Mexico

Spain
Paraninfo Thomson Learning
Calle/Magallanes, 25
28015 Madrid, Spain

For Barbara
E.R.W.

Debbie
C.W.K.

Lori, Michael, and Meghan, and to my students
J.M.S

Summary Table of Contents

Contents

VIII PATTERN AND PROCESS IN AMERICAN FOREIGN POLICY **515**

15 AT THE DAWN OF A NEW MILLENIUM: THE FUTURE OF AMERICAN FOREIGN POLICY **517**

Focus Boxes, Maps, Illustrations, and Tables

FOCUS BOXES

MAPS

ILLUSTRATIONS

TABLES

Preface

As the twenty-first century unfolds, the United States finds itself in uncharted waters. Dramatic changes in the global political and economic systems over the past decade have altered the playing field on which American foreign policy takes place. Although the United States emerged by the end of the twentieth century as the world's unchallenged preeminent power—a hegemon—another hallmark of the new century is the greater complexity American policy makers face at home and abroad as they seek to chart a new course for the new century. The global contest with the Soviet Union that dominated the last half of the twentieth century became the cornerstone of American foreign policy. Finding a replacement for its guiding principles has proven elusive.

As policy makers today seek to define a new policy posture, we are reminded of the choices the immediate post–World War II generation faced, and how those choices shaped half a century of American foreign policy. Then, America's rise to globalism and the onset of the Cold War triggered sweeping changes in the nation's world role, supplying purpose (anticommunism), stimulating policy (containment), and sustaining recurrent patterns of action (globalism, militarism, and interventionism). The contest between capitalism and communism also provided the rationale for a substantially expanded foreign policy bureaucracy designed to pursue America's new world role. And relations between the White House and Congress were shaped during this time to support a foreign policy consensus that encouraged presidential preeminence and congressional deference in foreign policymaking.

Today, the foreign policy landscape lacks familiar features, thus prompting the need once again to face critical choices. The twenty-first century poses new challenges and new opportunities, but the altered context also embraces new imperatives and imposes new constraints. Absent the twentieth century's guideposts, today's purposes, policies, and patterns of foreign policy action have become the subjects of recurrent and deep-seated disagreements among American policy makers and within the larger community.

What path will the United States follow in this unfamiliar environment? Will it continue to embrace the internationalist path of the past or step instead toward isolationism? What interests, goals, and problems will emerge as challenges, prompting a determination of key priorities? How will American policy makers chart the country's foreign policy course in a domestic and global environment of competing and often conflicting interests? These simple questions lead to others:

- How and will American leaders balance the pursuit of power and the pursuit of principle?

- How and will the United States draw on its vast panoply of resources to achieve its preferences?

- How and will the increasingly complex voices and interests of the American polity and society affect its foreign policy?

- How and will the president exercise foreign policy leadership?

- How and will the Congress respond to the president?

- How and will the altered global environment affect the other institutions involved in the American foreign policy-making process?

- How and will the altered environment at home and abroad affect the requirements for leadership in the twenty-first century?

This, the sixth edition of *American Foreign Policy: Pattern and Process,* addresses these and related questions. As in previous editions, we rely on a proven and resilient conceptual framework that frames the examination of the different sources of American foreign policy. This new edition continues to place the contemporary issues, debates, challenges, and opportunities in their historical context in order to assess the changes of today's world in the broader sweep of

the nation's enduring principles, values, and interests: peace and prosperity, stability and security, democracy and defense. Our conceptual framework allows us to utilize relevant theories effectively, and our placement of the contemporary debates in their historical context allows students both to see and to assess the forces underlying continuity and change in American foreign policy.

Those familiar with the book will note that we have retained the overall structure and thematic thrust of previous editions, which effectively harness the conceptual, theoretical, and historical components appropriate for the analysis of American foreign policy. Our analytical framework stresses five foreign policy sources that collectively influence decisions about foreign policy goals and the means chosen to realize them: the *external* (global) environment, the *societal* environment of the nation, the *governmental* setting in which policy making occurs, the *roles* occupied by policy makers, and the *individual* characteristics of foreign policy-making elites.

After establishing the analytical approach of the text (Part I) and considering the broad patterns of goals and policy instruments (Part II), we elaborate on these five sources in the nine chapters comprising Parts III through VII. Our final section and chapter (Part VIII) returns to the challenges of the new century and considers the direction and consequences of American choices and the sources and resources that will shape them. Here and elsewhere, we address in particular the challenge of transnational terrorism brought home to Americans with the September 2001 attacks on the World Trade Center and the Pentagon.

Those familiar with the book also will find much that is similar in the content and approach of this new edition. This should not hide the fact that it has been thoroughly updated and substantially revised to sharpen the historical and analytical content to reflect the foreign policy developments and recent scholarship on American foreign policy since publication of the last edition.

As we tackled the task of bringing our text into the new century, we made countless changes and revisions in each part. Among them, our readers will find the following:

- Part I introduces globalization as a key concept to which we return throughout the book. It also encourages readers to assess the contemporary debates about twenty-first century American foreign policy in terms of primacy, selective engagement, neo-isolationism, and cooperative security, and to locate the debates in the centuries-old discussion between liberalism/idealism and realism (Chapter 1). Additionally, the analytical framework around which we organize the book (Chapter 2) is presented more sharply and concisely, yet it retains its compelling logic.

- Part II has been substantially revised and updated. In Chapter 3, our discussion of goals now emphasizes *pragmatism* as well as power and principle. The concepts of internationalism and isolationism, realism and idealism, and power, principle, and pragmatism are designed to help students understand not only the post–World War II contest between East and West but also recent debates about the wisdom of promoting democracy and international values within the context of international relations theory and practice.

  Chapter 4 focuses entirely on military power and intervention, taking special care to consider the debate over the role of military force in a contemporary environment challenged by issues like humanitarian intervention, the proliferation of nuclear arms and other weapons of mass destruction, and arms control. Our discussion includes recent debates about when and how to use force.

  Chapter 5 has been revised and reoriented to focus exclusively on all nonmilitary forms of interventionism. It provides both the historical development and contempo-

rary debates about covert action (now including a review of the challenges to and purposes of contemporary covert action), economic and military aid (now including consideration of the declining support for aid programs), sanctions (stressing the widespread tendency to employ sanctions rather than military force), and public diplomacy (including the challenges posed by the information age). Throughout each of the chapters in this part, we reflect on the utility and effectiveness of both old and new goals and instruments.

- In Part III, we survey the international political and economic environments in their historical and contemporary variants as a source of American foreign policy. In Chapter 6 we consider how the characteristics of the political system shape American foreign policy choices. Our discussion reflects explicitly on the current setting, in which the United States enjoys primacy but must contend with emergent power threats, globalization, and increasing transnationalism. We reflect more thoroughly in this edition on critical global demographic and environmental challenges that extend beyond traditional great power politics and also on the activities of nonstate actors. These discussions are linked to American foreign policy strategies, including unilateralism, neo-isolationism, bilateralism, and multilateralism.

  In Chapter 7, we stress America's continuing centrality in the world political economy and the profound challenges and changes that globalization poses to its economic hegemony. Recent efforts to preserve and extend U.S. preponderance and the responses of others to them are examined. Our discussion concentrates on monetary and trade policy and employs the insights of hegemonic stability theory to help understand the system and American leadership in it.

- In Part IV, we assess the dynamics of the societal sources of American foreign policy. In Chapter 8 we address the nation's political culture and public opinion toward American foreign policy in an environment undergoing rapid political and demographic change. We update the impact of the changing face of the United States on the world around it, as well as the nature, role, and impact of public opinion in light of the changing views and perspectives of the American public about its twenty-first century world role. We also address the worrisome gap separating the foreign policy beliefs and preferences of foreign policy elites and other Americans.

  In Chapter 9, we concentrate on the nature, role, and influence of interest groups. The analysis includes compelling new evidence about the changing nature of the politics of defense policy making that continues to reinforce the veracity of long-standing theories about the influence of interests on the still largest nonentitlement discretionary spending item in the multi-trillion dollar federal budget.

- In Part V we focus on the governmental sources of American foreign policy. We examine the president's role and cluster of factors that affect presidential leadership in Chapter 10, including the setting (Constitution, courts, and other factors) and the structures that presidents use to exercise policy leadership. Our discussion of the institutional presidency covers the Clinton presidency and the first years of the Bush presidency. It highlights varying uses, problems, and factors that condition the president's ability to use the National Security Council system to exercise foreign policy leadership. Our revised focus on "presidential leadership" instead of "presidential preeminence" allows us to better grapple with the factors that promote and constrain or limit the central role of the president in foreign policy.

  Revisions of Chapter 11 update recent developments in the bureaucracy comprising the foreign affairs government. The continuing pertinence of the Cold War assumptions on which the principles and programs of many of these organizations were based inform much of the discussion.

  Chapter 12 deals with Congress. Substantially revised and reorganized, it now better reflects the role of Congress as a potential challenger to presidential leadership. Drawing on recent scholarship, it thoroughly explores the avenues of congressional influence—formal and informal, direct and indirect—to better assess the Congress's impact on foreign policy. We discuss treaty politics, war powers, and the power of the purse in this context and update the discussion to reflect the policy battles over these issues during the recent past. Our look into the twenty-first century context stresses the increasing ideological and partisan assertiveness of members of Congress.

- In Part VI we consider roles as sources of American foreign policy. Chapter 13 examines decision making with an emphasis on the impact of position on policy preferences and policy making. In this context, we assess rational actor and bureaucratic politics models. Our revised discussion of bureaucratic politics reflects recent scholarship and updates our discussion of the nature, sources, characteristics, and consequences of bureaucratic politics in light of the increasing complexity of an intensively interdependent world and the foreign policy involvement of more departments and agencies in executive branch policy making.

- In Part VII we focus on individual sources, stressing the characteristics of leaders. Chapter 14 includes consideration of the character, style, and personality of foreign policymakers, as well as the conditions in which their individual idiosyncrasies matter most. Our revision updates our discussion of President Clinton's character and style and includes a new case study on George W. Bush. New sketches of other leaders of recent years, including Madeleine Albright and Colin Powell, help us to explore the influence of personality, style, and personal background on foreign policy.

- In Part VIII we reflect on the future of American foreign policy and the prospects for a Second American Century. Our concluding thoughts make some tentative assessments of the administration of George W. Bush, using them to ponder what the new century might portend.

In addition to these substantive revisions, we have continued our determination to make the new edition accessible and conducive to effective teaching and learning. Our readers will find more organizational breaks and sections in each chapter designed to assist the student and help to structure readings and discussions. We have also continued our efforts to strengthen the readability of the text, while controlling its length. The book retains the glossary and textual highlights of glossary terms of the previous edition. To further its pedagogical value, we have added a list of key terms for each chapter. Tables, figures, and focus boxes have also been updated throughout to reflect recent developments. Finally, we remain committed to connecting our historical and contemporary discussions to broader themes, concepts, and theories. Doing so promotes greater critical and analytical thinking, better explanation and evaluation, and a more coherent consideration of the pattern and process of American foreign policy.

This overview captures just a few of the many changes, large and small, in this edition of *American Foreign Policy: Pattern and Process*. Our text now reflects a vision of the unfolding new century. But just as change and continuity describe the reality of contemporary American foreign policy, our book continues to be shaped by the many people who have contributed to it since its first edition in 1979 to the present. The contributions have come from our professional colleagues and critics, from "comment cards" sent to our publisher, ideas shared with our sales representatives, student evaluations, and other means. All have shaped our efforts to provide superior scholarship and an effective teaching and learning tool.

Those who have made suggestions for this edition, including thirteen professional colleagues who reviewed the previous edition and made extensive comments and suggestions for this edition, deserve a twenty-first-century thanks. They are Daniel Caldwell, James E. Campbell, David H. Clark, Scott Crichlow, C. James Delaet, James A. Garand, Emily O. Goldman, Robert Harkavy, Robert A. Hart, Jr., Margaret G. Hermann, Richard K. Herrmann, Christopher M. Jones, Jason LeBlanc, Lawrence LeBlanc, James M. McCormick, John Owen, IV, A. Robert McMullen, Ole R. Holsti, Todd Parker, James F. Pasley, Thomas Preston, George Quester, Curtis Reithel, Priscilla L. Southwell, and Stephen Wrage. One reviewer of the previous revision chose to remain anonymous, perhaps because he thought his comments were biting. We found them constructive, something true of all of the reviews, for which we are appreciative.

We also wish to acknowledge the contributions of the many others whose ideas, insights, and suggestions have contributed to the success of this book since its inception. At the risk of overlooking someone—and certainly recognizing we are slighting the hundreds of students who have shared often complimentary but also often constructively critical comments about the book over the years—we thank: Morris Blachman, Paul Blackstock, Linda P. Brady, Leann Brown, Dan Caldwell, William A. Clark, Oliver E. Clubb, Alfred B. Clubok, Roger Coate, Ellen C. Collier, William D. Coplin, Gene Crofts, Alfonso J. Damico, Vincent Davis, Mark J. DeHaven, Joseph DiCroce, Dan Driesbach, Timothy Duning, Beth Evatt, John Fairlamb, Robert W. Gregg, Joe D. Hagan, Lee Jane Hevener, Stephen Hibbard, James B. Holderman, James G. Holland, Robert Holley, Steven W. Hook, P. Terrence Hopmann, Muhammed Islam, Paul Kattenburg, Christopher Kautz, John Kegley, William Kreml, James A. Kuhlman, Dave Layman, Michael

Maggiotto, Pat McGowan, Raymond Moore, William Mould, Betsy Myett, Michael K. O'Leary, Christina Payne, Hazel Pridgen, Lucia Wren Rawls, Gregory A. Raymond, Barry Rich, James Roherty, Mac Rood, Robert Rood, James N. Rosenau, Loren Rudolf, Daniel Sabia, Lars Schoultz, Peter Sederberg, Ray Sexton, Chaitram Singh, Anne Sloan, Gordon Smith, Harvey Starr, William Stinchcombe, John Stolarek, Van Sturgeon, William Taylor, Robert Thompson, Victor A. Thompson, Mark Tompkins, Robert Trice, William Vocke, Brian Wallace, William Watts, Donald Weatherbee, Charles Wentworth, Bob Wislinski, Barbara J. Wittkopf, and Jonathan T. Wittkopf.

The professionals at our publisher also earn our thanks for their dedication to our efforts and for their friendship: Doug Bell, Emily Berleth, Thomas V. Broadbent, Glenn Cowley, Peter Dougherty, Marilea Fried, James Headley. Bertrand W. Lummus, Don Reisman, Anita Samen, Rachel L. Siegel, Jean Smith, Richard Steins, Dolores Wolfe, and Bob Woodbury.

Colleagues, friends, neighbors—they are both the easiest and the hardest to thank. They are the social safety-net when things are not going well and the cheerleaders when they are. Without naming names, as some have moved elsewhere professionally and others have departed, we thank them all.

Our wives and children are the most important among the social safety-net/cheerleader circle. Critics, editors, and always faithful believers in what we are trying to accomplish, this book would not have been possible without their optimistic encouragement, tireless support, and endless patience.

                 Eugene R. Wittkopf
                 Charles W. Kegley, Jr.
                 James M. Scott

About the Authors

Eugene R. Wittkopf is the R. Downs Poindexter Distinguished Professor of Political Science at Louisiana State University. A graduate of Valparaiso and Syracuse Universities, Wittkopf is a past president of the Florida Political Science Association and of the International Studies Association/South. He has also held appointments at the University of Florida and the University of North Carolina at Chapel Hill.

Wittkopf is the author of *Faces of Internationalism: Public Opinion and American Foreign Policy* (Duke University Press, 1990), and, with Charles W. Kegley, Jr., coauthor of *American Foreign Policy: Pattern and Process* (5th edition, St. Martin's Press, 1996) and, *World Politics: Trend and Transformation* (8th edition, Bedford/St. Martin's 2001). He has also edited or coedited several other books, including *The Global Agenda: Issues and Perspectives, The Nuclear Reader: Strategy, Weapons, War* (both with Charles W. Kegley, Jr.), *The Future of American Foreign Policy* (with Christopher M. Jones), and *The Domestic Sources of American Foreign Policy: Insights and Evidence* (with James M.

McCormick). His articles have appeared in the *American Political Science Review, American Politics Quarterly, International Organization, International Studies Quarterly, International Organization, Journal of Conflict Resolution, Journal of Politics, Polity, Social Science Quarterly,* and the *Washington Quarterly,* among other professional journals.

Wittkopf is the recipient of grants from the United States National Science Foundation to support his research on the foreign policy beliefs and preferences of the American people. In 1997 he received the highest award given by Louisiana State University in recognition of faculty contributions to research and scholarship when he was named the LSU Distinguished Research Master of Arts, Humanities, and Social Sciences. In 2002 he was named Distinguished Scholar by the Foreign Policy Analysis section of the International Strategies Association.

A past President of the International Studies Association, **Charles W. Kegley, Jr.** is the Pearce Professor of International Relations at the

University of South Carolina. A graduate of the American University and Syracuse University, Kegley has served as chairman of the Department of Government and International Studies at USC, and also has taught at Georgetown University, the University of Texas, Rutgers University as the Moses and Annuta Back Peace Scholar, and the People's University of China. In addition, he was a Pew Fellow at the John F. Kennedy School of Government at Harvard University and is a member of the Board of Trustees of the Carnegie Council on Ethics and International Affairs.

The editor of Prentice-Hall Studies in International Relations: Enduring Questions in Changing Times, Kegley's four dozen book publications include *The New Global Terrorism: Characteristics, Causes, Controls* (2003) and, with Gregory A. Raymond, *From War to Peace: Fateful Decisions in International Politics* (2002), *Exorcising the Ghost of Westphalia: Building World Order in the New Millennium* (2002), *How Nations Make Peace* (1999), *A Multipolar Peace? Great-Power Politics in the Twenty-First Century* (1994), and *When Trust Breaks Down: Alliance Norms and World Politics* (1990). In addition, with Eugene R. Wittkopf, Professor Kegley has published *World Politics: Trend and Transformation* (8th ed., 2001), *The Global Agenda* (6th ed., 2001), and *The Nuclear Reader: Strategy, Weapons, War*, 2nd ed. (1989). Kegley has also published *Controversies in International Relations Theory: Realism and the Neoliberal Challenge* (1995); *The Long Postwar Peace: Contending Explanations and Projections* (1991); and *After the Cold War: Questioning the Morality of Nuclear Deterrence* (1991). His articles have appeared in a wide range of scholarly journals, including the *Journal of Peace Research*, the *Journal of Conflict Resoltuion*, *International Studies Quarterly*, *Ethics and International Affairs*, *Bulletin of Peace Proposals*, *Alternatives*, *USA Today*, *Harvard International Review*, *Presidential Studies Quarterly*, *Comparative Political Studies*, *Conflict Management and Peace Science*, *International Interactions*, the *Journal of Politics*, and the *Political Research Quarterly*.

James M. Scott is associate professor and chair of the Department of Political Science at the University of Nebraska at Kearney. He is author of *Deciding to Intervene: The Reagan Doctrine and American Foreign Policy* (Duke University Press, 1996) and editor of *After the End: Making U.S. Foreign Policy in the Post–Cold War* (Duke University Press, 1998). With teaching and research interests in American foreign policy, he has published numerous book chapters and articles in professional journals such as *Congress and the Presidency*, *Political Science Quarterly*, *Presidential Studies Quarterly*, *Democratization*, *Global Society*, *The Journal of Political and Military Sociology*, *Southeastern Political Review*, *Futures Research Quarterly*, *PS: Political Science and Politics*, and *Review of Public Personnel Administration*. A graduate of Wheaton College and Northern Illinois University, he served as president of the International Studies Association-Midwest and of the Foreign Policy Analysis section of the International Studies Association in 2000–2001. In 2000, he received the University of Nebraska at Kearney's highest award for faculty research and creative activity when he received the Pratt-Heins Award For Outstanding Research and Scholarship.

❖

PART I

Analytical and Thematic Perspectives on American Foreign Policy

Chapter 1
In Search of American Foreign Policy:
A Thematic Introduction

Chapter 2
Pattern and Process in American Foreign Policy:
An Analytical Perspective

CHAPTER 1

In Search of American Foreign Policy

A Thematic Introduction

There are times when only America can make the difference between war and peace, between freedom and repression, between hope and fear.

PRESIDENT WILLIAM JEFFERSON CLINTON, 1996

Just as Pearl Harbor awakened this country from the notion that we could somehow avoid the call of duty and defend freedom in Europe and Asia in World War II, so, too, should this most recent surprise attack erase the concept in some quarters that America can somehow go it alone in the fight against terrorism or in anything else for that matter.

PRESIDENT GEORGE W. BUSH, 2001

America the invincible. Long a part of the nation's political heritage, that description is no longer accurate—if it ever was. On September 11, 2001, armed with only a few knives and a handful of airplanes packed with jet fuel and unwitting passengers and crew, four commercial airliners slammed into the World Trade Center (WTC), the Pentagon, and the hills of Pennsylvania. The casualty toll may never be known, but it certainly surpasses any previous terrorist attack against the United States, including those against the USS Cole and the American embassies in Kenya and Tanzania. Indeed, it was only the second time the continental United States had been struck (the first was in 1993, when the WTC was also attacked), surpassing December 7, 1941 as a day when Americans found themselves riveted to news about their nation's future. In turn, and spurred on by the media, the Bush administration declared that America was at war with terrorism and those who would perpetrate it.

As President Bush prepared the nation for a long-term search for and destruction of terrorist havens not only in southwest Asia but elsewhere, he pursued often time-worn policies. In the twentieth century alone three great wars have animated the great powers, and their outcome has profoundly shaped the world in which we live today. In many ways the war against terrorism is a replay of prior conflicts, as the struggle over principle and power remains central to the conflicts of interest dividing the antagonists and protagonists.

Differences in the war against terrorism are also evident, of course. Religious and nationalist fanaticism often animate the actors, and differences in their capabilities are evident, ranging from high-tech weapons designed to protect American troops abroad during the 1970s and 1980s to World War I vintage weapons that animate efforts to enhance the goals of the weak against the strong. What remains the same is a determination to use fear and force of arms to achieve political objectives.

In 1941 Henry Luce, the noted editor and publisher of *Time, Life,* and *Fortune* magazines, envisioned his time as the dawn of the *American Century*. He based his prediction on the conviction that "only America can effectively state the aims of this war," meaning World War II. These aims included "a vital international economy" and "an international moral order." In many ways Luce's prediction proved prophetic, not just as it applied to World War II but also to the decades-long Cold War contest with the Soviet Union that quickly followed. But even he might be surprised that the twenty-first century looks to be an even more thoroughly American century than his. In the early years of the new millennium, the facts are simple and irrefutable: Compared with all other nations, the United States today is in a class by itself. No one else can match the health and productivity of our economy, the extent of our scientific and technological resources, our ability to sustain massive levels of defense spending, or the power, sophistication, and global reach of our armed forces. The terrorist attacks on the American homeland on September 11, 2001, did considerable harm to the economy and jolted the ethos of invincibility, but it did not fundamentally change the relative ranking of the United States among the world's states. Indeed, the attacks were a boon to the military, helping to settle priorities along lines preferred by the Republicans. Hence the terrorist attacks did little to affect the critical point on which Henry Luce had based his judgment.

American power extends beyond traditional measures Luce considered as well, encompassing a wealth of less tangible assets broadly conceived as *soft power* (Nye 1990). They include the attraction of its culture and political beliefs and the ability of the United States to establish rules and institutions it favors. Thus the United States continues to set the agenda in the international organizations it helped to establish in the 1940s; democracy and market economies have spread throughout the world; and American culture—ranging from pop music, blue jeans, and McDonald's to PCs, Windows 2000, and Internet communications in English—exhibits nearly universal appeal in our rapidly globalizing world. Impressed with the global reach of America's soft power, one analyst observed that "One has to go back to the Roman Empire for a similar instance of cultural hegemony. . . . We live in an 'American age,' meaning that American values and arrangements are most closely in tune with the new Zeitgeist" (Joffe 1997).

THE AMERICAN CENTURY AND BEYOND

Powerful as the United States may be, America's "second" century will still be profoundly shaped by the three global wars of the twentieth century. Three times in eighty years—in World War I, World War II, and the Cold War—the world experienced international contests for power and position of global proportions and with global consequences, forcing the United States to confront its role as its political, economic, and military importance grew. All of them will cast their shadows across the contours of world politics as the twenty-first century unfolds.

The American presidents who occupied the White House during these contests shared a common vision of the nation's future, grounded in *liberalism* and *idealism*. Woodrow Wilson, under whose leadership the United States entered the war against Germany in 1917 and fought to create "a world safe for democracy," called for an association of nations that he promised would guarantee the "political independence and territorial integrity [of] great and small states alike." Franklin D. Roosevelt, president during World War II until his death in April 1945, portrayed the moral basis for American involvement in World War II as an effort to secure *four freedoms*—freedom of speech and expression, freedom of worship, freedom from want, and freedom from fear. He, too, supported creation of a new association of the United Nations, as the allies were called, to secure and maintain the structure of peace once the war against Germany and Japan was ended. And like Wilson, Roosevelt's vision of the postwar world embraced the principles of self-determination and an open international marketplace. Harry S. Truman, Roosevelt's successor, carried much of Roosevelt's vision forward, eventually adapting its principles to his own definition of the post–World War II world order.

George Bush perpetuated the liberal tradition following the third twentieth century contest for power and position. It ended in November 1989 when the Berlin Wall came tumbling down. For nearly thirty years the wall had stood as perhaps the most emotional symbol of the division between East and West and of the Cold War that had raged between the United States and the Soviet Union since World War II. Less than a year later Iraq invaded the tiny desert kingdom of Kuwait. The United States, now with the unprecedented support of the Soviet Union in the United Nations Security Council, took the lead in organizing a military response to Iraq's aggression based on the same principle of collective security that Wilson, Roosevelt, and Truman had embraced. George H. W. Bush evoked images of the "next American century" and a "new world order" in which the "rule of law" would reign supreme. He extolled America's leadership role, urging that "only the United States of America has the moral leadership and the means to back it up."

Once before, however, the United States had rejected the call for leadership and responsibility. Wilson failed in his bid to have the United States join the League of Nations, of which he had been the principal architect. In this and other ways the United States turned away from the challenge of international involvement that World War I had posed. Instead, it opted to return to its historic pattern of isolation from the machinations it associated with Europe's power politics, which Wilson had characterized as an "old and evil order," one marked by "an arrangement of power and suspicion and dread." The strategy contributed to the breakdown of order and stability in the decades following World War I, thus setting the stage for the twentieth century's second global contest for international power and position.

World War II was geographically more widespread and militarily more destructive than World War I. And it transformed world politics irrevocably. The place of the United States in the structure of world politics also was altered dramatically as it emerged from the war with unparalleled capabilities. In 1947 British author Harold J. Laski described the new world political circumstances:

> America bestrides the world like a colossus; neither Rome at the height of its power nor Great Britain in the period of its economic supremacy enjoyed an influence so direct, so profound, or so pervasive. It has half the wealth of the world today in its hands, it has rather more than half of the world's productive capacity, and it exports more than twice as much as it imports. Today literally hundreds of millions of Europeans and Asiatics know that both the quality and the rhythm of their lives depend upon decisions made in Washington. On the wisdom of those decisions hangs the fate of the next generation.
>
> (LASKI 1947, 641)

World War II not only propelled the United States into the status of an emergent superpower but also transformed the way it responded to the challenges of the postwar world. *Isolationism* was now the victim, as American leaders and eventually the American people embraced *internationalism*—a new vision predicated on assumptions about international politics derived from their experience in world war and the turmoil that preceded it. Wilsonian idealism gave way to the doctrine of *political realism,* which focused on power, not ideals. Containment became the preferred strategy for dealing with the Soviet Union in the latest contest for power and position, demanding resources and commitment beyond anything the nation had previously experienced. Some forty years later the United States would emerge "victorious" in this contest, as first the Soviet external empire and then the Soviet Union itself disintegrated. The ideology of communism also fell into widespread disrepute.

Ironically, the end of the Cold War removed the very things that gave structure and purpose to post–World War II American foreign policy: fear of communism, fear of the Soviet Union, and a determination to contain both. These convictions also stimulated the internationalist ethos embraced by the American people and especially their leaders following World War II. Absent them, today there is widespread debate about the ends and means of American foreign policy—not unlike that which occurred after World Wars I and II—reflecting the absence of an overarching foreign policy paradigm. Hence, throughout the two Clinton terms and into George W. Bush's administration, the role and purposes of the United States in the world were the subject of much discussion and disagreement.

Even as the United States debates its global role, forces unleashed during the past decade are dramatically reshaping the global environment. The spread of democracy to nearly every corner of the world has given millions of people freedom to control their own destinies in ways only recently deemed imaginable. Because democracies rarely engage in violent conflict with one another, *global democratization* gives rise to the hope that this century will be less marked by violence, warfare, and bloodshed than the last. Furthermore, democracy is often accompanied by the spread of *economic liberalism.* As market forces are unleashed, greater economic opportunity and rising affluence hold out the promise of improved living standards and an enhanced quality of life.

The globalization of the world political economy has accompanied the spread of political democracy and market economies, contributing to a homogenization of social and cultural forces worldwide. ***Globalization*** refers to the rapid intensification and integration of states' economies not only in terms of markets but also ideas, information, and technology, which is having a profound impact on political, social, and cultural relations across borders. The economic side of globalization dominates the headlines of financial pages and computer trade journals. But the causes and consequences of globalization extend beyond economics (see Focus 1.1). Globalization stems from "the onrush of economic and ecological forces that demand integration and uniformity and that mesmerize the world with fast music, fast computers, and fast food—with MTV, Macintosh, and McDonald's, pressing nations into one commercially homogenous global network: one McWorld tied together by technology, ecology, communications, and commerce" (Barber 1992). This is the environment that led an admiring German journalist to ask us to "Think of the United States as a gambler who can play simultaneously at each and every table that matters—and with more chips than anybody else. Whichever heap you choose, America sits on top of it" (Joffe 1997).

Still, because the political boundaries separating states are transparent to the cross-border trends unleashed by globalization, they pose challenges to the United States at home and abroad. Domestically, globalization "is exposing a deep fault line between groups who have the skills and mobility to flourish in global markets and those who either don't have these advantages or perceive the expansion of unregulated markets as inimical to social stability and deeply held norms." Understandably, this results in "severe tension

FOCUS 1.1   The Shrinking World

Contacts between the world's people are widening and deepening as natural and artificial barriers fall. Huge declines in transport and communication costs have reduced natural barriers. Shipping is much cheaper: between 1920 and 1990 maritime transport costs fell by more than two-thirds. Between 1960 and 1990 operating costs per mile for the world's airlines fell by 60%.

Communication is also much easier and cheaper. Between 1940 and 1970 the cost of an international telephone call fell by more than 80%, and between 1970 and 1990 by 90%. In the 1980s telecommunication traffic was expanding by 20% a year. The Internet, the take-off point for the information superhighway, is now used by 50 million people, with the number of subscribers tapping into it doubling every year.

Toppling Trade Barriers

Artificial barriers have been eased with the reduction in trade barriers (tariffs, quotas and so on) and exchange controls. In 1947 the average tariff on manufactured imports was 47%; by 1980 it was only 6%, and with full implementation of the Uruguay Round, it should fall to 3%.

Other artificial barriers were removed with the resolution of political conflicts that have divided the world for decades, such as the cold war and the apartheid system in South Africa.

Spurred by the fall of barriers, global trade grew 12-fold in the postwar period. Now more than $4 trillion a year, it is expected to grow 6% annually for the next 10 years.

The Rising Tide of Finance

The expansion of capital flows has been even more dramatic. Flows of foreign direct investment in 1995 reached $315 billion, nearly a sixfold increase over the level for 1981–85. Over the same period world trade increased by little more than half.

Less visible, but infinitely more powerful, are the world's financial markets. Between the mid-1970s and 1996 the daily turnover in the world's foreign exchange markets increased from around $1 billion to $1.2 trillion. Most private capital flows went to industrial countries, but a growing share is going to developing countries. Between 1987 and 1994 the flows to developing countries

rose from $25 billion to $172 billion, and in 1995 they received a third of the global foreign direct investment flows.

These changes are significant, but need to be placed in historical context. Much of this has happened before. For 17 industrial countries for which there are data, exports as a share of GDP in 1913 were 12.9%, not much below the 1993 level of 14.5%. And capital transfers as a share of industrial country GDP are still smaller than in the 1890s. Earlier eras of globalization also saw far greater movement of people around the world. Today immigration is more restricted.

The modern era of globalization is distinguished less by the scale of the flows than by their character. In trade, for example, a much smaller share by value consists of commodities (partly a reflection of lower prices relative to manufactures) and a larger share is services and intracompany trade. Finance too is different: net flows may be similar, but gross flows are larger—and the flows come from a wider variety of sources. And multinational corporations are leaders in mobilizing capital and generating technology.

Global Technology . . .

Some of the changes in international trade and finance reflect advances in technology. The lightning speed of transactions means that countries and companies now must respond rapidly if they are not to be left behind.

Technological change is also affecting the nature of investment. Previously, high-technology production had been limited to rich countries with high wages. Today technology is more easily tranferred to developing countries, where sophisticated production can be combined with relatively low wages.

The increasing ease with which technology can accompany capital across borders threatens to break the links between high productivity, high technology and high wages. For example, Mexico's worker productivity rose from a fifth to a third of the US level between 1989 and 1993, in part as a consequence of increased foreign investment and sophisticated technology geared towards production for the US market. But the

Continued

---

average wage gap has narrowed far more slowly, with the Mexican wage still only a sixth of the US wage. The availability of higher levels of technology all over the world is putting pressure on the wages and employment of low-skilled workers.

. . . And a Global Culture

Normally, globalization refers to the international flow of trade and capital. But the international spread of cultures has been at least as important as the spread of economic processes. Today a global culture is emerging. Through many media—from music to movies to books—international ideas and values are being mixed with, and superimposed on, national identities. The spread of ideas through television and video has seen revolutionary developments. There now are more than 1.2 billion TV sets around the world. The United States exports more than 120,000 hours of television programming a year to Europe alone, and the global trade in programming is growing by more than 15% a year.

Popular culture exerts more powerful pressure than ever before. From Manila to Managua, Beirut to Beijing, in the East, West, North and South, styles in dress (jeans, hair-dos, t-shirts), sports, music, eating habits and social and cultural attitudes have become global trends. Even crimes—whether relating to drugs, abuse of women, embezzlement or corruption—transcend frontiers and have become similar everywhere. In so many ways, the world has shrunk.

SOURCE: From Human Development Report 1997 by United Nations Development Programme, copyright © 1997 by the United Nations Development Programme. Used by permission of Oxford University Press, Inc.

---

between the market and social groups such as workers, pensioners, and environmentalists, with governments stuck in the middle" (Rodrik 1997).

Internationally, the forces unleashed by globalization are also "producing a powerful backlash from those brutalized or left behind in the new system," which is defined by an "inexorable integration of markets, nation-states, and technologies to a degree never witnessed before (Friedman 1999). Thus globalization may be a force beyond states' control. As World Bank vice president Ismail Serageldin observed, "The political boundaries of sovereign states have become permeable, whether we are dealing with the commerce of ideas or capital." And he worries that "people . . . no longer believe governments can master destiny, as they once believed" (de Borchgrave 1996).

There are other troublesome developments during the last decade of the twentieth century; including widespread *intranational conflict* fed by ethnic and religious feuds often centuries old, and transnational terrorist networks lashing out against the dominant power of the United States and the pervasiveness of its culture. As a global power, the United States has repeatedly found itself confronted with difficult questions about whether and how to respond to these often bloody confrontations.

Thus, as the forces that will define the twenty-first century unfold, American policy makers must deal with global trends and transformations that both challenge and transcend the nation-state, the very foundation of the contemporary world political order. They must also cope with the domestic political, social, and economic consequences that these trends and transformations inevitably portend.

ON AMERICA'S PURPOSES AND ROLE IN THE TWENTY-FIRST CENTURY: RETROSPECT AND PROSPECT

Little more than a decade ago social scientists and policy makers worried that the United States had suffered a decline in power, sapping its willingness to exercise influence abroad and encouraging those who would refocus the nation's agenda on domestic priorities. With the United States now the world's unchallenged military superpower, and with its economy revitalized by reduced inflation, productivity gains, and technological innovations, the *declinists* are in retreat. Still, the debate between the priorities that should be attached to the world environment compared with the domestic remains controversial. Thus it is not surprising that Presidents Bush and Clinton rationalized the nation's continuing engagement in the emerging new era using rhetoric strikingly similar to that of their predecessors. Just as George H. W. Bush harkened back to Wilsonian idealism at the time of the Gulf War, Bill Clinton referred to the task Harry Truman faced late in 1940s when he observed in his first inaugural address that "we need to design a new strategy for protecting American interests by laying the foundations for a more just and stable world."

What are those interests and foundations? Now, just as in the late 1940s and before, they are peace and prosperity, stability and security, democracy and defense. And now as previously, most American leaders believe these qualities rest on American *leadership* and *global activism,* as indicated by the rhetoric that presidents, and most of those who aspire to the presidency, typically embrace. It is not surprising, therefore, that the parameters of American foreign policy established in the last half of the twentieth century are resistant to change as we enter the twenty-first century. Still, critics and supporters alike remain concerned about the seeming lack of direction and the absence of a rationale underlying today's American foreign policy. At issue is the precise set of initiatives that will best secure those foundations and interests.

For forty years *containment* of the Soviet Union defined America's foreign policy. During the Clinton administration the concept animated strategy for dealing with Iran and Iraq, two of the so-called "rogue" states (later called "states of concern"), and is also sometimes used to frame U.S. policy toward China. Intervention into the affairs of others—with others, if possible, as in Kosovo; alone if necessary, as in Iraq—remains a favored

instrument of policy, now also joined by a widespread willingness to use sanctions where force of arms is unpopular. Military spending remains the highest in the world, permitting modernization of weapons systems to combat twenty-first century villains now only dimly perceived. The rhetoric of democratic promotion, economic liberalism, and the promotion of international values continues to be espoused but also continues to be corrupted in practice. What is lacking is an overall design or vision—a ***grand strategy***—that would give coherence and purpose to America's involvement abroad. Such a design is now more important in the wake of the September 11 attacks because, in the words of one observer, "the Post-Cold War world of easy preeminence, controlled low cost wars, budgetary plenty, and choices avoided is over" (Posen 2001/2002).

Policy analysts have debated the merits and shortcomings of a broad panoply of competing grand strategies.[1] Some urge that the United States take advantage of its position as the "sole superpower" to pursue a strategy of ***primacy.*** Advocates of primacy (*primacists*) have been concerned primarily with the reemergence of Russia as a military threat and with the challenge posed by possible future great powers. Among them are Japan, where the threat posed may be economic rather than military, and China, where the threat may be both. In the context of a 21st century war against terrorism, primacists have recommended a broad campaign against many targets to "further consolidate an already dominant U.S. power position" (Posen 2001/2002). A strategy of primacy urges that the aspirations of emerging challengers be thwarted and recommends the United States expend whatever treasure may be required to meet the challenge. Its advocates recognize that resources may be more limited than in the past, but they believe "the problem is not a lack of resources . . . but a lack of public will and support" (Posen and Ross 1997). They also are wary of contributions that international organizations like the United Nations can make to cope with contemporary security challenges, urging instead that the United States be prepared to act *unilaterally* (alone) in pursuit of its foreign policy goals and interests.[2]

Neo-isolationism occupies the other end of the spectrum. *Neo-isolationists* share with primacists an overriding concern with the role of power in the global arena, but they place a decidedly different spin on its meaning for today's American foreign policy. Who, they ask, poses a realistic challenge to America's overwhelming military power? They concede that "nuclear weapons have increased the sheer capacity of others to threaten the safety of the United States," but they also argue that the U.S. nuclear arsenal makes it "nearly inconceivable" that any other state could seriously challenge the United States militarily (Posen and Ross 1997). As one group of analysts put it, "isolationism in the 1920s was inappropriate, because conquest on a continental scale was then possible. Now, nuclear weapons assure great power sovereignty—and certainly America's defense" (Gholz, Press, and Sapolsky 1997). Even after 2001's terrorist strikes, such advocates argue that "the U.S. should do less in the world. If the U.S. is less involved, it will be less of a target" (Posen 2001/2002).

To be sure, if the United States is drawn into conflicts around the world, it will become the hated object of machinations by others, including those who practice terrorism or seek to develop biological and chemical as well as nuclear weapons of mass destruction. But the prescription for neo-isolationists that follows is the same as the nation's first president recommended two centuries ago: avoid foreign entanglements. Today this includes distancing the United States from the United Nations and other international organizations when they seek to make or enforce peace in roiling conflicts, thus positioning neo-isolationists close to primacists on the critical issue of whether to act alone or with others to promote its policy ends. The two groups differ, however, on the resources required to promote and protect the nation's interests, as the strategy of neo-isolationism is clearly less costly than primacy.

Neo-isolationists believe that cost savings can be realized by reducing American commitments abroad. An argument popular in the 1980s among the prophets of America's decline is that the United States had become "overcommitted," with obligations abroad exceeding its resources, a classic symptom of *imperial overstretch* (Kennedy 1987). Neo-isolationists find the solution in dramatic reductions in military forces abroad. Correspondingly, priorities may now be shifted to the domestic issues and problems often ignored during the long struggle with Soviet communism. Still, most advocates of neo-isolationism do not propose total withdrawal from the world. Even journalist and Reform Party presidential hopeful Pat Buchanan's (1990) popular call that America should be "first—and second, and third" does not prescribe that. Nor does military retrenchment necessarily imply a resort to economic nationalism, as "a vigorous trade with other nations and the thriving commerce of ideas" are not incompatible with military restraint (Gholz, Press, and Sapolsky 1997). Thus American national interests remain unchanged: "The United States still seeks peace and prosperity. But now this preferred state is best obtained by restraining America's great power, a power unmatched by any rival and unchallenged in any important dimension. Rather than lead a new crusade, America should absorb itself in the somewhat delayed task of addressing imperfections in its own society" (Gholz, Press, and Sapolsky 1997).

Advocates of *selective engagement* sit somewhere between the primacists and neo-isolationists. Like primacists, *selective engagers* focus on U.S. relations with the great powers, believing that "the purpose of U.S. engagement should be to affect directly the propensity of these powers to go to war with one another. . . . The argument is that Eurasia sinks into warfare when the United States is absent, not when it is present; and once it does, we ultimately regret it" (Posen and Ross 1997). And like neo-isolationists, they would reduce the costs associated with foreign involvements. They share with both skepticism about the utility of international organizations in serving American foreign policy interests. Where they differ from both is on the level and focus of U.S. global activism.

They are sensitive to the broad menu of challenges the United States now faces: transnational terrorism, conflicts sparked by ethnonationalism, the proliferation of biological, chemical, and nuclear weapons, regional conflicts among rival powers at the "second tier," and the compelling needs of millions of people in the *Global South* who live in poverty and without hope. While some would focus on *pivotal states* in the Global South to ensure stability there (Chase, Hill, and Kennedy 1996), generally selective engagers offer no overarching guidelines for dealing with the challenges. Instead, the United States must be "selective," guided by a pragmatic determination of where its true national interests lie.[3] A key objective is "stable, peaceful, and relatively open political and economic relations in the part of the world that contains important concentrations of economic and military resources: Eurasia." Here, in the context of an anti-terror campaign or some other 21st century challenge, U.S. power should "reassure the vulnerable and deter the ambitious" (Posen 2001/2001). One advocate of selective engagement describes those interests this way:

> (1) preventing an attack on the American homeland, primarily by keeping out of the wrong hands nuclear, biological, and chemical (NBC) weapons . . . ; (2) preventing great power wars and destructive security competitions among the Eurasian great powers; (3) maintaining secure oil supplies at stable prices . . . ; (4) preserving an open international economic order; (5) fostering the spread of democracy and respect for human rights, and preventing mass murder and genocide; and (6) protecting the global environment from the adverse effects of global warming and ozone depletion.
>
> (ART 1998–1999, 80)

He adds that the first three are "vital" interests," while the last three are "desirable."

Primacy, neo-isolationism, and selective engagement are all grounded in the doctrine of political realism, whose precepts we will explore in greater detail in the chapters that follow. There is another grand strategy grounded in Wilsonian idealism, which we can label *cooperative security*. Whereas the other proposed strategies emphasize that the United States will often have to act alone (unilaterally), cooperative security rests on the assumption that the United States will act *multilaterally*—in concert with many others (and typically on the basis of some general principle). Indeed, in responding to the 2001 terrorist attacks, cooperative security advocates tended to emphasize the process of the campaign: involving the UN, adhering to law, controlling the use of force, and relying on diplomacy and sanctions (Posen 2001/2002).

Building on United States' experience in the Persian Gulf War, advocates of cooperative security (*collectivists*) see international organizations, like the United Nations, as critical elements in global strategies designed "to convince all prospective aggressors that they will regularly be met with decisive countervailing power" if they break existing rules of international governance (Posen and Ross 1997). Collectivists also view regional conflicts and violent intranational disputes, like the ethnic warfare Europe and Africa have experienced in recent years, with alarm, believing they may spill into wider warfare. Frequent U.S. military intervention abroad may thus prove necessary. "It is not the subtle diplomacy of the United States that proves critical, but rather its military reputation, which depends on large, diverse, technologically sophisticated, and lushly supplied military forces capable of decisive operations. At least initially, the United States would have to provide disproportionate military power to launch a global cooperative security regime" (Posen and Ross 1997). Thus the prospects for building an effective cooperative security system imply a long-term U.S. commitment to active involvement in constructing the structures of peace now absent in the global arena.

TOWARD EXPLANATION

Primacy, neo-isolationism, selective engagement, and cooperative security are but four of a larger array of prospective grand strategies that now vie for the attention of American leaders.[4] Despite their differences, all share in common a concern for a definition of U.S. interests in the changing global environment, of the challenges the nation faces now or may face in the future, and of the prospects for linking American traditions and values to its foreign policy goals.

Despite these commonalities, we can safely predict that none of the competing strategies will guide American foreign policy in the new millennium in quite the way its advocates would like. The reason is simple: American foreign policy is not the product of a mechanical calculus of the nation's interests. Instead, determination of those interests is the product of a complex political process anchored in tradition and colored by contemporary developments at home and abroad. As Secretary of State Dean Rusk remarked some years ago, "the central themes of American foreign policy are more or less constant. They derive from the kind of people we are . . . and from the shape of the world situation."

Building on this notion, some critics of American foreign policy also argue that the seeming inability of the United States to design a new grand strategy for the new era has roots in the changed and changing character of the United States itself ("the kind of people we are"). They argue that the nation that faced the threat of Soviet communism is today a much different nation. In the words of one analyst,

Over the years, especially since the Vietnam War and now accelerating again with the absence of the Soviet threat, U.S. policy has lacked focus; it has become more politicized, more partisan, and more conflicted. . . . The divisions are basic, and they are deep. . . . They reflect the more divided, fragmented, and politically discordant society that America has become. The United States has always had disagreements over foreign policy—that is the price paid for living in a democratic and pluralist country. But now these differences are sharper and often more intense, and they frequently lead to paralysis of policy. (WIARDA 1996, 1–2)

As these ruminations suggest, if we are to anticipate the shape of American foreign policy in the new century we must understand much about the world, about the United States and its system of government, about the behavior of political leaders and others responsible for its foreign policy, and about the competing world views that animate the American people and their leaders. We must also understand how these forces have interacted in the past to create today's American foreign policy, as the United States finds itself bound by history even as many of the fears and strategies that once shaped it have dissipated. These are our purposes in this book.

KEY TERMS RELATED TO AMERICAN FOREIGN POLICY THEMES

American Century	**globalization**	**neo-isolationism** *(neo-isolationists)*
containment	**grand strategy**	
cooperative security *(collectivists)*	*idealism*	*pivotal states*
	imperial overstretch	*political realism*
declinists	*internationalism*	**primacy** *(primacists)*
economic liberalism	*intranational conflict*	**selective engagement** *(selective engagers)*
four freedoms	*isolationism*	
global activism	*liberalism*	**soft power**
global democratization	**multilaterally** *(multilateral)*	**unilaterally** *(unilateral)*
Global South		

SUGGESTIONS FOR FURTHER READING

Art, Robert J. "Geopolitics Updated: The Strategy of Selective Engagement," *International Security* 23 (Winter 1998/99): 79–113.

Berger, Sandy. "A Foreign Policy for the Global Age," *Foreign Affairs* 79 (November–December 2000): 22–39.

Brzezinski, Zbigniew. *The Grand Chessboard: American Primacy and Its Geostrategic Imperatives.* New York: HarperCollins, 1998.

Calleo, David P. "A New Era of Overstretch? American Policy in Europe and Asia," *World Policy Journal* 15 (Spring 1998): 11–25.

Dizard, Wilson P. *Digital Diplomacy: U.S. Foreign Policy in the Information Age.* Westport, CT: Greenwood, 2001.

Gholz, Eugene, Daryl G. Press, and Harvey M. Sapolsky. "Come Home, America: The Strategy of Restraint in the Face of Temptation," *International Security* 21 (Spring 1997): 5–48.

Haass, Richard. "What to Do With American Primacy," *Foreign Affairs* 78 (September/October 1999): 37–49.

Joffe, Josef. "America the Inescapable," *New York Times Magazine,* 8 June 1997, 38–43.

Laqueur, Walter. *The New Terrorism: Fanaticism and the Arms of Mass Destruction.* New York: Oxford University Press, 2000.

Ninkovich, Frank A. *The Wilsonian Century: U.S. Foreign Policy Since 1900.* Chicago: University of Chicago Press, 1999.

Nye, Joseph, S. "Redefining the National Interest," *Foreign Affairs* 78 (July–August 1999): 22–35.

Schwarz, Benjamin, and Christopher Layne. "A Grand New Strategy." *The Atlantic Monthly* (January 2002): 36–42.

The United States Commission on National Security/ 21st Century. *New World Coming: American Security in the 21st Century.* Phase I Report on the Emerging Global Security Environment for the First Quarter of the 21st Century. Washington, DC, United States Commission on National Security/ 21st Century, 1999.

Wittkopf, Eugene R., and Christopher M. Jones, eds., *The Future of American Foreign Policy.* New York: Worth/St. Martin's, 1999.

White, Donald W. *The American Century: The Rise and Decline of the United States as a World Power.* New Haven, CT: Yale University Press, 1996.

NOTES

1. Except as noted, the following brief summary of competing grand strategies is based on the overview in Posen and Ross (1997).

2. Michael Mastanduno (1997) argues that primacy is the strategy the United States pursued in the 1990s. Posen and Ross (1996–1997) are more qualified in their assessment, viewing the Clinton administration's grand strategy as one of "selective, but cooperative, primacy."

3. The essays in Nolan (1994) make a case for global engagement. See also Art (1991, 1998–1999) and Van Evera (1990).

4. See, for example, Richard N. Haass (1995), former director of foreign policy studies at the Brookings Institution, who links the ends of foreign policy to its means. The ends, he argues, are Wilsonianism, economism, realism, humanitarianism, and minimalism. The means are similar to those discussed above: unilateralism, neo-isolationism, and U.S. leadership. Alexander Nacht (1995) usefully summarizes the central arguments of a wide range of alternative foreign policy strategies associated with different schools of thought in international politics.

CHAPTER 2

Pattern and Process
in American Foreign Policy

An Analytical Perspective

A long-term consistency of behavior is bound to burden American
democracy when the country rises to the stature of a great power.

FRENCH POLITICAL SOCIOLOGIST ALEXIS DE TOCQUEVILLE, 1835

Decisions and actions in the international arena can be understood, predicted, and
manipulated only in so far as the factors influencing the decisions can be identified.

AMERICAN POLITICAL SCIENTIST ARNOLD WOLFERS, 1962

oreign policy embraces the goals that the nation's officials seek to attain abroad, the values that give rise to those objectives, and the
means or instruments used to pursue them. We
try in this book to understand how and why the
interaction of values, ends, and means shapes
American foreign policy—sometimes stimulating
change and promoting innovation, sometimes
constraining the nation's ability to respond inno-
vatively to new challenges, even when circumstances demand it. We direct particular attention
to the more than half century since World
War II, when the United States emerged as the
dominant power in world politics and the Amer-

ican people rejected isolationism in favor of
global activism. We argue that the adaptations in
American for-eign policy that occurred during
the Cold War (roughly 1947 to 1989) were confined largely to the means used to achieve persistent ends sustained by immutable values. We
also argue that the confluence of values and political forces that sustained American foreign policy during the Cold War persists to the present,
even in the absence of an overarching foreign
policy paradigm which once united the American people.

Our hypothesis that the values and goals underlying American foreign policy are resistant to

14

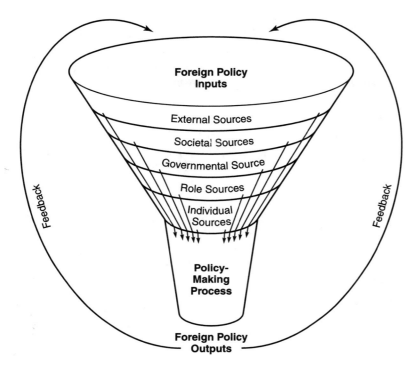

FIGURE 2.1 The Sources of American Foreign Policy as a Funnel of Causality

change prompts consideration of the reasons why. To answer this seemingly simple question we adapt a framework for analysis first proposed by political scientist James N. Rosenau (1966, 1980). The framework postulates that all of the factors that explain why states behave as they do in international politics can be grouped into five broad **source categories:** the *external* (global) environment, the *societal* environment of the nation, the *governmental* setting in which policy making occurs, the *roles* occupied by policymakers, and the *individual* characteristics of foreign policy-making elites. Clearly each of these categories encompasses a much larger group of more discrete variables, but together they help us to think systematically about the forces that shape America's foreign policy. Thus they suggest guidelines for assessing the performance of the United States in world politics and the conditions that will determine its course in the new millennium.

THE SOURCES OF AMERICAN FOREIGN POLICY

Our analytical framework says that each of the broadly defined sources of American foreign policy is a *causal agent* that helps to explain why the United States behaves in world politics as it does. The five causal agents together paint this portrait, as illustrated in Figure 2.1. It describes a theoretical *funnel of causality*[1] that shows how the five sources collectively shape what the United States does abroad.

The figure depicts the *inputs* to the foreign policy-making process as the external, societal, governmental, role, and individual categories that make up the analytical framework. The inputs give shape and direction to the actions the United States pursues abroad, which can be thought of as the *outputs* of the foreign *policy-making process*. In the language of scientific inquiry, the foreign policy behavior of the United States is the **dependent variable**—*what* we hope to explain—and the source categories and the variables they comprise the **independent variables**—*how* we hope to explain it.

Note, however, that whether we are attempting to explain a single foreign policy event or a sequence of related behaviors, no source category by itself fully determines foreign policy behavior. Instead, the categories are interrelated and *collectively* determine foreign policy decisions, and hence foreign policy outputs. They do so in two ways:

1. by generating the necessity for foreign policy decisions that result in foreign policy action, and

2. by influencing the decision-making process that converts inputs into outputs.

The policy-making process is what converts inputs into outputs. Here is where those responsible for the nation's foreign policy make the actual choices that affect its destiny. The process is complex because of its many participants and because policy-making procedures cannot be divorced from all of the multiple sources that shape decision makers' responses to situations demanding action. Still, we can think of the foreign policy-making process as the *intervening variable* that links foreign policy inputs (independent variables) into outputs (dependent variables). Although it is sometimes difficult to separate the process from the resulting product, once that conversion has been made we can begin to examine the recurring behaviors that describe and explain how the United States responds to the world around it.

Figure 2.1 also tells us something about the constraints under which policy makers must operate, as each of the interrelated sources of American foreign policy is "nested" within an ever-larger set of variables. The framework views individual decision makers as constrained by their policy-making roles, which typically are defined by their positions within the policy-making institutions comprising the governmental source category. Those governmental variables in turn are cast within their more encompassing societal setting, which is nested within an even larger international environment consisting of other states, nonstate actors, and global trends and issues to which the United States, as a global actor, believes it must respond.

EXPLAINING POLICY PATTERNS

Our framework's attention to the multiple sources of American foreign policy implicitly rejects the widespread impulse to search for its single cause, whose simplicity most of us intuitively find satisfying. Political pundits who seek to shape policy opinion often use the rhetoric of particular explanations to promote their political causes. For some, the seemingly dictatorial powers of private interest groups, who are often thought to put their personal gain ahead of the national interest, explain what the United States does abroad, and why. For others, the predatory characteristics of its capitalist economic system explain the nation's global impulses. Both "explanations" of American foreign policy may contain kernels of truth, and under some circumstances they may account for certain aspects of policy more accurately than competing explanations. However, because foreign policy actions almost invariably result from multiple sources, we are well advised to think in *multicausal* terms if our goal is to move beyond rhetoric toward an understanding of the complex reality underlying the nation's foreign policy.

Our antipathy toward single-factor explanations of American foreign policy is based in part on empirical observation and in part on the logic underlying the analytical framework we employ. Let us turn, therefore, to a fuller explication of the source categories that organize and inform our later analyses.

External Sources

The **external source category** refers to the attributes of the international system and to the characteristics and behaviors of the state and non-state actors comprising it. It includes all "aspects of America's external environment or any actions occurring abroad that condition or otherwise influence the choices made by its officials." "Geographical 'realities' and ideological challenges from potential aggressors" that shape the decisions of foreign policy officials are obvious examples (Rosenau 1980), as are more structural elements such as changing distributions of power, rising interdependence, expansive globalization, and the like. Thus the external source category draws attention to the characteristics of other states, how they act toward the United States, and how their attributes and actions influence American foreign policy behavior. Broadly speaking, then, the external category refers to the impact of the state of the world on the United States.

The idea that a nation's foreign policy is conditioned by the world around it enjoys a long tradition and wide following. *Political realists* in particular argue that the distribution of power in the international system, more than anything else, influences how its member states act. States in turn are motivated to acquire power to their own advantage. Because all states are assumed to be motivated by the same drives, the principal way to understand international politics and foreign policy, according to this perspective, is to monitor the interactions of states in the international arena or, in other words, to focus on the external source category.

Political realists' perspective is compelling and will inform much of our analyses in the chapters that follow, especially in Chapters 6 and 7. Still, we must be cautious before accepting the proposition that the external environment alone dictates foreign policy. Instead, it is more reasonable to assume that "factors external to the actor can become determinants only as they affect the mind, the heart, and the will of the decision maker. A human decision to act in a specific way . . . necessarily represents the last link in the chain of antecedents of any act of policy. A geographical set of conditions, for instance, can affect the behavior of a nation only as specific persons perceive and interpret these conditions" (Wolfers 1962). Thus external factors alone cannot determine how the United States behaves in world politics, but they do exert a powerful influence.

Societal Sources

The *societal source category* comprises those characteristics of the domestic social and political system that shape its orientation toward the world. Robert Dallek's *The American Style of Foreign Policy: Cultural Politics and Foreign Affairs* (1983) and Richard Payne's *The Clash with Distant Cultures: Values, Interests, and Force in American Foreign Policy* (1995) are illustrative interpretations of American foreign policy that rest on societal explanations. Neo-Marxist critics of American foreign policy, whose once popular views identified its driving forces as the nation's capitalist economic system and its need to safeguard foreign markets for American economic exploitation, also rely on societal variables. Similarly, if we recall how American territorial expansion and imperialism in the nineteenth century were often rationalized by references to *manifest destiny* and the belief that Americans were a "chosen people" with a divine right to expand, we find many accounts that argue that American ideological preferences influenced American policies toward peoples outside the state's territorial jurisdiction.

Because American foreign policy is deeply rooted in its history and culture, the impact of societal forces is potentially strong. As one analyst pointedly argued, "To change [America's] foreign policy, its internal structure must change" (Isaak 1977). In Chapters 8 and 9 we will give special attention to the impact of societal variables on American foreign policy.

Governmental Sources

Richard Nixon once noted "If we were to establish a new foreign policy for the era to come, we had to begin with a basic restructuring of the process by which policy is made." Jimmy Carter echoed this theme repeatedly in his 1976 presidential campaign by maintaining that to change policy one must first change the machinery that produces it. Ronald Reagan offered a variant on that theme in 1980, arguing that the greatest policy failures in the past could be attributed to the "excessive growth and unnecessary size of government." Bill Clinton's "reinventing government" program continued in that tradition, seeking to implement more successful foreign and domestic policies by making government work more efficiently.

The assumption underlying these viewpoints is that the way the U.S. government is organized for making foreign policy decisions affects the substance of American policy. This is the core notion of a governmental influence on foreign policy. Thus the *governmental source category* refers "to those aspects of a government's structure that limit or enhance the foreign policy choices made by decision makers" (Rosenau 1980).

Notable is that the new Bush administration came into office committed to pursuing a lower government profile than had the Clinton administration. However, it found that the traumatic impact of the September 2001 terrorist attacks required a dramatic infusion of government spending, with subsidies directed to the beleaguered airline industry in particular. Often, war is a boon to the American economy. In this case it forecast a bust, requiring the president to abandon his personal preferences to the demands of role-induced restraints designed to ensure a careful monitoring of monetary and fiscal restraint during times of economic crisis.

Governmental variables are more likely to constrain what the United States can do abroad and the speed with which it can do it than to enhance its ability to act with innovation and dispatch. The constitutional division of power between the executive and legislative branches of government stands out. It promotes policy compromise and incrementalism over policy innovation. As the French political sociologist Alexis de Tocqueville ([1835] 1969) observed, "Foreign politics demand scarcely any of those qualities which a democracy possesses; and they require, on the contrary, the perfect use of almost all those faculties in which it is deficient." We will examine governmental source variables in Chapters 10, 11, and 12.

Role Sources

The structure of government and the roles that people occupy within it are closely intertwined. The *role source category* refers to the impact of the office on the behavior of its occupant. Roles are important because decision makers indisputably are influenced by the socially prescribed behaviors and legally sanctioned norms attached to the positions they occupy. Because the positions they occupy shape their behavior, policy outcomes are inevitably influenced by the roles extant in the policy-making arena.

Role theory goes far in explaining why, for example, American presidents act, once in office, so much like their predecessors and why each has come to view American interests and goals in terms so similar to the images maintained by previous occupants of the Oval Office. Roles, it seems, determine behavior more than do the qualities of individuals.[2] Perhaps this explains why Jimmy Carter proved to be a less liberal president than many Democrats had expected, why Ronald Reagan was not as conservative a president as many Republicans had hoped, why Bill Clinton seemed to vacillate from one side of the political spectrum to the other, and why George W. Bush embraced "compassionate conservativism" to capture the middle of the political spectrum.

The role concept is also useful in explaining the kinds of policy decisions habitually made by and within the large bureaucratic organizations. Role pressures typically lead to attitudinal conformity within bureaucracies and to deference to their orthodox views. "To get along, go along" is a time-worn aphorism from which few in bureaucratic settings are immune. Because the "system" places a premium on behavioral consistency and constrains the capacity of individuals to make a policy impact, people at every level of government find it difficult to escape their roles by rocking the boat and challenging conventional thinking. Thus role restraints on policy innovation go a long way in explaining the resistance of American foreign policy to change even as the world changes. We examine their impact more completely in Chapter 13.

Individual Sources

Finally, our explanatory framework identifies as a fifth policy source the individual characteristics of decision makers—the skills, personalities, beliefs, and psychological predispositions that define the kind of people they are and the types of behavior they exhibit. The *individual source category* embraces the values, talents, and prior experiences that distinguish one policy maker from another and that distinguishes his or her foreign policy choices from others.

Clearly every individual is unique, so it is not difficult to accept the argument that what they might do in foreign policy settings will differ. Consider the following questions:

- Why did Secretary of State Dulles publicly insult Chou En-Lai of the People's Republic of China by refusing at the 1954 Geneva Conference to shake Chou's extended hand? Could it be that he viewed the Chinese leader as a symbol of an atheistic doctrine so abhorrent to his own values that he chose to scorn the symbol?

- Why did the United States persist in bombing North Vietnam for so long in the face of clear evidence that the policy of bombing the North Vietnamese into submission was failing and, if anything, was hardening their resolve to continue fighting? Could it be that President Johnson could not admit failure, and that he had a psychological need to preserve his positive self-image by "being right"?

- Why did the first President Bush personalize the war against Iraq following its invasion of Kuwait, demonizing Saddam Hussein as "another Hitler"? Did his belief that "history is biography" and his penchant for personal diplomacy cause him to view the war a contest between individual leaders rather than a conflict between competing national interests?

- Why, after campaigning vigorously in 1992 for a forceful U.S. response to ethnic cleansing in Bosnia, did Bill Clinton act so cautiously once he became president? Was his

reluctance a product of the Vietnam War, not only his lack of personal military experience at that time but also of the belief embraced by many of the Vietnam generation that negotiation and compromise are sometimes preferable to the use of force, even when dealing with aggressors?

- Why after such "low-expectations" for his presidency did George W. Bush rise to a leadership role as the nation's most self-assured "wartime president" since Franklin Roosevelt?

- Would leadership strategies have turned out differently if Al Gore had picked up the few errant Florida voters that would have led the Supreme Court to select him, not George W., as the nation's 43rd president?

Theories emphasizing the personal characteristics and experiences of political leaders enjoy considerable popularity. This is partly because democratic theory leads us to expect that individuals elected to high public office will be able either to sustain or to change public policy to accord with popular preferences, and because the electoral system compels aspirants for office to emphasize how their administration will be different from that of their opponents. However, in the same way that other single-factor explanations of American foreign policy are suspect, we must be wary of ascribing too much importance to the impact of individuals. Individuals may matter, and in some instances they clearly do, but the mechanisms through which individuals influence foreign policy outcomes are likely to be much more subtle than popular impressions would have us believe. This is the subject of Chapter 14.

THE MULTIPLE SOURCES OF AMERICAN FOREIGN POLICY

The explicitly multicausal perspective of our analytical framework begins with the premise that we must look in different places if we want to find the origins of American foreign policy; and it tells us where to look, thus providing a helpful guide to understand policy and how it is made. We can illustrate its utility using a strategy common among historians known as **counterfactual reasoning.** The strategy poses a series of questions which effectively drop a key variable from the equation and then asks us to speculate about what might have been. Regardless of how we might respond to the counterfactual questions, the simple act of posing them facilitates appreciation of the numerous forces shaping foreign policy. We can use counterfactual reasoning to highlight how we might assess the dominant theme of American foreign policy since World War II: the *containment* of the Soviet Union. Why was it so durable? Why did change come so gradually even as changes in world politics seemed to demand innovation?

To answer these questions, we must look in a variety of places. At the level of the international system, for instance, the advent of nuclear weapons and the subsequent fear of destruction from a Soviet nuclear attack promoted a status quo American policy designed primarily to deal with this paramount fear. Would the United States have acted differently over the fifty years of Cold War history had international circumstances been different? What if plans proposed by the United States immediately following World War II to establish an international authority to control nuclear know-how had succeeded? Might the Cold War never have started (Chace 1996)? What if Soviet leaders had decided against putting offensive nuclear weapons in Cuba in 1962, which precipitated the most dangerous crisis of the Cold War era? Would the absence of this challenge to United States' preeminence in the Western Hemisphere have reduced the superpowers' tendency in the years that followed to rely on nuclear deterrence and a strategy of *mutual assured destruction* to preserve peace? Might the Cold War have ended earlier by exposing nonmilitary weaknesses in the Soviet system, which reliance on military might to carry on the Cold War competition masked (Gaddis 1997)?

Consider also what might have occurred in the Cold War contest had developments in the United States unfolded differently. Would the preoccupation with Soviet communism have endured so long had nationalistic sentiments ("my country, right or wrong!") dissipated as the nation rapidly urbanized and its foreign-born population came increasingly from non-European countries? Or if a mobilized American public freed of fear of external enemies had revolted against the burdens of monstrously high levels of peacetime military expenditures? Or if the anticommunist, witch-hunting tactics Senator Joseph McCarthy initiated shortly after communist forces came to power in China in 1949 had been discredited from the start rather than later?

Or turn instead to the governmental sector. Would American foreign policy have changed more rapidly had foreign policy making not become dominated by the president and the presidency—if instead the balance between the executive and legislative branches anticipated in the Constitution had been preserved throughout the 1960s? Indeed, would American foreign policy have been different and more flexible if "Cold Warriors" had not populated the innermost circle of presidential advisers in the 1950s and 1960s and if career professionals within the foreign affairs bureaucracy had successfully challenged their singular outlook?

Then consider whether the seemingly ideological orthodoxy America's anticommunist foreign policy of those responsible for it had experienced fewer pressures for conformity. Would the decisions reached during the Cold War decades have been different had decision-making roles been less institutionalized, encouraging advocacy of more diverse opinions? Might American policy makers have sought more energetically to move, in George Bush's words "beyond containment," prior to his presidency had policy making roles encouraged more long-range planning and less timidity in responding to new opportunities?

Finally, consider the hypothetical prospects for change in American policy had other individuals risen to positions of power during this period. Would the cornerstone of American postwar policy have been so virulently anticommunist if

Franklin Roosevelt had lived out his fourth term in office? If Adlai Stevenson and not Dwight Eisenhower had been responsible for American policy throughout the 1950s? If Kennedy's attempt to improve relations with the Soviets had not been terminated by an assassin's bullet? If Hubert Humphrey had managed to obtain the 400,000 extra votes in 1968 that would have made him, and not Nixon, president? If George McGovern's call for America to "come home" had enabled him to keep Nixon from a second term? If Ronald Reagan's bid to turn Jimmy Carter out of office in 1980 had failed? If the 1988 election—a time of dramatic developments in Eastern Europe and the Soviet Union—had put Michael Dukakis in the Oval Office instead of George Bush?

Moving beyond the Cold War, would the United States' response to Iraq's invasion of Kuwait have been the same if Bill Clinton—the first American president born after World War II and whose formative years included the war in Vietnam—had been in the White House instead of George Bush, a World War II Navy combat pilot? Or would Clinton, too, have found that the responsibilities of his office moved him inexorably in the direction of a military response to Iraq's aggressive challenge? In short, would different policy makers with different personalities, psychological needs, and political dispositions have made a difference in American foreign policy during the Cold War and its immediate aftermath?

Counterfactual historiography based on "what-if" questions rarely reveals clearcut answers about "what might have been." Asking the questions, however, makes us more aware of the problem of tracing causation by forcing us to consider different possibilities and influences. Thus, to answer even partially the question "Why does the United States act the way it does in its foreign policy relations?" we need to examine each of its major sources. Collectively, these identify the many constraints and stimuli facing the nation's decision makers, thus providing insight into the factors that promote continuity and change in America's relations with others.

LOOKING AHEAD

We begin our inquiry into the pattern and process of American foreign policy in Part II, where we examine the goals and instruments of policy. We will show there that the central themes of American foreign policy and the enduring patterns of behavior that both reveal and sustain them are marked by persistence and continuity, even in the face of dramatic changes and challenges at home and abroad. The values of freedom, democracy, peace, and prosperity that animate American foreign policy have not always resulted in similar goals and tactics in the face of changing circumstances at home or abroad. But they have endured, thus contributing to a long-term consistency in American foreign policy.

Then, recognizing that the multiple sources of American foreign policy constrain decision makers' latitude, we will conduct our exploration of the causes of America's foreign policy persistence and continuity in descending order of the "spatial magnitude" of each of the explanatory categories. We turn first to the external environment (Part III), the most comprehensive of the categories influencing decision makers. Next we will examine societal sources (Part IV) and then proceed to the way in which the American political system is organized for foreign policy making (Part V). From there we will shift focus again to role sources (Part VI), which partly flow from and are closely associated with the governmental setting. Finally, we will consider the importance of individual personalities, preferences, and predispositions in explaining foreign policy outcomes (Part VII).

By looking at external, societal, governmental, role, and individual sources of American policy independently, we can examine the causal impact that each exerts on America's behavior toward the rest of the world. Our survey will show that certain factors are more important in some instances than in others. In Chapter 15, where we probe the future of American foreign policy, we will speculate about how interrelationships among the sources of American foreign policy might affect its course in the new century.

KEY TERMS RELATED TO ANALYTICAL PERSPECTIVES
ON AMERICAN FOREIGN POLICY

causal agent

counterfactual reasoning

dependent variable

external source category

foreign policy

funnel of causality

governmental source category

independent variables

individual source category

intervening variable

Manifest Destiny

multicausal

political realists

role source category

societal source category

source categories

SUGGESTIONS FOR FURTHER READING

Brown, Seyom. *The Faces of Power: Constancy and Change in United States Foreign Policy from Truman to Clinton.* New York: Columbia University Press, 1994.

Bucklin, Steven J. *Realism and American Foreign Policy: Wilsonians and the Kennan-Morgenthau Thesis.* Westport, CT: Praeger Publishers, 2000.

Greenstein, Fred I. and John P. Burke. *How Presidents Test Reality: Decisions on Vietnam, 1954 and 1965.* New York: Russell Sage Foundation, 1989.

Hermann, Charles F. "Changing Course: When Governments Choose to Redirect Foreign Policy," *International Studies Quarterly* 34 (March 1990): 3–21.

Hogan, Michael J., and Thomas G. Paterson, eds., *Explaining the History of American Foreign Relations.* New York: Cambridge, 1991.

Hudson, Valerie M. "Foreign Policy Analysis Yesterday, Today, and Tomorrow," *Mershon International Studies Review* 39 (October 1995): 209–238.

Ikenberry, G. John. *American Foreign Policy: Theoretical Essays.* New York: Longman, 1999.

Mastanduno, Michael, David A. Lake, and G. John Ikenberry. "Toward a Realist Theory of State Action," *International Studies Quarterly* 33 (December 1989): 457–74.

Neack, Laura, Jeanne A. K. Hey, and Patrick J. Haney, eds., *Foreign Policy Analysis: Continuity and Change in Its Second Generation.* Englewood Cliffs, NJ: Prentice Hall, 1995.

Smith, Steven M. *Foreign Policy Adaptation.* New York: Nichols, 1981.

Zelikow, Philip. "Foreign Policy Engineering: From Theory to Practice and Back Again," *International Security* 18 (Spring 1994): 143–71.

NOTES

1. The funnel metaphor draws on the classic study of the American voter by Angus Campbell, Philip E. Converse, Warren E. Miller, and Donald E. Stokes (1960).

2. The view that the office makes the person has been expressed thus:

If we accept the proposition . . . that certain fundamentals stand at the core of American foreign policy, we could argue that any president is bound, even dictated to, by those basic beliefs and needs. In other words, he has little freedom to make choices wherein his distinctive style, personality, experience, and intellect shape America's role and position in international relations in a way that is uniquely his. It might be suggested that a person's behavior is a function not of his individual traits but rather of the office that he holds and that the office is circumscribed by the larger demands of the national interest, rendering individuality inconsequential.

(PATERSON 1979, 93)

PART II

Patterns of American Foreign Policy

CHAPTER 3

Principle, Power, and Pragmatism:

The Goals of American Foreign Policy in Historical Perspective

The ultimate test of our foreign policy is how well our actions measure up to our ideals. . . . Freedom is America's purpose.
SECRETARY OF STATE MADELEINE K. ALBRIGHT, 1998

We have a place, all of us, in a long story . . . of a new world that became a friend and liberator of the old, a story of a slave-holding society that became a servant of freedom, the story of a power that went into the world to protect but not possess, to defend but not to conquer.
PRESIDENT GEORGE W. BUSH, 2001

Peace and prosperity, stability and security, democracy and defense—these are the enduring values and interests of American foreign policy. Freedom from the dictates of others, commercial advantage, and promotion of American ideas and ideals are among the persistent foreign policy goals tied to these values and interests. *Isolationism* and *internationalism* are competing strategies the nation has tried during its two-century history as means to its policy ends. Historically these strategies have also been closely intertwined with *idealism* and *realism,*

competing visions of the nature of humankind, of international politics and states' foreign policy motivations, and of the problems and prospects for achieving a peaceful and just world order.

During World War I Woodrow Wilson articulated the premises of *idealism,* summarizing them in a famous speech before Congress in January 1918 which contained fourteen points. They included a call for open diplomacy, freedom of the seas, removal of barriers to trade, self-determination, general disarmament, and, most importantly, abandonment of the balance-of-power system of international politics—an "arrangement of power and of suspicion and of dread"—in favor of a new, **collective security** system grounded in an international organization, the League of Nations. Under the system envisioned by Wilson, states would pledge themselves to join together to oppose aggression by any state whenever and wherever it occurred. Together, Wilson's revolutionary ideas called for a new world order completely alien to the experiences of the European powers which lay exhausted from four years of bitter war.

Europe's bloody history led its leaders to embrace **political realism,** not idealism, as an approach the problem of war. For them *realpolitik,* as realism is sometimes called, translated into a foreign policy based on rational calculations of power and the national interest. The approach built on the political philosophy of the sixteenth-century Italian theorist Niccolò Machiavelli, who emphasized in *The Prince* a political calculus based on interest, prudence, and expediency above all else, notably morality. Moral crusades, like "making the world safe for democracy," as Wilson had sought with U.S. entry into World War I, are anathema to realist thinking. Similarly, "realists view conflict as a natural state of affairs rather than a consequence that can be attributed to historical circumstances, evil leaders, flawed sociopolitical systems, or inadequate international understanding and education" (Holsti 1995).[1] In contrast, "Wilson's idea of world order derived from Americans' faith in the essentially peaceful nature of man and an underlying harmony of the world. It followed that democratic nations were, by definition, peaceful; people granted self-determination would no longer have reason to go to war or to oppress others. Once all the peoples of the world had tasted of the blessings of peace and democracy, they would surely rise as one to defend their gains" (Kissinger 1994a).

American history and American foreign policy have never been free of the debate between idealists and realists or from contentions about the role of ideals and self-interest. As one former policy maker observed in the aftermath of the Persian Gulf War, "we and the British . . . are still divided about whether the foreign policy of a democracy should be concerned primarily with the structure and dynamics of world politics, the balance of power, and the causes of war, or whether we should leave such cold and dangerous issues to less virtuous and more cynical peoples, and concentrate only on the vindication of liberty and democracy" (Rostow 1993).

In Part II of *American Foreign Policy: Pattern and Process* we examine the goals and instruments of American foreign policy over the course of the nation's history and the strategies and tactics used to realize them. We begin in this chapter with a brief look at the nation's philosophy and behavior as it first sought to ensure its independence and then expanded to become a continental nation and eventually an imperial power. *Isolationism* dominated thinking (if not always action) during this period, and it reasserted itself between World Wars I and II, interludes when the United States, contrary to isolationist warnings, participated actively in European balance-of-power politics. We then turn to the decades-long Cold War contest between the United States and the Soviet Union. This was a time of *internationalism,* indeed, *global activism,* as the United States actively sought to shape the structure of world peace and security. We conclude with a discussion of contemporary issues that illustrate the continuing contention among power, principle, and pragmatism as the United States faces a new century.

We continue our inquiry in Chapters 4 and 5, where we direct primary attention to America's rise to globalism in the decades following World War II. We will examine how military might and interventionism were brought into the service of America's foreign policy goals during the Cold War and ask about their continued relevance.

PRINCIPLE AND PRAGMATISM, 1776–1941: ISOLATIONISM, EXPANSIONISM, AND IMPERIALISM

Two motivations stimulated the colonists who came to America two centuries ago: "material advantages and utopian hopes" (Gilbert 1961). Freedom from England and, more broadly, from the machinations of Europe's great powers became necessary for their realization. Thomas Paine, a revolutionary pamphleteer famed for his *Common Sense,* expressed shock that "America, without the right of asking why, must be brought into all the wars of another, whether the measure be right or wrong, or whether she will or not." The seeds of nonentanglement and isolationism were sown in this environment. Paine again: "It is the true interest of America to steer clear of European contentions, which she never can do, while, by her dependence on Britain, she is made the make-weight in the scale of British politics."

Paine also worried that freedom was at stake. "The New World had become 'the asylum for the persecuted lovers of civil and religious liberty,' while in England 'a corrupt and faithless court' abused liberty, and elsewhere in the Old World liberty was simply denied. Americans were thus marked out as the keepers of the flickering flame of liberty" (Hunt 1987). John Winthrop, leader of Massachusetts Bay colonists of the early 1600s, urged that his followers consider themselves as a "city upon a hill"—a phrase used repeatedly by American leaders from the founding of the Republic to Ronald Reagan two centuries later—to affirm the view that the new nation was somehow different from all others. Thus was born a critical element in the nation's cherished political mythology—not only was it separate from the rest of the world, but it was also a model for others to emulate.

John Adams, another revolutionary patriot and the new nation's second president, urged that "we should separate ourselves, as far as possible and as long as possible, from all European politics and wars." George Washington had enshrined that reasoning in the nation's enduring convictions when he warned the nation in his farewell address to "steer clear of permanent alliances with any portion of the foreign world." "Why," he asked, "by interweaving our destiny with that of any part of Europe, entangle our peace and prosperity in the toils of European ambition, rivalship, interest, humor, or caprice?" He worried that participation in balance-of-power politics with untrustworthy and despotic European governments would lead to danger abroad and the loss of democratic freedoms at home. If the country interacted with corrupt governments it would become like them: Lie down with dogs, get up with fleas. Ironically, however, an alliance with France was the critical ingredient in ensuring the success of the American revolution.

Hamilton, Jefferson, and American Continentalism

With freedom won, the new Americans now had to preserve it. Thomas Jefferson and Alexander Hamilton posed alternative postures to meet the challenge and to move the nation beyond it—toward greatness.[2] Jefferson, Washington's secretary of state and the nation's third president, saw the preservation of liberty as the new nation's quintessential goal. For him, a policy of aloofness—*isolationism*—was the best way to preserve and develop the nation as a free people. He echoed Washington's concern as the United States faced a second war with Britain: "We especially ought to pray that the powers of Europe may be so poised and counterpoised among themselves that their own security may require the presence of all their forces at home leaving the other parts of the world in undisturbed tranquility."

Jefferson recognized that foreign trade was necessary to secure markets for American agricultural exports and essential imports. Thus he was prepared to negotiate commercial treaties with others and to protect the nation's ability to trade. "For that, however, the country needed no more than a few diplomats and a small navy. 'To aim at such a navy as the greater nations of Europe possess, would be a foolish and wicked waste of the energies of our countrymen'" (Hunt 1987).

Hamilton, the first secretary of the Treasury, offered quite different prescriptions. Beginning with assumptions about human nature central to the perspective of classical realism—that, in his words, "men are ambitious, vindictive, and rapacious"—Hamilton concluded pessimistically that "conflict was the law of life. States no less than men were bound to collide over those ancient objects of ambition: wealth and glory" (Hunt 1987). Thus the goals of American foreign policy were clear: develop the capabilities necessary to enable the United States to be (again in Hamilton's own words) "ascendant in the system of American affairs . . . and able to dictate the terms of the connection between the old and the new world!"

Hamilton's immediate impact on American political life ended when he was fatally wounded in a duel with Aaron Burr in 1804, but the influence of his ideas on foreign and domestic policy and the perceived need for strong executive leadership continued. As president, for example, Jefferson himself acted in Hamiltonian ways: He threatened an alliance with Britain to counter France's reacquisition of the Louisiana territory ceded to Spain in the 1763 Treaty of Paris and, having acquired it, threatened to take the Floridas from Spain. The power of the presidency grew accordingly.

Jefferson was more interested in the port of New Orleans as a vehicle to promote commercialism abroad than in all of the vast Louisiana territory, but the territorial expansion of the United States continued in the half-century following the Louisiana Purchase. The Floridas and portions of Canada were annexed next, followed by Texas, the Pacific Northwest, and California and portions of the present-day southwestern United States. The war with Mexico, precipitated by President James K. Polk, led to Mexico's cession of the vast California territory. Polk's threatened military action over the Oregon Country also helped to add the Northwest to the new nation. The expansionist spirit that animated these episodes is reflected in the policy rhetoric of their proponents. In 1846, for example, William H. Seward, who later became secretary of state, pledged, "I will engage to give you the possession of the American continent and the control of the world."

By mid-century the United States had expanded from sea to shining sea (see Map 3.1). *Manifest Destiny,* the widespread belief that it was the destiny of the United States to spread across the continent, captured the nation's mood. In the process, however, conflict over how to treat the issue of slavery in the newly acquired territories rended American society and politics. Four years of civil war suspended the progress of America's manifest destiny. It also resulted in more American casualties than any other conflict in the nation's history.

A Nation Apart

Beginning in 1796, the Napoleonic Wars raged in Europe intermittently for nearly two decades. Although the War of 1812, the North American theater of this conflict, briefly involved the United States in the Europeans' competition for "wealth and glory," the years following it saw isolationism take on the trappings of "a divine privilege, the perceived outcome of American national wisdom and superior virtue" (Serfaty 1972). Manifest destiny embodied the conviction that Americans had a higher purpose to serve in the world than others. Theirs was not only a special privilege but also a special charge: to protect liberty and to promote freedom. That purpose was served best by isolating the American republic from the rest of the world, not becoming involved in it.

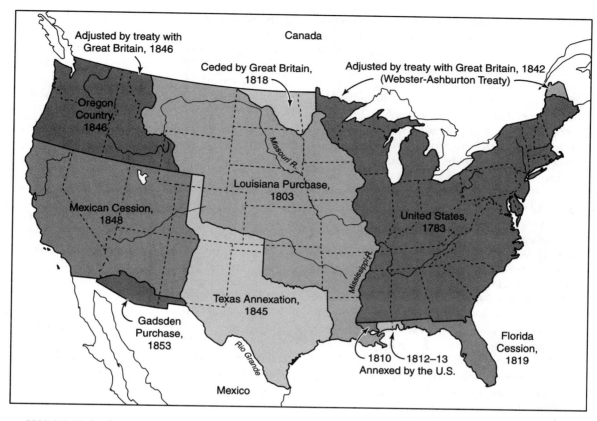

MAP 3.1 Birth of a Continental Nation: U.S. Territorial Expansion by the Mid-Nineteenth Century

Source: Walter LaFeber, *The American Age: United States Foreign Policy at Home and Abroad*, 2nd ed. New York: Norton, 1994, 132.

In 1823, President James Monroe sought to remove the United States from Europe's intrigues by distancing himself from its ongoing quarrels. In a message to Congress he declared the Western Hemisphere "hands off" from European encroachment: "We owe it . . . to candor and to the amicable relations existing between the United States and [European] powers to declare that we should consider any attempt on their part to extend their system to any portion of this hemisphere as dangerous to our peace and safety." What would later be known as the ***Monroe Doctrine*** in effect said that the New World would not be subject to the same forces of colonization perpetrated by the Europeans on others.

Little noticed at the time, Monroe's declaration shaped thinking about interventionism and the role and responsibilities of the United States toward its hemispheric neighbors well into the twentieth century.

Intrigue with foreign powers punctuated the contest between North and South during the Civil War, but in its aftermath the state turned inward—a pattern repeated in the twentieth century. Even as it focused on reconstruction, however, the nation's expansionist drive continued. Alaska was purchased from Russia in the 1860s, and Native Americans in the West were systematically subdued as the United States consolidated its continental domain. Here Manifest Destiny was little more than a crude euphemism for a policy of expulsion and extermination of Native Americans who were, in contemporary terminology, "nonstate nations." Thereafter, the advocates of expansionism increasingly coveted Cuba, Latin America, Hawaii, and various Asian lands. Not until the end of the nineteenth century, however, would the United States assert its Manifest Destiny beyond the North American continent—this time in pursuit of empire. By then, moralism had become closely intertwined with the Americans' perception that they were a nation apart, one with a special mission in world politics.

Democratic promotion—to *make the world safe for democracy*—would dominate much of American foreign policy in the twentieth century, but in the nineteenth it sought liberty. Equality and democracy were not typically within its purview. Democracy refers to political processes. Today we describe a country as democratic if "nearly everyone can vote, elections are freely contested, and the chief executive is chosen by popular vote or by an elected parliament, and civil rights and civil liberties are substantially guaranteed" (Russett 1998). *Liberty* (individual freedom) and *liberalism* (the advocacy of liberty) instead focus on individual freedom. Not until the 1830s, with the election of Andrew Jackson, could the United States begin to be properly called a democracy. At that time *Alexis de Tocqueville,* a French political sociologist, published his famous treatise *Democracy in America,* which focused on the role that ordinary people played in its political processes as he described America's uniqueness.

Although the American republic was the champion of liberty in its first century, its approach was *passive,* not active. It chose to act as an example, "a beacon of light on liberty," demonstrating to the world how a free society could run its affairs and holding itself as a model for others to emulate. But the United States would *not* assume responsibility for the world, even in the name of freedom; it would *not* be an agent of international reform, seeking to impose on others its way of life. Secretary of State John Quincy Adams prescribed the nation's appropriate world role in an often-quoted speech, delivered on July 4, 1821. "Wherever the standard of freedom and independence has been or shall be unfurled, there will [America's] heart, her benedictions, and her prayers be. But she goes not abroad in search of monsters to destroy" (see also Kennan 1995).

The United States was not unengaged, however. Even as its ideals colored its self-perceptions, pragmatism dictated the exercise of power. Crises and military engagements with European powers and Native Americans were recurrent as the nation expanded across the continent. Elsewhere the rule was **unilateralism,** not acting in concert with others. Thus the United States alone fostered the creation of Liberia in the 1820s, opened Japan to commercial relations in the 1850s, and scrambled to control Samoa in the 1880s. Then, in 1895, it asserted its self-proclaimed Monroe Doctrine prerogatives against the British in a dispute involving Venezuela. The United States now effectively claimed that it alone enjoyed supremacy in the Western Hemisphere, and it was evident that the United States had the capability to back its claim. In the decades following the Civil War the United States emerged as the world's major industrial power. By 1900 it had surpassed Great Britain as the world's leading producer of coal, iron, steel, and textiles. The stage was being set for the United States to assume Britain's mantle as the world's leading economic power and rule maker—a global hegemon.

Isolationism under Siege: Imperialism and Interventionism

Diplomatic historians credit jingoistic "yellow journalism" (press sensationalism) with a role in provoking the United States to declare war against Spain in 1898. In fact, multiple motives—all centered on Cuba, which for several years had engaged in insurrection against Spain—caused President William McKinley to seek congressional authorization for the use of force to end the Cuban war. They ranged from humanitarian concerns to commercial interests and growing expansionist sentiments. Senator Albert Beveridge, speaking in 1898, for example, referred to Americans as "a conquering race." "We must obey our blood," he urged, "and occupy new markets and if necessary new lands."

With victory in the "splendid little war" with Spain, the United States gained a primary goal: suzerainty over Cuba. The Philippines now also became a U.S. territory in the Pacific, joining Hawaii, which had been annexed in 1898. Puerto Rico and Guam also joined the new imperium. The United States was suddenly transformed into an imperial power rivaling the great powers of Europe. Thus the Spanish-American War is properly regarded as a watershed in American foreign policy, as it opened a new era in America's relations with the rest of the world.

McKinley eschewed outright annexation of Cuba, but the Philippines posed a more vexing choice. McKinley was interested principally in the port at Manila, and he worried about the problem of governing the Filipinos. The popular story of how McKinley decided to colonize the Philippines came from his revelation before church leaders in 1899:

> I walked the floor of the White House night after night until midnight; and I am not ashamed to tell you . . . that I went down on my knees and prayed Almighty God for light and guidance more than one night. And one night it came to me. . . . [T]here was nothing left to do but take them all, and educate the Filipinos, and uplift and civilize them as our fellow-men. . . . And then I went to bed, and . . . slept soundly.
>
> (LAFEBER 1994, 213)

Although historians are skeptical of this story, they do not deny that the United States then embarked on a project that persists until the present—to sponsor democracy elsewhere. First, however, it was necessary to put down a Filipino rebellion, which proved to be a bloody, four-year battle, "the first of many antirevolutionary wars fought by the United States in the twentieth century"

(LaFeber 1994). Only then could the United States concern itself with the Philippines' internal political processes. Attention to Philippine political development meant that democratic promotion—not just the abstraction of liberty—was now America's concern (Smith 1994a).

The McKinley administration is also credited with advancing American interests in China. In 1899 John Hay, McKinley's secretary of state, sought to enlist European support for the traditional nineteenth-century (unilateral) American policy of free competition for trade with China—that is, an **Open Door policy** toward China. In 1900 he advised European powers in the second of his "open-door notes" that the United States would not tolerate the division of China into "spheres of influence," insisting instead that its territorial integrity be respected. Regarded by some as an expression of the United States' growing foreign commercial interests and by others as an expression of American moralism and naiveté about balance-of-power politics, the Open Door was also based on a pragmatic appraisal of American power. Hay himself advised McKinley in terms Alexander Hamilton would surely have approved: "The inherent weakness of our position is this: we do not want to rob China ourselves, and our public opinion will not permit us to interfere, with an army, to prevent others from robbing her. Besides, we have no army. The talk of the papers about 'our preeminent moral position giving the authority to dictate to the world' is mere flap-doodle" (LaFeber 1994).

Foreign policy issues figured prominently in the election of 1900. William Jennings Bryan, the Democratic Party candidate and later Woodrow Wilson's secretary of state, carried the anti-imperialist banner. Theodore (Teddy) Roosevelt, McKinley's vice presidential running mate, was the champion of imperialism. Roosevelt had served in the Navy Department early in the McKinley administration and, with Captain Alfred Mahan, an early geopolitical strategic thinker, had promoted the development of sea power as a route to American greatness. Roosevelt succeeded to the presidency when an assassin's bullet felled McKinley. The shooting occurred only one day after McKinley claimed, in a speech on America's new world role, that "isolation is no longer possible or desirable."

Roosevelt is remembered for speaking softly while carrying a big stick. A leader of the "Rough Riders" during the Spanish-American War as well as an advocate of strong naval power, Roosevelt's presidency (1901–1909) was marked by a series of power assertions and interventions, primarily in Latin America. The United States forced Haiti to clear its debts with European powers, fomented insurrection in Panama to win its independence from Colombia and secure American rights for a trans-isthmian canal, established a financial protectorate over the Dominican Republic, and occupied Cuba. Roosevelt also mediated the end of the Russo-Japanese War (1904–1905), from which Japan emerged as an increasingly aggressive Far Eastern power.

Many of Roosevelt's specific actions were rationalized in his corollary to the Monroe Doctrine. In 1904, in response to economic chaos in the Dominican Republic which threatened foreign involvement, Roosevelt announced to Congress that "the adherence of the United States to the Monroe Doctrine may force the United States, however reluctantly, . . . to the exercise of international police power." In fact, however, the *Roosevelt Corollary* went well beyond Monroe's initial intentions (LaFeber 1994). The United States would now oppose Latin American revolutions, not support them. It would not only oppose European intervention into hemispheric affairs but support its own. It would use American power to bring hemispheric economic affairs under its tutelage. And it would now use military force to set hemispheric affairs straight, unlike Monroe who saw no need to flex military muscle. Thus the Roosevelt Corollary to the Monroe Doctrine set the stage for a new era in U.S. relations with its southern neighbors— most of whom came to resent the colossus to the North.

Roosevelt's rhetoric and behavior accorded well with the tenets of political realism as an imperial America faced the new century. Indeed, Roosevelt was the first U.S. president to embrace unambiguously the principles of power politics central to the realist view of international politics. Henry Kissinger, himself a prominent realist, describes Roosevelt's foreign policy approach approvingly:

> Like his predecessors, Roosevelt was convinced of America's beneficent role in the world. But unlike them, Roosevelt held that America had real foreign policy interests that went far beyond its interest in remaining unentangled. Roosevelt started from the premise that the United States was a power like any other, not a singular incarnation of virtue. If its interests collided with those of other countries, America had the obligation to draw on its strengths to prevail. . . . No other president defined America's world role so completely in terms of national interest, or identified the national interest so comprehensively with the balance of power.
>
> (KISSINGER 1994A, 38–39)

Dollar diplomacy describes the period from 1900 to 1913. As American business interests in the Caribbean and Central America mushroomed, the United States flexed its Roosevelt-Corollary principles and corresponding muscles to protect them. Roosevelt's interventionist tactics were continued by his successor, William Howard Taft, who at one point described his administration's policies as "substituting dollars for bullets." Hence the term "dollar diplomacy."

Little changed with Woodrow Wilson's election in 1912, as the data in Focus 3.1 make clear. Until the outbreak of war in Europe, Wilson was consumed by foreign policy challenges in China, Mexico, and the Caribbean, often resorting to military intervention to achieve his ends. "Determined to help other peoples become democratic and orderly, Wilson himself became the greatest military interventionist in U.S. history. By the time he left office in 1921, he had ordered troops into Russia and half a dozen Latin American upheavals" (LaFeber 1994). Intervention

---

FOCUS 3.1   Dawn of a New Millennium: The Use of American Armed Forces Abroad Initiated during the Roosevelt, Taft, and Wilson Administrations, 1901–1921

Theodore Roosevelt

1901 Columbia (State of Panama). U.S. troops protect American property and keep transit lines open on the isthmus during revolutionary disturbances.

1902 Colombia. U.S. forces protect American lives and property at Bocas del Toro during civil war.

1902 Colombia (State of Panama). U.S. troops are used to keep railroads running and to prevent the landing of Colombian troops in Panama.

1903 Honduras. U.S. forces protect the American consulate at Puerto Cortez.

1903 Dominican Republic. Marines land at Santo Domingo to protect American interests.

1903 Syria. U.S. forces protect the consulate in Beirut.

1903–1904 Abyssinia. Marines protect the U.S. Consul General during treaty negotiations.

1903–1914 Panama. U.S. forces protect American interests and lives following the revolution for independence for construction of the Panama canal.

1904 Dominican Republic. American and British forces establish a no-fighting zone and protect American lives and interests during revolutionary fighting.

1904 Tangier, Morocco. A marine guard lands to protect the consul general.

1904 Panama. U.S. troops protect American interests and lives at Ancon during a threatened insurrection.

1904–1905 Korea. A marine guard is sent to protect the American legation at Seoul during the Russo-Japanese War.

1906–1909 Cuba. U.S. forces seek to restore order, protect foreigners, and establish a stable government.

1907 Honduras. U.S. troops protect American interests in Trujillo, Ceiba, Puerto Cortez, San Pedro, Laguna, and Choloma during war between Honduras and Nicaragua.

William Howard Taft

1910 Nicaragua. U.S. forces protect American interests at Bluefields.

1911 Honduras. American troops protect American lives and interests during civil war.

1911 China. U.S. troops dispatched at various sites as the nationalist revolution approaches.

1912 Honduras. A small U.S. force temporarily lands at Puerto Cortez.

1912 Panama. U.S. troops supervise Panamanian elections outside the canal zone.

1912 Cuba. U.S. forces protect American interests in the province of Oriente and Havana.

1912 China. U.S. troops protect American lives and interests during revolutionary activities.

1912 Turkey. U.S. forces guard the American legation at Constantinople during the Balkan War.

1912–1925 Nicaragua. U.S. forces dispatched to protect American interests remain to promote peace and stability.

1912–1941 China. U.S. troops engage in continuing protective action following disorders that began with the Kuomintang rebellion.

Woodrow Wilson

1913 Mexico. U.S. marines evacuate American citizens and others.

1914 Haiti. U.S. forces protect American nationals.

1914 Dominican Republic. U.S. forces protect Puerto Plata and Santo Domingo City.

1914–1917 Mexico. Undeclared Mexican-American hostilities.

1915–1934 Haiti. U.S. forces maintain order during chronic threatened threatened insurrection.

1916 China. U.S. forces land to quell rioting on American property in Nanking.

1916–1924 Dominican Republic. U.S. forces maintain order during chronic threatened insurrection.

Continued

FOCUS 3.1   Continued

1917 China. U.S. troops land to protect American lives at Chungking.

1917–1918 Germany and Austria-Hungary. World War I.

1917–1922 Cuba. U.S. forces protect American interests during and following insurrection.

1918–1919 Mexico. U.S. troops enter Mexico pursuing bandits and fight Mexican troops at Nogales.

1918–1920 Panama. U.S. troops act as police during election disturbances and later.

1918–1920 Soviet Russia. U.S. troops protect the American consulate at Vladivostok and remain as part of an allied occupation force; later American troops intervene at Archangel in response to the Bolshevik revolution.

1919 Dalmatia. U.S. forces act as police in feud between Italians and Serbs.

1919 Turkey. U.S. marines protect the American consulate during the Greek occupation of Constantinople.

1919 Honduras. U.S. troops maintain order during attempted revolution.

1920 China. U.S. troops protect lives during a disturbance at Kiukiang.

1920 Guatemala. U.S. troops protect the American legation and interests.

1920–1922 Russia (Siberia). U.S. marines sent to protect U.S. radio station and property on Russian Island, Bay of Vladivostok.

SOURCE: Adapted from Ellen C. Collier, "Instances of Use of United States Armed Forces Abroad, 1778–1993," *CRS Report for Congress*, October 7, 1993.

---

arguably was not inconsistent with Wilsonian idealism, but in some sense it reflected its failure. "Wilson wanted elections, real change, order, and no foreign interventions—all at once," observes historian Walter LaFeber (1994). "He never discovered how to pull off such a miracle."

In May 1915 a German submarine torpedoed the *Lusitania,* pride of the British merchant marine. Nearly 1,200 lives were lost, including 128 Americans. The attack precipitated a crisis with the United States on the issue of neutrals' rights on the high seas. Wilson's attention now shifted from Asia and the Western Hemisphere to Europe, leading to U.S. intervention in World War I. Wilson also began to call for a new collective security system to replace the war-prone balance of power and for other fundamental reforms in international relations. However, Wilson's efforts to implement his vision failed during his lifetime. The refusal of the United States Senate to approve the Versailles peace settlement and U.S. membership in the League of Nations was a particularly devastating personal defeat for Wilson. Without American participation, the League itself was doomed to failure. Still, the principles

of Wilsonian idealism have never been extinguished. Indeed, the distinguished historian Walter LaFeber (1994) writes that Wilson was the first American president "to face the full blast of twentieth-century revolutions," and that his "responses made his policies the most influential in twentieth-century American foreign policy. 'Wilsonianism' became a term to describe later policies that emphasized internationalism and moralism and that were dedicated to extending democracy." We will return to that insight later in this chapter.

Isolationism Resurgent: Interwar Idealism and Withdrawal

The League of Nations as an American foreign policy program died in the presidential election of 1920. Warren G. Harding defeated Wilson, who was stricken with a debilitating stroke while campaigning for the League. Harding's foreign policy program called for a *return to normalcy,* effectively one that sought "relief from the burdens that international engagement brings" (Mandelbaum 1994).

Disillusionment with American involvement in World War I would eventually set in, undermining Americans' "confidence in the old symbols of internationalism and altruistic diplomacy" and their "assurance that America's mission should be one of magnanimous service to the rest of the world" (Osgood 1953). Disillusionment became especially prevalent in the 1930s, as isolationism again emerged as the dominant American foreign policy strategy. Initially, however, idealism was still accepted, perhaps out of popular indifference. Military intervention in Latin America and China also perpetuated the unilateralist thrust of American foreign policy evident even before the turn of the century.

Although the United States practiced interventionism during the 1920s, thus perpetuating a now firmly established policy pattern, American policy makers also enthusiastically pursued key elements of the idealist paradigm. With the Washington Naval Conference of 1921 the United States sought, through arms limitations, to curb a triangular naval arms race involving the United States, Japan, and Britain. A series of treaties designed to maintain the status quo in the Far East followed. The program conformed to idealist precepts, but no enforcement provisions were included. Thus realists argue that "the transient thrill afforded by the Washington Conference was miserable preparation for the test of political leadership provided by the ominous events that undermined the Far Eastern settlement a decade later" (Osgood 1953).

Realists also criticize the 1928 Pact of Paris, popularly known as the ***Kellogg-Briand Pact*** (after the U.S. secretary of state, Frank B. Kellogg, and the French foreign minister, Aristide Briand, who negotiated it). The agreement sought to deal with the problem of war by making it illegal. Realists thus regard it as "the perfect expression of the utopian idealism which dominated America's attempts to compose international conflicts and banish the threat of war in the interwar period. . . . The Pact of Paris simply declared that its signatories renounced war as an instrument of national policy. . . . It contained

absolutely no obligation for any nation to do anything under any circumstances" (Osgood 1953).[3]

The German reparations issue involved the United States intimately, but even here the United States sought detachment, not involvement in world affairs. During World War I the United States emerged as a *creditor nation*—that is, it sold more abroad than it bought (which remained true until the early 1970s). To finance sales to Britain and France during the war, it granted credits to the allied powers. After the war it insisted that the debts be repaid. Eventually debts became linked to German reparations, required under the punitive elements of the Treaty of Versailles which held Germany responsible for starting World War I. Various schemes were devised to settle the debt-reparations issue, but none proved satisfactory. The issue helped to estrange the United States from the European democracies as the economic depression of the 1930s set in and war clouds again overshadowed Europe.

As fascism rose during the 1930s and the world political economy fell into deep depression, neither the outlawry of war nor the principle of collective security stemmed the onslaught of renewed militarism. Germany, Italy, and Japan repeatedly challenged the post–World War I order, Britain and France seemed powerless to stop them, and the United States retreated into an isolationist shell. In the U.S. Senate a special committee chaired by the extreme isolationist Gerald P. Nye held hearings that attributed American entry into World War I to war profiteers— "merchants of death" they were called. Congress passed a series of neutrality acts between 1935 and 1937 whose purpose was to steer America clear of the emerging European conflict. The immediate application came in Spain, where General Francisco Franco, with the help of Hitler, sought to overthrow the Spanish republic and replace it with a fascist regime. The neutrality acts effectively barred the United States from assisting the antifascist forces.

The Great Depression reinforced isolationist sentiments in the United States. As noted earlier, Britain was the world's preeminent economic power in the nineteenth century. As the preponderant power in politics as well as economics—a global hegemon—it promoted an open international economic system based on free trade. Its power began to wane in the late nineteenth century, however. Following World War I, Britain's ability to exercise the leadership role necessary to maintain the open world political economy was severely strained. The United States was the logical candidate to assume this role, but it refused.[4] Britain's inability to exercise leadership and the United States' unwillingness to do so were primary causes of the Great Depression. Economic nationalism now became the norm. Tariffs erected by one nation to protect its economy from foreign inroads led to retaliation by others. The volume of international trade contracted dramatically, causing reduced living standards and rising economic hardship. Policy makers who sought to create a new world order following World War II would conclude that economic nationalism was a major cause of the breakdown of international peace. Indeed, the perceived connectedness of peace and prosperity is one of the major *lessons of the 1930s* that continues to inform American foreign policy even today.

Another lesson was learned when Britain's policy of trying to appease Hitler failed. In September 1938—meeting in Munich, Germany—Britain and France made an agreement with Hitler that permitted Nazi Germany to annex a large part of Czechoslovakia in return for what British Prime Minister Neville Chamberlain called "peace in our time." Instead, on September 1, 1939, Hitler attacked Poland. Britain and France, honoring their pledge to defend the Poles, declared war on Germany two days later. World War II had begun. The lesson drawn from the **Munich Conference**—that *aggressors cannot be appeased*—would also inform policy makers' thinking for decades to come.

In the two years that followed Hitler's initial onslaught against Poland—years that saw German attacks on France, Britain, and the Soviet Union—Franklin Roosevelt deftly nudged the United States away from its isolationist policies in support of the Western democracies. Germany's blatant exercise of machtpolitik (power politics) challenged the precepts of idealism that had buttressed the isolationism of the 1930s. Still, Roosevelt was careful not to jettison idealism as he prepared the nation for the coming conflict. He understood "that only a threat to their security could motivate [the American people] to support military preparedness. But to take them into a war, he knew he needed to appeal to their idealism in much the same way that Wilson had. . . . What he sought was to bring about a world community compatible with America's democratic and social ideals as the best guarantee of peace" (Kissinger 1994a).

In the spring of 1941 Congress passed and Roosevelt signed the **Lend–Lease Act.** The act permitted the United States to assist others deemed vital to the United States, thus committing the United States to the Allied cause against the Axis powers, Germany and Italy. The proposal provoked a bitter controversy in the United States. Senator Arthur Vandenberg, then a staunch isolationist (converted to internationalism after the war), remarked that Lend-Lease was the death-knell of isolationism: "We have tossed Washington's Farewell Address into the discard," he wrote in his diary. "We have thrown ourselves squarely into the power politics and the power wars of Europe, Asia, and Africa. We have taken a first step upon a course from which we can never hereafter retreat" (Serfaty 1972). The next step occurred when Japan attacked Pearl Harbor on December 7, 1941. No longer could America's geographic isolation from the world support its political isolation.

Technological change—the ability of Japan to strike at vital American interests thousands of miles from its own homeland—destroyed the rationale of isolationism. The diplomatic record of America's first century and a half does not, however, support the view that isolationism was an inappropriate policy. Isolationism is given a bad name, perhaps, because its practice during the 1930s removed the United States as an effective player in the European balance of power. Had it been involved—had it followed the prescriptions of realism or Wilsonian idealism—it might have helped avert the catastrophe of World War II. Still, it is important to emphasize that isolationism "never meant total isolation from the world," only "political detachment" (Deibel 1992). That it successfully nurtured the United States to the status of a great power is not easily dismissed—which is why even today (neo)isolationism continues its appeal.

With the onset of World War II, however, the United States began to reject its isolationist past. The ethos of *liberal internationalism*—"the intellectual and political tradition that believes in the necessity of leadership by liberal democracies in the construction of a peaceful world order through multilateral cooperation and effective international organizations" (Gardner 1990)—now animated the American people and their leaders as they embarked on a period of global activism not previously witnessed.

POWER AND PRINCIPLE, 1946–1989: GLOBAL ACTIVISM, ANTICOMMUNISM, AND CONTAINMENT

"Every war in American history," writes historian Arthur Schlesinger (1986), "has been followed in due course by skeptical reassessments of supposedly sacred assumptions." World War II, more than any other, served such a purpose. It crystallized a mood and acted as a catalyst for it, resolved contradictions and helped clarify values, and produced a consensus about the nation's world role. Most leaders were now convinced that the United States should not, and could not, retreat from world affairs as it had after World War I. The isolationist heritage was pushed aside as American policy makers enthusiastically plunged into the task of shaping the world to American preferences. Thus a new epoch in American diplomacy unfolded as—with

missionary zeal—the United States once more sought to build a new world order on the ashes of Dresden and Berlin, Hiroshima and Nagasaki.

In 1947 President Truman set the tone of postwar American policy in the doctrine that bears his name: "The free peoples of the world look to us for support in maintaining their freedoms. . . . If we falter in our leadership, we may endanger the peace of the world—and we shall surely endanger the welfare of our own nation." Later policy pronouncements prescribed America's missionary role. "Our nation," John F. Kennedy asserted in 1962, was "commissioned by history to be either an observer of freedom's failure or the cause of its success." Ronald Reagan echoed that sentiment nearly two decades later: "We in this country, in this generation, are, by destiny rather than choice, the watchmen on the walls of world freedom."

Internationalism Resurgent

Former State Dean Rusk declared in 1967 that "Other nations have interests. The United States has responsibilities." Consistent with its new sense of global responsibility in the emergent Cold War era, the United States actively sought to orchestrate nearly every significant global initiative. It was a primary sponsor and supporter of the United Nations. It engineered creation of regional institutions, such as the Organization of American States, and promoted American hegemony in areas regarded as American spheres of influence. It pushed hard for the expansion of foreign trade and the development of new markets for American business abroad.[5] It launched an ambitious foreign aid program. And it built a complex network of military alliances, both formal and informal. Its pursuit of these ambitious foreign policy objectives created a vast American "empire" circling the globe. Focus 3.2 summarizes the scope of America's commitments and involvements abroad in 1991, when the United States emerged as the world's sole remaining superpower—and exactly half a century after the Japanese attack on Pearl Harbor. Against this

---

FOCUS 3.2   America's Half Century: Nonmilitary and Military Dimensions of Global Activism at the End of the Cold War

Nonmilitary Involvements

- The United States maintained diplomatic offices in 160 nations and participated in over fifty major international organizations and eight hundred international conferences.
- U.S. broadcasting services promoted America's message and world view in forty-eight languages beamed throughout the world.
- The value of U.S. exports reached $421.7 billion, while its imports from abroad stood at $487.1 billion. In 1941 total U.S. trade with the rest of the world—exports plus imports—totaled $8.8 billion.
- U.S. economic aid to ninety countries exceeded $11.0 billion, bringing to $246.1 billion the total amount of foreign economic assistance granted to other countries since World War II. From June 1941 through June 1945 the United States spent $49 billion on foreign aid, all for military objectives.
- U.S. direct investment abroad stood at $361.5 billion.

Military Involvements

- Bilateral and multilateral treaties, executive agreements, and policy declarations committed the United States to the defense of over forty nations.
- In 1990, prior to the Persian Gulf buildup, 435,000 troops were stationed at 395 major military bases and hundreds of minor bases in thirty-five foreign countries. In 1940, one year

before the Lend-Lease Act was passed, the entire U.S. Army consisted of 269,000 officers and enlisted personnel.

- 47,000 Navy and Marine Corps personnel were aboard ships outside U.S. territorial waters. Another 10,000 were stationed at military bases on American territories in the Pacific. In 1940, one year before Pearl Harbor was attacked, the entire U.S. Navy consisted of 54,000 officers and enlisted personnel.
- 12,000 strategic nuclear warheads were deployed on 1,600 intercontinental and sea-based missiles and 260 intercontinental bombers.
- Nonstrategic forces levels included more than 8,000 tactical nuclear weapons, 16,000 battle tanks, 7,000 combat aircraft, 2,000 attack helicopters, and 300 aircraft carriers and major ships.
- The United States agreed to sell $20.9 billion of military equipment to other nations, bringing the total value of sales since the Korean War to $210 billion. Another $81.6 billion was spent in other forms of military aid and training.
- The nation's budget for military preparedness stood at $320.9 billion—a figure that exceeded the gross national product (GNP) of all but a handful of the world's other nations. In 1940—the same year that Nazi Germany attacked and occupied Belgium, the Netherlands, and France—the combined budgets of the Army and Navy departments was nearly $1.8 billion—1.8 percent of the nation's GNP.

---

background, "the first global society," a phrase used by Zbigniew Brzezinski, President Carter's national security assistant, accurately described the United States. Indeed, for half a century few aspirants to the White House would risk challenging the nation's active leadership role. Had they done so, they would have attacked a widely accepted and deeply ingrained national self-image that both led to and was sustained by extensive global interests and involvements.

Global activism is the first of three tenets uppermost in the minds of American policy

makers following World War II. The others focused on the challenge of Soviet communism. Together the three tenets defined a new orthodoxy that not only replaced the isolationist mood of the 1930s but also shaped a half-century of American foreign policy. The trilogy summarized below describes the new orthodoxy:

- The United States must reject isolationism and embrace an active responsibility for the direction of international affairs.

- Communism represents a dangerous ideological force in the world, and the United States should combat its spread.

- Because the Soviet Union is the spearhead of the communist challenge, American foreign policy must contain Soviet expansionism and influence.

The Communist Challenge to American Ideas and Ideals

Fear of communism—and an unequivocal rejection of it—played a major part in shaping the way the United States perceived the world throughout the Cold War. Communism was widely seen as a doctrinaire belief system diametrically opposed to "the American way of life," one intent on converting the entire world to its own vision. Because communism was perceived as inherently totalitarian, antidemocratic, and anticapitalist, it also was perceived as a potent threat to freedom, liberty, and prosperity throughout the world. Combating this threatening, adversarial ideology became an obsession—to the point, some argued, that American foreign policy itself became ideological (Commager 1983; Parenti 1969). The United States now often defined its mission as much in terms of the beliefs it opposed as those it supported. In words and deeds, America seemingly stood less *for* something, as in the nineteenth century, than *against* something: the communist ideology of Marxism-Leninism.

Official pronouncements about America's global objectives as they developed in the formative decade following World War II routinely stressed the menace posed by Marxist-Leninist (communist) doctrine. "The actions resulting from the communist philosophy," charged Harry Truman in 1949, "are a threat." President Eisenhower later warned that "We face a hostile ideology—global in scope, atheistic in character, ruthless in purpose, and insidious in method." "Unhappily," he continued, "the danger it poses promises to be of indefinite duration."

One popular view of "the beast" that helped sustain the anticommunist impulse was the belief that communism was a cohesive monolith to which all adherents were bound in united solidarity. The passage of time steadily reduced the cogency of that viewpoint, as communism revealed itself to be more *polycentric* than *monolithic*. Communist Party leaders became increasingly vocal about their own divisions and disagreements concerning communism's fundamental beliefs. The greatest fear that some felt were the motives of other communist states. Moreover, even if communism was in spirit an expansionist movement, it proved to be more flexible than initially assumed, with no timetable for the conversion of nonbelievers. Regardless, the perception of communism as a global monolith was a driving force behind America's Soviet-centric foreign policy.

A related conviction saw communism as endowed with powers and appeals that would encourage its continued spread. The view of communism as an expansionist, crusading force intent on converting the entire world to its beliefs, whose doctrines, however evil, might command widespread appeal was a potent argument. The **domino theory,** a metaphor popular in the 1960s, asserted that one country's fall to communism would stimulate the fall of those adjacent to it. Like a row of falling dominoes, an unstoppable chain reaction would unfold, bringing increasing portions of the world's population under the domination of totalitarian, communist governments. "Communism is on the move. It is out to win. It is playing an offensive game," warned Richard Nixon in 1963. Earlier in his political career Nixon had chastised Truman's secretary of state, calling him the "dean of the cowardly college of Communist containment" and recommended "dealing with this great Communist offensive" by pushing back the Iron Curtain with force. The lesson implied by the domino metaphor is that only American resistance could abate the seemingly inevitable communist onslaught. Reinforced by the image of communism as a monolithic force, it was especially potent in explaining America's resolve to fight in Vietnam.

The anticommunist goal became a bedrock of the foreign policy consensus that emerged after World War II. From the late 1940s until the United States became mired in the Vietnam War, few in the American foreign policy establishment challenged this consensus. Policy debates centered largely on how to implement the anticommunist drive, not on whether communism posed a threat. Some of the ideological fervor of American rhetoric receded during the 1970s with the Nixon-Kissinger effort to limit communist influence through a strategy of *détente.* References in policy statements to communism itself as a force in world politics also declined. President Carter went so far as to declare that "we are now free of that inordinate fear of communism which once led us to embrace any dictator who joined us in our fear."

But the anticommunist underpinnings of American foreign policy did not vanish. Instead, the belief that "communism is the principal danger" gained renewed emphasis under Ronald Reagan, whose Manichean world view depicted the world as a place where the noncommunist "free world," led by the United States, engaged in continuous battle with the communist world led by the Soviet Union, which he described as an "evil empire." Later, as domestic change in Eastern Europe and the Soviet Union itself accelerated, the more virulent forms of anticommunism waned. Richard Schifter, an assistant secretary of state in the Bush administration, declared that "communism has proven itself to be a false god." Rejected gods do not need to be condemned. The first Bush administration nonetheless chose to emphasize a worldwide transition to democracy inspired by the desire to extirpate the curse of communist ideology from the world. Secretary of State Baker: "Our idea is to replace the dangerous period of the Cold War with a democratic peace—a peace built on the twin pillars of political and economic freedom."

The historical import of anticommunism should be neither minimized nor forgotten, as the impact of the beliefs about communism in the American policy-making community was enormous. Successful opposition to communism became one of America's most important interests, coloring not only what happened abroad but also much of what took place at home, requiring the expenditure of enormous psychological and material treasure—and sometimes threatening cherished domestic values.

The Containment of Soviet Influence

As the physically strongest and the most vocal Marxist-Leninist state, the Soviet Union stood at the vanguard of the communist challenge. Hence the third tenet of the new orthodoxy emergent after World War II: The United States must contain Soviet expansionism and influence.

Four corollary beliefs buttressed the determination to contain Soviet communism:

- The Soviet Union is an expansionist power, intent on maximizing communist power through military conquest and "exported" revolutions.

- The Soviet goal of world domination is permanent and will succeed unless blocked by vigorous counteraction.

- The United States, leader of the "free world," is the only nation able to repel Soviet aggression.

- Appeasement will not work: Force must be met with force if Soviet expansionism is to be stopped.

A *Soviet-centric foreign policy* flowed from this interrelated set of beliefs, whose durability persisted for decades. Furthermore, the precepts of *political realism,* which focus on power, not principle, now came to dominate American foreign policy, as the purpose of the **containment** strategy was the preservation of the security of the United States "through the maintenance of a balance of power in the world" (Gaddis 1992; see also Gaddis 1982 and Kissinger 1994b). As one scholar put it, "[political] realists sought to reorient United States policy so that American policy makers could cope with Soviet attempts at domination without either lapsing into passive unwillingness to use force or engaging in destructive and quixotic crusades to 'make the world safe for democracy.' Their ideas were greeted warmly by policy makers, who sought . . . to 'exorcise isolationism, justify a permanent and global involvement in world affairs, [and] rationalize the accumulation of power'" (Keohane 1986a).[6]

To understand what brought about these durable assumptions, the containment strategy derived from them, and the doctrine of political realism that sustained them, it is useful to trace briefly alternative interpretations of the origins of the Cold War and, following that, the strategies of containment that America's Cold War presidents pursued.

The Origins of the Cold War: Competing Hypotheses Three hypotheses compete for attention as we seek to explain the origins of the Cold War: *conflicts of interest, ideological incompatibilities,* and *misperceptions.*

A Conflict of Interests In 1835 de Tocqueville predicted that the United States and Russia were destined by fate and historical circumstance to become rivals. He argued that "there are today two great peoples which, starting out from different points of departure, advance toward the same goal—the Americans and the Russians. . . . Each of them will one day hold in its hands the destinies of half of mankind." Tocqueville could not foresee the advent of Marxism-Leninism or the possibility that ideological differences would contribute to the dispute he regarded as inevitable. Instead, his prediction was based on the logic of *realpolitik.* From this perspective, rivalry between the emergent superpowers following World War II was inescapable. The status of the United States and the Soviet Union at the top of the international hierarchy made each suspicious of the other. And each had reasons to counter the other's potential global hegemony.

> The principal cause of the Cold War was the essential duopoly of power left by World War II, a duopoly that quite naturally

resulted in the filling of a vacuum (Europe) that had once been the center of the international system and the control of which would have conferred great, and perhaps decisive, power advantage to its possessor. . . . The root cause of the conflict was to be found in the structural circumstances that characterized the international system at the close of World War II.

(TUCKER 1990, 94)

But was the competition necessary? During World War II the United States and the Soviet Union had both demonstrated an ability to subordinate their ideological differences and competition for power to larger purposes—the destruction of Hitler's Germany. Neither relentlessly sought unilateral advantage. Instead, both practiced accommodation to protect their mutual interest. Their success in remaining alliance partners suggests that Cold War rivalry was not predetermined, that continued collaboration was possible.

After the war, American and Soviet leaders both expressed their hope that wartime collaboration would continue (Gaddis 1972). Harry Hopkins, for example, a close adviser to President Roosevelt, reported that "The Russians had proved that they could be reasonable and farseeing and there wasn't any doubt in the minds of the President or any of us that we could live with them and get along with them peacefully for as far into the future as any of us could imagine."

Roosevelt argued that it would be possible to preserve the accommodative atmosphere the great powers achieved during the war if the United States and the Soviet Union each respected the other's national interests. He predicated his belief on an informal agreement that suggested each great power would enjoy dominant influence in its own *sphere of influence* and not oppose the others in their areas of influence (Morgenthau 1969; Schlesinger 1967). As presidential policy adviser John Foster Dulles noted in January 1945, "The three great powers which at Moscow agreed upon the 'closest cooperation' about European questions have shifted to a practice of separate, regional responsibility." Agreements about the role of the Security Council in the new United Nations (in which each great power would enjoy a veto) obligated the United States and the Soviet Union to share responsibility for preserving world peace, further symbolizing the expectation of continued cooperation.

If these were the superpowers' hopes and aspirations when World War II ended, why did they fail? To answer that question, we must go beyond the logic of *realpolitik* and probe other explanations of the origins of the Cold War.

Ideological Incompatibilities Another interpretation holds that the Cold War was simply an extension of the superpowers' mutual disdain for each other's political system and way of life—in short, *ideological incompatibilities.* Secretary of State James F. Byrnes embraced this thesis following World War II. He argued that "there is too much difference in the ideologies of the United States and Russia to work out a long term program of cooperation." Thus the Cold War was a conflict "not only between two powerful states, but also between two different social systems" (Jervis 1991).

The interpretation of the Cold War as a battle between diametrically opposed systems of belief contrasts sharply with the view that the emergent superpowers' differences stemmed from discordant interests. Although the adversaries may have viewed "ideology more as a justification for action than as a guide to action," once the interests they shared disappeared, "ideology did become the chief means which differentiated friend from foe" (Gaddis 1983). From this perspective, the Cold War centered less on a conflict of interests between rivals for global power and prestige than on a contest between opposing belief systems about alternative ways of life. Such contests allow no room for compromise, as they pit right against wrong, good against evil; diametrically opposed belief systems require victory. Adherents, animated by the righteousness of their cause, view the world as an arena for religious war—a battle for the allegiance of people's minds. Thus American policy rhetoric—like that employed to justify past religious wars and religious persecutions—advocated "sleepless hostility to Communism—even preventive war" (Commager 1965). Such an outlook virtually guarantees pure conflict: Intolerance of competing belief systems is rife, and cooperation or conciliation with the ideological foe entails no virtue. Instead, adversaries view the world in *zero-sum* terms: When one side wins converts, the other side necessarily loses them.

Lenin thus described the predicament—prophetically, it happened: "As long as capitalism and socialism exist, we cannot live in peace; in the end, either one or the other will triumph—a funeral dirge will be sung either over the Soviet Republic or over world capitalism."

Misperceptions A third explanation sees the Cold War rooted in psychological factors, particularly the superpowers' *misperceptions* of each other's motives, which their conflicting interests and ideologies reinforced. Mistrustful parties see in their own actions only virtue and in those of their adversaries only malice. Hostility is inevitable in the face of such "we-they," "we're OK, you're not" mirror images. Moreover, as a nation's perceptions of its adversary's evil intentions become accepted as dogma, its prophecies also become self-fulfilling (White 1984).

A month before Roosevelt died, he expressed to Stalin his desire, above all, to prevent "mutual distrust." Yet, as noted, mistrust soon developed. Indeed, its genesis could be traced to pre-war years, particularly in the minds of Soviet leaders, who recalled American participation in the 1918–1919 Allied military intervention in Russia, which turned from its initial mission of keeping weapons out of German hands into an anti-Bolshevik undertaking. They also were sensitive to United States' failure to recognize the Soviet Union diplomatically until 1933 in the midst of a depression (perceived as a sign of capitalism's weakness and its ultimate collapse).

The wartime experience did little to assuage Soviet leaders; rather, their anxieties were fueled by disquieting memories:

- U.S. procrastination before entering the war against the fascists

- America's refusal to inform the Soviets of the Manhattan atomic bomb project or to apprise them of wartime strategy to the same extent as the British

- The delay in sending promised Lend-Lease supplies

- The failure to open up the second front (leading Stalin to suspect that American policy was to let the Russians and Germans destroy each other)

- The use of the atomic bomb against Japan, perhaps perceived as a maneuver to prevent Soviet involvement in the Pacific peace settlement

Those suspicions were later reinforced by the willingness of the United States to support previous Nazi collaborators in American-occupied countries, notably Italy, and by its pressure on the Soviet Union to abide by its promise to allow free elections in areas vital to Soviet national security, notably Poland. Soviet leaders also were resentful of America's abrupt cancellation of promised Lend-Lease assistance, which Stalin had counted on to facilitate the postwar recovery. Thus Soviet distrust of American intentions stemmed in part from fears of American encirclement that were exacerbated by America's past hostility.

To the United States, on the other hand, numerous indications of growing Soviet belligerence warranted distrust. They included:

- Stalin's announcement in February 1946 that the Soviet Union was not going to demilitarize its armed forces, at the very time that the United States was engaged in the largest demobilization by a victorious power in world history

- The Soviet Union's unwillingness to permit democratic elections in the territories it had liberated from the Nazis

- Its refusal to assist in postwar reconstruction in regions outside of Soviet control

- Its removal of supplies and infrastructure from Soviet-occupied areas

- Its selfish and often obstructive behavior in the fledgling new international organizations

- Its occasional opportunistic disregard for international law and violation of agreements and treaties

- Its infiltration of Western labor movements

Harry Truman typified the environment of distrust. Upon assuming the presidency after Roosevelt's death he declared: "If the Russians did not wish to join us they could go to hell" (Tugwell 1971). In this climate of suspicion and distrust, the Cold War grew (see Focus 3.3). "Each side thought that it was compelled by the very existence of the other to engage in zero-sum competition, and each saw the unfolding history of the Cold War as confirming its view" (Garthoff 1994; see also Kennan 1976).

Historians have long been intrigued about the origins of the Cold War and the weights that should be attached to competing explanations. Their task was made more difficult because nearly all sources of information came from the United States and the other western countries. Now, however, Russian authorities have begun to open Soviet archives from the early Cold War years, permitting new insights. Interestingly, the new evidence tends to confirm that the United States responded defensively to recurrent patterns of Soviet belligerence. Reinforcing this interpretation are historians' findings that Joseph Stalin's perceptions of and antipathy toward the west may have precluded the possibility of avoiding an East-West confrontation. Although the United States may have believed that the atomic bomb gave it the "the ultimate weapon" for dealing with Soviet intransigence on the issues unresolved

---

FOCUS 3.3   Mirror Images: The Onset of the Cold War

The Soviet Image of the United States

- **They (the rulers) are bad.** The Wall Street bankers, politicians, and militaries want a war because they fear loss of wealth and power in a communist revolution.
  They are surrounding us with military bases. They send spies (in U-2 planes and otherwise) to destroy the workers' fatherland.
  They are like the Nazis—rearming the Germans against us.
- **They are imperialistic.** The capitalist nations dominate colonial areas, keep them in submission.
  The Latin-American regimes (except Cuba) are puppets of the USA.
- **They exploit their own people.** All capitalist live in luxury by exploiting workers, who suffer insecurity, unemployment, and so on.
- **They are against democracy.** Democratic forms are mere pretense; people can vote only for capitalist candidates.
  Rulers control organs of propaganda, education, and communication. They persecute anyone favoring communist ideas.
- **They distort the truth.** They falsely accuse the USSR of desiring to impose ideology by force.
- **They are immoral, materialist, selfishly individualistic.** They are only out for money.
- **They (the people) are good.** The American people want peace.

The American Image of the Soviet Union

- **They (the rulers) are bad.** The men in the Kremlin are aggressive, power-seeking, brutal in suppressing Hungary, ruthless in dealing with their people.
  They are infiltrating the western hemisphere to attact us.
  They engage in espionage and sabotage to wreck our country.
  They are like the Nazis—an aggressive expansionist dictatorship.
- **They are imperialistic.** The communists want to dominate the world.
  They rigidly control the satellite puppet governments.
- **They exploit their own people.** They hold down consumer goods, keep standards of living low except for communist bureaucrats.
- **They are against democracy.** Democratic forms are mere pretense; people can vote only for communist canditates.
  Rulers control organs of propaganda, education, and communication. They persecute anyone favoring western democracy.
- **They distort the truth.** They pose as a friend of colonial people in order to enslave them.
- **They are immortal, materialistic.** They are preventing freedom of religion.
- **They (the people) are good.** The Soviet people want peace.

SOURCE: Ralph K. White, *New York Times*, 5 September 1961, 5.

---

in 1945, archival research now challenges that conclusion. Indeed, it shows that Stalin regarded the United States and its allies as wimps. Illustrative is Stalin's remark in December 1949 that "America, though it screams of war, is actually afraid of war more than anything else" (Haslam 1997). It is notable that his remark came shortly after the United States signed the North Atlantic Treaty forming the *NATO alliance* and less than a year before North Korea—with Soviet support—attacked South Korea, precipitating the Korean War.

Stalin's centrality in explaining the origins of the Cold War is reinforced by other recent findings. John Lewis Gaddis, America's preeminent historian of the Cold War, concludes on the basis of the new evidence that the possibility of continued U.S.-Soviet cooperation following World War II was but a pipe dream. Stalin had precipitated a series of "purges" in the Soviet Union during the 1930s, whose purpose was to eliminate all who may have opposed his autocratic regime. Tens of millions died. For Stalin, the incipient conflict with the United States was an extension of the conflict he visited on his own people, which set him apart from others in power when the Cold War began. In Gaddis's words,

> He [Stalin] alone pursued personal security by depriving everyone else of it: no Western leader relied on terror to the extent that he did. He alone had transformed his country into an extension of himself: no Western leader could have succeeded at such a feat, and none attempted it. He alone saw war and revolutions as acceptable means with which to pursue ultimate ends: no Western leader associated violence with progress to the extend that he did.
>
> (GADDIS 1997, 25).

Thus Gaddis concludes that "as long as Stalin was running the Soviet Union a cold war was unavoidable." Gaddis recognizes the role that power and ideology played in fomenting the Cold War. Still, he argues that neither *ensured* that conflict would follow. Instead, Stalin was the critical ingredient:

> For the more we learn, the less sense it makes to distinguish Stalin's foreign policies from his domestic practices or even his personal behavior. . . . Stalin . . . functioned in much the same manner whether operating within the international system, within his alliances, within his country, within his party, within his personal entourage, or even within his family. The Soviet leader waged cold wars on all these fronts. The Cold War *we* came to know was only one of many from *his* point of view.
>
> (GADDIS 1997, 293)

Historians may eventually alter their first impressions about the origins of the Cold War as now revealed in their newly acquired information from Russian archives.[7] Unlikely to change is the conclusion that a combination of power, principle, and pragmatism colored the way political leaders on both sides of the *Iron Curtain* played out this global contest for power and position. From the perspective of American foreign policy, the key issue was how best to apply the strategy of containment to curtail expansion of Soviet power and influence.

America's Containment Strategies: Evolutionary Phases The history of American foreign policy since World War II is largely the story of how the containment doctrine was interpreted and applied. Figure 3.1 illustrates the pattern of conflict and cooperation the United States directed toward the Soviet Union during the Cold War and the Soviets' responses. The information charted summarizes hundreds of verbal and physical actions the two powers directed toward one another as revealed in systematic analyses of media accounts of their behavior. The evidence reveals three patterns of Soviet-American interactions during the Cold War:

1. Conflict was the characteristic mode of Soviet-American interactions.

2. The acts of conflict and cooperation directed by one power toward the other were typically responded to in kind. Periods when the United States directed friendly initiatives toward the Soviets were also periods when the Soviets acted with friendliness toward the United States; periods of U.S. belligerence were periods of Soviet belligerence. Thus *reciprocity* describes the powers' patterns of behavior toward one another.

3. Although different presidents are identified with periodic shifts in the pattern of conflict and cooperation toward the Soviet Union during the Cold War, the historical record reveals "no detectable systematic differences in the way administrations regularly [built] on their own past behavior or in the way they [responded] to the Soviet Union" (Dixon and Gaarder 1992). Instead, regardless of the party affiliation or political ideology of those in the Oval Office, continuity rather than change is the hallmark of America's Cold War behavior toward the Soviet Union.

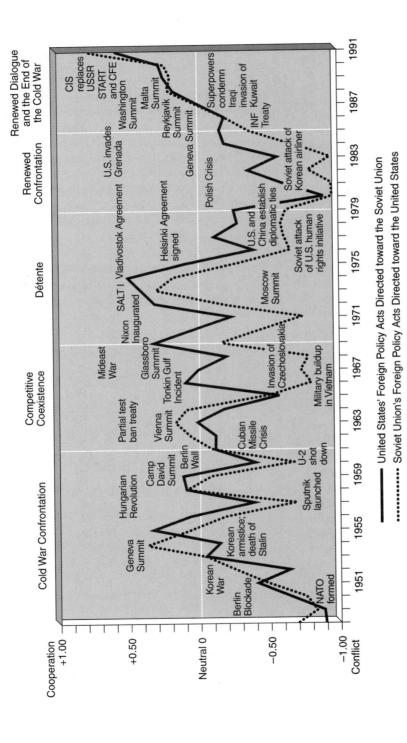

FIGURE 3.1 Soviet-American Relations, 1948–1991

Note: The index is the net proportion of cooperative acts and conflictual acts.

Source: Adapted from Edward E. Azar and Thomas J. Sloan, *Dimensions of Interaction* (Pittsburgh: Center for International Studies, 1973), and supplemented with data from the Conflict and Peace Data Bank. Data for 1966–1991 are from the World Event Interaction Survey, as compiled by Rodney G. Tomlinson.

For analytical purposes the history of the policy of containment can be divided into five chronologically ordered phases, as depicted in Figure 3.1.

Cold War Confrontation, 1947–1962 A brief period of wary friendship preceded the onset of Cold War confrontation, but by 1947 all pretense of collaboration ceased, as the antagonists' vital security interests collided over the issues surrounding the structure of post–World War II European politics.

In February 1946 Stalin gave a speech in which he spoke of the inevitability of conflict with the capitalist powers. Urging the Soviet people not to be deluded that the end of the war with Germany meant the state could relax, he called for intensified efforts by the Soviet people to strengthen and defend their homeland. Many Western leaders saw Stalin's first major post-war address as a declaration of World War III. Shortly after this, George F. Kennan, then a U.S. diplomat in Moscow, sent to Washington his famous "long telegram" assessing the sources of Soviet conduct. Kennan's conclusions were ominous: "We have here a political force committed fanatically to the belief that with [the] United States there can be no permanent modus vivendi, that it is desirable and necessary that the internal harmony of our society be disrupted, our traditional way of life be destroyed, the international authority of our state be broken, if Soviet power is to be secure."

Kennan's ideas were circulated widely when, in 1947, the influential journal *Foreign Affairs* published his ideas in an anonymous article he signed "X." In it, Kennan argued that Soviet leaders would forever feel insecure about their political ability to maintain power against forces both within Soviet society and the outside world. Their insecurity would lead to an activist—and perhaps aggressive—Soviet foreign policy. Yet it was within the power of the United States to increase the strain on the Soviet leadership, which eventually could lead to a gradual mellowing or final end of Soviet power. "In these

circumstances" Kennan concluded, "it is clear that the main element of any United States policy toward the Soviet Union must be that of a long-term, patient but firm and vigilant *containment* of Russian expansive tendencies" (Kennan 1947, emphasis added).

Not long after that, Harry Truman made this prescription the cornerstone of American postwar policy. Provoked in part by domestic turmoil in Turkey and Greece—which he and others believed to be communist inspired—Truman responded: "I believe that it must be the policy of the United States to support free peoples who are resisting attempted subjugation by armed minorities or by outside pressures."

Few declarations in American history were as powerful and important as this one, which eventually became known as the **Truman Doctrine.** "In a single sentence Truman had defined American policy for the next generation and beyond. Whenever and wherever an anti-Communist government was threatened, by indigenous insurgents, foreign invasion, or even diplomatic pressure . . . , the United States would supply political, economic, and, most of all, military aid" (Ambrose 1993).

Whether the policy of containment was appropriate, even at the time of its origination, remains controversial. Journalist Walter Lippmann wrote a series of articles in the *New York Herald Tribune,* later collected in a short book called *The Cold War* (Lippmann 1947), in which he argued that global containment would be costly for the United States, that it would militarize American foreign policy, and that eventually the United States would have to support any regime that professed anticommunism, regardless how distasteful it might be. Henry Wallace, a third-party candidate who opposed Harry Truman for the presidency, joined in Lippmann's concern when he warned of the dilemma the United States would eventually face: "Once America stands for opposition to change, we are lost. America will become the most hated nation in the world."

Lippmann's critique proved prophetic in all its details. Before the Cold War had run its course, the United States had spent trillions of dollars on national defense, had developed permanent peacetime military alliances circling the globe, and had found itself supporting some of the most ruthless dictatorship in the world—in Argentina, Brazil, Cuba, the Dominican Republic, Guatemala, Greece, Haiti, Iran, Nicaragua, Paraguay, the Philippines, Portugal, South Korea, South Vietnam, Spain, and Taiwan—whose only shared characteristic was their opposition to communism. In the process America's revolutionary heritage as a beacon of liberty often was set aside as the nation found itself opposing social and political change elsewhere, choosing instead to preserve the status quo in the face of potentially disruptive revolutions.

George Kennan, too, became alarmed at the way he felt his celebrated statement was taken out of context and misinterpreted, so that "containment" became an "indestructible myth," a doctrine "which was then identified with the foreign policy of the Truman administration."

> I . . . naturally went to great lengths to disclaim the view, imputed to me by implication . . . that containment was a matter of stationing military forces around the Soviet borders and preventing any outbreak of Soviet military aggressiveness. I protested . . . against the implication that the Russians were aspiring to invade other areas and that the task of American policy was to prevent them from doing so. The Russians don't want, I insisted, to invade anyone. It is not in their tradition. They tried it once in Finland and got their fingers burned. They don't want war of any kind. Above all, they don't want the open responsibility that official invasion brings with it.
>
> (KENNAN 1967, 361)

As Kennan later lamented, "the image of a Stalinist Russia poised and yearning to attack the West, and deterred only by [America's] possession of atomic weapons, was largely a creation of the Western imagination." Cautioning against "demonizing the adversary, overestimating

enemy strength and overmilitarizing the Western response" (Talbott 1990), Kennan recommended a political and economic rather than military approach to the containment of Soviet expansionism. Despite that advice, the belief that defeating Soviet communism required a militantly confrontational approach became the guiding premise behind post–World War II American foreign policy.

The inability of the superpowers to maintain the sphere-of-influence posture tacitly agreed to earlier contributed to their propensity to interpret crises as the product of the other's program for global domination. When the Soviets moved into portions of eastern Europe, American leaders interpreted this as confirmation that they sought world conquest.

The Soviet Union, however, perhaps had reason to think that the Americans would readily accede to Soviet domination in eastern Europe. In 1945, for example, Secretary of State James Byrnes stated that the "Soviet Union has a right to friendly governments along its borders." Under Secretary of State Dean Acheson spoke of "a Monroe Doctrine for eastern Europe." These viewpoints and others implied in the Yalta agreements, reinforced the Soviet belief that the western powers would accept the Soviets' need for a buffer zone in eastern Europe, which had been the common invasion route into Russia for more than three centuries. Hence, when the U.S. government began to challenge Soviet supremacy in eastern Germany and elsewhere in eastern Europe, the Soviet Union felt that previous understandings had been violated and that the West harbored "imperialist designs" (see also Focus 3.3).

A seemingly unending eruption of Cold War crises followed. They included the Soviet refusal to withdraw troops from Iran in 1946, the communist coup d'état in Czechoslovakia in 1948, the Soviet blockade of West Berlin in June of that year, the communist acquisition of power on the Chinese mainland in 1949, the outbreak of the Korean War in 1950, the Chinese invasion of Tibet in 1950, and the on-again, off-again Taiwan Straits crises that followed. Hence the "war" was not simply "cold"; it became an embittered worldwide quarrel that threatened to escalate into open warfare, as the two powers positioned themselves to prevent the other from achieving preponderant power.

The United States enjoyed clear military superiority at the strategic level until 1949, for it alone possessed the ultimate "winning weapon" and the means to deliver it. The Soviets broke the American atomic monopoly that year, much sooner than American scientists and policy makers had anticipated. Thereafter, the Soviet quest for military equality and the superpowers' eventual relative strategic strengths influenced the entire range of their relations. As the distribution of world power became **bipolar**—with the United States and its allies comprising one pole, the Soviet Union and its allies the other—the character of superpower relations took on a different cast, sometimes more collaborative, sometimes more conflictual.

Europe, where the Cold War first erupted, was the focal point of the jockeying for influence. The principal European allies of the superpowers divided into the North Atlantic Treaty Organization (NATO) and the Warsaw Treaty Organization (WTO). These alliances became the cornerstones of the superpowers' external policies, as the European members of the Eastern and Western alliances willingly acceded to the leadership of their respective patrons.

To a lesser extent, alliance formation also enveloped states outside of Europe. The United States in particular sought to contain Soviet (and Chinese) influence on the Eurasian landmass by building a ring of pro-American allies on the very borders of the communist world. In return, the United States promised to protect its growing number of clients from external attack. Thus the Cold War extended across the entire globe.

In the rigid two-bloc system of the 1950s the superpowers talked as if war were imminent, but in deeds (especially after the Korean War) both acted cautiously. President Eisenhower and his secretary of state, John Foster Dulles, promised a "rollback" of the Iron Curtain and the "liberation" of the "captive nations" of Eastern Europe. They pledged to respond to aggression with "massive retaliation." And they criticized the allegedly "soft" and "reactive" Truman Doctrine, claiming to reject containment in favor of an ambitious "winning" strategy that would finally end the confrontation with "godless communism." But communism was not rolled back in Eastern Europe, and containment was not replaced by a more assertive strategy. In 1956, for example, the United States failed to respond to Hungary's call for assistance in its revolt against Soviet control. American policy makers, despite their threatening language, promised more than they delivered. "'We can never rest,' Eisenhower swore in the 1952 presidential campaign, 'until the enslaved nations of the world have in the fullness of freedom the right to choose their own path.' But rest they did, except in their speeches" (Ambrose 1993).

Nikita Khrushchev assumed the top Soviet leadership position after Stalin's death in 1953. He claimed to accept *peaceful coexistence* with capitalism, and in 1955 the two superpowers met at the Geneva summit in a first, tentative step toward a mutual discussion of world problems. But the Soviet Union also continued, however cautiously, to exploit opportunities for advancing Soviet power wherever it perceived them to exist, as in Cuba in the early 1960s. Thus the period following Stalin's death was punctuated by a continuing crises and confrontations. Now—in addition to Hungary—Cuba, Egypt, and Berlin became the flash points. In 1960 there was even a crisis resulting from the downing of an American U-2 spy plane deep over Soviet territory. *Nuclear brinkmanship* and *massive retaliation* were symptomatic of the strategies of containment through which the United States at this time hoped to balance Soviet power and perhaps force the Soviets into submission.

Competitive Coexistence, 1962–1969 The Soviets' surreptitious placement of missiles in Cuba in 1962, the onset of the Vietnam War at about the same time, and the beginning of a seemingly unrestrained arms race cast a shadow over the possibility of superpower coexistence. The most serious test of the ability of the United States and the Soviet Union to avert catastrophe and to manage confrontation peacefully was the 1962 *Cuban missile crisis*—a catalytic event that transformed thinking about how the Cold War could be waged and expanded awareness of the suicidal consequences of a nuclear war. The superpowers stood eyeball to eyeball. Fortunately, one blinked.

At the American University commencement exercises in 1963, President Kennedy explained why tension reduction had become imperative and war could not be risked.

> Among the many traits the people of [the United States and the Soviet Union] have in common, none is stronger than our mutual abhorrence of war. Almost unique among the major world powers, we have never been at war with each other. . . .
>
> Today, should total war ever break out again—no matter how—our two countries would become the primary targets. It is an ironical but accurate fact that the two strongest powers are the two in the most danger of devastation. . . . We are both caught up in a vicious and dangerous cycle in which suspicion on one side breeds suspicion on the other and new weapons beget counterweapons.
>
> In short, both the United States and its allies, and the Soviet Union and its allies, have a mutually deep interest in a just and genuine peace and in halting the arms race. . . .
>
> So let us not be blind to our differences, but let us also direct attention to our common interests and to the means by which those differences can be resolved. And if we cannot end now our differences, at least we can help make the world safe for diversity.

Kennedy is also remembered for his clarion inaugural address two years earlier. "Let every nation know, whether it wishes us well or ill, that we shall pay any price, bear any burden, meet any hardship, support any friend, oppose any foe to assure the survival and the success of liberty." For some, the challenge was a renewal of America's Cold War challenge to the Soviet Union. For others, it was an expression of America's idealist heritage.[8] "Kennedy's eloquent peroration was the reverse of Palmerston's dictum, that Great Britain had no friends, only interests; America, in pursuit of liberty, had no interests, only friends" (Kissinger 1994a).

Kennedy's inaugural address defined an approach as resolutely anti-Soviet as that of his predecessors, but—especially following the missile crisis—his administration began in both style and tone to depart from the confrontational tactics of the past. Thus competition for advantage and influence continued, but the preservation of the status quo was also tacitly accepted, as neither superpower proved willing to launch a new war to secure new geostrategic gains. As the growing parity of American and Soviet military capabilities made coexistence or nonexistence the alternatives, finding ways to adjust their differences became compelling. This alleviated the danger posed by some issues and opened the door for new initiatives in other areas. For example, the Geneva (1955) and Camp David (1959) experiments in summit diplomacy set precedents for other tension-reduction activities. Installation of the "hot line," a direct communication link between the White House and the Kremlin, followed in 1963. So did the 1967 Glassboro summit and several negotiated agreements, including the 1963 Partial Test Ban Treaty, the 1967 Outer Space Treaty, and the 1968 Nuclear Nonproliferation Treaty. In addition, the United States tacitly accepted a divided Germany and Soviet hegemony in Eastern Europe, as illustrated by the failure of the United States to respond forcefully to the Warsaw Pact invasion of Czechoslovakia in 1968.

Détente, 1969–1979 With the inauguration of Richard Nixon as president and the appointment of Henry Kissinger as his national security adviser, the United States tried a new approach toward containment, officially labeled **détente.** In Kissinger's words, détente sought to create "a vested interest in cooperation and restraint," "an environment in which competitors can regulate and restrain their differences and ultimately move from competition to cooperation." Several considerations prompted the new approach, including recognition that a nuclear attack would prove mutually suicidal, a growing sensitivity to the security requirements of both superpowers, and their shared concern for an increasingly powerful and assertive China.

To engineer the relaxation of superpower tensions, Nixon and Kissinger fashioned the **linkage theory.** Predicated on the expectation that the development of economic, political, and strategic ties between the United States and the Soviet Union would bind the two in a common fate, linkage would foster mutually rewarding exchanges. In this way, it would lessen the superpowers' incentives for war. Linkage also made the entire range of Soviet-American relations interdependent, which made cooperation in one policy area (such as arms control) contingent on acceptable conduct in others (intervention outside traditional spheres of influence).

As both a goal of and a strategy for expanding the superpowers' mutual interest in restraint, détente symbolized an important shift in their global relationship. In diplomatic jargon, relations between the Soviets and Americans were "normalized," as the expectation of war receded. In terms of containment, on the other hand, the strategy now shifted more toward self-containment on the Soviets' part than American militant containment. As one observer put it, "Détente did not mean global reconciliation with the Soviet Union. . . . Instead, détente implied the selective continuation of containment by economic and political inducement and at the price of accommodation through concessions that were more or less balanced" (Serfaty 1978). When militarily superior, the United States had practiced containment by coercion and force.

From a new position of parity, containment was now practiced by seduction. Thus détente was "part of the Cold War, not an alternative to it" (Goodman 1975).

Paralleling its conviction to normalize relations with the Soviet Union, the Nixon administration sought to terminate the long, costly, and unpopular war in Vietnam. U.S. involvement escalated in the mid-1960s, but the war became increasingly unpopular at home as casualties mounted and the purposes of U.S. engagement remained vague and unconvincing. Thus the Vietnam War coincided with—indeed, caused—popular pleas for a U.S. retreat from world affairs. President Nixon's declaration in 1970—later known as the **Nixon Doctrine**—that "America cannot—and will not—conceive all the plans, design all the programs, execute all the decisions, and undertake all the defense of the free nations of the world" took cognizance of a resurgent isolationist mood at home.

Securing Soviet support in extricating itself from Vietnam was a salient American goal sought through the détente process, but arms control stood at the center of the new dialogue. The **Strategic Arms Limitation Talks (SALT)** became the test of détente's viability. Initiated in 1969, the SALT negotiations sought to restrain the threatening, expensive, and spiraling arms race. They produced two sets of agreements, the first in 1972 (SALT I) and the second in 1979 (SALT II). With their signing, each of the superpowers gained the principal objective it had sought in détente. The Soviet Union gained recognition of its status as the United States' equal; the United States gained a commitment from the Soviet Union to moderate its quest for preeminent power in the world.

The SALT II agreement was not brought to fruition, however. It was signed but never ratified by the United States. The failure underscored the real differences that still separated the superpowers. By the end of the 1970s, détente lost nearly all of its momentum and much of the hope it had symbolized only a few years earlier. During the SALT II treaty ratification hearings, the U.S. Senate expressed concern about an agreement with a rival that continued high levels of military spending, that sent arms to states outside its traditional sphere of influence (Algeria, Angola, Egypt, Ethiopia, Somalia, Syria, Vietnam, and elsewhere), and that stationed military forces in Cuba. These complaints all spoke to the persistence of Americans' deep-seated distrust of the Soviet Union and their understandable concern about Soviet intentions.

Renewed Confrontation, 1979–1985 The Soviet invasion of Afghanistan in 1979 ended the Senate's consideration of SALT II—and détente. "Soviet aggression in Afghanistan—unless checked—confronts all the world with the most serious strategic challenge since the Cold War began," declared President Jimmy Carter. In response the United States initiated a series of countermoves, including enunciation of the **Carter Doctrine** declaring the willingness of the United States to use military force to protect its interests in the Persian Gulf region. Thus antagonism and hostility once more dominated, and once more the pursuit of power dominated the nation's strategy of containment as Eisenhower's tough talk, Kennedy's competitiveness, and even Truman's belligerence were rekindled. Before Afghanistan, Carter had embarked on a worldwide campaign for human rights, an initiative steeped in Wilsonian idealism directed as much toward the Soviet Union as others. This, too, now fell victim to the primacy of power over principle.

Following his election in 1980, President Ronald Reagan and his Soviet counterparts delivered a barrage of confrontational rhetoric reminiscent of the 1950s. In one interview, Reagan went so far as to say "Let's not delude ourselves, the Soviet Union underlies all the unrest that is going on. If they weren't engaged in this game of dominoes, there wouldn't be any hot spots in the world." In another speech before the British parliament, he implored the nations of the free world to join one another to promote worldwide democracy. That ambitious call reflected

Wilsonian idealism and long-standing moralistic strains in American foreign policy. It also implied renewal of the challenge to Soviet communism that British Prime Minister Winston Churchill launched in Fulton, Missouri, in 1946, where he declared "an Iron Curtain has descended" across Europe and called for the English-speaking nations to join together for the coming "trial of strength" with the communist world. Reagan policy adviser Richard Pipe's bold charge in 1981 that the Soviets would have to choose between "peacefully changing their Communist system . . . or going to war" punctuated the tense atmosphere.

In many respects the early 1980s were like the 1950s, as tough talk was not matched by aggressive action. But the first Reagan term did witness some assertive action, notably resumption of the arms race. The United States now placed a massive rearmament program above all other priorities, including domestic economic problems. American policy makers also spoke loosely about the "winnability" of a nuclear war through a "prevailing" military strategy, which included the threat of a "first use" of nuclear weapons should a conventional war break out.

The superpowers also extended their confrontation to new territory, such as Central America, and renewed their public diplomacy (propaganda) efforts to extol the ascribed virtues of their respective systems throughout the world. A series of events punctuated the renewal of conflict:

- The Soviets destroyed Korean Airlines flight 007 in 1983

- Shortly thereafter the United States invaded Grenada

- Arms control talks then ruptured

- The Soviets boycotted the 1984 Olympic Games in Los Angeles (in retaliation for the U.S. boycott of the 1980 Moscow Olympics)

The Reagan administration also embarked on a new program, the **Reagan Doctrine,** which pledged U.S. support of anticommunist insurgents (euphemistically described as "freedom fighters") who sought to overthrow Soviet-supported governments in Afghanistan, Angola, and Nicaragua (Scott 1996). The strategy "expressed the conviction that communism could be defeated, not merely contained." Thus "Reagan took Wilsonianism to its ultimate conclusion. America would not wait passively for free institutions to evolve, nor would it confine itself to resisting direct threats to its security. Instead, it would actively promote democracy" (Kissinger 1994a).

Understandably, relations between the United States and the Soviet Union were increasingly strained by the compound impact of these moves, countermoves, and rhetorical flourishes. The new Soviet leader, Mikhail Gorbachev, summarized the alarming state of superpower relations in the fall of 1985 by fretting that "The situation is very complex, very tense. I would even go so far as to say it is explosive." The situation did not explode, however. Instead, the superpowers resumed their dialogue and laid the basis for a new phase in their relations.

Renewed Dialogue and the End of the Cold War, 1985–1991 Prospects for a more constructive phase improved measurably under Gorbachev. At first his goals were hard to discern, but it soon became clear that he felt it imperative for the Soviet Union to reconcile its differences with the capitalist West if it wanted any chance of reversing the deterioration of its economy and international position. In Gorbachev's words, these goals dictated "the need for a fundamental break with many customary approaches to foreign policy." Shortly thereafter, he chose the path of domestic reform, one marked by political democratization and a transition to a market economy. And he proclaimed the need for "new thinking" in foreign and defense policy to relax superpower tensions.

To carry out "new thinking," in 1986 Gorbachev abrogated the long-standing Soviet ideological commitment to aid national liberation movements struggling to overthrow capitalism.

"It is inadmissible and futile to encourage revolution from abroad," he declared. He also for the first time embraced **mutual security,** proclaiming that a diminution of the national security of one's adversary reduces one's own security. Soviet spokesperson Georgy Arbatov went as far as to tell the United States that "we are going to do a terrible thing to you—we are going to deprive you of an enemy."

Gorbachev acknowledged that the Soviet Union could no longer afford guns and butter. To reduce the financial burdens of defense and the dangers of an arms race, he offered unprecedented unilateral arms reductions. "We understand," Gorbachev lamented, "that the arms race . . . serves objectives whose essence is to exhaust the Soviet Union economically." He then went even further, proclaiming his desire to end the Cold War altogether. "We realize that we are divided by profound historical, ideological, socioeconomic, and cultural differences," Gorbachev noted during his first visit to the United States in 1987. "But the wisdom of politics today lies in not using those differences as a pretext for confrontation, enmity, and the arms race."

The premises underlying containment appeared increasingly irrelevant in the context of these promising pronouncements and opportunities. As Strobe Talbott (1990), later deputy secretary of state in the Clinton administration, put it, "Gorbachev's initiatives . . . made containment sound like such an anachronism that the need to move beyond it is self-evident." Still, the premises of the past continued to exert a powerful grip. Fears that Gorbachev's reforms might fail, that Gorbachev himself was an evil genius conning the West, or that his promises could not be trusted were uppermost in the minds of Ronald Reagan and, later, George Bush. "The Soviet Union," Bush warned in May 1989, had "promised a more cooperative relationship before—only to reverse course and return to militarism." Thus, although claiming in May 1989 its desire to move "beyond containment," the Bush administration did not abandon containment. Instead, it resurrected the linkage strategy.

Surprisingly, demands of linkage were soon met. Soviet troops were withdrawn from Afghanistan in 1989. A year later the United States sought and received Soviet support for Operation Desert Shield. Gorbachev then announced that the Soviet Union would terminate its aid to and presence in Cuba, and he promised that it would liberalize its emigration policies, and allow greater political and religious freedom.

The normalization of Soviet-American relations now moved rapidly apace.[9] The Cold War, which had begun in Europe and centered there for forty-five years, ended there. All the communist governments in the Soviet "bloc" in Eastern Europe permitted democratic elections, in which Communist party candidates routinely lost. Capitalist free market principles also replaced socialism. To the surprise of nearly everyone, the Soviet Union acquiesced in these revolutionary changes. Without resistance, the Berlin Wall was dismantled, the Germanies united, and the Warsaw Pact ended. As these seismic changes shook the world, the Soviet Union itself sped its reforms to promote democracy and a market economy, and eagerly sought cooperation with and economic assistance from the West.

The failed conservative coup against Gorbachev in August 1991 put the final nail in the coffin of Communist Party control in Moscow, the very heartland of the international communist movement. By that Christmas, the Soviet Union has ceased to exist, replaced instead by Russia and fourteen *newly-independent states* (including Ukraine, Belarus, Kazakhstan, Georgia, and others). With communism now in retreat everywhere, the face of world politics was transformed irrevocably, setting the stage for a post-containment American foreign policy.

The End of the Cold War: Competing Hypotheses With the end of the Cold War the proposition that George Kennan advanced in his famous 1947 "X" article appeared prophetic. "The United States has it in its power," he wrote, "to increase enormously the strains under which Soviet policy must operate, to force upon the Kremlin a far greater degree of moderation and circumspection than it has had to observe in recent years, and in this way to promote tendencies which must eventually find their outlet in either the breakup of or the gradual mellowing of Soviet power." That was precisely what *did* happen—over forty years later.

Left unsettled, however, were the causes of this "victory" over communism. Did *militant containment* force the Soviet Union into submission? If so, nuclear weapons played a critical role in producing what historian John Gaddis (1986) has called "the long peace." The drive to produce them also may have helped to bankrupt the Soviet planned economy. In particular, the Reagan administration's "Star Wars" program—officially known as the Strategic Defense Initiative (SDI)—arguably convinced Gorbachev and his advisers that they could not compete with the United States (Fitzgerald 2000). From this perspective *power* played a key role in causing the end of the Cold War. People on the conservative side of the political spectrum in the United States were quick to embrace this view, thus crediting Ronald Reagan and his policies with having "won" the Cold War.

Others, particularly on the liberal side of the spectrum, placed greater emphasis elsewhere. They saw Soviet leaders succumbing to the inherent *political* and *economic* weaknesses of their own system, which left them unable to conduct an imperial policy abroad or retain communist control at home. This is much like the demise of Soviet power Kennan envisioned decades earlier. Recall that Soviet leaders were convinced they were the vanguard of a socialist-communist movement that would ultimately prevail over the West. This provided the ideological framework within which the geostrategic conflict with the United States took place. Only when Soviet leaders themselves repudiated this framework—as Gorbachev did—was it possible to end the Cold War. From this perspective

the West did not . . . win the Cold War through geopolitical containment and military deterrence. Still less was the Cold War won by the Reagan military buildup and the Reagan doctrine. . . . Instead, "victory" came when a new generation of Soviet leaders realized how badly their system at home and their policies abroad had failed. What containment did do was to preclude any temptations on the part of Moscow to advance Soviet hegemony by military means. . . . Because the Cold War rested on Marxist-Leninist assumptions of inevitable world conflict, only a Soviet leader could have ended it. And Gorbachev set out deliberately to do just that.

(GARTHOFF 1994, 11–12; SEE ALSO PORTER 1992; BUT COMPARE PIPES 1995.)

Just as historians have debated the causes of the Cold War for decades, explaining its demise quickly became a growth industry.[10] The reasons are clear and compelling: If we can learn the causes of the Cold War's rise and demise, we will learn much about the role of power and principle, about ideals and self-interest, as the United States devises new foreign policy strategies for a new century. Clearly, however, a historical watershed is now behind us.

IN SEARCH OF A RATIONALE: FROM THE 1990S INTO THE TWENTY-FIRST CENTURY

At the conclusion of the Persian Gulf War, George Bush proclaimed that "we can see a new world coming into view. . . . In the words of Winston Churchill, a world order in which 'the principles of justice and fair play protect the weak against the strong. . . . ' A world where the United Nations—freed from Cold War stalemate—is poised to fulfill the historic vision of its founders. A world in which freedom and respect for human rights find a home among all nations." He also punctuated the necessity of American leadership: "In a world where we are the only remaining superpower, it is the role of the United States to marshal its moral and material resources to promote a democratic peace. It is our responsibility . . . to lead." Thus "Bush anticipated American dominance that would be both legitimate and, to some extent, welcomed by the global community" (Brilmayer 1994). In short, this would be a *New World Order.*

Bush's vision punctuated the continuing appeal of *Wilsonian idealism.* To be sure, power was the overriding element in the Cold War strategy of containment—to the point that principles themselves were sometimes bastardized. Nonetheless, Henry Kissinger, himself an ardent realist, recounts in his book *Diplomacy* (1994a) how elements of the idealist paradigm punctuated the policies of presidents from Franklin Roosevelt to Bill Clinton. He concludes that at the twilight of the twentieth century "Wilsonianism seemed triumphant. . . . For the third time in this century, America thus proclaimed its intention to build a new world order by applying its domestic values to the world at large."

Clinton went to Washington on the strength of his domestic policy program, but his foreign policy agenda was also ambitious. "There was scarcely any item on the wish-list of contemporary American internationalism—preventing aggression, stopping nuclear proliferation, vigorously promoting human rights and democracy, redressing the humanitarian disasters that normally attend civil wars—where Clinton promised a more modest U.S. role [than Bush]. On the contrary, the gravamen of the critique was that Bush had done too little, not too much" (Hendrickson 1994).

The Clinton agenda reflected the view that the end of the Cold War had opened a pandora's box of new challenges to America's enduring values and interests. Clinton described them in a 1994 address to the United Nations:

The dangers we face are less stark and more diffuse than those of the Cold War, but they are still formidable—the ethnic conflicts that drive millions from their homes; the despots ready to repress their own people or conquer their neighbors; the proliferation of weapons of mass destruction; the terrorists wielding their deadly arms; the criminal syndicates selling those arms or drugs or infiltrating the very institutions of a fragile democracy; a global economy that offers great promise but also deep insecurity and, in many places, declining opportunity; diseases like AIDS that threaten to decimate nations; the combined dangers of population explosion and economic decline . . . ; [and] global and local environmental threats.

As *globalization* gained momentum, in 1999 Clinton told the American Society of Newspaper Editors that those new challenges involved " . . . a great battle between the forces of integration and the forces of disintegration; the forces of globalism versus tribalism; of oppression against empowerment." Shortly before that Secretary of State Madeleine Albright affirmed that "Our strategic goal is to bring the nations of the world closer together around fundamental principles of democracy and law, open markets, and a commitment to peace."

At the very end of his administration, Clinton identified five areas of concern for "a foreign policy for a global age": maintaining strong alliances with our key friends in Europe and Asia (and expanding them to include new friends and partners); building and maintaining constructive relationships with Russia and China, while helping them to integrate into the global political and economic system; attending to local conflicts before they escalate or spill over into other areas; addressing emerging threats becoming more problematic in a globalizing world (for example, proliferation, terrorism, climate change, disease); and working toward continued economic integration and expansion of free markets, while also addressing the inequalities and other negative consequences often accompanying these forces. Let us briefly explore these ideas here before we elaborate on them in later chapters.

Promoting Democracy

During Clinton's first term, no goal seemed more important than promoting democracy. "In a new era of peril and opportunity," Clinton declared in 1993, "our overriding purpose must be to expand and strengthen the world's community of market-based democracies." Anthony Lake, then his national security adviser, urged that "the successor to a doctrine of containment must be a *strategy of enlargement*—enlargement of the world's free community of market economies."[11]

The centrality of *democracy promotion* rested squarely on the belief that democracies are more peaceful than other political systems. That conviction, a bedrock of Wilsonian idealism, enjoys a long heritage going back at least to Immanuel Kant's eighteenth-century treatise *Perpetual Peace*. Democracies are as willing and capable of waging war as others, but scholarly inquiry demonstrates conclusively what Kant argued two centuries ago: democracies do not engage in war with one another. Furthermore, democracies are more likely to use nonviolent forms of conflict resolution than others.[12] Thus Clinton and others in his administration would repeatedly defend the goal of democratic promotion by noting that *democracies don't wage war on each other*. Indeed, "they . . . converted that proposition into a security policy manifesto. Given that democracies do not make war with each other, . . . the United States should seek to guarantee its security by promoting democracy abroad" (Carothers 1994a).[13]

Initially the determination to promote democracy was most evident in Russia and the other **New Independent States** (former republics of the Union of Soviet Socialist Republics [USSR]). By conjoining democratic promotion with reform of former adversaries, Clinton embraced a timeworn foreign policy tradition. In each of four previous watersheds in America's response to victory in war—the Civil War, the Spanish-American War, and World Wars I and II—promoting democracy among the vanquished became paramount.

When Wilson said he would "make the world safe for democracy," he was but repeating with a global perspective Abraham Lincoln's assertion in 1858 that this country could not live "half slave and half free." Roosevelt and Truman later echoed Wilson, first when they doubted that America could survive alone in a world dominated by fascism and, later, after 1945, when they attempted to promote democracy in Eastern Europe so as to block the expansionist aims of a hostile Soviet Union and . . . insisted that the democratization of Japan and Germany would be the primary aim of American occupation policy.

(SMITH 1994C, 92–93).

In a larger sense democratic promotion also played to the heritage of liberty long evident in American foreign policy. Defending the Clinton project, Clinton's Deputy Secretary of State Strobe Talbott put it this way:

The American people want their country's foreign policy rooted in idealpolitik as well as realpolitik. The United States is uniquely and self-consciously a country founded on a set of ideas, and ideals, applicable to people everywhere. The Founding Fathers declared that all were created equal—not just those in Britain's thirteen American colonies—and that to ensure the "unalienable rights" of life, liberty, and the pursuit of happiness, people had the right to establish governments that derive "their just powers from the consent of the governed."

(TALBOTT 1996, 49–50; SEE HARPER [1997] FOR A REJOINDER.)

Despite the appeal of democracy, its centrality as a pillar of American foreign policy proved ephemeral. Almost immediately critics complained that "democratic enlargement" "had no connection to reality and . . . was an aspiration rather than a strategy." (Brinkley 1997). Another evaluation stressed that while democracy promotion was a generally useful element of U.S. foreign policy, "It is . . . only one of several. . . . It does not and cannot serve as a controlling framework or central organizing principle" (Carothers 1995).[14]

To be sure, some progress occurred. For example, the Clinton administration formalized certain institutional structures and processes to elevate democracy promotion in the policy process, and the U.S. Agency for International Democracy took advantage of its role in policy implementation to elevate democracy promotion to one of four core purposes in U.S. foreign aid policy (see Travis 1998).

Nevertheless, later events seemed to prove the critics right. Political turmoil and economic setbacks in Russia stalled efforts to build a new democratic state.[15] Strained relations over issues involving Iran, the Middle East, and the Balkans also dampened U.S. enthusiasm for aiding its former adversary. Interventions in Haiti and Bosnia designed to promote democracy quickly confronted the realities of grinding poverty and ethnic animosities that had prevented democracy and civil society in the first place. In the Middle East, the United States faced the uncomfortable fact that its security and economic interests were closely linked to authoritarian states, where democratic promotion might produce instability, not peace. In Africa, the one region where democratic promotion activities were emphasized most, the typically low priority of the region worked against substantial efforts or expenditures toward the goal.

Elsewhere the early enthusiasm that accompanied the rapid spread of democracy following the Cold War cooled in the face of setbacks and retrenchment. One of them involved the substantial opposition in Congress to committing U.S. resources for such purposes, especially after the Republican victories leading their majorities in both houses in 1994. Another involved questions about the seemingly positive and optimistic trend toward democratization. As one observer wrote in early 1997, "The headlines announcing that country after country was shrugging off dictatorial rule and embarking on a democratic path have given way to an intermittent but rising stream of troubling reports: a coup in Gambia, civil strife in the Central African Republic, flawed elections in Albania, a deposed government in

Pakistan, returning authoritarianism in Zambia, the shedding of democratic forms in Kazakstan, sabotaged elections in Armenia, eroding human rights in Cambodia" (Carothers 1997; see also Wright 1997). Still another involved the rather lukewarm results of policy implementation evaluations, many of which suggested that efforts to promote democracy were "usually modestly positive, sometimes negligible, and occasionally negative" (Carothers 1999). Not surprisingly, then, Clinton ended his administration with much less emphasis on democracy promotion than at the start. Increasingly, his administration soft-peddled its once outspoken advocacy of democratic enlargement, as pragmatism, not idealism, increasingly characterized its approach. Indeed, as one analyst argued, democracy promotion was increasingly subsumed into efforts to promote market economics (Brinkley 1997).

Promoting Open Markets

Clinton's 1992 drive for the White House emphasized economics. His agenda included domestic economic rejuvenation, enhanced competitiveness in foreign markets, and the promotion of sustainable development in the Global South. Then Under Secretary of the Treasury Lawrence H. Summers highlighted the intersection of Clinton's security and economic priorities when he observed that "the two key pillars of any viable foreign policy are the maintenance of security and the maintenance of prosperity." Meanwhile, the Commerce Department, normally a backwater in the foreign affairs government, brimmed with activity as it sought to return the United States to an era when "the business of America is business." Even the State Department shed some of its traditional aversion to commercial diplomacy. "For a long time secretaries of state thought of economics as 'low policy,' while they dealt only with high science like arms control," averred Secretary of State Warren Christopher. "I make no apologies for putting economics at the top of our foreign-policy agenda."

Clinton's foreign economic agenda focused on four general categories of issues. First, he worked to build an overall "architecture" of *rules and institutions* through renewal of the **General Agreement on Tariffs and Trade** (GATT), which included provisions for a new **World Trade Organization** (WTO), as well as additional efforts toward financial coordination. He also worked toward regional trade arrangements to *expand U.S. markets, reduce barriers to trade,* and *integrate economies* through such efforts as the North American Free Trade Agreement (NAFTA) linking the United States, Canada, and Mexico in a free trade zone and initiatives toward free trade zones in the Western Hemisphere and the Pacific Basin. The Clinton Administration also focused on bilateral approaches toward specific trade partners, including Japan, Europe, China, and the so-called "Big Emerging Markets" around the world. In addition to tough negotiating postures toward Japan, and the European Union on salient trade issues, Clinton negotiated an agreement for Permanent Normal Trade Relations with China and that country's accession to the World Trade Organization. In fact, by the time the Clinton Administration ended, it could claim some three hundred market-opening agreements with other countries. Finally, the Clinton Administration also took steps to improve the infrastructure and policies for U.S. exports and export promotion, streamlining export assistance and licensing procedures and expanding government efforts to advocate for U.S. exporters overseas (see Scott 1997, 1998).

Clinton's emphasis on shoring up the U.S. position in the world economy arguably produced some of his administration's most notable achievements (Walt 2000). The initiatives also fit well into the tapestry of *economic liberalism* (the existence or development of market economies) central to Wilsonian ideals. Indeed, the promotion of *democratic capitalism* almost invariably came coupled with the goal of democratic enlargement (Brinkley 1997). Hence creating market economies was not only good for business, it was also good for peace. As Deputy Secretary of State Talbott (1996) said in defending the administration's objectives, "The larger and more close-knit the community of nations that choose democratic forms of government, the safer and more prosperous Americans will be."

Still, there was a difference between Clintonism and Wilsonianism. As political scientist Stanley Hoffmann (1995) observed, "the main Clinton objective [was not] free trade per se, but a return to growth, hence to fuller employment at home. The president [was] more interested in the liberal vision at home than the liberal vision abroad. Or rather, the latter serves the former." Furthermore, democracy may not be able to thrive in the absence of economic liberalism. Because the correlation between democracy and economic liberalism in the United States is clear, analysts wonder if the former can exist without the latter (Gurr 1991).[16] If not, what political scientist Samuel Huntington (1991) describes as the latest wave of democratization may fall victim to the more difficult task of promoting market economies where none existed previously.

Promoting International Values

In 1992 candidate Bill Clinton criticized President George Bush for doing too little to stop ethnic conflict in Bosnia, where a systematic pattern of genocide widely described as *ethnic cleansing* was unfolding. In 1993 President Bill Clinton chose not to become involved in the Balkans' roiling ethnic conflict. Not until 1995 did the United States actively seek a settlement of the bloody dispute. Four years later Clinton would move more forcefully in support of a military response to civil conflict in the Serbian province of Kosovo. Together with its NATO partners, the United States launched a sustained military attack on Serbia designed to ensure the autonomy of Kosovo and to stanch the bloodletting perpetrated there on ethnic Albanians by Serbian military, paramilitary, and police forces.

Some analysts, drawing on statements President Clinton sounded following NATO's intervention, characterized the rationale underlying the campaign as the ***Clinton Doctrine***.[17] Speaking during the ***G-8*** (the seven largest western industrialized states plus Russia) summit in Germany in 1999, Clinton remarked that "We may never have a world that is without hatred or tyranny or conflict, but at least instead of ending this century with helpless indignation in the face of it, we instead begin a new century and a new millennium with a hopeful affirmation of human rights and human dignity." Then, speaking before KFOR (Kosovo Force) troops in Macedonia, Clinton defined in dramatically more assertive terms America's role in enforcing *international values*:

> People should not be killed, uprooted or destroyed because of their race, their ethnic background or the way they worship God. . . . Never forget if we can do this here [the Balkans], and if we can then say to the people of the world, whether you live in Africa, or Central Europe, or any other place, if somebody comes after innocent civilians and tries to kill them en masse because of their race, their ethnic background or their religion, and it's within our power to stop it, we will stop it.

We will examine the Clinton Doctrine and other ideas regarding the proper use of force in greater detail in Chapter 4. Here, however, it is significant as an example of the Clinton Administration's commitment to intervention for the purpose of upholding key values like human rights and key principles of international law. According to Clinton's National Security Adviser Sandy Berger (2000), such engagement is critical in preserving the ability of the United States to exercise leadership in the twenty-first century.

As in the case of promoting democracy, promoting international values, especially through military force, may fade with time. Whatever its end purpose, the Kosovo campaign was a "war by committee." Keeping the NATO allies united proved difficult, as a combination of domestic and international concerns within its member countries colored their commitment. In part to maintain cohesion, military operations were constrained in ways designed to minimize NATO casualties. But as the air campaign lengthened into weeks and then months, the target list was expanded to include what military strategists call "dual use" (military and civilian) infrastructure, such as bridges, television stations, electric power grids, and water supply systems. Arguably these are primarily civilian facilities which existing laws of warfare (the 1949 Geneva Convention and its 1977 protocol) seek to exempt so as to protect noncombatants.

As the bombing campaign intensified, so did the number of casualties on the ground.[18] Thus one journalist on the scene wrote the following: "As depicted by NATO briefers, the air campaign was an almost clinical exercise, of 'surgical hits' by 'precision-guided weaponry.' As seen from the ground, it was a much messier affair, in which real people died . . . From the point of view of ordinary Serbs, the distinction between Western behavior and Serbian behavior [seemed] more one of degree than one of kind" (Dobbs 1999). Former Secretary of State Henry Kissinger punctuated that viewpoint, saying that "When the only way to win is to make the population of the adversary suffer for it, that is a strange definition of morality and of humanity" (*Sunday Advocate* [Baton Rouge, La.], 11 July 1999). His concern echos an often-quoted phrase uttered by an American military officer during the Vietnam War: "We had to destroy the village to save it." Meanwhile, the war strained NATO to the point that it seemed unlikely to soon engage in another "out of area" exercise to promote international values. In the words of one Italian policy maker, "Obviously, nobody in his right mind would look with relish at the prospect of repeating this experience" (Gellman 1999).

Promoting Security and Stability

The security environment of the United States changed markedly in the years following the Cold War, prompting the Clinton administration to grapple with a mix of old and new problems. In addition to traditional state-centric concerns, the U.S. found it necessary to address an increasingly complex security context encompassing both state and nonstate actors, friends, former enemies, and rogues, and environmental forces previously ignored in security calculations.

Europe and Beyond? President Clinton noted late in his second term that maintaining and adapting U.S. alliances, forged chiefly in the Cold War, remains a central security challenge. Nowhere is this more obvious than in Europe, where the end of Cold War played with the central security alliance of post–World War II era: NATO. Long considered essential for security and stability in Europe and between Europe and the United States, NATO faced a number of critical challenges that President Clinton attempted to address: (1) who its members should be in an altered European landscape; (2) what its role and mission should be in the absence of the threat that spurred its creation; and (3) what its relationship should be with its erstwhile enemy.

On the first issue, Clinton sought expansion to the East to include former members of the Warsaw Pact. NATO comprised twelve members when it was created by the 1949. By the time of the fiftieth anniversary celebration, it embraced nineteen countries. Hungary, Poland, and the Czech Republic—all former members of the Warsaw Pact—were its latest signatories, joining only months before the Kosovo campaign.[19] A new Strategic Concept endorsed by alliance members also underscored "NATO's continued openness to new members and [its] commitment to enlargement as part of a broader effort to enhance peace and stability throughout the Euro-Atlantic community." Enlarging the alliance reflected the Clinton administration's vision of a unified, democratic, and peaceful Europe in which NATO would play a pivotal role. As one official put it in 1997, the administration anticipated building a security network stretching "from Vancouver to Vladivostok, the long way" (Apple 1997).

Indeed, many former communist states had sought membership. Instead, building on ideas first advanced during the Bush presidency, the Clinton administration pursued a "Partnership for Peace" program which enables former Warsaw Pact and other states to participate with NATO in a broad range of military activities—including joint military planning and training exercises, peacekeeping activities, and crisis management—but which does not provide security guarantees to the "partner" states or automatic membership at some future date. Nearly thirty "partners" participated in the first session of the Euro-Atlantic Partnership Council when it convened in mid-1997.

What, exactly, this new, expanded NATO would do was another question. Ironically, NATO celebrated its fiftieth anniversary in Washington at precisely the time it found itself engaged in its first-ever combat activity. The search for a new strategic vision to guide the Atlantic alliance in the twenty-first century dominated the anniversary agenda. "Out of area or out of business" encapsulated the vision of some, notably the United States, which has global interests and a global reach. "From this perspective, NATO's fundamental purpose should shift . . . from defending common territory to defending the common interests of Alliance members." Presumably that means NATO should be sensitive not only to geostrategic threats but also to other challenges, like the proliferation of weapons of mass destruction and transnational terrorism. "But for most European allies—including even those, like Great Britain and France, whose interests extend well beyond Europe—the Atlantic Alliance remains a quintessential European security organization, whose fundamental purpose is to provide security in and for Europe" (Daalder 1999; see also Kamp 1999).

The new Strategic Concept document adopted by the Atlantic allies reflected the concerns of both the Americans and the Europeans. With NATO warplanes actively engaged in Kosovo and peace enforcers already on the ground in Bosnia, the Balkans now clearly fell within NATO's embrace. But how NATO would respond to threats beyond the Balkans and its traditional geographic reach remained vague.

The relationship between this new NATO and its former enemy also generated security concerns. Sensitivity to Russian security concerns combined with fear of Russia renewing its security threat to the West has long animated the debate about NATO's future. The Partnership for Peace program put Russia on the same footing as other former Soviet and Warsaw Pact states when it joined the program in 1994. However, the decision to push NATO into eastern Europe in 1999 rankled Russia. Efforts to cushion the decision by reassuring the Russians that the newly expanding NATO was not aimed at them only partly succeeded. Relations quickly chilled significantly. Cooperation slowed, arms control treaties stalled in the Russian Duma, and other signs of friction appeared. Russian even turned to China to condemn the expansion as confrontational "blocism," and even worked to draft a formal treaty of peace and friendship, raising fears of a Sino-Russian partnership.

One approach to NATO's future leaves open the possibility of Russian entry into the alliance while simultaneously strengthening the NATO-Russia Council. Such attempts at rapprochement remain limited, however. Senator Sam Nunn, chair of the influential Senate Committee on Armed Services when the Partnership for Peace program was put into place, remarked, "The day when NATO takes in Russia as a member will be the day when NATO is no longer needed as a threat-based security alliance. A stable, democratic, market-oriented Russia operating within the precepts of international law and respecting the borders of its neighbors will obviate the need for NATO as we have known it." Unless, of course, NATO finds a new purpose.

Nonproliferation No security goal figured more prominently on the Clinton agenda than stopping the spread of weapons of mass destruction—nuclear, chemical, and biological—and the ballistic missile technology that might carry them.

FOCUS 3.4   Enlarging NATO: Why Bigger Is Better

Too often, the debate about NATO's future reduces the alliance's past to a one-dimensional caricature that discounts its relevance to today's European challenges. Certainly, NATO's cold war task was to contain the Soviet threat. But that is not all it did. It provided the confidence and security that shattered economies needed to rebuild themselves. It helped France and Germany become reconciled, making European integration possible. With other institutions, it brought Italy, then Germany, and eventually Spain back into the families of European democracies. It denationalised allied defence policies. It has stabilised relations between Greece and Turkey. All without firing a shot.

Now the new NATO can do for Europe's east what the old NATO did for Europe's west: vanquish old hatreds, promote integration, create a secure environment for prosperity, and deter violence in the region where two world wars and the cold war began. . . .

President Clinton observed in his [1997] state-of-the-union address that a child born today will have almost no memory of the twentieth century. Just the same, the children of the transatlantic community who are born today have the chance to grow up knowing a very different Europe. In that new Europe, they will know Checkpoint Charlie only as a museum, Yalta as just a provincial city in a sovereign Ukraine, Sarajevo as a peaceful mountain resort in the heart of Europe. The children of the next century will come of age knowing a very different NATO—one that masses its energies on behalf of integration, rather than massing its forces on the borders of division.

SOURCE: From Madeline K. Albright, "Enlarging NATO: Why Bigger is Better," *The Economist,* February 15, 1997, 22–23. © The Economist Newspaper Group, Inc. Reprinted with permission. Future reproduction prohibited. www.economist.com.

The United States has long been a chief advocate of the *nuclear nonproliferation regime* centered on the 1968 nuclear *Non-Proliferation Treaty (NPT),* to which nearly all states have since subscribed. (The United States also supports international controls on biological and chemical weapons, but these are less well developed.) The regime seeks to inhibit the spread of weapons technology by permitting now-nuclear states to share their knowledge of peaceful atomic energy uses with nonnuclear states at the same time that they are prevented from sharing technology related to weapons production. Controls on the export of existing technology to potential buyers are a crucial element of the regime. A primary objective is to permit less developed countries to have access to commercial nuclear power plants without allowing their by-products to be funneled into bombs. The *International Atomic Energy Agency (IAEA)* is charged with ensuring compliance with the NPT principles.

Evidence suggests that North Korea—and Iraq before it—came close to producing nuclear bombs not by diverting materials from peaceful purposes to weapons production but by building their own nuclear infrastructures, much like the United States did when it first built atomic weapons in the 1940s. The existing nonproliferation regime, with IAEA as its enforcement arm, cannot cope with this kind of proliferation, for which it was never designed.

North Korea's drive to obtain the bomb boldly challenged Clinton's priorities. In 1994 Defense Secretary Perry and others implied that nothing short of military action would blunt the forward momentum of the "rogue" state's weapons program, in violation of the nonproliferation treaty to which it is a signatory. Thus the United States positioned itself to engage in *counterproliferation,* an ambiguous yet threatening concept with origins in the first Bush administration's post–Persian Gulf thinking about the Pentagon's future mission. Counterproliferation, at least as first proffered by the Clinton administration, implied that "the United States intended to establish itself as global judge, jury, and executioner against weapons of mass destruction" (Müller and Reiss 1995; see also Pilat and Kirchner 1995).

A military crisis with North Korea was eventually averted, but at great cost to the United States. In a carefully crafted agreement, the United States, with the support of Japan and South Korea, agreed to supply North Korea with two new, proliferation-resistant nuclear reactors (plus enormous amounts of oil), in return for which North Korea would dismantle its nuclear facilities—but without guaranteed IAEA inspections for at least some time. Critics argued the agreement also was costly to the nonproliferation regime, as it encouraged other "rogue" states to keep alive their dreams of an atomic future in the expectation the United States would eventually reward them for not living up to their treaty obligations (Sanger 1994). Meanwhile, North Korea continued to develop ballistic missile technology with which it might someday be able to deliver an atomic device against a distant target. By decade's end Japan was increasingly concerned about its own security, causing many Japanese to wonder whether its pacifist profile, adopted after World War II, written into the Japanese constitution, and sustained by the U.S. nuclear umbrella, remained appropriate to developing security challenges in the Far East.

India and Pakistan also posed vexing challenges to the nonproliferation regime. While other states that once pursued the nuclear option, such as Argentina, Brazil, and South Africa, abandoned them, India and Pakistan pushed forward. Neither had signed the NPT, and their own rivalry combined with India's fear of China propelled their nuclear programs forward. India first tested a nuclear device in 1974. By the mid-1980s it was clear that Pakistan also enjoyed a nuclear capability built through largely clandestine means. Then, in May 1998, both carried out a series of underground nuclear tests, shocking the world with their "in-your-face" defiance of prevailing global sentiments and the long-standing global testing moratorium.

India has long maintained that the goal of nuclear nonproliferation can never be attained as long as some states reserve to themselves the right to possess these weapons.[20] Responding to criticisms (and the imposition of sanctions by the United States) following its 1998 tests, former foreign minister Natwar Singh asserted that "No one has the right to tell us we cannot have the nuclear option." He added that by sanctioning India while ignoring China's nuclear program, the United States was "pampering a dictatorship and pestering a democracy." An Islamic leader in Pakistan joined the chorus of protest to western reactions to its tests: "Do the United States, England, France have orders from God that they should be nuclear powers, and not us?" (Constable 1998).

India and Pakistan also are developing ballistic missiles, which could move their small cache of atomic weapons into launch-ready nuclear arsenals. This, too, is troubling to nonproliferation advocates. In 1987, seven of the world's most advanced suppliers of missile-related technology established the *Missile Technology Control Regime (MTCR)* in an effort to slow the development of missiles capable of delivering weapons of mass destruction. A decade later, more than thirty countries subscribed to its principles. However, the MTCR remains an informal, voluntary arrangement. The Clinton administration advocated transforming the export regime into a more formal institution with binding legal obligations, but this has not happened. Thus the MTCR remains at best an irritant against further missile development. Notably, the United States determined in the early 1990s that, despite the MTCR ground rules, China had provided missile technology to Pakistan—a message not lost in New Delhi (Singh 1999).

The Clinton administration did notch some victories on the nonproliferation front. In 1995, 175 countries agreed to extend the NPT indefinitely. Deputy Secretary of State Strobe Talbott (1999) explained that "The nonnuclear-weapons states that signed the NPT did so because they believed it would spare them the expense of having to compete with one another in nuclear weaponry and because it would prevent their neighbors from being able to threaten them with nuclear weapons. The overwhelming majority of states continues to believe that the spread of such weapons would add perilously to regional and global tensions." Earlier the administration also persuaded the New Independent States of Belarus, Kazakhstan, and Ukraine to return Soviet nuclear weapons on their soil to Russia for dismantlement. Additionally, in 1997, the administration gained ratification of the **Chemical Weapons Convention** in the Senate, which ensured that the United States would join over 160 countries in banning the development, production, acquisition, transfer, stockpiling, and use of chemical weapons. Furthermore, the United States helped to persuade China to join both of these agreements and the **Biological Weapons Convention** while curtailing some of its support for nuclear programs in Iran and Pakistan (Berger 2000).

Despite these victories, the battle against the proliferation of weapons of mass destruction continues. Of particular concern to many observers is the changing nature of the problem. As one analyst put it "Rogue nations and 'clientless' states, terrorist groups, religious cults, ethnic minorities, disaffected political groups, and even individuals appear to have joined a new arms race toward mass destruction," for which the United States is fundamentally unprepared (Sopko 1996–97). Indeed, some skeptics argue that "the spread of nuclear weapons and the means to deliver them has already advanced so far that the important question is no longer how to stop their proliferation, but rather how to prevent them from being used" (Cropsey 1994).

Low-Intensity Conflict and Neo-Containment
Early in the first Clinton term National Security Adviser Anthony Lake talked about the "enemies of the tolerant society," using the term "chaos" to describe post–Cold War challenges posed by "extreme nationalists and tribalists, terrorists, organized criminals, coup plotters, rogue states." Collectively, these kinds of threats were once encompassed

under the concept **low-intensity conflict:** violence and warfare that fall short of full-scale conventional combat or nuclear confrontation (see Snow 1998). Ethnic conflict in Bosnia and Kosovo, tribal warfare in Rwanda and Somalia, instability in Russia's "near abroad (terrorism at home and abroad)" terrorism in East Africa, anarchy in Sierra Leone, drug trafficking in South and Central America—all are examples of the challenges and often bloody consequences of low-intensity conflict. Economic sanctions and various kinds of military intervention are sometimes used to cope with such threats and to contain their contagion (see Barnet 1990). Most challenges posed by low-intensity conflict occur within rather than between nations, however, which limits the capacity of traditional foreign policy instruments to affect outcomes—and may help explain the checkered record of dealing with them during the past decade.

Iran and Iraq were thought to pose more traditional challenges, even as they were sometimes also linked to low-intensity threats. To deal with these so-called "rogue" or "backlash states," the Clinton administration proposed a policy of *dual containment.* Using language strikingly reminiscent of Kennan's famous "X" article, in which he called for containment of the Soviet Union, Anthony Lake (1994), also writing in *Foreign Affairs,* urged that "the United States has a special responsibility for developing a strategy to neutralize, contain and, through selective pressure, perhaps eventually transform these backlash states into constructive members of the international community."

Dual containment built on priorities that have long guided U.S.-Middle East policy, some going back to the early Cold War years, if not before: protecting Israel's security and independence, ensuring a continuing flow of oil to the world at reasonable prices, and keeping other powers from supplanting American dominance in the region. The growing perception of Islamic fundamentalism as a threat, much of it emanating from Southwest Asia (as recently), a fault line in what Samuel Huntington (1993a) calls a coming *clash of civilizations,* added a renewed sense of urgency to these long-standing goals. Nonetheless, there was something different: "Dual containment committed the United States to holding the ring against the two most powerful states in the Gulf. That was new. Even the British during their long ascendency over the region had always counted on a neutral or friendly regime in either Baghdad or Tehran" (Sicherman 1997).

Dual containment proved controversial from the beginning. Although built on the principles of *realpolitik,* critics challenged "the unstated assumption that the regional status quo in the Gulf can be maintained over the coming years, and that any changes there can be stage-managed by Washington" (Gause 1994). To be successful, two conditions had to be met. "First, decisive U.S. military power had to be available on short notice, and Washington had to be prepared to use it. Secondly, the key members of the [Persian Gulf War] coalition had to support a strategy of containment against both Iraq and Iran" (Sicherman 1997). Neither condition was met.

The United States did frequently use force against Iraq as reprisals for various transgressions, particularly its refusal to cooperate with the arms inspectors of the United Nations Special Commission (UNSCOM), who were charged with dismantling Saddam's capability to produce weapons of mass destruction. But the exercise of force was often tentative, not decisive. Thus one critic charged that "the administration's posture fit a familiar pattern of speaking grandly and deploying underwhelming force" (Garfinkle 1998; see also Kay 1998). Meanwhile, on the sanctions front, the United States found itself increasingly isolated as other coalition partners found them ineffectual and sought to regain commercial advantages by trading with Iraq. The United States also faced growing restiveness among other Arab states who once supported its policies but now became apprehensive about their own security in the face of disenchantment with U.S.-Middle Eastern policies.

The United States found itself out of step on sanctions toward Iran as well. In 1995 the Clinton administration imposed a comprehensive ban on all U.S. trade with Iran. Two years later it tried to impose secondary sanctions on foreign companies

investing in Iranian oil and gas industries. Meanwhile, China, France, and Russia stepped into the breech, supplying Iran with nuclear reactors and investments in other energy technologies from which American firms had hoped to profit. Once more, critics found American policy misguided: "A growing consensus now argues that containment of any nation, especially one with petrodollars, is increasingly difficult in an era of globalization when borders are more porous and competition for markets unprecedented. . . . Meanwhile, containment has had no appreciable effect on Iranian behavior in the areas Washington deems most critical—weapons of mass destruction, the Arab-Israeli peace process, and support for extremist Islamic movements" (Wright and Bakhas 1997; see also Sick 1999).

In 1997 the Iranian electorate unexpectedly chose Mohammed Khatami as Iran's new president. Widely perceived as a mandate for change in the Islamic Republic, Khatami's election raised hopes in some circles that steps might be taken to defuse the tense U.S.-Iranian relations. The Clinton administration did take some halting steps in this direction, as did the Khatami government, but with little noticeable effect. Once more, critics worried that U.S. policy was dysfunctional. One Iranian expert, who served on the National Security Council staff during Iran's radical Islamic revolution in 1979, put it this way:

> It is difficult . . . to make a logical connection between our objections to Iran's policies and the web of punitive sanctions that remain on the books. We have serious differences with China as well, but U.S. officials maintain that those differences can best be resolved by engagement and persuasion, not by hostility and estrangement. . . . We owe Iran no favors. But if our actions are harming our political and economic interests in the Persian Gulf, while not addressing our policy concerns, something is wrong. . . . Yet U.S. policy continues to be driven by inertia and old political habits.

(SICK 1999, 23)

The phrase "dual containment" was little used during the second Clinton term. However, what to do about Saddam Hussein's authoritarian regime and the security challenges it posed to its neighbors and U.S. interests remained a key concern. Growing domestic political sentiment favored overthrowing Saddam Hussein, not just isolating him. As Senate Majority Leader Trent Lott put it, "The doctrine here has to be rollback, not containment." Both concepts harken back to the 1950s, when the Eisenhower administration promised to abandon the allegedly defensive containment strategy for dealing with Soviet communism in favor of a proactive posture that would "roll back" the communist challenge to the very walls of the Kremlin. In the case of Iraq, Congress in late 1998 appropriated $97 million for the purpose of aiding Iraqi resistence groups in their efforts to topple the existing regime. A former under secretary of defense supported the sentiment this way: " Toppling Saddam is the only outcome that can satisfy the vital U.S. interest in a stable and secure Gulf region" (Byman, Pollack, and Rose 1999).

Others challenged that viewpoint. "Even if rollback were desirable," responded three prominent policy analysts, "any policy to achieve it would have to pass three tests to be considered seriously. It would have to be militarily feasible, amenable to American allies whose cooperation would be required for implementation, and acceptable to the American people" (Byman, Pollack, and Rose 1999). Their conclusion? None of the tests could be passed.

A New Problem Agenda? Alongside these security issues, the Clinton Administration began also to raise a host of new items driven to the forefront largely by the processes of globalization and interdependence. In addition to such transnational issues as terrorism and drug trafficking, Clinton began to direct attention to other newly-emerging security issues as major security challenges of the twenty-first century. For example, increasing dependence on electronic networks in the global information age makes those networks a potential target for *cyberterrorists*. In response,

the administration initiated a national strategy to protect computer systems and information infrastructure. Furthermore, the administration sought to elevate environmental and health threats to the level of national security concerns as well. Included in this group were concerns about global climate change and the spread of infectious diseases. As the 1999 National Security Strategy noted, "Environmental threats such as climate change . . . directly threaten the health and well-being of U.S. citizens. . . . Diseases and health risks can no longer be viewed solely as a domestic concern. With the movement of millions of people per day across international borders and the expansion of international trade, health issues as diverse as importation of dangerous infectious diseases and bioterrorism preparedness profoundly affect our national security."

Return to Realism? George W. Bush made it clear in his inaugural address that he would protect and promote the enduring values and interests of the United States. In his words, "The enemies of liberty and our country should make no mistake: America remains engaged in the world by history and by choice, shaping a balance of power that favors freedom. We will defend our allies and our interests. We will show purpose without arrogance. We will meet aggression and bad faith with resolve and strength. And to all nations, we will speak for the values that gave our nation birth."

However, the second Bush presidency faced a complex, globalizing world where borders matter less and issues more. It found it must chart a course without the advantage of an overarching foreign policy paradigm to guide policy choices. Finally, it was forced to adjust its initial approach to the post-September 11 world. What blend of principle, power, and pragmatism, then, will guide the Bush administration as it steers its way into the twenty-first century?

Early indicators suggest an effort to return to realism as a general orientation, along with an emphasis on more traditional foreign policy concerns than those which animated the Clinton administration and a somewhat reduced role in various international arenas.

Before his controversial victory in the 2000 election, George W. Bush's future national security adviser, Condoleezza Rice, hinted at a foreign policy approach based squarely on the tenets of realism. According to Rice (2000), the new administration "should refocus the United States on the national interest and the pursuit of key priorities." Another future administration official, Robert B. Zoellick (later named U.S. Trade Representative) argued that modern Republican foreign policy would be "premised on a respect for power, being neither ashamed to pursue America's national interests nor too quick to use the country's might" (Zoellick 2000). These statements clearly hinted at a less multilateral and more cautious approach to international engagement.

Throughout the election campaign, Bush officials emphasized the need for increased military spending to counter what they argued were the excessive reductions of the Clinton era. The American military, they argued, was dangerously unprepared and over-committed. Hence, they also argued for a reduction in overseas military commitments. The president-elect and those who would become his national security advisers signaled their intention to reduce the U.S. role in peacekeeping missions like that in the Balkans. Bush noted in this respect that U.S. troops would not be engaged in *nation-building,* an obvious effort to distance his administration from his predecessor's commitment to supporting such efforts (Sanger 2001). Such comments were met with disapproval among NATO allies, concerned that they indicated Bush would not fulfill U.S. commitments. This, of course, raised concerns about U.S. relations with its NATO allies. One observer suggested that Bush might soon discover that, with the United States doing less, he might find that NATO was "doing more than he would like" (*New York Times,* 20 January 2001, 19).

Similarly, the administration signaled that it would be less accommodating to both China and Russia. Continued financial aid to Russia was to be made contingent on greater Russian progress on its reform efforts. Bush's commitment to a missile defense system likewise indicated a tougher stance toward the former Cold War rival, perhaps complicating the relationship. Bush also promised to treat China more as a rival than a *strategic partner,* as Clinton had sought to characterize U.S. relations with the Asian giant. Bush also promised to provide stronger support to Taiwan, a position sure to add complexity to an already delicate and intricate relationship. China's opposition to Bush's determination to build a missile defense system, something shared in common with its erstwhile competitor Russia, added fuel to the simmering conflict that threatened to grow hotter.

In the economic arena, the Bush Administration appeared less likely to depart from its predecessor's approach. Free trade and the expansion of open markets remained priorities. Still, Bush signaled during his campaign he was less supportive of the efforts of institutions like the International Monetary Fund. But he moved to build on Clinton's efforts to integrate foreign and economic policy by establishing a staff coordinated by both his national security adviser and his chief economic adviser to work on international economic policy and economic crises. Given the imperatives of the globalizing economy, that decision was not surprising.

After the September 11, 2001, terrorist attacks, the Bush administration accelerated its reliance on the language of enduring values and international engagement, but reduced its emphasis on self-interest and unilateralism. The requirements of a campaign against terror, first in Afghanistan and then elsewhere, demanded international cooperation. As one observer noted "Allies are essential for success in the war on terrorism, which helps to explain the determination of President George W. Bush and his administration to build a broad coalition" (Posen 2001/2002). Russia and China both enjoyed much warmer relations as the administration concentrated its policy efforts on the anti-terror campaign. The Bush administration's initial instincts to act "against the interests of others in pursuit of relatively modest gains" (Posen 2001/2002) began to yield to its need to mobilize other countries, including its European allies. Its post–September 2001 foreign policy reflected this, as an observer aptly commented: "The United States needs friends, and thus must prioritize among its many foreign policy and defence policy initiatives, because these initiatives have frequently antagonized other governments and peoples" (Posen 2001/2002). Consequently, in the terms we used in the first chapter, George W. Bush's administration moved toward "selective engagement" in its approach to the world. Nonetheless, as the immediate urgency of the anti-terror war in Afghanistan recedes, the challenge of maintaining America's role as a global leader while achieving a more limited, self-interested foreign policy agenda will remain.

PRINCIPLE, POWER, OR PRAGMATISM?

As the policy of dual containment evolved during the 1990s, the United States often found itself acting alone, not in concert with its allies. Its behavior thus paralleled much of its nineteenth century foreign policy posture, when it typically preferred unilateralism over multilateralism as it pursued its enduring values and interests: peace and prosperity, stability and security, democracy and defense. As it entered the twenty-first century, however, its behavior as the only superpower caused consternation elsewhere. Across a broad range of issues—from expansion of NATO and the containment of Iraq to trading with Cuba and banning land mines—the United States took positions at variance with those of its closest, long-time friends and allies. This smacked of an arrogance of power many found offensive.

Potential adversaries like China and Russia also worried about the seemingly raw exercise of U.S. hegemonic power. Thus China refused to accept the explanation that the bombing of its embassy in Belgrade during the Kosovo war was accidental. Instead, it saw it as a purposeful act antagonistic to Chinese interests. Increasingly,

then, whether by design or default, the United States found itself isolated (Drozdiak 1997; Hendrickson 1994; Huntington 1999; Sanger 1999). One would not have expected this in the heady days following the Persian Gulf War, when President George H. W. Bush embraced the vision of a new world order founded on Wilsonianism and multilateralism. Early returns from the second Bush president, George W. Bush, seemed to promise an increase, not diminution, of such concern.

During the 1990s both Clinton and his Secretary of State Madeleine Albright would repeatedly describe the United States as the *indispensable nation*. Despite this apparent sense of triumphalism—which spurred "a rationale for mistrust and resistence" elsewhere in the world (Sanger 1999)—at home the United States remained unsure of its global role. As political scientist Samuel Huntington (1999) observed, "Neither the Clinton administration nor Congress nor the public is willing to pay the costs and accept the risks of unilateral global leadership." Elsewhere (1997) he has argued that while the Cold War fostered "a common identity between American people and government," the end of that global contest also eroded that bond. In its place we have witnessed "the displacement of national interests by commercial and ethnic interests" and a "foreign policy of particularism."

As the presidency of George H. W. Bush neared what would be its final year, Deputy Secretary of State Lawrence S. Eagleburger observed that "What is peculiar to the United States is that every generation or so we debate not only the merits of this or that policy, but the existential purpose of American foreign policy itself. Such a debate would be almost unthinkable in most other countries, where foreign policy is deemed to serve national interests, which themselves are seen as timeless and immutable." But in the United States, "we have tended to believe that our foreign policy must serve a moral purpose."

Today, no single moral purpose—not the promotion of democracy and market reform, not the protection of international values, not anit-terrorism—has emerged to galvanize the American polity toward global involvement in the way anticommunism and anti-Sovietism did. Thus it is not surprising that particularistic interests often dominate. As Leslie Gelb (1994), president of the prestigious Council on Foreign Relations, has observed, "Americans will not embark on a new crusade to make the world safe for democracy and free markets. These aims are worthy. But most Americans now understand that democracy is a state of grace not readily attained and not within their power to impose. Nor are they eager to expend lives and treasure to transform sink-holes into free enterprise paradises."

Thus the debate about power and principle, about ideals and self-interest, continues. It is as old as the republic itself, dating to the contest between Hamilton and Jefferson over which vision of national greatness would animate the nation's foreign policy in their new century. Thus contention about the appropriate role of the United States in world affairs, which has energized American foreign policy throughout its history, again marks its entry into a new century and a new millennium.

KEY TERMS RELATED TO THE GOALS OF AMERICAN FOREIGN POLICY

aggressors cannot be appeased
Alexis de Tocqueville
Biological Weapons Convention
bipolar
Carter Doctrine
Chemical Weapons Convention
clash of civilizations
Clinton Doctrine
collective security
conflicts of interest
containment
counterproliferation
creditor nation
Cuban missile crisis
cyberterrorists
democratic capitalism
democratic promotion
détente
dollar diplomacy
domino theory
dual containment
economic liberalism
ethnic cleansing

fear of communism
G-8
General Agreement on Tariffs and Trade (GATT)
global activism
globalization
idealism
ideological incompatibilities
indispensable nation
International Atomic Energy Agency (IAEA)
international values
Iron Curtain
isolationism
Kellogg-Briand Pact
Lend-Lease Act
lessons of the 1930s
liberal internationalism
liberalism
liberty
linkage theory
low-intensity conflict
make the world safe for democracy

Manifest Destiny
massive retaliation
militant containment
misperceptions
Missile Technology Control Regime (MTCR)
monolithic
Monroe Doctrine
Munich Conference
mutual security
NATO alliance
nation-building
New Independent States
New World Order
Nixon Doctrine
Non-Proliferation Treaty (NPT)
nuclear brinkmanship
nuclear nonproliferation regime
Open Door policy
peaceful coexistence
political realism
polycentric

Reagan Doctrine

realpolitik

reciprocity

return to normalcy

Roosevelt Corollary

Soviet-centric foreign policy

sphere of influence

Strategic Arms Limitation Talks (SALT)

strategy of enlargement

Truman Doctrine

unilateralism

Wilsonian idealism

World Trade Organization (WTO)

zero-sum

SUGGESTIONS FOR FURTHER READING

Ambrose, Stephen E., and Douglas G. Brinkley. *Rise to Globalism: American Foreign Policy since 1938,* 8th ed. New York: Penguin, 1997.

Boren, David L., and Edward J. Perkins, (eds.), *Preparing America's Foreign Policy for the Twenty-First Century.* Norman, OK: University of Oklahoma Press, 2000.

Bush, George, and Brent Scowcroft. *A World Transformed.* New York: Knopf, 1998.

Fromkin, David. *In the Time of the Americans: FDR, Truman, Eisenhower, Marshall, MacArthur—The Generation that Changed America's World Role.* New York: Knopf, 1995.

Gaddis, John Lewis. *Strategies of Containment: A Critical Appraisal of Postwar American National Security Policy.* New York: Oxford University Press, 1982.

Garthoff, Raymond L. *The Great Transition: American-Soviet Relations and the End of the Cold War.* Washington, DC: The Brookings Institution, 1994.

Halberstam, David. *War in a Time of Peace: Bush, Clinton, and the Generals.* New York: Scribners, 2001.

Hendrickson, David C. "In Our Own Image: The Sources of American Conduct in World Affairs," *The National Interest* 50 (Winter 1997–1998): 9–21.

Lieber, Robert J. *Eagle Rules? Foreign Policy and American Primacy in the Twenty-First Century.* Upper Saddle River, NJ: Prentice-Hall, 2002.

McDougall, Walter A. *Promised Land, Crusader State: The American Encounter with the World Since 1776.* Boston: Houghton Mifflin, 1997.

Melanson, Richard A. *American Foreign Policy Since the Vietnam War: The Search for Consensus from Nixon to Clinton.* Armonk, NY: M. E. Sharpe, 2000.

Ninkovich, Frank A. *The Wilsonian Century: U.S. Foreign Policy Since 1900.* Chicago: University of Chicago Press, 1999.

Ruggie, John Gerard. *Winning the Peace: America and World Order in the New Era.* New York: Columbia University Press, 1996.

Smith, Tony. *America's Mission: The United States and the Worldwide Struggle for Democracy in the Twentieth Century.* Princeton: Princeton University Press, 1994.

The United States Commission on National Security/ 21st Century. *Seeking National Strategy: A Concert for Preserving Security and Promoting Freedom.* Phase II Report on a U.S. National Security Strategy for the 21st Century. Washington, DC: United States Commission on National Security/ 21st Century, 2000.

NOTES

1. The classic statements of realism as an explicit theory can be found in Carr (1939), Kennan (1954), Morgenthau (1985), Niebuhr (1947), and Thompson (1960). Classical realism today is challenged by "neorealism," or "structural realism." This variant of realism focuses not on humankind's innate lust for power—a central construct in classical realism—but instead on states' drive for security in an anarchical world which causes them to behave in similar ways, resulting in efforts to secure power for survival. In this chapter we build primarily on classical realism as we focus on the contest of ideas about international politics as it has informed American foreign policy. In Chapter 6 we will draw on structural (neo)realism to

explain how the external environment now and in the past informs our understanding of American foreign policy. For critical discussions of both classical and structural (neo)realism, see Kegley (1995), Keohane (1986b), Mansbach and Vasquez (1981), Smith (1987), Vasquez (1983), and Waltz (1979).

2. The discussion of the Jefferson and Hamilton models for coping with the challenges the new Americans faced draws on Hunt (1987), especially pages 22–28.

3. "Legalism" is often treated with moral idealism as characteristic of the American world view (Kennan 1951). Its manifestations are the tendencies of American leaders to justify foreign policy actions by citing legal precedents, to assume that disputes necessarily involve legal principles, to rely on legal reasoning to define the limits of permissible behavior for states, and to seek legal remedies for conflicts. Thus, when confronted with a policy predicament, American policy makers are prone to ask not "What alternative best serves the national interest?" but instead, "What is the legal thing to do?"

4. Herman M. Schwartz (1994) argues that U.S. international economic policy in the 1920s and 1930s was deadlocked by two domestic economic groups, "nationalists," who were oriented toward the domestic market, and "internationalists," who, while also oriented toward the domestic market, were competitive in the international marketplace. The inability of either group to achieve dominance made U.S. efforts to realize a larger international role "only hesitant and erratic." After World War II the United States shifted its policy toward leadership, in part because the nationalists shifted their own calculation. Policy also shifted, Schwartz argues, because of the emergence of a third, small but influential group, "security internationalists." Fervently anti-communist and supporters of expanded military spending, the security internationalists joined other internationalists in favoring an expanded overseas presence, but like the nationalists, they feared strong labor unions at home. "This emerging third group resolved the old prewar deadlock, for now two groups could line up along a common axis of interests against the remaining group."

5. The popular aphorism (coined by Calvin Coolidge) that "the business of America is business" captures the belief that American foreign policy is often dominated by business interests and capitalistic impulses. While that view, typically ascribed to "revisionists" (see, for example, Kolko [1969], Magdoff [1969], and Williams [1972, 1980]), was once popular, others dispute its veracity. Political scientist Ronald Steel (1994), for example, categorically asserts

that "It is simply not possible to explain U.S. foreign policy in essentially economic terms. The oscillation between isolation and intervention, the persistent emphasis on morality, the obsession with freedom and democracy, the relentless proselytization cannot be stuffed into an economic straightjacket. American foreign policy may often be naive or hypocritical, but it cannot be confined to a balance sheet." See also Garthoff (1994).

Economic revisionism, which is referred to here, is not to be confused with other revisionist accounts that address the expansionist tendencies of the United States. Economic revisionists see the United States expanding in search of world markets for the surpluses of capitalism, whereas the diplomatic revisionist school sees the creation of an American imperium as the product of the American pursuit of national power or of its quest to impose its political system on others. For discussions of empire as a component of America's efforts to achieve political, not economic, preeminence, see Blachman and Puchala (1991), Hoffmann (1978), Liska (1978), and Lundestad (1990).

6. Realist critics warn of the dangers of a foreign policy rooted in messianic idealism, as moral absolutes rationalize the harshest punishment of international sinners, without limit or restraint, to the detriment of American interests (Kennan 1951). Arthur Schlesinger (1977), an adviser in the Kennedy administration, observes worriedly that "All nations succumb to fantasies of innate superiority. When they act on those fantasies . . . they become international menaces."

7. Research on the origins and evolution of the Cold War, always extensive, has grown dramatically in recent years. In addition to Gaddis (1997), examples include Holloway's (1994) *Stalin and the Bomb* and the essays on *The Origins of the Cold War in Europe* in Reynolds (1994). The Spring 1997 issue of *Diplomatic History* is a useful summary of new insights based on recent historiography. Melvyn P. Leffler (1996) reviews several studies and reaches conclusions from them somewhat at variance with those of other scholars. Earlier works include Gaddis (1972), Kolko (1968), Melanson (1983), Schlesinger (1986), Spanier (1988), Ulam (1985), and Yergin (1978).

8. See Bostdorff and Goldzwig (1994) for an analysis of Kennedy's often simultaneous use of idealist and pragmatic rhetoric, with special emphasis on Vietnam.

9. For a lively account of the end of the Cold War that focuses on Bush, Gorbachev, and their advisers, see Beschloss and Talbott (1993).

10. Kegley (1994) provides a useful overview of competing arguments.

11. These ideas were developed at some length in the Clinton's July 1994 report to Congress entitled *A National Security Strategy of Engagement and Enlargement,* leading one analyst to speculate that future historians may remember the principle of "democratic enlargement" as the "Clinton Doctrine" (Brinkley 1997).

12. For useful overviews and a sampling of the burgeoning scholarly literature on the democratic peace, see Chan (1997), Doyle (1986, 1995), Gowa (1999), Owen (1994), Ray (1995), Russett and Oneal (2000), and Spiro (1994).

13. See Hendrickson (1994–1995) for a trenchant critique of democratic promotion and related elements of the Clinton strategy of enlargement.

14. See also Thomas Carothers (1999) and Larry Diamond (1999) for appraisals of democracy promotion efforts in U.S. foreign policy. Gideon Rose (2000–2001) evaluates their analyses in the context of a broad review of related literature.

15. In 1999 British writer John Lloyd (1999), who spent five years in Moscow as bureau chief for *The Financial Times,* would write an article asking "who lost Russia?" The phrase is emotionally charged in American politics, as it refers to the "loss of China" in 1949 when communist forces took over the mainland. Not long after that Senator Joseph McCarthy of Wisconsin launched an anti-communist purge directed at the State Department and others in the foreign affairs government alleged to have been responsible for the "loss."

Ironically, the United States today finds itself divided by the same contentious judicial and constitutional challenges it once pursued as it sought to protect itself domestically from communism's challenges to the American way of life. Racial profiling—the identification of people not by what they may have done but how they look—has become a popular yet controversial approach law enforcement agencies now used to deal with potentially criminal elements in American society. The line separating domestic liberal and conservative values seems to have changed little in the process.

16. It has long been argued that economic development is a "requisite" to democracy (Lipset 1959); also see (Dahl 1989). Empirical studies that examine this proposition cross-nationally include Arat (1988), Bollen (1979), Burkhart and Lewis-Beck (1994), and Jackman (1973).

17. *Newsweek* reported in its July 26, 1999, issue that the president had planned to make a speech outlining a "Clinton Doctrine" for humanitarian intervention. It delayed the event after analyses of the effectiveness of the air campaign against Kosovo began to be questioned and other elements of the intervention, including in particular the conduct of "war by committee" (referring to the nineteen-member NATO alliance), raised doubts about applicability of the Kosovo experience elsewhere.

18. Journalist Michael Dobbs, who covered the NATO campaign from Kosovo and Belgrade for the *Washington Post,* wrote shortly after it ended that

I am reasonably confident that the number of Serbian civilian casualties was significantly higher than the number of Serbian military casualties. The official Serbian figure for their military casualties—576—may be too low, but the NATO estimates of between 5,000 and 10,000 Serb soldiers dead are almost certainly too high. . . . My estimate, based on extrapolations from independent sources, is perhaps 1,600 civilian and 1,000 military casualties.
(DOBBS 1999, 23)

19. On the decision to and process of expanding NATO to include members from Eastern and Central Europe, see Goldgeier (1999), Grayson (1999), and Yost (1998).

20. For an elaboration of India's policy position on its nuclear program and related proliferation issues, see Singh (1999). Clinton's Deputy Secretary of State Strobe Talbott articulates on the U.S. policy response in Talbott (1999).

CHAPTER 4

Instruments of Global Influence

Military Might and Interventionism

> Military power is an essential part of diplomacy.
> LAWRENCE S. EAGLEBURGER, 1984
> UNDER SECRETARY OF STATE

> If we have to use force, it is because we are America;
> we are the indispensable nation.
> MADELEINE K. ALBRIGHT, 1998
> SECRETARY OF STATE

In April 1950, about a year after the Soviet Union successfully tested an atomic bomb, the **National Security Council (NSC),** a top-level interagency body that advises the president on foreign policy matters, completed a policy review and issued its now-famous, top-secret memorandum known as **NSC 68.** This document set in motion the militarization of American foreign policy and the *containment* strategy that would persist for decades. A decisive sentence in NSC 68 asserted that "Without superior aggregate military strength, in being and readily mobilizable, a policy of 'containment' . . . is no more than a policy of bluff." NSC 68 also called for a nonmilitary counteroffensive against the Soviet Union, which included covert economic, political, and psychological warfare designed to foment unrest and revolt in Soviet bloc countries. Soon American foreign policy would become highly dependent on a range of powerful—but often controversial—military, paramilitary, and related instruments to pursue fundamental goals. America's domestic priorities also would be shaped by its preference for military might and interventionism, as defense spending would for decades comprise the largest share of discretionary (nonentitlement) federal expenditures.

As the Cold War ended, some analysts, recalling the NSC 68 as an example of successful strategic planning that made U.S. "victory" in the Cold War possible, called for a similar planning effort to guide the nation into the twenty-first century. One particularly significant aspect of the needed planning, many argued, was the place military instruments of policy would occupy in the dramatically changing global environment. As of yet, no such strategic plan has emerged despite the apparent growing military threat from various quarters of the world.

Our purpose in this chapter and the next is to examine the *instruments* of American foreign policy captured in the themes of military might and interventionism. These comprise the *means* used to achieve the political objectives of foreign policy. They include the threatened use of force, war and other forms of military intervention, propaganda, clandestine operations, military aid, the sale of arms, economic sanctions, and economic assistance. Here, in Chapter 4, our primary concern is the role that the actual and threatened use of military force, conventional and nuclear, have played during the past half century as instruments of both compellence and deterrence designed to defend homeland security and the survival of the United States and its allies. We will also assess their continuing relevance in a changed and changing world. Since foreign policy refers to the sum of objectives and programs the government uses to cope with its external environment, our attention is on that subset of foreign policy known as **national security policy**—the weapons and strategies the United States relies on to ensure security and survival in an uncertain, dangerous, and often hostile global environment.

THE COMMON DEFENSE: MILITARY GLOBALISM AND CONVENTIONAL FORCES

The logic of *realpolitik* encourages the practice of coercive behavior abroad. The potential dominance of military thinking on foreign policy planning is one symptom of that instinct. The *militarization* of American foreign policy following World War II occurred in part because the nation's policy makers routinely defined international political problems in terms of military solutions.[1] Not until they digested the painful Vietnam experience did many Americans begin to understand that military firepower and political influence are not synonymous.

American leaders' rhetoric consistently emphasizes the martial outlook derived from the assumptions of political realism. Indeed, the premises underlying the martial spirit have been reiterated so often that they have become dogma (see Focus 4.1).

The unexpectedly rapid diminution of clearly defined threats to the United States and its allies in the Cold War's wake called into question this martial spirit. Adjusting the nation's military capabilities to new challenges demanded new introspection. Inevitably that means we must understand past patterns of military preparedness and interventionist practices, which both inform and constrain future possibilities. We begin by considering the role of conventional military power in promoting and protecting the nation's interests.

Conventional Military Power during the Cold War

When the United States determined in 1990 to counter Iraq's invasion of Kuwait, it maintained a network of more than four hundred overseas military bases with nearly half a million soldiers and sailors assigned to posts and ships outside the

---

**FOCUS 4.1   The Militarization of American Foreign Policy:
Fifty Years of Policy Pronouncements**

"We must continue to be a military nation if we are to maintain leadership among other nations."

HARRY S. TRUMAN, 1945

"Regardless of the consequences, the nation's military security will take first priority in my calculations."

DWIGHT D. EISENHOWER, 1953

"Only when our arms are sufficient beyond doubt can we be certain beyond doubt that they shall never be employed."

JOHN F. KENNEDY, 1961

"United States military strength now exceeds the combined military might of all nations in history, stronger than any adversary or combination of adversaries. . . . Against such force the combined destructive power of every battle ever fought by man is like a firecracker thrown against the sun."

LYNDON B. JOHNSON, 1964

"Peace requires strength. So long as there are those who would threaten our vital interests and those of our allies with military force, we must be strong. American weakness could tempt would-be aggressors to make dangerous miscalculations."

RICHARD M. NIXON, 1970

"Our military forces are capable and ready. Our military power is without equal. And I intend to keep it that way."

GERALD R. FORD, 1976

"In the dangerous and uncertain world of today, the keystone of our national security is still military strength—strength that is clearly recognized by Americans, by our Allies, and by any potential adversary."

JIMMY CARTER, 1979

"Peace through strength is not a slogan; it's a fact of life—and we will not return to the days of hand wringing, defeatism, decline and despair."

RONALD REAGAN, 1984

"As we seek peace, we must also remain strong. The purpose of our military might is . . . to deter war. It is to defend ourselves and our allies."

GEORGE BUSH, 1989

"We cannot sustain our leadership role without maintaining a defense capability strong enough to underwrite our commitments credibly."

BILL CLINTON, 1994

"And I am certain of this, a dangerous and uncertain world requires America to have a sharpened sword."

GEORGE W. BUSH, 2000

United States itself. They reflected a national commitment to perceived global responsibilities shaped by a nearly half-century commitment to the containment of communism.

The importance of U.S. overseas troop deployments to American security has been greater nowhere more than in Western Europe, where the United States has maintained thousands of troops since the 1950s as a bulwark against a possible hostile encroachment. At one time they

acted as a *trip wire:* in the event of an attack by Warsaw Pact forces against Western Europe, the mere presence of American troops virtually ensured that some would be killed. In this way the "wire" ensuring an American retaliation would be "tripped"—and by the other (Soviet) side—because American policy makers would have "no choice" but to respond. The trip wire was an integral element of the Eisenhower administration's national security strategy. The logic supporting the presence of American troops in Western Europe later took on various colorations, but the essential function remained the same—to avert a hostile attack against Western Europe by making credible America's pledge to its allies.

Later, the Kennedy administration's strategy of *flexible response,* adopted as the official defense posture in 1967, became the means for credibly coping with conventional war threats. The strategy implied that the United States and its allies possessed the capabilities (and will) to respond to an attack by hostile forces at whatever level might be appropriate, ranging from conventional to nuclear weapons. Indeed, the NATO alliance reserved the right of *first use* of nuclear weapons if that proved necessary to repel a Soviet attack against the West. *Theater nuclear forces*—those directed toward regional rather than global threats—provided the link between U.S. conventional and strategic nuclear forces, thus tying American nuclear capabilities to the defense of its allies. The term itself suggested the possibility of theaterwide conflict (as in Europe during World War II) involving *tactical nuclear weapons* (weapons designed for the direct support of combat operations) without an escalation to global conflagration involving *strategic weapons* (nuclear and other weapons of mass destruction capable of annihilating an adversary).

The strategy of flexible response envisioned increased conventional war capabilities as a substitute for reliance on strategic nuclear weapons to deter Soviet aggression. In 1962 the ability to wage "two and one-half wars" at once became official policy. The United States would prepare to fight simultaneously a conventional war in Europe with the Soviet Union, an Asian war, and a lesser engagement elsewhere.

Conventional and tactical nuclear forces would now meet a major communist attack in *either* Europe *or* Asia and contend with a lesser contingency elsewhere. The reorientation of military doctrine was part of the reordering of the nation's world role envisioned in the *Nixon Doctrine,* which called for a lower American profile in the post-Vietnam era and for greater participation by U.S. allies in their own defense. Simultaneously, the United States adopted a *Twin Pillars strategy* toward the Middle East, a region of growing importance to the nation's vital interests as its dependence on imported oil grew. The strategy sought to protect American interests by building up the political and military stature of both Iran and Saudi Arabia. The sale of billions of dollars of highly sophisticated U.S. military equipment to both figured prominently in those plans.

The Carter administration did not markedly alter Nixon's determination to reduce America's presence abroad, but events in Afghanistan and the Persian Gulf in 1979 and 1980 did undermine the Twin Pillars strategy. They also spurred plans already in the works to develop a Rapid Deployment Force (later responsible as the U.S. Central Command for Operations Desert Shield and Desert Storm in the Persian Gulf) capable of intervening quickly in world trouble spots. The *Carter Doctrine,* enunciated in the president's 1980 State of the Union address, affirmed the determination of the United States to intervene in the Middle East militarily, if necessary, to safeguard American security interests.

In the European theater, the United States committed itself to deploy a new generation of *intermediate-range nuclear force (INF) weapons.* The decision was a direct response to the Soviet Union's growing medium-range nuclear capability, which was beyond the scope of the Soviet-American arms control negotiations that had been underway for many years. It reflected growing concern about the credibility of America's commitment to defend Europe from a Soviet attack, captured in the concept *extended deterrence.* Was the United States, European allies worried, truly willing to risk its own destruction to defend Western Europe? The INF action sought to guarantee that U.S. strategic forces remained "coupled" to the defense of Western Europe.

The prospect of deploying intermediate-range nuclear missiles became increasingly controversial after Ronald Reagan assumed the reigns of power and a "peace movement" emerged on both sides of the Atlantic, which sought to stop deployment of the INF weapons and otherwise reverse the nuclear arms race. Reagan sharpened the growing concerns with rhetoric suggesting that the United States might stand aside in the event of a nuclear war in Europe, implying he could "see where you could have an exchange of tactical weapons against troops in the field without it bringing either one of the major powers to pushing buttons." In an environment of renewed Soviet-American hostility, on the other hand, the Soviet Union chose to boycott further arms control negotiations, thus stalling productive talks for several years. The INF issue was finally settled in 1987, when the superpowers agreed to eliminate the weapons from Europe completely. Never before had they made an agreement to actually *disarm*.

As with the INF deployment, the Reagan administration continued some of Carter's policies, but it adopted a more assertive posture toward the nation's global aspirations. It jettisoned the belief that any conventional war with the Soviet Union would be short and settled either by negotiation or escalation to a nuclear confrontation. Instead, military planners now assumed that such a war would be protracted and global in scope, with fighting in numerous locations around the world but without necessarily precipitating a nuclear catastrophe. The aggressive posture fostered the development of new defensive concepts in Europe, such as the *Air-Land Battle*, which anticipated close air force support of army combat maneuvers on the ground—a style of warfare vividly illustrated (via CNN) in the Persian Gulf War. The administration also adopted a more aggressive posture toward conflict situations outside the European core area, notably in Africa, Central America, and Southwest Asia.

On the Soviet side, change was in the wind. In a speech before the United Nations in 1988, Soviet President Mikhail Gorbachev announced large-scale unilateral reductions in Soviet military forces that went far beyond what Western military planners only a short time earlier had dreamed possible. Before long, renewed negotiations between NATO and the Warsaw Pact on

European conventional forces resulted in a treaty that called for eliminating thousands of tanks, artillery pieces, armored personnel carriers, infantry fighting vehicles, and heavy armament combat vehicles.

On another front, the United States and the Soviet Union in 1990 agreed to stop production and significantly reduce their stockpiles of chemical weapons. Each also pledged further reductions once a multilateral agreement banning chemical weapons was reached. That promise was realized in 1992 with the *Chemical Weapons Convention*. The agreement came into force in 1997, thus bringing the world's major chemical arsenals under a modicum of international control.

Conventional Military Power for a New Era

In early 1990 the first Bush administration issued a new defense planning document designed to shape the military strategy necessary to cope with threats the United States might face in the next few years. The Bush plan recognized that the security environment in Europe was less threatening due to the revolutionary changes that had occurred in Eastern Europe. Thus the administration sought to reduce each superpower's armed forces in the "central zone" of Europe to 195,000. It also laid the groundwork for the 1991 decision to remove tactical nuclear weapons from Europe and Korea and from U.S. warships and submarines. Gorbachev followed Bush's lead, thus further reducing the once awesome levels of conventional military and tactical nuclear power deployed in Europe. However, despite the dramatic changes unfolding in the force postures of the NATO and Warsaw Pact alliances, the planning document anticipated continued Soviet-American rivalry. Critics therefore charged that the administration was blind to new, rapidly unfolding opportunities.

The Persian Gulf War provided the United States with a unique opportunity to test the weapons and strategies that for decades had been designed for, but untested in, Europe. Iraq had been armed with Soviet weapons and schooled in its military thinking. The result for Iraq was disastrous—and humiliating for Soviet military strategy. "Arguably, the Iraqis were inept in exercising Soviet plans with Soviet equipment," observed one analyst, "but many Russians privately [expressed] their dismay at the mismatch and [wondered] how much better they might have fared" (Snow 1998).

The Bush administration moved cautiously in assimilating the lessons of the forty-two day Persian Gulf War—viewed by many as a precursor to the renewal of the U.S. global policeman role in disrepute since Vietnam—and in adjusting to the collapse of the Soviet Union, which came less than a year after the Gulf victory. In early 1992, news media reported that a working version of the Pentagon's periodic planning document known as the Defense Policy Guidance was being developed, whose purpose was to "set the nation's direction for the next century." It laid out the rationale for a *Base Force* of 1.6 million active-duty troops (compared with 2.1 million at the time). The Defense Policy Guidance also asserted that the United States should prevent the emergence of a rival superpower by maintaining military dominance capable of "deterring potential competitors from even aspiring to a larger regional or global role" (Gellman 1992b); see also Gellman (1992a). A decade later, as the United States pursued a policy in Kosovo antagonistic to Russian interests, it seemed to some observers that the "sole superpower" philosophy embraced years earlier remained very much alive.

Despite criticisms, the Base Force proposal became the Bush administration's military blueprint for the post-Cold War era. The United States would now prepare for more military contingencies, not fewer. Colin Powell, chairman of the Joint Chiefs of Staff, defended the new plan. "The central idea in the [new national military] strategy is the change from a focus on global warfighting to a focus on regional contingencies," he wrote in *Foreign Affairs*. "When we were confronted by an all-defining, single, overwhelming threat—the Soviet Union—we could focus on that threat as the yardstick in our strategy, tactics, weapons, and budget. . . . [Now] we must concentrate on the capabilities of our armed forces to meet a host of threats and not a single threat" (Powell 1992–1993).

Following his election in 1992, Bill Clinton promised a rigorous *Bottom Up Review* of the nation's defense posture and its future needs. Even before it was completed, however, military spending cuts were announced that constrained what the Pentagon might otherwise have projected. Furthermore, although the Bottom Up Review set U.S. military strategy and force levels for the remainder of the decade, it did not deviate dramatically from Bush's Base Force plan. In particular, the focus on regional conflicts remained. U.S. forces would still be called on to fight two *major regional conflicts (MRCs)* on the scale of the Persian Gulf War nearly simultaneously. Thus the review emphasized that highly trained and well equipped forces should be retained to meet regional contingencies rapidly and without prior warning. It also anticipated that American forces would have to be prepared to fight in these conflicts without major support from U.S. allies.

Critics of Clinton's Bottom Up Review questioned its underlying premises. They doubted, for example, that two regional conflicts would: (1) occur simultaneously, (2) come without warning, and (3) be serious national security threats yet ones in which U.S. allies would choose to stand aside. They also noted that the military power of the United States, its state of readiness, and the level of its military spending far surpassed that of almost any combination of foreign foes that might be imagined. Finally, they questioned the assumption that future conflicts would be on the order of the Persian Gulf War. Instead, they predicted humanitarian intervention, counterterrorism, and other forms of military involvement arising out of ethnopolitical conflict and the proliferation of nuclear and technologically sophisticated conventional weapons. As events unfolded in the late 1990s and early 21st century, many of these arguments proved prophetic.

In 1997 the Pentagon released its Quadrennial Defense Review, a series mandated by Congress to assess periodically the nation's future military strategy, force structure, and the resources necessary to support them. The review anticipated five future dangers to the United States: (1) regional challenges, including attacks on friendly nations, ethnic conflict, religious wars, and state sponsored terrorism; (2) weapons of mass destruction, including Russian nuclear arms and the global proliferation of biological, chemical, and nuclear weapons; (3) transnational dangers, such as terrorism, drug trafficking, organized crime, and uncontrolled migration; (4) asymmetric attacks, including terrorism, information warfare, the use of unconventional weapons, and environmental sabotage; and (5) "wild card" scenarios, such as a new technological threat or the takeover of a friendly nation by anti-American factions (Cohen 1997). The two-MRCs concept remained a central element in the defense review, even as it called for a further streamlining of U.S. military forces to levels fully one-third less than during the Cold War. The review did, however, place greater emphasis on weapons modernization than earlier, thus ending the so-called "procurement holiday" to permit replacement of weapons acquired during the defense build-up of the 1980s.

In late 2001, George W. Bush's Defense Department completed the second Quadrennial Defense Review. This review, led by Defense Secretary Donald Rumsfeld, sought a more fundamental transformation of American military forces. Geared toward operating in an international environment characterized by a greater degree of uncertainty regarding the origin of security threats, the review sought to shift U.S. national security planning from "threat-based" to "capabilities-based" calculations. Such planning would focus on how potential adversaries might act, rather than on the potential adversary. Capabilities-based planning would therefore stress the resources and capabilities necessary to counter or preempt such actions. High among the list of such potential threats, even before the

September 11, 2001 attacks on the United States, were "asymmetric threats" such as terrorism, biological, chemical, and nuclear attacks, and cyberattacks (see the *Quadrennial Defense Review Report,* September 30, 2001). Additionally, the 2001 QDR moved national security planning away from the two-MRCs approach, stressing instead a force structure capable of meeting a range of threats. The 2001 QDR stressed first the capacity to address threats across the spectrum of potential conflicts, regardless of region, and secondarily "regionally-tailored" forces stationed in Europe, Asia, and the Middle East that would be capable of decisively defeating an adversary in one theater while repelling aggression ("deter forward") in another.

Throughout the QDR efforts, national security planners took steps to implement reports from the Joint Chiefs of Staff (*Joint Vision 2010,* and *Joint Vision 2020*) designed to improve the integration of the country's armed forces and to realize the fundamental transformation in warfare referred to as a revolution in military affairs.

A ***revolution in military affairs (RMA)*** can be defined as "a rapid and radical increase in the effectiveness of military units that alters the nature of warfare and changes the strategic environment." Today it is conventional wisdom that the U.S. military will undergo such a transformation in the twenty-first century as continued advances in weapons, computer, and information technology will afford it "increased stealth, mobility, and dispersion, and a higher tempo of operations, all under the shield of information superiority" (Metz 1997); see also Cohen (1996) and Nye and Owens (1996). The Pentagon has been particularly receptive to this vision because it sees the RMA concept as a way to cope with fewer resources and to reduce the number of lives lost in future wars, which is a matter of considerable political sensitivity today.

The world caught a glimpse of the changing nature of warfare stimulated by technological advances in the Persian Gulf War, when, following a massive bombing campaign, Iraq's army, believed to have been the fourth largest in the world, was routed in only 100 hours of combat. Particularly impressive was the far greater accuracy of *precision-guided munitions* ("smart" weapons) fired by stealthy F-117A fighters compared with older-design aircraft using unguided bombs (Orme 1997–1998).

The effectiveness of NATO's air campaign against Serbia eight years later was even more striking. NATO aircraft flew more than 34,000 sorties and dropped some 22,000 bombs, many guided to their targets by lasers and satellites after being launched from aircraft and ships hundreds of miles away.[2] Remarkably, NATO did not suffer a single casualty in the seventy-eight day bombardment. Some civilian casualties were sustained due to "collateral damage" or by errant bombs, but in the annals of modern warfare, their numbers were small indeed. Operations against Afghanistan in October 2001 further revealed the potential for RMA-driven warfare. According to RMA expert Eliot Cohen, "this war is going to give you the revolution in military affairs" (Ricks 2001). Not only did U.S. forces rely on precision-guided munitions deployed by most of its attack aircraft, but other new technologies were also used. For example, unmanned drones provided battlefield video to both air and ground forces, while some were outfitted with antitank missiles enabling the drones to not only survey targets for others, but also to fire at the emerging targets (Ricks 2001). In these recent operations, the mobility, range, and firepower of U.S. forces represented a qualitative shift from past military operations.

Defense analysts have long vigorously debated the many ramifications of pursuing the RMA, including its relationship to traditional modes of warfare such as the use of ground forces (Betts 1996; O'Hanlon 1998–1999; Orme 1997–1998). As the military's missions multiplied in the 1990s to include peacekeeping, peace enforcement, drug interdiction, counter-terrorism, and quelling domestic disturbances, concern also mounted that the military was being asked to prepare for multiple threats in a still-dangerous world without sufficient resources. Indeed, the Kosovo campaign "strained" U.S. forces to the point that their ability to fight two major regional conflicts simultaneously with existing weaponry and personnel began to be questioned (Myers 1999). During the 2000 election campaign, George W. Bush warned that U.S. defense spending was failing to keep pace with U.S. defense needs and missions. In an October speech in Wisconsin, for instance, he argued that "our investment in national security is at the lowest point it has been since Pearl Harbor. Overall, in the armed services, commitments around the world have tripled, while our forces have been reduced by nearly forty percent. The [Clinton] administration's own chairman of the Joint Chiefs recently said, 'We are doing much more than we were doing ten years ago, and we are doing it with much less.' The military has begun to feel the strain."

Clinton's Bottom Up Review anticipated that defense spending by 1999 would total $1.2 trillion (compared with $2 trillion spent during the first seven years of the Reagan administration) to support an active-duty military force sharply "down-sized" from its Cold War levels. (By 2001 the active-duty force had dropped to less than 1.4 million compared with 2.1 million in 1989.) Republican members of Congress repeatedly pressed for more resources, particularly after gaining control of Congress in the 1994 congressional elections. Dramatic increases in projected federal budget surpluses to the year 2015 (compared with dire deficit predictions only a few years earlier) enabled Clinton in mid-1999 to promise substantial increases in defense spending in the next decade. In 2002, George W. Bush's administration requested nearly $50 billion in additional funds.

Even as the United States continued to debate its defense priorities—as it has for decades—the import of its already remarkable conventional military capabilities has not been lost on others. Russia, once a formidable military competitor to the United States, was particularly impressed (disturbed?) by the high-tech weapons NATO unleashed on the former Yugoslavia during its air war in 1999.

> What . . . caught the eye of Russian military experts is the way Western high-precision conventional weapons have advanced to the point that they can substitute for nuclear ones in preemptive attacks. The differences between a tactical, or short-range, nuclear missile and a conventional high-precision weapon have been blurred. . . . Without a nuclear blast, deadly accurate conventional weapons can punch out the eyes of command and control sites, or extinguish electric power at radar stations or submarine bases. In the Cold War, at least, this kind of surprise attack would have been expected to be nuclear.
>
> (HOFFMAN 1999, 18)

Meanwhile, Russian President Boris Yeltsin wondered why, as a nuclear power, Russia's loud protests could not halt the NATO assault. Reportedly he demanded to know "Why are they not afraid of us?" (Hoffman 1999). The success of the high-tech campaign against the Al Qaeda terrorists and their Taliban hosts in Afghanistan had similar effects on other observers.

As the United States pursues the RMA, other states can be expected to respond with varying defensive strategies. The more wealthy of the industrial states may pursue RMAs of their own. Others who cannot afford to develop sophisticated information-based weapons may instead choose weapons of mass destruction (WMD)—particularly the so-called **NBC weapons** (nuclear, biological, and chemical). (Following the Persian Gulf War, an Indian general was asked what he learned about how to deal with the United States militarily. He reputably remarked: "If you have nuclear weapons, use them early and often.") Alternatively, *information warfare* of the sort now practiced by computer hackers may help level the playing field. Furthermore, multiple forms of terrorist attacks on the United States itself, including the possible use of weapons of mass destruction,

for which it is ill-prepared would constitute a third option, one made more pressing by the September 11, 2001 strikes in New York and Washington, D.C. (Betts 1998; Carter, Deutch, and Zelikow 1998). Ironically, then, the pursuit of a high-tech conventional weapons posture may stimulate a new "arms race" or open an already open society to new forms of unconventional threats.

Military Force and Political Purposes

The discussions of conventional war planning here and of strategic doctrine later in this chapter suggest that *prevention* is a primary purpose of American military might: to *deter* someone else's use of military force. In addition to prevention, American military forces have been used to *change* the behavior of others (often called **compellence**). NATO's U.S.-led Kosovo air campaign and the campaign against terrorism that began in 2001 are prime examples. When Serbian President Slobodan Milošević refused in late 1998 to agree to an accord negotiated in the French city of Rambouillet, which would have preserved Kosovo's autonomy as a province within the Serbian republic, NATO responded with devastating force. Its purpose: to force Milošević to do its bidding.

The Kosovo campaign is a rare example of an extreme application of coercion to achieve political purposes that falls somewhere "between war and peace." American efforts to deal with challenges from Iraq in the aftermath of the Persian Gulf War also fall somewhere between war and peace, despite enormously destructive and sometimes deadly consequences. In December 1998 the United States and Britain launched Operation Desert Fox, a seventy-hour aerial bombardment designed to punish Saddam Hussein for his refusal to let UN observer teams continue their efforts to root out Iraq's ability to develop weapons of mass destruction.

The U.S.-led campaign against terrorism—Operation Enduring Freedom—constitutes an application of force with its own distinctive characteristics. In the wake of the September attacks on the United States, the U.S. began a campaign targeted against Afghanistan for its support of the Al Qaeda terrorist network led by Osama bin Laden. Using a variety of forces dispatched to the area, including naval, air, and ground units, the U.S. campaign started with air strikes with cruise missiles, strategic bombers, and tactical aircraft targeting key communications, infrastructures, and military sites in order to establish freedom of movement (Balz 2001; DeYoung and Sipress 2001; Loeb 2001). It then proceeded to include ground operations primarily using a variety of elite and special forces and covert operatives in precision raids and other ground operations that senior administration officials characterized as "a series of arduous ground actions, including reconnaissance missions, small commando raids, and higher profile helicopter assaults against various targets" (Ricks and Loeb 2001; Graham and Ricks 2001).

Although the campaign had many facets, one of its key purposes was to topple the Taliban regime, which provided safe haven for the terrorists' network, and to apprehend bin Laden and other leaders of the network. Indeed, the campaign was "constrained, if not determined, as much by political and diplomatic calculations as by the Bush administration's primary goal of dismantling the terrorist network of Saudi-born militant Osama bin Laden and the ruling Taliban militia" (Ricks and Sipress 2001). Among the political and diplomatic concerns: winning defections among Taliban supporters; balancing competing interests of different ethnic groups in Afghanistan (i.e, the primarily Tajiki and Uzbeki "Northern Alliance" and the primarily Pashtun southern region); protecting the interests of key ally Pakistan; and addressing the broad concerns of the Islamic world.

In all of these cases, military power was used for political purposes. Far more frequent are less deadly uses of military power which, however, have the same purpose: to change the behavior of an adversary. Such uses of military power are frequently labeled *gunboat diplomacy*.

Examples of America's reliance on *force-short-of-war* as an instrument of influence illustrate the modern tactic of gunboat diplomacy. Following the Soviet invasion of Afghanistan in 1979, the United States augmented its Indian Ocean naval patrols as a signal to the Soviet Union not to extend its invasion westward. In 1983 the United States stationed a carrier task force in the Mediterranean to dissuade Libyan dictator Muammar Qaddafi from launching an attack on Sudan. In the same year it staged naval maneuvers on both sides of the Honduran isthmus in hopes of intimidating leftist guerrillas active in Central America and deterring Cuba, Nicaragua, and the Soviet Union from supporting them. In 1989 additional U.S. troops were sent to Panama following General Manuel Noriega's disregard of the results of the Panamanian election, a signal to Noriega that the United States might take further action. In 1994 the United States sent 35,000 troops to the Persian Gulf to deter Saddam Hussein from hostile maneuvers that might have been a prelude to the resumption of warfare over Kuwait. In 1996 a U.S. aircraft carrier battle group steamed into the Taiwan Strait in response to Chinese military exercises near the island state it considers a rogue province, but which the United States is legally bound to support. On these and many other occasions, the practice of gunboat diplomacy was designed for purposes other than protecting the immediate physical security of the nation or its allies. Instead, the purpose was to influence the behavior of others.

Figure 4.1 charts the frequency of these displays of force short of war—*forceful persuasion*—in the half century from 1946 to 1994. The data show that the United States subtly but surely threatened to unleash its military might to influence the decisions of other states nearly 400 times.[3] They also point to two peaks in American gunboat diplomacy during the Cold War, one extending from 1957 to 1965, the second from 1981 to 1986. The first coincides with the series of crises that culminated with the 1962

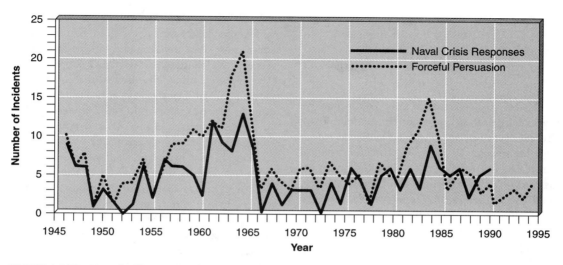

FIGURE 4.1 The Use of Military Force for Political Purposes, 1946–1994

Source: Adapted from Barry M. Blechman and Stephen S. Kaplan, *Force Without War,* Washington, DC: Brookings Institution, 1978, 547–53; Philip Zelikow, "The United States and the Use of Force: A Historical Summary," in George K. Osborn, Asa A. Clark IV, Daniel J. Kaufman, and Douglas E. Lute, eds., *Democracy, Strategy, and Vietnam,* Lexington, MA: Lexington Books, 1987, 34–36; and Adam B. Siegel, *The Use of Naval Forces in the Post-War Era: U.S. Navy and U.S. Marine Corps Crisis Response Activity, 1946–1990,* Alexandria, VA: Center for Naval Analyses, 1991, 7–11.

Cuban missile crisis and the onset of the Vietnam conflict that quickly followed; the second with the renewed conflict that accompanied the Reagan administration's bellicose posture toward Soviet "adventurism" in the years prior to the renewal of dialogue begun with Mikhail Gorbachev's assumption of power in 1985. The trough between them corresponds to the Vietnam War and its aftermath, a period of restraint on the use of force encapsulated in the phrase *Vietnam syndrome.*

There is a third notable peak during the first two years of the Clinton administration. Although often criticized for his own lack of military experience, Clinton's record suggests he was just as willing as his predecessors to use military force for political purposes. As Madeleine Albright, a central proponent of limited uses of force, reportedly stated in an argument with then Joint Chiefs Chairman Colin Powell in 1993, "What's the point of having this superb military you're always talking about if we can't use it?" (Isaacson 1999). Policy actions, including those

in Haiti, Bosnia, Iraq, and Kosovo, guided by sentiments such as these have caused some to fear that the United States is too prone to use its miliary power. Using continuing challenges from Iraq and a 1998 terrorist bombing of the U.S. embassies in Kenya and Tanzania as background, one analyst shared others' concerns:

Coming in rapid succession three recent events—last August's [1998] cruise missile attacks against targets in Afghanistan and Sudan, the resumption in December 1998 of hostilities with Iraq, and the launching, after fits and starts, of this [1999] spring's air campaign against Yugoslavia—have cast in sharp relief the centrality of military power to present-day American foreign policy. Offering the apparent prospect of clean, quick, and affordable solutions to vexing problems, force has become the preferred instrument of American statecraft. The deployment of U.S. forces into harm's way, once thought to be fraught with hazard and certain to generate controversy, has become common-place. The result has been the renewed, intensified—and perhaps irreversible—militarization of American foreign policy.

(BACEVICH 1999, 5)

The electoral victory in 2000 by George W. Bush, along with his appointment of Colin Powell as Secretary of State, seemed to herald somewhat less reliance on the use of force for political purposes. Not only was Powell well-known for his cautious views on the use of military force, but Bush argued throughout the fall and into early 2001 that U.S. forces should be used for fighting and winning wars, not for political purposes, peacekeeping or peace enforcing, or for nation building. As one observer noted, the combination of these views led many to expect the new administration to tilt military policy away from the interventionist tendencies of the Clinton administration" (Hancock 2000). However, the terrorist attacks on the U.S. in September 2001 dramatically changed both the playing field and such expectations. In the aftermath of the bombings, the Bush administration embarked on a sweeping antiterrorist campaign involving substantial applications of military force of many kinds. Clearly, the administration defined the situation as war, and therefore contemplated a range of military actions and interventions it would not have previously considered.

Military Intervention

The maintenance of a high military profile abroad and displays of force-short-of-war are two elements of the interventionist thrust of America's globalist foreign policy posture. A third is outright military intervention. Here, too, there has been a striking consistency in the willingness of American commanders-in-chief to intervene in the affairs of others. On ten conspicuous occasions—in Korea (1950), Lebanon (1958), Vietnam (1962), the Dominican Republic (1965), Grenada (1983), Panama (1989), Iraq (1991), Haiti (1994), Serbia (1999) and Afghanistan (2001)—the United States intervened overtly with

military power in another country to accomplish its foreign policy objectives. The first four account more than anything else for the label *interventionist* widely used to describe America's Cold War foreign policy. The next three are widely viewed abroad if not always at home as expressions of America's pursuit of *global hegemony*. The latter represent the American response to the emerging asymmetric threats of the 21st century.

The intervention in the Middle East in 1990–1991, which culminated in the Persian Gulf War, stands apart from the others in many respects. More American troops were sent there than to Vietnam (750,000 troops from the United States and elsewhere comprised the coalition marshaled against Iraq), yet remarkably few casualties were sustained in a high-tech war that lasted only forty-three days. (In contrast, the Vietnam Veterans Memorial on the Mall in the nation's capital commemorates the more than 58,000 Americans who lost their lives in a war that spanned two Republican and two Democratic administrations.) Moreover, it was the first overt intervention since World War II that enjoyed the acquiescence of the Soviet Union. Thus it was a clear instance of **collective security,** with enforcement measures approved by the UN Security Council against an aggressor on behalf of the world community. Also, the intervention was not rationalized in anticommunist terms.

The Kosovo air war also is remarkable for the absence of casualties, as we noted earlier. Like the Persian Gulf War, it, too, was a multilateral effort, but in this case the action was not sanctioned by the United Nations, a contentious point which impeded efforts to negotiate an end to the prolonged bombardment.[4] Instead, NATO, in its first-ever combat activity, was the enforcer. Still, the United States supplied most of the firepower. At the height of the bombing campaign some 800 U.S. aircraft and 37,500 troops were committed to the fight.

What explains decisions to intervene militarily? The anticommunist impulse was evident in Korea, Lebanon, Vietnam, the Dominican

Republic, and Grenada. Interestingly, however, there are a far-larger number of Cold War situations in which the United States might have been expected to intervene but did not. For example, it decided *not* to bail out the French in Indochina in 1954 when they faced defeat at the hands of Vietnamese communist forces at Dienbienphu, for example. And it decided *not* to use overt military force to remove the leftist Sandinista regime from power in Nicaragua in the 1980s. How can we reconcile such facts with the interventionist stigma?

Answers to these questions can be found only through an examination of the multiple sources of American foreign policy we outlined in Chapter 2, as different external, societal, governmental, and individual factors combine to shape each decision. Still, several consistent correlates governed the pattern of U.S. interventionism during the Cold War. More than 150 situations invited American intervention, but the contrast between the many potential interventions and the actual number may be explained by the presence of *inhibiting* factors. Critical to the choice *not* to intervene were the perceived need to use nuclear weapons, the prior presence of Soviet troops, the absence of armed conflict, the absence of a specific request for intervention, or the willingness of the president to let someone else, like Congress, veto an intervention decision. But "on those occasions when a Communist threat was thought to exist and when none of the other restraints was operative, intervention . . . followed" (Tillema 1973); see also Tillema (1989). Thus anticommunism was compelling if not determinant.

If this was the case, the Cold War's end should have led to a denouement of American interventionist behavior. Clearly that did not happen. Instead, new definitions of American interests have dictated perpetuation of this time-worn policy instrument.[5] The purpose of the U.S. intervention into Panama was, in the words of the U.S. ambassador to the United Nations, "to safeguard the lives of Americans, to defend democracy in Panama, to combat drug trafficking, and to protect the integrity of the Panama Canal Treaty." In the Persian Gulf, President Bush appealed to a higher purpose—to defend a weak state against the aggressive designs of a Hitler-like predator—but few doubted that access to Middle Eastern oil motivated the United States and others. In short, its purpose, as in Panama, was to defend American interests.

Still, the absence of a clear challenge to the United States since communism's demise plagued policy makers efforts to explain where and why American troops should be put in harm's way. The Clinton administration, sensitive to charges early in its first term that it had failed to credibly link diplomacy and the use of force, eventually drew a distinction between *vital* and *important* interests. According to the 1999 *National Security Strategy for a New Century,* for example, "the decision whether to use force is dictated first and foremost by our national interest. In those specific areas where our vital interests are at stake, our use of force will be decisive and, if necessary, unilateral" (see also Nye 1996). Such vital interests include defense of U.S. territory and allies, safety of U.S. citizens, the economic well-being of the United States, and the integrity of critical U.S infrastructure. For example, in sending troops to the Middle East to defend against a new Iraqi onslaught against Kuwait, then, as it did in 1994, the administration said the president was protecting a vital interest.

Important national interests, in contrast, "do not affect our national survival, but they do affect our national well-being and the character of the world in which we live." Incorporating general concerns for regions with friends or U.S. economic interests, the global environment, and crises that could generate destabilizing refugee flows, the use of force for such interests "should be selective and limited, reflecting the importance of the interests at stake. . . . [and] in concert with the international community whenever possible." One example of such concerns was defending democracy in Haiti. In such cases, explained General John Shalikashvili, chairman of the Joint Chiefs of Staff, "we are willing to use our military power primarily for coercive purposes in support of our diplomacy." This is forceful persuasion: the use of force-short-of-war. Former assistant secretary of defense Joseph S. Nye (1996) went further, saying "When U.S. interests are important but not vital, the United States has to weigh the costs and risks of using force, and must also consider more carefully whether it can bring together a multinational coalition rather than acting alone."

Initially, the administration of George W. Bush hardened the distinction between vital and other interests in opting for the use of force. Bush himself decried the "open-ended deployments and unclear military missions" of many of his predecessor's applications of force. Consequently, he promised to "replace diffuse commitments with focused ones," warning that the United States "must be selective in the use of [its] military" (Hancock 2000). However, when faced with an attack on U.S. territory and citizens, the administration did not hesitate to initiate military action.

The theory of political realism dictates that states will protect their interests. Thus intervention abroad should be regarded as neither unexpected nor reprehensible. Noteworthy is that the frequency of U.S. intervention prior to World War II and during the Cold War era is strikingly similar (see Figure 4.2). Nor has its pace slackened in the new era. What may be different is how American leaders defined "interests" in each of these periods.

The New Interventionism

Arguably the last decade of the twentieth century has witnessed greater sensitivity to humanitarian values as a reason to join military power to diplomacy. Britain's Prime Minister Tony Blair made that case in Kosovo, describing NATO's intervention there as "a moral cause." The most proactive supporter of the Atlantic alliance's military actions asserted that "We are fighting for a world where dictators are no longer able to visit horrific punishments on their own peoples in order to stay in power." In fact, in addition to vital and important interests that

might require the application of U.S. force, the 1999 U.S. *National Security Strategy for a New Century* also posited a third category of "humanitarian and other interests," which included human rights concerns and support for democratization. In these cases, the strategy suggested, U.S. military intervention *may* be appropriate to respond to, relieve, and/or restrict the consequences of the humanitarian catastrophe. A willingness to intervene in such conflicts, especially those *within* states, is the defining characteristic of the **new interventionism.**

The underpinnings for this approach rest in the Clinton Administration's efforts in several crises dating back to its first term, including Somalia, Rwanda, Haiti, and Bosnia. Presidential Decision Directive 56 (May 1997) on "Complex Contingency Operations" also shaped policy by establishing some general guidelines and processes for designing such an intervention. Some analysts, drawing on statements by President Clinton around the time of NATO's intervention in Kosovo, characterized the new interventionism as the **Clinton Doctrine.**[6] For example, Charles Krauthammer (1999) called attention to a March 23, 1999 speech in which Clinton stated "I want us to live in a world where we get along with each other, with all of our differences, and where we don't have to worry about seeing scenes every night for the next 40 years of ethnic cleansing in some part of the world." Others note a June 22, 1999 speech before KFOR (Kosovo Force) troops in Macedonia, in which Clinton put it even more bluntly:

> People should not be killed, uprooted, or destroyed because of their race, their ethnic background, or the way they worship God. . . . If somebody comes after innocent civilians and tries to kill them en masse because of their race, their ethnic background, or their religion, and it's within our power to stop it, we will stop it.

The use of troops for purposes of *peacekeeping* (keeping contending parties apart) and *peace enforcement* (imposing a settlement on disputants)

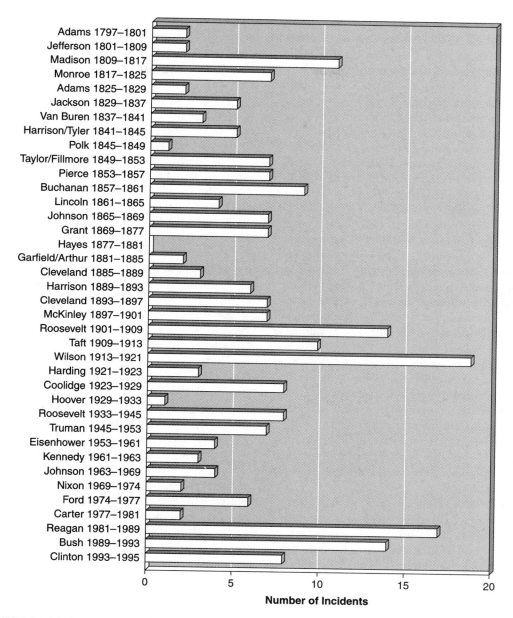

FIGURE 4.2 Initiation of the Use of U.S. Forces Abroad, by President, 1797–1995

Source: Adapted from Ellen C. Collier, "Instances of Use of United States Armed Forces Abroad, 1778–1993," *CRS Report for Congress,* October 7, 1993.

is the key policy instrument underlying the new interventionism. The Persian Gulf experience in collective security first ignited enthusiasm for using the United Nations as an instrument of both peacekeeping and peace enforcement. Within a short time thousands of troops were carrying out more UN operations than at any other time. The United States eagerly supported many of these operations, whose interests they served. Eventually, however, its enthusiastic embrace of multilateralism waned, blunted by its experience in Somalia where eighteen American lives were claimed in combat.[7]

The first Bush administration had initiated the Somalia intervention (called Operation Restore Hope), hoping to bring relief from famine to thousands of starving Somalis. Earlier it had launched Operation Provide Comfort, another multilateral initiative designed to protect the Kurdish people in Iraq from death and destruction at the hands of Saddam Hussein following the Persian Gulf War. Both were distinguished from other interventions by serving *humanitarian* purposes, not overtly political ones. Under Clinton, the Somalia intervention gradually escalated until American troops were involved in military activities against one of the factions. In October 1993, when American forces took casualties on one such operation, public and congressional outcries persuaded the administration to end the U.S. deployment.

In 1994 the Clinton administration participated in another—albeit much more limited—humanitarian intervention in Rwanda, where hundreds of thousands of refugees faced intolerable conditions following months of genocidal, ethnic bloodletting. Shortly after that former President Jimmy Carter negotiated the safe passage of Haiti's military leaders to Panama, paving the way for a U.S.-led multinational force to return Haiti's elected president to power. By ridding Haiti of its military regime, Operation Restore Democracy also sought to eliminate the human rights abuses the military regime had perpetrated on its own people.

Just as enthusiasm for multilateralism followed in the wake of the successful collective security effort in the Persian Gulf, support for humanitarian intervention grew as civil and ethnic conflict erupted elsewhere. It also flowed naturally from the apparent "triumph" of Wilsonian liberalism at the conclusion of the Cold War. As one analyst put it, "The new interventionism has its roots in long-standing tendencies of American foreign policy—missionary zeal, bewilderment when the world refuses to conform to American expectations, and a belief that for every problem there is a quick and easy solution" (Stedman 1992–1993). Thus the new interventionism combined "an awareness that civil war is a legitimate issue of international security with a sentiment for crusading liberal internationalism." A more skeptical characterization referred to it as "foreign policy as social work" (Mandelbaum 1996).

Laudable as they may be, humanitarian interventions raise troublesome moral, political, and legal questions. What level of human suffering is necessary before intervention is warranted? If intervention is required to relieve human suffering in Somalia and Rwanda, then why not in countless other places—the Sudan, Sri Lanka, Cambodia, Liberia, Tadjikistan—where poverty, starvation, ethnic violence, and the inhumanity of governments toward their own people are daily occurrences? Is the restoration of law and order a legitimate reason to intervene? To protect—or promote—democracy? What obligation, and for how long, does the intervener have to ensure that its stated goals are achieved?

Peace enforcement operations are plagued by many of the same questions as humanitarian interventions designed to keep peace by separating the antagonists. The Balkans' interventions in Bosnia and Kosovo stand out.

Conflict erupted in Bosnia-Herzegovina between ethnic Muslims and Serbs following the breakup in 1992 of Yugoslavia, of which it had been a part. The United Nations sent a peacekeeping force to the country believing it could contain the violence, but it proved ineffectual.

Ethnic cleansing, the practice by one side (notably Bosnian Serbs backed by the Yugoslav military from the republic of Serbia) to kill or drive from their homes people of the other side (Bosnian Muslims), became rampant. In April 1994, NATO launched air strikes against Bosnian Serbs, hoping to protect UN forces. Later the following year it launched a sustained bombing campaign designed to force negotiations between the antagonists. Finally, in late 1995, Assistant Secretary of State Richard Holbrooke brokered a cease-fire and an agreement designed to stop the ethnic conflict. Known as the *Dayton Peace Accords* (named after the Ohio city where the negotiators met), the agreement called for intervention by an Implementation Force (IFOR), whose purpose was to enforce the Dayton agreement. Keeping Bosnia as a separate state was a central element of the peace settlement. Negotiators rejected the alternative of partitioning it along ethnic lines reflecting the power positions of the antagonists.

President Clinton promised that U.S. forces would be in Bosnia for no more than a year. Three years later 6,000 American troops remained as part of the NATO-led peace enforcers, now renamed SFOR (for Stabilization Force), and their stay was extended indefinitely. By then some success in promoting democracy and reconstruction could be claimed, but the bitter antagonisms between rival ethnic groups remained rampant, dimming prospects for building a multi-ethnic Bosnian state. And Radovan Kardzić, the Bosnian Serb president indicted for genocide by the International War Crimes Tribunal in the Hague for his role in perpetrating ethnic cleansing during the long years of violence, remained at large.

The war crimes tribunal later indicted Slobodan Milošević for his role in the ethnic cleansing of Kosovar Albanians carried out by Serbian military, paramilitary, and police forces (which actually increased once the NATO bombing campaign against Serbia began). Ironically, ending that conflict required negotiating with the alleged criminal. And when the hundreds of thousands of ethnic Albanians who had been driven from their homeland by Serbs returned, widespread violent revenge took place. Now, it seemed, was the time for the Serbs to leave Kosovo—and thousands did. Although the NATO-led force of 50,000 troops (7,000 from the United States) came committed to maintaining the province's multi-ethnic composition, the prospects for achieving that goal seemed remote. Indeed, some critics of U.S. and NATO actions predicted an "occupation" of Kosovo that could last decades.

Although the nature and causes of the ethnic violence in Bosnia and Kosovo and the peace efforts to resolve them were similar, there was one important difference. Bosnia had been recognized by the United States and the members of the European Union as a sovereign state. Kosovo never was. No one doubted its status as a province of the Republic of Serbia, even though it was overwhelmingly populated by ethnic Albanians whose embrace of Islam, not the Eastern Orthodox Christianity of the Serbs, fueled separatist sentiments. Milošević rose to power in part on his pledge to strip Kosovo of its autonomy. The failed Rambouillet agreement sought to restore that autonomy. Regardless, the United States and its NATO partners never challenged Serbia's sovereignty over the province.

The use of force in the campaign against terrorism organized by George W. Bush in response to the 2001 attacks on the Pentagon and World Trade Center represents another aspect of this "new interventionism." In what many labeled the *Bush Doctrine,* the president told the public when the attacks began that "Today we focus on Afghanistan, but the battle is broader. Every nation has a choice to make. In this conflict there is no neutral ground. If any government sponsors the outlaws and killers of innocents, they have become outlaws and murderers themselves and they will take that lonely path at their own peril." Similarly, a senior foreign policy adviser explained: "We must eliminate the scourge of international terrorism. In order to do that, we need not only to eliminate the terrorists and their networks, but also those who harbor them" (quoted in De Young 2001). Such statements clearly provide the rationale for further intervention—in additional countries beyond Afghanistan—as part of the effort to address the terrorism threat. One common thread running through the Kosovo and anti-terrorism campaigns concerns their encroachment on the principle of sovereignty.

Sovereignty is a cardinal principle in international law and politics. It protects the territorial inviolability of the state, its freedom from interference by others, and its authority to rule its own population. The United Nations is predicated on the sovereign equality of its members. Article two, section seven of the charter specifically states that nothing in the charter should be construed to permit interference in matters essentially within the domestic jurisdiction of member states.

Still, some legal scholars believe that "humanitarian intervention is legally permissible in instances when a government abuses its people so egregiously that the conscience of humankind is shocked." From this perspective, the humanitarian interventions in Iraq and Somalia "represented the triumph over national sovereignty of international law designed to protect the fundamental human rights of citizens in every state" (Joyner 1993); see also Joyner (1992) and Fixdal and Smith (1998), but compare Stedman (1995) and Lund (1995). In this context, the campaign against terrorism that began in October 2001 raises some difficult questions. With Al Qaeda, the terrorist organization responsible for the attacks on the U.S., a non-state actor, American efforts to destroy the sprawling network are fundamentally interventionist and an intrusion on the principle of sovereignty. Moreover, they also constitute, as a putative general rule, an effort to hold governments responsible for the actions of individuals or groups within their borders. Furthermore, approval of the Kurdish, Somali, and Afghanistan interventions by the United Nations added legitimacy to the operations and the role of American forces in them.

Others worry that, however laudable stanching domestic injustice and bloodletting may be, discarding existing rules prohibiting intervention in states' internal affairs is troublesome without safeguards against abuse. With Kosovo as the background, a former legal counsel to the Senate Foreign Relations committee made the following unsettling observations:

> The United States and NATO—with little discussion and less fanfare—have effectively abandoned the old UN Charter rules that strictly limit international intervention in local conflicts. They have done so in favor of a vague new system that is more tolerant of military intervention but has few hard and fast rules. What rules do exist seem more the product of after-the-fact rationalizations by the West than of deliberation and pre-agreement. . . . No one, as yet, has devised safeguards sufficient to guarantee that power will not be misdirected to undermine the values it was established to protect.

(GLENNON 1999, 2, 5); SEE ALSO (RIEFF 1999 AND FRANCK 1999)

Finally, just as there are differences of opinion about where to intervene, there are differences about what is at stake. Journalist Michael Elliott put the issue succinctly: "'Values are a slippery concept on which to base the expenditure of blood and treasure. Reasonable, civilized men and women can disagree about which values are worth dying for" (*Newsweek,* 26 April 1999, 37).

To Intervene or Not to Intervene?

In the aftermath of the divisive Vietnam War, American policy makers worried about intervening in world trouble spots. Constrained by the *Vietnam syndrome,* they feared that prolonged involvement requiring substantial economic costs and many casualties would undermine support in Congress and among the American public. The death of 241 Marines in Beirut in 1983, who had been sent to Lebanon as part of a multinational peacekeeping force during the Lebanese civil war, and the death of another eighteen American soldiers in Somalia in 1983 reinforced their reluctance to intervene abroad militarily—especially with combat troops. Bill Clinton reflected that thinking when he stated emphatically at the outset of NATO's campaign against Serbia that "I do not intend to put our troops in Kosovo to fight a war."[8]

Ironically, eliminating the invasion option from the beginning may actually have intensified Milošević's resolve to stand up to NATO, thus prolonging the destructive conflict. As a study of the threat and actual use of force during the Bush and Clinton administrations (prior to Kosovo) concluded,

> There is a generation of political leaders throughout the world whose basic perception of U.S. military power and political will is one of weakness, who enter any situation with a fundamental belief that the United States can be defeated or driven away. This point of view was expressed explicitly and concisely by Mohamed Farah Aideed, leader of a key Somali faction, to Ambassador Robert Oakly, U.S. special envoy to Somalia, during the disastrous U.S. involvement there in 1993–1995: "We have studied Vietnam and Lebanon and know how to get rid of Americans, by killing them so that public opinion will put an end to things."
>
> (BLECHMAN AND WITTES 1999, 5)[9]

Ironically, then, an unwillingness to incur casualties may actually diminish the effectiveness of U.S. military threats, thus requiring the actual use of force, as during the Persian Gulf War. A study of eight post–Cold War cases in which "the United States utilized its armed forces demonstratively in support of political objectives" found that George H. W. Bush and Bill Clinton both had acted timidly, "taking some action but not the most effective possible action to challenge the foreign leaders threatening the United States." The authors conclude that "until U.S. Presidents show a greater ability to lead on this issue, or until the American people demonstrate a greater

willingness to step up to the challenges of exercising military dominance on a global scale, foreign leaders in many situations will likely continue to see American threats more as signs of weakness than as potent expressions of America's true military power" (Blechman and Wittes 1999). Efforts by the Bush administration to build support for U.S. operations against terrorism in Afghanistan and elsewhere seemed guided by this point, as administration officials carefully used the language of sacrifice "to prepare the public to accept the loss of American lives in combat" DeYoung and Milbank 2001).

Whether the United States *should* try to exercise military dominance on a global scale, and how it should decide when to intervene in conflict or humanitarian crises around the world are further questions for which different answers have been offered. Following the disaster in Lebanon early in the Reagan administration, Secretary of Defense Caspar Weinberger articulated a set of principles to govern the use of force abroad. Among other things, he stated that force should be used only when vital national interests are at stake, that clearly defined objectives and a commitment to winning were necessary, that support for the use of force by Congress and the American people should be expected, and that force should be used only as a last resort, suggesting that force and diplomacy operate on separate tracks. A decade later Colin Powell, in what is widely referred to as the **Powell Doctrine,** synthesized these ideas. "Powell stressed the importance of going into a conflict with all the forces at hand and winning quickly and decisively. Like Weinberger's six tests, the Powell Doctrine aimed at keeping U.S. troops out of wars to which the nation was not fully committed" (Jordan, Taylor, and Mazarr 1999). The Persian Gulf War fit the parameters of the Powell Doctrine; the Bosnia conflict, which erupted shortly thereafter, apparently did not. As the first Bush's Secretary of State James Baker reportedly said, "We don't have a dog in that fight."

Bosnia fit precisely the kinds of situations the United States has faced most often in the past decade. These are situations "where there is little precedent for American action, where American interests are more abstract than tangible, where the battle lines are uncertain, and where none of the contending parties wears a particularly friendly face" (Blechman and Wittes 1999). Is there a role for American military intervention in these situations? Does the United States still have interests that can be advanced best through intervention? Is the menu of interests broader or narrower than during the Cold War? If the United States does intervene, can it stay the course, as great powers historically have done (Luttwak 1994)? Or do the domestic political costs of prolonged engagement outweigh the foreign policy benefits?

The Clinton Administration's early efforts to grapple with these questions involved a concept called *assertive multilateralism,* which sought to develop greater coordination and cooperation with the United Nations, initially even by putting U.S. troops under foreign commanders in certain situations. These efforts failed with the Somalia debacle (see Daalder 1994; Sterling-Folker 1998).

In the wake of Somalia, Presidential Decision Directive 25 (May 1994) sought to establish criteria to guide decisions of these kinds. Overall, U.S. support for UN interventions would require a threat to international peace and security (including humanitarian crises like starving civilians), gross abuses of human rights, or a violent overthrow of a democratically elected government. For U.S. participation, an intervention must involve American interests and clear objectives, availability of troops and funds, the necessity for U.S. participation, congressional approval, a clear date for withdrawal, appropriate command and control arrangements, consent of the parties, and a realistic exit strategy. Because of these restrictive conditions, PDD-25 was widely regarded as a list of possible excuses for not intervening.

Subsequent national security strategy statements (for example, the 1999 *National Security Strategy for a New Century*) endorsed the use of force for humanitarian purposes, but sought to allay public and congressional concerns by emphasizing not only that force was generally not the best tool for such situations, but also that U.S. military involvement must be commensurate with U.S. interests, should involve others from the international community, and should be limited, clearly defined, and entail manageable risks and costs. In early 1999, an administration official suggested a relatively simple, three part consideration: if there is a moral justification for the use of force (for example, ethnic cleansing); if the area is of strategic significance to the United States; if the operation does not entail a heavy price. According to this official, these criteria would form the basis of the Clinton Doctrine on the matter (*Time,* 28 June 1999, 25).

Whatever weight a presidential "doctrine" carries, this one did not impress Clinton's successor. Apart from uses of force in defense of obviously vital interests, key members of the Bush Administration seemed, at least initially, to view "the military option only as a last and most distasteful resort" (Hancock 2000). With the author of the Powell Doctrine as Secretary of State, the administration was expected to view "humanitarian military intervention as a death warrant for GIs" (Hancock 2000). Moreover, Bush himself laid out significantly more demanding criteria for the use of force. For example, in a presidential debate held on October 3, 2000, Bush, echoing both the Weinberger and Powell doctrines—explained when he would commit U.S. troops:

> Well, if it's in our vital national interests. And that means whether or not our territory—our territory is threatened, our people could be harmed, whether or not our alliances—our defense alliances are threatened, whether or not our friends in the Middle East are threatened. That would be a time to seriously consider the use of force. Secondly, whether or not the mission was

clear, whether or not it was a clear understanding as to what the mission would be. Thirdly, whether or not we were prepared and trained to win, whether or not our forces were of high morale and high standing and well-equipped. And finally, whether or not there was an exit strategy. . . . I would be guarded in my approach. I don't think we can be all things to all people in the world. I think we've got to be very careful when we commit our troops. . . . I believe the role of the military is to fight and win war and, therefore, prevent war from happening in the first place.

While the U.S. response to the September 2001 terrorist strikes seemed to meet this more exacting standard, the criteria would appear to limit the use of force to a relatively few situations. As a recent Council on Foreign Relations analysis of humanitarian intervention suggested, this position is "tantamount to an intervention policy that [treats] any and all 'humanitarian' [considerations] as superfluous, and of refusing to participate in virtually any and every case of humanitarian intervention" (Frye 2000).

The range of views on these questions is wide indeed—reflecting both the absence of organizing principles for American national security policy as we begin a new century, and the differences of opinion within the American polity on the interests and threats at stake in the post–Cold War world.[10]

- Some neoisolationists argue that there are no present or prospective external threats to our interest great enough to justify intervention

- Others would limit our actions to steps that directly affect a narrow domestic agenda, for example, by forcing Japan to buy more American good and services

- Still others would use intervention to create the kind of stable and prosperous world they believe offers the greatest chance for peace and prosperity at home

- Finally, some believe that we should intervene to promote American values of democracy and human rights, as well as to relieve suffering and prevent "ethnic cleansing," even if there is no direct security impact on the United States.

(BROOKS AND KANTER 1994, 22–23)[11]

We can confidently predict that resolving the differences of opinion inherent in these alternative postures toward the means of American foreign policy will not come easily, as they mirror the same long-standing debates about idealism and realism, power and principle, and isolationism and internationalism that animate differences about the goals of American foreign policy we saw in Chapter 3.

STRATEGIC DOCTRINE THEN AND NOW: NUCLEAR WEAPONS AS INSTRUMENTS OF COMPELLENCE AND DETERRENCE

The clocks of Hiroshima stopped at 8:15 on the morning of August 6, 1945, when, in the blinding flash of a single weapon and the shadow of its mushroom cloud, the international arena was transformed from a balance-of-power to a balance-of-terror system. No other event marked more dramatically the change in world politics that would shape the next half century. The United States has not used atomic weapons in anger since August 1945, but it sought throughout the Cold War to gain bargaining leverage by relying heavily on nuclear force as an instrument of strategic defense (the defense of its homeland) and as a means "to defend its interests wherever they existed" (Gaddis 1987–1988). The latter implied its willingness not only to threaten but actually to use nuclear weapons. Even today nuclear weapons figure prominently in the design of American national security policy. As the Pentagon stated in its 1993 report on the roles and missions of American military forces after the Cold War, nuclear forces "truly do safeguard our way of life."

Strategic Doctrine during America's Atomic Monopoly, 1945–1949

The seeds of the atomic age were planted in 1939 when the United States launched the Manhattan Project, a program at the cutting edge of science and technology designed to construct a superweapon that could be used successfully in war. J. Robert Oppenheimer, the atomic physicist who directed the Los Alamos, New Mexico, laboratory during the development of the A-bomb, observed that "We always assumed if [atomic bombs] were needed they would be used." Thus the rationale was established for a military strategy based on, and backed by, extraordinary means of destruction with which to deal with enemies. President Truman's decision to drop the A-bomb on Hiroshima and, three days later, on Nagasaki was the culmination of that thinking. "When you have to deal with a beast you have to treat him as a beast," Truman reasoned.

Why did the United States use the bomb, which demolished two Japanese cities and took over one hundred thousand lives?[12] The official explanation is simple: The bomb was dropped "in order to end the war in the shortest possible time and to avoid the enormous losses of human life which otherwise confronted us" (Stimson and Bundy 1947). Whether the bomb was necessary to end the war remains in dispute, however. Hiroshima and Nagasaki were largely civilian, not military, targets, and there is now credible evidence that the Japanese wanted to surrender to the United States on acceptable terms.

Many historians now contend that the real motivation behind the bomb's use was preventing the expansion of the Soviet Union's postwar influence in the Far East, not a desire to save lives, whether American or Japanese.[13] A parallel interpretation contends that the United States wanted to impress Soviet leaders with the awesome power of its new weapon and America's willingness to exploit the advantages it now gave them. Regardless of its true motivations, the use of weapons of mass destruction against Japan marked the beginning of an era in which the instruments of war would be used not as means to military ends, but instead for the psychological purpose of molding others' behavior.

During the period of America's atomic monopoly, the concept of *compellence* (Schelling 1966) described the new American view of nuclear weapons: they would not be used to fight but rather to get others to do what they might not otherwise do. Thus nuclear weapons became instruments of *coercive diplomacy,* the ultimate means of forceful persuasion (George 1992).

President Truman and Secretary of War Henry L. Stimson counted on the new weapon to elicit Soviet acceptance of American terms for settling outstanding war issues, particularly in eastern and central Europe. Truman could confidently advocate "winning through intimidation" and facing "Russia with an iron fist and strong language," because the United States alone possessed the greatest intimidator of them all—the bomb. Stimson was persuaded that the United States should "use the bomb to pry the Soviets out of Eastern Europe" (LaFeber 1976). Although Stimson soon would reverse his position,[14] his first instincts anticipated the direction American strategic thinking would take during this formative period, which NSC 68 finally crystallized. The memorandum rationalized "increasing American military and allied military capabilities across the board both in nuclear and conventional weapons [and] making it clear that whenever threats to the international balance of power manifested themselves, the United States could respond" (Gaddis 1987–1988). Should it prove necessary, the bomb was a tool that could be used.[15]

Strategic Doctrine under Conditions of Nuclear Superiority, 1949–1960

The monopoly on atomic weapons the United States once enjoyed gave way to superiority in 1949, when, as we have noted, the Soviet Union also acquired the bomb. The assumption that America's adversaries could be made to bend to American wishes through atomic black-mail nonetheless became a cornerstone of the Eisenhower containment strategy, particularly as conceived by its chief architect, Secretary of State John Foster Dulles. Dulles sought to re-shape the strategy of containment around three concepts: rollback, brinkmanship, and massive retaliation, all of which revealed the perceived utility of nuclear weapons as instruments of co-ercive diplomacy

Rollback identified the goal: reject passive containment of the spread of communist influ-ence and, instead, "roll back" the Iron Curtain by liberating communist-dominated areas. Dulles pledged that the United States would practice rollback—and not merely promise it—by em-ploying "all means necessary to secure the libera-tion of Eastern Europe."

Brinkmanship sought to harness American strategic superiority to its foreign policy goals. In defining this concept, Dulles explained how atomic power could be used for bargaining purposes:

> You have to take chances for peace, just as you must take chances in war. Some say that we were brought to the verge of war. Of course we were brought to the verge of war. The ability to get to the verge without get-ting into the war is the necessary art. . . . If you try to run away from it, if you are scared to go to the brink, you are lost. . . . We walked to the brink and we looked it in the face. We took strong action.

(DULLES 1952, 146)

Massive retaliation became the strategic doc-trine determined to convince America's adver-saries it was both willing and able to carry out its threats. Labeled the "New Look" to distinguish it from Truman's strategy, massive retaliation was a **countervalue** nuclear weapons strategy designed to provide "the maximum deterrent at bearable cost" by threatening mass destruction of the things the Soviet leaders were perceived to value most—their population and military/industrial centers. The doctrine grew out of the Eisenhower admin-istration's simultaneous impulses to save money and to challenge the perception that American foreign policy had become largely a reflexive re-action to communist initiatives. No longer would containment be restricted to retaliation against lo-calized communist initiatives. Instead, it would target the very center of communist power to ac-complish foreign policy goals.

Despite its bold posturing, the Eisenhower administration, for the most part, proceeded cau-tiously. If it did sometimes threaten to use nu-clear weapons, it never carried out the threats; nor did it roll back the iron curtain, most notably when it failed to assist Hungarian revolutionaries who rose up against Soviet power in 1956. Nev-ertheless, faith in the utility of nuclear weapons as instruments of coercive diplomacy defined the 1950s, as the United States artfully pursued a compellent strategy.

Strategic Doctrine in Transition, 1961–1992

A shift from compellence toward a strategy of **de-terrence** began in the late 1950s and became read-ily discernible in the Kennedy and Johnson administrations. The Soviet Union's growing strategic capability helped stimulate the change. The development of intercontinental ballistic missiles (ICBMs) in particular caused alarm, as the United States now saw itself as being as vulnera-ble to Soviet attack as the Soviet Union was to an American strike. "On the day the Soviets ac-quired [the bomb as] an instrument and the means to deliver it," Kennedy adviser George Ball (1984) observed, "the bomb lost its military utility and became merely a means of mutual suicide . . . [for] there are no political objectives commensurate with the costs of an all-out nuclear exchange."

Kennedy himself felt it necessary to educate the world to the new strategic reality, warning of its dangers in a 1961 speech to the United Nations General Assembly:

> Today, every inhabitant of this planet must contemplate the day when this planet may no longer be habitable. Every man, woman, and child lives under a nuclear sword of Damocles, hanging by the slenderest of threads, capable of being cut at any moment by accident or miscalculation or by madness. The weapons of war must be abolished before they abolish us.
>
> Men no longer debate whether armaments are a symptom or cause of tension. The mere existence of modern weapons—ten million times more powerful than any that the world has ever seen, and only minutes away from any target on earth—is a source of horror, and discord and distrust.

From Compellence to Deterrence *Deterrence* means discouraging an adversary from using force by convincing the adversary that the costs of such action outweigh the potential gains. As a practical matter, strategic deterrence denotes the threatened use of weapons of mass destruction to impose unacceptably high costs directly on the homeland of a potential aggressor. To ensure that such costs can be imposed, a *second-strike capability* is necessary. This means that offensive strategic forces must be able to withstand an adversary's initial strike and retain the capacity to respond with a devastating second blow. In this way the aggressor will be assured of destruction, thus deterring the initial preemptive attack. Hence strategic deterrence implies sensitivity to the survivability of American strategic forces. In practice, the United States has sought survivability through a *triad of strategic weapons* consisting of manned bombers and land- and sea-based intercontinental ballistic missiles. It continues to do so today.

The Kennedy administration's doctrine of strategic deterrence rested on the principle of *assured destruction*—a condition realized if the country can survive an aggressor's worst possible attack with sufficient firepower to inflict unacceptable damage on the attacker in retaliation. It differed from massive retaliation in that the latter presupposed U.S. strategic superiority, which enabled the United States to choose the time and place where nuclear weapons might be used in response to an act of Soviet aggression (as defined by the United States). In contrast, the principle of assured destruction pledged that a direct attack against the United States (or perhaps its allies) would automatically result in a devastating American retaliatory nuclear strike. Hence this strategy of survival through nuclear attack avoidance depended critically on the rational behavior of Soviet leaders who, it was assumed, would not attack first if convinced that a first strike against the United States (or perhaps its NATO allies) would lead to its own destruction.

As the Soviet arsenal grew, American strategic doctrine increasingly stressed that what held for American deterrence of Soviet aggression also held for Soviet deterrence of American assertiveness. Hence *mutual deterrence,* based on the principle of *mutual assured destruction (MAD),* soon described the superpowers' strategic relationship. A "balance of terror" based on the military potential for, and psychological expectation of, widespread death and destruction for *both* combatants in the event of a nuclear exchange now governed the superpowers' strategic relationship. In this sense mutual deterrence "is like a gun with two barrels, of which one points ahead and the other points back at the gun's holder," writes Jonathan Schell (1984). "If a burglar should enter your house, it might make sense to threaten him with this gun, but it could never make sense to fire it." Yet preservation of a MAD world was eagerly sought: Because the price of an attack by one state on its adversary would be its own destruction, ironically the very weapons of war encouraged stability and war avoidance.

From Countervalue to Counterforce The principle of assured destruction emerged in an environment characterized by American strategic superiority. By the end of the 1960s, however, it became clear that the Soviets had an arsenal roughly equivalent to that of the United States. American policy makers now confronted gnawing questions about the utility of continually attempting to enhance the destructive capabilities of the United States. As Henry Kissinger, Nixon's national security adviser and later secretary of state, observed: "The paradox of contemporary military strength is that a gargantuan increase in power has eroded its relationship to policy. . . . [Military] power no longer translates automatically into influence."

By the time the first strategic arms limitations (SALT) agreements were signed in 1972, a new nuclear weapons orthodoxy began to emerge: Their purpose was to prevent war, not to wage it. Robert McNamara (1983), secretary of defense under Kennedy and Johnson, put it simply: "Nuclear weapons serve no military purpose whatsoever. They are totally useless—except only to deter one's opponent from using them." Such reasoning stimulated growing support in the 1980s for a "no first use" declaratory policy, even though such a policy would run counter to NATO doctrine, which maintained that nuclear weapons would be used if NATO conventional forces faced defeat on the battlefield.

Although the SALT arms control negotiations sought to restrain the superpowers' strategic competition, qualitative improvements in their weapons systems continued unabated. Inevitably this provoked new challenges to the emerging orthodoxy about nuclear weapons as instruments of policy. The continuing strategic debate now centered on the issues of targeting policy and warfighting strategies.

Like massive retaliation, the principle of assured destruction rested on the belief that deterrence could be realized by directing nuclear weapons at targets believed to be of greatest value to an adversary, namely, its population and industrial centers. The countervalue targeting doctrine joined the civilian and industrial centers of both Cold War adversaries in a mutual hostage relationship.

As early as 1962 Secretary of Defense McNamara suggested that the United States ought instead to adopt a **counterforce** strategy, one that targeted American destructive power on the enemy's military forces and weapons. A decade later the United States would take significant strides in this direction as it began to develop a "limited nuclear options" policy and the corresponding weapons capability to destroy heavily protected Soviet military targets. The new direction invited the addition of another lurid acronym to the arcane language of strategic planning: **NUTs**—variously defined as "nuclear utilization target selection" or "nuclear utilization theory."

President Carter extended the counterforce option in the 1980s, when he signed Presidential Directive (PD) 59. Known in official circles as the **countervailing** or **war-fighting strategy,** the new posture sought to enhance deterrence by targeting military forces *and* weapons, and population and industrial centers in the Soviet Union. It was incorporated into the top-secret master plan for waging nuclear war known as the **SIOP (Single Integrated Operational Plan),** which operationalizes strategic doctrine by selecting the military and nonmilitary targets to be attacked in the event of war (see Ball and Toth 1990; Hall 1998).

Even as the United States modified its plans for coping with the Soviet threat, the Soviet Union continued a massive program initiated in the 1960s to enlarge and modernize Soviet strategic forces. Advantages in numbers of missiles, missile warheads, and missile throw-weight accrued to the Soviets, stimulating a growing chorus of alarm that moved the United States away from the accommodationist policies of the 1970s toward a decidedly more militant posture (see also Chapter 3). "Our ability to deter war and protect our security declined dangerously during the 1970s," scolded Ronald Reagan, setting the stage for the largest peace time military buildup in the nation's history. The Reagan administration feared in particular that Soviet technological developments had rendered the land-based leg of the strategic triad vulnerable to a devastating first strike (which would undermine the U.S. second-strike capability but not eliminate it due to its submarine-based forces). Further, it became convinced that the Soviet Union could no longer be deterred simply with the threat of assured destruction. It therefore pledged to develop capabilities sufficient not only to ensure the survival of U.S. strategic forces in the event of a first strike (so that a devastating second strike could be launched), but also to deter a second strike by threatening a third. Reagan officials claimed that making nuclear weapons more usable would enhance deterrence by making the nuclear threat more credible.

Critics disagreed, charging that making nuclear war less unthinkable made it more likely. They often pointed to the vulnerability of the nation's command, control, communications, and intelligence (C³I) capabilities. A Soviet attack by comparatively few weapons would effectively "decapitate" the United States by killing its political leaders and destroying the communication links necessary to ensure a coordinated and coherent U.S. retaliation (Ball 1989; Schneider 1989). Such dangers undermined the feasibility of conducting a limited (protracted) nuclear war, they warned. Hence, critics of Reagan's policies concluded that a strategy premised on the usability of nuclear weapons in war would actually increase the probability of nuclear conflict, not reduce it.

The first Bush administration was not explicit about its strategic assumptions. However, while it stressed publicly that America's nuclear weapons were primarily for deterrence, it quietly continued to pursue a nuclear war-fighting capability. President Bush approved changes in the SIOP that would enhance U.S. capabilities to paralyze Soviet war-making abilities in the opening hours of conflict by "decapitating" the Soviet leadership. Critics, who averred that Bush's revised SIOP took "war fighting to dangerous extremes" (Ball and Toth 1990; see also Glaser 1992; Mazarr 1990; Toth 1989), again worried

that plans to blitz Soviet leaders at the beginning of hostilities would increase rather than decrease the risk of nuclear holocaust. Because these changes were made at the very time that the Soviet threat was diminishing, they gave testimony to the persistence of old ways of thinking about national security and strategy. Indeed, Secretary of State Baker asserted shortly before the Berlin Wall crumbled that "We are not on the verge of a perpetual peace in which war is no longer possible. We cannot disinvent nuclear weapons nor the need for continued deterrence."

From Offense to Defense Ronald Reagan launched perhaps the greatest challenge to the orthodox view of the utility of nuclear weapons with a dramatic call for a high-tech, "Star Wars" *ballistic missile defense (BMD)* system, designed to render nuclear missiles "impotent and obsolete." The *Strategic Defense Initiative (SDI),* as it was officially known, sought to create a "defense dominant" strategy. Believing the principle of mutual assured destruction "morally unacceptable," Reagan's program foreshadowed a distant future in which the United States would interdict offensive weapons launched toward the United States in fear or anger. The knowledge that the United States was invulnerable would also reduce the probability of war.

SDI became an object of criticism from the start, stimulating a debate that continues even today. Many experts felt that the program created expectations that technology could not fulfill until well into the next century, if ever. Still, advocates of a defense-dominant strategy maintained that "defending through active defense is preferable to defending through terrorism—the ultimate mechanism by which deterrence through threat of retaliation operates" (Congressional Research Service 1989). Thus research on various conceptualizations of a ballistic missile defense system continued for more than a decade, with $40 to $50 billion dollars expended on the effort.

Eventually the notion of establishing an impenetrable shield that would render incoming missiles "impotent and obsolete" was abandoned in favor of a less ambitious system. As the Soviet Union imploded and the Cold War fizzled, "scenarios of a Third World strike, a renegade Russian submarine missile attack, or an accidental or unauthorized launch became the primary justifications for the system" (Han 1992–1993). Today, the BMD debate has moved in divergent, yet related directions politically if not always technologically. One is known as *theater missile defense (TMD),* the other as *national missile defense (NMD).* The former seeks to protect U.S. allies in their local settings; the latter hopes to protect the United States itself.

The Persian Gulf War stimulated the search for theater defense systems, as the perceived success of the Patriot antimissile missile during the conflict gave impetus to the possibility of a successful defense against ballistic missiles. (The actual performance of the Patriot in that war is a controversial matter; [Hersh 1994; Postol 1991–1992; but compare Ranger 1993].) The army and navy are now actively engaged in research designed to overcome the technological challenges necessary to demonstrate the combat readiness of forward-based missile defenses. The air force also is actively pursing its own BMD program.

The development of a *national* missile defense system has been the source of continuing controversy, now spreading beyond two decades. Congressional Republicans in particular vigorously pursued the objective, while the Democrat-controlled White House generally stalled their efforts. In 1996 Clinton agreed to develop a program capable of being deployed by 2003 *if* a ballistic missile threat seemed imminent. At the time that seemed unlikely. Then North Korea tested missiles whose anticipated capabilities would permit attacks on the U.S. heartland (for example, Chicago). At about the same time China was shown to have engaged in espionage at U.S. nuclear facilities for many years, which may have significantly advanced its nuclear capabilities.[16]

By the end of his administration, Clinton moved in the Republican direction, finally agreeing in 1999 that the United States would field a national missile defense system against a "limited

missile attack" as soon as it was "technologically feasible," initially indicating his support for ground-based interceptors based in Alaska. On September 1, 2000, however, under significant pressure from both sides of the debate, President Clinton announced that, while "the NMD program is sufficiently promising and affordable to justify continued development," he would defer the decision to move forward with early deployment to his successor.

The man who assumed the White House in January 2001 was less hesitant. Throughout the 2000 campaign, George W. Bush promised to "defend U.S. citizens, not outdated treaties," and committed his administration to an early deployment of a comprehensive NMD system with land, sea, and space components. In May, 2000, Bush coupled his plan for NMD with a proposal to reduce—possibly unilaterally—U.S. nuclear arsenals to the "lowest possible number consistent with our national security," and less than the thresholds established in the START II accord. After his election, he reiterated his commitment, and began to lay the groundwork with American allies as well as China and Russia. Bush made it clear, however, that the U.S. decision would not be driven by opposition from those quarters (see *New York Times,* 20 January 2001, A19; Eckholm 2001). Bush's choice for defense secretary—Donald Rumsfeld—was also an ardent proponent of a comprehensive NMD system.

As indicated by immediate opposition from Russia and China (as well as a very lukewarm reception from NATO), whether the United States should build a BMD system is a contentious issue not only at home but also abroad.[17] The 1972 Antiballistic Missile Treaty (ABM) negotiated with the former Soviet Union arguably prohibits the United States from developing a missile defense system. At the Helsinki summit in 1997, following years of contention, Clinton won Russian President Boris Yeltsin's acceptance of the notion that, within certain performance parameters, theater BMD systems differ from the ABM systems envisioned decades earlier; thus paving the way for a "clarified" ABM treaty permitting deployment of forward-based missile defensive systems. Then, in the immediate aftermath of the Kosovo intervention, Soviet President Boris Yeltsin also agreed to discuss revisions to the 1972 ABM treaty that might permit development of a national missile defense system. Presumably this would be a "limited" or "thin" system designed to protect against an accidental or unauthorized use by a rogue state, like Iraq or North Korea. In October 2001, Bush and Vladimer Putin (Yeltsin's successor) reached agreement to allow the ABM treaty to be modified to permit NMD. Shortly thereafter, the administration announced it would go ahead with NMD and effectively abandon the ABM treaty.

Still, although the long-standing political obstacles to missile defense now seem to be inching toward resolution, the formidable technological challenges remain. Russia remains hesitant, and China is opposed (Eckholm 2001). Among the key concerns are the possibilities that "the creation of a national antimissile defense system would also have negative international consequences that would destabilize not only Russia-U.S. relations but others as well. China could be expected to take countermeasures. A new nuclear arms race could be expected in South Asia and other parts of the world. Europe would be affected, too" (Ivanov 2000). While the September 2001 terrorist strikes against the U.S. improved the chances for NMD (both by reducing domestic opposition and by revitalizing U.S. international leadership), the second Bush administration will have its hands full at home and abroad as it seeks to deploy this controversial system. Indeed, Bush's description during his 2002 State of the Union Address of North Korea, Iran, and Iraq as an "axis of crisis" promised to make resolution of his "war on terrorism" more difficult, not less.

Strategic Doctrine for a New Era

Late in 1997, and with little ceremony, Bill Clinton signed a new Presidential Decision Directive redefining existing nuclear weapons policy and strategy. The product of a Nuclear Posture Review begun years earlier, it replaced the last presidential guidance on the use of nuclear weapons in war, which Ronald Reagan had approved in 1981. That document anticipated that nuclear war would be protracted, that the president should have a menu of nuclear options from which to pick, and that limited nuclear exchanges might permit pauses during which negotiations could occur. The Soviet Union and its Eastern European allies were, of course, the prime targets, with some reports suggesting that at the Cold War's peak 40,000 targets in the communist world had been marked for destruction (Ottaway and Coll 1995).[18]

The Clinton guidelines dramatically reduced (but did not eliminate) potential nuclear targets in the former Soviet Union. Apparently, it did not abandon the notion that a protracted nuclear war might be fought (Hall 1998), but it did shift the emphasis to a more diffuse set of threats—not just a nuclear threat from a single, powerful antagonist but to general threats caused by "instability." Included are anticipated challenges by those who might possess not only nuclear but also biological and chemical weapons of mass destruction, in particular rogue states and rising powers such as China. The common thread with previous policy is clear: Nuclear weapons are designed to dissuade an adversary from attacking the United States (or its allies) by putting at risk whatever that adversary holds dear.

Although the Clinton administration's revised nuclear guidelines shifted to what some analysts regarded as a more realistic assessment of the challenges the United States now faces, critics were quick to seize on a number of unresolved issues. How many nuclear warheads are required for deterrence? Can prevention of their accidental use be assured? And can they guarantee against nonnuclear threats? The prestigious Henry L. Stimson Center addressed these issues in a series of reports on the evolving U.S. nuclear posture, which included the views of many of the nation's most knowledgeable defense experts (Goodpaster 1995, 1997). Interestingly, the center's conclusions raised doubts about the ability of nuclear weapons to deter biological or chemical weapons and recommended that the ultimate goal of U.S. policy should be a nuclear-free world.

This debate stimulated by the Hiroshima bomb more than half a century ago about the wisdom of having developed weapons of mass destruction and their utility as instruments of foreign policy continues.

ARMS CONTROL AND NATIONAL SECURITY

The end of the Cold War witnessed a flurry of dramatic arms control and disarmament initiatives considered unimaginable less than two decades earlier. By then negotiated arms control agreements had become not only a generally accepted dimension of U.S. national security policy, but also an integral element of strategic deterrence. As George Shultz, Ronald Reagan's secretary of state, explained, "The arms control process has always had as a main goal to ensure deterrence by enhancing stability and balance in the strategic relationship."

From SALT to START

The *Strategic Arms Limitation Talks (SALT)* negotiations were a joint effort by the Cold War adversaries to prevent the collapse of the fragile balance of terror that supported mutual assured destruction. The SALT agreements reached in 1972 (SALT I) attempted to guarantee each superpower's second-strike capability and thereby preserve the fear of retaliation on which *stable deterrence* presumably rested.

The first SALT agreement consisted of (1) a treaty that restricted the deployment of antiballistic missile defense (ABM) systems by the United States and the Soviet Union to equal and very low levels, and (2) a five-year interim accord on strategic offensive arms, which restricted the number of inter-continental ballistic missile (ICBM) and submarine ballistic missile (SLBM) launchers that each side was permitted to have.

The interim agreement on offensive weapons was essentially a confidence-building, stopgap measure that anticipated a comprehensive, long-term treaty limiting strategic weapons. The ABM accord is more problematic and was repudiated by both of the ABM signatories.

The SALT II treaty, signed in 1979 (but never ratified), sought that objective by substantially revising the quantitative restrictions of SALT I and by placing certain qualitative constraints on the superpowers' strategic arsenals. When SALT II was signed, these limits were expected to dampen dramatically the momentum of the superpowers' arms race. Although they may have kept the total number of strategic weapons below what otherwise would have been produced, the spiral of weapons production—notably deliverable warheads—continued.

The Reagan administration followed the "dual track" of its predecessors by pursuing simultaneously arms control talks and a military buildup. Early in its first term the Reagan team showed little willingness to discuss arms limitations, but a combination of domestic and international pressure gave impetus to two sets of negotiations—the *Strategic Arms Reduction Talks (START)*, aimed at *reducing*, not just capping, the superpowers' strategic forces, and the *intermediate-range nuclear force (INF) talks*, designed to limit theater nuclear weapons in Europe. As noted earlier, the superpowers reached a historic agreement in 1987 when they signed the INF treaty banning intermediate-range nuclear forces from Europe. Although the accord required dismantling less than five percent of the world's nuclear arsenals, it set the stage for, as British Foreign Secretary Sir Geoffrey Howe put it, "the beginning of the beginning of the whole arms control process."

On the strategic front, negotiations first stalled and then proceeded cautiously. In 1985 the superpowers finally agreed that "deep cuts" in their nuclear forces were desirable. They differed substantially in how those cuts should be accomplished, however, as their force compositions influenced their negotiating positions. As a traditional land power, the Soviet Union placed heavy reliance on land-based missiles. The United States sought to reduce their number, viewing them as the gravest threat to U.S. land-based forces. Conversely, the Soviets, facing an American strategic force more widely dispersed among the three legs of its strategic triad, sought cutbacks that would directly offset U.S. areas of superiority.

Eventually the principle of "deep cuts" became the mutually accepted goal. In 1991, after nine years of bargaining, the negotiators overcame their differences and concluded the START I treaty, committing each side to reduce its strategic forces by one-third. The treaty also provided a baseline for future reductions in the two sides' strategic capabilities.

In September 1991, responding to widespread complaints that the START I agreement barely began the kinds of arms reductions possible now that the threat of a Soviet attack had vanished President Bush declared that the United States must seize "the historic opportunity now before us." He called long-range bombers off twenty-four-hour alert, canceled plans to deploy the long-range MX missile on rail cars, and offered to negotiate sharp reductions in the most dangerous kinds of globe-spanning missiles. Not long after that, the new Russian President Boris Yeltsin declared that Russia "no longer considers the United States our potential adversary" and announced it would stop targeting American cities with nuclear missiles. Bush responded with a series of unilateral arms cuts to which Yeltsin quickly replied. He recommended that the two powers reduce their nuclear arsenals to only 2,000 to 2,500 warheads each—far below the cuts called for in START I and almost fifty percent greater than the reductions Bush had proposed.

At the June 1992 Washington summit, Bush and Yeltsin made the surprise announcement that Russia and the United States would make additional deep cuts in their strategic arsenals. The addendum to the START accord, which would become START II, called for a sixty percent reduction of the two powers' combined total nu-

clear arsenals—from about 15,000 warheads to 6,500 by the year 2003. Even more dramatically, the START II agreement, signed in early 1993, not only cut the number of warheads beyond earlier projections but also altered drastically the kinds of weapons each country could stockpile. Russia and the United States agreed to give up all multiple warheads on their land-based ICBM missiles—a particularly dangerous, "silo-busting" capability. They also pledged to reduce the number of submarine-launched ballistic missile warheads to no more than 1,750. President Bush described the hopeful future that START II portended: "With this agreement the nuclear nightmare recedes more and more for ourselves, for our children, and for our grandchildren."

Strategic Defense and Arms Control in the New Era

START II faced several nettlesome problems from the beginning. They included the presence of nuclear weapons on the territories of three other of the former Soviet republics (Belarus, Kazakhstan, and Ukraine) and stiff opposition from ardent Russian nationalists and communists in the Duma, the Russian parliament whose approval was required. Under the terms of the agreement, Russia would have to undertake expensive efforts to build new single warhead missiles to maintain strategic parity with the United States—an issue important to Russians committed to retaining its superpower status. And in the United States, congressional conservatives concerned about denuding America's nuclear capabilities were implacably opposed to the agreement. Thus START II remained unratified nearly ten years after it was signed.

Bill Clinton promised a thorough reevaluation of the nation's strategic posture paralleling the Bottom Up Review of conventional weapons. While it was underway, Clinton and Yeltsin agreed to detarget their respective strategic nuclear weapons. This meant, as Deputy Secretary of State Strobe Talbott put it, that "the pistols we have aimed at each other's heads will no longer be on hair trigger." When the

**Table 4.1 Strategic Nuclear Force Levels (Warheads)
of the United States and the Former Soviet Union, 1990–2007**

	UNITED STATES			RUSSIA		
	1990	**1998**	**2007**[a]	**1990**[b]	**1998**	**2007**[a]
ICBMs	2,450	2,451	300	6,612	4,144	385
SLBMs	5,760	3,776	1,008	2,804	2,480	1,016
Bombers	2,353	1,755	700	855	2,480	1,016
Total	10,563	7,982	2,008	10,271	7,430	1,969

[a]Assumes START II is in place and START III has been successfully negotiated.

[b]Includes weapons in Belarus, Kazakhstan, Russia, and Ukraine.

SOURCE: Adapted from Arms Control Association at www.armscontrol.org. © 2001 Arms Control Association. Reprinted with permission.

strategic posture review was completed in the fall of 1994, however, it reaffirmed previous policies but did little else. A disappointment to those who sought further reductions in strategic arms, no new initiatives were announced that would cut U.S. and Russian weapons below the 3,500/ 3,000 balance projected in the START II accord. Furthermore, the United States would continue to deploy nearly 500 nuclear weapons in Europe to deter an attack on American allies. And the long-standing doctrine of a "first use" of nuclear weapons was retained rather than adopting a no-first-use declaratory policy. As during the Cold War, this meant that the United States might draw the nuclear sword to fend off nonnuclear challenges, including those posed by biological and chemical weapons. Finally, Clinton approved a military plan to install more accurate missiles equipped with nuclear warheads on U.S. sub-marines. It was in this environment that an anonymous advocate of further reductions in offensive nuclear weapons worried that "the clay of history is beginning to harden again" (quoted in Smith 1994b; for a contrasting viewpoint, see Bailey 1995).

With START II stalled and U.S. strategic doctrine seemingly stuck in the clay of history, Clinton and Yeltsin met in Helsinki, Finland, in 1997, where they laid the basis for START III. The leaders agreed that by 2007 the two sides would limit their nuclear arms to between 2,000

and 2,500 strategic nuclear warheads. This would reduce by about 1,000 the number permitted under START II. (The agreement also anticipates parallel negotiations on tactical nuclear weapons and the disposition of warheads and fissile material.) They also agreed to a protocol to START II that would extend the target date for realizing its provisions. If the target is met, the end result of these complex negotiations and agreements would substantially reduce U.S. and Russian strategic nuclear forces beyond their early post–Cold War levels, as shown in Table 4.1. In October 2001, George W. Bush and Vladimir Putin concluded a handshake deal to further reduce nuclear arms, disagreeing only over whether to do so in a formal treaty or a simple executive agreement.

How many strategic nuclear weapons are necessary for effective deterrence? No one is sure, but some analysts—we can call them *minimalists*—advocate that a START IV treaty should seek reductions to 200 warheads for all of the major nuclear powers (see, for example, von Hippel 1997). Minimalists worry that the very existence of large numbers of nuclear weapons invites their eventual use. Notable in this regard is that while both the United States and Russia are proud to declare that neither any longer targets nuclear weapons at the other, each could easily retarget them in just a few seconds or minutes. Furthermore, it is not widely understood that the various SALT and START agreements refer to *deployed* nuclear weapons, not their total number, which includes hundreds, perhaps thousands more in storage; and the deployed weapons are horrendously destructive. "At any given time, the United States has on alert more than 2,300 warheads, delivering a combined explosive power of about 550 megatons (550 million tons) of TNT—the equivalent, to use a popular measure, of 44,000 Hiroshimas. This is the 'overkill' that has been an element of the popular myth about nuclear weapons for decades" (Hall 1998, 45). Finally, and at considerable cost, the United States continues to refine its nuclear arsenal, often dedicated to improving its counterforce capabilities to fulfill the Reagan administration's determination that the United States should be prepared to fight a protracted nuclear war. Reportedly, as we noted previously, the Clinton administration's nuclear guidance directive issued in 1997 did not alter this strategic posture significantly (Hall 1998).

Others who share the goals of minimalists note that the capability of American conventional weapons today is sufficient for deterrence. In particular, the revolution in military affairs promises that American security interests would be better served *without* nuclear weapons than *with* them. Les Aspin, long-time chair of the House Armed Services Committee and Bill Clinton's first secretary of defense, anticipated that future when he wondered about the wisdom of having developed nuclear weapons in the first place. His words:

> Nuclear weapons were the big equalizer—the means by which the United States equalized the military advantage of its adversaries. But now the Soviet Union has collapsed. The United States is the biggest conventional power in the world. There is no longer any need for the United States to have nuclear weapons as an equalizer against other powers.
>
> If we were to get another crack at the magic wand, we'd wave it in a nanosecond. A world without nuclear weapons would not be disadvantageous to the United States. In

fact, a world without nuclear weapons would actually be better. Nuclear weapons are still the big equalizer but now the United States is not the equalizer but the equalizee.

Other analysts—we can call them *maximalists*—believe that a deterrent force in the range of the START II force levels is necessary. Their conviction derives from the belief that Russia will be resurgent, eventually again posing a nuclear threat to the United States. More generally, the disparity in minimalists' and maximalists' perceptions turns are their view of America's appropriate global role (Jordan, Taylor, and Mazarr 1999; Posen and Ross 1997). Minimalists tend toward the neo-isolationist side of the spectrum. For them, a small cache of nuclear weapons is all that is necessary to ensure U.S. security in a world where it plays a markedly reduced role. Maximalists, on the other hand, tend to be either primacists or selective engagers (see Chapter 1). For them, nuclear weapons remain a source of both security and influence in an uncertain and dangerous world.

There is some common ground between minimalists and maximalists. They share the conviction that the stockpile of nuclear weapons should be dramatically reduced from Cold War levels. This also implies that the role of nuclear weapons in the new century will be dramatically different than that ushered in by Hiroshima's devastation (Jordan, Taylor, and Mazarr 1999).

Meanwhile, the arms control agenda remains unfulfilled. Stopping nuclear testing as a way to deal with proliferation remains an enduring objective. In 1996 President Clinton signed the *Comprehensive Test Ban Treaty (CTBT)*, calling it "the longest-sought, hardest-fought prize in arms control history." As the name implies, the treaty sought to stall further nuclear proliferation by banning completely all nuclear tests, including the underground tests permitted under the 1993 test ban treaty signed in the immediate aftermath of the Cuban missile crisis. More than ninety states joined the United States in signing the new treaty, including all of the then-declared nuclear powers

(Britain, China, France, Russian, and the United States). Notably absent were India and Pakistan, two of the three (Israel is the other) "nondeclared" nuclear states. Because of the way it was drafted, the CTBT cannot come into force until India, which refuses even to sign the treaty, ratifies it. Furthermore, although the United States is a signatory of the treaty, the Republican controlled Senate blocked its ratification. In November 1999, amidst frantic efforts by the administration to defer the vote, the Senate rejected the CTBT as fifty-one Republicans voted against ratification (Lowry 1999). This defeat, coupled with the failure of the Russian Duma to pass START II and the pressure to revise or even abrogate the ABM Treaty led many to ask "Is arms control dead?" (see Brown 2000; Cambone 2000).

At the level of conventional weapons, the agreement signed in 1990 to limit conventional forces in Europe (the *Conventional Forces in Europe Treaty,* or CFE), to which we alluded earlier, has led to a dramatic reduction in former Cold War antagonists' conventional European-based arsenals. By 1998 the 160,000 pieces of heavy Soviet equipment once deployed west of the Ural mountains had been reduced to about 25,000 (Mendelsohn 1997). The treaty's success made it a model for crafting the arms control settlement in the former Yugoslavia embodied in the Dayton Peace Accords (Mendelsohn 1997).

In late 1997 more than one hundred countries gathered in Ottawa, Canada, where they signed a treaty to ban the production and use of anti-personnel weapons, commonly referred to as land mines. Britain's Princess Diana campaigned against these widely used weapons, which often kill or maim not just military personnel but also noncombatants long after the overt violence that precipitated their use has ended. At the time of the Ottawa gathering analysts estimated that "anywhere from 80 million to 110 million land mines are buried in 68 nations, from Angola to Bosnia, Nicaragua to Cambodia" (Myers 1997). The United States agreed to participate in the negotiations but in the end

refused to sign the *Ottawa Landmine Treaty* (formally the Convention on the Prohibition of the Use, Stockpiling, Production and Transfer of Anti-Personnel Mines and on Their Destruction). The Pentagon vigorously opposed the treaty, reasoning that anti-personnel weapons are among the most effective in protecting South Korea from a North Korean invasion. Ironically, countless land mines left behind by retreating Serbian forces posed one of the gravest dangers to NATO peacekeepers following the Kosovo air bombardment.

The land mine debate reveals how difficult reconciling arms control with larger national security concerns often is. Still, the United States remains committed to the principle of integrating the control of weapons of war into its overall military posture. Coping with weapons of mass destruction will command primary attention, but, as illustrated with the land mines case, other weapons may also be scrutinized. Instructively, the United States joined African and European states in Oslo, Norway, in 1998, where they endorsed measures to control the spread of light weapons, the major cause of death in today's wars.

POWER AND PRINCIPLE: IN PURSUIT OF THE NATIONAL INTEREST

The world has changed dramatically in the past decade, but the means of American foreign policy—captured in the themes of military might and interventionism—remain durable patterns. Adjustments have been made, to be sure, but they have been confined largely to tactics, not fundamental reassessments of basic purposes or strategies. Thus we find that the nation's conventional military forces remain poised for global engagement and that nuclear weapons are still believed to provide security from attack through the threat of attack. Without a new framework for policy, old ways of thinking persist.

The outlines of a new framework remain unclear. Ultimately they will be dictated by the leadership path the United States pursues in the twenty-first century. Contention over the appropriate path will doubtless persist well into the new century. But to many this is the dawn of a new *American century*—and that presupposes a policy of *primacy*. Despite all the fits and starts and second thoughts, Bill Clinton put the United States on that track in the last decade of the "first" American century. George W. Bush promises to keep it on the same track in the first decade of the "second" American century.

KEY TERMS RELATED TO MILITARY MIGHT
AND INTERVENTIONISM IN AMERICAN FOREIGN POLICY

Air-Land Battle

assertive multilateralism

assured destruction

ballistic missile defense (BMD)

Base Force

Bottom Up Review

brinkmanship

Bush Doctrine

Carter Doctrine

Chemical Weapons Convention

Clinton Doctrine

coercive diplomacy

collective security

compellence

Comprehensive Test Ban Treaty (CTBT)

containment

Conventional Forces in Europe Treaty (CFE)

counterforce

countervalue

Dayton Peace Accords

deterrence

ethnic cleansing

extended deterrence

first use

flexible response

forceful persuasion

force-short-of-war

global hegemony

gunboat diplomacy

information warfare

instruments of American foreign policy

intermediate-range nuclear force (INF) weapons

interventionist

major regional conflicts (MRCs)

massive retaliation

maximalists

militarization of American foreign policy

minimalists

mutual assured destruction (MAD)

mutual deterrence

NSC 68

national missile defense (NMD)

National Security Council (NSC)

national security policy

NBC weapons

new interventionism

Nixon Doctrine

Ottawa Landmine Treaty

peace enforcement

peacekeeping

Powell Doctrine

precision-guided munitions

realpolitik

revolution in military affairs (RMA)

rollback

second-strike capability

SIOP (Single Integrated Operational Plan)

sovereignty

Strategic Arms Limitation Talks (SALT)

Strategic Arms Reduction Talks (START)

Strategic Defense Initiative (SDI)

strategic weapons

tactical nuclear weapons

theater missile defense (TMD)

theater nuclear forces

triad of strategic weapons

trip wire

Twin Pillars strategy

Vietnam syndrome

SUGGESTIONS FOR FURTHER READING

Alperovitz, Gar. *The Decision to Use the Atomic Bomb: And the Architecture of an American Myth.* New York: Knopf, 1995.

Brands, H. W. *The Use of Force After the Cold War.* College Station, TX: Texas A and M University Press, 2000.

Clark, Wesley K. *Waging Modern War: Bosnia, Kosovo & The Future of Combat.* New York: Public Affairs Books, 2001.

Daalder, Ivo H., and Michael O'Hanlon. *Winning Ugly: NATO's War to Save Kosovo.* Washington, DC: Brookings Institution, 2000.

De Young, Karen. "Allies Are Cautious on 'Bush Doctrine.'" *Washington Post,* October 16, 2001, p. A1.

George, Alexander L. *The Limits of Coercive Diplomacy.* Boulder, CO: Westview, 1994.

Haass, Richard N. *Intervention: The Use of American Military Force in the Post–Cold World.* Washington, DC: Carnegie Endowment, 1998.

Jordan, Amos A., William J. Taylor, and Michael J. Mazzar. *American National Security: Policy and Process.* Baltimore: Johns Hopkins University Press, 1998.

Kanter, Arnold, and Linton F. Brooks, eds., *U.S. Intervention Policy for the Post–Cold War World: New Challenges and New Responses.* New York: Norton, 1994.

Kegley, Charles W., Jr., and Eugene R. Wittkopf, eds., *The Nuclear Reader: Strategy, Weapons, War.* New York: St. Martin's, 1989.

MacKinnon, Michael. *The Evolution of U.S. Peacekeeping Policy Under Clinton.* London: Frank Cass Publishers, 1999.

Nye, Joseph S. "Seven Tests: Between Concert and Unilateralism," *The National Interest* 66 (Winter 2001–2002): 5–13.

Roberts, Adam. *Humanitarian Action in War: Aid Protection and Impartiality in a Vacuum.* New York: Oxford University Press, 1997.

Schell, Jonathan. *The Gift of Time: The Case for Abolishing Nuclear Weapons Now.* New York: Metropolitan, 1998.

Snow, Donald M. *National Security: Defense Policy for a Changed International Order.* New York: St. Martin's, 1999.

Snow, Donald M. *When America Fights: The Uses of U.S. Military Force.* Washington, DC: Congressional Quarterly Press, 2000.

NOTES

1. The militarization of American foreign policy occurred not because professional military leaders assumed policy-making roles (although some, such as George Marshall, did), but because civilian leaders tended to embrace military approaches to political problems (Yarmolinsky 1970–1971, 1971). Richard J. Walton (cited in Donovan [1974]) astutely observed that "Civilian control versus military control is a distinction without a difference if the civilians think the same way the military does."

2. Once NATO forces entered Kosovo, evidence revealed that many of the targets hit by "smart" weapons were decoys fabricated by the Yugoslav army, which the weapons' sensors and the pilots flying the bombing missions were unable to distinguish from real targets. NATO forces also were hampered at

times by heavy cloud cover and other adverse weather conditions, pointing out the need for greater all-weather capabilities.

3. Military forces can also be used to attain desired ends directly. The inventories drawn on here focus on those instances where the force itself does not obtain the objective, but rather affects the perceptions of others, thereby influencing their decision(s). The Kosovo air war properly falls within the category where force itself was used to achieve an objective. U.S. military action in the Persian Gulf War, designed to force Iraq to withdraw from Kuwait, is a similar event and hence was excluded from the data inventory.

4. Some NATO countries, notably France and to a lesser extent Germany, believe that only the United Nations can authorize the resort to force for purposes

other than self-defense. The United States, on the other hand, objects to holding NATO "hostage" to the UN Security Council, where Russia and China could veto the use of force (Daalder 1999).

5. On the use of force after the Cold War, see Brands (2000) and MacKinnon (1999).

6. *Newsweek* reported in its July 26, 1999, issue that the president had planned to make a speech outlining a "Clinton Doctrine" for humanitarian intervention. He delayed the event after analyses of the effectiveness of the air campaign against Kosovo began to be questioned and other elements of the intervention, including in particular the conduct of "war by committee" (referring to the nineteen-member NATO alliance), raised doubts about applicability of the Kosovo experience elsewhere.

7. On the Somalia intervention, see Schraeder (1998), Stevenson (1995), Brune (1999), and Clarke and Herbst (1997).

8. Writing before the Kosovo campaign, John A. Gentry (1998), a retired U.S. Army Reserve officer who spent time in Bosnia and at NATO headquarters working on Bosnia-related issues, wrote a scathing article entitled "Military Force in an Age of National Cowardice." He argues that "the United States presents a schizophrenic posture to the world: we crow about being the world's only superpower and claim the perquisites of that status, including the world's obeisance under the threat of sanctions, but radiate fear about using power if our people are likely to be hurt."

9. Research on public attitudes toward casualties suffered in Lebanon and in the humanitarian intervention in Somalia lends only limited support to the hypotheses that suffering casualties will cause public support of peacekeeping operations to dissipate (Burk 1999).

10. Interesting recent discussions of this question include O'Hanlon (2000) and Frye (2000). The latter is a Council on Foreign Relations study consisting of three memoranda to the president advocating different approaches and criteria.

11. Analyses and critiques of American interventionist policies and practices in the recent past and proposed for

the future can be found in Betts (1994), Crocker (1995), Haass (1994a; 1994b), Kanter and Brooks (1994), Maynes (1995), Schraeder (1992), Shalom (1993), T. Smith (1994b), and Van Evera (1990b).

12. For a vivid description of the human and physical damage, see Schell (1982).

13. See Alperovitz (1985, 1989), Bernstein (1995), Miles (1985). For rebuttals, see Alsop and Joravsky (1980), Bundy (1988), and Weinberg (1994).

14. Stimson actually became an early advocate of efforts to negotiate an agreement with the Soviet Union that might have limited the nuclear arms spiral that soon followed (Chace 1996).

15. Alperovitz and Bird (1994) discuss the role of the atomic bomb in the militarization of post–World War II American foreign policy.

16. In May 1999 the House of Representatives released a three-volume, declassified version of the report by its Select Committee on U.S. National Security and Military/Commercial Concerns with the People's Republic of China, chaired by Representative Christopher Cox (Republican, California). The report concluded that for twenty years China had carried out a successful espionage program that included information about all types of nuclear weapons currently deployed in the U.S. arsenal.

17. The literature on ballistic missile defense, both technical and political, is voluminous. For a sampling of recent commentary, see Cirincione (1997), Hartung (1998), Frye (1996), Gronlund and Wright (1997), Robb (1999), and Sloss (1999).

18. The fall of the Berlin Wall in 1989 caused Dick Cheney, Secretary of Defense in the first Bush administration and vice president in the second, to question the objectives of the SIOP and ultimately to dramatically reduce the number of its nuclear targets. Assumptions underlying the SIOP also began to be questioned. General George Lee Butler, who became commander of U.S. nuclear forces in 1991, would later become a vigorous advocate of the complete abolition of nuclear weapons (Smith 1997); see also Hall (1998).

CHAPTER 5

Instruments of Global Influence

Covert Activities, Foreign Aid, Sanctions, and Public Diplomacy

Intervention can be physical, spiritual, bilateral, multilateral, direct action,
skills transfer, institution building; it can be so many things—a fabulous menu!

CHESTER A. CROCKER,
CHAIR, BOARD OF DIRECTORS, U.S. INSTITUTE FOR PEACE, 1994

If we're just involved a little bit, we can make a huge difference.

PRESIDENT BILL CLINTON, 2000

In 1947, President Harry Truman enunciated the **Truman Doctrine,** thus committing the United States to an active, internationalist role in the post–World War II era. Congress passed a new National Security Act, which not only created the Department of Defense and the Joint Chiefs of Staff to coordinate the country's military establishment, but also the *Central Intelligence Agency (CIA)* to strengthen the ability of the United States to gather information and prevent recurrence of a catastrophe like Pearl Harbor. On June 5, 1947, at a Harvard University commencement address, Secretary of State George C. Marshall set forth the commitment of the United States to assist in the reconstruction of war-torn Europe as a basic principle of American foreign policy. Two years later, in Point Four of his inaugural address, President Truman called for "a bold new program for making the benefits of our scientific advances and industrial progress available for the improvement and growth of underdeveloped areas," making foreign aid programs major instruments of American foreign policy. A few years later, in 1953, the United States Information Agency was established, creating an institutional home for World War II's Voice of America and other broadcasting and information programs meant to promote American ideas and interests around the globe. Along with the opportunity to use trade and access to the huge American market for foreign policy purposes, the innovations of these few years thereby established the outlines of the main instruments on which American foreign policy would rely for the next half-century.

As the last chapter suggested, military might soon assumed a central role as a means to achieve post-war American objectives. However, American policy makers have also relied on other less coercive, but still interventionist, means to achieve their strategic and political goals. In this chapter, we examine covert activities, foreign assistance, sanctions, and public diplomacy, and provide background on their historical uses and consider the challenges and dilemmas the twenty-first century poses to their continued relevance and utility.

COVERT INTERVENTION: INTELLIGENCE COLLECTION AND COVERT ACTION

The *intelligence community* performs a range of functions, including collecting and analyzing information (discussed more thoroughly in chapter 11) and covert action. In terms of instruments of global influence, however, it is the covert activities of the United States government that provide a means of affecting events around the world and the policies of others. The United States' persistent covert involvement in the affairs of other nations contributed measurably to the interventionist label attached to post–World War II American foreign policy. *NSC 68,* the National Security Council document so essential to the militarization of American foreign policy, helped push the United States in that direction. As noted in Chapter 4, it called for a nonmilitary counteroffensive against the Soviet Union designed to foment unrest and revolt in Soviet bloc countries.

At least some in Washington soon recognized that such undertakings could be accomplished only by the establishment of a worldwide structure for covert action (*Final Report of the Select Committee to Study Governmental Operations with Respect to Intelligence Activities,* Vol. IV, 1976; hereafter cited as *Final Report,* I–IV, 1976).

To be sure, nations have always gathered information about one another, which often means engaging in **espionage**—spying to obtain secret government information. The United States is no exception (see, for example, Andrew 1995). Indeed, during the American revolution, the British hanged Nathan Hale, an American soldier, for spying. According to tradition, Hale's last words were "I only regret that I have one life to lose for my country." Today, Hale's statue stands outside the entry to CIA headquarters in Langley, Virginia.

Nevertheless, prior to World War II covert activities by the United States were very limited, usually involving efforts to collect information. During World War I intercepting and decoding enemy cable and radio messages—*cryptanalysis*—brought the application of modern technology to intelligence work. The "Black Chamber," a small U.S. military intelligence unit responsible for this activity, continued to function after the war, only to be terminated by President Hoover's secretary of state in 1929, who found the Black Chamber's activities abhorrent to America's idealist values. During the 1930s, Franklin Roosevelt and his advisers received specialized intelligence briefings about Japan and Germany from a broad array of information sources (Kahn 1986), but the United States did not have secret agents operating abroad. That also meant that it could not practice **counterintelligence**—"operations undertaken against foreign intelligence services . . . directed specifically against the espionage efforts of such services" (Holt 1995).

The immediate precursor to the CIA was the Office of Strategic Services (OSS), created by President Roosevelt during World War II. Headed by General William J. "Wild Bill"

Donovan, the OSS carried out covert intelligence operations against the Axis powers, marking the first time the United States moved beyond merely collecting information to actively shaping events in other countries. After World War II, the United States converted the OSS into a specialized intelligence agency charged with collecting and analyzing information and carrying out "special activities" as directed by the president.

In the years that followed, the CIA became infamous worldwide. According to a well-known congressional investigation of the CIA undertaken in the mid-1970s, "The CIA has been accused of interfering in the internal political affairs of nations ranging from Iran to Chile, from Tibet to Guatemala, from Libya to Laos, from Greece to Indonesia. Assassinations, coups d'état, vote buying, economic warfare— all have been laid at the doorstep of the CIA. Few political crises take place in the world today in which CIA involvement is not alleged" (*Final Report,* I, 1976). A growing volume of declassified documents and revelations flowing from the now-defunct Soviet empire show such characterizations of U.S. covert action to be mostly accurate.

The Definition and Types of Covert Action

As specified in a 1991 law, **covert action** is "an activity or activities of the United States Government to influence political, economic, or military conditions abroad, where it is intended that the role of the United States Government will not be apparent or acknowledged publicly." Early in the Cold War, American policy makers embraced covert actions like those described above as instruments of influence chiefly because of their alleged utility as a so-called "middle option," less risky than direct military action, but more aggressive than diplomatic pressure; hence, the instrument appealed to many as "a prudent alternative to doing nothing" (Berkowitz and Goodman 1998).

Over time, the United States has relied on a number of such "special actions" in its foreign policy. A 1954 National Security Council directive identified the breadth of such acts:

> propaganda; political action; economic warfare; escape and evasion and evacuation measures; subversion against hostile states or groups including assistance to underground resistance movements, guerrillas, and refugee liberation groups; support of indigenous and anticommunist elements in threatened countries of the free world; deception plans and operations; and all activities compatible with this directive necessary to accomplish the foregoing.
>
> (QUOTED IN GADDIS 1982, 158).

In the 1970s, it became clear that assassination was also part of this repertoire. Later, various forms of high-tech information warfare or "cyberwar" also joined the list.

Covert Intervention in the Early Cold War

In the early years of the Cold War, the use of covert action rested on a general consensus regarding the nature of the competition with the Soviet Union. As the 1954 Doolittle Report (*Report on the Covert Activities of the Central Intelligence Agency,* named for its head, Lieutenant General James Doolittle) insisted,

> It is now clear that we are facing an implacable enemy whose avowed object is world domination by whatever means and at whatever cost. There are no rules in such a game. Hitherto acceptable norms of human conduct do not apply. . . . We must . . . learn to subvert, sabotage, and destroy our enemies by more clever, more sophisticated, and more effective methods than those used against us.
>
> (QUOTED IN RANELAGH 1987, 277)

Driven by this view, American policy makers increasingly turned to covert interventions. Two of the CIA's boldest and most spectacular operations—the overthrow of Premier Mohammed Mossadegh in Iran in 1953 and the coup that ousted President Jacobo Arbenz of Guatemala in 1954 (see Andrew 1995; Gasiorowski 1987; Immerman 1982; Treverton 1987)[1]—resulted in the quick and virtually bloodless removal of two allegedly procommunist leaders. Consequently, both the agency and Washington policy makers acquired a sense of confidence in the CIA's capacity for operational success. Eventually, this reputation for results led to an enviable situation in which the CIA provided information, recommended policy programs, and then implemented them.

The invasion of Cuba at the Bay of Pigs in 1961 by a band of CIA-trained and financed Cuban exiles stands out as a classic case of CIA prominence in policy making. The CIA saw the Bay of Pigs operation as a way to eliminate the "problem" posed by Castro. Although engineered along the lines of the successful 1954 Guatemalan operation, the defeat suffered by the Cuban exiles tarnished the agency's reputation and cost Allen Dulles, the CIA director, his job.[2] Still, covert operations remained an accepted policy option. *Operation Mongoose* reflected that perspective. It consisted of paramilitary, sabotage, and political propaganda activities directed against Castro's Cuba in the aftermath of the Bay of Pigs, but with much the same purpose as the 1961 invasion. The Church committee's Senate hearings in the 1970s even revealed that the CIA once tried to humiliate Fidel Castro by dusting the Cuban leader's shoes with a substance that would make his hair fall out! Less humorously, the investigation reported that Castro had survived at least eight CIA-sponsored assassination plots.

Many additional examples of the use of covert operations during the Cold War could be cited. For instance, during the 1960s, the United States launched a covert action against Cheddi Jagan, prime minister of then British Guiana, believing him to be a communist. Thirty years later Jagan was elected president of the now-independent Guyana. Not knowing of the earlier clandestine action, the Clinton administration was embarrassed to learn that its nominee as ambassador to Guyana, William C. Doherty, Jr., had participated in the effort to unseat Jagan. From the 1950s to the 1970s, the agency also made payments to Japan's conservative political party, the Liberal Democratic Party (LDP), which dominated Japanese politics for more than a generation, hoping to stave off a challenge by Japanese socialists. *Paramilitary operations* were also initiated in Southeast Asia. In Laos, over 30,000 tribesmen were organized into a kind of private CIA army. In Vietnam, where a CIA analyst would later admit that the agency "assassinated a lot of the wrong damn people" (Carr 1994), a CIA operation known as Phoenix killed over 20,000 suspected Vietcong in less than four years (Lewy 1978; Marchetti and Marks 1974).

Although the CIA was (and is) prohibited by law from directing its actions toward American citizens, Americans were nevertheless targeted. The Church committee hearings revealed that in 1959 CIA agents tested the hallucinogenic drug LSD on a houseful of unwitting people in San Francisco. Recent declassified documents reveal that from the end of World War II to well into the 1970s, the Atomic Energy Commission, the Defense Department, the military services, the CIA, and other agencies used prisoners, drug addicts, mental patients, college students, soldiers, even bar patrons, in a vast range of government-run experiments to test the effects of everything from radiation, LSD, and nerve gas to intense electric shocks and prolonged "sensory deprivation." Why did the United States conduct these "experiments" so eerily reminiscent of the horrific medical experiments performed on innocent victims by the likes of Germany's Dr. Josef Mengele and Japan's General Shoro Ishii? "In the life-and-death struggle with communism, America could not afford to leave any scientific avenue unexplored" (*U.S. News and World Report* 24 January 1994, 33).

The catalog of proven and alleged CIA involvement in the internal affairs of other nations could be broadened extensively, but we cannot understand the reliance on either covert or military forms of intervention without recognizing how much the fear of communism and the drive to contain it motivated policy makers. According to Victor Marchetti and John Marks (1974), "covert intervention may seem to be an easier solution to a particular problem than to allow events to follow their natural course or to seek a tortuous diplomatic settlement. . . . The temptation to interfere in another country's internal affairs can be almost irresistible, when the means are at hand." Not surprisingly, then, as the Doolittle Report argued, policy makers used the same tools as the other side, no matter how repugnant they might have been. A higher purpose—the "national security"—was being served.

Covert Actions in the 1970s and 1980s

During the 1970s, covert actions were described simply as those secret activities designed to further American policies and programs abroad. Chile became an early target.[3] Beginning in the 1950s, the United States mounted a concerted effort in Chile to prevent the leftist politician Salvador Allende from first gaining and then exercising political power. By the 1970s American efforts included (1) covert activities; (2) a close working relationship between the government and giant United States-based multinational corporations doing business in Chile, whose corporate interests were threatened; and (3) pressure on multilateral lending institutions to do America's bidding. Anticommunist thinking contributed to the eventual overthrow of the Allende government, but the story also illustrated American willingness to use a range of instruments to oppose those willing to experiment in leftist domestic political programs.

The revelation of these activities and others led to growing concern about the use (and misuse) of covert activities. Both the president and Congress imposed restraints on the foreign and domestic activities of the intelligence community.

Senate hearings on intelligence activities, chaired by Frank Church (D-Idaho), revealed the CIA had tried to assassinate (murder for political purposes) foreign leaders and engaged in other questionable acts. As Church colorfully characterized it in the hearings, "Covert action is a semantic disguise for murder, coercion, blackmail, bribery, [and] the spreading of lies." This led President Ford to issue an executive order—still in force today—outlawing assassination and, as Congress became increasingly involved in the oversight of intelligence activities, to more refined definitions of and reporting requirements on covert actions (sometimes called "special activities") to ensure that presidents brought all proposed activities to the attention of appropriate congressional committees. For instance, the 1980 Intelligence Oversight Act established congressional intelligence oversight committees and required the submission of *presidential findings*—justifications of need, purposes, and (general) means—authorizing covert action.

The Reagan administration's determination to exorcise the ghost of Vietnam, and to challenge this increased congressional assertiveness, was especially apparent in its drive to "unleash" the CIA (Woodward 1987). Its capacity for covert actions in terms of staff and budget were greatly reenergized under William Casey, Reagan's CIA director. Casey also enjoyed wide latitude in conducting secret wars against American enemies, virtually running his own State and Defense departments out of the CIA (Scott 1996). In addition to covert actions in places like Iran, Chad, Ethiopia, Liberia, and the Sudan, his missions included implementation of the *Reagan Doctrine.*

As stated in National Security Decision Direction 75 (January 17, 1983), the *Reagan Doctrine* directed American policy "to . . . weaken and, where possible, undermine the existing links between [Soviet Third World allies] and the Soviet Union. U.S. policy will include active efforts to encourage democratic movements and forces to bring about political change inside these countries." As President Reagan said in 1985, "We must not break faith with those who are risking their lives on every continent from Afghanistan to Nicaragua to defy Soviet supported aggression and secure rights which have been ours from birth."

Afghanistan and Nicaragua became the most celebrated applications of the newly enunciated doctrine (which also included Angola and Cambodia). Using Pakistan as a gateway, the CIA provided the anti-Marxist *mujaheddin,* (the Islamic guerrillas challenging Soviet troops and the pro-Soviet regime in Afghanistan) with more than $3 billion in guns, ammunition, and other support, including a shoulder-fired anti-aircraft missile known as the Stinger, which proved enormously successful and may have played a critical role in the Soviet Union's withdrawal from Afghanistan (Scott 1996).[4]

In Nicaragua the CIA supported the contras (so-called counterrevolutionaries who were themselves a creation of the agency) with arms, aid, and support for naval blockades, air strikes, espionage, and propaganda operations. Eventually, the American role in Nicaragua figured prominently in the *Iran-contra affair,* a domestic scandal that rekindled fears of an abuse of power in the name of national security reminiscent of the Watergate affair a decade earlier. A central issue was whether funds diverted from the sale of arms to Iran in a secret arms-for-hostages deal violated a legal prohibition against continued CIA support of the contras' activities. The last two years of the Reagan administration were dominated by investigations of this scandal, not to mention renewed charges that the covert arms of the United States government were in need of more careful control.

Hence, as the Cold War came to a close, serious questions about the nature and desirability of covert interventions were being raised in many quarters. Because the Cold War's end took with it the basic rationale for most of the intelligence activities in which the United States had engaged, including covert interventions, many wondered

what place such activities would play in the absence of the Soviet threat.

In Search of a Rationale: Intelligence and Covert Action beyond the Cold War

Since the end of the Cold War, "The CIA . . . is . . . in search of a mission. . . . The end of the Cold War has rendered . . . largely irrelevant . . . the great covert action programs that were established in the 1950s to battle communism around the world" (Ignatius 1994). While most policy makers and policy analysts agree that intelligence must be collected and analyzed, the need for a continued covert action capability has been more controversial. In many respects, reform of the intelligence community was the theme of the 1990s. Initial efforts, which included tighter controls over covert action, followed the Iran-contra investigations, but collapsed when President Bush vetoed the legislation (see, for example, Boren 1992, and his critique in *Foreign Affairs*). By mid-decade, the House of Representatives had made its own study, recommending reforms for the twenty-first century (*Intelligence Community in the 21st Century,* Permanent Select Committee on Intelligence, U.S. House of Representatives, 104th Congress, 1996). Then, under pressure from Congress, the Clinton administration launched its own bipartisan review of the intelligence community (*Preparing for the 21st Century: An Appraisal of U.S. Intelligence,* Commission on the Roles and Capabilities of the United States Intelligence Community, 1996). Organizations outside the government also got in on the act (for example, *Making Intelligence Smarter: The Future of U.S. Intelligence,* Report of an Independent Task Force for the Council on Foreign Relations, 1996; and *In From the Cold: The Report of the Twentieth Century Fund Task Force on the Future of U.S. Intelligence,* 1996).

We will take up the issue of intelligence reform in Chapter 11; here, we note only that what to do with covert operations remains very much in dispute. With the end of the Cold War and the victory over Soviet communism—the principal adversary against whom covert action was directed for more than four decades—some wondered if the agency should even continue. Former Senator Daniel Patrick Moynihan, for example, proposed legislation to eliminate the CIA and fold its intelligence function into the State Department. In contrast, others maintained that, with new threats such as terrorism, covert intervention "offers today, no less than during the Cold War, an effective alternative to the unacceptable risks and costs of military operations" (Henriksen 2000). The shocking attacks on the United States in September 2001 crystallized the dilemma, exposing both the need for and limits of covert intelligence activities.

In the face of these pressures for reform, declining budgets, and a much more complex and intractable international environment, what place does covert intervention now have in American efforts to exert global influence? While this has been a central question for over a decade, the range of answers looks very different in the aftermath of the September 2001 attacks on the United States. Prior to the attacks, skepticism abounded on the continuing relevance of covert action to U.S. foreign policy. After the strikes, the CIA found itself reinvingorated, with counterterrorism and other operations related to the campaign against terrorism seeming to fill the void left by the end of the Cold War and the disappearance of the Cold War mission. Counterterrorism is not the only focus of the twenty-first century CIA, but it seems likely to be the primary mission for both intelligence and covert action for the foreseeable future. Supplementing this focus on counterterrorism, the CIA has also been active in drugs and narco-terrorism, high-tech "info war," economic espionage, enviro-intelligence, and traditional state threats.[5] We discuss these briefly and then turn to the emerging focus on counterterrorism.

The War on Drugs With congressional encouragement, the CIA has expanded its covert operations in the drugs and *narco-terrorism* arena, working with the Drug Enforcement Agency. As in counterterrorism, the CIA gathers information, conducts surveillance and infiltration, and provides personnel, training, resources, and operations support while the DEA makes the arrests. Recent examples include the CIA covert assistance to the Peruvian government in the apprehension of a leader of the Shining Path rebel groups (engaged in narco-terrorism), CIA penetration of a Venezuelan drug ring, and efforts along with the Mexican authorities to break up the Arellano-Felix cartel (Cantlupe 2000; Keller 2000; Lane 2000).

A concern should be noted here; as suggested by one observer, "drugs and the CIA are a bad mix" (Ignatius 1994). A steady stream of revelations in the past decade point to highly questionable alliances between the CIA and individuals connected to the drug trade in Laos, Vietnam, Afghanistan, Nicaragua, Guatemala, and others reaching at least as far back as the 1960s, some of which have been substantiated.[6] Even the operation in Peru noted previously has carried with it serious concerns about the unsavory characters with whom the CIA cooperates in pursuit of American interests (Keller 2000).

Economic Intelligence The CIA has also devoted more resources to *economic intelligence*. As reported by one knowledgeable observer, "the proportion of collection and analysis resources allocated to economic intelligence rose from less than 10% to 40% in the immediate post–Cold War period" (Johnson 2000b, 20). Former CIA director James Woolsey also testified at his confirmation hearings in 1993 that intelligence efforts in this area are "the hottest topic in intelligence policy." Intelligence actions might involve intelligence gathering on trade practices and negotiating positions, efforts to counter the industrial espionage of others, and even the covert theft of trade secrets (Kober 1998). The United States has also increased its use of businesses as cover for its agents abroad, and its contacts with the United States business community, both to gather information and disseminate it (Dreyfus 1998).[7]

In addition to being a hot topic, this is also a controversial one: there is a difference between gathering economic information and stealing trade secrets for America's corporations. Some policymakers would agree with former Arizona senator Dennis DeConcini, who argued that the CIA should assist American businesses in gaining or maintaining a competitive edge: "But it is very important, if Mitsubishi is building a new semiconductor that is three generations out, to have some kind of idea what it is and to get what you can [about it], even if necessary through some surreptitious activities" (Mann 1993). Such policymakers point out that American competitors like Britain and France are already active in this kind of covert effort. Others disagree, warning of the severe practical and ethical issues involved: "Intelligence cannot be provided in fairness to one U.S. company over another; yet widely distributing secrets risks the disclosure of sensitive sources and methods. . . . And if the CIA were caught with its hands in a Toyota safe at midnight, would that risk be worth the likely setback in U.S. Japanese relations?" (Johnson 2000b).

Information Warfare and Enviro-Intelligence The CIA has undertaken new covert efforts in two additional areas that reflect the changing nature of the world as we enter a new century. According to Berkowitz and Goodman (1998), *information warfare,* or "cyberwar" as it is sometime called, which is the use of or attacks on information systems for political and/or military advantage, is a critical area of national security in which the CIA is increasingly involved. Not only is the agency recruiting individuals with the specialized computer skills that would be useful in intelligence gathering and analysis related to such warfare, it is also developing "techno-spies as field-deployed case officers" (*Time,* April 10, 2000, p. 51). Covert "cyber-actions" involving these individuals include efforts to deter and track down hackers, prevent attacks on information

systems, detect and prevent "bugs" embedded in important information hardware and software, and operations to employ such tactics against others (Berkowitz 1998). An example is the cyber-effort to "hack" Slobodan Milošević's bank accounts to drain his funds in 1999. Increasingly, the CIA seeks "a few good geeks," as one account colorfully characterized the situation (*Time,* April 10, 2000, p. 51). Also, the CIA recently started up a Silicon Valley venture capital firm ("In-Q-Tel") to invest in high-tech start-ups to maintain the American advantage in the "gizmos and gadgets" on which the intelligence community depends (Breslau 2000).

Under President Clinton, the CIA also became increasingly involved in what some have called *enviro-intelligence* (Auster 1998b). These efforts chiefly involve intelligence-gathering and monitoring efforts that employ the nation's satellites and other technical resources to monitor and forecast crises. However, the CIA also monitors compliance with international environmental treaties, and began, in 1998, to target other countries to learn their negotiating positions on environmental issues such as the Kyoto agreement (Auster 1998b). To do so, it has established an environmental center and has tasked its operatives to penetrate the negotiating teams of other countries. An indicator of the significance of this area for future covert efforts is the National Intelligence Council report, *Global Trends 2015,* which details a host of emerging environmental issues (and consequences) that will impact the United States. The most striking aspect of this report is its departure from previous reports on "national security."

Targeting States Although the use of covert operations declined substantially after the end of the Cold War, the United States has kept up its use of covert operations against states it has identified as threats. Such uses of this instrument closely resemble the traditional applications of the Cold War, albeit on a smaller scale. One example is the six-year operation directed against Saddam Hussein and Iraq. When Iraq invaded

Kuwait in August 1990, President Bush ordered the CIA to prepare a covert action plan to destabilize Iraq by undermining the Iraqi economy, fomenting discontent within its military forces, and supporting internal and external resistance to Saddam. Bush submitted a *presidential finding* to Congress to that effect, which was immediately approved by the intelligence committees (Fletcher 1990). CIA efforts included propaganda in the form of broadcasts, leaflets, and video/audio cassettes, as well as attempts to support military officers planning a coup attempt (Kurkjian 1991; Oberdorfer 1993).

President Clinton continued the operation, enlarging CIA support for the Kurdish rebels in the northern region of Iraq, and helping to establish the "Iraqi National Congress"—a coalition of anti-Saddam groups. In 1995, under pressure from the Republican Congress to take stronger covert action against Iraq, the United States accelerated its support to include substantial military assistance. Together the Bush and Clinton administrations spent about $120 million through 1996 on the action (Thomas 1998). Unfortunately, in September 1996 the effort collapsed as the Kurds disintegrated into rival factions and Hussein launched a military strike into the region. A similar action based in Jordan, supporting the Iraqi National Accord (mostly former Iraqi military officers), also collapsed about the same time when Hussein's security forces infiltrated the organization (Risen 2000). The CIA was routed and its Kurdish allies were annihilated in what two long-time analysts of CIA activities called "possibly the greatest covert action debacle since Vietnam. . . . Having relied on covert action because it was unwilling to confront Iraq overtly, America appeared weak as well as naive in the wake of the operation's failure" (Berkowitz 1998). Efforts to revive the activities in 1998 largely failed. However, with suspicion of Iraq's support for the Al Qaeda terrorist network and the September 2001 attacks on the United States, new attempts to undermine Saddam Hussein's regime began in the fall of 2001.

Another example of these more traditional efforts began in the spring of 1999 when the Clinton administration launched a covert operation against Serbia and Slobodan Milošević. Having rejected an opportunity early in the decade to support a coup against Milošević by members of his inner circle and Yugoslav military officers (Vistica 1999), the Clinton administration turned to the option in May 1999. An intelligence finding issued in that month authorized the CIA to begin a range of efforts "to find other ways to get at Milošević" (*Newsweek,* May 31, 1999, 38). In addition to propaganda broadcasts from sites ringing Serbia, the CIA also reportedly funneled cash to opposition groups inside Serbia and worked to recruit dissidents in the government and military for a coup attempt. The agency also trained and equipped Kosovar rebels for sabotage inside Serbia. Furthermore, "techno-spies" tried to "hack" into foreign banks to access Milošević's accounts to drain their contents (*Time,* July 12, 1999, 37). It is as yet unclear how much effect this operation had on the removal of Milošević from power; who was voted out of office by the Serbian people in the fall of 2000.

Another example of this kind of covert action overlaps with the growing counterterrorism efforts discussed below and concerns CIA activities in Afghanistan after the September 2001 strikes against the United States. Targeted both at the Taliban regime and the Al Qaeda terrorist network led by Osama bin Laden, this covert action was described by one insider as "the most sweeping and lethal covert action since the founding of the agency in 1947" (Woodward 2001). Almost immediately after the attacks on New York and Washington, DC, George W. Bush signed an intelligence finding authorizing actions against the Taliban regime and the destruction of Osama bin Laden and his Al Qaeda network (Cushman 2001). As a senior official described it, "the gloves are off. The president has given the agency the green light to do whatever is necessary. Lethal operations that were unthinkable pre-September 11 are now underway" (Woodward 2001).

Coordinated by the CIA's Counterterrorism center, the CIA operation began with several objectives, including locating and targeting leaders of the Taliban and Al Qaeda, attacking the infrastructure and the communications and security apparatus of the Afghan regime and the terrorist network, and recruiting "defectors" from the Pashtun leaders in the southern areas of Afghanistan in order to remove the Taliban from power (Sipress and Loeb 2001). In addition to more than $1 billion in new funds for the covert action, the covert operation had additional muscle through its close collaboration with the U.S. military's special forces and other units in an unprecedented display of coordination (Woodward 2001). The CIA also operated armed, unmanned drones which produced live video and could be dispatched to fire on emerging targets. Plans were in place to use other, longer-range drones in similar ways (Ricks 2001). The Bush administration's commitment to extend the campaign against terrorism beyond the immediate goals in Afghanistan promised to lead to additional covert action in other countries as well.

Counterterrorism Even before the September 11 attacks on the United States, counterterrorist covert operations involving the CIA and FBI had expanded in recent years. A new Counterterrorism Center at CIA headquarters in Langley, Virginia staffed by both agencies brought CIA's ability to gather intelligence and engage in covert actions together with the FBI's investigative and law enforcement strengths. Also, the FBI has the authority to take action within American borders (the CIA does not). Prior to September 2001, the partnership had some successes, including the arrests of Mir Aimal Kansi (who assassinated two CIA employees outside CIA headquarters in 1993) and Mohammed Rashid (for bombing a Pan Am flight from Hawaii to Japan in 1982); the apprehension of Tsutomu Shirosaki (who attacked the United States embassy in Indonesia); the apprehension and prosecution of those who bombed the World Trade Center in 1993; and the investigation of the 1998 bombings

of United States embassies in Kenya and Tanzania (Kitfield 2000).

Perhaps the most extensive of these operations has been the effort to break up and apprehend the Al Qaeda network organized and financed by wealthy Saudi expatriate and zealous Islamic revolutionary Osama bin Laden.[8] Since 1995, when bin Laden's network first became a major target, the CIA has tried to infiltrate the network, track, arrest, and detain its members ("disruption operations"), and thwart attacks on the United States (Loeb 1998). At one point in 1998, CIA operatives were also prepared to fight their way into Afghanistan from Pakistan in an attempt to "snatch" bin Laden from a base at which he was staying, but the operation was canceled at the last minute. The CIA and FBI also claim that their "millenium operation" preempted numerous terrorist attacks planned in 2000 (Kitfield 2000). In late 2000, the Clinton administration began a "CounterIntelligence 21" program to extend this cooperation even further.

The September 11 strikes organized by Al Qaeda revealed the limited success of this counterterrorism effort and generated a new sense of urgency and mission for future actions. In addition to prompting calls for an investigation into the intelligence and law enforcement failure the attacks represented (Mitchell and Purdum 2001), the changed environment also produced an acceleration of the counterterrorism emphasis in the CIA and other intelligence and law enforcement agencies. The counterterrorism center at the CIA doubled in size after the attacks, and became the hub for planning operations in Afghanistan (and elsewhere) and for directing clandestine activities against terrorism (Pincus 2001). CIA director George Tenet took steps to break down barriers to coordination among different parts of the agency (analysts and operations personnel) and between the agency and others (especially the FBI). Additionally, George W. Bush increased the CIA budget by more than $1 billion for the war on terrorism (Woodward 2001). Furthermore, new personnel, both in intelligence analysis and in operations, were recruited and new attention was given in Congress to the idea of a unified counterterrorism budget coordinated centrally (McCallister 2001). Finally, a wide array of operations reminiscent of Cold War covert actions—intelligence gathering, destabilization campaigns, even assassination efforts[9]—were developed and implemented. In many ways, the anti-terrorism mission had replaced the anti-communist mission of the previous era.

Challenges for Covert Intervention in the Twenty-First Century

During George W. Bush's first term, the United States has faced a number of critical challenges regarding the use of covert action in the new century. First, to play an effective and central role in twenty-first century foreign policy, the agency has had to confront the long-term decline in the legitimacy of covert intervention. While the newly revitalized sense of mission stemming from the post-September 2001 campaign against terrorism will surely help, the CIA has reeled from unflattering revelations of questionable activities and associations that have dribbled to the press during the past decade. From association with drug dealers to death squad operators, recent revelations have scarred the agency's reputation. As important, the 1994 arrest of Aldrich Ames—the long-feared "mole" within the CIA—further seared the agency. His traitorous acts—he sold classified information about CIA activities to the Soviet Union from 1985 on—resulted in the widespread disruption of American clandestine activities generally, and the virtual destruction of CIA operations in Moscow. In 1994 he pleaded guilty to espionage and was sentenced to life in prison. During the same period (July 1994), *U.S. News & World Report* published a stinging indictment of the CIA that revealed, among other things, the (second) collapse of the United States spy network in Iran. It also revealed that nearly all of the American agents in East Germany were in fact double agents working for the communists. The

fallout from these shocks led many senior members to leave the agency; by one account, by 2005 nearly half the agents will have less than five years experience (Johnson 2001). Consequently, the CIA's capability to engage in covert intervention has suffered.

Second, the Bush administration has had to contend with the new demands placed on the agency by the nature of twenty-first century challenges. The agency's operations culture has largely lost its edge and its technological advantages are eroding. Budget cuts in the 1990s exacerbated the problem substantially. Dramatic failures like its operation in Iraq have led to "an aversion to risky espionage operations" (Risen 2000), and its failure to predict, much less prevent, the September 2001 attacks on the United States are certain to raise new questions about its activities. New tasks and targets for its covert operators require difficult-to-attract new recruits with new skills and specializations relevant to problems of the new century.

Finally, the major challenge concerns the fundamental shift in mission inherent in the transition from Cold War to twenty-first century worlds. At first, it seemed that the CIA had lost its mandate for covert intervention with the end of the Cold War. By one account, the agency "bounced from one small mission to another, from Bosnia to Korea, from drug-runners to international terrorists. These days, it seems, the CIA is as likely to be supporting other federal agencies—like the FBI in the case of counterterrorism, or the Drug Enforcement Administration in the case of counternarcotics—as it is to be out on its own" (Aizenman 1999). While the rise of counterterrorism has given the agency a new intelligence polestar, it has also presented a new set of (perhaps even greater) challenges to be met. In the twenty-first century, the agency faces "myriad and elusive small non-state groups or rogue regimes" difficult to pin down. Moreover, the targets "tend to shift rapidly from one hot spot to another," thereby stressing resources, logistics, and capabilities (Aizenman 1999). A long-time

**Table 5.1 Expenditures on Foreign Economic Aid
(Loans and Grants), 1946–2000 (In billions of dollars by fiscal year)**

Postwar Relief Period (1946–1948)	$12.5
Marshall Plan Period (1949–1952)	$18.6
Mutual Security Act Period (1953–1961)	$24.1
Foreign Assistance Act Period (1962–2000)	$299.9
Grand total	**$348.5**

Note: Numbers do not add to total due to different reporting concepts in the pre- and post-1995 periods.

SOURCE: Adapted from *U.S. Overseas Loans and Grants and Assistance from International Organizations, Obligations and Loan Authorizations, July 1, 1945–September 30, 1997*, Washington, DC: Agency for International Development, 1998, 4; supplemented with AID Congressional Presentations for FY 1999–2001

insider has warned that, while "the new intelligence war presents the CIA with an opportunity to excel . . . the campaign is also fraught with risk" (Woodward 2001). A CIA veteran notes that "the agency is being assigned a monumental task for which it is not fully equipped or trained" (cited in Woodward 2001). Since covert activities have been on the decline for a decade, the CIA has "been out of the business of funding and managing major lethal covert action" and will need to improve its capabilities rapidly (Woodward 2001). Among the key issues related to this challenge, discussed more fully in chapter 11, is the personnel needs of both the intelligence and operations divisions of the agency. The preference for clandestine operations demonstrated by every president since the onset of World War II and the nature of the counterterrorism mission in the twenty-first century suggest that this instrument of American foreign policy will remain in demand at the White House. However, the question remains as to whether the Bush administration will have finely honed tools at its disposal when it opts for covert intervention.

FOREIGN ASSISTANCE: INTERVENTION WITHOUT COERCION

Another instrument for exerting global influence short of military intervention is foreign assistance, both economic and military. Both power and principle have driven the use of aid over the past fifty years. However, since the end of the Cold War, the logic that sustained these programs has dissipated and their use as foreign policy tools has been heavily scrutinized.

Economic Assistance

Since World War II the United States has provided nearly $350 billion in *foreign economic aid*—loans and grants—to other countries (see Table 5.1). This is a large amount, but by no means the mammoth "giveaway" ascribed to foreign aid in the popular mind. On average, the sum is about $6.5 billion annually, substantially less than Americans spend each year on cigarettes and alcoholic beverages or commercial entertainment. In constant (noninflated) dollars, moreover, the amount of aid given today is dramatically less than forty years ago. In 1949 alone, the United States provided (in 1994 dollars) more than $50 billion in aid, most in the form of *Marshall Plan* assistance to rebuild Western Europe (*Congressional Quarterly Weekly Report,* 17 December 1994, 3568). Moreover, most foreign aid (military as well as economic) is "tied" to purchases of goods and services in the United States: according to the U.S. Agency for International Development, which oversees much of the foreign economic aid provided by the United States, about eighty percent of American economic aid is used to purchase American products or services (see also Dobbs [2001]).

Purposes and Programs Why give foreign aid at all? For much for the post–World War II period, most policy makers accepted the need and utility of economic assistance as an instrument of national interest and of principle. For most of the Cold War, economic assistance rested on the premise that it contributed to American security by supporting friends, providing for markets, and containing communist influence. "The security rationale provided a general and often compelling justification for U.S. foreign aid as a whole because aid for development and other purposes, it was argued, also supported U.S. security" (Lancaster 2000a). However, in addition to self-interest, United States aid policy was also built on the belief that helping poorer countries develop and providing humanitarian relief in times of disaster and crisis were principled actions on their own merits.

In practice, therefore, during the Cold War America's foreign aid programs satisfied both realists who would focus on self-interest and security concerns, and idealists, who would also stress humanitarian concerns (Tisch and Wallace 1994). Hence, as long as the security and humanitarian values ran parallel, most policy makers supported economic assistance. As we will see, after the Cold War, uncertainty over the contribution of aid to American security interests and economic development destroyed the consensus and raised doubts about the continued utility of the foreign economic aid tool.

To accomplish the purposes for which United States foreign economic aid is provided, the United States has relied on a number of different agencies since World War II. Since 1961, the *Agency for International Development (AID)* has been responsible for administering most American economic assistance programs. The aid it provides falls into three main categories: economic support funds, development assistance, and Food for Peace, although several others were added in the 1990s. Additional support is provided through subscriptions to multilateral lending agencies, such as the International Monetary Fund, the World Bank, and the International Development Association (IDA), the so-called "soft loan window" of the World Bank.

Economic support funds (ESF) are dollars granted or loaned to countries of special political significance to the United States. These funds are used for "enhancing political stability, promoting economic reforms important to long-term development, promoting economic stabilization through budget and balance of payments support, and assisting countries that allow the United States to maintain military bases on their soil" (Zimmerman 1993). Because of their political and strategic significance, ESF funds are provided by the State Department and managed by AID. Prior to 1978, the Philippines, Thailand, and Vietnam were the largest ESF recipients. Egypt and Israel have been the largest recipients of economic aid since the *Camp David Accords* of 1978. In 2000, they received more than $2.7 billion in ESF support (www.info.usaid. gov/press/releases/2000/budget2001.html).

Development assistance provides grants and loans to support social and economic development. Aid is typically provided to specific countries for specific projects like health, education, agriculture, and rural development. *Disaster relief assistance* also often falls under the rubric of development assistance. In 2000, the United States provided just over $2.5 billion in assistance for development, children, health, and disaster assistance (www.info.usaid.gov/press/releases/2000/budget2001.html).

Food aid is provided through the **Food for Peace program,** perhaps more widely known as PL (public law) 480 in reference to the Agricultural Trade Development and Assistance Act of 1954 which created it. The objectives of the Food for Peace program are "to expand exports of U.S. agricultural commodities, to combat hunger and malnutrition, to encourage economic development in developing countries, and to promote the foreign policy interests of the United States" (Zimmerman 1993). The program, in which the Department of Agriculture now plays a major role, sells agricultural commodities on credit terms and makes grants for emergency relief. The Food for

Table 5.2 Economic Cooperation with Russia, 1992–1998 (In billions of dollars)

Donor	Amount
United States Bilateral	$5.7
World Bank	$9.8
IMF	$36.1
Total	**$51.6**

SOURCE: "The Former Soviet Union and U.S. Foreign Assistance," *CRS Report for Congress IB95077*, 15 June 2000; supplemented by data at: www.foreignpolicy-infocus.org/briefs/vol3/v3n25fsu_body.html and www.state.gov/www/background_notes/russia_9810_bgn.html

Table 5.3 Cumulative Expenditures of Aid to Eastern Europe and the New Independent States, FY1992–FY1999 (In billions of dollars)

Recipient	Amount
Russia	$6.225
Other Former Soviet Republics	$5.794
NIS-Regional	$1.0
Total	**$13.019**

SOURCE: *U.S. Government Assistance to and Cooperative Activities with the New Independent States of the Former Soviet Union,* report for 1999 at http://www.state.gov/www/regions/nis/nis_assist_index.html

Peace program totaled about $60 billion by 2000, or about a fifth of all economic aid granted since PL 480 was passed. In 2000, about $800 million in food aid was administered by AID (www.info.usaid.gov/press/releases/2000/budget2001.html).

Economic aid is also channeled through American contributions to multilateral lending agencies, to which the United States has relegated large-scale *infrastructure projects* (basic facilities and systems like roads and regional irrigation systems) since the 1970s. It has also looked to them to provide much of the aid now given to Russia and the other New Independent States (see Table 5.2). Such assistance may have fewer political strings (being multilateral, although, as we will see in Chapter 7, the economic conditions are often onerous), but has long been unpopular in Congress because of the impression that these institutions' largesse is too readily accessible to those who oppose the United States. Since the end of the Cold War, the United States has also provided bilateral assistance to Eastern Europe through the Support for Eastern European Democracy Act (1989), and to the New Independent States through the Freedom Support Act (1992), both of which are administered by AID. In 2000, these programs received $533 and $836 million respectively (www.info.usaid.gov/press/releases/2000/budget2001.html; see also Table 5.3).

Given the variety of programs for American foreign aid, it should come as no surprise that foreign aid has evolved over time in its form and its purposes. In fact, as the following historical sketch of foreign aid policy suggests, different administrations have emphasized different objectives. Moreover, new purposes have arisen in the changing environment of the past decade. At the same time, the broad consensus on the security, economic, developmental, and humanitarian benefits of foreign aid has collapsed. Our review first examines the Cold War and the consensus it fostered, and then the years leading to the search for a new foreign aid focus.[10]

Economic Aid in the Cold War As noted earlier, the first major peacetime effort to utilize foreign aid as an instrument of foreign policy was the remarkably successful ***Marshall Plan,*** formally known as the European Recovery Program. Directed toward war-ravaged Western European countries, the Marshall Plan used American capital to rebuild the economic, social, and political infrastructures of European societies to enhance Europe's ability to resist communism and support a market for American products. After the outbreak of the Korean War, the ***Mutual Security Act*** of 1953 became the governing legislation for foreign aid. The emphasis now shifted from recovery to containment, and from Europe to Asia.

In 1961, the *Foreign Assistance Act* replaced the Mutual Security Act and created AID as the administering agency for economic assistance. Development capital and technical assistance were given greater emphasis than defense support aid, and the Alliance for Progress was launched in an attack on incipient revolution and communism in the Western Hemisphere. The prevailing thought was that aid would contribute to economic development in the newly emerging nations of the Third World (as the Global South was then called), which would foster stable democratic governments. Yet even as political development doctrines emerged to explain why foreign aid was in the United States' long-run interest, Cold War considerations—including the Vietnam War—continued to dominate the actual allocation of foreign economic aid during the 1960s. By the end of the decade, seventy percent of all American economic aid was directed to Asia and the Near East.

Official thinking about foreign aid took a new direction with the end of the Vietnam War. Development assistance shifted from social infrastructure projects to programs designed to meet *basic human needs,* as attention focused on alleviating poverty. In part that decision was related to the growing concern of Congress and the Carter administration with linking aid allocations to the human rights practices of developing countries comprising the Third World. Concerned that orthodox economic development theories led to "dualism" in developing societies—with one modern, growing sector and one traditional, stagnant sector—the basic needs perspective focused on assisting the poor as directly as possible. The basic human needs approach stressed food and nutrition, population planning and health, and education and human resource development in specific problems areas. Regionally, AID shifted its efforts to the poorest countries; for example, AID missions in Africa increased from eight in 1973 to twenty-eight in 1980 (Ruttan 1996).

By the end of the 1970s, security concerns reemerged as the driving factors behind United States foreign aid as the Reagan administration "sought to restore foreign economic assistance to what it regarded as its traditional role as an instrument of national security policy" (Ruttan 1996). Not only did the Reagan administration emphasize bilateral aid over multilateral aid (easier to link to American interests) and security assistance over economic assistance, but basic human needs, funded with development assistance, took a back seat to the use of economic support funds for strategic purposes (Payaslian 1996).

The consequences of the shift in approach were readily apparent. States like Guatemala, El Salvador, and Pakistan, who found themselves on the front line of the **Reagan Doctrine,** received large infusions of ESF aid.[11] Similarly, strategic considerations motivated its ambitious 1984 *Caribbean Basin Initiative (CBI),* a program of tariff reductions and tax incentives to promote industry and trade in Central America and the Caribbean as a way of thwarting the economic conditions on which Marxist revolutionaries thrive. As the Bush administration confronted the end of the Cold War, it supplemented its predecessor's emphasis with new support for political and economic transitions in the formerly socialist countries of Eastern Europe and, eventually, the former Soviet Union (see Zveli & Ruttan 1996; Lancaster 2000a). However, the Reagan administration sought unsuccessfully (Kegley and Hook 1991) to link foreign aid allocations to the voting behavior of Third World nations in the United Nations (a practice the Republican-controlled Congress of 1994–2000 wished to resurrect).

Aid to America's Cold War adversaries began in 1990 when the *Support for Eastern European Democracy Act* authorized assistance to Poland and Hungary and then, in 1992, to all of eastern and central Europe. In 1991, a bipartisan coalition in Congress approved $400 million to help the Soviet Union dismantle and store its chemical and nuclear weapons. A year later the *Freedom Support Act* authorized $425 million in assistance to the republics of the now former Soviet Union. In 1993 another $2.5 billion was authorized for Russia and the Ukraine, and in 1994 $1.25 billion more was added. Thus, in a very short time, former adversaries consumed a very large share—as much as twenty percent—of a shrinking foreign aid budget (Table 5.3; see also *Congressional Quarterly Weekly Report,* 17 December 1994, 3568).

Economic Aid into the Twenty-First Century: In Search of a Rationale A series of factors contributed to the decline in foreign economic assistance after the end of the Cold War, as well as the multiple efforts to re-target it at objectives that would enjoy broad support. The end of the Cold War removed the security rationale that sustained aid for over forty years, while the budgetary constraints of ballooning deficits and debt at the outset of the Clinton administration tested the political will of those responsible for providing aid to other countries.

In 1995, public opinion polls showed that as many as sixty-five percent of Americans thought foreign aid should be reduced (Program on International Policy Attitudes 2001). Additional political pressure developed from studies showing that aid had not produced much in the way of economic growth (for example, World Bank 1998; O'Hanlon and Graham 1997). The dramatic surge of overseas private investment, coupled with the apparent triumph of the neo-liberal consensus on the efficacy of market solutions, sapped the force of the argument for development assistance even further. Thus, Patrick Leahy, Democratic Senator from Vermont, concluded that aid policies were "exhausted intellectually, conceptually, and politically. [The foreign aid program] has no widely understood and agreed set of goals, it lacks coherence and vision, and there is a very real question whether parts of it actually serve broadly accepted United States national interests any longer" (quoted in *The Independent Group on the Future of U.S. Development Cooperation* 1992).

Declining support for and delivery of foreign economic assistance led to numerous efforts to restructure, reform, and refocus the economic aid instrument; as yet, none has garnered the kind of broad-gauged support that would ensure the effective use of the foreign policy tool in the twenty-first century. The controversy swirled over two interrelated issues: the structural and institutional mechanisms that administered aid and the purposes and targets of the aid. On the first issue, by 1994 AID was under pressure from many quarters. Outside the government policy analysts called for consolidation of AID with the State Department, its break-up into smaller, functionally oriented agencies, and its outright elimination (see Eagleburger and Barry 1996; Ruttan 1996; Lancaster 2000a). In 1998, Congress passed, and President Clinton signed into law, the *Foreign Affairs Reform and Restructuring Act,* which placed AID under the direct authority and foreign policy direction of the Secretary of State, even though it left the agency structurally separate. Just a few years later, at the outset of George W. Bush's administration, Senator Jesse Helms (R–NC) called for the outright elimination of AID, to be replaced with a quasi-governmental "International Development Foundation" that would deliver grants to nongovernmental organizations (NGOs), directly (Schmitt 2001b).

On the broader question of the purposes of foreign aid, a wide variety of possibilities arose. The most extreme involved the elimination of foreign aid as an instrument of foreign policy. The Cato Institute, the Heritage Foundation, and Senator Jesse Helms were leading advocates of this approach.[12] Doug Bandow (1996) of the Cato Institute, for example, called for "death to foreign aid," while the Heritage Foundation has regularly called for a transition to a policy of "trade, not aid" (Hoy 1998). According to Senator Helms, "the foreign aid program has spent an estimated two trillion dollars of the American taxpayers' money, much of it going down foreign ratholes, to countries that constantly oppose us in the United Nations, and many which rejected concepts of freedom. We must stop this stupid business of giving away the taxpayers' money willy-nilly" (quoted in Bandow 1996). Helms' solution? Abolish AID and instead stress private voluntary organizations and the Overseas Private Investment Corporation (OPIC), which guarantees risky private investment by American investors. In fact, Helms was so adamant that he virtually shut down the foreign policy activities of Congress and parts of the executive branch in 1995–1996 (Hook 1998). Ultimately, his determination led to the adoption of the 1998 *Foreign Affairs Reform and Restructuring Act,* noted earlier.

But not everyone was so determined to end the use of foreign aid as an instrument of foreign policy. The Clinton administration and others sought to revitalize foreign aid as an instrument of global influence by re-targeting it toward new purposes. Early efforts involved several interrelated ideas: *sustainable development, chaos* and *crisis prevention, and democracy promotion.* A major step toward new purposes occurred in September 1993, when the Task Force to Reform AID and the International Affairs Budget issued its report, *Revitalizing the AID and Foreign Assistance in the Post—Cold War Era.* The "Wharton Report" (named for Deputy Secretary of State Clifton Wharton, who chaired the commission) recommended a new global rationale to replace the conflicting demands placed on foreign aid. Recommending less military and more economic aid, the report stressed global issues such as the environment, drug trafficking, disease, population growth, and migration, among others, as the appropriate target for foreign aid policy (Nijman 1998).

Building on this report, and previous work by such organizations as the Overseas Development Council, a Washington-based private policy-planning organization, the Clinton administration advanced its vision of a renewed and refocused foreign program. Speaking before the Overseas Development Council, National Security Adviser Anthony Lake argued that aid policies should stress "the goals of democracy and a form of market development that is both politically and environmentally sustainable," along with "a humanitarian agenda toward the poorest nations . . . and . . . conflict resolution [as] a part of that agenda." Under Secretary of State for Global Affairs Timothy Wirth cited environmental degradation, poverty, disease, and emigration driven by civil conflict as "the primary threats to human security." AID Administrator Brian Atwood identified food insecurity and population growth as twin threats to security and "major contributors to conflict and to the chaos that we worry about so much."

Although AID was not successful in Congress, it took advantage of its role in implementing policy to build the strategy into its efforts.[13] AID guided its plans and budget requests with the sustainable development prism. A good example of the effort is the commitment to democracy promotion, previously discussed in Chapter 3. As Table 5.4 shows, the agency devoted increasing resources to this purpose, despite congressional ambivalence, and even opposition, to the idea (see also Auer 1998). In spite of such changes, the Clinton administration's effort to inject new life and purpose into foreign assistance suffered additional setbacks during its second term.

Early in George W. Bush's administration, the outlines of a new approach seemed to take shape (see Focus 5.1). To be sure, critics of foreign aid policy continued to exert pressure (for example, Schmitt 2001b), but greater agreement began to form around a two-tiered approach. In the first tier, aid purposes that more closely matched the twenty-first century environment received growing support among policy makers. These include *peacemaking* (targeting the civil conflicts that have characterized the past decade or so); *transnational issues* (targeting the increasingly urgent problems of disease, population, prosperity, drug trafficking, and the global environment);[14] *humanitarian relief* (targeting international disasters); and *humane concerns* (targeting the plight of children, women, and other vulnerable groups) (Lancaster 2000a). After September 11, 2001, aid to members of anti-terror coalitions also became a priority.

**Table 5.4 Promoting Democracy for Sustainable Development:
USAID Budget Requests, 1993–2000 (In millions of dollars by fiscal year)**

Region	1993	1994	1995	1996	1997	1998	1999	2000
Africa	72.3	103.2	84.7	77.8	66.3	67.2	100.5	120.6
Asia	30.4	25.7	41.1	77.4	76.3	79.0	86.4	113.7
Europe/NIS	68.6	156.4	156.2	147.9	175.0	212.8	160.9	148.4
L. America	132.8	75.6	115.3	75.3	95.5	92.3	112.7	110.4
Total	**304.1**	**360.9**	**397.3**	**368.4**	**413.1**	**451.3**	**460.5**	**493.1**

SOURCE: *U.S. Agency for International Development Congressional Presentations*, FY 1994–2001

FOCUS 5.1   From the Heartland: Do Members of Congress from Colorado Reflect a New Consensus on United States Foreign Economic Assistance?

"In my mind, engagement can take place most profitably with private businesses operating privately, operating on their own, with a president and a secretary of state who clearly articulate American interests, narrowly define them, and aggressively pursue them."

REP. TOM TANCREDO, REPUBLICAN, LITTLETON, COLORADO

"I am supportive of efforts to bring Third World countries into the global economy."

SEN. WAYNE ALLARD, REPUBLICAN, LOVELAND, COLORADO

. . . favor spending increases for proven disaster relief, micro-credit and family planning programs.

REP. DIANA DEGETTE, DEMOCRAT, DENVER, COLORADO, AS REPORTED BY BRUCE FINLEY

" . . . would support additional expenditures for our State Department diplomatic corps. I am for a robust American strategy of engagement."

REP. BOB SCHAFFER, REPUBLICAN, FORT COLLINS, COLORADO

"A no-brainer. It's in our self-interest to increase foreign assistance funding. In the process, we provide markets for our own good. We promote peace in the world."

REP. MARK UDALL, DEMOCRAT, BOULDER, COLORADO

SOURCE: Bruce Finley, "Increased Foreign Aid Advocated by Envoy," *Denver Post*, 8 February 2001, C1.

In the second tier, ongoing concerns with economic and social development and democracy support and promotion remain significant, but less salient given the record of aid on development and the progress on democratization (which makes it less urgent, while still important). Development concerns are increasingly addressed by multilateral institutions, who may be guided by the insights of previous studies that recommend more selective targeting on countries with sound institutional and policy frameworks, and more selective support for infrastructure and public goods not usually the focus of private investment (see O'Hanlon and Graham 1997; World Bank 1998; Collier and Dollar 1999; Wren 2001).

To be sure, other developments suggest continued struggles. George W. Bush's decision that American multilateral assistance would not be provided to agencies who worked through family-planning groups, whose services include counseling on abortion (*Christian Science Monitor*, 26 January 2001, 10), caused concerns about the American approach to addressing global population issues. Secretary of State Colin Powell's call for increased international affairs funding, including foreign assistance, was greeted by Senator

Jesse Helms' reply that he, as chair of the Senate Foreign Relations Committee, would support increased aid as long as AID was eliminated and replaced by a granting foundation that would funnel assistance to NGOs (Schmitt 2001b).

However, for advocates of aid there is some cause for optimism. Not only has Congress directed increasingly large portions of foreign aid to transnational, humanitarian, and humane problems, but many of these targets have actually received increased funding overall (Lancaster 2000a). Indeed, aid to children, for example, increased by over twenty percent between 1998 and 2001. Also, after a devastating earthquake rocked India in early 2001, Jesse Helms and eleven other prominent senators called on the new Bush administration to provide substantial emergency assistance and disaster relief. Moreover, it appears the American public has become less hostile to the idea of foreign aid: in 1995, sixty-five percent of the public thought aid should be reduced, but in 2000 that number had fallen to forty percent (Program on International Policy Attitudes 2001). Additionally, just before George W. Bush took office, Congress and the Clinton administration agreed to provide $435 million for debt relief to Africa. Perhaps the foreign aid instrument is finding a new rationale and foundation for support in the twenty-first century.

American economic aid programs were born and sustained in an environment when the perceptions of threats to American national interests were widely shared. Sharp differences of opinion marked debates about the appropriateness of foreign aid as a means to meet and parry those threats, but the goals themselves were rarely in dispute. That is no longer the case. Foreign and domestic priorities now compete with one another. Tax dollars spent to prevent crises in Africa are dollars needed by American cities. At the beginning of the twenty-first century, without the sense of threat that led to the Marshall Plan in 1947 and Point Four, foreign economic aid as an instrument of American foreign policy will remain controversial, and efforts to rebuild a consensus for its use will face continuing challenges.

Military Assistance

Foreign military aid, like its economic counterpart, is now a standard instrument of American foreign policy. In this case, however, political realism, with its focus on power and the national interest, is the dominant underlying rationale. Beginning with the Korean War, grants of military aid to other countries became an essential element of Cold War defense and security planning and a tool used to pursue several national security and foreign policy goals.[15] Sales of military equipment would later join grants, and then surpass them, as the major element of American arms transfer programs.

Purposes and Programs Foreign military grants and sales plus economic support funds (discussed earlier) comprise a broad category called *security assistance,* whose purpose is related to a multitude of United States policy objectives. Its goals were enumerated by Assistant Secretary of State H. Allen Holmes, testifying before Congress in 1989:

- Enhancing the ability of American security partners to deter and defend against aggression and instability

- Maintaining the cohesion and strength of our alliances

- Developing sound military-to-military relations that support our diplomatic strategy and enhance American influence and prestige

- Promoting regional stability

- Contributing to our access to military bases and facilities abroad, thereby maintaining the strategic mobility of American forces

- Strengthening the economics of key countries that are attempting to adjust to heavy debt, depressed commodity export prices, and startling changes in the global economic environment

- Providing support for emerging democracies while defending existing democratic institutions and values in other countries

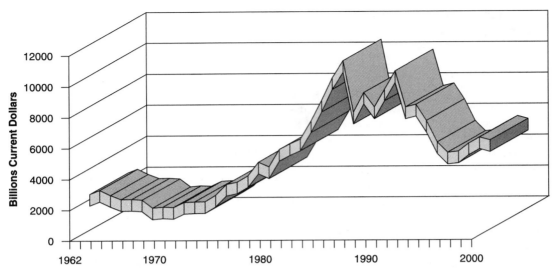

FIGURE 5.1 United States Security Assistance, 1962–2000

Source: *Budget of the United States Government, Fiscal Year 2001,* Historical Tables, Federal Government Outlays by Function at http://w3. access.gpo.gov/usbudget/fy2001/hist.html#h3

Table 5.5 Expenditures on Foreign Military Aid and Sales, 1950–1999 (In billions of dollars by fiscal year)

Military Assistance Program (MAP) and MAP Merger Funds	$61.7
International Military Education and Training Program	$2.8
Foreign Military Sales (FMS) and FMS Construction Agreements	$332.3
Commercial Exports Licensed under the Arms Export Control Act	$77.8
Excess Defense Articles	$6.5
Grand total	**$481.1**

SOURCE: Adapted from *Foreign Military Sales, Foreign Military Construction Sales, and Military Assistance Facts,* Washington, DC: Defense Security Assistance Agency, 2000, 2ff.

At least rhetorically, despite the dramatic changes in context from 1989 to the present, these objectives still officially drive military assistance policy. However, the need to support the defense industrial base by enabling arms manufacturers to export weapons in order to maintain their production lines has become relatively more important since 1989 and is now a key element underpinning military aid programs.

Figure 5.1 and Table 5.5 provide information on the provision of security assistance over time.

As Table 5.5 shows, nearly $500 billion in American military aid has been extended to other nations since the onset of the Korean War (including commercial sales approved by the government). Even that figure is likely to be on the conservative side, as it is based on unclassified information.

Historically, the *Military Assistance Program (MAP)* served as the principal mechanism for transferring United States defense articles, services, and training to other countries. The assistance took the forms of grants, requiring no repayment on the part of recipients. Since the mid-1970s the *International Military Education and Training Program (IMET)* has governed foreign military training, whose personnel by 1994 exceeded 576,000. By the turn of the century, according to the State Department, IMET included 2000 courses at 150 military schools for over 8000 foreign students annually (www.state.gov.www.global/arms/fmtrain/prog_desc.html). In her 2000 report to Congress on foreign military training, Secretary of State Madeleine Albright characterized IMET as "a low-cost, highly effective component of U.S. security assistance . . . to . . . further the goal of regional stability . . . augment the capabilities of the military forces of participant nations to support combined operations and inter-operability with U.S. forces . . . and increase the ability of foreign military and civilian personnel to instill and maintain basic democratic values and protect internationally recognized human rights."

Today *Foreign Military Sales (FMS)* are the most important American arms transfer program. In the fifteen years leading up to 2000, FMS accounted for nearly $180 billion, or more than seventy percent, of military aid (including commercial sales) to other countries. Even more striking is that the sales during this period substantially surpassed the total sales accumulated over the preceding thirty-five years. 1993 was the peak, with $32.9 billion in new agreements. Sales declined substantially after that, falling below $9 billion in 1997 and 1998, but surged again in the last two years of the century, exceeding $12 billion in both (Capaccio 2000). In 2000, U.S. arms sales jumped again, to $18.6 billion (Shanker 2001). Most of these government-to-government sales are in cash, but the Defense Department also provides credits toward foreign military purchases, repayment of which has often been waived.

The recipients of these weapons are predominantly from the Middle East, but the latter part of the twentieth century saw some diffusion. As part of the 1978 Camp David Middle East peace accords, noted in our earlier discussion of foreign economic aid, Egypt and Israel account for two-thirds of foreign military sales and credits. Saudi Arabia also accounts for a large proportion of military sales. In 1993 alone Saudi Arabia entered agreements to buy $11.8 billion in new weapons, bringing its total over the life of the FMS program to more than $60 billion. By 2000, its purchases had declined to less than $2 billion, however. Tiny Kuwait also made nearly $3 billion in purchases in 1993 as it modernized its military forces after the Persian Gulf War. Later in the decade, Turkey and Greece stepped up their purchases, and in Asia, Taiwan emerged as a major purchaser of American arms (in fact, the largest purchaser of arms in the world at the end of the 1990s). Sales increased elsewhere too, including a number of Latin American countries.

Driven by the demise of the Soviet Union, once the dominant arms sale competitor to the United States, and the dramatic display of new American weapons technology during the Gulf War, the 1990s have been an arms bonanza for the U.S. defense industry. According to the Stockholm International Peace Research Institute, by the end of the 20th century American arms sales exceeded fifty percent of the world's total, with sales increasing even as overall world sales decreased. Hence, military assistance and arms sales appear to be thriving as the United States enters a new century. A review of post–World War II military aid policies helps to explain why.[16]

Military Aid during the Cold War During the Cold War, American military aid flowed chiefly to Europe for the first decade, and then to East Asia (which fell off after Vietnam) and the Middle East (which continues to be the biggest recipient). Additionally, what began as grant aid shifted to military sales in the early 1960s as the Kennedy administration began to use sales as an alternative to grants due chiefly to adverse American balance of payments. Finally, by the late 1960s, United States military aid had shifted from the industrial world to the developing world. The driving purposes of military assistance were securing allies, cementing alliances, rewarding patrons, and renting overseas bases.

From Korea to Vietnam The containment policy provided a rationale for military aid to others, justified on the grounds that it augmented the capabilities of American allies to resist Soviet and Soviet-backed expansionism. The NATO and SEATO (Southeast Asia Treaty Organization) alliances thus received special attention, as did those with bilateral defensive arrangements with the United States, like Taiwan. Military aid also was used for the "rental" of base rights in places like Spain and for landing rights for ships and planes elsewhere. Economic support funds were also often used for this purpose, as in the Philippines, where sizable "side payments" were required to retain access to two large military bases, Clark Air Base and the naval facility at Subic Bay. The latter in particular increased in importance following the American withdrawal from Vietnam and the loss of the port facility at Cam Ranh Bay.

Vietnam affected other calculations as well. Between 1966 and 1975 the aid program increasingly targeted "friends" (Semmel 1983), as developing nations in the then Third World commanded greater attention. During the decade ending in 1975, South Vietnam, Cambodia, Laos, Pakistan, South Korea, and Taiwan—all bordering directly on the communist world and bound to the United States in defensive arrangements (see Map 5.1)—more than doubled their military aid receipts. Similar attention characterized the economic aid program, as we noted previously.

After Vietnam The Vietnam imbroglio triggered some serious concerns about U.S. military assistance policy. Some critics argued that military aid "is the 'slippery slope' that leads eventually to an over-extension of commitments and to a greater likelihood of military involvement" (Frank and Baird 1975). Others argued that American programs might have contributed to the maintenance of authoritarian regimes throughout the world since, regardless of their intentions, the programs' consequences included

a greater chance that military groups in recipient countries intervene in or maintain their grip on the politics of those nations (Rowe 1974). In the mid-1970s, for example, more than half of the recipients of American arms were dictatorships. Concern over this problem led some to try to adjust military assistance policy, but, as Figure 5.1 shows, security assistance continued to grow during this period.

The flow of arms to the Middle East achieved massive proportions during the Nixon and Ford administrations, stimulated by the Arab-Israeli conflict, the new financial resources available to Middle Eastern oil exporters from the sharp upsurge in world oil prices from 1973 to 1974, and the **Nixon Doctrine**—the pledge that the United States would provide military and economic assistance to its friends and allies but that those nations would be responsible for protecting their own security. As Figure 5.1 indicates, this is when the major acceleration of security assistance begins, driven chiefly by arms sales. Moreover, although the United States still sought to realize foreign policy objectives, the dramatic shift from grants to sales that occurred at this time also reflected the increasing importance of the economic gains accrued from arms sales. These benefits included maintenance of the domestic defense industry, reduction in the per unit cost of defense articles, and balance-of-trade and payments benefits.

During the 1976 presidential election, Jimmy Carter raised concern about the consistency between massive arms sales and the nation's avowed goal of seeking world peace. Once elected, he announced a new policy of "restraint" designed to curb the explosive arms trade, but Carter found it difficult to curb the use of military aid and sales to benefit American allies and friends, and rival arms exporters saw no reason to rein in their own profitable trade in arms. Thus the only serious attempt to curb the growing trade in sophisticated American weapons of war ended in failure. Indeed, part of a major accomplishment of the Carter administration—the 1978 Camp David Accords—involved increased military aid

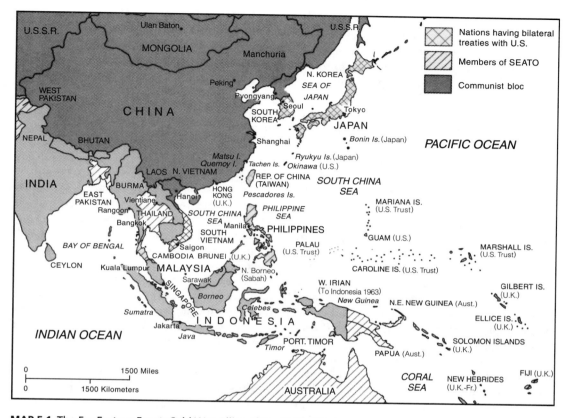

MAP 5.1 The Far Eastern Front: Cold War Allies of the United States

Note: Cambodia, Laos, and South Vietnam were granted security guarantees by the SEATO alliance, although they were not formally members of it.
Source: Walter LaFeber, *The American Age: United States Foreign Policy at Home and Abroad*, Vol. 1, 2nd ed. Copyright © 1994, 1989 by W. W. Norton & Company, Inc. Used by permission of W. W. Norton & Company, Inc.

and sales to Israel and Egypt. In practice, then, the acceleration of security assistance begun under Nixon continued apace.

The Reagan administration cast aside all pretense of restraint, declaring that "the United States views the transfer of conventional arms and other defense articles as an indispensable component of its foreign policy." Reagan also decide to increase the proportion of security assistance in the overall mix of foreign aid (Clarke 1997; Payaslian 1996). As before, and similar to his administration's approach to foreign economic aid, anticommunism and the perceived security threats to the nation dictated the flow of funds. Among the preferred targets was Cen-

tral America: although the Reagan administration never received all of the aid it sought—including military and other aid for the contras—aid levels did grow dramatically, to the point that on a per capita basis Central American nations became among the most heavily funded of all aid recipients. Elsewhere, Pakistan received several hundreds of millions in security assistance to facilitate (and reward) its support of anti-Marxist guerrillas fighting in Afghanistan. In all, the so-called "front line friends" of the United States were the recipients of dramatically increased military assistance. Overall, as Figure 5.1 shows, security assistance increased dramatically under Reagan's policies.

Hence, despite the concerns raised by Vietnam, the FMS program continued to grow during the 1970s and 1980s. Some critics worried that transfers of advanced military technology to countries and regions where conflict was frequent, as in the Middle East, would actually contribute to local aggression, not deter it (compare Kapstein 1994). As one Pentagon official described the situation in Somalia in 1992, when the Bush administration launched its humanitarian intervention there: "Between the stuff the Russians and we stuck in there during the great Cold War, there are enough arms in Somalia to fuel hostility for one hundred years" (cited in Barnet 1993). Some also pointed out how today's allies had a way of becoming tomorrow's enemies: "Much of the bitterness felt by Iranians toward the United States is traceable to twenty-five years of massive arms shipments to the Shah, much of it for use against Iranians—clubs, tear gas, and guns, and training for the dreaded secret police in how to use them" (Barnet 1993; Klare 1984).

Following the Coalition's victory over Iraq in the Persian Gulf War, George H. W. Bush determined that the time was again ripe to seek restraints on the global arms trade, particularly in the Middle East. He invited the five permanent members of the UN Security Council (who also are the world's largest arms merchants: Britain, France, China, and Russia, and the United States) to negotiate curbs on future arms sales and to prevent the kinds of technology transfers that made Iraq's war machine possible. Even as the discussions among the so-called "P-5" proceeded, however, the sale of new arms to Middle Eastern buyers skyrocketed. However, as Figure 5.1 shows, security assistance tumbled markedly in Bush's first year, before climbing after 1990.

Obviously the Gulf War was a major reason for the increases, but other factors also contributed to the growing numbers. In 1992, as Bush faced a tough reelection bid, the president broke with past practice, seeking to capitalize politically not on his arms restraint program but on the domestic benefits of arms sales abroad. In September and October 1992, he announced

$20 billion in new arms sales to such countries as Taiwan and Saudi Arabia as symbols of his commitment to "do everything I can to keep Americans at work" (Hartung 1993). Bill Clinton did not object, but the Chinese ended their participation in the P-5 arms restraint talks, marking the end of only the second serious effort in two decades to restrain the dangerous—if profitable—global trade in the weapons of war.

Military Aid into the Twenty-First Century
At the end of the twentieth century, U.S. security assistance, especially in the form of arms transfers and sales, was still thriving. Even as global defense spending declined, and global arms sales fell, American arms sales continued to be substantial. After a decline in the Clinton administration's first term, foreign military sales in 2000 increased by nearly fifty percent over 1997 levels, with further increases expected (see Figure 5.1). Unquestionably, the United States was the leading supplier of arms and military aid around the world. At issue, however, is the relationship between the continued practice of arms sales and security assistance and the foreign policy interests of the United States. In the early years of the second Bush presidency, questions about both power and principle were at stake, all of them sharp by three broad trends stemming from the 1990s.

One question turns on the utility of military aid (chiefly in the form of foreign military sales) for relatively traditional purposes, including securing and assisting allies and projecting American influence. Clearly that was the case during the 1990s. Much of the spike in security aid in 1993 came as a consequence of sharp increases of foreign military sales. American friends and allies in the Middle East were anxious to acquire American weapons to protect themselves against the possibility of renewed conflict with Iraq. Other friends and allies acquired American arms for similar reasons: Egypt and Israel kept up their steady diet (indeed, in 1999 and 2000, Israel agreed to reduce its take of economic assistance in return for additional military aid); Taiwan quickly accelerated its purchase, as did others in

Asia (for example, Thailand) with concerns about the rise of China's influence as well as the escalation of the India–Pakistan conflict; additional opportunities arose in Latin America when various restrictions on aid to that region (or specific countries in that region) were eased.

Turkey and Taiwan stand out as key illustrations of the logic as well as the troubling dilemmas it raises. In 1998, Turkey accelerated its already substantial purchases of American arms, first buying F-16 fighters and then a large shipment of attack helicopters. The Clinton administration approved its NATO ally's request, seeking to shore up relations and to deepen its connections with the Turkish military (to gain a measure of influence over its practices in the areas of human rights and democratic governance) (*America,* 23 September 2000, 3). The dilemma? Turkey has been embroiled in conflict with the Kurdish population in its southeastern region and has regularly engaged in repression and other violations of their human rights, sometimes brutally. Critics argued that the sales violated the provisions of both the Foreign Assistance Act and the Clinton administration's own Presidential Decision Directive 34 of February 1995 against military aid to violators of human rights (see Hartung 1995; Gabelnick 1999). Moreover, since the Central Intelligence Agency had already named Turkey as a state in danger of collapse and since the Turkish arms sales also prompted efforts by Greece to acquire more weapons of its own, the wisdom of continuing to use military aid for traditional purposes in Turkey is questionable (Gabelnick 1999).

Taiwan presents a similar question mark. The Clinton administration supported this friend and ally in Asia by supplying a large part of the $13.3 billion in arms imports it acquired in the last half of the 1990s to defend against threats from the People's Republic of China (see, for example, McLaran 2000). The administration of George W. Bush faced similar pressure early in his presidency, as Taiwan's president requested advanced weapons, including destroyers, almost immediately after Bush took office. Of course,

the United States' decision in this case affected its relations with China on many fronts.

A second question arises from trend during the 1990s toward applying military aid to deal with the emerging problems of the globalizing twenty-first century world. As security threats change from traditional, state-centric concerns to the less obvious transnational concerns we have discussed elsewhere, policy makers are struggling to use military assistance to meet the new challenges. The Clinton administration brought military assistance to bear on such problems as weapons proliferation (for example, the Cooperative Threat Reduction policy that provided aid to Russia to help control its nuclear arsenal), terrorism, drugs, and others. George W. Bush began to direct security assistance to members of the anti-terrorism coalition.

An interesting illustration of the use, and the challenge of its application, is the recent plan *Colombia* launched in the final year of the Clinton administration and continued by George W. Bush. Congress and Clinton agreed in the summer of 2000 to provide $1.3 billion to Colombia. Its purpose was to assist that country's efforts to combat the drug trade and narco-terrorism and to contend with a rapidly deteriorating security situation caused by leftist insurgents also engaged in the drug trade. In addition to economic aid, the package included $390.5 million for counter-narcotics operations, which included the provision of 105 attack helicopters and the creation and training of a special unit in the Colombian military. Additionally, the package provided another $245 billion for interdiction efforts and support of the Colombian National Police (*United States Support for Colombia,* Fact Sheet released by the Bureau of Western Hemisphere Affairs, U.S. Department of State, July 19, 2000). As an effort to address a growing security problem (drug trafficking and narco-terrorism), this application of military assistance nevertheless raises some concerns, including its appropriateness as a tool to address the American drug problem, its capacity for embroiling the United States in a festering civil war (the drug traffickers are also leftist guerrillas threatening the Colombian government), and its risk of making Americans the target of narco-terrorists (see Jenkins 2000–2001); *The Economist,* 2 September 2000, 32).

A third, and critically important question, arises from the trend toward usng arms sales for economic purposes. Global defense spending has been declining since the mid-1980s. Defense budgets fell by nearly forty percent from 1985 to 1995 (Markusen 1999), from nearly four percent of world gross domestic product to three percent (Arora and Bayoumi 1994). The productive overcapacity that resulted translated into fierce competition among weapons producers for markets to protect against threats to jobs and defense industrial bases in supplier countries (on the impact on jobs, see Thomson [1998]).[17]

Like Bush before him, Bill Clinton was especially sensitive to role of jobs in the weapons export equation. Consequently, it should not be surprising that the Clinton administration's use of foreign military sales was driven at least as much by domestic economic concerns as by security interests. In fact, the administration's long-awaited conventional arms transfer policy, issued as Presidential Decision Directive 34 in February 1995, explicitly stated among its goals a desire "to enhance the ability of the U.S. defense industrial base to meet U.S. defense requirements and maintain long-term military technological superiority at lower costs." Benefits from what some characterize as an "all come, all served" approach include export revenues, reduced unit costs for Defense Department purchases (the more units an arms maker manufactures, the lower the cost for each one), sustained assembly lines for the defense industrial base (which can produce existing weapons while gearing up for the next generation), substantial profits for the defense industry, and, of course, jobs for American workers employed in defense industries.

As sales rise (see Figure 5.1, for example), American military equipment appears in more and more hands. In its first term, the Clinton administration "delivered 1,625 tanks, 2091 ar-

mored personnel carriers, 318 combat aircraft, 203 helicopters and 1443 surface-to-air missiles around the world" (Broder 1997). The matériel is increasingly sophisticated as well, as restrictions on high-tech weapons exports are falling fast (for example, in 1997 the Clinton administration lifted the ban on high-tech weapons exports to Latin America) (Goozner 1997). However, according defense policy analyst William Hartung, "these sales are being subsidized and pushed for economic reasons with little regard to foreign policy or social concerns" (quoted in Goozner 1997). Thus, as Clinton left office, new concerns were raised about the role of the military in fueling regional conflict, instability, and civil wars, supporting repressive regimes, and diffusing advanced technology too widely, thereby assisting would-be challengers and raising the costs of American involvement in the world.

Concern over these and other issues led some members of Congress to press for a *code of conduct on arms transfers.* Rep. Cynthia McKinney (D-Georgia) led the efforts in the House of Representatives beginning in 1995. Her proposed code would prohibit arms sales to countries unless they: (1) had a democratic form of government; (2) respected citizens' rights; (3) refrained from aggression against other states; and (4) fully participated in the UN Register of Conventional Arms. In 1999, her bill had ninety-four co-sponsors and was passed by the House, only to die in the Senate. It is likely to reappear.

Consequently, Bill Clinton left George W. Bush some difficult questions. One of the key issues is reconciling competing goals as they relate to the use of foreign military sales and military assistance. Can security assistance be used to achieve power and prosperity, while still supporting American principles? For example, as noted earlier, democracy promotion is on the long list of security assistance objectives. Thus we might expect foreign military sales under the Clinton administration to have been directed more toward emerging and established democracies than others. In actuality, however, there is virtually no relationship between the kind of political regime a country has and how much (if any) U.S. military sales aid it receives (Kegley and Blanton 1994). This raises anew concerns of the nature of American friends and partners.[18]

Additionally, critics of the arms-exports-for-prosperity-and-jobs argument embraced by the Clinton administration, would note that the number of jobs produced for every dollar invested in the civilian sector is greater than in the military sector (Hartung 1994b); *The Defense Monitor* 23 (6) 1994; see also Chan and Mintz (1992). Money spent on the military is also money that cannot be spent elsewhere. Moreover, the taxpayer subsidizes arms exports through government credits and expenditures of millions for the Pentagon's arms export staff and programs (Hartung 1994b). Even the exports are often balanced by "offsets," or licensing agreements that permit buyers to participate in production of the weapon system, thereby "taking business from American companies and giving it to foreign suppliers" (Hartung 1994b).

The new Bush administration also had to contend with the globalization of the arms industry. Not only are a growing number of weapons being produced by co-development and co-production schemes, in which two or more countries develop new weapons systems collaboratively, but "arms manufacturers are following the lead of their commercial counterparts and going global, pursuing transnational mergers and alliances and establishing design, production, and marketing operations abroad" (Markusen 1999). This globalization stresses the U.S. economy and impacts weapons proliferation, technology diffusion, defense procurement, and national security.

Combined with concerns about the stimulus of weapons sales to violent conflict, civil war, regional instability, and the spread of increasingly advanced weaponry, such challenges will continue to arise as the Clinton administration and its successors seek to apply the military aid instrument. Its place in practice is not at issue—

military aid and arms sales are alive and well. At issue is the relationship between the use of this instrument and the values and interests of the United States in the twenty-first century.

SANCTIONS: COERCION WITHOUT INTERVENTION?

Within a week after Iraq's tanks lumbered into Kuwait in August 1990, the world community imposed strict economic sanctions on Iraq, cutting off Iraqi oil shipments and all other forms of trade. Two years later, in May 1992, the Security Council again imposed mandatory sanctions, this time against Serbia and Montenegro following the outbreak of war in Bosnia-Herzegovina. And in May 1993, the Security Council imposed an embargo on oil and weapons sales to Haiti, then still under the leadership of a military regime. In all, the United Nations imposed mandatory sanctions eight times between 1991 and 1994 (Pape 1997)—six more than in all of its previous history. The United States played a principal role in each of these actions, and many other sanctions episodes over the ensuing years, making the 1990 "the sanctions decade" (Cortright and Lopez 2000).

The Nature and Purposes of Sanctions

The enthusiasm for sanctions during the past decade is explained in part by the search for new instruments of foreign policy influence in a domestic environment characterized by limited support for military options. *Sanctions*—defined as "deliberate government actions to inflict economic deprivation on a target state or society, through the limitation or cessation of customary economic relations" (Leyton-Brown 1987)—are often seen as alternatives to military force that still permit the initiating state to express outrage at some particular action and to change the behavior of the target state. Sanctions may include boycotts (refusal to buy a nation's products) and embargoes (refusal to sell to a nation), among other actions. As Woodrow Wilson trumpeted in 1919, "A nation boycotted is a nation that is in sight of surrender. Apply this economic, peaceful, silent deadly remedy and there will be no need for force" (Hufbauer 1998). Thus sanctions occupy a middle ground between comparatively benign diplomatic action, on one hand, and forceful persuasion or overt military intervention, on the other.

The use of sanctions is not new. The United States was a key player in two-thirds of the more than 100 sanction attempts begun between the end of World War I and 1990. In four out of every five, the United States effectively acted by itself, with only minor support from other states (Elliott 1993). What is distinctive about the sanctions applied against Iraq, the former Yugoslavia, and Haiti is that they were multilateral. The United Nations charter has always allowed imposition of *multilateral sanctions* against international sinners, but, as noted, this has rarely been done. Sanctions applied against the white-minority regimes in Rhodesia in 1966 and South Africa in 1977 are the only UN-sponsored initiatives taken before the action against Iraq in 1990. The difficulty in securing broad agreement for action, particularly evident during the Cold War, and the equally difficult task of maintaining discipline among the sanctioning states over a period of time, help explain the paucity of broad-based multilateral initiatives.

Iraq is a good example of the difficulty. The purpose of the sanctions against Iraq varied over the years, ranging from forcing Iraq from Kuwait to the destruction of Iraq's military capabilities and creating sufficient domestic discontent to oust Saddam Hussein from power. A decade later, however, none of these objectives had been achieved. Sanctions remained in place after the Gulf War to ensure Iraq's compliance with UN mandates requiring inspection of its weapons facilities and the dismemberment of its nuclear, chemical, and biological weapons programs.

However, those most affected (Turkey and Jordan, for example) or who wished to resume normal commercial intercourse (such as France, China, and Russia) became increasingly restive. Even the United States eventually (if only tacitly) abandoned the weapons inspection objective, preferring instead the selective application of force to cope with Iraq's defiance of the international community and its potential for a continuing military threat (Gause 1999).

The evident failure of sanctions in Iraq raises troubling questions. Are they effective? Who are their victims?

The Effectiveness of Sanctions

Determining whether sanctions are effective is difficult, as "the correlation between economic pressure and changes in political or military behavior is rarely direct" (Christiansen and Powers 1993). Even in South Africa—where for two decades economic pressure was applied on the white-minority regime to bring an end to the segregationist *apartheid* system and open the way for black majority rule—the precise role that economic sanctions played in the endgame remains elusive. Analysts do generally agree, however, that sanctions were important if not determinative (see, for example, Davis 1993; Minter 1986–1987; but compare Doxey 1990). The same qualified success applies to Libya. In 1999, after a decade of international pressure on Libyan dictator Muammar Qaddafi for his role in sponsoring terrorism, he finally turned over to western powers for trial two Libyans alleged to have blown up Pan Am flight 103 over Scotland in 1988, killing all 280 of its passengers.

Cuba is a case where economic coercion failed. The United States placed sanctions on the Castro regime shortly after it assumed power in 1960. It soon banned all trade with Cuba and pressured other countries to follow suit. Its goals were twofold. The United States hoped to overthrow the Castro government. Failing that, from about 1964 onward it tried to contain the Castro revolution and Cuban interventionism elsewhere in the Western Hemisphere and in Africa. The major accomplishment, however, was largely confined to "increasing the cost to Cuba of surviving and developing as a socialist country and of pursuing an international commitment" (Roca 1987).

Several factors explain Cuba's ability to withstand American pressure. The support Cuba received from the Soviet Union was especially important, but the United States' inability to persuade its allies to curtail their economic ties with Cuba counted heavily, as did Castro's charismatic leadership and popular support. Once Soviet support of Cuba ended, the United States redoubled its efforts to topple Castro through economic coercion. (This dismayed much of the rest of the world, which reproached the United States in the United Nations with a resounding repudiation of the United States embargo.) Still, Castro survived. And he made the United States "pay" for its project by permitting large numbers of disgruntled Cubans to emigrate to Florida, where the state and federal governments had to care for them.

When the Clinton administration eventually took a few halting steps to ease the decades of bitter relations with the Castro regime conservative Republicans in Congress defended a more vigorous anti-Castro policy and passed the *Helms-Burton act,* whose purpose was to punish foreign firms doing business with Cuba. By threatening *secondary sanctions* against others, the law set off a storm of protest in Canada, Europe, and elsewhere, arguably affecting American foreign policy interests far beyond Cuba (Haass 1997); see also Morici (1997). Meanwhile, as other countries continued to invest in and trade with Cuba, American companies pressured Clinton to lift the embargo, hoping to profit themselves.

As the Cuban case shows, sanctions often fail because other states refuse to enforce them. Systematic evidence on the use of sanctions since World War I indicates that the United States achieved its objective in only one of three cases (Elliott 1993); see also Hufbauer, Schott and Elliott (1990).[19] During the Cold War, offsetting

aid from the Soviet Union often undermined American efforts, but even today unilateral sanctions rarely prove effective.

> In most instances, other governments . . . value commercial interaction more than the United States does and are less willing to forfeit it. . . . Such thinking makes achieving multilateral support for sanctions more difficult for the United States. It usually takes something truly egregious, like Saddam Hussein's occupation of Kuwait, to overcome this anti-sanctions bias.
>
> (HAASS 1997, 78)

If others do not go along, can *unilateral sanctions* work? Here the record is even more dismal. Between 1970 and 1990, "just five of thirty-nine unilateral U.S. sanctions [achieved] any success at all" (Elliott 1998). Furthermore, the dramatic changes in the world political economy accompanying globalization have reduced even further the number of targets vulnerable to unilateral economic coercion. Yet sanctions have become a preferred instrument of American foreign policy. A controversial 1997 study by the National Association of Manufacturers (NAM) determined that thirty-five countries had become the target of American sanctions between 1993 and 1996 alone, bringing some forty percent of the world's population under American wrath. Even President Clinton joined the chorus of protest, lamenting that the United States had become "sanctions happy." Although Jesse Helms, chair of the Senate Foreign Relations Committee, disputed both Clinton's claim and the NAM's numbers (Helms 1999), a former member of the Bush administration's first national security council staff called sanctions "the United States' policy tool of choice" even though they "contribute little to American foreign policy goals while being costly and even counterproductive" (Haass 1997). Many of Helms' own colleagues also disagree with the widespread area of sanction: since 1996, many members of the Senate have supported various restrictions on sanctions, as well as more general reviews of the use of sanctions as a foreign policy tool. To date, however, they have yet to enact any substantive legislation.

Still, sanctions do sometimes succeed. Success is most likely when the goal is modest, the target is politically unstable, the initiator and target are generally friendly and carry on substantial trade with each other, the initiator is able to avoid substantial domestic costs, and the sanctions are imposed quickly and decisively (Elliott 1993). Clearly these conditions are difficult to realize, but they are not beyond reach. One other factor is important—and may be the determining one. The initiator must not rule out the next level: "the possibility must be clearly communicated to the target that force will be used if necessary—to enforce the sanctions, to strategically buttress their effects, or as a last resort if sanctions fail. Sanctions imposed as an alternative to force because the political will to use force is lacking are not likely to be credible and therefore not likely to be successful" (Elliott 1998).

The Victims of Sanctions

Who are sanctions' victims? The implication of the lobbying effort of the National Association of Manufacturers is that the United States itself suffers. A study done at the Institute for International Economics in Washington estimated that economic sanctions in place in the mid-1990s "cost the United States some $20 billion in lost exports annually, depriving American workers of some 200,000 well-paid jobs." One of its principal authors added that "It would be one thing if these costs were compensated from the public purse, so that everyone shared the burden; it is quite another when the costs are concentrated episodically on individual American firms and communities" (Hufbauer 1998).

But while individual Americans and their communities may suffer economically, people in the targeted states typically suffer infinitely more. Two political scientists recently concluded that economic sanctions "may have contributed to

more deaths during the post–Cold War era than all weapons of mass destruction throughout history" (Mueller and Mueller 1999). In Iraq alone, the United Nations estimates that some 400,000 people may have died as a result of UN imposed sanctions. This number eclipses the fatalities suffered in the atomic bombings of Hiroshima and Nagasaki. The social costs that sanctions exacted have also been high. A former UN official responsible for the oil-for-food program in Iraq dramatized them this way:

> Iraqi families and Islamic family values have been damaged. Children have been forced to work, to become street kids, to beg, and engage in crime. Young women have been forced into prostitution by the destitution of their families. Fathers have abandoned their families. The many problems single mothers already faced in the aftermath of the Iran-Iraq war have been compounded. Workplace progress that professional and other women had achieved in recent decades has been lost. The education system has collapsed, with thousands of teachers leaving their posts because they are unable to work under existing conditions, and a dropout rate of some thirty percent at the primary and secondary levels. The health services are unable to handle the most basic preventable diseases—such as diarrhea, gastroenteritis, respiratory tract infections, polio—and curtail their spread to epidemic proportions. Hospitals attempt to function with collapsed water and sewage systems, without even the basic supplies for hygiene and minimal care.

(HALLIDAY 1999, 66; SEE ALSO AMUZEGAR 1997; GAUSE 1999)

Thus sanctions pose a moral dilemma: "the more effective they are, the more likely that they will harm those least responsible for the wrongdoing and least able to bring about change: civilians" (Christiansen and Powers 1993).

Grim as this description is, it cannot hide a central fact: ruling elites are typically immune from sanctions' effects. This is especially true in authoritarian regimes. Thus Saddam Hussein,

Muammar Qaddafi, Slobodan Milošević, and the military leaders in Haiti were able to pad their own existence as their peoples suffered. Indeed, in spite of a war and a decade of sanctions, Saddam Hussein greeted George W. Bush and his new secretary of state, Colin Powell, with a cocky assertiveness stemming from his ability to survive ten years of international isolation.

Political leaders in sanctioned societies may actually benefit from external economic pressure. One reason is that the typical response to economic coercion is a heightened sense of nationalism, a *laager mentality* (circle the ox wagons to face oncoming enemies), to use a phrase from the Afrikaners in South Africa. Nationalism stimulates resistance in the target state and encourages leaders to blame all hardships on outsiders. In the case of Serbia, for example, sanctions probably strengthened the nationalist extremists and helped to keep Milošević in power (Christiansen and Powers 1993; see also Woodward 1993).

Despite their checkered record of success and the troublesome dilemma they pose by increasing the suffering of innocent victims, sanctions will continue to be used as foreign policy instruments, particularly in instances where the United States (and others) are unwilling to use overt military force. Indeed, as the Bush administration engages in the twenty-first century campaign against terrorism, countries supporting terrorists will likely face a wide range of sanctions, among other policy actions. If nothing else, sanctions have symbolic value: They demonstrate to foreign and domestic audiences a resolve to act decisively, but short of war (Eland 1993; Lindsay 1986).

PUBLIC DIPLOMACY: USING INFORMATION AND IDEAS TO INTERVENE

United States public diplomacy is qualitatively different than interventions through clandestine intelligence operations, economic and military assistance programs, and sanctions on which the United States has relied to exercise influence over others. However, they are still a part of the informal penetrations of other societies and are therefore still part of the interventionist strategy generally employed by the United States. With the end of the Cold War, however, the logic that once sustained these programs has dissipated, much as it has in the case of other policy instruments. Thus, public diplomacy's institutional independence has been eliminated and its programs restructured and integrated into other institutions.

Public Diplomacy: Purposes and Programs

Public diplomacy is a polite term for what many would regard as straightforward propaganda (the methodical spreading of information to influence public opinion). According to the executive director of the United States advisory commission on public diplomacy, it "seeks to inculcate others with American values, promotes mutual understanding between the United States and other societies . . . reduces the potential for conflict . . . and dispels negative notions about the United States" (Kramer 2000). For most of last fifty years or so the *United States Information Agency (USIA)* was in charge of American public diplomacy efforts aimed at winning support around the world for America and its foreign policy.[20] Its instruments were information and cultural activities directed overseas at both masses and elites.

The USIA carried out its tasks through a worldwide network using a variety of media tools, including radio, television, films, libraries, and exhibitions. Among the best known are the Voice of America (VOA), which broadcasts news, political journalism, music, and cultural programs in many different languages to various parts of the globe, and Radio Free Europe and Radio Liberty (RFE/RL, both established by the CIA), which, during the Cold War, broadcast to Eastern Europe and the Soviet Union, respectively. The Reagan administration added Radio Marti and TV Marti, which direct their messages to Cuba, and WORLDNET, a television and film service downlinked via satellite to United States embassies, television stations, and cable systems around the world. In 1994, Clinton authorized Radio Free Asia. USIA also administered a variety of cultural *exchange programs* supporting travel abroad by American athletes, artists, dramatists, musicians, and scholars and travel to the United States by foreign political leaders, students, and educators for study tours or other educational purposes. In 1999, these tasks were parceled out between the State Department (for the public diplomacy and cultural programs) and a new, independent Broadcasting Board of Governors (for VOA and the other broadcasting programs).

Information and cultural programs are pursued in the expectation that specialized communications can be used to make the United States' image in the world more favorable. Opinion varies widely, however, regarding the propriety and effectiveness of public diplomacy as a policy instrument. Should such efforts be designed only to provide information? Should public diplomacy aggressively promote American culture and its values? Should it be linked intimately to the political contests in which the United States becomes engaged? In practice, each role has been dominant at one time or another.

Public Diplomacy in the Cold War

The USIA strongly advocated the anticommunist containment policy during the 1950s, and it later tried to justify American intervention during the Vietnam War. The Carter administration tried to shift the emphasis to cultural exchange programs, which "evoke more cooperative sentiments" when compared with information activities that have "the image of a more confrontational posture" (Adelman 1981). Reagan, however, moved sharply toward confrontation, as the USIA sought vigorously to promote United States policies abroad and to engage in the "war of ideas" with the nation's adversaries. Charles Z. Wick, USIA director under Reagan, proudly observed "The only war the United States has fought in the past

four years has been the propaganda war." But that bold approach to "telling America's story to the world" (USIA's motto) politicized the agency's cultural and exchange programs. Tension between these two aspects of USIA's mission— one policy-oriented, the other not—was never resolved.

Even if it was possible to agree on the nature and role of public diplomacy, evaluating its impact is difficult. During the Polish labor turmoil of 1980, the Soviet Union criticized American broadcasts beamed at Poland as "provocative and instigatory" and as "aimed at generating among the Polish population unfriendly sentiments with regard to the Soviet Union" (cited in Adelman 1981). Did these complaints prove that such broadcasts served American interests or harmed them?

If that situation seems ambiguous, an earlier one does not. In 1956 Hungarian freedom fighters revolting against Soviet domination received messages from Radio Free Europe implying that American assistance was on its way. It never came. Even the exchange programs that are a part of public diplomacy seem to yield ambiguous results. Although perhaps a quarter of a million scholars and teachers have participated in the well-known Fulbright Program, some of the most vociferous foreign critics of America visited the country under the sponsorship of the United States government.

Public Diplomacy in the 1990s

"For more than four decades, public diplomatists . . . convincingly portrayed themselves to the United States public as strike forces in the Cold War's 'war of ideas' " (Blackburn 1992). With the Cold War now history, what of the next four decades? Budgetary stringency renewed concern about how best to promote America's idea and ideals using the broadcast media (Elliott 1989–1990). USIA's seeming inability to redirect its programming to encourage the process of democratic change sweeping

Eastern Europe during the first Bush administration raised eyebrows. Others saw bureaucratic inertia, including an unwillingness to abandon traditional Cold War views, as a force preventing the United States from using its public diplomacy capabilities more aggressively.

Supporters of public diplomacy countered that American values need promotion, and that "The limits of military and economic power have become all too obvious of late. To dismantle the remaining instrument of U.S. foreign policy [public diplomacy] at this time seems more than a little foolish" (Laqueur 1994). Advocates also contended that cultural diplomacy in its broadest sense, which includes high-tech competition for global audiences, has become more important compared with traditional diplomatic and military approaches to the kinds of problems and issues the United States now faces.

Nevertheless, bureaucratic inertia, congressional restraints, and presidential disinterest combined to hasten the eventual demise of USIA by the end of the decade. In particular, the Republican Congress singled out the foreign affairs budget, which includes public diplomacy, for significant pruning. Senator Jesse Helms held foreign policy hostage for over a year in the middle of the 1990s, demanding that the USIA (and other international affairs agencies) be eliminated or integrated into the State Department (Hook 1998). Meanwhile, the Clinton administration forced Radio Free Europe and Radio Liberty to consolidate with the Voice of America and to move from Munich, Germany, where they had been located since 1951, to Prague, where the Czech Republic will help subsidize them. In 1998, Congress passed and Clinton signed the *Foreign Affairs Reform and Restructuring Act,* which ordered the abolition of USIA on October 1, 1999, separating the information and broadcasting elements of public diplomacy (made independent) from the political and policy elements (integrated into the State Department) in order to allow both to flourish.[21]

Public Diplomacy into the Twenty-First Century

In some ways, public diplomacy would seem to occupy a strengthened position as a policy tool for the twenty-first century. First, the broadcasting arms have been separated from the remainder and provided independence under the Broadcasting Board of Governors. This change would appear to insulate them from the political pressures that have dogged their operations throughout the past half-century. The Voice of America, for instance, has always claimed a commitment to be accurate, objective, and comprehensive in its broadcasts of news and analysis, even while it attempts to represent United States policies and values. The position it now occupies with the rest of the broadcast programs may serve it well in that effort.

However, as the United States Advisory Commission on Public Diplomacy noted as early as 1996, audiences for broadcasts—especially radio broadcasts—are falling, even while the VOA and others expand their operations. Hence, the administration of George W. Bush immediately faced a dilemma: the broadcast arms of public diplomacy were probably more extensive and capable than ever, but they were no longer as useful in the ways they once were. American policy makers will have to address this potential anachronism by continuing to reshape this instrument for the high-tech information age by stressing television, video, and Internet/online applications.

The other two elements of the public diplomacy suite—cultural exchanges and the public diplomacy officers and programs of USIA—would also seem to be well-poised for effective use in the twenty-first century. These elements of the USIA have been folded into the State Department where they can be directed toward key foreign policy issues and also be involved in the process of policy formulation and implementation. Presidential Decision Directive 68 ("International Public Information," April 30, 1999) claimed the consolidation was "to enhance the use of international public information as a key instrument for preventing and mitigating foreign crises and advancing U.S. interests around the world."

To accomplish this improvement, the integration involved the creation of a new under secretary of state for public diplomacy and public affairs, who oversees a bureau for educational and cultural affairs, a bureau of public affairs, and an office of international information programs. The first manages the cultural exchange programs (the entire bureau was in USIA until 1999 and was simply moved), while the latter acts as the "operational arm" by producing Web products, reports, videos, and other information packages on events, American policy, official speeches, and the like. Additionally, public diplomacy officers have been placed in each of the State Department's regional (that is, African, European, Near Eastern, Western Hemisphere, East Asian and Pacific, South Asian, and International Organization affairs) and functional bureaus (that is, Economics and Business; Arms Control; Nonproliferation; Political-Military; Democracy, Human Rights, and Labor; International Narcotics and Law Enforcement; Oceans and International Environmental and Scientific; and Population, Refugees, and Migration affairs) to integrate them into the day-to-day foreign policy process. Thus, when George W. Bush moved into the White House, it looked as if he would have a more useful and accessible public diplomacy instrument.

He was disappointed. This potentially useful instrument by which information and ideas (soft power) can be harnessed to American interests has actually been marginalized, not integrated. The program-driven public diplomacy officers do not mesh well in the policy-driven, centralized, and hierarchic State Department. Moreover, as an area of specialization and as special offices in the bureaus, public diplomacy is still considered decidedly "second tier" and has not been uniformly integrated (nor welcomed). Further in some cases, the public diplomacy offices remain in another building, while the under secretary and regional bureau personnel work in the main State Department building in the area in Washington, DC, known as Foggy Bottom. Even when they do occupy the same building, as in the case of most regional and functional bureaus, the public diplomacy sections are usually isolated on separate floors. To date, only the Office of International Information Programs has made the transition well; its products are uniformly valued throughout the building. As the United States Advisory Commission on Public Diplomacy recently concluded, "it will take several years before public diplomacy becomes an accepted 'cone' in the Department and is recognized for the value it brings to U.S. foreign policy goals and objectives" (www.state.gov/r/adcompd). Thus, even as "a new diplomacy for the information age" that targets foreign publics and NGOs as well as foreign governments becomes more possible, perhaps even more necessary, the Bush administration found the instrument difficult to wield.

USING THE INSTRUMENTS OF GLOBAL INFLUENCE IN THE TWENTY-FIRST CENTURY

The foreign policy agenda of the twenty-first century is becoming increasingly globalized and transnationalized. This has already generated problems for foreign policy makers as they have sought to apply the instruments of global influence in pursuit of American values and interests. In Chapter 4, we saw how the use of military force to achieve foreign policy objectives is becoming increasingly difficult and complex. Naturally, United States policy makers have turned to other tools to achieve their goals, such as the instruments reviewed in this chapter: covert action, economic and military aid, sanctions, and public diplomacy.

However, as our examination of these tools indicates, difficulty and complexity abound for them as well as for military force. As the new century began, policy makers increasingly found the levers of influence hard to find, hard to apply, and hard to control. In the years immediately following the end of World War II, American leaders grappled with the pressing question of how to design appropriate policy instruments to enable the United States to achieve its objectives in the Cold War. In the early years of the twenty-first century, the United States struggles to adapt the instruments created for another kind of international environment. Whether these levers of influence can be tuned to the globalizing world remains to be seen.

KEY TERMS RELATED TO COVERT ACTIVITIES, FOREIGN AID, SANCTIONS, AND PUBLIC DIPLOMACY

Agency for International Development (AID)

apartheid

basic human needs

Bay of Pigs

Camp David Accords (1978)

Caribbean Basin Initiative (CBI)

Central Intelligence Agency (CIA)

code of conduct on arms transfers

Columbia initiative

counterintelligence

counterterrorism

covert action

crisis prevention

cryptanalysis

democracy promotion

development assistance

disaster relief assistance

economic intelligence

economic support funds (ESF)

enviro-intelligence

espionage

exchange programs

Food for Peace program

Foreign Affairs Reform and Restructuring Act

Foreign Assistance Act

foreign economic aid

Foreign Military Sales (FMS)

Freedom Support Act

Helms-Burton Act

humanitarian relief

information warfare

infrastructure projects

intelligence community

International Military Education and Training Program (IMET)

Iran-contra affair

laager mentality

Marshall Plan

Military Assistance Program (MAP)

multilateral sanctions

Mutual Security Act

NSC 68

narco-terrorism

Nixon Doctrine

Office of Strategic Services (OSS)

Operation Mongoose

paramilitary operations

peacemaking

presidential findings

public diplomacy

Reagan Doctrine

sanctions

secondary sanctions

security assistance

soft power

Support for Eastern European Democracy Act

sustainable development

transnational issues

Truman Doctrine

unilateral sanctions

United States Information Agency (USIA)

SUGGESTION FOR FURTHER READING

Andrew, Christopher. *For the President's Eyes Only: Secret Intelligence and the American Presidency from Washington to Bush*. New York: HarperCollins, 1995.

Berkowitz, Bruce D., and Allan E. Goodman. *Best Truth: Intelligence in the Information Age*. New Haven: Yale University Press, 2000.

Clarke, Duncan. *Send Guns and Money: Security Assistance and U.S. Foreign Policy*. Westport, CT: Praeger Publishers, 1997.

Cortright, David, and George A. Lopez, eds. *The Sanctions Decade: Assessing UN Strategies in the 1990s*. Boulder, CO: Lynne Rienner, 2000.

Godson, Roy S. *Dirty Tricks or Trump Cards: U.S. Covert Action and Counterintelligence*. New Brunswick, NJ: Transaction Publishers, 2000.

Haass, Richard N., and Meghan L. O'Sullivan, eds. *Honey and Vinegar: Incentives, Sanctions, and Foreign Policy*. Washington, DC: Brookings Institution, 2000.

Hartung, William D. *And Arms for All*. New York: HarperCollins, 1994.

Johnson, Loch K. *Bombs, Bugs, Drugs, and Thugs: Intelligence and America's Quest for Security*. New York: New York University Press, 2000.

Lancaster, Carol. *Transforming Foreign Aid: United States Assistance in the Twenty-first Century*. Washington, DC: Institute for International Economics, 2000.

O'Hanlon, Michael, and Carol Graham. *A Half Penny on the Federal Dollar: The Future of Development Aid*. Washington, DC: Brookings Institution Press, 1997.

Richelson, Jeffrey T. *A Century of Spies: Intelligence in the Twentieth Century*. New York: Oxford University Press, 1997.

Romm, Joseph J. *Defining National Security: The Nonmilitary Aspects*. New York: Council on Foreign Relations, 1993.

Ruttan, Vernon W. *United States Development Assistance Policy: The Domestic Politics of Foreign Aid*. Baltimore, MD: Johns Hopkins University Press, 1996.

Tisch, Sarah J., and Michael B. Wallace. *Dilemmas of Development Assistance: The What, Why, and Who of Foreign Aid*. Boulder, CO: Westview, 1994.

Zimmerman, Robert F. *Dollars, Diplomacy, and Dependency: Dilemmas of U.S. Economic Aid*. Boulder, CO: Lynne Rienner, 1993.

NOTES

1. In April 2000, the CIA released a report on the action to overthrow Mossadegh. See the *New York Times Special* (http://www.nytimes.com/library/world/mideast/041600iran-cia-index.html) for coverage. See also "The Secret CIA History of the Iran Coup, 1953" at the National Security Archive (http://www.odci.gov/cia/publications/chile/index.html).

2. On the Bay of Pigs, see the CIA's own internal report, a scathing criticism of virtually all involved. Long classified and believed destroyed, the report was acquired by the National Security Archive and published in Kornbluh (1998).

3. The "facts" of the events in Chile between 1970 and 1973 are controversial. From 1998 to 2000, a series of CIA documents on the Chile operation were declassified, shedding substantial light on the extent of the American effort to first defeat and then destabilize the Allende regime. See the "Chile Documentation Project," directed by Peter Kornbluh at the National Security Archive (http://www.gwu.edu/~nsarchiv/latin_america/chile.htm), and the CIA report, "CIA Activities in Chile" released September 18, 2000 (http://www.odci.gov/cia/publications/chile/index.html).

4. But see Kuperman (1999), who argues that the effect of the Stingers has been exaggerated. Following the Soviets' withdrawal from Afghanistan the CIA launched a covert program to buy back unused Stinger missiles. Congress reportedly provided $65 million for the program—double the cost of the roughly one thousand missiles the United States provided the mujaheddin. However, only a fraction of the missiles were recovered, because the CIA does not know who controls them (Moore 1994). In 2001, stingers were fired by Taliban forces during the U.S. air attacks on Afghanistan.

5. Another telling indicator of the direction the CIA is taking, with both its intelligence-gathering analysis and its operations, is the National Intelligence Council report *Global Trends 2015* (at http://www.odci. gov/cia/publications/globaltrends2015/index.html). This report targets the intelligence community's attention on non-traditional aspects of world politics and national security. On the new agenda for the intelligence community, see Godson (2000), Godson, May and Schmitt (1995) and Johnson (2000a).

6. On the issue of the CIA-drug connection, see Johnson (2000a), Nelson (1995), and P. Scott (1998), as well as the CIA's own *The Inspector General's Report of Investigation regarding allegations of connections between CIA and the Contras in cocaine trafficking to the United States* (at http://www.odci.gov/cia/publications/ pubs.html).

7. On economic espionage and economic intelligence, see Schweizer (1993); Foley (1994); and Witkow (2000); and *Economic Espionage: Joint Hearing before the Senate Select Committee on Intelligence and the Subcommittee on Terrorism, Technology, and Government Information of the Senate Judiciary Committee,* 104th Congress, 1996.

8. On efforts to disrupt the bin Laden terrorism plans, see Kitfield (2000), Waller (1998), Loeb (1999), Newman (1998), and *Time* (October 19, 1998, pp. 46–48).

9. Although President Ford's executive order prohibits political assassinations, terrorist leaders such as Osama bin Laden are not covered by the ban. Moreover, White House and CIA lawyers have generally argued that the ban on assassination does not apply to wartime targeting of command and control assets, including, it would seem, leaders. The attacks on the United States prompted new consideration of modifying the ban through a new executive order as well.

10. For a review of United States foreign aid policy, see Ruttan (1996). Zimmerman (1993) is also useful, and Meernik and Poe (1996) offer an empirical analysis of the factors shaping United States aid decisions.

11. Pakistan was troublesome, as the Symington amendment to the Foreign Assistance Act in the late 1970s prohibited assistance to that nation as long as it pursued a nuclear weapons program. The Reagan administration sidestepped the prohibition using a common practice: it "certified" that Pakistan was not pursuing the development of nuclear weapons. Once the covert war against Russian forces in Afghanistan ended, the Bush administration dropped the certification and aid to Pakistan ended. Since the initiation of the "war against terrorism," aid to Pakistan has resumed in several forms.

12. See also Maren (1997), a former Peace Corp volunteer and AID official, whose devastating attack on the efficacy of foreign aid gave support to policy makers and analysts seeking its elimination.

13. See http://www.usaid.gov/about/overview.htm for a current statement of AID efforts toward a "sustainable development strategy" organized largely around the six goals noted above. Also, detailed strategic plans and evaluation reports emphasizing the outcomes of AID's efforts in these areas may be found at http://www.dec.org/usaid_eval. Other material on AID programs and expenditures may be found at http://www.usaid.gov/pubs/.

14. At least two recent studies advocate focusing foreign aid around the provision of "public goods" in these areas on the grounds that they constitute global threats to human well-being. See Kaul and Grunberg et. al (1999) and Kanbur, Sandler and Morrison (1999).

15. The Mutual Security Act became the umbrella legislation for economic and military aid after the onset of Korea. Foreign military sales are now governed by the Arms Export Control Act, first passed in 1968. As of early 1995, the Foreign Assistance Act (as amended) continues to govern other military aid programs. Economic assistance is authorized by both statutes.

16. See Clarke (1997) for an overview of United States security assistance organized by each presidential administration.

17. For a more detailed treatment of arms transfer see Bitzinger (1994); Grimmett (1995); Klare (1994–1995); Pierre and Conway-Lanz (1994–1995); and Spear (1994–1995).

18. This is by no means limited to arms sales, either. Indeed, a criticism of the IMET program has been its problematic embrace of repressive military officers. Arguments in favor of the program stress its contribution to professionalization and the commitment to civilian government (for example, Nye 1996). In no case has this been more controversial than the School of the Americas, which has trained military officers from Latin America for several decades. Unfortunately, many of the officers have been among the most repressive in their respective countries. For example, it was IMET-funded, School of the Americas trained soldiers in El Salvador who were guilty of the massacre of El Salvadoran civilians at El Mozote in 1981 and of the brutal murder of El Salvadoran Jesuit priests in 1989.

19. Robert A. Pape challenges even this number, arguing that Hufbauer, Schott, and Elliott are too

generous in their definition of "success." He argues that of 115 cases examined by Hufbauer, Scholl, and Elliott "only five cases are appropriately considered successes" (Pape 1997). For rejoinders, see Elliott (1998) and Pape (1998). See also Kaempfer and Lowenberg (1999) and the essays in Haass (1998).

20. Public diplomacy is normally thought to target foreign audiences, but the Reagan administration targeted the American public in a sustained effort to build support for its Central American policies, particularly aid to the contras. The efforts were carried out by the White House Office of Public Liaison and the State Department Office of Public Diplomacy. The latter eventually came under fire from Congress, which cut off funds for its operation. See Parry and Kornbluh (1988) for a critical view of the State Department's operation, and the letters to the editor in the Winter 1988–1989 issue of *Foreign Policy* for a rejoinder.

21. On the restructuring and consolidation of USIA into the State Department, see the Foreign Affairs Reform and Restructuring Act of 1998 (Public Law 105-277), the Reorganization Plan and Report of March 1999, and the October 2000 report of the United States Advisory Commission On Public Diplomacy, *Consolidation of the USIA Into the State Department: An Assessment After One Year*.

PART III

External Sources of American Foreign Policy

CHAPTER 6

Principle and Power
in a New Century

The International Political
System in Transition

Our well-being as a country depends . . . on the structural
conditions of the international system that help determine whether
we are fundamentally secure, whether the world economy is sound.

SECRETARY OF STATE GEORGE SHULTZ, 1984

The twenty-first century world is going to be
about more than great power politics.

PRESIDENT BILL CLINTON, 2000

Early in October 1994 U.S. satellite reconnaissance revealed that a division of Iraq's elite Republican Guard was moving toward the border with Kuwait. Within days over 60,000 Iraqi troops and an armada of powerful weapons—a military force larger than the one used four years earlier to invade Kuwait and proclaim it Iraq's nineteenth province—again stood within striking distance of the tiny oil sheikdom.

President Clinton warned Saddam Hussein that "it would be a grave mistake . . . to believe that for any reason the United States would have weakened its resolve on the same issues that involved us in the conflict just a few years ago." Accordingly, he ordered additional air, naval, and ground forces to the Persian Gulf to bolster those already deployed in the oil-rich region. The United States also worked closely with its allies in Europe and the Middle East to ensure their continued support of American policies.

The U.S. response to Iraq's provocation is a classic illustration of state behavior as explained by the theory of *political realism*. Perceiving its interests threatened by the aggressive behavior of an adversary seeking to upset the status quo, the

United States took action to *balance* Iraq's military power. Its behavior followed the injunction of *self-help* in a system characterized by the absence of central institutions capable of conflict management and resolution. It shows how the external environment acts as a source of American foreign policy, providing both stimulants to action and constraints on its ability to realize preferred goals. We examine these external effects in this chapter and the next.

Here, in Chapter 6, we probe how the distribution of power among the world's great and lesser powers, critical global problems and developments, and the activities of nonstate actors shape American foreign policy. In Chapter 7 we shift attention to the world political economy. There we examine the United States' role in managing the Liberal International Economic Order and inquire into the global and national effects of changes in the world political economy. The concepts *power* and *hegemony* punctuate our analyses in both chapters.

THE DISTRIBUTION OF POWER AS A SOURCE OF AMERICAN FOREIGN POLICY

The theory of political realism holds that the distribution of power among states defines the structure of the international system. In turn the structure determines states' behavior in world politics. Kenneth Waltz (1979), a leading proponent of *structural realism* argues that only two types of systems existed between the birth of the nation-state at the Peace of Westphalia in 1648: (1) a *multipolar* system, which existed until the end of World War II; and (2) a *bipolar* system, which characterized the distribution of power until the late twentieth century. In both, states protected their interests against external threats by balancing power with power.

Coalitions—alliances—were critical in the multipolar system. States that perceived one among them as seeking *hegemony* (preponderance) joined together in a balancing coalition to preserve their own existence (national self-interest). Wars were recurrent and often determined who among existing and aspiring hegemons would define the world order. The United States itself was born in a contest between Britain and France over who would dominate Europe and the New World. And the historical record shows that the architects of the new American republic were acutely aware of the perquisites and perils of power that buffeted the new nation, as we saw in Chapter 3.

The situation after World War II was quite different. Now only two powers contended for preponderance. Each still sought to balance power with power, as suggested by the strategies of containment the United States pursued to parry Soviet challenges (Gaddis 1982), but alliances were comparatively unimportant to their own survival. To be sure, the United States and the Soviet Union both tried to recruit allies to their cause. They repeatedly intervened abroad using military and other means to counter the threat each posed to the other's clients. The *North Atlantic Treaty Organization (NATO)* and the *Warsaw Pact* were pillars of their foreign policies.

Each also mirrored the behavior of the other as both developed ever-more-sophisticated weapons of destruction. But, structural realists argue, it was the weapons themselves—nuclear weapons in particular—that balanced the antagonists' power. As long as both enjoyed a *second-strike nuclear capability,* neither could dominate or destroy the other. As Waltz put it, "Nuclear weapons produced an underlying stillness at the center of international politics that made the sometimes frenzied military preparations of the United States and the Soviet Union pointless, and efforts to devise scenarios for the use of their nuclear weapons bizarre" (Waltz 1993; see also Gaddis 1986; Mearsheimer 1990a, 1990b; Waltz 1964).

The structural realist argument is not beyond dispute. Still, it usefully orients us toward an examination of historical configurations of international power and their effects on American foreign policy behavior, both in the past and in the new century.

Multipolarity and the Birth of the American Republic

From today's perspective it is difficult to believe that little more than two centuries ago the United States was a small, fledgling state whose very existence was perpetually jeopardized. With only about three million inhabitants, the thirteen colonies that proclaimed their independence from Britain were dwarfed by Europe's great powers: Britain, an island power, and France, Russia, Austria, and Prussia on the continent. Preserving the independence won at Yorktown in 1781 thus became a preoccupation. "It was the genius of America's first diplomats in this unemotional age that they realized the nature of their international opposition—which included all of the powers of the day, not excepting France—and adroitly maneuvered their country's case through the snares and traps of Europe's diplomatic coalitions until they irrevocably had secured national independence" (Ferrell 1988); see also Gilbert (1961).

The colonists' alliance with France was critical to their successful rebellion against England. France supported the United States to regain a foothold on the North American continent following an earlier defeat at the hands of the British. France and England had fought a series of wars in a century-old rivalry for preponderance in Europe and control of North America. The Seven Year's War in Europe, known as the French and Indian War in America, was the most recent. With the French defeat, the 1763 Treaty of Paris assured France's virtual elimination from North America. Canada and the Ohio Valley were ceded to the British. Louisiana was relinquished to Spain, which in turn ceded the Floridas to England. England sought to consolidate control of its empire in the years that followed. The famed Boston Tea Party was brewed by England's effort to squeeze more resources out of the colonies.

France reemerged as a principal security concern of the newly independent confederation of American states. Its policy makers were acutely aware that French support would last only as long as it served French interests. Indeed, an undeclared war erupted between the American and French navies in 1797. Ironically, however, the French Revolution and the rise of Napoleon Bonaparte, whose ambitions centered on Europe, contributed to the continental expansion of the United States. Talleyrand (Charles Maurice de Talleyrand-Périgord), the wily French foreign minister during the Reign of Terror, hoped to regain the Louisiana territory from Spain as part of a plan to recreate France's North American empire. Napoleon later became interested in the project but, facing renewed war against England, dropped it. Focused on Europe, not on recreating an empire far from the continent, he sold to the United States the vast tract of land which doubled its size. Diplomatic historian Robert Ferrell (1988) notes that "The 1803 sale of Louisiana to America was no mark of French friendship for the United States but the fortuitous result of a train of events that, but for the old world ambitions of Napoleon, would have drastically constricted American territorial expansion and might have extinguished American independence."

Napoleon's drive for European hegemony sparked more than a decade of protracted conflict and war, which finally ended in 1815 with the *Congress of Vienna* and the restoration of the Bourbon monarchy to the French throne. The War of 1812 was part of that system-wide conflict. The United States entered the fray against Britain, asserting its trading rights as neutral during wartime. A century later Woodrow Wilson would use similar principles to rationalize American involvement in World War I. However, unlike its position in 1917—by which time the United States had emerged as a major industrial power—in 1812 the United States was still struggling to secure its independence. History records the War of 1812 as a second American victory over the English; often forgotten is that the British successfully attacked and burned

Washington, DC, forcing President James Madison to flee the capital.

In 1823 President James Monroe enunciated what would later be called the *Monroe Doctrine*. Monroe's statement declared that the Americas were for Americans, as we noted in Chapter 3. Although enshrined as part of the nation's isolationist heritage necessary to preserve its liberty, the United States lacked the power to make good on its implicit threat to the European powers who were its targets. Instead, Britain's power—particularly its command of the high seas—effectively "enforced" the Monroe Doctrine for nearly seventy years. Its sea power kept other European states out of the New World and permitted the United States to develop from an agrarian society into an industrial power.

The Spanish-American War, which transformed the United States into an imperial power, had little impact on the global balance of power. In Europe, however, Germany was ascendant, challenging the French for continental hegemony in the Franco-Prussian War of 1870–1871 and posing a potential threat to England, the island power (see Kissinger 1994a). By 1914 the alliance structures of the *multipolar balance-of-power system* had rigidified. The guns of August that ignited World War I ended a century of great-power peace. Three years later the United States entered the war on the side of the British, French, and Russians against Germany and the Austro-Hungarian and Ottoman empires. As in the War of 1812, the legal principle of neutral rights on the high seas figured prominently in the decision for war. But political realists argue that more than principle was at stake: It was nothing less than the European balance of power, which posed potentially serious threats to American interests and security.

> America entered the European war when the aggressive continental land power of Germany was about to achieve hegemony in Europe by defeating the British sea power and to acquire simultaneously the mastery of the Atlantic Ocean. The very month that war was declared by America, Britain lost 880,000 gross tons of shipping, several times more than it could possibly replace. In that same month, mutinies in the French army made France's future in the war questionable. Russia, the third member of Europe's Triple Entente, was but a few months away from its internal collapse.

(SERFATY 1972, 7–8)

The United States reverted to isolationism after World War I, choosing not to become embroiled in the machinations of European power politics. But just as its balancing behavior turned the tide against German hegemonic ambitions at the turn of the century, its power proved critical in turning back the German and Japanese challenges mounted in the 1930s and 1940s. Guided by Wilsonian idealism, the United States had hoped to replace the "ugly" balance-of-power politics of the Old World with a new collective security system, embodied in the League of Nations. When that failed, it found that it had to resort to the same strategies it once deplored: joining Britain and the Soviet Union in a balancing coalition designed to prevent the Axis powers from achieving world hegemony. Once the death and destruction ceased and the ashes began to settle, the United States found that it alone had emerged largely unscathed from the ravages of a world war that claimed 50 million lives.

Hegemonic Dominance: A Unipolar World

World War II transformed the American economy, which now stood preeminent in the world political economy. The gross national product (GNP), agricultural production, and civilian consumption of goods and services all rose dramatically. In contrast, Europe lay exhausted and destroyed. Even the Soviet Union, whose armies pushed the Nazis from Stalingrad to Berlin, had suffered grievously. Its industrial, agricultural, and transportation systems had either been destroyed or severely damaged. Nearly 7 million Soviet civilians are thought to have perished in the war. Another 11 million soldiers were killed or missing in action. Although the United States had suffered some 405,000 killed or missing in action (Ellis 1993), it had virtually no civilian casualties. Thus the ratio of Soviet to American war deaths was more than to forty to one.

The Soviet Union had, of course, secured control over much of eastern Europe following the war, and it was over this issue that Soviet-American conflict centered. On balance, however, the United States was clearly in the superior position—a true hegemonic power. In 1947 the United States alone accounted for nearly half the world's total production of goods and services. And the nation's monopoly of the atomic bomb gave it military predominance. Only against this background can we begin to see how fundamental the shifts in the international distribution of power have been during the past five decades.

The post–World War II era began with the United States possessing the capability (if not the will) to exercise greater control over world affairs than perhaps any previous nation. It alone possessed the military and economic might to defend unilaterally its security and sovereignty. Its unparalleled supremacy transformed the system during this interlude into a unipolar one. Perhaps his anticipation of this environment is what led Henry Luce in 1941 to predict an *American century*—a prolonged period in which American power would shape the world to its interests.

Others worried that the United States might overextend itself. Political commentator and journalist Walter Lippmann (1943) observed that "foreign policy consists of bringing into balance . . . the nation's commitments and the nation's power." Thus "solvency" was, for Lippmann, a critical concern as the United States embarked on its rise to globalism. He later criticized the containment foreign policy strategy, arguing among other things that the regimentation required to combat Soviet communism would hurt the economy. Lippmann's concerns and criticisms anticipated the intense debate about the decline of American power that would occur four decades later. During the 1940s, however, the American century imagery was more compelling than solvency.

Still, the **unipolar moment** the United States enjoyed in the immediate aftermath of World War II began to change almost as soon as it emerged. The Soviets cracked the American monopoly of the atom bomb with a successful atomic test in 1949. Then, in 1953 they exploded a thermonuclear device, less than a year after the United States. And in 1957 they shocked the Western World as they became the first country to successfully test an intercontinental ballistic missile (ICBM) and to orbit a space satellite—feats that also signaled their ability to deliver a nuclear warhead far from mother Russia.

The Bipolar System

Bipolarity describes the concentration of power in the hands of the United States and the Soviet Union from the late 1940s until the 1962 Cuban missile crisis (see also Wagner 1993). The less-powerful nations looked to one or the other superpower for protection, and the two world leaders energetically competed for their allegiance. NATO, which linked the United States to the defense of Western Europe, and the Warsaw Pact, which tied the Soviet Union in a formal alliance to its Eastern European satellites, were the two major products of this early competition. The division of Europe into competing blocs also provided a solution to the German question—an implicit alliance between East and West against the center. As Lord Ismay, the first Secretary General of NATO, put it, the purpose of the Atlantic Alliance was "to keep the Russians out, the Americans in, and the Germans down."

By grouping the nations of the system into two blocs, each led by a predominant power, the bipolar structure bred insecurity throughout. Believing that the power balance was constantly at stake, each side perceived a gain by one as a loss for the other—a situation known in the mathematics of game theory as a *zero-sum* outcome. Recruiting new friends and allies was thus of utmost importance, while fear that an old ally might desert the fold was ever present. The bipolar structure provided little room for compromise.

Every maneuver seemed like a new initiative toward world conquest; hence, every act was perceived as hostile and required a retaliatory act. Because the antagonists believed conciliation was impossible, at best only momentary pauses in the exchange of threats, tests of resolve, and challenges to the territorial status quo could be expected (Spanier 1990). Repeated great power interventions in the Global South and recurrent crises at the brink of great power war characterized bipolarity.

Despite endemic threats and recurring crises, major war between the great powers did not occur. Instead, historian John Gaddis (1986) calls the Cold War era the *long peace*. The phrase describes the paradox that the perpetual competition and the concentration of enormous destructive power in the hands of the contestants produced caution and stability rather than recklessness and war. Gaddis along with structural realists attribute that caution and stability to nuclear weapons.

The Bipolycentric System

A looser structure began to replace bipolarity in the wake of the Cuban missile crisis, as the superpowers stepped back from the nuclear precipice and eventually pursued a policy of détente. Both now accepted that nuclear parity preserved strategic stability, as signaled by the SALT agreements. Their intermittent pledges to avert use of nuclear weapons to settle their differences and their growing conviction that the destructiveness of modern weapons also reduced the utility of defensive alliances. Rapid technological advances in their weapons systems catalyzed further changes in the increasingly fluid international polarity structure. ICBMs in particular decreased the need for forward bases—especially important to the United States—from which to strike the adversary.

As rigid bipolarity eroded, *bipolycentrism* characterized the emerging structure. The concept emphasizes the continued military superiority of the United States and the Soviet Union at this time

and the continuing reliance of the weaker alliance partners on their respective superpower patrons for security. The new system also permitted measurably greater maneuverability on the part of weaker states. Hence the suffix "polycentrism," connoting the possibility of many centers of power and diverse relationships among those subordinate to the major powers. In the bipolycentric system, each superpower sought closer ties with the secondary powers formally aligned with its adversary (like those once nurtured between the United States and Romania and between France and the Soviet Union). The secondary powers in turn exploited those ties as they sought to enhance their bargaining position within their own alliance by establishing relationships among themselves (for example, between Poland and West Germany). While the superpowers remained militarily dominant, greater diplomatic fluidity became evident.

The Fragmentation of the Atlantic Alliance

The convergence of Soviet and American military capabilities accelerated these developments, as it reduced the credibility of the superpowers' commitment to sacrifice their own security for their allies' defense. In a system shaped by a *balance-of-terror*, European members of NATO in particular worried that the United States might not willingly sacrifice New York City for Paris or Bonn. Mounting uncertainties about the credibility of the U.S. deterrent threat led France to develop its own nuclear force and later to withdraw from the integrated NATO command. Even the *flexible response* policy adopted as official NATO strategy during the Johnson administration did not restore European confidence in American promises. The policy tried to extend to Europe the principle of assured destruction of the Soviet Union should the Warsaw Pact attack Western Europe. For many Europeans, however, it simply signaled the United States' reluctance to expose itself to destruction to ensure its allies' security.

These concerns accelerated the polycentric divisions already evident. Talk of "decoupling" Europe from American protection prompted the decision to deploy in Europe a new class of U.S. intermediate-range nuclear missiles, thus enhancing the credibility of *extended deterrence*. Uneasiness persisted, however. Peace groups on both sides of the Atlantic challenged the "Atlanticist" orientation that bound the United States and Western Europe together. Increasingly European public opinion swung toward neutralism and pacifism, even as the United States undertook a massive rearmament program designed to enhance its ability to deter Soviet aggression. The specter of Europe devastated in a *limited response nuclear exchange*—a nuclear attack confined to the European theater without escalating to general war between the superpowers—inspired the European quest for a new security architecture that would prevent it from becoming a nuclear battleground.

Changes in the distribution of economic strength coincided with these geostrategic developments. Already by the 1960s and 1970s many U.S. allies were vibrant economic entities, no longer weak dependents. By the end of the 1980s the combined output of Japan and the twelve members of the European Community exceeded U.S. output by nearly a trillion dollars. Thirty years earlier, in 1960, it did not even equal U.S. output. Enhanced capabilities encouraged Europe and Japan to be more assertive and accelerated the erosion of America's ability to impose its own chosen solutions on nonmilitary questions. Thus the "century" of American hegemony Henry Luce had predicted in the early 1940s gradually appeared to have been short-lived.

The Splintering of the Soviet Bloc The fragmentation of the rigid bipolar Cold War alliances occurred in the East as well as the West. The Sino-Soviet split, dating to the 1950s, highlighted the breakup of what was thought to be a communist monolith. Reflecting ideological differences and security concerns befitting two giant neighbors, by the 1960s the dispute was elevated to rivalry for leadership of the world communist movement. This opened a new era of

Washington-Moscow-Beijing triangular politics. President Nixon's historic visit to China in February 1972 is the most celebrated symbol of triangular diplomacy of the period. "Playing the China card" thereafter became a favorite U.S. maneuver in its efforts to moderate Soviet behavior around the globe.

Periodic assertions of independence also marked the behavior of the communist regimes of East Germany, Poland, and Hungary during the 1950s. In the 1960s Czechoslovakia actually pursued a democratic experiment briefly, only to have it abruptly terminated by Warsaw Pact military intervention in 1968. Fearing possible defection from the communist fold, Kremlin leaders proclaimed the **Brezhnev Doctrine** (named after the Soviet Premier Leonid Brezhnev) to justify the invasion and to put on notice other communist states tempted to experiment with domestic reform.

Despite that warning, East European assertions of independence from "Moscow's line" grew in the 1970s and early 1980s, presaging the far-reaching domestic and foreign policy reforms that later swept the region. In 1989, Hungary became the first socialist country in Eastern Europe to schedule free elections, Poland elected a noncommunist prime minister, East Germany's communist leadership resigned and their successors permitted destruction of the Berlin Wall, and Czechoslovakia formed a new cabinet with a noncommunist majority.

Gorbachev's radical reforms under glasnost required new thinking in the Soviet Union's policy toward its former Eastern European satellites, as reform at home licensed reform of communist mismanagement abroad. Hesitant to deny Soviet allies the liberalization required to save his own country, Gorbachev repudiated the Brezhnev Doctrine in favor of the "Sinatra Doctrine," which decreed that satellite states would be permitted to "do it their way." This signaled the end of the Soviet empire in Eastern Europe. In quick succession members of the Warsaw Pact renounced communist rule and endorsed free market democracies.

With Europe now poised at the dawn of new era, Brent Scowcroft, President Bush's national security adviser, exclaimed that the surge of reform in Eastern Europe and the Soviet Union had brought about "a fundamental change in the whole international structure."

Toward Multipolarity: A Structural Realist Perspective on the Twenty-First Century

Changes in the structure of the international system begin with changes within states. "We know from structural theory," explains structural realist Kenneth Waltz, "that states strive to maintain their positions in the system. Thus, in their twilight years great powers try to arrest or reverse their decline. . . . For a combination of internal and external reasons, Soviet leaders tried to reverse their country's precipitous fall in international standing but did not succeed" (see also Gilpin 1981; Kennedy 1987). Thus the end of the Cold War inevitably raised questions about future power configurations and the constraints and opportunities they might portend.

In one sense, of course, the nature of international politics remained largely unchanged with the passing of bipolarity. As political scientist Robert Jervis cautioned shortly after the implosion of the Soviet Union,

> Many of the basic generalizations of international politics remain unaltered: It is still anarchic in the sense that there is no international sovereign that can make and enforce laws and agreements. The security dilemma remains as well, with the problems it creates for states who would like to cooperate but whose security requirements do not mesh. Many specific causes of conflict also remain, including desires for greater prestige, economic rivalries, hostile nationalisms, divergent perspectives on and incompatible standards of legitimacy, religious animosities, and territorial ambitions.

(JERVIS 1991–1992, 46)

Still, the passing of Cold War bipolarity portended a very different configuration of power and possibilities, prompting scholars and policy analysts to contemplate alternative images to portray the shape of the emergent international system. A three-bloc geoeconomics model, a reinvigorated multipolar balance-of-power model, a clash of civilizations model, a zones-of-peace/zones-of-turmoil model, and a global village image are among them (Harkavy 1997). *Unipolarity* also competed for attention, as the United States now found itself "the sole superpower."

In the afterglow of the Persian Gulf War syndicated columnist Charles Krauthammer (1991) made the case not only for unipolarity as a description of system structure but also as a prescription for others' behavior. "The center of world power is the unchallenged superpower, the United States," he wrote. "There is but one first-rate power and no prospect in the immediate future of any power to rival it. . . . American preeminence is based on the fact that it is the only country with the military, diplomatic, political, and economic assets to be a decisive player in any conflict in whatever part of the world it chooses to involve itself." He predicted that other states would turn to the United States for leadership, as they did in organizing a response to Iraqi's invasion of Kuwait and, later, in the interventions in Somalia and Kosovo. "The unipolar moment means that with the close of the century's three great Northern civil wars (World War I, World War II, and the Cold War) an ideologically pacified North seeks security and order by aligning its foreign policy behind that of the United States," Krauthammer argued. "It is the shape of things to come."

The distribution of economic and military capabilities among the major powers during the 1990s supports the unipolar description, as Figure 6.1 illustrates. For comparative purposes the figure also shows the distribution in 1950. The difference between the two time periods is striking. In 1950 the United States and the Soviet Union accounted for two-thirds of the economic output of the major powers and nearly ninety percent on their military expenditures. Clearly bipolarity aptly described the distribution of power. By the 1990s and early twenty-first century, however, no other power rivaled the United States. Japan and China were its closest competitors economically, but each could claim only about a fifth of the total economic output of the major powers while the U.S. share was twice that. No one rivaled the United States militarily, whose expenditures accounted for half of all military outlays among the major powers. Against this background plus related considerations having to do with the United States' unique geographical position, political scientist William Wohlforth (1999) concluded that "The distribution of material capabilities at the end of the twentieth century is unprecedented. . . . We are living in the modern world's first unipolar system. And unipolarity is not a 'moment.' It is a deeply embedded material condition of world politics that has the potential to last for many decades."

Others challenge that view. In the words of one analyst, "To assume that international order can indefinitely rest on American hegemony is both illusory and dangerous" (Kupchan 1998). While those who embrace this competing viewpoint concede the centrality of the United States, they also argue that even now it cannot act with impunity. Sketching alternative power configurations experienced throughout history, political scientist Samuel Huntington put it this way:

There is now only one superpower. But that does not mean the world is *unipolar*. A unipolar system would have one superpower, no significant major powers, and many minor powers. As a result, the superpower could effectively resolve important international issues alone, and no combination of other states would have the power to prevent it from doing so. For several centuries the classical world under Rome, and at times East Asia under China, approximated this

model. A *bipolar* system like the Cold War has two superpowers, and the relations between them are central to international politics. Each superpower dominates a coalition of allied states and competes with the other superpower for influence among nonaligned countries. A *multipolar* system has several major powers of comparable strength that cooperate and compete with each other in shifting patterns. A coalition of major states is necessary to resolve important issues. European politics approximated this model for several centuries.

(HUNTINGTON 1999, 35–36)

Huntington continues, saying that "contemporary international politics does not fit any of these three models. It is instead a strange hybrid, a **uni-multipolar** system with one superpower and several major powers." The United States has the capacity to "veto" actions initiated by other states. On the other hand, coping with "key international issues" requires its participation, "but always with some combination of other states." This contrasts sharply with the unipolar moment Krauthammer anticipated in the aftermath of the Persian Gulf War, when the United States could impose its will on others.

Although Huntington's uni-multipolarity concept focuses on power, which is central to realist theory, it shares similarities with Joseph Nye's (1992) concept of **multilevel interdependence,** which adds attention to the integrative and disintegrative forces central to liberal theory. Nye argues that "No single hierarchy describes adequately a world politics with multiple structures. The distribution of power in world politics has become like a layer cake. The top military layer is largely unipolar, for there is no other military power comparable to the United States. The economic middle layer is *tripolar* and has been for two decades. The bottom layer of *transnational interdependence* shows a diffusion of power." Nye postulates that the "layers" of world power have an important impact on American foreign policy.

a. **Pax Britannica, 1870–1872**

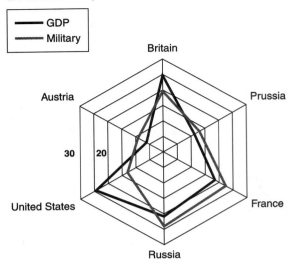

Country	GDP	Military
Britain	24	20
Prussia	11	13
France	18	22
Russia	21	24
United States	24	13
Austria	6	9

b. **Early Bipolarity, 1950**

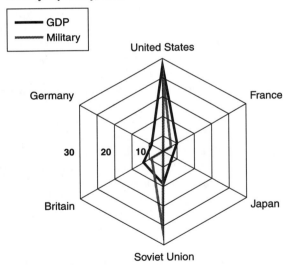

Country	GDP	Military
United States	50	43
France	8	4
Japan	5	0
Soviet Union	18	46
Britain	12	7
Germany	7	0

FIGURE 6.1 Comparing Concentrations of Power, 1870–1872, 1950, 1985, and 1996–1997.

Source: William C. Wohlforth, "The Stability of the Unipolar World," *International Security* 24 (Summer 1999): 14–15.

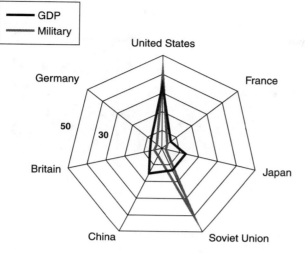

c. **Late Bipolarity, 1985**

— GDP
— Military

Country	GDP	Military
United States	33	40
France	6	3
Japan	13	2
Soviet Union	13	44
China	15	4
Britain	6	4
Germany	7	3

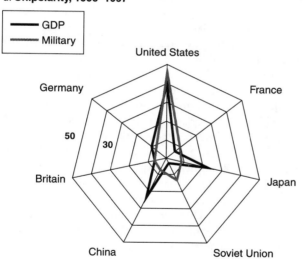

d. **Unipolarity, 1996–1997**

— GDP
— Military

Country	GDP	Military
United States	40	50
France	6	9
Japan	22	8
Russia	3	13
China	21	7
Britain	6	6
Germany	9	7

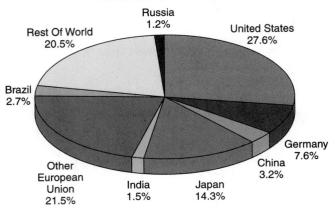

FIGURE 6.2 Shares of Gross World Product, 1998

Source: Adapted from *The World Bank Atlas 2000* Washington, DC: The World Bank, 2000, 42–43.

Writing a decade ago, he argued that "the United States is better placed with a more diversified portfolio of power resources than any other country," but he concluded that the post–Cold War world would "not be an era of American hegemony."

If these descriptions and prognoses are correct, we should expect that unipolarity will gradually give way to **multipolarity,** an international system structure not unlike that which existed before World War I in which power was diffused among a comparatively small number of major powers and a somewhat larger number of secondary powers aspiring to great power status. The United States, Japan, China, Russia, and Germany (either alone or within a united Europe) are widely regarded as the likely great powers in the system. Brazil and India are often mentioned as secondary powers who may seek great power status. Already these states account for the lion's share of gross world product, as Figure 6.2 illustrates.

The processes that will lead to the often anticipated multipolar world may take decades to unfold. Certainly a politically and militarily united Europe remains more a hope than a reality. Similarly, there is only a remote prospect that an economically dynamic power may rise to challenge the United States in the near term,

as *power transition theory* predicts (Organski and Kugler 1980). Japan, the world's second largest industrial power, suffered repeated economic setbacks during the past decade. And China, often predicted to surpass the United States as the largest economic power in the world in the next decades, simply does not enjoy the technological prowess that will enable it to soon challenge the United States, whose command of information technologies is overwhelming. Finally, no conceivable coalition of major powers will arise in the near-term to counter the preponderant power the United States now enjoys. Hence the prognosis that unipolarity is not a "moment" but a "material condition of world politics that has the potential to last for many decades" (Wohlforth 1999).

That said, structural realism and the long history of the rise and fall of great powers encourage us to contemplate alternative scenarios that may affect America's foreign policy future. Structural theory argues, for example, that great power status and its responsibilities are not easily shunned. This is even true for Germany and Japan, whose experience in World War II (and postwar pressures from the United States) caused both to foreswear nuclear weapons. "For a country to choose not to become a great power is a structural anomaly. For that reason, the choice is a difficult one to sustain. Sooner or later, usually sooner, the international status of countries has risen in step with their material resources. . . . Japanese and German nuclear inhibitions arising from World War II will not last indefinitely; one might expect them to expire as generational memories fade" (Waltz 1993).

The United States will remain the most powerful actor for the foreseeable future, even in a multipolar system in which Germany and Japan might possess nuclear weapons. (China, India, and Pakistan already do.) The United States, then, will be the power others will seek to *balance*. As one analyst put it, "Up to a point it is a good thing for a state to be powerful. But it is not good for a state to become *too* powerful because it frightens others" (Layne 1998). Hence the structural realist proposition that "unbalanced power, whoever wields it, is a potential danger to others" (Waltz 1997). The contrast with Krauthammer's prognosis is striking: America's leadership is something that will be feared, not sought. In the emergent multipolar system others will seek to check the dominant power, not *bandwagon* (ally) with it (Layne 1993, 1998; Walt 1990).

Ironically, the spread of democracy during the past decade, which has propelled an enthusiastic embrace of the democratic peace proposition as the road to a more peaceful world, may contribute to others' concern. Structural realist Kenneth Waltz explains:

> When democracy is ascendant, a condition that in the twentieth century attended the winning of hot wars and cold ones, the interventionist spirit flourishes. The effect is heightened when one democratic state becomes dominant, as the United States is now. Peace is the noblest cause of war. If the conditions of peace are lacking, then the country with a capability of creating them may be tempted to do so. . . . States having a surplus of power are tempted to use it, and weaker states fear their doing so.
>
> (WALTZ 2000A, 12)

In a way reminiscent of the declinists' arguments advanced in the 1980s, Waltz also cautions about the strain American leadership may place on the United States itself. He writes that "The vice to which great powers easily succumb in a multipolar world is inattention; in a bipolar world, overreaction; in a unipolar world, overextension." Thus "the American effort to freeze historical development by working to keep the world unipolar is doomed. In the not very long run, the task will exceed America's economic, military, demographic, and political resources; and the very effort to maintain a hegemonic position is the surest way to undermine it. The effort to maintain dominance stimulates some countries to work to overcome it" (Waltz 2000a).

Others' apprehension about American power is already clear, as we saw in Chapters 3 and 4. Whether the issue is military reprisals against Iraq, sanctions against Cuba and secondary sanctions against others, defending Taiwan against power incursions by China, intervening militarily in Haiti, browbeating Japan on numerical trade targets and Europe on bananas, or supporting tough standards on the distribution of international aid to economies in trouble, the United States has repeatedly found itself as "the lonely superpower at the top" in what is arguably a uni-multipolar world.

Against this background, it is by no means clear how the United States should respond to the challenges of the new century in which it, not others, may be feared—and reviled. We will return to this issue in Chapter 15, where we examine the second Bush administration and the future of American foreign policy at the dawn of a new millenium.

THE GLOBAL SOUTH IN A NEW ERA AND A NEW CENTURY

The distribution of power among the world's most economically, militarily, and politically capable states is not the only feature of the international political system that affects American foreign policy. Another that promises to grow more significant in the future is the relationship between the United States and the less developed countries of the world.

At the end of the World War II in 1945, fewer than sixty independent states joined the new United Nations, named for the allied coalition victorious in the long and destructive war against the Axis powers. Sixty years later more than three times that number would claim seats in the world organization. Some were products of the breakup of the Soviet Union, but many others grew out of the twentieth century end of other empires: the British, French, Belgian, Dutch, Spanish, and Portuguese colonial territories in Africa and Asia amassed since the 1400s but especially during a particularly vicious wave of imperialism that swept the world in the late nineteenth century. That colonial experience helps to define what today are commonly called the *developing countries*. During the Cold War it also became commonplace to refer to these states as the **Third World,** a concept used to distinguish them from the Western industrialized states, often called the **First World**.[1] Many Third World countries also embraced *nonalignment* foreign policy strategy, as they determined to strike a neutral course in the Cold War contest.

With the end of the Cold War, the term "Third World" is at once less accurate and less useful. **Global South** better distinguishes the states of the First World—now properly thought of as the **Global North**—from the rest of the world. As always, placement of particular states within these categories is sometimes problematic. Russia is an obvious example, as are the emerging market economies in eastern Europe and the *New Independent States* comprising the former republics of the Soviet Union. Still, the confluence of particular characteristics along four dimensions distinguish the North from the South: politics, technology, wealth, and demography.

States comprising the Global North are democratic, technologically inventive, wealthy, and aging, as their societies tend toward zero population growth. Some in the Global South share some of these characteristics, but none share all of them. Saudi Arabia is rich but not democratic; China is technologically inventive but not wealthy; India is democratic and increasingly technologically inventive but burdened with a burgeoning population that now exceeds a billion people; Singapore is both wealthy and technologically innovative, has a comparatively modest population growth rate, but is not democratic. Beyond these are many that are not democratic, technologically innovative, or wealthy, but whose demographics project a rapidly growing population that increasingly will strain already over-taxed social and ecological systems with too few economic resources and political capabilities to match the challenge. Many are in Africa south of the Sahara.

Scholars tried to capture the differences between North and South during the new world (dis)order that emerged as the Cold War ended. Focus 6.1 encapsulates some of their ideas—and displays a remarkable degree of consensus. The vision is that of a profoundly divided world which places the United States and its closest democratic friends, political allies, and economic partners on one side of a fault line separating them from most of the rest of the world. Although the rapid globalization of the world political economy and the spread of democracy in the past decade have blurred some of these distinctions as they apply to particular countries, the portrayal continues to show that the United States faces challenges for which many of the foreign policy instruments of balance-of-power politics are largely irrelevant.

Along the Demographic Divide: Population and Development

The demographic divide is central to the differences between the Global North and the Global South. Nearly eighty percent of the world's wealth is concentrated in the North, while more

---

FOCUS 6.1   Fault Line: The Global North versus the Global South

There is today a vast demographic-technological fault line appearing across our planet. On one side of this line are the fast-growing, adolescent, under-resourced, under-capitalized, under-educated societies; on the other side are the rich, technologically inventive yet demographically moribund, aging populations. . . . The greatest challenge global society faces today is preventing this fault line from erupting into a world-shaking crisis.

PAUL KENNEDY (1994, 4–5)

The key to understanding the real world order is to separate the world into two parts. One part is zones of peace, wealth, and democracy. The other part is zones of turmoil, war, and development. . . . Unfortunately, only fifteen percent of the world's population lives in the zones of peace and democracy. Most people now live in zones of turmoil and development, where poverty, war, tyranny, and anarchy will continue to devastate lives.

MAX SINGER AND AARON WILDAVSKY (1993, 3–7)

Nation-states will remain the most powerful actors in world affairs, but the principal conflicts of global politics will occur between nations and groups of different civilizations.

The clash of civilizations will dominate global politics. The fault lines between civilizations will be the battle lines of the future. . . . The world will be shaped in large measure by the interactions among seven or eight major civilizations. These include Western, Confucian, Japanese, Islamic, Hindu, Slavic-Orthodox, Latin America and possibly African civilization.

SAMUEL P. HUNTINGTON (1993A, 22–25)

The future of the Third World is hardly all bad news. . . . But the failures . . . will greatly outweigh the successes. . . . The global dilemmas and ills capable of coalescing into a specific body of political discontent and hostility will therefore challenge the current international system and constitute the next ideological challenge. . . . "Civilization clash" is not so much over Jesus Christ, Confucius, or the Prophet Muhammad as it is over the unequal distribution of world power, wealth, and influence, and the perceived historical lack of respect accorded to small states and peoples by larger ones.

GRAHAM FULLER (1995, 146–154)

---

than eighty percent of its people are in the South (see Figure 6.3). The unequal distribution of wealth and people translates into sharply different living standards, crudely measured by differences in per capita gross national product. As illustrated in Figure 6.4, the average annual income in Japan is more than fifty times greater than the average income in India, home of one-sixth of the world's more than 6 billion people. And the U.S. income is fourteen times that of the other countries comprising the Global South.[2]

These disparities—which in many other individual cases are even more stark—will widen, not narrow, in the future. At the end of the nineteenth century the ratio of average income in the richest country in the world to the poorest stood at nine to one. At the end of the twentieth century, the gap had widened to sixty to one (Birdsall 1998). Even in the unlikely event that North and South were to grow economically at the same rate, the comparatively higher population growth rates in the South will erode income gains at a faster rate than in the North. Thus, as one analyst wryly observed, "the old saw is still correct: The rich get richer and the poor get children" (Birdsall 1998).

Although fertility rates are declining worldwide, which portends a host of problems that will have to be addressed in the second half of this century (Eberstadt 2001), the first half will witness a continued march toward a more crowded and stressed world. Due to *population momentum* as well as other factors, the world's current population of more than 6 billion people will grow to

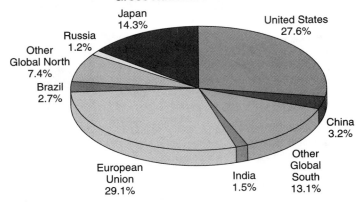

Gross National Product

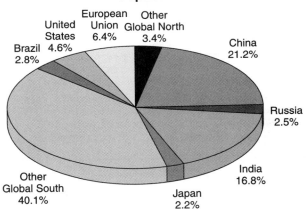

Population

FIGURE 6.3 Shares of Gross World Product and Population, 1998

Source: Adapted from *The World Bank Atlas 2000,* Washington, DC: The World Bank, 2000, 24–25, 42–43.

7.8 billion by 2025 and more than 9 billion by the time today's college students reach retirement age. Such dramatic growth is simply *unprecedented*. It took an entire century for world population to grow from 1 billion to 2 billion, but only one decade to add its last billion. By the end of the day that you read this page, the world will have added another 210,000 people to its already burgeoning number. Furthermore, as noted, nearly all of this growth will occur in the Global South (see Figure 6.5). Central America's 136 million people will double in size in 33 years, South America's 345 million in 42 years. The 577 million people living in the swath of the African continent cut-

ting through its center from East to West will multiply to nearly 1.5 billion before mid-century. And in South Central Asia, which includes India, the region's 1,475 million people will explode to twice that number well before we reach mid-century (Population Reference Bureau, *2000 Population Data Sheet*). The result? A world a third more populated than today in only half a century.

Some countries in the Global South will escape the economic stagnation associated with a rapidly rising population. Already South Korea, Taiwan, Hong Kong, and Singapore—which, with others, belong to a group of *Newly Industrialized Economies (NIEs)*—enjoy per capita in-

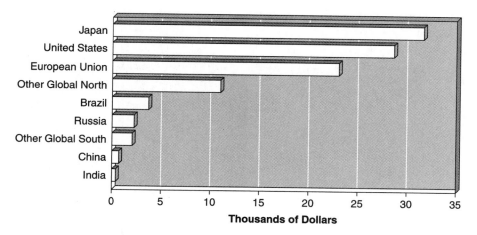

FIGURE 6.4 Global Variations in Per Capita Gross Domestic Product, 1998

Source: Adapted from *The World Bank Atlas 2000,* Washington, DC: The World Bank, 2000, 24–25, 42–43.

comes comparable to many Northern countries. The reason is that their economic growth rates during much of the 1980s and 1990s far surpassed their population growth rates. Rising living standards followed.

The experience of South Korea, Taiwan, Hong Kong, and Singapore (once commonly called the "Asian tigers") has been enjoyed elsewhere in the Global South as the precepts of democratic capitalism have spread during the past decade. Liberal political economists attribute these states' success to policies that promoted a vigorous expansion of global exports and cutbacks in domestic imports. The process was spurred by the so-called *Washington Consensus,* which refers to a common outlook shared by the U.S. government, the International Monetary Fund, and the World Bank that encouraged privatization of industries and other institutions, financial deregulation, and reductions of barriers to trade as the path to economic development. Arguably the precepts of the Washington Consensus contributed importantly to the globalization process witnessed during the past decade. (See also Chapter 7.)

The Global North (or many within it) has benefited handsomely from globalization. And some in the Global South have as well. As the prestigious World Watch Institute noted in its annual state-of-the-world report for 2001,

> The economic boom of the last decade has not been confined to the rich countries of the North. Much of the growth is occurring in the developing nations of Asia and Latin America, where economic reforms, lowered trade barrier, and a surge in foreign capital have fueled investment and consumption. Between 1990 and 1998, Brazil's economy grew 30 percent, India's expanded 60 percent, and China's mushroomed by a remarkable 130 percent. China now has the world's third largest economy (second if measured in terms of purchasing power parity), and a booming middle class who work in offices, eat fast food, watch color television, and surf the Internet.[3]

(FLAVIN 2001, 6)

But there is a dark side to globalization, as we noted in Chapter 1. Just as disparities in income between rich and poor widened during the twentieth century, the disparities between the Global North and South across a variety of measures remained stark during the economic boom of the 1990s. Worldwide over a billion people remain malnourished; 1.2 billion do not have access to clean water; and nearly 3 billion—almost half of

FIGURE 6.5 The Shape of the World's Population—Present and Future

Source: Adapted from Population Reference Bureau, *2000 Population Data Sheet.*

the world's population—survive on less than $2 a day (Flavin 2001). These statistics lead many observers to conclude that globalization has all too frequently produced growth without progress.

Population growth helps explain the disparate economic experiences of the world's states today and their projection into the future. Differences in history, politics, economics, and culture also play a role and are intermixed in complex and often poorly understood ways. Moreover, many Americans have the sense that world population growth is "someone else's problem, not ours." Although the population of the United States increased by more than eighty percent between 1950 and 2000, from 152 million to 276 million, much of this growth occurred through immigration, not high birth rates. To some, then, the way to halt the growth of U.S. population, which is projected to increase by nearly twenty-five percent in the first quarter of the twenty-first century, is to halt immigration (see also Chapter 8).

Increasingly, however, it is clear that the momentum of global population growth poses challenges to global and national security that will affect all of the world's inhabitants, including Americans. Indeed, immigration itself is a result of the *push* factors that make people want to leave their own homelands, and the *pull* factors that make the United States and other countries attractive. Thus, as John D. Steinbruner (1995), a former director of the Brookings Institution's Foreign Policy Studies program, surmised, "Both the scale and composition of this population surge will have consequences powerful enough not just to affect, but perhaps even to dominate, conceptions of international security."

Correlates and Consequences of the Demographic Divide

Conceptions of what constitutes "security" have changed dramatically since the Berlin Wall fell in 1989, as explained not only in the scholarly literature (see, for example, Klare and Thomas 1998; Nye 1999) but also in the reports of the U.S. Commission on National Security, popularly known as the Hart-Rudman Commission (www.nssg.gov). The essence of these analyses is that the twenty-first century portends dangers as well as opportunities. In a rapidly globalizing world, the Global South with its burgeoning population will figure prominently in those perils and promises.

Food Security Hunger is closely associated with poverty and population growth. Two centuries ago the Reverend Thomas Malthus predicted that the world's population would eventually outstrip its capacity to produce enough food to sustain its growing numbers. That has not happened, largely due to unprecedented increases in agricultural production since World War II. But the rate of growth in food production has slowed in recent

years, and the prospects for expanding food supplies by bringing more acreage under cultivation are limited. Furthermore, degradation of soils already under cultivation caused by modern farming methods, including widespread use of agricultural chemicals and poor water management practices, has begun to take a toll on the existing production platform (Brown 2001; *World Resources 1998–99*).

Against this background, achieving national and global food security, a long-standing goal of the international community, remains problematic. Global food supplies are abundant globally, and the proportion of people who go to bed hungry has declined in the past two decades, particularly in East Asia and Latin American (Brown 2001). But where population growth remains persistently high, hunger also persists because food often does not reach those most in need. The reason is simple: Many simply cannot afford to buy food because they lack the necessary income and employment opportunities. Politics and civil conflict also impede the ability of some to acquire adequate nutrition. That reality prompted the United States to launch its humanitarian intervention into Somalia in late 1992, and it continues to haunt international efforts to help those impoverished and starving in Sudan.

Poverty and inadequate food nutrition go hand in hand. The World Bank estimates that 1.2 billion people live on $1 a day (*World Development Report 2000/2001*). Not only does this limit their access to food, it also means no access to safe water, sanitation, health services, and economic opportunity. In the midst of a world of plenty, a fifth of humanity continues to live in **absolute poverty**.

Poverty and Urbanization As rural poverty persists, people migrate from the countryside to cities. *Urbanization* is a global phenomenon, but it is especially ubiquitous in the Global South (see Figure 6.6). In 1950, New York was the only city with a population of 10 million or more. Today another eighteen cities share that distinction. Fifteen of them are in the Global South.

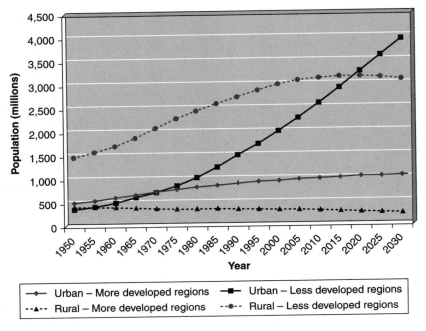

FIGURE 6.6 Estimated and Projected Urban and Rural Population of the More and Less Developed Regions, 1950–2030

Note: "More developed regions" conforms generally to the Global North, and "Less developed regions" to the Global South.
Source: United Nations, *World Urbanization Prospects: the 1999 Revision,* summary of findings, at www.www.undp.org/popin.

Lagos, the capital of Nigeria which today claims 13.4 million inhabitants, illustrates the relentless mathematics of urbanization. In 1950 Lagos had less than 3 million inhabitants. By 2015 it will have over 23 million. Cities like Jakarta, Indonesia, with 11 million now will swell with more than 4 million residents each year for the next decade and a half, and Karachi, Pakistan, will grow from 11.8 million to 19.2 by 2015 (United Nations, *World Urbanization Prospects: The 1999 Revision,* summary of findings, at www.undp.org/popin).

The rapid urbanization of the Global South adds pressure on already stretched agricultural systems and demands for imported food. Also, already over-taxed municipalities are often unable to respond to needs for expanded social services and increased investments in social infrastructure. Environmental degradation, social unrest, and political turmoil frequently exceed governments' capacities.

Emigration and Immigration People migrate to urban areas for many reasons, but jobs are uppermost. And jobs are few and hard to find, particularly where the ratio of dependent children to working-age adults is high—a natural consequence of rapidly growing populations, when the number of young people grows more rapidly than those who die. Today, educational and health systems in much of the Global South are burdened. These and other demands on governmental and social services encourage the immediate consumption of economic resources rather than their reinvestment to promote future economic growth. As the demand for new jobs, housing, and other human needs multiplies, however, the resources to meet the demand are often scarce and typically inadequate. Before long, the Global South will also be forced to address problems like those currently facing the Global North, where increased longevity and near zero-population growth threaten to overwhelm retirement and health-care systems, with potentially catastrophic economic, social, and political consequences (Peterson 1999). Modern science and medicine seem likely to continue to extend their life-saving and life-enhancing technologies worldwide, generating a similar crisis in the less developed world.

Without jobs at home, people are encouraged to emigrate. The International Labor Organization (ILO) estimates that 437 million young people will seek jobs in the Global South during the first decade of the twenty-first century (International Labor Organization, "Overview," *World Employment Report 2001,* www.ilo.org). Two-thirds will be in Asia. Sadly, however, the ILO also expects that the number of jobseekers in Africa will be less than previously projected because of the **AIDS** (acquired immune deficiency syndrome caused by the human immunodeficiency virus, or HIV) pandemic. As the organization notes in its *World Employment Report 2001,* the greatest long-run cost of the HIV infection in Africa "will be the loss of human capital. . . . Losses are disproportionately high among skilled, professional, and managerial workers. The epidemic will not only reduce the stock of such workers, but also reduce the capacity to maintain future flows of trained people." As AIDS spreads to Asia and elsewhere in the Global South, others will face similar threats (see also Population Reference Bureau, "Despair and Hope: The HIV/AIDS Epidemic," www.prb.org/pubs/wpds2000/Despair_and_Hope.htm). Secretary of State Colin Powell described AIDS this way: "I was a soldier, but I know of no enemy in war more insidious or vicious than AIDS, an enemy that poses a clear and present danger to the world."

If jobs fail to materialize at home, outward pressure is inevitable. Nowhere is the connection between population pressures in the South and their social and political consequences in the

North more evident. The United States has long been especially concerned about Mexico, the source of large numbers of illegal immigrants. Although the flow of illegal immigrants has slowed in recent years as the prospects of economic growth and a better life in Mexico have increased, for many the urge to go North remains irresistible. As one Mexican official put it in the early 1990s, "The consequences of not creating (at least) 15 million jobs in the next 15 years are unthinkable. The youths who do not find them will have only three options: the United States, the streets, or revolution" (cited in Moffett 1994).[4]

The Digital Divide Interestingly, the *digital divide* may also encourage outmigration from the Global South among those equipped with today's information technology skills, as they find the *pull* of opportunity in the Global North more attractive than opportunities at home. Countries in the North facing a steady-state population in turn often find attractive people in the South with technical skills as they seek to fill emerging skill shortages in their own economies.

The ***digital divide*** refers broadly to the access that people have to **information and communications technology (ICT).** The demographic, economic, and social patterns that explain the digital divide are not surprising. In the United States, for example, ICT access is greatest among young urban men in higher income groups. And because educational attainment is closely correlated with income and urban residence, level of education is the single most powerful determinant of ICT access and use.

The patterns evident in the United States are matched not only elsewhere in the technologically sophisticated North but also in the Global South. But because education and income are in short supply in the South, it also is not surprising the *global digital divide* closely tracks the inverse of the *global demographic divide.* (See Map 6.1.) The International Labor Organization in its *World Employment Report 2001* ("Overview," www.ilo.org) estimates that "barely six percent of the world's people have ever logged onto the

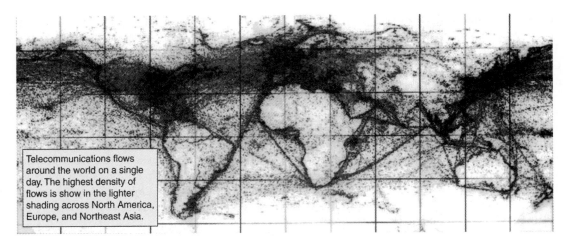

Telecommunications flows around the world on a single day. The highest density of flows is show in the lighter shading across North America, Europe, and Northeast Asia.

MAP 6.1 The Digital Divide

Source: Flanagan, Frost, and Kugler (2001, 24)

Internet and eighty-five to ninety percent of them are in the industrialized countries" (see also "Measuring Globalization" 2001). Much the same holds for other ICT access devices, which include personal computers, wired and wireless telephones, and other consumer electronics, such as televisions. But the digital divide is also explained by the capacity (or incapacity) of the public and private sectors to provide financial access to ICT services and by the cognitive processes education encourages, including an ability to process and evaluate the information that information and communications technologies offer (Ernest J. Wilson III, "Closing the Digital Divide: An Initial Review," www.internetpolicy.org/briefing/ErnestWilson0700.html).

ICT technologies hold great promise for many of the poorer countries of the world, as they may permit them to "leapfrog" technologies in which the Global North invested heavily as they developed economically. Wireless phones, for example, enjoy both popularity and promise in many developing countries, where the cost of stringing lines from pole to pole for traditional wired phones is often prohibitive. But because the individual, social, economic, and geographic factors that have created and perpetu-

ated the digital divide are complex, narrowing it will prove difficult and illusive.

Environmental Stress Increasingly many migrants (internal as well as international) can be thought of as *environmental refugees,* people forced to abandon lands no longer fit for human habitation due to environmental degradation. Their number is thought to be at least 10 million, which makes them the world's largest group of displaced persons, a term that also includes victims of political instability and ethnic conflict. Some become environmental refugees as a result of catastrophic events, such as the explosion of the nuclear power plant at Chernobyl in the Ukraine in 1986. Others suffer the consequences of long-term environmental stress, such as excessive land use that results in *desertification* (a sustained decline in land productivity), often caused by population growth. But increasingly environmental refugees are the victims of *global climate change* caused by *global warming.*

Global Warming By 2050 there may be as many as 150 million environmental refugees. The *Intergovernmental Panel on Climate Change (IPCC)* believes that global warming will be a

Worse Than It Looks

Because greenhouse gases stick around over time, global warming will continue even if all accumulation stops. Depending on future emissions, . scientists project a global mean temperature rise of 1.9 to 2.9 degrees Celsius between 1990 and 2100, with a corresponding rise in sea level of 46 to 58 centimeters.

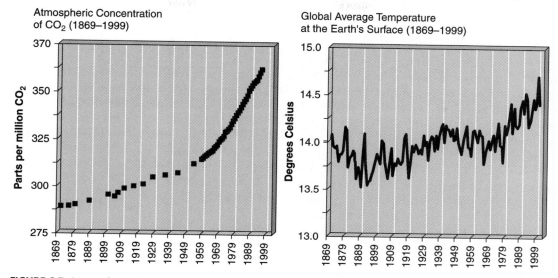

FIGURE 6.7 Atmospheric Concentrations of CO_2 and Global Temperatures, 1869–1999.

Source: Foreign Policy, November–December 2000, 30. Based on data from the Carbon Dioxide Information Analysis Center, NASA Institute for Space Studies.

primary culprit behind the movement of millions, as drought, floods, earthquakes, epidemics, and severe weather caused by global climate change, ranging from blizzards to an increased frequency of violent hurricanes, force people from their homes.

The IPCC comprises a network of hundreds of scientists from around the world who, under the auspices of the United Nations, have drawn on scientific analyses to advise governments on global climate change and strategies for dealing with it. *Global warming* has been the center of its attention. The term refers to a gradual rise in the earth's temperature that occurs when gases emitted from earth are trapped by the upper atmosphere, creating the equivalent of a "greenhouse roof" by trapping heat that would otherwise escape into space. Carbon dioxide (CO_2), which is emitted by burning fossil fuels like oil and coal, is believed to be a major cause

of global warming, with methane gas, nitrous oxide, and various halocarbon gases also among the suspects. Most greenhouse gases originate in the Global North, but China and others in the South are increasing their emissions rapidly. The Center for Strategic and International Studies recently concluded that world energy demand will increase by fifty percent by 2020, and that at some point the Global South, led by China, will consume more than the North (Nunn and Schlesinger 2000).

That the earth's temperature has climbed since the industrial revolution is widely accepted (see Figure 6.7). In the twentieth century alone, the average temperature of the earth's surface rose by .6 degrees Celsius. And the 1990s was the hottest decade on record. However, even though the IPCC has concluded that the concentration of CO_2 in the atmosphere has increased by more than thirty percent since 1750, the hypothesis that human activity is the cause of the rise in temperature remains contentious. So do proposals for dealing with global warming, even though the IPCC predicts that in this century temperatures can be expected to rise another two to three degrees Celsius.

Part of the controversy turns on the fact that over the long course of history, the earth's temperature has oscillated between eras of warmth and cold, as during the ice age. Motivated by self-interest, the global energy and petrochemical firms and countries that depend for their livelihoods on the export of fossil fuels are especially vigorous advocates of the view that temperature changes experienced in the past century and a half fit temperature patterns experienced over many millenniums, rejecting the view that human activity is the cause of global warming.

Small island states in the Pacific and elsewhere are among the equally vigorous challengers of fossil fuel proponents' views. Self-interest also motivates them. Global warming threatens to cause a rise in sea levels as polar ice caps melt, which could completely inundate the island states and obliterate their peoples and cultures. Already the mean height of sea levels has risen in recent years, and evidence mounts that the ice in the polar regions is melting. In 1990 a huge chunk of Antarctica's Pine Island Glacier measuring 100 miles wide and 30 miles long broke off and disappeared. A decade later, scientists determined that the Arctic ice cap is thinner—and thinning more rapidly—than once thought. And Russian scientists happened onto open water in an area typically covered year round by several meters of ice.

These and other findings lead to predictions of a gradual rise in sea levels due to global warming. If that happens, coastal areas from South Carolina and Florida to Louisiana and Bangladesh would disappear—along with the small Pacific island states. And the traditional weather patterns experienced in recent centuries would be disrupted dramatically.

The IPCC, first formed in 1988, has long been reluctant to attribute global warming to human activity, but in its second assessment report, completed in 1995, it stated conclusively its belief that global climate trends are "unlikely to be entirely due to natural causes." Instead, "the balance of evidence . . . suggests a discernible human influence on global climate." Six years later, it released a new report that stated even more emphatically that global warming was a man-made occurrence already well in place. "The debate is over," said Peter Gleick, president of the California-based Pacific Institute for Studies in Development, Environment, and Security. "No matter what we do to reduce greenhouse gas emissions, we will not be able to avoid some impacts of climate change" (cited in *U.S. News and World Report,* 5 February 2001). (See Map 6.2).

Deforestation and Biodiversity Deforestation often causes desertification and soil erosion. Unhappily, current trends point toward rapid deforestation worldwide. The destruction of tropical rain forests to make room for farms and ranches and to acquire exotic woods and wood products for sale in the global marketplace—as in the Amazon basin of Brazil, Indonesia, Malaysia, and Sri Lanka—is a matter of special international concern, as it contributes markedly to global warming through the greenhouse effect. Forests are "sinks" for carbon dioxide because they routinely remove CO_2 from the atmosphere during photosynthesis. When forests are cut down, these natural processes are erupted and destroyed, and, as the forests decay or are burned, they increase the amount of CO_2 discharged into the atmosphere. This makes deforestation doubly destructive.

Forests are also disappearing at a rapid rate in temperate regions as urbanization and commercial activities of various kinds lead to a loss of forests and surrounding ecosystems. With that comes degradation of watersheds, contributing to the growing shortage of fresh water around the world. And many of the remaining forests are themselves degraded by air pollution. *Acid rain* (precipitation made acidic through contact with oxides of sulfur and nitrogen), for example, has

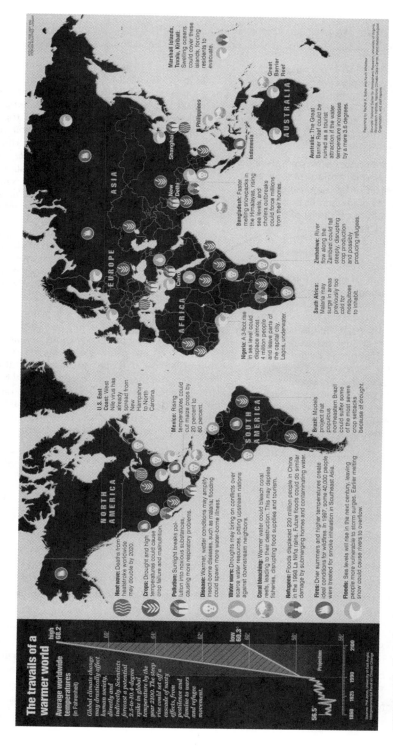

MAP 6.2 The Travails of a Warmer World

Source: U.S. News and World Report, 5 February 2001, 46–47. Copyright 2001. U.S. News and World Report, L. P. Reprinted with permission.

FOCUS 6.2   Biological Diversity

With an estimated 13 million species on Earth (UNEP 1995:118), few people take notice of an extinction of a variety of wheat, a breed of sheep, or an insect. Yet it is the very abundance of species on Earth that helps ecosystems work at their maximum potential. Each species makes a unique contribution to life.

- Species diversity influences ecosystem stability and undergirds essential ecological services. From water purification to the cycling of carbon, a variety of plant species is essential to achieving maximum efficiency of these processes. Diversity also bolsters resilience—an ecosystem's ability to respond to pressures—offering "insurance" against climate change, drought, and other stresses.
- The genetic diversity of plants, animals, insects, and microorganisms determines agroecosystems' productivity, resistance to pests and disease, and, ultimately, food security for humans. Extractions from the genetic library area credited with annual increases in crop productivity worth about $1 billion per year (WCMC 1992:433); yet the trend in agroecosystems is toward the replacement of polycultures with monocultures and diverse plant seed varieties with uniform seed varieties (Thrupp 1998:23–24). For example, more than 2,000 rice varieties were found in

Sri Lanka in 1959, but just five major varieties in the 1980s (WCMC 1992:427).

- Genetic diversity is fundamental to human health. From high cholesterol to bacteria fighters, 42 percent of the world's 25 topselling drugs in 1997 were derived from natural sources. The global market value of pharmaceuticals derived from genetic resources is estimated at $75–$150 billion. Botanical medicines like ginseng and echinacea represent an annual market of another $20–$40 billion, with about 440,000 tons of plant material in trade, much of it originating in the developing world. Not fully captured by this commercial data is the value of plant diversity to the 75 percent off the world's population that relies on traditional medicine for primary health care (ten Kate and Laird 1999:1–2, 34, 101, 334–335).

The threat to biodiversity is growing. Among birds and mammals, rates may be 100–1,000 times what they would be without human-induced pressures—overexploitation, invasive species, pollution, global warming, habitat loss, fragmentation, and conversion (Reid and Miller, 1989). Regional extinctions, particularly the loss of populations of some species in tropical forests, may be occurring 3–8 times faster than global species extinctions (Hughes et al. 1997:691).

---

damaged forests extensively in North America and Europe. It also has degraded lakes and streams (and buildings) for many years. Although progress has been made in mitigating the causes of acid rain in the Global North, the pollutant is on the rise in the Global South, especially in Asia. Much of the region's surge in energy consumption in recent years (and projected for the future) has been fueled by burning sulfur-containing coal (especially in China) and oil, the primary sources of acid emissions. "An estimated 34 million metric tons of SO_2 [sulfur dioxide] were emitted in the Asia region in 1990, over forty percent more than in North America" (*World Resources 1998–1999*).

Destruction of forests, particularly tropical rains forests, also destroys humankind's genetic heritage,

as plant and animal species become extinct even before they are identified and classified. The world's *biodiversity*—its genetic, species, and ecosystem diversity—is the inevitable victim (see Focus 6.2). Some experts worry that, due mainly to human activities, "the world is on the verge of an episode of major species extinction, rivaling five other documented periods over the past half-billion years during which a significant portion of the global fauna and flora were wiped out," each time requiring "ten million years or more for the number of species to return to the level of diversity existing prior to the event" (*World Resources 1994–1995*).

Habitat loss is the major threat to biodiversity. Ironically, perhaps, **bioinvasions** are now the second greatest threat to biodiversity (*World*

Origins of Top 150 Prescription Drugs in the United States of America

ORIGIN	TOTAL NUMBER OF COMPOUNDS	NATURAL PRODUCT	SEMI-SYNTHETIC	SYNTHETIC	PERCENT
Animal	27	6	21	—	23
Plant	34	9	25	—	18
Fungus	17	4	13	—	11
Bacteria	6	5	1	—	4
Marine	2	2	0	—	1
Synthetic	64	—	—	64	43
Totals	150	26	60	64	100

Such localized extinctions may be just as significant as the extinction of an entire species worldwide. Most of the benefits and services provided by species working together in an ecosystem are local and regional. If a keystone species is lost in an area, a dramatic reorganization of the ecosystem can occur. For example, elephants disperse seeds, create water holes, and trample vegetation through their movements and foraging. The extinction of elephants in a piece of savanna can cause the habitat to become less diverse and open and cause water holes to silt up, which would have dramatic repercussions on other species in the region (Goudie 2000:67).

Vascular Plants Threatened on a Global Scale
Of the estimated 250,000–270,000 species of plants in the world, only 751 are known or suspected to be extinct. But an enormous number—33,047, or 12.5 percent—are threatened on a global scale. Even that grim statistic may be an underestimate because much information about plants is incomplete, particularly in the tropics

SOURCE: *World Resources 2000–2001* Washington, DC: World Resources Institute, 2000, 14.

Resources 1998–1999). The term refers to the introduction of species native to one area of the world into another. The process is the inevitable consequence of global trade and tourism, both elements of the rapid globalization witnessed in the past decade. Although the introduction of new species in various parts of the world has for centuries proved economically beneficial, increasingly the consequences are malign. The deliberate import of exotic species for commercial purposes or agricultural production, for example, often results in a kind of "biological pollution" that results in the destruction of both aquatic and terrestrial life. "Some ecologists predict that as the number of potential invaders increases and the supply of undisturbed natural areas declines,

biological pollution by alien invaders may become the leading factor of ecological disintegration" (*World Resources 1998–1999*).

The spread of disease is caused by the same trade and travel that have increased the threat biological pollution poses to biodiversity. Millions of people travel across international borders every week. "And as people move, unwanted microbial hitchhikers tag along. . . . In the age of jet travel . . . a person incubating a disease such as Ebola can board a plane, travel twelve thousand miles, pass unnoticed through customs and immigration, take a domestic carrier to a remote destination, and still not develop symptoms for several days, infecting many other people before his condition is noticeable" (Garrett 2001).

The processes of globalization doubtless explain the rapid spread of mad cow and foot and mouth diseases throughout Europe and elsewhere in recent years. It may also explain the discovery of the West Nile virus in New York in 1999. The virus is commonly found in people, birds, and other animals in Africa, parts of Europe and Asia, and the Middle East, but had not previously been documented in the Western Hemisphere. The virus can cause encephalitis—an inflammation of the brain—which interferes with the normal functioning of the central nervous system.

International and Intranational Conflict

Not all threats to the global environment can be blamed on population growth. Rising consumption is also a culprit. Indeed, when it comes to finger pointing, the Global South dramatizes not its own population growth but the enormous—and disproportionate—consumption of global resources by the North (see Brown 1998; Lang 2001; Mitchell 2001; but compare Sagoff 2001). As the United Nations Development Programme notes, "on average, someone living in the developed world spends nearly $16,000 . . . on private consumption each year, compared with less than $350 spent by someone in South Asia and sub-Saharan Africa (*World Resources 2000–2001*). But population and consumption are intertwined in complex ways. As the demand for food increases because of population growth *and* changes in dietary habits associated with rising affluence, run-off from pesticides and fertilizers used to increase agricultural productivity pollutes waterways and contributes to the destruction of delicate coral reefs. As more energy is consumed to sustain a growing population and rising affluence, environmental degradation continues at a rapid and often accelerating pace.

As changing demographic patterns and lifestyle preferences test political wills and the ability of the earth's delicate life-support systems to support the world's six-plus billion people, the obvious question to ask is whether these developments are caldrons brewing violent international conflicts.

War inflicts human suffering that is often difficult to comprehend. But it also sometimes precipitates enormous desecration of the environment. Rome sowed salt on a defeated Carthage to prevent its resurgence. The Dutch breached their own dikes to allow ocean saltwater to flood fertile farmlands, hoping to stop the advancing German armies during World War II. The United States used defoliants on the dense jungles in Vietnam in an effort to expose enemy guerrillas. And Iraq engaged in acts of "environmental terrorism" when it released millions of gallons of oil into the Persian Gulf during the war over Kuwait. But is the reverse true? Does desecration of the environment precipitate violent conflict?

On the surface the answer would appear to be yes, but this may be too facile a conclusion. Systematic inquiry by Thomas F. Homer-Dixon (1999) and his associates into the relationship between scarcities of critical environmental resources and violent conflict in Africa, Asia, and elsewhere leads to the conclusion that environmental scarcities "do not cause wars between countries, but they can generate severe social stresses within countries, helping to stimulate subnational insurgencies, ethnic clashes, and urban unrest." These dynamics are especially acute in the Global South, whose societies are generally "highly dependent on environmental resources and less able to buffer themselves from the social crises that environmental scarcities cause."

Homer-Dixon acknowledges that many of the violent conflicts the world has witnessed in the past decade cannot be attributed to environmental scarcities, but he predicts pessimistically that "we can expect [scarcity] to become a more important influence in coming decades because of larger populations and higher per capita resource consumption rates." He adds that if a group of states he calls "pivotal" (see also Chase, Hill, and Kennedy 1996) fall on the wrong side of the "ingenuity gap"—the ability to adapt to environmental scarcity and avoid violent conflict—humanity's overall prospects will dramatically worsen. "Such a world will be neither environmentally sustainable nor politically stable.

The rich will be unable to fully isolate themselves from the crises of the poor, and there will be little prospect of building the sense of global community needed to address the array of grave problems—economic, political, as well as ecological—that humanity faces."

THE NORTH–SOUTH DIVIDE: CONFLICT OR COOPERATION?

In September 2000, 147 heads of state or government leaders of 191 countries—the largest world gathering of world leaders ever—met in New York at the historic UN Millennium Summit. Brainchild of UN Secretary-General Kofi Annan, the leaders gathered to set priorities for the United Nations in the new century and to assess how it might be retooled to best meet them. Quickly, however, nearly all of the policy statements and discussions boiled down to two themes common in the decades-long dispute between the Global North and South: peace and development. "Whether they were full of prose and poetry or brutally blunt, the speeches varied only in the particular aspects of the two issues that they stressed: globalization, armed conflict human rights, HIV/AIDS, environmental degradation, nuclear weapons, education, fairer economic systems, religious and ethnic tolerance, gender equality, and corruption" (White 2000). Bill Clinton was especially forceful in drawing the connection between peace and development. In an appearance before the UN Security Council, his last as president, he argued compellingly that "Until we confront the iron link between deprivation, disease, and war, we will never be able to create the peace that the founders of the United Nations dreamed of." That theme reflected, of course, many of the foreign policy priorities his administration had pursued during the 1990s.

The Millennium Summit was only the most recent in a series of world conferences on peace, development, and differences between North and South that convened during the past several decades. The *G-8* (the Group of Eight, comprising the world's seven largest industrialized countries plus Russia) have also from time to time discussed issues at the nexus of the North–South divide. Shortly before the Millennium Summit, for example, the G-8 concluded that closing the global digital divide was essential to bridging the gulf between the rich and poor nations. Amid controversy, an agreement was hammered out that created an information technology charter and a task force whose purpose is to investigate how Global South access to the Internet might be enhanced. Controversy arose when some leaders urged that issues such as debt relief, lack of food, housing, and basic amenities in impoverished countries deserved priority over Internet access. Proponents of the tech-thrust responded that access to technology promised an escape from the conditions of poverty that plague so many in the Global South.

Globalization also figures prominently in the most recent variant of the continuing North–South controversy, as we will note later. Globalization has once more pushed *equity* to the forefront of the North–South agenda. As argued by Theo-Ben Gurirab, Namibia's foreign minister who served as president of the UN General Assembly as the Millennium summit took shape, "Globalization is seen by some as a force for social change, that it will help to close the gap between the rich and the poor, the industrialized North and the developing South. But it is also is being seen as a destructive force because it is being driven by the very people, the colonial powers, who launched a global campaign of imperial control of peoples and resources in what we call now the third world. Can we trust them?"

Globalization and the technology themes related to it are among the most recent issues on the global agenda that relate to the millennium themes of peace and development. We will explore briefly other developments related to them during the recent past. All constitute challenges to American foreign policy provoked by the challenges and constraints of the international system.

The Earth Summit and Beyond

In 1992 the world community convened the *United Nations Conference on the Environment and Development (UNCED)* in Rio de Janeiro. Popularly known as the *Earth Summit,* it was the largest-ever world meeting of its kind, bringing together more than 150 nations, 1,400 nongovernmental organizations, and some 800 journalists. UNCED addressed how environmental and developmental issues interact with one another—something not done before, as the two issues previously had been treated on separate tracks. Statements of principles on the management of the earth's forests, conventions on climate change and biodiversity, and a program of action—*Agenda 21*—which embodied a political commitment to the realization of a broad range of environmental and development goals (see Sitarz 1993), were among UNCED's achievements.

Sustainable development, a concept encapsulating the belief that the world must work toward a model of economic development that also protects the delicate environmental systems on which humanity depends for its existence, encapsulated much of UNCED's thrust. The concept has important intergenerational implications. As first articulated in *Our Common Future,* the 1987 report of the World Commission on Environment and Development, popularly known as the Brundtland Commission after the Norwegian Prime Minister who was its chair, a *sustainable society* is one that "meets the needs of the present without compromising the ability of future generations to meet their own needs."

Population and Development In 1994, two years after UNCED, the United Nations sponsored the World Population and Development Conference, thus carrying forward the theme of interrelationships on which sustainability depends. Family-planning programs designed to check excessive population growth were among the conference's contentious topics, but it also addressed measures to reduce poverty and improve educational opportunities with a view toward enhanced sustainability. An emphasis on the rights, opportunities, and economic roles of women—all proven critical in reducing population growth rate—was a distinctive feature of the conference.

American foreign policy toward population and environmental issues has fluctuated widely during the past quarter-century. During the first United Nations population conference, held in Bucharest, Romania, in 1974, North and South quarreled about the very existence of a population problem. The United States and other rich countries embraced the view that the "population explosion" (Ehrlich and Ehrlich 1990) so impeded the economic advancement of Third World countries that nothing less than a frontal attack on the causes of population growth could cure their development illnesses. Developing nations responded that the prescription was little more than another attempt by the world's rich nations to perpetuate the underdog status of the world's poor. They also pointed with anger at the consumption patterns of the North, noting that these—not population growth in the South—were the real causes of pressures on global resources.

Ten years later, at a second global population conference in Mexico City, the United States again found itself out of step with majority sentiments, but now for very different reasons. By this time the Third World had accepted the proposition that unrestrained population growth impeded progress toward economic development. They now sought more vigorous efforts by the United Nations, other multilateral agencies, and individual countries in the North to help with family planning and other programs designed to contain the "explosion." The Reagan administration, however—which at home courted the growing chorus of antiabortion sentiments—announced that population growth was not a problem. It abruptly canceled support of family-planning programs, of which the United States had long been a champion. The about-face included termination of U.S. support for the United Nations Population Fund, a prohibition that continued into the Bush administration.

By the time of the 1994 Population and Development Conference, which met in Cairo, the Democrats had seized control of the White House, placing domestic antiabortionist forces on the defensive. The United States now sought again to play a leading role in addressing global population issues. As we saw in Chapter 5, the Clinton administration viewed uncontrolled population growth as a cause of the chaos and crises that often engulf states in the Global South. Thus the Agency for International Development prepared for a vigorous population stabilization program, and the United States once more became a champion of the efforts by the United Nations and other governmental and nongovernmental agencies to promote family-planning programs abroad.

History seemed to repeat itself in early 2001. Just as the Clinton administration moved early to reinvigorate U.S. support of population planning programs abroad shortly after Clinton was inaugurated in 1993, President Bush moved early in his presidency to restrict U.S. support for global family-planning programs designed to address global population issues.

Global Climate Change The United States has long been out of step with much of the rest of the world on *climate change issues*. During the 1992 Earth Summit, the United States worked hard to water down a global *Framework Convention on Climate Change,* but its endorsement by others set the stage for later meetings designed to address curbs on the causes of global warming and related issues.

In 1997 states met in Japan, where they initialed the **Kyoto Protocol to the 1992 Framework Convention.** It was the first international accord on climate change since the Earth Summit. The protocol sought to stabilize and then reduce the concentration of greenhouse gases in the atmosphere. Vice President Al Gore played a critical role in bringing the Kyoto negotiations to a conclusion satisfactory to the United States, but the U.S. Senate refused to ratify the agreement, in part because it failed to include emissions re-

straints on many countries in the Global South, notably China. (As of 2000, only thirty countries were parties to the Kyoto agreement, although more than a hundred had signed but not yet ratified the protocol.) Moreover, the agreement lacked "muscle."

Later negotiations designed to add muscle proved fruitless. Talks with European nations in 2000, for example, failed when the Europeans, with a long history of greater concern with energy efficiency than Americans, refused to accept U.S. proposals for "trading" greenhouse pollutants for forest cover (CO_2 sinks) in the United States and Global South countries with whom the United States (or others) might strike bargains. And post-Kyoto negotiations which established voluntary restraints on greenhouse gas emissions principles proved ineffectual. Meanwhile, as noted earlier, powerful domestic interests in the United States remained adamantly opposed to moving aggressively forward. Concerns about the domestic costs perceived to result from curbs on the burning of fossil fuels, notably gasoline, explained many of their objections.

The election of George W. Bush did not bode well for advocates of a tougher U.S. position on climate change and other global environmental issues. He campaigned on a sensitive environmental issue in supporting oil exploration in protected habitats in Alaska and moved to implement that pledge shortly after his election. He quickly sought to suspend Clinton administration efforts to prevent road construction and logging in millions of acres of sensitive old-forest and other federal lands. And he renounced his campaign promise to cut carbon dioxide emissions from power plants, a central element in the Kyoto Protocol. Critics concluded this could be the death knell of Kyoto efforts to establish targets for cutting CO_2 and other greenhouse gas emissions in the coming years.

Biodiversity, Biotechnology, and Deforestation When UNCED met in Rio de Janeiro, the United States found itself out of step with much of the world not only with regard to global warming but also biodiversity. The first Bush administration refused to sign the Convention on Biodiversity. The Clinton administration reversed that decision, but the Senate refused to ratify the agreement.

Despite U.S. absence, 180 countries are now party to the Convention on Biodiversity. Served by the secretariat of the convention in Montreal, the convention seeks to promote sustainable development and a comprehensive approach to protecting the world's delicate ecosystems and their biodiversity. Signatories of the convention meet periodically to share ideas about policies and practices for the conservation and sustainable use of biodiversity with an ecosystem approach. Recent initiatives include a Biosafety Protocol, which recognizes that advances of genetically engineered plants and animals simultaneously enhance the quality of life through new plants, animals, and medicines, but also pose risks. As the biodiversity secretariat has noted, "in some countries, genetically altered agricultural products have been sold without much debate, while in others, there have been vocal protests against their use, particularly when they are sold without being identified as genetically modified."

As a leader in biotechnology, American agribusinesses have been impacted by both the promise and problems of biotechnology. European nations, for example, have protested the use of hormone-injected cattle to produce hamburger meat for foreign export. They also have curtailed the import of genetically engineered corn originally intended for animal feedlots that inadvertently ended up in corn flake cereals and other foods consumed domestically and produced for export.

American pharmaceutical firms have also been impacted by biodiversity issues. Part of the drive to protect tropical forests where thousands of yet unnamed species thrive is because of their potential benefit in developing drugs to treat today's medical maladies. In the past many Global South countries missed out on the profits reaped

from the exotic plants and animals within their borders made possible when Northern companies "mined" their resources. The classic example comes from Madagascar. The rosy periwinkle native to tropical forests of that African island country is the source of a drug developed by Eli Lilly that was used in a revolutionary treatment of leukemia in children. Eli Lilly enjoyed profits in the tens of millions of dollars. Madagascar shared in none of them.

The Biodiversity Convention seeks to reverse this unequal exchange between North and South. Parties to the treaty recognize states' sovereignty over their natural resources and agree that access to valuable biological resources must be based on their mutual agreement and that the state of origin must share in any benefits their exploitation may yield. Cooperation might range from outright payments to sharing of biotechnical resources to profit-sharing plans.

The steps toward protecting biodiversity are halting and, as with the climate change treaty, often unenforceable. But steps are being taken—even without the formal participation of the United States in global efforts to protect the world's genetic heritage. The United States can ill afford to flaunt the will of the global community on this issue, nor has it. Despite not being a formal party to the biodiversity agreement, it continues to foster and follow policies consistent with the treaty's objectives and the goals of the world community.

Domestically, the United States has sponsored efforts to reforest areas once denuded of their natural covers. Globally, the United States shares with other industrialized countries an effort to rebuild forests lost to misuse, urban growth, and environmental degradation. The results have been encouraging. The United Nations Food and Agriculture Organization (FAO) reported in early 2001 that the rate of deforestation had declined measurably. As reported in its latest assessment, it concludes that the rate of forest loss slowed by twenty percent between 1995 and the onset of the new century. Reforestation in the Global North accounts for much of the decline. But deforestation continues unabated in the South. The FAO reports that forest destruction remains pervasive in much of Africa and Latin America. If there is a hopeful sign, it is in Asia, where deforestation has largely been compensated with reforestation programs. As a whole, however, the world community has yet to move beyond the statement of principles on the management of the earth's forests approved at the Earth Summit in 1992.

The Foreign Policy Interests and Strategies of the Global South

We noted earlier that environmental stress and resource scarcities are expected to fuel social strains that may ignite violent conflict. Violence is already pervasive in much of the Global South and figures prominently in Southern states' pursuit of their foreign policy interests and strategies. The policy choices the Global South makes in responding to its problems and opportunities have important implications for American foreign policy.

During the Cold War the developing countries of the Third World embraced three identifiable strategies: (1) reform the world political economy to make it more amenable to their interests; (2) steer clear of Cold War political-military alignments; and (3) acquire modern military capabilities to protect their sovereignty and independence. This, of course, is an oversimplification; few in the Third World pursued all of these goals simultaneously, while many others sought goals specifically tailored to their own perceptions of their unique national interests. Still, they remain part of the legacy that informs North-South relations in the new century and that take us beyond the demographic divide in which population and development figure so prominently. A brief sketch illustrates the historic context of these strategies, the interests that motivated them, and their continuing relevance.

Reform—and Resentment Third World efforts to reform the world political economy grew out of a perceptual lens in international politics known as *dependency theory* that originated in Latin America and was quickly embraced elsewhere. Dependency theorists argued that the relationship between the rich and poor countries—the *core* and *periphery,* respectively—explained the persistent underdevelopment of the developing countries. Galvanized by this logic and the evident commodity power demonstrated by the *Organization of Petroleum Exporting Countries (OPEC)* in the 1970s, the developing countries pressed the Northern countries to replace the rules governing the *Liberal International Economic Order (LIEO)* (discussed in detail in Chapter 7) with a new set of rules that would create a *New World Economic Order (NIEO)* designed to reverse the dependency relationships of the past. State intervention into markets marked many of their proposals. Although pressed vigorously in a variety of international forums into the early years of the Reagan administration, the dialogue between the Global North and South over the NIEO quickly degenerated into a dialogue of the deaf.

Today little remains of Southern efforts to reform the world political economy. Instead, it continues to operate according to rules governing capital, monetary, and trade flows set by the Global North. Indeed, as political democracy spread following the Cold War, it demanded the parallel development of market economies. Thus *privatization* became the buzzword of the 1990s. If there is a common thread joining these efforts with the NIEO drive, it is how to integrate the developing economies into the world political economy—on terms, the Global South would say, still dictated by the North, and the United States in particular.

A one-superpower world is the context in which many in the Global South now seethe at the rapid advancement of globalization, which not only undermines its cultures and values but also its ability to compete in the face of rules governing commerce, labor, and the environment set in the North. In early 2000, Malaysia's Prime Minister Mahathir Mohamad, an outspoken leader among the Asian developing countries, pointedly reflected the concerns of many in the Global South:

> What I see happening today as a result of globalization is an attempt to set up worldwide monopolies of certain businesses by a few giant corporations mainly from the West. In the future there will be at the most five banks, five automotive companies, five hypermarkets, five hotel chains, five restaurant chains and so on, all operating worldwide. All the small- and medium-sized companies in these fields and maybe others too will be absorbed by these Western-owned international giants. These monopolies would, it is claimed, bring about efficiency and thus lower cost through economies of scale. The raw materials the world needs will also be produced by giant mining and plantation companies operating in poor countries, and will be carried by air and sea freighters belonging to giant transportation companies, to be processed and resold throughout the world. Some, of course, will use cheap labor in the poor countries in order to reduce costs.
>
> It is the dream world of the supercapitalists come true. Others will merely work for the capitalists. They will earn more but they will own nothing that they can call their own. Quite obviously the great capitalists will wield immeasurable power. And they will become corrupted as they manipulate governments and international agencies so as to enable them to make more and more money for themselves.
>
> When the Cold War ended with the defeat of communism, it was not democracy that won. It was capitalism with a big capital C. The advent of communism and socialism in the early years of the twentieth century forced capitalism to adopt a more human face. Monopolies were broken up and

curbed. Today, without the challenge of communism, the true ugliness of capitalism has revealed itself. This time it will not permit any opposition or restriction.

> Democracy, the rule of the majority and the concern for the poor and the small must not stand in the way of world-girdling unbridled capitalism. Through the IMF, the World Trade Organization, the international media and the might of the most powerful and richest country on Earth, capitalism will assert its power. Before this juggernaut all must fall.
>
> The question is, do we resist now before it is too late or do we wait until, like communism, millions have been sacrificed before we rise in rebellion?

Nonalignment—and Neglect Diversity has always characterized the Global South. The Cold War gave it coherence, however—at least as seen through the eyes of the conflict's antagonists. Many in the Third World fed that perception through their foreign policy strategy of *nonalignment,* the purpose of which was to steer clear of Cold War political-military alignments.

Because Third World nations could not materially affect the outcome of the Cold War, they tried through nonalignment to maximize their own gains while minimizing their costs. The strategy, as preached with firebrand rhetoric at periodic summits first convened in 1961, stimulated keen efforts by each of the two superpowers to woo the uncommitted to its own side while preventing their alignment with the other. Nonalignment in effect enabled developing countries to play one side against the other in order to gain advantage for themselves. The Cold War competitors—in keeping with the sensitivity each manifested toward the other in the context of the bipolar distribution of power, perceived as a zero-sum contest—were willing players in the game.

Foreign aid was a favored foreign policy instrument the United States used to prevent defection of the nonaligned to "the other side." Between the end of the Korean War (when U.S. foreign aid efforts turned increasingly to the Third World) and 1990, the United States expended some $200 billion in foreign economic aid. Although the motivations behind these vast sums often took into account the welfare of the recipients, security concerns and an overriding emphasis on the containment of communism were the driving forces (see Chapter 5).

Soviet and Soviet bloc aid never rivaled that of the United States, and much of what was once committed apparently never actually made it to recipient countries. Nonetheless, the Soviet Union and its allies were eager competitors. Like the United States, the historic pattern of Soviet bloc aid followed the path of its strategic and geopolitical interests, with much of it concentrated in the Middle East, Southeast Asia, and the Western Hemisphere (notably Cuba and Nicaragua).

Beginning in the 1970s, members of OPEC also became major contributors of foreign aid to developing states, although their actual sums dropped measurably during the 1980s as world oil prices plummeted. Since the 1960s, however, and even more markedly since the end of the Cold War, the United States and the other industrial economies of the Global North have been the principal sources of development assistance, which Southern states receive directly from individual donor countries (bilateral aid) or from international financial institutions (multilateral aid).

With the end of the Cold War, the flow of aid slowed markedly, even as the demands for assistance to Russia and the New Independent States and to war-ravaged states like Afghanistan, Cambodia, and others grew. Although the great powers continue to rely on foreign aid as an instrument of statecraft, the United States, historically the most generous donor in dollar terms, is today the least generous as measured by the percentage of its wealth devoted to foreign assistance. A long-established international norm is that the rich countries give .7 percent of their gross national product (GNP) to the poor countries. Today, among the twenty-one major foreign aid donors in the Global North, the United States is *dead last*. Its assistance to poor countries is but a fraction of the money Americans spend annually on alcoholic beverages, tickets to sporting events and rock concerts, and weight reduction plans.

The end of the Cold War not only dissipated much of the rationale that sustained foreign aid in the past; it also removed whatever facade of strength nonalignment may once have provided the Global South. "This political device is now lost to [the states of the South]. Nonalignment died with the Cold War. More than that, the way the East-West rivalry ended, with the values and systems of the West vindicated and triumphant, undermined the very basis of the nonaligned movement, which had adopted as its foundation a moral neutrality between the two blocs" (Chubin 1993).

Still, the residue of resentment stemming from a colonial past and an underdog status in the global hierarchy persists. In a one-superpower world, the Global South is particularly sensitive to the elitist character of the United Nations Security Council, and how profoundly decisions there—where the Global South has virtually no voice but in which the United States is now dominant—can affect its future (Chubin 1993; Korany 1994). Indeed, for the Global South, the post–Gulf War world seems to reveal "the reemergence of a more open and explicit form of imperialism, in which national sovereignty is more readily overridden by a hegemonic power pursuing its own self-defined national interest" (Bienefeld 1994).

Sovereign Independence—and Intranational and International Challenges to It Global South states have always been acutely sensitive about their independence and sovereignty. Thus the increased concern in the United Nations Security Council with humanitarian intervention to protect human rights, promote democracy, and enhance other arguably legitimate values

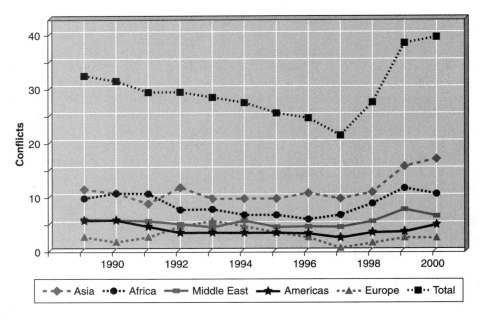

FIGURE 6.8 A World at War, 1989–2000

Source: The Defense Monitor 30 (January 2000): 1. Based on data from Sipri Yearbook 2000; Upsala University Conflict Project; Center of Defense Information.

often is perceived as a threat to their independence and integrity.

It is important to note that the benefits Southern states may once have enjoyed as a consequence of Soviet and American efforts to win their allegiance also had their costs. More often than not, the Third World was the battleground on which the superpowers' covert activities, paramilitary operations, and proxy wars were played out. Almost all civil wars in the Cold War era occurred on Third World "killing fields," where the number of casualties ran into the tens of millions (Singer 1991). And the pattern continues: Of the nearly forty active violent conflicts at the onset of the twenty-first century, almost all were in the Global South (see Figure 6.8).

Most of these conflicts are grounded in often ravaging and bloody enthopolitical disputes, to which traditional foreign policy instruments as well as traditional international relations theory grounded in realism and idealism are of dubious relevance. The main problem in many countries in the former Soviet Union and the Global

South, explains K.J. Holsti (1998), "is not between communities within the state, but between the regime and those communities. . . . The state, rather than ethnic communities, has often been the main threat to the lives and security of its own citizens." Holsti notes, for example, that "it was the government-trained and organized militia in Rwanda in 1994 that launched the genocide of the Tutsis." Thus a basic, underlying condition of ethnopolitical conflict "is the systematic exclusion of individuals and groups from access to government positions, influence, and allocations. There is, in brief, differential treatment of specified groups by governments, which means that there are fundamental problems of justice underlying armed conflict." Robert Kaplan (2000) likewise worries pessimistically that "the coming anarchy" will be propelled by a breakdown of authority in much of the Global South. Indeed, *failed states*—states whose governments are ineffective in coping with internal rebellion and threatened domestic anarchy—are increasingly evident.

Elsewhere in the Global South, long-standing *security dilemmas* continue to propel apprehensions, suspicions, and violent conflict. The Middle East, where bitter differences about religion and territory between Jews and Arabs are rife, is a prominent example. So is the drive among South Asian countries to acquire nuclear weapons. China first acquired weapons of mass destruction in the 1960s. India responded with its own nuclear test in the 1970s. Pakistan followed in the 1990s. Arguably each of the triangular nuclear competitors armed for defense, not offense, but their potential adversaries perceived malevolence and responded accordingly. The result smacks of the Cold War competition between the United States and the Soviet Union: a classic arms race precipitated by competing belief systems, conflicts of interest, and potential misperceptions of the intentions of "the other side."

Traditional instruments of statecraft might be better suited to dealing with the Asian security dilemma and analogous situations elsewhere in the Global South, but, as we saw in Chapter 4, Southern states often resist the entreaties of the United States and others in the Global North, viewing them as an unwarranted interference into their sovereign independence. That conclusion is nowhere more evident than in the Middle East, where, despite repeated initiatives by the Clinton administration and its predecessors, the United States has routinely been perceived as favoring Jews over Muslims, angering not only Arabs but also the followers of Islam throughout the world.

Faced with seemingly endless conflict at home or abroad, it is not surprising that political elites in much of the Global South, like those in China, India, and Pakistan, would join the rest of the world in a quest to acquire modern military capabilities. Often this has meant that the *burden of military spending*—as measured by the ratio of military expenditures to GNP—is highest among those least able to bear it.

Since the end of the Cold War, military expenditures have dropped dramatically. So has their burden. In the decade ending in 1997, the military burden worldwide dropped by half, from 5.2 percent to 2.6 percent. But the decline in the Global South has been somewhat smaller, falling from 4.9 percent to 2.7 percent (U.S. Arms Control and Disarmament Agency 2000). And some remain heavily burdened. North Korea, for example, continues to spend a tenth of its GNP on the weapons of war, even as its people face starvation requiring humanitarian assistance from others to survive. Thus the societal costs of military spending—which typically exceed expenditures on health and education—bear little relationship to the level of development.[5] Whether a state is embroiled in war with its neighbors or threatened by ethnic, religious, or tribal strife at home remains a potent explanation.

Arms imported from abroad, whether surreptitiously or openly, fuel the conflicts of a world at war. True, the value of arms purchased from foreign suppliers declined dramatically in the past decade, paralleling the worldwide decline in the burden of military spending. Nonetheless, demand for the weapons of war remains high in many places.

The United States figures prominently in the practice of selling arms to others. Indeed, it emerged in the wake of the implosion of the Soviet empire as the world's principal supplier state, accounting for roughly $60 of every $100 in arms exports by the end of the 1990s (U.S. Arms Control and Disarmament Agency 2000). And the Global South accounted for $78 of every $100 of conventional arms delivered between 1995 and 1998 (Grimmett 1999). Saudi Arabia topped the list of arms purchasers during this period, accounting for some twelve percent of global arms purchases from all sources. In 1998 alone, it received nearly $9 billion in arms deliveries (Grimmett 1999). Surprisingly, Taiwan ranked second, doubtless a concern to leaders on China's mainland.

The conventional weapons sold to arms buyers include the standards: tanks, self-propelled guns, armored cars, artillery pieces, combat aircraft, surface-to-air missiles, and the like. Increasingly, the export of small arms—"man-portable firearms and their ammunition primarily designed for individual use by military forces as lethal

Table 6.1 Current UN Peacekeeping Missions, 1948–2000

Mission Name and Location	Acronym	Starting Date
UN Truce Supervision Organization—Middle East	UNTSO	June 1948
UN Military Observer Group in India-Pakistan—Kashmir	UNMOGIP	January 1949
UN Peacekeeping Force in Cyprus	UNFICYP	March 1964
UN Disengagement Observer Force—Golan Heights	UNDOF	June 1974
UN Interim Force in Lebanon	UNIFIL	March 1978
UN Mission for the Referendum in Western Sahara	MINURSO	April 1991
UN Iraq-Kuwait Observation Mission	UNIKOM	April 1991
UN Observer Mission in Georgia	UNOMIG	August 1993
UN Mission in Bosnia Herzegovina	UNMIBH	December 1995
UN Mission of Observers in Prevlaka—Croatia	UNMOP	January 1996
UN Interim Administration in Kosovo	UNMIK	June 1999
UN Mission in Sierra Leone	UNAMSIL	October 1999
UN Transitional Administration in East Timor	UNTAET	October 1999
UN Organizational Mission in the Democratic Republic of the Congo	MONUC	November 1999
UN Mission in Ethiopia and Eritrea	UNMEE	July 2000

SOURCE: Adapted from United Nations Department of Peacekeeping Operations.

weapons," including "revolvers and self-loading pistols, rifles and carbines, assault rifles, and light machine guns" (U.S. Arms Control and Disarmament Agency 2000)—also has become a major concern (see also Klare 1994–1995). Trafficking in small arms has increased in sync with the rise of enthnopolitical conflict. Although the United Nations, in concert with the United States, has taken steps to stem the flow of small arms across borders, a "comprehensive resolution [of this problem] is unlikely in the near future" (U.S. Arms Control and Disarmament Agency 2000),

Meanwhile, the United Nations finds itself increasingly mired in bitter disputes in much of the Global South. Of the fifty-four UN peacekeeping, humanitarian, and observer missions undertaken since its birth, thirty-five were initiated in the 1990s (*The Defense Monitor,* January 2001, p. 6). By the end of the decade, nearly half of those were still in operation (see Table 6.1). Some people argue that UN peacekeeping operations have the untoward effect of postponing political settlements of underlying disputes; other

respond that the United Nations has played a critical role in saving lives. Regardless, unhappiness with the United Nations and other international institutions is rife in the United States.

Transnational Interdependence: Agents of Challenge and Change

Earlier we cited Joseph Nye's concept of a layer cake as a metaphor for the emergent global structure in which the United States now finds itself. "The bottom layer of transnational interdependence," he explained, "shows a diffusion of power" (Nye 1992). Of what does that bottom layer consist? It consists of a multitude of actors who know no national boundaries but who nonetheless profoundly impact the established entities that claim sovereignty in world politics (states and nation-states) and the people who live in them. These nonstate actors are increasingly important in shaping contemporary global politics. International organizations and multinational corporations are the most ubiquitous among them. Transnational terrorist groups, ethnopolitical movements, and criminal entities comprise other, less-benign types. We touch on each of them briefly in this section.

International Organizations: An Overview

The United Nations is probably the most widely known of all international organizations. It is a multipurpose organization embracing a broad array of other organizations, centers, commissions, and institutes. The distinguishing characteristic of the UN family of organizations is that governments are their members. Hence they are known as international *intergovernmental organizations (IGOs)*. There are nearly three hundred IGOs in existence, and their concerns embrace the entire range of political, economic, social, and cultural affairs that are the responsibilities of modern governments.

In addition to IGOs, the transnational layer of international politics also embraces international *nongovernmental organizations (NGOs)*. Their number grew explosively in the 1990s, from an estimated 5000 in 1990 to perhaps five times that number by the end of the decade (*The Economist,* 11 December 1999, p.20). The members of these international organizations (such as the International Federation of Red Cross and Red Crescent Societies) are individuals or societal groups, not governments. NGOs also deal with the entire panoply of transnational activities. It is useful to think of them as intersocietal organizations that help facilitate the achievement and maintenance of agreements among countries regarding elements of international public policy (Jacobson 1984). For example, making rules regarding security at international airports and the treatment of hijackers would not be possible without the cooperation of the International Federation of Air Line Pilots' Associations; thus NGOs have an impact on the rules governing different policies. Their influence is arguably greatest in the Global North, where democratic institutions invite the participation of interest groups in the policy-making process. They have been particularly vigorous and visible on environmental and trade issues in recent years. Thus NGOs help to blur the distinction between domestic and foreign policy issues.

NGOs and IGOs alike mirror the same elements of conflict and cooperation that characterize international politics generally. Accordingly, not all are appropriately conceived as agents of interdependence. NATO, for example, historically has been a collective defense arrangement. Although an international organization, until recent years it depended for its very existence on the presence of a credible adversary, whose hostility induced cooperation among the alliance's members.

The United States was a primary mover behind the creation of NATO, the United Nations, and a multitude of other international organizations launched in the decades following World War II. It also encouraged the economic integration of Western Europe, which in 1957 culminated in the Treaty of Rome, creating the European Economic Community comprising France, Germany, Italy, Belgium, the Netherlands, and Luxembourg. The community has since been renamed the *European Union (EU)* and embraces fifteen European countries, with further expansion promised.[6] Although the EU counts political and security functions among its charge, its greatest successes have come in moving Europe toward a single, integrated regional economy. Today the EU has its own currency, the *euro;* is the largest market in the world; and is a major competitor as well as partner of the United States in the world political economy (see Figure 6.1).

U.S. support for an integrated Europe and other international organizations flowed naturally from the international ethos that animated America's global activism following World War II. As the nature of the international system and the United States' role within it changed, however, so did American attitudes. That is nowhere more apparent than in the response of the United States to the changing United Nations.

International Organizations: The Uneasy U.S.–UN Relationship

American idealism was a motivating force behind creation of the United Nations during the waning days of World War II.

American values shaped the world organization, whose political institutions were molded after its own. Almost immediately, however, the United Nations mirrored the increasingly antagonistic Cold War competition between the United States and the Soviet Union. Thus the United States sought—with considerable success—to utilize its position as the leader of the dominant Western majority in the UN to turn the organization in the direction of its own preferred foreign policy goals. That became more difficult with the passage of time, however—especially as the decolonization process unfolded and the United States found itself on the defensive along with its European allies (most of which had been colonial powers) in the face of a hostile Third World coalition with which the Soviet bloc typically aligned. In 1975 that coalition succeeded in passing a General Assembly resolution over vigorous U.S. protest that branded Zionism "a form of racism and racial discrimination." The vote outraged Daniel P. Moynihan, then U.S. ambassador to the United Nations, who lashed out vehemently against "the tyranny of the UN's 'new majority.'"

In the years that followed, U.S. attitudes toward the United Nations and many of its affiliated organizations ranged from circumspection to outright hostility. The Carter administration withdrew from the International Labor Organization (ILO) to protest what it regarded as the organization's anti-Western bias. The Reagan administration followed by withdrawing from the United Nations Educational, Scientific, and Cultural Organization (UNESCO). The administration's disenchantment with multilateralism also found expression in its indifference to and attack on the World Court and its decision to selectively withhold funds for various UN activities—a tactic the United States had long decried when the Soviet Union chose it to protest UN policies and operations it found inimical to its interests. The United States also became wary of turning to the United Nations to cope with various regional conflict situations, as it had previously done.

By the end of the Reagan administration the once-prevalent retreat from multilateralism, often accompanied by a preference for a unilateral, go-it-alone posture toward global issues, began to wane. The decision of the Soviet Union under Mikhail Gorbachev's leadership to pay its own overdue UN bills and, in the wake of its misadventure in Afghanistan, to turn (or return) to the UN Security Council to deal with conflict situations in a manner recalling the original intended purpose of the UN, helped to stimulate the reassessment of U.S. policy toward the United Nations. That set the stage for Soviet-American cooperation in responding to Iraq's invasion of Kuwait.

In the years that followed, the Security Council authorized several new peacekeeping and peace enforcement operations, far outpacing any previous period in the organization's history, as we saw earlier. UN Secretary-General Boutros Boutros-Ghali championed an even broader role for the UN in what President George H. W. Bush described as a new world order, proposing the creation of a volunteer force that would "enable the United Nations to deploy troops quickly to enforce a ceasefire by taking coercive action against either party, or both, if they violate it" (Boutros-Ghali 1992–1993, 1992). The rapid deployment units would go into action when authorized by the Security Council and serve under the command of the secretary-general and his designees.

This and other ideas put forward by the proactive secretary-general proved controversial, however. So, too, did the growing number of UN operations around the world. As their costs—both financial and political—mounted, disenchantment in the United States (long a critic of the UN's excessive bureaucracy and penchant toward mismanagement) also grew. The Clinton administration, as we saw in previous chapters, now elaborated rules that would sharply constrain U.S. participation in UN military operations. Secretary of State Madeleine Albright led the charge to oust Boutros-Ghali as UN Secretary General in favor of Kofi Annan. And the new

Republican majority in the House of Representatives, acting on the single foreign policy item in its "Contract with America" program put forth during the 1994 mid-term elections, passed legislation that would curtail funds available for UN peacekeeping or enforcement operations and prohibit U.S. forces from serving under the command of a non-U.S. officer.

Bitter disputes between the Clinton administration and the Republican controlled Congress would follow. U.S. arrears in its financial obligations to the United Nations mounted, topping $1 billion by the time the General Assembly opened its annual session in September 1999, putting it on the verge of losing its voting privileges. Clinton and Congress would repeatedly seek compromises permitting the debts to be paid, only to see them fall victim to partisan and ideological rancor. Senator Jesse Helms (R-North Carolina), chair of the powerful Senate Foreign Relations Committee and a spokesperson for American conservatives, effectively held the entire U.S. foreign affairs budget hostage in a continuing dispute with the administration about the role of international institutions in world politics and the challenges to U.S. sovereignty he thought they posed. An article Helms published in *The National Interest* (Helms 2000–2001) as Clinton was leaving office encapsulates his ideas and arguments. His remarks were stimulated by an earlier speech by Secretary-General Kofi Annan, "in which he declared that 'the last right of states cannot and must not be the right to enslave, prosecute, or torture their own citizens.' The peoples of the world, he said, have 'rights beyond borders.'" Annan also declared that the UN Security Council "is the 'sole source of legitimacy on the use of force' in the world."

Drawing on the historical legacy that warns of "entangling alliances," Helms responded that "Americans look with alarm upon the UN's claim to a monopoly on international moral legitimacy. They see this a threat to the freedom of the American people, a claim of political authority over America and its elected leaders." He said

"we want to ensure that the United States of America remains the sole judge of its own international affairs, that the United Nations is not allowed to restrict the individual rights of U.S. citizens, and the United States retains sole authority over the deployment of U.S. forces around the world." And he concluded with a warning: "If the United Nations does not respect American sovereignty, if it seeks to impose its presumed authority over the American people without their consent, then it begs for confrontation and . . . eventual U.S. withdrawal."

Responding in part to the pressures of Helms and others—including many embedded in Helms-Biden legislation passed by Congress in 1999 that demanded UN reforms—U.S. Ambassador to the United Nations Richard Holbrooke brokered a deal only days before Clinton vacated the White House that would reduce U.S. contributions to the United Nations regular budget to twenty percent from twenty-five percent. The reduction was made possible only because other states agreed to increase their fees—and only because American media mogul Ted Turner agreed to contribute over $30 million to the United Nations to bridge a short-term budget deficit. The scale of assessments for peacekeeping operations was also revised. The U.S. share would drop from more than thirty percent to less than twenty-eight percent beginning in 2001 and then progressively fall to about twenty-five percent in later years.[7]

When the new Bush administration assumed the reigns of power in January 2001, it faced a world angry and disgusted with what the French rather derisively call the world's "hyperpower." The derision derives from U.S. recalcitrance about what are, after all, rather paltry sums of money by almost any standard (like the cost of fifty cruise missiles fired against Iraq). The reason, of course, is that money is not the critical issue.[8] It is a matter of who controls the destiny of states' foreign policies, including that of the United States. And on this, as Senator Helms pointedly reminds us, there is wide and deep disagreement in a world—and a world organization—comprising nearly 200 sovereign states with widely different capabilities and divergent interests.

Robert A. Pastor, an aide to former president Jimmy Carter, summarizes this viewpoint as seen though the eyes of American policy makers:

> The United States has always been ambivalent about whether it wanted to strengthen or limit the United Nations. Its position at any given time depended, not surprisingly, on whether it viewed a specific action as serving its interests. Even in the case of the Gulf War, President George Bush did not consult the United Nations in making his decision to drive Saddam Hussein from Kuwait; he decided first and then sought international legitimacy and support. President Bill Clinton's request in July 1994 for a UN Security Council resolution to restore constitutional government to Haiti was similarly motivated: It was intended not to strengthen the United Nations but to support a U.S. initiative. In the case of Kosovo, NATO decided to begin the bombing of Serbia without United Nations authorization because of the opposition of Russia and China.

(PASTOR 1999, 11)

Thus the twenty-first century promises to be no different than the ones that have gone before, as the incentives to maximize individual gains rather than subordinate them to the collectivity persist.

Multinational Corporations Since World War II multinational corporations have grown enormously in size and influence, thereby dramatically changing patterns of global investment, production, and marketing. (Multinational corporations [MNCs] are business enterprises organized in one society with activities abroad growing out of direct investment as opposed to portfolio investment through shareholding.) The United Nations Programme on Transnational Corporations (United Nations Programme on Transnational Corporations 1993, 99–100) esti-

mates that in the early 1990s some 37,000 MNCs controlled assets in two or more countries and that they were responsible for marketing roughly ninety percent of Northern countries' trade. Moreover, a comparison of countries and corporations according to the size of their gross economic product shows that half of the world's top one hundred economic entities (in 1998) were multinational corporations. Among the top fifty entities, MNCs account for only fourteen, but in the next fifty they account for thirty-six (Kegley and Wittkopf 2001, 231).

Although Global South countries have spawned some multinational corporations, most remain headquartered in the developed world, where the great majority of MNC activities originate. Historically, the United States has been the home country of the largest proportion of multinational parent companies, followed by Britain and Germany. The outward stocks and flows of foreign direct investment from the United States would steadily decline in the following decades. By the 1990s the investment world appeared "tripolar," with the United States, Europe, and Japan the key actors. Unexpected at the beginning of the decade, tripolarity grew out of the convergence of three interrelated trends: (1) the rapid integration of Europe, which made it possible to treat the European Community as a single investment entity; (2) the growing importance of Japan as a source of foreign direct investment; and (3) the declining role of the United States as a source of investments and its corresponding rise as a host country.

By mid-decade, however, American dominance in the MNC world remained unassailable. In 1996 it headquartered a third of the world's 500 largest corporations. Other liberal democracies followed in its train, as (in order) Japan, France, Germany, and Britain continued to dominate the multinational world (*Fortune,* 4 August 1997, F1.)

The dominance of MNCs located and directed from the Global North underlies much of the resentment toward globalization noted earlier in this chapter. Nonetheless, the process of extending the tentacles of these giant corporations so vividly decried by Malaysia's Prime Minister Mahathir Mohamad (and others) continues relentlessly.

Although most MNCs are headquartered in the Global North, they pose little direct threat to the economies or the policy-making institutions in these large, complex societies. Not so in the case of the Global South, where the economic power and reach of multinational firms—typically American—have enabled them to become a global extension of Northern societies, serving as an engine not only for the transfer of investment, technology, and managerial skills but also of cultural values; hence Prime Minister Mahathir's concern and anger.

Although such transboundary transfers may be beneficial, in the past they have posed serious threats to the very integrity of sovereign states. Perhaps the most notorious example occurred in Chile in the early 1970s. There, International Telephone and Telegraph (ITT) sought to protect its interests in the profitable Chiltelco telephone company by seeking to prevent Marxist-oriented Salvador Allende from being elected president and subsequently by seeking his overthrow. ITT's efforts to undermine Allende included giving monetary support to his political opponents and, once Allende was elected, attempting to induce the American government to launch a program designed to disrupt the Chilean economy. Eventually Allende was killed and his government overturned. Only today, as U.S. government documents from this period are being declassified, are we beginning to understand the extent of U.S. involvement in Chilean internal affairs.

In some instances, MNCs engage in practices that may be embarrassing to home countries—as when the West German government found that a German firm had sold mustard-gas manufacturing equipment to Libya. Or they may seem to defy their home countries—as when the French subsidiary of Dresser Industries of Dallas, Texas, exported energy technology to the Soviet Union in defiance of the Reagan administration. Ultimately behavior such as this and the ITT case raise the question of whether multinational corporations are beyond the control of governments. In practice, the question has been more salient in the Global South than the North. Furthermore, most efforts at control have evolved nationally rather than internationally (see Spero and Hart 1997).

Today the Global South, although worried about the effects of globalization, is less fearful of the untoward effects of MNCs' involvement in their political systems than about its own ability (or inability) to attract MNC investment capital and the other perquisites that flow from it. MNCs are especially important to those who seek to emulate the economic success of the *Newly Industrialized Economies (NIEs)*, which depends on an ability to sustain growth in exports. Foreign capital is critical in this process, even though it often comes at a high price, as suggested by the untoward effects of the *Washington Consensus* (see also Broad and Cavanagh 1988; Wiarda 1997).

Critics of multinationals—sometimes called "imperial corporations" (Barnet and Cavanagh 1994)—contend that they exact a cost on the Global North as well as the Global South. They note that while corporate executives often have a "broad vision and understanding of global issues," they have little appreciation of, or concern for, "the long-term social or political consequences of what their companies make or what they do" (Barnet and Cavanagh 1994); see also Barnet and Müller (1974) and Kefalas (1992). These allegedly include a host of maladies, including environmental degradation, a maldistribution of global resources, and social disintegration. Beyond this, critics worry that MNCs are beyond the control of national political leaders.

The formidable power and mobility of global corporations are undermining the effectiveness of national governments to carry out essential policies on behalf of their people. Leaders of nation-states are losing much of the control over their own territory they once had. More and more, they must conform to the demands of the outside world because the outsiders are already inside the gates. Business enterprises that routinely operate across borders are linking far-flung pieces of territory into a new world economy that bypasses all sorts of established political arrangements and conventions.

(BARNET AND CAVANAGH 1994, 19)

The United States is not immune from these processes. "Although still the largest national economy and by far the world's greatest military power, [it] is increasingly subject to the vicissitudes of a world no nation can dominate" (Barnet and Cavanagh 1994). Meanwhile, some corporate visionaries extol multinational corporations' transnational virtues. "There are no longer any national flag carriers," in the words of Kenichi Ohmae, a prominent Japanese management consultant. "Corporations must serve their customers, not governments."

International Regimes During the 1960s and 1970s multinational corporations were the object of considerable animosity due to their size and "global reach" (Barnet and Müller 1974). Today they are widely recognized as key players in the globalization processes that engulf people everywhere. Indeed, it is inconceivable to think how the international economic system might function without them, just as it is inconceivable to think that international commerce or other forms of interaction could occur in the absence of government rules regulating their exchanges. Thus states and nonstate actors coalesce to form *international regimes* that facilitate cooperative international relations.

International regimes can be thought as "sets of implicit or explicit principles, norms, rules, and decision-making procedures around which actors' expectations converge in a given issue area of international relations" (Krasner 1982). They are important in understanding the regularized patterns of collaboration widely evident in international politics. The international political system may appear anarchical (a central concept underlying the logic of political realism), but it is nonetheless an ordered anarchy. Regimes help explain that apparent anomaly.

The global monetary and trade systems created during and after World War II are clear examples of international regimes. Both evolved under the leadership of the United States, the hegemonic power in the postwar world political economy. Together the two regimes helped define the Liberal International Economic Order (LIEO), which embraced a combination of principles, rules, norms, and decision-making procedures that limited government intervention in the international economy and otherwise facilitated the free flow of capital and goods across national boundaries. The global system governing the extraction and distribution of oil is another example. Here governments, multinational corporations, and two international organizations, the Organization of Petroleum Exporting Countries (OPEC) and International Energy Agency (IEA), collectively play critical roles in supplying an energy-hungry world with a critical resource (see Keohane 1984).

These and other examples show that nonstate actors help to build and broaden the foreign policy agendas of national decision makers by serving as "transmission belts of policy sensitivities across national boundaries." They help to shape attitudes among mass and elite publics, they link national interest groups in transnational structures, and they create instruments of influence enabling some governments to carry out more effectively their wishes when dealing with other governments (Keohane and Nye 1975). International regimes facilitate all of these processes. Thus in concert with nonstate actors, they play critical roles in the maintenance of international equilibrium.

Transnational Terrorism, Ethnopolitical Movements, and Trans-Border Criminal Operations Transnational terrorists, ethnopolitical movements, and the activities of transborder criminal elements are exceptions to this

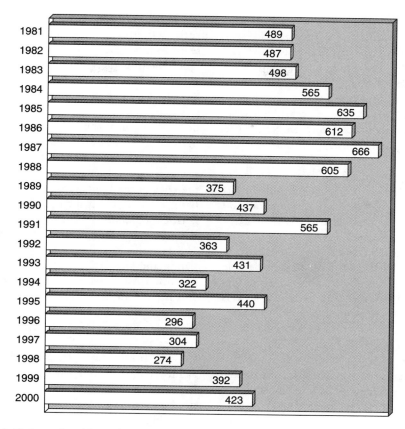

FIGURE 6.9 Total International Terrorist Attacks, 1981–2000

Source: U.S. Department of State, *Patterns of Global Terrorism: 2000,* Washington, DC: Department of State, 2001.

bold and optimistic conclusion. Their consequence and perhaps objective as nonstate actors is chaos, not equilibrium. Thus they pose vexing challenges to states generally and to the United States in particular.

In its annual *Patterns of Global Terrorism: 2000,* released in 2001, the State Department recorded 473 terrorist incidents. Bombings were the predominant terrorist mode, accounting for 179 incidents in 2000 against U.S. citizens or assets. Since the State Department began keeping records in the late 1960s, "more than 7,000 terrorist bombings have occurred worldwide" (*Patterns of Global Terrorism: 1999*). Accordingly, the United States has devoted considerable attention to terrorism and terrorist threats in recent years.

The attacks on the USS Cole in Yemen, military barracks in Saudi Arabia, and American embassies in Kenya and Tanzania, all of which resulted in considerable loss of life, are among the recent deadly terrorist attacks on U.S. interests and assets around the world leading up to September 11. The strikes against the World Trade Center and the Pentagon, larger in scale than any previous terrorist attacks, dramatically altered the situation, however, leading to substantially greater attention and resource commitment.

The number of international terrorist incidents declined in the 1990s compared with the previous decade (see Figure 6.9), as did the number of attacks on American interests and personnel. The trends are not unrelated to the end of the Cold War, as the Soviet Union and the Communist states in Eastern Europe had provided both support and safe haven for terrorist groups. However, the attacks have gotten closer to home. In 1993 two CIA employees were murdered as they drove into a parking lot in Langley, Virginia. In the same year, terrorists bombed the World Trade Center in New York City, killing six Americans and wounding more than a thousand. Several of the alleged culprits were quickly apprehended and later found guilty in U.S. courts. In early 1995, the purported ringleader of the attack was arrested in Pakistan and hustled to New York to face trial. Soon after that two U.S. consular employees in Karachi were gunned down as they carpooled to work. Since then the United States has focused considerable attention on Saudi Arabian millionaire and terrorist suspect Osama bin Ladin, whose followers are believed to be responsible for the bombings of the USS Cole and the American embassies in Africa. In 1999 both the United States and the United Nations leveled sanctions against the Taliban government of Afghanistan for its suspected role in harboring bin Ladin and his global terrorist network. None of these things could have prepared Americans for September 11, however. After the attacks, as it became increasingly clear that Al Qaeda and its Taliban benefactors were behind the actions, George W. Bush announced the U.S. response: a campaign against terrorism targeted against Afghanistan and the Al Qaeda terrorist network that involved a variety of resources such as intelligence assets and military forces, including naval, air, and ground units.

Traditionally, terrorism has been a tactic of the powerless directed against the powerful. Thus political or social minorities and ethnopolitical movements often perpetrated acts of terrorism to seize the media limelight and promote their causes. Those seeking independence and sovereign statehood—like the Palestinians in the Middle East and the Basques in Spain—typified the kinds of aspirations that often animated terrorist activity.

Recently, however, as illustrated by the terrorist activities of bin Laden and his followers, terrorism has become something more than "propaganda by deed" (Laqueur 1998). It has become a weapon used to inflict not just "noise," but to cause "the greatest number of casualties as possible." Bin Laden's sprawling, transnational network of jihadists is committed to advancing a narrow view of Islam and recruiting disaffected Muslims into creating "Islamic Republics" throughout the Islamic world. The policies and presence of the United States in the Middle East has made it a principal target of these "religious fanatics" (Laqueur 1998); see also (Doran 2001). According to bin Laden, the presence of U.S. troops in Saudi Arabia's Muslim Holy Lands, and U.S. policies toward Iraq and Israel, and other issues warrants "the judgment to kill and fight Americans and their allies, whether civilian or military" as "an obligation for every Muslim who is able to do so in any country" (quoted in Bergen 2001).

The Bush administration's global struggle against terrorism is a prime example of low-intensity conflict. Fulfilling its commitment will not be easy, however. Terrorists have perfected their ability not only to withstand urban conflict, as in Somalia, but also to stand up to the weapons of war radical Muslims believe the infidels have used against them. Often they have been actively assisted by states, who find nonstate actors like Al Qaeda useful outlets for pursuing their own interests. Although radical Islamic fundamentalists are widely identified with today's international terrorist activities, a broader conception of terrorism would also incorporate government activities such as those of Serbia, which during much of the 1990s supported mass rapes and killings in Bosnia, Herzegovina, and its own province of Kosovo. "It's a war," explained one State Department official as the conflict in the Balkans raged. He added, however, that the "issue of definition is an extremely thorny and difficult one."

Thorny definitional issues aside, the spread of ethnonational movements in the past decade encouraged the weak to visit terrorism on the strong. Today it is evident that many people do not pledge their primary allegiance to the state and the government that rules them. Instead, they regard themselves as members of their nationality first and their own state second. That belief encourages the cultural, religious, ethnic, and linguistic communities within today's politco-territorial states to express their own individuality. Even the United States—a "melting pot" of immigrants from around the world—today finds "multiculturalism" a growing challenge to the dominant political culture (see Chapter 8). Violence has sometimes accompanied expressions of multiculturalism within the United States. Often it invites expression abroad through terrorism, both within states and transnationally.

Finally, we must acknowledge that criminal organizations also pose new dangers to the established state system and the equilibrium traditional IGOs and NGOs provide. No accounting of Russia's efforts to establish democratic capitalism during the 1990s would be complete without an understanding of how deeply ingrained criminal elements have become in its politics, economics, and society; and the consequences extend beyond Russian borders. American banks, for example, have sometimes been alleged to have unwittingly become agents of money laundering by Russian criminal elements.

On another front, the United States has for more than a decade been involved in a "war against drugs." It has been a costly war which, most recently, has resulted in the pledge of several billions of dollars to stanch the flow of drugs into the United States by targeting with military means the activities of Columbian drug lords. The second Bush administration has questioned the wisdom of dealing with the *supply side* of drug trafficking (stopping drugs at the source, which was the war-against-drugs policy launched in the first Bush administration), and instead to focus more attention on the *demand side* of the problem, meaning drug consumption in the United States.

There is no obvious answer to coping with drugs, or, indeed, other criminal activities. Globalization is part of the reason. By opening states borders to an increasingly free flow of capital and goods, all states are vulnerable to those elements in society who would take illegal advantage of others. The United States is especially vulnerable, since freedom—political and economic, the cornerstone of American society—is easily penetrated by others. Thus it should come as no surprise that following Nafta's launch in 1993, which sought to create a free-trade zone across the North American continent, the flow of drugs through Mexico northward would also rise dramatically (Andreas 1996).[9] Meanwhile, the growing use of computers, the Internet, and other information technologies promises that *cyberterrorism* will become an increasingly dangerous force in the twenty-first century.

AMERICAN FOREIGN POLICY AT THE DAWN OF A NEW CENTURY

The years immediately following World War II were fraught with opportunity for the United States as it actively embraced global responsibilities and pursued an assertive foreign policy that shaped a world compatible with the American vision. Thus the character of the international political system in the decades following World War II was largely a product of the policies and programs the United States engineered and the choices it made in responding to the challenges posed by others.

The role that the United States will play in shaping the world of the twenty-first century now unfolding is uncertain. As the world's sole superpower, the United States has a greater capacity than anyone to create a world order that once more is compatible with its interests and values. Paradoxically, however, the United States also today finds itself burdened with responsibilities. The institutions it promoted and once supported without reservation are sometimes the unwelcome symbols of an inhospitable and intractable international system. The emerging configuration of world power portends new challenges that already have proved more vexing than managing the Soviet menace. Many of those outside the circle of great powers remain skeptical of the impact of American power on their own interests and values, even as developments within those societies spill onto the larger global stage. And many within the circle of great powers now fear American capabilities and intentions, even as they find they must deal with an economic and military gorilla whose shadow blankets them all. Meanwhile, the relentless march of globalization poses new threats to even a superpower's ability to manage the forces that define its security and well-being.

Historically the United States has responded to external challenges either with detachment or through assertiveness. Today we live in a transitional period—one in which the old world order has passed but the shape of the new order has yet to be determined. Whether detachment or assertiveness will characterize America's response to the challenges of the new century must still be decided.

KEY TERMS RELATED TO THE INTERNATIONAL POLITICAL SYSTEM AND AMERICAN FOREIGN POLICY

acid rain

America First

American century

balance

bandwagon

biodiversity

bioinvasions

bipolar international political system

bipolarity

bipolycentrism

Brezhnev Doctrine

burden of military spending

Congress of Vienna

cyberterrorism

decentralized international political system

deforestation

dependency theory

Earth Summit (United Nations Conference on the Environment and Development, UNCED)

euro

European Union (EU)

extended deterrence

failed states

flexible response

G-8 (Group of Eight)

hegemony

intergovernmental organizations (IGOs)

international regimes

Kyoto Protocol to the 1992 Framework Convention

Liberal International Economic Order (LIEO)

limited response nuclear exchange

long peace

Monroe Doctrine

multilateralism

multilevel interdependence

multipolar balance-of-power system

multipolarity

multipolar international political system

neo-isolationism (as grand foreign policy strategy)

New World Economic Order (NIEO)

Newly Industrialized Economies (NIEs)

nonalignment

nongovernmental organizations (NGOs)

North Atlantic Treaty Organization (NATO)

Organization of Petroleum Exporting Countries (OPEC)

periphery	*self-help*	**unipolarity**
political realism	*security dilemmas*	**unipolar moment**
power	*special relationship (United States and Britain)*	*United Nations Conference on the Environment and Development (UNCED)*
power transition theory		
rapid reaction force	**structural realism**	*Warsaw Pact*
second-strike nuclear capability	**sustainable development**	**zero-sum**
selective engagement (as grand foreign policy strategy)	*transnational interdependence*	
	uni-multipolar	

SUGGESTIONS FOR FURTHER READING

Barnet, Richard J., and John Cavanagh. *Global Dreams: Imperial Corporations and the New World Order.* New York. Simon and Schuster, 1994.

Brown, Seyom. *New Forces, Old Forces, and the Future of World Politics.* New York: HarperCollins, 1995.

Haass, Richard N. "What to Do with American Primacy," *Foreign Affairs* 78 (September/October 1999): 37–49.

Homer-Dixon, Thomas. "The Rise of Complex Terrorism," Foreign Policy (January/February 2002): 54–59.

Huntington, Samuel P. *The Clash of Civilizations and the Remaking of World Order.* New York: Simon and Schuster, 1996.

Kennedy, Paul. *Preparing for the Twenty-First Century.* New York: Random House, 1993.

Keohane, Robert O., and Joseph S. Nye, Jr. *Power and Interdependence: World Politics in Transition,* 3rd ed. Glenview, IL: Addison-Wesley, Brown, 2000.

Kupchan, Charles A. "After Pax Americana: Benign Power, Regional Integration, and the Sources of Stable Multipolarity," *International Security* 23 (Fall 1998): 40–96.

Neuman, Stephanie G., ed., *International Relations Theory and the Third World.* New York: St. Martin's, 1998.

Pastor, Robert A., ed., *A Century's Journey: How the Great Powers Shape the World.* New York: Basic Books, 1999.

Sen, Amartya. *Development As Freedom.* New York: Knopf, 1999.

Singer, Max, and Aaron Wildavsky. *The Real World Order: Zones of Peace/Zones of Turmoil.* Rev. ed. Chatham, NJ: Chatham House, 1996.

"The South in the New World (Dis)Order," *Third World Quarterly,* Special Issue, 15 (March 1994): 1–176.

Waltz, Kenneth. "Structural Realism after the Cold War," *International Security* 25 (Summer 2000): 5–41.

World Resources 2000-2001. Washington, DC: World Resources Institute, 2000.

NOTES

1. The *Second World* in this scheme comprised the Soviet Union, its allies, and other communist societies. For them, a commitment to planned economic practices, rather than reliance on market forces to determine the supply of and demand for goods and services, was the distinguishing characteristic.

2. Averages obscure as well as illuminate. Thus the "other Global North" and "other Global South" aggregates contain widely varying figures. Within the North, for example, Switzerland's per capita GDP in 1998 was $39,983—which surpasses even Japan's—while the figure for the Slovak Republic stood at only $3,699. And within the South, Singapore's average income stood at $30,168, compared with only $145 in Sierra Leone. The differences in growth between them is also striking. Singapore's income grew by nearly $11,000 between 1993 and 1998, while Sierra Leone's grew a minuscule $5.

3. "Purchasing power parity" (PPP) is an index now often used by multilateral financial institutions that calculates the true rate of exchange among currencies when parity—when what can be purchased remains the same—is the same. The index measures what can be bought with a unit of each currency.

4. See Eberstadt (1991), Foster (1989), and Wattenberg (1989) for discussions of the security implications of demographic trends.

5. As in the advanced industrial societies of the North, military expenditures by Global South countries are sometimes justified on grounds that they produce economic benefits. As the *World Development Report 1988* points out, "military spending can have positive spinoff effects, such as fostering technological innovation, training personnel who later move into civilian work, providing employment opportunities, building domestic institutions, stimulating a country's tax effort, and promoting more intensive use of existing resources. Furthermore, military industries can be a focus of industrialization activities." However, the same report observes that their positive effects often are counterbalanced by long-term costs.

6. In addition to the original six, the EU includes Austria, Britain, Denmark, Finland, Greece, Ireland, Portugal, Spain, and Sweden.

7. Renegotiation of peacekeeping assessments was part of a larger effort on reforms of UN peacekeeping operations known as the Brahimi Report, named after Algerian Ambassador Lakhdar Brahimi who chaired the panel. The panel conducted a rigorous review of all aspects of UN peacekeeping operations in an effort to make them more efficient and effective. The report was released in August 2000.

8. With the new Bush administration's endorsement, Senator Helms in early 2001 introduced legislation in Congress that would release nearly $600 billion dollars in funds owed to the United Nations.

9. Goods other than drugs are also often traded illicitly. Among them are ozone-depleting chemicals (chlorofluorcarbons known as CFCs) used in refrigerants and other products that have been banned due to their adverse effects on the atmosphere's protective ozone layer and certain animal products, like ivory from elephant tusks. See French and Mastny (2001).

CHAPTER 7

The World Political Economy in Transition

Opportunities and Constraints in a Globalizing World Political Economy

It's our challenge to succeed as the first outward-looking, nonimperialist, continental superpower.

LAWRENCE H. SUMMERS,
U.S. SECRETARY OF THE TREASURY, 1999

[We will] work with our neighbors to build a Western Hemisphere of freedom and prosperity—a hemisphere bound together by shared ideals and free trade.

PRESIDENT GEORGE W. BUSH, 2001

"Propelled by a number of political, economic, and technological developments, the world has moved from the sharply divided international economy of the Cold War to an increasingly integrated global capitalist system. . . . Enormous increases in international trade, financial flows, and the activities of multinational corporations integrated more and more economies into the global economic system in a process now familiarly known as 'globalization.'" These concise yet prescient observations by political economist Robert Gilpin (2000) encapsulate the profound changes the world political economy has experienced in the past decade. We have moved beyond "interdependence." Today we live in a tightly integrated world political economy in which no state is immune from the economic challenges and changes other states face.

The United States sits center stage in the globalization process (compare Dunn 2001). As we discussed in Chapter 1, *globalization* refers to the rapid intensification and integration of state's economies not only in terms of markets but also ideas, information, and technology, which is having a profound impact on political, social, and cultural relations across borders. Symbolized by the Internet and fueled by the revolution in computers and telecommunications, its most visible manifestations are found in the global reach of Coca Cola and McDonald's, of shopping centers that look the same whether they are in London or Hong Kong, Chicago or Rio de Janeiro, of rock music and designer jeans that know no political boundaries, contributing to the development of a global culture in which national identities are often submerged. As a result of these processes, the U.S. economy and American values have penetrated virtually every corner of the world. Some states and peoples accept this. Others are resentful. Regardless, the American "gorilla" is not easily dismissed.

The nation's gigantic gross national product (GNP), now in excess of $8 trillion, overshadows that of all others. American output is close to thirty percent of all of the world's production of goods and services—nearly six times its proportion of world population. The consequence of the enormous size of the U.S. economy is that little can be done in the United States without repercussions abroad. Interest rates in the United States influence interest rates abroad; domestic inflation is shared elsewhere; the general health of the U.S. economy is a worldwide concern. Once it could be said that when the United States sneezes the rest of the world catches pneumonia. That is no longer true. What remains true is that "when the United States sneezes the rest of the world catches cold" (Cooper 1988). The global importance of the American economy stems from the international position of the U.S. dollar and the United States' dominant position in the global network of trade relationships. Dollars are used by governments and private investors as reserves and for international trade and capital transactions. Today some countries (for example, Ecuador and Panama) even use the dollar as their own currency. In 1999 the United States exported nearly $700 billion in merchandise to the rest of the world. And, remarkably, American consumers bought over $1 trillion in goods from other countries. Little wonder that access to the U.S. market—the largest in the world—is so valued by other countries and is a common talking point in U.S. trade negotiations with other states.

The dominance of the United States in the world political economy was even greater in the years immediately following World War II than it is today. In 1947 the country accounted for fifty percent of the gross world product. It also was the world's preeminent manufacturing center and was unchallenged as its leading exporter. For at least the next twenty-five years the United States enjoyed a preponderance of power and influence so great as to warrant the label **hegemon.** Although there is no commonly accepted definition of hegemony, political scientist Joshua Goldstein (1988) suggests "hegemony essentially consists of being able to dictate, or at least dominate, the rules and arrangements by which international relations, political and economic, are conducted."[1]

The atomic bomb symbolized the nation's awesome capabilities in the politico-military sphere, and remained largely unchallenged until the 1962 Cuban missile crisis. In the world political economy the United States derived its hegemonic status from a preponderance of material resources, of which four sets are especially important: control over markets, raw materials, and sources of capital, and a competitive advantage in the production of highly valued goods (Keohane 1984).

The enviable position the United States enjoyed in the early post–World War II years would inevitably change as Europe and Japan recovered from the ravages of war. By 1970 its proportion of gross world product had declined to about twenty-five percent. That would not have been especially worrisome had it not been accompanied by other developments. Although the U.S. proportion of gross world product stabilized, its share of both old manufactures ("sunset industries"), such as steel and automobiles, and new manufactures ("sunrise industries"), such as microelectronics and computers, continued to decline. Moreover, labor productivity in other countries often exceeded that in the United

States, where personal saving rates and levels of educational achievement also fell short of others' achievements. The United States' share of international financial reserves declined precipitously. And its dependence on foreign energy sources, first evident in the early 1970s, continued unabated for decades. Thus in all the areas essential to hegemony—control over raw materials, capital, and markets, and competitive advantages in production—American preponderance waned.

In this chapter we examine the role the United States has played in building and maintaining the *Liberal International Economic Order* the Western industrial nations created during and following World War II and have sought to maintain since. We also discuss the special responsibilities the United States exercises in the monetary and trade systems and how its changing power position has both affected and been affected by changes in the world political economy.

AMERICA'S HEGEMONIC ROLE IN THE LIBERAL INTERNATIONAL ECONOMIC ORDER: AN OVERVIEW

In 1944 the United States and its wartime allies met in the resort community of Bretton Woods, New Hampshire, to shape a new international economic structure. The lessons they drew from the Great Depression of the 1930s influenced their deliberations even as they continued their military contest with the Axis powers. The main lesson was that the United States could not safely isolate itself from world affairs as it had after World War I. Recognizing that, the United States now actively led in the creation of the rules and institutions that were to govern post–World War II economic relations. The *Liberal International Economic Order (LIEO)* was the product. The *Bretton Woods system,* as the LIEO is commonly called, promised to reduce barriers to the free flow of trade and capital, thus promoting today's tightly intertwined world political economy.

The postwar Liberal International Economic Order rested on three political bases: "the concentration of power in a small number of states, the existence of a cluster of important interests shared by those states, and the presence of a dominant power willing and able to assume a leadership role" (Spero 1990). Economic power was concentrated in the developed countries of Western Europe and North America. Neither Japan nor the Third World (today's Global South) posed an effective challenge to Western dominance, and the participation of the then-communist states of Eastern Europe and the Soviet Union in the international economy was limited. The concentration of power restricted the number of states whose agreement was necessary to make the system operate effectively.

The *shared interests* among these states that facilitated the operation of the system included a preference for an open economic system—one based on free trade—combined with a commitment to limited government intervention, if this proved necessary. Hence the term *liberal economic order* (see also Gilpin 1987).

The onset of the Cold War was a powerful force cementing Western cohesion on economic issues. Faced with a common external enemy, the Western nations thought economic cooperation as necessary not only for prosperity but also for security. The perception contributed to a willingness to share economic burdens. It also was an important catalyst for the assumption of leadership by only one state—the United States—and for the acceptance of that leadership role by others (see also Ikenberry 1989).

Economist Charles Kindleberger (1973) articulated the importance of leadership in maintaining a viable international economy. Kindleberger was among the first to theorize about the order and stability that preponderant powers provide as he sought to explain the Great Depression of the 1930s. He concluded that "the international economic and monetary system needs leadership, a country which is prepared, consciously or unconsciously, . . . to set standards of conduct for other countries; and to seek to get others to follow them, to take on an undue share of the burdens of the system, and in particular to take on its support in adversity." Britain played this role from the Congress of Vienna in 1815 until the outbreak of World War I in 1914; the United States assumed the British mantle in the decades immediately following World War II. In the interwar years, however, Britain was unable to play the role of leader. And the United States, although capable of leadership, was unwilling to exercise it. The vacuum, Kindleberger concluded, was a principal cause of the national and international economic traumas of the 1930s.

Hegemonic Stability Theory

Kindleberger's insights are widely regarded as a cornerstone of *hegemonic stability theory.* This theory contrasts sharply with political realism, which sees order and stability in the otherwise anarchical international political system as the product of power balances designed to thwart the aspirations of dominance-seeking states. Hegemonic stability theory, however, focuses on the role that the preponderant power of only one state—the hegemon—plays in stabilizing the system. It also captures the special roles and responsibilities of the major economic powers in a commercial order based on market forces.

From their vantage points as preponderant powers, hegemons may range from *benevolent* (most interested in general benefits for all) to *coercive* (more exploitative and self-interested). Either type is able to promote rules for the system as a whole. In general, capitalist hegemons, like Britain in the nineteenth century and the United States in the twentieth century, prefer open systems because their comparatively greater control of technology, capital, and raw materials gives them more opportunities to profit from a system free of nonmarket restraints. But capitalist hegemons also have special responsibilities. They must make sure that nations facing balance-of-payments deficits can find the credits necessary to

finance their deficits and otherwise lubricate the world political economy. If the most powerful states cannot do this, they themselves are likely to move toward more *closed* (protected or regulated) domestic economies, which may undermine the open (liberal) system otherwise advantageous to them. Hence, those most able to both benefit from and influence the system also have the greatest responsibility to ensure its effective operation.

As hegemons exercise their responsibilities they confer benefits known as public or *collective goods.* Collective goods are benefits everyone shares, as they cannot be excluded on a selective basis. National security is a collective good that governments provide all their citizens, regardless of the resources that individuals contribute through taxation. In international politics, "security, monetary stability, and an open international economy, with relatively free and predictable ability to move goods, services, and capital are all seen as desirable public goods. . . . More generally, international economic order is to be preferred to disorder" (Gill and Law 1988). States (like individuals) who enjoy the benefits of collective goods but pay little or nothing for them are *free riders.* Hegemons typically tolerate free riders, partly because the benefits they provide encourage other states to accept their dictates; thus both gain something.

All states worry about their *absolute power,* but hegemonic powers (especially benevolent ones) typically exhibit less concern about their relative power position than others. That is, they are less likely than others to "worry that a decrease in their power capabilities relative to those of other nation-states will compromise their political autonomy, expose them to the influence attempts of others, or lessen their ability to prevail in political disputes with allies and adversaries" (Mastanduno 1991). And they are less likely to behave defensively on international economic policy issues compared with an aspiring hegemon or with those that feel their relative power position deteriorating—hence hegemons' greater willingness to tolerate free riders. As a hegemon's preponderance erodes, however, its behavior on trade and monetary issues can be expected to change. Arguably this happened with the United States after the Cold War, explaining its growing unwillingness to tolerate free-riding by its allies in the absence of the glue that earlier cemented them together in a common, anticommunist, anti-Soviet cause (Mastanduno 1991).

Beyond Hegemony

Why does a hegemon's power decline? Is erosion inevitable, or is it the product of lack of foresight and ill-conceived policies at home and abroad? A variety of answers have been suggested. All suggest that what happens at home and abroad are tightly interconnected.

Growing concern about the United States' ability to continue its leadership role in international politics received national attention with the 1987 publication of historian Paul Kennedy's treatise, *The Rise and Fall of the Great Powers,* in which he wrote:

> Although the United States is at present still in a class of its own economically and perhaps even militarily, it cannot avoid confronting the two great tests which challenge the longevity of every major power that occupies the "number one" position in international affairs: whether it can preserve a reasonable balance between the nation's perceived defense requirements and the means it possesses to maintain those commitments; and whether . . . it can preserve the technological and economic bases of its power from relative erosion in the face of ever-shifting patterns of global production.

(KENNEDY 1987, 514–515)

The danger, which Kennedy called *imperial overstretch,* is similar to that faced by hegemonic powers in earlier periods—notably the Spanish at the turn of the seventeenth century and the British at the turn of the twentieth. "The United States now runs the risk," he warned, "that the sum total of [its] global interests and obligations is nowadays

far larger than the country's power to defend them all simultaneously." He reiterated that theme shortly after the United States and its coalition partners attacked Iraq in January 1991: "The theory of 'imperial overstretch' . . . rests upon a truism, that a power that wants to remain number one for generation after generation requires not just military capability, not just national will, but also a flourishing and efficient economic base, strong finances, and a healthy social fabric, for it is upon such foundations that the country's military strength rests in the long term" (Kennedy 1992).

Conservative critics argued *imperial overstretch* was a ruse designed to deprecate the defense-spending initiatives of the Reagan administration. The relationship between the health of the economy and American foreign policy is not easily dismissed, however. Indeed, a variety of commentators from both sides of the political spectrum would weigh in on the "declinist" argument, all saying that if the United States collapsed into a second-rate power, it would likely be for domestic, not foreign reasons (see Krauthammer 1991; Luttwak 1993; Nunn and Domenici 1992).

Still, the foreign dimension also could not easily be dismissed. Can the United States compete with Europe and Japan? Today the answer appears self-evident, as businesses and entrepreneurs have largely reengineered the U.S. economy with sophisticated technological advances, in turn producing dramatically increased productivity among American workers. Some, in fact, have spoken so glowingly about the "new economy" that they predicted the classical business cycles of the "old economy"—characterized by periods of prosperity and low unemployment followed inevitably by inflation resulting in rising unemployment and depressed economic activity— were now confined to the ashbin of history (see, for example, Weber 1997). Whether the "new economy" can withstand their own predictions coming out of the terrorist bombing remains to be seen, however.

Before the extended prosperity of the 1990s, others worried that the United States might not be able to compete with Europe, Japan, and others not just because of what happens at home but also because of the transnational processes that erode hegemonic power (see, for example, Thurow 1992). Success in maintaining an economic order based on free trade will itself eventually undermine the power of the preponderant state. "An open international economy facilitates the diffusion of the very leading-sector cluster and managerial technologies that constitute the hegemon's advantage. As its advantage erodes, the costs of maintaining collective goods that support an open economy begin to outweigh the benefits. The hegemon's commitment to free trade decays in the train" (Schwartz 1994). The growing cries for protection against foreign competition heard from domestic groups disadvantaged by free trade—voiced shrilly in the 1980s and again in Seattle, Washington, and Quebec in the 1990s as political leaders talked of further expanding the liberal economic order—reflect persistent doubts about free trade, placing pressure on the lead state to close the open economic order from which it otherwise benefits.

Empirical evidence that supports the central tenets of hegemonic stability theory remains inconclusive (see Isaak 1995; Schwartz 1994). The theory is not without critics. Still, as our discussion of the U.S. role in the management of the international monetary and trade systems will show, hegemonic stability theory provides important insight into the dynamics of America's opportunities and constraints in a rapidly globalizing world political economy.

AMERICA'S ROLE
IN THE MANAGEMENT
OF THE INTERNATIONAL
MONETARY SYSTEM

The agreements crafted at Bretton Woods in 1944 sought to build a postwar international monetary system characterized by stability, predictability, and orderly growth.[2] The wartime

allies created the *International Monetary Fund (IMF)* to assist states in dealing with such matters as maintaining stability in their financial inflows and outflows (their balance of payments) and *exchange rates* (the rate used by one nation to exchange its currency for another's). More generally, the IMF sought to ensure international monetary cooperation and the expansion of trade—a role, among others, that it continues to play as one of the most influential international organizations created during and after World War II. The wartime allies meeting at Bretton Woods also created the *World Bank*. Its charge was to assist in postwar reconstruction and development by facilitating the transnational flow of investment capital. Today, it is a principal means used to channel multilateral development assistance to the Global South.

In the immediate postwar years, however, the IMF and the World Bank proved unable to manage postwar economic recovery. They were given too little authority and too few resources to cope with the enormous economic devastation that Europe and Japan suffered during the war. The United States, now both willing and able to lead, stepped into the breach.[3]

Hegemony Unchallenged

The dollar became the key to the role that the United States assumed as manager of the international monetary system. Backed by a vigorous and healthy economy, a fixed relationship between gold and the dollar (the value of an ounce of gold was set at $35), and a government commitment to exchange gold for dollars at any time—known as *dollar convertibility*—the dollar became "as good as gold." In fact, it was better than gold for other countries to use to manage their balance-of-payments and savings accounts. Dollars, unlike gold, earned interest, incurred no storage or insurance costs, and were in demand elsewhere, where they were needed to buy goods necessary for postwar reconstruction. Thus the postwar economic system was not simply a modified gold standard system: It was a dollar-based system.

Bretton Woods obligated each country to maintain the value of its own national currency in relation to the U.S. dollar (and through it to all others) within the confines of the mutually-agreed exchange rate. Thus Bretton Woods was a *fixed exchange rate system.* In such a monetary system, governments maintain the value of their currencies at a fixed rate in relation to the currencies of other states. Governments in turn are required to intervene in the monetary market to preserve the value of their own currency by buying or selling others' currency.

Because the dollar was universally accepted, it became the vehicle for system preservation. Central banks in other countries either bought or sold U.S. dollars to raise or depress the value of their own currencies. Their purpose was to stabilize and render predictable the value of the monies needed to conduct international financial transactions.

A central problem of the immediate postwar years was how to get dollars into the hands of those who needed them most. One vehicle was the Marshall Plan, which provided Western European nations with $17 billion in assistance to buy the U.S. goods necessary to rebuild their war-torn economies. The United States also encouraged deficits in its own balance of payments as a way of providing *international liquidity* (reserve assets used to settle international accounts) in the form of dollars.

In addition to providing liquidity, the United States assumed a disproportionate share of the burden of rejuvenating Western Europe and Japan by supporting various forms of trade competitiveness and condoning discrimination against the dollar. It willingly incurred these short-run costs because the growth that they sought to stimulate in Europe and Japan was expected eventually to provide widening markets for U.S. exports.[4] The perceived political benefits of strengthening the Western World against the threat of communism helped to rationalize acceptance of these economic costs. In short, the United States purposely tolerated free riding by others. Everyone benefitted in this encouraging

environment. Europe and Japan recovered from the war and eventually prospered. The U.S. economy also prospered, as the outflow of U.S. dollars encouraged others to buy good and services from the United States (Spero and Hart 1997). Furthermore, the dollar's top currency role facilitated the ability of the United States to pursue a globalist foreign policy. Business interests could readily expand abroad because U.S. foreign investments were often considered desirable, and American tourists could spend their dollars with few restrictions. In effect, the United States operated as the world's banker. Other countries had to balance their financial inflows and outflows. In contrast, the United States enjoyed the advantages of operating internationally without the constraints of limited finances. Through the ubiquitous dollar, the United States came to exert considerable influence on the political and economic affairs of most other nations (Kunz 1997).

By the late 1950s concern mounted about the long-term viability of an international monetary system based on the dollar (see Triffin 1978–1979). Analysts worried about the ability of such a system to provide the world with the monetary reserves necessary to ensure continuing economic growth. They also feared that the number of foreign-held dollars would eventually overwhelm the American promise to convert them into gold on demand, undermining the confidence others had in the soundness of the dollar and the U.S. economy. In a sense, then, the dependence of the Bretton Woods system on the United States contained the seeds of it own destruction.

Hegemony under Stress

Too few dollars (lack of liquidity) was the problem in the immediate postwar years. Too many dollars became the problem in the 1960s, which led to pressure on the value of the dollar and to trade deficits. Eventually, American leaders took action to shift some of the costs of maintaining the international monetary system onto other industrialized countries in Europe and Asia.

Beginning in the 1960s, extensive American military activities, including the war in Vietnam, foreign economic and military aid, and massive private investments produced increasing balance-of-payments deficits. Although encouraged earlier, the deficits were now out of control. Furthermore, U.S. gold holdings fell precipitously relative to the growing number of foreign-held dollars, undermining the ability of the United States to guarantee dollar convertibility. In these circumstances, others lost confidence in the dollar, becoming less willing to hold it as a reserve currency for fear that the United States might devalue it. France, under the leadership of Charles de Gaulle, went so far as to insist on exchanging dollars for gold—although arguably for reasons related as much to French nationalism as to the viability of the U.S. economy.

Along with the glut of dollars, the increasing monetary interdependence of the world's industrial economies led to massive transnational movements of capital. The internationalization of banking, the internationalization of production via multinational corporations, and the development of currency markets outside direct state control all accelerated this interconnectedness—progenitors of the process we now call "globalization" (Keohane and Nye 2000). An increasingly complex relationship between the economic policies engineered in one country and their effects on another resulted.

Changes in the world political economy also helped to undermine Bretton Woods. By the 1960s the European and Japanese recoveries from World War II were complete, symbolized by their currencies' return to convertibility. Recovery meant that America's monetary dominance and the dollar's privileged position were increasingly unacceptable politically, while the return of convertibility meant that alternatives to the dollar (such as the German mark and Japanese yen) as a medium of savings and exchange were now available. The United States nonetheless continued to exercise a disproportionate influence over these other states, even while it was unreceptive to their criticisms of its foreign economic and national security policies (such as the war in Vietnam).

From its position as the preponderant state, the United States came to see its own economic health and that of the world political economy as one and the same. In the monetary regime in particular, American leaders treasured the dollar's status as the top currency and interpreted attacks on it as attacks on international economic stability. That view clearly reflected the interests and prerogatives of a hegemon. It did not reflect the reality of a world political economy in transition: "The fundamental contradiction was that the United States had created an international monetary order that worked only when American political and economic dominance in the capitalist world was absolute. . . . With the fading of the absolute dominance, the international monetary order began to crumble" (Block 1977).

The United States sought to stave off challenges to its leadership role, but its own deteriorating economic situation made that increasingly difficult. Mounting inflation—caused in part by the unwillingness of the Johnson administration to raise taxes to pay either for the Vietnam War or the Great Society at home—was particularly troublesome. As long as the value of others' currencies relative to the dollar remained fixed, the rising cost of goods produced in the United States reduced their relative competitiveness overseas. In 1971, for the first time in the twentieth century, the United States actually suffered a modest (extraordinarily modest by today's standards) trade deficit (of $2 billion), which worsened the next year. Predictably, demands grew from industrial, labor, and agricultural interests for protectionist trade measures designed to insulate them from foreign economic competition. Policy makers, correctly or not, laid partial blame for the trade deficit at the doorstep of major U.S. trading partners. The United States now sought aggressively to shore up its sagging position in the world political economy. In 1971 President Nixon abruptly announced that the United States would no longer exchange dollars for gold. He also imposed a surcharge on imports into the

United States as part of a strategy designed to force a realignment of others' currency exchange rates. These startling and unexpected decisions— which came as a shock to the other Western industrial nations, who had not been consulted— marked the end of the Bretton Woods regime.

With the price of gold no longer fixed and dollar convertibility no longer guaranteed, the Bretton Woods system gave way to a system of *free-floating exchange rates.* Market forces rather than government intervention were now expected to determine currency values. The theory underlying the system is that a country experiencing adverse economic conditions will see the value of its currency in the marketplace decline in response to the choices of traders, bankers, and businesspeople. This will make its exports cheaper and its imports more expensive, which in turn will pull the value of its currency back toward equilibrium—all without the need for central bankers to support their currencies. In this way it was hoped that the politically humiliating devaluations of the past could be avoided. However, policy makers did not foresee that the new system would introduce an unparalleled degree of uncertainty and unpredictability into international monetary affairs.

Hegemony in Decline

Hegemonic stability theory says that international economic stability is a collective good preponderant powers provide. As a hegemon's power wanes—as arguably the relative power of the United States did in the 1970s and 1980s— economic instability should follow. It did: Two *oil shocks* induced by the *Organization of Petroleum Exporting Nations (OPEC)* and the subsequent debt crisis faced by many Global South countries and others created a new sense of apprehension and concern about the viability of the existing international economic order. The United States, no longer able, or even willing, unilaterally to pay the costs of monetary stability, struggled to respond to challenges.

Coping with the OPEC Decade The first oil shock came in 1973–1974, shortly after the Yom Kippur War in the Middle East, when the price of oil increased fourfold. The second occurred in 1979–1980 in the wake of the revolution in Iran and resulted in an even more dramatic jump in the world price of oil. The impact of the two oil shocks on the United States, the world's largest energy consumer, was especially pronounced— all the more so as each coincided with a decline in domestic energy production and a rise in consumption. A dramatic increase in U.S. dependence on foreign sources of energy to fuel its advanced industrial economy and a sharp rise in the overall cost of U.S. imports resulted. As dollars flowed abroad to purchase energy resources (a record $40 billion in 1977 and $74 billion in 1980), U.S. foreign indebtedness, also known as "dollar overhang," grew enormously and became "undoubtedly the biggest factor in triggering the worst global inflation in history" (Triffin 1978–1979). Others now worried about the dollar's value—which augmented its marked decline on foreign exchange markets in the late 1970s and early 1980s, as illustrated in Figure 7.1.

Global economic recession followed each oil shock. Ironically, however, inflation persisted. *Stagflation*—a term coined to describe a stagnant economy accompanied by rising unemployment and high inflation—entered the lexicon of policy discourse. Moreover, the changing fortunes of the dollar in the early post–Bretton Woods monetary system reflected in part the way the leading industrial powers chose to cope with the two oil-induced recessions. In response to the first, they relied on fiscal and monetary adjustments to stimulate economic recovery and to avoid unemployment levels deemed politically unacceptable. In response to the second, which proved to be the longest and most severe economic downturn since the Great Depression of the 1930s, they shifted their efforts to controlling inflation through strict *monetarist policies* (that is, policies designed to reduce the money supply in the economy in order to control inflation). Large fiscal deficits and sharply higher interest rates

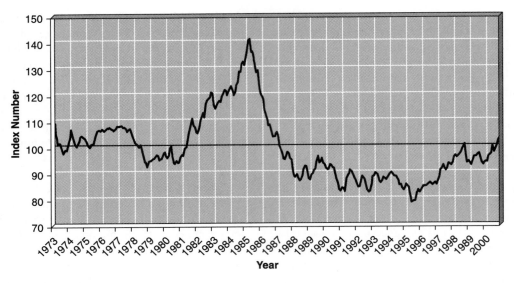

FIGURE 7.1 The Value of the Dollar, 1973–2000 (March 1973 = 100)

Note: The data are the *Major Currencies Index.* It is a weighted average of the foreign exchange values of the U.S. dollar against a subset of currencies in the broad index that circulate widely outside the country of issue. The weights are derived from those in the broad index. The *Broad Currencies Index* is a weighted average of the foreign exchange values of the U.S. dollar against the currencies of a large group of major U.S. trading partners. The index weights, which change over time, are derived from U.S. export shares and from U.S. and foreign import shares. For details, see Michael P. Leahy, 1998. "New Summary Measures of the Foreign Exchange Value of the Dollar," *Federal Reserve Bulletin* 84 (October 1998): 811–818.
Source: www.federalreserve.gov/releases/H10/Summary/

resulted. Both were particularly apparent in the United States. The other industrial nations also experienced higher levels of unemployment than they previously had been willing to tolerate. World inflation already was on the rise prior to the first oil shock and may have prompted OPEC's action, but rising oil prices accentuated inflationary pressures.

The Debt Crisis By the mid-1980s many Global South countries and others owed enormous debts to Western banks and governments. Because these debts were often denominated in dollars and the interest rates charged on them tied to rates in the lending countries, rising interest rates in the United States and elsewhere caused their debt obligations to ratchet upward, with devastating results. A "debt crisis" soon followed, leading to what effectively became the "debt decade" (Nowzad 1990).

The specific event that triggered the debt crisis was the threat in 1982 that Mexico would default on its loans. Like Mexico, others with the largest debts, including Poland, Argentina, and Brazil, required special treatment to keep them from going into default when they announced they did not have the cash needed to pay their creditors. Their plight was caused by heavy private and public borrowing during the 1970s, which caused private loans and investments and public loans at (nonconcessional) market rates to become more important than public foreign aid for all but the poorest of countries (Burki 1983).

The first oil shock gave impetus to the "privatization" of Global South capital flows. As dollars flowed from oil consumers in the West to oil producers in the Middle East and elsewhere, the latter—unable to invest all of their newfound wealth at home—"recycled" their petrodollars by investing in the industrial states, who were them-

---

FOCUS 7.1   How the IMF Works

The International Monetary Fund (IMF) and the World Bank—known as the Bretton Woods institutions—were established in 1944. The purpose of the IMF was to promote international monetary cooperation, exchange rate stability, and the expansion of international trade by acting as a lender of last resort when a member country faced an economic crisis.

In principle, the IMF has a structure akin to a financial cooperative. A member country's contributions to the IMF (called "quotas") are based on its weight in the global economy. This weight also determines its voting power and borrowing capacity (called "drawings"). Quotas amount to an exchange of assets with little direct cost to taxpayers. For instance, in the case of the United States, its contributions entitle it to an equal amount of U.S. claims on other currencies. That is, just as other countries can draw U.S. dollars from

the IMF in times of need (such as pressures on the U.S. dollar), the United States can draw on their currencies (be it the Japanese yen or the German mark) for itself. In fact, the United States has drawn on the IMF on twenty-eight different occasions. . . . By approaching the IMF, a member country facing a financial crisis has access to the fund's resources and advice. As a country's drawings become larger relative to its quotas, it must meet more exacting standards or "conditionalities," which typically mean significant changes in economic policies to ensure that the country's domestic and external deficits are drastically lowered or even eliminated. Failure to meet those conditions results in suspension, renegotiation, or even cancellation of the program.

SOURCE: Devesh Kapur. "The IMF: A Cure or A Curse?" *Foreign Policy* 111 (Summer 1998): 116.

---

selves the largest consumers of oil. In the process the funds available to private banks for lending to others increased substantially (see Spiro 1999).

Many of the non–oil-exporting developing nations became the willing consumers of the private banks' investment funds. The fourfold rise in oil prices induced by the OPEC cartel hit these nations particularly hard. To pay for the sharply increased cost of oil along with their other imports, many chose to borrow from abroad to sustain their economic growth and pay for needed imports. Private banks were willing lenders, as they believed *sovereign risk*—the risk that governments might default—was virtually nonexistent, while the returns on their investments in the Global South were higher than in the industrial world. For several reasons, however, the debtor nations found repayment of their loans increasingly difficult. Rising interest rates were the most important factor. Sovereign risk suddenly became an ominous reality.

The IMF assumed a leadership role in securing debt relief for many debtor countries, thus keeping them from defaulting on their loans, but

it did so at the cost of imposing strict conditions for domestic reform on individual debtors. Included were programs designed to curb inflation, limit imports, restrict public spending, expose protected industries, and the like. It also typically urged those it helped to increase their exports, meaning it sought an *export-led adjustment* to the debt problem.

The IMF austerity program—vigorously pushed with strong U.S. backing until 1985—could claim considerable success from a strictly financial viewpoint (see Amuzegar 1987), but its domestic burdens and political costs simply proved overwhelming (Sachs 1989). Analysts blamed *IMF conditionality* for the overthrow of the Sudanese government of President Jaafar Nimeri in 1985, for example. (See Focus 7.1). Debt and related financial issues also inflamed domestic political conflict in many other heavily indebted countries, including Argentina, Brazil, Chile, Mexico, and Nigeria. All of this encouraged political leaders in the debtor countries to adopt a more defiant posture toward the predicament they faced (see the essays in Riley 1993).[5]

In this emotionally charged atmosphere the United States first adopted an arm's-length policy on the debt issue, refusing to perform the hegemon's classic stabilizer role due to its ideological antipathy toward intervention in the marketplace (Grieve 1993). Eventually, however, it would offer different plans designed to defuse a financial crisis with potentially catastrophic global proportions. Still, in the mid-1990s it would again find it necessary to arrange with the IMF a financial bailout of the Mexican economy due to a currency crisis there. Later in the decade it would seek to stimulate its own economy as a way of coping with a series of roiling Asian currency crises that plunged as much as forty percent of the world into recession, and which again required several multi-billion dollar bailouts. Even today, more than two decades after the onset of the "debt crisis" of the early 1980s, debt relief remains a primary issue on the North-South global agenda.

Toward Macroeconomic Policy Coordination

The Reagan administration's initiatives in dealing with debt crisis marked an abrupt end to what had been its *passive unilateralism*—commonly referred to as "benign neglect"—toward international monetary and macroeconomic policy issues. Passive unilateralism now gave way to various manifestations of *pluralistic cooperation* (Bergsten 1988). The latter was especially evident in the 1985 Plaza Agreement for coping with the soaring dollar. American efforts thus began to stress more multilateral coordination to shore up the international monetary system, but largely failed in the face of often competing national interests as well as powerful domestic pressures.

Passive Unilateralism, 1981–1985 The increase in U.S. interest rates which so burdened the Global South debtor countries in the early to mid-1980s also contributed to the changing fortunes of the dollar (see Figure 7.1). Deficit spending by the federal government contributed to

rising interest rates, as the United States itself now borrowed in capital markets to cover military and other expenditures. Beyond this, three other factors helped to restore faith in the dollar: renewed economic growth in the United States; a sharp reduction in inflation (both stimulated by a decline in oil prices caused by a global oil glut); and the perception that the United States was a safe haven for financial investments in a world otherwise marked by political instability and violence. Foreign investors therefore rushed to acquire the dollars necessary to take advantage of profitable investment opportunities in the United States. This situation contrasted sharply with the 1970s, when the huge foreign indebtedness of the United States was a principal fear.

The appreciation of the dollar was a mixed blessing for the United States. It reduced the cost of imported oil (whose price first eased and then plummeted in 1986), but it increased the cost of U.S. exports to foreign buyers, thus reducing the competitiveness of American products in overseas markets. This meant the loss of tens of thousands of jobs in industries that produced for export. A series of record trade deficits followed—$160 billion in 1987 alone—as imports became relatively cheaper and hence more attractive to American consumers.

The federal budget deficit also reached record portions at this time, topping $200 billion annually. Simultaneously, the United States became a debtor nation for the first time in more than a half-century, as it moved in only five years from being the world's biggest creditor to being its largest debtor. The debt legacy would eventually constrain the government's policy choices in dealing with later economic downturns, as happened with the prolonged recession of 1990 to 1992. It also raised the prospect of a long-term decline in Americans' unusually high standard of living, as money spent tomorrow to pay today's bills would not be available to meet future problems or finance future growth. By 1991 interest payments on the national debt (the accumulation of past deficits) constituted fourteen percent of all federal outlays, the third largest category of expenditures (following entitlements and defense spending). Within a few years interest payments were projected to exceed defense spending (Nunn and Domenici 1992). Not until the economy turned around and the annual budget deficits reversed in the mid-to-late 1990s would Americans begin to actually pay down the long-accumulating national debt.

In a normally functioning market, the combination of a strong dollar and severe trade imbalance would set in motion self-corrective processes that would return the dollar to its equilibrium value. Growing U.S. imports, for example—though beneficial to America's trade partners in generating jobs and thus stimulating their return to economic growth—should create upward pressure on the value of others' currencies. Conversely, a drop in American exports should ease the demand for dollars, thereby reducing the dollar's value in exchange markets. These mechanisms did not work, however, because of persistently high interest rates in the United States.

Pluralistic Cooperation, 1985–1988 Historically, the United States had been loath to intervene in the international marketplace to affect the value of the dollar. By 1985, however, the erosion of American trade competitiveness in overseas markets due to the overvalued dollar had become domestically unpalatable. In response, the *Group of Five (G-5)* (the United States, Britain, France, Japan, and West Germany) met secretly in the Plaza Hotel in New York and decided on a coordinated effort to bring down the dollar's value. The landmark agreement also committed the major economic powers to work with one another to manage exchange rates internationally and interest rates domestically. And it signaled the emergence of Japan as a full partner in international monetary management (Spero and Hart 1997), which led to the formation of the *Group of Seven,* commonly called the **G-7** (the G-5 plus Canada and Italy).

When the Plaza agreement failed, the industrialized states sought other ways to manage their currencies, but the important goal of macroeconomic policy coordination remained unfulfilled (see Mead 1988–1989, 1989). The United States' inability to devise a politically acceptable budget-deficit reduction strategy was a critical factor in its failure. Eventually, however, the chronic trade and budget deficits became overwhelming, helping to precipitate the dollar's long slide from the lofty heights it had achieved by mid-decade (see Figure 7.1).

The Failure of Pluralistic Cooperation, 1989–1993 After the Bush administration assumed power in 1989, it showed little enthusiasm for multilateral venues for dealing with economic policy issues. Instead, it was content to permit the dollar to fall to levels believed by some experts to have been below its actual purchasing power—a policy akin to the "benign neglect" of Reagan's first term.

Maintaining a weak dollar was designed to enhance the competitiveness of U.S. exports in overseas markets, but it also attracted renewed concern about economic fundamentals in the United States.[6] Simultaneously, U.S. dependence on foreign energy sources again grew to ominous proportions, contributing not only to the trade deficit but also to the nation's vulnerability to oil-supply or price disruptions caused by some kind of crisis—which struck in August 1990 when Iraq invaded Kuwait. Ominously, perhaps, the value of the dollar in the international marketplace declined sharply in the early weeks of the Persian Gulf crisis. Normally a country viewed as a "safe haven" for investments during times of crisis will see the value of its currency appreciate. This had been the United States' typical role. In the Persian Gulf case, however, investors concluded Europe and Japan were better bets. While the Bush administration practiced passive unilateralism toward the dollar, Germany's central bank—the Bundesbank—maintained high interest rates in an aggressive effort to contain inflationary pressures generated by the cost of unifying the former East and West Germanies. Mimicking the effects on the dollar during Reagan's first term, the mark's value soared as investors now chose to hold marks rather than dollars; this further weakened a dollar already suffering from the effects of recession at home.

The dollar was dealt another blow by the Bush administration when the president proclaimed at the 1992 Republican nominating convention that the budget agreement he had worked out with Congress in 1990 to cope with the federal budget deficit was a mistake he would not repeat. Renewed fear about further growth in the already burgeoning deficit caused the dollar to plunge even further. Almost simultaneously a currency crisis in Europe—stimulated again by German monetary policy—threatened the European Union's European Monetary System, a semifixed exchange rate system established in 1979 which sought to create a "zone of monetary stability" (Spero and Hart 1997) among Europe's currencies as a precursor to a single European currency.

As in the monetary crises of the 1960s and 1970s, existing mechanisms of macroeconomic policy coordination proved ineffective. Even the G–7, which had begun to hold annual economic summits (and now includes Russia, making it the *Group of Eight [G–8]*) proved inadequate "as a mechanism for synchronizing economic policy to exert leadership over the world economy" (Ikenberry 1993). Its failure (which continues) stems from "the inability of the major industrial states to make hard economic choices at home. Each government's emphasis on dealing with seemingly intractable domestic problems . . . constrains joint efforts to stimulate global economic growth or to manage monetary and trade relations, preventing G–7 governments from pursuing disciplined and synchronized fiscal and monetary policies" (Ikenberry 1993; see also Smyser 1993).

Hegemony Resurgent

By the end of the 1990s world leaders would again be talking about new ways to manage the international monetary system. The Asian currency crises of 1997 to 1998 were the principal catalysts, but, as before, as the twenty-first century approached, macroeconomic policy coordination among the world's largest economic powers remained an elusive goal. For the United States, however, the 1990s became the longest period of sustained economic growth in its history. Still, the renewed strength of the American economy did not translate into a restoration of international economic stability, nor did it restore the American leadership of the 1950s and 1960s.

Clinton's First Term Bill Clinton went to Washington determined to be the "economic president." Although verbally committed to a greater degree of multilateral policy making than the Bush team, the Clinton team continued the policy of benign neglect toward the sagging dollar—this time as a mechanism of righting the trade imbalance between the United States and Japan. But there was no noticeable effect on U.S. trade with Japan—indeed, the deficit persisted despite several years in which the dollar was comparatively weak. Finally, in May 1994, the administration reversed course as it coordinated a massive, sixteen-nation intervention into currency markets in an effort to prop up the sagging dollar. Additional interventions followed.

Although the Clinton administration abandoned its policy of benign neglect, its efforts to halt a further decline in the dollar fell short. The causes of the sagging dollar, which weakened against the German mark and reached postwar lows against the Japanese yen, were baffling, as the U.S. economy was generally sound and growing, conditions that normally would cause the value of a currency to rise. Arguably globalization was an underlying cause. The growing volume of world trade and the activities of currency speculators, who use sophisticated electronic means to carry out their transnational exchanges, could already significantly affect national currency values in the early 1990s. Over $1.5 trillion in currency trading occurs each day. This exceeds the total value of foreign exchange held in countries' central banks (*New York Times*, 25 September 1992, 1; *Washington Post National Weekly Edition*, 1 March 1999, 7).

Some cited the continuing trade and government budget deficits as the causal factors. Others saw the Clinton administration's policies and performance as the primary culprit. As one senior Clinton adviser explained, "The value of the dollar on any given day is like a global referendum on all the policies of the Clinton administration combined. It is as though the world were having a huge discussion on the Internet, and the dollar's value is a snapshot of that discussion." Still others suggested that the problem lay not with the dollar but with the yen. What the Japanese called *endaka* (strong yen crisis) was, according to this reasoning, propelled by the imbalance of Japan's financial transactions with the rest of the world, leading to increased demand for the yen and hence its higher price.

Clinton's Second Term   Over the long-term, states' economic health affects the value of their currencies. During the 1990s the U.S. economy thrived, Japan's fell into a prolonged recession (see Gilpin 2000), and Europeans and others worried that the European Union's planned launch of a single European currency, the euro, would create uncertainty about the future—especially so since the German mark, Europe's top currency, would disappear.

Collectively, these forces contributed to a strong revival of the dollar. By the end of the decade it was priced at levels last seen in 1986 (see Figure 7.1). Now others' concern was not so much a weak dollar, but a strong dollar. Japan, for instance, would benefit from a strong dollar, because Japanese exporters could keep their prices low compared with American producers and thus compete for a greater share of the U.S. market. And, indeed, U.S. imports surged in the 1990s, as Americans consumed foreign-produced goods and services at breathtaking, record levels (over $1 trillion, in 1999, for example). Still, the Japanese worried that the soaring dollar would cause Japanese investors to invest not in Japan, which was seeking to stimulate its own economy with low interest rates, but in the United States, which promised much greater investment returns. Eu-

ropean investors uncertain about the euro also looked once more to the United States as a safe investment haven. Again, foreign investments in the United States surged during the 1990s, especially in domestic stock markets, which experienced unparalleled capitalization growth.

Clinton's Secretary of the Treasury, Robert Rubin, unrelentingly supported the dollar as its value surged. "A strong dollar is in the interest of the United States," he said repeatedly. But domestically, not everyone agreed. As in the 1980s, a strong dollar hurts American firms that produce for export by making them less competitive. U.S. automakers in particular worried that the gains in domestic market share they had made through quality improvements and substantial investments in plant and equipment would once more be eroded by foreign competition. Thus it is not surprising that labor unions and other workers were visible in the anti-globalization protests at recent meetings of the IMF, World Bank, World Trade Organization, and the 2001 Summit of the Americas, where the second Bush administration hoped to launch a hemisphere-wide free trade zone.

American consumers, on the other hand, generally benefit from a strong dollar. Tourists get more value for their money when they travel abroad. At home, foreign-produced goods are cheaper, which in turn makes them attractive to consumers. Lower-priced imports also help to keep inflation low, as domestic producers are unable to increase prices.

So what is the "proper" value of the dollar? There is no clear-cut answer to that question. There are winners and losers domestically. And there are winners and losers in other countries. Globalization has added to that uncertainty, as the currency crises of 1997 to 1998 demonstrated.

Globalization Again

Alan Greenspan, chair of the Federal Reserve System, remarked in testimony before Congress in the mid-1990s that the ability of the Federal Reserve System to prop up the dollar by buying it in foreign exchange markets "is extraordinarily limited and probably in a realistic sense nonexistent." The internationalization of finance and the removal of barriers to transnational capital flows also have, in Greenspan's words, "[exposed] national economies to shocks from new and unexpected sources, with little if any lag." They came with a vengeance later in the decade, as the globalization of finance led to an era of "mad money" largely outside the control of governments (Strange 1998).

The Asian Financial Crisis The susceptibility of states to global financial shocks became painfully obvious during exchange rate crises in Central and South American, in East Asia, and in Russia at various times during the 1990s. These crises not only destabilized the economies of the immediately affected countries, but also sent shock waves throughout the entire world economy. Indeed, the crises that pummeled East Asia, Latin America, and Russia toward the end of the decade were often cited as posing the most serious challenge to global economic stability since the Great Depression of the 1930s. The utility of the international institutions created after World War II now also came under close scrutiny.

The crisis began in Thailand, an attractive investment opportunity among the Asian NIEs. *New York Times* foreign economic correspondent Thomas L. Friedman describes what happened:

> On the morning of December 8, 1997, the government of Thailand announced that it was closing fifty-six of the country's fifty-eight top finance houses. Almost overnight, these private banks had been bankrupted by the crash of the Thai currency, the baht. The finance houses had borrowed heavily in U.S. dollars and lent those dollars out to Thai businesses for the building of hotels, office blocks, luxury apartments, and factories. The finance houses all thought they were safe because the Thai government was committed to keeping the Thai baht at a fixed rate against the dollar. But when the government failed to do so, in the wake of massive global speculation against the baht—triggered by a daring awareness that the Thai economy was not a strong as previously believed—the Thai currency plummeted by thirty percent. This meant that businesses that had borrowed dollars had to come up with thirty percent more Thai baht to pay back each one dollar of loans. Many businesses couldn't pay the finance houses back, many finance houses couldn't repay their foreign lenders and the whole system went into gridlock, putting 20,000 white-collar employees out of work.
>
> (FRIEDMAN 1999, IX; SEE ALSO LEWIS 1998)

These processes would soon be repeated elsewhere in Asia, then Latin America and Russia.

With the support of the United States (which, as we noted earlier, reduced its own interest rates to stimulate economic recovery elsewhere), the IMF stepped forward to help the ailing economies in Asia and elsewhere—but with the expectation they would follow IMF advice on reforms that could prevent recurrence of the financial collapses. The IMF itself became the object of criticism for not having foreseen the impending debacle (see, for example Kapur 1998).

Part of the controversy surrounding the IMF concerns what is often described as the *moral hazard* problem (Kapstein 1999). The term refers to the willingness of private investors to make risky choices when investing in emerging markets based on their expectation that the IMF or someone else (the United States?) will bail them out if the countries in which they invest face economic instability or, worse, collapse. In short, if private investors are protected from failure by public authorities, they are likely to take higher risks (with other people's money) than would otherwise be warranted. In the end, the public (taxpayers) foots the bill for private investors' failed choices, who in effect bear none of the costs of failure.

Toward a New Financial Architecture? The Asian contagion and the criticism of the IMF that followed spurred widespread negotiations among policy makers about how to create a new financial architecture. At the level of states, policy makers and scholars debated the wisdom of *dollarization*. Dollarization proposes that other countries abandon their own currencies and adopt the U.S. dollar for all of their financial transactions. Some argue that by adopting the dollar as their own as Ecuador did, others can avoid the unsettling swings in currency values that inevitably seem to plague weaker currencies (and weaker economies) (see, for example, Hausmann 1999). Others counter that this would make other states' economies subject to monetary policies in the United States dictated by the Federal Reserve Board not on the basis of their welfare, but on economic considerations in the United States. Hence "dollarization is an extreme solution to market instability, applicable in only the most extreme cases. The opposite approach—a flexible exchange rate between the national currency and the dollar—is much more prudent for most developing countries" (Sachs and Larrain 1999).

At the international level, various proposals for reform were made, ranging from scuttling the IMF, to improving private and public financial institutions in developing countries and other emerging markets, to simply generating better data on economic conditions. The last alternative is sometimes called "transparency" (see Florini 1998), which means providing open information akin to what financial analysts call "market efficiency" when they talk about access to information about publically traded stocks and bonds.

Treasury Secretary Robert Rubin became heavily involved in discussions about a new financial architecture and a leading spokesperson for transparency. Others were vocal in their antagonism toward the IMF. "Led by the unlikely team of former Secretary of State George Shultz, former Treasury Secretary William Simon, and former Citicorp chairman Walter Wriston, the IMF's critics call the organization 'ineffective, unnecessary, and obsolete.' They claim that 'it is the IMF's promise of massive intervention that has spurred a global meltdown of financial markets'" (Kapstein 1999).

In the end, changing the system proved too difficult.[7] Even Rubin conceded there are "no easy answers and no magic wands for overhauling financial institutions to make the world safe for capitalism." Paraphrasing a famous remark by Winston Churchill about democracy, Rubin also surmised that "the floating exchange rate system is the worst possible system, except for all others."

Although the IMF weathered the storm, it remains jostled in the rough sea that marks a world political economy in transition. Early in the new Bush administration, Treasury Secretary Paul O'Neil said the agency must do more to prevent, not simply respond to, crises. In his words, "I envision that the IMF, while sharpening its ability to respond to financial disruptions swiftly and appropriately, does so less frequently because it has succeeded in preventing crises from developing in the first place."

As its largest financial contributor, the United States is in a position to nudge the IMF toward reform. Indeed, responding to U.S. concerns, the IMF policy-setting committee declared in April 2001 that "strong and effective crisis preventions" should be a top priority of the fund. Although critical of the current practices of the organization, it is noteworthy that the new Bush administration did not call for its abolition. Perhaps it is heeding the opinions of those who believe the role of the IMF cannot be minimized. In the words of one analyst, "should the IMF fade into irrelevance, new institutions to stabilize the world economy will be needed" (Kapstein 1999).

AMERICA'S ROLE IN THE MANAGEMENT OF THE INTERNATIONAL TRADE SYSTEM

The volume and value of international trade have increased exponentially during the past half century. Over this period states have vacillated between erecting barriers to trade designed to meet their domestic economic goals and opening their borders to realize the benefits that free trade promises.

Globalization is a product of the vanishing borders free trade implies, but it also has provoked increasingly vocal criticism in the United States and elsewhere among people and groups who believe the costs of globalization outweigh its benefits. Some states also worry, as during the Asian currency crisis, that globalization threatens their sovereign prerogatives (see also Chapter 6). Thus, ironically, the very success of the LIEO and its open, multilateral trade regime has stimulated the backlash that encourages its closure.

An Overview of the International Trade Regime

Management responsibilities in the postwar economic system as envisaged at Bretton Woods were to have been entrusted not only to the IMF and the World Bank but also to an International Trade Organization (ITO), whose purpose was to lower restrictions on trade and set rules of commerce. Policy planners hoped that these three organizations could assist in avoiding repetition of the international economic catastrophe that followed World War I.

In particular, the zero-sum, *beggar-thy-neighbor policies* associated with the intensely competitive economic nationalism of the interwar period were widely regarded as a major cause of the economic catastrophe of the 1930s, which ended in global warfare. (Beggar-thy-neighbor policies are efforts by one country to reduce its unemployment through currency devaluations, tariffs, quotas, export subsidies, and other strategies that enhance domestic welfare by promoting trade surpluses that can only be realized at another's expense.) Thus priority was assigned to *trade liberalization,* which means removing barriers to trade, particularly tariffs. Implementing this essential objective was to have been ITO's charge, but it was stillborn, as its charter became so watered down by other countries' demands for exemptions from the generalized rules that Congress re-

fused to approve it. In its place, the United States sponsored the *General Agreement on Tariffs and Trade (GATT).* Although initially designed as a provisional arrangement, GATT became the cornerstone of the liberalized trading scheme originally embodied in the ITO.

Trade liberalization was to occur through the mechanism of free and unfettered international trade, of which the United States has been a strong advocate for half a century. Free trade rests on the *normal-trade-relations (NTR)* principle, until recently known as the *most-favored-nation (MFN)* principle. Both principles say that the tariff preferences granted to one nation must be granted to all others exporting the same product. The principle ensures equality in a state's treatment of its trade partners. Thus *nondiscrimination* is a central norm of the trade regime.

Under the aegis of GATT and the most-favored-nation principle, states undertook a series of multilateral trade negotiations, called "rounds," aimed at reducing tariffs and resolving related issues. The eighth and most recent session, the Uruguay Round, completed in 1993, replaced GATT with a new *World Trade Organization (WTO),* thus resurrecting the half-century-old vision of a global trade organization "with teeth." The excruciatingly long, often contentious Uruguay negotiations reflected increasing strain on the liberal trading regime, particularly as states moved beyond the goal of tariff reduction to confront more ubiquitous and less tractable forms of *new protectionism* that have become widespread.[8] *Nontariff barriers* are among the most ubiquitous.

Nontariff barriers (NTBs) to trade cover a wide range of government regulations that have the effect of reducing or distorting international trade, including health and safety regulations, restrictions on the quality of goods that may be imported, government procurement policies, domestic subsidies, and antidumping regulations (designed to prevent foreign producers from selling their goods for less abroad than they cost domestically).[9] NTBs comprise one of several new protectionist challenges to the principle of free trade often called **neomercantilist** challenges. (**Neomercantilism** is state intervention in economic affairs to enhance national economic fortunes. More precisely, it is "a trade policy whereby a state seeks to maintain a balance-of-trade surplus and to promote domestic production and employment by reducing imports, stimulating home production, and promoting exports" (Walters and Blake 1992). Neomercantilist practices have assumed greater prominence in American foreign economic policy in recent decades. They are also evident in other countries, as witnessed by the concern among America's trade partners about the consequences of genetically engineered agricultural products, of which the United States is the leading exporter (see Paarlberg 2000).

Hegemony Unchallenged

The United States was the principal stimulant to all eight multilateral negotiating sessions designed to reduce trade barriers. From the end of World War II until at least the 1960s, it also willingly accepted fewer immediate benefits than its trading partners in anticipation of the longer-term benefits of freer international trade. In effect, the United States was the locomotive of expanding world production and trade. By stimulating its own growth, the United States became an attractive market for others' exports, and the outflow of dollars stimulated their economic growth as well. Evidence supports the wisdom of this strategy: As the average duty levied on imports to the United States declined by more than half between the late 1940s and the early 1960s, world exports nearly tripled.

On the Periphery in the Global South Not all shared in the prosperity of the U.S.-backed LIEO. Many states in the emerging Global South failed to grow economically or otherwise to share in the benefits of economic liberalism. Instead, their economies remained closely tied to their former colonizers. Holdovers from the imperial period of the late 1800s, time-worn trade patterns perpetuated unequal exchanges that did little to break the newly independent nations out of the yoke of their colonial past. Thus the developing states on the periphery[10] were largely irrelevant as the new economic order emerged. They enjoyed too little power to shape effectively the rules of the game, which nonetheless seriously affected their own well-being.

The Second World The Soviet Union and its socialist allies in Eastern Europe were also outside the decision-making circle—but largely by choice. During World War II, Western planners anticipated the Soviet Union's participation in the postwar international economic system, just as they originally anticipated Soviet cooperation in maintaining the postwar political order. But enthusiasm for establishing closer economic ties between East and West began to wane once the war ended. 1947 was the critical year, as President Truman then effectively committed the United States to an anticommunist foreign policy strategy and Secretary of State George Marshall committed the United States to aid the economic recovery of Europe. Although American policy makers thought the Soviet Union might participate in the Marshall Plan, much of the congressional debate over the plan was framed in terms of the onslaught of communism—rhetoric that certainly did not endear the recovery program to Soviet policy makers.

Furthermore, Soviet leaders were determined to pursue a policy of economic autarky that would eliminate any dependence on other countries. Thus they rejected the offer of American aid. They also refused to permit Eastern European countries to accept Marshall Plan assistance. Thereafter East and West developed essentially separate economic systems which excluded one another. Meanwhile, the United States moved to exclude the communist countries from most-favored-nation trade treatment. With its allies, it also restricted exports of goods that might bolster Soviet military capabilities or those of its allies, thus threatening Western security. Many would remain in place until they began to be dismantled in the 1990s (see Cupitt 2000).

Hegemony under Stress

Domestically, four major statutes (as amended) have framed the U.S. approach to international trade issues and the multilateral negotiations that flowed from them: (1) the Reciprocal Trade Agreements Act of 1934; (2) the Trade Expansion Act of 1962; (3) the Trade Act of 1974; and (4) the Omnibus Trade and Competitiveness Act of 1988. Beginning in 1974 and reaffirmed until 1994, Congress (is responsible under the Constitution for trade policy) also granted the president *fast-track authority* to negotiate trade agreements with other countries.

Fast-track authority does not guarantee that Congress will approve a trade agreement negotiated by the president, but it does promise that Congress will consider the agreement in a timely fashion and will either vote it up or down, without making any amendments.[11] Presidents for two decades found fast-track procedures to their liking, but in 1994 Congress permitted that authority to expire. Clinton sought to renew it in 1997 in an effort to move beyond Nafta toward a hemispheric-wide *Free Trade Area of the Americas (FTAA)*. "At issue," Clinton argued with some justification, "is America's leadership and credibility in the eyes of our competitors." Nonetheless, Congress rebuffed him. A year later Republican Speaker of the House of Representatives Newt Gingrich would again seek to renew that authority, and again Congress refused. By this time labor and environmental interests had become outspoken critics of the costs of free trade stimulated by globalization (Destler 1999), as we will discuss more fully later. Interestingly, President Bush would later ask for the same authority from the Republican Congress that it denied Clinton, also with the intent of creating a Free Trade Area of the Americas.

The European Union The Kennedy Round of negotiations in the mid-1960s marked the high point of the movement toward a liberalized trade regime. The negotiations grew out of the 1962 Trade Expansion Act. The rhetoric surrounding the act's passage cloaked trade liberalization in the mantle of national security, and the act itself was described as an essential weapon in the Cold War struggle with Soviet communism. Nonetheless, it was motivated in part by concern for maintaining U.S. export markets in the face of growing economic competition from the European Economic Community (EEC). It specifically granted the president broad power to negotiate tariff rates with EEC members.

Today, as during most of the past quarter century, the *European Union (EU),* of which the EEC is a progenitor, figures prominently in U.S. trade policy. With Canada, Japan, and, most recently, Mexico, it is among the most important U.S. trade partners (see Figure 7.2). Although the United States has officially supported European efforts to create an integrated economic union, transatlantic relations have not always been smooth, as the devil is in the details. Agricultural issues have proved especially vexing.

The Kennedy Round made progress on industrial tariffs, to the point that by 1975, when the Tokyo Round began, the United States and the European Community had reduced tariff rates on industrial products to negligible levels; but on the important question of agricultural commodities little headway was made. Although agricultural trade fell beyond the purview of GATT as originally conceived, it became a matter of growing importance to the United States. Europe's *Common Agricultural Policy (CAP)* posed the immediate challenge. Initiated in 1966—and still a centerpiece of EU policy—CAP was (is) a protectionist tariff wall designed to maintain politically acceptable but artificially high prices for farm products produced within the European Community. That curtailed American agricultural exports to the region. The lack of progress and later disagreements on this issue began to raise doubts among American policy makers about the wisdom of promoting expansionist economic policies from which others benefitted. Even today, agricultural issues remain among the

Exports

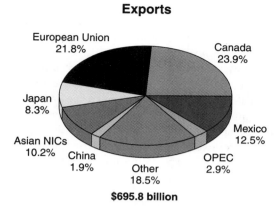

Canada 23.9%
European Union 21.8%
Japan 8.3%
Asian NICs 10.2%
China 1.9%
Other 18.5%
OPEC 2.9%
Mexico 12.5%

$695.8 billion

Imports

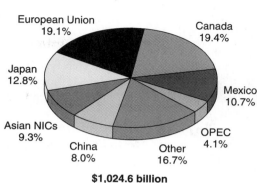

Canada 19.4%
European Union 19.1%
Japan 12.8%
Asian NICs 9.3%
China 8.0%
Other 16.7%
OPEC 4.1%
Mexico 10.7%

$1,024.6 billion

FIGURE 7.2 U.S. Trade Partners, 1999

Source: Adapted from U.S. Bureau of the Census
www.census.gov/foreign-trade/Press-Release/99_press_release
Accessed April 28, 2001.

most troublesome in U.S.-EU trade relations. By the time the Tokyo Round commenced in 1975, trade negotiators found themselves in a radically different environment from that of the previous GATT sessions. Trade volume had grown exponentially worldwide, economic interdependence among the world's leading industrial powers had reached unprecedented levels, tariffs were no longer the principal barriers to trade, and the United States was no longer an unfaltering economic giant. In this new environment, reducing barriers to the free flow of agricultural products and coping with nontariff barriers to trade received increased emphasis.

A measure of success was achieved on NTBs. No progress was made on agriculture, however. This shortcoming "probably more than any other single factor . . . helped to undermine the integrity and credibility of the trading system" (Low 1993). Thus, in the years between the end of the Tokyo Round and the beginning of the Uruguay Round, GATT's rules seemed increasingly irrelevant to state practices. Protectionism in violation of the principle of nondiscrimination became increasingly rife. Growing concern about the challenge of the more economically advanced developing nations was also apparent.

Challenge from the Global South As noted earlier, the postwar international monetary and multilateral trading systems evolved primarily under the aegis of the Western industrial states, whose interests and objectives they served. Developing countries on the periphery were largely outside the privileged circle. Many came to view the existing international economic structure as a cause of their underdog status. Their challenge was especially vigorous in the immediate aftermath of the first OPEC-induced oil shock, but eventually subsided in the 1980s as more and more developing countries sought to integrate into the globalizing economy.

During the 1950s developing states began to devise a unified posture toward others on security issues and to press for consideration of their special problems and needs in the context of the global economic structure, as we saw in Chapter 6. It would take almost another decade before their efforts bore fruit. Then, during the 1964 United Nations Conference on Trade and Development (UNCTAD), called at the behest of the developing countries, the ***Group of 77 (G-77)*** was formed as a coalition of the world's poor to press for concessions from the world's rich. The G-77 today numbers over one hundred and thirty and remains a significant voice in pressing the interests of the South in its dialogue with the North. At a summit in Havana in 2000, for example, the G-77 called for a New Global Human Order designed to spread the world's wealth and power.

The G-77 scored a major victory with the Sixth Special Session of the United Nations General Assembly, held in 1974, when it used its superior numbers to secure passage of the Declaration on the Establishment of a *New International Economic Order (NIEO)*. Inspired in the wake of OPEC's price squeeze by the belief that "commodity power" endowed the Global South with the political strength necessary to challenge the industrial North, the South pressed for more rapid economic development, increased transfers of resources from industrialized to developing nations, and a more favorable distribution of global economic benefits. More fundamentally, the G-77 sought a substantial alteration of the rules and institutional structures governing the transnational flow of goods, services, capital, and technology. Simply put, the New International Economic Order sought regime change—a revision of the rules, norms, and procedures of the Liberal International Economic Order to serve the interests of the South rather than the North (Krasner 1985).

The Global South's drive for regime change derived from its belief that the structure of the world political economy perpetuates developing states' underdog status. International economic institutions, such as the IMF and GATT, were (are) widely perceived as "deeply biased against developing countries in their global distribution of income and influence" (Hansen 1980). The perception was buttressed—then and now—by a legacy of colonial exploitation, the continued existence of levels of poverty and deprivation unheard of in the Global North, and a conviction that relief from many of the economic and associated political ills of the South can result only from changes in the policies of the North, in whose hands responsibility for prevailing conditions and the means to correct them were (are) thought to lie.

The Global North—then and now—rejected those views. Accepting them would have been tantamount to relinquishing control over key international institutions and a fundamental redistribution of global resources—two unlikely prospects. Instead, it located the cause of the Global South's economic woes in the domestic systems of developing countries themselves (see, for example, Bissell 1990). Thus proposals to radically alter existing international economic institutions, as well as the more modest elements of the program advanced during the 1970s and early 1980s, met with resistance and resentment. The United States was especially intransigent, as it continued to view the Global South primarily through an East-West prism, showing little interest in those aspects of Southern objectives related to transforming the Liberal International Economic Order.

As the unifying force of commodity power receded and different countries were affected in different ways by the changing economic climate of the 1980s, latent fissures within the G-77 became evident. As a result, the Global South no longer spoke with a unified voice. The differences between the *Newly Industrializing Economies (NIEs)* and the least developed of the less developed countries had the effect of dividing the G-77 into competing groups rather than uniting them behind a common cause.

Today the Global South's determination to replace the LIEO with a New International Economic Order is little more than a footnote to the history of the continuing contest between the world's rich and poor countries. Still, many of the issues raised retain their relevance. Central among them is the role of the state in managing international economic transactions. Whereas the LIEO rests on the premise of limited government intervention, *economic nationalists* or mercantilists assign the state a more aggressive role in fostering national economic welfare. Economic nationalism (mercantilism) undergirded the "Asian Miracle," a term widely used to describe the spectacular economic performance of Hong Kong, Singapore, South Korea, and Taiwan, often called the "Asian Tigers," that began in the 1970s and then spread elsewhere in the region as export-led growth gained popularity and momentum. In the wake of the Asian contagion of the late 1990s, however, mercantilism once more came under criticism. "Crony capitalism" symbolized the difference between liberalism and mercantilism.

Crony capitalism refers to the tightly knit relationships among corporate and other economic agents in Asian societies, including government officials, that often dictate their economic decisions, regardless of economic imperatives. Family-and-friend ties are especially prominent, as in Indonesia, where the Suharto government (and family) fell victim to the Asian currency crises of the late 1990s.

Analysts are not agreed on whether the economic development models of western capitalism or the Asian models, which embrace strong state roles in the economy (neomercantilism) and cultural values (such as crony capitalism), have won the day (Lim 2001). A decade ago the United States and other Western countries marveled at the Japanese economic miracle and sought to understand its underlying logic. Today Japan is experiencing economic doldrums, and the *Washington Consensus,* although increasingly under attack (see Naim 2000), animates thinking in the most powerful states. Ironically, however, the United States finds itself under even greater pressure to stimulate global economic growth than was true prior to the WTC and Pentagon terrorist attacks which had significant adverse effects on the global economic activity.

As a principal driving force behind the Washington Consensus (see Chapter 6), the United States figures prominently in any discussion of North-South relations. Trade is among the persistent issues. As the largest economy in the world, the Global South sees access to the U.S. market as a key to its economic success. Although the United States from time to time has sought to accommodate Southern objectives, it retains significant barriers to imports from the Global South. NTBs sometimes figure in these exclusions.

More broadly, the new drive of the United States—strongly supported by some domestic groups—to impose on Global South exporters similar labor and environmental standards to those in the United States, poses significant challenges to new entrants to U.S. markets (see Destler and Balint 1999). Not only are these standards seen as inapplicable in labor markets where labor is cheap and capital dear, environmental standards like those in the United States tax government resources in developing countries beyond their capabilities. Not surprisingly, then, the contention over the costs and benefits of globalization have taken on a global flavor, as U.S. efforts to extend its own environmental and labor standards are viewed in the Global South as thinly veiled forms of protectionism.

The Second World Again   The economic isolation of East from West that began in the early Cold War continued for more than a decade. Not until the late 1960s and early 1970s did the Soviets and the Americans begin to significantly shift their views about commercial ties with "the other side." The change was especially evident once détente became official policy on both sides of the Cold War divide. Trade now became part of a series of concrete agreements across a range of issues that would contribute to what Nixon's national security adviser Henry Kissinger described as the superpowers' "vested interest in mutual restraint." For their part, the Soviets saw expanded commercial intercourse as an opportunity to gain access to the Western credits and technology necessary to rejuvenate the sluggish Soviet economy. In addition, grain imports from the United States enabled the Soviets to supplement shortfalls in their own agricultural production. The contrast with the 1950s was striking.

The high point of détente was reached at the 1972 Moscow summit, when the two Cold War antagonists initialed the first Strategic Arms Limitation Talks (SALT) agreement. SALT was the cornerstone of détente, but expanded East-West trade was part of the mortar. A joint commercial commission was established at the summit, whose purpose was to pave the way for the granting of most-favored-nation status to the Soviet Union and the extension of U.S. government-backed credits to the Soviet regime. Neither happened as envisioned. Over the objection of President Ford and Secretary of State Kissinger, Congress made MFN status contingent on the liberalization of communist policies regarding Jewish emigration. (Congress did not limit the provisions of the law to the Soviet Union or to Jews, so they also applied to others, including China, into the 1990s.) Restrictions were also placed on Soviet (and Eastern European) access to American government-backed credits. These further strained the economic ties détente once sought to nurture and contributed to a mounting Eastern debt to the West (see Stevenson and Frye 1989). Eventually Soviet leaders repudiated the 1972 trade agreement in response to what they regarded as an unwarranted intrusion into Soviet domestic affairs.

In part because of congressional constraints, East-West trade stagnated in the second half of the 1970s. Furthermore, the Carter administration's commitment to a worldwide human rights campaign often led to American attacks on the Soviet Union's human rights policies. Carter also tried to use trade to moderate objectionable Soviet behavior in the Global South and to sanction the Soviets for their invasion of Afghanistan in 1979. Reagan would follow a similar path, with the added twist that his administration saw trade as a stick that could be used to punish Soviet leaders for unwanted behavior (Spero and Hart 1997). Still, there was no measurable change in Soviet behavior.

A recurring feature of this period is that U.S. allies did not always share U.S. views on how to deal with the Soviet Union in the economic sphere. For example, many Europeans saw U.S. policy as hypocritical in that it attempted to pressure its allies into not selling the Soviets energy technology at the same time as the United States sold them grain. Other examples could be cited.

Against this background, today's European views of U.S. attitudes toward Russia have a distinctly familiar ring. Bush's national security adviser Condoleezza Rice took Germany's chief diplomatic aide to Germany's Chancellor Gerhard Schröder by surprise when she advised him to "be tough" with the Russians. (*New York Times*, 7 May 2001). For Europeans, smoother relations with Russia are preferred, and moving forward on addressing global environmental concerns, on which the new Bush administration proved intransigent, were more salient. The gulf in the policy positions of the transatlantic allies was reminiscent of the earlier 1980s, when they tussled over the wisdom of supporting the construction of a Soviet energy pipeline into Europe. The Reagan administration worried that this would increase European dependence on Soviet energy supplies. Europeans viewed it as an opportunity to increase access to scarce energy resources.

Meanwhile, the future of Russia itself remains in doubt. *Mayfiya* groups have subverted government efforts to modernize the economy (Handelman 1994). The quality of life is deteriorating, as witnessed by decreased life-expectancy rates. And democratization is threatened, as media sources and political groups that do not toe the government line are systematically harassed. These and other conditions led the prestigious *Atlantic Monthly* to publish an article in mid-2001 titled "Russia Is Finished" (Tayler 2001). The article's topic line was especially ominous: "The unstoppable descent of a once great power into social catastrophe and strategic irrelevance." Even as Russia struggles politically and economically, it has expressed an interest in joining the World Trade Organization, which would help to integrate it further into the capitalist world political economy. Doing so, however, will require difficult internal Russian reforms. President Clinton urged that these changes be made in a June 2000 speech before the Duma, the Russian legislature. He said that "Russia should not be the only major industrialized country standing outside this global trading system."

Meanwhile, countries in Eastern Europe have made enormous strides in converting from socialist command economies to capitalist market economies. Several have also joined the WTO and hope to join the European Union. "The former communist countries sought to integrate themselves into the capitalist world economy not only to benefit from trade and investment but also as part of a larger effort to make their political and economic transitions irreversible" (Spero and Hart 1997).

From Free Trade to Fair Trade

Historically, the United States has espoused a laissez-faire attitude toward trade issues, believing that market forces are best able to stimulate entrepreneurial initiatives and investment choices. During the 1980s, however, it came to believe that "the playing field is tilted." This implies that American businesspeople are unable to compete on the same basis as others—notably the continental European states, Japan, and the more advanced developing countries, where governments, playing the role of economic nationalists, routinely intervene in their economies and play entrepreneurial and developmental roles directly. Senator Lloyd M. Bentsen, a long-time advocate of free trade and later Secretary of the Treasury in the Clinton administration, captured the shifting sentiment toward free trade during the debate over the 1988 omnibus trade act: "I think in theory, it's a great theory. But it's not being practiced, and for us to practice free trade in a world where there's much government-directed trade makes as much sense as unilateral disarmament with the Russians."

Not only were sentiments toward free trade shifting rapidly in the United States—at one time during the 1980s some 300 hundred bills were pending before Congress that offered protection to almost every industrial sector—but signs of closure characterized the trade system itself. By the time the Uruguay Round of trade negotiations began in 1986, the system was rife with restrictive barriers, subsidies, invisible import restraints, standards for domestic products that foreign producers could not meet, and other unfair trade practices that went beyond GATT's principles (see also Anjaria 1986). To cope with

the changing environment at home and abroad, the United States mounted a series of responses. *Multilateralism* was one.

The Multilateral Venue Other nations were not quick to accept the United States' analogy of an uneven playing field skewed to its disadvantage. As one observer put it caustically, "the more inefficient and backward an American industry is, the more likely the U.S. government will blame foreign countries for its problems" (Bovard 1991). Still, other countries were sensitive to the need to keep protectionist sentiments in the United States at bay. Because U.S. imports stimulated the economic growth of its trade partners, they conceded that new trade talks (the Uruguay Round) should not only consider traditional tariff issues and the new protectionism but also issues traditionally outside the GATT framework of special concern to the United States due to its comparative advantages.

The new issues included barriers to trade in services (insurance, for example), intellectual property rights (such as copyrights on computer software, music, and movies), and investments (stocks and bonds). Agriculture also remained a paramount issue, as the economic well-being of American agriculture depends more heavily on exports than do other sectors of the economy.[12]

Because world trade in agriculture evolved outside of the main GATT framework, it was not subject to the same liberalizing influences as industrial products (Low 1993; Spero and Hart 1997). Agricultural trade policy is especially controversial because it is deeply enmeshed in the domestic politics of producing states, particularly those, like the United States and some members of the European Union, for which the global market is an outlet for surplus production. The enormous subsidies that governments of some leading producers pay farmers to keep them competitive internationally are at the core of differences. The perceived need for subsidies reflects fundamental structural changes in the global system of food production. New competitors have emerged among Global South producers, and markets traditionally supplied by Northern producers have shrunk as a consequence of technological innovations enabling expanded agricultural production in countries that previously experienced food deficits.

During the Uruguay Round the United States aggressively proposed to phase out all agricultural subsidies and farm trade protection programs within a decade. It gained some support from others but faced stiff opposition from Europeans (particularly France), which viewed it as unrealistic. Sharp differences on the issue led to an impasse in the Uruguay Round negotiations, delaying conclusion of the talks beyond the original 1990 target date.

Three years later, when the talks finally concluded, the United States could claim a measure of success, as the European Union (then called the European Community) and others agreed to new (but limited) rules on export subsidies, domestic subsidies, and market access. Some domestic groups in the United States worried that increased agricultural efficiency would eventually drive small American farmers out of business; but for the industry as a whole, liberalization was perceived as more beneficial to American farmers than to producers elsewhere due to the Americans' greater efficiency.

Liberalization of agricultural trade was also expected to benefit agricultural exporters in the Global South by providing them with greater access to agricultural markets in the Global North. (The anticipated dismantling of the Multifiber Arrangement, a vast market-sharing arrangement among textile-producing countries that effectively denied access to others, would also benefit textile exporters in the Global South.) This was expected to encourage them to open their own economies to other products produced in the Global North, for whom the South had already become an important market that would grow even more prodigiously in the 1990s.

By the time of the Uruguay Round many developing states had initiated trade liberalization on their own, thus coming to participate more fully in the GATT trade regime. In some areas,

however, long-standing North–South differences continued to color issues of importance to the United States (see the essays in Tussie and Glover 1993). Trade-related intellectual property rights (TRIPs)—one of the new issues confronted at Uruguay—was among them. The United States (and other Northern states) wanted protection of copyrights, patents, trademarks, microprocessor designs, and trade secrets, as well as prohibitions on unfair competition. (TRIPS would figure prominently in future U.S. trade talks with China.) Developing states vigorously resisted these efforts along with the concept of "standardized intellectual property norms and regulations throughout the world" (Low 1993).[13] Thus little significant headway was made on TRIPs. U.S. efforts regarding trade-related investment measures (TRIMs) and services (such as banking and insurance) and the Clinton administration's efforts to abolish European restrictions on non–European produced movies and television programs (read "American") also met widespread resistance.

The United States did realize a long-standing goal when the World Trade Organization was approved as GATT's replacement. Proponents of the WTO saw it as a useful element in states' efforts to keep the instrumentalities of the liberal trade regime consonant with state practices in the increasingly complex world political economy. It was not without detractors, however. Critics were especially antagonistic to WTO's dispute settlement procedures. They were concerned that the findings of its arbitration panels would be binding on the domestic laws of participating states. More broadly, the very title of the new organization suggested potential threats to American decision-making prerogatives which sparked the ire of conservative critics in particular. Presidential hopeful Pat Buchanan's reaction is illustrative: "The glittering bribe the globalists are extending to us is this: enhanced access to global markets—in exchange for our national sovereignty" (Rabkin 1994). Environmentalists—often on the other end of the political spectrum—also worried about the WTO. They feared it would further erode their ability to protect hard-won domestic victories against the charge that environmental protection laws restrict free trade.[14] GATT's controversial rulings that a U.S. ban on the import of tuna caught by merchants who also ensnare encircling dolphins is illegal—popularly known as the "GATTzilla versus Flipper" debate—symbolized their apprehensiveness. Environmentalists worried that the World Trade Organization would perpetuate the "elitist" character of GATT (dispute panelists are appointed, not elected, and make their decisions behind closed doors), and that controls in a wide range of areas with environmental implications would be expanded and nontariff trade barriers designed purposely to protect the environment (including dolphins) disallowed. In short, they argued that the environment and sustainable development were given insufficient attention in the design of the WTO (French 1993). Their fears were reaffirmed in 1998, when the WTO in a case similar to the dolphin-tuna controversy overturned U.S. policies designed to keep shrimp caught in nets without turtle-excluder devises out of U.S. markets (Destler and Balint 1999).

Aggressive Unilateralism At the same time that the Clinton administration pushed the Uruguay Round to successful conclusion it pursued policies toward Europe, Japan, and others with means best characterized as *aggressive unilateralism*. The approach contrasted sharply with the laissez-faire attitudes of the previous Bush administration, captured with the quip allegedly made by one of its economic advisers: "Potato chips, computer chips, what's the difference. They're all chips. A hundred dollars of one or a hundred dollars of the other is still a hundred dollars."

Aggressive unilateralism says it matters very much what an economy produces. As practiced by the Clinton administration during its first term, its elements included the following:

- Threatening South Korea with trade sanctions unless it permitted AT&T to compete equally with Korean firms in seeking equipment sales

- Threatening Japan with a 100 percent increase in tariffs on luxury cars exported to the United States unless it opened the Japanese market to U.S. manufacturers

- Accusing the European Community (predecessor of the EU) of unfairly subsidizing production of Airbus, rival of Boeing-built commercial jetliners

- Intervening on behalf of Boeing to secure a $6 billion contract for the sale of commercial jetliners to Saudi Arabia

- Redirecting Pentagon research monies to the private, commercial sector

- Reinstating Super 301 provisions of the 1988 omnibus trade act to permit rapid U.S. trade retaliation following the breakdown of trade talks with Japan

- Threatening to withdraw China's most-favored-nation trade status unless specific criteria for respecting human rights were met

The administration's posture toward China fulfilled a campaign promise that smacked of Cold War tactics—the belief that tough economic pressure can secure explicitly political ends. Carter and Reagan had both tried this, and both failed. In the end, so did Clinton.

Clinton had tried to meet strong congressional dissatisfaction with China's human rights policies in the aftermath of the 1989 Tiananmen Square massacre of prodemocracy demonstrators by spelling out in a 1993 executive order the conditions China would have to meet to retain its preferred trade status. As the deadline approached a year later, it was clear that little had been done to meet those conditions and that various face-saving gestures had also failed.

Faced with the reality that China had become one of the nation's most important trade partners (see Figure 7.3), the administration unabashedly abandoned its human rights posture and earlier campaign promise. Secretary of State Warren Christopher announced that a policy of "comprehensive engagement" would become the focus of U.S. policy, calling it "the best way to

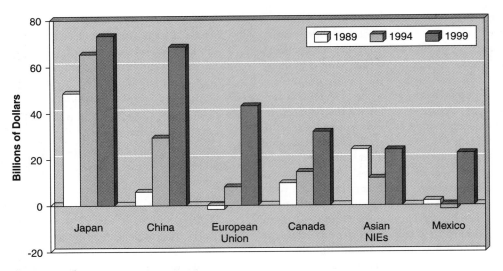

FIGURE 7.3 U.S. Trade Deficit with Principle Trading Partners, 1989, 1994, and 1999

Source: Adapted from U.S. Department of Commerce, "United States Foreign Trade, Summary of U.S. Export and Important Merchandise Trade," FT-900. February 1990: 5–6; U.S. Department of Commerce, "U.S. International Trade in Goods and Services," FT-900 Supplement, December 1994: 8–17; and U.S. Bureau of the Census www.census.gov/foreign-trade/Press-Release/99_press_release
Accessed April 28, 2001.

influence China's development." The purported change echoed the senior Bush administration's earlier emphasis on market incentives toward political liberalization—an approach Clinton viciously attacked during the 1992 presidential campaign. Meanwhile, critics charged that profits had won out over principles. Later, however, Clinton could claim victory when, after threatening to impose higher tariffs on Chinese goods, he won a commitment from the Chinese to halt their piracy of compact discs and other items in violation of intellectual property rights standards.

The administration's trade policies toward Europe, Japan, and Korea bore some resemblance to its China policies in that they rested on the premise that economic security and national security would go hand in hand in the post–Cold War world. As Clinton declared early in his administration, "It is time for us to make trade a priority element of American security." "Security" and "war" would often punctuate administration rhetoric and others' interpretations of it

(see Friedman 1994a). In the fight during his second term to win congressional approval for granting China normal-trade-relations status, which paved the way for its entry into the WTO, Clinton and National Security Adviser Sandy Berger would often invoke the national security symbol as the administration pursued its goal.

During its first term, however, its actions are best understood through the lens of *fair trade, managed trade,* and *strategic trade.* Together they infused American trade policies with a distinctly neomercantilist cast.

Fair Trade Fair trade implies that American exporters should be given the same access to foreign markets that foreign producers enjoy in the United States (see also Prestowitz 1992). As Clinton put it, "We will continue to welcome foreign products and services into our market, but insist that our products and services be able to enter theirs on equal terms." Fair trade is often closely associated with "reciprocity," which increasingly in recent years has meant "equal market access in terms of outcomes rather than equality of opportunities." Together the two concepts lay the basis for an interventionist trade policy (Low 1993).

Section 301 of the 1974 Trade Act embodies this interventionist thrust. It permits the United States to retaliate against others engaged in "unreasonable" or "unjustifiable" trade policies that threaten American interests. Liberalization, however—not retaliation—is the primary purpose of Section 301, and this was achieved in about one-third of the cases raised between 1975 and 1990. Retaliation occurred in about one-tenth of them (Low 1993).

Frustrated with the tedious process of resolving disputes under Section 301, but especially with what it regarded as trade practices believed responsible for the persistent U.S. trade deficits of the 1980s, Congress incorporated "Super 301" in the 1988 Omnibus Trade and Competitiveness Act. Unlike the earlier provision, Super 301 *required* that the president identify countries engaged in unfair trade practices and either seek negotiated remedies or threaten them with U.S. retaliation. Although Super 301 was "almost unanimously viewed abroad as a clear violation of the GATT" (Walters and Blake 1992), Congress's resentment of the trade policies of Japan and the four Asian NIEs was glaring.

Japan was often viewed in the United States as the preeminent neomercantilist power, based on the belief that its persistent balance-of-trade and payments surpluses resulted from an intimate government-business alliance that tilted the playing field in its favor. The continuing trade imbalance between Japan and the United States—which runs into the tens of billions of dollars each year, as Figure 7.3 shows—reinforces the belief that Japan's trade policies are inherently detrimental to American business interests (see Fallows 1994); for a contrasting view, see (Emmott 1994; also Bergsten and Noland 1993).

There is little doubt that Japan's protectionist trade policies inhibit penetration of its market by American firms. Japanese business practices, including cross-share holding patterns known as *keiretsu* which result in informal corporate bargains, also make foreign penetration difficult regardless of government policies. American consumers, however, continue to show marked preferences for Japanese products not shared by their counterparts on the other side of the Pacific Basin, where cultural traditions reinforce the view that foreign products are ill-suited to the Japanese consumer. It is a perception American producers sometimes feed—as with American automakers' practice until recently of building only cars with the steering wheel on the left rather the right, which fits the British driving pattern followed in Japan.

American exports to Japan have increased considerably in recent years, in part a product of continuing negotiations between the two countries. Among them was the Structural Impediments Initiative (SII), launched in 1989 shortly after Japan was named as one of three countries engaged in unfair trade practices under Super 301 (Brazil and India were the others). Despite a $49 billion trade deficit with Japan, the Bush administration chose not to retaliate against Japan the following year, as Super 301 permitted.

The Bush administration was clearly uncomfortable with the confrontational, unilateralist thrust of Super 301—not one case of retaliation was initiated (see Low 1993)—and thus was pleased to see it expire after 1990. Four years later the Clinton administration revived the section's provisions via executive agreement following the breakdown of the latest series of Japanese-American trade negotiations known as the "framework" talks.

Managed Trade The framework agreement was reached at the 1993 Tokyo G-7 summit. Once the negotiations began, the United States insisted on using certain quantitative indicators to monitor whether Japan was in fact opening its markets in various sectors, including autos, telecommunications, insurance, and medical equipment. Its intransigence on the issue led to a breakdown of negotiations in early in 1994, as the Japanese retorted that numerical standards would require Japan to engage in *managed trade*—in effect responding to a demand for a minimum U.S. share of the Japanese market. (In a free trade system, the government's role is limited to making rules governing commerce, whose direction is then determined by market forces. In a managed trade system, the government intervenes to steer trade relations in a predetermined direction as determined by the government itself.)

Clinton would later deny that the United States ever demanded numerical import quota commitments from Japan. All the United States sought, according to U.S. Trade Representative Mickey Kantor, was an agreement on "objective criteria" to show progress in opening up Japan's markets to all foreign (not just American) goods. Japan did eventually agree that quantitative measures could be used to measure progress in opening Japanese markets in insurance, glass, and medical and telecommunications equipment, but it refused to guarantee the United States any specific market shares—thus side-stepping the contentious issue of "numerical targets." Furthermore, no agreement was reached on automobiles and auto parts. To keep pressure on the Japanese in these markets, the Clinton administration promptly set in motion the process that could lead to sanctions, although it chose to use Section 301 of the 1974 Trade Act rather than the more aggressive Super 301 provision. It then threatened stiff tariff increases on luxury Japanese automobiles produced for the U.S. market unless U.S. car companies and spare-parts manufacturers were guaranteed greater access to the Japanese market.

An eleventh-hour agreement was reached in mid-1995. Both sides claimed victory. The United States said the agreement set "numerical benchmarks" that would yield measurable results in opening the Japanese market; Japanese negotiators replied they had agreed to no numbers and would bear no responsibility for achieving any numerical targets. Thus, that round in the often tense U.S.-Japanese trade

dispute ended without a definitive deal—as had happened so often in the past.

Managed trade between the United States and Japan as pursued by the Clinton administration was not without precedent. In 1986 the Reagan administration made an agreement with Japan to guarantee foreign companies a share of the Japanese semiconductor market. President Bush renewed it in 1991. He also led a trade mission to Japan that included a contingent of American auto executives, thus giving it an unabashedly neomercantilist coloration. The mission seemed to confirm the view expressed by Leon Britain, competition commissioner of the European Community, that the Bush administration was "drifting toward a preference for managed trade" and that it sought "a certain share of the Japanese market on political rather than commercial grounds." The mission accomplished little, but it left the distinct impression that the United States was just another "ordinary" power: "For the leader of the free world to travel to Tokyo with his nation's businessmen in tow was a jarring sight. This was not a leader with a vision of a New World Order; it was merely a man out to make a buck for this country" (Murray 1992–1993). Shortly thereafter the speaker of the Japanese Diet (parliament), Yoshio Sakurauchi, described the United States as "Japan's subcontractor" and American workers as lazy and illiterate. "Japan bashing" in turn became a popular American sport.

Despite the Reagan-Bush precedents, the Clinton administration was sensitive to criticisms of its tactics and objectives. Deputy Treasury Secretary Roger C. Altman (1994) defended them in *Foreign Affairs,* charging that "The Japanese government that berates the United States on charges of managed trade has long been in the business of targeting market outcomes itself."

Despite Altman's spirited—even hawkish— defense, other nations were suspicious of U.S. motives, fearing that the United States sought a bilateral deal with Japan that would come at their expense. European governments were especially critical of the determination of the United States to threaten unilateral sanctions in the auto industry dispute rather than let the new World Trade Organization settle the issue. Similarly, Peter Sutherland, head of GATT, warned of the dangers of managed trade: "Governments should interfere in the conduct of trade as little as possible. Once bureaucrats become involved in managing trade flows, the potential for misguided decisions rises greatly."

Strategic Trade Sutherland's views arguably apply even more strongly to the application of strategic trade to "level the playing field." **Strategic trade** is a form of industrial policy that seeks to create comparative advantages by targeting government subsidies toward particular industries. The strategy challenges the premises of classical trade theory and its touchstone, the principle of comparative advantage.

Classical theory shows how international trade contributes to the welfare of trading partners. It attributes the basis for trade to underlying differences among states: Some are better suited to the production of agricultural products, such as coffee, because they have vast tracts of fertile land, while others are better suited to the production of labor-intensive goods, such as consumer electronics, because they have an abundance of cheap labor.

Economists now recognize, however, that comparative advantages take on a life of their own.

Much international trade . . . reflects national advantages that are created by historical circumstance, and that then persist or grow because of other advantages to large scale either in development or production. For example, the development effort required to launch a new passenger jet aircraft is so large that the world market will support only one or two profitable firms. Once the United States had a head start in producing aircraft, its position as the world's leading exporter became self-reinforcing. So if you

want to explain why the United States exports aircraft, you should not look for underlying aspects of the U.S. economy; you should study the historical circumstances that gave the United States a head start in the industry.

(KRUGMAN 1990, 109)

If the contemporary pattern of international trade reflects historical circumstances, states may conclude it is in their interests to try to create advantages that will redound to the long-run benefit of their economies. Curiously, then, the logic of comparative advantage can itself be used to justify government intervention in the economy. Although the returns on strategic trade policies are often marginal (Krugman 1990), the fact that some states engage in such practices encourages others to do likewise. Indeed, the United States became increasingly sensitive to the logic of strategic trade as the Soviet threat ended and its own power position compared with Japan and Germany, among others, declined, thus making it more aware of the costs of free-riding by its Cold War allies and principal economic partners (Mastanduno 1991; see also Snidal 1991).

The Clinton administration's early decision to grant tax breaks and redirect government spending to high-tech industries to enhance their competitive advantages demonstrated its willingness to follow the path of others. Clinton's attack on the EU's subsidies for the Airbus shortly after his first inauguration marked in dramatic style the approach and was likely influenced by the thinking of his newly chosen chair of the Council of Economic Advisers, Laura D'Andrea Tyson. Tyson's book, *Who's Bashing Whom? Trade Conflict in High-Technology Industries* (1992)—which includes a detailed examination of the aircraft industry, among others—articulates a "cautious activist agenda" for enhancing American competitiveness along the lines strategic trade theory prescribes. Moreover, the Clinton administration's "National Export Strategy" and the "Big Emerging Sectors" component of its "Big

Emerging Markets" initiative were organized in part around the idea that government-industry cooperation and support in key sectors of the economy were vital to "compete and win in the global marketplace" (see Scott 1997a; Scott 1998a). Similarly, the administration's efforts to relax export controls on high-tech products stemmed largely from this sense of competition (see Cupitt 2000).

The success of government efforts to target subsidies toward particular ("strategic") industries is, as noted, mixed. While the record of Pacific Rim countries is arguably positive, it is also marked by some conspicuous failures. Notable among them is "the Japanese government's reluctance in the 1950s to support a little start-up company named Tokyo Tsushin Kogyo. The company is now known as Sony Corporation" (Blustein 1993). The key issue, then, is the ability of governments to pick "winners and losers."

In the particular case of the aircraft industry, Europeans are especially critical of the proposition that they grant subsidies while the United States does not. They correctly note that the commercial sector in the United States benefitted enormously from the billions of dollars in military aerospace research and development the Pentagon spent during the Cold War, which helped to create an unequaled aerospace industry—commercial as well as military. Moreover, as the theory of strategic trade suggests, Europe's ability to compete in the industry is severely circumscribed by the advantages historical circumstances conferred on the United States.

A concern for *competitiveness* ties together many of the Clinton administration's initial trade policy thrusts. Clinton pledged repeatedly during and after his 1992 campaign to create more "high wage, high skill" jobs for Americans. Government intervention in the economy—neomercantilism—flows naturally from that pledge. Thus in early 1994, after Clinton personally played a role in nudging Saudi Arabia toward a $6 billion commercial aircraft deal with Boeing Company and McDonnell Douglas Corporation rather than the European Airbus Industry consor-

tium, the president would crow that this proves "that we can compete" (see also Barnes 1994).

Implicit in the concern for competitiveness was the notion that trade competition from others—particularly Japan and low-wage producers on the Pacific Rim—had diminished the living standards of American workers. The policy implications were clear: Only an aggressive campaign to enhance U.S. competitiveness could reverse the trends.

Not everyone agreed with that viewpoint. Economist Paul Krugman, whose challenges to the assumptions of classical trade theory form much of the basis of current thinking about strategic trade, was especially critical of what he called the "dangerous obsession" with "competitiveness" (Krugman 1994a, 1994b). In particular, he criticized the view that "the nation's real income [had] lagged as a result of the inability of many U.S. firms to sell in world markets" (Krugman and Lawrence 1994). He noted that almost all of the decline in American living standards between 1973 and 1990 could be explained by a decline in domestic productivity. The same was true in Europe and Japan. "The moral," Krugman continued, "is clear":

> As a practical, empirical matter the major nations of the world are not to any significant degree in economic competition with each other. Of course, there is always a rivalry for status and power—countries that grow faster will see their political rank rise. So it is always interesting to compare countries. But asserting that Japanese growth diminishes U.S. status is very different from saying that it reduces the U.S. standard of living—and it is the latter that the rhetoric of competitiveness asserts.
>
> (KRUGMAN 1994A, 35)[15]

Globalization Again

The fracas with Japan over automobiles and auto parts—and competitiveness—would pass as the economic fortunes of Japan and the United States reversed course during the 1990s. As we have noted, Japan stumbled into a prolonged economic slump while the U.S. economy soared. Interestingly, dramatic increases in the productivity of American workers widely attributed to the spread of information and communications technologies undergirded the prolonged period of prosperity and growth.

It is notable that the growing trade imbalances of the United States with its principal trading partners between 1994 and the end of the decade (see Figure 7.3) were not accompanied by the harsh, protectionist politics of the 1980s and early 1990s. Prosperity at home explained this. Who was threatened? Also notable is that the product mix coming from abroad in the latter-half of the 1990s was notably different than earlier. By the end of the decade, for example, China rivaled Japan as having the largest trade imbalance with the United States. Still, this did not provoke the vociferous criticism from domestic political interests that the automobile controversy with Japan ignited. Arguably one reason is that the products China exports to the United States are no longer products in which American producers choose to compete.

Globalization also matters. Today many products imported from abroad are produced by American companies. So it is difficult to determine who benefits from trade liberalization and who pays for trade competition. Indeed, "made in America" is an increasingly rare find. Even American automobiles (like Chrysler) are produced by foreign-owned companies; and companies that are not foreign-owned buy many of their components from foreign producers or make them in co-production schemes with foreign companies.

The foundations of globalization are lodged in part in the regionally-based initiatives the United States launched in the 1980s and 1990s. Ironically, those regional schemes may also threaten the perpetuation of globalization processes.

Regionalism In addition to multilateralism and aggressive unilateralism, *regionalism* figures promi-

nently in American policy makers' responses to the changes and challenges of a world political economy in transition. Notable manifestations include the Caribbean Basin Initiative, a program of tariff reductions and tax incentives designed to promote industry and trade in Central America and the Caribbean launched in 1984; and the North American Free Trade Agreement (NAFTA), approved in 1993, which links the United States with Canada and Mexico in a free-trade area. Post-Nafta initiatives include the *Asia-Pacific Economic Cooperation (APEC)* forum, which seeks creation of a Pacific Rim free trade scheme by the year 2020, and the *Free Trade Area of the Americas (FTAA)*, which anticipates a free-trade area encompassing the Western hemisphere much earlier than that.

The particulars on these schemes differ, but they share a common goal: trade liberalization. By reducing barriers to trade, all parties expect to benefit from liberalization, which promises greater efficiencies through specialization and hence potential benefits not only to producers but also to consumers that will enhance their living standards—at least that is the theory. Hegemonic theory also tells us that the United States will benefit handsomely, as its greater control of capital and technology gives it advantageous access to both opportunities and rewards.

NAFTA's purpose was to intertwine Mexico and Canada with the United States as a prelude to a wider Western Hemispheric economic partnership, embodied in the senior Bush administration's Enterprise for the Americas Initiative. The agreement itself was an emotionally charged, high-profile issue during the 1992 presidential campaign and later, as Congress faced its approval. Third-party candidate Ross Perot made a big splash with the charge that a "giant sucking sound" would be heard as American jobs rushed to Mexico should NAFTA be approved. Journalist and presidential hopeful Pat Buchanan (1993) charged that "NAFTA is not really a trade treaty at all, but the architecture of the New World Order. . . . NAFTA would supersede state laws and diminish U.S. sovereignty." In the end

---

FOCUS 7.2   Top Currencies? The Euro and the Dollar

Elementary monetary economics teaches that within a single economy, money fulfills three basic functions—it serves as a medium of exchange, a unit of account, and a store of value. An international currency used among economic agents—that is, persons engaging in financial transactions—in multiple economies serves the same functions. . . . There is, however, one fundamental difference between the use of money in a single economy and the use of an international currency in a multieconomy setting. In the former contexts, governments typically declare (by fiat) the currency that is used as legal tender within their jurisdictions. For example, when receiving tax receipts, the Swiss government demands to be paid in Swiss francs and not in, say, Mexican pesos. In the international setting, however, the choice of currencies responds predominantly to market forces, whose consequences are ratified more than guided by international agreements. . . .

A fundamental distinction [exists] between the dollar and the euro. The former is issued by a single political jurisdiction, while the euro [is] issued by a union made up of multiple jurisdictions. . . . Political stability is an important determinant of international currency use. Differences between, say, the states of Alabama and Massachusetts over the stance and mix of monetary and fiscal policies are unheard of, as are threats of any state to secede from the U.S. monetary union. Differences between, for example, Germany and Italy over macroeconomic policy issues cannot, however, be ruled out a priori. . . .

. . . The euro certainly possesses the potential to challenge the hegemonic role now played by the U.S. dollar in international transactions. Whether the euro will fulfill that role or go the route of other challengers to the dollar will, to a large extent, depend upon the credibility—both in terms of inflation performance and political cohesion—garnered by the EMU [European Monetary Union] in the years [ahead].

SOURCE: George S. Tavlas, "The International Use of Currencies: The U.S. Dollar and the Euro," *Finance and Development* 35 (June 1998): 46–49.

Congress approved the pact, in part because of side agreements on labor and environmental issues the Clinton administration initiated. These agreements, as we note later, have led to important if unintended consequences.

NAFTA was directed in part (as was Buchanan's invective) against the European Union. Since the 1950s European leaders have tried methodically to build a more united Europe, beginning especially in the economic sphere with a European-wide common market. In the mid-1980s they boldly committed themselves to create a single market by 1992 and, later, a single European currency, the euro. They also promised closer cooperation on foreign political and military affairs.

The latter goal has proven elusive, particularly as the conflicts in the Balkans during the 1990s tested the EU's political resolve. On the economic front, however, Europe now comprises the largest market in the world. The euro has been successfully inaugurated as a replacement for the multiple national currencies of many of its members. (Informally called "Euroland," the countries adopting the euro are Austria, Belgium, Finland, France, Germany, Ireland, Italy, Luxembourg, the Netherlands, Portugal, and Spain.) Eventually the euro may challenge the top currency role of the dollar (see Focus 7.2). The EU anticipates expanding further to include the democratic states in Eastern Europe.[16] Hence it continues its relentless push to create a continent-wide economic union with Brussels as its centerpiece (but compare Martin and George 1999).

Increasingly the EU's economic clout has caused friction with the United States. C. Fred Bergsten, director of the Institute of International

Economics, worries that the United States and Europe "are on the brink of a major trade and economic conflict."

> Washington has already retaliated against European import restrictions on American beef and bananas—each retaliation accounting for a $100 million or so of annual trade—and has rejected all European efforts to resolve these disputes. . . .
>
> . . . In addition, a major dispute over commercial aircraft is brewing as the two sides quarrel over whether direct European governmental subsidies for Airbus or indirect Pentagon subsidies for Boeing are more egregious. Europe's outcry over U.S. sanctions against European firms that deal with American adversaries such as Cuba and Iran has only been swept under the rug. And just over the horizon lies the biggest battle of all: the debates over farm subsidies, genetically modified products, and overall agricultural trade that will explode . . . when the U.S.-EU "peace clause" (a moratorium on new complaints in the agricultural sector) expires.
>
> (BERGSTEN 2001, 17)

The range of actual and potential controversies goes beyond these issues. Bergsten notes that the views of the United States and the EU on the appropriate agenda for a new round of global trade negotiations are vastly different. They contributed to the breakdown of the 1999 ministerial meeting of the WTO in Seattle, where the United States hoped to launch new multilateral talks. Furthermore, in 1999 delegates from forty-eight European and Latin American countries met in Brazil to talk about their common interests in creating a free trade zone between the two regions. The EU has entered an association agreement with Mexico, and it has begun negotiations with Mercosur, the southern cone trade bloc comprising Argentina, Brazil, Paraguay, and Uruguay (Bergsten 2001). Europe and the United States also differ markedly on global warming issues, as we saw in Chapter 6. Those issues have

important implications for a wider array of energy and related environmental policies.

Regional concerns extend beyond Europe. Japan has long been the dominant economic power in Asia. The United States, viewing itself as a Pacific power, took the initiative in creating the Asia-Pacific Economic Cooperation forum, hoping to play a leading role in shaping the future of Asian economic relations in the global competition for regional economic power (see also Bergsten 1994).

For years scholars and policy makers have speculated about the possible emergence of three large currency and trade blocs, one in Europe centered on the EU and the German mark; one in the Western Hemisphere centered on the United States and the U.S. dollar; and the third in Asia centered on Japan and the Japanese yen. (Note that such a tripolar system would exclude many countries in the Global South.) As the United Nations wrote in its 1991 *World Economic Survey,* "today the question is not whether these blocs will be formed, but rather how encompassing they will be and how to ensure that they will not harm the [global] trading system."

Japan, however, showed little interest in playing a leadership role in creating an Asian economic area with Tokyo as the leader. Indeed, Japan's imperial past continues to ignite passionate resentment and fear throughout much of Asia. Recently, however, Japan has negotiated a series of bilateral trade agreements with other Asian states, eschewing the global multilateral forums it preferred in the past. The region as a whole is moving toward preferential trading arrangements not unlike those undergirding the European Union and its associated states, and steps are being taken toward coordinating currency values in the way the predecessors of the present day EU first began their currency links (Bergsten 2001). Thus the possibility of a tripolar trading and currency world remains very much alive.

The implications of a regionally oriented political economy centered on Asia, Europe, and North America remain unclear (see, for example, Kahler 1995; Mansfield and Milner 1997; Trade

Blocs 2000). Although NAFTA and related regional initiatives in Africa, Asia, and Latin America were thought by some to be consistent with GATT's rules, other analysts worried that they violated the principle of nondiscrimination underlying the liberal trade system, thus taking it one more step toward closure. The same is true with the vast array of new, regionally-based schemes now in sight (see Trade Blocs 2000). Although such cooperative arrangements might lead to trade liberalization *within* each region, they arguably would promote that liberalization by discriminating against those *outside* the region. This has long been a complaint lodged against the European Union. Already a substantial portion of trade in Asia, Europe, and North American derives from imports and exports among the countries comprising the three regions.

Others are concerned with the impact that transforming economic relationships into regional centers may have on security relationships. One line of reasoning suggests that "bitter economic rivalry" is a likely outcome of a triangular world political economy because of fear that "there can be enduring national winners and losers from trade competition" (Borrus, et al. 1992)—which is the logic underlying strategic trade theory. Strategic trade practices combined with the way technology develops and the changing relationship between civilian and military research and development will tempt states to " 'grab' key technologies and markets before others can: Doing so would guarantee domestic availability of the industrial resources needed to field state-of-the-art military forces and eliminate the need to make unacceptable concessions." The result? Mercantile rivalry among the world's principal trading blocs, in which "fear of one another" may be the only force binding them together (Borrus, et al. 1992).

The Politics of U.S. Trade Policy We have referred repeatedly in this chapter to the way that labor and environmental groups have become energized on trade issues in recent years at one time. Labor was a champion of free trade, and environmental interests were focused largely at home. Neither is true today. Hence the politics of U.S. trade policy has changed in ways that have important consequences for a world political economy in transition, but one in which the United States remains a key player (see Hockin 2001; Das 2001; Rothgeb 2001). Indeed, environmental and labor issues arguably now comprise the "new protectionism" (Stokes 1999–2000).

During the early post–World War II decades a broad domestic consensus supported trade liberalization, but labor groups began to defect in the 1970s and 1980s, as the declining competitiveness of U.S. exports and the loss of jobs to foreign competitors affected them adversely. American workers' income also began to stagnate in the 1970s, a trend that persisted into the 1990s. Meanwhile, workers' rights related to workshop conditions (such as child labor and "sweatshops") and unionization in other countries where organized labor is weak gained importance (see Kapstein 1996; Newland 1999), as did related issues, such as China's human rights practices. Globalization was behind these developments. By 1993, labor, a backbone of support for the Democratic party, had become even more antagonistic to trade liberalization issues, leading it to oppose NAFTA. Clinton won that fight only with the strong support of congressional Republicans and their business allies.

Globalization also animated environmentalists' interests in trade issues. We have noted some of their concerns as they relate to the ability of the WTO (and GATT before it) to overturn hard-won domestic environmental victories in the name of free trade. Hence labor and environmentalists, otherwise odd political bedfellows, were seen marching together in globalization protests in Seattle, Washington, DC, and Quebec (see Cohen 2001).

I. M. Destler and Peter Balint (1999) use the phrase "trade and . . . " to encapsulate how American trade politics have moved beyond simply reconciling competing commercial interests to accommodating a wider array of issues that globalization has magnified. They describe the "trade and . . ." issues as those that "involve not the balance to be struck *among* US commercial interests, but the proper balance *between* these interests and others that society values." Principal among them, as we have noted, are issues that "involve labor and environmental standards enforced (or not enforced) by U.S. trading partners and the impact that the global trade regime may have on U.S. capacity to strengthen or maintain prolabor and proenvironmental measures here at home."

The side agreements the Clinton administration negotiated to win approval of NAFTA stimulated much of the debate over "trade and . . ." issues. Three agreements related to environmental enforcement and workers' rights were deemed important to winning approval of the agreement. Faced with opposition within his own party, Clinton would later seek to make these issues a centerpiece of future efforts to devise new trade liberalization rules. Other countries, however, were not pleased. Many in the Global South, for example, viewed the extension of American labor standards through multilateral trade agreements as yet another form of Northern trade protectionism. Environmentalists continued to worry about the erosion of domestic laws in the face of others' rulings. Business interests, on the other hand, worried that labors' and environmentalists' demands would erode their ability to compete in the world marketplace.

Dissension over "trade and . . ." issues has figured prominently in the unwillingness of Congress to grant the president renewal of fast-track authority, as this would permit him to negotiate agreements with other countries that would either include or exclude these items as he saw fit, without the ability to Congress to make changes in those agreements. Yet fast-track authority is viewed by pro-trade internationalists as essential to the ability of the United States to continue to exercise a leadership role in the world political economy. Without that leadership, they argue,

regionalism, mercantilism, protectionism—all anathema to the LIEO—will surge.

Recognizing these realities, President George W. Bush asked Congress shortly after the Third Summit of the Americas in Quebec to grant him fast-track authority that would enable the United States to move toward creation a Free Trade Area of the Americas. His proposal sought to placate the competing interests evident in the trade fights Clinton faced by suggesting a "labor and environmental toolbox" that could be used by international organizations to urge countries to comply with international labor standards and environmental practices. The implication is that the agreements the Bush administration might negotiate would not include enforceable labor or environmental standards, as none would be linked directly to the new agreements. Not surprisingly, among Democrats, for whom these issues have become salient, the reception was less than warm. "The toolbox is empty," is the one way one Democratic congressman responded.

AN OUTWARD-LOOKING, NON-IMPERIALIST, CONTINENTAL SUPERPOWER?

American leadership in the world political economy and in the international political system has long been prized not only in the United States but also in other countries. Increasingly, however, others are concerned about the exercise of American leadership. Concepts and terms we have used in this and previous chapters and others we will introduce in Chapter 8 suggest something about the apprehension of others. Primacy, aggressive unilateralism, hardline, hyper-power, neomercantilism—these are among the phrases that other states often associate with an arrogance of power. Our theories of international politics predict that an arrogance of power will lead to balancing behavior by others, not the bandwagoning witnessed during the Cold War. Certainly many of the behaviors of other states in the world political economy during recent years are consistent with balancing behavior.

Globalization has enhanced the soft power of the United States. It has also opened states' borders to forces over which they sometimes have little control. The United States is not immune from the vanishing borders phenomenon, as we have seen. Liberal internationalists believe that further liberalization of the world political economy is necessary if the fruits of progress experienced in the 1990s are to be sustained in the new century. They also believe that American leadership is essential to that process. American policy makers, on the other hand, can no longer count on broad-based domestic support for liberalization. Instead, they must balance domestic and in-

ternational interests. Often this offends one or the other, sometimes both.

Repeated calls for new institutions to cope with new realities have been heard. Certainly the rules guiding the economic institutions operating today are vastly different from the way they looked when the Bretton Woods system was launched in the 1940s. But it seems unlikely institutions whose purposes depart radically from those already in place will be launched. Thus we find ourselves in a challenging world political economy in transition in which only incremental adjustments can be expected. In the words of one analyst commenting at the time of the 1997–1998 global currency crises (Kapstein 1999), "the best we can expect for the foreseeable future is a muddle-through strategy based on existing cooperative frameworks."

KEY TERMS RELATED TO THE WORLD POLITICAL ECONOMY
AND AMERICAN FOREIGN POLICY

absolute power

aggressive unilateralism

Asia-Pacific Economic Cooperation (APEC)

beggar-thy-neighbor policies

Bretton Woods system

collective goods

Common Agricultural Policy (CAP)

crony capitalism

dollar convertibility

dollarization

economic nationalists

European Union (EU)

exchange rates

export-led adjustment

fair trade

fast-track authority

fixed exchange rate system

free-floating exchange rates

free riders

Free Trade Area of the Americas (FTAA)

General Agreement on Tariffs and Trade (GATT)

globalization

Group of 77 (G-77)

Group of Eight (G-8)

Group of Five (G-5)

Group of Seven (G-7)

hegemon

hegemonic stability theory

imperial overstretch

international liquidity

International Monetary Fund (IMF)

Liberal International Economic Order (LIEO)

managed trade

monetarist policies

moral hazard

most-favored-nation (MFN)

multilateralism

neomercantilist (neomercantilism)

New International Economic Order (NIEO)

New Protectionism

Newly Industrializing Economies (NIEs)

nondiscrimination

nontariff barriers (NTBs)

normal trade relations (NTR)

oil shocks

Organization of Petroleum Exporting Nations (OPEC)

parallel currency

passive unilateralism	*stagflation*	*World Bank*
pluralistic cooperation	**strategic trade**	**World Trade Organization (WTO)**
sovereign risk	**Washington consensus**	

SUGGESTIONS FOR FURTHER READING

Bhagwati, Jagdish . *The Wind of a Hundred Days: How Washington Mismanaged Globalization.* Cambridge, MA: MIT Press, 2001.

Destler, I. M., and Peter J. Balint. *The New Politics of American Trade: Trade, Labor, and the Environment.* Washington, DC: Institute for International Economics, 1999.

Eichengreen, Barry. *Toward a New Financial Architecture: A Practical Post-Asia Agenda* Washington, DC. Institute for International Economics, 1999.

Friedman, Thomas L. *The Lexus and the Olive Tree: Understanding Globalization.* New York: Farrar, Straus, Giroux, 1999.

Gilpin, Robert. *The Challenge of the Global Capitalism: The World Economy in the 21st Century.* Princeton, NJ: Princeton University Press, 2000.

Kunz, Diane B. *Butter and Guns: America's Cold War Economic Diplomacy.* New York: Free Press, 1997.

Kegley, Charles W., Jr., and Eugene R. Wittkopf, eds., *The Global Agenda: Issues and Perspectives.* Boston: McGraw-Hill, 2001.

Langhorne, Richard. *The Coming of Globalization: Its Evolution and Contemporary Consequences.* New York: MacMillan. 2000.

Mansfield, Edward D., and Helen V. Milner, eds., *The Political Economy of Regionalism.* New York: Columbia University Press, 1997.

Nye, Joseph S., and John D. Donahue, eds., *Governance in a Globalizing World.* Washington, DC: Brookings, 2000.

Rothgeb, John M., Jr. *U.S. Trade Policy: Balancing Economic Dreams and Political Realities.* Washington, DC: CQ Press, 2001.

Yergin, Daniel, and Joseph Stanislaw. *The Commanding Heights: The Battle Between Government and the Market Place That Is Remaking the Modern World.* New York: Simon and Schuster, 1999.

NOTES

1. We confine the use of "hegemony" to America's role in the world political economy, recognizing, however, that there is a close interaction between economic and political dominance. As one analyst put it, "Hegemonic capacity has a military side as well as an economic one. In order to function, businesses need security and stability—the assurance that goods shipped will arrive, that contracts will be enforced, and that the world in general is predictable" (Schwartz 1994). For further discussions and contrasting viewpoints, see Friedberg (1989), Gilpin (1987), Huntington (1988–1989), Kennedy (1987), Rosecrance (1990), and Strange (1987). For a critique of the concept of hegemony, including Goldstein's definition, see Nye (1990). For a discussion of why "primacy" may or may not matter, see Huntington (1993b) and Jervis (1993).

2. For a concise overview of the international monetary system that places the Bretton Woods system in the broader context of the nineteenth and early twentieth centuries, as well as the post–Bretton Woods period after 1973, see Eichengreen (1998).

3. Our discussion of the international monetary and trade systems draws on Spero (1990) and Spero and Hart (1997). See also Schwartz (1994) and Walters and Blake (1992).

4. Declassified documents from the Truman and Eisenhower administrations clarify the role the United States played in encouraging aggressive Japanese exports to the United States. They also reveal how concern for communism in Asia stimulated choices based on political rather than economic criteria, whose consequences contributed to the ability of

Japan to challenge the United States economically decades later. See Auerbach (1993) for a summary.

5. On the IMF's Structural Adjustment Programs, as the austerity measures are known, see Mohan (2000); Sahn, Dorosh, and Younger (1999); and Schydlowsky (1995).

6. "The theology in government that a gradually declining dollar is good for U.S. competitiveness is a dangerous oversimplification," argued Jeffrey E. Garten, investment banker and author of *A Cold Peace: America, Japan, and Germany and the Struggle for Supremacy*. He added that "there is no precedent in history where a major industrial power has been competitive while its currency was depreciating" (cited in Mufson 1992).

7. The G-77 did agree in early 1999 to establish a modest forum whose purpose would be to foster consultations on exchange rate fluctuations and other problems to the Asian contagion, including movements in international hedge funds (*New York Times*, 21 February 1999, 14).

8. As is often the case, the meaning of "new protectionism" has changed and today encompasses concerns about environmental issues and labor standards that we discuss later in this chapter. See Stokes (1999–2000).

9. *Voluntary export restrictions (VERs)* are another form of protection that have been especially popular with the United States. VERs are export quotas that place quantitative restrictions on certain products, such as autos, steel, textiles, and footwear. Because they are imposed by the exporting country following negotiations, VERs are "hands-off" forms of protection that require no action on the part of the importing country. VERs were prohibited in the Uruguay Round of GATT agreements.

10. The concept is from dependency theory, which classifies states into core (industrialized countries) and periphery (developing countries), according to their position in the international division of labor. For discussions, see Caporaso (1978); Shannon (1989); and Sklair (1991).

11. Trade policy expert I. M. Destler explains:

Fast-track is Washington's solution to a bedrock constitutional dilemma. The president and the executive branch can negotiate all they like, but Congress makes U.S. trade law. Other nations know that our highly independent legislature will not necessarily deliver on executive promises. So in negotiations where broad-ranging commitments to open markets are exchanged, they refuse to bargain seriously unless U.S. officials can assure that Congress will write their concessions into U.S. statutes. Fast-track offers that assurance, with its promise that Congress will vote up or down, within a defined time period, on legislation submitted by the president or implement specific trade agreements. (Destler 1999, 27).

12. The "Cairns group," a coalition of fourteen industrial and developing-nation agricultural exporters first organized in 1986 to press for trade liberalization in agriculture, also urged U.S. action (see Tussie 1993).

13. Developing states had earlier opposed inclusion of counterfeiting on the GATT agenda. The practice—which involves such things as Rolex watches, Apple computers, and photo-reproduced college textbooks—is widespread in much of the Global South. The United States has been especially critical of China, arguing that it engages in widespread piracy of computer software, musical compact discs, and video laser discs. Such practices were alleged when the Uruguay Rounded ended to have cost American companies as much as $1 billion a year (*New York Times*, 24 July 1994, 8).

14. The environmental consequences of free trade are subject to often vigorous dispute. For contrasting viewpoints, see Bhagwati (1993, 2001); Daly (1993); Destler and Balint (1999); Esty (1994); and French (1993).

15. For a critique of Krugman's arguments and a rejoinder, see especially the essays by Clyde V. Prestowitz, Jr., Lester C. Thurow, Stephen S. Cohen, and Krugman in the July/August 1994 issue of *Foreign Affairs*.

16. In the 1997 Treaty of Amsterdam, designed to revise the Maastricht Treaty, EU negotiators agreed to widening and deepening of the EU by beginning accession talks with Cyprus, Poland, Hungary, the Czech Republic, Estonia, and Slovenia.

❖

PART IV

Societal Sources of American Foreign Policy

Chapter 8
Americans' Values, Beliefs, and Preferences:
Political Culture and Public Opinion in Foreign Policy

Chapter 9
The Transmission of Values, Beliefs, and Preferences:
Interest Groups, Mass Media, and Presidential Elections

CHAPTER 8

Americans' Values, Beliefs, and Preferences

Political Culture and Public Opinion in Foreign Policy

America has never been united by blood or birth or soil. We are bound by ideals
that move us beyond our backgrounds, lift us above our interests
and teach us what it means to be citizens.

PRESIDENT GEORGE W. BUSH, 2001

Nobody can know what it means for a President to be sitting in that White House
working late at night and to have hundreds of thousands of demonstrators
charging through the streets. Not even earplugs could block the noise.

PRESIDENT RICHARD M. NIXON, 1977

Foreign policy is often seen as "above politics." Domestic interests are subservient to national interests, according to this viewpoint. When the security of the nation is at stake, Americans lay aside their partisan differences and support their leaders as they make the tough choices necessary to promote and protect the national interest in an anarchical world. Politics, in short, stops at the water's edge.

Is this viewpoint, firmly embedded in the nation's political mythology, realistic? Are domestic partisan and ideological differences put aside when leaders make foreign and national security policy decisions affecting the nation's vital interests? Or are their choices influenced measurably by the anticipated effect on their popularity and power at home?

Picture for a moment the following scenario: The president's day begins in the Oval Office at 7:00 A.M. with briefings from his principal advisers. His chief domestic adviser opens with reports of rising inflation, increasing unemployment, and growing volatility in stock and bond markets. He also describes a worsening balance-of-trade picture as the value of the dollar soars, the euro plummets, and oil prices rise even as the California energy crisis widens. The latest polls show that economic concerns and the smell of domestic political scandal have caused the president's popularity with the American people to weaken. On top of this, the opposition party in the impending mid-term congressional elections have accused the president of pursuing a "wishy-washy" policy toward the nation's Middle East allies.

The national security adviser is next, warning that CIA reports indicate a likely increase in terrorist attacks on U.S. military and civilian assets by militant Islamic fundamentalists in the Middle East. She strongly urges immediate action to protect American interests and investments in the region. A strategy session is quickly crammed into the day's agenda that includes separate consultations with representatives from the American Petroleum Institute and from groups calling themselves "Friends of Israel" and "Citizens for Arab Justice." The last group voices concerns about what they say is a pro-Israeli foreign policy and accuses the administration of "racial profiling" of Arab Americans.

What factors will most influence a president confronted by such circumstances? Although we cannot get into a president's mind, we can guess what calculations are likely to shape his choices. When forced to reach a decision, we can reasonably assume that he will ask himself, "What is the likely domestic repercussion of option X or Y? Will it enhance or erode my public standing? Will it undermine the strength of my partisan supporters? And might it, perhaps overnight, turn those supporters into antagonists?" Countless questions about the likely response of America's allies and adversaries in the Middle East and elsewhere can also be anticipated, but the urge to give priority to the domestic consequences of foreign policy decisions may be irresistible. As one former policy maker lamented,

> [American leaders have shown a] tendency to make statements and take actions with regard not to their effect on the international scene to which they are ostensibly addressed but rather to their effect on those echelons of American opinion . . . to which the respective [leaders] are anxious to appeal. The questions, in these circumstances, [become] not: How effective is what I am doing in terms of the impact it makes on our world environment? but rather: How do I look, in the mirror of domestic American opinion, as I do it? Do I look shrewd, determined, defiantly patriotic, imbued with the necessary vigilance before the wiles of foreign governments? If so, this is what I do, even though it may prove meaningless, or even counterproductive, when applied to the realities of the external situation.
> (KENNAN 1967, 53)

This viewpoint suggests that foreign policy decisions are likely to be guided more by a concern for the reactions they will provoke at home than abroad. Preserving one's power base and the psychological desire to be admired encourage foreign policy decisions designed to elicit favorable domestic responses. At the extreme, theater substitutes for rational policy choice; spin control becomes an overriding preoccupation.

Our purpose in this chapter and the next is to explore how American foreign policy is conditioned by the nation's internal or societal characteristics. Here we probe how America's *political culture*—Americans' beliefs about their political system and the way it operates—and the public's foreign policy attitudes and preferences—*public opinion*—affect American foreign policy. Then, in Chapter 9, we explore the roles that interest groups, the mass media, and presidential elections play in transmitting beliefs, attitudes, and preferences into the policy-making process. Throughout, we seek to understand how these societal forces constrain leaders' foreign policy behavior and when and how they encourage policy change.

We begin our inquiry by considering how the national attributes of and domestic conditions in the United States compare with other countries.

AMERICA IN THE COMMUNITY OF NATIONS: AN EXCEPTIONAL CASE?

The characteristics that make the United States the kind of nation it is shape Americans' self-images and their perceptions of their nation's proper world role. In the waning days of the Cold War many analysts worried that the relative decline of the United States in the world community would make it more like an "ordinary" country. Today, however, it is clear the United States remains far from a typical society in the international community. As the data in Table 8.1 show, it is the world's fourth-largest country in geographical size and third in population. It is endowed with vast natural resources, wealth, technology, and mobilized military power—a "hyper-power" among the democratic market economies comprising the Global North. Although the nation's economic growth, saving, investment, and energy efficiency rates are comparatively low, the nation as a whole is materially well off. Americans comprise less than five percent of the world's population, but in any given year they produce (and consume) a quarter or more of its total economic output. Personal wealth is far from equally distributed, but the "average" American is better off than his or her counterpart living almost anywhere else in the world. Comparatively speaking, the American people also are highly urbanized, well educated, and have easy access to sophisticated communications systems. In short, American society and the quality of life the American people enjoy are quite unlike any other in the world.

There also is a downside evident in the United States. Violent crime, although reduced dramatically during the 1990s, remains commonplace on American streets. The United States began that decade ranked number one in intentional homicides in the Global North. It also ranked number one in reported rapes, divorces, and percentage of the population in prison and Number two in drug crimes (*Human Development Report 1993,* 191–92). Such data point to a strained social fabric and a diminished quality of life. Comparable cross-national data at the end of 1990s are not available, but many Americans continue to say they are afraid to walk on the streets of their own neighborhoods at night and fear for the safety of their children in school.

It is tempting to assume that America's *national attributes*—particularly its enormous capabilities and resources—dictate its foreign policy objectives, but direct causal linkages are unwarranted. For example, simplistic, single-factor propositions such as "large, populous countries inevitably are imperialistic," "educated societies pursue peaceful foreign polices," or "militarized countries are necessarily expansionist" cannot be substantiated empirically. Too many counter-examples exist. Even the behavioral "law" that democracies do not wage war against one another requires some qualification (note the combatants in the War of 1812 and the American Civil War). Moreover, most societal conditions remain stable for years, so they seldom precipitate policy change. More appropriately, then, national attributes such as size, resources, and economic conditions are best conceived as background factors that make some foreign policy options possible while limiting the feasibility of others. We can also think of societal factors as data forming part of decision makers' perceptual maps of the world and their state's place within it. Because images of American society may shape policy makers' thinking more strongly than some tangible conditions do (Dallek 1983), changes in American society—be they in demography, lifestyle, consumer habits, import dependence, domestic savings and investments, public and private indebtedness, or environmental quality—also may shape their views about the nation's proper international role and ultimately influence the kinds of policies and programs they propose.

The bases on which these perceptions of American society and its world role rest also are rooted in policy makers' prior beliefs and experiences, as the nation's leaders are creatures of its political culture and cannot escape its influence. A closer examination of that culture is thus warranted.

**Table 8.1 American Society in the World Community:
The Comparative U.S. Rank in the Late Twentieth Century**

National Attributes and Indicators	Date of U.S. Observation	U.S. Rank Among Other Countries
Economic Status		
Gross national product (GNP)	1998	1
GNP per capita	1998	6
Percent of exports in gross domestic product (GDP)	1998	43
Domestic savings as percent of GDP	1998	73
Military Power		
Military expenditures (dollars)	1997	1
Military expenditures per capita	1997	7
Military expenditures as percent of GNP	1997	55
Resources		
Population	1998	3
Commercial energy consumption per capita	1997	8
Percent urban population	1998	31
Education		
Adult literacy rate	1998	5
Percent of secondary school-age population enrolled 1997	1997	13
Public expenditures as percent of GNP	1995–1997	38
Public expenditures as percent of total gov. expenditures	1995–1997	66
Social		
Index of human development (life expectancy, adult literacy rate, school enrollments, per capita income)	1998	3
Under-five mortality rate	1992	9
Public health expenditure as percent of GDP	1996–1998	11
Life expectancy at birth (years)	1998	28
Doctors per 1000 population	1992–1995	35
Urban population (percent of total population)	1998	40
Information Technology		
Televisions per 1000 people	1996–1998	1
Personal computers per 1000 people	1996–1998	1
Internet hosts per 1000 people	1998	1
Cellular mobile subscribers per 1000 people	1996–1998	16
Governmental		
Central government expenditures (dollars)	1997	1
Central government expenditures as percentage of GNP	1997	122

SOURCE: U.S. Arms Control and Disarmament Agency, *World Military Expenditures and Arms Transfers 1998.* Washington, DC: ACDA, 2000, 51; United Nations Development Programme, *Human Development Report 2000.* New York: Oxford University Press, 2000, 157–160, 186–217, 223–230.

POLITICAL CULTURE
AND FOREIGN POLICY

The *political culture* of the United States refers to the political values, cognitions, ideas, and ideals about American society and politics held by the American people. Because these are both deep-seated and widely shared—as surely they are since most Americans have been socialized by the same cultural influences—the political culture concept taps a potentially important domestic source of American foreign policy. Indeed, it is common-place to observe that "the nation was explicitly founded on particular sets of values, and these made the United States view itself as different from the nations of the Old World from which it originated" (McCormick 1992). In short, American foreign policy may be different from the policies of other states because the United States itself is unique.

What are the core values widely embraced in American society? Analysts' opinions on this question vary (see Elazar 1994; Kingdon 1999; Lipset 1996; McClosky and Zaller 1984; Morgan 1988; Parenti 1981), not only because political subcultures and alienated groups make it difficult to generalize safely about the degree to which some values are universally embraced, but also because the nation's "loosely bounded culture" (Merelman 1984) is fluid and pluralistic. It allows the individual citizen freedom to practice his or her own philosophy while still upholding a commitment to the nation. Thus the American political tradition emphasizes majoritarianism but simultaneously tolerates disagreement, parochial loyalties, and counterallegiances.

The Liberal Tradition

Despite diversity, and respect for it, certain norms dominate. There are values and principles to which most Americans respond regardless of the particular political philosophy they espouse. Although no single definition adequately captures its essence, the complementary assumptions that comprise "mainstream" American political beliefs may be labeled *liberalism.* Basic to the liberal legacy is Thomas Jefferson's belief, enshrined in the Declaration of Independence, that the purpose of government is to secure for its citizens their inalienable rights to life, liberty, and the pursuit of happiness. The "social contract" among those who created the American experiment, which sought to safeguard these rights, is sacred. So, too, is the people's right to revolt against the government should it breach the contract. "Whenever any form of government becomes destructive of those ends," Jefferson concluded, "it is the right of the people to alter or abolish it."

In the liberal creed, as Jefferson affirmed, legitimate political power arises only from the consent of the governed, whose participation in decisions affecting public policy and the quality of life is guaranteed. Other principles and values embellish the liberal tradition, rooted in the seventeenth-century political philosophy of the English thinker *John Locke.* Among them are individual liberty, equality of treatment and opportunity before the law ("all men are created equal"), due process, self-determination, free enterprise, inalienable (natural) rights, majority rule and minority rights, freedom of expression, federalism, the separation of powers within government, equal opportunity to participate in public affairs, and legalism ("a government of laws, not of men"). All are consistent with Locke's belief that government should be limited to the protection of the individual's life, liberty, and property through popular consent.

Together, these tenets form the basis of *popular sovereignty,* which holds that "the only true source of political authority is the will of those who are ruled, in short the doctrine that all power arises from the people" (Thomas 1988). Abraham Lincoln's embrace of government of, by, and for the people affirms this fundamental principle. Because the American ethos subscribes enthusiastically to this principle, Americans think of themselves as a "free people."

American leaders—regardless of their partisan or philosophical labels—routinely reaffirm the convictions basic to the *Lockean liberal tradition,* as do the documents Americans celebrate on national holidays. Even those who regard themselves as political conservatives are in fact "traditional liberals who have kept faith with liberalism as it was propounded two hundred years ago" (Lipsitz and Speak 1989). Thus it is not surprising that other nations typically see few differences in the principles on which American foreign policy rests, even when political power shifts from one president to another or from one political party to the other.

Liberalism and American Foreign Policy Behavior

In a classic treatise on *The Liberal Tradition in America,* Louis Hartz (1955) argues that Lockean liberalism has become so embedded in American life that Americans may be blind to what it really is—namely, an ideology. The basis for the ideology of liberalism, so the reasoning holds, is the *exceptional American experience.* It includes the absence of pronounced class and religious strife at the time of the nation's founding, complemented by the fortuitous gift of geographic isolation from European political and military turmoil.

To mobilize public support for U.S. actions abroad and endow policy decisions with moral value, American leaders often have cloaked their actions in the rhetoric of the ideological precepts of American exceptionalism and Lockean liberalism. Principles such as self-determination and self-preservation are continually invoked to justify policy action, as "concern with wealth, power, status, moral virtue, and the freedom of mankind were successfully transformed into a single set of mutually reinforcing values by the paradigm of Lockean liberalism" (Weisband 1973).

Remaking the world in America's image also springs from the nation's cultural traditions. As President Ronald Reagan once put it, "our democracy encompasses many freedoms—freedom of speech, of religion, of assembly, and of so many other liberties that we often take for granted. These are rights that should be shared by all mankind." Accordingly, Reagan in 1983 launched the *National Endowment for Democracy (NED),* a controversial program whose purpose is to encourage worldwide the development of autonomous political, economic, social, and cultural institutions to serve as the foundations of democracy and the guarantors of individual rights and freedoms (see Carothers 1994b).

An important synergism related to the promotion of democracy abroad is the set of beliefs that forges the premises of both classical democratic theory and capitalism into a deeply entrenched ideology of *democratic capitalism.* While democracy and capitalism have common historical and philosophical roots, at home they have sometimes been in conflict, as capitalism in particular has led to great inequalities in income and wealth. Indeed, during the last quarter of the twentieth century the incomes of Americans in the bottom tenth percentile fell by seven percent, while the incomes of those in the top tenth percentile grew by thirty-eight percent (Danziger and Reed 1999).[1] Abroad, however, the premises of democratic capitalism embedded in the American culture certainly help explain Americans' distaste for socialism and why they viewed Soviet communism as a threat to "the American way of life."

The cultural ethos that supports *equality of opportunity,* not *equality of outcome,* may also explain what appears to be public indifference to the plight of so many poor people around the world. Noteworthy is that "the spread of democracy has made more visible the problem of income gaps, which can no longer be blamed on poor politics—not on communism in Eastern Europe and the former Soviet Union nor on military authoritarianism in Latin America. Regularly invoked as the handmaiden of open markets, democracy looks more and more like their accomplice in a vicious cycle of inequality and injustice" (Birdsall 1998; see also *World Development Report 2000/2001*).

Despite its seemingly negative consequences for inequality of outcome, the liberal tradition continues to influence in other ways how the

United States seeks to promote democratic capitalism abroad.

> Guided by faith in the liberal tradition's nostrums and by the mechanistic notion learned in civics class that a community is built by balancing competing interests, American foreign policy experts urge societies riven by conflict to play nice: to avoid "winner takes all" politics and to guarantee that, regardless of election results, the weaker party will have a voice in national political and cultural affairs. To accomplish this, coalition governments, the guaranteed division of key offices, and a system of "mutual vetoes," are always recommended.
>
> (SCHWARZ 1998, 69)

A political system constructed this way is expected to ameliorate conflict, much as Americans believe their own balance-of-power political system does.

The American way of war also has roots in the liberal tradition. Among the industrialized countries, more Americans than anywhere else are churchgoers and profess that religion is an important part of their life (Morin 1998). Not surprisingly, then, in every war America's side is God's side (Lipset 1996). Less flattering is the argument that the American penchant to resort to military force abroad is sustained by a culture of violence at home (Payne 1996).

Other illustrations can be found linking foreign policy predispositions to the influence of American values. It seems, then, that the question is not whether there is a relationship between culture and foreign policy, but how it operates. Precise answers to that question remain elusive, but one probable link can be found in the *law of anticipated reactions*. The "law" posits that decision makers screen out certain alternatives because they anticipate that some options will be adversely received—an anticipation born of their intrinsic image of the American political culture which helps to define in their minds the range of permissible foreign policy goals and options. As one analyst put it, political culture's influence "lies in its power to set reasonably fixed limits to political behavior and provide subliminal direction for political action . . . all the more effective because of [the] subtlety whereby those limited are unaware of the limitations placed on them" (Elazar 1970). Robert Kennedy's argument against using an air strike to destroy the missiles the Soviet Union surreptitiously placed in Cuba in 1962 illustrates this subtle screening process. As he himself described it:

> Whatever validity the military and political arguments were for an attack in preference to a blockade, America's traditions and history would not permit such a course of action. Whatever military reasons [former Secretary of State Dean Acheson] and others could marshal, they were nevertheless, in the last analysis, advocating a surprise attack by a very large nation against a very small one. This, I said, could not be undertaken by the U.S. if we were to maintain our moral position at home and around the globe. Our struggle against communism throughout the world was far more than physical survival—it had as its essence our heritage and our ideals, and these we must not destroy.[2]
>
> (KENNEDY 1971, 16–17; SEE ALSO EVAN 2000)

This screening process has sometimes failed, of course—especially when principle clashes with power. Thus fear of communism helps to explain how a country committed to individual rights and liberties sometimes suppressed them in the name of national security. Similarly, the ascent of the United States to the status of a global power after World War II helps to explain how a nation committed to "limited government" nonetheless could permit the rise of an "imperial presidency," undeterred by the constitutional system of checks and balances, and justify the creation and maintenance of a gigantic peacetime military establishment (see Deudney and Ikenberry 1994).

We also must acknowledge that the ideas and ideals comprising the political culture are open to competing interpretations and are often in flux. Demographic and other developments coalesce to generate changes in otherwise durable values and beliefs (McClosky and Zaller 1984; Citrin et al. 1994). Because the political culture is not immutable, policy makers may feel less constrained by anticipated adverse reactions to their policy choices.

Political Culture in a Changing Society

Consider what happened to the 1960s' generation. Raised to believe that the United States was a splendidly virtuous country, young Americans found—through the Bay of Pigs invasion; racial discrimination in Selma, Alabama, and elsewhere; the assassinations of President Kennedy, his brother Robert, and Martin Luther King Jr.; and then Vietnam—that ideals were prostituted in practice. Outraged, large numbers of alienated Americans protested the abuses that undermined seemingly sacred assumptions. Simultaneously, the faith the American people placed in their political and other social institutions declined precipitously. They also began to question traditional American values.

With the political culture in flux, the climate of opinion encouraged policy change. A war ended ignominiously. Two American presidents were toppled: one (Lyndon Johnson) in the face of intense political pressure, the other (Richard Nixon) in disgrace. Legal barriers to racial equality were dismantled. New constraints were placed on the use of American force abroad, both overt and covert, and the range of permissible action was reduced in ways that continue to shape policy thinking today. Thus it appears that changes in the political culture—whether they stem from public disillusionment, policy failure, or other causes—can affect the kinds of policies that leaders propose and the ways they are later carried out.

Today the core values comprising American society and its political culture continue to be split along lines that mirror the 1960s and 1970s. The "baby boomers" who came of age politically during these decades evince a greater tolerance "for groups such as homosexuals that have suffered discrimination and toward practices ranging from interracial marriage to premarital sex that once might have been condemned. That tolerance also extends to the free expression of controversial views" (Broder and Morin 1999). Arguably these changes colored the debate over President Clinton's impeachment. Research shows the nation was split nearly evenly between those who think the president has a greater responsibility than others for setting a high moral standard and those who believe evaluations of job performance are more important than judgments about a president's personal life (Broder and Morin 1999).

The political culture also faces a new challenge that promises to further test its tolerance and other core values: *multiculturalism.* "At the core of multiculturalism . . . is an insistence on the primacy of ethnicity over the individual's shared and equal status as a citizen in shaping his or her identity and, derivatively, his or her interests."

> Multiculturalism is based on the conviction that the image of America as a land of equal opportunity is not just exaggerated, but fraudulent. . . . An important purpose of multiculturalism is to justify the claims of subordinate ethnic groups to a larger share of society's goods, both tangible and intangible. From this ideological perspective, ethnicity should determine the allocation of all important benefits, such as jobs, government contracts, places in universities, legislative seats, control of the curriculum in schools and colleges, time on public television, and so forth.
>
> (CITRIN ET AL. 1994, 9; SEE ALSO GILPIN 1995)

Thus multiculturalism promotes *communal rights,* whereas liberalism rejects them in favor of *individual rights* and equal opportunity.

Multiculturalism clearly challenges the conception of the United States as a pluralistic society, one embodied in the nation's motto *e pluribus unum*—out of many, one. The motto reflects

Americans' immigrant heritage which led President Reagan to describe the United States as an "island of freedom," a land placed here by "divine Providence" as a "refuge for all those people in the world who yearn to breathe free." It also reflects the conviction that diversity itself can be a source of national pride and unity, something no other nation has ever tried or claimed. This is what makes the American effort to build a multiethnic society "a bolder experiment than we sometimes remember" (Schlesinger 1992). The *melting pot* became a popular metaphor to describe the process that assimilated the newly-arrived into the dominant social and political ethos—that combination of ideas and ideals Swedish social scientist Gunnar Myrdal (1944) described over a half-century ago as "the American Creed."

The 1980s and 1990s saw a larger immigration into the United States than at any time since the early twentieth century, and its composition was dramatically different. In the early twentieth century the vast majority of immigrants came from Europe. In the late twentieth century most came from Asia and Central and South America. These changes are reflected in the composition of foreign-born Americans (which includes all residents not born in the United States, not just recent immigrants). According to the U.S. Census Bureau, in 1999 more than 26 million foreign-born people now live in the United States, comprising nearly ten percent of the total population. Half came from the Caribbean and Central and South America, more than a quarter from Asia. Only sixteen percent came from Europe (Bureau of the Census 2000). Combined with other demographic trends, it is now possible to foresee a future in which Americans of European stock will no longer comprise a majority. Indeed, as President Clinton observed in commemorating Martin Luther King day in the waning days of his presidency, "America is undergoing one of the great demographic transformations in our history. . . . Today there is no majority racial or ethnic group in Hawaii or California or

Houston or New York City. In a little more than fifty years, there will be no majority race in America" (see also Maharidge 1996).

Ironically, today's immigrant Americans often advocate multiculturalism and consequently challenge the European—and especially British—heritage on which the nation's civic culture rests. Many of these non-Europeans "bring with them a resentment, in some cases a hatred, of Europe and the West provoked by generations of Western colonialism, racism, condescension, contempt, and cruel exploitation," observes Arthur Schlesinger, Jr. (1992). From this perspective, "the spread of Western culture is due not to any innate quality but simply to the spread of Western power. Thus the popularity of European classical music around the world—and, one supposes, of American jazz and rock, too—is evidence not of wide appeal but of 'the pattern of imperialism, in which the conquered culture adopts that of the conqueror.'"

With the American creed under stress, the nation's immigration policy also is under attack. Where migrants of European origin were once given preferential access, today the emphasis is on the skills migrants will bring with them, not their national origin. Meanwhile, many Americans have jettisoned the melting pot metaphor. A 1993 *Newsweek* poll (9 August 1993) found that only twenty percent of the American people believed the United States is still a melting pot, compared with two-thirds who felt that today's immigrants "maintain their national identity more strongly." Sixty percent also expressed the view that immigration today is bad for the country, compared with a similar proportion who felt it had been good for the country in the past.

These stark changes reflect, among other things, fear that immigrants threaten Americans' jobs and the widespread belief that many of them end up on states' welfare rolls. Seven years after the *Newsweek* poll, during a time of booming economic activity, the Pew Research Center for The People and The Press (2000) found that nearly forty percent of the American people embraced the view that "immigrants today are a burden on our country because they take our jobs, housing, and health care." Interestingly, however, this was down from sixty-three percent who held that view in 1994. In that environment of anti-immigrant resentment, the Republican-controlled House of Representatives introduced legislation modeled after California's Proposition 187, which sought to exclude illegal immigrants from such publicly funded services as education and health care. Two years later President Clinton signed into law the "Illegal Immigration Reform and Immigrant Responsibility Act," which restricted public benefits for foreign nationals.

The foreign policy implications of multiculturalism are not easily assessed, largely because those in positions of power continue to subscribe to the still-dominant liberal ethos. As American society and culture change, however, leaders may find it increasingly difficult to build and maintain coalitions of support for internationalism and for particular elements of the internationalist paradigm, such as multilateral institutions or intervention on behalf of democracy. Thus multiculturalism poses yet another challenge to the maintenance of global activism in the new millenium. Noteworthy is that the Cold War actually facilitated its blossoming. "The long war" against communism strengthened Americans' national identity, providing a "unifying dynamic [that] helped overcome ethnic and sectional differences and the ideological heritage of individualism" (Deudney and Ikenberry 1994). Its end in turn encouraged reemergence of ethnic and sectional differences previously muted in the anticommunist struggle. Thus, more than in the past, American policy must be "based on compromises among the advocates of rival ideologies and on shifting coalitions of supporters." This portends "a greater degree of instability and unpredictability with respect to the commitment of national energy and resources to foreign affairs" (Citrin et al. 1994; see also DeConde 1992; De La Garza and Pachon 2000; Krenn 1999).

As this conclusion suggests, the potential impact of changes in the dominant political culture on American foreign policy depends critically on American leaders. It depends on how those in positions of power perceive those changes and how their perceptions affect their corresponding political calculations. Thus a direct correspondence between principles and American diplomatic practice may not exist. Instead, cultural changes shape an atmosphere that makes new practices more acceptable and old ones less so. Americans' foreign policy beliefs and the opinions they express on the issues policy makers must grapple with daily help to define what is acceptable and what is not, as the changes in attitudes that we have noted toward immigration illustrate. It is appropriate, therefore, that we direct attention to the nature and impact of public opinion.

PUBLIC OPINION AND FOREIGN POLICY: AN OVERVIEW

Like America's diplomatic history, public attitudes toward the nation's world role have alternated between periods of introversion and extroversion, between isolation from the world's problems and active involvement in shaping them to fit American preferences. Public support for global activism dominated the Cold War era. The nature of internationalism has undergone fundamental changes, however, especially during and since the Vietnam War. Internationalism is now also under challenge in some quarters, as the world's sole superpower seeks to balance priorities at home and its purposes abroad.

Coming to grips with the twenty-first century world will be difficult, as the American people embrace sometimes competing foreign policy goals:

- They favor global activism but oppose sending economic and military aid to other nations

- They yearn for peace through strength but are wary of international institutions

- They fear nuclear weapons and their proliferation and support efforts to reach negotiated arms agreements with the nation's present and former adversaries

- They oppose the use of force abroad but back presidents when they choose force of arms and prefer military victory to limited war
- They worry about the impact of free trade on their jobs but believe globalization has been good for the country

Little wonder that the role public opinion plays in shaping the nation's conduct is poorly understood and often suspect, and why policy makers sometimes disparage it. John F. Kennedy's view, as described by his aide, Theodore C. Sorensen (1963), is a timeless insider's view: "Public opinion is often erratic, inconsistent, arbitrary, and unreasonable—with a compulsion to make mistakes. . . . It rarely considers the needs of the next generation or the history of the last. . . . It is frequently hampered by myths and misinformation, by stereotypes and shibboleths, and by an innate resistance to innovation."

Despite this viewpoint—whether accurate or not—a vast coterie of media, political, and private groups now spend millions of dollars every year to determine what the American people think and what they are thinking about. Although modern polling ranges far beyond politics to touch virtually every aspect of Americans' private and public lives, political polling is extraordinarily pervasive (and intrusive). The seemingly axiomatic importance of political attitudes in today's world explains the compulsion to measure, manipulate, and master public opinion. As one observer put it, "Politicians court it; statesmen appeal to it; philosophers extol or condemn it; merchants cater to it; military leaders fear it; sociologists analyze it; statisticians measure it; and constitution-makers try to make it sovereign" (Childs 1965).

FOREIGN POLICY OPINION AND ITS IMPACT

Democratic theory presupposes that citizens will make informed choices about the issues of the day and ultimately about who will best represent their beliefs in the councils of government. The American people in turn expect their views to be considered when political leaders contemplate new policies or revise old ones, because leaders are chosen to represent and serve the interests of their constituents. The Constitution affirms the centrality of American citizens by beginning with the words "We the people."[3]

The notion that public opinion somehow conditions public policy is appealing, but it raises troublesome questions. Do public preferences lead American foreign policy, as democratic theory would have us believe, or is the relationship more subtle and complicated? Do changes in foreign policy result from shifts in American public attitudes? Or is the relationship one of policy first and opinion second? Indeed, are the American people capable of exercising the responsibilities expected of them?

The Nature of American Public Opinion

The premise of democratic theory—that the American people will make informed policy choices—does not hold up well under scrutiny. That most Americans do not possess even the most elementary knowledge about their own political system, much less international affairs, is an inescapable fact. Moreover, people's "information" is often so inaccurate that it might better be labeled "misinformation." The following reveal the often startling levels of ignorance:

- In 1985, twenty-eight percent of those surveyed thought that the Soviet Union and the United States fought each other in World War II; forty-four percent did not know the two were allies at that time
- In 1979, the year the SALT II treaty was signed, only twenty-three percent of the adult population knew the two countries involved in the SALT negotiations.
- In 1964, only fifty-eight percent of the American public thought that the United States was a member of NATO; almost two-fifths believed the Soviet Union was a member
- In 1997, as the Clinton administration pushed for expanding NATO, eight in

ten Americans knew the United States was a member of the alliance, but less than sixty percent knew that Russia was not; twenty-three percent assumed that Russia was a member. After Hungary, Poland, and the Czech Republic were invited to join NATO, only one in ten Americans could recall the names of any of the invitees

- In 1983, forty-five percent of the American people thought the United States supported the Sandinista government in Nicaragua, not the contras; a nearly identical number indicated they had not heard or read about the fighting between the Sandinistas and the rebels

- In 1993, after more than year of bitter conflict in the former Yugoslavia, only twenty-five percent of the American people could correctly identify the ethnic group that had conquered much of Bosnia and surrounded the capital city of Sarajevo—this despite reports that half or more of them had followed events in the region

- In 1994, forty-six percent of the electorate believed that foreign aid, which accounts for less than one percent of the federal budget, was one of its two biggest items (welfare was the other)

- In 1999, just as the United States embarked on a military campaign aginst Serbia, only thirty-seven percent of the American people knew the United States was supporting the Albanian Kosovars in the conflict

- In 1985, only sixty-three percent of the public knew that the United States supported South Vietnam in the Vietnam War, a violent conflict that cost 58,000 thousand American lives

Evidence demonstrating the extent of political misunderstanding and ignorance about basic issues could be expanded considerably, but it would only reinforce the picture of a citizenry ill-informed about major issues of public policy and ill-equipped to evaluate government policy

making. Noteworthy is that the issues about which the public is persistently ignorant are not fleeting current events but typically ones that have long figured prominently on the national or global political agendas.

The absence of basic foreign affairs knowledge does not stem from deficiencies in U.S. educational institutions. It stems from disinterest. Public ignorance is a function of public inattention, for people are knowledgeable about what is important to them. More Americans are concerned about the outcome of major sporting events than with the shape of the political system. Again, consider some evidence:

- *Inattention to public issues:* In 1990, as tens of thousands of U.S. troops were poised for battle in Middle Eastern deserts, only fifty-three percent of the American public indicated they were "very interested" in following news about relations between the United States and other countries. The proportion of those closely following specific foreign policy issues or events was even lower (Rielly 1991)

- *Apathy and voter turnout:* In comparison with turnout rates in other democratic countries, American voters are apathetic. The percentage of eligible voters who voted in the fourteen presidential elections since World War II has ranged from forty-nine percent (1996) to sixty-three percent (1960). Ronald Reagan in 1980 and George Bush in 1988 were both elected president by only a third of the eligible electorate. For Bill Clinton the calculation was even starker: In 1992 only fifty-five percent of eligible voters elected to vote; of those, only forty-three percent voted for him. Four years later voter turnout dropped below fifty percent for the first time since 1925. And in 2000, George W. Bush and Al Gore split almost evenly the fifty percent of the voting age population who participated in the election. Strikingly, among modern presidents "only [Lyndon] Johnson . . .

won his first election by more than fifty-five percent of the two-party vote" (Brace and Hinckley 1993)

- *Other forms of political nonparticipation:* Between 1952 and 1998 the proportion of Americans who profess to have worked for a political party or candidate during a congressional or presidential campaign never exceeded seven percent (Conway 2000). In 1998, only two percent of the entire population indicated they had written or spoken to a public official about a foreign affairs issue in the preceding three or four years (Gallup Poll survey for the Chicago Council on Foreign Relations)

In short, the United States purports to be a participatory system of democratic governance, but few are deeply involved in politics and most lack the interest and motivation to become involved.[4] Furthermore, most Americans are more interested in domestic affairs than in foreign policy (although concern on both counts is low). This fact led Gabriel A. Almond (1960) to conclude in his classic study, *The American People and Foreign Policy,* that public opinion toward foreign policy is appropriately thought of as "moods" that "undergo frequent alteration in response to changes in events," instead of resting on some kind of "intellectual structure." He argued that, "the characteristic response to questions of foreign policy is one of indifference. A foreign policy crisis, short of the immediate threat of war, may transform indifference to vague apprehension, to fatalism, to anger; but the reaction is still a mood, a superficial and fluctuating response."

Are Interest and Information Important?

Almond's conclusion has long been regarded as conventional wisdom, but there are important reasons to question it (Caspary 1970; Holsti 1996). Most Americans may be uninformed about and seemingly indifferent to the details of policy, but they are still able to discriminate among issues and to identify those that are salient.

Foreign and national security policy issues are typically among them. When other concerns dominate, there are good reasons for it.

Consider the responses given to opinion pollsters' question, "What do you think is the most important problem facing the country today?" International issues were prominent in Americans' thinking during the height of the Cold War in the 1950s and early 1960s, typically dominating their concerns except for an occasional interruption caused by economic recessions. Not surprisingly, Vietnam emerged paramount in many of the polls taken between 1964 and 1972. Economic needs and issues headed the list of most important problems during the remainder of the 1970s. The national energy "crisis" (fundamentally a foreign policy problem) was among them. However, not until early 1980, in response to events in Iran, did an explicitly foreign policy issue emerge as the single most important concern of the American people.

Unemployment and related economic problems remained paramount after the Iranian hostage crisis. Then, in late 1983, the fear of war and international tensions emerged as salient. They figured prominently in the concerns of the American people as they went to the polls in November 1984. Eventually the issue dissipated, as the Reagan administration began to pursue a more conciliatory posture toward the Soviet Union. Concern for drugs emerged as the most salient issue soon after George Bush became president—doubtless a product of the new administration's own priorities, as evident in its determination to use military force to oust Panama's leader and alleged drug dealer, Manuel Noriega.

The fall of the Berlin Wall understandably dampened Americans' concern for foreign and national security policy issues. The crisis over Kuwait and the war that followed rekindled interest in these issues, but with victory in hand the American people increasingly expressed concern about deficits, debts, recession, and unemployment—in short, the economy. That issue would dominate public concern during the 1992 presidential election and much of the early Clinton presidency. By 1994, as economic growth was rekindled, concern for crime emerged on the agenda as the nation's most important problem. Thereafter, with vibrant economic activity at home and few immediate threats abroad, no single issue dominated the public consciousness, although crime did remain important in the eyes of the American people.

The evidence thus supports the conclusion that the public holds firm opinions on issues it cares about and that those opinions are often stable over time, but if conditions change, public opinion also changes. We can extend that insight even further and suggest that the American people know what matters, and *they learn*. Again, consider some evidence.

- *Public opinion on salient questions is unwavering*—the American people know what matters: In late 1969, when the United States was still mired in Vietnam, two-fifths of the American people felt the war was morally wrong. The proportion grew to nearly two-thirds two years later and remained at that level for more than a decade. Similarly, in 1984 only thirty percent of the American people supported U.S. military aid to the contras fighting the Nicaraguan government. The percentage was unchanged four years later, despite concerted presidential efforts to win public approval for the policy. Furthermore, large numbers of Americans attributed the causes of conflict in Central America to indigenous poverty and injustice, not, as the Reagan administration argued, to outside (read Soviet and Cuban) interference

- *Public attitudes change in response to new conditions— the American people learn.* In 1945, shortly after the war against Japan ended, sixty-nine percent of the American people believed development of the atomic bomb was a good thing. That proportion dropped markedly following the successful Soviet test of an atomic weapon

in 1949. By 1955 twenty-seven percent of the American people believed that nuclear war between the United States and the Soviet Union would result in the complete destruction of humankind; and in 1987, eighty-three percent believed that the United States and the Soviet Union would both be completely destroyed in an all-out nuclear war. A decade later, in 1998, sixty-one percent believed the development of the atomic bomb had been a bad thing; and most thought another country was likely to use the bomb in the near future

The overall record thus suggests that Americans are discerning as they contemplate the world around them. Sometimes they see foreign policy and national security issues as primary concerns. At other times they accord domestic matters priority. They seem to engage in learning, transferring experiences in one situation or historical circumstance to another. Furthermore, their opinions about who will best handle these issues historically have been important predictors of presidential election outcomes. Strike a blow for democratic theory!

If the conclusion that the American people are indifferent to foreign policy is questionable— which it is—the relevance of their lack of knowledge is also suspect. Few people, including corporate executives, legislative aides, and political science majors and their professors would perform uniformly well on the kinds of knowledge and information questions pollsters and journalists pose to measure how well the general public is informed.

More important than interest and knowledge is whether the American people are able, in the aggregate, to hold politically relevant foreign policy beliefs. These beliefs and the corresponding attitudes that both inform and spring from them may not satisfy political analysts when they evaluate the theory and practice of American democracy. Comparatively unsophisticated foreign policy beliefs may nonetheless be both coherent and germane to the political process. Two examples, one on either side of a use-of-force issue, make the point.

- *In Central America:* Many Americans proved unable during the 1980s to identify where in Central America El Salvador and Nicaragua are or who the United States supported in the long-simmering conflicts there. But they were nonetheless unwavering in their firm conviction that young Americans should not be sent to fight in the region. From the perspective of policy makers in Washington, the latter was the important political fact

- *In the Middle East:* Few Americans could correctly identify Kuwait or Saudi Arabia as monarchies rather than democratic political systems, but they were still willing to send American men and women to protect them and to help them win their "freedom." To policy makers in the first Bush administration, the latter point was the politically relevant one

To understand the frequent discrepancy between what Americans know, on the one hand, and how they respond to what they care about, on the other, it is useful to explore the differences between opinions and beliefs.

Foreign Policy Opinions

The Gallup Poll Organization routinely asks Americans what they think about many subjects. In a July 2000 survey, at a time the Clinton administration was actively seeking to broker an agreement between Israel and the Palestinians governing the status of Jerusalem, Gallup found that forty-one percent of Americans said their sympathies rested with the Israelis; only fourteen percent sided with the Palestinians. In May of that year, as tensions between China and Taiwan mounted, by a six percent margin more Americans opposed the use of American military force to defend Taiwan than supported it. In the same month, by a margin of fifty-six to thirty-seven percent, they favored Congress passing a law that

would grant China normal trade relations, permitting its admission to the World Trade Organization. A year earlier, in June 1999 as the United States and its NATO allies wrapped up a successful air bombardment against Serbia's "ethnic cleansing" of Kosovar Albanians, four in ten Americans thought the United States had made a mistake in sending military forces to fight in the Balkans, but two in three also favored U.S. participation in an international peacekeeping force in Kosovo. And as the 2000 presidential election heated up, more than half of the American people supported building a national missile defense system favored by both major political parties (although they differed on details). (These data may be accessed at www.gallup.com/poll/releases.)

These poll data capture what we normally think of as *public opinion*. Often the opinions (attitudes) reflected are highly volatile—and some may in fact be *nonattitudes* (the term refers to the fact that individuals often do not have opinions on matters of interest to pollsters, yet, when asked, they will offer an opinion). The character of the issue, the pace of events, new information, or a friend's opinion may provoke change. So may "herd instincts": Attitude change is stimulated by the desire to conform to what others may be thinking—especially opinion leaders and "political pundits." Indeed, it is perhaps ironic that those who are most attuned to foreign policy issues are often the most supportive of global activism and what policy makers or other opinion influentials want (Zaller 1992). Hence Americans' opinions about specific issues appear susceptible to quick and frequent turnabouts as they respond to cues and events in the world around them.

Public attitudes change, but even in the short run they are less erratic than often presumed. Stability rather than change is demonstrably the characteristic response of the American people to foreign and national security policy issues (Shapiro and Page 1988).[5] Furthermore, even changes observed over long stretches of time are predictable and understandable—not "formless

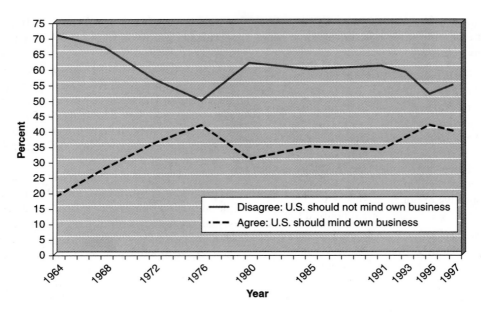

FIGURE 8.1 Isolationist Sentiments, 1964–1997

Note: Responses are to the question "The U.S. should mind its own business internationally and let other countries get along the best they can on their own."
Source: Pew Research for The People and The Press, *America's Place in the World II* Washington, DC: Pew Research Center, 1997, 15.

and plastic," as Almond once described them. Consider two issues that stretched across the last half of the twentieth century: *global activism* and the *costs of global involvement.*

Opinions about Global Activism *Internationalism,* broadly defined as the conviction that the United States should take an active role in world affairs, enjoyed persistent public support throughout the forty-plus years of the Cold War. Even so, measurable fluctuations are evident. During the 1960s and 1970s, in particular, support for internationalism declined. It reached its ebb during the mid–1970s as a combination of worrisome concerns undermined the international ethos. The wrenching Vietnam experience challenged the assumption that military power by itself could achieve American foreign policy objectives; détente called into question the wisdom of the containment foreign policy strategy; and Watergate challenged the convictions that American politi-

cal institutions were uniquely virtuous and that a presidency preeminent in foreign policy continued to be necessary. Despite these concerns, support for internationalism rebounded in the decade following Vietnam.

That picture has remained largely unchanged since, despite the frequent claim that the American people turned inward following the fall of the Berlin Wall as a combination of concern for domestic priorities and indifference toward the rest of the world shaped their thinking. Polling data refute that argument. The data in Figure 8.1, for example, show a slight decline in the proportion of internationalists in the early 1990s compared with the mid–1980s, but by September 1997, only two in five Americans agreed that the United States "should mind its own business and let other countries get along the best they can on their own." Furthermore, since the 1940s various pollsters have asked Americans if they "think it will be best for the future of the country if we take an active part in world affairs or if we stay out." In October 1945, seventy-one percent said active involvement would be best; in mid-1999, sixty-one percent echoed that sentiment (Sobel 2001). Support, decline, and resurgence are thus evident. If today internationalism seems less well-anchored than in the past, public apathy, not public antagonism, is the explanation (Lindsay 2000a, 2000b).

Opinions about the Costs of Interventionism
War and interventionism as instruments of policy have commanded considerable attention in recent years. Public approval of war appears to occur just prior to and after its inception, followed—predictably perhaps—by a gradual but steady decline in bellicose attitudes and a concomitant rise in pacific sentiments. The wars in Korea and Vietnam illustrate the patterns. During each, enthusiasm closely tracked casualty rates: As the casualty rates went up, support for the wars declined (Mueller 1971). The pattern suggests that American attitudes toward war are episodic rather than steady: In the context of actual war involvement, public attitudes range from initial acceptance to ultimate disfavor (Campbell and Cain 1965).

The swift victory of the United States and its Coalition partners in the Persian Gulf War perhaps stanched the cyclical reactions among Americans evident in other wars. Even in that case, however, many people later questioned the wisdom of the war as Iraq's Saddam Hussein—whom George Bush had likened to Hitler—remained in power. Moreover, it is now "conventional wisdom," which is supported by compelling evidence (Larson 1996), that the American people will not support military interventions if America's military men and women are likely to suffer.

However, a close examination of the evidence relating to the peacekeeping and peace enforcement operations commonplace since the end of the Cold War in the past decade raises doubts about that conventional view. The American people have proven to be "pretty prudent" when it comes to assessing the circumstances that might call for military intervention (Kohut and Toth 1994; Jentleson 1992; 1998), and they are not unwilling to support multilateral intervention even if American lives are at risk but the purposes convincing (Burk 1999). As scholars concluded following a recent survey that systematically probed the casualty "myth," "a majority of the American people will accept combat deaths—so long as the mission has the potential to be successful. The public can distinguish between suffering defeat and suffering" (Feaver and Gelpi 1999). As with internationalism, then, the reasons underlying Americans' alternating views on war and other forms of violent foreign conflict are compelling—suggesting once more that they are better able to make prudent political judgments than political pundits would sometimes have us believe.

Foreign Policy Beliefs

The stability of public attitudes and the learning they demonstrate are intimately related to changes that have occurred at home and abroad, thus giving rise to new *foreign policy beliefs*. Although support for active involvement in world affairs rebounded in the 1980s from its nadir in the 1970s, internationalism in the wake of the Vietnam tragedy came to wear two faces—a cooperative one and a militant one. ***Cooperative*** and ***militant internationalism*** grow out of differences among the American people not only on the question of whether the United States ought to be involved in the world (a central tenet of classical internationalism), but also on how it should be involved (Wittkopf 1990).

The domestic consensus favoring classical internationalism captured elements of both conflict and cooperation, of unilateralism and multilateralism. The United States was willing to cooperate with others to solve global as well as national problems; but if need be, it would also intervene in the affairs of others, unilaterally and with military force, if necessary, to defend its self-perceived vital national interests. In the years following World War II, a consensus emerged in support of these forms of involvement, but in the wake of Vietnam, concern about conflict and cooperation came to divide rather than unite Americans. Attitudes toward communism, the use of American troops abroad, and relations with the Soviet Union distinguished proponents and opponents of the alternative forms of internationalism.

Four identifiable belief systems flowed from these concerns, which inhered among elites as well as the mass of the American people (Holsti and Rosenau 1990; Wittkopf 1990):

- *Internationalists* supported active American involvement in international affairs, favoring a combination of conciliatory and conflictual strategies reminiscent of the pre-Vietnam internationalist foreign policy paradigm

- *Isolationists* opposed both types of international involvement, as the term implies

- *Hardliners* tended to view communism as a threat to the United States, to oppose détente with the Soviet Union, and to embrace an interventionist predisposition

- *Accommodationists* emphasized cooperative ties with other nations, particularly détente with the Soviet Union, and rejected the view that the United States could assume a unilateralist, go-it-alone posture in the world

Although accommodationists and hardliners are appropriately described as "internationalists," it is clear their prescriptions for the United States' world role often diverged markedly. This undermined the broad-based domestic support for foreign policy initiatives that presidents in the Cold War era counted on, and made the task of coalition building, which more recent presidents have faced, more difficult.

Beliefs are important in understanding why public attitudes are often less fickle than might be expected. A *belief system* acts as "a set of lenses through which information concerning the physical and social environment is received. It orients the individual to his environment, defining it for him and identifying for him its salient characteristics" (Holsti 1962).

Belief systems also establish goals and order preferences. They enable people to relate systematically information about one idea to others. Importantly, this ability is not a function of information or knowledge; in fact, *social cognition theory* demonstrates that individuals use information short-cuts, based on their beliefs, to cope with ambiguous messages about the external environment. Paradoxically, then, ordinary citizens hold coherent attitude structures *not because* they possess detailed knowledge about foreign policy but because they lack it: "A paucity of information does not impede structure and consistency; on the contrary, it motivates the development and employment of structure. [Individuals attempt] to cope with an extraordinarily confusing world . . . by structuring views about specific foreign policies according to their more general and abstract beliefs" (Hurwitz and Peffley 1987).

Because of their nature, beliefs are remarkably stable. Most images concerning foreign affairs are formed during adolescence and remain more or less fixed unless somehow disturbed. Peer group influences and authority figures may exert a modifying impact on images, but only the most dramatic of international events (war, for example) have the capacity to completely alter foreign policy beliefs (Deutsch and Merritt 1965). Relevant here is philosopher Charles Sanders Pierce's instructive comment on the dynamics of image change: "Surprise is your only teacher." Thus core beliefs, formed through early learning experiences, serve as *perceptual filters* through which individuals orient themselves to their environment and structure how they interpret international events they encounter later in life. If beliefs do change, they are likely to be replaced by new images that continue to simplify the world, albeit in new terms (William James's adage that "most people think they are thinking when they replace one set of prejudices for another" may be appropriate here).

World War II, and the events that led to it, indelibly imprinted the world views of many Americans—including an entire generation of policy makers (Neustadt and May 1986). For the

Munich generation, the message was clear: Aggressors cannot be appeased. To others, Vietnam was an equally traumatic event (Holsti and Rosenau 1984). For the *Vietnam generation,* the lesson was equally simple: There are limits to American power and the utility of military force in international politics. (A dramatically different but now popular view holds that war, once begun, should not be prosecuted "with one arm tied behind the our back.") The emergence of the distinctive beliefs associated with cooperative and militant internationalism in the wake of Vietnam thus conforms to our understanding of how beliefs change.

Did the end of the Cold War—dramatized by the crumbling of the Berlin Wall, long a symbol of the bitter East-West conflict—have a similar effect on Americans' foreign policy beliefs? Do cooperative and militant internationalism, whose Cold War roots include fear of communism and dissension over how to deal with the now moribund Soviet Union, continue to describe differences among the American people about whether and how to be involved in the world? The evidence shows they do.[6]

Individuals often ignore information that might cause them to change their beliefs or to engage in purposeful or inadvertent behavior that would otherwise reorient their perceptions to new realities.[7] Beyond this, the alternative internationalist orientations are not bound to the specific historical circumstances of the Cold War but transcend it (see Murray 1994; Russett, Hartley, and Murray 1994). The two faces of internationalism closely track *idealism* and *realism* (Holsti 1992)—competing visions of how best to deal with transnational problems, which predate the Cold War and persist as new issues compete for attention in the post–Cold War era, as we have seen in previous chapters. Thus in the 1990s, proponents of militant internationalism (particularly hardliners) were more likely than others to support the use of U.S. troops in places like Europe, the Middle East, and Korea, and to approve of CIA intervention abroad—including spying on friends as well as foes. Proponents of cooperative internationalism (particularly accommodationists), on the other hand, expressed greater support for extending NATO's protective umbrella eastward, normalizing relations with Cuba, Iran, Iraq, and Vietnam, supporting international institutions financially, and backing U.S. participation in UN and other multilateral peacekeeping and peace enforcement operations (Wittkopf 1994c, 1996, 2000; see also Holsti and Rosenau 1999a, 1999b). The varying preferences track long-standing differences in realist and idealist prescriptions for coping with security challenges.

How do Americans' foreign policy beliefs find expression in the nation's policies? Causation is difficult to trace, but the consistency of public beliefs with the internationalist faces of American foreign policy since Vietnam is undeniable. Many of the policies pursued by the Nixon, Ford, and Carter administrations represented more accommodationist than hardline positions. President Carter asserted in 1977, for example, that the previously "inordinate fear of communism" had been lifted. That viewpoint epitomized the shift to a conciliatory internationalism that tolerated diversity, and détente was its manifestation. The shift in thinking included the beliefs that military power was no longer a viable instrument of policy, that the Soviet Union had become a status quo power, that the United States should assist the "forces of change" in the Third World, and that a deepening of cooperation ("trilateralism") should come to characterize U.S. relations with Europe and Japan.

By the end of Carter's term in office, however, the emphasis on accommodation shifted back to a hardline posture.[8] The Soviet Union's intervention in Afghanistan in December 1979 served as a catalyst to change. With that, and with Ronald Reagan's election in 1980, any remaining semblance of détente was lost. Reagan pursued a vigorous anti-Soviet and interventionist foreign policy that epitomized hardline foreign policy beliefs. Still, he was unable to overcome the accommodationists' opposition to some of his policies. Witness Central America, where despite concerted presidential efforts to win congressional and public support for a more belligerent approach to the Sandinista regime in Nicaragua, the administration came up short. The example illustrates well how public opinion sometimes constrains presidential initiatives in foreign policy (see Wittkopf and McCormick 1993; Sobel 2001). Moreover, during his second term in office Reagan adopted a more conciliatory posture toward the Soviet Union, reminiscent of the accommodationist orientation he earlier had so vigorously rejected. The administration also retreated from the unilateralist orientation that had led some to worry about the end of internationalism, finding solace instead in the multilateralism historically central to the liberal internationalist ethos.

George Bush came to the White House determined to manage the Cold War competition with the Soviet Union, but as Mikhail Gorbachev pursued one conciliatory initiative after another, the president often found himself in the odd situation of having to defend himself against charges that he had done too little to stimulate the kinds of changes Soviet leaders seemed so desperately to want. Lacking what he himself called "the vision thing," Bush embarked on a policy of "status quo plus," which pleased neither his supporters nor his critics. Not until the Kuwait crisis was Bush able to seize the high ground on the national security issues for which he was uniquely prepared. As noted in previous chapters, the president spoke repeatedly in a State of the Union Address that followed shortly on the heels of the initiation of war against Iraq of the "next American century," in which the "rule of law" would reign supreme in the *new world order.* Bush's vision embraced the tradition of moral idealism long evident in American foreign policy, but especially since Woodrow Wilson sought early in this century to create a "world safe for democracy."

Ironically, however, even as the vision of a new world order was premised on idealism, the question of how to deal with Saddam Hussein's aggressive behavior again pitted realists (militant internationalists) and idealists (cooperative internationalists) against one another. The dichotomy was sharply displayed in the congressional debate between the proponents of force and those of sanctions, as also mirrored in public opinion polls.

Force or sanctions? The issue punctuated the debate early in the Clinton administration about how best to respond to the *ethnic cleansing* perpetrated by Bosnian Serbs on their Muslim neighbors in the former Yugoslavia. As in the debate over Iraq, hardliners and accommodationists were clearly identifiable in Congress—especially after the Republicans gained control—and elsewhere. If there was a new twist, it was that Democrats and liberals—previously among the strongest supporters of cooperative internationalism—who were now supporters of intervention, while Republicans and conservatives—previously among the strongest supporters of militant internationalism—were now more cautious. The shift from Republican to Democratic control of the White House doubtless contributed to these changing preferences. Clearly the American polity remained divided about whether and how the United States should be involved in the world along lines that parallel the classic tenets of realism and idealism. The divisions persisted into the second Clinton term, when, with America's NATO allies, Clinton launched a military operation in Kosovo. They were also evident on nonintervention issues, including normalizing relations with Vietnam, bringing China into the World Trade Organization, and easing restrictions on U.S. ties with Castro's Cuba.

When a new Republican administration took over the reigns of power in 2001, a reversion to previous partisan positions on internationalism, with Republicans favoring hardline policies and Democrats accommodationist ones, quickly became evident on such issues as missile defense and global warming. Thus, as the nation embarks on a new century, it is clear internationalism continues to wear two faces: one cooperative, the other militant.

The Public "Temperament": Permissive, Nationalistic, and Acquiescent

The responsiveness of the American people—for better or worse—to events and the political information directed at them is nowhere more apparent than in the support they accord their political leaders during times of crisis and peril. Like the citizens of other nations, Americans embrace nationalist sentiments: They value loyalty and devotion to their own nation and promotion of its culture and interests as opposed to those of other nations. Nationalism sometimes includes the ethnocentric belief that the United States is (or should be recognized as) superior to others, and should therefore serve as a model for them to emulate.

Although no one would argue that all Americans always think nationalistically on foreign issues, generally they perceive international problems in terms of "in-group loyalty and out-group competition" (Rosenberg 1965). In the extreme, nationalism results in a world view that accepts the doctrine, "my country, right or wrong." And because citizens often equate loyalty to the nation with loyalty to the current leadership, they sometimes confuse admiration for their representatives in government with affection for country and its symbols: "my president, right or wrong."

The public's nationalistic temperament stems in part from its tendency to view "things foreign" with hostility and fear. International politics often appears esoteric, secret, complicated, and unfamiliar—a cacophony of problems better left to "experts" who allegedly "know better" (and who, in turn, are quite willing to perpetuate the notion)—rendering public attitudes in the realm of foreign policy vulnerable to manipulation. People who feel threatened are prone to seek strong leadership to deal with the perceived threatening agent, a tendency policy makers have long recognized. Nazi leader Hermann Goering expressed this idea, contending "Voice or no voice, the people can always be brought to do the bidding of the leaders. That is easy. All you have to do is to tell them they are being attacked and denounce the pacifists for lack of patriotism."

Nationalistic sentiments find expression in the way Americans respond to the initiatives of their leaders during crises or threats from abroad, where the public's response is typically *permissive*. Presidents frequently realize their widest freedom of action in such circumstances, because the American people typically acquiesce in and support the decisions of their leaders.

The impact of dramatic foreign policy events and initiatives on presidential performance evaluations reveals clear evidence of the permissiveness of public attitudes. Typically such events produce *rally-round-the-flag* effects that boost a president's popularity with the public. Examples abound:

- George W. Bush's approval rating ticked up five percentage points after he ordered an air attack on Iraq following its alleged threat to U.S.-British planes patrolling a no-flight zone in southern Iraq

- Bill Clinton's popularity with the American people spurted eleven percentage points following the June 1993 American cruise missile attack on Iraqi intelligence headquarters in Baghdad and nine points following the occupation of Haiti a year later

- George H.W. Bush's popularity climbed by eighteen points following the initiation of military action against Iraq in January 1991

- Ronald Reagan's approval notched upward by six points following the bombing of Libya in April 1986

- Jimmy Carter's popularity jumped by thirteen points following the Camp David Middle East accords in September 1978

- Bill Clinton's popularity ticked up three points following U.S. air strikes against suspected terrorist facilities in Afghanistan and the Sudan—even as he faced the prospect of an impeachment trial at home

- George W. Bush's popularity jumped a remarkable 35% after the terrorist attack of September 2001. His popularity skyrocketed from 55% to 90%, the highest popularity rating ever recorded, even surpassing his father's 89% rating following the military action against Irag in early 1990.

Such changes are evident across a broad range of foreign policy events, including wars, crises, peace initiatives, and summit conferences—all of which demonstrate the *permissive, nationalistic* and *acquiescent* responses of the American people to their leaders' policy initiatives.

But the American people are also discriminating. Ronald Reagan's popularity plummeted by sixteen percentage points following the Iran-contra revelations in late 1986, the largest drop ever recorded by the Gallup Poll (other polls recorded even steeper declines). Contrast this with John Kennedy's experience, who found that his public approval actually rose to its peak (eighty-three percent) following the Bay of Pigs fiasco. Both involved mistakes in judgment, but the way each president handled his mistake appears to have significantly affected public perceptions of him. (In the Iran-contra affair, not only did the American people disapprove of the sale of arms to Iran, they disbelieved the president's version of what happened and thought the administration was engaged in a cover-up similar to the Watergate affair [Ostrom and Simon 1989].) More typically, international crises are *approval-enhancing* events, whereas political scandals are *approval-diminishing* events (Ostrom and Simon 1989).

The Politics of Prestige

Presidents care about their popularity with the American people because it affects their ability to work their will with others involved in the policy process. Richard Neustadt (1980) explains the underlying logic in his classic book *Presidential Power*: "The Washingtonians who watch a President have more to think about than his professional reputation. They also have to think about his standing with the public outside of Washington. They have to gauge his popular prestige. Because they think about it, public standing is a source of [presidential] influence." In short, the more popular a president is, the more likely he is to accomplish his political agenda. This is the essence of what Dennis M. Simon and Charles W. Ostrom (1988) call the *politics of prestige*.

Presidents also care about their popularity because it affects their political latitude. Both the absolute and relative levels of presidents' popularity, evidence suggests, are important in explaining America's postwar political use of force short of war: The more popular presidents are, the more they are "freed" from domestic constraints to do as they wish abroad (Ostrom and Job 1986; also James and Oneal 1991; compare Lian and Oneal 1993; Meernik 1994). As one member of Congress commented on Bush's popularity following the invasion of Panama in 1989, "If the President's popularity is at eighty percent, I think [he] can do whatever he wants."

Rally-round-the-flag events, like the invasion of Panama or missile attacks on Iraq and Afghanistan, significantly affect presidents' popularity. Indeed, one presidential scholar (Lowi 1985a) argues that foreign policy comprises the only arena available to presidents that permits them to improve their popularity ratings once in office. The *state of the economy* is the most potent (environmental) predictor of presidential popularity. It was the principal factor that undermined the Bush presidency and caused his 1992 reelection bid to fail. Still, the American people want *peace* as well as *prosperity*. Thus foreign policy sometimes figures prominently in the long-term erosion of support as well as the short-term boosts that most presidents experience. For Truman, the Korean War was the significant factor explaining the dramatic loss of public confidence in his leadership; for Johnson, the Vietnam War and riots in the cities were critical; for Nixon, it was the continuation of the Vietnam War and Watergate; and for Carter, it was his inability to secure the release of Americans held hostage in Iran.

Trends in presidential popularity are described in Figure 8.2. Presidents historically have begun their presidencies with a *honeymoon*—a crucial first few months after an election, in which the president is relatively free of harsh public criticism—only to find that in the long-term their popularity declines. Interestingly, however, none of the four most recent presidents experienced very enthusiastic honeymoons. The

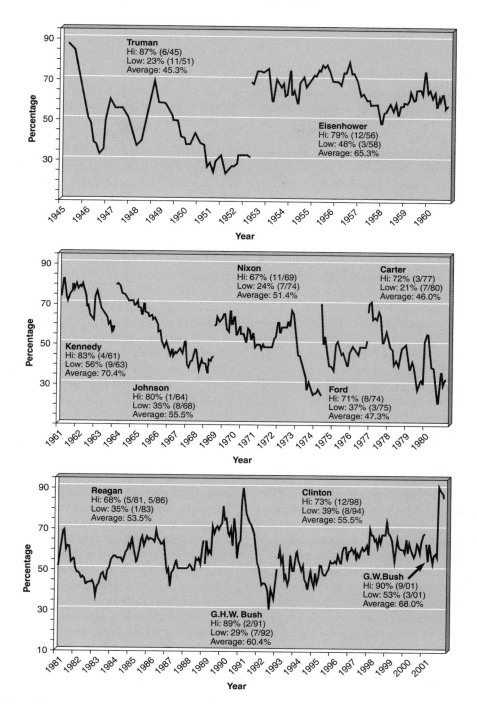

FIGURE 8.2 Public Approval of Presidential Performance, 1945–2001

Note: Data appear in monthly intervals beginning in June 1945 and ending in January 2002. In months with multiple polls, the last poll is used. In months where no poll was taken, the data are extrapolated using preceding and/or succeeding monthly data. The panels in the figure contain unequal numbers of monthly intervals.

Source: Adapted from *The Gallup Opinion Index,* October–November 1980; various issues of *The Gallup Report* and *The Gallup Poll Monthly,* and Gallup poll data available at www.gallup.com/poll/releas

specific reasons vary, but the closeness of their electoral victories combined with increasingly bitter partisan polarization in the country doubtless undermined their early influence with Congress and elsewhere.

As noted, specific events often cause erosion of presidential support, but it may also be stimulated by growing public dissatisfaction and lost patience with unfulfilled campaign promises, or perhaps by the adage that "familiarity breeds contempt."[9] With every presidential decision (or "nondecision"), opposition forms or becomes more vocal, Congress looks increasingly to its own parochial concerns, and the president's support seems to ooze away imperceptibly but steadily in what one scholar has described as a "cycle of decreasing influence" (Light 1991; see also Brace and Hinckley 1992). The tendency is symptomatic of the difficulties of running a government, managing a complex economy, and executing the nation's foreign policy in a manner satisfactory to a majority of Americans.

The experiences of George H.W. Bush and Bill Clinton deserve special comment—Bush because he failed in his reelection bid in 1992 despite having achieved the highest approval ratings ever given a president since modern polling began more than half a century ago; Bill Clinton because he left office with the highest approval ratings since modern polling began despite being only the second president in American history to have been impeached.

George Bush experienced the devastating effect of a declining economy on a president's popularity, which led to his defeat by Bill Clinton in 1992. The intriguing question is why Bush could not parlay his extraordinarily high popularity levels—eighty-nine percent according to the Gallup Poll in March 1991—into political survival and longevity. The evidence suggests two answers to the question.

First, Bush's popularity manifested far wider gyrations than any of his predecessors over comparable periods in office. Ronald Reagan's popularity changed by more than five percentage points only twice during his first three years in office, but

Bush's changed by this amount nearly seven times as often, leading modern presidents in this kind of fluctuation (Brace and Hinckley 1993).

Second, Bush's sometimes unusually high but wildly fluctuating approval ratings did not sustain him because they were "tied less to George Bush the individual and more to a remarkable clustering of events" (Brace and Hinckley 1993). Most of these were international events, including the invasion of Panama, the crisis over Kuwait and the Persian Gulf War, the fall of the Berlin Wall, and the demise of communism in Eastern Europe. The White House played on each of these developments with considerable political drama, but it paid scant attention to the domestic economic policy. Thus Bush's popularity appears to have been sustained almost entirely by international events of comparatively low salience to most Americans (Edwards, Mitchell, and Welch 1995). This made his popularity unstable and highly susceptible to damaging negative events. "With approval maintained at an artificial high point through a series of dramatic positive events," argue political scientists Paul Brace and Barbara Hinckley (1993), "any other events and presidential activities drove the polls down." In short, Bush's approval rating with the American people was not only higher than other presidents, it was also more vulnerable to losses.

Bill Clinton's story is less easily explained. The honeymoon during his first term was neither as long nor his approval rating as high as some of his predecessors, a reflection perhaps not only of his comparatively weak electoral base but also his controversial decision to focus immediate attention on the issue of homosexuals in the military. Partisan disputes over his economic program and proposed tax increases and continuing concern about the state of the economy also plagued the new president. Moreover, the media cut him little slack. During his first eighteen months in office, nearly two-thirds of television news evaluations of Clinton were negative, compared with the evenly balanced coverage Bush had received previously. Press coverage was also markedly less positive than Clinton's approval ratings with the mass public

("They're No Friends of Bill: TV News Coverage of the Clinton Administration" 1994).

Gradually, however, Clinton's popularity gained momentum. No single foreign policy event explained this; instead, it was the increasingly vibrant state of the U.S. economy. But unlike many of his predecessors, Clinton experienced no discernible honeymoon boost at the beginning of his second term, as Figure 8.2 shows. The enigma of Clinton's second term is that the domestic scandals that dogged him throughout his presidency, leading to his impeachment in December 1998, cost him very little in the polls. Again, the bubbling U.S. economy contributed to his continued positive job approval ratings.[10] As Alan Greenspan, the powerful chairman of the Federal Reserve Board, chirped in a May 1998 meeting with the president, "This is the best economy I've ever seen in fifty years of studying it" (Woodward 2000). At the time, Clinton's approval rating stood at sixty-four percent, well above the fifty-seven percent he experienced shortly after his second inauguration. Remarkably, this was after four months of investigations into Clinton's dalliance with a White House intern by Whitewater independent counsel Kenneth Starr. Starr pursued his investigation relentlessly. In August 1998 Clinton found himself before a federal grand jury, a first for a president, answering difficult questions about his affair with the intern and other matters. Four months later he was impeached by the House of Representatives on perjury and obstruction of justice charges. Clinton's approval rating was sixty-six percent the day after his grand jury testimony. Shortly after his impeachment it stood at a stunning seventy-three percent, an all time high. And two years later, his sixty-seven percent approval rating ranked as the highest of any outgoing president since modern polling began—even surpassing Dwight Eisenhower and Ronald Reagan.

Faced with such penetrating domestic scandal and partisan invective, how is it possible to explain Clinton's remarkably resilient popularity? "It's the economy, stupid!"—Clinton's 1992 campaign rallying cry—comes readily to mind.

But is that answer sufficient? The historical record is replete with examples of presidents' undoing in the face of a potentially disapproval-enhancing scandal. But Clinton was immune. The reason, it appears, is because, as we noted earlier, the American people seem willing to separate private morality from their assessment of a person's job performance. As two veteran Washington reporters wrote at the time of Clinton's grand jury testimony, the public "sees two very different Bill Clintons: The president whose stewardship of the nation's economy and decisiveness in foreign affairs they continue to applaud, and the man whose scandal-plagued personal life is viewed with increased disgust, embarrassment, and even sadness" (Broder and Morin 1998; see also Kernell 1999). Interestingly, the apparent separation of private life and professional competence may have benefitted George W. Bush: Just before the 2000 presidential election news accounts reported that Bush had been arrested in 1976 for driving under the influence of alcohol, but the revelation had no discernible impact on voters' evaluations of his qualifications for the presidency.

Public Opinion and Foreign Policy: An Addendum

The preceding discussion could be expanded in several ways. Here we add only a few additional observations: Americans' confidence in their political institutions, the components of the concept *public opinion*, and the political and sociodemographic correlates of foreign policy attitudes and beliefs.

Confidence in Political Leaders and Institutions The confidence that Americans place in the nation's political, economic, and social institutions is closely related to the other developments in public attitudes described above. Jimmy Carter dramatized ingredients symptomatic of the changing "public voice" when, in a 1979 nationwide speech, he spoke of "a fundamental threat to American democracy." The threat, he said, was a "crisis of confidence," reflected in "a growing disrespect for government and for churches and for schools, the news media and other institutions." Among the trends was a decline in Americans' sense of political efficacy and a general feeling of despair, alienation, and powerlessness regarding the future. An American public that once appeared to be naive, simplistic, and *jingoistic* (ultrapatriotic) now appeared more aware of and cynical about foreign policy issues. Noteworthy is that the decline in confidence was—and continues to be—matched by a dramatic decline in *social capital* across a broad range of indicators, including political participation and involvement in private civic associations (Putnam 2000). The concept refers broadly to the ability of people to work together, which has both private and public benefits (Nye, Zelikow, and King 1997; Putnam 2000). "Networking," a common social practice that builds friendships and careers, is an example of the kinds of social bonds that bind individuals and societies.

Public disclosures of the half-truths regarding American involvement in Vietnam and revelations about what was undertaken in the name of national security by presidential staffers, military organizations, and intelligence agencies contributed to Americans' growing cynicism and, arguably, to the corresponding erosion of social capital in the last quarter of the twentieth century. Deep-seated cynicism became especially evident during and immediately after the Vietnam War. Ronald Reagan helped to rebuild public confidence in political leaders (but not social institutions generally). However, it was dealt another blow by the revelations of the Iran-contra affair (Lipset and Schneider 1987; see also Craig 1993; Sussman 1988), which once more raised concerns about the abuse of power in the name of national security. Questions about whether George H.W. Bush was completely honest about his role in the Iran-contra affair dogged his presidency to the very end—when he pardoned former Secretary of Defense Caspar Weinberger and other Iran-contra principals for any wrongdoing.

The military is one institution to have enjoyed a dramatic rebound in confidence with the American people in more recent years—explained in part by its success in the Persian Gulf War. And it sustained that confidence throughout the 1990s. Among the three branches of the federal government, confidence in the 1990s was highest for the Supreme Court, followed by the presidency and, at some distance, Congress. Whether the Supreme Court will continue to command respect in the wake of its sharply divided decision in *Bush vs. Gore,* which determined the outcome of the 2000 presidential election, is, however, problematic. As Justice Stevens wrote in a dissenting opinion, "Although we may never know with complete certainty the identity of the winner of this year's Presidential election, the identity of the loser is perfectly clear. It is the Nation's confidence in the judge as an impartial guardian of the rule of law."

The Public Opinion Pyramid American society is structured like a pyramid, with a very small proportion of *policy influentials* (people who are knowledgeable about foreign affairs and who have access to decision makers) and decision makers at the top, followed by a larger component comprising the *attentive public* (those knowledgeable about foreign affairs but not necessarily with access to decision makers), with the bulk of the population making up the "mass public." The pyramid represents the three strata that make up the aggregate concept *public opinion.* While estimates vary about the distribution of Americans among the three groups, most suggest that the elite comprise less than two percent of the population, the attentive public between five and ten percent, and the mass public, by definition, the rest.

One of the sharpest distinctions in public attitudes occurs between elites, on the one hand, and the mass public, on the other. Support for *liberal internationalism*—defined by U.S. Ambassador Richard Gardner (1990) as "the intellectual and political tradition that believes in the necessity of leadership by liberal democracies in the construction of a peaceful world order through multilateral cooperation and effective international organizations"—is demonstrably greater among elites than the general public. For example, a 1997 survey by Pew Research Center (Pew Research Center for The People and The Press 1997) revealed that "The public feels the United States should be no more or less active than any other country, restrained in its commitment of troops and resources to foreign adventures. In contrast, a majority of influential Americans ranging from union leaders to national security experts believes the U.S. role should be prominent and forceful" (Kohut and Toth 1998). Analysts Andrew Kohut and Robert Toth (1998) conclude that "Never before has the difference on such a fundamental issue as America's place in the world been so wide."

Table 8.2 illustrates this and other differences between elites—decision makers, policy influentials, and opinion leaders—and most other Americans. The data show that elites are markedly more supportive of active involvement in the world than is the mass public, whether that be in a shared context or unilaterally. They attach somewhat less salience to potential threats to the United States but are more willing to intervene with troops to protect its interests. Still, they are less hawkish than most Americans when it comes to dealing with terrorists and are more reticent about using sanctions as an instrument of policy. They also warmly embrace globalization and the principle of free trade and oppose economic protectionism, basic pillars of liberal internationalism.

Several factors explain the yawning gap between elites and masses on particular foreign policy issues and on general postures. Interest in foreign affairs, access to information about what is happening in the world, and socialization experiences are among them. Some also argue that the gap is a product of elites' failure to understand what most Americans really think (Kull and Destler 1999).

But it is also true that American leaders and the mass public share much in common. In particular, elites and masses differ in similar ways on the question of how the United States should be involved in the world. The belief systems derived from the cooperative and militant orientations toward global activism used earlier to describe mass foreign policy attitudes apply to American leaders as well. Thus elite and mass preferences diverge on specifics, but they converge on cooperative and militant internationalism as alternative orientations toward the elements comprising America's foreign policy ends and means. The similarities and differences between the specifics and the general manifest themselves this way: "Elites consistently subscribe to internationalist and accommodationist values in greater proportions than the mass public. The mass public," on the other hand, "is more likely to embrace hardline values" (Holsti and Rosenau 1990, 1999a; Wittkopf 1990, 1994c, 2000). Thus the structure of elite and mass attitudes is similar, even as the specific policy preferences of each diverge.

Political and Sociodemographic Correlates of Foreign Policy Attitudes

Partisanship and political ideology (conservative versus liberal) are important correlates of foreign policy beliefs. As noted earlier, Republicans and conservatives are more likely to be hardliners while Democrats and liberals tend to be accommodationists. In addition to these differences, public attitudes on specific foreign policy issues often vary by such factors as age, educational level, gender, income, occupation, racial background, religious identification, and region of the country (see, for example, Wilcox, Ferrara, and Allsop 1993; Holsti 1996). For policy makers, knowledge about these variations is important politically, because it allows them to court some groups while ignoring others.

Income, occupation, and education are typically important in distinguishing the attentive public from the mass public. People in higher income groups, in professional occupations, and with more education are typically better informed about international affairs than their counterparts in other societal groups. These are the people most likely to support what foreign

Table 8.2 Differences in the Foreign Policy Preferences of American Leaders and the Mass of the American People, 1997–1998 (percentages)

	Leaders	Public	Gap*
America's World Role			
Best for U.S. future if it plays an active world role	97	85	+12
The United States should assume a shared leadership role but also be the most active among the leading nations	50	22	+28
The United States should act in international crises even without the support of its allies	48	23	+25
Military Spending			
Increase defense spending	26	30	−4
Possible Critical Threats to U.S. Vital Interests			
Unfriendly countries becoming nuclear powers	67	78	−11
Chemical and biological weapons	64	79	−15
International terrorism	61	86	−25
Development of China as a world power	57	60	−3
Aids, Ebola, epidemics	34	74	−40
Islamic fundamentalism	31	43	−12
Global warming	27	46	−19
Military power of Russia	19	35	−16
Immigrants and refugees into U.S.	18	57	−39
Economic competition from Europe	16	27	−11
Economic competition from low wage countries	16	42	−26
Economic competition from Japan	14	47	−33
Regional ethnic conflicts	26	36	−10
Use of Military Force—Favor Using Troops If:			
Iraq invades Saudi Arabia	80	52	+28
North Korea invades South Korea	75	34	+41
Arab forces invade Israel	71	44	+27
Russia invades Poland	60	34	+26
Serbs kill Kosovar Albanians	56	44	+12
China invades Taiwan	52	32	+20
Cubans attempt to overthrow Castro	19	43	−24
Very Important U.S. Foreign Policy Goals			
Prevent the spread of nuclear weapons	85	84	+1
Combat international terrorism	74	81	−7
Maintain military superiority	58	62	−4
Defend allies' security	58	47	+11
Stop the flow of illegal drugs into the United States	57	84	−27
Combat world hunger	56	64	−8

Table 8.2 Continued

	Leaders	Public	Gap*
Very Important U.S. Foreign Policy Goals—Cont.			
Secure adequate supplies of energy	56	67	−11
Improve the global environment	47	56	−9
Protect the jobs of American workers	45	83	−38
Promote and defend human rights	41	41	0
Improve living standards in less developed countries	37	30	+7
Promote market economies	36	36	0
Reduce trade deficit with foreign countries	34	53	−19
Strengthen the United Nations	33	48	−15
Protect weak nations against aggression	30	34	−4
Bring democracy to other nations	27	31	−4
Control illegal immigration	21	58	−37
Favor Sanctions Against:			
Iraq	77	75	+2
North Korea	66	68	−2
Iran	55	71	−16
China	37	62	−25
Cuba	37	66	−29
Options for Coping with Terrorists			
Diplomacy to apprehend suspects	98	90	+8
Improve relations with adversary	97	86	+11
Trial in International Criminal Court	90	90	0
Air strikes	79	80	−1
U.S. ground troops	60	63	−3
Assassination	35	61	−26
Economic Issues			
Globalization is good for the United States	88	60	+28
Japan practices unfair trade	77	64	+13
European Union practices unfair trade	20	31	−11
Tariffs are necessary to protect jobs	36	60	−24
Multilateralism			
The United States should contribute more to the IMF	84	33	+51

*Leaders minus public. All percentages based on those holding an opinion except for the second entry (the United States should be the most active leading nation), which includes "don't know" responses.

SOURCE: Data on the most active of leading nations from *America's Place in the World II*. Pew Research Center for The People and The Press, 1997, 27. All other data are adapted from data files summarized in John E. Rielly, ed., *American Public Opinion and U.S. Foreign Policy 1999*. Chicago: Chicago Council on Foreign Relations, 1999.

policy leaders want. In March 1999, for example, the Gallup Organization found Americans ambivalent about U.S. participation in NATO air strikes against Serbia (forty-six percent favor, forty-three percent oppose). But among the thirty-six percent who indicated they were following the situation in Kosovo closely, fifty-eight percent supported what by then was U.S. policy (*Poll Releases,* March 24, 1999). Similarly, in late 1994 only forty-two percent of the mass public supported NATO's expansion into Eastern Europe—a central tenet of the Clinton administration's Partnership for Peace program—but the move was supported by fifty-five percent of those who closely followed news about U.S. foreign relations (based on a Gallup Poll survey for the Chicago Council on Foreign Relations).

Gender differences on foreign policy issues, particularly those related to the use of force, are among the correlates of foreign policy attitudes that have attracted attention in recent years. A "gender gap" first became evident in the 1980 election, when Ronald Reagan was found to enjoy markedly less support among female voters than among male voters. The differences, which were repeated four years later, appear to have been related to a greater fear among women of Reagan's bellicose foreign policy pronouncements and concerns about his ability to manage the risks of war (Frankovic 1982).[11]

Evidence from early in the 1988 presidential campaign indicated that Bush inherited women's distrust of Reagan, but by the time of the election in November 1988 gender differences had largely dissipated (Farah and Klein 1989; Taylor 1988; compare Bendyna and Lake 1995). With the onset of the crisis and war in the Persian Gulf, however, wide differences between men and women on use-of-force issues were again revealed. An August 1990 survey showed, for example, that seventy-nine percent of the male respondents would support sending U.S. troops to defend Saudi Arabia against a possible Iraqi attack, but only fifty-one percent of the females would. Five months later, as the United Nations

deadline for Iraq's withdrawal from Kuwait approached, another survey asked whether the United States should go to war against Iraq if it failed to comply. Of the women fifty-four percent said yes, compared with seventy-three percent of the men. Women were also less likely than men to approve of Bush's handling of the crisis in Kuwait. Whether these differences had an effect on the 1992 presidential election is problematic, but it is clear that Bill Clinton was sensitive to gender-based issues as he mounted his campaign with the promise to make the composition of his administration "look like American society"; and comparatively larger numbers of women did vote for him than for Bush or Perot. (Single women, who "often believed that they had been harmed by Reagan and Bush's policies" were especially prone to vote for Clinton [Abramson, Aldrich and Rohde 1994].) Two years later white males voted overwhelmingly for Republican congressional candidates, helping to secure the new Republican majority, but in 1996 Clinton again earned the votes of a disproportionately higher number women than did Bob Dole. And that pattern would be repeated in the 2000 election, as Al Gore received twelve percent more of the female vote than George W. Bush (*New York Times,* 12 November 2000, www.nytimes.com/2000/11/12/politics).

Generational changes also deserve consideration. Earlier, in commenting on the impact of Vietnam, a contrast was drawn between the Munich generation and the Vietnam generation. The electoral battle between George Bush, a World War II veteran, and Bill Clinton, a Vietnam War dissenter, epitomizes the generational changes now taking place in American policy-making circles. With it comes potentially important implications for the foreign policy thinking that the next generation of policy makers may bring into positions of power (see Holsti and Rosenau 1980, 1984). The cyclical swings between global activism and withdrawal in American diplomatic history, argues Frank L. Klingberg (1983, 1990), are largely generational in nature, with oscillations between each mood occurring every

---

FOCUS 8.1   Cycles of Introversion (Isolationism) and Extroversion (Internationalism) in America's Foreign Policy

American policy makers historically have been unable to reconcile the advantages of withdrawing from the world with the benefits of reforming it. Hence the nation's global posture has alternated between periods of *introversion* and *extroversion*—that is, between periods of isolationist withdrawal and global involvement. Periods of extroversion are marked by a "willingness to use direct pressure (economic, diplomatic, or military) on other nations, while introversion stresses domestic concerns as well as normal economic, diplomatic, and humanitarian relations with other nations" (Klingberg 1996).

Debates among policy makers as to which role best serves the national interest have never been resolved conclusively. America's vacillation between introversion (isolationism) and extroversion (internationalism) appears to fluctuate in rhythmic *cycles*, with each taking twenty-five to thirty years (a political generation) to run its course, as summarized below.

INTROVERSION	EXTROVERSION
1776–1798	1798–1824
1824–1844	1844–1871
1871–1891	1891–1919
1919–1940	1940–1967
1967–1987	1987–?

---

twenty-five to thirty years quite independently of public dissatisfaction with particular experiments (such as Vietnam or humanitarian intervention). Although detailed evidence supporting the generational thesis remains elusive, the long history of swings between introversion and extroversion identified by Klingberg and others (summarized in Focus 8.1) suggests that generational effects may be especially potent as the United States turns toward the new century. They may be particularly important in explaining the gulf in attitudes between the men and women with military service and a growing cadre of political leaders without that experience (Holsti 1998–1999; Ricks 1997).

A PUBLIC IMPACT ON AMERICAN FOREIGN POLICY?

"Polls are not only part of the news today, they are news. They not only sample public opinion, they define it." That observation by Kathleen A. Frankovic (1998), director of polling at CBS News, underscores not only the ubiquity but also the importance of public opinion polls in contemporary America.

Policy makers are acutely aware of the importance of polling. The unceasing presidential job approval question asked by many media and other polling organizations effectively subjects the president to a *perpetual election;* and presidents are, for good reason, sensitive to where they stand in that "election," as we have seen. Does this also mean that policy makers "pander" to the public?

That policy makers are guided by public whim rather than principled conviction is a widely accepted belief. It is not warranted. Although there is a close correspondence between public preferences and public policy, the fit has widened, not narrowed, in recent years (Monroe 1998). The gulf between public preferences and public behavior was no more evident than during the impeachment trial of President Clinton. Survey data showed unambiguously that the majority of Americans preferred not to see Clinton removed from office, despite his transgressions, but the Republican controlled Congress continued to press ahead anyway.

Systematic evidence compiled by political scientists Lawrence Jacobs and Robert Shapiro

(2000), much of it based on interviews with Washington policy makers, shows that politicians use public opinion but are not abused by it. "The irony of contemporary politics," they write, "is that politicians both slavishly track public opinion and, contrary to the myth of 'pandering,' studiously avoid simply conforming policy to what the public wants." Instead of conforming to pubic preferences, they themselves use systematic polling to decide what they want to do; "their purpose [is] to exert the 'leadership skills to shape public opinion' and 'educate the people'" (compare Harris 2001). That conclusion affirms the viewpoint of Kennedy adviser Theodore Sorensen (1963), who some years ago put it this way: "No president is obliged to abide by the dictates of public opinion. . . . He has a responsibility to lead public opinion as well as respect it—to shape it, to inform it, to woo it, and win it. It can be his sword as well as his compass."

The notion that policy makers see public opinion as something to be shaped, not followed, is understandable when we recall the tendency of the public to acquiesce to government decisions. The propensity to accede to leaders' choices and not to mobilize to alter them minimizes the impact on foreign policy that the public can exert. Government's responsiveness to public preferences is further reduced by the public's usual passivity. The conclusion that follows is that the American public participates (through elections, for example) without exercising power. It is involved but does not have influence.

Rather than asking if there is a direct causal connection between public opinion and the content of foreign policy, then, it may be better to inquire into the functions of public attitudes in the process itself.

Public Opinion as a Constraint on Foreign Policy Innovation

One of the reasons American foreign policy has proved so resistant to change since World War II is that public images of international politics are themselves resistant to change. As we have already noted, fundamental beliefs regarding foreign relations are typically inflexible:

> Almost nothing in the world seems to be able to shift the images of forty percent of the population in most countries, even within one or two decades. Combinations of events that shift the images and attitudes even of the remaining fifty or sixty percent of the population are extremely rare, and these rare occasions require the combination and mutual reinforcement of cumulative events with spectacular events and substantial governmental efforts as well as the absence of sizable cross-pressures.
>
> (DEUTSCH AND MERRITT 1965, 183)

Public opinion thus acts as a brake on policy change, not by stopping innovations but by limiting modifications because of policy makers' perceptions of the inflexibility and unpredictability of public opinion.

The constraining impact of the *Vietnam syndrome* illustrates the tendency. If decision makers think the public voice will not permit certain initiatives and fear that the public may become mobilized against innovations, that in itself may restrict the kinds of alternatives considered. As one pollster put it, political leaders regard public opinion "as the great gorilla in the political jungle, a beast that must be kept calm" (Sussman 1988). Their task, then, is to "keep things quiet," which means they seek "to stifle public debate on matters that people care about, or should care about." It is perhaps for these political and psychological reasons that American foreign policy is perceived by so many analysts and political leaders to be constrained by public attitudes: "Mass opinion may set general limits, themselves subject to change over time, within which government may act" because the "opinion context . . . fixes the limitations within which action may be taken" (Key 1961). "Fear of electoral punishment," even if unrealistic, serves to limit what decision makers are likely to do—if for no other reason than their (often erroneous) assumption that "the public will never stand for it" (Waltz 1971).

Richard Sobel examines the impact of public opinion on American foreign policy in four interventionist episodes: (1) Vietnam, beginning with the Johnson administration and extending through Nixon's; (2) Nicaragua, where during the Reagan administration the United States sought through support of counterrevolutionary forces to topple the government of the pro-Marxist Sandinista regime; (3) the Persian Gulf War, prosecuted to successful battlefield conclusion during the Bush administration; and (4) Bosnia, where initial U.S. humanitarian intervention during the Bush administration culminated in multilateral intervention under U.S. leadership during the Clinton administration.

Based on systematic evidence as well as interviews with key policy makers during each of these conflict situations, Sobel's conclusions reinforce the long-standing argument that public opinion limits the range of policy makers' foreign policy choices. But his conclusions also extend another long-standing observation: that public opinion may constrain policy makers' latitude, but it does not shackle them. "The public's attitudes set the limits within which policy makers may operate," Sobel (2001) writes. "Within those parameters of permissive consensus, decision makers may operate with less or more political costs and relative discretion about which policies to choose." He also adds "That discretion is wider when conflicts are less salient and [public] support is higher."

Public permissiveness invites presidents to act first and create support later. Often they are successful. Two examples related to the rally-round-the-flag phenomenon make the point. Before Johnson announced his Vietnam policy in 1965, which called for a dramatic escalation of U.S. direct involvement, only forty-two percent of the public favored such an approach; after the announcement, seventy-two percent favored it. Before Bush invaded Panama in December 1989 in an effort to overthrow General Manuel Noriega, fifty-nine percent of the public opposed it; fol-

lowing the military action, eighty percent viewed it as justified.

The public's historical tendency to follow decision makers' leads encourages them to think that if they do not enjoy a climate of public support for their actions, they can create it. Theodore Roosevelt put it bluntly: "I did not 'divine' what the people were going to think. I simply made up my mind what they ought to think and then did my best to get them to think it." Similarly, George Elsey, an adviser to President Truman, confided that "The president's job is to lead public opinion, not to be a blind follower. You can't sit around and wait for public opinion to tell you what to do. . . . You must decide what you're going to do and do it, and attempt to educate the public to the reasons for your action."

Public Opinion as a Stimulus to Foreign Policy Innovation

Exceptions to the general rule of public acquiesce and passivity may be rare, but there are instances when changes in public opinion precede rather than follow changes in policy.

Consider the issue of American policy toward Mainland China's admission to the United Nations. A growing proportion of the public favored admission at the same time that influential segments of the policy-making community remained in rigid opposition to it. In 1950 no more than fifteen percent of the American public favored admission, but by 1969 more than half supported it (Mueller 1973), a level of that may have made the eventual U.S. decision not to block admission possible. In much the same way, support for the diplomatic recognition of China by the United States rose dramatically in the decade before President Carter extended it in 1978 (Shapiro and Page 1988).[12]

Another instance where changes in public attitudes were ahead of policy shifts was the Vietnam imbroglio, where public disaffection with continued intervention was often deeper and more vocal than among government leaders. Similarly, public demonstrations of outrage in 1985 toward South Africa's racial policy of *apartheid* by a small group of activists appeared to rally public opinion and to be critical in bringing congressional pressure to bear on the administration to abandon its South Africa policy known as "constructive engagement." It also may have contributed to the congressional decision a year later to override a presidential veto to place sanctions on South Africa.

More recently, a plurality of the general public and an even larger number of opinion leaders supported normalization of relations with Vietnam long before the Clinton administration took this initiative (Rielly 1991, 1995). Large numbers also support entering into negotiations with Cuba and North Korea toward this end (Rielly 1995). Public support of multilateral intervention in Bosnia also was higher than unilateral action before the Clinton administration embraced NATO's active involvement in the conflict (Sobel 2001, 1998).

In these cases, it appears that public preferences laid the basis for foreign policy innovation or change. But we must be careful not to assert that public opinion *caused* policy innovation or change. It is probably more accurate to argue that the public can influence the course of policy, even when it is mobilized, only indirectly, by changing "the image of public opinion held by persons capable of affecting policy decisions" or by altering "the image of public opinion held by the public itself" (Rosenberg 1965). In this way public opinion affects how policy makers think about the international environment, the climate of domestic opinion, and the latitude available for their decisions within an otherwise constraining environment.

Public Opinion as a Resource in International Bargaining

Ironically, the constraining influence of public opinion may sometimes work to the United States' advantage in dealing with other states. American diplomats, for instance, may enhance their ability to get their way at the bargaining table by claiming that "the American people will never tolerate this." By describing themselves as victims of popular preferences, diplomatic negotiators may indeed gain considerable bargaining

leverage. "The fact that this decisional process may not in reality originate in the will of the people does not diminish the significance or usefulness of symbolically casting the threshold of national tolerance in terms of public opinion" (Fagen 1960; see also Putnam 1988).

In practice, of course, Congress is often the expression of public opinion on diplomatic matters. Knowing this, presidents sometimes seek to portray their policies at home as supported by "the American people," in effect using their opinions not only as bargaining leverage with other governments but also with Congress. Sometimes their strategies are successful, sometimes not. Clinton, for example was able to parlay broad public support for establishing normal trade relations with China into a wider margin of victory in Congress than initially thought possible. But he was not able convince key segments of American society or Congress to support the Kyoto Protocol to the Framework Convention on Climate Change.

The Opinion-Policy Nexus: Correlation or Causation?

The foregoing observations about the functions of public opinion demonstrate the complexity of linkages between Americans' preferences and the nation's foreign policy behavior. "A democratic myth" is what Gabriel Almond (1960) called the notion "that the people are inherently wise and just, and that they are the real rulers of the republic." That conclusion is unassailable as far as it goes. It is also true, however, that the complex, still poorly understood relationship between opinion and policy is affected by a cluster of intervening factors, including the nature of the issue, the leadership, policy makers' perceptions, and the international and domestic circumstances prevailing at the time of decision.

To this we should add that over time there is a strong correspondence between public preferences and the foreign policy ends and means American leaders choose.[13] That may seem paradoxical, since much evidence supports the existence of short-run discrepancies between preferences and policies. Yet the paradox itself speaks to an enduring question: How is it that "a policy-making system which has mastered all the modes of resistance to outside opinion nevertheless seems, from a long-run perspective, to accommodate to it" (Cohen 1973)?

We have already suggested some answers to this puzzle, particularly in the ability of presidents to mold public opinion to fit their preferred policy choices. Still, when presidents mount what Theodore Roosevelt called "the bully pulpit," they may risk later becoming prisoners of their own past efforts. Public opinion is thus typically a conservative force, a source of inertia that acts as a restraint on policy innovation. Or, as Alan Monroe (Monroe 1979) concludes in a comparative study of consistency between public preferences and public policy, the policy-making system makes it "more difficult to pass publicly approved changes than to maintain the status quo."

POLITICAL CULTURE, PUBLIC OPINION, AND AMERICAN FOREIGN POLICY

The nature of American society and politics is conducive to strong domestic influences on its foreign policy behavior. Comparatively speaking, the United States is a *society-dominant system* (Friedberg 1992; Katzenstein 1977; RisseKappen 1991). Thus, unlike, say, France and Germany, which are state-dominated political systems, the nature of domestic structures in the United States—buttressed by a political culture that emphasizes individualism and pluralism—facilitates the expression of public opinion on foreign policy issues. It provides multiple access points to decision makers. It also demands that policy makers monitor that opinion as they maneuver to build coalitions supportive of their policies. President George H. W. Bush's determined effort to build and maintain public support in Congress and elsewhere for his policies in the Persian Gulf—which were haunted by the dreaded Vietnam syndrome—illustrates how even in the area of national security (long believed to be "above politics"), societal forces often exert a profound impact on American foreign policy. Indeed, some lament that "foreign policy is essentially politics-driven," with seemingly greater attention given to poll results than to policy effectiveness (Schneider 1990). Still, the "limits" to permissible behavior may be elastic, but they cannot be ignored completely without risking policy failure. Johnson learned that in Vietnam, as did Nixon in the Watergate affair, Reagan during the Iran-contra scandal, and George H.W. Bush in his neglect of the domestic economy despite an enviable record of foreign policy successes.

In Chapter 9 we will look more closely at the access points through which public opinion and the political culture are sometimes expressed. These include interest groups and the electoral process. We will also examine the role of the mass media, an increasingly visible transmission belt through which politically relevant ideas circulate in the American polity.

KEY TERMS RELATED TO POLITICAL CULTURE AND PUBLIC OPINION IN AMERICAN FOREIGN POLICY

accommodationists	*belief system*	*equality of opportunity*
acquiescent	*communal rights*	*equality of outcome*
approval-diminishing events	**cooperative internationalism**	**exceptional American experience**
approval-enhancing events	**democratic capitalism**	**hardliners**
attentive public	*e pluribus unum*	*honeymoon*

idealism	*militant internationalism*	*politics of prestige*
individual rights	*multiculturalism*	*popular sovereignty*
internationalists	*Munich generation*	*public opinion*
isolationists	*national attributes*	*rally-round-the-flag*
jingoistic	*nationalistic*	*realism*
John Locke	*New World Order*	*social capital*
law of anticipated reactions	*nonattitudes*	*social cognition theory*
liberal internationalism	*perceptual filters*	*society–dominant system*
liberalism	*permissive*	*Vietnam generation*
Lockean liberal tradition	*policy influentials*	*Vietnam syndrome*
melting pot	*political culture*	

SUGGESTIONS FOR FURTHER READING

Almond, Gabriel A. *The American People and Foreign Policy.* New York: Praeger, 1960.

Dallek, Robert. *The American Style of Foreign Policy: Cultural Politics and Foreign Affairs.* New York: Knopf, 1983.

Holsti, Ole R. *Public Opinion and American Foreign Policy.* Ann Arbor, MI: University of Michigan Press, 1996.

Kennedy, David M. "Can We Still Afford to Be a Nation of Immigrants?" *The Atlantic Monthly,* 278 (November 1996): 52–68.

Kull, Steven, and I. M. Destler. *Misreading the Public: The Myth of a New Isolationism.* Washington, DC: Brookings Institution Press, 1999.

Lind, Michael. *The Next American Nation: The New Nationalism and the Fourth American Revolution.* New York: Free Press, 1995.

Page, Benjamin I., and Robert Y. Shapiro. *The Rational Public: Fifty Years of Trends in Americans' Policy Preferences.* Chicago: The University of Chicago Press, 1992.

Small, Melvin. *Democracy and Diplomacy: The Impact of Domestic Politics on U.S. Foreign Policy, 1789–1994.* Baltimore: Johns Hopkins University Press, 1996.

Sobel, Richard. *The Impact of Public Opinion on U.S. Foreign Policy Since Vietnam: Constraining the Colossus.* New York: Oxford University Press, 2001.

Wittkopf, Eugene R. *Faces of Internationalism: Public Opinion and American Foreign Policy.* Durham, NC: Duke University Press, 1990.

Wolfe, Alan. *One Nation, After All: What Middle Class Americans Really Think About God, Country, Family, Poverty, Racism, Welfare, Homosexuality, Immigration, the Left, the Right, and Each Other.* New York: Viking, 1999.

Zaller, John R. *The Nature and Origins of Mass Opinion.* New York: Cambridge University Press, 1992.

NOTES

1. The U.S. Census Bureau estimates in its periodic "Small Area Income and Poverty Estimates" that the proportion of Americans living below federally defined poverty levels in the 1990s varied between 15.1 percent in 1993 (39.3 million people) and 11.8 percent in 1999 (32.3 million people).

2. Although this is the orthodox interpretation of Robert Kennedy's role during the deliberations over the Cuban missiles, transcripts of taped conversations during those meetings suggest that Kennedy was actually a proponent of the invasion option, of which air strikes would obviously be a part (see White

House Tapes and the Minutes of the Cuban Missile Crises 1985; May and Zelikow 1997).

3. The meaning of democracy, and the democratic premise, is captured by its Greek root: demokratia 5 *demos* (people) 1 *kratia* (power).

4. Such findings invite a negative estimate of the intelligence of the American people and their importance in the political system by suggesting, as Friedrich Nietzsche concluded, that "the masses are asses." It also invites the conclusion that leaders should ignore the opinions of the masses, along the lines of Oscar Wilde's famous adage that "those who try to lead the people can only do so by following the mob." Although some may be attracted to these viewpoints, neither conclusion is warranted by the evidence, as we will demonstrate in the next section.

5. See also Graham (1986), Russett and Graham (1988), Wittkopf (1990) and, for a contrasting viewpoint, Holsti (1987).

6. See Hinckley (1993), Holsti (1994), Holsti and Rosenau (1994), and Wittkopf (1994c, 1996, 2000).

7. The classic study of belief system rigidity is Ole R. Holsti's (1962) examination of John Foster Dulles' image of the Soviet Union. Other studies that address the factors influencing the development of political attitudes and beliefs among mass and elite publics and why they are often resistant to change include Conover and Feldman (1984), Converse (1964), Festinger (1957), Herrmann (1986), Hirshberg (1993), Hurwitz and Peffley (1987, 1990, 1992), Larson (1985), Neuman (1986), and Zaller (1992).

8. Carter's foreign policy is often thought to have been "weak" and his policies and policy-making procedures characterized by inconsistencies and incoherence. Skidmore (1993–1994) offers an alternative view that emphasizes contradictions between internal and international pressures. "International incentives, arising from the dynamics of U.S. decline, initially pulled the administration toward a strategy of adjustment to external change. Domestic constraints favoring policy rigidity, however, eventually forced Carter to abandon much of his early reformist approach in an effort to salvage his dwindling domestic popularity." See also Hoffmann (1979–1980) and Rosati (1993).

9. Much of the literature that seeks to explain fluctuations in presidential popularity focuses on the impact of economic variables. The pioneering work incorporating foreign policy was done by John Mueller (1973). Ostrom and Simon's (1985, 1989) extension of that work to the impact of political drama generally is especially illuminating.

10. A *New York Times*/CBS News survey in February 1998 found that the public's approval of Clinton's handling of the economy exceeded his overall approval rating, something that had not happened for two decades except for one month of the Reagan presidency in 1983.

11. See also Fite, Genest, and Wilcox (1990), Shapiro and Mahajan (1986), and Smith (1984).

12. Relevant case studies on the impact of public opinion in the foreign policy domain include Gilboa (1987), Kusnitz (1984), Leigh (1976), and Levering (1976). Powlick (1991) also shows that American foreign policy officials generally accord greater weight to public opinion than is sometimes thought, and that when opposition to a decision emerges, they try to change public opinion by "educating" it to their preferences.

13. See Monroe (1979, 1998), Page (1994), Page and Shapiro (1992), and Stimson, MacKuen, and Erikson (1994).

CHAPTER 9

The Transmission of Values, Beliefs, and Preferences

Interest Groups, Mass Media, and Presidential Elections

> The government of the United States . . . is a foster child of special interests.
>
> PRESIDENT WOODROW WILSON, 1913

> We in the media do not focus on the national interest, but on what interests the nation.
> It's the policy makers who must keep the national interest clear.
>
> TED KOPPEL,
> *NIGHTLINE* ANCHOR AND MANAGING EDITOR, ABC NEWS, 1995

According to liberal democratic theory, leaders are chosen to reflect societal values by converting public preferences into policy. By extension, American foreign policy ultimately is an expression of Americans' sentiments. As James Schlesinger, a former presidential adviser and secretary of defense put it, "foreign policy does not rest upon a definition of the national interest. It rests on public opinion."

How realistic is that viewpoint? We concluded in the last chapter that, because the United States is a society-dominant political system, public opinion is likely to play a more important role in shaping American foreign policy

than in other political systems, where the power of both the state and societal groups is more centralized than in the United States. Still, it is not clear whose opinions are heard. Often the disjunction between elite and mass preferences is large. Moreover, the American political system may be premised on the value that "all men are created equal," but clearly that is not the case. Some people have more access to policy makers than others, and some have more influence. Such disparities within the American polity raise important questions about who really controls American foreign policy and policy making. Do elected and appointed leaders indeed devise policies that reflect public preferences? Or do they instead pursue policies that cater to a privileged elite from which the leaders themselves are drawn? Or policies that appeal to specialized interests? In short, what is the correspondence between the theory and practice of democratic liberalism in America?

We seek an answer to that question in this chapter by focusing on the access points through which public opinion and the political culture may be expressed. Specifically, we examine the social background characteristics of American leaders, the nature and influence of special interest groups on American foreign policy, the role of the mass media in shaping and transmitting information and opinions, and finally, the impact of foreign policy attitudes and issues on presidential elections.

DEMOCRATIC LIBERALISM IN THEORY AND PRACTICE

Two models compete to explain how societal preferences are translated into the political process: *elitism* and *pluralism*. As summarized in Focus 9.1, elitism emphasizes the influence of a few, pluralism emphasizes how a broader array of preferences are translated into the policy process. Both models provide important insights into the societal sources of American foreign policy, but each also raises troublesome questions in a political culture premised on "we the people." We begin this chapter by focusing on those questions as they relate to American foreign policy.

Does a Power Elite Control American Foreign Policy?

The United States is undeniably a democratic society. The complication with that description is that it is also a special-interest society (as well as a bureaucratic, mass consumption, and information society). In particular, when we ask whether those who make American foreign policy share the characteristics and convictions of Americans generally, perplexing findings emerge.

Who Is Chosen to Lead? Who is chosen to lead? In terms of numbers, not many. Only a few thousand individuals out of the more than 275 million Americans decide issues of war and peace. In principle, everyone is eligible. In practice, few are. People are selectively recruited, and those outside the mainstream are denied access and the opportunity to serve. At the top levels—because of family connections, income, and education—foreign policy makers are not drawn proportionately from a cross-section of American society. The result is an *elite*—not only in the sense that a small minority controls policy-making power but also because America's foreign policy managers are typically drawn from an unrepresentative national coterie.

The elitist character of foreign policy making becomes apparent when policy makers' backgrounds are cataloged. Remarkably similar characteristics describe America's foreign policy establishment since its rise to globalism. Consistent with the meaning of "elite," the group is comparatively small and its composition enduring, having changed little in at least half a century. Since World War II (and even more so before), the top positions have been filled by people from the upper class who were educated at the nation's best schools. They are, as the title of a prize-winning book put it, *The Best and the Brightest* (Halberstam 1972).[1] Furthermore, they have generally come from predominantly white, Anglo-Saxon, Protestant (WASP) backgrounds; a disproportionate number have been trained in law; and many have had extensive experience in big business. Indeed, most policy makers' prior careers were spent as managers or owners of major corporations and financial institutions or on the faculties of the nation's elite universities. More often than not, they served in appointed rather than elected positions while in government (Brownstein and Easton 1983; Burch 1980). In essence, the presence of this governing elite makes popular sovereignty fictional—a myth

FOCUS 9.1   How Elitism and Pluralism Differ in Their Views of Power and Society

	ELITE THEORY	PLURALIST THEORY
Most Important Political Division(s) in Society	*Elites* who have power, and *masses* who do not.	*Multiple competing groups* (economic racial, religious, ideological, etc.) that make demands upon government.
Structure of Power	*Hierarchical,* with power concentrated in a relatively small set of institutional leaders who make key society decisions.	*Polyarchal,* with power dispersed among multiple leadership groups who bargain and compromise over key societal decisions.
Interaction among Leaders	*Consensus over values and goals* for society, with disagreements largely limited to means of achieving common goals.	*Conflict and competition over values and goals* as well as means of achieving them.
Sources of Leadership	*Common backgrounds and experiences* in control of institutional resources; wealth, education, upper socioeconomic status; slow continuous absorption of persons who accept prevailing values.	*Diversity in backgrounds and experiences* and activism in organizations; continuous formation of new groups and organizations; skills in organizational activity and gaining access to government.
Principal Institutions of Power	Corporations, banks, investment firms, media giants, foundations, "think tanks," and other *private organizations, as well as government.*	Interest groups, parties, and the legislative, executive, and judicial branches of *government*
Principal Direction of Political Influence	*Downward* from elites to masses through mass media, education, civic, and cultural organizations.	*Upward* from masses to elites through interest groups, parties, elections, opinion polls, etc.
View of Public Policy	Public policy reflects *elite preferences,* as modified by both altruism and desire to preserve the political system from mass unrest; policy changes occur incrementally when elites redefine their own interests.	Public policy reflects *balance of competing interest groups;* policy changes occur when interest groups gain or lose influence, including mass support.
Principal Protection for Democratic Values	*Elite commitments* to individual liberty, free enterprise, and tolerance of diversity, and their desire to preserve the existing political system.	*Competition among groups;* countervailing centers of power each checking the ambitions of others.

SOURCE: Thomas R. Dye and Harmon Zeigler, *The Irony of Democracy: An Uncommon Introduction to America Politics* . Copyright © The Wadsworth Group, a division of Thomson Learning.

used "to legitimate the rule not of the people, but of a small and privileged elite" (Thomas 1988).

The evidence from 1961 to 1988 on the career experience of executive officials in the "inner cabinet" (the secretaries of State, Defense, and Treasury and the Attorney General) confirms this viewpoint. Eight of ten previously served in the national government, nearly half worked in private business, three-fifths were attorneys, and over a quarter had academic careers (Lowi and Ginsberg 1990). The pattern continued into the first Bush administration. Of its cabinet-level appointees ninety percent held previous government posts, thirty-five percent had corporate positions, forty percent had careers in law, and half were educated in the Ivy League (Dye and Zeigler 1990).

Bill Clinton campaigned in 1992 on the promise that he would make his administration "look like America," but the picture that later emerged was quite different. Clinton did appoint a larger number of women and minorities to top jobs in his administration than his predecessors had. He also relied more heavily on people who had held government positions before (many in elected offices) and were trained in law, but he picked few with backgrounds in business or the military. Thus Thomas R. Dye surmised that if the Clinton administration looked like America, "then America has become a nation of lawyers and lobbyists" (Dye 1995).

In other ways, however, the Clinton administration looked very much like its predecessors: "Its appointees [were] drawn overwhelmingly from among the most privileged, best educated, well connected, upper- and upper-middle-class segments of America. There [was] very little 'diversity' in the educational and social backgrounds of top Clinton advisors" (Dye 1995).

Meritocracy is how one observer characterized the unusually high levels of educational attainment of Clinton's first-term appointees: "Perhaps more than any in our history, Clinton's is a government of smart people." It was also "the most networked. Friendships formed at elite colleges and law schools [were] sustained through an archipelago of think tanks, foundations, councils, and associations" (Ignatius 1994).

George W. Bush, Clinton's Oval Office successor, continued the tradition of appointing women and minorities to high level positions. But the distinctive characteristic of his administration was the extraordinary number of appointees who had served in prior Republican administrations, including his father's. Dick Cheney (vice president) and Colin Powell (secretary of state) stand out. Both had served as architects of the senior Bush's Persian Gulf standoff of Saddam Hussein,

arguably his crowning foreign policy achievement. Secretary of Defense Donald Rumsfeld previously served in that same position during the Ford administration. Secretary of the Treasury Paul O'Neill at that time worked in the Office of Management and Budget. Furthermore, the second Bush president, like his father and grandfather before him, graduated from Yale, among the nation's most prestigious private universities. He would later add Harvard to his resumé with a graduate degree in business administration before seeking his fortune in the Texas oil patch.

It is also noteworthy that the women who have become increasingly visible in the nation's institutional elite, particularly in government, themselves share social characteristics much like their predominantly male predecessors. Women, too, are educated in disproportionate number at the nation's most prestigious private colleges, have advanced graduate degrees, and, in the case of those in higher-level government positions, are recruited more often from within government than without (Dye 1995).

African-Americans, on the other hand, have yet to penetrate the institutional elite in sufficient numbers to warrant broad characterizations (see Dye 1995). Still, it is noteworthy that the most visible minority appointees in the Clinton administration typically had law or other advanced graduate degrees. Clinton's Commerce Secretary Ron Brown, among the most prominent African-Americans appointed by Clinton to a top job, had extensive political experience which included chairing the National Democratic Party as it sought to capture the White House in 1992. Colin Powell, like Brown, grew up in Harlem, but unlike Brown his career took a military route that led rapidly to the rank of general. Eventually, however, he too would become a political appointee, serving during the Reagan and first Bush administrations as national security adviser and, later, as Chairman of the Joint Chiefs of Staff during the late Bush and early Clinton administrations.

More recently, Alabama native Condoleeza Rice, George W. Bush's national security adviser, rose through academic ranks with a Ph.D. from the University of Denver's Graduate School of International Studies as an expert on Eastern Europe and the Soviet Union. This led eventually to a prestigious Council on Foreign Relations fellowship and then a position on the first Bush National Security Council staff. She would later return to Stanford University, also a prestigious private university, where she became provost. She left Stanford to join the campaign trail of the man who would become the first president elected in the twenty-first century.

Interestingly, Rice also shared another characteristic reminiscent of the traditional, pre-Clinton foreign policy elite: close corporate connections. Rice was a member of the board of directors of three multinational companies: Charles Schwab, Chevron, and Transamerica Corporation. The Center for Responsive Politics reports that Chevron's board was "so charmed" by Rice that they named one of their tankers after her.

Vice president Dick Cheney also enjoyed close ties with the oil industry. After leaving the first Bush administration he became CEO of Halliburton, the world's largest oil field services company. That company, through its European subsidiaries, sold spare parts to Iraq's oil industry, in violation of UN sanctions against that country.

Many other Bush appointees enjoyed close ties with key American industrial and financial interests. The corporate connections of members of Bush's "inner cabinet" are summarized in Focus 9.2. To a man (underscore man), each of them brought to his new position a rich and extensive involvement with corporate America.

What do these career and socialization experiences tell us about foreign policy making? Commonality of experience—reinforced by the short line of elites in front of the revolving door between government service and the private sector and prestigious universities—fosters uniformity in foreign policy attitudes. The continuity of American foreign policy during the Cold War can be traced in part to the shared characteristics of the self-selecting, self-recruiting, and self-perpetuating "governing elite" in charge. Like-

minded individuals "guarded" American foreign policy by instructing incumbent administrations on similar policy principles (Domhoff 1984). More recently, observers skeptical of the second Bush administration's reemphasis of traditional national security issues—which included a national missile defense system, enhanced military spending, and a reduced interest in and concern about the kinds of post-Cold War security issues that animated the Clinton administration—wondered if that reorientation might be explained by the recall of Cheney, Powell, Rumsfeld, and others steeped in the ethos of their administrative experiences serving Cold War presidents. Critics also worried that the administration's "tilt" on other issues, notably environmental protection, reflected its close corporate connections.

All of George W. Bush's inner circle of advisers are part of the foreign policy elite that has shaped American foreign policy since World War II and before. Often called *the Establishment* or the *Wise Men*, these (for the most part) men believed they possessed the training and experience necessary to make the right foreign policy decisions—and that public opinion would support their choices. The roster of names is lengthy. Excluding presidents and appointees to the new Bush administration, it includes Robert Lovett, John McCloy, Robert McNamara, Henry Stimson, Averell Harriman, James F. Byrnes, Allen and John Foster Dulles, George F. Kennan, Dean Acheson, Clark Clifford, Paul Nitze, Nelson Rockefeller, Paul Warnke, William and McGeorge Bundy, Dean Rusk, Elliot Richardson, George Ball, Eugene and Walt Rostow, Henry Kissinger, Zbigniew Brzezinski, James Schlesinger, Cyrus Vance, George Shultz, Alexander Haig, William Casey, Caspar Weinberger, James A. Baker, Brent Scowcroft, Lawrence Eagleburger, Warren Christopher, Leslie Gelb, Anthony Lake, Joseph Nye, and Samuel Berger. Many more could be added.

Every American president since World War II found himself dependent on this coterie of elites and its advice. Perhaps this is what led John F.

FOCUS 9.2   George W. Bush's Inner Cabinet: The Corporate Connection

	CORPORATE CONNECTIONS
Secretary of State Colin Powell	America Online/Time Warner
	General Dynamics
	Gulfstream Aerospace
Secretary of Defense Donald Rumsfeld	Allstate
	Amylin Parmaceuticals Company
	Asea Brown Boven
	G. D. Searle
	General Dynamics
	General Instrument
	Gilead Sciences
	Gulfstream Aerospace
	Kellogg
	Motorola
	Pharmacia
	Sears, Roebuck & Company
	Tribune Company
Secretary of the Treasury Paul O'Neill	Alcoa
	Eastman Kodak
	International Paper
	Lucent Technologies
Attorney General John Ashcroft	AT&T
	Enterprise Rent-A-Car
	Microsoft
	Monsanto
	Schering-Plough

SOURCE: "Political Profile: George W. Bush's Cabinet," Center for Responsive Politics, *www.opensecrets.org* April 13, 2001.

Kennedy to respond, when urged during his 1960 campaign to hit his critics harder: "That is not a very good idea. I'll need them all to run this country."

The Council on Foreign Relations The recruitment and advisory roles of the *Council on Foreign Relations* illuminate the channels through which American elites and their preferences have often been funneled into the foreign policy-making process. The Council has been described as "the most influential policy-planning group in for-eign affairs" (Dye 1990) and its journal, *Foreign Affairs,* described by *Time* magazine as the most influential magazine in the country. Its limited membership is drawn from among the most prestigious and best connected of the nation's financial and corporate institutions, universities, foundations, media, and government bodies. Its members (who are gatekeepers for new entrants), past and present, include most of those previously named as having moved through the revolving door of government service. "Every person of influence in foreign affairs" has been a member, including presidents (Dye 1990).

The Council sees its role as building elite consensus on important foreign policy issues. "It initiates new policy directions by first commissioning scholars to undertake investigations of foreign policy questions. . . . Upon their completion, the [Council] holds seminars and discussions among its members and between its members and top government officials." Furthermore, *Foreign Affairs* is "considered throughout the world to be the unofficial mouthpiece of U.S. foreign policy. Few important initiatives in U.S. policy have not been first outlined in articles in this publication" (Dye 1995).

The consistency between studies and reports initiated by the Council and articles appearing in *Foreign Affairs* and actual American foreign policy since World War II is remarkable. The Council does not actively advocate particular policies, but through its initiatives, publications, and other consensus-building strategies it has played a key role in the development of such policies as containment, the NATO agreement, the Marshall Plan, the International Monetary Fund and World Bank, and diplomatic relations with China. It also effectively advocated major initiatives in American military strategy. It proposed *flexible response* as a substitute for the doctrine of *massive retaliation,* for example, and it supported military involvement in Vietnam and, later, withdrawal. Its 1980s Project paved the way for a number of the Carter administration initiatives in human rights, nuclear nonproliferation, arms sales, and North-South relations.

Similarly, through the Council on Foreign Relations, the foreign policy elite called in the late 1970s for a fundamental reevaluation of Soviet-American relations in response to a perceived Soviet military buildup which Ronald Reagan made a centerpiece of his foreign policy. Later, the Council would urge a relaxation of tensions in Soviet-American relations, and it became involved in the initiation of the Strategic Arms Reduction Talks (START) and the intermediate-range nuclear forces (INF) arms control talks with the Soviet Union and embraced

the "no first use" principle regarding nuclear weapons. Following Mikhail Gorbachev's assumption of power in the Soviet Union, it supported the thaw in Cold War relations that would lead to the end of that global contest.

Today the Council is probing new directions for American foreign policy in the absence of an overarching security threat including the task of terrorism to home and security. It also remains a voice for liberal internationalism and the corollary principle that American leadership is essential.

Other Policy Planning Groups The Council on Foreign Relations is the most important private policy-planning entity linking the elite in American society to the government, but it is not alone. An array of private policy-planning organizations and "think tanks" seek to exercise influence across the broad spectrum of American foreign policy, including national security and foreign economic policy. Among them are the Brookings Institution, the Carnegie Endowment for International Peace, the Cato Institute, the Center for Strategic and International Studies, the Committee for Economic Development, the Business Roundtable, the American Enterprise Institute, the Institute for International Economics, the Heritage Foundation, the Overseas Development Council, the Center for Defense Information, the Population Reference Bureau, and the Worldwatch Institute.

The Aspen Institute, a policy discussion group, recently figured prominently in knitting together the Clinton administration's foreign policy team, once regarded as successors to the generation of Wise Men. The Aspen Strategy Group, established in the early 1980s to discuss contentious arms control issues, counted nearly every senior foreign policy official among its members. The Group's broad goal as it met through the years "was to rebuild, through regular social and intellectual exchanges, the kind of bipartisan foreign policy elite that steered the nation during the early Cold War years. It was, in that sense, a social club for smart people" (Ignatius 1994).

The socialization experiences of the new Bush administration's foreign policy team tracked neither the Aspen Strategy Group nor any other upstart elitist group but, instead, the contours of the traditional foreign policy Establishment, as we have noted. Surprisingly, however, the president himself came to the White House with only limited exposure to international affairs and no foreign policy experience—despite the fact that his father is widely regarded as having assumed the Oval Office more experienced in foreign affairs than any other president.

But George W. Bush and others outside his "inner cabinet" of foreign policy officials in another sense mirrored trends that have moved the country in a more politically conservative direction since Vietnam. Terms like "counter establishment" (Blumenthal 1988) and "counterculture" (Atlas 1995) have been used to describe the shift toward conservative values among the nation's leaders. The conservative Federalist Society is one group that lends cohesion to many in the Bush administration at the cabinet and subcabinet levels, which individuals are committed to bringing their conservative ideas into mainstream legal thought. Small chapters of the Federalist Society have been active on college campuses for many years, where they have focused on the current state of the legal order. The society "is founded on the principles that the state exists to preserve freedom, that the separation of governmental powers is central to our Constitution and that it is emphatically the province and duty of the judiciary to say what the law is, not which it should be" (Edsall 2001). Thus, for example, members of the society are determined "to completely undo the landmark civil rights and civil liberties decisions of the last half of the 20th century." The thrust of these beliefs is evident not only in American foreign policy but also especially in many of the domestic policy positions the new Bush administration has pursued.

Elites have long played a prominent role in foreign policy making. They will continue to do so. But whether the outlook of the Establishment's Wise Men and its conservative variants derived from a commonality of training, experience, and beliefs can be sustained in the new century is problematic.

Elite Attitudes and Behavior Democracy encourages the participation of different people and the expression of their often divergent preferences. Therefore, the consistency between government policy and the recommendations of a cadre of statesmen-advisers-financiers outside of government does not necessarily pose a problem for liberal democratic theory. But what if we ask the related questions: Are the values and outlook of foreign policy-making elites and others with influence different from those of the American people they presumably represent? If leaders are different from those they lead, does a small minority actually control the majority?

Evidence on these questions is mixed. Elites generally have been *public regarding,* perceiving themselves as "guardians of the public good." Indeed, they are vigorous protectors of the public weal as embraced in the liberal ethos of the prevailing political culture. That includes "a willingness to take the welfare of others into account as part of one's own well-being and a willingness to use governmental power to correct perceived wrongs done to others. It is a philosophy of noblesse oblige—elite responsibility for the welfare of the poor and downtrodden, particularly blacks" (Dye and Zeigler 2000).

Although "average" Americans have generally registered approval of elites' policies (a notable exception is Vietnam), elites' views of the wisdom of "the people" are not flattering. Moreover, the liberal ethos when applied elsewhere in the world, which means extending (imposing?) American values about liberty and democratic capitalism to others, has led to a continuing record of intervention into the affairs of others who do not share American ideas and ideals. Violent conflict and bloodshed have often resulted.

Furthermore, there are limits to elites' commitment to liberal democratic values as they promote their self-interests. That is particularly evident in a globalizing world political economy.

Corporate elites sacrifice long-term economic growth for short-term, windfall, paper profits, knowing that the nation's competitive position in the world is undermined by shortsighted "bottom-line" policies. Elites move factories and jobs out of the United States in search of low-paid workers and higher profits. Global trade and unchecked immigration lower the real wages of American workers. Inequality in America increases, and elites and masses grow further apart (Dye and Zeigler 2000).

Ironically, elites' self-interest is also the glue that keeps the social/economic/political system together. "The only effective check on irresponsible elite behavior is their own realization that the system itself will become endangered if such behavior continues unrestrained. So periodically elites undertake reforms, mutually agreeing to curb the most flagrant abuses of the system" (Dye and Zeigler 2000). Reforms are typically incremental rather than revolutionary, however. Elites' willingness to change policies is tempered by their zeal to protect their interests. So existing policies may be reformed, but they are seldom replaced.

Does a Military-Industrial Complex Control American Foreign Policy?

The argument that American foreign policy is democratic because the foreign policy elite represents the public at large is challenged by those who see elite opinion diverging from that of the mass public. Indeed, a *power elite* (Mills 1956) consisting of a select few allegedly governs America without direction from the majority. Actual government authority does not reside with the people—the Lockean liberal tradition and the doctrine of popular sovereignty notwithstanding. Instead, it rests in the hands of a select minority who exercise substantial power over foreign policy making and public policy in general. In short, the American political system gives the public participation (elections, for example) without power and involvement without influence, while a small set of elites, acting both openly and behind closed doors, makes the important decisions.

This discrepancy between the theory and practice of democratic governance is most visible wherever power is concentrated— allegedly a defining characteristic of the *military-industrial complex.*

The Theory President Eisenhower, a highly decorated World War II general, first brought national attention to the existence of a military-industrial complex when he warned, in an often quoted passage from his farewell address given on January 17, 1961:

> This conjunction of an immense military establishment and a large arms industry is new in the American experience. The total influence— economic, political, even spiritual—is felt in every city, every statehouse, every office of the Federal Government. We recognize the imperative need for this development. Yet we must not fail to comprehend its grave implications. Our toil, resources, and livelihood are all involved; so is the very structure of our society.
>
> In the councils of government we must guard against the acquisition of unwarranted influence, whether sought or unsought, by the military-industrial complex. The potential for the disastrous rise of misplaced power exists and will persist.

Eisenhower worried that the military-industrial complex was a threat because its vast power undermined the countervailing forces that would otherwise keep the abuse of power in check. "We must never let the weight of this combination endanger our liberties or democratic processes," he cautioned.

Eisenhower's warning came at about the same time as Harold D. Lasswell (1962) prophesied that a "garrison state" governed by "specialists in violence" would arise to dominate policy making and as C. Wright Mills (1956) argued that a power elite promoted policies designed to serve its own, rather than the nation's, interests. Mills, using a somewhat different label than Eisenhower, described the military-industrial partnership this way:

> The "Washington military clique" is not composed merely of military men, and it does not prevail merely in Washington. Its members exist all over the country, and it is a coalition of generals in the roles of corporation executives, of politicians masquerading as admirals, of corporation executives acting like politicians, of civil servants who become majors, of vice-admirals who are also the

assistants to a cabinet officer, who is himself, by the way, really a member of the managerial elite (Mills 1956).

According to Mills, the partnership among these interests was more a natural coalition than a conspiracy. The interests might occasionally join forces to strive for the same self-serving ends, but not necessarily by design and infrequently through coordinated activities. "The power elite," wrote Mills, "is composed of political, economic, and military [personnel], but this institutionalized elite is frequently in some tension: it comes together only on certain coinciding points and only on certain occasions of 'crisis.'" Later theorists would describe the military-industrial complex as a partnership of "(1) the professional soldiers, (2) managers and . . . owners of industries heavily engaged in military supply, (3) top government officials whose careers and interests are tied to military expenditure, and (4) legislators whose districts benefit from defense procurement" (Rosen 1973).

It is not surprising that members of this elite lacked a unified voice on key issues. Nonetheless, its entrenched (if disorganized) power was believed to derive naturally from a capitalist economic system dependent on foreign involvement for economic benefit. In particular, the post–World War II arms race and the high level of U.S. military spending during the period were often attributed to the self-aggrandizing activities of the military and industrial sectors, which (so the reasoning goes) propagated policies favorable to its interests. As a "peddler of crisis" (Sanders 1983) that benefitted from trouble abroad, the complex justified its existence during the Cold War by provoking fear of the Soviet menace and the need for vigilance in order "to wage a war against cutbacks and not the Soviets" (Thompson 1990). External dangers were allegedly exaggerated to rationalize unnecessary weapons programs and ensure that the military budget would continue to grow "regardless of whether there is war or peace" (Parenti 1988). In so doing, it promoted policies beneficial to itself but arguably detrimental to the nation as a whole.

Even now, critics fear that money spent to continue research, development, and procurement of weapons is money that cannot be used for investments targeted at critical domestic needs.

Adherents to the thesis of a powerful military-industrial force in American society stress that its combined components outweigh other, potentially countervailing domestic forces. Thus the complex is able to predominate over other societal groups (compare Friedberg 1992). "Each institutional component of the military-industrial complex has plausible reasons for continuing to exist and expand. Each promotes and protects its own interests and in doing so reinforces the interests of every other. That is what a 'complex' is—a set of integrated institutions that act to maximize their collective power" (Barnet 1969). As Eisenhower put it,

> The Congressman who seeks a new defense establishment in his district; the company in Los Angeles, Denver, or Baltimore that wants an order for more airplanes; the services which want them, the armies of scientists who want so terribly to test their newest views; put all of these together and you have a lobby.

In short, the military-industrial partnership is so influential because it permeates the whole of American society.

The Evidence—Part I: The Cold War Years
The belief that the interests of the military-industrial complex have been unfairly served to the possible detriment of the national interest is buttressed by considerable circumstantial evidence; some of which, drawn from the waning Cold War years is described below.

- "In the mid-1980s, at the height of the Reagan administration's planned $2.3 trillion defense buildup, the Pentagon was spending an average of $28 million an hour. . . . By 1990 . . . the total defense-spending boom for the Cold War years [would] total $3.7 trillion in constant 1972 dollars—nearly enough 'to buy everything in the United States except the land: every house, factory, train, plane and refrigerator'" (Ignatius 1988)

- One of every sixteen American workers relied directly on the military-industrial complex for his or her paycheck, and millions more were indirectly dependent on them as customers (Thompson 1990). "More than thirty percent of mathematicians, twenty-five percent of physicists, forty-seven percent of aeronautical engineers, and eleven percent of computer programmers work in the military-industrial complex" (Lipsitz and Speak 1989). "For every billion dollars that the Pentagon cuts from its arms budget, almost 30,000 jobs will be lost by industry" (Reifenberg 1990)

- The list of top fifteen companies receiving prime contract awards from the Pentagon remained remarkably stable since World War II, especially among aerospace manufacturers. "Six of the eight aerospace production lines have had a continuous contracting relationship with one military service . . . in most cases back to World War II" (Kurth 1989)

- The prime aerospace contractors typically receive a new contract as a current production line phases out an existing award according to the *follow-on imperative,* which holds that "a large and established aerospace production line is a national resource" (Kurth 1989)

- "The imperatives of the industrial structure are reinforced . . . by the imperatives of the political system. Four of the major production lines are located in states that loom large in the Electoral College: California (Rockwell and Lockheed-Missiles and Space), Texas (General Dynamics), and New York (Grumman). Three others are located in states that for many years had a senator who ranked high in the Senate Armed Services Committee or Appropriations Committee" (Kurth 1989)

- The Pentagon's 20,000 prime contractors and 150,000 subcontractors and vendors "labor" under a noncompetitive "funny form of capitalism," which subsidizes corporate profits and cushions contractors "from the impact of their inefficiency" by a process known as "contract nourishment" (Atkinson

and Hiatt 1985). One study concluded that "virtually all large military contracts have cost overruns from 300 to 700 percent" (Parenti 1988)

- Fraud, waste, bribery, and corruption have been chronic in military contracting, as attested by procurement abuses in the 1980s that included "$748 . . . for a pair of $7.61 pliers, a $7,000 coffee pot, and $600 toilet seats" (Meier 1987). In the wake of such disclosures "the military . . . added 7,000 additional staffers to solve its spare-parts problems" (Reich 1985)

- Universities do substantial basic research for the Pentagon. Seduced into partnership, they no longer serve as a countervailing balance to the military-industrial community. "Our job," one MIT researcher noted, "is not to advance knowledge but to advance the military" (cited in Parenti 1988)

- Numerous private "consulting firms" and "nonprofit" think tanks compete for a share of military "research monies." "Few civilian analysts are to be found" in the employment of these firms, popularly known as the "beltway bandits" (because of the proximity of their offices to the interstate beltway around Washington, DC). Instead, they are populated with former Pentagon personnel and retired officers (Pincus 1985). "Studies that challenge higher authority, that deviate much in either tone or color from the represented service's pitch or uniform hue" are few and far between (Brewer and Bracken 1984)

- Support for Rand Corporation and other federally funded research and development centers (FFRDCs) that design and test weapon systems and devise war-fighting strategies increased by thirty percent between 1987 and 1991 (Pearlstein 1994). The centers receive Pentagon contracts without competitive bidding

- Defense spending consistently accounted for a high percentage of federal outlays. Even under conditions of massive budget deficits, federal debt, and a diminishing Soviet threat, the Bush administration in 1990 sought a

$7 billion increase in military spending for 1991 and further increases each year thereafter through 1995. As a Pentagon budget official wryly noted, "Only over here do we call a $1 billion hike—we wanted a $10 billion hike—a $9 billion cut" (Thompson 1990)

These anecdotes and insights provide empirical support for the alleged existence of a complex of military-industrial interests—at least during the Cold War—but its influence on American foreign policy is easily overestimated. It may be true that pressures for increasing or continuing defense spending were (and are) brought to bear by some lobbyists and defense contractors, but it does not follow that the military-industrial partnership single-mindedly pursued this objective above all others. Indeed, the profits of many American industries that did (and do) contract work for the Pentagon do not depend heavily on it. Furthermore, war and foreign adventure, alleged by the more radical versions of the military-industrial construct to have been critical to its survival, actually threatened the financial interests of corporate America and the lives (though not the prospects for promotion) of military officers.

Thus the military-industrial complex undoubtedly colored much activity during the Cold War abroad and at home, particularly the structure of defense spending and the shape of the nation's military capabilities. Nevertheless, we cannot safely conclude that U.S. Cold War initiatives derived solely from the pressures of the faceless MIC. Where there is interest, there is not necessarily influence.

The Evidence—Part II: Since the Cold War The end of the Cold War portended important changes in the politics of defense spending as first the Bush and then the Clinton administrations cut actual or projected defense spending and down-sized the military. Critics of the military industrial complex theory argue that these changes demonstrate it was "at best, inadequate and, at worst, inaccurate. The power of the military-industrial complex, if it was real, ought to have been sufficient to prevent severe budget

decline, hardware cancellation, and base closings, the very events [that took place] in the 1990s" (Adams 1994; see also Anton and Thomas 1999). Certainly there is merit in this critique, but it overstates the extensiveness of the changes that have taken place since the Berlin Wall fell and, in particular, the political dynamics that sustain defense procurement and production.

Pork-Barrel Politics and the New Industrial Policy As the post–Cold War military build-down gained momentum during the first Bush administration, defense advocates offered several arguments designed to slow its pace, including protecting the nation's "defense industrial base" and maintaining "excess capacity" that could be brought into production in the event of a major war. At the same time, sales of U.S. military equipment to other nations increased dramatically. Liberal Democrats in Congress, who previously opposed such arms transfers, now supported them, as concern about jobs back home and related presumed economic benefits took precedence (see Renner 1994).

The sale of seventy-two advanced F-15 aircraft to Saudi Arabia in 1992 was particularly notable, as it enjoyed the support not only of congressional Democrats but also of presidential hopefuls George Bush and Bill Clinton. The Bush administration earlier had shelved the Saudi request, but Bush revived it during the campaign to keep production lines at McDonnell Douglas Corporation going and to preserve an estimated 7,000 jobs.

Clinton went a step further, supporting two weapons systems the Bush administration wanted to ax: the Seawolf submarine and the V-22 Osprey tilt-rotor aircraft. Meanwhile, the Pentagon began to pick up costs military contractors had previously paid as they sought to sell U.S. military hardware in trade shows around the world.

The Bush administration's ill-fated effort to kill the V-22 Osprey—a vertical takeoff transport plane ordered by the Marine Corps but opposed by top-level Pentagon officials (including Dick Cheney, then secretary of defense) as unnecessary and too expensive—illustrates how the ***iron triangles*** inside the defense policy process preserve weapons systems even in the face of stiff opposition. The concept refers to the bonds that link defense contractors and interest groups (the private sector), defense bureaucrats (the Defense Department), and members of Congress (the legislative branch) into a single entity that is exceedingly difficult to break. In the case of the Osprey, one side of the triangle was shaky—defense bureaucrats at the top. But they faced determined opposition from the two other sides of the triangle as well as opposition from within the Pentagon itself.

The interest-group side was represented by the aerospace companies (led by Boeing) and unions (led by United Auto Workers) that produced the plane. They mobilized a national network of workers and supplier companies with a toll-free hotline to Congress, and a national "Tilt Rotor Appreciation Day" capped off by a flight demonstration in Washington. Members of Congress whose districts would lose jobs and money were brought on board. Several members began weekly strategy sessions with lobbyists, and one representative hosted a cocktail party that drew 200 lobbyists and industry officials, checkbooks at the ready. Defense PACs [political action committees] vowed to step up contributions to members of key congressional committees who had already received $2 million the year before. And the bureaucratic side of the triangle, working inside the Pentagon, was the Marine Corps, which wanted the program. (Bennett 1994a)

The Osprey survived—helped in part by the support it received in the presidential campaign. Thus, by the time Bill Clinton was sworn into office, the pattern was clear: "Politicians of all stripes [had become] preoccupied with keeping military spending high for economic and political reasons" (*The Defense Monitor,* 22 [2] 1993). But tragedy lurked in the background: More than one of the Osprey crashed after production began, killing dozens of young Marines. In a now highly politicized environment, the Osprey's future had to be faced again. Ironically, Vice President Dick Cheney would be among those responsible for a decision. Meanwhile, the commander of the Osprey squadron was fined after it was revealed he ordered subordinate officers to lie about the Osprey's maintenance records.

The Seawolf nuclear attack submarine, whose construction Clinton supported, was projected to cost $2.4 billion, making it among the most expensive weapons systems ever built. Its primary mission was to defeat the Soviet Union, which by 1992 had imploded. Moreover, construction of a newer, less costly submarine was projected to begin before the end of the decade. Political support for the nuclear submarine by the Pentagon, in Congress, and elsewhere was, however, vigorous. By the mid-1990s the Submarine Industrial Base Preservation Council could report that the Navy had granted construction subcontracts to firms in forty-five of the fifty states (Priest and Mintz 1995). Senator Bob Dole, who earlier had voted against the Seawolf, came out in support of it as he positioned himself for a run at the presidency. House Speaker Newt Gingrich, other members of Congress, and many governors also supported construction of the submarine out of obvious concern for protecting defense jobs in their constituencies.

Supporters of the weapon system also introduced "industrial policy" into the debate. They argued that if the Seawolf was not funded, General Dynamics' Electric Boat Division, which had long produced submarines at its Groton, Connecticut facility, would likely close shop. This would leave only one shipbuilder capable of producing nuclear ships or submarines, a situation perceived dangerous for national security (Priest and Mintz 1995). Navy Secretary John H. Dalton defended that viewpoint, saying "We live in an uncertain world. . . . Two shipyards capable of building nuclear submarines are important because 'we may need a surge capacity to build more than one submarine a year.'" Senator John McCain (R-Arizona), an influential member of the Senate Arms Services Committee and among the Seawolf critics, did not buy that argument: "This whole thing reminds me of 'Let's Make a Deal' and the taxpayer gets to pay. We've kept the shipyards in business well into the next century."

A combination of Cold War thinking, pork-barrel politics, and industrial policy also punctuated debate about two other expensive weapons systems: the air force's F-22 Raptor stealth fighter now in advanced stages of development and near ready for production; the other the proposed Joint Strike Fighter plane, which is still in early stages of research and development.

The F-22 was conceived in the early 1980s as a next-generation replacement for the F-15 fighter, long the mainstay of the U.S. fighter force and arguably still the most sophisticated plane of its kind. Development of the F-22 has taken two decades. Much has changed in that time. Not only has the Cold War ended, but technical problems and cost overruns have pushed the estimated cost of each copy of the plane to $200 million, which translates into $70 billion for the fleet of over three hundred jets the air force wants. Critics also argue that the F-15 will continue to dominate the skies for many years into the future, and that other planes planned by the Pentagon obviate the need for the F-22.

Supporters counter that the F-15 has been sold to many other countries, which levels the playing field between the United States and potential adversaries. The F-22 is therefore necessary if the United States is to maintain air superiority. Supporters also note that production of the plane would lead to 21,000 jobs throughout the United States. Although Congress remained skeptical, the Clinton administration supported production of sixteen F-22s to determine if required performance tests could be met. (Clinton, also in the waning days his administration, promised Israel that it would be the first to receive the new fighter.)

The Joint Strike Fighter is conceived as a new aircraft that will replace aging air force, navy, and marine fighters with a single, cost-effective plane that would fit each of the service's needs (something not done previously). The Pentagon initially made the decision to award the contract to only one company. Boeing and Lockheed Martin were the competitors and the stakes were enormous. The Pentagon anticipates that 5,000 copies of the plane will be built at a cost ranging from $28 million to $38 million each, making it the single most expensive weapons system ever (Wayne 1999).

Boeing and Lockheed Martin became locked in fierce competition, hoping to win the lucrative contract. Early in 2000, however, journalists reported that the Pentagon was rethinking awarding the contract to just one company (Wayne 2000). In testimony before Congress, Air Force Secretary Whitten Peters expressed concern that "given the current state of the defense industry, going to a singe contractor at this time could effectively leave us with a single contractor for many years." And that, as in the case of the Seawolf, is perceived by some as dangerous for the nation's security. (Eventually Lockheed Martin won the contract, but some members of Congress continued to question the Pentagon's winner-take-all strategy for awarding the contract.)

Demise of the Military-Industrial Complex? Fear that the widespread consolidation of the defense industry in the 1990s could have an adverse long-term impact on the ability of the United States to maintain its security raises perplexing questions about the continued utility of the military-industrial construct. Has the downsizing of the defense industry reduced the ability of the United States to produce sophisticated weapons of war? Has the absence of a single, overarching security threat reduced the financial incentives of corporate America to produce the weapons necessary to combat twenty-first century security threats? Eugene Gholz and Harvey Sapolsky (1999–2000), defense policy analysts at the Massachusetts Institute of Technology, have addressed issues directly related to these questions. Their findings are instructive. First, their analysis supports the conclusion that the congressional-business-bureaucratic *iron triangle* remains highly effective.

The politics of jobs and congressional districts that many analysts thought governed the Cold War have triumphed in its aftermath. Today, years after the collapse of the Soviet Union, not one Cold War weapon platform line has been closed in the United States. The same factories still produce the same aircraft, ships, and armored vehicles (or their incremental descents). (See Table 9.1)

Table 9.1 Active Post-Cold War Production Lines

	Current Product	Likely Follow-on
Aircraft		
Lockheed—Marietta, Ga.	C-130	C-130J, F-22
Lockheed—Fort Worth, Tex.	F-16	Joint Strike Fighter
Lockheed—Palmdale, Calif.	Aurora[a]	Another secret aircraft
Northrop—Palmdale, Calif.	B-2	B-X
Northrop—Lake Charles, La.	JSTARS	Small surveillance aircraft
Northrop—St. Augustine, Fla.	E-2C	New Navy support aircraft
Boeing—St. Louis, Mo.	F-15, F/A-18C/D, AV-8B, T-45	F/A-18 E/F
Boeing—Long Beach, Calif.	C-17	C-17
Helicopters		
United Technologies-Sikorsky—Stratford, Conn.	UH-60 Blackhawk	CH-60, UH-60 Upgrade, Comanche
Boeing-Vertol—Philadelphia, Pa.	V-22	V-22, Comanche
Textron-Bell—Fort Worth, Tex.	OH-58D Kiowa Warrior, V-22	V-22
Boeing-Hughes—Mesa, Ariz.	AH-64D Apache Longbow	AH-64D
Kaman—Bloomfield, Conn.	SH-2 Seasprite (export)	SH-2G Super Seasprite (export)
Shipyards		
Newport News Shipbuilding—Newport News, Va.	CVN-77	CVNX, NSSN
Litton Ingalls—Pascagoula, Miss.	DDG-51, LHD	DD-21, LHD
General Dynamics-Bath Ironworks—Bath, Me.	DDG-51	DD-21, LPD-17
General Dynamics—Electric Boat—Groton, Conn.	SSN 21 (Seawolf)	NSSN
Litton-Avondale—Avondale, La.	LMSR, LPD-17	LPD-17, T-ADC(X)
General Dynamics-NASSCO—San Diego, Calif.	LMSR	T-ADC(X), JCC
Armored Vehicles		
General Dynamics—Lima, Ohio	M1A2	M1A3
General Dynamics—Woodbridge, Va.	AAAV Design	AAAV
United Defense—York, Pa.	Hercules, Grizzly, M2 Bradley	Crusader
General Motors—London, Ontario	LAV	LAV

[a]Aurora is allegedly a secret reconnaissance airplane built in Lockheed's Skunk Works. It is not officially acknowledged by the U.S. Air Force or DoD, but there is reason to believe that Skunk Works has a substantial project.

SOURCE: Gholz, Eugene and Harvey M. Sapolsky. "Restructuring the U.S. Defense Industry," *International Security* 24 (Winter 1999–2000):13.

The drawdown after the Cold War is often portrayed as one of the harshest when compared to the defense cuts after other wars fought by the United States. It has actually been the gentlest; more than a decade after the defense budget cuts started, government contracts still support 2.1 million private defense-sector employees—400,000 more than at the budgetary low point of the Cold War (Gholz and Sapolsky 1999–2000).

They also note that pressures for further defense spending cuts faded by the late 1990s, as federal budget surpluses took pressure off Congress and the president to continue downsizing the military. The process in fact began early in the decade. Following the Pentagon's "bottom-up review" of the military, Clinton declared in only his second State of the Union message "We must not cut defense further." Congress applauded loudly.

Second, Gholz and Sapolsky dispute the argument advanced by MIC theorists that the defense industry enjoyed a cozy relationship with government during the Cold War that minimized their risks. Pointing to more than a dozen prime contractor production lines closed between the early 1950s and the early 1990s, the analysts suggest that in fact defense contracting was a high-risk venture during the Cold War resulting from the political and technological uncertainty the defense industry faced. They further argue prime contractors' ability to please their customer, namely the Pentagon, is the reason why the same ones won awards year after year. "The way to please the customer was often to promise still more enhancements, which compounded technological uncertainty. . . . Responsiveness to the military customers rather than to Congress was a highly prized, contract-winning trait during the Cold War" (Gholz and Sapolsky 1999–2000).

Today, however, with a diminished external threat, politics reigns supreme. Members of Congress, as we have seen, are sensitive to the impact of defense spending in their own states and districts. Intense lobbying by a highly effective industry lobby is also a potent force. In 1997, for example, an off-election year, Boeing made

$424,000 in campaign contributions, and McDonnell Douglas (later acquired by Boeing) contributed $331,000 (Wayne 1998).

The financial mergers of many of the large defense contractors in recent year has enhanced their already powerful voices. By the end of the 1990s, just three companies, Boeing, Lockheed Martin, and Raytheon, controlled seventy percent of U.S. defense business and a growing share of markets abroad (Wayne 1998). A consolidated defense industry likewise faces less competition, which reduces its risks. "The contractors no longer have to cut each other's throat to compete," observed the director of the Center for Defense Information. "Now they are giants who are beefing up their case for more spending" (cited in Wayne 1998).

Gholz and Sapolsky use stock market data to ascertain the risks faced by defense contractors. They use a standard Wall Street measure that balances the risks and rewards that affect the rate of return on particular stocks. The assumption is that investors prefer stocks which minimize variations in their rate of return.

Evidence from this analysis shows that the volatility of defense stocks has declined measurably since the mid-1970s. With that, so has the risk of investing in the defense industry. The sharpest decline is evident between 1989, when the Berlin Wall fell, and 1993, when Clinton announced no further cuts in defense spending (see Figure 9.1). The implication is that the defense industry has enjoyed a more predictable investment climate since politics has dominated defense spending decisions than when it was governed by the threat posed by Soviet Communism.

Clearly elements underlying the military-industrial-complex construct remain compelling in the post–Cold War environment, even if particular aspects of it do not. Indeed, Gholz and Sapolsky (1999–2000) conclude domestic politics is even more evident today than previously, making it the most compelling explanation of defense budgeting. "The Cold War is over. U.S. defense budgets are being absorbed in producing wasteful political benefits. Despite the appearance of a

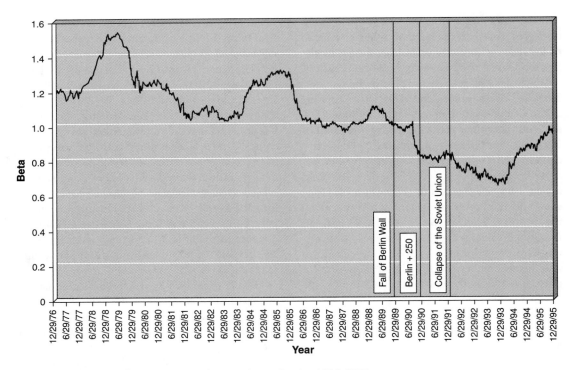

FIGURE 9.1 The Risk of Investing in Defense Industry Stocks, 1976–1995

Note: Beta is a measure of systematic risk based on the rate of return of a stock or group of stocks relative to the entire stock market.
Source: Gholz, Eugene and Harvey M. Sapolsky. "Restructuring the U.S. Defense Industry," *International Security* 24 (Winter 1999–2000): 39.

post–Cold War drawdown—and even a so-called procurement holiday—political pressures keep government expenditure on the defense industry at Cold War levels."

Do Special Interest Groups Control American Foreign Policy?

The power-elite thesis and the corollary military-industrial-complex construct challenge the theoretical tenets of liberal democracy. If in practice an elite indeed rules, then "democratic" policy formation is a political myth. Foreign policy making under such conditions is little more than a reflection of the motives and interests of a privileged few.

Juxtaposed to this is an alternative view—that "average" Americans influence policy by orga-

nizing themselves into groups to petition the government on behalf of their shared interests and values. James Madison, one the three contributors to *The Federalist Papers* designed to win support for the Constitution, worried that a single interest (which he called a "faction") might tyrannize others. To counter that, Madison supported a Constitution that would encourage multiple interests that would counter one another.

If Madison were alive today, he might at first blush applaud the description of the United States as an interest group society. These groups are the bedrock of American *pluralism*. From the pluralist perspective, interest groups serve the public interest by lubricating the system of checks and balances the nation's founders devised. Indeed, interest groups are a key element defining the United States as a society-dominated political system. Still, pluralism also raises perplexing questions about democracy in practice, as we will see. After looking a second time, Madison might himself be perplexed and troubled.

Types of Interest Groups Today thousands of organizations purport to represent Americans' interests. Often represented by the more than 20,000 registered lobbyists who seek to influence members of Congress, lobbyists in 1999 spent an average of $2.7 million on every congressional member—a record total of $1.42 billion in federal lobbying alone that promises to grow even further (Center for Responsive Politics, *Influence Inc.* at *www.opensecrets.org,* April 13, 2001).

The interest groups themselves range from those representing comparatively heterogeneous constituencies, such as AARP (formerly the American Association of Retired Persons), the largest interest group in the nation, to smaller, more homogeneous groups organized around rather specific issues, such as the Sierra Club. Most are concerned primarily with *economic* issues and seek to promote policies that benefit the special interests of their members. The AFL-CIO is an example in the area of organized labor, as is the American Farm Bureau in agriculture.

Among the smaller proportion of noneconomic groups, two types stand out: *public interest groups* and *ideological/single-issue groups*. **Public interest groups** differ from the economic interest groups in that they seek to represent the interests of society as a whole and to realize benefits that are often less tangible. Common Cause, the League of Women Voters, and Ralph Nader's Public Citizen are among the most visible public interest groups. **Ideological/single-issue groups** seek to influence policy in more narrowly defined arenas. Examples again include the Sierra Club, which concentrates on environmental protection issues, the National Rifle Association, which opposes restrictions on gun ownership, and the United Nations Association of America, which seeks to influence U.S. policy toward the UN. Various ethnic interest groups with special foreign policy concerns are also properly

regarded as single-issue groups. Often, however, their activities are not distinguishable from groups that emphasize a particular philosophical viewpoint. Americans for Democratic Action and Empower America are clear examples of ideologically motivated groups. They support liberal and conservative positions, respectively, in foreign and domestic policy. Some religious groups, notably the conservative Christian right, also combine a particular political viewpoint with their religious message as they seek to influence U.S. foreign policies (Martin 1999).

Three other types of actors should be regarded as interest groups broadly defined. First, foreign governments hire lobbyists in an effort to influence the decisions of American policy makers on salient issues. Between 1977 and 1996, the number of countries with representation in Washington grew from 110 to 150, and the number of the firms or individuals who represent them from 220 to more than 1,100 (McCormick 1998). European and Asian countries in particular have stepped up their activities. Japan has been especially active in promoting its interests and protecting itself from attacks on its trade policies. In addition to hiring lobbyists, it has supported various think tanks and academic institutions. In 1988 and 1989 Japanese government agencies, corporations, and foundations spent $400 million "trying to win American 'hearts and minds'" (Judis 1990; see also Choate 1990). Several other Asian countries either directly or indirectly contributed vast sums to the Democratic party in 1996, trying to influence the outcome of the presidential election. The contributions, some in contravention of U.S. law, provoked considerable controversy, congressional investigations, and grist for Senator John McCain's (R-Arizona) drive four years later to make campaign finance reform a centerpiece of his campaign for the Republican party presidential nomination.

Second, departments and agencies of the U.S. government act much like interest groups. They have their own conceptions of appropriate policy and take steps to ensure their views are represented in decision-making circles. The Pentagon, for example, historically has employed (using taxpayers' dollars) hundreds of "congressional liaisons" whose purpose is to secure legislation favorable to itself. Iron triangles are not confined to defense issues but are widely evident in other policy areas as well. Often called *issue networks* rather than iron triangles, they comprise government officials, lobbyists, and policy specialists whose shared interest and expertise in a particular "issue" bring them together.

Third, both state and local governments conduct their own foreign economic policies. Their activities (often in competition with one another) in the solicitation of foreign direct investment resemble those of special interest groups generally (see Goldsborough 1993; Kline 1983; Tolchin and Tolchin 1988).

Interest Groups and Foreign Policy However reassuring to democratic theory the pluralist interpretation may be, in the foreign policy arena, where the questions at issue are often technical and remote from the daily lives of Americans, the presence of organized interests raises the specter of policy domination by narrow vested interests.

Because interest-group activities are not always visible or attended by the press, interest groups are often assumed to be working secretly behind the scenes to devise policies that serve their own interests, not those of the nation. Indeed, many people firmly believe that foreign policy is determined by special interests. Their beliefs are reinforced by some dramatic evidence. For instance, the American Israel Public Affairs Committee (AIPAC)—a key cog in the so-called "Jewish" or "pro-Israeli" lobby—is often thought to control America's Middle East policy (see Bard 1994; Tivnan 1987; Uslaner 1998). U.S. recognition of Israel only eleven minutes after it declared its independence; congressional passage of the Jackson-Vanik amendment denying the Soviet Union promised trade benefits unless it changed its policies governing the emigration of Soviet Jews; and the continuing flow of enormous sums of military aid to Israel lend credence

to the supposition. AIPAC is believed to be so powerful that its detractors claim it has made Israel "America's fifty-first state."

Ethnic interest groups—representing Americans of Arab, Armenian, Greek, Irish, and Jewish descent, and those with ancestry in the so-called Captive European Nations (the former communist states in Eastern Europe), among others—have long played an active role in seeking to shape American foreign policy (understandable in a nation of immigrants). African and Cuban Americans have also recently emerged as visible proponents of their special interests and perspectives (see Uslaner 1998). The African-American lobby Trans-Africa played a visible role in the politics surrounding the decision to intervene militarily in Haiti during the Clinton administration. Earlier it contributed importantly to shaping the sanctions policies toward South Africa believed to have contributed to the demise of its Apartheid regime (McCormick 1998).

In the case of Cuba, several organizations since Castro seized power in the early 1960s have pressured Washington to keep sanctions against Cuba in hopes of toppling Castro's leftist regime. The conservatively oriented Cuban American National Foundation is the most visible among them and has been credited with largely dictating U.S.-Cuban policy during the Reagan and first Bush years (Haney and Vanderbush 1999). It also has shaped the major political parties' approach to Cuban policies (McCormick 1998), particularly in Florida where conservatively oriented ethnic Cubans are concentrated.

The Republican Party has generally benefitted from Cuban-Americans' support, but in 1996 large numbers of them defected to the Democratic party, helping Bill Clinton carry the state against Republican Bob Dole. Four years later, as the campaign season unfolded, a young boy, Elian Gonzalez, ended up in Florida after his mother was lost at sea while seeking to escape Cuba. Whether to return him to his father became an emotionally charged issue that captivated the nation's attention for weeks. Al Gore sought resolution of the issue in family court. George W.

Bush from the start supported Cuban-Americans' conviction that the boy should remain in the United States. Bush's narrow and controversial victory in the state, which sealed the election in his favor, may have been decided by the state's Cuban-American community.

The ubiquity and seeming influence of ethnic groups caused long-time Senator Charles McC Mathias to worry some years ago that the effects of their lobbying may be more harmful than beneficial:

> Ethnic politics . . . have generated both unnecessary animosities and illusions of common interest where little or none exists. There are also baneful domestic effects: fueled as they are by passion and strong feelings about justice and rectitude, debates relating to the interplay of the national interest with the specific policies favored by organized ethnic groups generate fractious controversy and bitter recrimination.

(MATHIAS 1981, 997)

Two decades later political scientist Samuel Huntington (1997) would echo Mathias' lament: "America remains involved in the world, but its involvement is now directed at commercial and ethnic interests rather than national interests. Economic and ethnic particularism define the current American role in the world. . . . Increasingly people are arguing that these are precisely the interests foreign policy should serve."[2]

As Huntington suggests, economic policy and particularly trade issues stimulate considerable interest group activity—because jobs and profits are at stake. Congress is the favored target of these organized efforts. Historically the Chamber of Commerce and the AFL-CIO have figured prominently in these efforts. A veritable cacophony of more narrowly focused interest groups also have often been vocal contestants.

Economic interest groups were especially visible in the fight over NAFTA during the early Clinton administration, when scores of groups contended on both sides of the issue and millions of dollars were spent to influence not simply the

final outcome but also the details of the agreement (Avery 1998; Cohen, Paul, and Blecker 1996; Rothgeb 2001). Near the end of the Clinton administration, intense lobbying would again characterize the fight over granting normal trade relations (NTR) to China. The unexpectedly lopsided vote in favor of NTR may have been the product of "The New China Lobby" (Bernstein and Munro 1999), which knits in close partnership business and consulting interests on both sides of the Pacific.

Interestingly, however, organized labor, once a champion of free trade, increasingly has sided with environmental and other groups opposed to trade liberalization and, more broadly, globalization. It believes globalization encourages the export of jobs to low-wage countries at the expense of American workers while corporate executives profit. In the words of Robert Reich, Secretary of Labor in the Clinton administration, "Even though the business cycle in recent years has improved things for the country as a whole, labor does not feel that it has really shared in the expansion. It feels that manufacturing jobs are still vanishing—whether because of technology or globalization and free trade" (see Mazur 2000; Newland 1999).

Despite the ubiquity of ethnic interest groups and those involved in trade policy, which often turns as much on domestic as foreign policy concerns, the interest groups involved in other foreign policy issues historically have not figured prominently in policy debates. (There are some notable exceptions, such as the "old" China lobby, which for two decades sought to prevent U.S. diplomatic recognition of communist China.) Recently defense policy questions have emerged as an important exception. U.S. policy toward Central America during the Reagan administration also did not fit the historical mold. In both cases, ideological/single issue groups sought to influence policy using the tactics normally associated with domestic interest group activity, including writing letters to members of Congress, testifying at congressional hearings, meeting with members of the media, publicizing the voting records of candidates for office, working in electoral campaigns, engaging in protests and demonstrations, and the like.

During the early phases of détente, for example, several well-known lobbying groups (the Arms Control Association, Center for Defense Information, Council for a Liveable World, Committee for a Sane Nuclear Policy, United Nations Association, and the Women's Strike for Peace, among others) were active proponents of U.S. efforts to relax tensions with the Soviet Union. Equally prominent groups opposed their efforts: the AFL-CIO, American Legion, American Enterprise Institute, American Security Council, Heritage Foundation, National Conservative Political Action Coalition, Veterans of Foreign Wars, and various ethnic interest groups (Cox 1976). Eventually, the Committee on the Present Danger emerged as an especially visible and vocal critic of détente, and the 1979 SALT II treaty in particular, doubtless playing a critical role in creating a domestic political environment inhospitable to its ratification (see Caldwell 1991; Sanders 1983).

In the case of Central America, the Reagan administration confronted a broad array of organized opponents, in which various religious groups figured prominently, but it also enjoyed the support of a countercoalition of groups, which at one time numbered more than fifty (Arnson and Brenner 1993). The opponents enjoyed the upper hand, however. This was especially evident in Congress where the administration's policies toward Nicaragua were never popular, as witnessed by the administration's own organized White House and the State Department efforts to build public support for its policies (see Parry and Kornbluh 1988).

The Reagan administration's decision to launch its own domestic "public diplomacy" efforts on behalf of its Central American policies implies that organized interest groups do indeed have the ability to affect foreign policy. Lending further credence to that view, Reagan complained six weeks prior to leaving the presidency that an "iron triangle" in a "Washington colony" comprising Congress, the news media, and special interest groups was "attempting to rule the nation according to its interests and desires more than the nation's." He lamented in his memoirs that "one of the greatest frustrations during those eight years was my inability to communicate to the American people and to Congress the seriousness of the threat we faced in Central America" (Reagan 1990).

Are Interest Groups Influential? Asking whether interest groups are influential may seem curious, as we have already given several examples where the answer seems clear-cut. Still, as with the military-industrial complex, we must remind ourselves that where there is interest, there is not necessarily influence. Research on the foreign policy influence of interest groups during the Cold War shows that. Briefly, those findings show the following.

- Interest groups exert a greater impact on domestic than on foreign policy issues, where the foreign policy elite are relatively immune from domestic pressures due to national security considerations

- Interest group influence during crises is rare, as the president has enormous power to shape public opinion and receives little effective challenge from others

- Interest groups exert their greatest influence on nonsecurity issues that entail economic considerations commanding attention over long periods

- The impact of interest groups varies with the issue; the less important the issue, the greater the likelihood of interest group influence

- Interest groups most effectively exercise power over policy through Congress

- When congressional interest in a foreign policy issue mounts, interest group activity and influence increase

- Interest group influences increase during election years, when candidates for office are most prone to open channels of access and communication

- Interest groups are most influential when only a narrow segment of society is affected and the issue is not in the public spotlight, attended by the mass media. "A lobby is like a night flower," observed AIPAC's director of foreign policy issues. "It thrives in the dark and dies in the sun" (cited in Grove 1991)

- Influence between the government and interest groups is reciprocal. However, government officials are more likely to manipulate interest groups than the latter are to shape government policy

- Single-interest groups have more influence than large, national, multipurpose organizations, but their influence is limited to their special policy interest

- Interest groups often attempt to influence public opinion rather than policy itself, but mass attitudes are seldom amenable to manipulation by interest group efforts

- Interest groups sometimes seek inaction and maintenance of the status quo; such efforts are generally more successful than efforts to bring about policy change. Thus interest groups act as "veto groups" that inhibit policy change

This summary of findings shows that while interest groups seek to persuade, their mere presence, indeed, ubiquity, does not guarantee their penetration of the foreign policy-making process. Interest groups may be effective on certain special issues. More often, foreign policy making is relatively immune to interest group influence. An important reason is that, within the policy-making arena, interest group influences often counterbalance one another. Many of these generalizations drawn from the Cold War era remain compelling, but changes at home and abroad that the new era has spawned may also have stimulated the tremendous growth in interest group and lobbying activity witnessed in the recent past. James McCormick (1998), a preeminent scholar of Congress and foreign policy, suggests several that have had the effect of encouraging greater

interest group influence. Among them are (1) congressional reforms that have encouraged greater interest group access; (2) the growth of partisan and ideological divisions among the American people, which have stimulated interest group interests and enhanced opportunities to exercise foreign policy influence; (3) the rise of new groups with foreign policy concerns— "foreign lobbies, some religious lobbies, think tanks, and scattered single-issue lobbies"; (4) the increased salience of trade and related issues compared with traditional national security issues; (5) a changing locus of decision making away from the small groups that make crisis decisions toward broader involvement by others interested in structural decisions (for example, goals and tactics of defense policy); and (6) procedural requirements imposed on the executive by Congress that have opened new points of access to others seeking to shape foreign policy preferences.

McCormick offers evidence to support each of these ideas, but his conclusions are compelling: "While involvement and access may arguably be necessary conditions for policy influence, they are not sufficient ones. . . . Significant barriers still hamper interest groups from working their will on foreign policy making even as these groups are increasingly involved in the process. . . . The usual judgment that interest groups can be more effective in stopping action than in changing directions remains as accurate in the foreign policy arena as it does in the domestic arena."

The Politics of Policy Making: Elitism and Pluralism Revisited

The popularity of the pluralist model of policy making rests on the democratic belief that the public good is served when each group in a society of diverse interests seeks to maximize its own interests, much as Adam Smith hypothesized in his classic *The Wealth of Nations* that the invisible hand of the marketplace driven by self-interest would serve the public interest. In the marketplace of ideas and self-interest, the ability of any one group to exert disproportionate influence is offset by the tendency for *countervailing powers* to materialize. When an interest group seeks vigorously to push policy in one direction, another (or a coalition of others aroused by perceived threats to their interests) will be stimulated to push policy in the opposite direction. Indeed, today's losers often become tomorrow's winners.

The positive side of this picture is that no one interest dominates policy. That was the wish and intent of the nation's founders. The negative side is *gridlock,* a popular description of the Washington policy-making scene in recent years as Democrats and Republicans repeatedly found themselves at loggerheads. When the pursuit of one group's interests are balanced by another's, can anything be accomplished?

Political economist Mancur Olson addressed this dilemma and its consequences in two classic works, *The Logic of Collective Action* (1965) and *The Rise and Decline of Nations* (1982). His arguments draw on the theory of collective goods and the "free-rider" problem we discussed in Chapter 7. With respect to interest groups, Olson argues that small, private organizations (such as trade associations) often have an advantage over others as they seek to promote their interests, because larger groups (the American consumer) are unorganized. Individuals also have an incentive to free ride on organized interest groups, because they benefit from their activities even if they fail to share in the costs (nonunion labor, for instance, often enjoys the benefits that unionized labor has won through collective bargaining).

Building on the logic of these arguments, writer/journalist Jonathan Rauch (1994) argues that "demosclerosis" is the result: Democratic government can accomplish little that is meaningful, because each of the organized interests in American society seeks a share of the government's pie (taxes), even if this means redistributing wealth from one segment of society to another. "We have met the special interests and they are us," Rauch observes (see also Lowi 1979).

The pervasiveness of countervailing interests in American society contributes to demosclerosis. Money not only fuels group lobbying activities, it also funds elections. The 2000 presidential campaign cost more than any other in history— at least $3 billion according to Federal Election Commission data—and the number promises to grow even higher. A variety of sources contribute money, including *political action committees (PACs)* representing interests of corporations and groups (limited to $5,000 each) and *soft money* contributions from corporations, labor unions, and wealthy individuals (in unlimited increments of $100,000, $250,000 or more).

Policy makers routinely complain about the power of interest groups and promise to reign them in. Campaign finance reform was at the centerpiece of John McCain's bid for the White House in 2000, as we noted earlier, and he returned to the Senate determined to pursue his goals there. Earlier proposals for reform have been adopted, but they have not always had the intended effect. For example, Congress passed election reform legislation in the 1970s designed to limit individuals' financial donations to candidates for political office. Inadvertently, Congress's action compounded the problem by making it easier to form PACs and enabling them to solicit voluntary contributions that could be channeled to particular candidates or to political parties. PACS are now a major source of campaign funds, with aerospace, defense, pro-Israeli, and "New Right" PACs near the top of the list of contributors in recent years.

There is little doubt that money has altered the character of contemporary campaign politics. Still, in some sense campaign finance patterns reinforce the veracity of pluralism as they reinforce the image of policy making as a taffy-pull among countervailing forces. Average Americans are able to contribute to the causes of the groups that represent their interests, pool their resources, and use them to influence electoral outcomes and, hence, policy choices. But few Americans are able to give the vast sums that the most wealthy contribute (their contributions exceed PACs').

So the taffy-pull becomes another arena of competition among the elite.

So which model of the politics of policy making is correct? The answer favors the elitist model, lending credence to Richard Barnet's (1972) observation that American foreign policy is "an elite preserve . . . made for the benefit of that elite." "The flaw in the pluralist heaven," writes E. E. Schattschneider in his classic study, *The Semisovereign People* (1960), "is that the heavenly chorus sings with a strong upper-class bias." In fact, the elitist and pluralist accounts both depict a process in which the ordinary citizen matters very little in any direct sense when it comes to foreign policy making.

THE ROLE OF THE MASS MEDIA IN THE OPINION-INTEREST-POLICY PROCESS

If anyone is in a position to challenge the power of the privileged in American society, arguably it is the mass media. The communications industry—print, radio, and television—plays two pivotal roles. First, public attitudes may be influenced (created, some would say) by the information the media disseminates. Second, the behavior of policy makers themselves may be affected by the news the media reports and by the images of the world it conveys. From either perspective, the media is an important link in the causal chain that transmits Americans' values, beliefs, and preferences into the foreign policy process. Indeed, it seemingly is in a position to exert a potent influence on the shape of American foreign policy itself.

Many Americans are apparently taken with the notion the media shapes public opinion. Some might even say that the media is public opinion. Government officials likewise attribute vast powers to the media. They may be right, as the evidence suggests that policy makers are able to use the mass media to mold public preferences to support their policies.

Policy makers themselves, however, are typically less than sanguine about the media. Their views have ranged from awe and fear to downright hatred. Nearly every president has come to believe his administration is victimized by the media.[3] (John F. Kennedy may be the exception.) Such views are captured in Oscar Wilde's famous remark that "the President reigns for four years, but Journalism reigns forever." Thus many consider the mass media as a *fourth branch of the government,* also often called the *fourth estate.* It is no accident, therefore, that presidents actively court the media's favor and ascribe to it the power to make or break government policy.

Research shows that mass media has a profound effect both on public opinion and on the shape of policy choices decision makers face. Still, the notion that the media is somehow able to "determine" either foreign policy or even foreign policy attitudes is questionable. The relationship between media influences and other societal sources of foreign policy behavior is more complex than this simple view suggests.

A preferable hypothesis is that the mass media performs a mediating role, helping to shape both foreign policy attitudes and choices but not determining them. The hypothesis contrasts with the typical views of the media, which tend to embrace one of two alternatives: "The media either take foreign policy out of the hands of the elite and open the process to an ill-informed public or they are indentured servants of the foreign policy elite" (Kovach 1996). Neither of those polar extremes is without veracity, but neither is completely accurate either. We can learn why by examining, first, the relationship between the mass media and the public and, second, the relationship between the mass media and policy makers.

The Mass Media and the Public

The proposition that the mass media shapes public attitudes is tempting if for no other reason than that it comprises the primary vehicle for the transmission of knowledge; and "knowledge is power." The institutions that provide Americans with political information are pervasive and sophisticated. Over ninety-eight percent of all American households own at least one television set (seventy-five percent own two or more); and they view it an average of seven hours a day. There are over 1,400 daily newspapers in the United States, with total daily circulations exceeding 55 million. The three major weekly news magazines also claim nearly 10 million readers. This extraordinary establishment has the ability to determine "what the news is," to define behaviors as important actions, and thereby to make them into events.

The *agenda-setting* role of the mass media is particularly important (McCombs and Shaw 1972). Most people may be inattentive to foreign or other issues of public policy most of the time, but when they do show interest or are exposed to issues, the mass media tells them what to care about. Put succinctly, "the mass media may not be successful in telling people what to think, but [they] are stunningly successful in telling their audience what to think about" (Cohen 1963). By telling us what to think about, however, the media also provides cues as to what to think, precisely because of its capacity to determine what we think about (Entman 1989).

The media's ability to set the agenda and to influence thinking in other ways is greatest among those who are neither interested nor involved in politics and hence lack political sophistication. Because many who comprise the mass public have no prior information to draw on in forming attitudes about new developments, the media exert a potentially powerful impact on perceptions about events simply because the information it supplies is new—and is often presented in a sensational way in an effort to influence "appropriate" preferences. Noteworthy is that nearly forty percent of Americans report that the media is their source of information about important international problems, compared with twenty-five percent who turn to it when it comes to domestic issues (Wittkopf and Hinckley 2000).

Furthermore, the attention the media gives to different issues may contribute to its symbolic significance. During 1987, for example, the United States became increasingly involved in the Persian Gulf war between Iran and Iraq. However, news about its air attack on Iranian bases in the gulf region and the destruction of an Iranian domestic airliner by the USS Vincennes in October of that year was dwarfed by news of the dramatic Wall Street stock market crash, the steepest since the infamous crash of 1929. In "calmer times," Doris A. Graber (1993) observes, the Persian Gulf incidents "would have been the top stories."

The ability of public officials to *frame* the way policy issues are presented by the media further enhances the media's capacity to shape individuals' thoughts and opinions. During the continuing conflict in the Balkans during the 1990s, the media failed to report high levels of public support for U.S. involvement there. Instead, the media framed the issue in terms of opposition to involvement, which may have had the effect of misdirecting policy away from public preferences (Sobel 1998). We can also surmise that this meant many Americans came to believe U.S. interests were not at stake in that troubled region.

The media not only sets the agenda and frames the issues, it also functions as a *gatekeeper* by filtering the news and shaping how it is reported.[4] The media's gatekeeping role is especially pronounced in foreign affairs, as the menu of foreign affairs coverage offered the American people comes from remarkably few sources. Principal among them are three prestigious *newspapers of record* (the *New York Times, Washington Post,* and *Los Angeles Times*), two wire services (the Associated Press [AP] and United Press International [UPI]), and four national television networks (ABC, CBS, CNN, and NBC). Furthermore, newspapers such as the *New York Times* provide news to other newspapers, which typically follow its lead in the way they present news stories about foreign affairs to local audiences.

The *New York Times'* motto promises "all the news that's fit to print," but in fact there is too much news even for it. Thus, in choosing what to print, the media gatekeepers also shape the values to which Americans are exposed. Over the long run "the media tend to reinforce mainstream social values. They transmit 'normal' or legitimate issues and ideas to the public and [filter] out new, radical, or threatening perspectives" (Bennett 1980). Similarly, *pack journalism*—a troublesome phenomenon in which reporters follow the lead of one or a few others in deciding what is (or is not) news and how it should be interpreted—often leads to remarkably similar news accounts, particularly among the national print and electronic media (Graber 1997).

Clearly, as the foregoing ideas suggest, the media plays a powerful role in American society. Why, then, is its impact on the public's foreign policy attitudes less direct and pervasive than might be expected?

Media Inattention to Foreign Affairs The mass media's ability to shape foreign policy attitudes is undermined in part by its relative inattention to foreign affairs and its comparatively greater concern for domestic news. Few reporters are paid to cover foreign affairs, and television programming is overwhelmingly oriented toward local, not national or international news.

By some standards coverage of foreign affairs is not inconsequential. Doris Graber (1993) reports that major Chicago newspapers devote about six percent of their space to international news and that national television networks give about twenty percent of their time to it. Still, foreign affairs certainly do not command overwhelming attention. In part this is due to the absence of a mass market for foreign policy news in the face of industry efforts to boost profits.[5] A survey of newspaper reading habits sponsored by the *Washington Post* led to the conclusion that "local news is the franchise for America's newspapers. . . . It is why people buy newspapers." Whereas nearly two-thirds of the respondents said they were very interested in local news, less than one in five said they were interested in foreign news—"a snore for most Americans," according to the *Post* (Morin 1996).

Newspapers also suffer a competitive disadvantage compared with television. Seven of ten Americans report that television is their primary source of all news (Morin 1996). In the post–Cold War environment, however, even network televison news has turned decidedly inward. Garrick Utley, longtime foreign correspondent for several major TV news networks, reports that the "total foreign coverage of network nightly news programs has declined precipitously, from 3,733 minutes in 1989 to 1,838 minutes in 1996 at ABC, the leader, and from 3,351 minutes to 1,175 minutes at third-place NBC" (Utley 1997). The number of minutes devoted to foreign policy coverage in particular, always a smaller subset of foreign news, has also declined. Similarly, Pippa Norris (1997) shows a dramatic decline in TV network coverage of international news during the transition to the post Cold War world and since.

If television challenges the print media, the Internet challenges TV. Today the Internet is a major source of news for many Americans. Data gathered by the *Pew Research Center for The People and The Press* (opinion survey conducted April 20–May 13, 2000 at *www.press-people.org*) show that one in three Americans goes online every week in search of news; about half that number log on everyday. At the same time, regular viewership of network broadcast news dropped during the 1990s from thirty-eight to thirty percent, and local news viewership from sixty-four to fifty-six percent. Furthermore, the trends promise to continue in the future, as today's younger Americans are more likely to turn to the Internet for news than their predecessors.

An exception to the comparatively scant attention other media give to foreign affairs is the coverage it receives in the national newspapers of record, sometimes called the *prestige press*. A study done some years ago showed that the *New York*

Times allotted over forty percent of its total national and international coverage to foreign news (Frank 1973). That proportion may have changed in recent years, but the *Times* remains an important source of international news. How many people consume that coverage remains problematic, however, as the circulation of the *Times* constitutes but a fraction of the nation's newspaper subscribers. Perhaps in response to that reality, and certainly in deference to the electronic information age, the *Times* and the other newspapers of record all offer access to their news via the Internet, often at no charge.

CNN, the twenty-four hour Cable News Network, occupies a place providing world news that sets it apart from others. It maintains a global network of news-gathering offices, and its news broadcasts from around the world are seen around the world. Thus, courtesy of CNN, millions of Americans and others (including Saddam Hussein in Baghdad!) viewed at close range the dramatic aerial bombardment of Iraq at the onset of the 1991 Persian Gulf War. Two years earlier they witnessed the Chinese government's bloody suppression of pro-democracy forces on Tiananmen Square. Then-CNN anchor Bernard Shaw captured the drama unfolding in China this way: "Unbelievably, we all came here to cover a summit, and we walked into a revolution."

The *CNN effect* captures the presumed impact of CNN's new coverage. The phrase was especially popular in the early 1990s, when television news coverage of developments in Somalia were credited by some as having "forced" the Bush administration to intervene there to stem widespread starvation and death. Broadly conceived, the CNN effect can be described as "a loss of policy control on the part of policy makers because of the power of the media, a power they can do nothing about" (Strobel 1999). Research has largely discredited the CNN effect, but the mere fact that it enjoyed such popular attention and considerable scholarly inquiry is testimony to the presumed impact of television news broadcasting on both policymakers and other Americans.

Today, even CNN finds itself challenged. Changing preferences in favor of more commentary and "human interest" broadcasts championed by other cable companies have pressured CNN to steer a new course in today's highly competitive media environment. The stream of 24-hour news coverage long the mainstay of CNN has begun to give way to other programming formats as a result.

Finally, there is another way that cable television has impacted political news. Theodore Roosevelt early in the last century described the presidency as a *bully pulpit*. By that he meant the president could use the power of his office to cajole, to persuade, to get others inside and outside of government to support his policies and programs. The advent of television encouraged that process, as presidents could largely control their access to the media, whether through periodic press conferences or releasing "breaking news" that would break just in time for the evening news broadcasts. Today, however, the president can no longer count on media exposure. One *Washington Post* editorial board member put it rather caustically:

> Technological advances now undermine the bully pulpit rather than amplify it. The rise of cable TV has changed television from a presidential megaphone into a presidential scourge. The three big networks—ABC, CBS, NBC—which once carried all presidential press conferences live, and which reported respectfully on initiatives emanating from the White House, have been displaced by new cable channels that compete for reviewers by eschewing such deference. Rather than televise the president, these cable channels churn out irreverent talk shows. The bully pulpit has been drowned out by bullying pundits.
>
> (MALLABY 2000)

Public Inattention to Foreign Affairs Most Americans are uninterested in and ill-informed about foreign affairs, as we learned in Chapter 8.

In late 1990, for example, as the Cold War was winding down and the United States was in the midst of the crisis over Kuwait, only thirty-six percent of the American people said they were very interested in following news about other countries and barely more than half were very interested in news of U.S. relations with other countries (Rielly 1991). By the end of the decade the proportions in all cases had dropped even further (Rielly 1999). An earlier study found that three-quarters of the public claimed they paid attention to government and public affairs, but only about a third had above-average knowledge on these matters. Over forty percent were poorly informed. This led the authors to conclude that, "while seventy-six percent of the people say they pay attention to politics, they clearly aren't taking notes" (Ornstein, Kohut, and McCarthy 1988).

If the American people fail to listen to or digest news, then obviously the media are not influencing their opinions. Given a choice, Doris A. Graber observes, Americans "do not seek out foreign policy news." In December 1987, for example, as the United States and the Soviet Union prepared for a meeting designed to reduce the danger of war, NBC News broadcast an hour-long, prime-time interview with Soviet president Mikhail Gorbachev. "Only fifteen percent of the national audience tuned in. Half of the viewers who at that time ordinarily watch NBC's entertainment programs switched to other networks" (Graber 1997).

The Imperviousness of Beliefs Research grounded in social psychology shows that most people do not easily change their beliefs, as we saw in Chapter 8. Popular myths notwithstanding, what they read in print and see and hear on television does not alter what they think.[6] Instead, they use information short-cuts that cause them to interpret new information in ways that reinforce, not restructure, prevailing attitudes. *Selective perception* is also a pervasive human tendency: People search for "comfortable" information that "fits" with preexisting beliefs; they screen out or reject information with which they

disagree. In short, we see what we want to see, we hear what we want to hear.

Selective perception is partially subconscious, stemming from the nearly universal need to maintain stable images when confronted with inconsistent and confusing information. In the parlance of psychology, everyone seeks to maintain *cognitive balance* (Festinger 1957), either by screening out information that runs counter to cherished beliefs or by suppressing information that challenges preexisting images. An individual subscribing to the simplistic belief that all civil disturbances are inspired by Islamic fundamentalists, for instance, is likely to reject or block out information that contradicts that theory, such as reports that civil conflict in Rwanda stems from poverty and long-standing ethnic disputes.

Selective perception is also pervasive because people are prone to avoid information with which they disagree. Most people read magazines and listen to news programs that reinforce interpretations consistent with their preconceptions. Few seek out information that challenges them. How many, for instance, routinely read magazines that reflect liberal views, such as *The Nation,* and also conservative ones, like *National Review?*

Individuals' lack of receptivity to wide-ranging ideas that challenge existing prejudices and stereotypes inhibits the mass media's ability to influence attitude change. *Selective recall* is a related tendency that reinforces attitude consistency. Even among those who are relatively sophisticated politically, long-standing ideological predispositions toward conservative or liberal perspectives shape interpretations of events communicated by the media.

Television's Inadvertent Audience The pervasiveness of television in the homes and daily lives of millions of Americans requires that we add important caveats to the foregoing conclusions. Television has provided the mass of the American people with an infusion of foreign policy information that most neither like nor want. Instead, because most who watch television news see what does not interest them as well as what does—they don't "edit" the information television journalists supply by walking away from the set or turning it off—they have become an *inadvertent audience* (Ranney 1983). Even when the American people are attentive to foreign affairs, as clearly many were during the Persian Gulf War, the impact on their political knowledge of exposure to information remains slight (Bennett 1992).

What are the consequences of the intrusive force of television? First, television may explain the decline of confidence in the nation's institutional leadership witnessed during recent decades. As William Schneider (1982), a well-known political analyst, observes, "negative news makes good video. Consequently, television presents much of the news as conflict, criticism, and controversy. . . . The public responds to this large volume of polarized information by becoming more cynical, more negative, and more critical of leadership and institutions." Less patience with foreign policy initiatives by individuals and institutions about which Americans are cynical and distrustful may be a related consequence of exposure to American involvement in world affairs, which television brings home but which most Americans find confusing and unnecessary. Others argue, however, that the news itself is what matters: "The confidence gap is more properly understood as a product of . . . bad news than as a reflection of the manner in which it is communicated to a gullible public by cynical, headline-seeking reporters" (Craig 1993).

Second, members of the inadvertent audience, being uninterested, are unlikely to have convictions as strong about issues as do those who regularly follow foreign policy concerns. "When people with weak opinions are exposed to new information, the impact of that information is very strong. They form new opinions, and if the information they receive is negative or critical, their opinions will develop in that direction" (Schneider 1982). As Kennedy adviser Theodore Sorensen (1994) observed, members of the inadvertent audience, who watch "the screen by the hour instead of by program, . . . often find their attention unintentionally engaged by the

picture unfolding before them, their interest inadvertently aroused, their opinions almost involuntarily formed, and their actions as well as reactions as voters and citizens spontaneously motivated." Still, "there is no evidence that television changes the nature of the public's concerns in the area of foreign policy," observes Schneider (1984). "These concerns remain what they always have been: peace and strength. Television simply intensifies these concerns and creates more negative and unstable public moods."

Third, television has also affected the relationship between the mass public and policy makers in important ways. Members of Congress who wish to make names for themselves (read all), for example, are induced to frame their foreign policy ideas in "one-liners" that will fit into the thirty-, sixty-, or ninety-second slots the evening news allocates to such issues. For the electorate television has meant that "a Presidential candidate without much prior international experience can come to office with a collection of half-minute clichés in his head masquerading as foreign policies" (Destler, Gelb and Lake 1984). The compelling importance of television in shaping electoral outcomes magnifies the impact of these "sound bites."

The Internet The remarkably rapid spread of the Internet in the past decade and its growing significance as a source of news inevitably challenges further our ideas about the role of the media in the opinion-policy process. Certainly one of the medium's defining characteristics is the absence of gatekeepers. Virtually anyone can transmit information on the Internet. In the absence of gatekeepers to filter the information and separate the wheat from the chaff, there are few ways to assess the accuracy or authoritativeness of the source. Nonetheless, Internet information often has important political content. And it may preempt more established news media. The *Drudge Report,* for example, was among the first sources of information about the events that led to President Clinton's impeachment trial. Scholars are only now beginning to understand the impact of the Internet on political attitudes and for-eign policy thinking. Because younger Americans are more prone than others to rely on the Internet as a source of political news, this promises to be an intriguing avenue of inquiry for many years. Meanwhile, we already know that the Internet, like television, challenges long-standing theories about how attitudes change.

How Do Attitudes Change? Mass foreign policy attitudes are resistant to change, but they do change. How? Television, we have suggested, plays a role, especially among those with little knowledge about or interest in foreign policy. The relationship between elites and masses also has a bearing on attitudes in the general population. When those most attuned to foreign policy adjust their beliefs to accommodate new foreign policy realities, the changes can be expected to filter throughout society.

The classic explanation of the opinion-making and opinion-circulating process is known as the *two-step flow theory of communications.* As originally formulated, it says that "ideas often flow from radio and print to opinion leaders and from these to the less-active sections of the population" (Katz 1957). The dynamics of attitude change are best explained, the hypothesis holds, through the crucial channel of face-to-face contact. Members of the mass public do not actually sit down and exchange ideas with governing elites or those close to policy makers, of course. Instead, ideas become meaningful only after they have been transmitted to members of the mass public from opinion leaders such as teachers, members of the clergy, local political leaders, and others who have an above-average interest in public affairs and occupy positions allowing them to communicate frequently with others. Attitude change, according to this view, stems from changes in the thinking of the policy elite and those attentive to public affairs, with society at large following sometime later. Face-to-face contacts with opinion leaders are a crucial link in the diffusion process. Hence, the mass media is not the primary transmitters of ideas; nor is it the pri-mary stimulus of mass attitude change. Instead, it is the conduits through which attitudes are first connected to the political system and then trans-mitted through interpersonal contact.

Television complicates this view. There are few or no apparent face-to-face intermediaries between evening news anchors and the con-sumers of their messages. The two-step flow the-ory is thus overly simple in today's world. Some analysts suggest that a *multistep flow* theory is preferable, as it provides a more accurate de-scription of the opinion-making and opinion-circulating process in an age of mass electronic communication. The multistep flow seeks to draw attention to the multiple channels through which ideas and opinions are circulated in Amer-ica's complex society (Sandman, Rubin, and Sachsman 1982).

Clearly, though, even with a multistep flow of communications, the media play a crucial role in the transmission of opinions within the politi-cal system. Hence they are pivotal in the process of opinion making and opinion diffusion. Syndi-cated columnist William Safire has drawn partic-ular attention to the opinion-shaping role of the "Opinion Mafia"—those whom others might call "political pundits"—in his own retrospective comment on the original two-step flow theory. Arguing that in an environment where "political leaders tend to play it safe and consult polls be-fore taking positions," more people turn to "those multimedia commentators who are ready to pound beliefs into shape while the iron of con-troversy and crisis is red hot" (Safire 1990).

The Mass Media and Policy Makers

Ordinary Americans may be impervious to the media's influence because they tune out its mes-sages. On the other hand, those at the top of the public opinion pyramid—policy makers, policy influentials, and the attentive public—often rely heavily on the information the communications industry disseminates. Television has a leveling effect in that even those indifferent to foreign af-fairs get some information about it while those making up the elite and attentive public take advantage of a broader array of information—virtually all of it from publicly available media sources, including the Internet. On the surface, then, it appears that the media may be most influential with those who have the most influence.

Policy Makers, Policy Influentials, and the Media   To suggest that policy makers rely on the media—instead of the intelligence community, for instance—as a primary source of information may appear to be an exaggeration, but it is true. A study of roughly 100 officials in policy positions found that nearly two-thirds reported the media was generally their most rapid source of information in crisis situations, and over four-fifths indicated the media was an important source of policy-relevant information (O'Heffernan 1991).

This is the case partly because media reports about world developments are more timely and readable than official reports and are often perceived to be less biased than those of government agencies that gather data with a bureaucratic agenda in mind. Hodding Carter, a former State Department spokesperson, explained: "Most policy people, when they are not out there posturing and beating their chest in public about the effects of the media, would be happy to tell you how often they get information faster, quicker, and more accurately from the media than they get it from their official sources" (O'Heffernan 1991).

Policy influentials likewise depend on media reports. An often cited example comes from conservative writer William F. Buckley (1970)—no admirer of the news establishment of which he is a part—who admitted that after hearing a radio bulletin of Egyptian President Gamal Abdel Nasser's death, "I slipped off to telephone the *New York Times* to see if the report was correct (one always telephones the *New York Times* in emergencies). The State Department called the *New York Times,* back in 1956, to ask if it was true that Russian tanks were pouring into Budapest." John Kenneth Galbraith (1969), a former American ambassador to India, has also testified to the accuracy of the nation's elite newspapers: "I've said many times that I never learned from a classified document anything I couldn't get earlier or later from the *New York Times.*"

Bernard Cohen, a careful student of the subject, put the special role of the *prestige press* in a way that retains a timeless ring (as foreign policy professionals will readily admit):

> [The *New York Times*] is read by virtually everyone in the government who has an interest or responsibility in foreign affairs. . . . One frequently runs across the familiar story: "It is often said that Foreign Service Officers get to their desks early in the morning to read the *New York Times,* so they can brief their bosses on what is going on." This canard is easily buried: The "bosses" are there early, too, reading the *New York Times* for themselves. . . . The *Times* is uniformly regarded as the authoritative paper in the foreign policy field. In the words of a State Department official in the public affairs field, "You can't work in the State Department without the *New York Times.* You can get along without the overnight telegrams sooner."
>
> (COHEN 1961)

More recent evidence suggests that policy makers now also ascribe special importance to television news accounts (see Larson 1990). This is especially evident in insiders' and other accounts of the way they monitor the development of international crises in the White House Situation Room, where multiple television sets feed continuous electronic news coverage into the crisis nerve center. The long-popular television series *West Wing* provides a glimpse into what others describe.

Media Vulnerability to Government Manipulation   To a considerable extent the media reflects, rather than balances, the attitudes of the government. During the 1979 Iranian hostage crisis, for example, the media rarely strayed from the government's line about what was happening

(Larson 1990). Similarly, the media generally accepts the government's definition of America's friends and foes. When those definitions change, the media reflects the changes. Even during the Vietnam War the media continued to the very end to give the administration's account of the conflict considerable attention. (This is not to deny that the media contributed to the public's distaste for that unhappy and disconcerting venture.)

By deferring to the government the media encourages public acceptance of the government's view of the world; basically this means the viewpoints of the president and the executive branch, which remain the primary sources of foreign policy information. Therefore, it is able most of the time to "set the agenda of coverage and frame stories to reflect official perspectives" (Graber 1993).

The crisis over Kuwait that led to the Persian Gulf War illustrates how the media and government together often shape opinion—and perhaps policy. Market research showed that the best way to frame the issue was to depict Saddam Hussein as an enemy of the American people and to use George Bush to accomplish that end. Once the issue was cast and sold in this way, some policy options became more acceptable and others less so. In particular, "the Saddam framing . . . made it possible to dismiss the leading policy alternative of economic sanctions against Iraq long before there was any empirical basis for doing so (That is, long before it was reasonable to determine whether sanctions were working)" (Bennett 1994b). It is not surprising, then, that Bill Clinton would also invoke the Hitler image to describe Serbian President Slobodan Milošević as NATO war planes launched their air attack on Kosovo. What much of this suggests is that the media frequently operates as a conduit for the transmission of information from the governing elite to the American people rather than as a truly independent source of information about what the government is doing. Some years ago political journalist Theodore Draper described the "game of politics and propaganda" between government officials and media repre-

sentatives as one that "has become as stylized as an eighteenth-century dance."

First the officials hand out privileged information to favored journalists ("U.S. intelligence flatly reported that . . ."). Then the journalists pass out the same information, with or without attribution, to their readers. Finally, pro-administration congressmen fill pages of the Congressional Record with the same articles to prove that the officials were right (Draper 1968).

The seeming collusion between media and government, whether conscious or unconscious, stems from a variety of sources, including the media's dependence on government news releases, its inability to obtain classified information, media self-censure, the government's use of "privileged" and "on background" briefings, and the fact that self-restraint is often in the media's self-interest.

Even the familiar news "leak," often used by incumbent administrations to float "trial balloons," by competing factions within the government to fight their bureaucratic battles publicly through the media, or by individuals to protect their political backsides, does not alter that conclusion. Indeed, it reinforces it. In addition to being required by their professional code of ethics to protect the confidentiality of "high government sources," reporters typically must offer such protection in order to be assured of receiving future news stories. It is clear that "high government officials" (meaning White House staffers and members of the Cabinet) are often the source of government "leaks." To cite but one example: Soon after James Baker resigned as secretary of state to take over the senior George Bush's sagging re-election campaign "stories started suggesting that the campaign was in shambles and a loss would not be Baker's fault" (Kurtz 1993). In short, the leak is an American political institution, a practice rooted in tradition and employed routinely by officials in every branch and at every level of government. Because of their interdependence, the media are vulnerable to government manipulation. News, in government parlance, is "manageable." Because what is reported often depends on what is leaked for public consumption rather than on what has actually occurred behind closed doors, public relations and the art of governance are increasingly intertwined. Public officials themselves now engage in agenda setting and strive to place the correct "spin" on news stories that cast doubt on policy makers and their policies. The Clinton administration, in particular, elevated *spin control* to a near art form. Clinton's media spokesperson Mike McCurry was admired by foes as well as friends for his deftness in deflecting media inquiries into the myriad of scandals and sordid details that long plagued Clinton's presidency. *Washington Post* media reporter Howard Kurtz (1998) has even suggested that Clinton and his administration were so adept at spin control they were able to harness it for political advantage.

In the extreme, the government effectively censors the news. Censorship is anathema to democratic principles. It occurs nonetheless, especially during periods of crisis and peril, when the nation's vital interests or security are believed to be at stake. Thus the Reagan administration denied reporters permission to observe the Grenada assault force in 1983, an intervention later revealed to be fraught with mistakes. Journalists covering the 1989 invasion of Panama also complained that the military deliberately kept them away from the action. The "pool" arrangement used during the Persian Gulf War had a similarly constraining impact. Only limited numbers of reporters were allowed to accompany military units. Their reports could only be passed on, even to journalists left behind, after having been "screened" by military authorities. Such scrutiny (censorship?) was defended as being necessary to ensure that news reports would not jeopardize U.S. forces in the region. Secretary of Defense Rumsfeld has rekindled much of the information/censorship conflict, as he has maintained a strong hold on Pentagon information about the war in Afghanistan, and, in particular, has kept the media from gaining direct access to the soldier in the field.

The control of information during the Persian Gulf War and later reflected the Pentagon's determination "never again to lose a public rela-

tions war." As political scientist W. Lance Bennett explains, "Many policy officials in the Defense Department and the State Department became convinced that the U.S. military defeat and eventual withdrawal from Vietnam resulted, in part, from critical media coverage of battlefield activities and sympathetic coverage of domestic opposition to government policies back home." The Gulf War gave the military a new lease on life, which they turned into "a public relations bonus" that paid huge dividends to Bush's popularity with the American people (Bennett 1994b).

Disclosures about government lies during Watergate and in areas that the government at one time routinely but liberally defined as matters of "national security" appear to have enhanced the mass media's ability to function as a check on government control. Furthermore, one of the clear lessons of the Iran-contra scandal is that covert foreign policy actions cannot long remain secret, despite the government's efforts to hide them. Still, the fact that abuses of power seem to remain concealed for extended periods is perplexing. (For example, it was the foreign press, not the U.S. media, that first disclosed the Iranian arms-for-hostages deal.)

Although Vietnam, Watergate, and the Iran-contra scandal stimulated a more aggressive and critical posture in parts of the fourth estate, the media and the government remain intertwined to a considerable extent in a process that invites collusion. The government's proven ability to manage the news, combined with the media's dependence on the government to get the news, perpetuates a symbiotic relationship between the two institutions (see Hess 1984). As one observer put it, "correspondents, editors, pundits, and publishers who work for major media outlets tend to see themselves as members of an opinion-making elite. They consider themselves on an intellectual and social par with high-level policy makers, an attribute that increases the prospect of their being co-opted by ambitious and determined policy makers" (Carpenter 1995).

Because news derived from the government itself compromises the media's capacity to scrutinize government actions in the foreign policy domain, it may be appropriate to ask not whether the media controls public opinion in America but whether the government uses the media to create and manipulate public opinion (see Parenti 1986).

The Foreign Policy Agenda and "Press Politics" Often it appears as if the media are in control, not the government. Public officials' distaste for and fear of the media seems to reflect this. They are particularly wary of television and the ability of highly visible and respected journalists, such as TV news anchors, to undermine their policies or influence. "A sixty-second verbal barrage on the evening news or a few embarrassing questions can destroy programs, politicians, and the reputations of major organizations. Political leaders fear this media power, because they often are unable to blunt it or repair the damage" (Graber 1993; see also Jordan and Page 1992).

Ironically, the media also increasingly sets the *policy-making agenda*. One knowledgeable Washingtonian commented: "Ever since the breakup of the Soviet Union, it has become clear to anyone who cares to notice that in Washington the real agenda-setters for foreign policy sit not in the White House but in editorial rooms and press cubicles" (Maynes 1993–1994). Others have echoed that sentiment, arguing that a "chorus of congressional leaders, political pundits, television commentators, and print journalists" urged U.S. involvement in Somalia and elsewhere, while television images of conflict and despair have thrust the new interventionism on behalf of humanitarian values to the top of America's foreign policy agenda (Hoge 1994; see also Stedman 1992–1993; compare Gowing 1994). The Cold War emphasis on Soviet expansionism and the containment of communism provided the media with "a gauge for determining the importance of events by how much they affected America's security," which tended to focus on the means but not ends of policy. Now, "in the shapeless aftermath of a clear-cut superpower rivalry the impact of media's immediacy is magnified" (Hoge 1994); see also Perlmutter (1998).

Policy makers' reliance on media information enhances the media's importance as an agent in the foreign policy process. Patrick O'Heffernan's (1991) survey of policy-making officials found that a majority rely most heavily on media information during the early stages of the policy cycle. This is a critical period, as the definition of the situation will dictate the response (see Chapter 13). By controlling the information, the media help to frame the issue.

The increasingly rapid pace of electronic news and television's global coverage also shorten the time frame for policy responses to new developments abroad—often called the *news cycle*. In 1961, when the Berlin Wall went up, President Kennedy took eight days to respond to the provocative action. In 1989, when the wall came down, President Bush was forced to respond overnight. Now, more than a decade later, the news cycle has been shortened from hours to minutes. Moreover, by publicizing foreign events or other international developments, the media draws attention to them. Journalist Marvin Kalb has used the term *press politics* to describe the growing "inseparability of foreign policy from its management in the news" (Bennett 1994b).

There are instances where journalists themselves or the media more generally have become agents in the diplomatic process. In 1977, for example, CBS anchor Walter Cronkite was able to secure public pledges from Egyptian and Israeli leaders that paved the way for Anwar Sadat's historic visit to Jerusalem and the Camp David accord mediated by President Carter a year later. Similarly, there is little question that CNN provided an important communications node between the United States and Iraq during the Persian Gulf War.

In summary, the relationship between the media and policy makers is both subtle and complex, with no easy conclusions about who influences whom in what circumstances. Television has quickened the pace of news and inevitably shaped the way policy makers use the media and respond to events abroad, but it by no means determines American foreign policy. It is clear nonetheless that the fourth estate is a powerful institution that affects multiple facets of American political life. Theodore White, focusing once more on the media's ability to set the agenda, usefully summarizes the media's importance:

> The power of the press in America is a primordial one. It sets the agenda of public discussion; and this sweeping political power is unrestrained by any law. It determines what people will talk and think about—an authority that in other nations is reserved for tyrants, priests, parties, and mandarins. No major act of the American Congress, no foreign adventure, no act of diplomacy, no great social reform can succeed in the United States unless the press prepares the public mind.
>
> (WHITE 1973, 327)

THE IMPACT OF FOREIGN POLICY ATTITUDES AND ISSUES ON PRESIDENTIAL ELECTIONS

The press and public conventionally view elections as opportunities for policy change, if only for their potential to bring about new leadership. However, elections may also enable voters' preferences on foreign policy issues to be translated into policies that reflect those preferences. The important question, then, is whether voting is a viable means of expressing the public's policy preferences and thus translating them into policy.

It seems plausible that decision makers' fear of electoral punishment would lead them to propose policies designed to maintain their popularity and thus enhance their prospects for winning office. However, the "apparent immunity of the foreign policy establishment to electoral accountability" (Cohen 1973) is notable. Research on the two rival propositions has been extensive, and on the whole, the results have "not . . . been

kind to democratic theory." They show "that policy voting is quite rare" and that, for a variety of reasons, citizens fail to vote for candidates on the basis of policy preferences. "In short, voters are incapable of policy rationality" (Page and Brody 1972).

The Electoral Impact of Foreign Policy Issues

Although controversial and not always consistent, evidence abounds to support the *issueless politics* hypothesis—that voter choice is determined neither by the nature of the issues nor candidates' positions on them (see Asher 1992). Foreign policy is no exception.

The role of the Vietnam War in 1968 is a classic case in point. The massive U.S. escalation of the war began in 1965. By 1968, as the war continued and its casualty lists grew, support declined. Campus unrest, mass demonstrations against the war, increasingly vocal minority opposition, including challenges from within the president's own party, were indicative of the changing climate of opinion. Johnson's decision not to run for a second full presidential term was widely interpreted as a direct result of this domestic opposition. We would expect, therefore, that voters would have treated the election as a referendum on Vietnam, but they didn't. They didn't because they (correctly) perceived little difference between the positions of the candidates (Richard Nixon and Vice President Hubert Humphrey) on Vietnam policy. In short, from voters' perspective, the 1968 election, despite the centrality of Vietnam in American politics and society, was an issueless campaign (Page and Brody 1972).

Americans clearly do hold opinions about foreign policy matters, but they are not transmitted into the policy-formation system through the electoral process (compare Aldrich, Sullivan, and Borgida 1989). How do we account for such a failure?

One inviting explanation is that many Americans may regard foreign policy issues as among the most important facing the nation, but they fail to arouse the depth of personal concern raised by issues closer to their daily lives. In addition, foreign policy issues are not the ones that "divide the populace into contending groups. . . . In general foreign issues, involving as they do the United States versus others, tend to blur or reduce differences domestically" (Nie, Verba, and Petrocik 1976).

That does not mean, however, that party outcomes are unaffected by foreign policy issues during presidential elections. Public views of foreign policy have been related to the partisan votes cast in each election between 1952 and 1988 (Asher 1992). Republicans benefitted from those perceptions in eight of the ten elections.

The 1964 election was the only one in which voter preferences on foreign policy issues clearly favored the Democrats. Although Democrats benefitted from public fears of nuclear war in 1984, the Republicans benefitted on the issue of war prevention.[7] By 1988, however, the Republicans could claim the high ground on both peace and prosperity. Michael Dukakis and the Democratic Party lost in a landslide—and the Republicans claimed the White House for the seventh time out of eleven Cold War presidential elections.

Four years later George H. W. Bush found himself on the defensive. Peace was in hand—indeed, after a half-century of bitter conflict, the United States had "won" the Cold War with the Soviet Union and turned the tide against Iraq's aggression—but prosperity was not. The nation's economy was in recession, concern for debts and deficits punctuated campaign rhetoric, and Bill Clinton was determined to focus attention on domestic ills, not foreign policy challenges. A sign in his Arkansas campaign headquarters proclaiming it's "The Economy, Stupid!" reflected Democratic leaders' single-minded determination to stress domestic policy.

The end of the Cold War and the departure of virulent anticommunism from the domestic political agenda played to their strategy, while the partisan advantages Republicans once enjoyed on foreign policy mattered little this time (Weisberg and Kimball 1995). "Throughout the Cold War the Republican Party's reason for existence was anticommunism," observes Leon Sigal (1992–1993) in a retrospective look at what he calls "the last Cold War election" (see also Deudney and Ikenberry 1994). "Republicans could be counted on to shield America from the Red Menace, at home and abroad. . . . Now that the [Russian] bear has disappeared, what else does the G.O.P. stand for?"

As we demonstrated in Chapter 8, the state of the economy is a powerful predictor of how Americans evaluate presidential performance. It is not surprising, therefore, that George Bush attracted their ire. Clinton, on the other hand, was quick to tie the state of the economy to the United States' continuing ability to play an active role in world affairs. "America must regain its economic strength to play a proper role as leader of the world," he declared. "And we must have a president who attends to prosperity at home if our people are to sustain their support for engagement abroad." But domestic policy was Clinton's strong suit, and he played to it repeatedly.

Admittedly weak on domestic policy issues, Bush also proved vulnerable on the very issues perceived to be his long suit. The "foreign policy president" largely confined himself to "tidying up the details of the old agenda. . . . He failed by and large to assist eastern Europe and the Soviet Union in their perilous transitions, to devise a foreign policy squaring national self-determination with state sovereignty and minority rights, to stanch bloodletting in Bosnia, and to prevent the proliferation of all arms, not just weapons of mass destruction." For most Americans these were not issues of burning significance.[8] Even the brief euphoria sparked by victory in the Persian Gulf War soon gave way to "more pressing subjects" (Omestad 1992–1993). Indeed, Bush's decision to stop the war before Iraq's leader was driven from power eventually soured the views of many as they wondered whether the war had been worth the effort. A popular bumper sticker captured the irony of Bush's situation: "Saddam Hussein still has his job. What about you?"

By 1996 Bill Clinton was in a surprisingly strong position on foreign policy. Although Republican standard-bearer Bob Dole attacked Clinton's policies toward Iraq, North Korea, Bosnia, and China, arguing that he (Dole) would provide more aggressive leadership, public opinion polls showed that a majority of Americans regarded Clinton as a strong leader in foreign policy (see also Ladd 1997). Indeed, for Clinton foreign policy "became a surprisingly useful forum for refuting . . . GOP charges that [he] was feckless and lacked backbone" (Omestad 1996–1997).

More importantly, perhaps, the U.S. economy was bubbling and Americans were enjoying the prosperity of sharply reduced inflation and unemployment compared with four years earlier. So we should expect that the state of the economy would have "made it difficult for any challenger to get political traction from criticizing Clinton's foreign policy." Furthermore, on foreign policy 1996 seemed like a classic "issueless, me-too-ism" campaign, as "voters strained to see any major difference on foreign and security policy between two mainstream internationalists, Clinton and Dole" (Omestad 1996–1997; see also Dionne 1996).

Al Gore and George W. Bush were also internationalists. Using the belief-system framework described in Chapter 8, Gore's platform and champaign leaned toward the accommodationist side of the internationalist/isolationist divide, while Bush's tipped toward the hardline. Gore was a champion of the Kyoto accord designed to cope with global warming; Bush was more circumspect, although he did promise to seek to lower CO_2 emissions (a pledge broken shortly after he was elected). Gore endorsed the Clinton plan for a limited national ballistic defense system that would cover the territorial United States; Bush pledged a more ambitious system that would include U.S. allies in the anticipated defense umbrella. Gore supported the downsizing of the U.S. military that had taken place during the 1990s; Bush attacked the Clinton-Gore defense posture as inadequate for meeting the challenges of the new century and

promised to build a new generation of high-tech weapons to meet them.

Analysts have yet to determine what impact, if any, these foreign and national security policy postures had on the final presidential vote in 2000. Usually it is difficult to determine the separate effects of particular foreign policy questions on citizens' voting behavior. Because most elections involve a variety of often overlapping issues, some of those who vote for the winning candidate do so because of the candidate's stance on particular issues; others do so in spite of it. Foreign policy issues thus become part of a mix of considerations. Typically they are a less important ingredient than domestic political issues or judgments of past performance (Abramson, Aldrich, and Rohde 1986, 1990; Fiorina 1981). As a result, voters' behavior is more likely an aggregate judgment about prior performance than a guide to future action. This is known as *retrospective voting.*

Foreign Policy and Retrospective Voting

Consider President Carter's electoral fate. The public generally gave Carter high marks on personal attributes but low marks on performance. Evaluations of his foreign policy performance were especially critical. Carter's popularity surged in late 1979 in the immediate aftermath of the seizure of American embassy personnel in Teheran, but his inability to secure their release fueled public dissatisfaction with his overall performance. His challenger, Ronald Reagan, criticized the policy of détente Carter and his predecessors had promoted, called for sharply increased defense spending, and hammered away at the theme of alleged American impotence in international affairs. In this context, "the continuing crisis in Iran came to be seen as a living symbol and constant reminder of all that Reagan had been saying" (Hess and Nelson 1985).

Four years later, Reagan's reputation for leadership proved a strong force motivating voters to choose the incumbent president over his challenger, Walter Mondale. Elements of Reagan's foreign policy record could easily be criticized, but four years of relative peace had put to rest fears about Reagan's recklessness. "No longer fearful that the President's policies might lead to war, the public had no compelling reason to abandon him" (Keeter 1985). In many respects the Bush candidacy became a retrospective judgment on the Reagan years. Peace and prosperity thus redounded to Bush's benefit, as noted. Moreover, because Reagan had moved during his second term toward an accommodationist foreign policy posture and away from his "evil empire" approach to the Soviet Union, the ideological differences on foreign policy issues that bore on the electoral outcomes in 1980 and 1984 tended to disappear in 1988. Still, to the extent that voters perceived differences between the candidates on foreign policy issues, particularly their willingness to "stand up for America" (Pomper 1989), they favored Bush.

We have already commented on Bush and Clinton. Clinton swamped Bush on domestic policy, with foreign policy a distinctly secondary issue in spite of Bush's distinguished foreign policy record. Clinton again swamped Dole on domestic policy. The irony, perhaps, is that Gore would not capitalize on the state of the economy during the Clinton-Gore years to put him in the White House (in part because of his determination to distance himself from other aspects of the Clinton presidency); but in the absence of an overriding foreign policy issue in 2000, Gore could not capitalize on his slim margin of support among voters to carry the day.

Despite the acknowledged importance of retrospective voting, history invites the conclusion that "elections are primarily a symbolic exercise that . . . offer the masses an opportunity to participate in the political system, but electoral participation does not enable them to determine public policy." "Parties do not offer clear policy alternatives," and a "candidate's election does not imply a policy choice by the electorate" (Dye and Zeigler 1990). Noteworthy is that Ralph Nader charged during the 2000 election that Republican and Democratic candidates Bush and Gore did not differ on the environmental issues central to Nader's presidential campaign. Nader's percent of the presidential vote barely registered on the national scale.

Ironically, even when parties would seem to offer distinct alternatives, elections still do not set the course of foreign policy. That is nowhere more clear than in the 1964 presidential contest, when Vietnam became a major foreign policy issue. Republican challenger Barry Goldwater campaigned on the pledge to pursue "victory" against communism in all quarters of the globe, but especially in Vietnam "by any means necessary." The incumbent Lyndon Johnson campaigned on a theme of greater restraint in Vietnam, and his landslide victory was widely interpreted that way. Yet it was Johnson, armed with the Gulf of Tonkin Resolution passed by Congress, who would soon escalate the war in Southeast Asia. Why? Because, despite popular impressions of the foreign policy alternatives the electorate faced, the results of the election as they related to popular support for various Vietnam options were so ambiguous as to lead to the conclusion "that the 1964 vote . . . could have told [Johnson] anything he cared to believe" (Boyd 1972; see also Pomper 1968).

Despite evidence to the contrary, particularly in the foreign policy domain, policy makers nonetheless act as though voters make choices on the basis of their policy preferences. Hence, they pay attention to the anticipated responses of voters in shaping their policy choices. So elections do matter, particularly in shaping the character of the personnel a new president appoints to key positions in a new administration.

LINKAGES BETWEEN SOCIETAL SOURCES AND AMERICAN FOREIGN POLICY

The question posed at the outset of this and the preceding chapter—"In what ways do societal factors influence American foreign policy?"—

has invited a series of additional questions, and, inevitably, provoked a variety of answers. It is clear, however, that the view of the United States as a society-dominated political system provides insight into the potential impact of the political culture, public opinion, elites and masses, the media, and presidential elections. The ability of citizens "to mobilize support for their demands and to organize themselves" is a characteristic feature of society-dominant systems (Risse-Kappen 1991). Similarly, elections and interest groups help to channel mass preferences and private interests into public policy in the United States, where, as we noted at the outset of this chapter, the power of both the state and societal groups is more decentralized than in many other industrial societies. Thus elites are unable to dictate completely what American foreign policy will be—which is the "top-down" view of policy making akin to the elitist model described earlier. Similarly, the mass of the American people do not determine American foreign policy from the "bottom up," a view that parallels the pluralist model. Instead, there is a constant interaction between policy makers and the public, elites and masses alike, much of it promoted through the media and the electoral system. American foreign policy emerges out of this continuing interaction. Still, policy makers and other elites enjoy a competitive advantage in shaping the agenda and are ultimately responsible for final decisions; important caveats and

qualifications must be attached to the role that mass preferences and private interests play in shaping policy. Still, we have seen that societal factors do indeed intrude upon the policy-making process and thus serve as a source of American foreign policy.

Societal factors explain more about the process of formulating American policies toward the external environment than about the objectives of those actions and the particular means chosen to achieve them. Moreover, it is difficult to isolate causal connections between particular societal variables and particular actions abroad. Thus societal factors rarely if ever "determine" foreign policy actions. Instead, they exert influence primarily as part of the context within which decisions are formulated. In particular, they operate more as forces constraining foreign policy than as forces stimulating radical departures from the past.

To pinpoint better the sources of American foreign policy decisions and initiatives, we need to turn from considering factors within American society to examining the political institutions from which most foreign policy initiatives spring. As we will discover in the next three chapters, these institutions—part of the domestic structures of the American political system—are comparatively decentralized into competing power centers, thus providing multiple access points to those in the society-dominated American political system who seek to shape American foreign policy.

KEY TERMS RELATED TO THE TRANSMISSION OF VALUES, BELIEFS, AND PREFERENCES

agenda-setting	*the Establishment*	*gatekeepers*
bully pulpit	*follow-on imperative*	*iron triangles*
CNN effect	*Foreign Affairs*	*issue networks*
cognitive balance	*fourth branch of the government*	*issueless politics*
Council on Foreign Relations	*fourth estate*	*meritocracy*
elitism	*frame issues*	*military-industrial complex*

newspapers of record	*power elite*	**selective perception**
pack journalism	*press politics*	*soft money*
pluralism	*public regarding*	*spin control*
political action committees (PACs)	**retrospective voting**	*Wise Men*

SUGGESTIONS FOR FURTHER READING

Carpenter, Ted Galen. *The Captive Press: Foreign Policy Crises and the First Amendment.* Washington, DC: Cato Institute, 1995.

Cohen, Bernard C. *The Press and Foreign Policy.* Princeton, NJ: Princeton University Press, 1963.

Grose, Peter. *Continuing the Inquiry: The Council on Foreign Relations from 1921 to 1966.* New York: Council on Foreign Relations Press, 1996.

Haney, Patrick J., and Walt Vanderbush. "The Role of Ethnic Interest Groups in U.S. Foreign Policy: The Case of the Cuban American Foundation," *International Studies Quarterly* 43 (June 1999): 341–361.

Jeffreys-Jones, Rhodri. *Changing Differences: Women and the Shaping of American Foreign Policy, 1917–1994.* New Brunswick, NJ: Rutgers University Press, 1995.

Judis, John B. *The Paradox of American Democracy: Elites, Special Interests, and the Betrayal of Public Trust.* New York: Pantheon, 2000.

Kotz, Nick. *Wild Blue Yonder: Money, Politics, and the B-1 Bomber.* Princeton, NJ: Princeton University Press, 1988.

O'Heffernan, Patrick. *Mass Media and American Foreign Policy: Insider Perspectives on Global Journalism and the Foreign Policy Process.* Norwood, NJ: Ablex, 1991.

Patterson, Thomas E. *Out of Order.* New York: Vintage, 1994.

Roberts, Priscilla. "All the Right People: The Historiography of the American Foreign Policy Establishment," *Journal of American Studies* 26 (December 1992): 409–454.

Skidmore, David, and Valerie M. Hudson, eds., *The Limits of State Autonomy: Societal Groups and Foreign Policy Formulation.* Boulder, CO: Westview, 1993.

Strobel, Warren P. *Late-Breaking Foreign Policy: The News Media's Influence on Peace Operations.* Washington, DC: U.S. Institute for Peace, 1997.

Vernon, Raymond, Debora L. Spar, and Glenn Tobin. *Iron Triangles and Revolving Doors: Cases in U.S. Foreign Economic Policymaking.* New York: Praeger, 1991.

Wittkopf, Eugene R., and James M. McCormick, eds., *The Domestic Sources of American Foreign Policy: Insights and Evidence.* Lanham, MD: Roman and Littlefield, 1999.

NOTES

1. Education and training do not guaranteed that foolish policy decisions will not be made. Indeed, one of the main points of Halberstam's book is that intelligent people are capable of making wicked and stupid decisions.

2. Others have joined in this chorus. Morris P. Fiorina (2001), a prominent congressional scholar, argues that "The political class today allows national problems to fester because its members insist on having the entire loaf, not just a portion, because they would rather have an election issue than incremental progress, and because parties that have only shallow roots in the population at large are increasingly dependent on specific constituencies whose interests are not shared by the general population."

3. Despite policy makers' views, recent research on the role of the media based on the 1992 presidential election reveals that media coverage of presidential candidates is balanced and hence fair. As described by Russell Dalton, Paul Beck, and Robert Huckfeldt (1998), "Contemporary journalistic norms encourage . . . diversity of views and moderation in overall political content: the days of a highly partisan American press are gone. . . .

The attempt of most newspapers to be fair in their coverage of the campaign ironically may explain why the media have received so much criticism from both partisan camps and why this is likely to continue. . . . The evidence . . . may explain why it seems nearly everyone agrees the media is biased—they just disagree on its direction." Groeling and Kernell (1998) also conclude from research into the way ABC, CBS, and NBC report polling data on presidential popularity that "the charges of reckless bias that presidents are sometimes inclined to make" enjoy some support but are "neither so consistent nor strong as to sustain the charges."

4. The media is widely believed to be dominated by "liberals," and there is some historical evidence to support that view (Lichter and Rothman 1981; Schneider and Lewis 1985). Interestingly, however, newspapers routinely endorse Republican presidential candidates far more frequently than Democratic candidates. In 2000, for example, George W. Bush received 173 newspaper endorsements, while Al Gore, his more liberal challenger, received 111 (*Editor and Publisher* www.editorandpublisher.com). An exception to the general rule was 1992, when Bill Clinton enjoyed the endorsement of 183 daily newspapers compared with 138 for Bush (*Editor and Publisher,* 7 November 1992, 15). Furthermore, the radio airwaves and television talk shows, including those on cable TV, overwhelming tilt to the conservative and often far right of the political spectrum, with few, if any, liberals represented (Kurtz 1996).

5. Market considerations may have other untoward effects. Commenting on media coverage of stock markets, economist Robert Shiller (2001) notes that because "the news media are in constant competition to capture the public's attention . . . the media often seem to disseminate and reinforce ideas that are not supported by real evidence. . . . Too often the media are swayed by competitive presures to skew their presentations toward ideas best left alone."

6. Evidence and critiques of the "minimal-effects" thesis can be found in Dalton, Beck, and Huckfeldt (1998), Iyengar, Peters, and Kinder (1982), and Page, Shapiro, and Dempsey (1987).

7. Long-standing political lore holds that Republicans produce "peace with poverty," while Democrats bring "war with wealth." These perceptions are no longer clear-cut, as the Democrats made significant inroads on both issues during the 1990s. Gallup poll data from the mid-1970s through the early 1990s show that the Democratic Party was more often perceived as the party of peace than the Republican Party. Since 1992, the Democrats also have more often been perceived as the party of "peace with wealth." (The Gallup Poll www.gallup.com/poll/surveys).

8. Empirical research shows that compared with other issues, Bush's widely acclaimed handling of foreign policy issues during his presidency had "a limited substantive importance to voters' decisions at the polls" (Miller and Shanks 1996).

PART V

❖

Governmental Sources
of American Foreign Policy

CHAPTER 10

Presidential Leadership
in Foreign Policy Making

In the areas of defense and foreign affairs, the nation must speak
with one voice, and only the president is capable of providing that voice.

PRESIDENT RONALD REAGAN, 1984

I would welcome the support of the Congress [for military action in Haiti]
and I would hope that I will have that. Like my predecessors,
I have not agreed that I was constitutionally mandated to get it.

PRESIDENT BILL CLINTON, 1994

Observing President George W. Bush respond to the September 11 terrorist attacks on the United States, building an international coalition, dispatching emissaries and troops, and initiating a "war on terrorism," it is easy to understand why the president of the United States is widely regarded at home and abroad as the most powerful individual in the world. The president is commander-in-chief of the world's most powerful military forces and the leader of the world's most prosperous and advanced economy. The increasing global popularity of the political ideas often associated with the United States provides the U.S. president with additional influence. Also, the advantages of the presidential form of government over other democratic systems such as the British parliamentary system allow the president to respond quickly and pragmatically to emergent challenges (Waltz 1967).

Furthermore, a half-century of Cold War competition with the Soviet Union and the ideological challenge of communism contributed measurably to presumption of presidential preeminence in foreign policy making. Indeed, prior to Vietnam it was commonplace to argue that

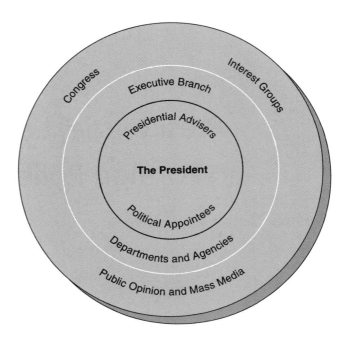

FIGURE 10.1 The Institutional Setting:
The Concentric Circles of Policy Making

Source: Adapted from Roger Hilsman, *To Move a Nation.* New York: Doubleday, 1967, 541–544.

"the United States has one president, but it has two presidencies." As political scientist Aaron Wildavsky (Wildavsky 1966) argued in a classic essay, "The president's normal problem with domestic policy is to get congressional support for the programs he prefers. In foreign affairs, in contrast, he can almost always get support for policies that he believes will protect the nation."

Since the Vietnam War, however, the premise of *presidential preeminence* has been questioned as Congress more vigorously asserted its foreign policy prerogatives. With the demise of the Cold War and the associated changes in both the international and domestic policy environment, Congress continued its activism and other foreign policy actors now also challenged the premises of presidential leadership. As one columnist wrote, "The end of the Cold War has changed the stature of the president—moving him off the imperial heights of the 'most powerful man in the world' to the mundane level of a political leader struggling over incremental domestic policy questions" (Lauter 1994).

In this chapter we examine the forces giving rise to the power of the presidency, particularly during the past half-century, the efforts of presidents to enhance their control over the machinery of government responsible for making and executing the nation's foreign policy, and the factors that shape ***presidential leadership,*** including recent challenges to the premise of presidential preeminence.

Our probe draws on Roger Hilsman's (1967) conceptualization of the foreign policy-making process as a series of concentric circles (Figure 10.1). In Hilsman's conceptualization, the innermost circle in the policy-making process consists of the president, his or her immediate personal advisers, and such important political appointees as the secretaries of state and defense, the director of the Central Intelligence Agency (CIA), and various under and assistant secretaries who bear responsibility for carrying out policy decisions.

Outside this core, the second circle contains the various departments and agencies of the executive branch or, more specifically, the career professionals of those agencies who provide continuity in the implementation of policy from one administration to the next, regardless of who occupies the White House. Their primary task—in theory—is to provide top-level policy makers with the information necessary to make decisions and then to carry those decisions out. The outermost circle is what Hilsman called the "public one," consisting of Congress, interest groups, public opinion, and the mass media. According to Hilsman's image, the institutions, groups, and individuals at this level are least involved in the day-to-day foreign policy process. The clear implication is that important decisions involving the fate of the nation are made within the innermost circle; when it comes to policy leadership, the role and influence of various players involved in policy making declines with their distance from the center.

Using this conceptualization as a starting point, we will describe the foreign affairs government in three phases. First, in this chapter, as noted, we will examine the factors that affect presidential leadership in the foreign policy domain. We direct particular attention to the rise of the National Security Council system and the role of the president's national security adviser as a more White House-centered policy process has evolved over the past fifty years. Second, in Chapter 11 we consider the foreign policy bureaucracy and its information-gathering and policy-implementation roles. The structural characteristics of the foreign affairs government, which define authority and divide the labor among those responsible for making and executing foreign policy, influence presidential decisions, policy implementation, and policy performance. The impact of this structure therefore requires examination. Finally, in Chapter 12 we examine the role of Congress in the policy-making process, investigating the tools available to Congress to influence foreign policy, the ways members exert that influence, and some of the patterns of congressional influence and legislative-executive relations that occur.[1]

THE SETTING OF PRESIDENTIAL LEADERSHIP

The U.S. Constitution shapes the president's role in foreign policy by empowering the president to lead, but it also creates constraints and challenges to that leadership. The Constitution does not assign "the foreign policy power" to any branch, but forces them to share responsibility by breaking foreign policy power into pieces and assigning various portions to the Congress and to the executive. Because the Constitution does not specify which branch is to lead, it provides the political branches an *"invitation to struggle"* (Corwin 1948).

Foreign Affairs and the Constitution

For the president, constitutional foreign policy power derives from Article II which assigns the general executive power and the roles of *commander in chief, chief negotiator* ("He shall have the power, by and with the advice and consent of the Senate, to make treaties"), and *chief diplomat* (" . . . shall appoint ambassadors . . . and shall receive ambassadors and other public ministers") to the president.[2] Clearly, the specific grants of constitutional authority are limited. The president has important opportunities, but not unambiguous authority, to lead.

These limits are even more obvious when the Constitution's treatment of congressional foreign policy powers is considered. In Article I, Congress is entrusted with the general legislative power ("all legislative powers herein granted shall be vested in a Congress of the United States"), which empowers it to make laws and appropriate funds ("no money shall be drawn from the Treasury but in consequence of appropriations made by law"). Together, the general legislative power and "power of the purse" grant Congress nearly limitless authority to affect the flow and form of foreign relations.

The Constitution further forces the sharing of the war power by countering the president's power as commander in chief with the congressional injunction to provide for the common defense, to declare war, to raise and support armies, to provide and maintain a Navy, to make rules for the government and regulation of the land and naval forces, and to organize, arm, discipline, and call forth the militia. The president's diplomatic powers are constrained by the Senate's constitutionally-mandated role to "advise and consent" on treaties as well as the appointment of ambassadors and other executive branch personnel. Additionally, Congress is to regulate international commerce and immigration, to define and punish piracies, to grant letters of marque and reprisal, to make rules concerning capture on land and water, and to "make all laws necessary and proper for carrying into execution the foregoing powers."

It would seem then, far from concentrating foreign policy authority, that the Constitution disperses it and forces it to be shared. Were the Constitution itself the only basis for presidential leadership, Hilsman's conception of decision-making authority over foreign affairs shown in Figure 10.1 would be hard to sustain. As one observer once noted, "it seems incredible that these few meager grants support the most powerful office in the world and the multi-varied, wide-flung webwork of foreign activity of the most powerful nation in the world" (Henkin 1972). However, other important factors help to develop the leadership role of the president.

First, the Constitution's provisions have combined with practice to expand, over time, the central role of the president in the formulation as well as execution of American foreign policy. Presidents have undeniably taken advantage of their ability to act decisively and set the foreign policy bureaucracy in motion. By concluding treaties and other agreements with foreign nations; by public declarations; by recognizing or not recognizing new governments; by attending international conferences; by deploying military power here or there; by encouraging or denouncing the actions of other nations, and so forth; presidents have established the precedent

of presidential leadership. Moreover, Congress has acquiesced in such exercises of power and has even delegated further responsibilities to the president (including some specifically assigned to Congress by the Constitution), thereby increasing the force behind presidential leadership. Examples of such delegation include the responsibility to propose budgets to Congress as required by the 1921 budget reforms (thus strengthening the president's ability to set the spending agenda) as well as the power to conclude trade agreements (often without congressional approval) established by the 1934 Reciprocal Trade Agreements Act. Additionally, the post–World War II growth of executive foreign policy institutions, most notably the Department of Defense, the Central Intelligence Agency, and the National Security Council established by the 1947 National Security Act, gave the president even greater tools with which to take foreign policy action.

The U.S. role in a changing international environment further expanded the role of the president. The ability of the president to act assertively and decisively in the crisis-ridden atmosphere of the post–World War II period dramatically increased the foreign policy powers of the presidency. The widely shared consensus that the international environment demanded an active American world role contributed to the belief that strong presidential leadership was needed. Hence, because most members of Congress fundamentally agreed on the requirements of Cold War foreign policy, the president's policy decisions went largely unchallenged. The Vandenberg Resolution (1949), in which Congress supported a permanent American alliance with European nations (which later became NATO), and the Formosa Strait (1955), Middle East (1957), Cuban (1962), Berlin (1962), and Gulf of Tonkin (1964) resolutions, in which Congress gave the president broad power to deal with external conflict situations, fostered presidential supremacy by demonstrating a unity of purpose between the president and Congress. Together these factors eventually gave rise to what Arthur M. Schlesinger, Jr. (1973) labeled an *imperial presidency.*

The Role of the Courts

The judicial branch has also contributed to the enhancement of presidential leadership. Generally, the courts have refrained from involvement in foreign policy issues. When the judiciary has addressed such issues, it has tended to support presidential claims of authority, which has solidified the president's foreign policy-making role. In a seminal case in 1936, for instance, the Supreme Court ruled in *United States v. Curtiss-Wright Export Corporation,* that the president acts "as the sole organ of the federal government in the field of international relations." With few exceptions, the courts, in this and other cases, have repeatedly conferred on the president broad powers in foreign affairs.[3]

The courts have furthered presidential leadership with nondecisions as well. The Supreme Court has usually avoided refereeing contests between the executive and legislative branches because it considers the issues involved as political rather than legal. Frequently, the court does this by use of the **doctrine of political questions,** a judicial construct that enables the courts to sidestep politically contentious foreign policy issues. Three recent cases illustrate the effects of this long-standing tradition. In 1981, several members of Congress brought suit against President Reagan, arguing that he had violated the Constitution and the War Powers Resolution by sending military advisers to El Salvador.[4] The court dismissed the suit with the ruling that a determination of whether U.S. forces in El Salvador were involved in actual or potential hostilities was a political, not a judicial, finding.

Six years later, as U.S. forces reflagged Kuwaiti ships with American flags to protect them in the Persian Gulf, members of Congress again asked the court to enter the war powers fracas by declaring that the president should submit a report to Congress under the War Powers Resolution. Again the court concluded the issue was a nonjusticiable political question.[5]

The third case also involved the Persian Gulf. In late 1990 fifty-four Democratic members of Congress sought to derail further Bush administration military deployments and action in the Persian Gulf.[6] They argued that the Constitution required that Congress debate and authorize a declaration of war before the president could initiate hostilities. This time the (U.S. district) court left open the door to a possible ruling against the president's war-making power without congressional involvement—but it also waffled: "It would be both premature and presumptuous for the court to render a decision on the issue of whether a declaration of war is required . . . when the Congress itself has provided no indication whether it deems such a declaration either necessary, on the one hand, or imprudent, on the other."

While this pattern of judicial support for presidential leadership is dominant, there are some limitations that should be noted as well. For example, in the 1952 case of *Youngstown Sheet and Tube Co. et al. v. Sawyer,* the Supreme Court determined that presidential authority was greatest when explicitly authorized by Congress and circumscribed when explicitly prohibited by Congress. In the "zones of twilight" between them, authority is less certain and possibly shared with Congress. Also, in two cases during the Nixon administration (*New York Times v. United States,* 1971, and *U.S. v. Nixon,* 1974), the Supreme Court limited the president's ability to control information on the grounds of national security or executive privilege.

The investigations into the Whitewater affair, the Paula Jones sexual harassment case, and the Monica Lewinsky episode, coupled with the subsequent impeachment and trial of President Clinton further weakened some presidential powers. In a number of decisions, the courts ruled: (1) sitting presidents may be sued while in office; (2) government lawyers may be compelled to testify regarding their counsel and advice to a president; (3) presidents' conversations with advisers may not be protected by executive privilege; (4) presidential security forces may be required to testify about presidential behavior. Clinton also become the first president to testify before a grand jury while in office (see, for example, Holmes 1998). Many observers argue that these cases have weakened the presidency, although others note that none involved presidential national security claims.

Based on these characteristics of U.S. foreign policy making, Hilsman's conception placing the president at its core seems to be both justified and accurate. However, developments after the Vietnam War pose a counterpoint to the expansion of presidential leadership just described. Since Vietnam, White House leadership has come under increasing scrutiny. As discussed more thoroughly in Chapter 12, many observers argue that Congress and its members have become more assertive. Of particular concern to Congress was the question of control over American commitments and the president's war powers. A series of legislative efforts to circumscribe the executive's authority resulted: the National Commitments Resolution (1969), the repeal of the Gulf of Tonkin Resolution (1970), the Case Act (1972), and the War Powers Resolution (1973), to name a few. They tried to make it more difficult for presidents to initiate war single-handedly and to otherwise circumscribe their foreign policy latitude.

Such congressional challenges continued after the end of the Cold War as well. Important examples include congressional resistance to the Clinton administration's efforts to construct a strategy of "assertive multilateralism" that would commit the United States to more substantial involvement in peacekeeping and peacemaking operations through the United Nations; its challenge to the administration's efforts to raise democracy promotion to a more prominent role in U.S. foreign policy strategy; its refusal to provide fast-track authority for trade negotiations; and its challenges to foreign aid and other international assistance programs (see, for example, Scott 1998a). Thus, continued challenges to and limits on presidential leadership throughout the Clinton Administration suggest that Hilsman's image may not fully capture the shifting roles and influence of the president, Congress, and other players.

THE STRUCTURES OF PRESIDENTIAL LEADERSHIP

The president's greatest resource—at least in principle—in exercising policy leadership is the vast executive establishment. Most of the federal government's work force of 3.1 million civilians work in the executive branch, where collectively they bear responsibility for making and implementing the full range of America's domestic and foreign policies. The obvious challenge for a president is to harness the structures and personnel of the executive agencies to his or her foreign policy agenda. While their resources, expertise, and control over day-to-day policy provide the president with substantial assets, the numbers comprising the federal work force, diffusion, and their longevity also present challenges for leadership.

The Cabinet

The president is nominally "boss" of the employees who staff the executive departments and agencies of the foreign affairs government, but the president by no means *controls* them. That truism led Richard Neustadt (Neustadt 1980) to describe the president's power as the *"power to persuade."* The interests of executive branch organizations are not always synonymous with the interests of the president. The people who staff them commonly hold their positions long before and long after any given president's term in office. To them the president is often a "transient meddler in their business" (Destler 1974).

The tension between the White House and the executive agencies is a reason for the president's appointment of department and agency heads, who together form the **cabinet.** In principle, these appointed officials represent the president's authority over and need to harness the executive departments. Once George Washington established the principle of meeting with these department heads, for the next 140 years or so the cabinet served as the chief advisory body for the president in both foreign and domestic affairs. Strong cabinets were the norm in this period, as department heads had their own political capital and clout on Capitol Hill. For a variety of reasons, however, the cabinet declined in importance in the twentieth century. For example, the 1921 budget reforms placed greater power over department budgets in the hands of the White House, while the expansion of the bureaucracy enlarged the size of the cabinet, making it less useful as an advisory body. Other reforms gave rise to an expanded White House staff more closely aligned with the president.

As important, department chiefs often become captives of the interests of the departments they administer and of the positions advanced by career professionals within them. Because chiefs are necessarily advocates for the departments they head, they are often in conflict with one another and sometimes even with the president. Indeed, "one of the strengths of cabinet members, namely their capacity to make a compelling case for their programs, has proved to be their chief liability with presidents" (Cronin 1973). Members of the cabinet thus quickly come to be viewed as the president's "natural enemies." Cabinet decision making is usually the casualty, and the cabinet itself is a "perennial loser" (Allison and Szanton 1976). Indeed, in spite of the occasional call for a return to "Cabinet Government," there has been a marked decrease in the influence of the cabinet since World War II, especially as it relates to foreign policy.

The erosion of cabinet policy making stems in part from "the cross cutting nature of most presidential policy issues." These require "advice from a broader perspective than that of individual department heads" (Pfiffner 1990). It also grows from the disdain of bureaucrats and the permanent bureaucracy most presidents nurture. *Adhocracy*—a system of decision making that "'minimizes reliance on regularized and systematic patterns of providing advice and instead relies heavily on the president to distribute assignments and select whom he listens to and when'" (Haass 1994a; see also Watson 1993)—is often the result. A common aspect of adhocracy is that "it neither trusts nor respects standing bureaucracies. They are viewed as slow, unimaginative, and disloyal" (Haass 1994a).

Such *"government by inner circle"* now commonly describes presidential policy making. Although cabinet members may sometimes be members of the circles, it is typically because of their individual ties with presidents, not their institutional roles. Prominent recent examples include Defense Secretary Dick Cheney and Secretary of State James Baker during the first Bush administration, and Secretary of the Treasury Robert Rubin during the Clinton administration.

The Presidential Subsystem

Despite what some see as its untoward effects, every American president since World War II has relied increasingly on his personal staff and the Executive Office of the President for advice and assistance in the development of policies and programs. A *presidential subsystem* within the executive branch is the result, which often leads to differences between the presidency, on the one hand, and the established bureaucracies comprising the second concentric circle of policy making, on the other.

The institutionalization of the presidency began with the Executive Reorganization Act of 1939, which authorized President Roosevelt to create the Executive Office, consisting of the *White House Office* and the *Bureau of the Budget.* The former unit was to house the president's personal assistants and their staffs. The latter, created in 1921 under the jurisdiction of the Treasury Department, was to ensure presidential control over budgetary matters and later over the president's entire legislative program.

Since 1939 the *Executive Office of the President (EOP)* has included a plethora of other offices and councils. The lists and labels change continually, reflecting both presidential preferences and policy priorities. At the end of the Clinton administration, for example, the EOP included, among others, the National Economic Council, the National Security Council, the Council of Economic Advisers, the Council on Sustainable Development, the Foreign Intelligence Advisory Board, the Office of Management and Budget, the Office of Policy Development, the Domestic Policy Council, the Office of Science and Technology Policy, the Council on Environmental Quality, the Office of the United States Trade Representative, the Office of National AIDs Policy, and the Office of National Drug Control Policy.

With new offices and functions have come more people and demands for more money. During the Clinton Administration, the EOP consisted of a staff of nearly 1,800 and a budget of over $250 million. The *institutionalized presidency* is now "a powerful inner sanctum of government, isolated from traditional, constitutional checks and balances" (Cronin 1984). Moreover, an enlarged White House staff designed to increase presidential control of the executive branch becomes, in the eyes of critics, "a screen" between the executive and legislative branches that "[cuts] off the president from the government and the government from the president. The staff becomes a shock absorber around the president, shielding him from reality" (Arthur Schlesinger, in *The Wall Street Journal,* 7 January 1981).

The Chief of Staff As the size of the presidential subsystem has increased, most presidents have eventually concluded they must rely on a ***chief of staff*** to ensure presidential leadership and to bring order to an otherwise potentially chaotic White House staff operation. This was one of the hallmarks of the Nixon administration, where H. R. Haldeman and John Ehrlichman played critical staff roles. Carter began his presidency with the pledge that he would never operate as Nixon had, but he, too, eventually found a strong chief of staff necessary for effective governance. Reagan and Bush also began this way; eventually Clinton came to the same conclusion.

Clinton was renowned early in his presidency for others' easy yet time-consuming access to him, and especially for endless but inconclusive meetings ("schmooze-a-thons") involving large numbers of staff and cabinet members. Although Clinton was the first Democratic president to

start with a chief of staff, his first appointment—Thomas "Mack the Nice" McLarty, an outgoing business person and lifelong friend—did little to institute the kind of central control associated with the position.

Corrective action was taken midway through the Clinton presidency with the appointment of Leon Panetta as chief of staff. A former member of Congress and director of the Office of Management and Budget, Panetta sought a more orderly White House operation. To accomplish this, Panetta constructed a system that established himself as the sole *gatekeeper* for the president. All the various offices and departments in the White House reported to Panetta (or his deputies) and no one other than Panetta was given "walk-in" privileges to the president, not even the National Security Adviser or the president's personal advisers. Panetta also took control of the president's schedule and instituted weekly "long-term planning" meetings to encourage broader goals and strategies for the administration. Finally, and most important for foreign policy, while bringing first-term National Security Adviser Anthony Lake into the president's daily 7:30 meeting to raise foreign policy issues to a more prominent level within the White House, Panetta also strengthened his influence on the National Security Council, adding himself to its top-level "Principals Committee" (Drew 1994). These moves greatly enhanced the centralization of the White House staff and substantially elevated the importance of the chief of staff in all policy matters.

When Panetta departed the administration at the end of Clinton's first term, he left a system that was substantially more centralized, but also significantly more personalized. His replacement, Erskine Bowles, sought to retain the organization and centralization, but also to revitalize the formal policy structures of the White House. Hence, structures such as the National Economic Council, the National Security Council, and the Domestic Policy Council were given more weight, and the tightly controlled access to the president was loosened somewhat (Solomon 1997). When Bowles departed in 1999, he was replaced by his deputy, John Podesta, who retained Bowles' system.

George W. Bush is no exception to the trend toward strong chiefs of staff. Stressing a highly centralized and structured White House staff, his appointment was Andrew Card, who served in both the Reagan and the first Bush White Houses. Card's role stemmed from Bush's preference for a corporate model that delegates responsibility to subordinates (Berke 2001). Interestingly, however, George W. Bush often seemed to rely on his vice president, Dick Cheney, to perform roles played by such chiefs of staff as Panetta. According to observers, Cheney established a powerful staff closely integrated into the president's staff (Schmitt 2001b). Moreover, Bush delegated chief of staff-like responsibilities on such issues as the budget to the vice president as well (Berke 2001).

As might be concluded from examples such as Leon Panetta, strong chiefs of staff have proven necessary to bring order to White House decision-making processes, but they also contribute to the view that the White House staff itself distances the president from the rest of the executive branch of government. This is especially true if, as in the Nixon administration, staff members like Henry Kissinger, H. R. Haldeman, and John Ehrlichman are more powerful than the secretaries of state or defense or the domestic department heads. In these situations, the staff serves not as channels of communication between the president and his "line" departments and agencies, but as an independent layer of decision-making authority between the president and the rest of the executive branch.

The National Security Adviser The *National Security Council (NSC)* is the institutional umbrella within the presidential subsystem bearing primary responsibility for foreign policy. This council—and especially its staff—has grown from its creation in 1947 to be the center of most foreign policy making in most administrations. For example, it was as head of the NSC and its staff that Kissinger acquired greater influence than the

secretaries of state or defense. Ever since, the national security adviser's role and relationship with the president have been closely scrutinized.

Kissinger's formal title was Special Assistant for National Security Affairs. The world "special" has since been dropped, and the position is sometimes referred to loosely as simply *national security adviser* (NSA). Others had occupied the post in previous administrations—Robert Cutler and later Gordon Gray under Eisenhower; McGeorge Bundy under Kennedy; and Bundy and Walt W. Rostow under Lyndon Johnson. While the role of the NSA grew steadily through his tenure, none had achieved the same level of prominence and influence in the foreign affairs government as did Kissinger. Zbigniew Brzezinski, Kissinger's successor in the Carter administration, was somewhat less dominant, but he, too, emerged as his boss's key foreign policy adviser. Although President Reagan initially sought to downgrade the role of the national security adviser—six different men held the position in Reagan's eight-year presidency—the Iran-contra affair demonstrated that the national security adviser and his staff had embarked on operational activities that expanded the role of the NSC system in new and uncharted directions. In his final two years, Reagan turned to Frank Carlucci and Colin Powell to restore the centrality of the NSA and the NSC system.

Brent Scowcroft, Bush's national security adviser, eschewed operational activities and pursued a role more akin to his pre-Reagan predecessors but without the publicity. Thus he played an active managerial role in the administration. Anthony Lake, Clinton's first NSA, assumed a low-profile role and worked within the system to build support for Clinton's foreign policy and to brief reporters "on background" (not for attribution) about it. His deputy was Samuel (Sandy) Berger, who took over as NSA when Lake stepped down as NSA at the end of the first Clinton term. While maintaining a collegial relationship with Defense Secretary William Cohen and Secretary of State Madeleine Albright, by most accounts Berger gradually assumed the central role in foreign policy making that was by then becoming the norm for the National Security Adviser (see Heilbrunn 1998; Perlez 1999).

George W. Bush's choice for national security adviser was forty-six-year-old Condoleeza Rice, a former NSC staff member for George H. W. Bush. A close adviser to George W. Bush during the 2000 campaign, Rice seemed destined to adopt a low-key approach stressing coordination and management in the face of more assertive and high profile advisers such as Colin Powell (Secretary of State), Donald Rumsfeld (Secretary of Defense), and Vice President Dick Cheney. In fact, one observer predicted early in the second Bush administration that Cheney would be the "arbiter" and the "player to make [the system] work" (*Business Week,* 29 January 2001, 28). Indeed, Cheney asserted himself on defense and foreign policy and attended the regular meetings held by Rice, Powell, and Rumsfeld (McGeary 2001). Rice, however, eventually developed her personal relationship with the president into a more central role as "traffic cop," spokesperson and personal adviser (McGeary 2001).

Presidential preferences explain in part the variations in how different presidents draw on and interact with their in-house foreign policy advisers.[7] Still, all recent presidents, regardless of their initial predilections, have found it necessary to exert political control over foreign policy making by institutionalizing it within the White House. According to Theodore Sorensen (1987–1988), a White House staff member during the Kennedy administration, "since the days when Dean Acheson could serve as both secretary of state and Truman's personal adviser and coordinator, the overlap between national and international issues, the number and speed of thermonuclear missiles, and the foreign policy pressures from Congress, the press, and public, have all mounted to a point where no president can conscientiously delegate to anyone his constitutional responsibilities in foreign affairs."

We can gain an appreciation of how presidential style and external pressures encourage the centralization of foreign policy in the White House through a historical examination of the way different presidents have used the National Security Council (NSC) and its staff. By reviewing roles, structures, and operations of each administration's NSC system, we will gain insight into the endemic differences between the institutionalized presidency comprising the innermost circle of foreign policy making and the career professionals comprising the second concentric circle.

Organizing for Foreign Policy: The National Security Council System

Created by the National Security Act of 1947,[8] the purpose of the *National Security Council* is to "advise the president with respect to the integration of domestic, foreign, and military policies relating to the national security." Statutory members of the council include the president (as chair), vice president, and secretaries of state and defense. The director of central intelligence and the chairman of the joint chiefs of staff (JCS) are statutory advisers. Because presidents can include anyone they wish, others often participate, including the secretary of the treasury, the attorney general, the U.S. ambassador to the United Nations, the director of the Office of Management and Budget (OMB), heads of such organizations as the Arms Control and Disarmament Agency (ACDA), and the Agency for International Development (AID), and various presidential advisers and assistants, depending on the issues and presidential predilections.

The president is free to use the NSC as much or as little as he or she desires, and its deliberations and decisions are purely advisory. Still, over time it has become the primary mechanism for tackling problems all presidents face: acquiring information, identifying issues, coping with crises, making decisions, coordinating actions, and ensuring agency compliance with presidential wishes. Through the development of formal *interagency processes,* it has become the principal formal mechanism for coordinating the vast federal structure on foreign policy.

Institutionalizing the NSC System, 1947–1961
Although created during his administration, President Truman did not use the NSC extensively, fearing it might encroach on his constitutional prerogatives by imposing a parliamentary-type cabinet system over foreign policy decision making. In fact, Truman did not even attend NSC meetings before the outbreak of the Korean War in 1950. As a result, the council's role was largely perfunctory. With the outbreak of the Korean War, however, Truman recognized the wisdom of better coordination of policy and action. He therefore directed that major national security policy recommendations come to him via the council and he also instituted weekly meetings. Nevertheless, the State Department remained at the core of foreign policy: the secretary of state was even named the ranking member of the NSC in Truman's absence. In fact, the famous NSC 68 memorandum was coordinated chiefly by the State Department and outside formal NSC channels (see Chapter 4). Nevertheless, by the end of his term Truman also had begun to use the NSC staff for interagency planning purposes.

As an instrument of presidential leadership, the NSC system developed substantially under President Dwight D. Eisenhower. Coming from a professional background that emphasized the need for staff work and overall coordination, former General Eisenhower took the largely undeveloped NSC structure he had inherited from Truman and transformed it into a highly formalized system which he viewed as "the central vehicle for formulating and promulgating policy" and "the primary means of imparting presidential direction and over-all coherence to the activities of the departments and agencies" (Clark and Legere 1969). An interagency planning board and operations coordinating board made up of mid-level officials from the relevant foreign policy bureaucracies, both eventually chaired by the special assistant for national security affairs (the now-familiar position created by Eisenhower and filled initially by Robert Cutler), became part of Eisenhower's NSC system. They were charged, respectively, with generating policy recommen-

dations for consideration by the full NSC and with overseeing the implementation of presidential decisions (Greenstein 2000). Eisenhower attended (and chaired) 326 of the NSC's 366 meeting during his two terms and made these meetings the largest item on his weekly agenda (U.S. Department of State 1997). Still, formal council meetings were often followed by more intimate "rump" sessions, or the president would convene meetings of a small group of advisers outside the formal NSC structure to deal with urgent matters.[9]

Personalizing the Staff, 1961–1969 By the time Eisenhower left office the highly institutionalized National Security Council system was being criticized as an excessively bureaucratized system that stifled innovation and diluted policy decisions (Jackson 1965; Henderson 1988; Prados 1991). Reacting to criticisms of Eisenhower's "paper mill," President Kennedy moved initially to dismantle most of the machinery. Shortly after his election in 1960 he appointed McGeorge Bundy as his special assistant for national security affairs and announced that the purpose of Bundy's staff would be "to assist me in obtaining advice from, and coordinating operations of, the government agencies concerned with national security." He also announced his intention to strengthen the role of the secretary of state in the area of interagency coordination.

Insiders' accounts of the Kennedy administration indicate that Kennedy was quickly disappointed with the docile role assumed by Dean Rusk, Kennedy's choice as secretary of state, in an otherwise action-oriented administration. The State Department as an organization also proved too sluggish for White House officials. When this happened, the White House staff stepped into the perceived vacuum—not only Bundy's staff but also other members of Kennedy's personal "team," most of whom were specifically recruited for his administration rather than drawn from careerists in established bureaucracies.

The National Security Council itself remained largely moribund, however. Preferring informality and personal control, Kennedy relied instead on ad hoc interagency task forces designed to serve presidential needs rather than the agencies they represented. The 1961 Bay of Pigs fiasco, from which Kennedy learned "never to rely on the experts," contributed much to his reliance on decision-making groups formulated without regard for the institutional affiliations of their members. The most celebrated of these smaller, ad hoc groups was the so-called *Ex Com (Executive Committee of the NSC)*, initially comprising some thirteen advisers on whom Kennedy relied heavily in devising a response to the surreptitious installation of Soviet offensive weapons in Cuba in October 1962. Similar but less well-known ad hoc groups dealt with crises in Berlin and Laos, paramilitary experiments being tried in Vietnam, and covert intelligence operations directed against Cuba. Bundy served on most of the informal groups and his staff acted aggressively as a sort of "president's personal State Department."

Another key innovation was the establishment of the White House *Situation Room* next to Bundy's office in the basement. Linked to the communication channels of the foreign policy bureaucracy, the Situation Room allowed Bundy and the NSC staff to become increasingly central to foreign policy making. It was expanded in each subsequent administration. Hence, while the NSC itself proved far less important in ensuring presidential control than these less formal groups, the National Security Council staff assumed a more significant role, as did the NSA.

Kennedy's assassination in November 1963 brought to the White House a man with little interest and less experience in foreign affairs. Johnson's approach to national security matters was even less formal than Kennedy's. The NSC as a formal deliberative mechanism languished—a fact that, in the view of one of Johnson's critics, contributed to the Vietnam morass.

> The decisions and actions that marked our large-scale military entry into the Vietnam War in early 1965 reflected the piecemeal consideration of interrelated issues, . . . the natural consequence of a fragmented NSC and a general inattention to long-range policy planning. Consultation, even knowledge of the basic facts, was confined to a tight circle of presidential advisers, and there appears to have been little systematic debate outside that group.

(HOOPES 1973B, 7)

Informal meetings of the tight inner circle—the famed *Tuesday Lunch* gatherings—substituted for more formal meetings. At these meetings of the president, the secretaries of state and defense (Rusk and Robert McNamara), the national security adviser (first McGeorge Bundy, then Walt W. Rostow, who replaced Bundy in 1966), and eventually the director of the CIA, the chairman of the joint chiefs, and the president's press secretary, Vietnam was the principal luncheon topic. Indeed, Vietnam gradually consumed more and more of the administration's attention. While it preserved personal control and organizational flexibility, the cost of Johnson's highly personal and informal approach was the exclusion of subordinates on whom the president and his close circle of advisers depended for implementation of top-level decisions. While the NSA and NSC staff remained key foreign policy players, Johnson utilized them as his personal staff and not as coordinators of the policy process. The informality and lack of structure impaired the Johnson administration's ability to plan, prepare, assess, and implement policy in a coordinated fashion. Moreover, when Walt W. Rostow took over the position of National Security Adviser, he continued to manage the flow of information to the president, to communicate presidential wishes to the bureaucracy, and to provide policy analysis and advice. But he did much less to encourage the free flow of ideas and alternatives to the president than had his predecessor. The result was bureaucratic distrust of Rostow's ability to present departmental viewpoints to Johnson objectively, which further hampered effective policy making (Hoopes 1973b; Mulcahy 1995).

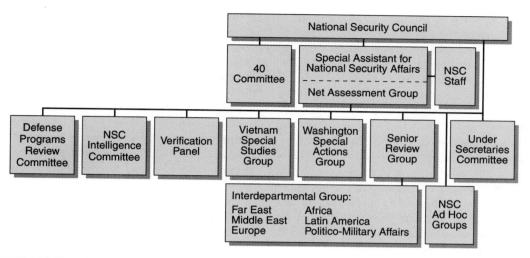

FIGURE 10.2 The Nixon Administration's National Security Council System

The White House Ascendant, 1969–1989
Noncoherence describes the policy-making legacy Nixon inherited from a divided and demoralized Johnson administration in January 1969. The outgoing administration's "policy-making institutions, formal and informal, had little that would recommend them to its successor" (Destler 1974). Hence, Nixon, and subsequently his successors, worked to construct more organized NSC systems, each of which, ultimately, resulted in a White House-centered structure and process.

The Nixon Administration Nixon moved rapidly to restore coherence by rebuilding a more formal NSC system and placing it at the hub of foreign policy making. Eschewing the informality and sloppiness of the preceding administrations while preserving the personalization of the NSC staff, Nixon named Harvard political scientist Henry Kissinger as his special assistant for national security affairs and directed Kissinger to establish an "Eisenhower NSC system" but "without the concurrences" (Destler 1974). According to

Morton Halperin, who helped devise the system, the goal was to ensure presidential control and conduct of foreign policy (National Security Council Project 1998).

The system that Nixon and Kissinger established located decision-making authority in the White House. Kissinger tripled the NSC staff and organized a system around a number of top-level interagency committees—nearly all directed by Kissinger—whose jurisdictions covered the entire waterfront of American foreign policy, from arms control negotiations with the Soviet Union (the Verification Panel), to crisis management (the Washington Special Actions Group), to covert operations (the 40 Committee, named for the National Security Decision Memorandum that set it up). Their task was to develop alternatives for consideration by the president and the full NSC. Because Kissinger directed nearly all of them (the Under Secretaries Committee chaired by the Deputy Secretary of State was the exception, and it was soon marginalized), his role in the NSC system was pivotal (see Figure 10.2). The working committees served the top-level "Review Group," also chaired by Kissinger, which screened all interagency papers prior to their consideration by the NSC (U.S. Department of State 1997).

The system fit Richard Nixon's preferred operating style. In contrast to Eisenhower's approach (which encouraged the NSC system to focus on compromises among departments and agencies), and in contrast to the Kennedy and Johnson styles (which saw NSC meetings as forums for its members to advocate views), Nixon wanted all policy options to be laid out for his subsequent consideration and, above all, to maintain his flexibility. Kissinger's influence in the system derived in part from Nixon's preference for solo decision making. The president's trust in Kissinger further enhanced his influence. Indeed, Kissinger himself has written that "in the final analysis the influence of a Presidential Assistant derives almost exclusively from the confidence of the President, not from administrative arrangements" (Kissinger 1979, 40).[10]

Two additional developments characterized the operations of the Nixon system. First, President Nixon increasingly used Kissinger to implement foreign policy, thereby expanding the role of the national security adviser into operational responsibilities. Kissinger's activism produced some spectacular diplomatic successes in China, the Soviet Union, the Middle East, and elsewhere, and culminated in Kissinger's appointment as secretary of state, an assignment he held concurrently with his White House role. Second, even as Kissinger's personal influence rose, his elaborate NSC system atrophied. The decisions that led to the 1970 Cambodia incursion, for example, were a product of "catch-as-catch-can" gatherings between Nixon and his advisers outside the formal NSC framework (Destler 1974). Other major foreign policy initiatives involving China, the Middle East, and Vietnam also evolved outside the system. The "back channel" to the Soviet leadership that Kissinger established is perhaps his most celebrated bureaucratic end-run. It led to a breakthrough in the strategic arms negotiations with the Soviets even while formal negotiations between the two sides' delegations (the "front channel") continued (see Talbott 1979).

The Ford and Carter Administrations   One of Gerald Ford's first moves on the eve of his inauguration as the first nonelected president was to ask Kissinger to remain as his secretary of state and national security adviser. In his dual capacity Kissinger continued to operate what some felt was a one-man foreign policy show, one all the more apparent because the president he served was a relative novice in international affairs. As public and congressional disapproval of the concentration of power in one adviser's hands grew, Kissinger's star and the popularity of the policies he engineered gradually waned. In response, Ford appointed Brent Scowcroft to the NSA slot. Scowcroft restored a less elaborate version of the Nixon-Kissinger NSC system, but limited his own role to managing the process. Kissinger remained the primary foreign policy adviser with unlimited access to President Ford, while the NSC worked to present President Ford with policy analysis and alternatives.

When Jimmy Carter took office after his defeat of Gerald Ford in 1976, he sought to construct an NSC system that would avoid concentrating foreign policy power into one individual's hands, while preserving the White House role in coordinating the foreign policy bureaucracy and ensuring that a broad spectrum of idea and a vigorous debate over policy alternatives occurred. President Carter's designation of Zbigniew Brzezinski as assistant for national security affairs (which came before he named his secretary of state), reaffirmed the determination of the White House to exercise foreign policy control. The elaborate NSC system of the preceding years was replaced with one based on two committees: a Policy Review Committee (PRC) responsible chiefly for long-term projects, to be chaired by a cabinet member whose department had the greatest stake in a given issue; and a Special Coordinating Committee (SCC) chiefly responsible for short-term projects (including covert intelligence operations and crisis management), to be chaired by the national security adviser.

The latter committee eventually emerged as the most influential body within the NSC structure. Brzezinski also emerged as the pivotal foreign policy adviser, and eventually expanded his role into operational activities as well. Initially one of a "collegium" of key advisers that included Secretary of State Cyrus Vance, Secretary of Defense Harold Brown, and UN Ambassador Andrew Young, Brzezinski transformed his role through his control over the SCC, his easy access to the president, and Carter's practice of avoiding formal NSC meetings in favor of more informal meetings of some of the key principals (the NSC met only ten times in his administration).

Fundamental conflict between the secretary and the president's national security adviser on foreign policy also emerged as a major problem. Although the principal members worked reasonably well together for the first half of the administration, by the second some serious fissures had developed. Brzezinski stressed a hardline posture toward the Soviet Union and focused on the East–West conflict. Vance and Young stressed détente and appeared more sensitive to North–South relations and global-order issues. For a time, Carter seemed unable to reconcile the often conflicting thrusts of his principal advisers. However, Young resigned when his contacts with the Palestine Liberation Organization (in violation of established policy) were disclosed. Vance resigned in the spring of 1980 to protest the president's abortive military rescue of American hostages in Iran, the first time in sixty years a secretary of state resigned because of a policy dispute with the president. The White House–State Department rift did not end with Vance's departure, either. Carter named Senator Edmund S. Muskie as Vance's successor, but he was barely confirmed in office when Carter signed PD 59, which moved U.S. strategic doctrine in the direction of an explicit counterforce posture—and without ever consulting the new secretary of state.

The rift between Brzezinski and Vance perpetuated what by 1980 had become a recurrent concern. Should the national security adviser be primarily a manager of the decision process or primarily a personal adviser and "resident intellectual" to the president? What is the proper relationship between the national security adviser and the secretary of state? Based on the experiences of the five presidents who occupied the Oval Office in the 1960s and 1970s, a degree of consensus emerged among practitioners and scholars about what the national security adviser should—and should not—be doing (Destler 1983b; "The National Security Adviser: Role and Accountability" 1980). Their activities fall along a continuum between an *"inside management" role,* where the adviser performs the role of facilitator, and a "leadership" role, which often places him in the potential position as a second secretary of state. The thrust of the consensus that emerged toward the end of the Carter administration is that the NSA should emphasize the "inside" role and eschew the "outside." Exemplary tasks associated with each role are listed in Focus 10.2, which also suggests that some activities midway between the "inside" and "outside" orientations may be acceptable.

The Reagan Administration Ronald Reagan's efforts to address the lessons of previous administrations produced an NSC system that began as a cabinet-style approach and ended in a more White House-centered structure. Initially preferring to restore the cabinet and National Security Council per se, redress the balance between the White House and the State Department, and deemphasize the role of the NSC staff and national security adviser, Reagan constructed a system whose problems eventually led him to replace it.

Reagan's initial system revolved around strong department heads and a weak national security adviser. Reagan's choice of Alexander Haig as secretary of state was spotlighted as an indication of the president's desire to relocate primary control over foreign policy making in the State Department. The former NATO commander had been schooled in the ways of the White

FOCUS 10.1   The National Security Assistant: The Professionals' Job Description

YES ("Inside Management")	OKAY In Moderation	NO ("Outside Leadership")
Briefing the president, handling foreign policy in-box	Discreet advice/advocacy	Conducting particular diplomatic negotiations
Analyzing issues and choices:	Encouraging advocacy by NSC staff subordinates	Fixed operational assignments
a. Ordering information/ intelligence	Information and "background" communicating with press, Congress, foreign officials	Public spokesperson
b. Managing interagency studies		Strong, visible internal advocacy (except of already established presidential priorities)
Managing presidential decision processes		Making policy decisions
Communicating presidential decisions and monitoring their implementation		
General interagency brokering, circuit-connecting, crisis management		

SOURCE: I. M. Destler, "The Rise of the National Security Assistant," in Charles W. Kegley, Jr., and Eugene R. Wittkopf, eds., *Perspectives on American Foreign Policy: Selected Readings.* New York: St. Martin's, 1983, 262.

House as an assistant to Henry Kissinger and later as chief of staff during the final, embattled days of the Nixon White House. Reagan also selected Casper Weinberger, formerly the director of the Office of Management and Budget under Nixon, to serve as secretary of defense. Richard V. Allen was selected as the National Security Adviser. Reagan publicly stated that the secretary of state was going to be his "primary adviser . . . [and] the chief formulator and spokesman for foreign policy for this administration."

Haig's initial attempts to act on this premise, including his proposal, submitted on inauguration day, to establish himself as the administration's "foreign policy vicar," were rebuffed. No clearly defined organizational structure for the management of foreign policy emerged during the administration's first year, as it gave priority to domestic rather than foreign policy. In February 1981, top officials did agree to establish Senior Interdepartmental Groups (SIGs) on foreign, defense, and intelligence issues (chaired by the heads of the relevant agencies) and a series of In-

terdepartmental Groups (IGs) at the assistant secretary level, each chaired by the agency most responsible for the issue. These groups would report to the NSC. Later that year, the National Security Planning Group (NSPG) was established to strengthen planning and policy coordination. A smaller and less formal body, the NSPG included the original statutory members and advisers to the NSC designated in the 1947 National Security Act and held regular weekly meetings with the president.

This initial system soon broke down for at least two reasons. First, with a weak NSA, no mechanism for resolving disagreements among the leading executive agencies and departments existed. Second, as Robert C. McFarlane, who became Reagan's national security adviser late in 1983, would later testify before Congress, the system was characterized by the absence of an organizational framework within which to engage in a "thorough and concerted governmentwide analysis" of critical foreign policy proposals (McFarlane 1994).

In early 1982, Reagan replaced Allen with William Clark (a former California Supreme Court Justice and then deputy secretary of state) and issued a presidential directive to establish a more organized NSC system. Although it preserved the secretary of state's responsibility for the "overall direction, coordination, and supervision of the interdepartmental activities incident to foreign policy formulation," it also made NSA Clark responsible for "developing, coordinating, and monitoring national security policy" (U.S. Department of State 1997). Shortly thereafter, Haig resigned as secretary of state, to be replaced with George Shultz. Unfortunately, these changes did little to solve the personality conflicts and internecine warfare that were occurring. The newly-formalized system did not make a dramatic improvement because of its hybrid combination of White House-centered coordination and department-centered structures.

In fact, while Clark first sought to operate as an **honest broker** for others in the foreign affairs government, he eventually concluded that "Cabinet secretaries are all parochial, so you've got to decide yourself what to do." Thus he played an increasingly active role, enhancing the policy-making role of the NSC staff generally and increasing the number of professional staff serving the council to a level greater than at any time since Kissinger's tenure (Destler 1983a). Consequently, by the summer of 1983, Clark was widely regarded as having become the most influential foreign policy figure in the White House. As the most conservative of the president's inner circle of advisers, he also came into conflict with other, more pragmatic White House staffers, particularly Chief of Staff James Baker. The squabbling (especially on the issue of defense spending) may have contributed to Clark's sudden and unexpected departure for the Interior Department in October 1983.

Clark's successors presided over three years of increasingly incoherent, fragmented, contentious, and uncoordinated foreign policy efforts complicated by the president's unwillingness to correct the underlying problems with the system that gave rise to these results. His immediate successor was Robert C. "Bud" McFarlane, a former NSC staffer under Kissinger and Scowcroft and a troubleshooter for Secretary of State Haig, who inherited an elaborate, but still incoherent NSC organizational structure and sought to use it to contend with the centrifugal forces of *cabinet government* and a relatively inattentive president.

McFarlane enjoyed some successes as national security adviser, but he resigned in late 1985 after becoming "overwhelmed by 'Cabinet government'" and his inability to resolve interminable squabbles among key administration officials (Cannon 1988). MacFarlane was replaced by his deputy, Rear Admiral John Poindexter, who lasted just over a year in the position before he was forced to retire over the Iran-Contra scandal in late 1986.

Iran-contra represented the failure of President Reagan's NSC system and illuminates many of the problems and deficiencies that system entailed. The "Iran initiative," as the special commission led by former Senator John Tower, former Secretary of State Ed Muskie, and former NSA Brent Scowcroft (the Tower Board) called it, included an attempted strategic opening to Iran, the sale of arms to Iran via Israel and by the United States itself in an effort to secure the release of hostages held in Lebanon, and, ultimately, the diversion of profits from the arms sales to the contras fighting the Sandinista regime in Nicaragua. Because the record indicates, for example, that Secretary of State Shultz and Secretary of Defense Weinberger vigorously opposed the transfer of arms to Iran, that key covert action findings that authorized the arms-for-hostages swap were approved by the president without their knowledge, and that John Poindexter authorized the transfer of arms profits to the contras without the president's knowledge, the Tower Board concluded that the proper use of existing structures might have averted the single most damaging foreign policy failure of the Reagan presidency.

Such problems led Colin Powell to reaffirm the truism that an effective process is critical to a sound policy. "Issues come and go," observed Powell. "Process is always important." Perhaps recognition of Powell's observation finally led the Reagan White House to address the incoherence of its NSC system, because Poindexter's immediate successor—Frank Carlucci—quickly "set out to restore the credibility of the institution, to restore it to its proper role as an interagency body . . . That is its 'honest broker' role, and we set out to reestablish it. We took the NSC out of operations." Carlucci also established the national security adviser as a more central coordinator rather than another policy advocate. When he left the position in December 1987 to replace Weinberger as secretary of defense, his deputy, General Colin Powell, assumed the role. Under their leadership, the NSC played an important and positive role in preparing for the Washington and Moscow superpower summits, and the NSA once more emerged as an effective facilitator of the foreign affairs policy process (Cannon 1988; Kirschten 1987).

White House Centralization: The Bush and Clinton Administrations When George H. W. Bush moved from vice president to president through his 1988 election victory, he constructed an NSC system that reflected his experiences in the Reagan Administration. His system had several characteristics. First, it was *White House-centered;* the NSA and NSC staff managed the process and coordinated policy, while the stakeholders from the foreign policy bureaucracy worked through an interagency process to formulate policy options. Also, while Bush placed great weight on the role of the departments of State and Defense, the key interagency committees designed to serve the NSC were chaired by the NSA and Deputy NSA, placing the White House in a position to control bureaucratic differences. Further, Bush selected his top-level advisers to create a collegial team that would work well together with the president, who would play an active and attentive role in making foreign policy decisions. Hence, Bush essentially sought to counter the key deficiencies of the early Rea-

gan system: its decentralized cabinet government approach; its lack of White House coordination; its personal and bureaucratic divisions; and its lack of presidential attentiveness.

The structure of the Bush NSC system had three layers. At the top was the *Principals Committee,* consisting of the national security assistant (as chair), the secretaries of state and defense, the director of central intelligence, the chairman of the Joint Chiefs of Staff, and the president's chief of staff, with participation by the attorney general and treasury secretary when issues required. The Principals Committee was charged with reviewing, coordinating, and monitoring the development and implementation of national security policy. Serving the Principals Committee was the *Deputies Committee,* chaired by the deputy national security adviser, with participants at the rank of under secretary. This committee coordinated and reviewed the work of the third layer and had the responsibility for preparing policy issues, papers, and recommendations for the Principals Committee. A series of *Policy Coordinating Committees* (PCCs), consisting of eight permanent regional and functional committees, and others on an ad hoc basis, were responsible for initially developing policy options and for overseeing policy implementation. These PCCs consisted of representatives from across the foreign policy bureaucracy at the assistant secretary level.

To knit the system together, Bush assembled an experienced team of advisers with collegial relationships. James Baker, a friend of Bush who ran his 1988 presidential campaign and also served as Reagan's chief of staff and secretary of the treasury, was named secretary of state. Former congressman Dick Cheney became secretary of defense after Bush failed to win Senate approval of former Senator John Tower for the job. Earlier Cheney had served President Ford as chief of staff. Colin Powell returned to active military duty at the end of the Reagan administration and was named chairman of the Joint Chiefs of Staff. As his national security adviser, Bush selected Brent Scowcroft, who had occupied that role in the Ford administration and was, as noted, a member of the Tower Board which investigated the Iran-contra affair. Bush himself played a critical role, participating in virtually every high-level meeting of his administration (National Security Council Project 1999a).

As the NSA, Scowcroft tried, apparently successfully, to involve the secretaries of state and defense in the policy process and to himself maintain close contact with the president. Baker and Scowcroft agreed at the outset that "Baker would have the lead on foreign policy, Scowcroft and the NSC would have no operational role, and Scowcroft himself would be a low-profile 'honest broker' within the administration." With this they hoped to avoid "niggling disagreements over public speeches, television interviews, ambassadorial visits, and the like" (Gergen 1989). According to two NSC staff members who served the Bush White House, "it was Scowcroft's job to make the government work, using his staff in policy development and engaging Baker, Cheney, and Powell until a coherent and shared policy direction emerged" (Zelikow and Rice 1995). As another observer explained late in the Bush presidency, Scowcroft "managed both to be a highly influential adviser to the president and to coordinate effectively the debate among the president's top foreign policy officials. Scowcroft was able to combine these two functions because he lacked the insatiable drive toward power and fame that has crippled previous National Security Council heads" (Judis 1992).

Paralleling this NSC system, however, was a less formal advisory "structure" on which Bush relied heavily. This informal advisory process, centered around the president himself, usually included Scowcroft, Cheney, Baker, Powell, and Chief of Staff John Sununu. Stressing teamwork and solidarity, this small group supplemented, and at times supplanted, the more formal NSC system. It reflected Bush's preference for a tight inner circle of confidants chosen on the basis of loyalty and friendship, not institutional ties. A similar informal system evolved at the deputies level as well, with key officials from different agencies working closely and collegially together (National Security Council Project 1999a).

Most observers believe the first Bush administration system to be a model in terms of structure and in terms of the role and behavior of the NSA (for example, National Security Council Project 1999a; 1999b). Indeed, subsequent administrations have essentially adopted the structures and procedures put in place by the first Bush administration. In most policy areas the formal and informal advisory systems complemented each other well. Former members of the NSC staff pointed to German unification, the end of the Cold War, most of the Gulf War policy making, the Middle East peace process, and a few others as good examples of the structure and process at work (National Security Council Project 1999a; Zelikow and Rice 1995).

There were, of course, a few problems. Heavy reliance on the formal structures in the early months heightened the influence of Reagan Administration holdovers in the bureaucracy resulting in a "strategic review" of foreign and national security policy that delivered little that was new or innovative: a cautious "status quo plus" policy. Some argue that Bush's responses to Soviet initiatives were shaped more by the "highest levels" than by the NSC system (Beschloss and Talbott 1993). Also, while military actions in Panama and the Persian Gulf were largely successful, they both involved far less systematic policy review than might have been expected. With regard to Panama, "so far as is . . . evident, there was . . . no NSC meeting in connection with Bush's most ambitious foreign policy move of his first year . . ." (Prados 1991). The decision process that led to the defense of Saudi Arabia in August 1990 and, later, to the war against Iraq also indicates that the decision making leading up to the Gulf War was less formal than it should have been, and that the decisions to end the war were taken with little formal review (Gordon and Trainor 1995; see also journalist Bob Woodward's glimpse of that process as seen through the eyes of Colin Powell in Focus 10.3.) Finally, Bush's decision to dispatch U.S. troops to Somalia was

---

FOCUS 10.2   Reflections on the Gulf War Decision-Making Process

Powell recalled vividly the efforts he had made to present all the options in the Persian Gulf—including containment of Iraq—to the president, to make sure the full range of possibilities had been considered. It had been hard. . . .

One Friday afternoon in early October . . . Cheney and Powell had gone to the Oval Office to see Bush and Scowcroft. The sun was streaming in. For some reason the atmosphere wasn't right. There were interruptions; it was the president's office, the wrong place for this kind of discussion, Powell felt. He preferred the formality of the Situation Room, where Bush could stay focused. The mood in the Oval Office was too relaxed, too convivial—the boys sitting around shooting the shit before the weekend. . . .

Powell . . . had become increasingly disenchanted with the National Security Council procedures and meetings. Scowcroft seemed unable, or unwilling, to coordinate and make sense of all the components of the Gulf policy—military, diplomatic, public affairs, economic, the United Nations. When the principals met, Bush liked to keep everyone around the table smiling—jokes, camaraderie, the conviviality of old friends. Positions and alternatives were not completely discussed. Interruptions were common. Clear decisions rarely emerged. Often Powell and

Cheney returned from these gatherings and said to each other, now what did that mean? What are we supposed to do? Frequently, they had to wait to hear the answer later from Scowcroft or on television.

The operation needed a field marshal—someone of the highest rank who was the day-to-day manager, Powell felt. The president, given his other domestic and political responsibilities, couldn't be the chief coordinator. It should be the national security advisor. Instead, Scowcroft had become the First Companion and all-purpose playmate to the president on golf, fishing, and weekend outings. He was regularly failing in his larger duty to ensure that policy was carefully debated and formulated. . . .

"We are at a 'Y' in the road," Scowcroft began. The policy could continue to be deter-and-defend, or it could switch to developing the office option.

Powell was struck once again by the informality of the rolling discussion among these . . . men who had been friends for years. There was no real organization to the proceedings as they weighed options. Ideas bounced back and forth as one thought or another occurred to one of them.

SOURCE: Bob Woodward, *The Commanders*. New York: Simon and Schuster, 1991, 41, 301–302, 318.

---

curiously disconnected to careful NSC consideration. While his Deputies Committee prepared options and the NSC met to consider them on November 25, 1992, Bush's decision to pursue the most interventionist of the options did not reflect the analysis of the NSC or the preferences of the major stakeholders in the review process (Schraeder 1998).

According to James Steinberg, who later became the Deputy NSA, President Clinton's team concurred that the Bush NSC system had been highly successful and so sought to preserve it (National Security Council Project 2000). Hence the incoming administration retained much of

the previous administration's system, adopting the same three-layered structure: a Principals Committee, a Deputies Committee, and a series of *Interagency Working Groups* (IWGs), the equivalent of the Bush administration's Policy Coordinating Committees, to "review and coordinate the implementation of presidential decisions in their respective policy areas" (U.S. Department of State 1997). The Clinton NSC system was also White House-centered, with the national security adviser and the deputy national security adviser chairing the Principals Committee and the Deputies Committee respectively. While retaining the fundamental structure, the administration made several important, if incremental, changes. First, the membership of the Principals Committee was expanded to include the secretary of the treasury, the ambassador to the UN, the assistant to the president for economic policy (head of the National Economic Council), and the director of the Office of Management and Budget. Other officials, including the attorney general and the director of the Office of National Drug Control Policy, attended as necessary. Hence, key advisers on areas of foreign economic policy were included in the system (in conjunction with the National Economic Council, discussed later).

The composition and responsibilities of the Deputies Committee also changed. To the typical members of this committee, the Clinton administration added the deputy assistant for Economic Policy and the national security adviser to the vice president. Additionally, this committee's responsibilities in assigning and overseeing the work of the IWGs were strengthened: it "served as the senior subcabinet interagency forum for considering policy issues affecting national security and for reviewing and monitoring the work of the NSC interagency process" (U.S. Department of State 1997). According to James Steinberg, who chaired the Deputies Committee in the administration's second term, it was "the principal daily operating committee of the interagency process" (National Security Council Project 2000).

The Clinton Administration's NSC staff mirrored the by-now familiar structure of regional and functional offices that parallel the structure of the State Department, although this bureaucracy of the NSC system was somewhat reorganized to reflect the realities of the post–Cold War world. Initially downsized from the Bush Administration, the NSC staff was subsequently expanded in the second Clinton term.

To staff his NSC system, President Clinton drew chiefly on individuals with foreign policy experience from the 1970s, especially in the Carter Administration. For his first secretary of state, Clinton tapped Warren Christopher, who had served as deputy secretary of state in the Carter administration (where he negotiated the release of American diplomats held hostage in Iran in 1980). For Defense, Clinton first selected former House member Les Aspin, whose expertise was developed on the House Armed Services Committee. Aspin lasted less than a year in office, and was subsequently replaced by William Perry, a veteran of the Carter Defense Department. For his national security adviser, Clinton turned to Anthony Lake, the man who had coauthored the following description of the NSA role, reminiscent of the "insider management" role described in Focus 10.1:

> If the assistant is to be the director of policy formation, he should be strictly an inside operator. To avoid the massive confusion of the last decade or more, the adviser should not speak publicly, engage in diplomacy, nor undermine the secretary [of state] with Congress and the news media. A president who cannot demand that of the adviser and an adviser who cannot so forbear are simply asking for catastrophe for their administration. But while enforcing these constraints, the president must also make it clear that the assistant is the person in charge.

(DESTLER, GELB, AND LAKE 1984, 277)

Lake's experience included service on Kissinger's NSC staff and in Carter's State Department. Having witnessed Kissinger and Brzezinski firsthand, Lake was determined on becoming NSA himself to avoid the foreign policy flareups and pitfalls each of them experienced. He described his conception of the NSA's task shortly after his selection as making sure that Clinton "gets the wide array of alternatives, the concise information, and the broad range of advice [for decision making] that he requires."

For all its formal coherence and promise, the evidence indicates that the Clinton NSC system did not function well for much of his first term. Although Clinton announced at the outset of his

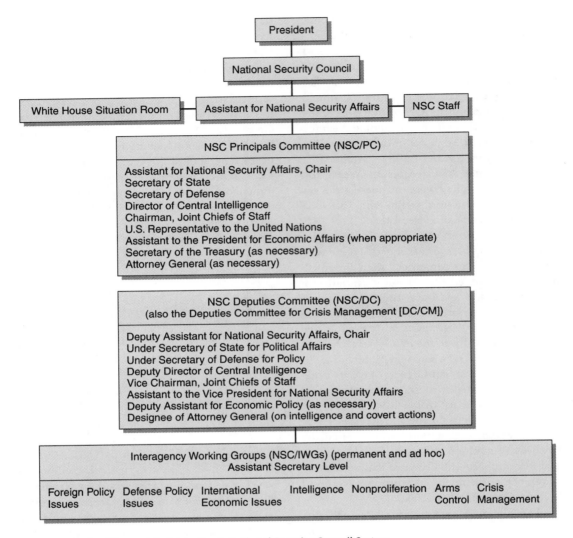

FIGURE 10.3 The Clinton Administration's National Security Council System

Note: The White House chief of staff later became a member of the NSC Principals Committee.
Source: Adapted from Presidential Decision Directive (PDD) 2, January 20, 1993.

presidency his intention to make foreign policy in the White House and to turn to the State Department for its implementation, neither end of that equation worked out well. First, Clinton showed little interest in foreign policy issues and even less in the formal policy-making structures outlined in Figure 10.3. For example, formal NSC meetings were never held to discuss his policies toward Russia—arguably among the positive achievements early in his administration. Instead, Russia policy was discussed in less-structured settings among the administration's foreign policy "principals" (Lake, Christopher, Albright, the secretary of defense, director of the CIA, chairman of the Joint Chiefs of Staff, and, later, White House chief of staff). Formal NSC meetings on other topics were also infrequent. (For additional discussion see Halberstam 2001.)

Anthony Lake also failed to perform the NSA tasks effectively. One observer noted that he was "so low key that he . . . failed to enunciate the Administration's policies clearly" (Pine 1994). Policy makers at State and Defense criticized Lake for being "inscrutable and complained privately that he was not giving their views a fair hearing with Clinton" (Harris 1997b). According to another observer, "Lake became famous for chairing deliberations that never arrived at conclusions. Participants in NSC meetings still say that the meetings only ran smoothly and produced coherent results when they were headed by Lake's former deputy, Sandy Berger" (Heilbrunn 1997). The administration's propensity to "adhocracy" also helped little. Indeed, the "lines of authority" in the Clinton White House were likened to "a plate of spaghetti: Everyone seems to be in charge of everyone so that no one is held accountable, there is little hierarchy, and there are loops of influence and access that collide, coincide or work in blissful ignorance of one another until some fiasco looms" (Devroy 1994). Further complicating Lake's performance as NSA was the fact that he had not developed a close, comfortable relationship with the one person with whom such a relationship was critical: Bill Clinton. Described by one observer as "quite stiff," the relationship became increasingly strained as President Clinton eventually came to see Lake as simply a "talented briefer" and turned more and more to Sandy Berger, Lake's deputy, for advice (Halberstam 2001).

Outside the White House, the foreign policy team was not much more effective. Defense Secretary Aspin's blunders on Somalia led to his resignation, while Warren Christopher proved capable and diligent as an implementor, but not overly effective as a policy maker,

a strategist, or even a manager of the State Department. Lacking effective White House coordination and leadership, what emerged was a "division of labor on foreign policy. Lake was interested in issues such as Africa and Northern Ireland. The State Department, by contrast, handled Bosnia, North Korea, and the Middle East and, together with the Pentagon, developed the Partnership for Peace proposal" (Heilbrunn 1998).

Examples of both the president's failure to attend to foreign policy and the White House's failure to coordinate effectively include a series of highly publicized failures in Somalia in 1993, as well as the botched effort to forge a strategy for peace keeping and peace-enforcement (Daalder 1994); the two-year equivocation over Bosnia (Sterling-Folker 1998); and the disorganized and unsystematic fashion by which the decision to seek NATO enlargement occurred (Goldgeier 1998). While the system yielded an effort to chart a new strategy for the post–Cold War world as promulgated in the 1994 White House document *A National Security Strategy of Engagement and Enlargement,* that effort was widely ridiculed as overly general and ambiguous.

By mid-1994, improvements began. Lake asserted himself more as a central coordinator for foreign policy. New White House Chief of Staff Leon Panetta brought greater discipline to the process—and to the president himself—forcing regular foreign policy meetings. Deputy National Security Adviser Sandy Berger strengthened the role and activities of the Deputies Committee to instill greater direction to the administration's foreign policy efforts. Other steps initiated in hopes of shoring up the administration's foreign policy performance included elevating Vice President Gore to an increasingly visible foreign policy role in the months that followed (Devroy and Barr 1995; Sciolino and Purdum 1995). The efforts paid off as President Clinton was able to complete his first term with a series of foreign policy achievements (North Korea, Haiti, trade, the Dayton

Accords) that contrasted well with the miscues of the first eighteen months.

With the onset of a second term, Christopher, Lake and Perry all departed, to be replaced by Madeleine Albright, the first female secretary of state, Berger, who moved up from Deputy NSA to NSA, and William Cohen, the former maverick Republican Senator from Maine, who took over the defense secretary's position. This *"ABC" club* moved quickly to solidify a more effective NSC system.

While the essential structures remained constant, several changes prompted most observers to agree that the administration had corrected many of the problems of the first term. One major change was simply Clinton's improved discipline and engagement on foreign policy matters. Albright and Cohen also helped to strengthen the system. As secretary of state, Albright was more aggressive than Christopher, and was also a much better public spokesperson. At the same time, Albright generally supported Berger's strong role, noting at one point "As far as I am concerned, a strong national security adviser is very important for a strong secretary of state" (Perlez 1999). Cohen's experience and reputation, as well as his bipartisan appeal, provided effective leadership at the Pentagon and in NSC meetings. In addition to his cautious, steady approach to security matters, Cohen also worked well with NSA Berger and Secretary of State Albright, although he and Albright frequently disagreed on issues related to the use of U.S. military force, as in Bosnia and Kosovo (Harris 1997b; Lancaster 2000).

The most significant change, however, involved the new NSA. Berger and his first deputy, James Steinberg, substantially improved the functioning and central coordination of the NSC system. Stressing process and consensus-building, Berger soon emerged as the steady hand behind the wheel. According to administration officials, behind the public profiles of Albright and Cohen, Berger became "the most influential policy maker on a day-to-day basis" (Harris 1999). Another former official called him "chief coordinator and adviser to the president . . . the glue that holds the foreign policy team together" (Heilbrunn 1998). Fundamental to this greater control and coordination was Berger's "insistence on involvement in virtually every important detail of foreign policy" (Harris 1999). Consistent with this change, the Principals Committee became a more central locus of decision making than before (National Security Council Project 2000).

Berger's emergence as the linchpin to the improved NSC system rested on several actions. First, he began his leadership of the system by ordering a review of the administration's foreign policy principles and goals in order to instill a sense of direction (Heilbrunn 1998). Building on his own experiences as deputy national security adviser in the first term, Berger also improved policy coordination and planning by strengthening the activities of the Deputies Committee (National Security Council Project 2000). Regarded in the second term as the "chief operating committee for American foreign policy," this committee held daily meetings chaired by Steinberg, a practice that continued under Steinberg's successor, Lieutenant General Donald L. Kerrick (a veteran of the NSC staff). Related to this, the NSC staff itself was expanded to over 200 proessionals spread among nineteen regional and functional offices in order to increase its ability to coordinate and oversee policy (Patterson 2000).

The rise of Berger and his NSC staff as the locus of foreign policy was accompanied by waning policy influence from the foreign policy bureaucracy, especially the State Department. Most observers agreed that, while Albright began the second term with the highest profile of the foreign policy team, her influence declined dramatically thereafter. Despite her continued visibility on foreign policy issues, her role in policy formulation was much more limited. A former member of Clinton's NSC staff asserted that "her weight as secretary of state in the determination of foreign policy appears less than at any time in the Clinton Administration, including Secretary of State Warren Christopher's term" (quoted in

Perlez 1999). Another observer suggested that Albright had "become the errand boy of foreign policy rather than the conceptualizer of it" (quoted in Lancaster 2000). This diminished role became especially apparent after the Kosovo operations in the spring of 1999 (Perlez 1999; Lancaster 2000). Consequently, another challenge for Berger was to maintain collegial and cooperative relationships with Albright and Cohen even as he asserted himself in foreign policy. Signs of tension, especially between Albright and Berger, were apparent, especially after Kosovo, as Albright was increasingly bypassed in policy making, appearances before the press, interaction with members of Congress, and, eventually, in policy implementation (for example, Harris 1999; Perlez 1999; Lancaster 2000). To control these tensions, Berger took several steps to nurture the "ABC" relationship. In addition to regular meetings of the Principals Committee, Berger, Albright, and Cohen met at least once a week for lunch together, and held a breakfast meeting with other members of the Principals Committee every week as well. During significant events, they also held "near daily strategy sessions," always at the White House and always chaired by Berger (Harris 1997b; Harris 1999). In addition, the three worked out a set of principles to guide their work together and in the public eye; these principles emphasized respect, public solidarity, and open, direct communication (Patterson 2000).

These efforts aided Berger immeasurably to control "the historic antagonism between national security advisers and secretaries of State and Defense" as he consolidated decision making in the White House and placed himself at the center of the NSC system (Harris 1999). The consequence was a smoother, more focused policy-making process based on Clinton's engagement and Berger's management skills and consensus-building. To the extent that the Clinton Administration could point to a record of progress at the end of its second term on issues such as peace in the Middle East and Northern Ireland, conflict in the Balkans, engagement with China, revitalizing and enlarging NATO, and other areas, it was in large measure due the greater competence of the NSC system in the second term.

The Past as Prologue At the start of 2001, the son of the forty-first president assumed the office of the presidency. In a contentious election, George W. Bush, former Governor of Texas, narrowly defeated Vice President Al Gore in the Electoral College (having lost the popular vote to Gore) and assembled a foreign policy team for the twenty-first century. The new president leaned heavily on his father's foreign policy personnel, first selecting former Secretary of Defense Dick Cheney as his vice president. Cheney also headed his transition team. As his national security adviser, Bush named a member of his father's NSC staff, Condoleeza Rice. Rice, a foreign policy adviser to Bush during the 2000 campaign, was reputed to be " a good manager and an honest broker of ideas" (Sciolino 2000). For his secretary of state, Bush selected Colin Powell, former NSA for Reagan and chair of the Joint Chiefs of Staff for Bush and the first year of the Clinton Administration. Well-known for his conservative views on the uses of the American military, Powell tackled the challenge of integrating the political and economic aspects of U.S. foreign policy into his expertise on security. As secretary of defense Bush named Donald Rumsfeld, who had served in that capacity under President Gerald Ford.

Unsurprisingly, in National Security Presidential Directive 1 (February 13, 2001), the new Bush Administration structured its foreign policy system along the lines of the first Bush Administration. Like Clinton, along with the usual NSC members, Bush also included the secretary of the treasury, U.S. representative to the United Nations, the assistant to the president for economic policy, the chief of staff, and the counsel to the president. Serving this council was the now-traditional three-tiered interagency structure centralized in the White House:

a Principals Committee, a Deputies Committee, and a series of eleven regional and functional policy coordinating committees. The president or vice president chairs the NSC meeting, the National Security Adviser or her deputy chairs the Principals and Deputies committees, and different personnel at the assistant secretary rank chair the policy coordinating committees.

However, the overall size of the NSC staff was reduced by over thirty percent (to 70 staffers) and the structure was initially simplified. The Clinton administration practice of having a legislative affairs and communications function in the NSC staff was ended, with both handled by the political staff of the White House. Finally, a new deputy national security adviser for international economic issues was appointed and tasked with coordinating with the National Economic Council (Daalder and Destler 2001).

Over its first year, the Bush NSC system experienced several changes. One concerned the role of Condoleeza Rice. Rice initially described her "insider" role as "working the seams, stitching the connections together tightly. . . providing the glue for many, many agencies and instruments the United States is now deploying around the world" (Daalder and Destler 2001). Over time, however, Rice took up a more visible and operational role, including a highly assertive presence in the public arena. Additionally, she played her position just down the hall from the Oval Office into a role that went beyond the "traffic cop" description she initially offered. As one observer noted: "Bush wants his info whittled down to one-page memos, and she writes them; he likes one-person oral briefings, and she provides them. He doesn't want to hear a cacophony of competing voices; she ensures that disputes are resolved before they reach him. And Rice hangs out with the First Family" (McGeary 2001). Hence, while a number of observers thought that Rice was taking a back seat to others early in the administration, by the end of the first year she had carved out a more traditional position as NSA.

One of those individuals to whom Rice was said to be taking a back seat was Vice President Dick Cheney, who emerged as a critical force in the Bush NSC system. With the president's blessing, Cheney assembled a sort of mini-NSC staff in his own office, and was delegated far greater influence on foreign policy than previous vice presidents (Schmitt 2001b). In fact, within the first month of the administration, rumors circulated that Cheney might even chair the Principals Committee, effectively removing that key role from the national security adviser's control. However, in National Security Presidential Directive 1, Bush placed Rice in that role. Nevertheless, "Cheney installed himself as overseer of defense and foreign policy portfolios, and sits in on the weekly lunches held by Rice, Rumsfeld, and Powell" (McGeary 2001). President Bush viewed Cheney as an honest broker—like most NSAs—and relied on him more heavily in foreign affairs than most previous presidents.

Another development involved the emergence of rivals in the upper echelon of administration officials. We discuss this in more detail in chapter 11, but the issue is worth noting briefly here as well, as it impacted the functioning of the NSC system. Early in the administration's first year, disagreements and struggles for role and influence emerged, with Powell and Rumsfeld the principal antagonists (Perlez 2001c; Wastell 2001). Throughout the spring of 2001, for example, Colin Powell was dealt a series of embarrassments on issues such as sanctions on Iraq, relations between North and South Korea, and the Kyoto accords on global climate change as the White House endorsed the positions held by others in the administration and backed away from his policy statements (Wastell 2001). Powell also initially appeared to be outside the loop on the administration's commitment to national missile defense. Rumsfeld, supported by Cheney and Rice, consistently pressed for firmer, often more unilateralist, positions. While the September 11 attacks dampened the disputes, it did not eliminate them entirely (see chapter 11 for more discussion of this point). One observer even suggested that George W. Bush's administration resembled a hybrid of his father's and Ronald Reagan's: a collegial group (like the first Bush administration) divided into moderate and hard-line factions (like Reagan's) (Perlez 2001c).

The September 11 attacks had other effects on the NSC system as well. First, the administration's embrace of a military response led to an even greater role and voice for Rumsfeld and the Defense Department. The new-found focus on terrorism also led to some shuffling and reorganization designed to bring that issue into greater focus. A new NSC office for counterterrorism was established to better coordinate U.S. policy efforts, while an Office of Homeland Defense headed by former Pensylvania Governor Tim Ridge was also established in the White House to coordinate overall U.S. homeland security efforts. Parallel to that step, a Homeland Security Council, chaired by the director of the Office of Homeland Security, was also developed to mirror the National Security Council and bring together the major agencies and other stakeholders to manage the development and implementation of homeland security policies. Additionally, the Bush administration's penchant for orderly, deliberate procedures and structures gave way to more informal machinery, in much the same way that the first Bush administration had supplemented its formal with an informal system. As Paul Light observed late in 2001, the more improvisational system was "an organized ad hocracy." Interwoven coalitions handled shared tasks and clear lines of authority eroded (Milbank and Graham 2001).

Consequently, the challenges facing Rice as the NSA formally tasked with running the system were substantial. Even with her increased visibility and role, an assertive vice president, an experienced secretary of defense, and a high-profile secretary of state challenged her ability to control and coordinate foreign policy. Rivalries between advisers and agencies constituted formidable obstacles for an effective system. New voices in the war on terrorism further complicated matters. Maintaining an organized structure and process to ensure careful formulation and implementation of foreign policy became even more difficult.

Summary: Presidential Leadership and the NSC System As the preceding review suggests, the evolving NSC system has become the central structure for presidential leadership in U.S. foreign policymaking. Among the patterns that emerge, several stand out. First, the NSC system is very much a creature of presidential preference. Over time, it has been tailored and personalized to individual styles and needs, reflecting its central role as an extension of presidential authority over the foreign policy bureaucracy. As Colin Powell has explained, "at the end of the day, the duty of the National Security Council staff and the [NSA] is to mold themselves to the personality of the president. And that is why it has to remain a flexible organization with no statutory organization or devices in it. . . . The NSC has to mold itself to the will and desire and feelings of the president. . . . [I]f he's satisfied, that's all that counts" (National Security Council Project 1999b). At the same time, the development suggests that the system works best with an attentive president who is engaged in the process. As former NSA Brent Scowcroft observed, "the NSC system was really developed to serve an activist president in foreign policy. . . . I don't know that the system works all that well when you don't have the president there all the time, because by himself the national security adviser can't really do it" (National Security Council Project 1999b).

Additionally, the NSC system has grown substantially as a White House institution, especially through the evolution of the NSC staff into the president's personal foreign policy advisers and coordinators. From its early days as a little-used advisory board with a tiny staff to handle paperwork, an *NSC bureaucracy* has evolved to serve the needs of presidential decision making and policy coordination. Far from the collection of cabinet officials that originally comprised the NSC, the "system" that evolved instead relies on the national security adviser and a professional staff to manage a complex interagency process. Despite some inclinations to the contrary (for example, Reagan and Carter), this *personal State Department* has become the core of foreign policy making in every administration since Johnson. Indeed, two experienced observers recently suggested that "the NSC has become more like an agency than a presidential staff," to the detriment of both (Daalder and Destler 2000).

As the role of the NSA and NSC staff has grown with the development of the NSC system, a number of tensions have arisen that have required attention. Most notable of these are the persistent rivalries among key members, including those between the NSA and the secretary of state and between the NSC staff and the State Department. Although the NSC was established in part to manage the rivalries between departments and agencies, it has fueled these new tensions. Reflecting on the development of the NSC since the 1950s, Frank Carlucci asserted, "these tensions between the national security adviser and the secretary [of] state seem to run through every administration." Brent Scowcroft concurs, noting "they're inevitable in a way" (National Security Council Project 1999b).

Those tensions bring us back to the issue of the role of the NSA. As suggested earlier, a kind of consensus has developed over the preferred nature of that role (see Focus 10.1), but it is still hard to implement. A recent gathering of former national security advisers confirmed the consensus, stressing the need for a low-profile honest broker committed to the process first and to advising second, and out of the business of operational activities. According to Scowcroft, "My sense is that in order for the system to work, you first have to establish yourself in the confidence of your colleagues to convince them you are not going to pull fast ones on them. That means

when you are in there with the president alone, which you are more than anybody else, that you will represent them fairly. . . . And after you have done that, then you are free to be an adviser" (National Security Council Project 1999b). A former NSC staff member from the first Bush administration put it this way: "The NSA has to have two hats. . . . [T]he first has to be the management hat, and everyone has to feel the process is legitimate. . . . His first responsibility has got to be the whole. But he can still have his own voice so long as everyone around there has confidence that he doesn't get so persuaded by his own voice that he's no longer a legitimate broker" (National Security Council Project 1999a). Easier said than done, if history is any guide.

The evolution of the NSC system suggests a kind of pendulum of reactions as succeeding administrations responded to the problems, strengths, and weaknesses of the systems utilized by their predecessors. Inexorably, it seems, these pendulum swings zeroed in on the need for a White House-centered approach to ensure presidential foreign policy leadership, the need for a strong but collegial national security adviser to manage the process and act as honest-broker, and the need for presidential attention and engagement. The NSC itself today bears little resemblance to its ancestry. "Today most people asked about the NSC would think of the national security *adviser* and his small *staff* in the West Wing and Old Executive Office Building. In Ike's day the NSC was the president in council or, at a minimum, a reference to the NSC principals—the vice president and the secretaries of state and defense" (Prados 1991). What today is better conceived as the *National Security Council system* is nonetheless critically important. How to make both the council and the assistant for national security affairs most effective is now the issue, as neither the wisdom nor determination of presidents to exercise control over American foreign policy from the White House is any longer in question.

Other Executive Office Functions: Managing Economic Affairs

Before leaving the presidential subsystem, mention should be made of other units within the Executive Office which, along with the NSC, are at the immediate disposal of the president and thus contribute to presidential leadership in foreign policy making. Principal among them are the offices and personnel responsible for economic and budgetary decision making, policy arenas that the end of the Cold War and budgetary issues have pushed to the forefront of the presidential subsystem's agenda.

Managing the Budget The largest, with over 500 staff members, is the *Office of Management and Budget* (OMB). OMB has responsibility for reviewing budgetary and other legislative requests coming from departments and agencies and for examining legislation passed by Congress before it is signed into law by the president. It also assists in devising plans for the organization and management of executive branch functions. Those tasks assign the OMB a potentially critical voice in ensuring that agencies' plans and programs are consistent with presidential priorities.

Different presidents have employed different budgetary and management techniques to realize their objectives. In the early 1960s, after Robert McNamara introduced the Planning, Programming, and Budgeting System (PPBS) into the Defense Department, Lyndon Johnson ordered that PPBS be applied throughout the government as a procedure for making more-informed budgetary choices. President Nixon emphasized "management by objectives." The approach entailed assigning priorities to competing objectives and choosing some programs over others. As concern for restraining public spending mounted, Jimmy Carter implemented zero-based budgeting (ZBB), which required that each program be justified anew each year. It did not prove effective, however, in stemming the flow of public spending.

Fueled in part by the priority the Reagan administration gave to rebuilding the nation's defensive posture, budget deficits by the mid-1980s topped $200 billion annually. As the OMB attempted to cope with the deficit, it found that the largest item in the budget—national defense—involved other players with a stronger suit. Rather than challenge a steamroller, the politically wise strategy was to trim at the margins rather than launch a frontal attack. The result, however, is that the OMB was notably less effective in imposing a presidential imprimatur on the nation's foreign policy spending priorities during the 1980s than might have been expected.

By the time George H. W. Bush moved into the Oval Office the government's flow of red ink was too great to ignore. Despite a "no new taxes" campaign pledge, Bush found it necessary to reach a politically contentious (and eventually costly) budget agreement with Congress. Designed to curb federal spending, it exposed defense as well as social programs to the budgetary ax. Bush's controversial OMB director, Richard G. Darman, often found himself in the unenviable position of the messenger people wanted to kill.

During the Clinton Administration, the OMB was directed first by Leon E. Panetta, and then by Alice M. Rivlin, Panetta's deputy until 1994 when the former congressman became Clinton's chief of staff. Jacob J. Lew, Rivlin's deputy, succeeded her as director in May 1998. These directors became leading advocates of strict budgetary discipline in an administration that promised budget reductions but found them difficult (see Woodward 1994). Meanwhile, the "management" side of the OMB, already a low priority, was dealt twin blows as proposed reforms of the office promised to merge its dual functions into one and as the administration's "reinventing government" initiative promised dramatic reductions in the size of the federal bureaucracy. "Total Quality Management" (TQM) became the core concept in this latest effort to reform management practices in the federal government (see also Chapter 13). Vice President Al

Gore, architect of the management reform effort, promoted technological innovation as the key to a more responsive government.

In 2001, George W. Bush named Mitchell Daniels to be director of the OMB. A former staffer for Senator Richard Lugar and vice president for Eli Lilly and Company, Daniels also served in the Reagan White House. Under Daniels' leadership, the Bush OMB was charged with a role in all budget, policy, legislative, regulatory, procurement, and management issues. These responsibilities, the size of the federal budget, the burgeoning costs of existing entitlement programs, and the continuing demands for new expenditures assure that the OMB will remain a major player in the presidential subsystem.

Managing Economic Policy Over time, economics has become a more central element of U.S. foreign policy. The White House has turned to several different components of the presidential subsystem to formulate and coordinate economic policy.

The Council of Economic Advisers To assist in the economics of economic policy making, the president has relied on the *Council of Economic Advisers* (CEA). Together with officials from the OMB and the Treasury Department, the council makes economic forecasts on which the income and expenditures of the federal government are based. It has no operational responsibilities. Instead, it serves exclusively in an advisory capacity to the president (Porter 1983). The council itself comprises three presidential appointees, usually drawn from the ranks of the most respected academic economists. The council's chairperson becomes the administration's senior economist and is responsible for establishing the positions the council takes. One of two remaining members is typically assigned international responsibilities.

Created in 1946 with an eye toward short-run economic stabilization, today the CEA advises the president on the entire range of domestic and foreign economic policy issues; the value of the dollar and the U.S. trade balance are among them. The council also plays a role in managing the delicate relationship between the president and the Federal Reserve Board, an independent federal agency with broad powers over monetary policy (Feldstein 1992; Solomon 1994). As we saw in Chapter 7, monetary policy exerts a direct impact on the dollar and trade balance. Channels of influence available to the CEA include face-to-face meetings between the president and the chair of the council, interaction with the secretary of the treasury and other senior personnel, membership on the National Economic Council, involvement of the CEA members and its staff in interagency groups, testimony before Congress, and public commentary (Feldstein 1992). The CEA also prepares the influential *Economic Report of the President,* presented annually to Congress, which is widely used inside and outside of government.

The Office of the United States Trade Representative For assistance in trade policy, presidents have relied on the *Office of the United States Trade Representative.* Headed by a presidential appointee who carries the rank of ambassador as well as membership in the cabinet, the U.S. trade representative (USTR) exercises primary responsibility for developing and coordinating the implementation of international trade policy and acting as the principal trade spokesperson in the U.S. government. The office directs American participation in trade negotiations with other nations, including bilateral talks, such as the Structural Impediments Initiative and "framework" negotiations with Japan, and multilateral ventures, such as the Uruguay Round of GATT negotiations concluded in 1993.

The trade representative originated in the Kennedy administration as the Special Trade Representative. The USTR achieved cabinet status during the Ford administration, when it wrested control over multilateral trade affairs from the State Department, and the office became a major player in multilateral negotiations during the Carter administration. A subsequent reorganization of the trade office in 1980 gave the USTR a greater voice among the many government agencies involved in determining overall American trade policy. President Reagan pledged that his trade representative would continue to play a dominant role in orchestrating the nation's trade policies. Growing trade deficits led to efforts to negotiate voluntary export restrictions (VERs) covering particular products with Japan and others in an effort to ameliorate the adverse effects of the strong dollar (see Chapter 7). Although Reagan had announced his trade representative would play the dominate role in orchestrating U.S. trade policy, in practice the USTR proved too weak to do anything more than negotiate market-sharing agreements with others. Instead, benign neglect characterized the administration's general approach to trade policy as "needed coordination of monetary, trade, and industrial policy between the Treasury Department, the USTR, and the Commerce Department [was] sorely lacking" (Stokes 1992–1993).

Congress became increasingly agitated with Reagan's unwillingness to take corrective action to deal with the nation's burgeoning trade deficit. In 1986 it began consideration of a new trade bill which eventually became the Omnibus Trade and Competitiveness Act of 1988. This assertiveness reflected congressional sensitivity to the changing American position in the world political economy. The effort also required broad involvement of many players: the drafting of the 1988 Omnibus Trade and Competitiveness Act, for example, included 23 committees and subcommittees in 17 subconferences and involved 199 conferees, more than a third of Congress (Stokes 1994, 1430).

The new trade law contained no radical new departures from existing U.S. trade policy, despite many highly protectionist measures figuring prominently in the deliberations during its long gestation period. The *Super 301* provision was perhaps the exception. As noted in Chapter 7,

Super 301 required the president to identify countries engaged in unfair trade practices and negotiate remedies with them. The USTR was charged with that responsibility, effectively solidifying the office's role as the government's principal trade policy actor in a way not previously done.

Because the Bush administration was uncomfortable with the confrontational, unilateralist thrust of Super 301 and did little to push it, Bush's USTR (Carla A. Hills) fared little better than Reagan's (Clayton Yeutter) in devising a governmentwide response to the trade challenges the United States faced. However, "rather than leading trade policy, a bureaucratically weak and directionless USTR . . . often [became] a victim of the political pressures around it." That "reactive stance" often resulted in "bad trade policy" in which "U.S. interests . . . suffered" (Stokes 1992–1993).

Given President Clinton's emphasis on economic policy, both domestic and foreign, trade policy was destined to be an administration priority. Clinton named Mickey Kantor, a California attorney skilled in regulatory problems and chair of the Clinton-Gore 1992 campaign, as his trade representative. Kantor quickly assumed a high-profile role in a series of contentious trade issues involving the European Union, NAFTA, the Uruguay Round, and Japan. His assertive personal style and aggressive policy postures offended some both within the United States and abroad, but he had a reputation for loyalty to the president and reflected the administration's preference for a posture of aggressive unilateralism on trade issues. Kantor was replaced in 1996 with long-time USTR staff member Charlene Barshevsky. Under Barshevsky's leadership, the office of the USTR continued its aggressive efforts in bilateral trade relations with Japan, Europe, and others. Barshevsky was also a principal proponent of and decision maker in the efforts to extend U.S.-Chinese trade relations. She played a pivotal roles in engineering the Permanent Normal Trade Relations agreement with China in 1999, selling it to the

U.S. Congress in 2000, and negotiating China's entry into the World Trade Organization.

George W. Bush turned to Robert Zoellick for the USTR position. Zoellick formerly served the first Bush Administration as Under Secretary of State for Economic and Business Affairs and Counselor to the Secretary, and the Reagan Administration's Department of the Treasury. Under Bush, Zoellick was given cabinet rank and made the lead policy maker and spokesperson for American trade policy. Reputed to be a "master strategist and policy analyst," Zoellick devoted his initial efforts at securing fast-track authority from the Congress for the rapid negotiation of additional trade agreements (Blustein 2001), and coordinating the start of a new round of trade talks in the World Trade Organization.

The National Economic Council Different presidents have devised different means to seek top-level coordination of foreign economic policy making (see Cohen 1994). President Clinton's major innovation was the *National Economic Council* (NEC), created by executive order as the economic policy counterpart to the National Security Council. Creation of the council symbolized Clinton's determination to show that economic policy would be at least equal in importance to national security policy during his administration.

The NEC built on efforts by previous presidents. Twenty years earlier President Nixon had launched a Council on International Economic Policy in an unsuccessful effort to centralize control over foreign economic policy making. Ford created an Economic Policy Board, chaired by the secretary of the treasury, whose purpose was to oversee the entire range of foreign and domestic economic policy. Carter followed with a similarly structured Economic Policy Group, but eventually relied on a special presidential representative to facilitate policy coordination. During the Reagan administration the Cabinet Council on Economic Affairs was given responsibility over economic policy, and the administration's

NSC apparatus eventually contained a Senior Interagency Group for International Economic Policy. The Bush administration adopted similar practices.

Clinton's National Economic Council was therefore simply the most ambitious mechanism for top-level coordination of foreign economic policy making. As one observer noted, prior to Clinton the tendency was to subordinate trade concerns to foreign policy or strategic interests. In contrast, "With the creation of the National Economic Council in 1993, America's international economic interests have become a major pillar of U.S. foreign policy" (Stokes 1994).

Like the National Security Council, the National Economic Council was intended to coordinate the cabinet departments and agencies with interests and responsibilities in economic policy; to advise the president on economic policy decisions; and to monitor their implementation. To accomplish these tasks, the NEC relied on a staff of about thirty to manage its responsibilities in both the domestic and foreign economic policy arenas. Moreover, since the assistant and deputy assistant had roles on the NSC's Principals Committee and Deputies Committee, the NEC and NSC staff cooperated. In fact, to facilitate that cooperation, Robert E. Rubin, head of the NEC and and then-National Security Adviser Anthony Lake agreed to share staff for international economic matters, who would then report to both men (Destler 1996). Also, like Lake, Rubin viewed his role as an "honest broker" in representing the views of executive branch departments and agencies in White House decision making. Rubin was succeeded in 1995 by Laura D'Andrea Tyson (former chair of the Council of Economic Advisers), who gave way to Gene Sperling in 1996.

In practice, much of the NEC's work, like that of the National Security Council, occurred below the level of "the principals" (cabinet and other members of the NEC) by their deputies and in interagency working groups dealing with particular issues. These ranged from energy economics to trade and technology policy and beyond. In much of this the NEC's role was to ensure that political considerations were aired along with economic ones. "The NEC gives me a sense of where politics are going both internally and externally," declared OMB director Leon Panetta. That is not always an easy task, however. As NEC deputy W. Bowman Cutter put it, "It is a law that the economics of an issue always run exactly counter to the politics."

During Clinton's first term, the NEC was central to several foreign economic policy issues, including the North American Free Trade Agreement in 1993 and the completion of the Uruguay Round in 1994. After initially taking a back seat to the State Department on China and its most-favored-nation (MFN) status in 1993, the NEC assumed a central role in 1994. It was also key in U.S.-Japan relations in this period.

When Rubin moved on to take up the position of Secretary of the Treasury, his successor, Laura Tyson, had much less success. A slow transition and several months of suspended meetings forced the NEC out if its modest role into the background. In the breach, other offices stepped forward to handle such crises as the Mexican peso collapse in late 1994. Moreover, Rubin continued to assert himself on international economic matters from his new position, making Tyson's role even more difficult. By most accounts, the NEC simply receded into the background until Tyson managed to carve out a role on trade issues in mid-1996 (Destler 1996).

When Tyson stepped down, Gene Sperling took over. Most observers expected the NEC role to again decline, but, instead, Sperling helped solidify its place on matters of both domestic and international policy. For instance, Sperling and the NEC were the central coordinators for the U.S. response to the Asian financial crises of 1997–1998, working closely with Treasury Secretary Bob Rubin. Additionally, Sperling worked closely with USTR Charlene Barshevsky on the China-WTO-Permanent

Normal Trade Relations agreements in 1999–2000. Along with these contributions, Sperling's NEC was the locus of the administration's efforts on the budget and overall economic policy in the second term as well.

The prominence of Clinton's NEC was in part a function of Clinton's own preferences and priorities. For Clinton, "the interplay between trade, technology, educational training, economics and jobs [seemed to engage him] intellectually and animate him politically" (Friedman 1994b). Still, the rapid globalization of the world political economy, which Clinton's policies encouraged, has elevated the importance of economic issues and blurred the distinction between foreign and domestic economic policy. Today, more departments and agencies with important domestic roots and often powerful congressional allies have a greater stake in international economic policy. Clinton sought to give clear and consistent direction on economic issues from the White House, thus managing interagency politics that otherwise would dominate the process and the outcome.

George W. Bush found the same imperative when he assumed the office of the presidency. He retained the NEC and named Lawrence Lindsay, former member of Reagan's Council of Economic Advisers and George H. W. Bush's White House policy staff, as assistant to the president for economic policy. Additionally, he established a new deputy national security adviser for international economic policy to coordinate with the NEC. Under Lindsay, while keeping a low profile, the NEC for the Bush administration coordinated economic policy making on domestic and international issues and monitored economic policy implementation to ensure its consistency with the White House agenda. For example, after the September 11 attacks on the United States, Lindsay played the key role in monitoring the impact of the attacks on the U.S. economy and recommending responses to the problems faced by New York City and a number of industries.

PRESIDENTIAL LEADERSHIP IN THE TWENTY-FIRST CENTURY

The president and the presidency are central to U.S. foreign policy making. No other governmental source of foreign policy has the combination of stature, resources, authority, and opportunity. But, will the presumption of presidential leadership with which we began this chapter persist into the new century?

There are good reasons to expect continued foreign policy leadership by the president. As suggested at the outset of this chapter, the broad powers and opportunities granted to the chief executive will continue to allow the president to act on constitutional roles as chief executive, commander-in-chief, and chief diplomat, and the less formal, but still vital roles of *chief communicator, chief legislator,* and, perhaps, *chief lobbyist.* Together these will provide occasion for presidents' efforts to forge foreign policy. Furthermore, regardless of the occupant of the position, the president is likely to play a vital role in foreign policy agenda-setting—the process of identifying problems, setting priorities, and the like. As our review of the NSC system indicates, ordering policy reviews, requiring the development of options on one issue and not another, and assigning responsibilities to certain executive branch structures and agencies rather than others give the president the capability to influence heavily the "list of subjects or problems to which government officials, and people outside of government closely associated with those officials, are paying some serious attention at any given time" (Kingdon 1995). Although other players can influence the agenda, if the president chooses to address an issue, others must as well.

Just as clearly, presidential command of the foreign policy departments, agencies, and personnel, along with the continued importance of the United States in the international system, provide the White House with the ability to initiate action. Although this is closely related to the *agenda-setting power* possessed by the White House, this capability to take action enables the White House to force other players to respond, and constitutes another source of presidential leadership not likely to disappear in the twenty-first century. George W. Bush's leadership in response to the September 11 attacks nicely illustrates this capacity.

Some would argue that the fundamental nature of the international system itself supports continued presidential leadership in the twenty-first century. According to this view, the rise of presidential leadership occurred in response to demands, foreign and domestic, to which the other branches of government, notably Congress, could not respond adequately. That was most emphatically true in the foreign policy domain—and it remains so. The reasons inhere in the nature of the international system, the central element in the theory of political realism evident in American foreign policy thinking since its founding, but especially so since World War II, during which presidential government and the imperial presidency became the operative norms (and constitutional challenges). As one analyst argued:

> The role played by the executive in foreign affairs . . . is rooted in the requirements imposed on the nation-state by the potentially anarchic quality of the international system. . . . Policy takes precedence over politics because the international system both severely limits the sensible choices a country can make and shapes the processes by which these decisions are reached.
>
> (PETERSON 1994, 231–232)

According to this logic, the very structure of the international system may alter the agenda of American politics and priorities, but it will not alter the responsibility of the president to respond to the challenges and opportunities posed by the external environment. Again the changed international content after September 11 supports this observation.

There are, however, other aspects of the policy-making environment that would seem to limit presidential leadership, or at least generate challenges to it. Given the fundamentally fragmented nature of power in the American political system (that is, the governmental sources), one could also argue that the ability of the president to lead during the past years depended as much on policy agreement among the different actors as anything else. Hence, during the first two decades of the Cold War, the fundamental agreement embodied in the Cold War foreign policy consensus generated a much greater tendency toward executive branch (especially White House) foreign policy leadership in the making of U.S. foreign policy than previously had been the case. As one analyst concluded, "congressional acquiescence to executive initiative during the Cold War was often the result of policy agreement" (Carter 1998). Once that basic policy agreement—on the roles, threat, interests, and instruments—began to erode roughly two decades into the Cold War, White House leadership also diminished. In particular, the Vietnam experience destroyed much of the Cold War consensus, and the ensuing policy disagreements largely ended the so-called "era of bipartisanship," making presidential leadership more difficult (Melanson 1996; Destler, Gelb, and Lake 1984; Holsti and Rosenau 1984).

Where does that leave us today? If the Cold War era contributed to consensus and executive leadership, during the past decade we have witnessed a greater fragmentation of leadership. The combination of additional voices from inside and outside government, less consensus, and more varied issues continued the pattern of challenges to presidential leadership by Congress. Interests are more difficult to define, much less agreed upon; issues are no longer clearly foreign or domestic, but are often *intermestic*—with both domestic and foreign content and consequences—which dramatically changes the stakes for stakeholders outside the White House. In short, the more subtle, varied, and complicated environment of a rapidly globalizing world in which threat is less readily recognizable would seem to prompt challenges to presidential leadership.

Finally, our discussion of the past fifty years or so of White House efforts to exercise foreign policy leadership suggests that other variables will condition the effectiveness of that leadership. Our review of the evolution of the NSC system drives the conclusion that part of the president's ability to lead depends, first, on establishing and using structures that allow leadership. Moreover, presidential leadership also depends on staffing those structures with the "right" people. Selection of appointees and staff, decision and advisory structures, management of time and information, and other aspects related to the management of the executive branch obviously matter. The record of the past half-century suggests that not every president succeeds in these areas; failure to do so inhibits leadership opportunities. Beyond structure and personnel, personality, style, attentiveness, interest, initiative, and other varying personal characteristics produce different results in the exercise of presidential leadership. (We address presidents' individual characteristics in greater detail in Chapter 14.) Our review of the NSC systems indicates that presidents must be engaged, attentive, and informed to exercise leadership. Indeed, our review may even suggest that no system will work *unless* the president is involved.

Factors related to the policy context or situation will also impact presidential leadership. For example, crisis situations tend to involve presidential leadership, while noncrisis situations tend to involve a broader set of policy actors. It is also widely agreed that intermestic issues are considerably less subject to presidential leadership, prompting instead the involvement of Congress, interest groups, and others. Moreover, variation in policy issue, say from military force to aid to trade to intelligence to others, also prompts changing patterns of role and influence, while different policy instruments also generate similar shifts. Finally, as suggested by Chapters 8 and 9, variation in public opinion, involvement of interest groups, and the media—all of which can stem from the international environment, policy context, and other sources—can also affect the president's ability to lead.

In sum, presidential leadership in twenty-first century foreign policy is not a foregone conclusion. Neither is it the constant that a simple interpretation of the Hilsman model with which we began this chapter would initially suggest. Certainly, continued and direct White House involvement in foreign policy is now a permanent feature of the governmental structures responsible for making and executing American foreign policy. Yet, just as the last century witnessed considerable shifts in foreign policy leadership, from decade to decade, administration to administration, and issue to issue, so too might we expect foreign policy to emerge in a similar fashion in the new century. As the United States continues to seek influence over complex external problems; as established departments and agencies continually strive to protect their own interests in coping with those problems; and as Congress involves itself in international and intermestic matters; the president will be central to, just not necessarily the center of, foreign policy making.

KEY TERMS RELATED TO PRESIDENTIAL LEADERSHIP IN FOREIGN POLICY MAKING

"ABC" club

adhocracy

agenda-setting power

assistant to the president for economic policy

Bureau of the Budget

cabinet

cabinet government

chief communicator

chief diplomat

chief legislator

chief lobbyist

chief negotiator

chief of staff

commander in chief

Council of Economic Advisers

Deputies Committee

doctrine of political questions

Ex Com (Executive Committee of the NSC)

Executive Office of the President (EOP)

gatekeeper

government by inner circle

honest broker

imperial presidency

"inside management" role

institutionalized presidency

interagency processes

interagency working groups (IWGs)

intermestic

invitation to struggle

National Economic Council

national security adviser

National Security Council

National Security Council system

NSC bureaucracy

Office of Management and Budget

"personal State Department"

Policy Coordinating Committees

power to persuade

presidential leadership

presidential preeminence

presidential subsystem

Principals Committee

Situation Room

"Tuesday Lunch"

United States Trade Representative

White House-centered

White House Office

SUGGESTIONS FOR FURTHER READING

Bock, Joseph G. *The White House Staff and the National Security Assistant: Friendship and Friction at the Water's Edge.* New York: Greenwood, 1987.

Bush, George H. W., and Brent Scowcroft. *A World Transformed: The Collapse of the Soviet Empire, the Unification of Germany, Tianenman Square, the Gulf War.* New York: Knopf, 1999.

Daalder, Ivo H. *Getting to Dayton: The Making of America's Bosnia Policy.* Washington, DC: Brookings Institution Press, 2000.

George, Alexander L. *Presidential Decisionmaking in Foreign Policy: The Effective Use of Information and Advice.* Boulder, CO: Westview, 1980.

Halberstam, David. *War in a Time of Peace.* New York: Scribner, 2001.

Haney, Patrick. *Organizing for Foreign Policy Crises: Presidents, Advisers, and the Management of Decision-Making.* Ann Arbor, MI: University of Michigan Press, 1997.

Hyland, William. *Clinton's World: Remaking American Foreign Policy.* Westport, CT: Praeger Publishers, 1999.

Koh, Harold H. *A The National Security Constitution: Sharing Power after the Iran-Contra Affair.* New Haven, CT: Yale University Press, 1990.

Michaels, Judith E. *The President's Call: Executive Leadership from FDR to George Bush.* Pittsburgh, PA: University of Pittsburgh Press, 1997.

Neustadt, Richard E. *Presidential Power and the Modern Presidents: The Politics of Leadership from Roosevelt to Reagan.* New York: Free Press, 1990.

Prados, John. *Keepers of the Keys: A History of the National Security Council from Truman to Bush.* New York: William Morrow, 1991.

Preston, Thomas. *The President and His Inner Circle: Leadership Style and the Advisory Process in Foreign Policy Making.* New York: Columbia University Press, 2001.

Renshon, Stanley A., ed, *The Clinton Presidency: Campaigning, Governing, and the Psychology of Leadership.* Boulder, CO: Westview, 1995.

Shoemaker, Christopher C. *The NSC Staff: Counseling the Council.* Boulder, CO: Westview, 1992.

NOTES

1. Because we discussed interest groups, the general public, and the mass media in Chapters 8 and 9, attention in Chapter 12 to Hilsman's outermost concentric circle will be confined to Congress.

2. Schlesinger (1989a) observes that the framers of the Constitution saw designation of the president as commander in chief "as conferring a merely ministerial function not as creating an independent and additional source of executive authority." As we will see in Chapter 12, this presidential power has figured prominently in the executive-legislative dispute over war powers, especially since the Vietnam war.

3. On constitutional issues, see Fisher (1991), Henkin (1990), Koh (1990), and J. Smith (1989).

4. Crockett v. Reagan, 558 F. Supp. 893 (D.D.C. 1982).

5. Lowry v. Reagan, 676 F. Supp. 333 (D.D.C. 1987).

6. Dellums v. Bush, 752 F. Supp. 1141 (D.D.C. 1990).

7. George (1980) identifies three different presidential management models: competitive, formalistic, and collegial. In the competitive model, the president purposely seeks to promote conflict and competition among his advisers, thus forcing problems to be brought to the president's attention for resolution and decision. Franklin Roosevelt is the only president to have clearly followed it.

Johnson began by emphasizing the competitive approach but gradually moved toward a formalistic model. This model seeks to establish clear lines of authority and to minimize the need for presidential involvement in the politicking among cabinet officials and key advisers. A "chief of staff" often provides a buffer between the president and cabinet heads. Nixon's approach to presidential management took the formalistic model to its extreme. However, Truman and Eisenhower also followed it, and Reagan began that way.

Kennedy is the best illustration of the collegial model, which emphasizes teamwork and group problem solving. The president operates like the hub of a wheel with spokes connecting to individual advisers and department heads, who often act as "generalists" rather than "functional specialists" concerned only with parts of particular problems. Bush and Clinton embraced styles akin to the collegial model.

8. As noted in earlier chapters, the CIA, the Department of Defense, and the Joint Chiefs of Staff were also created by the National Security Act.

9. These rump sessions may explain the apparent incongruity between Eisenhower's emphasis on the NSC system and the widespread belief that Secretary of State Dulles operated as the chief architect of American foreign policy during most of the Eisenhower years (in contrast, see Greenstein 1982, 1994). Dulles's biographer, Townsend Hoopes (1973a), also argues that the close working ties between Eisenhower and Dulles "compromised" Eisenhower's effort to use the NSC system to "orchestrate" the activities of the various foreign policy agencies into a coordinated foreign policy.

10. President Ford (1979) made a similar observation on why he eventually decided he needed a chief of staff: "Because power in Washington is measured by how much access a person has to the president, almost everyone wanted more access that I had access to give." For a study of the relationship between access and influence, see Link and Kegley (1993).

CHAPTER 11

The Foreign Policy Bureaucracy and Foreign Policy Making

The machinery of U.S. foreign policy making and implementation
is in a state of serious disrepair . . . [rendering] U.S. foreign policy
increasingly ill-equipped to shape and respond to the realities
and challenges of the twenty-first century.

STATE DEPARTMENT REFORM:
REPORT OF AN INDEPENDENT TASK FORCE COSPONSORED
BY THE COUNCIL ON FOREIGN RELATIONS
AND THE CENTER FOR STRATEGIC
AND INTERNATIONAL STUDIES, 2001

It's very hard to give policy advice and not somehow
become identified with the policy, or at least have an intellectual
stake in wanting that policy to succeed.

R. JAMES WOOLSEY,
DIRECTOR OF THE CENTRAL INTELLIGENCE AGENCY, 1994

Global activism is a pattern of American foreign policy. In response to international challenges such as the Cold War, the global economy, and, more recently, global terrorism, and in pursuit of U.S. political, economic, military, and social interests, the United States has constructed an elaborate complex of organizations and instruments through which to engage in the world. Recall from Chapters 4 and 5 the United States manifestations at the beginning of the twenty-first century: diplomatic relations with nearly every foreign government; participation in scores of international organizations; billions of dollars in economic and military assistance and sales; military deployments in many parts of the world, and the capacity to strike virtually anywhere else; leadership in a burgeoning international political and military coalition against terrorism; and trade and investment connections with other countries far beyond the nation's proportion of world population. Whose activities are reflected in such involvements? Whose responsibility is it to protect the interests they represent?

The *executive departments* of government, and the political appointees who head them, are at the core of the foreign policy-making process, particularly the Departments of State and Defense. The secretary of state, in principle at least, is the president's foremost foreign policy adviser and the State Department is the agency of government charged with coordinating U.S. activities overseas. The tense international political environment of the post–World War II period, which directed primary emphasis toward security considerations, also made the Defense Department and intelligence community particularly important. In the last two decades or so, other executive agencies have also gained importance in the foreign policy process. Most notably, agencies with responsibilities in international economic affairs, including the Commerce and Treasury departments, have gained greater voices in many foreign policy debates.

In Chapter 10 we drew a distinction between executive branch agencies comprising the second concentric circle of policy making and the presidential subsystem, which makes up the innermost circle. In practice the various secretaries of state, defense, and treasury who serve the nation are simultaneously members of the inner circle as well as heads of the large, complex organizations found in the second concentric circle. These organizations are critically important to those in the innermost circle. The president and his closest advisers must depend on them and on their thou-

sands of career professionals to manage America's day-to-day foreign relations and to implement the decisions of the president and presidential advisers. Hence the scope and magnitude of the responsibilities of major organizations in the second concentric circle require scrutiny.

THE DEPARTMENT OF STATE

As the "first among equals" in the foreign affairs government, the Department of State is the principal agent of the executive branch of government responsible for managing U.S. foreign relations. In 2001, it operated a network of more than 250 posts throughout the world (principally embassies and consulates), plus delegations and missions to international organizations. At home and through these field missions, the State Department engages in a wide range of activities. Its responsibility to coordinate U.S. overseas activity would seem to give it the leadership role in foreign policy. Yet, the most obvious pattern for the Department of State since World War II has been its loss of influence in the formulation of foreign policy. As we will see, there are several factors that account for this, but the department and its personnel continue to grapple with the foreign policy opportunities and challenges of the new century.

Structure and Mission

The State Department is organized in the hierarchical pattern typical of most large organizations, with the secretary of state perched on top of a series of more narrowly defined offices and bureaus that divide the labor within the department. As shown in Figure 11.1, that division reflects the department's orientation to the major geographic regions of the world through its *regional bureaus* under the direction of the under secretary of state for political affairs. Its *functional bureaus* show the necessity to cope with problems that transcend geographic boundaries, such as arms control, nonproliferation, political-military affairs, human

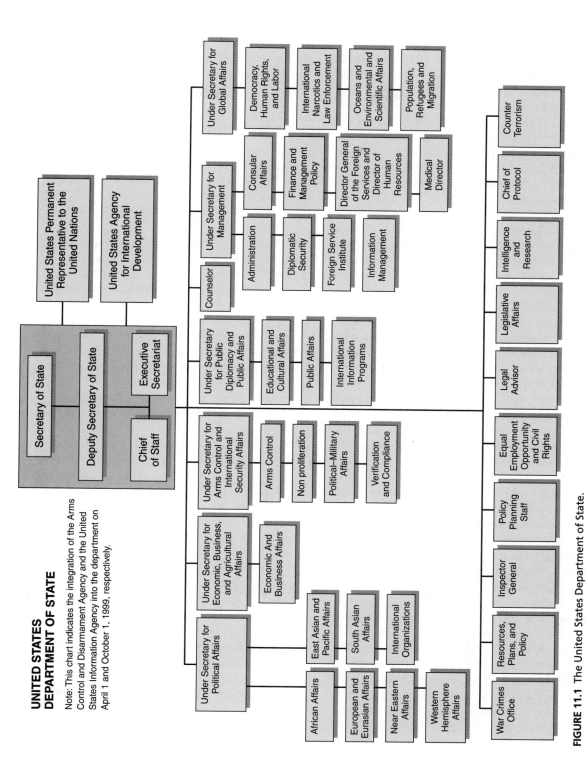

UNITED STATES
DEPARTMENT OF STATE

Note: This chart indicates the integration of the Arms Control and Disarmament Agency and the United States Information Agency into the department on April 1 and October 1, 1999, respectively.

FIGURE 11.1 The United States Department of State.

Source: Department of State website at www.state.gov/www/dept/org_chart.html

rights, international narcotics, the environment, and population and refugees. The department is further staffed through a series of "support" offices to aid in analysis, planning, public affairs, and legislative affairs. The boxes in the figure also account for the 1998 Foreign Affairs Restructuring Act, which folded the functions of the Arms Control and Disarmament Agency, the United States Information Agency, and the United States Agency for International Development into the department (see Chapter 5).

Decision-making responsibility within the State Department itself follows the hierarchical pattern of its organization chart. Indeed, a common criticism of the State Department when it comes to decision making is its rigid hierarchy. Decisions of greatest importance are made by the secretary, the deputy secretary, and the under secretaries who occupy the seventh floor of the State Department offices in the area of Washington, DC, known as Foggy Bottom and who frequently interact with the White House. Routine decisions, important more for policy implementation than development, are often made by the assistant and deputy assistant secretaries. Country directors and "desk officers" within each regional bureau arguably comprise the backbone of the State Department when it comes to coordinating U.S. policy toward particular countries abroad. In practice, however, the responsibilities of the regional bureaus have been greatly diluted by the involvement of several dozen other federal agencies in the management of foreign affairs, whose personnel also staff the overseas embassies (Warwick 1975; Wiarda 2000).

Through this hierarchical structure, department personnel manage much of the day-to-day foreign relations of the United States. They *represent* the United States to other countries as well as convey the viewpoints and preferences of foreign governments and other international actors to the United States; they *negotiate* with foreign and international diplomats; and they analyze and *report* on events and information overseas. Department personnel also *recommend policy,* providing advice in the formulation and reformulation

of initiatives through their participation in interagency groups. In short, the department manages, helps to shape, and implements many aspects of American foreign policy.

The Foreign Service and Its Subculture

Within the State Department itself, the individuals who matter most are the *Foreign Service officers (FSOs),* who accounted (in 2001) for less than 7,000 of the 17,000 employees of the department (it also employs nearly 10,000 foreign nationals working in field missions abroad). This elite corps of *professional diplomats* traditionally holds the most important positions within the State Department (outside of the political appointments made by the president) both at home and abroad.

The popular image of the Foreign Service, based partly on legend as well as historical fact, is that of a remarkably homogeneous diplomatic corps comprising upper-class men from the Northeast with degrees from Ivy League colleges. However, the Foreign Service officers corps has sought to open itself to a broader geographical, educational, ethnic, and socioeconomic spectrum. It has encouraged women and African-Americans to join its ranks, especially after female Foreign Service officers won a class action suit in 1989 against the State Department. The suit charged the department with discriminating against women by hiring more men for the Foreign Service and giving them better career assignments, performance ratings, and honors awards. "Still, if the Foreign Service is no longer a smug men's club, it is more like one than any other part of the U.S. government" (Rubin 1985; see also Holmes 1994; McGlen and Sarkees 1993).

One of the distinctive elements of the Foreign Service is its relatively powerful *organizational subculture,* which is, according to James Q. Wilson (1989), "a persistent, patterned way of thinking about the central tasks of and human relationships within an organization." In fact, this powerful subculture is one of the reasons for the waning of the department's influence since

World War II. It consists of several major characteristics. The first of these stems in part from the Foreign Service's personnel system, separate from the Civil Service to which most federal employees belong. This unique system leads to *elitism.* As a long-time observer noted, "FSOs see themselves as members of an elite corps of talented, nonpartisan, close-knit, and unjustly beleaguered professionals" (Clarke 1989). Consequently, other groups, such as State's Civil Service employees and employees of other agencies, are, by definition, nonelite. Thus the *State 2000* report insightfully cautioned that "We must break down the barriers that risk making us a series of fractured 'we/they' cultures, whether Foreign Service and Civil Service, women and men, or single officers and tandem couples" (U.S. Department of State 1992).

A second key element of the distinctive Foreign Service subculture is its *resistance to outside ideas.* As one officer put it, " 'The Foreign Service officer believes that his is an arcane craft which people on the outside cannot hope to understand.' We listen carefully and politely but seldom change our views" (*Diplomacy for the 70's: A Program of Management Reform for the Department of State* 1970). According to another observer, "the stock in trade of the regular foreign service officers . . . is a large supply of cold water with which to dash ideas that emanate elsewhere or which challenge prevailing professional perspectives" (Rockman 1981). It should come as no surprise that the combination of elitism and resistance to outside ideas work against effective participation in "the rough-and-tumble of bureaucratic politics" (Rockman 1981). Therefore, members of the State Department have been relatively less effective in the interagency working groups that have been so central to American foreign policy making.

A third characteristic of the Foreign Service subculture is the widely held belief that the only experience that is relevant to the activities of the Department of State is experience gained in the Foreign Service. This *parochialism* derives partly from the assignments of the typical Foreign Ser-

vice officer. Viewed as a generalist rather than a specialist, an FSO's career pattern usually involves two- or three-year tours of duty both in Washington and abroad in a variety of operating and functional positions (see Melbourne 1992). Its consequence, especially in combination with the elitism and resistance to outside ideas, is personnel who are overly dismissive, and often disdaining of, ideas, experiences, and expertise gained outside the service.

A fourth characteristic of the subculture is its emphasis on the essence or central *mission* of the department: negotiation, representation, and reporting. "It doesn't matter if it was a junior officer hoping for tenure, an FS-1 seeking to get into the Senior Foreign Service, or an ambassador or assistant secretary," observed one foreign service officer, "the qualities judged begin with reporting, analysis, and policy" (Bushnell 1989). Hence, Foreign Service personnel generally believe that overseas operations of the kind conducted by AID, USIA, the CIA, and the Department of Defense are peripheral to the main foreign policy task (Scott 1969; see also Clarke 1989). For example, as we discussed in Chapter 5, while the 1998 Foreign Affairs Restructuring Act integrated the United States Information Agency into the department to elevate the role and centrality of public diplomacy, this "program" and function is not part of the traditional mission and is hotly resisted by the careerists throughout the agency. Secretary of State Warren Christopher discovered this problem in another area when he attempted to expand the role of the State Department in advocating for American businesses abroad, a task also resisted by the foreign service (Scott 1997a).

The way the Foreign Service manages its personnel contributes to another characteristic of the subculture: its *cautiousness and risk-aversion.* The Foreign Service employs an *"up-or-out" promotion system,* under which a foreign service officer must advance beyond his or her present rank within a specified time or be "selected out." As a 2001 report on State Department reform overseen by the Council on Foreign Relations concluded, the system has "the unintended effect of forcing qualified personnel out of the service." In addition to generating a highly competitive environment, that principle, together with the exceptional importance of the efficiency rating, tends, as one department self-study put it, "to stifle creativity, discourage risk-taking, and reward conformity" (Diplomacy for the 70's: A Program of Management Reform for the Department of State 1970). Whether one's star is allowed to shine in an assignment to political affairs in Paris rather than to budgetary affairs in Ouagadougou is heavily dependent on the outcome of one's evaluation by superiors. Foreign Service Officers tend therefore to avoid rocking the boat and to eschew controversial views that may be viewed as challenges to the wisdom of one's superiors.

Over the years a number of developments both inside and outside the Foreign Service have disrupted the professional diplomatic corps, helping to reinforce this penchant for caution and traditionalism. Preeminent among them were the effects of **McCarthyism.** In the winter of 1950, Senator Joseph McCarthy claimed "I have in my hand a list of 205 that were known to the Secretary of State as being members of the Communist party and who, nevertheless, are still working and shaping the policy in the State Department." With those words, McCarthy launched an all-out attack against suspected—but never proven— "disloyalty" in the Foreign Service. The immediate thrust was directed against those charged with responsibility for the "loss" of China to communism in 1949. Eventually the entire corps of Foreign Service officers suffered the grueling humiliation of security investigations engendered by an atmosphere of hysterical anticommunism.

Among the serious consequences of McCarthyism for the State Department, two stand out. First, the devastating attacks promoted certain harmful values among its personnel: "the virtues inculcated were caution, conformity, discretion, and prudence" (Warwick 1975). Second, extraordinary security consciousness and an elaborate system of horizontal clearances resulted. The latter in particular has made State's operating procedures among the most complex of all federal agencies. The result is, according to many, a slowness and inefficiency in the department's processes, as well as "a most cautious way of doing business. It reflects an institutionalized desire to diffuse responsibility among many different offices and colleagues rather than to accept responsibility oneself" (Campbell 1971; see also U.S. Department of State 1992).[1]

Other factors since World War II contributed to the decline of the department's influence in the wider foreign policy circles. Among them were the increasing presidential interest in and control over foreign policy at the expense of the State Department, the issue agenda of the Cold War (which stressed security and military force, thereby elevating the importance of the Defense Department and the intelligence community), and the growing importance of economic and other "intermestic" issues to the foreign policy issue agenda (on which the State Department is ill-equipped and over which other agencies have gained influence).

The State Department in the Foreign Affairs Government

The combination of the subculture of the State Department and factors external to the organization are critical in explaining why a department that theoretically sits center-stage in the foreign affairs government is in fact ill-equipped to play a leadership role. Three additional factors circumscribe the State Department's ability to exercise leadership in the larger foreign affairs government: the role and orientation of secretaries of state; the tension between careerists and appointees; and the fact that the department is a bureaucratic pygmy among giants.

Secretaries of State and the State Department Secretaries of state may or may not be influential in foreign policy, despite their assumed role as the president's leading foreign policy adviser. Since the 1950s, most secretaries have had to choose between two basic role orientations: to maximize their relationship with the president and distance themselves from the department itself, or to maximize their leadership and use of the department, only to see their influence with the president wane. Few manage both; some manage neither.

Let us consider secretaries over the past fifty years or so. John Foster Dulles is widely regarded as one of the most influential secretaries of state in the twentieth century, but he did little to infuse the organization with a corresponding capacity to lead. Dulles reportedly told President Eisenhower he would accept the job only if he did not have to assume responsibility for managing the department and the Foreign Service. Dean Rusk was a less dramatic secretary and his personality and preoccupation with Vietnam prevented a more effective use of the department's expertise (Diplomacy for the 70s: A Program of Management Reform for the Department of State 1970).

Those who followed Dulles and Rusk—including Kissinger, Vance, Muskie, Haig, Shultz, Baker, and Christopher—did no more to build bridges between top officials and careerists in order to involve the latter more actively in policy making. Kissinger took many of his NSC staffers with him to Foggy Bottom when he left the White House, but largely ignored the department. Vance was apparently more popular at the State Department "partly due to memories of his predecessor—tales of Kissinger mistreating FSOs and ashtray-throwing tantrums [were] legion" (Rubin 1985)—but eventually Vance became enmeshed in a bureaucratic duel with the White House, which he ultimately lost. Alexander Haig, Reagan's first secretary of state, also resigned when he found himself outside the charmed circle of White House advisers in an administration otherwise known for its friction with the career staff. If there was an exception, it was George Shultz, Haig's successor, whose survival through the end of the Reagan era suggests he was better able to satisfy the competing demands of organization person and presidential adviser. Even Shultz found himself initially less influential as an

adviser, and often under attack by right-wing Reaganites who believed he had become a captive of the State Department's "liberal" Foreign Service establishment. Moreover, Shultz's influence over policy was considerably limited until the Iran-contra affair reduced the presence and role of other policy makers in the White House, CIA, and Defense Department.

In contrast, James A. Baker, Shultz's successor, reopened the chasm separating the secretary of state from the department's career professionals and attempted to keep himself inside George H. W. Bush's inner circle. Whereas Shultz "used the brightest stars of the career Foreign Service as the core of his policy-making team," Baker's style was to keep them at arm's length. "Many Foreign Service officers [complained] that Baker and his coterie of insiders . . . turned the department's seventh-floor executive suite into an inaccessible redoubt where even the most senior professional diplomats [felt] unwelcome and ignored" (Goshko 1989). "He's running a mini-NSC, not State," complained one senior diplomat. "We learn what our policy is when we read it in the newspapers."

Warren Christopher did not fare much better than Baker. Although he sometimes acted as a leading spokesperson for Clinton's foreign policy, and he did administer changes to the State Department (both structurally and procedurally), the White House generally regarded his public performances as ineffectual, particularly on such difficult issues as Bosnia. Indeed, its willingness to "subcontract" negotiations in North Korea and Haiti to former President Jimmy Carter reflected an even deeper dissatisfaction with Christopher and his top aides at the State Department. And they won no praise from senior and mid-level Foreign Service officers either, who believed that Christopher and those around him were "nice guys" who sincerely tried to do a good job but just proved ineffective. "The indictment they [leveled] against the Clinton team [which included members of the White House staff as well as Christopher] is that its policies frequently [were] so ill-defined or so prone to sudden flip-flops that they collectively . . . became known within the bureaucracy as 'the lurch'" (Goshko 1994).

When Madeleine Albright took over in January 1997 as the first woman to hold the position of secretary of state, she was initially hailed by most observers—including long-time State Department critic Jesse Helms, Republican chair of the Senate Foreign Relations Committee—as a major improvement over Christopher. Respected by the president and potentially able to add prestige to the department through her efforts, her highly visible role seemed to place her in a position to restore the secretary of state to an influential adviser role, as well as to elevate the department to a more prominent position.

Barely two years into her tenure, however, Albright had failed in both respects. According to one observer, "she remains a participant in the process. But her weight as secretary of state in the determination of foreign policy appears less than at any time in the Clinton Administration" (Perlez 1999). Another even less flattering appraisal concluded that "She has, in effect, become the errand boy of foreign policy rather than the conceptualizer of it" (quoted in Lancaster 2000). As we discussed in Chapter 10, Albright maintained good relations with National Security Adviser Sandy Berger and Defense Secretary William Cohen (the "ABC Club"), but her role in policy was more as an implementor, and her relationship to the president was formal, not close (Isaacson 1999).

Within the department, Albright had failed as well. Department officials allegedly viewed her as an "insecure, indifferent leader who [was] quick to anger and obsessed by her public image" (Lancaster 2000). The careerists grumbled about her lack of attention and leadership and her narrow interests. One foreign policy specialist concluded that "she has been largely unsuccessful in either getting control over her own building or her own policy generally" (quoted in Lancaster 2000). In short, in spite of a few instances of policy influence (the 1998–1999 Serbia-Kosovo policy, for instance), Albright succeeded in neither the organization person nor the presidential adviser orientation.

George W. Bush's choice for secretary of state began with even more accolades than Albright. Colin Powell was widely regarded as "the star" of the foreign policy team at the outset of the second Bush administration. One political analyst asserted that Powell was "uniquely positioned to become the most influential voice in foreign affairs within the Bush administration. . . . Powell will almost certainly emerge as a 'first among equals' within the Bush Cabinet" (Kitfield 2001a). Most observers, it seemed, expected Powell to use his "star power" and political clout to make the secretary of state the lead voice on foreign policy. Moreover, Powell's early comments at his confirmation hearings and in his initial talks with State Department employees suggested that he was determined also to lead the department effectively and to restore it to a more prominent position as well.

Toward the end of the Bush administration's first year, the picture looked quite different. To be sure, Powell continued to give every indication that he was committed to being a good "organization person." He "rallied the troops at State and rebuilt a demoralized institution" (McGeary 2001). He advocated persuasively for additional resources for the budget-starved department. He pressed hard within the administration to fill ambassadorships with career personnel rather than with campaign supporters, and he turned to careerists for many of the assistant secretary and deputy assistant secretary positions within the department. He also dismantled many of the special envoy positions used by the Clinton administration to handle important assignments and pushed the responsibilities back to the traditional bureaus and offices. Finally, he sent two desk officers to brief President Bush before his trip to Mexico— the first time that had occurred since the Cuban Missile Crisis—thereby displaying his confidence in the career Foreign Service officers (see Kaplan 2001a). Through actions like these and others, Powell paid careful attention to the department,

---

FOCUS 11.1   Warrior-Diplomat: Colin Powell at the State Department

[Secretary of State Colin] Powell . . . has reestablished the State Department at the forefront of foreign policy. During the Clinton years, much of the power had shifted to the White House. For U.S. diplomats overseas, accustomed to being overshadowed by special envoys dispatched from Washington, some of Powell's ideas seem almost revolutionary. One of his most popular lines about U.S. ambassadors: "They're right out there, and we're wrong here until proven otherwise."

. . . But it's his style—a crisp military efficiency and rock-star-like charisma—that has really energized the State Department. Already, his casual manner and disdain for red tape are legendary. Following reports that the Bush team frowned on ringing cell phones, Powell returned from a Florida trip to open a meeting by holding a conch shell up to his ear: "Shell phone," he said. Country desk officers, used to toiling in relative obscurity, have been astonished when Powell drops by unannounced. "He jumps over layers of bureaucracy to deal with people directly," says one State Department official. "It jazzes people up, either with excitement or fear."

His efforts to repair State Department morale couldn't come at a better time. Resignations by specialists have quadrupled since 1994. A former AOL board member, Powell was disturbed to learn that some employees can't even exchange E-mail. His first budget request included a boost in funding for technology.

SOURCE: *U.S. News and World Report*, 4 June, 2001, 31. Copyright 2001 U.S. News & World Report, L.P. Reprinted with permission.

---

earning favorable reviews from FSOs for his leadership (Kitfield 2001a).

However, even as Powell provided evidence that he would be an effective manager and leader of the State Department, his influence as a policy adviser appeared to wane. Late in 2001, *Time* (September 10, pp. 24–32) ran a cover story entitled "Odd Man Out," commenting on the impression that Powell had been less influential—even "invisible"—than expected. This concern stemmed from several developments. First, Powell appeared to be the victim of an alliance between Vice President Dick Cheney and Defense Secretary Donald Rumsfeld designed to "contain" his influence and assert their own predominance within the administration. Some observers, convinced that Cheney desired to be the "vicar" of foreign policy, believed that the Vice President was motivated by "anti-Powellism" (Kaplan 2001a). One indicator of this effort was a series of personnel decisions in the Defense Department, National Security Council, and the Vice President's office (as noted in Chapter 10) in which Powell's recommendations were ignored in favor of more hard-line appointees allied with

Cheney and Rumsfeld (Kaplan 2001a; 2001b). Even within his own department, Powell lost on certain personnel decisions. For example, he sought to eliminate the special envoy for the Iraqi resistance and retain the special envoy for war crimes; Cheney and the White House pressed for just the opposite and prevailed. Powell was also forced into accepting some individuals favored by Cheney and Rumsfeld that he did not want (for example, John Bolton for Under Secretary for Arm Control and International Security), complaining to friends that such individuals "were foisted upon him" (McGeary 2001).

Moreover, on a series of policy issues, Powell's preferences and public statements were reversed or contradicted by Cheney, Rumsfeld, or President Bush, often publicly. Among them were Powell's proposals to narrow Iraqi sanctions, continue the Clinton administration's engagement with North Korea to control that country's nuclear weapons program, support the development of a European defense force, and stay the course in the Kosovo commitment (see *Newsweek*, 12 March 2001, 42; Kettle 2001; Kaplan 2001a). President Bush was even said to have "reined in" Powell on one of these occasions (Wastell 2001; Perlez 2001c). A Senator on the Foreign Relations Committee commented that Powell had been "absolutely cut off at the knees with the early initiatives he took" (McGeary 2001).

To be sure, Powell had his successes. As one observer suggested, "The White House lets him run free on Africa and AIDS. . . . He fought Rice to get Bush to renege on his campaign promise to bring home U.S. troops from the Balkans. He moved Bush back toward talking to North Korea. He quelled hard-line rumbling when he took charge of retrieving the American spy plane crew from China; Pentagon officials seeking retaliation were forced to withdraw their announcement that the U.S. would sever ties with the Chinese military" (McGeary 2001). Even before the September 11 attacks on New York and Washington DC, Powell had pushed the administration to re-engage in the Middle East. After the attacks, Powell took the lead in this area, and in helping to build an international coalition against terrorism and in support of U.S. operations in Afghanistan, visiting countries throughout Europe, the Middle East, and South Asia, among others. These variations were, perhaps, the signs of an administration settling in. Or, they were indicators that the early promise of a secretary of state as both organization person and policy adviser in full gear was settling back into a familiar post-World War II pattern.

Careerists Versus Political Appointees Another tension in the role of the State Department (indeed, in any agency) that works against its ability to exercise effective leadership is the natural tension between career employees and the political appointees generally placed above them. Careerists frequently view political appointees as "in-and-outers," more concerned with political advantage and short-term results than good policy. Appointees, on the other hand, frequently view careerists as overly cautious and unresponsive to the White House and department leadership. Often, a contest ensues.

A major manifestation of this tension involves the mid-level positions and ambassadorships to which FSO careerists aspire and into which political appointments from outside the Foreign Service are frequently made.[2] Not only does this reduce the opportunities available to career officers at the prime of their careers, when their potential to make a meaningful contribution is greatest, but it also generates resentment among the most senior members of the Foreign Service toward the appointees. In George W. Bush's first year, for example, 1,700 people sought jobs in American embassies, mostly in Europe and the Caribbean (the "plum" postings). Two hundred became finalists, and a fortunate forty-nine were named. Not surprisingly, in addition to former politicians being rewarded for service (e.g., former Republican Senators Dan Coats of Indiana and Howard Baker of Tennessee, in line for the Germany and Japan postings), the list is heavily laden with major contributors to the George W. Bush election campaign. Few such rewards go to "hardship" postings in Latin America, Africa, and Asia, which tend to be designated for the careerists (Lacey and Bonner 2001).

Presidents have long used ambassadorial appointments to reward their political supporters, but the propensity to make political appointments also reflects their profound distrust of "careerists." Politicians often believe that careerists are not only disloyal to their policies but also actively seek to undermine them.[3] Often, however, the demands political appointees make on those expected to serve them are contradictory. They want the career staff to be detached, but accuse it of being bland; they demand discipline, but can brand this as lack of imagination; they require experienced judgment, but may call this negativism. One FSO complains, "Presidents and their aides need scapegoats. They can't blame the administration so they blame the secretary of state and if they can't blame the secretary of state they criticize the department's staff" (Rubin 1985).

Another manifestation of this tension can be seen in the Clinton administration's propensity to establish special envoys outside the department structure (using political appointees rather than career officials) to deal with major problems. Examples include special envoys and ambassadors like former Senator George Mitchell for Ireland, and other similar, if lower profile appointments for NATO enlargement, war crimes, the test ban treaty, and others. Such efforts illustrate the "adhocracy" discussed in Chapter 10 (and will be revisited in Chapter 13). They constitute efforts to work around the established bureaus and offices and better "control" career employees.

Without Bureaucratic Muscle A third reason for the State Department's inability to exercise greater leadership is its relative lack of resources and bureaucratic muscle in Washington's intensely political environment. As one Foreign Service officer put it more than two decades ago, the secretary of state "is [the] most senior of cabinet members, and is charged (in theory) with responsibility for the coordination of all foreign policy activities, [but] he presides over a bureaucratic midget" (Pringle 1977–1978). Nothing has changed since. The State Department's budget for 2000 was $8.4 billion compared with $280 billion for the Defense Department. The total international affairs budget ($20.6 billion in 2000) comprises less than 1.5 percent of all federal expenditures. Meanwhile, the expenditures of every other department in the executive branch exceed those of the State Department—a pygmy among giants.

Centralization of foreign policy making in the White House grows naturally out of the State Department's lack of leadership but typically results in the "exclusion of the bureaucracy from most of the serious, presidential foreign policy business" (Destler, Gelb, and Lake 1984). Both circumstances reflect the State Department's inattentiveness to presidential needs: "Once a president comes to believe that Foggy Bottom is not attuned to politics, they are doomed to being ignored" (Gelb 1983). Specific presidential complaints are that the State Department produces bad staff work and is slow to respond, resistant to change, reluctant to follow orders, and incapable

of putting its own house in order. Recognizing its own penchant toward parochialism, a State Department self-study concluded that "There should be little wonder that the top leadership in the White House and in the Department have tended over the years to create separate, smaller mechanisms to deal with the key foreign policy agenda items—leaving [the State Department] more and more marginalized" (U.S. Department of State 1992). The case of Madeleine Albright is instructive on this point. As discussed earlier and in Chapter 10, in spite of her initial "star power" and highly visible role, her influence quickly receded as Sandy Berger, the National Security Adviser, asserted control from the White House to ensure that Clinton's priorities (policy and political) were at the forefront. A group of former NSC staffers also pointed to this problem, noting how interagency groups chaired by the State Department tend to be bypassed or marginalized in favor of those reflecting greater White House control (National Security Council Project 1999a).

Part of the reason for the belief that the State Department is insensitive to a president's political needs is that the department necessarily represents in the councils of government the interests of other countries, who are its "clients." "From a White House perspective, efforts to accommodate the legitimate concerns of other countries are often viewed as coming at the expense of American interests, and the accommodationists are viewed as not being tough enough. Presidents usually do not have much patience with this kind of advice, find they cannot change State's penchant for it, and soon stop listening" (Gelb 1983; see also Clarke 1989). Within the interagency groups who play a key role in policy formulation, this *clientitis* is also damaging, causing other participants to discount the State department representative.

Twenty-First Century Challenges As the State Department faces the new century, it faces at least four challenges that will affect its ability to fulfill its responsibilities in American foreign policy.

1. The department's structure—with its regional and functional bureaus dividing up the world and its problems—seems ill-suited to provide effective leadership or even coordinated and coherent policy advice. As the United States Commission on National Security Twenty-First Century concluded in its February 2001 report (*Roadmap for National Security: Imperative for Change*), "the State Department's own effort to cover all the various aspects of national security policy . . . has produced an exceedingly complex organizational structure. Developing a distinct 'State' point of view is now extremely difficult and this, in turn, has reduced the department's ability to exercise any leadership." Restructuring to bring together economic, transnational, political, and security concerns would enable the State Department to formulate a more coherent approach to policy issues and better enable it to meet the challenges of the new century.

2. The department's personnel and subculture establish major obstacles for effective policy making. The department must take steps to attract the experts it needs to address the new policy agenda, and it must establish procedures that better support and reward effective policy behavior. In particular, the Foreign Service rules and procedures—including the "up-or-out" promotion system, must be overhauled.

3. The department desperately requires more resources in order to meet its obligations. Its budget is minuscule and barely supports a bare-bones set of operations. Moreover, as a 1998 report by the Henry L. Stimson Center indicates (*Equipped for the Future: Managing U.S. Foreign Affairs in the 21ˢᵗ Century*), "the means and methods used by U.S. diplomats to advocate our interests abroad are barely out of the quill-and-scroll stage."

4. Finally, the State Department will have to struggle with the impact of an issue agenda

that seems to diminish its centrality. Just as in the Cold War, military and security concerns reduced the dominance of the State Department while enhancing the roles of the defense and intelligence agencies, the twenty-first century problem agenda works against the State Department. The transnational and economic problems and issues of the new century invite influence by others and require coordination by the White House. The increased emphasis on counterterrorism and related security issues further diffuses influence away from the State Department toward others. In light of the 50-year trend away from State Department leadership, the department will have to grapple new challenges to its role.

In no small measure, whether the State Department can play a meaningful role in addressing the problems and prospects of the new century will depend on how George W. Bush's administration views the State Department's roles and responsibilities in the development and implementation of its foreign policy priorities.

THE DEPARTMENT OF DEFENSE

Given the international environment that has dominated much of the last fifty years, it is no surprise that the Department of Defense (DOD) has been an important voice in foreign policy making. The secretary of defense and the chairman of the Joint Chiefs of Staff bear the heaviest responsibility for advising the president on national security policy. Because the DOD is also thoroughly interwoven into the fabric of American social, political, and economic life, the defense secretary's recommendations greatly influence both the foreign and domestic environments.

Structure and Mission

As Figure 11.2 shows, the Defense Department is a complex agency. In truth, the Defense Depart-

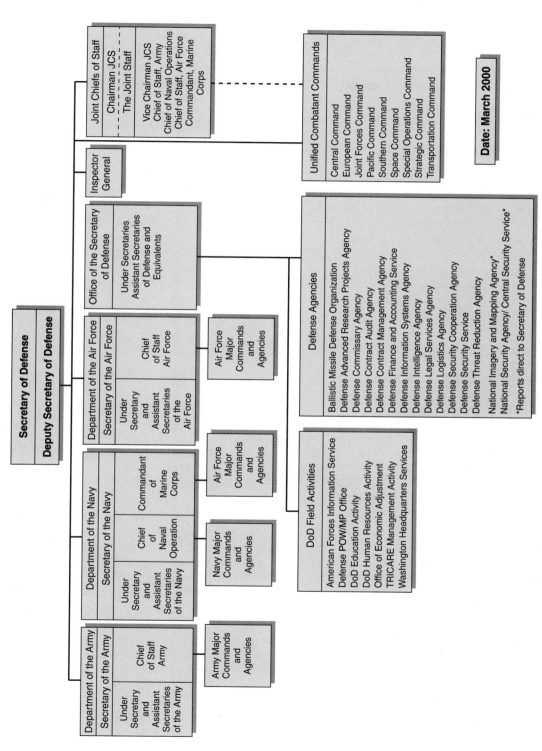

FIGURE 11.2 The United States Department of Defense

Source: Department of Defense website at www.defenselink.mil/pubs/ofg/dod.pdf

ment, popularly referred to simply as the **Penta-gon** because of the shape of its headquarters in Arlington, Virginia, is far more complex than the figure is able to convey. The organizational chart shows the formal relationship between the secretary of defense, the military departments, each of which is headed by a civilian, the military services that comprise them, and the Joint Chiefs of Staff. It also indicates the importance of civilian control of the military, as the defense secretary and the service secretaries are all civilians, an issue to which we will return in more detail later. However, it fails to fully reveal the complicated chain of command that exists on national security policy and the increasing commitment to and adoption of *"jointness,"* by which the services are more integrated in their forces, doctrines, and commands. It is clear, however, that the department is a massive agency.

The complex organization portrayed in Figure 11.2 performs four important roles in American national security policy (see also Jordan, Taylor and Mazarr 1999). First, it has a *policy* role, providing advice and analysis to the White House on national security matters. This function is chiefly performed by the secretary and the Office of the Secretary of Defense (OSD) along with the Joint Chiefs of Staff (JCS) and their chair, who is now the "principal military adviser" to the civilian leadership. Second, the DOD exercises *military command* over the nation's armed forces, under the overall authority of the president (who is commander in chief). This function is chiefly performed at the strategic level by the OSD, and at the tactical level by the services themselves, especially through their unified commands. The JCS is technically not in the operational chain-of-command, but also plays a role. Third, the DOD *administers* the military services, managing personnel and budgets, weapons and supplies and training forces. This function is performed chiefly by the services themselves, with general oversight and supervision by the OSD. Finally, the DOD *collects intelligence* for use in devising and reviewing policy through intelligence units of the services and the Defense Intelligence Agency. Thus,

implementing the role and mission of the department—providing policy advice and carrying out the security policy of the United States—is less easily coordinated and centralized than the organizational chart initially suggests.

The Secretary of Defense and the Office of the Secretary of Defense

The secretary of defense is the president's chief adviser on defense matters, including such issues as force size and structure and weapons procurement. The secretary is assisted in carrying out his or her responsibilities by the *Office of the Secretary of Defense,* comprising under secretaries, assistant secretaries, and other personnel responsible for more discrete issues, such as policy development, acquisitions and technology, personnel and readiness, and command, control, communications, and intelligence.

Managing the Military: Autonomy Versus Centralization   Like all bureaucratic organizations, the military services within the Defense Department prize their autonomy in what historically has been the "services-dominated architecture" of the defense establishment. As one analyst noted wryly in commenting on the 1986 defense reorganization proposals, "In more than two hundred years [the Navy Department] had never met a centralization proposal that [it] liked" (Davis 1987). Hence, secretaries of defense have their work cut out as they seek to lead the department in its foreign and national security functions.

Over time, different secretaries of defense have used different management strategies to coordinate the disparate military organizations. One strategy is *"decentralization."* This is the preferred strategy of the military services, because it means delegating authority for both resources and strategy to them (Hammond 1994). Secretary of Defense Caspar Weinberger pursued this management strategy which is best suited to a time of growing defense spending as during the 1980s. However, Bill Clinton's third Defense Secretary, former Republican Senator William Cohen, probably also falls into this category, much to the surprise of many observers who expected him to be more aggressive in managing the department. As one keen observer noted:

> Cohen's instincts in trying to run the Pentagon were more those of a politician than a CEO. . . . He made the day-to-day decisions with skill and nuance, but he backed off from the long-range force restructuring decisions that might have torn the Pentagon apart. . . . In general, Cohen's political instincts were quite good. But he was obviously very dependent on [Air Force General Joe] Ralston, the vice chair [of the Joint Chiefs of Staff], who knew the building and its interior politics better than most and would let Cohen know what decisions he had to make and when to make them (Halberstam 2001, 441).

A second strategy focuses on *"management of the acquisition process,"* including the development of new technologies and equipment. This strategy "permits the secretary of defense to have a major impact on the shape and functions of the armed services in the longer term by guiding their development and application of new technologies" (Hammond 1994). In this approach, the secretary of defense actively shapes key aspects of the resource planning and can shape overall strategy without imposing a blanket, top-down, managerial style in either resources or strategy. Harold Brown, defense secretary under President Carter, followed this route. William Perry, Clinton's second defense secretary, probably also falls into this category.

A third approach concentrates on developing overall strategy while delegating much of the resource management and planning. This *"top-down, directive planning guidance"* approach, which is promoted by the 1986 Defense Reorganization Act, prompts the military services to integrate their operations, and it encourages greater attention to "operational and contingency planning" and "long-range force . . . planning" (Ham-

mond 1994). Not surprisingly, many of the post-1986 defense secretaries adopted this approach, including Dick Cheney (for George H. W. Bush) and Les Aspin.

The final strategy is *"central resource management"* which concentrates both budgetary and strategic planning in the OSD. In this approach, which is best exemplified by Robert McNamara during the Kennedy and Johnson administrations and Frank Carlucci in the waning days of the Reagan administration, civilian control is most extensive. Under McNamara, for example, the Office of the Secretary of Defense was staffed with "acerbic, even arrogant, analytically brilliant men, most of whom had made their mark in business or academic life" (Nathan and Oliver 1994). McNamara and the OSD were "soon involved at virtually every level of national security management and military planning. Commanders in the Pacific and Europe were given less autonomy, and McNamara's centralized budgeting procedures led to his staff's preempting most traditional military planning" (Nathan and Oliver 1994).

Although the 1986 defense reforms expanding the role of the JCS has made this last approach less possible, by most accounts, George W. Bush's secretary of defense, Donald Rumsfeld, embraced it, seeking to exercise leadership across both strategy and resources management. Not only did Rumsfeld begin his tenure with a top-down strategic review run by a handful of officials in his office to "pursue dramatic reforms in the way the nation's armed forces are organized" and used (Ricks 2001a), he also tapped a group of former CEOs to install as the service chiefs, seeking to reassert civilian control and loosen the grip of the military on resource planning (see also Kitfield 2001b; Wilson 2001a, 2001b). The approach has drawn fire—one Republican defense aide noted early on, "I don't know of anybody, be it in the industry, the generals, or Congress that is happy with Rumsfeld" (cited in *The Straits Times,* 25 April 2001, 6) but Rumsfeld enjoyed some early success. Not only did he rebuild the Office of the Secretary of Defense into a more aggressive *policy shop* (see following), he also presided over a Quadrennial Defense Review plan to shift military strategy away from post-World War II conventions (see the Department of Defense *Quadrennial Defense Review Report,* September 30, 2001, also discussed in Chapter 4). After the terrorist strikes of September 11 drove home the need for a revised approach to national security, Rumsfeld also embarked on a plan to restructure the fundamental command structure of the Pentagon away from it focus on regional commands (see Ricks 200 1b).

The Policy Shop: The Office of the Secretary of Defense One of the major developments in the U.S. Foreign policy bureaucracy was the rise of the Office of the Secretary of Defense as a source of policy ideas. Beginning with Robert McNamara's tenure as secretary of defense in the 1960s, the OSD emerged as an important bureaucratic player often vying with bureaus in the State Department and offices in the NSC staff. The OSD is, technically, the staff of the secretary of defense. However, as Figure 11.3 indicates, this sizable staff is organized into a wide variety of offices. Some are designed to facilitate management over the defense department itself (for example, the offices of the undersecretary for personnel and readiness and for acquisition, technology, and logistics). However, within the OSD, the office of the undersecretary for policy houses a series of units designed to formulate and analyze policy options. Although the names and assignments have varied since McNamara built them up, historically these units of the "*policy shop*" have been among the most powerful in the department.

During the 1960s, for example, the *Office of International Security Affairs* (ISA) emerged as an influential Defense Department voice in the foreign affairs government. Called by many the "*little State Department,*" its influence stemmed from McNamara's ability to establish control over the sprawling military complex and the fact that Vietnam was the principal foreign policy problem of the era.

After the Johnson administration, the OSD declined in influence until the Reagan administration restored its significance. Under Reagan, the "policy shop," now divided into an International Security Affairs office and an International Security Policy (ISP) office, exercised a powerful voice in the Office of the Secretary of Defense and in the interagency groups used to formulate policy ideas. For example, during the Reagan administration, ISP was headed by Richard Perle, who was a powerful player in the internal struggles over arms control policy (Talbott 1984). Fred Iklé, Reagan's undersecretary of defense for policy, was also a major player on most foreign policy initiatives.

After declining in influence during the Bush administration, OSD and its key policy offices regained some of their clout in the Clinton administration. Following Clinton's election, Les Aspin, Clinton's first secretary of defense, sought an even greater role for policy, as he brought in a number of "defense intellectuals" whose tasks extended beyond traditional defense issues to encompass more novel threats to national security in the post–Cold War (dis)order. Aspin, whose tenure as secretary of defense was marked mostly by managerial failures, reorganized the OSD and the policy office to better reflect the emerging foreign policy and security environment. Indeed, by paralleling the State Department structure in many ways, and by adding such offices as environmental security and regional security, Aspin clearly set up the OSD to compete with the State Department. Aspin's successors, Perry and Cohen, further reorganized the OSD to reflect changing priorities, but Perry stripped away a number of Aspin's innovations by eliminating some of the newer offices.

George W. Bush's choice for defense secretary, Donald Rumsfeld, spent the first months of his tenure assembling a civilian team for the OSD drawn primarily from veterans of the Ford, Reagan, and the first Bush administrations. A well-known bureaucratic in-fighter, Rumsfeld assembled a team that would enable the OSD to compete effectively in foreign and national

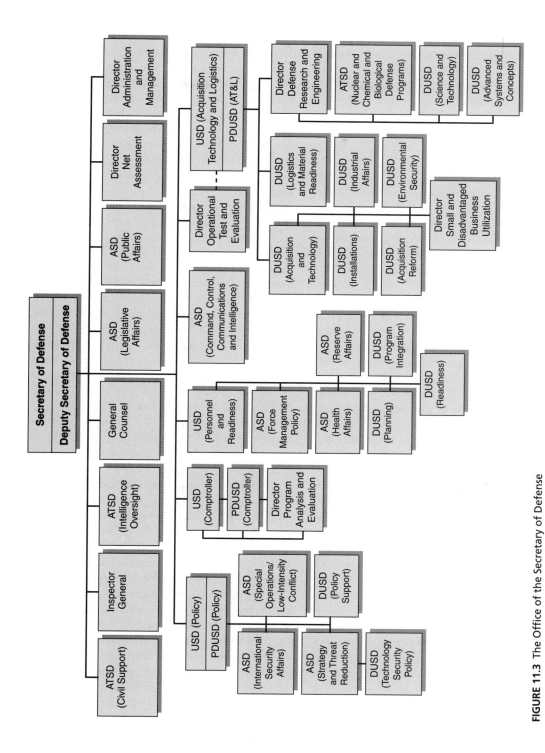

FIGURE 11.3 The Office of the Secretary of Defense

Source: Department of Defense website at www.defenselink.mil/pubs/ofg/ofsecdf.pdf

security policy circles. It is perhaps notable that, unlike Powell, Rumsfeld installed outsiders rather than careerists into key positions, hoping in that way to assert his own control. Ultimately, this is the key: the role and influence of the OSD, both within and outside the department, depends on the style and preferences of the secretary of defense.

The Joint Chiefs of Staff

The 1947 National Security Act created the *Joint Chiefs of Staff* **(JCS)** to provide military advice to the NSC. The *Defense Reorganization Act of 1986* further expanded the JCS to an even more prominent role in foreign and national security policy. This first major reorganization of the Defense Department since the 1950s, popularly known as the *Goldwater-Nichols Act* after its congressional architects, sought in particular to strengthen the role of the institutions associated with the Joint Chiefs of Staff and to ameliorate the *interservice rivalry* that has long plagued the defense establishment.[4] Since its implementation, the JCS has played an increasingly central role in both policy formulation and implementation. This is especially true, when the use of force is being considered but, ironically, less so once the decision to apply force is taken. Both the 1999 Kosovo campaign and the 2001 campaign against the Taliban regime and the Al Qaeda network in Afghanistan illustrate this well. In both situations, the chairmain of the Joint Chiefs was central to the decisions to use force, but lost influence to the theater commanders and the civilian command authority once the campaigns began (see, for example, Halberstam 2001).

The JCS consists of six officers—the senior military officer within each uniformed service and a chairman and vice chairman (a position added by Goldwater-Nichols) appointed by the president, The chairman of the JCS serves as the nation's chief military officer. Each service chief—the chief of staff of the Army, the chief of staff of the Air Force, the chief of naval operations, and the commandant of the Marine Corps—is responsible for advising his civilian

secretary on military matters and for maintaining the efficiency and operational readiness of the military forces under his command. Until the 1986 reorganization, the joint chiefs were assisted in that task by a joint staff comprising some 400 officers selected from each branch of the armed forces. Since 1986, however, the joint staff serves the chairman, operating solely under his direction, authority, and control.

Additionally, the Goldwater-Nichols act made three additional changes that have impacted policy formulation and implements. First, it stimulated the creation of a new "joint specialty" designed to make service on the joint staff more rewarding professionally. Since 1986, "jointness" has become a central aspect of the department. Second, it centralized and expanded the staff, which now numbers roughly 1,600, while also permitting civilians to serve. Finally, the act explicitly named the chairman of the joint chiefs as the principal military adviser to the president, the secretary of defense, and the National Security Council (but not a member, as some had proposed). Before the Goldwater-Nichols act, that task fell to the joint chiefs as a collective body. Now, in fact, the JCS chairman has "the right to give advice [to civilian policy makers] not only when asked, but also when not asked" (Perry 1989).

The law did not, however, make the chairman a commander with direct control over U.S. combat forces, a move many believed would have undermined the primacy of civilian control over the military. In fact, although the JCS system comprises the nation's senior military officers, they do not command combat forces in the field. Instead, they are essentially an administrative unit outside the operational chain of command. The actual command of combat forces in the field rests with nine commanders in chief (CINCs),[5] who receive their orders from the president as commander in chief through the secretary of defense. Thus, for example, in the 1999 Kosovo campaign, General Wesley Clark, commander in chief of the European theater (and Supreme Allied Commander in Europe), was more influential in the application of force that drove the Serbians from Albania than the JCS. Indeed, Clark, who sought to use American military might more aggressively than the JCS wished to do, was able to circumvent their obstruction and appeal directly to the civilian chain of command (see Halberstam 2001; Clark 2001).[6] A similar pattern occurred in the campaign against Afghanistan, where Chairman of the JCS General Hugh Shelton (and his successor Army General Richard Myers) was central to the initial planning only to see operational influence shift to Army General Tommy Franks, Commander in Chief of the Central Command.

Nevertheless, while the Goldwater-Nichols act moved tentatively on this issue, it did give the JCS authority to transmit orders from the president or the secretary of defense to the CINCs. It also authorized, per the defense secretary's discretion, the chair of the JCS to oversee the CINCs. The CINCs of unified commands in turn were given "operational command" but not complete command over forces assigned to them. Since the first Bush administration, the White House and the secretary of defense have, in practice, put the chair of the JCS into the command loop in this way.

Although the Defense Reorganization Act of 1986 did not accomplish all that its proponents had hoped, it has had major effects on both the formulation and implementation of military policy. For one, it has dramatically advanced the "jointness" concept and reduced (but not eliminated) interservice rivalries. By emphasizing, constructing and rewarding joint operations, Goldwater-Nichols has helped to transform the military. According to some, "the dominant norm for the JCS is no longer parochial protection of individual service interests, but a norm of jointness, in which service perspectives, forces, and doctrines are genuinely integrated" (Roman and Tarr 1998).[7] Indeed, JCS produced a *Joint Vision 2010* plan in 1996, and then developed the strategy even further in its 2001 plan entitled *Joint Vision 2020*. Operations in Kosovo (1999) and Afghaniston (2001) illustrate key aspects of the concept.

Second, it has dramatically enhanced the role of the chairman of the JCS and the joint staff at his command to plan, organize, and coordinate the nation's military forces and operations. No longer required to submit corporate advice, the chair is empowered to provide his or her own recommendations. This has therefore encouraged the other chiefs to work more closely with the chair because they know he or she can advise as desired (Roman and Tarr 1998). For example, Colin Powell remembered that, during his time as chairman he "did not have to take a vote among the chiefs before recommending anything. I did not even have to consult them, though it would have been foolish not to do so" (Powell 1995). Powell's successors—John Shalikashvili, Hugh Shelton, and Richard Myers— enjoyed the same advantage.

Third, the changes have transformed the chair's role within interagency processes as well. Not only is representation on interagency working groups the responsibility of the staff of the JCS, the chair's (and vice chair's) participation in meetings of the deputies and principals committees is "indistinguishable from that of the cabinet officers and other politicians who are members of that body. In this context, the chairman is a decision maker, not simply an adviser" (Roman and Tarr 1998). Consequently, "the participation of the military in public policy making has never in peacetime been more centralized, integrated, and effective than it is today" (Roman and Tarr 1998). David Halberstam's (2001) account of applications of force in the 1990s clearly reveals this transformation.

The recent past supports this conclusion. The first chairman to really take advantage of the reform was Colin Powell, schooled in the art of politics in part by his experience as national security adviser during the Reagan presidency. He became, in the words of defense specialist Richard Kohn (1994), "the most powerful military leader since George C. Marshall, the most popular since Dwight D. Eisenhower, and the most political since Douglas MacArthur." Worried that Powell had become too influential,

Kohn charged that during his tenure "civilian control eroded most since the rise of the military establishment in the 1940s and 1950s."

Further evidence can be found in Clinton's efforts to shape the JCS to better fit his administration's conception of the utility of force in "operations other than war." According to one observer, "Clinton's experience with Powell taught him that he would have to choose his next chairman carefully" (Worth 1998). He did so first by looking outside the current JCS to select General John Shalikashvili, CINC of Europe, who was considerably more supportive of nontraditional missions. He then replaced the remaining members of the JCS with like-minded chiefs. Finally, in July 1997, he named Army General Hugh Shelton, a former Special Operations commander-in-chief, as Shalikashvili's successor. While "some defense analysts claim that Clinton . . . 'packed' the JCS," the fact that such action was necessary to gain support for his foreign and military policies is instructive.

Twenty-First Century Challenges

As we look toward the end of the first decade of the new century, two key questions about the Defense Department's foreign policy role must be addressed. The first concerns the overall force posture, doctrines, and strategies of the department in light of the dramatically changed global environment. As the new century began, the American military looked remarkably similar to its Cold War version in spite of the dramatically different strategic and security environment. The need for reform and restructuring was punctuated sharply when three airliners piloted by terrorists crashed into the towers of the World Trade center and the Pentagon on September 11, 2001.

Critics had long been pressing for restructuring in light of the new threats and security concerns likely to face the country, stressing unconventional threats such as those revealed by the terrorist strikes. However, previous efforts to restructure forces and strategies in light of the al-

tered environment produced few major changes. For example, although a regular *Quadrennial Defense Review* (the first was completed in 1997) was initiated—with much fanfare—to plan for America's defense needs, its proposals continued to envision a force structure "to be built around aircraft carriers, combat jets, tanks, and other big-ticket weapons," all of which would require additional defense spending (Newman and Cooperman 1997). According to the Center for Strategic and Budgetary Assessment, a defense policy institute:

> The [1996] QDR [Quadrennial Defense Review] contains a number of serious strategic flaws, including: a facile assessment of future threats; a reliance on outdated models for force structure analysis; a threat assessment that is defined in terms of U.S. strategy; a narrow examination of plausible strategic alternatives; an overemphasis on Cold War measures of forward presence; a major disjuncture between strategic assessment and recommended force posture; and a dependence on a vision of future warfare that is both self-referential and unrealistic. . . . [T]he QDR provides ample evidence that DOD has yet to transcend its Cold War planning framework. The QDR opts for a strategy that focuses on near-term and familiar challenges when it should pursue a "transformation" strategy that focuses on the very different, and potentially far more serious, challenges likely to be faced over the long term. . . . As a result of the shortcomings in both the strategic and budgetary areas, it is clear that DOD will eventually have to revisit many of the issues and concerns that are raised—or, in some cases, avoided—in the QDR.
>
> (HTTP://WWW.CSBAONLINE.ORG/)

In 2001, Secretary of Defense Donald Rumsfeld and his director of the Office of Net Assessment, Andrew Marshall, initiated another review to make "significant changes in the weapons the

Defense Department buys and the way the military thinks about strategic challenges" (Ricks 2001). According to a Pentagon official, the review would eliminate the "two major regional contingency" doctrine of the 1990s and set the Defense Department on a course to meet the challenges of the new century. As we discussed in Chapter 4, Rumsfeld revealed the results in late September 2001, shortly after the terrorist attacks. The 2001 *Quadrennial Defense Review Report* stressed the critical challenges of terrorism, chemical and biological weapons, cyberattacks, and missile threats and oriented U.S. strategy away from the two "major regional contingency" approaches that had dominated force planning. Hence, in conjunction with *Joint Vision 2020* and Rumsfeld's subsequent plans for revamping the military's command structure, the Bush administration initiated its efforts to bring U.S. military forces into line with the twenty-first century environment. Of course, implementing the proposed changes will take time, and almost certainly prove more difficult than planning for them.

The second major concern involves **civil-military relations** in the new century. Civilian control of the military is a principle as old as the Republic itself and thoroughly interwoven into the nation's liberal political culture (Huntington 1957). As we have discussed, many believe that the uniformed military is more influential and capable in its policy role than ever before. Critics express concern that the balance between civilian and military control of the defense establishment now—to an alarming degree—tilts toward the military. In their view, augmenting the authority and independence of the chair of the joints chiefs under the Goldwater-Nichols act has had the unintended consequence of so dramatically enhancing the power of the armed services that they now challenge the very principle of civilian control of the military. John Lehman, Secretary of the Navy at the time of the 1986 reorganization act, has written that "In their understandable quest for efficiency, the military reformers have consolidated the power previously separated be-

tween the military departments, disenfranchised the civilian officials of each service, and created autocracy in the joint staff and arbitrary power in the person of the chairman" (Powell, et al. 1994).

This potential crisis in civil-military relations has several facets. First, the military has become more politicized, steadily more open in its political views and affiliations, and increasingly willing to manipulate political leaders and processes to secure their own preferences (Cohen 1997). Second, there is an increasing gap between the military and broader society, as fewer citizens serve in the armed forces and as recruits are drawn from an increasingly narrow segment (mostly from military families). This may indicate "a growing gap between military and societal values" (Cohen 1997). Finally, the rise of the centralized staff and the power of the JCS and its chair, as noted, shifts the balance between civilian and military officials (Cohen 1997; see also Holsti 1998–1999; Ricks 1997).

Will this combination of factors generate a civil-military crisis in the new century? The Goldwater-Nichols act does markedly enhance the capacity of the JCS chairman to exercise influence, but it does not guarantee that the exercise of influence will be successful: "Goldwater-Nichols assures that the nation's top military officers will be *heard* by civilian policy makers, but not that they be *heeded*" (Johnson and Metz 1995). If the current chapter in the continuing debate has distinctiveness, it is in the "activism of the military" in "helping define its relationship to civil authorities and to the American public" (Johnson and Metz 1995).

Having said that, we would also be remiss if we did not recall how frequently during the past half-century civilian leaders adopted military ways of thinking about political problems, as witnessed by the recurrent resort to force and other interventionist strategies the nation has long embraced. It is, perhaps, instructive that among Donald Rumsfeld's first efforts when he took over the role of secretary of defense was a systematic campaign to reestablish civilian control over the military.

THE INTELLIGENCE COMMUNITY

Like the military, the intelligence community has played a prominent role in American foreign policy for nearly half a century. Established to be "American's eyes and ears in a dangerous world" (Kober 1998), the intelligence community was, as a former chair of the House Permanent Select Committee on Intelligence suggested, "a spyglass focused on the Soviet Union, keeping track of Soviet military research and development and watching Soviet activities throughout the developing world" (McCurdy 1994). With the end of the Cold War, the intelligence community found itself increasingly challenged over its continuing relevance and its capabilities. As we discussed in Chapter 5, many critics called for major overhauls of the community.

When members of the Al Qaeda terrorist network successfully hijacked four airliners and crashed three of them into the World Trade Center and the Pentagon on September 11, 2001, the intelligence community found its new mission for the twenty-first century. However, its failure to warn of the attacks and to apprehend Osama bin Laden, the terrorist leader, ensure that questions and criticism will continue. How the intelligence community should serve American foreign policy and security interests remains a critical question. How it should be structured to do so is equally vital.

Since its inception, the intelligence community has engaged in four basic activities: *research and analysis* (CIA and most members), *espionage* (mostly CIA), *technical surveillance* (mostly non-CIA members), and *covert action* (mostly CIA) (Hilsman 1995). In the twenty-first century environment, with its new emphasis on non-state and transnational threats such as terrorism, these remain the central activities. The nature, extent, and objectives of these activities remain vital questions.

Structure and Mission

Foreign policy decision makers need *finished intelligence*—"data . . . which has been carefully collated and analyzed by substantive experts specifically to meet the needs of the national leadership" (Marchetti and Marks 1974)—to understand the varied military, economic, political, scientific, domestic, and foreign issues and events requisite to sound policy making. Such information comes from at least four sources. Much of what constitutes *raw intelligence* (the uncollated and unanalyzed data) must be sifted from *open sources*—reports of journalists and the publications of government agencies, private businesses, and scholars. Additional information is acquired through cloak-and-dagger escapades often called *human intelligence (HUMINT)* because it comes from human, not technical sources. *Imagery intelligence (IMINT)* (computer code that must be converted into images) from cryptanalysis and reconnaissance satellites and *signal intelligence (SIGINT)*—information gathered from interception and analysis of communications, electronic, and telemetry signals—are *technical sources* that provide a wealth of intelligence from around the world.

As Figure 11.4 indicates, gathering and analyzing these different forms of information occurs in and through a vast complex of agencies that together make up the intelligence community. Overall, responsibility for managing the community rests with the ***director of central intelligence (DCI),*** who is also director of the Central Intelligence Agency. The DCI exercises his or her authority through the *National Foreign Intelligence Board (NFIB)* and the *National Intelligence Council (NIC)*. These are bodies made up of the principals of operating agencies comprising the intelligence community and chaired by the DCI. The DCI, in turn, is responsible to the National Security Council, and through it, to the president. In practice, of course, the character of the "intelligence community" is much more decentralized and disorderly than this brief description suggests, and the director of central intelligence exercises much less central authority than the title seems to imply. "Indeed, tribal and feudal metaphors often seem more appropriate in describing how the various collection, processing, and analytic organizations interact with one another and with policy makers" (Flanagan 1985; see also Lowenthal

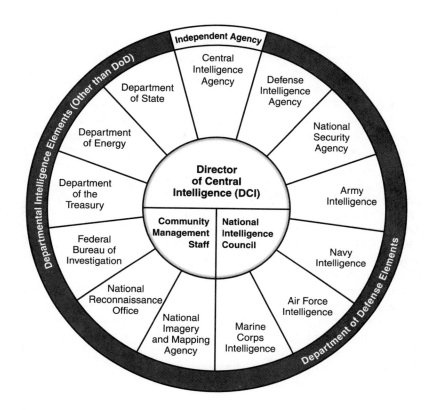

FIGURE 11.4 The United States Intelligence Community

Source: The Central Intelligence Agency website at www.odci.gov/ic/icroll.htm

1992). *Oversight* of the intelligence community is conducted by both branches. In the executive branch, in addition to the National Security Council, the *President's Foreign Intelligence Advisory Board (PFIAB)* gives general counsel on the conduct of the intelligence community, including the collection and evaluation of intelligence and the execution of intelligence policy. In 1993, President Clinton's Executive Order 12863 established the *Intelligence Oversight Board* as a standing committee for the PFIAB to focus specifically on the legality of intelligence activities. In practice, however, the PFIAB has not been a central player in the intelligence community, as presidents have viewed its utility quite differently (Holt 1995).

Congress developed its current oversight mechanisms in the late 1970s following revelations of abuses committed over the previous quarter-century by intelligence agencies. It established the House and Senate *Select Committees on Intelligence* to authorize appropriations for the intelligence community, receive reports on intelligence analysis and production, and oversee the conduct of covert activities once the president has presented a "finding" on the need for such activities. More broadly, the president is required by law to keep Congress "fully and currently informed" of all intelligence activities, and Congress as a whole appropriates all money for the intelligence community, including money for intelligence activities secretly tucked away in the Pentagon's budget.

Intelligence and the Department of Defense
The size of the intelligence community, in money and personnel, remains uncertain owing to the secrecy in which the community and its activities are shrouded. Budget estimates from the 1990s, which remain classified, indicate that

spending on intelligence reached $28 billion, fell to $26 billion, and then, at the end of the decade, climbed back to about $30 billion (see *Congress Daily/AM,* 28 April 2000; also Aizenman 1999). Figure 11.4 makes it clear that the Department of Defense (DOD) is the largest component of the intelligence community. Through the agencies and elements shown in the figure, the DOD consumes anywhere from two-thirds to three-fourths of the federal intelligence budget.

The *National Reconnaissance Office (NRO)* is the biggest spender. The NRO manages the nation's satellite reconnaissance programs at an annual cost (in 1999) of about $7 billion (*Defense Week,* 1 February 1999). Controlled jointly by the CIA and Defense Department, it operates under the "cover" of the Air Force, which reportedly pays the bills for the extremely costly photographic and electronic reconnaissance satellites and the rockets necessary to put them into orbit. The imaging (previously photographic) satellites for years provided enormous amounts of detailed information on military and related strategic developments in the Soviet Union and elsewhere. According to one anonymous source, the NRO imaging capability "could start with a satellite picture covering all of downtown Washington and get down so close you can almost read license plates on cars" (Pincus 1994). Given that, the failures of high-tech reconnaissance satellites to detect Iran's nuclear program and India's 1998 preparations for its nuclear test are troublesome.

The NRO was created in 1960 to replace the U-2 spy-plane program. Its existence was not revealed until 1973, when its name was inadvertently included in a declassified congressional document, and it remained officially unacknowledged until 1992. "The magic phrase '*national technical means*' was invented so that the parties could talk to each other about reconnaissance satellites without using those words" (Holt 1995). To better coordinate surveillance and imagery intelligence obtained from NRO satellites, the Central Imagery Office was created in 1993 (Holt 1995). In 1996, the National Imaging and Mapping Agency was established to manage all military and civilian surveillance and mapping operations. It combined the functions of the Defense Mapping Agency, the Central Imagery Office, the Defense Dissemination Program Office, and the CIA's National Photographic Interpretation Center, along with the imagery processing and dissemination functions of the Defense Intelligence Agency and the NRO. Its budget is also classified (Lais 1997).

Once the Cold War ended Congress became increasingly restive about the resources the NRO and its related agencies demanded. New fuel was added to the controversy when, in mid-1994, the Senate Intelligence Committee complained that the NRO had concealed from Congress a $310 million office building under construction near Dulles Airport in Washington. "The NRO 'is a Cold War organization that still operates under a rule that puts the taxpayer last and its requirements first,' is the way one twenty-year observer of the agency [put] it" (cited in Pincus 1994). To address this problem, Congress (in its 2000 intelligence authorization bill) established a "National Commission for the Review of the National Reconnaissance Office" to "evaluate the roles and mission, organizational structure, technical skills, contractor relationships, use of commercial imagery, acquisition of launch vehicles, launch services, and launch infrastructure, mission assurance, acquisition authorities, and relationship to other agencies and departments of the federal government in order to assure continuing success . . . " The commission completed its work in early 2001 and offered a series of recommendations for upgrading the operations and oversight of the NRO.

The *National Security Agency (NSA),* which is responsible for signals intelligence (SIGINT), communications security, and cryptology, follows the NRO as the second most expensive DOD intelligence agency, spending about $4 billion per year in the 1990s. It is also the largest agency, employing an estimated 38,000 people in 2000 (Strobel 2000).

NSA's operations are extraordinarily technology-intensive, requiring massive supercomputers to discharge its responsibilities. Created by a classified presidential directive in 1952, NSA was not generally acknowledged as a government organization until 1957 and, much like the NRO, did not acknowledge its own existence until 1991. Indeed, its legendary silence led people to joke that its initials stood for "No Such Agency."

Scrutiny has heightened in recent years, however. Publicity over a Cold War-era program known as *"Echelon,"* by which the NSA collected information from commercial communication satellites, led to concerns over an NSA role in stealing trade secrets from allies and invading the privacy of American citizens (Strobel 2000; Munro 2000). Early in 2000, its massive array of computers—nearly half the computing power in the entire world–crashed and remained shut down for three days. Although it is now believed that human error and computer glitches are responsible, the crash raised questions about the security of the NSA operations and the age and capability of its technology (Strobel 2000; Vistica 2000).

After a 1998 investigation by the Senate Intelligence Committee found the NSA "in desperate need of organizational restructuring and modernization of its information technology," NSA undertook reforms in both areas. In 2000, for example, its five traditional directorates (operations, information systems security, technology, corporate management, and support services) were reorganized into two directorates: Signals Intelligence (SIGINT) and Information Assurance. Other efforts by the agency's leadership to modernize and streamline the agency have been resisted by its career employees (Wolfe 2001; Strobel 2000). According to Representative Porter Goss (R–Florida), chair of the House Intelligence Committee, these and other concerns combine to make the NSA "the number one concern in the intelligence community right now in terms of capability."

Like NSA, the **Defense Intelligence Agency (DIA)** also operates under the authority of the secretary of defense, but it is the smallest of all DOD intelligence operations, with about 7,000 employees and a budget of approximately half a billion dollars. Created by Robert McNamara in 1961, the DIA was to consolidate in one agency the various intelligence units of the armed services. The latter—Army Intelligence, Air Force Intelligence, and the Office of Naval Intelligence—are involved in the collection of "departmental" intelligence as opposed to "national" intelligence—that is, in collecting information germane to their tactical (battlefield) missions. In so doing, however, their intelligence product has often been skewed in the direction preferred by their parent organizations for "budgeteering" purposes: the air force predicted a bomber gap; the navy predicted the expansion of Soviet naval power, and the army found Russian divisions that only existed on paper (Ransom 1970; see also Shulsky and Schmitt 1994–1995).

Designed to provide direct intelligence support to the secretary of defense and the Joint Chiefs of Staff (for whom the director of DIA is the principal intelligence adviser), the DIA's assignment was to improve coordination and management of Defense Department intelligence resources. For instance, the DIA represents the Defense Department on the National Foreign Intelligence Board and manages the defense attaché system (which places military representatives in U.S. field missions abroad). In 1995, the "Defense HUMINT Service" unit was formed, which collects the military's spies and clandestine operatives into single system (rather than one for each service) under the DIA (but, interestingly, overseen in the field by the CIA) to improve the coordination and analysis of military intelligence (Waller 1995).

Although the functions assigned the DIA appear to place it in a position superior to the army, navy, and air force, the DIA collects little information on its own, relying instead on the service intelligence agencies for its raw intelligence data. Moreover, the individual military departments send observers to the NFIB meetings and military attachés themselves are drawn from the armed services (Holt 1995). Hence the DIA has chiefly analyzed information collected by the DIA, the

Pentagon's satellites, and the embassy attachés, but has been less effective as a central coordinator (Waller 1995). These and other problems have led critics to question the need for DIA's continued existence, but as long as it enjoys the backing of the secretary of defense it will remain a formidable rival of other intelligence agencies.

Intelligence and the Department of State

The *Bureau of Intelligence and Research (INR)* is the State Department's representative in the intelligence community. The department's intelligence functions arise naturally out of its general foreign affairs responsibilities, and much of what the department routinely does in the way of analyzing and interpreting information might be regarded as intelligence work. INR is the unit through which the State Department makes its input into the various interagency committees that seek to guide intelligence operations (other than covert activities), including the National Foreign Intelligence Board. The director of INR is also the secretary of state's senior in-house intelligence adviser.

In addition to representing the State Department within the intelligence community, INR's primary objective is to introduce a "diplomatic sensitivity to intelligence reports"; and its own reports "are among the most highly regarded in the government—some say the best" (Johnson 1989). But INR does not independently collect intelligence except through normal cable traffic and reporting from overseas posts. Instead, it depends on input from other agencies, which its small staff then turns into finished intelligence reports. Within the intelligence community, therefore, the State Department has been more a consumer than a producer of intelligence. That fact combined with INR's comparatively small size lead to the suspicion that the State Department is in a relatively disadvantageous position in the highly competitive intelligence community.

Intelligence and Other Agencies The Treasury Department, the Energy Department, and the Federal Bureau of Investigation (FBI) are the remaining officially designated members of the intelligence community. Each plays an important role in intelligence operations, although none is concerned primarily with the collection of foreign intelligence.

Treasury's intelligence activities derive in part from the collection of foreign economic intelligence by its overseas attachés. More specific intelligence activities derive from the department's responsibilities for protecting (by the U.S. Secret Service) the president, presidential candidates, and certain foreign dignitaries; for controlling (through the Bureau of Alcohol, Tobacco, and Firearms and the U.S. Customs Service) illegal trafficking in alcohol, tobacco, firearms, and other articles entering international trade and for protecting against terrorism in international transportation facilities; and for ensuring compliance (through the Internal Revenue Service) with the Internal Revenue laws.

The Department of Energy maintains an Office of Intelligence responsible for the overt collection of intelligence on energy policies and developments abroad. As the department responsible for conducting nuclear weapons research, development, and production, it maintains counterintelligence capabilities regarding those weapons. It also participates with other government agencies in monitoring nonproliferation issues.

The Federal Bureau of Investigation (a Justice Department agency) is responsible for counterintelligence, and plays a key role in counterterrorism as well. The FBI's mandate is strictly domestic; therefore, it must work with the CIA, which bears responsibility for counterintelligence and counterterrorism abroad. However, the relationship between the two agencies has long been marked by conflict (Riebling 1994), fed in part by their different perspectives and responsibilities.

When the FBI catches spies, it thinks in terms of putting them in jail or, if they have diplomatic immunity, of expelling them from the country. When the CIA catches spies, it thinks in terms of turning them into double agents, that is, using them to spy on the government they have been working for (Holt 1995).

Recently, however, fueled in part by the Aldrich Ames spy case (which was characterized by a lack of cooperation between the FBI and the CIA) and emerging security threats like terrorism and drugs, the FBI and CIA have begun to co-operate more closely. The "Counterintelligence 21" project, for example (see Chapter 5), among other efforts to link the FBI more effectively, has facilitated better cooperation, as has the establishment of the counterterrorism center discussed in Chapter 5. Indeed, in the after-math of the September 11 strikes, the counter-terrorism center expanded its operations substantially, with FBI agents increasing their presence and activities accordingly. Moreover, when terrorist attacks occur against American targets overseas, as in the 1998 attacks against American embassies in the Sudan and Tanzania, or at home as in the 2001 attacks on New York and Washington, FBI officials are typically first on the scene, demonstrating both the centrality of the FBI and increasing cooperation between the FBI and CIA. However, the indictment and arrest of FBI counterintelligence officer Robert Hanssen, charged with fifteen years of passing secrets, identifying spies, and naming potential targets for recruitment, has extended the pall of the Ames debacle to the FBI as well (Risen 2001b, 2001c).

Although not formally designated a member of the intelligence community, mention should be made of the Justice Department's Drug Enforcement Administration (DEA), which does carry out some intelligence activities in connection with its responsibilities as a police force, with jurisdiction over foreign and domestic aspects of narcotics production and trafficking. Thus, although its activities sometimes overlap with the CIA, the two agencies, much like the FBI and CIA, have quite different perspectives on their bureaucratic roles. Indeed, many accounts indicate that the DEA's efforts to combat the drug trade in the 1980s and early 1990s came into direct conflict with the CIA's activities in Central and South American, especially in Nicaragua. Just as with the FBI, the DEA's role abroad has expanded in recent years, stimulated in part by the "war on drugs" and the heightened national concern with drug trafficking to which both the Bush and Clinton administrations responded (see Chapter 5).

The Central Intelligence Agency

When George Tenet took over the position of director of central intelligence in July 1997, he inherited an agency—perhaps an entire intelligence community—in crisis. The CIA continued to grope about in the post–Cold War environment for a role and purpose that would define and legitimize its activities (and budgets). Tenet's CIA was also rocked by scandals that threatened its morale and ability to function: the exposure of Aldrich Ames, a counterintelligence officer, as a "mole" for the Soviet Union/Russia (Wise 1995); the revelation that Tenet's predecessor, John Deutch, had violated security and compromised agency and intelligence community secrets (see *Bulletin of the Atomic Scientists,* November 2000, 37); and the allegations by female CIA officers of gender discrimination within the operations directorate (see Shannon 1995). Public criticism over many of the agency's predictions and its previous activities in places like Nicaragua, Guatemala, and elsewhere damaged its prestige and standing. A host of reform studies called for dramatic changes in its role, structure, and operations, including some that advocated its complete dismantling.[8] At the same time, coordinating across the sprawling intelligence community was increasingly challenging, and a series of highly-publicized intelligence analysis failures led many to question whether the agency and community could "get it right." Things did not get easier either. The 2001 terrorist attacks on the United States substantially raised the stakes for agency failure. In short, Tenet directed an agency in disarray, one facing challenges and problems in all its major responsibilities. Addressing these challenges—in management, in intelligence analysis, and in covert operations—and reshaping the agency (and the broader intelligence community) to respond to the new threats of the new century remains a critical requirement.

Organization and Responsibilities Largely out of concern for the quality of intelligence analysis available to policy makers—stemming in part from the surprise attack by the Japanese at Pearl Harbor in 1941—the United States created the CIA as part of the National Security Act of 1947. The CIA was assigned responsibilities for: (1) advising the National Security Council (NSC) on intelligence matters relating to national security; (2) making recommendations to the NSC for coordinating the intelligence activities of the various federal executive departments and agencies; (3) correlating and evaluating intelligence and providing for its dissemination; and (4) carrying out such additional services, functions, and duties relating to national security intelligence as the NSC might direct. Before long, covert psychological, political, paramilitary, and economic activities were added to the CIA's charge, which we examined in Chapter 5.

As we noted before, the Director of Central Intelligence is also the head of the Central Intelligence Agency. Assisted by a deputy director of central intelligence and another for intelligence community management, the director oversees the activities of the CIA's bureaucracy, which is shown in Figure 11.5. With a budget of just over $3 billion and around 20,000 employees (excluding contract employees and paid informants), the CIA currently constitutes about ten to fifteen percent of the intelligence community's expenditures and an even smaller percentage of its employees.

Although it clearly has many elements and support offices, the core of the CIA is its two main directorates: intelligence and operations. The *Directorate of Intelligence* is the analysis division of the CIA (see Figure 11.6). Its responsibilities are to sift through and analyze the vast quantity of data gathered from public and intelligence community sources and produce the CIA's intelligence assessments. Covert actions, clandestine intelligence collection, and counterintelligence are the responsibility of the CIA's *Directorate of Operations,* otherwise known as the clandestine services.

The CIA and the Management of Intelligence One major challenge that has always confronted the DCI and the broad intelligence community is coordination. The "central" in its name theoretically makes the CIA the hub of the intelligence community, as it seeks to exercise its responsibility for coordination of the intelligence community. However, the DCI exercises independent authority only over the CIA's budget. This puts the DCI at a competitive disadvantage in dealing with the other intelligence agencies, whose activities he or she is supposed to coordinate. Noting this, a congressional committee described the DCI's influence over the rest of the intelligence community as limited to that of "an interested critic" (cited in Bamford 1983).

Periodically, this weakness has engendered efforts to strengthen the central coordinating power of the DCI. President Nixon, for example, first charged the DCI with making recommendations for a consolidated national foreign intelligence budget. President Ford later tried to enhance the DCI's role in the allocation of national (but not tactical) intelligence resources. Carter went even further, giving the DCI "full and exclusive authority over approval of the National Intelligence Program budget submitted to the president." The Reagan administration backed away, deciding to "cast the DCI more in the role of a coordinator, rather than a manager, of community affairs" (Flanagan 1985). Moreover, while legislation introduced in 1992 called for greater power for the DCI, "to coordinate and set priorities for the entire intelligence community" (Boren 1992), it was shelved soon after Bill Clinton became president. Several subsequent proposals late in the 1990s recommending that the DCI be provided authority over a unified intelligence budget (see Prados 1996) fell victim to the tribal rivalries to which we referred earlier.

The most recent effort began in 2001. In May of the year, George W. Bush asked former national security adviser Brent Scowcroft—the head of Bush's Foreign Intelligence Advisory Board—to review the intelligence community

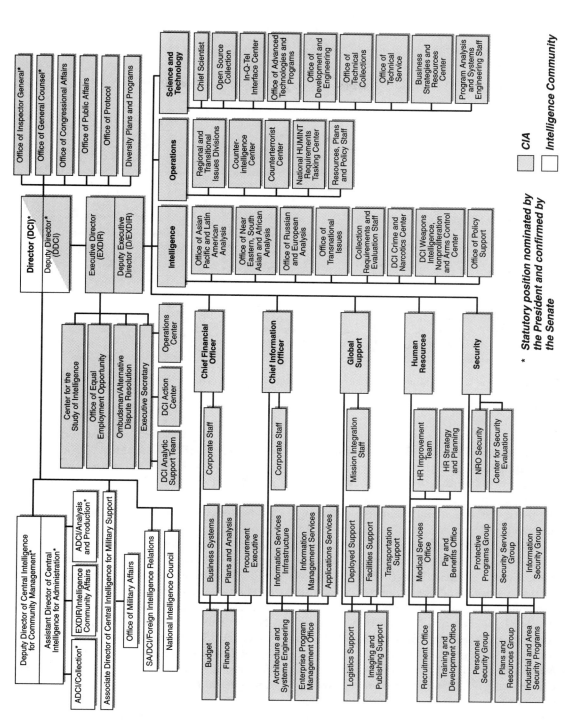

FIGURE 11.5 The Central Intelligence Agency

Source: The Central Intelligence Agency website at www.odci.gov/cia/publications/facttell/diagram.htm

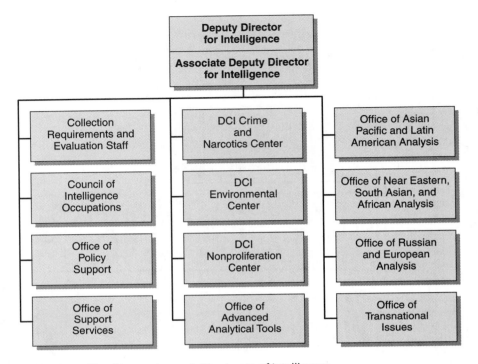

FIGURE 11.6 The Central Intelligence Agency's Directorate of Intelligence

Source: The Central Intelligence Agency website at www.odci.gov/cia/di/mission/orgchart.html

while CIA director George Tenet conducted a thorough internal review of the intelligence system. After the September 11 attacks exposed what many believed to be flaws in the system (and intelligence failures as well), the House Intelligence Committee issued a report criticizing the intelligence community and advocating "a fresh look at restructuring the CIA and the rest of the U.S. intelligence community." Committee Chairman Porter Goss (R-Florida) urged President Bush to be "bold, innovative and to think out of the box."

Shortly thereafter, in November, Scowcroft's committee recommended that the NRO, the National Imagery and Mapping Agency, and the NSA all be transferred from the Department of Defense to the CIA to be coordinated and directed by the director of central intelligence (Pincus 2001). Defense Secretary Rumsfeld opposed the change, as did the Pentagon and the Senate

and House Armed Services Committees, but commission members argued that "this is the moment in time when we need to do the right thing no matter who loses turf" (Pincus 2001). Another battle of tribal rivalries brewed.

Another coordinating mechanism at the disposal of the director of central intelligence flows from his or her responsibility to produce intelligence reports for the entire foreign affairs government. As noted earlier, the DCI chairs two units that bring together the other national intelligence agencies, the National Foreign Intelligence Board (NFIB) and the National Intelligence Council (NIC). Among their tasks is production of *National Intelligence Estimates (NIEs),* routinely prepared on various parts of the world, and *Special National Intelligence Estimates (SNIEs),* prepared in response to specific requests by top-level policy makers. These reports, signed by the DCI, are supposed to be the "best judgments" of the intelligence community on their respective subjects, and large numbers are typically produced every year. Their value, however, is suspect. One Senator described them as "overly cautious, caveated, and consensus-oriented" (Boren 1992). General Norman Schwarzkopf, who led U.S. forces during Operation Desert Storm in the Persian Gulf war, characterized the intelligence estimates as "unhelpful mush."

The CIA's intelligence analysis role faces at least three major challenges. The first concerns the problems associated with coordinating the disparate elements of the intelligence community as they work to create a unified estimate. The many perspectives and voices have a centrifugal effect on the estimates, working to either water them down to common denominators (the "mush" to which Schwarzkopf referred) or to weigh them down with exceptions, footnotes, alternate views, and the like, so that there is no true "estimate" involved but, rather, a series of agency-based positions. The second issue concerns the difficulty in generating timely estimates that extract the necessary information from the various agencies that collected it in such a way as to provide good information for policy makers. Information available to the government in its far-flung intelligence-gathering agencies does not always make it to policy makers. The final challenge is often referred to as the *"producer-consumer" challenge*. It refers to the difficulty in getting the information—accurate and objective—into key policy makers' hands in useful forms and at opportune moments.

Intelligence Gathering and Analysis The CIA plays a central role in both gathering and analyzing information, and then providing that potentially vital intelligence to policy makers who must make decisions. Intelligence is gathered by officers in both the intelligence (especially open, publicly available sources) and operations (especially HUMINT) directorates, and is then analyzed by the scientists, researchers, and scholars (many with Ph.D.s) in the intelligence directorate (see, for example, Nye 1994; Andrew 1995;

Berkowitz and Goodman 2000). As noted, both the intelligence directorate and the DCI play key roles in shaping community-wide assessments and estimates as well.

The CIA's role in gathering, analyzing, and disseminating intelligence continues to be a dilemma for the new century (see Berkowitz and Goodman 2000). Most information gathered by the intelligence community is from open sources or from technical sources. The CIA plays a role in each of these: open sources are examined chiefly in the intelligence directorate, but are also reported on by field agents. Technical sources often involve the CIA as well, in conjunction with other agencies such as the NRO and the NSA. Generally, however, the special contribution of the CIA in intelligence gathering involves HUMINT, which is the province of the operations directorate.

Recruiting and running spy networks in other countries is perhaps the signature effort of the CIA in the public's mind. Beginning immediately after World War II, the agency (and its forerunners) worked to cultivate well-placed human sources of information in foreign governments and societies who could provide critical information on key issue and events. Trained at "The Farm," Camp Peary in Virginia, espionage officers were assigned a variety of "covers" in American embassies and other positions which enabled them to perform their activities.

After the intelligence scandals of the 1970s, however, the Carter administration tried to reshape the intelligence community. Most significant for intelligence gathering, resources devoted to HUMINT were cut as the Carter administration chose to emphasize technical means of intelligence collection. Bobby Inman testified before Congress in 1982 that "the intelligence establishment" lost "forty percent of its personnel from 1964 to the mid-1970s." Later reports put the number of employees in the CIA's Directorate of Operations (DO) during the Carter administration at 3,000 (Ignatius 1995). Following Reagan's election, many restrictions imposed during the 1970s were lifted and the intelligence community, with the CIA at the vanguard, enjoyed a resurgence.

The number of workers in clandestine services grew to roughly 7,000 during the Reagan administration, "swollen by new recruits who were managing a global campaign of paramilitary operations against the Soviet Union" (Ignatius 1995).

Expanding numbers masked a more serious problem, however. According to an operations officer (writing under a pseudonym) who retired in disgust in 1993, the DO "has evolved into a sorry blend of Monty Python and Big Brother" (Shirley 1998). The culture that evolved inside the DO has become "sloppy" and "lackadaisical," staffed chiefly with personnel without the expertise that one would expect for someone specializing in, say, the Middle East (Shirley 1998). As the former officer noted, "the average senior officer rose through the hierarchy without ever learning much about the language, culture, or politics of the countries in which he served. . . . Not a single Iran desk chief during the eight years that I worked on Iran could speak or even read Persian. Not a single Near East Division chief knew Arabic, Persian, or Turkish, and only one could get along even in French" (Shirley 1998). This, in part, stemmed from the DO subculture nurtured by training at "the Farm," where instructors "told trainees that cultural distinctions did not matter . . . 'an op is an op'" (Shirley 1998).

Nowhere were these problems more evident than the consequences of a late 1970s decision to stress the recruitment of foreign nationals as a measure by which to evaluate the performance of intelligence officers (Shirley 1998; Aizenman 1999). This led to what many eventually characterized as the "*numbers game:*" recruiting as many foreign nationals as possible to spy for the United States as the key to career advancement within "The Company." As operations officers attempted to build their recruitment records—often without consideration of the quality or consequences of their efforts—this numbers game almost inevitably led to problems. As early as 1985, for example, "the vast majority of the CIA's foreign agents were mediocre assets at best, put on the payroll because case officers needed high recruitment numbers to get promoted" (Shirley 1998). In 1994

an investigative report by *U.S. News and World Report* (4 July 1994) determined that "the pressure from DO managers to recruit new agents is so great that many field officers exaggerate the value of their agents, claim State Department reporting as their own, try to compromise officials of friendly governments, and even claim to have recruited nonexistent agents."

To counter this problem DCI William Webster introduced an "Asset Validation System" late in the Reagan administration, which was expanded by his successors Robert Gates, James Woolsey, and John Deutch. However, it has mostly required a few more memoranda and a little more paperwork, without having much effect (Shirley 1998). In the middle of the Clinton administration, publicity on some of the questionable assets led to more serious attention. In 1996, a more thorough evaluation resulted in the dismissal of about 1,000 agents, including 100 who were murderers, torturers, or other types of criminals (Aizenman 1999). Meanwhile, disgruntled and disillusioned operations officers retired in droves, convinced that the real reforms on the directorate's operations and culture were unlikely. According to one former officer, "nearly three-quarters of the case officers from [the] 1985 class have quit the service" (Shirley 1998).

The September 11 terrorist attacks revealed another problem: the lack of HUMINT caused by the overreliance on technical means and the long-term decay of the CIA's human intelligence assets. The shocking success of the surprise attacks exposed the flip side of the HUMINT dilemma: such assets may be unsavory, but the lack of them can cause intelligence failures with devastating results. Addressing this problem, a former CIA counterterrorism expert argued "We have a major gap here. . . There's been a lot of emphasis on technical collection at the expense of human resources" (Freedberg 2001). Both the long-term emphasis on technical means and the more recent "human rights checks" on human assets have combined to create a deficient agency. Indeed, after the attacks President George W. Bush immediately increased the agency's funds partly to support better HUMINT. Former President Bush urged changes as well: "We have to free up the intelligence system from some of its constraints. . . . [It is] kind of a dirty business and you have to deal with a lot of unsavory characters" (McCallister 2001).

The difficulty, of course, is attracting the right personnel. Although the CIA enjoyed a dramatic increase in applications after the September 11 attacks, its needs are more difficult to meet. As a longtime analyst of intelligence affairs noted, "The ideal candidate is an Arab-American citizen, has knowledge about the culture and the Middle East, has language ability, and is willing to work for the CIA." An anonymous CIA officer added: you [also] need to put people in place and let them sit there for ten years" (quoted in Freedberg 2001). Such expertise is rare, and the agency does not have the luxury of such time.

A related aspect concerns counterintelligence, which involves efforts to secure America's secrets from foreign governments (see Godson 2000). Long focused on preventing and discovering Soviet spies, counterintelligence responsibilities were long the responsibility of CIA counterintelligence chief James Jesus Angleton, who headed the counterintelligence unit for two decades until his forced resignation in 1974. Convinced that the CIA had been penetrated by a "mole," Angleton ruthlessly pursued those he suspected of spying for others, isolated other agents, and sometimes destroyed their careers (Mangold 1991). His "legendary paranoia and incessant probing of valued CIA employees created 'hostility and a meanness of spirit . . . stifled ideas, and poisoned initiative'" (Smith 1994a).

Indeed, many argue that the climate left by Angleton resulted in the marginalization of CIA counterintelligence efforts and, ultimately, the Aldrich Ames scandal (Wise 1995). After Ames' activities were unearthed in 1994, the CIA's inspector general determined that his spying, which dated back to 1985, had led to the betrayal of fifty-five clandestine operations, nearly twice the number first thought. Virtually all CIA agents in Eastern Europe were either blown or double agents.

The Ames fiasco led the Clinton administration to make the FBI more centrally responsible for counterintelligence (Jones 1998) and, in early 2001, to issue an order establishing a new national counterintelligence executive, or "czar" to identify security threats and vulnerabilities (Risen 2001a). The February 2001 arrest of Robert Hanssen, an FBI counterintelligence officer, for alleged spying for the Soviet Union dating back to 1985, only heightened concerns about the ability of the intelligence community to protect the nation's secrets.

Analyzing intelligence—whether HUMINT or other kinds—is similarly problematic. Clearly assessing situations and providing policy makers with information is a vital role and responsibility of the CIA and the broader intelligence community (Berkowitz and Goodman 2000). One key role the CIA's intelligence directorate plays in this effort is the production of the *President's Daily Briefing* and the *National Intelligence Daily,* which provide daily descriptions and analyses of events and developments around the world of potential importance to policymakers. Other, longer term reports and papers are produced by the members of the intelligence directorate, whose officers sift through open sources, HUMINT, and technical sources to anticipate problems, trends, and developments. As Joseph Nye (1994) has described their efforts, "Intelligence analysts sift through reams of information, trying to sort the accurate from the erroneous, and when not enough facts are available, estimating what the picture would look like if all facts were available."

How good have these analyses been? Wide agreement exists on the high quality and usefulness of the daily intelligence documents, called by one intelligence officer the "most important product of the CIA." Many instances of timely, accurate papers and assessments exist and even critics acknowledge a body of excellent analyses (Goodman 1997). A recently released set of CIA estimates on Soviet spending and policy suggests a reasonably accurate set of documents (Berkowitz and Richelson 1995; Firth and Noren 1998; Fischer 1999; Haines and Leggett 2001).

However, others would argue that, on major questions, the CIA has repeatedly failed to provide good analysis. A listing would include its failure to: anticipate North Korea's invasion of South Korea in 1950 and the Chinese intervention later that year; the Soviet Union's placement of missiles in Cuba in 1962; the Soviet intervention in Czechoslovakia in 1968; the 1973 attack on Israel by Egypt and its allies; and the fall of the Shah of Iran and the Soviet invasion of Afghanistan in 1979. Accusations of poor performance on the issue of Vietnam have been leveled as well (see Adams 1994). More recently it would include its failure to anticipate Iraq's 1990 invasion of Kuwait and the 1998 test of nuclear weapons by India (see, for example, Goodman 1997; Pipes 1995).

Perhaps the most important of such alleged failures is the CIA's record on the Soviet Union. In spite of the positive assessments noted above, others have argued that the CIA failed to provide accurate assessments of Soviet strengths and weaknesses, Gorbachev's stated intentions, and the changes in Soviet military policy. As one critic stated, "prior to the Soviet collapse, the CIA, despite the agency's intense and decades-long preoccupation with Moscow, provided no strategic warning to U.S. policy makers that the Kremlin was changing and that our relations with Russia would never be the same" (Goodman 2000). If so, the failure was, as former DCI Stansfield Turner noted, "the greatest corporate failure in the agency's history" (cited in Goodman 2000).

Some would argue that the intelligence community's failure to warn against, much less prevent, the September 11 strikes on New York and Washington constitute another catastrophic failure. This one highlighted an additional weakness: not only is the CIA lacking in adequate HUMINT, it does not have sufficient analysts to sift through and make sense of the intelligence data it does collect. The House intelligence committee noted "At the National Security Agency and the Central Intelligence Agency, thousands of pieces of data were never analyzed, or were analyzed after the fact, because there are too few analysts; even fewer with the necessary language

skills. . . . Written materials can sit for months, and sometime years, before a linguist with proper security clearances can begin a translation." According to Loch Johnson (2001), writing before the September strikes, "between 1993 and 1997, fully 1,000 analysts retired from the CIA alone—a one third reduction, back to 1977 levels. By the year 2005, CIA director George Tenet anticipates that up to 40 percent of the workforce at the agency will have served for five years or less. As a result, the secret agencies lack enough talented interpreters of information to make sense of the data that flood their offices." The terrorist attacks on the United States in September underscore the need to reverse this trend and prevent future intelligence failures.

Another problem concerns the role of the DCI and the potential for *"politicization" of intelligence.* Politicization refers to the possibility that the DCI can use his or her position as adviser (or, in the case of some recent CIA directors, a member of the president's cabinet) to "slant" intelligence and reports to fit their own policy preferences. William Casey and his deputy Robert Gates are frequently singled out as the most problematic examples of politicization. Casey's role in the Reagan administration was especially controversial because he was the first DCI to enjoy cabinet rank, which simultaneously placed him in the position of advocating policy and providing assessments on which to base it. Notable examples of his alleged politicization include his efforts to ensure that CIA estimates blamed the Soviet Union for global terrorism and the 1981 assassination attempt against Pope. During confirmation hearings in 1991 leading to his appointment as the senior Bush's CIA director, Gates, too, was accused of slanting or suppressing intelligence during the 1980s to serve his (and Casey's) hard-line anti-Soviet views. Interestingly, after he was finally confirmed as CIA director, Gates launched an internal study of the "politicization" of intelligence. The task force found a "disturbing" degree of politicization within the agency but also concluded it was less pervasive than many critics alleged. This problem surfaced again during the Clinton administration when Cinton's second DCI, John Deutch, demanded and received cabinet rank to go along with his intelligence position (Waller 1996).

Management and Oversight of Covert Actions Because the CIA's responsibilities also include covert operations (discussed in Chapter 5) and espionage in other countries, which by their nature require secrecy, how to exercise control over such intelligence operations has been a regular concern for both the president and Congress. The National Security Council bears this responsibility in the presidential subsystem. Hence, the NSC apparatus has been ultimately responsible for approving covert actions and seeing that they meet applicable legal regulations (such as the prohibition against assassination of foreign political leaders).[9]

However, the concept of *plausible denial* complicates this relatively straightforward responsibility. Plausible denial means that the president is not appraised of current or pending covert actions in order to save him or her from the possible embarrassment of a "blown" operation. Hence, as the investigations of the 1970s showed, presidents can (and have) denied knowledge of covert operations undertaken on their behalf. As testimony during one of these investigations indicated, "one means of protecting the president from embarrassment was not to tell him about certain covert operations, at least formally" (*Final Report of the Select Committee to Study Governmental Operations with Respect to Intelligence Activities* 1976, I).

Partly as a result of such revelations in the 1970s, Congress has attempted to clarify the responsibility for the initiation and monitoring of covert operations. The Hughes-Ryan Amendment to the 1974 Foreign Assistance Act required that the president certify to Congress (that is, "find") that an executive-approved covert action is "important to the national interests of the United States." The law required that the DCI inform Congress of the *presidential finding* in a "timely manner," but also thereby required that the president be aware of and formally approve covert actions. In practice, the requirement

meant informing roughly forty-five to two hundred members of Congress in the House and Senate committees on intelligence, armed services, appropriations, and foreign affairs and relations. The 1980 Intelligence Oversight Act, which superceded the Hughes-Ryan requirements, cut the number of committees to only two (and, in some circumstances, allowed notification of just the speaker and minority leader in the House, the majority and minority leaders in the Senate, and the chairs and ranking members of the House and Senate intelligence committees). However, the act required prior notification of the action in most circumstances.

The evidence from the 1970s suggests other problems with top-level management of covert operations by the nation's elected officials. As one analyst observed in commenting on the Carter administration, "A tendency reportedly has grown within the CIA to forward only a few broad covert action categories to the president and make in-house decisions on all the supposedly routine ones . . . [which] permits the agency to bypass the White House and Congress" (Johnson 1980). Even when they are issued, the nature of the findings is also problematic. As some observers have indicated, they have often been too broad to be useful as instruments of control, management, and oversight (see Turner 1985; Holt 1995).

The Iran-Contra affair during the Reagan administration prompted another wave of concerns about managing covert actions. As many investigations and accounts indicate,[10] in its efforts to maintain support for the rebels fighting against the leftist Sandinista regime in Nicaragua, as well as to secure the release of American hostages held by terrorists with ties to Iran, the Reagan administration concealed the operations from Congress, failed to issue written findings, circumvented congressional restrictions on aid to the contras, and provided false and misleading information about its activities.

The Iran-contra revelations reinforced Congress's uneasiness about its oversight responsibilities with respect to covert actions and led to further changes. President Reagan issued an executive order in 1987 designed to address some of the problems. Among other things, it required all agencies to report on their activities; precluded the NSC staff from involvement in covert operations; and required written findings prior to the initiation of the operation, and access by all members of the NSC to those findings. The administration and Congress agreed to establish an independent inspector general for the CIA to improve the agency's ability to monitor itself. Congress pressed the administration even further, seeking to require written notification of all covert actions within specified time periods, thus closing the loophole the Reagan administration had used to ignore Congress as it pursued its Iranian initiative and support of the contras (Holt 1995). The legislation failed to pass the House and was then dropped when George H. W. Bush assumed the presidency. However, in 1991, Congress succeeded in passing legislation (as part of the intelligence authorization bill) that finally defined covert actions, required written findings in all cases, and banned retroactive findings.

Hence, while tension over control of covert action still exists, Congress has strengthened both its own and the president's responsibility to oversee these often controversial operations. Today they are more carefully supervised and overseen than ever (Johnson 2000a; Godson 2000). Nevertheless, revelations throughout the Clinton administration of the covert activities in which the United States has engaged (old operations in Guatemala and Chile, and new ones in Iraq and Serbia, for example) continue to raise questions about oversight and have led some to argue for the outright elimination of such activities (Hilsman 1995). New covert activities in the campaign against terrorism raise further concerns, especially since George W. Bush, determined that assassinations of terrorists is permissible under existing executive orders, and because he has authorized the CIA to "take the gloves off" in its efforts. An inherent tension exists between the principle of democratic governance, which depends on access to information so that citizens can make informed decisions, and on the secrecy that surrounds the collection of intelligence and covert intelligence operations. The question remains: Can a democratic society long absolve itself from responsibility for the conduct of its government officials without also running the risk of losing sight of who is serving whom, for what purpose, and in pursuit of what ideals? The question goes to the heart of a fundamental and persistent democratic dilemma.

ECONOMIC AGENTS IN GLOBALIZING WORLD

As our discussion in Chapters 6 and 7 suggested, substantial changes in the international political and economic systems have raised new challenges for American foreign policy. One involves the role and impact of chiefly domestically oriented departments and agencies on foreign policy. They had foreign policy roles before, but they tended to be played at the margins of key foreign and national security policy issues. However, with the end of the Cold War and the acceleration of globalization, these other executive departments and agencies have seen their role in foreign policy expand. Moreover, their primary domestic constituencies—finance for the Treasury Department, business for the Commerce Department, farmers for the Agriculture Department, and workers for the Labor Department—have become increasingly interested and engaged in international economic issues. As the issues addressed by these executive branch departments—such as trade, international finance, and economics—have become more important, a greater leadership role for those agencies principally responsible for them has ensued. And while they are increasingly involved in the interagency groups and committees that comprise the executive branch's coordinating bodies, they themselves have added complexity to the process of coordination.

Department of the Treasury

In the Eisenhower administration, Under Secretary of State Douglas Dillon played the key role in international economic policy and throughout the 1960s the National Security Council had the principal coordinating role; the trend since that time has been toward the rise of the *"economic complex"* (Destler 1994, 1998). Nobody better reflects this than the Treasury Department, which today may be the dominant voice on international economic policy.

Concern for the position of the U.S. dollar in the international monetary system gives the Treasury Department a keen interest in international affairs. Its responsibilities include tax policy, tariffs, the balance of trade and payments, exchange rate adjustments, and the public debt. Thus the Treasury is the principal department in which domestic and international financial and fiscal policy recommendations are formulated. Its ascendance in the area of international economic policy making may be "the outstanding organizational feature of U.S. international economic policy since the end of World War II" (Cohen 1994).

The importance of the Treasury Department has often brought the secretary of the treasury, who serves as the chief financial officer of the United States, into the most intimate circle of presidential advisers, where he has been able to influence foreign as well as domestic policy making. The roster of influentials would begin with Alexander Hamilton, the nation's first treasury secretary. In the past half-century it would include George M. Humphrey, Douglas Dillon, John Connally, William Simon, Michael Blumenthal, G. William Miller, James A. Baker, Nicholas F. Brady, Lloyd Bentsen, Robert Rubin, and Paul O'Neill among others.

Many recent department secretaries have participated in foreign policy making. In both the Clinton and the current Bush administrations, the secretary formally became not only a *designated member* of the National Security Council, but also of the NSC's Principals Committee (see Chapter 10). Moreover, Clinton's Treasury secretaries—Lloyd Bentson, Robert Rubin, and Lawrence Summers—were centrally involved with the National Economic Council, as is George W. Bush's Treasury Secretary, Paul O'Neill.

Other key roles for the Treasury secretary include the secretary's duties as the U.S. governor of the International Monetary Fund, the World Bank, and the Inter-American, Asian, and African development banks. Those assignments give the Treasury Secretary and Department a major voice in the often contentious decisions regarding United States participation in, and the level of contributions to, multilateral lending institutions, and in the complex issues involved in maintaining and operating of the international monetary system. During the Clinton administration, for example, it was the Treasury Department that took the lead in devising and implementing a solution to the Mexican financial crisis in 1995 and the 1997–1998 Asian financial crisis. Robert Rubin was the key policy maker in working out increased American support for the IMF in 1998 as well. During the Clinton administration, the Treasury Department was also more actively engaged in shaping trade policy than during the Reagan and Bush presidencies.

In George W. Bush's administration, Paul O'Neill took an active role on a number of issues. Reputed to be "an influential voice" on economic and other policies, O'Neill led the effort to ensure a successful re-opening of the U.S. stock markets after the September 11 terrorist attacks. Throughout the administration's first year, O'Neill met privately with Bush weekly and was reputed to be a favorite of the president. His overall impact may be indicated by the statement of an administration official: "long after a meeting has ended, O'Neill's comments often are the most memorable" (Kessler 2001). However, O'Neill frequently found himself at odds with Lawrence Lindsay, head of the National Economic Council (see Chapter 10), as both tried to assert supremacy over economic policy (Kessler 2001).

Within the department, the office of the under secretary for international affairs and the assistant secretary for international affairs are the main units that carry out the department's international responsibilities (see Figure 11.7). It is organized

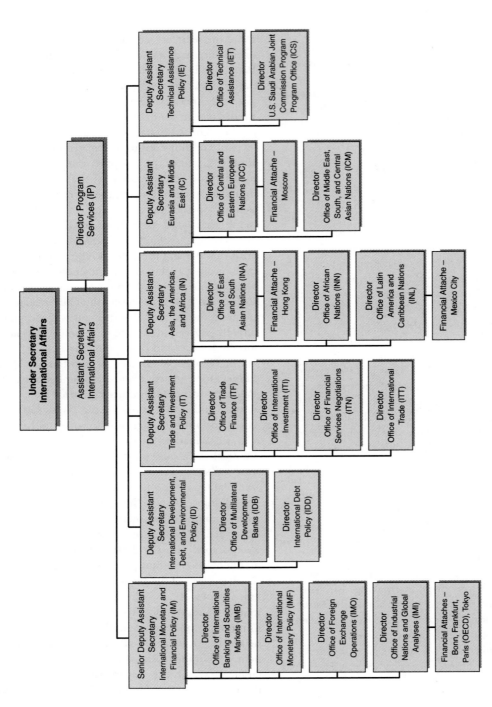

FIGURE 11.7 The Treasury Department's Office of International Affairs

Source: The Treasury Department website at www.ustreas.gov/oasia/orgchart.htm

into subunits responsible for international monetary affairs, trade and investment policy, technical assistance policy, international monetary and financial policy, international development, debt, and environmental policy, and regional areas (Asia, the Americas, and Africa; Eurasia and the Middle East). Through these units the office assists the secretary of the treasury and the under secretary for international affairs in the formulation and execution of international financial, monetary, commercial, energy, and trade policies and programs. It is now rare that an NSC interagency working does not have a participant from this office.

Department of Commerce

The Commerce Department is especially concerned with foreign economic policy issues that relate to the expansion and protection of American commerce abroad. Unlike the secretary of the treasury, however, the secretary of commerce and the Commerce Department as a whole historically have not been principal actors in foreign economic policy making. Instead, as indicated in Chapter 10, the United States Trade Representative plays the lead role in the *development* of trade policy. Since 1980, however, when the government's trade-related responsibilities were reorganized, the Commerce Department has been the principal agency for *implementing* trade policy (other than agricultural trade). Thus, as former Commerce Secretary Malcolm Baldrige (1983), observed, "trade is the only major cabinet function where policy is made in one department (the United States trade representative) and carried out in another (Department of Commerce)."

Specific trade responsibilities of the Commerce Department include all import-export programs: administration of countervailing duty and antidumping statutes,[11] foreign commercial representation and export promotion, trade policy analysis, and foreign compliance with trade agreements. Those duties are discharged by two subunits of the department: the International Trade Administration and the Bureau of Export Admin-

istration. The International Trade Administration is headed by the under secretary for international trade, whose charge relates to issues of import administration, international policy and programs, and trade development. This office also supports the *Trade Promotion Coordinating Committee,* an interagency committee established in 1992 to promote exports. Also headed by an under secretary, the *Bureau for Export Administration* (BXA) administers and enforces laws and regulations that govern exports. As its 2000 annual report indicated, the bureau oversees export of "dual-use commodities, technology and software from the United States has the responsibility of implementing the U.S. encryption policy and is responsible for compliance by the U.S. business community with the Chemical Weapons Convention. BXA investigates violations of export controls and implements the antiboycott provisions of the Export Administration Act and Export Administration Regulations. BXA is responsible for a variety of programs related to maintaining a strong U.S. defense industrial base. BXA also participates in the efforts of the U.S. Government to assist many of the newly independent states of the former Soviet Union, the Baltics, and Central Europe in developing effective export control systems."

As noted in Chapter 7, the Commerce Department began to play a substantially expanded role during the Clinton administration, which was more determined to fuse domestic and international economic policy into a single venue than any of its predecessors. This expanded role included responsibility for the country's first *"national export strategy,"* which was developed under Clinton's first Commerce Secretary, Ronald H. Brown, a former chair of the National Democratic Committee and an especially vigorous advocate of using Commerce to expand America's influence around the world. The national export strategy placed Commerce at the forefront of efforts to support and promote America's businesses seeking to export their products. Brown's chief lieutenant in this effort was his first undersecretary for international trade, Jeffrey Garten. Under their leadership, Commerce produced a highly developed strategy and set of structures to provide American businesses with information and export support, link them to export markets, advocate on their behalf, and monitor markets and trade practices around the world. A central piece of this approach targeted the so-called *"Big Emerging Markets,"* in Asia, Latin America, eastern and southern Europe, and Africa.[12]

Second, the Clinton administration also aggressively attacked the Cold War-era export controls to loosen restrictions on high technology exports (computers, telecommunications, satellites). The Commerce Department was the principal advocate for expanded exports in these areas and played a key role in both the formulation and the implementation of the new standards. However, with revelations that American companies had exported satellite technology to China, in 1999 Congress and the Clinton administration placed satellites under the control of the State Department, which was much less anxious to grant approval for the export of the technology.

Another aspect of Commerce's increasing role stems from the fact that since 1980 the Commerce Department, not the State Department, has been responsible for U.S. commercial representation abroad. The **U.S. and Foreign Commercial Service** seeks to enhance the competitiveness of American businesses abroad through an extensive network of district offices throughout the United States and posts located in more than sixty countries throughout the world. In conjunction with the domestic network of Export Assistance Centers created by the National Export Strategy and the expanded export centers in key markets overseas, Commerce personnel were well-placed to encourage and support American firms to sell abroad.

Department of Agriculture

The United States is one of the largest producers of agricultural products for the world marketplace. In 1999, for example, United States agricultural exports increased by fifteen percent in total volume from the previous year and amounted to $49 billion. Therefore, ensuring continued access to overseas markets continues to be a priority goal of American negotiators in all their trade talks, ranging from multilateral efforts during the Uruguay Round of GATT trade talks to discussions today in the World Trade Organization (WTO) and in bilateral efforts with individual countries. Export markets are critical to the welfare of American farmers, so the Agriculture Department has a major stake in the administration of foreign economic policy.

Most of Agriculture's foreign economic responsibilities are conducted under the direction of the under secretary for farm and foreign agricultural services out of the office with the same name. Particular departmental interests include promoting the sale of agricultural commodities abroad, including the sale or distribution of surplus commodities owned by the government under *Public Law 480* and the *Food for Peace Program,* allocating import quotas for certain agricultural commodities, and participating in international negotiations relating to world trade in agricultural products. These services are conducted principally by the Foreign Agricultural Service.

The **Foreign Agricultural Service (FAS),** operating under the authority of the under secretary for Farm and Foreign Agricultural Services, is the principal subdivision of the department concerned with international affairs. Its primary purpose is promoting sales of American agricultural commodities overseas. Toward that end, it maintains agricultural counselors and attachés in more than eighty-five American embassies abroad and a parallel group of international trade specialists in Washington. The FAS is responsible for formulating, administering, and coordinating Agriculture Department policies and programs as they relate to multilateral conventions and organizations, such as the WTO and the Food and Agriculture Organization (FAO) of the UN, and for providing support for U.S. agricultural representatives during international negotiations. Its overseas attachés also act as a worldwide agricultural intelligence and reporting system on supply, demand, and commercial trade conditions relating to agricultural products.

FAS also manages (in cooperation with the Agency for International Development) agricultural functions under PL 480, the *Food for Peace Program,* designed to meet immediate needs in countries of the Global South and improve their economies in the long run (while also enhancing market opportunities for American exporters). Included under PL 480 are long-term credit sales for American dollars, whereby the government dispenses commodity surpluses it purchases to support the American farmer. Humanitarian donations to foreign governments, voluntary relief agencies, and international institutions, such as the World Food Program of the UN, are included.

Department of Labor

Gathering information, proffering advice, administering selected programs, and participating in international negotiations (especially in the International Labor Organization [ILO], the World Trade Organization, and the Organization for Economic Cooperation and Development [OECD]) are also the international affairs functions of the Labor Department, but with a view toward their importance for the American wage earner rather than the agricultural, business, or financial communities. They are carried out by the *Bureau of International Labor Affairs* headed by the deputy under secretary for international affairs. The bureau carries out its functions through its offices of child labor, international economic affairs, and international organizations. During the Clinton administration, the bureau also frequently represented the department in interagency working groups in the NSC system. The department itself had a role in the National Economic Council.

Among other things, the department's authority traditionally has carried with it a special concern for immigrant labor and immigration policy, and for assessing the impact of trade agreements, such as NAFTA, on American workers. As the American economy has become increasingly dependent on foreign markets, for both imports and exports (now up to almost one-third of the gross domestic product), these efforts on behalf of American worker have become increasingly significant. For example, according to Bruce Stokes (2001), "In NAFTA's first five years, nearly 210,000 U.S. workers qualified for benefits because they lost their jobs due to competition from Canada and Mexico." In addition to these efforts, Labor has also been involved with the State Department in the provision of labor attachés for assignment abroad and with the Agency for International Development in the execution of technical assistance activities overseas. The department also bears responsibility for the administration of the trade adjustment assistance programs for workers under the Trade Act of 1974, which provides restitution to those adversely affected by foreign trade competition.

THE FOREIGN POLICY BUREAUCRACY AND THE POLITICS OF POLICY MAKING

The executive departments and agencies that comprise the foreign affairs government are so numerous and multifaceted that no brief description could adequately capture either the breadth of their interests or the depth of their involvement in matters of foreign policy. As a way of explicating governmental sources of American policy, however, the description provided here demonstrates a distinguishing characteristic of American foreign policy making—decision making by and within a disparate set of exceedingly large and complex organizational structures. Effecting control over them and dealing with the consequences of their behavior are important presidential concerns for political, legal, and other reasons. Still, presidents depend on the organizations and agencies comprising the foreign affairs government, without which it would be impossible to accomplish their foreign policy agendas. The organizations comprising the second concentric circle of policy making also often have their own agendas, as we have seen in this chapter. And they have the capacity to derail presidential preferences, an idea we will explore in more detail in Chapter 13. Since more of them are increasingly engaged in foreign policy concerns, the challenges for presidential leadership increase. Moreover, as we have seen in this and previous chapters, because the Cold War imperatives had such an impact on their structures, resources, personnel, and missions, the changing agenda of the new century raises questions about the suitability and continued relevance of many of these departments, agencies, or units within them.

It is, of course, the case that foreign policy is not solely determined by the White House and executive branch agencies. Congress and its members—another concentric circle in the scheme we introduced in Chapter 10 to organize our discussion—often plays a role. How, when, and to what extent are the subjects of our next chapter.

KEY TERMS RELATED TO THE FOREIGN POLICY BUREAUCRACY AND FOREIGN POLICY MAKING

Big Emerging Markets

Bureau for Export Administration

Bureau of Intelligence and Research (INR)

Bureau of International Labor Affairs

cautiousness and risk-aversion

central resource management

civil-military relations

"clientitis"

covert action

decentralization

Defense Intelligence Agency (DIA)

Defense Reorganization Act of 1986

director of central intelligence (DCI)

Directorate of Intelligence

Directorate of Operations

economic complex

elitism

espionage

executive departments

finished intelligence

Food for Peace program

Foreign Agricultural Service (FAS)

Foreign Service officers (FSOs)

functional bureaus

Goldwater-Nichols Act

human intelligence (HUMINT)

imagery intelligence (IMINT)

Intelligence Oversight Board

interservice rivalry

Joint Chiefs of Staff (JCS)

"jointness"

"little State Department"

management of the acquisition process

McCarthyism

mission

national export strategy

National Foreign Intelligence Board (NFIB)

National Intelligence Council (NIC)

National Intelligence Daily

National Intelligence Estimates (NIEs)

National Reconnaissance Office (NRO)

National Security Agency (NSA)

national technical means

"numbers game"

Office of International Security Affairs

Office of the Secretary of Defense

open sources

organizational subculture

oversight

parochialism

Pentagon

plausible denial

policy shop

politicization of intelligence

presidential finding

President's Daily Briefing

President's Foreign Intelligence Advisory Board (PFIAB)

"producer-consumer" challenge

professional diplomats

Quadrennial Defense Review

raw intelligence

regional bureaus

research and analysis

resistance to outside ideas

Select Committees on Intelligence

signal intelligence (SIGINT)

Special National Intelligence Estimates (SNIEs)

technical sources

technical surveillance

top-down, directive planning guidance

Trade Promotion Coordinating Committee

"up-or-out" promotion system

U.S. and Foreign Commercial Service

SUGGESTIONS FOR FURTHER READING

Carter, Ashton B., and John P. White. *Keeping the Edge: Managing Defense for the Future.* Cambridge, MA: MIT Press, 2001.

Clark, Wesley. *Waging Modern War.* New York: Public Affairs Press. 2001.

Cohen, Stephen D. *The Making of United States International Economic Policy: Principles, Problems, and Proposals for Reform,* 4th ed. Westport, CT: Praeger, 1994.

Dizard, Wilson P. *Digital Diplomacy: U.S. Foreign Policy in the Information Age.* Westport, CT: Greenwood Publishers, 2001.

Godson, Roy S. *Dirty Tricks or Trump Cards: U.S. Covert Action and Counterintelligence.* New Brunswick, NJ: Transaction Publishers, 2000.

Gordon, Michael, and Bernard Trainor. *The General's War: The Inside Story of the Conflict in the Gulf.* Boston, MA: Little, Brown, 1995.

Halberstam, David. *War in a Time of Peace.* New York: Scribners. 2001.

Holt, Pat M. *Secret Intelligence and Public Policy: A Dilemma of Democracy.* Washington, DC: CQ Press, 1995.

Johnson, Loch H. *Bombs, Bugs, Drugs, and Thugs: America's Quest for Security.* New York: New York University Press, 2000.

Johnson, Robert E. *Modern United States Civil Military Relations: Wielding the Terrible Swift Sword.* Washington, DC: United States Government Printing Office, 1997.

McGlen, Nancy E., and Meredith Reid Sarkees. *Women in Foreign Policy: The Insiders.* New York: Routledge, 1993.

Plischke, Elmer, ed., *U.S. Department of State: A Reference History.* Westport, CT: Greenwood Publishers, 1999.

Richelson, Jeffrey T. *A Century of Spies: Intelligence in the Twentieth Century.* New York: Oxford University Press, 1997.

Rubin, Barry. *Secrets of State: The State Department and the Struggle over U.S. Foreign Policy.* New York: Oxford University Press, 1985.

NOTES

1. Also, by driving out those with Asian expertise, the United States found itself without decision makers of expertise on Asia, including China as well as Vietnam, at the very time that it needed it most (McNamara 1995; Thomson 1972, 1994).

2. The 1980 Foreign Service Act specified that ambassadorial appointments will "normally" go to career officers, but the law has had little practical effect. Since the 1960s the number of political (noncareer) appointments has averaged about 30 percent. Carter had fewer than any other president (an average

of 24 percent during his presidency), and Kennedy and Reagan the most (33 percent). During the Clinton presidency the proportion stood at about 30 percent (data provided by the Presidential Appointments Staff, U.S. Department of State). At the beginning of George W. Bush's presidency, Secretary of State Colin Powell pressed for the appointment of career officers rather than others, but was not particularly successful.

3. A recent example is the efforts of the Iraqi desk, led by State Department employee Frank Ricciardone,

to block (successfully) the assistance Congress and the White House allocated for the Iraq National Congress as part of a plan to undermine and even overthrow Saddam Hussein. The State Department employees have stalled virtually all the aid since October 1998 (Timmerman 2001).

4. A principal issue giving impetus to the defense reform movement, which Congress spearheaded, was the quality of advice that the joint chiefs provided civilian leaders and, more broadly, their capacity to command the separate and powerful military services. For example, in his final testimony before Congress, General David C. Jones, chairman of the Joint Chiefs of Staff from 1978 to 1982, charged that "the fundamental balance of influence within the defense establishment is oriented too much toward the individual services." A 1985 study by the staff of the Senate Armed Services Committee blamed poor interservice coordination for the failure of the 1980 Iranian hostage rescue mission and for shortcomings in the 1983 invasion of Grenada. On the pre-reform context and the factors leading up to Goldwater-Nichols, see Roman and Tarr (1998).

5. There are currently four geographically oriented unified commands, the Central, European, Pacific, and Southern, and five others organized by function, the Joint Forces, Space, Special Operations, Strategic, and Transportation commands.

6. For his aggressive use of his powers, Clark was pushed out of the military in spite of his successful management of the Kosovo campaign. The JCS saw to it that he was replaced as commander in Europe and, with no higher assignment available, Clark retired prematurely at age 55.

7. But see Gordon and Trainor (1995), whose analysis of the Persian Gulf War concludes that interservice rivalries are alive and well in the Pentagon.

8. On the issue of CIA reforms, initial efforts, which included tighter controls over covert action, followed

the Iran-Contra investigations, but collapsed when President Bush vetoed the legislation (see, for example, Boren 1992), and the critique in May (1992). By mid-decade, the House of Representatives had made its own study, recommending reforms for the twenty-first century (*Intelligence Community in the 21st Century,* Permanent Select Committee on Intelligence, U.S. House of Representatives, 104th Congress, 1996). Then, under pressure from Congress, the Clinton administration launched its own bipartisan review of the intelligence community (*Preparing for the 21st Century: An Appraisal of U.S. Intelligence,* Commission on the Roles and Capabilities of the United States Intelligence Community, 1996). Organizations outside the government also got in on the act (see *Making Intelligence Smarter: The Future of U.S. Intelligence,* Report of an Independent Task Force for the Council on Foreign Relations, 1996; *In From the Cold: The Report of the Twentieth Century Fund Task Force on the Future of U.S. Intelligence,* 1996).

9. Recent reviews of covert operations and their oversight include Knott (1996), Godson (2000), and Johnson (2000a).

10. In addition to the reports of the Tower Board and the House and Senate Select Committees that investigated the Iran-Contra affair, see also Draper (1991), Walsh (1997), and the three volumes of the *Final Report of the Independent Counsel for Iran/Contra Matters.*

11. Countervailing duties are import taxes that offset subsidies provided by the exporting nation. Antidumping regulations are designed to make up for the advantage gained by selling exports for prices below those in the exporter's own domestic market.

12. On the National Export Strategy and the "Big Emerging Markets" initiative, see Stremlau (1994–1995), Scott (1997a), and Garten (1998).

CHAPTER 12

The Congress and Foreign Policy Making

Congress . . . could, should, and will have
an influence on the fashioning of foreign policy.

HENRY HYDE,
HOUSE INTERNATIONAL RELATIONS COMMITTEE CHAIR 2001

The preferred stance is to let the president make the decisions and,
if it goes well, praise him, and if it doesn't, criticize him.

LEE HAMILTON,
HOUSE FOREIGN AFFAIRS COMMITTEE CHAIR 1994

During the 1990s, the president saw his attempt to establish a new strategy for dealing with ethnic conflict in the Global
South blocked, his effort to redesign foreign aid
policy thwarted, his request for authority to negotiate expanded trade denied, his design for
curbing global warming ignored, and his commitment to ending nuclear testing rejected. At
the same time, he was forced to accept restructuring of the Department of State, restrictions on
funding the International Monetary Fund, and

substantially higher defense spending. All of these
actions resisted by the president were driven by
Congress. Similarly, in 2001, the president faced
opposition in Congress on several foreign policy
issues, including defense strategy and spending
and national missile defense. In contrast, when
terrorists attacked the United States, crashing airliners into the World Trade Center and the Pentagon on September 11, 2001, Congress rallied
behind the president, not only by handing him
broad authority to begin a campaign against

terrorism, but also by working out and muting differences on a variety of other issues, both foreign and domestic, in a bipartisan fashion. While few would argue that Congress makes foreign policy, these recent examples—and the contrast they reveal—suggests that Congress can have an impact. The actions and the contrast raise important questions. How and when do members of Congress assert themselves on foreign policy issues? What impact, on what issues, and in what situations, do members have?

The traditional view of Congress's role relegates it to the outer circle of the concentric circles of policy making we discussed in Chapter 10. Thus Congress's role is typically seen as primarily a negative one—to function as a public critic of the president and otherwise place limits on presidential behavior. Examples of bipartisanship—in which most members of Congress support the president's foreign policy regardless of their party affiliation—and congressional deference—in which presidents have their way—are legion, especially in the early Cold War years. Even today, most observers would argue that Congress looks to the president for leadership.

As we have seen in previous chapters, presidents' ability to exert foreign policy leadership is uneven. Some of that variability can be traced to Congress. Congress cannot replace the president as the central actor in American foreign policy making, but it often influences, shapes, and occasionally even determines foreign policy.

In this chapter we examine Congress's role in American foreign policy making. We begin with a look at the setting of congressional foreign policy behavior, briefly reviewing the Constitution's stipulations and ambiguities and the key players in Congress who affect foreign policy. Second, we examine the range of instruments and avenues of influence Congress uses to influence foreign policy. Third, we discuss the obstacles to congressional influence and survey the record of executive-legislative foreign policy interactions since World War II and their implications.

THE SETTING OF CONGRESSIONAL FOREIGN POLICY MAKING

Understanding the role and influence of Congress requires that we understand the powers and responsibilities the Constitution assigns it and and how Congress wields those powers and exercises those responsibilities.

The Constitution and Congress

As we saw in Chapter 10, the Constitution creates an uncertain playing field in its assignment of foreign policy powers.[1] In Article II, the president is made commander-in-chief and given the power to name ambassadors, receive foreign officials, and negotiate treaties, as well as the general executive power. By contrast, in Article I, Congress is granted more extensive responsibilities, including the general legislative power, the "power of the purse," the powers to declare war, to raise and support armies, to provide and maintain a Navy, to make rules for the government and regulation of the land and naval forces, and to organize, arm, discipline, and call forth the militia. Congress is also to regulate international commerce and immigration, to define and punish piracies, to grant letters of marque and reprisal, and to make rules concerning capture on land and water. Moreover, the U.S. Senate is constitutionally empowered to "advise and consent" on treaties as well as the appointment of ambassadors and other executive branch personnel. Finally, the Constitution directs Congress to "make all laws necessary and proper for carrying into execution the foregoing powers."

Just a cursory glance at these assignments suggests that Congress has considerable power and authority in foreign policy making if it chooses to act. Furthermore, the overlapping of several areas (for example, the war, diplomatic, and appointment powers) is the basis for the "invitation to struggle" description of executive-legislative relations, as it establishes a system of *separate institutions sharing power.*

Although these characteristics presage an environment of substantial congressional foreign policy activity, that has rarely been the case. Several factors explain this apparent paradox. We will discuss them in more detail later in this chapter, but we begin with a particularly important one: the congressional setting which permits many congressional actors to have a voice in foreign policy.

Congressional Foreign Policy Actors

When speaking of Congress and foreign policy it is important to recognize that many actors comprise the institution. Indeed, "Congress" need not act at all to affect American foreign policy; influence may flow from a variety of players without a formal action or output by the collective institution. Broadly speaking, Congress is:

- The institution, acting collectively through its procedures, when majorities can be mustered to take action on legislation and other activities

- Either of the two houses, acting collectively through their procedures

- One or the other of the two political parties in the institution

- Any of the many committees or subcommittees of either house, an increasing number of which are involved in some aspect of foreign policy

- *Congressional caucuses*—voluntary associations of legislators—many of which have foreign policy emphases (for example, the Senate Caucus on International Narcotics Control, the Congressional Black Caucus, the Arms Control and Foreign Policy Caucus, the Congressional Human Rights Caucus, and the Military Reform Caucus, to name a few)

- *Congressional leaders* such as the House Speaker and minority leader, the Senate majority and leaders, committee and subcommittee chairs and ranking members, and others, most of whose actions have become increasingly partisan (Sinclair 1993; Smith 1994)

- Individual members of Congress who become *foreign policy activists* and *foreign policy entrepreneurs* (Carter and Scott 2000a, 2001)

- Congressional staff and *"congressional bureaucracies"* composed of staff members and specialists (Carter 1998), such as the Congressional Research Service, the General Accounting Office, the Congressional Budget Office, and others

Any one or any combination of these congressional foreign policy actors can exercise influence on a given issue. This is one reason why Congress has a difficult time asserting itself on foreign policy: different actors may advocate different policies, making it difficult for any to succeed. Any one may interact with the executive branch or seek to engage the public, interest groups, and the media. Occasionally, some may even engage other countries' representatives. Finally, each actor also has access to other levers of policy influence. Indeed, because there are so many avenues of foreign policy influence, these congressional actors have far more routes to policy influence than the Constitution's formal assignments of responsibilities suggests.

AVENUES OF CONGRESSIONAL FOREIGN POLICY INFLUENCE

Along with recognition of the constitutional setting and the array of congressional actors who may or may not play a role on a given foreign policy issue, we must understand two more factors: (1) the avenues available for congressional

Table 12.1 Avenues of Congressional Influence

	Direct	**Indirect**
Legislative	Issue-Specific Legislation	Nonbinding Legislation
	Treaties (Senate)	Appointments (Senate)
	War Power	Procedural Legislation
	Appropriations	
	Foreign Commerce	
Nonlegislative	Informal Advice/Letters	Framing Opinion
	Consultations	Foreign Contacts
	Oversight/Hearings	
	Use of Courts	

SOURCE: Adapted from Scott (1997b).

foreign policy influence, and (2) all the avenues require interest, engagement, and activity on the part of the congressional players. The first indicates opportunity, the second that taking advantage of opportunity is, ultimately, a political issue. Members of Congress can act, but they must choose to act in order to have foreign policy influence of any kind. That they often do not is a reflection of their own political and policy interests, as well as some of the obstacles to the exercise of congressional influence that we will discuss later.

Categorizing the Avenues of Influence

There are many ways to categorize the avenues of influence available to members of Congress. One useful way is to distinguish between *legislative* and *nonlegislative* actions (Burgin 1997), and between *direct* and *indirect* efforts (Lindsay 1993). Legislative actions involve those related to the passage of specific laws or resolutions; nonlegislative actions are those that do not involve a legislative output. Direct actions are issue and case specific; indirect actions are aimed at influencing the broader political environment or climate of a debate. If these two dimensions are combined, then four categories of congressional influence avenues can be identified: direct-legislative, direct-nonlegislative, indirect-legislative, and indirect-nonlegislative (see, for example, Scott 1997b). These possibilities are summarized in Table 12.1. Significantly, members combine and link efforts across these categories, thereby amplifying their effects.

Direct-Legislative Avenues The direct-legislative foreign policy activities Congress may engage in are fairly impressive and are the most obvious and most scrutinized. They include the powers to declare war, to appropriate funds, and to regulate international commerce. The Senate also has the power to approve treaties. The key to this avenue of influence is *substantive legislation* developed through the institution's legislative procedures. Substantive legislation may involve treaty ratification, legislation regarding the use of force, trade and aid legislation, budget appropriations, and any other issue-specific legislation members of Congress are able to pass. Every year a long list of bills and amendments relating to foreign policy is considered in some fashion by one or both houses of Congress (Lindsay 1994b). While "major legislation" (for example, the *Comprehensive Anti-Apartheid Act of 1986,* by which Congress imposed sanctions against South Africa in spite of President Reagan's opposition . . . and veto) is less frequent (Hinckley 1994), "minor" legislative actions have abounded.

Other examples of Congress' use of this avenue of influence includes legislation late in the Clinton administration requiring changes in the way the United States and the International Monetary Fund address economic crises. Congress also relies on this avenue of influence when it attaches limits, restrictions, and conditions on foreign aid legislation. Examples include 1975 legislation cutting off American aid to Turkey for its invasion of Cyprus; amendments in the 1980s placing conditions on American aid to El Salvador; and restrictions on aid to various countries for reasons related to drug trafficking, support for terrorism, and nuclear proliferation issues in the 1990s. In 2000, for example, the foreign aid bill included $100 million for Serbia, but conditioned the assistance on cooperation by the Serbian government in apprehending and bringing to justice those individuals indicted for war crimes.

Numerous other examples from the past forty years related to human rights and democracy could also be cited, such as the 1974 Jackson-Vanik amendment prohibiting most-favored-nation trade status for countries restricting emigration. Note, too, that members can "earmark" funds to go to specific projects they favor, which also constitutes substantive legislation, as we discuss later. Substantive legislation of this sort also includes Senate actions on treaties. Recent examples include the ratification of the Chemical Weapons Treaty in 1997 and the rejection of the Comprehensive Test Ban Treaty in 1999.

Finally, congressional legislation regarding trade fits in this category. Congress has become increasingly involved in this area over the past twenty years as the American position in the world economy has changed (see Chapter 7). While members of Congress passed the Reciprocal Trade Agreements Act in 1934 to provide greater latitude for the president to conclude trade accords, the recent record has Congress becoming more involved. In 1988, for example, Congress passed the *Omnibus Trade and Competitiveness Act* which included numerous provisions and restrictions on American trade relations, including the *"Super 301"* measure to require retaliatory action against countries engaging in unfair trade practices. In 1993, after the Bush and Clinton Administration concluded negotiations for the North American Free Trade Agreement, the ratification struggle on Capitol Hill was intense and involved substantial additions, amendments, and special clauses to gain support (Scherlen 1998). The succeeding year's debate over passage of the Uruguay Round trade accord (which, among other things, established the World Trade Organization) was similarly difficult.

Likewise, in 2000, Congress took additional action on trade-related legislation. First, the Clinton administration negotiated with Congress to provide *permanent normal trade relations* (the successor term for "most-favored-nation") to China. In spite of heavy lobbying by opponents, the House passed the measure in May 2000 and the Senate, after overcoming the opposition of a handful of members, followed suit in September. Moreover, Congress passed the Trade and Development Act of 2000 which extended trade opportunities to Africa and offered the Caribbean Basin countries the trade advantages afforded to members of NAFTA. The act also included over $400 million in debt forgiveness to African countries, as well as a long list of industry-specific provisions sponsored by individual members of Congress.

A notable feature of the policy debates on NAFTA and the WTO is that, throughout, the president enjoyed *"fast-track" authority,* or "trade promotion authority" that is, congressionally-delegated authority to negotiate the trade arrangements, subject to consultation with Congress, after which the Congress agrees to vote the accord up or down without amendments. Even with this authority, President Clinton found his administration negotiating with Congress along the way of both agreements. Subsequent to the 1994 world trade agreement, however, fast-track authority expired. Repeated requests by Clinton over the next five years for renewal of fast-track authority were rebuffed. George W. Bush made renewing fast-track a high priority in his first year, but Democrats and a few key Republicans, stalled progress, even in the more accommodating bipartisan spirit after the September 11 attacks.

One last point should be made regarding substantive legislation. Members of Congress need not be successful in gaining passage of a particular piece of legislation for it to shape foreign policy. The mere *threat* of legislation may be used to trigger **anticipated reactions** whereby the White House incorporates congressional preferences into its policy proposals. Hence it is not simply successful legislation that matters. A member or members may get results without producing legislation. One example of this phenomenon is the Reagan administration's 1985 decision to enact a series of partial sanctions against South Africa, a policy action most of the administration had rejected until then. While Congress never actually passed legislation requiring sanctions, its legislative proposals prompted the administration to preempt congressional policy making (Baker 1989). More recently, the Clinton administration's 1994 "Presidential Decision Directive 25" bears the fingerprints of Congress as well. Although it was a presidential policy decision regarding the use of force under multilateral conditions, and although Congress did not pass legislation in 1993 or 1994 on the matter, the administration substantially revised its initial draft to accommodate legislative and other congressional signals about its content (Daalder 1994).

Direct-Nonlegislative Avenues Through the direct-nonlegislative avenues, members of Congress rely on activities other than legislation to exercise influence. Such efforts could include consultations and communications with the president and other administration officials, oversight activities like hearings and other investigations, fact-finding missions, and even lawsuits against the president or administration. Such efforts may be linked to legislative and other efforts as well.

Examples are numerous. In the 1960s, Senators Frank Church (D-Idaho) and William Fulbright (D-Arkansas) relied heavily on their ability to use oversight hearings to address foreign policy in the government operations and foreign relations committees respectively (see Johnson 1998–1999; Woods 1998). Senator Church's select committee investigation and hearings on CIA abuses in the 1970s are another example.[2] More recently, congressional intelligence committee hearings in the fall of 2001 to explore the intelligence community's performance leading up to the September 11 terrorist attacks led to recomendations for reform and restructuring the intelligence community.

Many members rely on letters and other communications with the White House or departments to express their policy views. In late 2000, for instance, Jesse Helms sent a letter to the Secretary of State stating that a proposal for U.S. participation in the new International Criminal Court would be "dead on arrival" in the Senate. Use of the courts includes efforts by Ron Dellums (D-California) in 1989 and Tom Campbell a decade later to hold the president accountable for the requirements of the War Powers Act.

Indirect-Legislative Avenues Members of Congress can also use legislative approaches to provide more indirect inputs to foreign policy. In these cases, the inputs are not issue and case specific. Thus the Senate has the ability to approve or not approve top administration personnel appointments, and both houses can introduce procedural or *prospective-procedural legislation* which alters processes or creates new institutions (Burgin 1997; Lindsay 1994b).

The Senate's appointment powers enable members to play a role in the president's selection of his foreign policy team. Generally the premise is that presidents should be entitled to their appointments, but the Senate has regularly intervened to block objectionable nominees. In 1989, for example, former Senator John Tower, President Bush's first choice for Secretary of Defense, was rejected by a majority of senators led by Georgia Democrat Sam Nunn. In 1997, Anthony Lake, President Clinton's selection for the

Director of Central Intelligence, was blocked by conservative senators led by Richard Shelby (R–Alabama). Senators increasingly scrutinize lower-level appointments as well, frequently blocking or holding hostage objectionable appointments. For instance, George W. Bush's nomination of Otto Reich as Assistant Secretary of State for the western hemisphere drew substantial opposition. Reich, whose service in the Reagan administration involved him in the Iran-Contra affair, was blocked by Senators John Kerry (D-Massachusetts) and Christopher Dodd (D-Connecticut).

Furthermore, key senators can use their ability to block appointments to exact policy concessions on other matters. In recent years, no one has been more active in this than Jesse Helms (R–North Carolina). In 1989 Helms held up numerous potential Bush appointments to gain policy concessions across a wide range of issues; and in 1995, as chair of the Foreign Relations Committee, he blocked several ambassadorial and other appointments to force administration support for his plan to reorganize the State Department and other foreign policy agencies (Hook 1998).

Increasingly, members use appointment-approval power to link to their interests in non–foreign policy issues. In 1999, for example, Senator James Inhofe (R-Oklahoma) blocked the appointments of Lawrence Summers to be treasury secretary and Richard Holbrooke to be UN Ambassador to protest the recess appointment (naming an official when the Senate is in recess in order to circumvent Senate confirmation) of an openly gay man, James Hormel, as ambassador to Luxembourg (Shenon 1999).

Congress frequently resorts to procedural legislation to ensure a voice in policy. This may involve creating new agencies, requiring specific processes or agency involvement in policy decisions, or requiring reports (Lindsay 1994b). Again, many examples exist. The 1973 War Powers Act is essentially a procedural policy, as it specifies a decision process for using force abroad. The 1976 Arms Export Control Act not only required certain reporting to Congress, but also specified that certain agencies must participate in the decision. The 1980 Intelligence Oversight act established congressional oversight committees and reporting requirements to better control the executive's use of the intelligence community. More recently, in 1998 Foreign Affairs Restructuring Act revised the relationships between the State Department and the Agency for International Development and eliminated the U.S. Information Agency and the Arms Control and Disarmament Agency, folding their operations into the State Department.

Through actions such as these, members of Congress seek to shape the way the executive branch formulates and implements policy, as well as to ensure that information on policy decisions is shared with Congress (Lindsay 1994c).

Indirect-Nonlegislative Avenues On the indirect-nonlegislative avenue of influence, members of Congress engage in the process of *framing*—trying to "change the climate of opinion surrounding the policy" (Lindsay 1994c). Increasing access to the media as well as increased opportunities for direct foreign contact make this venue a frequent means to exert congressional foreign policy activity and exercise influence. Through framing activities members both signal the White House of their preferences and help shape public opinion.

Such efforts include participation in media talk shows and writing opinion pieces for newspapers. The participation and subsequent arrest of members of Congress in 1985 protests over South Africa's apartheid are another. In 1988, members sought to frame trade policy debates by appearing on the steps of the Capitol and smashing an electronic device made by Toshiba in protest of that company's sale of sophisticated electronics to the Soviet Union. Representative Pete Geren's (D-Texas) role in getting a prototype of the V22 Osprey to land on the Capitol grounds in the early 1990s was also fundamentally a framing exercise.

The increasing prevalence of members of Congress meeting directly with foreign leaders offers another avenue for indirect-nonlegislative activities. For example, in 1997, Senator Jesse Helms met with UN Secretary-General Kofi Annan to discuss U.S.-UN relations. Two years later Helms delivered a speech before UN delegates. At about the same time then-House Speaker Newt Gingrich (R–Georgia) repeatedly attacked the Clinton Administration for pressuring the Israeli government to make concessions to the Palestinians in Mideast peace talks. The attacks followed numerous private meetings between Gingrich and then-Israeli Prime Minister Benjamin Netanyahu and a 1998 Gingrich speech before the Israeli Knesset. In 2001, Helms led members of the Senate Foreign Relations Committee to Mexico to meet newly-elected President Vicente Fox and to hold joint meetings with the Foreign Relations Committee of the Mexican Senate.

To summarize, these avenues of influence in combination with the Constitution's grants of authority would appear to make to make Congress a dominant power in the "invitation to struggle" with the president for a voice in foreign policy making. Its multiple avenues of influence would appear to enable Congress to set overall policy much like a board of directors does in private enterprise. Remember, though, that the availability of these avenues does not necessarily mean they are used. That depends, as noted previously, on the interest and activity of members of Congress. Hence, while Congress has *opportunities* to influence foreign policy, it may or may not take advantage of them.

Avenues of Influence in Practice: Treaties, War, and Money

We now review three areas in which Congress has an obvious role to play because of the Constitution: treaties, war, and money.[3] As we review these areas, we will assess whether the appearance of Congress as a foreign policy rival of the president matches the reality. We will use examples of how members of Congress use the avenues of influence just summarized to shape policy to fit their preferences.

Treaties   Treaty-making powers rest in the Senate, whose advice *and* consent by a two-thirds vote is necessary before the president can consummate (with the exchange of instruments of ratification) a treaty with another country. (This effectively gives control to only 34 of the 535 members of Congress.) The Senate Foreign Relations Committee bears primary responsibility for conducting the hearings and investigations on which senatorial advice and consent are based. These and related foreign affairs responsibilities once made the Foreign Relations Committee the most prestigious of all Senate committees.

In recent years, however, ideological divisions have prevented the committee from speaking with a single voice. More importantly, perhaps, it does not serve senators' other interests. According to Nebraska Republican Chuck Hagel, "Foreign Relations has been kind of a wasteland" (cited in Lindsay 2000b). In 1995, following the Republican victories in the midterm elections, Senate Majority Leader Bob Dole had to cajole four senators into taking seats on the committee (Sciolino 1995). As one member of the committee once put it: "Well, you know, it is fun to hobnob with foreign leaders and discuss world affairs, but it doesn't get me any place with my Senate colleagues. . . . Foreign Relations doesn't have much legislative jurisdiction that's important to other senators—it's nothing like Finance or Appropriations" (cited in Smith and Deering 1990). The committee nonetheless remains a primary forum for the discharge of Congress's foreign policy responsibilities.

Despite the importance of the Constitution's treaty clause, the precise mechanism through which the Senate proffers advice and consent to the president is ambiguous. In barest form the process consists of the president, in the capacity of the nation's chief diplomat, negotiating through representatives a treaty with another state, and the Senate then merely voting up or down. More frequently, advice and guidance is offered in a variety of communications between the executive branch and the legislature, including letters and even resolutions.

In 1997, for example, the Senate communicated its preferences on the global warming treaty under negotiation at Kyoto, Japan to President Clinton through the Byrd-Hagel resolution, named for West Virginia Democrat Robert Byrd and Nebraska Republican Chuck Hagel. The resolution, which passed ninety-five to zero, warned the administration that any global warming treaty that did not apply to developing nations as well as the developed world would face substantial opposition in the Senate.[4] Moreover, Senate opposition to the treaty, which would require a five percent reduction in 1990 greenhouse gas levels for all industrialized countries by 2012, continued even more strenuously after the Clinton administration signed the treaty in November 1998. The treaty languished without support on Capitol Hill until early 2001, when George W. Bush formally announced that he would not seek its ratification, thereby abandoning the agreement (to the chagrin of America's partners in Europe) (Andrews 2001).

Another form of advice involves naming members of the Senate to the negotiating team. This practice has been widespread ever since the Senate rejected the Versailles Treaty ending World War I, which was negotiated without senatorial representation on the Peace Commission headed by Woodrow Wilson. By incorporating members of the Senate into the negotiation team, presidents have often been able to circumvent Senate opposition and develop internal advocates for the agreements.

Consent to treaties is established by a two-thirds vote, but the Senate also often attaches **reservations** to treaties. These may take the form of amendments that require the executive to renegotiate the terms of the treaty with other signatories—a potentially inhibiting obstacle, particularly with the increase in the number of multilateral treaties. Alternatively, reservations or "conditions" may simply incorporate the Senate's

interpretation of the treaty without any binding effect on the parties to it. Other variants are reservations that apply only to the United States.

The most celebrated example is the so-called *Connally Amendment* to the Statute of the International Court of Justice. According to this reservation, the United States reserves the right to determine whether matters falling under the court's compulsory jurisdiction clause are essentially within the domestic jurisdiction of the United States, and hence beyond the Court's purview.

The Senate's role in the treaty-making process became the subject of a sharp dispute in 1987 between the Reagan administration and Congress over the administration's announced reinterpretation of the 1972 Anti-Ballistic Missile (ABM) treaty. The reinterpretation would have permitted the administration to test technology as part of its Strategic Defense Initiative (SDI), previously thought to be prohibited by the ABM treaty (Sofaer 1987). Senator Sam Nunn, chair of the powerful Armed Services Committee, concluded that the document submitted by the Nixon administration fifteen years earlier permitted only a narrow interpretation (Nunn 1987). Following Nunn's leadership, the Senate voted to restrict SDI tests and funds. Nunn and his colleagues also attached a reservation to another treaty—the ratification resolution for the Intermediate Nuclear Force Treaty—that reflected its sense of the Senate's role in any future reinterpretation of that treaty. Thus, through actions at the individual, committee, and chamber levels, members of the Senate linked together several different avenues of influence (treaty ratification, budgetary decisions, and oversight) to protect the Senate's treaty-making powers and ensure that its preferences were incorporated into the agreement.

The Clinton administration announced early on that it supported the narrow or traditional interpretation of the ABM treaty. After the 1994 congressional midterm elections that returned a Republican majority in both houses of Congress, the administration found itself under congressional pressure to develop a National Missile

Defense system—a part of the well-known "Contract with America" designed by Newt Gingrich. As discussed in Chapter 4, the administration and the Republican-led Congress debated the merits of both the system and the treaty frequently after the 1994 midterm elections, finding new questions about the system's consistency with the ABM treaty.[5] The discussion peaked in the summer of 2000 when the Clinton administration announced its decision to go forward with national missile defense (NMD). George W. Bush also signaled his support for national missile defense throughout the 2000 campaign, noting in many speeches that he would be committed to American interests, not "outdated treaty language." Hence, his administration pressed forward with NMD regardless of the implications for the ABM Treaty. Interestingly, after the September 11 attacks, the administration proceeded somewhat more carefully, especially with Russia, trying to find common ground and a way to preserve the treaty. Congress, too, muted its criticism and opposition, approving substantial funding for NMD in late 2001.

Until recently, the Senate's treaty ratification record has been quite positive. The most famous treaty failure occurred in 1920, when the Versailles Treaty came up short of the two-thirds majority that would have opened the way for U.S. membership in the League of Nations. From then until the end of the Cold War, the Senate rejected only three treaties, while two others that failed to receive a two-thirds majority were subject to reconsideration (*Treaties and Other International Agreements: The Role of the United States Senate,* 1993).

Since 1993, however, the record has been considerably more mixed. In fact, the Clinton administration was able to gain ratification of just two of five major treaties during its two terms. As noted, the administration signed but failed to gain ratification of the *Kyoto Protocol on Global Climate Change.*[6] It also negotiated a *Comprehensive Test Ban Treaty* that was rejected outright by the Senate in a highly partisan vote in November 1999.[7] Finally, although the administration

helped to design and supported a treaty for the establishment of an *International Criminal Court,* opposition by the Senate (and the Department of Defense) kept President Clinton from signing the treaty until December 31, 2000. When he did so, he declined to submit it to the Senate or even to recommend its ratification (see *Insight on the News,* 19 February 2001, 31; *National Journal,* 27 January 2001, 277).

Of the two successes, only one came relatively easy. On May 1, 1998, the administration acquired Senate ratification of the NATO expansion treaty paving the way for the eastward movement of the alliance to include, first, Poland, Hungary, and the Czech Republic, and then others in subsequent years (Goldgeier 1998, 1999; Grayson 1999; Yost 1998). Exhaustive meetings between members of the administration, Congress, and NATO allies laid the groundwork for the expansion. According to Senator Dan Coats (R-Indiana), the agreement was "one of the least partisan issues I've been involved with since I came here" (Lippmann and Dewar 1999).

The other—the April 1997 ratification of the *Chemical Weapons Convention* (originally negotiated by the Reagan and Bush administrations)—occurred only after a difficult and highly-charged political fight enabled the Clinton administration to win ratification with seventy-four votes in the Senate. However, it took complex maneuvering within the Senate to break loose the treaty from Foreign Relations Committee Chair Jesse Helms' hold inside the committee and then to assemble a coalition of supporters for the treaty on the Senate floor. Moreover, it took substantial bargaining between the White House and the Senate to gain passage. The White House had to agree to a long list of over two dozen conditions and to accede to demands for the restructuring of the foreign affairs agencies along lines advocated by Senator Helms. Ultimately, all forty-five Democratic senators voted in favor of the treaty, while members of the Republic Party split twenty-nine to twenty-six in favor of the accord originally negotiated by presidents of their own party.[8]

Hence, while much of the Cold War period attests simultaneously to congressional deference to presidential initiatives and to general agreement between the president and Congress on many foreign policy issues, those areas of agreement as they related to recent treaty approvals have narrowed substantially. Increasing policy disagreement and partisanship appear to have persuaded members of the Senate to wield the treaty ratification power more forcefully than in previous years. Moreover, individual members of the Senate seem quite willing to use the ratification power to exact concessions on other foreign policy issues. There are signs of increased partisanship and politicization as well (for examples, the CTBT).

What the historical record fails to show is also noteworthy. It does not reveal those occasions when treaties were not presented for a vote due to known legislative opposition. The Carter administration's decisions not to proceed with a comprehensive test ban treaty and to shelve the Threshold Test Ban Treaty and the Peaceful Nuclear Explosives Treaty are examples (Warburg 1989). Its decision to withdraw the SALT II treaty also fits the mold. In recent years, the Kyoto treaty stands as a good example of this phenomenon. The Senate did not reject the treaty outright: President Clinton withheld the treaty from the Senate because he could not secure the necessary two-thirds vote.

Executive agreements are the usual method presidents use to make international agreements that avoid the necessity of securing the advice and consent of the Senate. The Supreme Court has ruled that these government-to-government agreements have the same legal force as treaties, and thus become part of the "supreme law of the land," but they may be concluded without legislative scrutiny. Early examples include the agreements governing the Lend Lease Act of 1941, which enabled the United States to provide war materials to its World War II allies, and Truman's aid to Greece and Turkey in the late 1940s. Others include the Paris peace agreement on Ending the War and Restoring Peace in Vietnam (1973); the SALT I accord on offensive weapons (1972); and various bilateral agreements covering American military base rights in Spain, the Azores, Diego Garcia, Bahrain, and Iceland.

Of the nearly 8,000 international agreements concluded between 1946 and 1992, ninety-five percent were executive agreements (*Treaties and Other International Agreements: The Role of the United States Senate,* 1993) and hence not subject to the formal approval procedures of the Senate. Many of these were based on statutory directives, and others were entered into pursuant to treaty provisions, both of which require legislative input. Still, the vast number affirm the president's wide latitude to negotiate international agreements unrestrained by constitutional checks and balances.

Evidence that executive agreements pose a potential challenge to congressional oversight is seen in Congress's periodic attempts to block such maneuvers. One effort occurred in 1953–1954, when Republican Senator John Bricker's (Ohio) proposal for a constitutional amendment to restrict the president's treaty-making powers and ability to manage the day-to-day conduct of foreign affairs fell only one vote short of the two-thirds majority necessary for Senate approval. Two decades later, concern over the breadth and depth of overseas commitments the executive branch had entered into without Congress's knowledge led to a statute (known as the **Case Act** after its sponsor, Republican Senator Clifford Case of New Jersey) that required the president to submit to Congress all international agreements within sixty days of their execution.

Although the Case Act augmented Congress's capacity to be informed of executive agreements, the president remained the initiator of agreements with other nations, determining which are to be treaties and which executive agreements. Moreover, the law protected the secrecy of executive agreements by providing that they need be forwarded only to the relevant Senate and House committees if the president determines that public disclosure would endanger national security. Thus the statute may have complicated presidents' lives, but it has not substantially restricted their freedom.

War The Constitution is less than clear on where war-making powers lie. It states in Article I, Section 8 that "the Congress shall have power . . . to declare war." Elsewhere, however (Article II, Section 2), the Constitution also specifies that "the President shall be Commander-in-Chief of the Army and Navy of the United States." Of the two provisions, the latter has proven the more important, as the president has used that provision to justify stationing troops all over the world. Presidents have also used it to justify American military intervention in Korea (1950–1953), Lebanon (1958), the Dominican Republic (1965–1966), Vietnam (1965–1973), Grenada (1983), Panama (1989), the Persian Gulf (1990–1991 and 1994), Somalia (1992–1994), Bosnia (1995–present), Kosovo (1999) and Afghanistan (2001). Yet in none of those cases was military action accompanied by a formal declaration of war. In Kosovo, Congress refrained from any authorization while, two years later, in Afghanistan, it authorized the use of force in response to the September 11 strikes without actually declaring war.

Protracted American involvement in Vietnam prompted congressional efforts to redress the war-making balance. President Johnson argued that his authority rested on the *Gulf of Tonkin Resolution,* passed by Congress in August 1964. The joint resolution gave the president approval "to take all necessary measures to repel any armed attack against the forces of the United States and to prevent further aggression." As the quagmire of Vietnam deepened, the meaning of the Gulf of Tonkin Resolution became the source of intense debate. The Johnson administration insisted that the resolution was the "functional equivalent" of a declaration of war, but Congress eventually repudiated that interpretation when it repealed the Gulf of Tonkin Resolution in 1970. It then took concrete steps to limit future presidential war-making prerogatives, embodying them in the **War Powers Resolution,** passed in 1973 over President Nixon's veto.

The War Powers Resolution: Provisions and Dilemmas Several provisions in the War Powers Resolution (or Act) try to ensure congressional consent in decisions to deploy American troops abroad. First, the resolution stipulates that the president should inform Congress when he or she introduces forces "into hostilities or into situations where imminent involvement in hostilities is clearly indicated by the circumstances." This first provision triggers a second, which prohibits troop commitments from extending beyond sixty days without specific congressional authorization (although this period can be extended up to ninety days if the safety of American troops is at stake). Third, any time American forces become engaged in hostilities without a declaration of war or a specific congressional authorization, the law enables Congress to direct the president to disengage such troops by a concurrent resolution of the two houses of Congress. Because such a measure would not require the president's signature to take effect, it constitutes a **legislative veto** and may no longer be constitutional because of the Supreme Court's *INS v. Chadha* ruling in 1983. The sixty-day limit and various consulting and reporting requirements, however, remain intact.

President Nixon argued that the sixty-day limit and the concurrent resolution provisions "purport to take away, by a mere legislative act, authorities which the president has properly exercised under the Constitution for almost two hundred years." They are unconstitutional, he asserted, because "the only way in which the constitutional powers of a branch of government can be altered is by amending the Constitution—and any attempt to make such alterations by legislation alone is clearly without force." He also claimed the resolution would "seriously undermine the nation's ability to act decisively and convincingly in times of international crisis" and that it would "give every future Congress the ability to handcuff every future president." Although the Senate rejected Nixon's argument and overrode the veto to make the War Powers Resolution law, virtually every president since

Nixon has also questioned the constitutionality of the act. The courts' typical resort to the *doctrine of political questions* makes it unlikely that the constitutionality of the War Powers Resolution will ever be judicially tested. However, several other dilemmas regarding the provisions of that law also exist.

First, what are *consultations*? The War Powers Resolution seeks to ensure greater congressional participation in decisions authorizing the use of force by requiring consultation between the executive and legislative branches "in every possible instance" prior to committing U.S. forces to hostilities or to situations likely to result in such. Presidents generally claim to have met this requirement, but rarely has serious and meaningful debate between the two branches occurred prior to a presidential decision on the use of force. Indeed, most presidents resort to *notification* and *reporting* rather than consultation, which would seem to violate the spirit, if not the letter, of the War Powers Resolution.

For example, in 1986, after a surprise nighttime attack on Tripoli and Benghazi to punish Libyan leader Muammar Qaddafi's alleged support of international terrorism, Republican House leader Robert H. Michel, one of the dozen or so lawmakers briefed by the Reagan White House just before the Libyan raid, expressed the sentiment that "we really ought to have some sort of vehicle for getting Congress into the mix, so we're not left out in the cold."

In 1990, congressional leaders appointed a bipartisan consultative group comprising the Congress's leaders and key committee chairs in an effort to facilitate consultation on developments in the Persian Gulf region. Bush met with group occasionally, but he ignored it when he made the critical decision to send many thousands more troops to the region (Collier 1994b), which unequivocally moved the United States toward an offensive capability. The Clinton administration's decisions to launch attacks against Iraq repeatedly during the 1990s are also illustrative. In each instance, the administration reportedly notified congressional leaders shortly before the attacks but did not consult them on specific courses of action. Clinton's decisions to use force in Haiti, Bosnia, Iraq, and Kosovo also failed to involve serious consultations (Hendrickson forthcoming; Fisher 1998; Fisher and Adler 1998).

Hence, there is no agreed-on mechanism to ensure that the president will weigh congressional views before making a decision to use force. The consultations issue is critical to the effectiveness of the War Powers Act because once the decision to use force is implemented, Congress's power is severely circumscribed. Two examples make the point. President Bush informed members of Congress of his intention to invade Panama at 6:00 P.M. on December 19, 1989. The actual invasion began seven hours later, at 1:00 A.M., December 20. In 1999, President Clinton began meeting with members of Congress only six days in advance of the initiation of the Kosovo bombing campaign, seeking their support for the decision he had already made. While this "consultation" left members with time to initiate opposition to the action had they so desired, there is little to suggest that the president did much more than notify members of his plans and ask for their support. With the decisions made in both cases prior to the notification—and with additional pressure from NATO in the second instance—there would seem to be little that Congress could have done.

Second, what are *imminent hostilities?* Many U.S. force deployments since the passage of the War Powers Act have involved situations short of outright combat, leaving open the opportunity for presidents to define them as outside the arena of "imminent hostilities." This has greatly complicated the application of the act's provisions and, occasionally, triggered substantial political debates.

For example, in the Reagan administration's deployment of American forces in Lebanon (1983) and the Persian Gulf (1987), the question of whether American troops were placed in danger of "imminent hostilities" as envisaged by the

War Powers Resolution figured prominently in the congressional-executive contest. U.S. marines were first sent to Lebanon in 1982 as part of a multinational force with the expectation that their presence there would be brief. In August 1983 the marines suffered two fatalities and several casualties, prompting Reagan to seek congressional authorization for the deployment. Negotiations between Congress and the president resulted in a compromise resolution passed by both houses involving the War Powers Resolution but authorizing the marines to stay in Lebanon for eighteen months. When he signed the resolution, however, the president stated "I do not and cannot cede any of the authority vested in me under the Constitution as president and as commander in chief of the United States armed forces. Nor should my signing be viewed as any acknowledgment that the president's constitutional authority can be impermissibly infringed by statute." In the end, the October truck-bombing of marine headquarters in Beirut, which killed 241 marines and navy personnel, persuaded the administration to withdraw the troops. In February 1984 the marines were stationed on ships offshore and, shortly thereafter, a complete evacuation from Lebanon was ordered.

The definition of imminent hostilities also played a role in the debate over the war power and the dispatch of American troops to Somalia in 1992–1993. Billed as a humanitarian mission in December 1992 by the outgoing administration of George H. W. Bush, the continued deployment and expanding activities of the American troops later evoked substantial congressional debate and discussion, especially as the American forces became increasingly involved in military operations. Calls for the application of the War Powers Act, for President Clinton to seek congressional authorization for continued deployment, and for immediate withdrawal of the troops came from both sides of the aisle on Capitol Hill. Ultimately, when ninety-six American soldiers were killed or wounded in early October 1993, the criticism from Congress and elsewhere reached a crescendo and generated suf-

ficient pressure for the administration to announce it would withdraw American troops from the troubled country by the end of March 1994. Notably, the War Powers Act, while mentioned and threatened, was not formally invoked.

In contrast, there was little question about the nature of hostilities in September 2001. Just three days after terrorists from Osama bin Laden's Al Qaeda network attacked the United States, the U.S. Congress authorized the Bush administration to "use all necessary and appropriate force" in response. The authorization also specifically referenced the War Powers Act. Coming in the wake of the largest terrorist attack in history, and before the administration deployed any forces to retaliate, the authorization provided a broad grant of war-making authority to the administration. While congressional influence can be seen in each instance, the unevenness with which the War Powers Act has been applied, as illustrated by the preceding examples, raises the question of the effectiveness of the Act.

The War Powers Resolution: Impact and Effectiveness
The United States has engaged in significant and sizable uses of its armed forces abroad nearly two dozen times since the War Powers Resolution was passed, and it has deployed forces in relatively minor actions in nearly eighty other instances. While presidents have often submitted reports to Congress under the resolution (more than fifty times through the end of the Clinton administration), in none has it been fully implemented. In particular, Section 4(a)(1), which would set the sixty-day clock in motion, has almost never been cited; nor has reference been made to actual or imminent hostilities. For its part, Congress has invoked the provisions of the act only once, in 1983, when in connection with the deployment of U.S. marines to Lebanon, it declared that Section 4(a)(1) had become operative—but it went on to authorize the marines to stay in Lebanon for eighteen months. In the case of the Persian Gulf War, Congress stated that its authorization to use force against Iraq "constituted specific statutory authorization within the meaning of the

War Powers Resolution" (Collier 1994a), and its authorization for the 2001 campaign in Afghanistan contained similar language.

So has the War Powers Resolution had an effect on presidents and the use of U.S. force abroad? A brief review of some recent uses of force highlights the dilemmas that impinge upon the effectiveness of the law and assessments, pro and con, that have emerged among policy makers and scholars. First, although the act has been vigorously discussed in Congress and its application threatened, it has never been formally applied. Second, the political will of Congress to invoke the provisions of War Powers Resolution in conflict situations is questionable, because that would pose profound confrontation between Congress and the president. Third, the War Powers Resolution is poorly designed for dealing with uses of force short of large deployments of combat troops on the ground (that is, peacekeeping forces, air strikes, and other more limited applications), which are far more commonplace than overt uses of military force. On the other hand, Congress appears to have drawn on the power of the War Powers Resolution to shape presidential behavior in some conflict situations, even though it did not seek to apply the act formally. Consider the following examples.

When President Bush ordered military forces into Panama in December 1989, he submitted a report about the intervention to Congress "consistent with the War Powers Resolution" but neither cited the provision of the act that would limit the duration of force deployments nor recognized the legitimacy of the act itself. "I have an obligation as president to conduct the foreign policy of this country as I see fit," he exclaimed. He also announced, however, that U.S. troops were expected to be home in less than two months—within the sixty-day framework of the War Powers Resolution.

Bush adopted a similar posture during the crisis over Kuwait leading to the Persian Gulf War. A week after the invasion of Kuwait he submitted a report "consistent with the War Powers Resolution" indicating that he had deployed U.S. forces to the region to deter further Iraqi aggression. He did not cite section 4(a)(1) of the resolution, which would have started the sixty-day clock, and specifically stated "I do not believe involvement in hostilities is imminent." He reaffirmed that posture in November following the dispatch of an additional 150,000 troops to the region, claiming only that "The deployment will ensure that the coalition has an adequate offensive military option should that be necessary."

On November 29, 1990, the UN Security Council authorized the use of "all necessary means" to evict Saddam Hussein from Kuwait if he did not comply with UN mandates by January 15, 1991. The Bush administration maintained "that the president did not need any additional congressional authorization for this purpose" (Collier 1994b); see also (Moore 1994). Representative Ronald Dellums (D-California) and over fifty of his colleagues, fearing that the administration would press forward without congressional authorization, took the administration to court.[9] While the case was dismissed, the (U.S. district) court left open the door to a possible ruling against the president's war-making power without congressional involvement. In the end, of course, the Bush administration did seek congressional authorization, but the president insisted to the very end that he had a legal right to make war against Iraq "regardless of any action that Congress might or might not take" (Moore 1994). Nevertheless, it could be argued that congressional concerns, the suit brought by Dellums, and the threat of the War Powers Act combined to force the president to bring the decision to Congress before acting.

The Persian Gulf War and later interventions in Somalia, the Balkans, and Haiti have added new elements to the War Powers debate, as they invite questions about Congress's role in authorizing U.S. participation in United Nations military or peacekeeping operations. The issue was left unresolved at the United Nations' creation in 1945, when it was anticipated that member states would conclude agreements placing military forces at the disposal of the new organization. The

UN Participation Act, the implementing legislation for U.S. participation in the United Nations, makes it clear that congressional approval is required for any agreement designating U.S. military forces for United Nations use, but that further congressional approval would not be necessary before they could be made available to the UN Security Council for enforcement action.

Congress made attempts to play a larger role in defining the U.S. purpose and mission in Somalia, leading eventually, as we have noted, to the Clinton administration's pledge to remove U.S. forces from the African nation by March 31, 1994. The House of Representatives also passed a resolution that used the *legislative veto* section of the War Powers Resolution—presumed to have been a dead letter since the Supreme Court's *Chadha* ruling—to direct the president to remove U.S. troops from Somalia. The Senate did not act on the House proposal, but Congress did cut off funds for further operations in Somalia (unless Congress later authorized more). Again, while the act was not expressly applied, arguably Congress affected the policy.

Like Bush, Clinton looked increasingly to the United Nations Security Council for his authority to use force, not to Congress (or the Constitution?). As he honed the military option to unseat Haiti's military regime in 1994, for example, he said he "welcomed" congressional support for the contemplated action, but added: "Like my predecessors of both parties, I have not agreed that I was constitutionally mandated to get it." Shortly after that, "he told the American public that he was prepared to use military force to invade Haiti, referring to a UN Security Council [resolution] as authority and his willingness to lead a multilateral force 'to carry out the will of the United Nations'" (Fisher 1994–1995).

The climate for congressional acquiescence to presidential deployments seemed to shift significantly in 1995. The Republican Congress, which came into power in January, determined to reign in U.S. participation in UN operations. The *National Security Revitalization Act* passed by the House sought to increase congressional control over peacekeeping deployments. It also proposed to bar the president from placing U.S. forces under foreign command as part of a UN peacekeeping operation—a move opposed by Clinton officials as an affront to the president's powers—and to reduce U.S. contributions to UN operations by the amount the Defense Department spent supporting past peacekeeping activities. Republican presidential contender Senator Robert Dole also introduced the *Peace Powers Act.* While repealing much of the War Powers Act, it would have strengthened its consultation provisions and the congressional oversight of UN-sponsored peacekeeping missions (similar legislation was introduced and later defeated in the House). "It makes sense to untie the president's hands in the use of force to defend U.S. interests," Dole told the Senate Foreign Relations Committee, "but we need to rein in the blank check for UN peacekeeping."[10]

Nevertheless, in the fall of 1995 President Clinton committed 20,000 American troops to Bosnia-Herzogovina as part of the Dayton peace accords (Hendrickson 1998). Clinton's action followed his decisions to commit American forces to NATO enforcement of a UN-authorized "no-fly" zone over Bosnia and to dispatch roughly 350 U.S. troops to Macedonia to join a mission authorized by the UN Security Council intended to prevent a widening of the Balkan conflict. Clinton's decision took place in the climate of heightened congressional concern over force deployments generally and the president's authorization of NATO air-strikes against the Bosnian Serbs in August. In the months that followed the Dayton peace accords, Clinton pledged to consult with Congress before committing American troops to the peace enforcement mission. Instead, he basically presented Congress with his decisions and then asked Congress to support him. Despite some grumbling and opposition and complaints, both houses of Congress would pass resolutions supporting Clinton's actions. Congressman Henry Hyde (R-Illinois) lamented that "the die is cast, now we have to fall in line."

Four years later, in early 1999, Clinton committed additional American forces to another operation in the former Yugoslavia, this time engaging in a massive bombing campaign against Serbia in reaction to its actions in Kosovo, a autonomous Serbian province heavily populated by ethnic Albanians.[11] Secretary of Defense William Cohen and Secretary of State Madeleine Albright had asserted earlier that NATO had the authority to use force without either UN or congressional approval. That view was later challenged, leading to heated debates in the House of Representatives. But, in spite of the obvious opposition to Clinton's initiative, no substantive actions were taken to derail them.

Clinton did initiate discussions with Congress a few days before the start of the campaign, hoping to win members' support for the action. Under the leadership of several prominent Republican Senators, the Senate in March 1993 passed a resolution supporting the president's initiative. The House, however, was considerably more divided on the issue and failed to pass a similar resolution (Dionne 1999; Pianin 1999; Gugliotta 1999).

Then, three weeks into the Kosovo campaign, resolutions were introduced in the House calling for the withdrawal of all American troops from the conflict and for a declaration of war. Intense debates over war powers followed. Secretary of State Albright informed members of the House International Relations Committee that "we do not believe in a war powers resolution . . . there is a conflict going on . . . The President has, we believe, the constitutional authority to do what he is doing." When the issue went to the House, a series of resolutions that would have constrained Clinton's authority failed.

Not to be denied, Representative Thomas Campbell (R–California) filed a suit in court against President Clinton for violation of the War Powers Act. This case was dismissed for lack of standing, as well as court use of the political questions doctrine (see Chapter 10) (Fisher 2000b). So did Congress exercise influence, or was it denied? On the surface it appears that Congress

again failed to rein in the president, but it should be remembered that Clinton also seems to have responded to the congressional climate by publicly ruling out the use of American ground troops in the Balkans conflict.

In sharp contrast to the controversy surrounding U.S. applications of force in Somalia, Haiti, Bosnia, and Kosovo, substantial consensus characterized the climate around the use of force against the al-Queda network and the Taliban regime in Afghanistan. In response to the attacks on the United States, Congress moved swiftly to authorize the Bush administration to use force against the perpetrators of the attack. The resolution, which passed the House 420-1 and the Senate 98-0 just three days after the attacks, authorized the president to use "all necessary and appropriate force . . . against nations, organizations, or persons . . . [who] planned, authorized, committed, or aided" the attacks.

Clearly driven by the direct attack and its devastating consequences, the resolution nevertheless fell short of the authority requested by George W. Bush, who sought the power to respond to the September 11 attacks and any future attacks. Cognizant of mistakes like the Gulf of Tonkin Resolution of 1964, some members of Congress tried to avoid "blank check" grants of war-making authority. According to Democratic Senator John Kerry (D–Massachusetts), not only did the resolution require Bush to provide regular updates to Congress, it also stipulated that Congress had to vote on funding military actions.

Moreover, as Democratic Chair of the Foreign Relations Committee Joseph Biden (D–Colorado) argued, the resolution "was narrowly drawn to apply only to responses to [September 11] terrorist actions" and invoked the War Powers Act by requiring the president to return to Congress for a formal declaration of war if he desired to expand the U.S. action (Povich 2001). Other observers acknowledged the careful language and the fact that Congress had not provided Bush with a "blank check," but cautioned that the resolution probably did not substantially limit the president. For example, constitutional and national security law scholar Harold Koh of the Yale Law School stated "I think it is extremely broad because no nations are named, the nations are to be determined by the president and the president could theoretically name lots of nations. . . . There is also no time limit" (Lewis 2001).

And so the debate continues. In many respects, the historical record suggests that the War Powers Resolution has failed in its intention to redress the balance between Congress and the president. Quite simply, the president has not conceded he is bound by its provisions, and Congress cannot ensure enforcement. Many observers have endorsed this view (Fisher and Adler 1998; Lowi 1985b; Hendrickson forthcoming). Even congressional luminaries, including Bob Dole and Henry Hyde, have proposed its repeal.

Jacob K. Javits, architect of the War Powers Act, wrote shortly before his death that the resolution "did not, and does not, guarantee the end of presidential war, but it does present Congress with the means by which it can stop presidential war if it has the will to act" (Javits 1985). In most instances it appears that Congress lacks the will—in part because short, decisive military actions by the president (like the interventions in Grenada, Panama, and the Persian Gulf, and attacks on Libya and Iraq) tend to be politically popular at home. When they are unpopular, as came to be the case with the humanitarian intervention in Somalia, Congress shows more backbone.

Yet, other observers conclude that the act has, indeed, constrained presidential uses of force (see Gartzke 1996; Auerswald and Cowhey 1997). A recent analysis of uses of force before and after the War Powers Act concludes, for instance, that "The use of force after the Act is significantly different than it was before the Act, despite seeming congressional passivity" (Auerswald and Cowhey 1997). According to this analysis, presidents have, even while denouncing the act, engaged in more selective and careful applications of force. Moreover, Congress has, even while failing to invoke the act, generated anticipated reactions from presidents because of its provisions. Meanwhile, the president continues to enjoy considerable latitude in responding to international situations. Hence, while "presidential preeminence" is too strong a term, "presidential leadership" seems accurate; at the same time, "congressional deference" or "acquiescence" no longer appear to be accurate characterizations of its war-making role.

Money What about the *power of the purse?* Since Congress has the exclusive power to appropriate funds for foreign as well as domestic programs, we should expect that here, more than in any other area, Congress would assert its authority over foreign affairs; in many respects, that has been the case. A few examples include the 1976 Clark amendment barring the use of funds for any activities involving Angola; the Boland amendments of the 1980s barring or restricting aid to the Nicaraguan contras; the 1995 vote to cut off funds to enforce the arms embargo against Bosnia; a 1999 amendment to withhold half of American aid to Russia until that country ended its nuclear and ballistic missile cooperation with Iran.

It is also noteworthy that members of Congress are able to link the power of the purse to other avenues of influence. Indeed, the mere threat of a linking issue enables members to have an impact on policy. For example, the power of the purse enables them to conduct regular oversight hearings in conjunction with budgetary decisions. These hearings address military, diplomatic, trade, and intelligence issues, among others. Because budgeting is about voting, the process enables members to bargain for influence on one issue or another, frequently by tying apparently unrelated policy questions together. As members utilize this potentially powerful tool, they are guided by both policy and electoral concerns. The politics of defense and foreign aid budgeting highlight the dynamics.

Managing Foreign Aid Expenditures[12] Because it depends directly on Congress's appropriation of money, the perennially unpopular foreign aid program enables Congress to scrutinize the executive branch's conduct of foreign policy. "Here is where the specter of '535 secretaries of state' is inevitably raised by critics of an aggressive congressional role" (Warburg 1989). Congress frequently exercises its power of the purse by adjusting presidential requests and adding its own. For instance, in 1995, House Speaker Newt Gingrich added $18 million to the budget for efforts to overthrow Saddam Hussein. Additionally, Congress often *earmarks* foreign aid funds for particular countries or for particular programs. For example, in 1996, there were earmarks for Israel, Egypt, Turkey, Greece, Ireland, Ukraine, Armenia, Cyprus, and Burma, among others (McCormick 1998).[13]

In addition, *conditionality* has become a centerpiece of congressional-presidential struggles over foreign aid funding (see Turner 1988). Bans on aid to countries taking certain actions—such as human rights violations, seizing U.S. fishing vessels, granting sanctuary to terrorists, and the like—are commonplace. In the case of the Freedom Support Act of 1992, which authorized U.S. assistance for the republics of the former Soviet Union, Congress linked the flow of aid to the removal of Russian troops from the Baltic states. Aid also has been made conditional on recipients meeting certain standards, such as cooperating with the United States in the interdiction of drug trafficking, holding free elections, or supporting the United States on UN resolutions. In fact, Congress reportedly directs where half of all development loan funds and over ninety percent of all U.S. security assistance is to go (Kondracke 1990).

Congress also resorts to *reporting requirements* to ensure executive compliance with legislative restrictions. The pervasiveness of reporting is indicated by the explosion in the number of reporting requirements, from 200 in 1973 to more than 800 in 1988 (Collier 1989, 37). For example, the ratification resolution for the Chemical Weapons Treaty, discussed earlier, contained a variety of reporting requirements on compliance and others matters, which were attached as conditions by opponents of the treaty before it was passed by

the Senate. From Congress's point of view, reporting requirements provide Congress with information; promote consultation; focus attention on a problem; provide a means of control; and oversee implementation (Collier 1988).

Although reporting requirements are useful to Congress, their number is now so great that "Congress has difficulty keeping track of them" (Collier 1988). Moreover, the required reports and certifications may generate *micromanagement*—detailed legislative interference in the conduct of America's foreign relations. For example, in the late 1980s AID employees in Global South countries complained "that they spend so much time filling out reports to Congress that they have only an afternoon a week to help the poor" (Kondracke 1990). Republicans and Democrats are equally guilty. As Democratic Senator Joseph R. Biden caustically observed, "When the Republicans were in the White House, they kept on saying, 'Don't micromanage foreign policy.' But they have turned out to be the biggest micromanaging, tinkering fools around." (See Focus 12.1.)

Presidents can often avoid such situations by taking advantage of loopholes. Congress typically provides loopholes to permit the president flexibility to ignore restrictions that he believes compromise the United States' security interests. As Senator Richard Lugar (R-Indiana) commented in regard to Clinton's Haiti policies, "Any resolution that we can adopt won't really bind the administration. There'll always be an escape hatch." For example, the Freedom Support Act's requirement that tied U.S. aid to the withdrawal of Russian troops from the Baltic states is one that the president could waive. After the passage of the Helms-Burton Act in 1996—which requires secondary sanctions against foreign companies and individuals doing business with Cuba, as well as allowing legal action by Americans against such companies—the Clinton administration took advantage of the law's waiver provision and suspended key requirements for six months . . . and then another six months . . . and another . . . all the way through the end of his second term.

FOCUS 12.1   President Clinton Responds to the Republican Congress, May 1995

Legislation that Congress is considering . . . would place new restrictions on how America conducts its foreign policy and slash our budget in foreign affairs. I believe these bills threaten our ability to preserve America's global leadership and to safeguard the security and prosperity of the American people in the post–Cold War world. The world is still full of dangers but more full of opportunities, and the United States must be able to act aggressively to combat foreign threats and to make commitments and then to keep those commitments. These bills would deprive us of both those capabilities.

Supporters of the bills call them "necessary costcutting measures." But in reality, they are the most isolationist proposals to come before the United States Congress in the last fifty years. They are the product of those who argue passionately that America must be strong, and then turn around and refuse to pay the price of that strength or to give the presidency the means to assert that strength.

The price of conducting our foreign policy is, after all, not very high. Today slightly more than one percent of the budget. . . . That one percent, which includes contributions to the multilateral development banks, helps to dismantle nuclear weapons, saves lives by preventing famine, immunizing children, and combating terrorists and drug-traffickers.

Bills in both the House and the Senate place new restrictions on our ability to respond to these dangers, as well as to take advantage of all the opportunities that are out there for the United States. . . . . . These constraints represent nothing less than a frontal assault on the authority of the president to conduct the foreign policy of the United States and on our nations' ability to respond rapidly and effectively to threats to our security.

Repeatedly, I have said there are right ways and wrong ways to cut the deficit. This legislation is the wrong way. We did not win the Cold War to walk away and blow the opportunities of the peace on shortsighted, scattershotted budget cuts and attempts to micromange the United States' foreign policy.

The Bush and Clinton administrations sought unsuccessfully to overhaul the foreign aid program by sweeping away congressional restrictions. As discussed in Chapter 5, the most recent efforts occurred in 1994 when the Clinton administration proposed to appropriate aid not for specific countries or programs but in pursuit of broad foreign policy goals. Earmarks and distinctions between military and economic assistance would be eliminated. It quickly became clear that Congress was reluctant to relinquish its ability to influence aid allocations. "We will not give to an unelected bureaucracy . . . authority to spend dollars any way they want, so long as they call it 'pursuit of democracy' or 'expanding economic development,'" asserted David R. Obey of the House Appropriations Subcommittee on Foreign Operations. Republicans were even less interested when they assumed the reins of congressional leadership following the 1994 elections.

Instead, they targeted foreign aid for sharp budget cuts—and possible total elimination as an instrument of American foreign policy.

More recently, the centrality of Congress on the issue of aid and foreign affairs spending was highlighted by a series of confrontations with the White House. In addition to the three-year brawl over foreign aid and foreign affairs spending that eventually resulted in the shut-down of the Senate Foreign Relations Committee and severe cutbacks in the international affairs budget, Congress denied Clinton's request for funds to assist Mexico during its 1995 financial crisis (forcing the president to package some discretionary funds with IMF assistance instead). In 1998 amidst the Asian financial crisis, Congress resisted Clinton's request for $18 billion in additional IMF funds, acceding only when the president was able to build a coalition in the Senate and agreed to press a number of IMF reforms (Carter and Scott

2000b). Throughout the last half of the 1990s, Congress repeatedly held American contributions to the United Nations hostage to a variety demands, including UN reforms, reduced American dues, and even abortion policy. Shortly before it left office the Clinton administration did succeed in extracting funds from Congress to pay delinquent dues, but only after it had secured revisions to United States' UN assessments. George W. Bush ran into further trouble on this issue in 2001 when House Republicans led by Tom Delay (Texas) sought to tie payment to a UN exemption for the U.S. from jurisdiction of the International Criminal Court. Eventually the impasse was broken and $862 million in back dues was paid.

The confirmation hearings of Colin Powell as secretary of state and his early testimony before Congress provide further evidence of Congress' power of the purse. Powell's argument for increased aid and foreign affairs funding explicitly acknowledged the role of Congress on the matter. Moreover, his call for increased international affairs funding, including foreign assistance, was greeted by Senator Jesse Helms' reply that he, as chair of the Senate Foreign Relations Committee, would support increased aid as long as AID was eliminated and replaced by a granting foundation that would funnel assistance to NGOs (Schmitt 2001a). Helms' statement illustrates clearly how the power of the purse can be connected to other policy concerns.

Managing Military Expenditures Military spending is another budgetary area in which Congress can and does play a major role. During the 1950s and 1960s, Congress often voiced its views on the defense budget by appropriating *more* for defense than was asked for by the president. After that, Congress began cutting administration requests substantially, much as it did with foreign aid. Moreover, its micromanagement of the Pentagon increased steadily. A White Paper from the first Bush administration complained that "some thirty committees and seventy-seven subcommittees claim some degree of oversight . . .

and more than 1,500 congressional staffers devote nearly all of their time to defense issues" (*Wall Street Journal,* 18 December 1989, A10). The administration also complained that "the Pentagon alone spent $50 million and 500 'man-years' in fiscal 1989 writing reports to satisfy Congress" (cited in Burgin 1993). Meanwhile, Congress made an increasing number of changes in the president's defense budget requests. In 1970 Congress made 830 program changes during the annual budgetary cycle; by the end of the Cold War the number had grown to nearly 2,800 (Blechman 1990).

The motivation to micromanage is tied directly to the factors that differentiate the perspective of members of Congress on foreign and national security policy issues from that of the president. *Political grandstanding* for electoral purposes is a powerful incentive. For example Congress publically debated (and voted on) virtually all of the important strategic and many conventional weapons systems requiring production decisions during the Reagan administration's military build-up in the 1980s, when the incentives to micromanage were especially strong. The decisions Congress faced included the MX missile, the Strategic Defense Initiative (SDI), the Stealth bomber program, antisatellite systems, chemical weapons, the Trident II submarine, the B-1 bomber, cruise missiles, nuclear-powered aircraft carriers, and anti-aircraft guns and tactical aircraft. Before Reagan, decisions on them typically would have been made in congressional committees. As Senator Gaylord Nelson noted wryly, "the floor is being used as an instrument of political campaigning far more than it ever was before." Electoral incentives in the form of financial contributions and constituency support also multiplied as the guns-instead-of-butter spending priorities of the Reagan administration helped to politicize defense policy (Lindsay 1987).[14]

The same parochialism that motivates members of Congress to serve on committees fuels Congress's micromanagement of the defense budget, as members are alert to the impact of defense spending on their constituencies, as we saw in Chapter 9. As one defense expert observed caustically, "Politicians of both parties see the [defense] budget as a jobs program. No longer does the defense debate take place between hawks and doves, but between those who have defense facilities and those who don't" (Korb 1995a). Hence, immediate constituency interests promise to figure prominently in the calculations. A persistent question, then, is how to get Congress to focus on policy rather than micromanaging individual programs.

Defense "intellectuals" in Congress, notably Sam Nunn, chair of the Senate Armed Services Committee, and Les Aspin, chair of the House Armed Services Committee, did strike out in new strategic directions in the early post–Cold War years, believing, as Aspin put it, that 'there are new realities in the world, but no new thinking at home to match them'" (Stockton 1993). The two drafted their own defense budgets, setting out markedly different priorities from the Bush administration's budget requests.

Nunn's and Aspin's response to broad policy issues as the Cold War waned is not easily explained by the imperative of reelection or the demands of constituent service. A sense of "duty" and a belief that addressing policy issues is "part of their job" are perhaps better explanations (Stockton 1993). But Nunn and Aspin would soon leave Congress, and Congress throughout the Clinton years would continue micromanaging the defense budget. According to one accounting:

> Congress cut Bush's requests for HARM missiles (52 percent), high-speed cargo ships (49 percent), U.S. troops stationed in Europe after FY 1996 (33 percent), C-17 cargo planes (28 percent), Strategic Defense Initiative (SDI) funding (25 percent), FA-18 Aircraft (25 percent), and the development of a new Centurion-class nuclear submarine (14 percent). Bush was also forced to accept a total fleet of twenty B-2 Stealth bombers, rather than the seventy-five he had requested. . . . Congress increased funding

for modernization of M-1 tanks (492 percent), Bradley fighting vehicles (120 percent), JSTARS radar aircraft (65 percent), and a helicopter-borne laser for use as a minesweeper (50 percent). Members also added $1.2 billion for an unrequested helicopter carrier, continued to fund the V-22 Osprey air transport, and refused to stop the Seawolf submarine program after building only one such submarine. . . . Facing a Republican Congress . . . [President Clinton's] budget battles intensified. Congress tried to increase antimissile defense funding and gain more control over peacekeeping activities, but was unable to override Clinton's veto. Clinton also vetoed the Foreign Operations appropriations bill, as it cut his requests for Arms Control and Disarmament Agency (53 percent), UN peacekeeping costs (49 percent), U.S. Information Agency (16 percent), and the Department of State (13 percent). Congress was more successful in cutting multilateral aid requests by 48 percent, bilateral aid requests by 15 percent, and export assistance requests by 10 percent.

(CARTER 1998, 112–113)

Indeed, in each of the last four years of his term, Congress increased the defense budget beyond Clinton's request. Moreover, Congress was clearly the driving force behind the reincarnation of the Strategic Defense Initiative in its current form: National Missile Defense. It was Congress that sought additional funds for an expanded program beginning in 1995, Congress that voted to go forward with the program in 1999, and Congress that pressured Clinton to endorse NMD in 2000. In this context, the second Bush administration's commitment to NMD is merely the continuation of congressional policy.

Congress continued to use its *power of the purse* over military expenditures during George W. Bush's administration, although the nature of that use shifted in the wake of the September 2001 terrorist attacks on the United States. Prior to the attacks, Bush's budget faced congressional micromanagement similar to those of his predecessors. The overall amount, the specific programs, and, especially, the commitment to spending over $8 billion on national missile defense drew substantial congressional activism, especially after the Democrats assumed the majority in the Senate after Vermont Senator James Jeffords switched parties. For example, Carl Levin (D–Michigan), the chair of the Senate Armed Services Committee, indicated his intention to oppose missile defense spending. Joseph Biden appeared before the National Press Club the day before the terrorist strikes to announce in strong terms his opposition to missile defense.

In the wake of the attacks, the climate changed substantially. First, many of those most likely to oppose the Bush administration's budget proposals backed away from their opposition. Levin, for instance, decided to suspend plans to block missile defense spending in the interest of bipartisanship and unity (Hartung 2001). Moreover, Congress in general became more supportive toward military spending, agreeing to emergency funds and other increases. Furthermore, many members of both parties sought to expand spending rather than oppose the administration's requests.

Of course, that does not mean they abandoned use of the *power of the purse*. Instead, members used it to shape and increase spending in light of the campaign against terrorism. For example, the House Appropriations Committee added almost $2 billion to Bush's defense budget to increase counterterrorism spending. It also trimmed missile defense spending by $500 million (Morgan 2001). The Senate Armed Services Committee added $600 million to meet non-traditional threats (Roosevelt 2001). All told, with emergency funds and supplemental requests, the defense budget was expected to grow from the previous year by over $60 billion dollars to $375 billion in fiscal year 2002 (Hartung 2001). Buried in those funds were numerous examples of the spending parochialism we noted earlier: Curt Weldon's (R–Penn) continued advocacy of the V-22 Osprey tilt-rotor plane built in his dis-

tricts; Georgia and Texas delegates' continued advocacy for the Lockheed Martin F-22 fighter built in their states; and others (Hartung 2001).

Still, in some ways the end of the Cold War has added incentives to "strategize" as well as to micromanage: "While voters may have had little interest in such topics in the past, the demise of the Soviet threat allows legislators to link proposals on strategy to more immediate voter concerns" (Stockton 1995). The Defense Reorganization Act of 1986 (the Goldwater-Nichols Act) requires that each annual budget request to Congress be accompanied by a comprehensive report on overall national security strategy, enabling Congress to consider strategic concerns as well as budget lines. Moreover, in the National Defense Authorization Act of 1996, Congress did require *Quadrennial Defense Reviews* beginning in 1997, which were to include: "a comprehensive examination of the defense strategy, force structure, force modernization plans, infrastructure, budget plan, and other elements of the defense program and policies with a view toward determining and expressing the defense strategy of the United States and establishing a revised defense program through the year 2005." To be sure, both of these requirements place the White House in the position of conducting the studies, but they ensure that Congress has opportunities to review more than annual budgets.

Constraints on the Power of the Purse Congressional actions on the foreign aid and defense budgets demonstrate Congress's willingness to exercise its power of the purse, although its instruments for doing so are not finely honed and its motives sometimes suspect. Indeed, there are limits to Congress's ability use its fiscal powers. Briefly, they include:

- *Problems associated with political will and political costs.* On some issues, members of Congress are reluctant to challenge a president because of the potential costs involved. It is difficult to get even a majority of the 535 members of Congress organized into two competing political parties to agree on a particular policy priority, especially if it challenges the president. Nowhere is this more evident than in controlling the use of force. Members are reluctant to use the power of the purse to control uses of force for fear that they will be vulnerable to the criticism that they left American forces exposed. For example, in spite of the outcry over the 1970 American incursion into Cambodia order by the Nixon administration, Congress cut off Cambodian war funds only after (then known) U.S. military activity had ceased, and Congress never failed to appropriate the funds for the war that the Johnson and Nixon administrations sought. Two decades later Congress again cut off funds for a U.S. operation, this one in Somalia. Again, however, the target date was the one the administration had already announced for terminating the U.S. role

- *Problems associated with the instrument itself.* It is often noted that "policy is what gets funded." However, while the power of the purse is central to some foreign policy initiatives, its link to others is not. The extent to which money can be used to affect the nation's foreign policy is limited. Simply put, it is difficult to legislate foreign policy or to equate lawmaking with foreign policy making. Programs, but not necessarily policies, require appropriations. Hence, some of the most important aspects of America's foreign relations do not require specific and direct appropriations of money

- *Problems associated with the budget process.* The budget process itself is long, drawn-out, complex, and fragmented, which makes difficult the prospect of coordinating the process and policy. This problem is especially acute because, within each house of Congress, the substantive committees having jurisdiction over particular programs authorize expenditures, but another committee makes the actual appropriations. Moreover, opportunities for individuals to pursue their

own agendas and pressures for log rolling and compromises tend to blunt the sharp edge of the power of the purse

- *Problems associated with presidential discretion.* The president has important budgetary powers that also limit the ability of Congress to turn its power of the purse into direct policy results. For one, the 1921 budget reform act gave the president the agenda-setting power of proposing a budget to Congress. More significantly, presidents have opportunities to **impound** funds, or to refuse to spend money appropriated by Congress. Presidents also have **discretionary funds**—monies provided the president to deal with situations unforeseen at the time of the annual budget process—on which they can draw to evade congressional restrictions. For example, Johnson used $1.5 billion in contingency funds embedded in the Defense Department budget to finance military operations in Southeast Asia during 1965 and 1966 (Nathan and Oliver 1976). Similarly, the Reagan administration used $10 million in CIA discretionary funds to finance the contras during its first term (Copson 1988). The Clinton administration used discretionary funds to aid Mexico in 1995 during that country's financial crisis after Congress rejected its request for emergency assistance. George W. Bush used discretionary funds to support the CIA's expanded counter terrorist intelligence and covert activities

- **Reprogramming** permits funds within an appropriation category to be moved from one purpose to another (for example, from shipbuilding to submarine construction). Although the 1974 Budget and Impoundment Control Act sought to constrain such executive flexibility, it still specified that the president could order **deferrals** (temporary spending delays, which can extend up to twelve months) and **rescissions** (permanent efforts to cancel budget authority), subject to congressional review[15]

In summary, our review of the congressional power of the purse suggests that members of Congress use multiple instruments and opportunities to shape American foreign policy. These avenues range from substantive legislation to less direct means, all of which may be linked together to shape policy. Moreover, our review suggests that members may have influence even when the institution does not produce legislation, as presidents respond to congressional preferences, often through "anticipated reactions," and adjust policies accordingly. However, the president retains important advantages in foreign policy leadership, including control over the implementation of policy. Other presidential advantages stem from obstacles that obstruct congressional foreign policy making, to which we now turn.

OBSTACLES TO CONGRESSIONAL FOREIGN POLICY MAKING

Because of its access to powerful avenues of influence such as those discussed previously, Congress can, at times, play an assertive foreign policy role. However, as an institution, Congress suffers from some key disadvantages when it comes to competing effectively with the president over the direction of the nation's foreign relations. Three interrelated factors—parochialism, organizational weaknesses, and lack of expertise—help to explain this disadvantage and shed light on the reasons that members of Congress frequently fail to utilize its apparently powerful and numerous avenues of foreign policy influence.

Parochialism

Congress is more oriented toward domestic than foreign affairs. All 435 members of the House are up for reelection every two years, as is a third of the Senate. Continual preoccupation with reelection creates pressure to attend more to domestic than to international concerns. The pressure is especially acute on the House side, and perhaps explains why the ten provisions of the House Republicans' *Contract with America* during the 1994 election included only one foreign policy item. The president has a national constituency. In contrast, all 535 members of Congress have much more-narrowly construed electoral bases and correspondingly restricted constituency interests. Thus, in the words of former Under Secretary of State William D. Rogers (1979), "With the fate of the entire House and a third of the Senate in the hands of the voters every 730 days, Congress is beholden to every short-term swing of popular opinion. The temptation to pander to prejudice and emotion is overwhelming."

The twenty-first century environment arguably exacerbates these tendencies. For one, globalization and the concomitant rise of intermestic issues dramatically increase the range of constituency interests in issues formerly thought to be either purely domestic or purely international. Increased ethnic diversity may also heighten the concerns and interests of constituents (Shain 1994–1995). These developments present often powerful incentives for Congress to address specialized issues that relate to foreign policy. Moreover, the international threat environment plays a critical role in such calculations. Without pressing threats, constraints on foreign policy activism erode, as the costs related to narrow, often single-issue-driven policy concerns are diminished. The combination of more concerns and lowered political risks may simply encourage more members to act on their parochial interests. Conversely, when clear threats appear, as after September 11, 2001, members are more likely to control parochial urges.

Because senators and representatives depend for their survival on satisfying their constituents' parochial interests, "being national-minded can be a positive hazard to a legislative career" (Sundquist 1976). Thus a foreign policy problem may be viewed from a representative's Polish, Israeli, or Irish constituent viewpoint. Similarly, military needs may be weighed by the benefits of industries located within a senator's state or representative's district. "Asked one day whether it was true that the navy yard in his district was too small to accommodate the latest battleships," Henry Stimson (chair of the House Naval Affairs Committee early in the century) replied, 'That is true, and that is the reason I have always been in favor of small ships' (cited in Sundquist 1976).

The president's vantage point is much different. Having a nationwide constituency, the president's outlook on foreign policy problems is broader. The president can usually afford to alienate some local or narrow interests (by refusing to support a protective trade restriction, for example) without fear of electoral retribution; and while the president is rewarded for thinking in long-run terms rather than for the moment, a senator or representative is not. "With their excessively parochial orientation," former Senator J. William Fulbright explains, members of Congress "are acutely sensitive to the influence of private pressure and to the excesses and inadequacies of a public opinion that is all too often ignorant of the needs, the dangers, and the opportunities in our foreign relations." (Fulbright and two of his successors as chairs of the Senate Foreign Relations Committee, Frank Church of Idaho and Charles Percy of Illinois, lost reelection bids in part because they assumed leadership roles in foreign rather than domestic affairs.)

Interest in and attention to foreign policy issues by members of Congress is typically short-lived and strongly influenced by their newsworthiness (Crabb and Holt 1992). According to Republican Senator Daniel J. Evans of Washington, the legislative process has degenerated into "reading yesterday's headlines so that we can write today's amendments so that we can garner tomorrow's headlines." Often amendments are passed with little expectation of becoming law. As one Senate aide observed, "It has come to be an accepted part of the game that amendments are passed and press releases claiming credit are issued, with the understanding that most of these items will be tossed in the wastebasket when the bill goes to conference with the House." The *"hundred barons phenomenon"*—all senators want

to be seen as directing the nation's foreign policy—explains the seemingly pointless behavior (Oberdorfer and Dewar 1987).

The congressional committee system, where the institution's real work is done, reinforces parochialism. Members of Congress serve on committees to enhance their prospects for reelection, expand their influence within chambers, devise good public policy, and position themselves for new careers (Fenno 1973; see also Burgin 1993; Smith and Deering 1990). Although distinguished performance in congressional committees may further each of those goals, reelection depends primarily on *constituent service*. Such concerns deflect congressional attention from substantive policy issues. Gaining a committee assignment germane to the interests of people back home is therefore critical to the effective performance of constituent service. Congressional committees reflect these preferences, which in turn help to shape the legislative process.

> Farm state members want to deal with agriculture while city people do not, so the agriculture committees are rural and proagriculture in their composition. The military affairs committees are dominated by partisans of the military, urban affairs committees by members from the cities, interior committees by proreclamation westerners, and so on. By custom, the judiciary committees are made up exclusively of lawyers. Within each committee, there is further specialization of subcommittees and of individual members. . . . And through logrolling, the advocates of various local interests form coalitions of mutual support.
>
> (SUNDQUIST 1976, 600)

Given these incentives and the behaviors they encourage, congressional attention to foreign affairs is often fleeting and shallow. Indeed, "sacrificing overall consistency and coherence of national policy for narrow interests and short-term objectives . . . is the natural consequence of the political calculus that inevitably dominates congressional decision making" (Blechman 1990).

Table 12.2 Foreign Affairs Responsibilities of Committees in the House and Senate, 107th Congress (Number of Foreign Policy-Related Subcommittees in Parentheses)

Senate Committee	Foreign Affairs Responsibility	House Committee
Agriculture, Nutrition, and Forestry (1)	Foreign agricultural policy and assistance	Agriculture (2)
Appropriations (7)	Appropriation of revenues, rescission of appropriations	Appropriations (7)
Armed Services (6)	Defense, national security, national security aspects of nuclear energy, defense production,	Armed Services (5)
Banking, Housing, and Urban Affairs (2)	International economic policy, export and foreign trade promotion	Financial Services (2); Energy and Commerce (4); International Relations (6)
Budget	Budgetary matters, concurrent budget resolution	Budget
Commerce, Science, and Transportation (4)	Merchant marine, marine fisheries, oceans, coastal zone management, nonmilitary space sciences and aeronautics	Energy and Commerce (4); Resources (3); Science (3)
Energy and Natural Resources (2)	Energy policy, nonmilitary development of nuclear energy	Energy and Commerce (4); Science (3); Resources (3)
Environment and Public Works (2)	Environmental policy, regulation of nuclear energy, ocean dumping, environmental aspects of outer continental shelf lands	Science(3)
Finance (3)	Revenue measures, customs, foreign trade agreements, tariffs, import quotas	Ways and Means (1)
Foreign Relations (7)	Relations with foreign nations, treaties, executive agreements, international organizations, foreign assistance, international economic policy, trade and export promotion, intervention abroad, declarations of war, terrorism, international environmental and scientific affairs	International Relations (6)
Governmental Affairs (1)	Organization and reorganization of the executive branch, organization and management of nuclear export policy	Government Reform(3)
Intelligence	Intelligence activities, covert operations	Intelligence
Judiciary (2)	Immigration and refugees, terrorism, espionage	Judiciary (4)
Health, Education Labor and Pensions (1)	Regulation of foreign labor	Education and the Workforce (1)

SOURCE: www.senate.gov/committees/index.cfm and www.house.gov/house/CommitteeWWW.html
Note: Descriptions of the foreign affairs responsibilities are derived from the jurisdictions of the Senate committees in the 107th Congress, with the corresponding jurisdictions of House committees matched to those as closely as possible. All are standing committees of the respective houses of Congress except the Intelligence committees, both of which are select committees.

Organizational Weaknesses

Foreign policy influence by members of Congress is also hindered by the fragmentation of power and responsibility within Congress. President Truman's famous quip, "The buck stops here!" has no counterpart in Congress. Over half of the standing committees in both the House and Senate have broadly defined jurisdictions that give them some foreign affairs responsibility (see Table 12.2). Unlike the executive branch, where policy debates take place in private with a single individual, the president, often making the final choice, congressional debates are perforce public, with final choices made by counting yeas and nays, and with decision making diffuse. Under these conditions, policy consistency and coordination are most unlikely.

During the 1970s Congress undertook several procedural reforms that decentralized power from the committee to the subcommittee level, encouraged challenges to the seniority system, and reduced the importance of leadership positions.[16] As a consequence it became more difficult than ever to locate power and authority in Congress. "There are 165 different people in the House and Senate who can answer to the proud title 'Mr. Chairman,' having been given committees or subcommittees of their own" (Broder 1986). Accordingly, the congressional leadership cannot speak for the institution as a whole, and Congress rarely speaks with a single voice. Newt Gingrich reversed the trend toward fragmented leadership when he became speaker of the House by gathering and concentrating some powers and authority to the leadership. Overall, his success was marginal in an institution as decentralized and sprawling as the House of Representatives. In fact, the Republican decision to limit the tenure of any committee chair probably exacerbates the problem by reducing the impact of expertise (Gugliotta 1998).

The rise of *single-issue politics*—which subjects members of Congress to evaluation not on the basis of their entire record but only their performance on particular issues—magnifies the problems associated with the diffusion of power. Noting that the 385 committees and subcommittees of Congress are scouted by hundreds of registered lobbyists, one former official lamented that instead of a two-party system Capitol Hill resembles "a 385-party system" (cited in Crabb and Holt 1992). As the foreign-domestic policy divide has become increasingly porous, this effect has increasingly had foreign policy consequences. Business groups, ideological groups, ethnic groups, labor groups, environmental groups, and virtually every other special interest group seems to be able to find something "international" on which to focus their efforts.

The fragmentation of power and responsibility in Congress also frustrates executive-legislative consultation and coordination and makes Congress appear irresponsible. When facing a skeptical electorate, for example, these conditions enable individual senators and representatives to deflect criticism with the defense, "I didn't do it; it was everyone else."

Individual accountability is reduced further by the congressional penchant for dealing with issues in procedural terms rather than confronting them directly. A striking illustration occurred with the Senate's consideration of two controversial treaties to cede American control of the Panama Canal to Panama. Senators took record votes on over fifty amendments, nearly twenty reservations, a dozen understandings, and several conditions—nearly ninety proposals for change of one kind or another. Many of the proposed changes were billed as "improvements," which made it easier to vote for a politically unpopular document. (In the case of the Panama Canal, however, it is noteworthy that over half of the thirty-eight senators who supported the treaties lost in their next campaign for reelection.) Procedure therefore becomes a useful tool for coping with single-issue politics, allowing members of Congress to conceal their true positions, thereby avoiding direct confrontation with the president and deflecting potential electoral criticism.

> If done directly, a Congressional decision—for example, to disapprove money for a new aircraft carrier—would require that more than half of all Congressmen conclude that the Navy can do with fewer carriers. . . . This would involve a stark confrontation with expertise that would be very uncomfortable for a Congressman. If a showdown is reached on the carrier issue, the vote is almost certain to be cloaked in procedures (motions to table, and so on) that would allow the Congressman to justify his vote, if he needed to, on a procedural question rather than on the merits of the case.
>
> (ASPIN 1976, 165)

A different sort of Congress' seeming irresponsibility arises out of the very sluggishness of the legislative process. Slow, deliberative procedures may be inherent in a body charged with reconciling disparate views, but delays are prolonged by the dispersion of power and responsibility between two houses, their further fragmentation within a complex structure of committees and subcommittees (which slows the legislative process on major issues to "near paralysis" [Burgin 1993]), and the near absence of party discipline. The Senate's cloture rule, requiring an extraordinary majority for terminating debate, is another restraint on initiative. "The result is that any piece of legislation must surmount an obstacle course of unparalleled difficulty. . . . Few things happen quickly. Policies eventually adopted are often approved too late. . . . And in the process of overcoming the countless legislative hurdles, policies may be compromised to the point of ineffectiveness" (Sundquist 1976). Contrast that picture with the president's proven ability to act quickly and decisively, as rapidly moving international developments frequently require. "Presidents can procrastinate too," James L. Sundquist (1976) observes, "but unlike Congress they are not compelled to by any institutional structure."

A final form of irresponsibility is found in the frequent tendency of members of Congress to "leak" information. A glaring example of the recurrent problem took place in 1987, when the Senate Intelligence Committee voted not to make public a report on its closed-door hearings on the Iran-contra affair, only to have NBC News acquire the first half of it three days later. Within two weeks the other half appeared in the *New York Times*. Senator Patrick J. Leahy (D-VT) later resigned as vice chair of the committee when it was learned he had leaked the unclassified committee report—and at precisely the time the committee was trying to demonstrate that Reagan administration officials, not members of Congress, were most often responsible for leaking classified government information.

Recent violations occurred in 1995 and 2001. In 1995, when Representative Robert C. Torricelli, a Democrat from New Jersey, revealed

classified information allegedly implicating the CIA in a pair of murders in Guatemala—despite his oath "not [to] disclose any classified information received in the course of my service with the House of Representatives."[17] Such leaks arise from the independence that senators and representatives prize and from the benefits they can realize by placing issues in the mass media's spotlight. (Torricelli cited "moral obligation" in defending his behavior.) Unfortunately, one of the consequences is that the president often uses "executive privilege" to conceal information—particularly classified information—thus preventing congressional involvement in policy making. In 2001, George W. Bush restricted briefings of Congress on military actions around Afghanistan because of his frustration with congressional leaks of previous briefings.

Lack of Expertise

The third weakness limiting Congress's ability to exercise foreign policy leadership derives from the White House's comparatively greater command of *technical expertise* and from its ability to control the flow of information. We have already observed this in our discussion of the departments and agencies comprising the foreign policy bureaucracy, all of which are *executive* branch organizations. Although they sometimes resist presidential orders, as we will see in Chapter 13, these organizations contribute enormously to presidential leadership. Congress must often depend on the executive branch for the information critical to sound policy recommendations (see West and Cooper 1990).

Congress has tried to overcome its lack of expertise in several ways. First, Congress dramatically increased the size of the professional staff serving congressional committees and individual members of Congress. Growth exploded during the 1970s and continued throughout the 1980s, bringing the total number of personal and committee staff employees to more than 15,000 by 1991 (Mann and Ornstein 1993). In the mid-1990s, with the Republicans in the majority, the total number of congressional staff was trimmed by about twenty-five percent, with committee and support agency staff sustaining much larger reductions than personal staff. However, after 1996, personal and committee staff numbers began to increase. In the late 1990s, the combined totals again exceeded 14,000 (Moen and Copeland 1999).

Staff resources give Congress a greater capacity to assert an independent congressional position and the means to become involved in policy questions where congressional interest and expertise previously may have been lacking (Crabb and Holt 1992). Furthermore, in an atmosphere where knowledge is power, congressional staffs exercise greater influence over the direction of policy. The technical experts filling staff roles, and the networks of communications and coalitions that have developed among them, enable them to steer policy, operating as an "invisible force in American lawmaking" (Fox and Hammond 1977).

Second, Congress has, as noted previously, increased the reporting requirements on practically every bureaucratic agency, and has strengthened oversight since the mid-1970s as well. This has improved the ability of members to extract relevant information from the executive branch in a timely fashion.

Third, Congress has developed "congressional bureaucracies" to assist it in assembling information and analysis. For example, it has expanded the overseer role of the General Accounting Office periodically. In 1972, Congress created the Office of Technology Assessment to evaluate scientific and technical proposals, and in 1974 it added the Congressional Budget Office to assist in analyzing budget options and preparing the annual budget resolution. In 1995, the Republican majority attempted to reverse the growth of legislative staff and support agencies. Not only did it reduce staff (mostly those serving committees), it also eliminated the Office of Technology Assessment (parceling outs its re-

sponsibilities to the GAO and to the newly-established House Science Committee).

Individual members of Congress often develop considerable policy expertise. The committee system and the penchant to allocate positions of authority according to the rules of seniority mean that some senators and representatives often spend their entire legislative careers specializing in their committees' areas of jurisdiction. Because incumbents are returned to office more often than not, it is not uncommon to find congressional careers that span a quarter-century or more—much longer than any postwar president is even allowed by the Constitution to remain in office.

Historically, specialization by entrenched members of Congress has been especially prominent in the Senate and House Armed Services committees (the latter now called the Committee on National Security), where southern Democrats in particular have claimed considerable expertise on national security issues. Members of these committees now also receive large amounts of intelligence from the CIA, contributing to their ability to arrive at policy judgments independent of the president. Congress's committee and seniority systems also facilitate the patron-client relationships between Congress and the foreign policy bureaucracy described in the previous chapter. Such relationships sometimes subvert presidential interests, but they also provide Congress power vis-à-vis the executive branch.

Still, all members of Congress cannot be experts on all matters of policy. Moreover, members of Congress are especially ill-equipped to acquire the kinds of information that would enable them to better monitor, and hence influence, decision making in times of crisis. Following the Ford administration's use of marines to rescue the ship *Mayaguez* from its Cambodian captors in May 1975, for example, a survey revealed that the press was the principal source of information for many members of Congress. This was even true for a majority of

Table 12.3 Congressional Foreign Policy Assertiveness Since World War II

FOREIGN POLICY BEHAVIOR	TIME PERIODS		
	Cold War (1946–67)	Post-Vietnam (1968–88)	Post-Cold War (1989–97)
Compliant	42.4%	22.6%	23.7%
	(161)	(76)	(18)
Resistant	28.4%	38.4%	47.4%
	(108)	(129)	(36)
Rejection	8.2%	14.6%	2.6%
	(31)	(49)	(2)
Independent	21.0%	24.4%	26.3%
	(80)	(82)	(20)
	100.1%	100%	100%
	(380)	(336)	(76)

SOURCE: Scott and Carter (1999)

those serving on congressional committees directly concerned with foreign and national security policy. Little wonder that one (anonymous) member of Congress cynically observed, "the actions of the United States are not secret to other nations, only to Congress and the American people" (*Congressional Quarterly Weekly Report* 13 November 1976).

CONGRESS AND THE PRESIDENT

Having reviewed the setting, avenues of influence, and obstacles facing members of Congress on foreign policy issues, how do we assess broad patterns of congressional-executive interactions in the foreign policy domain? How do we make sense of the shifts between acquiescence and assertiveness? As we have noted, Congress has been active and deferential at different times. It also seems clear that congressional deference is not primarily a matter of lack of opportunity or instrument of influence. What, then, has been the post–World War II pattern of legislative-executive relations?

A key pattern that helps to explain the mixed accounts in our previous discussion concerns the willingness of members of Congress to follow the president's lead. As that discussion hinted, members of Congress seem to have been much more assertive in foreign policy since the Vietnam War. As indicated in Table 12.3, the percentage of congressional foreign policy behavior that is compliant with presidential leadership has dropped by nearly fifty percent from its Cold War level. During the Cold War, the president got all of what he wanted in foreign policy almost half the time. Since then, members were likely to give the president what he wanted less than a quarter of the time. Conversely, members of Congress are now almost twice as likely to resist the president and tend to engage in their own independent attempts to make foreign policy. Indeed, in the decade since the fall of Berlin, congressional members were more likely to push their own foreign policy preferences than to follow those of the president. Moreover, as we discuss later, a number of studies indicate that partisanship also increased across each period as well. (McCormick, Wittkopf, and Danna 1997; Carter and Scott 2001; Wittkopf and McCormick 1998).

The increasing assertiveness and partisanship are significant for our analysis for two reasons. First, they substantiate our argument that presidential leadership of Congress became more difficult after the Vietnam War. Second, they suggest continued challenges for the president in the new century. These two results help us bring into sharper relief the broad patterns characterizing the relationship between Congress and the President since World War II. Activism and deference both have been characteristic at different times and on different issues. To highlight these shifts, we now turn to a review of the phases in legislative-executive relations, and then examine the role of partisanship and bipartisanship, especially as it illuminates the climate of the new century.

Phases in the Relationship between Congress and the President

As we have suggested, the role and influence of Congress has varied over the post–World War II years. Broadly speaking, legislative-executive relations generally divides into three phases: the Cold War (1945–1968), post–Vietnam (1969–1989), and post–Cold War (1989–present). Each era has had some distinctive characteristics with respect to congressional foreign policy involvement and influence.[18]

The Cold War Phase The primary pattern of this phase was congressional deference to presidential leadership. This era, the so-called *era of bipartisanship,* was fundamentally characterized by foreign policy consensus over the goals and purposes and over the means of U.S. foreign policy. A key element of this period was the relative clarity—and therefore agreement about—the nature of the threats to U.S. interests. (see, for example, Holsti and Rosenau 1984; Melanson 1999). Congress therefore generally deferred to presidential leadership, in part because of the general policy agreement that existed.

Within this period, several different patterns developed. From World War II to roughly 1951, *accommodation* describes the pattern of relations between Congress and the President. The nation's goals of globalism, anticommunism, and containment of perceived Soviet expansionism were forged during that time through a variety of specific foreign policy initiatives and programs in which Congress willingly participated. Bipartisanship captures the essence of the accommodative atmosphere of the period.

Accommodation was followed by a brief period of *antagonism,* a phase that lasted from 1951 to 1955. McCarthyism fell within this period. So, too, did congressional recriminations over who "lost" China; disenchantment with "limited" war in Korea and the firing of a general (Douglas MacArthur) who independently sought to expand that war; and growing concern over the cost of foreign aid and Truman's commitment of troops to Europe. Efforts by the Senate to curb presidential treaty-making powers symbolized the antagonisms of the period. A period of congressional foreign policy *acquiescence* followed during the decade ending in 1965. In was then that Congress passed the "area resolutions" granting presidents broad authority to deal with conflict in the Middle East, Berlin, Cuba, the China straits, and Vietnam as they alone saw fit. A bipartisan spirit was again dominant as Congress agreed with most of the specific foreign policy decisions made by the three presidents who held office during the period. Any lingering doubts Congress may have had about some of them were "simply swallowed," as Congress preferred "not to share the responsibility of decision with the president" (Bax 1977). By backing presidential decisions in a manner that legitimated them to the public, Congress helped to build a broad-based, anticommunist foreign policy consensus.

Presidents, for their part, encouraged the acquiescent congressional mood, since a passive role made consultation with or deference to "mere legislators" unnecessary. Following the massive Vietnam buildup in 1965, however, congressional docility began to dissipate. Highly publicized Senate Foreign Relations Committee hearings, chaired by J. William Fulbright, fed the growing perception that the war in Vietnam was a major mistake. Still, Congress refused to exercise the constitutional prerogatives at its disposal to constrain presidential behavior. Congress was in a state of *ambiguity.*

Post–Vietnam Phase   In contrast to the relative deference of the Cold War phase, the post-Vietnam phase is generally characterized by congressional *activism* and assertiveness. With the Cold War consensus shattered by the Vietnam War, members of Congress began to re-assert congressional prerogatives and seek greater roles on shaping American foreign policy. Without common agreement on policy or common perspectives on the nature of the problems facing the United States, presidential leadership became more difficult, and members of Congress sought to rein in the excesses of the "imperial presidency" many observers argued had developed through the deference of Congress. As one observer suggested, "In no previous era of congressional ascendancy has the United States borne the burdens of world leadership. And in no previous era of presidential counterreformation has the White House confronted such a formidable array of procedural weapons at the legislature's disposal" (Warburg 1989). The following summaries of congressional action are characteristic of the post–Vietnam era:

- In 1970 Congress "repealed" the Gulf of Tonkin Resolution that gave President Johnson, as he interpreted it, a "blank check" for prosecuting undeclared war in Southeast Asia

- In 1973 Congress overrode President Nixon's veto to write the War Powers Resolution into law, thus requiring the president to consult Congress before dispatching troops abroad

- In 1974 Congress embargoed arms sales to Turkey in retaliation for its invasion of

Cyprus, despite the objectives of the Ford administration

- In 1974 Congress refused to permit the president to extend most-favored-nation (MFN) trade treatment to the Soviet Union by linking MFN to the emigration of Soviet Jews

- In 1975 Congress ensured American withdrawal from Vietnam by denying the president authority to provide the South Vietnamese government emergency military aid to forestall its imminent collapse in the face of communist forces

- In 1976 Congress prohibited continued CIA expenditures to bolster anti-Marxist forces fighting in Angola

- In 1978 the Senate adopted a reservation to the Panama Canal neutrality treaty permitting the United States to use military force to re-open the canal if it were closed for any reason

- In 1980 Congress passed legislation asserting its right to receive prior executive branch notice of impending covert intelligence activities

- In 1982 Congress denied the Defense Department and the CIA funds for the purpose of overthrowing Nicaragua's government

- In 1983 Congress invoked provisions of the War Powers Resolution to limit the time military forces could remain in Lebanon

- In 1985 Congress cut from two hundred to fifty the number of land-based MX missiles to be deployed in fixed silos

- In 1986 Congress overrode a presidential veto to place economic sanctions on South Africa

These examples of congressional activism in response to the so-called "imperial presidency" of the Vietnam era reflect Congress's effort to ensure itself a greater voice in foreign policy making. By writing certain conditions into legislation and otherwise placing a distinctively legislative stamp on American foreign policy, a sometimes submissive Congress raised its voice in shaping the nation's foreign affairs, often at the expense of the president. As Under Secretary of State William D. Rogers lamented in 1979, "foreign policy has become almost synonymous with law-making. The result is to place a straitjacket of legislation around the manifold complexity of our relations with other nations." Ronald Reagan echoed that sentiment in 1985, exclaiming, "We have got to get to the point where we can run a foreign policy without a committee of 535 telling us what we can do." Indeed, in the latter half of this phase, critics charged that Congress, not the president, was acting in an "imperial" fashion (Jones and Marini 1988; see also Califano 1994).

The impact of Vietnam and subsequent events in moving Congress from acquiescence toward assertiveness deserves emphasis. Acquiescence is possible only when a broad national consensus exists on the general purposes of policy and when the specific means the president chooses to pursue them are generally successful (Bax 1977). It seems most likely in an environment characterized by relatively clear—and significant—threats to U.S. interests. Those conditions crumbled in the wake of Vietnam. The experience borne of that war thus affirms an earlier historical pattern: An assertive congressional mood typically has coincided with and followed each major American war. The post–Civil War Reconstruction era, the post–World War I "return to normalcy" period, and the years following the Korean War provide striking parallels. Concerted congressional efforts to preempt presidential foreign policy prerogatives followed each of them.

Like the Cold War phase, the post–Vietnam period involved several different patterns as well. Richard Nixon's decision to expand the Vietnam War into Cambodia in the spring of 1970 transformed ambiguity into *acrimony*. During the next three years the Senate passed a variety of measures to curtail the president's ability to keep or use American troops in Indochina, but the House typically refused to support them. However, in 1971 both chambers adopted language that proscribed the use of funds authorized or appropriated by Congress "to finance the introduc-

tion of United States ground combat troops into Cambodia, or to provide United States advisors to or for Cambodian military forces in Cambodia." Significantly, the bill was passed only *after* the spring offensive of 1970 had been completed. Other efforts to restrict expenditures were also largely symbolic. Nevertheless, Congress had begun to participate in the termination of America's role in the tragic Indochina conflict.

The high point of congressional acrimony occurred in 1973, when Congress passed the War Powers Resolution over President Nixon's veto. As noted earlier, for at least a decade after this, congressional **assertiveness**—though subject to ebbs and flows—best describes how Congress sought to be heard and treated as a coequal in foreign policy making. While the Reagan administration challenged a broad array of reforms put into place by the "imperial Congress" to assert its own foreign policy prerogatives (Warburg 1989), Congress remained aggressive in its efforts to shape foreign policy. The trend continued until the end of the Cold War.

Between the fall of the Berlin Wall in 1989 and the Persian Gulf War in 1991, the first Bush administration contended with members of Congress in trying to adapt to the changing landscape. In some ways, Congress remained assertive and active: pushing for defense policy changes; pressing the administration for more proactive responses to the dissolution first of the Warsaw Pact and then of the Soviet Union itself; championing the promotion of democracy. However, Bush adopted an almost defiant posture toward Congress's foreign policy role. He "wielded the threat of a veto effectively, and even when signing important foreign policy legislation, made claims of executive power which implied that Congress did not have the same legislative authority in foreign policy as in other fields and that seemed to ignore the role of Congress in foreign policy granted by the Constitution" (*Congress and Foreign Policy 1991*).

The Post–Cold War Phase   The post–Cold War phase takes us into the twenty-first century. It mirrors in many ways the patterns that developed toward the end of the post–Vietnam phase: struggle between the president and the Congress over foreign policy. However, with all vestiges of the Cold War's guideposts swept away, the dissensus characterizing American foreign policy makers opened the door for even greater contests. The hallmark of this latest phase of congressional-executive relation is its *partisanship,* as politics has increasingly trumped policy.

Curiously, perhaps, in some regards the latest phase also invited greater participation by Congress in shaping an American foreign policy, at least initially. "As perceptions of external threat have receded," political scientist James M. Lindsay (1994a) observed, "the American public is now more likely to tolerate legislative dissent on foreign affairs. Faced with fewer electoral costs in opposing the president, members of Congress are more likely to deal the president public rebuffs." For example, the Democratic-led Congress passed legislation broadening the agenda for negotiation of a North American Free Trade Agreement to include such matters as environmental protection. It adopted conditions for continuing China's most-favored-nation (MFN) trade status (twice vetoed by Bush). It held hearings on U.S. policy toward Iraq prior to the Persian Gulf War that seemed to vindicate Congress's position that sanctions should have been imposed on Iraq long before Bush applied them. It proposed to initiate sanctions against those who would assist Iran or Iraq in developing weapons of mass destruction or advanced conventional weapons. Later the Republican-led Congress took steps to curtail the new interventionism on behalf of humanitarian values, notably in Somalia. It recommended lifting the trade embargo against Vietnam. It terminated funding for the enforcement of a United Nations embargo on the sale of arms to Bosnia and later demanded that the arms embargo be lifted. It launched a determined effort to hamstring American participation in future UN peacekeeping operations; to slash foreign affairs spending while increasing defense spending; and to defeat multilateral agreements on chemical weapons, global warming,

nuclear testing, and efforts to control genocide and other war crimes. To these examples, others could be added. In general though, while both Bush and Clinton had some success on big issues—the Gulf War for Bush, Russian aid (in 1993) and NATO expansion for Clinton (1996-1998)—but the overall pattern was sharply partisan and antagonistic.

At least initially, the pattern in George W. Bush's administration seemed destined to be consistent with that of his predecessors. The persistence of divided government (with Democrats taking control of the Senate after Senator Jeffords switched parties in the late spring of 2001), disagreements over the general course of the United States in its relations with friends and rivals (for example, over unilateralism and multilateralism, and between internationalism and selective engagement), and dissensus over policy goals in a variety of areas indicated continued *partisanship* and political strife consistent with the post-Vietnam trend. Much of that discord fell away after the September 11 attacks on the United States.

In the changed environment, *bipartisanship* was reasserted in many ways, driven in the short-term by the recognition of the clear threat facing the United States. Thus, as we have discussed, the Bush administration and Congress moved toward more cooperation and accommodation on a number of issues. At first blush, it appeared that presidential leadership and congressional deference had returned.

Certainly the partisan environment was muted considerably. However, a closer look indicates that substantial congressional activism and assertiveness remained. Even while being more supportive of the president, Congress still resisted *"fast-track" authority,* forced compromises in anti-terrorism legislation proposed by the administration, took actions on global warning and energy policy that diverged from the administration's preferences, balked at emergency powers for the president, and continued to resist some objectionable administration foreign policy appointments. Hence, even with a more urgent threat to American security driving greater cooperation, different interests and perspectives continued to drive members of Congress to resist presidential preferences.

In fact, even with unity and agreement triggered by the nation's response to the terrorist attacks, other factors suggest limits to the scope and duration of that more limited consensus. One is the persistence of divided government in the twenty-first century, which provides part of the context for disagreement between the White House and Congress. The combination of globalization and its attendant complexity; the increasing importance of intermestic issues, and the broader foreign policy agenda with items like the environment, disease, immigration and refugees, ethnic conflict, and others further limit the possibilities for consensus or a return to the congressional deference of the Cold War phase. Congressional activism and assertiveness, sometimes driven by *partisanship,* are likely to persist as part of the pattern of legislative-executive relations in the twenty-first century. In this light, we now turn to a consideration of the patterns and shifts between bipartisanship and partisanship since World War II.

Bipartisanship and Partisanship

The proposition that "politics stops at the water's edge"—long a part of the nation's cherished political mythology—was a sure victim of the changed and changing nature of executive-legislative relations in the post—Vietnam War era. Increasing partisanship—"foreign policy as a continuation of politics"—has been the dominant pattern ever since. Even the bipartisanship triggered by the terrorist attacks on the United States is not likely to eliminate it.

Bipartisanship is the practical application of the "water's edge" consensual ideal. As noted, it is often used to describe the cordial and cooperative relationship between Congress and the executive branch during much of the Roosevelt, Truman, and Eisenhower presidencies—the period when the United States rejected isolation-

ism, embraced internationalism, and developed the postwar strategy for containment of the Soviet Union. Congress and the president often acted as partners in these efforts, especially on matters involving Europe. The famous conversion of Arthur Vandenberg, Republican senator from Michigan who coined the "water's edge" aphorism, symbolized the emergent bipartisan spirit. Once a staunch isolationist, Vandenberg used his position as chair of the powerful Senate Foreign Relations Committee after World War II to engineer congressional support for NATO and the Marshall Plan.

To be sure, partisan and ideological differences between the president and Congress and within the latter were never absent during the heyday of bipartisanship. Republican Senator Robert A. Taft, for example, personified many of the elements of congressional antagonism between 1951 and 1955. He opposed NATO, criticized Truman for failing to declare war in Korea and concentrating too much power in the White House, and worried that containment would result in continuing U.S. involvement in world affairs, which he opposed. His neoisolationist sentiment and its associated criticisms were a minority voice, however—one that the anticommunist consensus muted as Congress moved from a posture of antagonism toward the president in the early 1950s to acquiescence in the latter half of the decade. Not until the Vietnam War challenged the premises of the anticommunist consensus were the premises of bipartisanship itself also questioned. Now foreign policy increasingly became the object of factional and partisan dispute. No longer did politics stop at the water's edge.

Presidents invariably appeal to bipartisanship to win political support for their programs. Often they use bipartisan commissions as a vehicle to that end. The commissions President Reagan appointed to seek alternative policies for Central America, strategic defense, and military base closings, are prominent examples, as is the bipartisan study of the CIA's future which the Clinton administration launched in 1995 (at Congress's insistence). George H. W. Bush also underscored the importance he attached to bipartisanship when he called in his inaugural address for "a new engagement . . . between the executive and the Congress." "There's grown a certain divisiveness," he lamented. "And our great parties have too often been far apart and untrusting of each other. It's been this way since Vietnam. That war cleaves us still." He continued, saying "A new breeze is blowing—and the old bipartisanship must be made new again."

As we have noted, however, Bush was openly antagonistic toward Congress' foreign policy role. Thus "gridlock" applied to foreign as well as domestic policy during his presidency. Beset by increasing partisanship during his terms, President Clinton sought to reduce it with respect to foreign policy, first by appointing William Cohen, a former Republican Senator from Maine, as Secretary of Defense for his second term. Late in his second term, Clinton sought to restore some bipartisanship by resorting to a commission much like those embraced by President Reagan. Led by former Democratic Senator Gary Hart and former Republican Senator Warren Rudman, the "Commission on National Security for the Twenty-First Century" worked throughout 1999 and 2000 to outline a blueprint for the new century that would rebuild a consensus.

The urge to restore bipartisanship to foreign policy making stems from a desire to restore the halcyon mood of the early post–World War II era. Beyond this, advocates of bipartisanship see it as a vehicle promoting the policy coherence and consistency necessary to an effective foreign policy (Kissinger and Vance 1988; Winik 1989). Such a view assumes a broad-based agreement within American society about the appropriate American role in world affairs, similar to that once provided by deeply held anticommunist values. It also seems to require a relatively clear and urgent threat environment.

Critics, on the other hand, argue that bipartisanship is a tool used to stifle the expression of divergent viewpoints which is the heart of democratic governance (Falk 1983; Nathan and Oliver 1994). Too often, they say, its appeal is motivated by the goal of blurring the separation of powers which assigns different foreign policy roles and responsibilities to Congress and the president. As one member of Congress put it, "calls for bipartisanship usually seek to have Congress follow the president, never the opposite" (Hamilton 1988). Yet, as Justice Louis Brandeis wrote (in *Myers v. United States* 1926), the purpose of the separation-of-powers doctrine is "not to avoid friction but . . . to save the people from autocracy."

Because the bipartisan concept itself is often used for partisan purposes, its precise meaning is unclear.[19] One simple, yet useful measure is how often a majority of Republicans and Democrats agree with the president's position on foreign policy issues that come before Congress. Figure 12.1 uses this measure to trace bipartisan behavior in each house of Congress from Truman to Clinton. It shows a gradual decline in bipartisanship following the Eisenhower presidency and an especially sharp decline in the House beginning with Ford. Clearly bipartisanship is in retreat, especially since Vietnam.

Shifts in the partisan and ideological support accorded different presidents underlie these changes. During the Cold War, Democratic presidents consistently enjoyed their greatest foreign policy support not only from their own partisans but also from liberals, regardless of party. Eisenhower, a Republican president, also enjoyed support from liberal Democrats as well as from members of his own party. This pattern underlies the "two presidencies" thesis which posits a domestic presidency confronted with numerous challenges and a foreign policy presidency enjoying support and deference from Congress (Wildavsky 1966).

Since Eisenhower, however, Republican presidents have received their greatest support from conservatives and comparatively little from liberals. The changing patterns of foreign policy voting

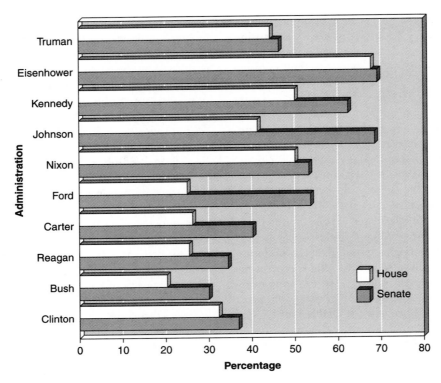

FIGURE 12.1 Congressional Support of Presidential Policy from Truman to Clinton

Note: Each bar represents the percentage of foreign policy votes on which a majority of both parties supported the president's position. Data for Clinton are for the 103rd Congress (1993–1994) only.
Source: Data through 1988 from James M. McCormick and Eugene R. Wittkopf, "Bipartisanship, Partisanship, and Ideology in Congressional-Executive Foreign Policy Relations, 1947–1988," *Journal of Politics* 52 (November 1990): 1085; data for the Bush and Clinton administrations compiled by McCormick and Wittkopf from various issues of the *Congressional Quarterly Weekly Report.*

in Congress suggest that partisan attachments and ideological predispositions now reinforce one another. Before Vietnam partisanship and ideology cross-cut one another, muting differences between Congress and the president. After Vietnam they magnified them. Republicans have become the party of conservative internationalism and Democrats the party of liberal internationalism, thus bringing both parties into alignment with their postures on domestic policy. In such a situation, as might be expected, the "two presidencies" thesis finds little support, as analyses of the post-Vietnam and post-cold war eras indicate (for example, Fleisher, Bond, & Krutz 2000).

The end of the Cold War might have been expected to moderate the partisan and ideological disputes characteristic of congressional-executive relations since Vietnam, as many of them played out in differing perceptions about how best to deal with the perceived Soviet threat. As perceptions of external threat receded, however, members of Congress also found incentives to distance themselves from presidential initiatives (Lindsay 1994a; see also McCormick and Wittkopf 1990b). Indeed, rather than receding, partisanship increased in just about every way imaginable. Party leaders have shown "increasingly partisan patterns in their support for presidential positions (Smith 1994). Congressional voting behavior on foreign and defense policy has also shown increasing partisanship (Carter 1998; McCormick, Wittkopf and Danna 1997; Rohde 1994; Sinclair 1993; Wittkopf and McCormick 1998). Those individual members of Congress who choose to make foreign policy a focus of their attention—foreign policy entrepreneurs—have also become increasingly partisan over the three phases discussed previously (Carter and Scott 2001). As we have suggested, the more obvious threat environment after September 11, 2001 reduced, but did not eliminate the general pattern.

CONGRESS AND TWENTY-FIRST CENTURY FOREIGN POLICY

The inauguration of George W. Bush in 2001 initially appeared to end six years of divided government. Its return, when the Democrats gained control of the Senate, renewed fears of "Gridlock," which popularly described the conflict and inaction that accompanied the partisan divisions between Congress and the president across a broad array of both foreign and domestic policy issues prior to that. The Iran-contra affair during the Reagan administration and the seemingly endless series of vetoes and veto threats during the first Bush presidency are testimony to the often bitter conflicts between the Republican presidents and the Democratic-controlled Congress evident for more than a decade. The government shutdown of 1995–1996 and the impeachment trial of Bill Clinton provide similar evidence from the 1990s.

The return of divided government further fueled the concerns of those who believed that the sources of conflict between Congress and the executive go beyond partisan divisions along Pennsylvania Avenue. How foreign policy will fare in the contest between Congress and the president today thus remains uncertain—a conclusion made all the more stark by the dramatic changes in the world's political and economic systems, the rise of intermestic issues and the forces of globalization, and the closely balanced divisions between Democrats and Republicans in American society that Congress mirrors. The unity of purpose generated by the nation's response to the terrorist attacks of September 2001 provided some cause for optimism, but other indications of continued dissensus limited such views.

Two intriguing questions remain. First, how active will members of Congress be on foreign policy in the new century? The dramatic changes just noted would seem to presage considerable activity. Second, how assertive will members of Congress be in the new century? Will they attempt to forge their own foreign policies and resist presidential leadership? The patterns of the past fifty years give us ambiguous guidance. The increasing levels of assertiveness seem to suggest that the current president will have his hands full. Much of the historical record suggests that it is policy consensus that smooths relations between the two branches; but is broad, sustained consensus possible in today's complex, globalized environment?

In all likelihood, the pattern is likely to be mixed. Foreign and defense policy issues are sometime described as falling into three categories: crisis policy, structural policy, and strategic policy (Ripley and Franklin 1991). Congress has virtually no role in crisis decision making, but it is a central component of the exceedingly complex institutional labyrinth in which structural and strategic policy is made.[20] We should expect more presidential leadership on some policy issues but less on others. The president may well remain the leading partner—if not always the senior partner—in devising responses to the challenges and opportunities the nation now faces. Still, as one recent analysis concluded, "Post–Cold War presidents should fasten their seat belts securely; foreign and defense policy making is likely to be an increasingly bumpy ride" (Carter 1998).

KEY TERMS RELATED TO CONGRESS AND FOREIGN POLICY

accommodation

acrimony

acquiescence

activism

advice and consent

ambiguity

antagonism

anticipated reactions

assertiveness

bipartisanship

Case Act

Chemical Weapons Convention

Comprehensive Anti-Apartheid Act of 1986

Comprehensive Test Ban Treaty

"congressional bureaucracies"

congressional caucuses

congressional leaders

constituent service

consultations

Contract with America

deferrals

direct-legislative avenues

direct-nonlegislative avenues

discretionary funds

earmarks

era of bipartisanship

executive agreements

"fast–track" authority

foreign policy activists

foreign policy entrepreneurs

framing

Gulf of Tonkin Resolution

"hundred barons phenomenon"

imminent hostilities

impound

indirect-nonlegislative avenues

indirect-legislative avenues

legislative veto

micromanagement

National Security Revitalization Act

notification

Omnibus Trade and Competitiveness Act

partisanship

permanent normal trade relations

political grandstanding

power of the purse

prospective-procedural legislation

Quadrennial Defense Reviews

reporting requirements

reprogramming

rescissions

reservations

separate institutions sharing power

single-issue politics

substantive legislation

"Super 301"

technical expertise

UN Participation Act

War Powers Resolution

SUGGESTIONS FOR FURTHER READING

Bacchus, William I. *The Price of Foreign Policy: Congress, the Executive and Foreign Affairs Funding.* College Park, PA: Pennsylvania State University Press, 1997.

Blechman, Barry M. *The Politics of National Security: Congress and U.S. Defense Policy.* New York: Oxford University Press, 1990.

Crabb, Cecil V., Glenn Antizzo, and Leila S. Sariedinne, *Congress and the Foreign Policy Process: Modes of Legislative Behavior.* Baton Rouge, LA: Louisiana State University Press, 2000.

Deibel, Terry L., and Karen M. Rohan, eds., *Clinton and Congress: The Politics of Foreign Policy.* New York: Foreign Policy Association, 2000.

Fisher, Louis. *Presidential War Power.* Lawrence, KS: University of Kansas Press, 1995.

Fleisher, Richard, Jon R. Bond, and Glen S. Krutz. "The Demise of the two Presidencies." *American Politics Quarterly.* 28:1 (Spring 2000), 3–25.

Franck, Thomas M., and Edward Weisband. *Foreign Policy by Congress.* New York: Oxford University Press, 1979.

Halberstam, David. *War In a Time of Peace: Bush, Clinton, & The Generals.* New York: Scribners, 2001.

Hersman, Rebecca K. C. *Friends and Foes: How Congress and the President Really Make Foreign Policy.* Washington, DC: Brookings Institution Press, 2000.

Lindsay, James M. *Congress and the Politics of U.S. Foreign Policy*. Baltimore: Johns Hopkins University Press, 1994.

Mann, Robert. *A Grand Delusion: America's Descent Into Vietnam*. New York: Basic Books, 2001.

Moskowitz, Eric, and Jeffrey S. Lantis. "The War In Kosovo: Coercive Diplomacy." pp. 59–87 in Ralph G. Carter, ed. *Contemporary cases in U.S. Foreign Policy. From Terrorism to Trade,* 2002.

Ripley, Randall B., and James M. Lindsay, eds., *Congress Resurgent: Foreign and Defense Policy on Capitol Hill*. Ann Arbor, MI: University of Michigan Press, 1993.

Warburg, Gerald Felix. *Conflict and Consensus: The Struggle between Congress and the President over Foreign Policymaking*. New York: Harper and Row, 1989.

Weissman, Stephen R. *A Culture of Deference: Congress's Failure of Leadership in Foreign Policy*. New York: Basic Books, 1995.

NOTES

1. On constitutional issues, see Fisher (1995, 1997), Henkin (1990), Koh (1990), Silverstein (1996), and J. Smith (1989).

2. Additional examples from the last several years of the Clinton administration include hearings on such topics as the Nigerian transition, Permanent Normal Trade Relations with China, trade and economic growth in Venezuela, the Clinton administration's foreign policy record, U.S. policy toward Iraq, U.S. trade policy, the African Growth and Opportunity Act, the U.S. trade deficit, unilateral trade sanctions, fast-track authority, and Japan's role in the international community, just to name a few.

3. A recent analysis of Congress and its role on war and money is Fisher (2000a).

4. On then-freshman Senator Chuck Hagel's concern about and strategy on the Kyoto agreement, see Zengerle (1998).

5. For an example of the recent debate, see the exchange between Senators Jesse Helms (R-North Carolina) and Byron Dorgan (D-North Dakota) in the *CQ Researcher* 8 September, 2000, 705; Deutch, Brown, and White (2000); and *The Economist* (3 June, 2000, 16.

6. On the Kyoto accord, see Andrews (2001), Cooper (1998), Eizenstadt (1998), Jacoby, Prinn, and Schmalensee (1998), Sheehan (1998), Zengerle (1998), and *The National Review* 18 May, 1998, 18.

7. On the Senate's rejection of the Comprehensive Test Ban Treaty, see Alter (1999), Cambone (2000), Howell (2000), Lowry (1999), Rodman (1999), Schell (1999), and Schwartz (2000).

8. Good accounts of the treaty and the ratification debate include Isaacs (1996, 1997), Smithson (1995),

and, especially, Krepon, Smithson, and Parachini (1997).

9. Dellums v. Bush, 752 F. Supp.1141 (D.D.C. 1990).

10. Interestingly, Bob Dole, then a freshman senator, co-sponsored the War Powers Resolution with Senator Jacob Javits.

11. Accounts of the Kosovo campaign and decision include Daalder and O'Hanlon (2000), Halberstam (2001), Hendrickson (forthcoming,) Mandelbaum (1999), Marcus (2000), and Moskowitz and Lantis (2002).

12. See Bacchus (1997) for an analysis of the tug of war between Congress and the president over foreign aid and international affairs spending.

13. Special-interest groups and ethnic lobbies are important in determining who gets how much, with the result that flexibility in the president's use of this long-standing policy instrument is severely impaired.

14. Defense procurement is typically regarded as a pork-barrel issue which members of Congress use to cultivate constituency support. During the debate on the B-1 bomber, for example, the Air Force and its industrial allies lobbied Congress with the argument that they would profit from the project with increased jobs and dollars in their states and congressional districts (Kotz 1988; Ornstein and Elder 1978). Interestingly, however, congressional votes on strategic-weapons issues are best explained not by constituency interests (as the military-industrial complex thesis would argue) but instead on the basis of Congress members' political ideology (Lindsay 1990). Although foreign and national security policy often are thought to be above politics, evidence abounds to show that

they are as frequently characterized by partisan and ideological disputes as are domestic issues. See Bernstein (1989), Bernstein and Anthony (1974), Fleisher (1985), McCormick (1985), McCormick and Black (1983), McCormick and Wittkopf (1990a, 1990b), Moyer (1973), Taylor and Rourke (1995), and Wayman (1985).

15. Court rulings in the aftermath of the *Chadha* decision on the legislative veto restricted the comprehensiveness of Congress's role in these matters compared with the intent of the 1974 budget law (Fisher 1991; Fisher 1993). Also, the Iran-contra affair suggests another area: "problems associated with 'creative policy funding.'" Presidents may be able to pursue policies with monies from third parties. For example, between $3 and $4 million in profits from the sale of arms to Iran in early 1986 and as much as $50 million from private contributors and foreign governments was supplied to the contras at precisely the time the Boland amendment banned U.S. government support for the guerrillas. Both Lieutenant Colonel Oliver North and Admiral John Poindexter, North's boss at the NSC, testified before Congress that they believed the withholding of appropriations by Congress did not prevent the president from pursuing his foreign policy objectives using private or foreign-donated funds. Congress debated, but ultimately defeated, a 1990 bill that would have explicitly legislated against such activities.

16. See Cavanagh (1982–1983), Pfiffner (1992), and Smith and Deering (1990) for examinations of changes in Congress since the 1960s, and Drischler (1985) and Lindsay (1987, 1988) for insight into their importance for the enactment of foreign affairs legislation.

17. The Torricelli incident is more complicated than it appears, as the information "leaked" by the representative actually came from a State Department employee, Richard Nuccio (*The Washington Post,*

12 September, 1997, A24; *New York Times,* 11 September, 1997, A30; Marks 1997). Whether one considers Nuccio a "whistleblower" or a "leaker," the example illustrates what many observers have been arguing for decades: the most prolific "leakers" in Washington are not members of Congress, but members of the executive branch.

18. In addition to the three-phase breakdown utilized here, this section also extends the chronology suggested by Frans R. Bax (1977) into six comparatively distinct subphases of executive-legislative relations during the past half-century.

19. One definition associates bipartisanship with "unity in foreign affairs" as reflected in "policy supported by majorities within each political party"; another depicts it as a set of "practices and procedures designed to bring about the desired unity" (Crabb 1957). For a review of the idea and practice of bipartisanship, see Collier (1989).

20. The difference between structural and strategic policy is not clear cut. Ripley and Franklin (1991) suggest that "structural policies and programs aim primarily at procuring, deploying, and organizing military personnel and materiel, presumably within the confines of previously determined strategic decisions." What they call "subgovernments"—typically "composed of members of the House and Senate, members of congressional staffs, bureaucrats, and representatives of [interested] private groups and organizations"—are principal actors in the structural policy arena. Strategic policies, on the other hand, "assert and implement the basic military and foreign policy stance of the United States toward other nations. Policy planning and proposals resulting from that planning stem primarily from executive branch activities. . . . Although congressional influence can be important, that influence is often used to respond supportively to executive branch agencies."

PART VI

Role Sources of American Foreign Policy

Chapter 13
The Process of Decision Making
Roles, Rationality, and the Impact of Bureaucratic Organizations

CHAPTER 13

The Process of Decision Making

Roles, Rationality, and the Impact of Bureaucratic Organizations

> As modern bureaucracy has grown, the understanding of change
> and the formulation of new purposes have become more difficult. Like men,
> governments find old ways hard to change and new paths difficult to discover.
>
> RICHARD M. NIXON,
> PRESIDENT, 1970

> [The foreign policy apparatus] was often a witches brew
> of intrigue, elbows, egos, and separate agendas.
>
> JAMES A. BAKER,
> FORMER SECRETARY OF STATE, 1995

In 1992, Bill Clinton made a more assertive American response to ethnic conflict and aggression in places such as the former Yugoslavia part of his campaign for the presidency. After his victory, he signed a Presidential Review Directive to initiate just such a policy change, calling for a policy shift to *assertive multilateralism*. It would expand U.S. cooperation with UN peace operations and devote more American military resources and personnel to multilateral efforts. Clinton even called for a standing UN force with American participation, and for American troops to serve under foreign commanders. Over a year later, the administration released Presidential Decision Directive 25 announcing the administration's policy on peace operations. Far from the policy shift initially advocated, PDD-25 instead rejected expanded American participation in and cooperation with UN operations, announcing instead a list of conditions that had to be met before the United States would agree to, much less support materially, such operations.[1]

How did the bold, aggressive policy of the first few months of the Clinton Administration evolve into the cautious, unimaginative policy announced in April 1994?

Understanding this American foreign policy decision, like understanding so many others, requires us to consider the many different people, widely dispersed throughout the agencies and institutions of the American government, who make American foreign policy. It also requires that we examine the decision-making process through which they interact to make such policy choices. Our inquiry in previous chapters gives a glimpse of what we can expect to find.

First, the very size of the government—the incredibly complex organizational structures into which the millions of federal employees fit and the maze of channels through which innovative ideas must pass before they become new policies—is likely to work against policy change and the formulation of new purposes. Apart from cabinet-level departments, the federal roster includes over sixty different departments and agencies and over 1,250 advisory boards and commissions. Add Congress—which, as we have seen, often acts more like 535 separate interests than one unified body—and we can begin to appreciate how the very size of government inhibits policy change in response to new realities.

Second, the politics of policy making within this maze of multiple and often overlapping institutions is more conducive to the status quo than to change. Money and personnel mean political power. Once acquired, institutions protect them. They oppose changes that threaten to erode their sources of influence. Incremental changes at the edge are acceptable, but fundamental reorientations that would require massive budgetary and personnel cuts must be resisted.

Hence, President's Clinton's choice to abandon the ambitious ideas of "assertive multilateralism" as a post–Cold War world foreign policy strategy was the consequence of a complex environment with multiple voices and stakeholders. It may have been rationally calculated to the emerging international (and domestic) environment. Perhaps, and more likely, it was a consequence of confrontation, bargaining, and compromise among competing individuals and agencies over the proper use of American military force. Surely it was conditioned by a variety of players, each of whom was influenced by the roles they occupy and the patterns of demands and expectations that define those roles.

In this chapter we reflect on the impact of roles and two interpretations of American decision-making procedures that embrace rival images of role-induced behavior—the *rational decision-making model* and the *bureaucratic politics model*. As we will see, the two offer sometimes competing, sometimes complementary views of roles as sources of American foreign policy.

ROLES AS A SOURCE OF FOREIGN POLICY

Role theory posits that the positions and the processes, rather than the characteristics of the people who decide, influence the behavior and choices of those responsible for making and executing the nation's foreign policy. As colorfully summarized in *Miles' Law,* role theory suggests that "where you stand (on a policy issue) depends on where you sit (in the bureaucracy)."[2] Each role (or position) carries with it social and psychological demands and expectations that shape perceptions of how it should be performed. These pressures, which include personal and peer pressures as well as those of "the boss," affect both attitudes and actions. They influence *anyone* filling a particular role, regardless of personal preferences. Thus every individual behaves similarly to others who have occupied the same role. Furthermore, changes in policy presumably result from changes in *role conceptions* rather than from changes in the individuals who occupy the roles. Individuals are not unimportant, from this perspective, but the institutional roles that individuals occupy mold their behavior and constrain their decision-making latitude.

Policy makers are not immune from this phenomenon. Each policy-making role carries with it certain expectations, obligations, and images of appropriate behavior—pressures that push the new occupant of an office to think and act like his or her predecessor. The newcomer's style and mannerisms may be markedly different from the predecessor's, but orientations toward crucial issues will be similar. "It's an old story in Washington that where you stand depends on where you sit. That's a practical acknowledgment of the fact that people's views change as they change responsibilities," political journalist David Broder observed.

There are limits to role theory's ability to explain policy-making behavior, of course. A forceful personality may actually redefine the role to extend the boundaries of permissible behavior, as Franklin Roosevelt did when he expanded the scope and authority of the presidency. Ronald Reagan's habit of taking many naps and frequent vacations—a propensity that reflected his relaxed style in an office that heretofore demanded sleepless attention to the duties of governance—also transcended customary role requirements, although in another direction. George W. Bush's penchant for retiring early at night fits that same pattern.

Particular roles may also permit more than one interpretation, and some have boundaries so wide and elastic that the behavior of individuals within them is almost unpredictable. Moreover, individuals, especially at higher levels of government, often have multiple roles whose conflicting pressures may pull an individual in multiple directions. Resolving such role conflicts may involve a number of factors, but surely indicates that, in some cases at least, "role by itself cannot explain positions taken by individual decision makers" (Vertzberger 1990).[3] Clearly the individual source category (discussed in Chapter 14) is a key place to look for additional explanation. Indeed, as Downs (1967) has argued, there are different types of decision makers (climbers, conservers, zealots, advocates, and statesmen) with different values and goals (power, personal secu-

rity, advancement of a few core goals, loyalty to the organization, desire for the best possible policy) who will react to and manipulate roles in different ways.[4]

Nevertheless, this line of reasoning has substantial implications for American foreign policy. Role theory's premise—that people's conduct conforms to their roles—means that if we are to understand the nature of American foreign policy we must examine the behavior most often associated with foreign policy-making roles in addition to examining individuals themselves. That focus also enables us to understand a potentially potent source of foreign policy change. Because roles shape goals, policy innovations may derive from changes in major policy-making roles or individuals' conceptions of them. If the decision-making system with its existing roles and their prevailing interpretations changes, then policy redirections may follow.

FOREIGN POLICY MAKING AS A RATIONAL PROCESS

President Carter's campaign strategists attempted to portray a particular image of their candidate when he was running for reelection in 1980. In an often-televised commercial, Carter was photographed in the Oval Office, working industriously late into the night, poring over documents. He was pictured as a deep thinker, intellectually absorbed in the tasks of the office—making the decisions that only he could make—formidable choices on which the nation's destiny would depend. Viewers (voters) were asked to compare his qualifications—his intelligence, experience, dedication, energy, and diligence—with those of his opponent.

The footage did more than attempt to sell the candidate, though. It also reinforced a popular view of the policy-making process at the nation's nerve center on Pennsylvania Avenue: that fateful decisions are made by rational actors engaged in orderly, contemplative processes. In this *rational decision-making model,* American foreign policy results from a deliberate intellectual process in which the central figures carefully choose what is best for the country and select tactics appropriately designed to promote its national interests.

Thus the question "Is foreign policy making rational?" is a curious one. We tend, almost instinctively, to think, "How could it be otherwise?" Indeed, where the stakes are the lives of millions of people and perhaps the survival of the nation itself, it is disconcerting to picture something as important as foreign policy choice as governed by incoherence, emotions, or irrational impulses. The notion of rational policy making is much more comforting. Political leaders also try to cultivate public images of themselves as decisive, unfettered by subconscious psychological drives, able to manage the stress and burden of their positions, endowed with boundless energy, and prepared to guide the country safely through crises while pursuing the nation's best interests. Their efforts are frequently successful because we prefer to think of our leaders' decisions as the product of rational deliberations.

What constitutes rationality as it applies to foreign policy decision making? Although "rationality" is loosely used in a variety of ways, it generally refers to "actions chosen by the nation . . . that will maximize strategic goals and objectives" (Allison 1971). This implies purposeful, goal-directed behavior that occurs when "the individual responding to an international event . . . uses the best information available and chooses from the universe of possible responses that alternative most likely to maximize his goals" (Verba 1969; see also Levi 1990; Moser 1990; Zagare 1990).

The Rational Actor Model

The *rational actor model* treats the nation-state as if it were a **unitary-actor,** a single, homogeneous entity, and presumes that all policy makers go through the same rational thought processes to make *value-maximizing choices* to define national interests and identify options.

"[The assumption] allows one to consider all decision makers to be alike. If they follow the [decision] rules, we need know nothing more about them. In essence, if the decision maker behaves rationally, the observer, knowing the rules of rationality, can rehearse the decisional process in his own mind and, if he knows the decision maker's goals, can both predict the decision and understand why that particular decision was made" (VERBA 1969, 225)

Scholars who study decision making and advise policy makers on ways to improve their policy-formulation skills describe the perfect rationality role model as a sequence of decision-making activities involving the following intellectual steps:

1. *Problem recognition and definition.* The necessity for choice begins when policy makers perceive an external problem and attempt to define objectively its distinguishing characteristics. Objectivity requires full information about the actions, motivations, and capabilities of other actors as well as the state of the international environment and trends within it. The search for information must be exhaustive, and all the facts relevant to the problem must be gathered.

2. *Goal selection.* Next, those responsible for making foreign policy choices must decide what they want to accomplish. This disarmingly simple requirement is often difficult. It requires the identification and ranking of *all* values (such as security, democracy, freedom, and economic well-being) in a hierarchy from most- to least-preferred.

3. *Identification of alternatives.* Rationality also requires the compilation of an exhaustive list of *all* available policy options and an estimation of the costs associated with each alternative course of action as it relates to the goals and values decision makers hope to realize.

4. *Choice.* Finally, rationality requires selecting from competing options the single alternative with the best chance of achieving the desired

goal(s). For this purpose, policy makers must conduct a rigorous means–ends, cost–benefit analysis, one guided by an accurate prediction of the probable success of each option.

Clearly, the requirements of perfect rationality are stringent. Nonetheless, elements of this idealized version of decision making have been approximated in some instances. The 1962 Cuban Missile Crisis—described by Secretary of State Dean Rusk as "the most dangerous crisis the world has ever seen"—illustrates several ways the deliberations of the key American policy makers conformed to a rational process.[5] Once Washington discovered the presence of Soviet missiles in Cuba, President Kennedy charged the crisis decision-making group he formed to "set aside all other tasks to make a prompt and intensive survey of the dangers and all possible courses of action." Six options were ultimately identified: Do nothing; exert diplomatic pressure; make a secret approach to Cuban leader Fidel Castro; invade Cuba; launch a surgical air strike against the missiles; and blockade Cuba. Goals had to be prioritized before a choice could be made among these six. Was removing the Soviet missiles, retaliating against Castro, or maintaining the balance of power the objective? Or did the missiles pose little threat to vital U.S. interests? "Do nothing" could not be eliminated as an option until the missiles were determined to pose a serious threat to national security.

More recently, the first Bush administration's decisions to apply force in the Persian Gulf crisis with Iraq (Smith 1992; Gordon and Trainor 1995; Bush and Scowcroft 1999) and to send ground troops to Somalia in late 1992—described in Focus 13.1—also illustrate the approximation of rationality often used to describe decision-making processes. Rational decision-making does not reflect the whole story of those decision processes, of course, but we do have a sense that they were punctuated by value priorities, efforts to relate means to ends, and preferred courses of action to cope with the situations—all central canons of rational choice.

Rationality and Reality: The Limits to Rational Choice

Despite the apparent application of rationality in these (and other) cases, the rational actor model is more an idealized standard used to evaluate behavior than an actual description of real-world behavior. One participant in the Cuban missile deliberations, Theodore Sorensen, suggested why rational procedures are difficult to follow:

> Each step cannot be taken in order. The facts may be in doubt or dispute. Several policies, all good, may conflict. Several means, all bad, may be all that are open. Value judgments may differ. Stated goals may be imprecise. There may be many interpretations of what is right, what is possible, and what is in the national interest.
>
> (SORENSEN 1963, 19–20)

Despite the virtues promised by rational choice, then, there are impediments. Some are human. They derive from deficiencies in the intelligence, capability, and psychological needs and aspirations of those who make foreign policy decisions under conditions of uncertainty. Others are organizational. Individuals meeting in groups make most policy decisions. As a result, most decisions require group agreement about the national interest and the wisest course of action to pursue. Reaching agreement is not easy, however, as reasonable people with different human characteristics and values understandably disagree about goals, preferences, and the probable results of alternative options. Thus the impediments to sound (rational) policy making are substantial. Let us examine them in greater detail.

Tardy Problem Recognition Decision makers often neglect evidence of an impending problem until it confronts them directly or reaches crisis proportions. People seldom foresee improbable events (Boffey 1983). Most are prone psychologically to deny the existence of troublesome problems (even when they might be partially

---

FOCUS 13.1   The Road to Somalia: The Bush Administration's Decision to Send U.S. Ground Troops

The Somali crisis was touched off by the ouster of the country's longtime dictator, President Mohamed Siad Barre, in January 1991. By early [1992], the collapse of all governmental authority combined with drought, the continuation of traditional clan warfare and growing chaos had led to mass starvation, and made Somalia [in the words of one AID official] "the most acute humanitarian tragedy in the world. . . . "

U.S. foreign policy making had gone into low gear during the presidential campaign, but after the election, pressure grew on several fronts for more dramatic action in Somalia [beyond the emergency food airlift Bush had ordered in August].

On November 12, Assistant Secretary of State Robert L. Gallucci, the department's chief of political-military affairs, recommended that the United States lead a coalition to save Somalia from starvation under a UN Security Council authorization to use "all necessary means," including armed forces. [Acting Secretary of Lawrence S. Eagleburger], convinced by Gallucci's arguments, became an advocate of more forceful U.S. action.

On November 16, senior representatives of U.S. relief organizations working in Somalia met with UN officials and appealed for more protection. About the same time a Senate delegation

headed by Democratic Senator Paul Simon of Illinois and a House delegation under Democratic Representative John Lewis of George were calling for more security after visits to Somalia.

The first of four NSC Deputies Committee [a National Security Council panel just below the cabinet level] meetings leading to Bush's decision to send ground troops convened at the White House on Friday, November 20. . . . Such meetings are normally secret, but news of this one was revealed the day before in the *New York Times* op-ed page and on the MacNeil-Lehrer News Hour. Both reports favorably cited recommendations for U.S. military action by Frederick C. Cuny, a relief expert who was an AID consultant in Somalia as he had been in the U.S. military relief for the Kurds in northern Iraq. Cuny advocated using 2,500 U.S. troops with air and naval support to open supply lines. At the time, this was considered a bold proposal.

In the first day of interagency discussion, Under Secretary of Defense Paul Wolfowitz hinted at the possibility of using U.S. ground troops, but the general representing the joint chiefs, the uniformed military, said little. . . . On November 21, the second day of discussions, [Admiral David Jeremiah, the vice chairman of

---

responsible for them), and often avoid facing information suggesting the necessity for difficult choices.

Inadequate Information Henry Kissinger once observed that "when the scope for action is greatest, the knowledge on which to base such action . . . is at a minimum." The information required to define a problem is often incomplete, outdated, or unavailable, and critical variables such as others' intentions are not open to scrutiny. In addition, "information overload"—the availability of too much information—may also undermine rationality. Discrepant and contradictory information makes distinguishing the significant from the irrelevant difficult.

Inaccurate Information The information on which decision makers' choices are based is screened, sorted, and rearranged by their advisers. Distortion is compounded by the tendency of advisers to tell their superiors what they want to hear rather than supplying them with the cold, hard facts, and by policy makers' all-too-human tendency to reject unfamiliar or disturbing information.

Deficient Information Gathering Policy makers rarely search for *all* pertinent information. Instead, they base decisions on partial information.[6] Rationality is compromised, because if an exhaustive search had generated additional information, conceivably a different set of policy

the Joint Chiefs of Staff], who coordinates with [JCS Chairman General Colin L. Powell] daily, startled the groups by saying that "if you think U.S. forces are needed" on land in Somalia, "we can do the job." . . . Jeremiah's statement transformed the use of U.S. ground troops—an option that previously had been considered "fantasy land" by nonmilitary policy makers—into a leading possibility.

What brought the shift in Pentagon thinking is a matter of speculation. . . . [One] official familiar with the thinking of Powell and Defense Secretary Richard B. Cheney says they were willing to "do more than put a Band-Aid on the problem" because the situation in Somalia is so stark and "what we do can make a big difference."

Presidential National Security Adviser Brent Scowcroft, who held several discussions with Bush, was among those in the administration receptive to a major U.S. military initiative. . . .

Two more Deputies Committee meetings were held at the White House on November 23 and 24. Meanwhile, Cheney and Powell were thinking harder about the dangers of U.S. military intervention, especially after a briefing . . . by Brigadier General Frank Libutti, commander of the U.S. airlift operations into Somalia. If the United States were not careful, he said, its troops would be in Somalia for ten or fifteen years.

When Bush met his senior advisers in the National Security Council on November 25, he began by declaring that "we want to do something about Somalia." He had three options before him: increased support for existing UN efforts, a U.S.-organized coalition effort without the participation of American ground troops, or a major U.S. effort to lead a multinational force in which U.S. ground troops took the leading role.

Powell . . . took no position on what should be done, but expressed concern about the use of ground troops and questioned whether conditions in Somalia would permit the smooth handoff of military responsibilities to a UN peacekeeping force.

After what one participant called "a broad discussion," Bush decided that if the UN Security Council agreed, and other nations would join the effort, U.S. combat troops would lead an international force to Somalia. . . .

SOURCE: Don Oberdorfer, "The Road to Somalia," *Washington Post National Weekly Edition*, December 14–20, 1992: 6–7.

---

choices would have been considered. Moreover, rather than admit error, leaders are prone to cling to bad decisions and to search energetically for new information that justifies their previous mistaken choices.

Ambiguous National Interests   When facing a policy problem it is not sufficient to insist that the national interest be served. That merely begs the question. The more difficult intellectual task requires "prioritizing" *all* possible goals according to their ability to promote the nation's welfare. Rationally identifying what is best is difficult because every goal has associated costs as well as possible unanticipated long-run consequences.

"Rational" goal selection, therefore, frequently means choosing the lesser of two evils. For instance, if a leader's goals include (1) normalizing relations with China and (2) providing Taiwan with advanced weapons to ensure its continued independence, one interest may be achieved only at the expense of the other. Or consider the goals of (1) promoting democracy in other countries and (2) supporting the principle of national self-determination. The former may undermine the latter by rationalizing suppression of minority ethnic groups.

The Constraint of Time Pressure   Because policy makers work constantly with overloaded agendas and short deadlines, time is rarely available for careful identification of possible courses of action and for a cool-headed assessment of their consequences. "There is little time for leaders to reflect. They are locked in an endless battle in which the urgent constantly gains on the important. The public life of every political figure is a continual struggle to rescue an element of choice from the pressure of circumstance" (Kissinger 1979).

Options that are not identified cannot be considered. As Thomas Schelling asks, "How do you make a list of things you would never have thought of?" (cited in Bloomfield 1974). In fact, instead of identifying options on their own, presidents usually are presented with an abbreviated list of "feasible" options by their advisers and by bureaucratic agencies. During a crisis in particular, the pressure to shorten the search for options is intense, which limits the range of alternatives considered to the first ones that come to mind (usually those derived from prior analogous situations).

Satisficing Rational decision making is compromised most by the way foreign policy *choices* are actually reached. Policy makers do not choose the option or set of options that has the maximum chance of realizing desired goals (Lindblom 1959; March and Simon 1958). Instead, they typically terminate their evaluation as soon as an alternative surfaces that appears superior to those already considered. Herbert Simon (1957) describes this as *satisficing* behavior. Rather than seeking optimal alternatives, decision makers are routinely content to select the choice that meets minimally acceptable standards. For this reason they frequently face "unresolvable" choices that preclude satisfaction across competing preferences; instead of "optimal" choices, often only "admissible" ones are available. Had they acted rationally by engaging in maximizing behavior, they would have chosen the one choice "best" able to produce preferred results.

The difficulties of correctly ascertaining the payoffs attached to available options reduce the prospects for rational choice (and promote satis-

ficing instead). Even in the best of circumstances—even if policy makers could obtain full information and were able to identify all the options available to realize the preferred goal—"guesstimates" about the relative utility and efficacy of each alternative still often guide the choice. Because determining the best (rational) choice is difficult, *"muddling through"* better describes how choices perceived to be feasible and pragmatic often win out. "A wise policy maker," Charles Lindblom (1959) surmises, "expects that his policies will achieve only part of what he hopes and at the same time will produce unanticipated consequences he would have preferred to avoid. If he proceeds through a succession of incremental changes, he avoids serious lasting mistakes." Some past leaders have been known to advocate this less-than-comprehensive, trial-and-error method for making difficult decisions. "It is common sense," noted Franklin D. Roosevelt, "to take a method and try it; if it fails, admit it frankly and try another."

Psychological Restraints Foreign policy is made not by states but by human beings acting on behalf of states. Hence, decision-making processes cannot be separated from psychodynamics (Simon 1985). Decisions therefore may be rooted less in logic than in the subconscious needs and drives of decision makers (see Chapter 14). The need to be liked, the desire to be popular, and the temptation to look decisive, even heroic, may interfere with rational judgment and ultimately sacrifice the nation's welfare. Decision makers also tend to be overconfident about their judgments and analytical skills and to overestimate their abilities and wisdom so as to maintain their "illusion of control" (Langer 1975).

Personal emotional needs and passions also may lead decision makers to confuse their own goals with those of the nation. If they come to see themselves as indispensable to the nation's welfare, they may equate what is good for them with what is good for the country. When this happens, policy may be driven by a leader's perceived need to maintain or strengthen his or her

---

FOCUS 13.2   Foreign Policy Decision Making in Theory and Practice

THE IDEAL PROCESS	ACTUAL PERFORMANCE
Accurate, comprehensive information	Distorted, incomplete information
Clear definition of national goals	National goals biased by personal motivations and organizational interests
Exhaustive analysis of all options	Limited number of options considered, none thoroughly analyzed
Selection of optimal course of action most capable of producing desired results	Selection of course of action by political bargaining and compromise
Effective statement of decision and its rationale to mobilize domestic support	Confusing and contradictory statements of decision, designed primarily for media
Instantaneous evaluation of consequences followed by correction of errors	Superficial policy evaluation, uncertain responsibility, poor follow-through, and delayed correction

---

power and popularity, possibly at the expense of the nation's interests.

The confusion of national and personal needs is sometimes used to show how irrefutably irrational many foreign policy choices have been. The classic example is Adolf Hitler, whose determination to seek military conquest of the entire European continent proved disastrous for Germany. More recent examples include Saddam Hussein's determination to fight the technologically (if not numerically) superior United States and its coalition of allies, facing sure defeat, rather than to withdraw from Kuwait, and Slobodan Miloševic's decision to use force against Kosovo and defy NATO, which proved devastating for both Serbia and Miloševic's own political career. In all three cases we can explain the apparent discrepancy between what is good for the nation and what is good for the nation's leaders by distinguishing between procedural rationality and instrumental rationality (Zagare 1990).

Procedural rationality is what we have described to this point. It is the kind of rationality that relates to the decision-making dynamics of small groups and large-scale bureaucratic organizations. It is the definition of rationality that underlies the theory of political realism, which sees all states as acting in fundamentally similar ways. Like the rational actor model we have described,

realism, too, sees states as single, unitary actors whose (rational) decision processes result in choices that seek to maximize benefits to national interests and minimize costs.

Instrumental rationality, on the other hand, is a more limited view of rationality. It says simply that individuals have preferences, and that when faced with two (or more) alternatives, they will choose the one that yields the preferred outcome—and this is rational behavior. Although we might dispute some individuals' preferences, we cannot dismiss them as "crazy" or their choices as "irrational" simply because they result in negative consequences for the nation as a whole or for the individuals themselves.

Our review of how policy makers actually make decisions warrants the conclusion that the ideal requirements of rational problem solving are seldom met in real life (see Focus 13.2). Preconceived notions pass for facts. Decisions are made to satisfy immediate, not long-term, needs. Decision makers avoid the task of formulating a coherent strategy. They have a natural reluctance to reach decisions and a strong temptation to pass the buck. They usually weigh only a few alternatives and ponder only a small number of consequences. Decision makers rarely achieve full knowledge, even though the volume of information may be staggering. Instead, they scan only the information they regard as most relevant to the decision. Often they reach a decision first and find reasons (information) to support it only later. The result is not rationality, with each step leading logically to a value-maximizing choice, but something quite different—a haphazard, trial-and-error, seat-of-the-pants process conducted in a rush based on "gut-it-out," best-guess calculations strongly influenced by social pressures (Anderson 1987). Thus the process looks decidedly indecisive and improvisational, and the degree of rationality in foreign policy decision making typically "bears little relationship to the world in which officials conduct their deliberations" (Rosenau 1980).

What are the implications of such a conclusion? If the nation's behavior is not the product of public officials laden with exceptional skills and cognitive powers, untiringly collecting accurate information and logically deriving conclusions to maximize the country's national interests, is the rational actor model completely irrelevant to the "real world"? And should we reject it out-of-hand in our quest to understand how American foreign policy is made?

In some respects the model of rational choice is little more than a caricature, a straw man easily destroyed by even superficial knowledge about how people and organizations make choices on a daily basis, as they must. Still, even if we know that rationality is more ideal than real, the rational actor model is useful in understanding how decision making occurs, all the more so because policy makers aspire to rational decision-making behavior, and on occasion may even approximate it. As one political scientist put it: "Officials have some notion, conscious or unconscious, of a priority of values; . . . they possess some conceptions, elegant or crude, of the means available and their potential effectiveness; . . . they engage in some effort, extensive or brief, to relate means to ends; and . . . therefore, at some point they select some alternative, clear-cut or confused, as the course of action that seems most likely to cope with the immediate situation" (Rosenau 1980).

Administrative Theory and Foreign Policy Rationality

The practical relevance of the rational model finds expression in administrative theory, which seeks to explain how bureaucratic organizations should be designed to serve the best interests of the state and its citizens. The theory is relevant in any modern organization, public or private, and nowhere more so than in American foreign policy making: Given America's incredibly varied global interests, large-scale bureaucracy is necessary. Neither sufficient time nor resources are available to manage foreign relations without the support of large organizations, which facilitate rational decision making in ways that would otherwise be impossible (Goodsell 1985). Before we reject the rational actor model completely, then, we must first consider a subsidary hypothesis: that the U.S. foreign policy-making machinery enhances the prospects for rational decision making, even if the ideal is not always realized.

The idea that modern bureaucracy—by virtue of the roles it creates—enhances the prospects for rational decision making stems from the German scholar Max Weber's (1864–1920) seminal theories. Large-scale bureaucracies contribute to efficient administration and rationality, Weber reasoned, by how they are organized and operate:

- Structured on the principle of division of labor, bureaucracies make each person in the machinery of government a specialist, even an expert, at her or his job; functional divisions among agencies as well as within them (as, for example, in the separation of diplomatic and defense responsibilities between the State and Defense departments) achieves *specialization* by assigning different tasks to different people qualified in different ways.

- Dividing authority among competing organizations enhances the probability that all policy options will be considered before decisions are reached. *Multiple advocacy* (George 1972) results from interagency bargaining, because the process requires defending positions and negotiation prevents any one agent from unilaterally making a critical policy decision.

- Authority is distributed hierarchically, and a clear *chain of command* delineates who is responsible for what and to whom. It is easier to get things done when everyone has a clear idea of who is subordinate to whom, who has authority over what, and what role each cog in the machinery should perform. Precious time does not have to be devoted to deciding who has the power to decide.

- Rules specify how each major function or task is to be performed and prescribe *standard operating procedures* for each task. Hence, rather than deliberating about the best method for handling a problem, the professional bureaucrat can concentrate on mastering those methods.

- Bureaucracies rely on a system of records, written documents systematically gathered and stored to facilitate intelligence retrieval, provide a data bank of past decisions, and increase the information available for making future decisions.

- In principle, bureaucracies recruit "the best and brightest" personnel on the basis of achievement and aptitude rather than on the basis of ascriptive criteria such as ethnicity, gender, wealth, or family background.

- Similarly, personnel are compensated and promoted on the basis of their achievements, thus placing decision-making responsibility in the hands of those deemed most competent. "Merit" determines who is "selected up" and who is "selected out," rather than criteria such as seniority, personal characteristics, ingratiation, or favors to superiors.

- Administrative norms allow some specialists the luxury of engaging in "forward planning." Unlike the president, whose role requires that attention be focused on the crisis of the moment, bureaucracies can consider long-term needs.

This brief overview of administrative theory portrays a bureaucratic policy process that contributes to rational decision making. There is considerable merit in that viewpoint. Still, before we jump to the conclusion that bureaucratic decision making is a modern panacea, these theoretical propositions, as with the rational actor model, tell us how bureaucratic decision making *should occur* but not necessarily how it *does occur*. The reality of bureaucratics practice suggests that bureaucracies *cause* problems as well as *solve* them.

THE CASE AGAINST BUREAUCRATIC FOREIGN POLICY MAKING

In principle, bureaucracies are expected to help the president carry out presidential policies. In practice, the president depends on the bureaucracies comprising the foreign affairs government to get things done. Thus, as Henry Kissinger advised, "to understand what the government is likely to do, one has to understand the bureaucratics of the problems."

What are some of the consequences of presidential dependency on bureaucracies? Does it limit the president's power over American foreign policy? Are bureaucracies "ruling servants," in control of policy by virtue of their power to impede? Indeed, does the bureaucracy rule while the president merely reigns? Those troublesome questions have been raised by past presidents' recurrent complaints that they were unable to persuade, even coerce, their own bureaucracy to support their policies. Subordinates have often appeared insubordinate; rather than helping to get things done, they have opposed presidential directives. "You know," Ronald Reagan once said, "one of the hardest things in a government this size is to know that down there, underneath, is that permanent structure that's resisting everything you're doing." Indeed, political scientist and former presidential adviser Richard E. Neustadt observed that, "to a degree, the needs of bureaucrats and president are incompatible. The better one is served, the worse will be the other."

Although it is an exaggeration to speak of the *bureaucratic captivity* of presidents, they are heavily dependent on the bureaucracy for information, for identifying problems, for advocating solutions and, most importantly, for implementing presidential orders. Correspondingly, presidents' leeway is markedly constrained by the government they are elected to run.

The very enormity of the federal bureaucracy is a constraint. The federal civilian workforce (excluding postal workers) totaled 1.8 million in 2000. Almost 1.5 million more were on active military duty in the uniformed military services. Federal employees are ensconced in roughly 2,000 separate but overlapping government agencies. Presidents come and go, but these millions of bureaucrats remain, providing continuity from one administration to the next. Just over 3,000 are "policy makers"—individuals appointed by and able to be fired by the president. The rest are career civil servants, whose independence and job security are protected by an elaborate system of rules and regulations. As a result, foreign policy decisions necessarily are made by many individuals within a massive but fragmented governmental structure, most of whom are beyond the immediate reach of elected public officials. As Woodrow Wilson put it in a timeless description, "Nobody stands responsible for the policy of government . . . a dozen men originate it; a dozen compromises twist and alter it; a dozen offices put it into execution."

Bureaucratic Behavior: Interorganizational Attributes

How do large bureaucratic organizations relate to one another? How do individuals behave within complex organizational settings? At least four interorganizational (how the organizations relate to each other) characteristics of administrative decision making are important to an understanding of bureaucratic behavior and its impact on foreign policy. Four other intraorganizational features (how the organizations shape the roles of the people within them), discussed in the next section combine to summarize the **bureaucratic politics model** of foreign policy decision making.[7]

Parochialism Bureaucracies are driven to protect their jurisdictions. They define issues and take stands on them to promote their self-interests. Indeed, "since a public bureaucracy is concerned with special and limited aspects of public policy, to a degree it resembles the ordinary private pressure group" (Freeman 1965). As James M. Fallows, President Carter's chief speechwriter, observed, "The chief force motivating most top bureaucrats, cabinet secretaries, and even some White House aides is job security—you can predict a bureaucrat's reaction to almost any issue by the way it will affect their job or fiefdom. That's what comes first."

Individuals who occupy bureaucratic roles are not immune to the **parochialism** that often places organizational interests ahead of national interests. A candid list of the criteria by which career bureaucrats judge their success would have to include a handsome salary, how many people are under their authority, measurable opportunities for advancement, and a large office near the parking garage. Consider the following description from an investigative report on the CIA by *U.S. News and World Report*:

> Current and retired members of the clandestine service say the CIA's darkest secret is the fact that the agency's sanctum sanctorum resembles the Department of Agriculture more than James Bond's MI6 or Jack Ryan's CIA. Too many operations officers, these critics charge, are more interested in chasing promotions than prying loose other nations' secrets. Says Richard Kerr, a former deputy

director of central intelligence . . . : "What they're doing today is good for the DO [clandestine services]—not for the country."

(JULY 4, 1994, 43)

In another example, the Pentagon has worked diligently for over a decade to acquire the V-22 Osprey, a tilt-rotor aircraft capable off and landing like a helicopter, but flying like an airplane. The Marines greatly desired the Osprey to ensure their ability to transport units swiftly and efficiently into faraway places. Thus, the Marine Corps and its supporters worked against the first Bush administration's repeated efforts (led by Defense Secretary Dick Cheney) to cancel the program for broader strategic and budgetary reasons. From the perspective of advocates of the Osprey, its contribution to Marine Corps interests and capabilities was paramount (Jones 2001). The success of the Marine Corps and its advocates during the first Bush administration—plans to purchase over 900 of the aircraft continued in spite of the White House decision to cancel the program—led to additional efforts later in 2001 when, in the face of rising costs, troubling maintenance and safety records, and several well-publicized crashes killing marines, high-ranking officers went so far as to falsify maintenance records to protect the program (Flaherty 2001; Marquis 2001).

Even more recently, it was revealed after the 2001 terrorist attacks on New York and Washington DC, that the "National Commission on Terrorism" established by President Clinton in 2000 had recommended a series of changes in the security, intelligence, and law enforcement communities to deal with a threat for which the commission found a dreadful lack of preparation (see Focus 13.3). Nearly every proposal was embraced by the White House and Congress after the 2001 attacks. Why not before? Virtually every agency head, including FBI director Louis Freeh, CIA director George Tenet, Secretary of State Madeleine Albright, and Attorney General Janet Reno, opposed parts of the report because "they

trespassed on [their] turf" (Foer 2001). As one observer noted, such agencies "proved more skillful at protecting themselves from bureaucratic encroachment than at protecting the country from Al Qaeda" (Foer 2001).

As Drezner (2000) notes; organizations "resist or subvert new tasks that are assigned to them, for fear that they will lose their cohesion and ability to function." White House efforts to centralize control over foreign policy making are partially a response to the problems parochialism poses.

Competitiveness   Far from impartial, neutral administrators that obediently carry out presidential orders, the departments and agencies comprising the foreign affairs government frequently compete with one another for influence. As a staff member of the Clinton administration's National Security Council once noted, organizations take stands on issues that advance their interests and maneuver to protect them against other organizations and senior officials, including the president (Halperin 1971). Although not intentionally malicious, many agency heads nonetheless confuse their organization's welfare with the nation's. The V-22 case just discussed is a good example that illustrates the following observation:

> National security managers have a personal investment in the health and aggrandizement of their own bureaucratic organizations. They equate the national interest and their organization's interest as a matter of course. They will fight to maintain an obsolete air base, build redundant weapons systems, proliferate arms around the world by certifying that the nation's "vital interests" are at stake when it is merely their own budgets.

(BARNET 1972, 122)

As Drezner (2000) argues "Agencies that prefer the status quo or fear losing power will resist the introduction of new ideas [or new players] into the policy mix and use any means at their disposal to avoid unpalatable ideas."

FOCUS 13.3   Bureaucracy and the Terrorist Threat

Prior to September 11, a major reason why a succession of government commissions and legislators called for organizational changes in the homeland security areas was to draw attention to the problem of terrorism and the need to respond. Advocates of change argued that terrorism constituted a very real threat to U.S. security—yet this threat did not receive the priority attention of the U.S. government that they believed it deserved. Consolidating homeland security functions would give it that priority—by creating what the General Accounting Office called a "focal point." Most proposed placing the new organization within the Executive Office of the President in an effort to make homeland security a White House priority.

Clearly, before terrorists turned commercial jetliners into conventional weapons of mass destruction and killed more than 5,000 people on U.S. soil, homeland security was not a top priority for the U.S. government. To be sure, successive presidents had talked about the threat of terrorism. Clinton frequently worried, often publicly, about a germ weapons attack by terrorists on U.S. soil. Bush mentioned the threat of terrorism during his campaign, and continued to talk about the threat as president (although often as an argument for developing missile defenses). Spending on counterterrorism activities also increased dramatically—from $6 billion in 1998 to well over $10 billion in 2001. And with the appointment of a national coordinator for security, infrastructure protection, and counterterrorism in 1998, there was an attempt to improve coordination among the myriad of agencies and interests involved in preparing for, preventing, and responding to terrorist attacks.

But even with heightened presidential interest, increased funding, and improved coordination, the terrorist threat had not moved to the top—or even near the top—of the daily agenda of the president and his senior national security advisers. The national coordinator was a special assistant to the president and senior director on the NSC staff, reporting to the national security adviser—not the president. And while the issue of terrorism was rising in importance in every agency with a role to play in guarding against the threat, terrorism remained just one among their many concerns. For the Pentagon, preparing to fight two major theater wars remained the priority—and in the distance loomed the rise of China and the acquisition of long-range missiles by nuclear-armed rogue states. The customs agents searched luggage and shipments coming across borders—to sniff out illegal drug shipments more than germ weapons. Foreign service officers working their first tour of duty in consular sections in U.S. embassies abroad, and Immigration and Naturalization Services personnel at U.S. ports of entry worried more about preventing entry of people who wished to stay for good than keeping out people who wished to do the United States. harm. The FBI tracked federal criminals at home and sought to garner evidence that could stand up in U.S. courts against terrorists abroad, but did not take the initiative to track people who might terrorize our nation. And the list goes on. In each and every case other critical agency functions were, for very understandable reasons, given priority over countering the terrorism threat.

Prepared statement of W. H. Daalder & I. M. Destler before the Committee on Governmental Affairs, U.S. Senate, October 12, 2001 (at http://www.brookings.edu/views/testimony/daalder/200110/02.htm accessed 11/17/2001.

Heads of bureaucratic organizations are not insensitive to the nation's interests, but they struggle over defining what is best for the country. For several years prior to the Persian Gulf War, for example, the United States authorized the sale of advanced-technology goods to Iraq (which, ironically, may have enhanced Iraq's ability to wage war against the United States). The Commerce Department, following its mandate to promote in-ternational trade, became a vigorous proponent of technology sales to Iraq. Commerce usually prevailed in the interorganizational policy process because it was able to build a "'winning' coalition in favor of liberal export controls" with the State Department, whose arguments extended beyond economics to an array of diplomatic concerns. Together the Commerce and State Departments blocked the Defense Department's objections.

Thus, "each agency's separate organizational mission led it to embrace a different conception of national security and, therefore, different reasons for supporting either trade promotion or trade control" (Jones 1999). More recently, before President Clinton became engaged on the issue, tentative plans for the expansion of NATO were stalled in a "NATO Interagency Working Group" due to bureaucratic wrangling and competition between a Defense Department opposed to the idea and a few policy makers from the State Department and elsewhere who supported the enlargement of NATO to include states from Central and Eastern Europe (Goldgeier 1999).

The effect of competition can also be seen in policy implementation, as American policy toward Mexico at the beginning of the new century suggests. According to one observer, "virtually every U.S. government agency [in Mexico] is pursuing its own policy there—usually several policies at once, which are often secret, contradictory, and conducted with varying levels of coordination with the ambassador. Although this means that each agency has a piece of the action and a vested interest in its own programs, the agencies lose overall coordination, harmony and focus on the larger goals" (Wiarda 2000).

The incidence with which agency officials propose and pursue policies that blatantly benefit their own organizations attests to the parochial outlook and selfish concerns that typically dominate bureaucratic thinking. Consider the following example. After the collapse of the Soviet Union, the CIA's clandestine services, officially known as the Directorate of Operations, shut down its operations there, believing that Russia no longer posed much of a threat. Less than two years later the decision was reversed by the CIA official responsible for operations in the former Soviet Union and Eastern Europe. Why? Because "a decision to stop targeting Russia would cost the agency 500 overseas jobs for case officers [those whose job is to recruit and oversee individuals who conduct espionage and provide information to the agency]" (*U.S. News and World Report,* 4 July 1994).

Another example comes from the fall of 2001. Following the terrorist attacks on New York and Washington DC, a special commission headed by former national security adviser Brent Scowcroft recommended that several Defense Department intelligence agencies—the National Reconnaissance Office, the National Imagery and Mapping Agency, and the National Security Agency—be transferred to the CIA for better intelligence coordination and analysis (see Chapter 5). Of course the CIA was in favor of the restructuring, but the Defense Department and Defense Secretary Donald Rumsfled were immediately opposed to the idea (Pincus 2001).

The reasons for competitive intergovernmental politics are numerous. Kissinger (1969) suggests one: "The decision maker will always be aware of the morale of his staff. . . . [He] cannot overrule it too frequently without impairing its efficiency. . . . Placating the staff then becomes a major preoccupation of the executive." Another reason is that most agency heads are not only tied *to* their own organization but also *by* it: "A secretary of a federal department almost invariably becomes more the agent of the permanent bureaucracy under his command than a free agent, mainly because he must rely upon the permanent officials for expert information and analysis" (MacMahon 1951). Thus, caught in the middle between higher-level elected officials and their advisers on one side, and the career professionals in an organization on the other, the typical agency head must try to satisfy both. The pressures encourage competition with other organizations for scarce resources and power. Policy success in such an atmosphere tends to be defined more in terms of *organizational interests* than of the national interest.

Imperialistic Task Expansion Driven to protect their own interests and promote their own influence, bureaucratic agencies invariably seek to enlarge their budgets and staffs, both absolutely and in relation to other agencies. Bureaucratic agencies also typically seek to increase their prerogatives and functional powers. Thus the

Defense Department (among others) sought aggressively to capture part of the CIA's $3 billion share of the intelligence budget at a time when the agency searched for a new post–Cold War mission in the face of intense scrutiny by Congress and others. At the same time, the CIA sought to defend its roles and budgets and to find new missions in the changing threat environment of the new century. Later, in 2001, the roles reversed as the CIA supported a proposal to give it three DOD intelligence agencies, while the DOD resisted. Another example may be Madeleine Albright's support in 1998 for the restructuring of the foreign affairs agencies that gave the State Department greater control over the Agency for International Development and immersed the US. Information Agency in the State Department (Broder 2001). The reasons are clear. Size is a sign of security, expansion an indicator of importance, and, to some extent, prestige and influence can be conferred only by growth. Other things being equal, larger bureaucracies have greater access, greater credibility, greater resources, greater durability—and greater influence. (Such organizations usually have more enemies as well!) Thus, most organizations strive to maintain and enhance their budgets and grow their personnel.

The raison d'être of administrative organization is efficiency through the performance of discrete tasks by independent units; a division of labor that clearly differentiates functions permits experts to specialize. This rationale led in 1947 to creation of a separate Central Intelligence Agency, whose ostensible purpose was to coordinate the gathering of foreign intelligence, and in 1961 to creation of the Agency for International Development (AID) to specialize in the administration of foreign aid and technical assistance.

Practice, however, frequently fails to conform to theory. Imperialistic bureaucracies seek to perform the tasks for which other agencies have been assigned responsibility. That inclination explains why the Council on International Economic Policy created by President Nixon did not become an effective coordinator of economic policy making: It became merely another competitor jockeying for a piece of the policy action among those preexisting units needing coordination. The Clinton administration's National Economic Council fared better, but still struggled with many of the same "turf wars," especially after Robert Rubin moved from the White House to the Treasury Department. George W. Bush has apparently experienced similar tension between his Treasury Department, headed by Paul O'Neill, and his NEC, headed by Lawrence Lindsay.

Bureaucratic imperialism also explains why so many different agencies are independently involved in gathering roughly the same intelligence information (for example, the State Department, the Defense Department, and the CIA, among others), and why the three military services have found it "absolutely essential" that each develop its own capabilities in areas where the other services specialize (as evidenced by the fact that the army at one time had more support aircraft than the air force). The result: Instead of a bureaucratic division of labor, functions are often duplicated.

The bureaucratic imperatives of the uniformed military services, which include not only imperialism but also competitiveness and endurance, are well illustrated by the activities and strategies advocated by the different branches in the run-up to the Persian Gulf War (Gordon and Trainor 1995; Holland 1999). They are also seen in the meaning that each branch attached to the Persian Gulf War as each positioned itself for the oncoming debate about the military's role in the post–Cold War world. Focus 13.4 provides a glimpse of how the war stimulated "new thinking" in the Pentagon and among its congressional and interest-group supporters shortly after its victorious conclusion.

Endurance Bureaucracies are survival-oriented. Both the number and size of administrative units responsible for promoting and protecting America's activist foreign policy interests have increased enormously. More new units have been created or expanded than phased out or cut back. Once in place, they usually persist and grow, even in the

---

**FOCUS 13.4 Bureaucratic Competitiveness and Task Expansion:
Military Rivalry in the Aftermath of Victory in the Persian Gulf**

As the Defense Department begins its most dramatic restructuring of the armed forces in decades, the services are in tough competition for declining dollars. Although such budget rivalries are hardly new, the Persian Gulf War is being used to reshape the debates on the future roles and missions of the military. . . . Senior U.S. military officials say they were most concerned during the initial days of the gulf crisis about the vulnerability of Saudi Arabia. . . . The only ground-based American forces aligned against Iraqi troops in late August were an airborne infantry division and marine units ill-equipped to battle heavy armor, plus an air force fighter wing with no more weapons than it could carry under its wings.

This experience has spurred the air force to create two special combat wings that, for the first time, would include a mix of fighter, bomber and attack planes that could be dispatched in crises. Until now, air force tactical wings have been composed of a single type of aircraft.

The army, with its thousands of tons of heavy armor and hundreds of thousands of combat troops, was hit hardest by the military's limited sealift and airlift capacity. Once content to let the navy and air force worry about such capacity, army officials now say they will press the other services to increase resources for sealift and airlift operations.

The army wants the navy, for instance, to be able to transport at least two divisions simultaneously within thirty days of call-up—not just one division, as the navy had planned. Navy officials readily agree that more of the Pentagon budget needs to be invested in transport ships. . . . The

Marine Corps, which has spent billions of dollars on amphibious landing operations, conducted no amphibious assaults against Iraq, but argues that this kind of war-fighting capability should not be abandoned because the fear of an amphibious attack kept several Iraqi divisions diverted toward the sea during the war.

All the services have appeared equally eager to use the Gulf War in sales pitches for more purchases of the kinds of weapons that proved most successful. The air force and navy, for instance, are using memories of the pinpoint strikes by "stealth" F-117A fighter-bombers to push for continuation of the stealth B-2 bomber and development of a stealth carrier-based plane for the navy.

At the same time, the services are pointing to the deficiencies that were evident in the war in arguing for improved and expanded new systems. The navy, for example, which dropped primarily "dumb bombs" and had only a limited number of high-technology, precision-guided missiles, is now using the success of the air force's "smart" weapons in lobbying to expand its own arsenal. . . . The navy, annoyed that it received so little credit for its aerial bombing attacks, discovered what officials believe is one of the reasons. "We didn't realize," says one naval official, "how lousy the video recorders were on our aircraft until we saw them side by side with the air force's. We had junk. The air force guys had nice clean pictures." Better recorders are sure to be on the navy's new shopping list.

SOURCE: Molly Moore, "The Armed Services and the Nibbling Rivalries," *Washington Post National Weekly Edition,* June 17–23, 1991, 31.

---

face of great adversity (see Kaufman 1976). The Agency for International Development, for example, whose primary purpose during the Cold War was to aid poor countries as a way of fighting communism, later found that America's own inner cities were environments ripe for sharing expertise first gained working abroad—which coincidentally helped to justify the agency's continued existence when members of Congress sought

to dismantle it in the 1990s (see Chapter 5 and *New York Times,* 26 June 1994).

Bureaucratic growth is arguably a response to new challenges and changing circumstances. With the end of the Cold War, for example, the State Department opened fourteen new embassies in the former Soviet Union and expected to increase its number of diplomats there by nearly half. The Commerce Department also quadrupled the number of trade promotion officials assigned to the region, the Treasury Department increased its economic analysts from three to eleven, and AID, traditionally oriented exclusively toward the Global South, created a twenty-five person team to speed delivery of technical and humanitarian assistance to the former Soviet Union (Priest 1992, 33). Historically, however, organizational "reforms" designed to streamline government have often created *new* organizations to coordinate and regulate the activities of existing ones (perhaps the Clinton Administration's NEC and the Bush administration's office of Homeland Security and Homeland Security Council are recent examples). The result is not enhanced efficiency, but rather the addition of new layers to a burgeoning bureaucracy. As Secretary of the Navy John Lehman complained in 1985, "It would be impossible for me or anyone to accurately describe to you the system with which, and within which, we must operate. There are thousands upon thousands of offices and entities and bureaus that have been created over the years to deal episodically with aspects of defense."

Bureaucratic Behavior: Intraorganizational Attributes

The interorganizational side of bureaucratic behavior just described is easily summarized: All bureaucratic organizations pursue their own purposes, promote their own power, enhance their own position in the governmental hierarchy, and strive to endure. Successful pursuit of those objectives flows in part from and in turn reinforces internal standard operating procedures and the way bureaucratic organizations mold the behavior of their role occupants.

Secrecy and Exclusiveness Bureaucratic agencies seek to minimize interference in and regulation of their operations. To the extent possible, they keep their proceedings secret from potential enemies—including the president—who might use such knowledge to attack their opera-

tions publicly, and they conceal activities that can injure their public image. Efforts by the Marines to falsify maintenance records for the V-22 Osprey are simply a more egregious form of this behavior. "There are no secrets in Washington," President Kennedy observed, "except the things I need to know." Conversely, bureaucratic secrets are "leaked" selectively for propaganda purposes when their release is politically advantageous.

Attitudinal Conformity Every bureaucracy eventually develops a *shared "mind set"* or dominant way of looking at reality, which few challenge. The process of recruitment and self-selection brings together individuals who already share many basic attitudes. The Foreign Service, for instance, has sought "young people they consider most like the successful officers already in the system" (Harr 1969). Free thinkers or people who might "rock the boat" or "make waves" are not welcomed; instead, those subscribing to the agency's dominant values are preferred.[8] Moreover, the State Department's *organizational subculture—* a common set of goals and norms shared by members of the organization—spreads quickly among its personnel creating patterned ways of thinking and acting (Wilson 1989; Scott 1969).

Attitudinal conformity is reinforced in small-group decision-making situations, where social pressures that reinforce group norms sometimes produce **groupthink,** a cohesiveness and solidarity of outlook that may lead to dysfunctional policy choices as the group's search for unanimity overrides the realistic appraisal of alternative policy choices (Janis 1982).[9] Indeed, several recent studies indicate that groupthink has been associated with poor outcomes in numerous foreign policy decisions (for example, Herek, Janis, and Huth 1987; Schafer and Crichlow 1996). President Johnson's habit of addressing Bill Moyers, his resident "dove" on Vietnam, as "Mr. Stop-the-Bombing" illustrates the pressures toward conformity small decision-making groups often generate.

The Kennedy administration's disastrous Bay of Pigs decision in 1961 contained numerous elements of groupthink (Janis 1982), as did the

Reagan administration's policy revisions regarding Iran and the Lebanese hostage crisis in 1985–1986 that led to the Iran-contra affair ('t Hart 1990). Even decision processes that lead to success, as those that brought about victory in the Gulf War, are susceptible to concurrence-seeking behavior and pressures toward attitudinal conformity. For example, even some in the "inner circle" of decision making, such as Secretary of State James A. Baker and JCS Chairman Colin Powell, were unwilling to challenge the dominant views articulated by President Bush and his national security adviser, Brent Scowcroft. To do so "would have meant undermining one's own political standing at the White House" (Hybel 1993). In 1998, when President Clinton and his advisers decided to retaliate with force against Osama bin Laden and Al Qaeda for the bombing of U.S. embassies in Africa, similar concurrence-seeking behavior occurred (see Russel 2000; Hendrickson 2002).

Once an individual joins a bureaucratic organization, socialization to its "mission" and its "essence" (Allison and Halperin 1972) reinforces conformity to the organization's central norms. Recruits are quickly educated into their role and the acceptable attitudes that go with it. Nonconformity can result in loss of influence or, in the extreme, one's job. On the other hand, those who conform to peer-group attitudes, who are perceived as team players, are rewarded. "Promotions are awards given to bureaucrats for accepting organizational myths" cynically describes this phenomenon.

Shared convictions about an organization's role and mission are important in maintaining organizational morale, but the line is not always clear between a healthy commitment to an organization's welfare and what is detrimental to larger purposes. Institutional mind sets discourage creativity, dissent, and independent thinking, undermining rational policy making. The Department of State, for instance, has found in numerous self-studies that pressures producing uniformity of thought and stifling creativity have been persistent problems.

Deference to Tradition Because decision making in complex organizations is conducted according to *rules*, bureaucrats are prone to defer to tradition and standard operating procedures rather than invent a new way to deal with a new problem. "A man comes to an assignment," Charles Frankel (1969) observed, "and he is told what policy is. He must find a way to navigate through the storms, to resist the pressures of people and events, and to turn over the policy to his successor in the same condition in which it was when he received it from his predecessor." A former staff member of the National Security Council dubbed this respect for ritual and precedent the *curator mentality* (Thomson 1994).

Reliance on Historical Analogies When a decision point is reached, policy makers are prone to search history impressionistically for parallels that suggest options for dealing with the emergent problem. That tendency—which often results in a misreading of historical lessons (Neustadt and May 1986; Khong 1992)—helps account for continuity in American foreign policy. The "Munich" analogy, for example, was drawn on by a generation of policy makers as evidence that it is impossible to appease aggressors. As noted in Chapter 3, the analogy refers to the 1938 British and French agreement that permitted Nazi Germany to annex a large part of Czechoslovakia in return for what British Prime Minister Neville Chamberlain called "peace in our time." Instead, war broke out in Europe a year later, with the apparent lesson that an aggressor cannot be stopped short of fighting it.[10]

Bill Clinton invoked the Hitler analogy to describe Serbian President Slobodan Milošević as NATO warplanes launched an extensive air attack in Kosovo in 1999. George Bush drew on the Munich analogy directly as he prepared the nation for war against Saddam Hussein, whom he also described as a modern-day Hitler. Indeed, so strong was his commitment to the analogy that it "acted as a barrier to the search for information that could have jeopardized its validity" (Hybel 1993). Heavy reliance on analogical thinking

FOCUS 13.5   Stereotyping: Pluses and Minuses

In the days since September 11, 2001, it has become increasingly evident that American policy makers, a large portion of the American people, Osama bin Laden, members of the Al Qaeda network, the Taliban, and many in the Muslim world are becoming caught up in the negative and self-perpetuating characteristics that are a concomitant of stereotyping. American political leaders talk about other countries being with us or against us and the Al Qaeda terrorist network and those who harbor its groups as evil. On the other side, Osama bin Laden considers all Americans infidels and has waged a *jihad* against Christians and Jews. There is no shade of gray in the depiction of the other. Such ethnocentrism allows each to believe they are right, good, and moral, and to dehumanize the other. By engaging in such stereotyping, we develop a consensual belief about the other group and how they are to be treated.

All stereotypes are developed around some grain of truth. After all, the evidence appears to be substantial that Osama bin Laden and his lieutenants plotted and financed the events of September 11; the bombing of the USS Cole, the bombing of two U.S. embassies, and the earlier attempt on the World Trade Center. And bin Laden would respond that the U.S. is responsible for the deaths of more than 5,000 children in Iraq and countless youth in the Palestinian lands, has defamed the Muslim holy spots in Saudi Arabia with its bases and troops, and has kept in power monarchs and dictators in the Arab and Muslim world who are insensitive to the suffering of their people. These incidents become the architecture around which the stereotypes are built, making it easy to prejudge others based on dress, religion, accents, and place of origin.

Stereotypes have consequences. They lead us to make the assumption that all members of the "enemy" or outgroup are homogeneous in their points of view and perspectives. *We* know that there are differences about *us*—Americans represent a mosaic of many different peoples, religions, and perspectives. But the differences among *them* are not noticed or differentiated; *they* are all alike. The outgroup is generally perceived to operate as a unit and to be capable of taking care of what is happening—indeed, they are viewed as the puppet master pulling the strings and calling the shots.

Stereotypes also lead us to become selective in our perception of information; facts and anecdotes that are incongruent with our stereotypes are reinterpreted to make them consistent with what we believe and facilitate us to maintain our impression of these others. Thus, members of each group exposed to the same information interpret it differently. The Taliban insist that American war planes were targeting civilians with a growing number of casualties while American generals report that civilian casualties were still too few in number given the intensity of the bombing campaign. There was a tendency for both parties to characterize data in terms that would strike a non-involved observer as biased and self-serving.

Moreover, stereotypes lead to proposals and concessions being diminished in value in the eyes of the recipient, particularly if they have come from the *enemy*. An offer or argument that may seem appropriate to *us* can be viewed as posturing, inadequate, or fostering a deliberate misunderstanding when posed by these *others*. The Taliban demand for evidence that Osama bin Laden was involved in the events of September 2001 as a condition for handing him over seemed quite reasonable to those involved in Al Qaeda and in many parts of the Muslim world, but a deliberate ploy to buy time by the American leadership. The U.S. food drop in Afghanistan [was] viewed suspiciously by the Taliban and others and viewed as merely a public relations ploy. *Who* takes an action becomes important in assessing its value.

As this discussion suggests, stereotypes influence what is perceived, how it is interpreted, and what worth it is assigned. Stereotypes become self-perpetuating and are difficult to change. The dilemma becomes how to keep the current war from turning into a broader clash of civilizations as each side considers the other more homogeneous and evil. With many near starvation, young Muslim recruits from countries throughout the region joining the Taliban, with ethnic differences dividing the various groups that could form a future Afghan government, with members of the Al Qaeda network spread from the region that it will leave when the going gets tough or its interests have been satisfied, the conflict is not black and white. To have any hope of diluting our stereotypes, it is critical to learn more about the peoples who are considered part of the other side and the events that have shaped the action, to become aware of the nuances and complexities that are found in so-called outgroups, and to seek out interactions where sharing perspectives rather than defending one's own position takes precedence.

SOURCE: Margaret G. Hermann, "Stereotypes Build Solidarity, but Limit Our Understanding," *Maxwell Perspective* 12 (Fall 2001), 10–11.

before and after Iraq's invasion of Kuwait limited the Bush administration's ability to follow the canons of procedural rationality, thus calling into question the instrumental rationality of its decisions, particularly the choice of war over containment through the sustained application of sanctions. By no means does this detract from the administration's success in bringing Iraq to its knees, but it does establish that "success does not prove rationality" (Hybel 1993).

Other attributes of bureaucratic behavior as it relates to foreign policy making could be added to this discussion, but they would not change the conclusion drawn from it: that the decision-making system profoundly influences the behavior of those who occupy institutionally defined decision-making roles. Given this, we now shift attention to some of the major policy consequences of those attributes.

POLICY CONSEQUENCES OF ORGANIZATIONAL DECISION MAKING

Because American foreign policy is a product of organizational decision-making processes, it is useful to consider how bureaucratic behavior shapes both policy and policy making. Some conspicuous repercussions of bureaucratic processes follow.

Bureaucratic Resistance to Change

In the realm of broad foreign policy conceptions and goals, the president and the executive bureaucracies may be natural enemies. Because many upper-echelon career officials have retained their positions for years, sometimes even decades, their long-held assumptions about American foreign policy may be as deeply entrenched as the bureaucracies for which they work. Fundamental assumptions—about Soviet motives during the Cold War and Russian imperialism since, about the continuing wisdom of globalism and the util-

ity of force, and about other themes that have defined American foreign policy for more than five decades—have become bureaucratic conventional wisdom, unworthy of further reexamination. Presidents intermittently come to power with fresh ideas about foreign policy essentials, eager to implement new approaches, only to find that old ways of thinking are firmly entrenched in agencies that are *resistant to change*.

The Carter administration found, for example, that many in the State Department were unresponsive to some of its early foreign policy initiatives on human rights and arms sales. "Some of the older generation of diplomats openly didn't . . . believe in the efficacy or wisdom of such notions as campaigns for human rights or restraint in arms sales abroad," observed one department insider. "They fully expected that most of the new initiatives would soon be dropped, and they did everything they could to see that the day of abandonment came sooner rather than later" (Carter 1981). The experience suggests that failures to change foreign policy can be attributed in part to a bureaucracy's refusal to support a new administration's new ideas.

Similarly, the end of the Cold War demanded a fresh appraisal of old ways of thinking, but many bureaucratic agencies continued to view the future through the prism of the past. The bureaucratic resistance in 2000–2001 to new counterterrorism approaches we discussed earlier is an example of this. Another is "the ghost in the Pentagon" (Iklé 1990), as a former under secretary of defense described the "enduring mind-set" of military planners as they contemplated the first evidence that the Cold War was indeed passing. This recognition is perhaps what prompted George Bush to pledge at the 1989 Malta summit that he would "kick our bureaucracy and push it as fast as I possibly can" to achieve a new arms control agreement with the Gorbachev regime. Similarly, in the opening episode of this chapter, President Clinton's desire to construct a new strategy of *assertive multilateralism* with which to approach conflicts in the developing world ran afoul of bureaucratic intransigence as the armed services, led by General Colin Powell, resisted the core elements of the policy initiative.

Even if new realities are recognized, however, reorienting standard operating procedures and reallocating existing resources to new problems is not easy. Nowhere is that more apparent than in the Pentagon, where decisions on weapons systems and their intended purposes often take decades to come to fruition. Thus when Clinton's first secretary of defense, Les Aspin, undertook a "bottom-up" review of the U.S. military, he confronted a simple yet enduring fact: "The military machine cannot turn around on a dime" (Sweetman 1994). The task, then, was to rethink the purpose and utility of Cold War weapons in a post–Cold War world while simultaneously reducing defense spending to the levels sought by the White House without threatening either the nation's security or its ability, as anticipated by Aspin, to fight and win two simultaneous regional conflicts. The order was too tall, as Aspin fell short in the ability to manage a complex organization in transition. He resigned less than a year after assuming an office for which he had arguably spent a lifetime preparing.

Even in 2001, with the need for change more apparent than ever, George W. Bush's administration ran into a similar problem. Throughout 2001, President Bush and Defense Secretary Donald Rumsfeld signaled their desire for a more fundamental change of strategy and planning to meet the challenges and imperatives of the new environment. However, Rumsfeld's much anticipated report, released in September 2001 (just after the September 11 terrorist strikes)—the 2001 Quadrennial Defense Review Report (see Chapters 4 and 11), was far less sweeping than expected. Moreover, even with the jarring reality of the terrorist attacks fresh in everyone's minds, initial proposals for the reorganization of the Pentagon's regional command structure to better promote cooperation and coordination against the terrorist threat were resisted. High-level officials, including Rumsfeld, concluded that "the current structure is too balkanized to execute a global campaign against terrorism," and that "transna-

tional concerns, such as terrorism and weapons proliferation have not received adequate attention from senior commanders" (Ricks 2001b). Nevertheless, plans for restructuring encountered fierce opposition from the services, especially the regional commanders-in-chief (CINCs), whose independence and influence in the current structure is substantial (Ricks 2001b).

Bureaucratic Competition and Foreign Policy Inertia

Bureaucratic competition encourages its own inertia as well as *policy inertia*. The overwhelming complexity of the foreign affairs machinery, with its entrenched and competing bureaucracies, limits what leaders can do and casts doubt on Washington's capacity to act expeditiously. Reaching consensus and taking decisive action is inhibited because policy is formulated and implemented by many individuals situated in a complex institutional arrangement. Bureaucrats in charge of the different agencies usually disagree: They want different policies and define situations differently because of their differing vantage points. The result is policy formulation that often comes down to a tug of war among competing agencies, a high-stakes political game in which differences are settled at the lowest common denominator. Henry Kissinger described the process this way:

> Each of the contending factions within the bureaucracy has a maximum incentive to state its case in its most extreme form because the ultimate outcome depends, to a considerable extent, on a bargaining process. The premium placed on advocacy turns decision making into a series of adjustments among special interests—a process more suited to domestic than to foreign policy. This procedure neglects the long-range because the future has no administrative constituency and is, therefore, without representation in the adversary proceedings. Problems tend to be slighted until some agency or department is made responsible for

them. . . . The outcome usually depends more on the pressures or the persuasiveness of the contending advocates than on a concept of over-all purpose.

(KISSINGER 1969, 268)

Two recent examples help to illustrate this general phenomenon. Bureaucratic disagreement and competition—notably between the State and Defense Departments—over the proper course of U.S. policy in the former Yugoslavia contributed heavily to the Clinton Administration's failure to forge an effective approach to the problem until 1995. Progress did not come until the State Department used internal policy reviews to enlist the support of Deputy National Security Adviser Sandy Berger to propose a more aggressive approach. With the help of National Security Adviser Tony Lake, who used his position as process manager to force the issue, this more aggressive approach prevailed in spite of continued Defense Department opposition when President Clinton opted for a more assertive U.S. effort (Daalder 2000).

A few years later, George W. Bush's team experienced a policy logjam over a fundamental dispute over how to deal with Iraq. Prior to the September 11 strikes, the administration was locked in a serious competition between the State and Defense departments over sanctions against Iraq. Colin Powell and his staff, including Richard Haass, Director of the Policy and Planning Staff, preferred a revision of U.S. policy to reduce the sanctions, while Donald Rumsfeld and his staff, including Deputy Defense Secretary Paul Wolfowitz preferred an even more aggressive effort to topple Saddam Hussein's regime. Both sides blocked the other, with the result that policy was locked in place (McGeary 2001; Perlez 2001c). After the September 11 strikes, the two sides squared off over Iraq again, with Wolfowitz advocating a widening of U.S. military action against Afghanistan to include attacks on Iraq with the ultimate purpose of eliminating Hussein's regime. Powell and his team, concerned about the need to build and preserve a broad coalition against Al Qaeda and the Taliban regime in Afghanistan, argued against widening the war (*Newsweek,* October 1, 2001, p. 26; Tyler and Sciolino 2001; Allen and Sipress 2001). Bush's decision to identify Iraq as part of an "axis of evil" (with Iran and North Korea) in his 2002 State of the Union address hinted at the direction of the U.S. anti-terror campaign after Afghanistan.

In addition, fundamental or far-reaching choices are discouraged by the conservative nature of organizational policy making. The inclination among career officials to "go along in order to get along" encourages acceptance of prevailing policies and the status quo. Furthermore, bureaucracies typically administer programs created by prior decisions. Most bureaucrats therefore see themselves as loyal, even unquestioning, implementors of past policies rather than the creators of their own. The greater the loyalty to specific administrative tasks, the greater the commitment to existing policy. "To try and believe in what one is doing, . . . to see broader problems in narrow terms derived from one's own specific activities," is a natural part of a bureaucrat's role, but the result is that "the information and judgments bureaucrats provide for use in the making of policies tend to be strongly biased in favor of the continuation, rather than the modification, much less the reversal, of existing policies. . . . Thus a bureaucracy inevitably comes down heavily on the side of established policies and strongly resists change" (Reischauer 1968). The Powell-led resistance to assertive multilateralism nicely punctuates this point. To this we might add the second Bush administration conviction that the Pentagon's continuing commitment to Cold War weapons has impaired the development of a new generation of high-tech weapons that would continue the Revolution in Military Affairs (RMA).

Bureaucratic Sabotage of Presidential Foreign Policy Initiatives

The popular impression that American foreign policy is little more than what the president says it is can be misleading. The president alone does not make foreign policy. Policy must not only be pronounced but also carried out, and for that task the chief executive must rely on the bureaucracies comprising the executive branch. Hence, what the government's departments and agencies choose to implement becomes American foreign policy: Policy is what is done, not just what is said.

Because bureaucracies are by nature exclusive, parochial, and interested primarily in protecting their own power and authority, we should not be surprised that few agencies cheerfully carry out presidential directives they perceive as harmful to their organizations. When threatened, bureaucrats are inclined to put themselves first and to defend their own welfare. The often intractable foreign affairs machinery is, therefore, capable of disloyalty to the president it ostensibly serves. And since change, or the prospect of change, usually threatens someone (because policy change almost invariably entails some redistribution of influence in the government hierarchy), bureaucratic agencies frequently resist top-level policy proposals. A Washington cliché says that "the only decision that's final is the one you agree with."

Nearly every president has complained at one time or another that the federal bureaucracy ostensibly designed to serve him undercut his policy by refusing to carry out orders expeditiously. Witness President Truman's prediction prior to General Eisenhower's succession to the White House: "He'll sit here and he'll say, 'Do this! Do that!' *And nothing will happen.* Poor Ike—it won't be a bit like the army. He'll find it very frustrating." Another example is President Kennedy's observation that giving the State Department an instruction was like dropping it in the dead-letter box. As Dick Cheney put it when he was President Ford's chief of staff, "There is a tendency before you get to the White House or when you're just observing it from the outside to say, 'Gee, that's a powerful position that person has.' The fact of the matter is that while you're here trying to do things, you are far more aware of the constraints than you are of the power. You spend most of your time trying to overcome obstacles to getting what the president wants done."

Bureaucratic inaction and *lack of responsiveness* often manifest themselves as lethargy. The government machinery grinds slowly. (To quote the tongue-in-cheek characterization of James H. Boren, founder of the International Association of Professional Bureaucrats, "One must always remember that freedom from action and freedom from purpose constitute the philosophical basis of creative bureaucracy.") Procrastination appears endemic and is easily interpreted as intentional when in fact it is often inadvertent. It takes time to move people, paper, and processes along, and completing even the simplest requests routinely involves delay. An impatient president can easily mistake the crawling pace for insubordination, even sedition (because the effect—braking or abrogating policy decisions—is the same). But we must be careful not to equate everyday bureaucratic inaction with intentional foot dragging and disobedient noncompliance.

Still, willful *bureaucratic sabotage* is not a mere figment of leaders' imaginations. It can take several forms. Bureaucracies can withhold or slant vital information. They can provide advice showing reasons why recommended policy changes will not work, and they can circulate that advice to those in a position to challenge the policy change. They can leak information to Congress or discreetly contact interest groups capable of mobilizing opposition to a directive the bureaucrats find intolerable. Or they can delay policy implementation by demanding time to study the problem thoroughly (to death, that is)—a tactic known as *paralysis by analysis*—or by complexifying it into incomprehensibility (violating the KISS principle: "Keep It Simple, Stupid!"). And bureaucracies can buck a presidential directive by interpreting it in such a way that it is administered differently than proposed or with a change in emphasis. The result, of course, is no results. It has been said in this context that bureaucracies never change the course of the ship of state— they just adjust the compass.

Sometimes bureaucratic sabotage can be direct and immediate, as President Kennedy discovered in the midst of the 1962 Cuban missile crisis. While Kennedy sought to orchestrate U.S. action and bargaining, his bureaucracy in general and the navy in particular were in fact controlling events by doing as they wished.

> [The bureaucracy chose] to obey the orders it liked and ignore or stretch others. Thus, after a tense argument with the navy, Kennedy ordered the blockade line moved closer to Cuba so that the Russians might have more time to draw back. Having lost the argument with the president, the navy simply ignored his order. Unbeknownst to Kennedy, the navy was also at work forcing Soviet submarines to surface long before Kennedy authorized any contact with Soviet ships. And despite the president's order to halt all provocative intelligence, an American U-2 plane entered Soviet airspace at the height of the crisis. When Kennedy began to realize that he was not in full control, he asked his secretary of defense to see if he could find out just what the navy was doing. McNamara then made his first visit to the navy command post in the Pentagon. In a heated exchange, the chief of naval operations suggested that McNamara return to his office and let the navy run the blockade.

(GELB AND HALPERIN 1973, 256)[11]

Another example of bureaucratic disobedience occurred during the tense period *preceding* the Cuban missile crisis in 1962. Kennedy had concluded in March 1961 that Jupiter missiles in Turkey should be removed. He felt they were obsolete and exacerbated Soviet fears of encirclement and possible American attack from just beyond the Soviet border. The president therefore instructed the State Department to negotiate withdrawal of the American missiles. Turkish officials disapproved, however, so the State Department reasoned that the diplomatic thing to do was to comply with the Turkish request that the

missiles stay until American Polaris submarines armed with nuclear missiles took their place. However, according to Robert Kennedy (1971), "the president believed he was president and that, his wishes having been made clear, they would be followed and the missiles removed." During the Cuban Missile Crisis, Kennedy therefore was surprised to discover that arrangements to remove the missiles had not been completed.[12]

President Clinton also experienced a form of bureaucratic sabotage of his policies toward Haiti and the former Yugoslavia. At the same time that he sought to return Jean-Bertrand Aristide to power, replacing Haiti's military regime with the nation's last popularly elected president, the CIA repeatedly told Congress that, according to its psychological profile of Aristide, he was mentally unfit to rule. As the Clinton administration considered options for deposing Haiti's military leader, it shunned covert action, as officials in both the White House and State Department did not trust the CIA to carry out its mission. They believed the agency was anti-Aristide, partly because of his leftist political platform (Devroy and Smith 1993).

The conflict between the administration and the CIA was particularly embarrassing to the president, whose policies toward Haiti were already widely under attack from various quarters, but it was a classic illustration of the different purposes and perspectives policy makers and intelligence analysts bring to policy problems. Indeed, intelligence consumers and producers rarely speak the same language. Instead, they characteristically appear like "two closely related tribes that believe, mistakenly, that they speak the same language and work in the same manner for agreed outcomes. . . . Indeed, one is often reminded of George Bernard Shaw's quip about Britons and Americans being divided by a common tongue" (Lowenthal 1992).

In the former Yugoslavia, after the Dayton peace accords in 1995, the U.S. military deployed to enforce the peace took advantage of ambiguity in the language of the agreement ("authority" rather than "responsibility") to avoid aggressive efforts to enforce the terms of the agreement. In particular, the military assiduously avoided efforts to apprehend suspected war criminals (Daalder 2000; Holbrooke 1998). Later, during the Kosovo campaign in 1999, the military—especially the Joint Chiefs of Staff—limited the air war in ways that frustrated the Clinton administration, while, at the same time, the theater commander, Wesley Clark, used his control over the campaign to press for wider action than the administration preferred (Halberstam 2001; Clark 2001).

Managing Bureaucratic Intransigence

The "bureaucratic captivity" of American foreign policy is easily exaggerated. Although bureaucracies have a grip on presidential policies, presidents are not powerless to respond. There are ways to handle recalcitrant agencies and obstructionist officials.

Consider Franklin D. Roosevelt, the "master" of managing federal bureaucracies. An astute politician, Roosevelt overcame policy-implementation obstacles through a divide-and-rule strategy. "Planned disorganization and confusion" aptly describes it.

> [He] deliberately organized—or disorganized—his system of command to insure that important decisions were passed on to the top. His favorite technique was to keep grants of authority incomplete, jurisdictions uncertain, charters overlapping. The result of this competitive theory of administration was often confusion and exasperation on the operating level; but no other method could so reliably insure that in a large bureaucracy, filled with ambitious men eager for power, the decisions, and the power to make them, would remain with the president. . . . Franklin allowed no one to discover the governing principle.

(SCHLESINGER 1958, 527; SEE ALSO GEORGE 1980)

In short, Roosevelt sought to control policy by denying control to those around him.

The "Kissinger solution" represents a second, rather blunt but highly effective strategy: Punish the disobedient agency by excluding it from future decision making or circumvent it by creating a smaller, substitute unit. Removing a bureaucracy from influence—especially on issues that vitally concern it—can have considerable therapeutic value, making a hostile agency less intent on opposing presidential policy every time its own parochial interests are at stake.

President Kennedy employed a third tactic: causing disturbance *within* a recalcitrant agency by skipping the normal chain of command and dealing directly with lower-echelon officials. By upsetting standard operating procedures and going through unusual channels of communication, Kennedy obtained needed information and avoided bureaucratic bottlenecks. A related Kennedy tactic was to encourage a recalcitrant official's voluntary resignation by hinting that he or she was no longer in favor. Kennedy "would plant newspaper reports that the official was planning to resign. After reading a sufficient number of these reports, the official would grasp what was happening and turn in his resignation" (Berkley 1978).

Richard Nixon practiced yet a fourth strategy, described best by his words to George Shultz when the latter was director of the Office of Management and Budget (OMB):

> You've got to get us some discipline, George. You've got to get it, and the only way you get it, is when a bureaucrat thumbs his nose, we're going to get him.
> . . . They've got to know that if they do it, something's going to happen to them, where anything can happen. I know the Civil Service pressure. But you can do a lot there. There are many unpleasant places where Civil Service people can be sent.

This punitive approach requires a stomach for vindictiveness, because dismissals, forced resignations, and demotions risk adverse publicity and are time-consuming. These obstacles may explain why the common approach is to remove an obstructionist employee by giving him or her a promotion or special assignment to a prestigious-sounding but meaningless position. To "squeeze" an intransigent bureaucrat from a position, the victim is "layered over" by assigning others to perform his or her duties.

President Carter practiced a fifth method by attacking causes instead of symptoms: He proposed to regain control of government by reorganizing it. "We must give top priority to a drastic and thorough revision and reorganizing of the federal bureaucracy." Reorganization attempts have been frequent and were implemented not only by Carter but also Truman, Johnson, Nixon, Reagan, Clinton, and now George W. Bush. Symptomatic of the magnitude of the problem—and indicative of why solutions are so intractable—is the fact that reorganization seldom demolishes existing organizations. As noted earlier, most entrenched bureaucracies have perfected survival tactics: In the words of former Secretary of State James F. Byrnes, the "nearest thing to immortality on Earth is a government bureau." Evidently reorganization (or even what Secretary of the Navy John Lehman termed "deorganization," not greater centralization and unification of authority, but decentralization and greater accountability) is not a final solution. Carter also sought revision of the regulations governing civil servants' employment with the Civil Service Reform Act, which put some 7,000 top bureaucrats into a Senior Executive Service, entitling them to earn bonuses for outstanding job performance but separating them from job tenure (a virtual guarantee of permanent employment). The reform permitted the chief executive and cabinet officers to reassign upper-middle management personnel and, where deemed necessary, to replace those not moving quickly enough or in the right direction. Similar reforms followed in the Foreign Service with the creation of Senior Foreign Service. These innovations augmented the president's managerial capabilities, but they did not guarantee agency responsiveness to presidential orders.

Like his predecessors, Ronald Reagan sought to exercise greater control over the federal bureaucracy. He campaigned for office by openly opposing the government he sought to run, berating its size and promising to reduce, reorganize, and streamline it. "Government is not the solution, it is the problem," Reagan declared in his first inaugural speech. To accomplish these changes, Reagan sought to control the bureaucracy by infiltrating it with political operatives. To gain a top government post candidates were required to pass an "ideological censorship" test (Barber 1985). The number of political appointees increased by a third, from roughly 2,200 to more than 3,300 (Struck 1985). The goal was driven by the perceived need, in the words of Navy Secretary Lehman, "to roll back the accretion of layers of centralized bureaucracy and restore a crisper accountability." In many ways, George W. Bush has approached the problem similarly. His use of appointments to place preferred personnel in management positions, and his establishment of "chief operating officers" in each department and agency—who also form a "President's Management Council" to ensure control—are designed to promote more effective management of bureaucracy.

Vice President Al Gore, point man of the Clinton administration's "reinventing government" initiative launched in 1993, echoed some of Reagan's earlier sentiments. "Our problems don't come from bad workers," he noted. "Rather we have good people trapped in bad systems." The Clinton administration thus proposed energizing the government by cutting red tape, making it more consumer-oriented, eliminating unnecessary programs and consolidating others, and making government workers more productive. The administration's goal, as described by Gore (1993), was to focus "on how well [the government] performs." ***Total Quality Management (TQM)*** became the buzzword. Drawing on the ideas of management consultant W. Edwards Deming, the core idea was to make the government operate more like a business.[13] At the same time, the Clinton plan called for the elimination of some 250,000 federal jobs, a work force reduction of about twelve percent. "We are sympathetic to the idea of more effective but smaller government," Gore declared. "We know that we need a government appropriate for this age of shrunken resources."

The Clinton plan won high praise for its objectives, but many, particularly in Congress, were skeptical of the administration's ability to achieve its lofty goals. Reagan's failure to live up to his promises may have colored their assessments. During Reagan's presidency big government got bigger, as federal spending went up, not down, and budget outlays as a percentage of the GNP rose to peacetime records. Moreover, while reductions in some agencies' personnel were implemented, overall the number of federal civilian and military employees grew by seven percent between 1980 and 1987, from to 4.9 million to 5.3 million. Under Clinton, however, civilian nonpostal employees fell from 2.2 million in 1993 to 1.8 million in 2000, while military personnel fell from just under 2 million to about 1.4 million in the same period. Still, some worried that, even as the number of employees was reduced, bureaucratic red tape remained, perpetuating what some management analysts dubbed "hollow government" (Carney 1994). George W. Bush addressed this problem in his first term, creating the President's Management Council noted earlier, and focusing on down-sizing, privatization, and competition to promote efficiency and effectiveness.

Thus the goal of making the federal bureaucracy responsive to presidential priorities and political preferences remains as elusive as ever. Indeed, whether the federal bureaucracy can be made measurably more tractable is questionable. A key problem is that most presidents serve for only four years, a few eight at most. It is impossible to reform a complex and recalcitrant bureaucracy so quickly. Whether the foreign affairs government's responsiveness and willingness to take direction can be increased thus also remains doubtful. "Those who think we're powerless to do anything about the greenhouse effect," presidential candidate George Bush warned in 1988, "are forgetting about the White House effect. As president, I intend to do something about it." But well into his presidency, Bush learned the power of the "bureaucratic effect" as his "Commerce and Interior departments waged constant guerrilla warfare against any effort to make good on the president's prior commitments" (Talbott 1989).

There exists a long history of failed efforts to control bureaucratic growth and reform the federal bureaucracy even in the face of determined presidential challenges. Arguably this is explained in part by Congress's unwillingness during much of the past half-century to trim federal programs and the agencies that administer them. The Republican Party promised to reverse that posture when it won majority control of Congress in 1994. Although it played a key role in the shift from deficits to surpluses in the federal budget, it had little else to show for its efforts at the beginning of the new century beyond a politically disastrous government shutdown in 1995 and, in the realm of foreign affairs, a modest reorganization of the State Department, the Agency for International Development, and the United States Information Agency (see Chapter 5). Time will tell if the combination of George W. Bush's administration and the Congress fare any better as they seek substantial reorganization of the Defense Department, intelligence community, and "homeland security" agencies in the wake of the September 11, 2001 terrorist strikes against the United States.

Compartmentalized Policy Making and Foreign Policy Inconsistency

Because each foreign affairs department and agency has its own definition of proper goals, the U.S. government sometimes pursues incompatible foreign policies. A former official gives a disturbing recollection of policy inconsistency that bureaucratic competition produced:

The Agency [CIA] supported Indonesian rebels against Sukarno while State was trying to work with Sukarno. It supplied and emboldened the anticommunist Chinese guerrillas in Burma over the protests of the Burmese government and the repeated protestations of the State Department in Washington and our ambassador in Burma that we were doing no such thing. . . . [The CIA] meddled elsewhere, to the consternation of the State Department and friendly governments. In the mid-1950s, its agents intruded awkwardly in Costa Rica, the most stable and democratic country in Latin America. While the agency was trying to oust José Figueres, the moderate socialist who became the Costa Rican president in a fair election in 1953, the State Department was working with him and our ambassador was urging President Eisenhower to invite him to the United States to enhance his prestige. So it went the world around.

(SIMPSON 1967, 103)

Another example is an incident that occurred during the Shah's final days in Iran, which set the stage for the taking of the American embassy and American diplomatic personnel. The American response to the unfolding drama was clouded by a quarrel between the National Security Council staff in Washington and the State Department's representatives in both Teheran and Washington. The divergent views, and the bickering and struggle that followed, led to a tragic outcome. William Sullivan, the U.S. Ambassador to Iran, concluded that the difference in views held by the competing bureaucracies in Washington extended to the "instructions that were sent to the embassy or, more often, to the absence of any instructions whatsoever. . . . By November 1978 [National Security Adviser] Brzezinski began to make his own policy and established his own 'embassy' in Iran." According to Sullivan (1980), the White House ignored his recommendation that, upon the Shah's fall from power, the United States. should not cast its fate with the successor

(Bakhtiar) government because, in his view, it "was a chimera the Shah had created to permit a dignified departure, that Bakhtiar himself was quixotic and would be swept aside by the arrival of Khomeini and his supporters in Teheran." As history records, the ambassador's dire predictions proved correct even while Brzezinski's policy prevailed. Iran fell into revolution, and American diplomats became its victims.

Another example comes from the first Bush administration, when differences about what to do with, for, and about Mikhail Gorbachev generated turf battles and the pursuit of incompatible objectives. While President Bush and Secretary of State Baker spent their time attempting to convince the Soviets (and the American public) that they truly wished Gorbachev's domestic reforms and foreign policy redirection to succeed, Secretary of Defense Cheney and Vice President Quayle publicly proclaimed their reservations about Gorbachev's prospects and peaceful intentions. Meanwhile, a secret team was established in the White House to discredit Gorbachev's credibility. Because the professed goal of "ending the Cold War" was not endorsed by all of the administration's factions, initiatives to end that conflict appeared timid, tardy, and inconsistent (see Beschloss and Talbott 1993).

American policy toward Mexico at the beginning of the new century also illustrates the problem. With an immense range of different agencies involved in various aspects of policy (over forty on drug policy alone), some in several different strands, struggle and inconsistency is virtually unavoidable. As Wiarda (2000) argues, "we do not have a single U.S. foreign policy in Mexico; instead we have approximately sixty-seven policies—one or several policies for each of the U.S. agencies operating there. . . . [T]he bureaucratic politics of U.S.-Mexican relations has now become so complex, so multilayered, so conflicting, that it hamstrings, frustrates, and often paralyzes policy and makes it virtually impossible for the United States to carry out a successful foreign policy

Bureaucratic Consensus-Seeking (groupthink at the extreme)	Indicators	Bureaucratic Confrontation (warfare at the extreme)
Limited	Number of Actors	High
Aligned	Positioning of Interests	Opposed
Closed Arena	Contingent Power Structure	Open Network
Collegial	Interaction by "pulling and hauling"	Competitive
Quick	Compromise Formation	Slow
Low	Implementation Slippage	High

FIGURE 13.1 The Continuum of Bureaucratic Politics

Source: Adapted from Thomas Preston and Paul 't Hart, "Understanding and Evaluating Bureaucratic Politics: The Nexus Between Political Leaders and Advisory Systems." *Political Psychology,* 20 (Spring 1999): 49–98.

there." Focus 13.3 provides another glimpse at the problem of compartmentalization, this time in the context of counterterrorism activities. George W. Bush's solution was to establish an Office of Homeland Security and a Homeland Security Council to pull the disparate agencies together.

Bureaucratic Pluralism and Foreign Policy Conflict and Compromise

Bureaucratic pressures diminish presidents' ability to assert control and lead. Rather than selecting policies from alternative recommendations and turning to the bureaucracy to implement them, presidents often choose among agreed-on bureaucratic solutions and then seek to mobilize their action on the decisions reached.

That image does not conform to the popular view of presidents determining policy goals through rational processes. However, most if not all presidential decisions are affected by the options that bureaucracies offer. Hence, policy determination is more realistically pictured as a product of bargaining through an accommodative, and sometimes conflictual political process. Policy results from competition, compromise, and even conflict, not necessarily the president's priorities. Presidents, rather than deciding, act as "power brokers" who resolve their competing agencies' conflicting demands.

Seen in this way, the nation's chief executive is an arbitrator of interagency disputes, and policy making entails settling jurisdictional struggles. In many ways the captive president's role is primarily to govern by managing his or her own bureaucracy. "The president is beset with too many often conflicting opinions," James Baker observed in 1987 while serving as Reagan's chief of staff. "He spends an inordinate time resolving differences among his advisers who are there because their existence has been legislated." How to get bureau chiefs, assistant secretaries, and agency heads to do what is needed and prevent their rebellion dominates presidents' attention. "Somehow a president must try to make a ministry out of what is at best a coalition" (Lowi 1967). George W. Bush's need to manage disputes between Colin Powell and Donald Rumsfeld is a stark illustration.

As portrayed in Figure 13.1, the result of this organizational setting is a continuum of policy making possibilities that ranges from the *consensus-seeking* characteristics of smaller groups, which sometimes exhibit groupthink, to the *bureaucratic confrontation* characteristic of the bureaucratic rivalries we have highlighted. As the figure suggests, movement along the continuum may be conditioned by any of several factors, including the number of actors involved, the positioning of interests, the contingent power structure, the nature of the "pulling and hauling" that occurs, and others. Presidents must grapple with the forces that pull in either of these directions to avoid the extreme versions of groupthink and turf wars at either end of the continuum.

When viewed from the perspective of the role any president must play, the reasons for compromise, incrementalism, and caution in policy making become apparent. The president is surrounded on a daily basis by advisers, including members of the cabinet, who so interpret their jobs as to make maximum claims on their agencies' behalf. Having heard from one supplicant the extreme of one side of a policy dispute, and then the other extreme from another, the president must forge the terms of settlement.

Permitting foes to save face is also an important part of this game. Because policy making involves constant struggle, with much give and take, "the profusion of so many centers of power makes building the kind of consensus necessary for positive action a formidable task" (Hilsman 1990). Ironically, then, American foreign policy's resistance to adaptive change may flow not from the concentration of power but from its diffusion. The jumble of policy-making centers and increases in their number decrease presidents' capacity to take visionary initiatives. Because policy directions are set through long-established intra- and interagency bargains that reflect an established distribution of influence, policy disruptions are unlikely unless the distribution of influence itself is changed. Perhaps it was this kind of environment that stimulated Dean Acheson's memorable remark that a secretary of state's most essential quality is "the killer instinct."

It is important, however, to remember that the president is not simply another actor in the process (Krasner 1972). When presidents assert themselves, they can prevail. Indeed, the evidence suggests that attentive and engaged presidents are capable of overcoming the most damaging aspects of bureaucratic politics. As Goldgeier (1999) has argued, "If the question is whether policy outcomes inside the executive branch reflect presidential dominance over the foreign policy apparatus or the pulling and haul-

ing of bureaucratic interests, the answer is: when the president gets involved he wins (unless the bureaucracy can get outside actors, for example Congress, to constrain him)." Recently, for example, the drift and stalemate over U.S. policy toward NATO expansion and intervention in Bosnia were largely resolved when President Clinton asserted himself in the process (see Goldgeier 1999; Daalder 2000). Disputes between Secretary of State Powell and other advisers during the first year of Bush's administration were largely resolved by Bush's policy choices: he sided with Defense Secretary Rumsfeld on some issues and Powell on others.

The president also has some key instruments that enable him to overcome the problems we have been discussing. Among the most critical are the White House-centered National Security Council system and interagency process discussed in Chapter 10. The effective use of the National Security Adviser is critical to this ability. Additionally, as former National Security Adviser (to Lyndon Johnson) Walt Rostow observed, "it takes a very strong president to insist that these people get along" (National Security Council Project 1999b). There is no substitute for an attentive president.

Other Effects of Bureaucratic Decision Making

The preceding discussion has identified some of the basic characteristics and consequences of bureaucratic policy-making behavior, but still others are discernible.

Among them is ***ad hoc decision making.*** Preoccupied with each day's immediate crisis, leaders rarely think long-term. Often, they confront only issues that have reached crisis proportions. Critics of the first Bush administration called attention to its penchant for ad hoc decision making, complaining that American policy appeared to react passively to others' decisions or issues as they arose, even at a time when vision seemed most necessary. Bush was not alone, however. As one State Department official described the Carter administration's decision making: "Adhocracy gone mad seemed too often to be the order of the day, with policy careening from crisis to crisis with no more certain guide than the decisions of the moment" (Carter 1981). The unattractive picture suggests policy by improvisation instead of planning. Rather than choices being made in light of carefully considered national goals, trial-and-error responses to policy problems as they surface seem more characteristic. A related consequence of bureaucratic behavior is *decision avoidance*. Most of us think of presidents as decisive—an image presidents willingly cultivate. Harry Truman (1966) put it this way: "The greatest part of the president's job is to make decisions—big ones and small ones. . . . The president—whoever he is—has to decide. He can't pass the buck to anybody. No one else can do the deciding for him. That's his job."

Unfortunately, few presidents adhere to Truman's advice. Many, quite proficient at passing the buck, manage not to decide. "Presidents are, in the eyes of bureaucrats, notorious for putting off decisions or changing their minds. They have enough decisions to make without looking for additional ones. In many cases, all the options look bad and they prefer to wait" (Gelb and Halperin 1973).

The psychological incentives to wait are enormous. Not taking direct action or letting the force of momentum determine policy avoids criticism and opposition. Especially in foreign policy, where the wrong decision can mean the difference between life and death for millions, it is tempting to seek refuge from decision-making burdens by simply denying that a problem exists.

A third potential effect of bureaucratic decision making is the so-called **risky-shift phenomenon**. People deciding in groups are reluctant to appear overly cautious or, worse, fearful. Hence they act differently together than they would alone. For psychological reasons they reach shift-to-risk decisions under peer-group pressure. Thus groups, it has been argued, are usually dominated by their most reckless (and neurotic) member. People will sacrifice themselves for and take chances on behalf of others that they would not normally take when acting for themselves alone. When decision responsibilities are shared, risky alternatives are more likely because no member of the group making the risky decision can be held personally responsible for proposing a policy that produces failure.

Bureaucracy generally encourages caution and restraint, as we have noted. However, when policy making becomes concentrated in the hands of a few, as it is prone to do when the nation faces an external threat, the penchant for caution may be overcome and even reversed. "Madness," Friedrich Nietzsche argued, "is the exception in individuals but the rule in groups."

Still another product of decision making in large, complex organizations is the increased likelihood of *unmanaged policy initiatives*. Some individuals occasionally have the opportunity to take unilateral initiatives. If policy making is really determined at the implementation stage and not at the declaratory stage (when the president or his staff proclaims the policy), then what bureaucrats actually do defines the real policy. In a sense, then, every bureaucrat has the opportunity to be a policy maker. "In the intricate sticky webs of paperwork, the principle of accountability flutters and expires. Responsibility gets diffused; finally it disappears. Everyone is responsible; therefore no one is responsible. It is 'the system'" (Kilpatrick 1985).

A revealing illustration occurred during the Vietnam War. After President Nixon finally declared a cessation of the bombing over North Vietnam in 1972 in the hope of encouraging bargaining concessions from the North Vietnamese, air force General John D. Lavelle took it on himself to order hundreds of pilots to attack North Vietnam. Over a three month period he continued to order dropping the bombs in clear violation of the president's official policy. To the North Vietnamese, not surprisingly, the president's policy proclamation mattered little: American policy had *not* changed.

The covert actions of Lt. Colonel Oliver North in the Iran-contra affair also fit this mold.

FOCUS 13.6   The Bureaucratic Politics of American Policy Toward Mexico

The bureaucratic politics of U.S. Mexican policy-making has now snowballed way beyond Allison's original formulation to encompass dozens of offices, departments, and agencies carrying out hundreds if not thousands of programs. The White House, the president, and the National Security Council are supposed to coordinate all these distinct programs but that is being done ineffectively or so superficially that each agency continues to follow its own route.

- A host of U.S. agencies—primarily domestic affairs agencies—have jurisdictions over and are interested and involved in U.S. policy toward Mexico. . . . [T]hey add to the bureaucratic politics—the jostling and even rivalries among agencies—that has long characterized and often frustrated the successful carrying out of U.S. policy.
- There are more U.S. government agencies assigned to the American Embassy in Mexico than to any other country in the world. . . . The bureaucratic politics of foreign policy making used to be confined to three main, sometimes rival agencies: State, DOD, and CIA. Now it includes more.
- Not only is there often rivalry and bureaucratic politics between cabinet departments, but there are other rivalries within departments—for instance between the army and navy within Defense, between Customs and INS within Treasury, between FBI and DEA within Justice. To say these agencies are not always on the same wavelength would be an understatement.
- Each U.S. agency operating in Mexico conducts a quasi-autonomous policy, which it may coordinate with the ambassador.

- A high priority has been placed on interagency cooperation in implementing policy regarding Mexico. . . . However, there is often less cooperation than meets the eye; the sharing of equipment and resources has not worked out very well, and there is often major, mean-spirited conflict and secrecy among agencies operating in Mexico.
- Virtually every U.S. government agency operating in Mexico is pursuing its own policy there—usually several policies at once, which are often secret, contradictory, and conducted with varying levels of coordination with the ambassador. . . . The United States does not have one single, well-thought-out policy that it arrived at through the rational actor model. Rather it has scores of policies toward Mexico. Ultimately, having so many policies means having no policy at all, and that is both dysfunctional and self-defeating.
- We do not have a single U.S. foreign policy in Mexico; instead we have approximately sixty-seven policies—one or several policies for each of the U.S. agencies operating there. . . . [T]he bureaucratic politics of U.S.-Mexico policy has now become so complex, so multilayered, so conflicting, that it hamstrings, frustrates, and often paralyzes policy and makes it virtually impossible for the United States to carry out a successful foreign policy there.

SOURCE: Howard J. Wiarda, "Beyond the Pale: The Bureaucratic Politics of United States Policy in Mexico," *World Affairs.* 162 (Spring 2000): 174–175f.f.

A gung-ho underling intoxicated with the desire to pursue Cold War confrontation by any means necessary, North "seized upon the 'neat idea' " of making clandestine arms sales to what Secretary of State George Shultz had termed a terrorist regime (the anti–American government of Iran) and using the profits to support the contras, opponents of the leftist Sandinista government in Nicaragua. Moving "under cover," North set up an illegal plan to divert secret funds from the arms sales in order to provide the contras clandestine military support. His operation established a "secret government" or "government within a government" to conduct a "secret war." This "junta" felt it had been forced to manipulate the real U.S. government to get what it wanted because it could not secure public approval or congressional authorization for its action (Draper 1990).

In the end the carefully crafted plan backfired at the same time that it jeopardized basic democratic principles. Convicted of lying to Congress (even though he claimed to have received the tacit approval of President Reagan), North was given a light sentence by presiding Judge Gesell, who, in pronouncing the sentence "reiterated the jurors' view that North was not a leader but a 'low-ranking subordinate' who presumably was not entirely responsible for what he did" (Fitzgerald 1989). His conviction was later set aside by a U.S. Appeals Court.

Finally, one last feature of bureaucratic policy making can be noted: its increasing complexity in today's globalizing world. As Focus 13.6 on U.S. foreign policy toward Mexico suggests, the end of the Cold War and the transition into the twenty-first century have brought substantial changes to the policy environment and issue agenda for American foreign policy. The increasing interconnectedness of societies like the United States and Mexico expands the "complex interdependence" described by Robert Keohane and Joseph Nye (2001) and drives an increasingly "intermestic" policy agenda. The consequence is an expanding array of agencies and interests involved in American foreign policy, with the attendant increase in many of the more negative features of bureaucratic policy making discussed in this chapter. As Howard Wiarda (2000) observes in Focus 13.6, the environment of the new century seems likely to contribute to more bureaucratic politics, not less.

ROLES AND THE PROCESS OF DECISION MAKING: CREDITS AND DEBITS

The impact of role-induced bureaucratic behavior on foreign policy making is seriously at odds with the rational actor model. Although the texts we are likely to read in a high school civics course make historical policy decisions sound

reasonable, the memoirs of past participants in the decision-making process—including presidents—and an objective treatment of the diplomatic record leave quite a different impression. To contemporary eyewitnesses and to others who have later probed the record of events, those happenings often did not look orderly or rational. At times they appear more like scenes from the theater of the absurd. To some, the American foreign policy-making process contributes to its recurrent failures (Etheredge 1985); to others, it makes the United States its "own worst enemy" (Destler, Gelb, and Lake 1984).

Still, we must be careful not to overstate or misrepresent the impact of large-scale organizations on American foreign policy making. "Bureaucrat" need not be a dirty word. (If a bureaucrat is anyone who works for a publicly funded organization at the federal, state, or local level, their numbers are very large indeed!) The negative side of the ledger must be balanced by the clear advantages of modern bureaucracy. In fact, the conduct of American foreign policy would not be possible without a modern bureaucracy and the kind of organizational support career professionals alone can provide. Though deficient in many respects, bureaucratic government is nonetheless indispensable to a great power's practices.

It is not the enormous size of the government that alone makes officials appear to be continually tripping over each other (although that is part of the problem); nor is the propensity for the policy-making system to stumble and blunder due merely to self-serving people (although they contribute to the problem as well). The formidable challenges posed by today's complex, globalizing world make bureaucratic government necessary even as they make it look unresponsive to a changing environment. "Inveighing against big government," observes syndicated columnist George Will, "ignores the fact that government, though big, is often too weak." The solution, therefore, is not to do away with bureaucratic government, but to run it efficiently and shape its power to national purposes. For that, vigorous leadership is required.

In the final analysis, then, bringing out the best that the foreign affairs government has to offer—and preventing the worst that it can produce—rests with the president and his or her principal advisers. But can they make a difference? Or was the eminent sociologist Max Weber correct when he argued, "In a modern state the actual ruler is necessarily and unavoidably the bureaucracy"? To address that question, we must examine the fifth and final source of American foreign policy: individual leaders.

KEY TERMS RELATED TO FOREIGN POLICY DECISION MAKING

ad hoc decision making

bureaucratic captivity

bureaucratic competition

bureaucratic confrontation

bureaucratic politics model

bureaucratic sabotage

consensus-seeking

curator mentality

decision avoidance

groupthink

instrumental rationality

Miles' Law

muddling through

"multiple advocacy"

organizational interests

organizational subculture

paralysis by analysis

parochialism

policy inertia

procedural rationality

rational actor model

rational decision-making model

resistant to change

risky-shift phenomenon

role conceptions

role theory

satisficing

specialization

standard operating procedures

Total Quality Management (TQM)

unitary-actor

unmanaged policy initiatives

value-maximizing choices

SUGGESTIONS FOR FURTHER READING

Allison, Graham T., and Philip Zelikow. *Essence of Decision: Explaining the Cuban Missile Crisis.* Boston: Little, Brown, 1998.

Daadler, Ivo. *Getting to Dayton: The Making of America's Bosnia Policy.* Washington, DC: Brookings Institution, 2000.

Garrison, Jean. *Games Advisers Play: Foreign Policy Advisers in the Influence Process.* College Station, TX: Texas A&M University Press, 1999.

Goldgeier, James M. *Not Whether but When: The U.S. Decision to Enlarge NATO.* Washington, DC: Brookings Institution Press, 1999.

Gordon, Michael, and Bernard Trainor. *The General's War: The Inside Story of the Conflict in the Gulf.* Boston: Little, Brown, 1995.

Janis, Irving L. *Groupthink: Psychological Studies of Policy Decisions and Fiascoes.* Boston: Houghton Mifflin, 1982.

Khong, Yuen Foong. *Analogies at War: Korea, Munich, Dien Bien Phu, and the Vietnam Decisions of 1965.* Princeton, NJ: Princeton University Press, 1992.

McNamara, Robert S. *The Tragedy and Lessons of Vietnam.* New York: Times Books, 1995.

Preston, Thomas. *The President and His Inner Circle: Leadership Style and the Advisory Process in Foreign Policy Making.* New York: Columbia University Press, 2001.

Snyder, Richard C., H. W. Bruck, and Burton Sapin, eds., *Foreign Policy Decision-Making: An Approach to the Study of International Politics.* New York: Free Press, 1962.

't Hart, Paul, Eric Stern, and Bengt Sundelius. *Beyond Groupthink: Political Group Dynamics and Foreign Policymaking.* Ann Arbor, MI: University of Michigan Press, 1997.

NOTES

1. For discussion and analysis of the decision-making on *assertive multilateralism* and the former Yugoslavia, see Sterling-Folker (1998) and Daalder (1994).

2. On *Miles' Law,* see Neustadt and May (1986) and Allison and Zelikow (1999).

3. An interesting exchange on the relative importance of roles, role conflicts, ideas, and interests focused on the preferences and policy behavior of the Chief of Naval Operations may be found in Rhodes (1994) and Mitchell (1999).

4. We are indebted to Scott Crichlow for these points.

5. For studies of the Cuban Missile Crisis, see Allison and Zelikow (1999); Blight (1990); Blight, Nye, and Welch (1987); Blight and Welch (1989); Brugioni (1993); Hilsman (1996); May and Zelikow (1997); and Nathan (1993).

6. This may not be entirely illogical. Anthony Downs (1957) suggests that the rational voter cannot afford to gather all the information available about all candidates prior to deciding for whom to vote: The costs involved are too high for the resultant payoff. Instead, voters base decisions on partial information such as the candidate's party label. Similar logic about the costs of acquiring information apply to a wide array of decision situations.

7. For further discussions of the bureaucratic political model, see Allison (1971); Allison and Halperin (1972); Allison and Zelikow (1999); Brower and Abolafia (1997); Hilsman (1990); Preston (2001); Preston and 't Hart (1999); Rosati (1981); Rosenthal, 't Hart, and Louzmin (1991); and Townsend (1982). For critiques, see Art (1973); Bendor and Hammond (1992); Caldwell (1977); Krasner (1972); Rhodes (1994); and Welch (1992). Recent applications of the model to examine policy decisions include Byrnes (1999); Holland (1999); Jones (1994); Kuperman (1999); Mitchell (1999); Stern and Verbeek (1998); and Wiarda (2000).

8. Some organization theorists note that *new* units within administrative agencies (for example, the State Department's Bureau of Human Rights in the Carter administration) recruit ideologues and risk takers, whereas old ones recruit cautious, security-conscious personnel who are more likely to protect their stakes in the status quo than to express their policy prefer-

ences and push reforms. See also Drezner (2000) on the clash between newer, ideas-based agencies and older, entrenched bureaucracies.

9. More recent formulations of the groupthink model include 't Hart (1990) and 't Hart, Stern and Sundelius (1997).

10. The lessons of the 1930s also led policy makers to conclusions about the appropriateness of interventionist and noninterventionist trade policy regarding manufactured and agricultural goods (Goldstein 1989). The result, as we noted in Chapter 7, is that international trade in the industrial and agricultural sectors developed quite differently.

11. Although this anecdote illustrates graphically the potential ability of bureaucratic agencies to defy political leaders, its historical accuracy has been questioned. For an examination of the events surrounding the account, see Caldwell (1978).

12. The Turkish missiles have long figured prominently in the Cuban missile story. Kennedy was believed to have been intransigent on the issue of trading U.S. missiles in Turkey for Soviet missiles in Cuba, but a transcript of a crucial meeting of the ExCom declassified twenty-five years after the event reveals that Kennedy was more willing to compromise on withdrawal of the U.S. missiles than previously thought. He apparently worried about how he could justify going to nuclear war over missiles his own advisers considered obsolete (Bundy and Blight 1987–1988; see also May and Zelikow 1997).

13. Deming's is "the philosophy of nonhierarchical management style, employee 'empowerment,' and customer satisfaction. . . . The problem with this 'entrepreneurial' model of government, its critics say, is that government is not and should not function like a business. Businesses respond to the bottom line; government is supposed to respond to laws written in the public interest" (Carney 1994). The effort to make government behave more like the private sector actually began during the first Bush administration. Richard G. Darman, Bush's director of OMB, was a primary catalyst behind the 1990 Chief Financial Officers Act, designed to improve government agencies' financial management. For a critical review of TQM as applied to government, see Wieseltier (1993).

PART VII

Individuals as Sources
of American Foreign Policy

Chapter 14
Leader Characteristics
and Foreign Policy Performance

CHAPTER 14

Leader Characteristics and Foreign Policy Performance[1]

If I have learned anything in a lifetime in politics and government,
it is the truth of the famous phrase, "History is biography"—that decisions
are made by people, and they make them based on what they know
of the world and how they understand it.

VICE PRESIDENT GEORGE H. W. BUSH, 1987

One of the most unsettling things for foreigners is the impression that
our foreign policy can be changed by any new president
on the basis of the president's personal preference.

HENRY KISSINGER,
FORMER SECRETARY OF STATE 1979

Picture a president sitting alone in the Oval Office, wrestling with a crisis that threatens the lives of thousands of Americans and non-Americans. Assume that this particular president is impulsively competitive, is prone to act brashly to attract attention, is inclined to take risks to exploit opportunities, views the world as a jungle in which one must perpetually claw and scratch for power, is distrustful of others, is contemptuous of his adversaries, and has a quick temper. Assume also that the president is driven by a fear of failure stemming from low self-esteem, a fear overcome in the past by dramatic and successful actions that restored his self-confidence. How is such a president likely to respond to the crisis he faces? Will he calculate rationally, considering only the interests of the United States? Or will his response be driven by his background, his beliefs, and his personality traits?

Properly speaking, states are incapable of acting or thinking. In reality, foreign policy decisions are made by a remarkably few people acting on behalf of states, most conspicuously the president and the president's inner circle of advisers. "The management of foreign affairs," Thomas Jefferson maintained, is "executive altogether." Harry Truman concurred, exclaiming "I make American foreign policy." For these reasons, the personal characteristics of those empowered to make decisions on behalf of the nation are crucial.

In this chapter we examine individuals as an important source of American foreign policy. We look at the people who occupy the decision-making roles at the highest echelons of government, particularly presidents, and explore whether and how their personal aspirations, anxieties, convictions, memories, and experiences influence American foreign policy.

INDIVIDUALS AS A SOURCE OF FOREIGN POLICY

Because of the president's power and preeminence, it is tempting to think of foreign policy as determined exclusively by presidential preferences and to personalize government by identifying a policy with its proponents. Ralph Waldo Emerson's aphorism, "There is properly no history, only biography," dramatizes the popular impression that individual leaders are the makers and movers of history. This *hero-in-history model*[2] of foreign policy making finds expression in the practice of routinely attributing foreign affairs successes and failures to the administration in which they occurred, not to mention attaching the names of presidents to the policies they promulgate (for example, the Clinton Doctrine, the Kennedy Round). The conviction that the individual who holds office makes a difference is also one of the major premises underlying the democratic electoral system, as new administrations seek to distinguish themselves from their predecessors. Hence leadership and policy are portrayed as synonymous, and changes in policy

and policy direction are often perceived as results of the predispositions of the leadership.

A consideration of the idiosyncratic characteristics of individuals draws attention to the psychological foundations of human conduct. Perceptions, personal needs, and drives are all important determinants of the way people act. Correspondingly, decision makers' inner traits influence how they respond to various situations. The cognitions and responses of decision makers are determined not by "the 'objective' facts of the situation . . . but [by] their 'image' of the situation;" that is, they "act according to the way the world appears . . . not necessarily according to the way it 'is' " (Boulding 1959). That principle correctly suggests that images shape foreign policy behavior.

Perceptions are not simple reflections of what is passively observed. Instead, they are influenced by the memories, values, needs, and beliefs the observer brings to the situation (see Falkowski 1979; Jönsson 1982; Vertzberger 1990). Everyone's perceptions are biased by personality predispositions and inner drives, as well as by prior experiences and future expectations. What occurs in decision makers' heads is therefore important.

As we shift attention from the way issues are debated to the debaters themselves, we must ask if contrasts among decision makers make a difference in policy—in content as well as in style. Do the particular personal qualities of the people holding policy positions determine the course a nation charts for itself in foreign affairs? Or would others holding those positions during the same period have acted similarly? Do changes in leadership stimulate changes in foreign policy? If so, in what ways, and under what conditions? We now turn to these intriguing questions.

INDIVIDUALS AND FOREIGN POLICY PERFORMANCE

No two individuals are identical; each person differs in some way from every other. This personal diversity is exhibited by the major figures in post–World War II American foreign policy. Compare "give 'em hell" Harry Truman, soft-spoken Ike Eisenhower, charismatic Jack Kennedy, "Tricky Dick" Nixon, "down-home" Jimmy Carter, Hollywood "Dutch" Reagan, "preppie" George Bush, and "Slick Willie" Clinton. Apparent differences in policy elites' personalities may nevertheless mask important similarities. The relevant question, therefore, is not how different are the individuals who make American foreign policy, but, instead, what impact do leaders' peculiar traits have on their decision-making behavior.

Although it is difficult to generalize, it is easy to demonstrate that policy makers' personal characteristics influence their behavior, as in-depth case studies of particular decision makers abound.[3] Many probe the life history of policy makers to describe their psychological makeup and world view. These *psychobiographies* invariably assume that leaders' personalities are determined by their early childhood experiences, their relationships with parents and peers, their self-concept, and the like. These background factors are presumed to mold the leaders' personalities and beliefs and their later *decision-making styles* and policy-making behavior.

Psychobiography: Personal Characteristics and Foreign Policy Behavior

Consider the psychological consequences of President Woodrow Wilson's stern and often punitive childhood. Wilson's inability to please his rigid father as a child is hypothesized to have created an all-consuming need in later life to attain self-esteem, which accounts for Wilson's failed approach to the realization of his idealistic policy programs. As president, Wilson compulsively strove to perform great deeds to compensate for his fear of rejection. Most notable was his intense battle to create the League of Nations, a passion explained by Wilson's overriding need to attain a puritanic "state of grace" (George and George 1964).

The first American secretary of defense, James Forrestal, is the object of another illustrative psychobiography (Rogow 1963). Driven and worri-some, Forrestal became obsessed by paranoiac fantasies. He not only feared foreigners but distrusted his own friends and coworkers. His career ended tragically in suicide.

John F. Kennedy The possible relationship between a leader's psychological profile and his or her policy behavior is suggested by investigations of the ways President Kennedy's personality may have been instrumental in the decisions he made during the Cuban missile crisis. According to one (controversial) interpretation (Mongar 1974), Kennedy suffered most of his life from a neurotic conflict between an overpowering fear of failure, on one hand, and an overwhelming need for assistance, on the other. The first stemmed from his inability to compete successfully with his older brother. Joe Kennedy Jr. was introduced by his father to friends as a future president of the United States, and his mother held him up as a model for the other children, especially Jack, giving him a free hand in disciplining them. In that atmosphere it became impossible for Jack to gain recognition and affection from his parents, which undermined the younger Kennedy's self-assurance. A succession of childhood illnesses permitted him to avoid fruitless competition, and he resorted to "the manipulation of fantasy to protect his [preferred self-] image of greatness." Thus self-deception served as a defense mechanism to protect him from his fears of weakness.

Maturity helped young Jack Kennedy strengthen his *self-image*. As his personality took shape, Kennedy still needed to prove his personal worth. His search for adventure, and his restlessness, intellectualism, and acceptance of difficult tasks reflected this abiding compulsion. To protect his preferred self-image, he habitually disarmed criticism "by modestly calling attention to minor shortcomings. This witty self-derision, which reflected a merciless introspection, undermined criticism early and simultaneously elicited reassurance and support from other people." Political problems, even foreign policy crises, became "games," opportunities to recover self-esteem. Kennedy's major decisions, Mongar argues, were shaped by his personal motives.

Is Kennedy's situation unique, or do emotional and personality needs strongly influence other policy makers' responses to foreign policy situations? Consider the case of Henry Kissinger, a decision maker whose extraordinary childhood deviated markedly from the typical route to power.

Henry A. Kissinger Kissinger escaped from Nazi persecution in his native Germany; studied in high school at night while working all day; was drafted into the army; attended college at Harvard; and then became a college professor and served as presidential foreign policy adviser, culminating in his appointment as the first Jewish secretary of state.

Kissinger arguably relied on ideas developed during his early experiences to deal with analogous personal and national problems later in life (Isaak 1975). Personally insecure, yet egocentric, Kissinger felt that uncertainty was the very essence of international politics. He consistently acted as a policy maker on his beliefs, first, that people are limited in what they can do, and second, that because of the complexity of life, many imponderables make history move. Ironically, however, the principle of uncertainty that supported his pessimistic world view may also have been the source of his successes, for Kissinger's achievements may be attributed in part to his ability to use ambiguity, negotiate compromise, and secrecy—as well as public relations strategies ingeniously devised to enhance his image—in his conduct of diplomacy.[4]

Kissinger's embrace of political realism as a theory of international politics also was shaped by his unusual past. *Realpolitik* stresses the expectation of conflict between states, not collaboration, the need to increase power relative to one's adversaries, the inadequacy of moral precepts as a guide to foreign affairs, and distrust of others' motives. Each of these finds a counterpart in the "lessons" Kissinger derived from his personal experiences during the crucial formative period of his political awakening. It seems, then, that Kissinger's disdain of moralism and his corresponding preference to ask not "What is right, and what is wrong?" but "Who is strong, and who is weak?" was rooted in his uncertain, insecure youth.

These brief synopses of Wilson, Forrestal, Kennedy, and Kissinger illustrate the varied personalities of those who have risen to positions of power in the American foreign policy establishment and the impact of their needs, background, and prior experiences on their later outlook and policy-making behavior. We can explore these ideas further by looking specifically at the relationship between presidential character and presidential performance. Here James David Barber's analysis of presidents' personal traits and leadership styles is particularly informative.[5]

Presidential Character: Types and Consequences

According to Barber, presidents can be understood best by observing their "*style*" (habitual ways of performing political roles), "*world view*" (politically relevant beliefs), and especially "*character*"—"the way the President orients himself toward life—not for the moment, but enduringly" (Barber 1992).

Two dimensions of **presidential character** are critical: the energy presidents put into the job (active or passive) and their personal satisfaction with their presidential duties (negative or positive). The first captures presidents' images of their job description. Active presidents are movers and shakers, energetically engaged in the challenge of leading, eagerly attentive to the responsibilities of office, and willing to accept the task of policy formulation and management. Conversely, passive presidents prefer to steer an even course, maintaining existing arrangements and avoiding the conflict that invariably accompanies changes in policy.

The second dimension reflects presidents' levels of contentment with their job. This varies because some presidents have not enjoyed the position they achieved and have looked with disfavor on the burden of awesome responsibility. Such negative types, Barber notes, tend to have had childhood experiences that make them duti-

PERSONAL SATISFACTION

Energy	Personal Satisfaction	
	Positive	Negative
Active	Franklin Roosevelt Harry Truman John Kennedy Gerald Ford Jimmy Carter George Bush Bill Clinton George W. Bush	Woodrow Wilson Herbert Hoover Lyndon Johnson Richard Nixon
Passive	William Taft Warren Harding Ronald Reagan	Calvin Coolidge Dwight Eisenhower

FIGURE 14.1 Barber's Classification of Twentieth Century Presidents by Their Character Type

fully accept but not enjoy the demands that go with holding power.

These two dimensions of presidential character create four categories: passive-negative, passive-positive, active-negative, and active-positive. Barber distinguishes among the four this way: "*Active-positive* presidents want most to achieve results. *Active-negatives* aim to get and keep power. *Passive-positives* are after love. *Passive-negatives* emphasize their civic virtue. The relation of activity to enjoyment in a president thus tends to outline a cluster of characteristics, to set apart the adapted from the compulsive, compliant, and withdrawn types."

Not surprisingly, Barber contends that presidents with active-positive characters are best equipped to direct the nation's foreign policy and to meet its challenges and crises. Active-positives are self-respecting and happy, open to new ideas, and able to learn from their mistakes. Their energies are no longer consumed with conquering the developmental traumas associated with youth but instead are directed outward toward achievement. As policy makers, therefore, active-positives have a greater capacity for growth and flexibility. Figure 14.1 identifies active-positive presidents as well as the other types comprising Barber's typology.

Barber's research shows that the behavior of leaders with similar skills and values can be quite different, depending on their character. A leader's inner self, and especially his or her degree of self-confidence and self-esteem, critically affect performance. Thus personality traits and emotional needs developed during childhood influence all decision makers' careers and conduct. Let us consider some vignettes from Barber's work[6] and then, emulating his methodology, extrapolate from it to assess the character of the nation's forty-second and forty-third presidents, William Jefferson Clinton and George Walker Bush.

Woodrow Wilson An active-negative president, Woodrow Wilson proved incapable of compromising with Senate irreconcilables and others disposed against the League of Nations. "'Accept or reject'—that was the way Wilson posed the question." In the end his "narrow insistence on a failing course of action" cost him what he cherished so deeply.

Warren G. Harding A passive-positive, Harding longed to be America's "best loved" president, but history remembers him as perhaps "'the worst President,' the zero point for all scales of 'presidential greatness.'" He came to power at the end of the first epic struggle of the twentieth century and set aside the national debate on the League of Nations in favor of a "return to normalcy" (read "isolationism") and then initiated the Washington

Conference on Naval Disarmament and related agreements designed to secure peace in the Pacific. But "his early success was based on illusions—illusions that helped to produce the debacle of the 1930s" (Wolfowitz 1994).

Harry S. Truman An active-positive president, Harry Truman took "massive initiatives at a time when such initiatives seemed unlikely, given the circumstances of his accession to office, his own qualifications, and the condition of the country." Why? Many of Truman's bold foreign policy actions—the Truman Doctrine, the Marshall Plan, NATO, and the Korean intervention—arguably stemmed from Truman's decisive personality.

Dwight D. Eisenhower Although Barber submits that Eisenhower is difficult to categorize, he concludes Ike was a passive-negative. Eisenhower "did not feel a duty to save the world or become a great hero, but simply to contribute what he could the best he was able." This was the passive side of his character. The negative side, observes Barber, was reflected in his feelings that he was imposed on by an unnecessarily heavy schedule. Indeed, Eisenhower claimed his heart attack in September 1955 was triggered "when he was repeatedly interrupted on the golf links by unnecessary phone calls from the State Department."

Lyndon B. Johnson Barber concludes that Johnson was, like Wilson, an active-negative president. The "fantastic pace of action in his presidency," motivated by humanitarian concerns and a commitment to the pursuit of happiness and creating a better world, revealed the activism in Johnson's character. The "tough, hard, militaristic" posture he assumed toward his enemies evinced his negativism. A 1952 statement while a member of the Senate, in which he declared that he was "prepared to reduce Moscow to rubble to stop communist aggression anywhere," revealed that side of his character.

Richard M. Nixon An active-negative president, Richard Nixon is a revealing contrast with

Truman and Kennedy. According to Barber, Nixon's decision to widen the Vietnam War by invading Cambodia in the spring of 1970 was symptomatic of this character: "To see in President Nixon the character of Richard Nixon—the character formed and set early in his life—one need only read over his speech on the Cambodian invasion, with its themes of power and control, its declaration of independence, its self-concern, its damning of doubters, and its coupling of humiliation with defeat" (Barber 1977). Nixon reached this critical decision without urging from his advisers, and the manner in which the president announced his decision "flabbergasted" his defense secretary, Melvin Laird. Extreme personal isolation ultimately destroyed the Nixon presidency.

Gerald R. Ford Entering office in the wake of the Watergate scandal and Nixon's resignation, Barber notes that Ford exceeded the low expectations many held for his presidency and showed a capacity to grow and learn. Although "a step-by-step thinker," Ford approached the task of policy making with the positive attitude and activism characteristic of active-positives: "Just as all the props were collapsing in Vietnam, he unrealistically called for hundreds of millions more in military aid. He turned foreign policy over to a wizard of dramatic negotiation [Henry Kissinger] whose ad hoc successes obscured deepening world chaos, and he stood as firm and fast as he could against all sorts of 'wild' schemes to spend the country out of recession, countering them with some tame schemes of his own."

Jimmy Carter Noting that Carter came to Washington full of high expectations at a time of low hopes, Barber predicted that the energetic, "up and at 'em" active-positive Carter would enjoy life in the Oval Office and would find that it could be fun. Barber also warned, however, that Carter's troubles would spring "from an excess of an active-positive virtue: the thirst for results." His prediction proved accurate. Carter's character eventually led him impatiently to pursue too many goals simultaneously—a penchant that lent credibility to the frequent charges that he was inconsistent and indecisive, that he lacked a clear sense of priorities, and that he abandoned policy objectives almost as soon as they were announced in favor of still newer objectives, which then also were shelved.

Ronald Reagan Reagan's personality and ideology reveal inconsistent traits, but his "take-it-easy" style and optimism made Reagan a passive-positive: "the receptive, compliant, other-directed character whose life is a search for affection as a reward for being agreeable and cooperative rather than personally assertive." Several facets of his passive-positive orientation stand out. First, Reagan's aides described him even during crisis situations "as 'uninvolved in the planning process,' 'secluded,' and 'disconcertedly disengaged'" (McElvaine 1984). As one scholar of the presidency recently observed, Reagan "was more dependent than any other modern president on others to accomplish his aims. As a result, the policies of Reagan's presidency were to a large extent a function of the shifting cast of aides who served him" (Greenstein 2000). Moreover, Reagan adhered to a simple "black and white" outlook and was uninterested in facts and unaffected by them (see Dallek 1984; Glad 1983). Finally, Reagan's thirty years of show business, following scripts written and directed by others, instilled a theatrical style in his performance. As he once revealingly commented: "Politics is just like show business. You have a hell of an opening, coast for a while, and then have a hell of a close."

George H. W. Bush Coming to office with a wealth of experience as a public servant—member of Congress, chair of the Republican National Committee, director of the CIA, envoy to China, ambassador to the United Nations, and vice president—George Herbert Walker Bush was an active-positive president. Noting that "Mr. Bush wants a mission . . . [and] sees himself as enlivened and inspired," Barber also worried, however, that "The basic question about Bush . . . is not character, but world view. What is his vision?" (Barber 1989) Many others asked the same question.

Bush himself disparaged "the vision thing," but it dogged his entire presidency. His preference for prudence and pragmatism seemed often to lead to a cautious—indeed, timid—response to the dramatic developments in Europe and the Soviet Union leading to the end of the Cold War.[7] However, Bush's active, hands-on style and character—neatly summed up in his own claim to have the responsibility "to conduct the foreign policy of this country in the way I see fit"—was illustrated in his leadership and style during the Persian Gulf War. Drawing on his extensive contacts with and courtship of world leaders, Bush personally engineered the Coalition that fought the war against Iraq, reflecting a long-standing preference for personal politics (Mullins and Wildavsky 1992). At home his preference for a small, inner circle of advisers chosen on the basis of personal ties and loyalty rather than expertise or independent thinking promoted secrecy that helped to conceal the president's thinking from Congress and the public. This style not only preserved the administration's flexibility, but also enhanced Bush's decision-making freedom.[8]

Bill Clinton On Bill Clinton's first inauguration, Barber wrote that "William Jefferson Clinton is politically active-positive, has strong political skills, and keeps working for what he believes is best" (*The News and Observer,* [Raleigh, NC] 17 January 1993, 10). Educated at Georgetown, Oxford, and Yale Universities, Clinton returned to Arkansas, where he lost a bid for Congress in 1974 but won the attorney general's office two years later. Five terms as governor followed, during which he garnered a reputation for active efforts in political leadership.

As president, in many ways Clinton was an ideal illustration of the active-positive character. His interest in politics and policy was unique among modern presidents, and his energy, enthusiasm, intelligence, and confidence dominated his public career.[9] A self-described "policy wonk," Clinton thoroughly relished a hands-on role in the political and policy process (see, for example, Drew 1994). Furthermore, his philosophy of government stressed activism, if by moderate means. His goal, as he told one of his chief speechwriters in 1998, was "to save government from its own excesses so it can again be a progressive force" (quoted in Weisberg 1999; see also Purdum 1996). Additionally, Clinton had a genuine enthusiasm for the political aspects of the presidency, thriving on the campaigning style adopted by his White House and relishing opportunities for personal contact with advisers, other policy makers, and the public. Intellectually, Clinton also seemed to savor debate and discussion of the ideas underlying policy and democratic governance, as exemplified by his penchant for "seminaring" on policy issues (see, for instance, Drew 1994; Daalder 1994) and his persistent engagement with academic and policy specialists throughout his presidency (see, for example, Barber 2001).

These characteristics and others certainly indicate the active-positive nature of Bill Clinton's character. However, other, frequently less flattering characteristics temper that assessment. There is, for example, Clinton's lack of discipline and tendency toward exaggeration and dishonesty (see Drew 1994; Purdum 1996; Maraniss 1995; Maraniss 1998a). An aspect of this trait is Clinton's well-publicized ability to make everyone believe he had agreed with them without actually doing so. Even during his time as governor of Arkansas, "Clinton began to garner a reputation . . . for slipperiness and waffling in excess of even the norm of politics" (Kelly 1994). Leaving aside the personal implications, in political terms these characteristics complicated his efforts to exercise policy leadership on such issues as Bosnia, Somalia, Haiti, China, and elsewhere. Frequently, promises were made and pledges taken, only to be revised, reversed, or remain unfulfilled. It soon became "the conventional diplomatic wisdom" that "the pledges of the president

of the United States are to be regarded more as well-meaning sentiments than actual commitments" (Kelly 1994).

In the wake of the Monica Lewinsky affair and the impeachment and trial of President Clinton in 1998–1999, these and other aspects of Clinton's character became even more salient.[10] As one of his biographers summed up, these characteristics included:

> His tendency to block things out, to compartmentalize different aspects of his life, to deny reality at times, to keep going no matter what obstacles face him, and to feel a constant hunger for affirmation. Other traits are more familiar to historians and psychiatrists as the generic characteristics of many powerful and ambitious men. These include an enormous appetite for life, a powerful sex drive . . . a lack of normal standards of self-control, an addiction to the privileges of public office and a reliance on aides to shield him from public scrutiny of private behavior.
>
> (MARANISS 1998B, 6)

Indeed, according to one specialist on addictive behaviors, this "Clinton Syndrome" rested on insecurity, low self-esteem and a need for affirmation and reassurance (Levin 1998). None of these is a trait generally associated with active-positive presidents.

Ultimately, Clinton's complex character may have been accurately summed up by his former political adviser, Dick Morris. According to Morris, Clinton was motivated by two inseparable goals: "to accomplish his [policy] agenda while maximizing his political power" (cited in Purdum 1996). As another put it, "Clinton's successes and failures happened because he wanted, more than anything in life, to get to [the White House], and because he wanted this, at least in part, in order to do good—and because the great goal of doing good gave him license to indulge in the everyday acts of minor corruption and compromise and falsity that the business of politics demands" (Kelly 1994).

George W. Bush The first president of the new century is somewhat difficult to classify according to Barber's scheme. By most accounts, George W. Bush's attitude toward the presidency and his duties and toward public service generally are positive, based on a sunny self-confidence and a substantial degree of satisfaction from his pursuits in the political arena. Less clear is his orientation toward the job in terms of his energy and involvement. Bush is almost certainly not passive, as he accepts the challenges of leadership and actively engages in efforts to enact his policy agenda. However, to an unusual degree he also tends to delegate responsibility and to rely on aides and advisers. Furthermore, he is notoriously uninterested in the details of policy or process. Hence, while George W. Bush can be fairly labeled an active-positive president, that description masks some significant differences between him and his recent predecessors. Finally, Bush's approach to the presidency changed somewhat after the September 11 terrorist strikes on the United States.

As James David Barber argues, the roots of presidential character are in the past. For George W. Bush, that past includes a family with an extensive public service record, the challenge of living up to the standard of his father, whose name (mostly) he shares, and the learning experiences offered by a failed business and run for Congress, and a stint as governor of one of the largest states in the country.

In spite of his success at portraying himself as an outsider, not to mention an average citizen, George W. Bush hails from a political family with a tradition of service and more than a little status. On his mother's side, he is a direct descendant of President Franklin Pierce. On his father's side, his grandfather, Prescott Bush, was a U.S. Senator, and his father, of course, had a thirty year political career that culminated in his service as vice president and then president. Consequently, a sense of civic duty (perhaps even opportunity) appears to run deep in George W. Bush and his family (see, for example, Kristof 2000d). As one observer suggested, George W., and perhaps the Bush family, trusts in its competence and management abilities, appearing to believe that "if someone has to run things it should be a Bush" (Bennet 2001).

Many observers have noted how closely the younger Bush's career steps matched those of his father.[11] Like his father, George W. was educated at Andover and then Yale University, where he also followed his father by being inducted into the elite Skull and Bones secret society. Like his father, he entered military service (in the younger Bush's case, the Air National Guard during the Vietnam War), where he became a jet pilot. After earning a master's degree from the Harvard Business School, George W. moved to Midland Texas to begin an oil company (which failed), just as his father had done twenty-seven years earlier. A year later, he ran unsuccessfully for a Texas seat in the United States House of Representatives; his father had successfully captured a seat in 1966 (but failed in a bid for the Senate in 1970). Just as the elder Bush ran successfully for president in 1988, George the younger ran and won in 2000. These parallel tracks have led many to speculate that George W. Bush's efforts are explained by his motivation to fill his father's shoes, or compete with his father's aspirations. It should be noted that, until his successful presidential run, the younger Bush had failed to match his father in each of these steps: the elder Bush did better in school, flew in combat, ran a successful oil company, and won a seat in the House of Representatives.

The comparison perhaps explains some of the other characteristics of George W.'s first forty years. By most accounts, the younger Bush showed little interest in public affairs or a political career until his unsuccessful run for the House seat. For example, a Yale classmate stated "If I had to go through my class, and pick five people who were going to run for president, it would never have occurred to me he would ever run" (Romano and Lardner 1999a). Indeed, George W. seems to have largely ignored the leading political issue of his time, namely Vietnam, instead developing a reputation in college and after as "a rabble-rouser of sorts" (Kristof 2000a), an undisciplined "Bombastic Bushkin" devoted to good times and parties (Romano and Lardner 1999a). If not an alcoholic, he was at least a frequent heavy drinker. Living up to the high standards and achievements of his father was difficult, generating a relationship some have characterized as "a shadow, a competition, [and] an opportunity" all at once (Romano and Lardner 1999a). Only at his fortieth birthday in 1986 did he break this pattern; since then George W. claims to have stopped drinking entirely.

That date also marks the beginning of his second effort at his own political career. First he served as an informal adviser and guardian of his father's presidency, acting as the elder Bush's "pit bull" to enforce loyalty (it was, for example, George W. who confronted his father's chief of staff, John Sununu, with the news that he would have to resign after the imperious Sununu had overstepped his authority one too many times) (Verhovek 1998). After advising his father during the painful 1992 electoral loss to Bill Clinton, the younger Bush defeated incumbent Texas Governor Ann Richards in 1994, and then won reelection in 1998 with sixty-nine percent of the vote, catapulting himself into the hunt for the Republican presidential nomination. After locking up the party's nomination in the summer of 2000, George W. successfully defeated Al Gore (in the electoral college), the sitting Vice President, to become the forty-third president of the United States.

This quick review of George W. Bush's past suggests that he has grown from an undisciplined, disinterested citizen to a more disciplined, focused leader. His campaigns in 1994, 1998, and 2000, along with his time in office in both Texas and Washington, DC, reveal him to be an enthusiastic, "methodical, disciplined candidate and officeholder" (Bennet 2001). Many aspects of his presidential character clearly support the placement of Bush into the active-positive category.

As we noted earlier, active-positives tend to be happy and self-respecting, open to new ideas, and able to learn from their mistakes, which

seems to characterize the forty-third president. For Bush, there is, first, his energy, enthusiasm, and charisma, which he has used to great effect as both governor and president. These characteristics also assisted him as he led the U.S. response to the September 2001 terrorist attacks (see Thomas and English 2001; Cohen 2001; Gellman and Allen 2001). Moreover, there is his deep reservoir of self-confidence—some say even arrogance—that supports him in all his efforts. A journalist characterized this trait as follows: "He is a cheery guy whose success has arisen not from self-doubt but from self-confidence, and when setbacks have arisen he has normally shrugged and moved on" (Kristof 2000c). Not only has this trait enabled Bush to accept compromise, and even defeat, but it has also made him comfortable in surrounding himself with high-quality, formidable advisers without fear that they will outshine him (Kristof 2000d). His self confidence was also apparent in his style as he rallied America and the world after the terrorist strikes (Thomas and English 2001; Gellman and Allen 2001). Bush also has relied on his extroverted personality and substantial charisma to garner support and achieve results. Furthermore, he has apparently learned from his failings, both in his personal life and in his political efforts (for example, the failed campaign for Congress and his father's failed campaign for the presidency in 1992).

In his public career since 1994, George W. Bush has also been focused and agenda-driven, holding fast to a set of priorities and managing his time and staff to see them realized. In his campaign for governor in Texas in 1994, for example, Bush ran on a four-part agenda (education reform, juvenile justice, welfare reform, and tort reform) unified by an emphasis on economic opportunity and development (Bennet 2001). As governor, he zeroed in on that agenda and devoted himself to applying his prodigious personal skills at "wooing legislators, the public, and the news media" in order to enact his agenda (Kristof 2000e). As president, he initally adopted a similar approach, emphasizing a relatively narrow range of issues and pressing for what he believed to be necessary changes from the policies of his predecessor (Walsh 2001; Bush 2001). After September 11, he shifted his administration, structure and all, to focus on the new war on terrorism (Allen and Sipress 2001; McManus and Gerstenzang 2001).

According to a White House aide, as a "conviction politician . . . the thing that is most gratifying to him is to be able to effectuate [his preferred] solutions" (Walsh 2001). This has required not only policy advocacy but also a willingness to compromise when necessary. Bush has shown that as both governor and president.

Additionally, Bush has usually insisted on a disciplined, organized structure and process that keeps his staff tightly focused on his themes and preferences. At an early meeting in his presidential life, for example, he chastised late-arriving aides by noting that "this is the on-time administration." Consistent with his Harvard Business School training, Bush has stressed a corporate model, with himself as the chair of the board. "Good management," he has said, "makes good politics." Announcing several nominees in January 2001, for example, Bush stressed the importance of recruiting good people, delegating responsibility, and holding them accountable, leaving himself free to concentrate on the "big picture." While aides stress that he "is very engaged" (Walsh 2001), they also acknowledge Bush's embrace of "a Reagan-style assertion of a chief executive's responsibility to dictate broad principles and then delegate minor matters" (Kristof 2000e). After September 11, however, Bush relied on a more "improvisational administration" (Milbank and Graham 2001) to respond to the challenges of the new war on terrorism (see Chapter 10).

In spite of this obviously positive and generally active character, there are indications that George W. Bush is different from other active-positive presidents. First, his "corporate" style of leadership and management has the effect of distancing him from the hands-on, day-to-day politics and policy process. George W. Bush is, simply put, not detail-oriented. Throughout his

2000 presidential campaign, for example, Bush frequently joked that he rarely read past the executive summary of any policy report or analysis. As president, he has kept what observers have critically characterized as "banker's hours," with frequent weekend holidays, a pattern that also held when he was governor of Texas. Others have described a "new phase in his own role," one with more vigor and public profile, but not necessarily a more detail-oriented approach (Engel 2001). Not only does this qualify the "active" designation, but it may involve political consequences in terms of public perceptions of his leadership. One observer noted that "the American public may not be as indulgent toward a fifty-something president who keeps banker's hours as it was to an ancient king like Reagan" (Bennet 2001).

Second, his preference for linear thinking, careful planning, tight time management, and focused attention on specific issues has led him to take a less visible role in many areas. Bush's self-avowed commitment to "the big picture" has led him to eschew the spotlight offered by many national and international developments (quite unlike his predecessor, who rarely missed a chance to take center stage). As presidential scholar Fred Greenstein has commented, "It's almost as if he doesn't realize that the president is the symbolic leader of the nation" (quoted in Harris 2001). Preferring to stay "on message," Bush therefore ignores opportunities to exercise symbolic leadership, which is generally inconsistent with active presidents. After September 11, this tendency revealed itself in Bush's focus on the war on terrorism to the exclusion of other domestic issues. Presidential counselor Karen Hughes agreed that "you won't find him issuing proclamations on every subject, and proudly so, because he wants to reserve his capital to use it where it helps implement his agenda" (Walsh 2001). However, a Republican strategist has suggested that Bush runs the risk of marginalizing himself and his leadership: "Americans expect their president to be more front and center, more activist than Bush has been" (quoted in Walsh 2001).

Finally, his philosophy of government differs from that of most active-positive presidents. Unlike Bill Clinton, for example, whose basic faith in the ability of government to promote social progress pervaded his public career, Bush embraces a more limited conception, which works against his inclination to actively address the nation's problems. In his words, "there's too much focus on central government. . . . The role of government is to free people to make decisions and choices on their own. There is a role for government, but it is to create an environment in which entrepreneurship can flourish." Hence, while George W. Bush is best characterized as an active-positive, he bears some striking similarities to the more passive-positive character of Ronald Reagan.

Leadership and the Impact of Leadership Styles

Leaders' personalities impact foreign policy performance in many ways, ranging from grand designs to their choice of advisers and way they organize their advisory systems. Alexander George (1988), for example, describes three different approaches presidents have evolved for managing the tasks they all face of mobilizing available information, expertise, and analytical resources for effective policy making: the formalistic, competitive, and collegial models. In a *formalistic model,* clear lines of authority minimize the need for presidential involvement in the inevitable politicking among cabinet officers and presidential advisers; in the *competitive model,* the president purposely seeks to promote conflict and competition among presidential advisers; and in the *collegial model,* teamwork and group problem solving are sought, with the president acting like the hub of a wheel with spokes connecting to individual advisers and agency heads. What approach a president chooses and how it operates in practice will be shaped by the president's personality: by his or her cognitive style (analogous

to world view), sense of efficacy and competence, and general orientation to political conflict.

Building on these and related ideas, Margaret G. Hermann and Thomas Preston (1999) argue that the authority patterns presidents use in dealing with their advisers derive from three fundamental factors: (1) the degree to which presidents want to be *involved* in the foreign policy making process based on their prior experience, which reflects their foreign policy interest and expertise; (2) the extent to which they believe they can *control* that process, which affects their tolerance for conflict among their advisers as policy goals are pursued; and (3) their *sensitivity* to the context in which policy choices must be made, which affects the kinds of information they will seek as they weigh policy options. The interactions among these three concepts reveal an eight-fold typology of possible foreign policy advisory systems. The typology collectively "indicates a kind of relationship between the president and the his [or her] advisers based on the president's leadership style" (Hermann and Preston 1999). The typology is shown in Figure 14.2 with examples in each cell.

Figure 14.3 in turn summarizes the presidential advisory systems associated with the leadership styles depicted in Figure 14.2. It suggests several interesting variations:

Presidents' advisory systems are more hierarchical and formal the higher the president's belief that what happens can be controlled. There is more centralization of authority in the president. Advisers' input to problem definition, options generalization, and planning is more valued the more sensitive the president is to the political context, while there is more emphasis on advisers who share the concerns, vision, and ideology of presidents who are less sensitive to the political context. The advisory systems are more open to outside influences the more sensitive and responsive the president is to contextual information (Hermann and Preston 1999).

FOCUS 14.1   Responding to Terrorism: The Shifting Approach of George W. Bush.

Lyndon B. Johnson chose bombing targets in Vietnam. George [H. W.] Bush rallied a Gulf War coalition but neglected the home front. Bill Clinton soaked up every detail of Bosnia and Kosovo.

What kind of war president is George [W.] Bush turning out to be? . . . [T]he president as CEO, delegating some roles to more-experienced advisors but keeping others to himself. In military planning, Bush has set the basic course but left much of the detailed work to a powerful—and sometimes divided—war cabinet. In diplomacy, he has hit the telephones with the diligence his father showed during the Persian Gulf War, talking with more than two dozen foreign leaders.

As chief salesman for his newly declared war on terrorism, Bush has spoken in public every day but one since Sept. 11, [2001] sometimes even eloquently—a switch for a man who long preferred one-on-one politicking to speechmaking.

And in domestic policy, Bush is about to turn attention to the slumping economy and education reform for the first time since the terrorist attack on New York and the Pentagon—mindful of charges that his father ignored domestic concerns. Still, the war will come first.

"This is now the focus of my administration," Bush has said, both publicly and privately.

Indeed, the unsought challenge of terrorism has given the president, whose domestic political agenda and popularity were eroding before Sept. 11, a new and clearer purpose.

Aides describe a decision-making process that is settling into an intense but regular routine: The National Security Council, which once met perhaps twice a month, now meets twice a day. The war is now "our normal state of being," one weary aide said.

Bush's daily schedule has been remade to reflect the new reality. He still arrives in the Oval Office at 7:00 A.M. and gets his customary intelli-

gence briefing from CIA Director George J. Tenet at 8:00 A.M. But he now also has a daily FBI briefing at 8:30 A.M. on the investigation into the terrorist networks that planned the attack. After that comes a regular 9:00 A.M. "Communications meeting" with political advisors Karen Hughes and Karl Rove. Later in the day come meetings of a new "domestic consequences" group of the war's effort on the home front, and a variety of other events.

But the main decision-making event is a 9:30 A.M. meeting of the full NSC: Bush, Vice President Dick Cheney, Secretary of State Colin L. Powell, Defense Secretary Donald H. Rumsfeld and National Security Advisor Condoleezza Rice, backed by a roomful of aides.

The same group, minus the president, meets again every evening in what is called a "principal meeting" to review the day's action and plan for the next 24 hours. Bush has used the morning NSC meetings to hear his Cabinet members hash out their debates on basic policy questions; one aide said it is a kind of crash course in counterterrorism options and a departure from the way he handled most earlier foreign policy decisions . . .

Normally, Cabinet members work though an issue at length, brief the president on their areas of agreement and offer him a few clear choices on issues where they disagree. But this time Bush has been more deeply engaged, aides say.

"From the very beginning, the president decided he wanted to chair the NSC meetings . . . because I think he didn't want a process where options were coming up to him, where we had said 'A thinks this, B thinks this, the consensus positions would be this,' " said one official who has attended.

Source: Doyle McManus, James Gerstenzang (and Times Staff Writers). 2001. "After the Attack; The Strategy: Bush Takes CEO Role in Waging War." *Los Angeles Times.* September 23, 2001, p. A1.

Presidents Clinton and the senior Bush illustrate aspects of the ideas summarized in Figures 14.2 and 14.3 (Hermann and Preston 1999). Bush, for example came to the White House with extensive foreign policy experience. Hence he largely ignored domestic policy (to his detri-

ment, as we saw in Chapter 8), choosing instead to concentrate on foreign policy issues. Bush generally preferred a collegial style relationship with his staff; indeed, as we saw in Chapter 10, loyalty was highly prized during his administration. Hermann and Preston also note that Bush

				Prior Experience in Foreign Policy Making	
				High	Low
Belief Can Control What Happens	**High**	Sensitivity to Context	Low	Direct (Nixon)	Arbitrate (Truman, Johnson[a])
			High	Guide (Eisenhower)	Coordinate (Carter, Clinton)
	Low	Sensitivity to Context	Low	Strategize	Monitor (Reagan[a])
			High	Consult (Kennedy, G.H.W. Bush[b])	Delegate (G.W. Bush)

[a]President's score was at or near mean for group on belief can control what happens.
[b]President's score was at or near mean for group on sensitivity to political context.

FIGURE 14.2 Proposed Influence of Presidential Leadership Style on their Advisory Process Based on the President's Leadership Style

Note: Presidents are placed in the cells on the basis of a "personality-at-a-glance technique." For details see Hermann 1987b; Hermann 1987c. Source: Margaret G. Hermann and Thomas Preston, "Presidents, Leadership Style, and the Advisory Process," updated by the authors from Eugene R. Wittkopf and James M. McCormick, eds., *The Domestic Sources of American Foreign Policy*, 3rd ed. Lanham, MD: Roman & Littlefield, 1999, 357. Updated by the author from Hermann and Preston.

became less sensitive to the political context and less inclusive of his advisors when he was under pressure and "the more he perceived a threat not only to the policies of his administration but to policies important to his political well-being and place in history." We also know that Bush could personalize issues, as during the crisis leading to the Gulf War. When backed into a corner, he personalized the situation, "tending to see the world in black and white terms. . . . Bush became a man with a mission wanting advisers who also shared his perspective on the problem. . . . Only advisers who had his vision concerning what was happening were included in the inner circle."

In contrast to Bush, Clinton chose to focus on domestic, not foreign policy. This led him to appoint people to staff positions and cabinet posts with foreign policy expertise, but also none who would eclipse his own power and authority. Clinton was notorious for deciding not to decide.

As we saw in Chapter 10, "talkathons" were commonplace, especially during his first term. (Interestingly, Clinton spoke admiringly of his successor's ability to run a tight ship and to keep everything on schedule.) Clinton was also the consummate politician. This meant that while he chose advisors with expertise, he also preferred those politically attuned to the issue at hand. Clearly Clinton was a successful politician. He was the first Democratic president to win reelection since Franklin Roosevelt. And he weathered his impeachment trial and assorted other charges lodged against him and other members of his administration.

As Focus 14.1 suggests, George W. Bush's style is a work in progress. Initially, he preferred a more detached, structured approach consistent with a corporate model or a CEO style. For example, his early (and relatively rare) NSC meetings tended to be structured around short

Focus of Policy Coordination	Authority Pattern	
	Formal	**Informal**
Focus on Political Process	• Loyalty Important • Advisers Used as Sounding Board • Interested in Focusing on Important Decisions • Interested in Evaluating Rather Than Generating Options • Leader-Dominated Group-Think Possible • Procedures Well-Defined and Highly Structured	• Advisers Seen as Part of Team • Sharing of Accountability • Group Cohesion is Valued • Advisors Provide Psychological Support • Options Sought that Minimize Conflict and Disagreement
Focus on Substance of Problem	• Select Advisers Who Share Cause/Concern/ Ideology • Advisers Seen as Implementors and Advocates • Advisers Tailor Information to Fit Biases • One or Two Advisers Play Gatekeeper Roles for Information and Access • Decisions Shaped by Shared Vision • Disagreements Center on Means Rather Than Ends	• Wants Experts as Advisers • Advisers Seen as Providing Information and Guidance • Open to Using Bureaucracy to Get Information • Time Spent on Generating Options and Considering Consequences • Seeks "Doable" Solution to Problem • Disagreement is Valued

FIGURE 14.3 The Influence of Presidential Leadership Style on the Selection and Organization of Advisers

Source: Margaret G. Hermann and Thomas Preston, "Presidents, Leadership Style, and the Advisory Process," updated by the authors from Eugene R. Wittkopf and James M. McCormick, eds., *The Domestic Sources of American Foreign Policy*, 3rd ed. Lanham, MD: Roman and Littlefield, 1999, 360.

summaries of adviser positions and presentations of a few previously agreed-upon options for Bush to consider. After the September 11 attacks on the United States, Bush adopted a less formal style and structure, a more engaged and active role for himself, and a more free-wheeling discussion and debate. On foreign policy, at least, Bush's initial style gave way to a more informal approach (Allen and Sipress 2001). However, Bush has consistently stressed delegation, preferring to concentrate on the bigger picture. As observers have noted, Bush continued his preferred management style: "Once the strategy was ordained, the execution of the war [was] left, to a remarkable extent, in the hands of the military" (Engel 2001). As Focus 14.1 suggests, Bush continued to rely on the CEO approach, "delegating some roles to more-experienced advisors but keeping others to himself" (McManus and Gerstenzang 2001).

Why are some leaders successful and others not? Presidential scholar Fred Greenstein (2000) argues that successful modern presidencies have rested on a president's communication skills, effective organization, political skills, vision, cognitive style, and emotional intelligence. David Gergen (2001), who has worked for and observed presidents since Nixon, argues that the "must-have list" includes personal integrity, a sense of mission, the ability to persuade, the ability to work with other politicians, skilled advisers, the ability to inspire, and a successful "honeymoon period" after inauguration.

Historian Garry Wills (1994a; 1994b; see also Hermann 1986) argues that followers are essential to leaders (their "first and all-encompassing need") and suggests that leaders and followers must share a common goal. "Followers do not submit to the person of the leader. They join him [or her] in pursuit of the goal" (Wills 1994b). The effective leader, then, "is one who mobilizes others toward a goal shared by leader and followers." In part, then, successful presidential leadership is determined by how presidents respond to the demands and expectations of presidential advisers, the departments and agencies that make up the foreign affairs government, Congress, other world leaders, and, of course, the electorate. In a democracy, Wills argues, this often means an effective leader must defer to the demands of public opinion and abandon principle for the sake of compromise—actions typically held in low regard but perhaps necessary to sustain followership, without which leaders cannot exist and leadership be sustained.

Others, however, are seemingly uncomfortable with this viewpoint, particularly when it comes to foreign policy and interactions with other nations, friend and foe. Henry Kissinger (1994a), a distinguished political historian as well as former policy maker, urges in his book *Diplomacy* that power, principle, and analytical thinking are the bedrock of successful foreign policy leadership throughout history. He specifically disparages modern political leaders "who measure their success by the reaction of the television evening news," which makes them prisoners of "the purely tactical, focusing on short-term objectives and immediate results."

THE IMPACT OF INDIVIDUALS' PERSONALITY AND COGNITIVE CHARACTERISTICS

Another way to assess the impact of individuals' personal characteristics on their foreign policy behavior is to investigate which behaviors and preferences are associated with particular personality traits and related beliefs. Individuals can be described using a variety of personal characteristics. The following eight concepts are among those that have been linked to the foreign policy attitudes, beliefs, and behavior of foreign policy elites.

- *Nationalism:* a state of mind that gives primary loyalty to one state to the exclusion of other possible objects of affection (such as other countries, family, or transnational entities like the European Union or a religion). Nationalists glorify their own state and exaggerate its virtues while denigrating others. Because nationalists develop an ego involvement with their own state, they tend to defend its acclaimed right to superiority (Stagner 1971)

- *Need for power:* an individual's need to have influence or prestige when interacting with others. This basically connotes the level of one's need for control over others. Political leaders with a high need for power typically hold strong nationalist sentiments (Hermann 1980; Hermann 1984). They also are more likely than others to engage in aggressive behavior. Thus different presidents' need for power has been found to predict to whether or not the United States engaged in war during their administrations (Winter 1987)

- *Need for affiliation:* an individual's level of concern with maintaining friendly relationships with others. The felt need for interpersonal warmth may affect foreign policy decision making in several ways. Leaders with a need for affiliation rely more than others on the opinions of friends than on those of experts (Winter and Carlson 1988). Additionally, individuals concerned with maintaining friendly relationships prefer to engage in cooperative relations with other states rather than pursue tougher policy options. A concern with cooperation and friendship, however, may also a cause leader to respond aggressively if he or she feels betrayed by a friend (Winter 1993)

- *Need for achievement:* an individual's level of concern with attaining excellence in whatever the person does. Political leaders with a high need for achievement are often motivated by a desire to make a favorable impact on history. This heightened concern affects foreign policy decision making by making leaders who experience it more likely to rely on the advice of experts when making policy decisions (Winter and Stewart 1977). It also increases their willingness to take risks if they see opportunities to leave a positive imprint on world events (McClelland 1961)

- *Distrust of others:* a personality characteristic that reflects an individual's suspicion of the motivations and actions of others. Individuals distrustful of others are reluctant to make commitments. Thus they are wary of the risks involved in engaging in cooperative international behavior and skeptical of its potential benefits. Distrustful leaders also typically embrace nationalist sentiments and tend to have an exaggerated need for power (Hermann 1980)

- *Conceptual compexity:* how leaders structure their views of the world. Those who see a great deal of ambiguity in their surroundings and believe that multiple factors explain particular events are more "conceptually complex" than leaders who see the world around them in terms of a few clearly defined characteristics. Those high in complexity generally see many possibilities and believe they can be flexible in their reactions to events, while those low in complexity usually prefer either–or choices (Hermann 1987). Less conceptually complex leaders see themselves as having comparatively few policy options and thus are more likely than more conceptually complex leaders to adopt conflictual policies (Hermann 1980; Hermann 1984; Hermann and Hermann 1989). They also are generally more likely than conceptually complex leaders to take risks and to test accepted norms of international behavior (Hermann and Kegley 1995). Fur-

thermore, variation in conceptual complexity leads to different advisory systems and structures (Preston 1997; Preston 2001). Interestingly, one study focusing on Civil War military leaders also suggests that the relative conceptual complexity of opposing battlefield commanders may predict which side will prevail in battle (Suedfeld, Corteen, and McCormick 1986)

- *Analogies.* Political leaders frequently structure their understanding of the world by relying on their interpretations of the **lessons of the past** (Neustadt and May 1986). They typically see current situations as analogous to previous events, essentially equating them with previous circumstances they perceive common to both. They then take the "lessons" they learned from the outcome of an earlier situation and use them as guides when making decisions dealing with the new, seemingly similar event. But which past events are deemed relevant to the new situation and the lessons an individual associates with those events depends critically on that person's perceptual lens. So determining which analogy someone chooses can provide important insight into his or her behavior (Jervis 1976; Khong 1992). As we have seen in previous chapters, "Munich" and "Vietnam" are popular analogies, and they can lead to quite different foreign policy choices.

- ***Operational Codes:*** a construct that includes several different personal characteristics relating to individuals' views about fundamental factors affecting the course of world affairs. Taken together in the form of an operational code, these provide insight into a person's basic beliefs about how the world operates (George 1969; Walker, Schafer, and Young 1998). Operational codes include an individual's beliefs about the basic nature of the person's (policy maker's) political environment. Does he or she see the world as basically cooperative or conflictual? Can an individual make an impact on history? Or is the course of world events beyond one's control? Those beliefs also include the individual's preferred foreign policy strategies and tactics. Does the person (policy maker) believe that engaging in cooperative acts is the most effective way to attain one's goals? Or does he or she prefer to rely on the use of threats?

Analyses of political leaders' operational codes show that they have an important influence on their own behavior (Holsti 1970; Johnson 1977; Starr 1984), and in some cases on their country's foreign policy behavior as well. One study of U.S. policy during the Vietnam War found that changes in American tactics over time closely mirrored predictions based on the operational code of Henry Kissinger (Walker 1977). Another found that changes in the foreign policies of the Carter administration reflected changes in Carter's operational code while he was president (Walker, Schafer, and Young 1998).

These eight concepts illustrate how individuals' personality traits and cognitive characteristics may influence foreign policy behavior. The list is not exhaustive, and some of these factors can work in tandem with others to affect leaders' behavior. But knowledge of these characteristics is important as they provide insight into leaders' policy choices when faced with particular international events. To illustrate how a leader's personal characteristics may influence his or her policy preferences, we turn to a well-known example.

John Foster Dulles and the Soviet Union

According to an authoritative interpretation (Holsti 1962), former Secretary of State John Foster Dulles's behavior toward the Soviet Union was driven by his prior beliefs rather than by Soviet conduct. "Built on the trinity of atheism, totalitarianism, and communism, capped by a deep belief that no enduring social order could be erected upon such foundations," his belief system was predicated on three strong convictions: (1) the Russian people were basically good, but Soviet leaders were irredeemably bad; (2) Soviet national interest, which sought to preserve the state, was good, in contrast with the implacably

bad, atheistic international communism; and (3) the Soviet state was good but the Communist Party was bad.

What were the sources of Dulles's beliefs? His perceptions were shaped in part by his childhood experiences, his relationship with his parents and his peer groups, and his psychological needs and personal predispositions—his basic personality. Dulles came from a celebrated, well-connected elite background that boasted two previous secretaries of state. He presumably inherited his moralistic, evangelic attitude toward most issues from his father, a stern Presbyterian minister. John Foster Dulles was perhaps the most unabashed moralist ever to sit in the office of the secretary of state (Barnet 1972); for him the purpose of policy was the pursuit of morality. He believed that the Cold War was essentially a moral rather than a political conflict. In his mind, the "insincere," "immoral," and "brutal" Soviet leadership was hateful because its creed was "godless." Two universal faiths competed, one good and the other evil.

Other aspects of Dulles's background also may have affected his later outlook. For instance, his early training and practice in business law may have inculcated an aggressive "can do" attitude, "an inspired ability to calculate risks and gamble on them," and a habit of mind that "carried over into his diplomacy, where countries 'were all instinctively rivals and opponents of his own client, America'" (Barnet 1972). Moreover, Dulles "was never in touch with people who knew hunger, poverty, or personal failure. Believing in addition that everyone must make the most of themselves in life and that those who do not have something wrong with them, he never seriously tried to understand the people whose misfortune it is to get left on the bottom rungs of the ladder" (cited in Barnet 1972).

As secretary of state, Dulles's rigid, doctrinaire beliefs and personality traits predetermined his reactions to the Soviets and led him to distort information so as to reduce any discrepancies between his knowledge and his perceptions (Holsti 1962). Dulles's psychological need for image maintenance led him to reject all information that conflicted with his preexisting belief that the Soviet Union could not be trusted. Friendly Soviet initiatives were seen as deception rather than true efforts to reduce tension. For example, Soviet military demobilizations were attributed to necessity (particularly economic weakness) and bad faith (the released men would be put to work on more lethal weapons). Similarly, the Austrian State Treaty—a Soviet initiative for the withdrawal of Soviet and American occupation forces from Austria in return for the promise that the Austrians would maintain a policy of neutrality in the East-West dispute—was explained as Soviet frustration (the failure of its European policy) and weakness (their system was "on the point of collapse") (Holsti 1962). Thus, in Dulles's image, the Soviets could do only harm and no good. If they acted cooperatively, it was either because they were dealing from a position of weakness or because they were trying to deceive the United States into a position of unpreparedness. When they did anything bad, it supported Dulles's prior image that the Soviets were incapable of virtuous behavior. The Cold War policies of John Foster Dulles, we may reasonably conclude, were derived from his entrenched negative beliefs—what Henry Kissinger (1962) termed an *"inherent bad faith"* model of the Soviet leadership.

Dulles's inflexible image and unwillingness to accept any uncomfortable information was reinforced by his extreme faith in his own judgment and lack of respect for that of others, whom he regarded as his inferiors. Dulles felt "he was uniquely qualified to assess the meaning of Soviet policy. This sense of indispensability carried over into the day-to-day operations of policy formulation, and during his tenure as secretary of state he showed a marked lack of receptivity to advice" (Holsti 1962).

Other Examples

The Dulles example makes a convincing case for the influence of individual variables on policy behavior, for it seems clear that Dulles's foreign policy behavior was firmly rooted in his belief system and personality traits. Other examples also reinforce that conclusion.

Madeleine Albright, the first women secretary of state, is another interesting example of a powerful person whose personality and socialization experiences colored her foreign policy approach. As illustrated in Focus 14.2, Albright's experience as a young refugee from the dictates of Stalinist Russia and Nazi Germany appears to have profoundly shaped her career choices and especially her beliefs about how the United States should respond to the Balkans' crises when they were beset by civil conflict and ethnic cleansing during her tenure as U.S. ambassador to the United Nations and, later, secretary of state.

Henry Kissinger was also a victim of Nazi Germany. The impact of that experience is not entirely clear, but celebrated elements of his personality were revealed during his tenure at Foggy Bottom. They included his need for personal acceptance, his reputed distrust of democratic foreign policy, his intolerance of dissent, his insistence on secrecy, his "taste for solo performances," and his substitution of private for public diplomacy (Starr 1984).

Similarly, L.B.J.'s intense need to be loved and feel in control of his fate fed his penchant during the Vietnam War to surround himself with advisers who provided him with information he wanted to hear (Kearns 1976). Johnson's immense ego involvement with affairs of state also led him to "personify" his policies, as illustrated by his statements regarding his Vietnam policies: "By 1965, Johnson was speaking of 'my Security Council,' 'my State Department,' 'my troops.' It was *his* war, *his* struggle; when the Vietcong attacked, they attacked *him*. On one occasion, a young soldier, escorting him to an army helicopter, said: 'This is your helicopter, sir.' 'They are *all* my helicopters, son,' Johnson replied" (Stoessinger 1985). "The White House machinery became the president's psyche writ large" (Kearns 1976).

Consider as well Harry Truman, a president who "was prone to back up his subordinates to an extent that was indiscriminate" (DeRivera 1968). A decisive person, Truman expected

Madeleine Albright learned how to throw everything out and start over almost from birth. . . . Her father, an up-and-coming Czech intellectual and diplomat, found himself on a political hit list after Hitler invaded. . . . Albright's mother Anna was born to a prosperous family and a comfortable life, educated, like Madeleine, in Switzerland. It was from her, Albright says, that she learned about resilience. . . . Albright's discipline and assiduousness, she says, came from her father. Josef Korbel was a formal man, a statesman turned professor, who learned to ski wearing his topcoat and tie. "He was a strict European parent," says [Albright's brother] John. . . . Her father was the first of the intellectual mentors who sharpened her skills and toughened her hide. . . . [Another was Zbigniew] Brzezinski, Albright's Ph.D. adviser at Columbia and later her boss at the National Security Council, [who] could fillet an unprepared student in a second. . . . Albright became a favorite of his, and it was here, as one of the few female students in his class, that she learned she had to be better prepared than the boys to be taken seriously. . . . [After serving on Brzezinski's NSC staff and Senator Ed Muskie's congressional staff], [i]t was during the 1980s that Albright reinvented herself . . . into a political star. . . . Albright took her years of experience at the White House and Senate and turned herself into one of the most popular professors at Georgetown's School of Foreign Service. . . . At the same time, Albright began another important ritual to incubate ideas and expand her network. She began playing host during dinners at her Georgetown home, to argue policy over cocktails and chicken-rice casseroles. "You never went to Madeleine's for the gourmet food," says a participant. "You went for the discussion." . . . By the time Clinton won in 1992, her profile in Washington made her a natural candidate for the UN job. Albright would joke later that someday she would write a book about her experience on the Security Council and title it Fourteen Suits and a Skirt. And she wasn't afraid to play off her gender. On Valentine's Day she placed sweets in red gift bags on the empty chairs of the fourteen other Security Council members in the council room, each with a note attached saying how proud she was "to sit with fourteen handsome young men". . . . But Albright is the first to say the UN was the perfect final training ground for any future Secretary of State. . . . White House foreign policy meetings in the first Clinton term were famous for dragging on forever. Albright had a penchant for efficiency. During one Saturday White House video conference on Bosnia in March 1995, Albright finally became exasperated with the abstract seminar Anthony Lake and State Department diplomats were holding forth on U.S. policy in the civil war. "Gentlemen," she said, "it's nice to think about all these things we hope to do or wish we could do," they heard Albright interrupt from the screen. "But you better start figuring out what we're going to do and whether we're going to send in troops to enforce a cease-fire."

Source: Nancy Gibbs, "The Many Lives of Madeleine," Time, 17 February 1997, 58–61. Copyright © 1999 Time, Inc. Reprinted by permission.

Even her critics acknowledge that the Czech born Albright, a refugee from Hitler and Stalin, has a strong internal compass on matters of democracy and human rights. She has been a consistent advocate for the use of military force in humanitarian crises and conflicts with "rogue" states such as Iraq, beating back efforts by the Pentagon, for example, to limit the deployment time for U.S. peacekeepers in Bosnia.

Source: John Lancaster, "No Clout Where it Counts," Washington Post National Weekly Edition 17 April 2000, 6.

It was early in Clinton's first term . . . that Albright showed her stripes on foreign policy. At a 1993 meeting with Joint Chiefs Chairman Colin Powell—who gave his name to the doctrine that the military should be used only after a clear political goal has been set, and then only with decisive force—she challenged the general: "What's the point of having this superb military that you're always talking about if we can't use it?" As Powell later recalled, "I thought I would have an aneurysm." Thus arose the Albright Doctrine that has held sway since her ascension to Secretary of State: a tough-talking, semimuscular interventionist that believes in using force—including limited force such as calibrated air power, if nothing heartier is possible, to back up a mix of strategic and moral objectives. In an administration that grew up gun-shy by reading and misreading the lessons of Vietnam, she's the one who grew up appeasement-shy by learning in painfully personal ways the lessons of Munich.

Source: Walter Isaacson, "Madeleine's War," Time, 17 May 1999, 28. Copyright © 1997 Time, Inc. Reprinted by permission.

loyalty and was intolerant of disrespect. Hence when he was confronted with blatant insubordination from General Douglas MacArthur (an authoritarian who wanted to call the shots and expand the war with the communists in Asia), the president dealt with the insubordination decisively: "You're fired!" Able to give loyalty himself, Truman expected it from others. President Eisenhower illustrates the difficulties of evaluating the psychological bases of diplomatic conduct, because his low-key approach produced results that were not at the time recognized as a part of his design. Historians have reevaluated his presidency and now see strength and command where previously they perceived inattention and indifference to the duties of office (see Ambrose 1990). Eisenhower's personality contributed to his "hidden hand" managerial approach and its quiet effectiveness (Greenstein 1982).

Richard Nixon and Bill Clinton also present perplexing cases. Some of Nixon's conduct, both in and out of office, appears explicable only in light of his private conflicts and emotional problems. Consider the portrayals of Nixon's character and personality offered by Summers and Summers (2000) and Abrahamsen (1977). These scholars diagnose Nixon as a disturbed personality, at war with himself since the traumatic events and parental disputes of his unhappy childhood. Those conflicts were never resolved, making Nixon unstable, indecisive, and, above all, self-consciously unsure of himself. They account for Nixon's obvious discomfort in the White House, his inability to maintain warm personal relationships, his paranoid distrust of those around him, his self-absorption, and his competitive, adversarial approach toward his political opponents. They almost certainly led him to conquer and destroy to become the "victor," and they may have subconsciously attracted Nixon to failure, because inwardly he felt inadequate and suspected that he did not deserve success. Decisions motivated by such personal factors may have contributed to the tragedies of Vietnam and Watergate.

Similarly, what one careful observer characterized as "the Clinton enigma" (Maraniss 1998a) can be traced to individual characteristics. For example, as Stanley Renshon (1998) and David Maraniss (1995; 1998a) have suggested, many aspects of Clinton's behavior, including his tendency to avoid decisions, his evasiveness, his license with the truth, and his lack of self-control, can be attributed to his personal ambition, his experiences in a troubled home, and the environment in which he learned his political behavior. According to Maraniss (1998a), for instance, "It was not difficult to find the darker corners of Clinton's life. He could be deceptive, and he came from a family in which lying and philandering were routine, two traits that he apparently had not overcome. As he grew older, the more tension he felt between idealism and ambition, the more he gave in to his ambition, sometimes at the expense of friends and causes that he had once believed in." Persistently troubling throughout his political career, these characteristics led to the Monica Lewinsky episode and, ultimately, Clinton's loss of effectiveness for much of his second term.

Our sketch of George W. Bush from earlier in this chapter suggests additional examples of such linkages. They show that the content and conduct of American foreign policy may in some instances be profoundly influenced by policy makers' personal characteristics. Still, both the occasions for the exercise of that influence and its extent are likely to be constrained by a variety of factors, to which we now turn.

LIMITS ON THE EXPLANATORY POWER OF INDIVIDUAL FACTORS

Can continuities and change in post–World War II American foreign policy be traced to leaders' personal attributes? As intuitively inviting as that interpretation might be, it ignores the fact that individuals are only one of several sources of American foreign policy, any of which can limit severely the impact that leaders exert on the direction of foreign policy. The question, then, is under what conditions are leaders' individual characteristics likely to be influential?

When Are Individual Factors Influential?

In general, the influence of personal characteristics on policy-making conduct *increases* in direct proportion to the following factors:

- The individual's level of advancement in the decision-making structure. The higher one climbs in the hierarchy of the foreign affairs government, the more the occupant's personality will affect policy

- The ambiguity and complexity of the decision-making situation. Because people respond to bewildering and uncertain situations emotionally rather than rationally and calmly, perceptions of circumstances are important. At least four types of such foreign policy situations bring psychological (nonlogical) drives into play: (1) new situations, where the individual has had little previous experience and few familiar cues to assist in the definition of the situation; (2) complex situations, involving a large number of different factors; (3) contradictory situations, which encompass many inconsistencies and incompatibilities; and (4) situations devoid of social sanctions, which permit freedom of choice because societal definitions of appropriate options are unclear (DiRenzo 1974)

- The level of self-confidence and ego in the individual. Decision makers' subjective faith in their own ability to control events—their self-esteem, self-confidence, and belief in themselves—strongly determines the extent to which they will dare to allow their own preferences to set policy directions (DeRivera 1968). Conversely, in the absence of such assurance (or narcissistic ego inflation), self-doubt will inhibit risk taking and leadership

- The level of the individual's personal involvement in the situation. When people believe their own interests and welfare are at stake, their response is governed primarily by their private psychological needs. They cease to appear cool and rational and begin to act emotionally. Compare student behavior when mechanically taking class notes during a lecture with behavior when called upon to recite or when negotiating with a professor over an exam grade. Likewise, when policy makers assume personal responsibility for policy management (and become ego-involved in outcomes), their reactions frequently display heightened emotion and their personalities are revealed. Contrast President Johnson's behavior with respect to Vietnam in 1963 (cautious) with his behavior in 1968 (excited, compulsive), by which time the war had become "his war"

- A scarcity of available information. When facing a decision in which pertinent information is unavailable, gut likes or dislikes tend to dictate policy choices. Conversely, "the more information an individual has about international affairs, the less likely is it that his [or her] behavior will be based upon nonlogical influences" (Verba 1969). Other things being equal, ample information reduces the probability that decisions will be based on psychological drives and personal needs

- Power having been assumed recently or under dramatic circumstances. When an individual first enters office, the formal requirements of the role are least likely to circumscribe what he or she can do. That holds true especially for newly elected presidents, who routinely enjoy a "honeymoon" period during which they are relatively free of criticism and extraordinary pressure. So, too, cabinet members and other top-level officials usually experience a brief period during which their personal freedom is great and their decisions encounter little resistance. Moreover, when a leader comes to office following a dramatic event (a landslide election or the assassination of a predecessor), "the new high-level political leader can institute his [or her] policies almost with a free hand. Constituency criticism is held in abeyance during this time" (Hermann 1976)

- Crisis conditions—although they capture only a fraction of the countless decisions made by members of the foreign affairs government—often bring together circumstances that enhance individuals' potential impact on the policy process. Because crises upset "business as usual," they typically upset the influences that otherwise affect how foreign policy is made, thus permitting individual factors to play a larger-than-usual role in affecting foreign policy decisions. It is not coincidental that the great leaders of history have customarily arisen during periods of extreme challenge. The moment may make the person rather than the person the moment, in the sense that crisis can liberate a gifted leader from the constraints that normally would inhibit his or her capacity to engineer change

- A foreign policy crisis is "a situation that (1) threatens high-priority goals of the decision-making unit: [for example, foreign policy makers]; (2) restricts the amount of time available for response before the decision is transformed; and (3) surprises the members of the decision-making unit by its occurrence" (Hermann 1972). When such a situation arises, several things typically happen (Hermann 1969):

  - The highest level of government officials will make the decision(s) (because of the perceived threat to national goals or interests)

  - Bureaucratic procedures usually involved in foreign policy making will be sidestepped (because high-ranking officials can commit the government to action without the normal deference to bureaucracies)

  - Information about the situation is at a premium (because time limits decision makers' ability to acquire new information)

- Selection among options is often based on something other than information about the immediate situation (for example, because of the short time, analogies with prior situations may be inaccessible)

- Personal antagonisms and disagreements among policy makers will remain subdued (because of the urgent need for consensus)

- Extreme responses are encouraged (because of limited information and the enhanced importance of the policy makers' personalities)

Especially noteworthy for our purposes is that crises encourage formation of ad hoc decision-making groups which are given broad authority (Hermann and Hermann 1989). In crises, then, decision-making elites truly govern. Bureaucratic procedures are short-circuited and decision responsibility is redistributed from the usual centers of government power. Hence, one of the greatest role-induced constraints on individual decision makers is circumvented.

Moreover, a "crisis alters organizational plans and objectives by disrupting the regular schedule of activities." As a result, "personnel assignments are reallocated and top-level decision makers focus their attention exclusively on the crisis, postponing action on other matters that may originally have had a higher priority on their scale of values" (Robinson 1972). During the Cuban missile crisis, for example, some of the members of the ad hoc crisis-management team were "relieved" of their organizational affiliations. Assigned the role of "skeptical generalists," "they were charged with examining the policy problem as a whole, rather than approaching the issues in the traditional bureaucratic way whereby each man confines his remarks to the special aspects in which he considers himself to be an expert and avoids arguing about issues on which others present are supposedly more expert than he" (Janis 1982).

Finally, evidence from case studies indicates that the domestic political implications of policy options are not given their usual intense consideration in crisis situations (Paige 1972; compare Hampson 1988). This further liberates individuals from their typical constraints, thus encouraging the expression of individual values and increasing the likelihood that decision makers' personal characteristics will imprint policy. Indeed, the individual leader's personality may now be determinative, as the usual institutional and societal barriers to decisive action are suspended. In a situation that simultaneously challenges a nation's will and the president's self-esteem, governmental decision processes can easily become fused with the chief executive's psychodynamic processes. Furthermore, the resolution of a policy crisis under such circumstances could depend ultimately on the outcome of a personal, emotional crisis (DiRenzo 1974). It is instructive to note in this context that the influence of personality on the decisions of American foreign policy makers has been especially strong when the use of force has been involved (Etheredge 1978)—and force is often the option chosen in crisis situations.

Are there other situations that elevate the potency of leaders' personal characteristics as policy determinants? One such situation may be when a decision centers on broad, abstract conceptions of the nation's basic policy goals. Unlike occasions when policy makers are asked to find a pragmatic solution to a specific problem, in this case attention focuses on doctrinal and ideological issues, thus making leaders' value preferences, fundamental beliefs, and inner needs especially influential.

Consider the divergent postures assumed by past presidents on the issue of containing communism. In the specific context of Indochina, where five different presidents were confronted with the necessity of deciding if and how a "war" with communism should be waged, personality became a visible influence on how each reacted. A former policy planner illustrates the phenomenon:

> Truman was obdurate, tough, and determined to demonstrate these traits in his policies. . . . [H]e felt challenged by the rise of communism in Southeast Asia and became determined to arrest it. Eisenhower, far more at ease in the office, accustomed to high command, and not in need of establishing his credentials as a tough leader with the Congress, was relatively relaxed and more aloof. He alone among the five presidents involved was able to absorb a defeat to communism in Indochina [that of the French] and to provide such a defeat with a domestic appearance of success by way of gradually increasing U.S. responsibility in Southeast Asia. . . . Kennedy was sophisticated, eager, and daring to the point of adventurousness. He accordingly did not shy away from undertaking new commitments. . . . Johnson suffered from the combination of an enormous inferiority complex in regard to handling affairs of state, and an enormous feeling of superiority, experience, and self-confidence in handling and manipulating the movers, shakers, and sleepers in American politics. His inferiority complex. . . . put him in wholly unwarranted awe of the national security and foreign affairs expert advisers he inherited from Kennedy [and] the intellectuals who surrounded him. . . . Accordingly, Johnson accepted the ill-conceived scenarios of the graduated escalation school of thought in regard to Vietnam. . . . Finally, Nixon's negative manipulative traits of a highly insecure (proto-paranoid) but extremely ambitious power-seeker . . . led him to deceive the public into believing he was withdrawing from Vietnam when in fact he was not only continuing but intensifying the war. . . . [H]e managed also to convince the public that he was turning defeat in Vietnam into standoff . . . by changing the most fundamental premise of American foreign policy, namely, the coequation in the U.S. public's mind of American security with the defeat of communism everywhere.

(KATTENBURG 1980, 227)

Knowing that different presidents responded differently to similar situations, another intriguing question follows: How different are the personalities of those comprising the decision-making elite?

Do Policy-Making Elites and Politicians Have Similar Personality Profiles?

In terms of background and experience, a remarkably homogeneous collection of people have made up America's postwar foreign policy establishment. Recall from Chapter 9 the similarities of those who have managed American foreign policy since 1945. When we carefully examine America's postwar foreign policy makers, we discover that—in spite of their varied personality predispositions and beliefs—they share a distinctive set of personal characteristics that set them apart from the average person. Those attracted to political careers conventionally are thought to possess an instinct for power. As power seekers, they pursue power "as a means of compensation against deprivation. *Power is expected to overcome low estimates of the self,* by either changing the traits of the self or of the environment in which it functions" (Lasswell 1974). Accordingly, politicians seek positions of power that confer attention and command deference, respect, and status to overcome their personal sense of inadequacy. Erich Fromm has argued in a similar vein that "the lust for power is rooted in weakness and not in strength, and that fundamentally this motive is a desperate attempt to gain secondary strength where genuine strength is lacking" (cited in DiRenzo 1974).

The disturbing suggestion here is that policy makers are power-hungry. Though they may claim they enter politics to do good and serve the public, in fact they subconsciously seek leadership to compensate for their personal insecurities and to bolster their own self-esteem by holding power over others. As Bruce Buchanan (1978) has argued, for example, "those who make the final presidential sweepstakes are [persons] of near fanatical personal ambition who show themselves willing to sacrifice health, family, peace of mind, and principle in order to win the prize."

This image of leaders' psychological motives can easily be exaggerated, as clear differences in motivation and belief are also evident. Generalizations about the *response* of people to the acquisition of power are less risky, perhaps. Those with power, whether conferred by election or appointment to high office, become personally absorbed in the roles they play, let their egos and identity become involved with it, and become intoxicated with the sense of power, purpose, and importance they derive from the experience. After all, they find themselves making history, attended by press and public.

Even the most self-assured individuals can easily confuse personal identity with the role played and mistake the power conferred by the position for personal power. The next step is to inflate one's own importance in the overall scheme of things: to think that one has made things happen when in fact things have happened only because of the power one controls, or to assume that, being powerful, one is indispensable. People become elite only because they occupy elite positions and not because, as they sometimes assume, they are inherently special. Individuals playing roles often become, in their own minds, the masks they wear. In this respect the impact of the office on the officeholder makes those in the foreign policy elite more alike than different.

Do Individuals Make a Difference? Psychological Limits on Policy Change

In a sense, I had known that "power" might feel like this, just as I had known, before I ever had a drink, that whiskey goes to the head. The taste of power, or whatever it was that I tasted that first day, went to my head too, but not quite as I had been warned it would. I had come into the office with projects and plans. And I was caught in an irresistible movement of paper, meetings, ceremonies, crises, trivialities. There were uncleared paragraphs and cleared ones, and people waiting for me to tell them what my plans were, and people doing things that had nothing to do with my plans. I had moved into the middle of a flow of business that I hadn't started and wouldn't be able to stop. There were people in place to handle this flow, and established machinery in operation to help me deal with it. The entire system was at my disposal. In a word, I had power. And power had me.

(FRANKEL 1969, 5–6)

This recollection by a new policy maker of his first day in office illuminates the connection between policy maker and policy position. The policy-making system influences the behavior of those who work within it. Although we cannot speak precisely about what makes a politician a politician, our discussion in the previous chapter documented the similarity of outlook among those who occupy roles within the foreign affairs government—regardless, by implication, of the idiosyncratic variations among the individuals themselves and their projects and plans. As individuals enter new groups, they experience enormous pressure to conform to the prevailing and preexisting views of that group. They find that they must "go along to get along." Rewarded for accepting the views of their superiors and predecessors, and punished or ostracized for questioning them, few resist. Authority and tradition are seldom challenged.

The psychological tendency to accept the views of those with whom we interact frequently is sobering. It suggests that certain types of situations elicit certain uniform behaviors regardless of the different personalities involved. Because people behave differently when in different groups and when engaged in different activities, it is uncommon for all but those with unusually strong personalities to resist group pressures and role demands. All people are inclined to adapt themselves and sometimes their personalities to their roles or positions (see Lieberman 1965), each of which has certain expected ways of behaving and attitudes associated with it. Often these are governed by preexisting decision norms

embedded in and reinforced by social processes within an institutional structure. All role occupants tend to conform to the rituals, vocabulary, and beliefs defined by these preexisting norms. As one review of research on this phenomenon concludes:

> If there has been one important lesson coming from all the research in social and personality psychology . . . it is that situations control behavior to an unprecedented degree. It is no longer meaningful, as it once was, to talk in terms of personality "types," of persons "low in ego strength," or of "authoritarians"—at least it is not meaningful if we wish to account for any substantial portion of an individual's behavior. . . . Rather, we must look to the situation in which the behavior was elicited and is maintained if we hope ever to find satisfactory explanations for it. The causes of behavior we have learned are more likely to reside in the nature of the environment than inside the person. And although the operation of situational forces can be subtle and complex in the control of behavior, it can also be extremely powerful. . . . Research . . . seems to indicate that . . . [in] "real life" we are often faced with a situation or role which demands behavior of a certain kind and, over a period of time, our beliefs are likely to change in a way consistent with this situation or role behavior.

(HANEY AND ZIMBARDO 1973, 40–42;
FOR A CONTRASTING VIEW, SEE GALLAGHER 1994)

This conclusion applies to the presidency as well, where the formal and informal norms of the office—the demands of the job, its constitutional obligations, and its public pressures—arguably permit less freedom of individual expression than many others. "Both its prominence and its symbolic functions make the presidential office a more important molder of its incumbents than any other in the nation" (Truman 1951). Indeed, "The historical consistency of the president's responsibilities produces a like consistency in the kinds of exposures he will encounter as he goes about the business of performing his functions" (Buchanan 1978). "The higher a man stands in the social scale," Leo Tolstoy observed, "the more manifest is the predetermination and inevitability of his every act."

These pressures provide a potent explanation for the persistence and continuity characteristic of American foreign policy during the Cold War and why even now adjustments to new realities seem so difficult: For nearly five decades the individuals comprising the policy-making establishment accepted the prevailing image of the world and bent their behavior, and ultimately their beliefs, to that of their predecessors. As James Rosenau (1980) concluded, "Even the president must function within narrowly prescribed limits, so much so that it would be easier to predict the behavior of any president from prior knowledge of the prevailing state of that role than from data pertaining to his past accomplishments, orientations, and experiences." The external environment, societal factors, governmental characteristics, and role-induced constraints restrict the range of permissible policy choices. Durable policy prescriptions were advanced for decades, despite changing international circumstances. The names of the actors may have changed as the Cold War was played out, but the script remained the same. Changing it now may be imperative, as the external world is radically different with the passing of the Cold War. But many of the individuals remain the same and, as we have seen, people are slow to adjust their thinking to new realities. Even those of the successor political generation, like Bill Clinton and George W. Bush, remain prisoners not only of their own political ambitions but also of the domestic and international forces that continue to mold the behavior of individuals once they rise to positions of prominence. As President Clinton once noted: "At least on the international front, I would say the problems are more difficult than I imagined them to be [as a candidate]."

Additional Restraints on Individual Initiative and Policy Innovation

In addition to the constraints discussed previously, other considerations properly falling within the individual source category also narrow the range of alternatives available to leaders. Among them are the following:

- The tendency of policy makers, like the general public, to maintain preexisting images and to view and interpret new information so as to preserve rather than change their perceptual models of reality

- The propensity of policy makers to avoid decision-making responsibilities altogether by relying on reassuring illusions and rationalizations (Janis 1989)

- The impact of "organizational norms, routines, and standard operating procedures [which] may . . . constrain the manner in which issues are defined, the range of options that may be considered, and the manner in which executive decisions are implemented by subordinates" (Holsti 1976)

- The legacy of past policies—in the form of treaties signed with other countries, previous budgetary decisions, prior commitments, and the like—which may reduce considerably the range of available choice and limit changes in existing policy to only incremental revisions

- The tendency of decision makers to feel subjective, if subconscious, loyalties toward pet programs (and the people associated with them), often resulting in a reluctance to withdraw support from them despite their diminishing utility

- The tendency for acquiescent personalities ("team players") to strive for positions of power and for "rugged individualists" and reformers to be systematically selected out

- The desire of policy makers to be loved and respected, together with their concern for earning a "place in history," which may instill the preference to do what is popular even if it is unwise

- The reliance of policy makers on established rules and procedures for decision making
- The stagnating effect promoted by length in public service. As President Nixon said in 1972, "It is inevitable [that] when an individual has been in a cabinet position or, for that matter, holds any position in government, after a certain length of time he becomes an advocate of the status quo; rather than running the bureaucracy, the bureaucracy runs him"

When these psychological and circumstantial restraints on policy initiatives are added to the many domestic and external factors discussed in the preceding chapters, we can appreciate why policy "change, as it occurs, does so in acts of renewing, repairing, or improving existing relationships or commencing new ones that correspond to familiar patterns [and why] diplomacy . . . normally resembles more the act of gardening than of bulldozing" (Seabury 1973).

QUESTIONABLE UTILITY OF THE "HERO-IN-HISTORY" THESIS

The interpretation at the beginning of this chapter articulated a potentially powerful source of change in American foreign policy: Since so much authority is concentrated in the hands of so few, it is logical to assume that the decision-making elite in charge of foreign policy can, with relative ease, choose to revise—indeed, revolutionize—America's foreign policy. Change the people in charge, it is assumed, and the policy itself will often change in turn. In short, change the leadership, and then look for a change in American foreign policy.

The theory and evidence summarized in this chapter force us to question the utility of this "hero-in-history" model of American foreign

policy making. At the very least, the thesis is much too simple. By attributing policy variation to a single source, it tries to explain everything and succeeds in explaining little.

Why? To recapitulate, we find that the people who make American foreign policy are not that different from one another after all. Only certain types of people seek positions of power, and top leaders are recruited from similar backgrounds and rise to the top in similar ways. Consequently, they share many attitudes and personality characteristics. Moreover, once in office, their behaviors are shaped by the positions they occupy; they typically see their options differently from within the system than they did outside it. Often they conform their beliefs to the beliefs of their peers and predecessors. The pressures imposed by the office and decision-making setting elicit similar policy responses from diverse personalities. The result: Different individuals often pursue their predecessors' policies and respond to international events consistently. American policy makers thus routinely display a propensity for incremental change, perpetuation of established routines of thought and action, and preservation of established policies.

This reasoning invites the conclusion that, even though the president and his or her immediate circle of advisers constitute one of the most powerful institutions in the world, and even though, in principle, they have the resources to bring about prompt and immediate change by the decisions they make, those powers are in fact seldom exercised. In today's complex world, it is difficult for great leaders to "emerge," and momentous decisions are rare. Personal characteristics influence the style with which decisions are reached, but the overall thrust of American foreign policy remains highly patterned and fixated on the past. As Ole Holsti (1973) puts it, "Names and faces may change, interests and policies do not." Thus Henry Kissinger's comment in 1976, as the nation prepared to elect a new president, remains a timeless and telling observation: "The essential outlines of U.S. policy will remain the same no matter who wins the U.S. presidential election."

KEY TERMS RELATED TO LEADER CHARACTERISTICS AND FOREIGN POLICY PERFORMANCE

active-negative	*decision-making styles*	*need for power*
active-positive	*distrust of others*	**operational codes**
analogies	**formalistic model**	*passive-negative*
character	**hero–in–history model**	*passive-positive*
chief executive officers	*inherent bad faith*	**presidential character**
collegial model	*lessons of the past*	*psychobiographies*
competitive model	**nationalism**	*self-image*
conceptual complexity	*need for achievement*	*style*
crisis conditions	*need for affiliation*	*world view*

SUGGESTIONS FOR FURTHER READING

Ambrose, Stephen E. *Eisenhower: Soldier and President.* New York: Simon and Schuster, 1990.

Etheredge, Lloyd S. *A World of Men: The Private Sources of American Foreign Policy.* Cambridge, MA: MIT Press, 1978.

George, Alexander L., and Juliette L. George. *Presidential Personality and Performance.* Boulder, CO: Westview, 1998.

Gergen, David R. *Eyewitness to Power: The Essence of Leadership from Nixon to Clinton.* New York: MacMillan, 2001.

Greenstein, Fred I. *The Presidential Difference: Leadership Style from FDR to Clinton.* New York: Free Press, 2000.

Hatfield, J. H. *Fortunate son: The Making of an American President.* New York: St Martin's LLC 1999.

Jones, Charles O. *The Trusteeship Presidency: Jimmy Carter and the United States Congress.* Baton Rouge, LA: Louisiana State University Press, 1988.

Maraniss, David. *The Clinton Enigma: A Four-and-a-Half Minute Speech Reveals This President's Entire Life.* New York: Simon and Schuster, 1998.

Preston, Thomas. *The President and His Inner Circle: Leadership Style and the Advisory Process in Foreign Policy Making.* New York: Columbia University Press, 2001.

Renshon, Stanley A. *High Hopes: The Clinton Presidency and the Politics of Ambition.* New York: Routledge, 1998.

Wills, Garry. *Certain Trumpets: The Call of Leaders.* New York: Simon and Schuster, 1994.

Wilson, Robert A., and Michael R. Beschloss, eds., *Power and the Presidency.* New York: MacMillan, 2000.

NOTES

1. Scott Crichlow contributed to the revision of this chapter for the current edition.

2. The terminology is borrowed from the timeless "great man" versus "Zeitgeist" debate. At the core of the controversy is the perhaps unanswerable question of whether the times must be conducive to the emergence of great leaders, or whether, instead, great people would have become famous leaders regardless of when and where they lived. For a discussion, see Greenstein (1969).

3. The studies by Barber (1992), Donovan (1985), and Stoessinger (1985) provide insights to the personalities and beliefs of the postwar presidents that are particularly relevant to foreign policy formulation.

4. Woodward and Bernstein (1979) provide a less-than-flattering glimpse of this man who otherwise was successful as a diplomat. Hersh (1983) and Isaacson (1993) offers additional critical appraisals. For overviews of Kissinger's world view and "operational code" and an assessment of their impact on his policy performance, see Caldwell (1983) and Walker (1977).

5. Additional recent examinations of presidential style and character include Gergen (2001), Greenstein (2000), Landy and Milkis (2000), Schlesinger (1997), and Wilson and Beschloss (2000).

6. Unless otherwise noted, all quotations from Barber in this section are from the fourth (1992) edition of his book.

7. See also Beschloss and Talbott (1993). However, Zelikow and Rice (1995) argue that Bush's management of the dramatic changes in Europe, including the reunification of Germany, was both effective and proactive.

8. See also Hermann (1989), Mullins and Wildavsky (1992), and Schneider (1990).

9. During Clinton's first term, observers frequently concluded that he had "the dreaded Carter disease—no focus, no continuity, confusing motion with accomplishment," in the words of one frustrated Democratic member of Congress (see also Greenstein 1993–1994). After the staffing changes late in his first term (discussed in Chapter 10), this criticism was less common, although others quickly took its place.

10. On the Lewinsky scandal and the investigation of the president by Independent Counsel Kenneth Starr, see Peter Baker (2000) and Richard A. Posner (2000).

11. On George W. Bush's life, see Minutaglio (1999); Hatfield (1999); Romano and Lardner (1999a, 1999b); Kristof (2000a, 2000b, 2000c, 2000d, 2000e); and Thomas (2000).

PART VIII

Pattern and Process in American Foreign Policy

Chapter 15
At the Dawn of a New Millenium:
The Future of American Foreign Policy

CHAPTER 15

At the Dawn
of a New Millenium

The Future of American
Foreign Policy

I've told the world we're going to have an active, internationalist
foreign policy with U.S. interests at its heart.

PRESIDENT GEORGE W. BUSH, 2001

I claim not to have controlled events,
but confess plainly that events have controlled me.

PRESIDENT ABRAHAM LINCOLN, 1864

The vision of three airliners piloted by terrorists slamming into U.S. buildings in New York and Washington, D.C. led many observers to define a new era for American foreign policy: the "post-Cold War" world would now be replaced by a post-September 11, 2001 world as a temporal demarcation of contemporary challenges to the United States and its foreign policy. "This changes everything" is a phrase embraced by many in the public, the media, and the government. But has it? Is the post-September 11, 2001, landscape that different? What new challenges did the events of that day unearth? The United States entered the

twenty-first century as the world's unchallenged political, military, and economic *hegemon*. "Sole superpower" no longer adequately captures its centrality in world politics. "Hyper-power," a derisive French term increasingly used throughout Europe, comes closer to describing the pre-eminent power position of the United States. Ironically, it is reminiscent of the description of America's global position British historian Harold Laski (1947) proffered in 1947, when, as we saw in Chapter 1, he wrote that "America bestrides the world like a colossus; neither Rome at the height of its power nor Great Britain in the period of its economic supremacy enjoyed an influence so direct, so profound, or so pervasive."

Today, even with the challenges of the post-September 11, 2001 environment, the United States appears to be in the early years of a second American century. Indeed, the sophistication and swiftness with which the United States responded to the terrorist strikes suggests that the question is not really whether the United States enjoys primacy. Instead, the question is what to do with it (Haass 1999), and for others, the question is what to do about it.

The widening gulf in capabilities and influence between the United States and its closest allies and adversaries during the past decade has thrust those questions to the forefront of international politics. Since the demise of the Soviet Union over a decade ago, the U.S. economy has prospered as the "New Economy" based on *information and communications technology (ICT)* dramatically increased productivity while the Japanese economy stagnated, the Russian economy declined, and the Europeans sought to cope with persistent unemployment and other problems related to consolidation of the European Union. Even with the terrorist bombings of the World Trade Center, the United States remains the central focus of the world political economy.

Militarily, the United States not only emerged from the Cold War as the preeminent military superpower, during the 1990s it also widened the gulf between itself and its nearest competitors. Its investments in defense exceeded the combined expenditures of all of the other major industrial powers. And its investments in military research and development, already unsurpassed, continued unabated. U.S. technological prowess was amply demonstrated during the air war in Kosovo and in the campaign against the Taliban and Al Qaeda in Afghanistan. Simultaneously, *globalization* propelled the spread of America's *soft power*. Today American ideas and values are sometimes shared and sometimes shunned around the world, but they cannot be ignored.

TOWARD A SECOND AMERICAN CENTURY: WHAT TO DO WITH AMERICAN PRIMACY?

Debates about the future of American foreign policy remain unabated, just as they have since the dawn of the republic and particularly during the twentieth century, when America's role in the world has been at issue. Today, as before, contention focuses on the priorities related to the enhancement and protection of American national security and interests.

American foreign policy since the nation's founding evinces identifiable cyclical swings between isolationism and internationalism. Because American policy makers historically have been unable to reconcile the advantages of withdrawing from the world with the benefits of reforming it, the nation's global posture has alternated between periods of global involvement and retrenchment. The relative value of each view has never been conclusively determined, as one conception has dominated at one time only to be replaced later by the other. We saw these themes played out in Chapter 3 and in many of the more specific issues in American foreign policy patterns and processes discussed in later chapters.

After World War II the United States embarked on a global foreign policy, which committed it to involvement in every corner of the world, however remote. Global activism reached its zenith in the Vietnam War, which in turn stimulated an inward turn and a growing neo-isolationist mood. Still, global activism continued to dominate the thinking of most elites, despite growing differences among them about the means of American foreign policy. With the end of the global contest between capitalism and communism, however, the timeless debate about the wisdom of global activism compared with the advantages of a retreat from its burdens has resurfaced and now animates elites as well as the mass

---

FOCUS 15.1   The "Golden Straitjacket"

To fit into the Golden Straitjacket a country must either adopt, or be seen as moving toward, the following golden rules: making the private sector the primary engine of its economic growth, maintaining a low rate of inflation and price stability, shrinking the size of its state bureaucracy, maintaining as close to a balanced budget as possible, if not a surplus, eliminating and lowering tariffs on imported goods, removing restrictions on foreign investment, getting rid of quotas and domestic monopolies, increasing exports, privatizing state-owned industries and utilities, deregulating capital markets, making its currency convertible, opening its industries, stock, and bond markets to direct foreign ownership and investment, deregulating its economy to promote as much domestic competition as possible, eliminating government corruption, subsidies and kickbacks as much as possible; opening its banking and telecommunications systems to private ownership and competition, and allowing its citizens to choose from an array of competing pension options and foreign-run pension and mutual funds. When you stitch all of these pieces together you have the Golden Straitjacket.

Unfortunately, this Golden Straitjacket is pretty much "one size fits all." So it pinches certain groups, squeezes others and keeps a society under pressure to constantly streamline its economic institutions and upgrade its performance. It leaves people behind quicker than ever if they shuck it off, and it helps them catch up quicker than ever if they wear it right. It is not always pretty or gentle or comfortable. But it's here and it's the only model on the rack this historical season.

SOURCE: Excerpt from "The Golden Straitjacket" from *The Lexus and the Olive Tree: Understanding Globalization* from Thomas Friedman. Copyright © 1999 by Thomas L. Friedman. Reprinted by permission of Farrar, Straus, Giroux, L. L. C.

---

of the American people. Thus the ends of American foreign policy, not just its means, are subjects of often intense debate and disagreement. Military intervention against extremists in Afghanistan and elsewhere may postpone the debate, but it is unlikely to resolve it conclusively.

How Best to Protect and Enhance American Security and Interests?

As we saw in Chapter 1, *primacy, neo-isolationism, selective engagement,* and *cooperative security* figure prominently in the most recent exchange of ideas as the United States enters a new century and a new millennium. Often the labels used by others are different from these and the nuances they suggest important. Charles Maynes (2001), for example, calls advocates of contending viewpoints *controllers, shapers,* and *abstainers.* He then overlays them with the liberal and conservative variants each school of thought embraces, thus creating a more complete and comprehensive picture of the current debate. Still, primacy, neo-isolationism, selective engagement, and cooperative security remain compelling ideas.

Primacists (Maynes' *controllers*) remain committed to maintenance of U.S. hegemony. To a large extent the second Bush administration embraces primacy and the hardline, unilateralist foreign policy beliefs and preferences that underlie it. As Maynes (2001) observes, those who embrace primacy "have decided that it is in America's interest to use its immense power not merely to make America the leader of the international system—its *primus inter pares*—but to dominate it." Treasure and blood may have to be expended to achieve the goal. Primacy will likely pass sometime in the future, but postponing that inevitability as long as possible is desirable.

Neo-isolationists remain a significant voice in the debate about America's foreign policy priorities. Maynes calls them *abstainers:* "Since America is no longer threatened by a major international foe, and as globalization is benign, America can comfortably scale down its active role in the world, trusting to natural balances the task of keeping the peace."

The liberal variant of the neo-isolationist or abstainer viewpoint emphasizes the magic of the marketplace, believing that "the growing strength of globalization, with its open borders and floating exchange rates, has put the market back in the driver's seat." Maynes adds that "With the loss of an external threat [as during the Cold War], the U.S. government was suddenly deprived of the argument that there was no foreign policy option other than internationalism."

New York Times foreign economic correspondent Thomas Friedman explicates the virtues of globalization in his popular book *The Lexus and the Olive Tree* (1999). He argues that states can only enjoy the benefits of globalization if they adopt the "Golden Straitjacket" implied by the *Washington consensus* (see Focus 15.1). The benefits are substantial: "your economy grows and your politics shrink." In short, economics trumps politics, much as Karl Marx theorized in the eighteenth century. But it is capitalism, not communism, that reigns supreme.

With markets reigning supreme, Friedman continues, "politics becomes just political engineering to implement decisions in the narrow space allowed you in this system." Markets also solve the security issue. Friedman explains with the "Golden Arches Theory of Conflict Prevention": "No two countries that both had McDonald's had fought a war against each other since each got its McDonald's." The reason is that "today's globalization system significantly raises the costs of countries using war as a means to pursue honor, react to fears, or advance their interests."

The argument that interdependence reduces the probability of war enjoys a long history, going back at least to Norman Angell's (1914) acclaimed book *The Great Illusion*. Although the integrative tendencies in the world political economy were interrupted by the twentieth century experiments in communism, socialism, and fascism, they have sharply accelerated over the last two or three decades. What is different today, Friedman writes, "is a difference of *degree*. Today's version of globalization . . . makes for a much stronger web of constraints on the foreign policy behavior of those nations which are plugged into the system. It increases the incentives for not making war and increases the costs of going to war in more ways than in any previous era in modern history."

The conservative variant of neo-isolationist/abstainer logic places little credence in the magic of the market. Indeed, its advocates see globalization as a threat to American interests, values, and freedom of choice. For them, the best way to protect the national interest is to thwart challenges to America's sovereign prerogatives. Conservative neo-isolationists thus oppose institutions like the World Trade Organization, which they fear will constrain America's sovereignty and freedom of action. Not surprisingly, those who embrace the conservative side of the neo-isolationist/abstainer viewpoint see a strong military posture and reliance on nuclear weapons as critical to U.S. survival.

As we saw in Chapter 1, primacists/controllers and conservative neo-isolationists continue to form a natural coalition around a common theme, even though they arrive there by different routes. "Each group wants to make sure that America remains the sole arbiter of its own fate, the former by keeping others subservient, the latter by staying out of their quarrels" (Maynes 2001).

The second Bush administration embraces not only the logic of primacy and unilateralism but also elements of *selective engagement*. Condoleezza Rice (2000), Bush's national security adviser, wrote during the 2000 presidential campaign that a Republican foreign policy should "refocus the United States on the national interest and the pursuit of key priorities." The refocused priorities would seek:

- To ensure that America's military can deter war, project power, and fight in defense of its interests if deterrence fails

- To promote economic growth and political openness by extending free trade and a stable international monetary system to all committed to these principles, including in the western hemisphere, which has too often been neglected as a vital area of U.S. national interest

- To renew strong and intimate relationships with allies who share American values and can thus share the burden of promoting peace, prosperity, and freedom

- To focus U.S. energies on comprehensive relationships with the big powers, particularly Russia and China, that can and will mold the character of the international political system

- To deal decisively with the threat of rogue regimes and hostile powers, which is increasingly taking the forms of the potential for terrorism and the development of weapons of mass destruction (WMD) (Rice 2000, 46–47)

Robert B. Zoellick, appointed United States Trade Representative in the second Bush administration who also held positions in the first Bush and Reagan administrations, wrote similarly that "a modern Republican foreign policy . . . is premised on a respect for power, being neither ashamed to pursue America's national interests nor too quick to use the country's might" (Zoellick 2000). Both Zoellick and Rice thus seemed to reject the humanitarian and international values that motivated many U.S. military interventions during the 1990s, beginning with the intervention in Somalia launched in late 1992 by the senior president Bush. Indeed, Rice (2000) scored those who would replace the "national interest" with "humanitarian interests" or the interests of the "international community." She chided Wilsonian idealism and its expression in the Clinton administration's foreign policy—including the so-called Clinton doctrine (see Chapter 4)—for "the belief that the United States is exercising power legitimately only when it is doing so on behalf of someone or something

else." However, in its efforts to combat terrorism in Afghanistan, the Bush administration adjusted its rhetoric and invoked both humanitarian and international values to mobilize international support for both military and rebuilding efforts. As the administration contemplated further action against others—including the "axis of evil" states (Iraq, Iran, and North Korea)—the primacy, unilateralism, and emphasis on the national interest once more moved to center stage.

The Bush administration's hardline-unilateralist-selective-engagement posture contrasts sharply with the views of cooperative security advocates. *Collectivists* (roughly equivalent to Maynes' *shapers* and those we described in Chapter 8 as accommodationists) "argue that, rather than engage in a futile and dangerous quest for hegemony, America should work with others to try to shape the international environment in a manner that serves not only its national interest, but that of others as well" (Maynes 2001).

Maynes suggests that Joseph S. Nye and Richard N. Haass represent conservative variants of the collectivist/shaper logic, calling them "prudent realists." Nye, Dean of the Kennedy School of Government at Harvard University and a former assistant secretary of defense in the Clinton administration, is a leading spokesperson for liberal international relations theory, which emphasizes both the virtues and constraints that interdependence, transnationalism, and globalization pose. In a *Foreign Affairs* article on *Redefining the National Interest* (1999), Nye recognizes that values are an important component of American foreign policy: "In a democracy, the national interest is simply the set of shared priorities regarding relations with the rest of the world. It is broader than strategic interests, though they are part of it. It can include values such as human rights and democracy. . . . A democratic definition of the national interest does not accept the distinction between a morality-based and an interest-based foreign policy."

Still, Nye worries that in the information age, in which ICT capabilities have the capacity to shape foreign policy preferences, priorities have become misdirected. Strategic challenges like those once posed by the Soviet Union should remain a top priority, he argues. "Imminent threats" to U.S. interests—those that do not threaten U.S. survival—are second order issues. And "important contingencies that indirectly affect U.S. security but do not directly threaten U.S. interests" would follow in last place. For Nye, many of the military intervention initiatives during the Clinton administration—in Haiti and Kosovo, for example—would fall in the third tier.

Also writing in *Foreign Affairs,* Richard N. Haass (1999) similarly argues that priorities must be reordered. Haass was appointed director of policy and planning in the State Department in the new Bush administration and served previously on the National Security Council staff as a chief Middle East adviser to the senior Bush during the Persian Gulf crisis and War.

In response to the question "What to do with American primacy?" Haass recognizes that America's preeminent power will inevitably erode. Thus he argues that

> The U.S. objective should be to persuade other centers of political, economic, and military power—including but not limited to nation-states—to believe it is in their self-interest to support constructive notions of how international society should be organized and should operate.
>
> The proper goal for American foreign policy, then, is to encourage a multipolarity characterized by cooperation and concert rather than competition and conflict. In such a world, order would not be limited to peace based on a balance of power or a fear of escalation, but would be founded in a broader agreement on global purposes and problems.
>
> (HAASS 1999, 38)

Arguably multilateralism flows naturally from Haass's vision, but he, like Nye, is decidedly skeptical of military interventions on behalf of in-ternational values. Arguably war against an illusive terrorist threat is no exception. Nye's prescription calls for "a limited doctrine of humanitarian intervention." Similarly, he is critical of the Clinton administration's program of democratic enlargement: "America simply lacks the means to shape the political culture and system of another country—short of long-term occupation, an option usually unavailable and not guaranteed to work, as demonstrated in Haiti. . . . A foreign policy informed by a universal humanitarian impulse would surely qualify as a case of what Paul Kennedy defines as 'imperial overstretch.'" Additionally, collectivists such as Haass urge restraint in the war against terrorism, especially in its post-Afghan phase. A major concern is the impact of wider operations on support both within the United States and among America's antiterrorist coalition.

The waning of support for humanitarian involvement in the aftermath of the Kosovo intervention can be explained in part because the "cost" of "winning" typically involves prolonged involvement to secure the peace.

> The basic aim of humanitarian intervention—from Somalia to Haiti to Kosovo—is to heal the rifts in a society—ethnic, class, partisan, tribal. Can it be done by the armed intervention of outsiders? Well, if we bulldoze the place—flatten it, destroy it, occupy it, as we did Germany and Japan in World War II—we can certainly reshape it and remake it in our image. But that is hardly what humanitarian interventions are meant to do.
> They are meant to halt the bloodletting, freeze the situation in place, mediate between the parties, and attempt a reconciliation. The logical end of all humanitarian intervention is peacekeeping. And the lesson of the last half-century is that peacekeeping works if the parties have had enough and merely want an outsider to provide assurance— . . . but peacekeeping in the absence of these conditions is an exercise in futility.
>
> (KRAUTHAMMER 1999, 8)

Hence some believe that humanitarian intervention "is an idea whose time has come, and gone" (Krauthammer 1999).

Collectivists and shapers share a vision of greater multilateral cooperation to solve national and global problems, but many, like Nye and Haass, are critical of what they see as the liberal, collectivist excesses of the Clinton administration, in part because of the Kosovo experience. Clearly the second Bush presidency embraced that skepticism. Although it defined a framework in which multilateralism appears prominently, its actions defied its words. Its unexpected unilateral rejection of the Kyoto Protocol designed to slow global warming, which it described as "fatally flawed in fundamental ways"; its expressed intention to withdraw American troops from the Balkans multilateral peace enforcement operations; its rejection of peace enforcement operations in general ("Don't expect any Chapter VII interventions from this administration" was how a Bush administration NSC staff member put it to one of the authors, referring to the section of the United Nations Charter empowering the Security Council to address threats to the peace); and its decisions to abrogate unilaterally the 1972 anti-ballistic missile treaty to pave the way for a missile defense system stand in sharp contrast to its pledge to pursue cooperative ties with others.

What Are the Threats the United States Faces?

The foreign policy debates of the past decade have focused on how best to promote and protect American interests, security, and values. What threatens them? Answers to that straightforward yet difficult question shape the choices American leaders and followers must make as they seek solutions to national and global challenges.

The litany of global challenges has been recited throughout previous chapters. It includes transnational terrorism, the proliferation of weapons of mass destruction, information warfare,

international trafficking in drugs and related criminal activities, outlaw states, failed states, and festering local, ethnopolitical, and regional conflicts that constantly threaten to erupt into wider wars. In the eyes of some, transnational terrorism is a phenomenon that has profoundly changed the character of international politics and America's role as a world leader.

As we enter a new century, several extensive studies have been undertaken that move beyond the present to contemplate the future and the long-term trends that will shape it. They include the Defense Department's *Joint Vision 2020,* the CIA's *Global Trends 2015,* and the State Department's strategic plan that looks far into the future. The report of the Bipartisan Commission on National Security/Twenty-First Century, popularly known as the Hart/Rudman Commission, figures prominently among these long-range studies. Called *New World Coming: American Security in the Twenty-First Century,* the report released in 1999 summarized its projections and concerns about the future in fourteen compelling prognoses.

- Americans will become increasingly vulnerable to hostile attack on our homeland, and our military superiority will not entirely protect us

- Rapid advances in information and biotechnologies will create new vulnerabilities for U.S. security

- New technologies will divide the world as well as draw it together

- The national security of all advanced states will be increasingly affected by the vulnerabilities of the evolving global economic infrastructure

- Energy will continue to have major strategic significance

- All borders will be more porous; some will bend and some will break

- The sovereignty of states will come under pressure, but will endure

- Fragmentation or failure of states will occur, with destabilizing effects on neighboring states
- Foreign crises will be replete with atrocities and the deliberate terrorizing of civilian populations
- Space will become a critical and competitive military environment
- The essence of war will not change
- U.S. intelligence will face more challenging adversaries, and even excellent intelligence will not prevent all surprises
- The United States will be called upon frequently to intervene militarily in a time of uncertain alliances and with the prospect of fewer forward-deployed forces
- The emerging security environment in the next quarter century will require different military and other national capabilities

Based on these prognoses and the evidence that sustains them, the Commission's conclusions for America and its foreign policy are unsettling: "For many years to come Americans will become increasingly less secure, and much less secure than they now believe themselves to be." Terrorism now faces that pessimistic conclusion. In the words of CIA director George Tenet, "the threat from terrorism is real, it is immediate, and it is evolving.

Taken together, the evidence suggests that threats to American security will be more diffuse, harder to anticipate, and more difficult to neutralize than ever before. Deterrence will not work as it once did; in many cases it may not work at all. There will be a blurring of boundaries: between homeland defense and foreign policy; between sovereign states and a plethora of protectorates and autonomous zones; between the pull of national loyalties on individual citizens and the pull of loyalties both more local and more global in nature.

Despite these dire predictions, the Commission ends on a familiar theme: the need for American leadership: "The American moment in world history will not last forever; nothing

wrought by man does. But for the time being a heavy responsibility rests on both its power and its values."

How Do Others See American Primacy?

How will others respond to a twenty-first century exercise of leadership so long promoted by American policy elites and, during much of twentieth century, embraced by others? The Hart/Rudman Commission was not insensitive to this sensitive question. It concluded that "a world amenable to our interests and values will not come into being by itself. Much of the world will resent and oppose us, if not for the simple fact of our preeminence, then for the fact that others often perceive the United States as exercising its power with arrogance and self-absorption." That prognosis is not only prophetic but also a current reality.

The manifestations of American arrogance and unilateralism so worrisome to others are many and familiar. They include:

- A determination to pursue the anti-terrorist war in other states regardless of their own wishes and with or without the support of U.S. allies.
- Unilateral military attacks on Afghanistan for its alleged complicity in terrorist attacks on American embassies in East Africa
- Conflicts with Japan and the European Union about strategic trade practices and market-opening initiatives for auto parts, bananas, corporate mergers, and genetically engineered foodstuffs
- Conflicts with China about intellectual property rights, human rights, and the future of Taiwan
- Cancellation of missile talks with North Korea initiated earlier, embarrassing its South Korean ally
- Initiation of trade protection measures against steel imports from emerging market states

- Rejection of the Ottawa Landmine Treaty and the Comprehensive Test Ban Treaty
- Refusal to participate in the creation of an International Criminal Court
- Withdrawal from participation in the Kyoto Protocol designed to curb global warming
- Initiation of a domestic energy policy that would vastly expand use of nuclear power and exploration for and burning of fossil fuels
- A determination to build a missile defense system applauded by few beyond American shores

Other examples that provoke the ire of American allies and adversaries alike could be added to the list. In some ways the Kosovo intervention stands as a watershed in others' attitudes toward U.S. foreign policy actions, which seem to "oscillate between the high-minded and what critics might call the high-handed" (Marcus 2000). The 1990s began with broad international support for U.S. initiatives in stemming Iraq's aggression against Kuwait. The decade ended with much more limited support for NATO intervention in the former Yugoslavia that was bitterly opposed by Russia and China. The promise of the *Clinton Doctrine*—that the United States would intervene wherever its military power could promote and protect international values—was unsettling to others whose polities are often less than paragons of human rights virtues.

The enormous power of the United States revealed in Kosovo challenged America's NATO allies, who were confronted once again with the uncomfortable fact that their own interests and security are heavily dependent on a militarily and technologically preeminent power with whom they increasingly disagree on a host of closely intertwined nonmilitary issues. Meanwhile, support continued to weaken among many Europeans and others for the U.S.-backed sanctions and coercive diplomacy efforts targeted toward Iraq to enforce the peace won in the Gulf War, fragmenting the once-vaunted victorious Coalition.

Worrisome to others is the penchant of the United States since the end of the Cold War to intervene abroad militarily with technologically sophisticated weapons that increasingly make the exercise of coercive force bloodless (for the intervener, at least). "Cruise-missile diplomacy" seems to have become the order of the day. International relations scholar Andrew Bacevich (1999) described the current coercive diplomacy fashion this way: "Offering the apparent prospect of clean, quick, and affordable solutions to vexing problems, force has become the preferred instrument of American statecraft. The deployment of U.S. forces into harm's way, once thought to be fraught with hazard and certain to generate controversy, has become commonplace. The result has been the renewed, intensified—and perhaps irreversible—militarization of U.S. foreign policy."

Ironically, the September 11, 2001 terrorist attacks on the United States have encouraged the militarization of American foreign policy and the spilling of blood on behalf of its interests. Whereas the 1990s was the decade of enlargement of democratic states, the twenty-first century has quickly reverted to a pattern reminiscent of the Cold War years. In this sense there has been a return to a (new) "normalcy" in international politics. In the words of one observer, "a year after the departure of President Bill Clinton, a new normalcy belies the best that was expected of the past decade and the worst that was anticipated for the new one" (Serfaty 2002).

Although the United States prevailed in the Cold War, today it "finds itself not more secure but less. With communism discredited and the Soviet Union having collapsed, American prosperity and well-being are now more precarious, held hostage to a world order that is susceptible to attack from any quarter. That is the logic of globalization" (Bacevich 1999).

Although globalization has its positive side, many also believe it disproportionately promotes American interests and values. As one scholar put it, "In countries around the world, many consider globalization a threat to their values, jobs, and ways of life. The view of globilization as U.S.-led,

U.S.-directed, and most beneficial to U.S. interests and companies" (Mazzar 2002). Hence, when combined with American economic, military, and technological prowess, U.S. power appears "unprecedented, unrestrained, and unpredictable." Indeed, "it is widely believed around the world today that the global distribution of power is dangerously out of balance" (Ikenberry 2001).

Hostile, anti-American rhetoric that speaks to this imbalance is widely evident. During Clinton's second term, the liberal German *Frankfurter Rundschau* "accused Americans of arrogant zealotry and a 'camouflaged neocolonialism'" (Kagan 1998). At Oxford University in 1999, students debated the proposition "Resolved, the United States is a rogue state" (Ikenberry 2001). Two years later, shortly before President Bush made his first trip to Europe, the German weekly *Der Spiegel* used the phrase "the snarling, ugly Americans" to refer to perceived U.S. arrogance.[1]

Hostile rhetoric has been equally shrill outside of Europe. The United States bore the brunt of this criticism in May 2001, when for the first time it was voted off the United Nations Human Rights Commission, whose purpose is to monitor and report on human rights abuses. The United States had been a member since the Commission's founding in 1947. Although the vote was secret, it quickly became clear that not only did Global South states opposed to U.S. policies vote against the United States, but also some of its friends in the North did as well. The unexpected vote was a stunning defeat for the United States. Sudan—a country widely accused of many human rights abuses, including slavery, during its prolonged civil war—was among those elected to membership on the Commission. "Beyond belief" was the shocked response of former UN ambassador and Secretary of State Madeleine Albright when she learned Sudan had been elected and the United States rejected.

For some in the United States, the immediate response was a reinvigoration of their long-prevalent anti-UN attitude. Members of Congress, for example, seized on the action as reason not go forward with a budget deal negotiated in the last days of the Clinton administration that would lead to U.S. payment of some of its back UN dues (see Chapter 6).

From a longer-term perspective, the (largely symbolic) action taken against the United States is a small indication of the balancing behavior ("counterhegemonic tendencies") other states are likely to exhibit toward America's preponderant power as we move farther into the twenty-first century. Balancing is a classic, time-worn strategy for dealing with hegemonic powers, as we saw in Chapter 6. As former Secretary of State Henry Kissinger (2001b) observes, "dominant power evokes nearly automatically a quest by other societies to achieve a greater voice over their decisions and to reduce the relative position of the strongest." He also adds a warning: "No matter how selfless America perceives its aims, an explicit insistence on predominance would gradually unite the world against the United States and force it into impositions that would eventually leave it isolated and drained."

American Leadership: Coercive or Benevolent Hegemony?

A persistent theme among advocates of various policy prescriptions in this chapter, as well as policy-making elites throughout much of twentieth century diplomatic history, is the need for American leadership in world affairs. During the Cold War, the United States became leader of the "free world." With that conflict's end, presidents Bush and Clinton worried that isolationist sentiments would again capture the country's imagination, as they had following World War I, so they continued to argue that creating a world safe for American security, interests, values, and, indeed, global justice, depended on American leadership. George W. Bush continued in that vein.

What does "leadership" in international politics mean? Historian Garry Wills, author of *Certain Trumpets: The Nature of Leadership* (1995), addresses that question and reaches disquieting conclusions. Noting that the United States became "leader of the free world" after World War II as the defender of freedom anywhere, Wills also recites how the arrogance of power led the United States to engage in often unsavory interventionist practices that led to the removal of "inauthentic leaders—the enemies of freedom—even when the people had chosen them," as in Chile in the 1970s. Indeed, as we saw in Chapters 4 and 5, the United States often engaged in overt and covert practices that bastardized its own cherished values.

This kind of leadership is best described in the contemporary context as *coercive hegemony*. The concept fits the pattern of much of the recent past, at least as seen from the perspective of other countries. Coercive hegemony tracks political realists' conception of international politics, which applauds the stabilizing influence of a dominant power. It also fits with more radical views of hegemony (known as Gramscian after the radical thinker and Italian Communist Party leader Antonio Gramsci), which see hegemony as the source of dominant social and cultural values in the international system.[2] Many fear that coercive hegemony will ultimately drive America's war against terrorism.

Benevolent hegemony is leadership of a different sort. It conforms to the farsighted leadership Charles Kindleberger talked about in his analysis of the causes of the Great Depression (see Chapter 7). Whereas coercive hegemons often "tax" their patrons to the benefit of the hegemon's interests, benevolent hegemons are more altruistic, providing public goods that create order, stability, and prosperity from which all can benefit (see also Snidal 1985).

Wills prefers benevolent to coercive hegemony. Leaders require followers—at home as well as abroad. Followership implies persuasion, not coercion. It implies openness not secrecy; consultation, not confrontation (see also Haass 2000). Too often, Wills argues, American elites have failed to lead the American people, resorting instead in the name of "national security" to the notion that they "know better," and too often they have chosen to dictate to other states rather than consult with them. "A framework of

mutually enriching exchanges protects far better than nuclear weapons in space."

America's unilateralist heritage is traceable as far back as George Washington and Thomas Jefferson, whose pleas to avoid "entangling alliances," militate against a consultative/cooperative posture toward others. Nonetheless, Wills argues that "until America's leaders address the American people and other nations with . . . respect, attention, and persuasion, we shall lack foreign policy leadership of any sort."

Others share that viewpoint. Ardent political realist Henry Kissinger (2001b), for example, challenges twenty-first century American foreign policy to embrace a posture that will "recognize its own preeminence but [will] conduct its policy as if it were still living in a world of many centers of power. In such a world, the United States will find partners not only for sharing the psychological burdens of leadership but also for shaping an international order consistent with freedom and democracy."

Similarly, former State Department official Robert Kagan cautions critics of American foreign policy arrogance. Describing the United States as "the benign empire," Kagan (1998) says "the truth is that the benevolent hegemony exercised by the United States is good for a vast portion of the world's population. It is certainly a better international arrangement than all realistic alternatives." And he quotes from political scientist Samuel Huntington (1993b) (before Huntington "joined the plethora of scholars disturbed by the 'arrogance' of American hegemony"): "'A world without U.S. primacy will be a world with more violence and disorder and less democracy and economic growth than a world where the United States continues to have more influence than any other country shaping world affairs.'" Kagan adds that the truth is no other state wants to assume even an equal share of responsibility for managing global crises or making the kinds of sacrifices hegemonic powers must make.

Noteworthy in Kagan's view is the continuing penchant of American policy makers to define the "national security" in terms that ex-

FOCUS 15.2   There's More to Right than Might

By sending Slobodan Milosevic to The Hague, the Serbian government . . . confirmed one of the oldest dictums of international relations. "The standard of justice depends on . . . the power to compel," wrote the Greek historian Thucydides about 2,400 years ago. "The strong do what they have the power to do and the weak accept what they have to accept." At the end of the day, justice is empty without force.

The War Crimes Tribunal at The Hague is a model of international jurisprudence. It has broad leigimacy and carefully designed procedures to ensure that every person accused, even Milosevic, will get a fair trial. Yet the tribunal has been ineffective until now. It took not lofty ideals but power—mostly American power—to make it work. Hundreds of pages of well-wrought indictments and warrants would have languished in filing cabinets had it not been for the decision by Washington . . . to block international aid to Yugoslavia until Milosevic was in a jail in the Netherlands. Might made right.

The day before Milosevic was extradited, another important event took place at The Hague. The International Court of Justice ruled 14 to 1 that the United States had broken international law when it executed two German citizens . . . in Arizona in 1999. America is bound by the Vienna protocol to inform foreign detainees that they have the right to seek help from their own embassies—a kind of international Miranda protection. It didn't. The United States also ignored the World Court's ruling requesting a last-minute stay of the executions. This decision, barely noted in the American media, made headlines all over Europe.

I can hear the angry objections from Washington. . . : What business does a court in the Netherlands have telling the democratic government of the United States what it should do? Well, what business does a court in the Netherlands have telling the democratic government of Yugoslavia what it should do? Here lies the central tension in American foreign policy today. The United States wants to create a world of universal values, rules, and institutions. But we can't abide the fact that they might apply to us. Over the past decade, with the rise of a world economy and without the constraints of a cold war, these global rules and institutions have been growing in number and scope. It is becoming increasingly clear that we can straddle the fence no longer. America must make up its mind about what sort of world it wants to live in.

Washington has pressed to set up UN tribunals for the former Yugoslavia, Rwanda, Cambodia, and Sierra Leone. . . . It has invoked international law often, capturing Manuel Noriega, fighting Saddam Hussein, arresting drug dealers and prosecuting terrorists. American

tend well beyond Fortress America. "Americans seem to have internalized and made second nature a conviction held only since World War II: Namely, that their own well-being depends fundamentally on the well-being of others; that American prosperity cannot occur in the absence of global prosperity; that American freedom depends on the survival and spread of freedom elsewhere; that aggression anywhere threatens the danger of aggression everywhere; and that American national security is impossible without a broad measure of international security."

Cementing America's benevolent leadership role implies a form of multilateralism similar to that described earlier by Richard Haass (1999):

"The proper goal for American foreign policy . . . is to encourage a multipolarity characterized by cooperation and concert rather than competition and conflict. In such a world, order would not be limited to peace based on a balance of power or a fear of escalation, but would be founded in a broader agreement on global purposes and problems." The international institutions the United States fostered during the post–World War II era contributed to those objectives in the latter half of the twentieth century. Perpetuating that vision into the twenty-first century may continue to serve the interests of all, not just Americans (Ikenberry 1989, 1999, Ikenberry 2001); see also Tucker 1999; but compare Maynes 1998). (See Focus 15.2.)

courts now routinely indict foreign statesmen, companies, and cartels for all kinds of violations of its laws (something unheard of twenty years ago). Most significant, Washington has established procedures and aribtration panels for trade that trump national laws. You can't have a global economy without global rules and courts.

And yet Washington resists paying its UN dues or signing on to the International Criminal Court, the Kyototo accords, the ban of land mines and various other inconvenient treaties and rulings. It objects when arbitrators rule against the United States and is horrified if a foreign court indicts an American citizen. In many cases, the United States has strong, sensible objections to international agreements. They reflect the reality that America is in a unique position as the world hegemon—its troops are spread around the world, it is the chief target of global terrorist and it is the country protesters would most like to embarrass.

But the answer to these concerns is not to walk away from the world but to sit down and negotiate. Most American objections could easily produce a workable compromise if both sides understood that they needed a deal. It would certainly be better for these world bodies, which without America are simply debating societies. "What is the point of having an International Criminal Court without the United States as a member? It would be utterly ineffective,' says Princeton's Gary Bass, the author of a noted book on war crimes. And while there are many important debates to be had about the specifics . . . on the whole, the move toward more civilized rules of conduct among and within states is a triumph.

It also has practical benefits for the United States. Around the world, American power is increasingly viewed as suspect. This is not because of anything the United States has done but rather because of what it is. Great strength breeds great resentment. If America can use international treaties to pursue its policies in such a climate, its policies will be doubly effective. If it can use international institutions to reflect its ideas and ideals, they will take root more easily and durably. Wisely used, international legitimacy can be a potent source of American power, building institutions that will preserve a world of peace and liberty long after American hegemony wanes. Recall another dictum of politics. "The strongest," wrote Rousseau, "is never strong enough to be always the master, unless he transform his strength into right and obedience into duty."

Source: Fareed Zakaria, "There's More to Right than Might: Milosevic in the dock should remind go-it-alone Americans why we need global rules and courts," *Newsweek*, July 9, 2000, p. 43.

Can that vision be projected into the future by a *society-dominant democracy* where domestic and foreign policy interests are often in seeming conflict?

THE SOURCES OF AMERICAN FOREIGN POLICY: CONTINUITY OR CHANGE?

The intrusion of domestic politics into foreign policy making in democratic polities is a disadvantage that—at least in the eyes of some—undermines their ability to deal effectively with foreign policy crises and other external challenges. French political sociologist Alexis de Tocqueville ([1835] 1969) argued more than a century ago that democracies are "decidedly inferior" to centralized governments in the management of foreign affairs because they are prone to "impulse rather than prudence." Democracies, according to this reasoning, are slow to respond to external dangers but, once aroused, they overreact to them.

George Kennan, intellectual father of the Cold War foreign policy strategy of containment and a strong proponent of realist thinking, reflected on democratic foreign policy performance this way:

I sometimes wonder whether a democracy is not uncomfortably similar to one of those

---

**FOCUS 15.3   The Influence of Domestic Politics
on Twenty-First Century American Foreign Policy**

The lack of national interests that command widespread support does not imply a return to isolationism. American remains involved in the world, but its involvement is now directed at commercial and ethnic interests rather than national interests. Economic and ethnic particularism define the current American role in the world. The institutions and capabilities—political, military, economic, intelligence—created to serve a grand national purpose in the Cold War are now being suborned and directed to serve narrow subnational, transnational, and even nonnational purposes.

SAMUEL P. HUNTINGTON (1997, 37)

Domestic politics is driving American foreign policy. . . . Congress not only legislates the tactics of foreign policy but also seeks to impose a code of conduct on other nations by a plethora of sanctions. . . . Successive administrations have acquiesced, in part as a compromise to gain approval of other programs, in part because, absent an immediate outside danger, domestic politics has become more important to political survival than the handling of foreign policy. . . .

Simultaneously, ubiquitous and clamorous media are transforming foreign policy into a subdivision of public entertainment. The intense competition for ratings produces an obsession with the crisis of the moment, generally presented as a morality play between good and evil. . . .

HENRY A. KISSINGER (2001A, 15–16)

---

prehistoric monsters with a body as long as this room and a brain the size of a pin: he lies there in his comfortable primeval mud and pays little attention to his environment; he is slow to wrath—in fact, you practically have to whack his tail off to make him aware that his interests are being disturbed; but, once he grasps this, he lays about him with such blind determination that he not only destroys his adversary but largely wrecks his native habitat. You wonder whether it would not have been wiser for him to have taken a little more interest in what was going on at an earlier date and to have seen whether he could not have prevented some of these situations from arising instead of proceeding from an undiscriminating indifference to a holy wrath equally undiscriminating.

(KENNAN 1951, 59)

Many scholars and policy makers have joined the long-standing chorus lamenting the role that domestic politics play in the American foreign policy process. Nearly all begin with the premise that domestic politics now figure more prominently due to the absence of a dominant external challenge and a corresponding foreign policy paradigm around which American elites and followers can unite. Focus 15.3 gives a sampling of their ideas.

Fear that the nature of the American polity reduces its capacity to adjust to changing conditions and new challenges lies at the center of concerns about its ability to adapt to the changes and challenges of a new century and a new millennium. Can America adjust to the twenty-first century world? Or will it fail to adapt, muddling through with a combination of (in Kennan's words) "little attention to [the] environment" and "blind determination" to have its way once it notices what is happening? Arguably the U.S. response to the terrorist attacks on its assets in New York and Washington, DC, reflects its "blind determination" to have its own way on the global response to terrorism.

Still, balance sheet on forces now at work at home and abroad on the broad range of opportunities and challenges to contemporary American foreign policy yields no firm conclusions. Yet our understanding of the sources of American foreign policy—the external environment, conditions within American society, the structural characteristics of the government, the roles occupied by decision makers, and the characteristics of decision makers themselves—leads us to conclude that only here, in the confluence of these forces, can we find the clues that will reveal the nation's response to the events and challenges of the new century.

Individuals as Sources of American Foreign Policy

Any administration's foreign policy reflects the character of the person sitting in the innermost sanctuary of power, the Oval Office. A president's *individual* or idiosyncratic qualities influence policy style, but many restraints reduce the impact of personality on policy itself. All recent presidents have found it necessary to bend strong convictions to the force of competing political pressures, because successful presidential performance requires a willingness to satisfy political constituents at home and abroad on whom their popularity and power depend. George W. Bush began to experience those pressures less than six months into office.

We have classified George W. Bush as an *active-positive president,* but his is also a laid back presidency. Unlike his predecessor, who sought media attention, Bush shuns it. Learning from Clinton's early mistakes, he runs a highly disciplined White House operation. Meetings start and end on time, neckties are required, and cell phones are not permitted. He also prefers a "CEO" management approach that heavily emphasizes delegation and distances him from the nitty-gritty of decision-making. Learning from his father's mistakes, he began his presidency determined to pay attention to a narrow range of primarily domestic policy issues, such as educational reform, which is not a traditional Republican priority, and to remain focused and disciplined.

Assessing Bush's first one hundred days, a former political director of the Democratic Congressional Campaign Committee concluded that "Bush learned all the right lessons from his father's administration, but he has come up with the wrong answers, that is, he's learned focus, focus, focus, but not breadth. . . . By focusing only on one specific part of solutions, he's given the impression that his policies lack depth" (cited in Cook 2001b).

Journalist Charles Cook (2001b) has labeled this "'the silver-bullet presidency.' For every major problem, the administration has a silver-bullet proposal to address it. Weakening economy? Cut taxes. Energy crisis? Drill in the ANWR [Arctic National Wildlife Refuge]. Inefficient, bureaucratic delivery of social services? Faith-based initiatives." Cook adds that "the obvious problem with this approach is the assumption that just one policy change will solve the problem. If that solution fails to be enacted, lacks public support, or is ineffective, the president's handling of the entire problem becomes the issue."

Bush is likely to change his approach as his presidency matures, the terrorists attacks of September 2001 certainly gave a rapid spurt to a new sene of maturity but the first hundred days also can be prophetic. Journalist and presidential adviser David Gergen writes that "in those fourteen weeks, more than any other time in his presidency, [the president] sets the stage for his entire stewardship. And, Gergen adds, "the public's judgment forms in a matter of weeks and, once formed, soon calcifies. It's a matter of public psychology" (Gergen 2000).

Early public opinion polls showed the American people viewed Bush as a person quite favorably. His policy decisions, however, were often seen as excessively pro-business. His defense of oil exploration and production in the environmentally-sensitive ANWR and his decision to withdraw from the Kyoto global warming protocol were among them. Some of Bush's early appointments and other decisions designed to shore up his support among the conservative, right wing of the Republican party also drew the ire of others.

Europeans were among those angered by the Kyoto decision, and they remain skeptical if not outright opposed to the Bush administration's proposed missile defense program. Bush's early announcement that he would withdraw American troops from the peace enforcement operations in the Balkans also did not sit well.

By the time Bush arrived in Europe for his first trip there, the National Academy of Sciences had issued a climate change report (which Bush had requested) in which it joined the chorus of other mainstream scientists saying human activity was largely responsible for causing global warming. Bush now changed his tune. Although he continued to oppose the Kyoto Protocol, he acknowledged that global warming was a problem. Later he promised increased research funds to deal with it, renewed the U.S. commitment to the 1992 Framework Convention on Climate Change, and pledged to work toward a new agreement that would be broadened to include the Global South. His administration also backed away from its newly minted energy policy report, which contained environmentally questionable postures.

Bush remained adamant on missile defense, but the planned defense program was now called simply "missile defense system." "National" was dropped from the title, as Bush sought to ensure the Europeans, including Russia, that the United States sought a missile shield that would protect American allies from missiles launched by rogue states, not just U.S. territory. He also came away from a meeting with Russian President Vladimir Putin, in which missile defense figured prominently, believing the two leaders had laid the basis for greater rapport in U.S.-Russian relations.

And there was little talk in Europe about the United States withdrawing from either the Balkans or NATO. Indeed, Defense Secretary Rumsfeld had visited Europe shortly before Bush and sought to assure NATO's allies that any realignment of American military strategies toward Asia would not come at the expense of the U.S. commitment to the Atlantic Alliance.

Following the September 2001 terrorist attacks on the United States, the Bush administration initiated efforts to build and sustain an antiterrorist coalition. Among its key features were a renewed dialogue with China, cooperation with Russia, and collaboration with NATO. In addition, the administration sought to construct partnerships with other states in the Middle East, Central and Southwest Asia, and elsewhere.

In all of these small changes and in other maneuvers (including quietly arranging economic bailouts of Argentina and Turkey of the sort Bush lambasted the Clinton administration for during the presidential campaign), the Bush administration was beginning to soften its ideologically-driven, hardline-unilateralist foreign policy edge and to look more pragmatic. At home, where earlier it had been shocked when a moderate Republican senator bolted from the party, the administration began a series of discussions on how better to accommodate the views of moderates in its own party as well as Democrats and to adjust its policy proposals accordingly. In the process the "silver-bullet presidency" may also have begun to look more pragmatic generally. It was a lesson Bill Clinton had to learn after his first two years in office, which led to his successful reelection bid in 1996. It is also a good indicator of the constraints on individual preferences presented by other sources of foreign policy, including roles.

Roles as Sources of American Foreign Policy

A president is not the personification of the state. George W. Bush, like all of his predecessors, discovered that his ability to move in new directions is restricted by his predecessors' prior commitments and policies, the actions and preferences of the individuals already in position to implement policy his own conception of how he was expected to perform the *role* of president, and external challenges and threats over which he has no immediate control.

Roles define patterns of expectations, and the constraints of the past are powerful. Presidents are free from neither. Presidents almost never end up meeting their own expectations and role conceptions. Foreign policy typically figures prominently in the changes they experience both personally and in the larger environment.

> Every president becomes what he did not want to be. Since 1945, the pattern has periodically repeated. Harry Truman initially had limited postwar foreign policy goals—mainly Europe and maybe Japan—but the Korean War set the stage for the globalist exuberance of the 1950s. John F. Kennedy was a charismatic cold warrior, until he discovered the need for détente after the 1962 Cuba missile crisis—too late, however, to get the nation out of the interventionist trap that buried Lyndon B. Johnson. After the 1972 Moscow summit, Richard Nixon returned to the joys of containment in the Middle East and central West Africa, and his successor, Gerald Ford, ultimately banned references to "détente" for the duration of the 1976 presidential campaign. Jimmy Carter viewed the Nixon-Henry Kissinger-Ford foreign policy as the anti Model of what he wanted to do, but relentless Soviet pressures in Iran, Afghanistan, and even Central America forced a reappraisal of his penchant for human rights. . . . Ronald Reagan, the staunch warmonger who dismissed the idea of negotiations with the "evil empire," left office as a peacemaker. Clinton, who had wanted to come home to attend to "the economy, stupid," made the world his new home after his unpresidential behavior took him away from his original emphasis on domestic themes and issues. [By the time he left office, Clinton had logged more miles and visited more countries than any other president.]

(SERFATY 2002, 210–211)

Geroge W. Bush could not have anticipated the profound havoc bin Laden and the Al Qaeda would wreak on his presidency. Indeed, no one could have predicted the unprecedented attack the terrorists visited on America's territorial virginity. George W. Bush has become an unlikely war president. Whereas he went to Washington determined to avoid the domestic lapses in his father's policy agenda, he has suddenly been pressed into a foreign policy role for which he arguably was ill prepared. Circumstances often dictate priorities and the roles needed to address them. Thus, Bush finds himself pursuing "a fight to save the civilized world and values common to the West, to Asia, [and] to Islam." "Freedom from fear" is now the overriding goal (Serfaty 2002). It is consistent with American interests and values since the beginning of the Republic more than two centuries ago. Ironically, "thanks to bin Laden and his followers, the exploding global resentment of globalization with a U.S. face has been interrupted, if only briefly. Terrorism has generated a surge of nostalgic sympathy for the United States and given a bad name to those who would tear it down" (Mazzar 2002).

The backgrounds of those appointed to fill foreign policy-making roles invariably shape the decisions that are made. It is noteworthy that many of George W. Bush's were veteran appointees of the Republican administrations of the 1970s and the 1980s, including his father's. Inevitably they brought well-worn conceptual baggage with them. These foreign policy managers were insiders, which helps to explain why Cold War precepts and related experiences often shaped their perspectives even as the new Bush administration sought to embrace a twenty-first century rhetoric. Familiar scripts are difficult to discard.

In many respects the first Clinton administration's immediate entourage shared similar, time-worn badges. However, Clinton more than any other president sought to shape a federal establishment that reflected "America." Thus more women and minorities were appointed to the cabinet and other policy-making roles—the 3,000 or so politically appointed positions in the federal government identified in the so-called "plum book" (because of the color of its cover)—than in any previous administration. At the next echelon, however, where millions of public employees are charged with the day-to-day management and implementation of the nation's public policy, domestic as well as foreign, the administration could do little to transform the face of bureaucracy. At the top tier of the "permanent government"—those "who run the country no matter who is president"—ninety percent of the posts continued to be held by white males, making it "look more like the United States Senate" than America (Weiner 1994). The "permanent government" (dare we add nonelected?) in the administration of George W. Bush, which likewise included many top-level slots occupied by women and minorities, also remained heavily populated by white males.

Here in the "permanent government" the role requirements that constrain individual latitude are particularly acute. "Bureaucratic politics" is the phrase we used to explain the how and why of individuals' behavior in the multitude of large-scale organizations that comprise the foreign affairs government. "Bureaucrat" is the way many Americans otherwise choose to disparage them. Either way, the fundamental premise is that the position (with its subculture and perspective) conditions and shapes an individual's policy preferences and perspectives. Because both the personnel and the perspectives are more enduring than the elected officials, they often act as a brake on policy innovation. These role conceptions may also condition the options that are considered by high-level officials, and they may come to "capture" appointees, even at the highest levels.

Governmental Sources of American Foreign Policy

Adaptations in America's foreign policy for the new century also will be shaped by the structure of the nation's system of government, in which the president and Congress share foreign policy responsibility. The president has been the preeminent player in the past, but as domestic and international forces increasingly challenge the president's once dominant position—"the most powerful person in the world"—exercising leadership over the direction of American foreign policy has become more difficult.

Presidents enjoy enormous advantages as they seek to exercise their leadership role. As we saw in Chapter 10, the advantages include constitutional and legal prerogatives, precedents set by previous presidents, and the power to persuade, which flows in part from president's role as chief executive and head of the White House-based presidential subsystem. However, the exercise of presidential leadership is not without constraints, as we have seen. Many are beyond the influence of the Oval Office and the control of the White House.

The overlapping organizations that comprise the foreign affairs government, while nominally at the president's command, are neither easily directed nor led, as the role requirements of career professionals reward caution, not innovation. Furthermore, new presidents—often viewed as "transient meddlers" in the business of the people who staff the foreign affairs government—frequently find that their preferences are not top priorities in an environment that equates organizational survival with individual survival. Thus, like his predecessors, George W. Bush faces a persistent problem: how to ensure that foreign affairs bureaucracy is responsive to the White House agenda and preferences.

Frequently, substantial bureaucratic resistance to White House direction complicates and confounds the exercise of presidential leadership. As political scientist Theodore Lowi aptly put it almost two decades ago:

> Presidents operate on the brink of failure and in ignorance of when, where, and how failure will come. They do not and cannot possibly know about even a small proportion of government activity that bears on their failure. They can only put out fires and smile

above the ashes. They don't know what's going on—yet they are responsible for it. And they feed that responsibility every time they take credit for good news not of their own making.

(LOWI 1985B, 190)

The influence of career professionals comprising the foreign affairs government on the formulation and implementation of policy is particularly evident today as the evolving agenda of global challenges and opportunities now engages more elements of the foreign affairs government than ever before, thereby raising more interests, voices, and perspectives. They also complicate the challenge of coordinating the increasingly sprawling and disparate stakeholders on any given issue. As the nation faces a complex environment fraught with dangers and opportunities that blur the distinction between foreign and domestic policy, the State Department and other traditional foreign policy agents typically find themselves joined by the Treasury, Commerce, Justice, and Agriculture Departments as well as other agencies, like the Drug Enforcement Agency and the Environmental Protection Agency, in the search for appropriate responses to unfolding problems.

Ironically, the changing nature of twenty-first century world politics calls into question the relevance of the missions and capabilities of the foreign affairs organizations created and shaped during America's twentieth-century rise to globalism. Virtually all of them were designed to address Cold War threats. Today, most struggle to adapt to the new context. Presidents and their appointees must in turn grapple with how to reorient entrenched bureaucracies toward new goals and purposes. Nowhere is this more evident than in recent efforts to reorganize and improve America's "homeland security," which have exposed the entrenched interests and even inappropriate structures of many defense, intelligence, and law enforcement agencies.

The challenge is formidable; few presidents have succeeded in the past. In many ways a "new

wine in old bottles" problem, the challenge is to move stubborn bureaucratic structures (and the traditions, born in another era, that sustain them) in a direction suitable for addressing twenty-first century problems while also jettisoning old mind-sets. Organizations, like individuals, are prone to cling to the past and the assumptions with which they are comfortable. Illustrative are the obstacles George W. Bush and his Secretary of Defense Donald Rumsfeld face as they seek to implement the president's bold campaign promise to discard Cold War premises and assumptions and reorient the Pentagon to meet twenty-first challenges in new and innovative ways.[3]

When Congress is added to this governmental source brew, we can easily understand how the structure of the American government can act as a brake on presidential leadership and policy innovation. During much of twentieth century bipartisanship, born of a broad foreign policy consensus supporting America's rise to global leadership, muted the Constitution's invitation for struggle. The new century, however, is marked more by dissensus and disagreement about the nation's interests, the threats it faces (terrorism excepted), and the posture that should shape America's world role. In this environment—first stimulated by the fractious Vietnam War and Watergate scandal more than two decades ago—Congress is often resolute in its own policy positions rather than deferential to presidential preferences. Like his father and like Bill Clinton before him, George W. Bush faces an assertive and independent-minded Congress unwilling to accede automatically to presidential initiatives.

Clinton's experience is illustrative of contemporary presidential-congressional relations. Although neither helpless nor without influence, Clinton watched as Congress scuttled his efforts to address the problem of global climate change, eliminate nuclear weapons testing, expand free trade arrangements, strengthen American involvement in multilateral peace operations, and reorient foreign aid policy. Clinton also found it necessary to accept congressional preferences on a host of issues not to his liking, including defense spending and national missile defense, among others. Congressional assertiveness is sure to impact the second Bush presidency as well.

The congressional challenge to presidential foreign policy leadership stems from a variety of sources. Three stand out. First, as noted earlier, the contemporary environment is characterized by intensified interdependence and globalization. Globalization encourages the presence and deepens the salience of *intermestic issues*. Members of Congress are more likely to be interested and involved in such issues. Second, the absence of an obvious and pressing strategic threat reduces the costs of challenging the president, thereby reducing the political risk to members of Congress who assert their individual preferences. The American people's comparative indifference to foreign policy issues actually encourages this tendency. "General public disinterest in foreign policy gives many members a lot of latitude to pursue particular foreign policy interests without fear of political backlash, even if their views do not correspond with mainstream America or even with their own constituents" (Hersman 2000). Third, with more voices in the executive branch involved in foreign affairs, more congressional committees and subcommittees and their members have a stake in foreign policy issues. Their ability to protect their stakes and promote their interests is enhanced by the informal as well as formal avenues of influence members of Congress enjoy (see Hersman 2000).

Partisanship and the ideological differences that accompany it exacerbates the divisions between the Congress and the president. The trend toward greater partisanship has been evident for some time and culminated in 1994, when Republicans won control of the House of Representatives after forty years of Democratic dominance driven by the New Deal coalition forged during the Great Depression. Divided government resulted and persists. Republicans won a narrow victory in the 2000 House elec-

tions, and the Senate became evenly divided. Vermont Senator James Jeffords later left the Republican fold due to policy and ideological differences with the White House. Although now an Independent, Jeffords announced he would caucus with the Democrats in choosing a majority leader and developing legislation, thus once more returning the executive and legislative branches to divided rule.

The complex structures and processes of the presidential form of government make presidential leadership in the absence of consensus difficult. Foreign policy becomes "more issue-based than vision-based" and is therefore more vulnerable to the effects of "porous and fragmented institutions, where policy is driven more powerfully by clusters of like-minded individuals" than anything else (Hersman 2000). This environment suggests that the model we used to organize our discussion of governmental sources (Figure 10.1 on page 322) exaggerates presidential preeminence in foreign policy making. Instead of concentric circles, the president, executive bureaucracy, and Congress may better be viewed as contenders for influence and leadership, and their relative influence may vary by issue, policy instrument, and context. This model suggests a series of "shifting constellations," as shown in Figure 15.1. It says that, within the international and societal contexts, the governmental sources (the White House, Congress, and foreign affairs government) are not neatly or hierarchically arranged, but frequently act as competitors with one another. In the context of this image, George W. Bush should expect to work hard to manage the executive branch and his relations with Congress.

Societal Sources of American Foreign Policy

Because the United States is a society-dominant political system, the ability of the president to work his will in Congress ultimately will be influenced by the support his policies enjoy among the American people. Indeed, the potential influ-

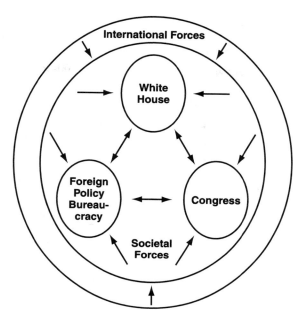

FIGURE 15.1   The Policy Making Environment as a Shifting Constellation of Powers

Source: James M. Scott, ed. *After the End: Making U.S. Foreign Policy in the Post-Cold War World.* Durham, NC: Duke University Press, 1998, 8.

ence of societal forces in a globalizing world is especially potent, as, in President Clinton's words, "there is no longer a clear, bright line dividing America's domestic concerns and America's foreign policy concerns." The State Department echoed that view in its 2000 Strategic Plan: "The intersection of domestic and foreign issues has expanded to affect every American and involve virtually the entire U.S. Government." In short, foreign policy is often little more than an extension of domestic policy; politics does not stop at the water's edge.

At a time of peace and prosperity and no imminent external threat, the American people's definition of national priorities understandably is driven by domestic concerns. Although it has been commonplace during the past decade to argue that the American people are turning inward, there is little evidence to suggest this is an isolationist plunge reminiscent of the period between the two twentieth century world wars. In-

stead, the American people want their leaders to prioritize issues and be selective, with greater attention now given to domestic over global concerns. Because Americans are less supportive of a "nonself-interested American foreign policy" than previously (Schneider 1997), it becomes more difficult for American leaders to devote limited resources to international purposes. Again, the war against terrorism is a notable exception.

If the American people seem to evince public apathy and, as has long been the case, misinformation about American foreign policy, the reasons are understandable. Doubtless this is worrisome from the perspective of democratic theory, which says that an informed citizenry will shape American leaders' policy choices. It also casts doubt on policy makers' claims when they profess they know what "the American people" want. Terrorism aside, the reality is that the preeminence of the United States in twenty-first century world politics leads most Americans to attach comparatively little salience to what happens beyond Fortress America. That also means presidents cannot ignore—without inviting political peril—the priorities that the American people now attach to the home front. It may also mean that leaders—including presidents—who seek to make foreign policy issues into major priorities make themselves vulnerable to political attack.

Instructive in this respect is that six months into his presidency, survey data showed that George W. Bush's determination to build a missile defense system ranked only eighth on a list of Americans' top nine policy priorities (www. gallup.com/poll/indicators/indpublic_cong.asp, accessed June 30, 2001).

Judging by the fact that a missile defense shield was then the single most prominent foreign and national security priority of the new administration, it appears that the gap between leaders and the mass of the American people, which we documented in Chapter 8, remains.

The meaning of that gap for democratic theory is not entirely clear, however. Public ignorance and misunderstanding is the obvious elitist interpretation of this persistent empirical finding. But the counterweight to that interpretation is the failure of some pursuits that American leaders favored despite public dissension that turned out to be fundamentally flawed. Vietnam heads the list, but it is not alone.

In a careful study of the gap between leaders and the general public, Benjamin Page and Jason Barabas conclude that:

> Taken as a whole, the gaps . . . between the foreign policy preferences of citizens and those of leaders do not appear . . . to result from a contrast between leaders' wisdom and expertise and the public's ignorance, misunderstanding, selfishness, or short-sightedness. In many cases public opinion may be reasonably well informed and deliberative, and the gaps may reflect differences between leaders and citizens with respect to values, goals, and interests. In such cases democratic theory

would seem to recommend responsiveness to what the citizens favor.

(PAGE AND BARABAS 2000, 362)

Still, others worry that the nature of contemporary American politics militates against the development of a coherent foreign policy framework to guide the United States in the new century. Henry Kissinger is among them. As we saw earlier (see Focus 15.2), he laments the way domestic politics has intruded on foreign policy making. Charles Maynes shares that concern:

> At the beginning of the last century, Americans interested in foreign policy had an advantage that those similarly interested today do not: Leading the debate over foreign policy choices were two exceptionally eloquent national figures—Theodore Roosevelt and Woodrow Wilson.
>
> By contrast, today's politics produce—perhaps require—political figures of narrow electoral calculation rather than lofty policy conviction. Since Reagan in the 1980s, no recent president or presidential candidate has been willing to make his vision of America's role in the world a major thrust of his message to the country. All have suffered from the lack of the "vision thing," and perhaps all agree in private that displaying it might prove politically lethal. [History will decide if George W. Bush follows the path of his predecessors.]

(MAYNES 2001, 57)

Even as the American people look inward rather than outward, pressures from powerful interests in the United States continue to dictate large expenditures on national defense. Defense spending declined each year in the decade ending in 1995, but since then, with the support of both Republicans and Democrats, it has been on an upward spiral. Today, as during the Cold War, defense spending consumes a lion's share of discretionary federal spending. A concern for jobs and an urge to keep the defense industrial base "warm" are potent domestic sources behind the urge to spend on the military. Meanwhile, expenditures on other foreign affairs activities remain minuscule (see Binnendijk 1997), even as the federal budget accumulated massive surpluses during a time of unparalleled economic prosperity in the 1990s.

Interest groups and political action committees continue to press their special causes, leading policy makers to navigate a middle course among the shoals of America's political pluralism. The changing face of America, documented in the 2000 census, promises to encourage even greater interest group activity. Clinton once remarked that "you can't be president anymore unless you understand the concerns of at least fifty different groups." For those fifty groups, the best way to have their concerns expressed is through organized political activity. Foreign governments also are taking advantage of channels of access and influence made possible by America's open political system. With the United States the world's preeminent power, others want to be sure their voices are heard. "Today Washington is . . . inundated by foreign diplomats and revolving-door lobbyists working to ensure that the interests of America's partners are not overlooked" (Ikenberry 2001; see also Huntington 1997).

The electronic media also seem to play an increasingly prominent role in shaping political agendas and causing policy makers to pander to public preferences. The *perpetual election*—constant polling to determine presidents' standing with the American people—arguably forces presidents to choose the path of convenience, not conscience, when faced with tough choices. Foreign policy challenges and crises often boost presidents' popularity at home, as witnessed by the marked increase in George W. Bush's popularity during the crisis with China over the downing of a U.S. Navy EP-3E surveillance plane early in his presidency. But the state of the economy typically exerts a more enduring impact. Even here, however, the challenges facing the United States in a rapidly changing world political economy have caused skittishness in the public mood, as witnessed not only by protests against globaliza-

tion but also by Al Gore's inability to reap the political gains normally associated with a healthy and growing economy.

Fear of "jobless growth" in the U.S. economy helped to explain much of the growing sentiment against immigrants evident in the early 1990s. That has since dissipated, as many Americans now realize the often positive contributions immigrants make to the nation's economy and culture. Still, *multiculturalism*—an expression of new immigrant groups' rejection of the "melting pot" metaphor long used to describe the process that assimilated new Americans into the established social system—promises to be a source of continuing debate about issues ranging from affirmative action to the use of Spanish in classrooms. The only certainty is that the urge to migrate to "the land of the free" will continue as population growth, environmental degradation, and religious and ethnic conflicts push millions from their homelands. Thus emergent challenges in American society itself will continue to focus attention on domestic challenges, undermining its ability to reach consensus on an appropriate world role for today and tomorrow.

The Cold War stimulated the cohesiveness that bound the American nation together for so long. As we noted in Chapter 8, the "the long war" against communism strengthened Americans' national identity, providing a "unifying dynamic [that] helped overcome ethnic and sectional differences and the ideological heritage of individualism" (Deudney and Ikenberry 1994). It also contributed immensely to the emergence of presidential preeminence in foreign policy. Paradoxically, then, the end of the third great war of the twentieth century eroded a principal pillar on which the legitimacy of presidential leadership had rested for half a century. Today the nation is almost evenly divided along party and ideological lines. The narrowness of the 2000 presidential election and the nearly equal balance between Republicans and Democrats in Congress are mirror images of contemporary American politics and society. "Although national elections are supposed to produce definitive winners and losers, this election was actually a tie. Politically speaking, America is split right down the middle" (Cook 2001a).

The 2000 presidential election was unusual in some respects, but it was not atypical. The electoral process rarely clarifies the range of public support for specific policies. Voter preferences, then, are a breeding ground for policy evolution, not revolution. Mapping a new foreign policy strategy for a new century in such an environment is nearly impossible.

External Sources of American Foreign Policy

As the world's preeminent power, the United States has a greater opportunity now than ever to shape a world consonant with its longstanding interests and values: peace and prosperity, stability and security, democracy and defense. Still, it is not unfettered by external influences on its preferences. Although a giant, like Gulliver it remains tied to others by many strings. Moreover, as we discussed at the outset of this chapter, the more the United States pursues policies that conflict with the values and preferences of other states, the more likely it is that they will engage in *balancing* behavior rather than *bandwagoning*.

China is a key actor in this equation. Most strategic analysts view China, the most populous of the emerging industrial economies, as the most likely strategic competitor and rival of the United States in the new century. The flashpoint in their relations is Taiwan. How China's rise to power and how the contentious Taiwan issue are handled will likely shape the entire panoply of security and nonsecurity issues in the Far East, including relations with Japan, the two Koreas, and perhaps others. And the repercussions will extend beyond Asia, helping to shape the contours of a new multipolar distribution of power widely believed to be on the distant horizon of the twenty-first century.

The first Bush administration pursued a policy of engagement toward China rather than confrontation. Bill Clinton criticized that strategy during the 1992 presidential campaign but would later adopt it as his own under the guise of *comprehensive engagement*. His administration first de-linked trade from human rights issues, and then ultimately became the champion of granting China *Permanent Normal Trade Relations (PNTR)*, paving the way for its entry into the World Trade Organization. It believed this is the best way to integrate China into the mainstream world political economy, thus opening the Chinese economy and society to external influences and the possibility these might in turn encourage the spread of democratizing forces in the communist country.

The George W. Bush administration did not, at least initially, follow the path of either of its predecessors. Instead, it viewed China not as a strategic partner but as a strategic threat. In the eyes of China's leaders, its hostile intent was affirmed when early in his presidency Bush submitted a bill to Congress calling for the sale of advanced weapons to Taiwan that China vigorously opposed. The president has also more clearly articulated, than had his predecessors, the determination of the United States to defend Taiwan against an armed attack. Previously what the United States would do in such an eventuality was purposely shrouded in ambiguity. China viewed the administration's determination to build a missile defense system as an offensive threat, encouraging it to engage in a military build-up of its own. It is perhaps notable that the administration devoted attention to the concerns expressed by both Europe and Russia on this issue, but virtually none expressed by China.

Beyond the strategic challenges China poses (as well as the possibility of other rivals in Europe and elsewhere), the whole of Asia confronts economic challenges that inevitably involve the United States, the world's unchallenged economic hegemon. Japan's economy after a decade of economic stagnation has yet to undertake the reforms the Clinton administration and others had urged for years. Elsewhere, particularly in Southeast Asia, growing religious conflicts and the hangover from the economic meltdown of

Singapore leads the rankings as the most global nation in the index, due in large part to its high trade levels, heavy international telephone traffic, and steady stream of international travelers. European nations round out the rest of the top five countries. Despite high levels of integration on various technological measures, the United States remains less integrated in economic terms, leaving it twelfth in the index.

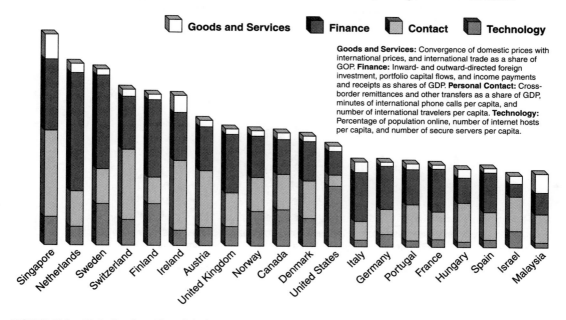

Goods and Services   **Finance**   **Contact**   **Technology**

Goods and Services: Convergence of domestic prices with international prices, and international trade as a share of GOP. **Finance:** Inward- and outward-directed foreign investment, portfolio capital flows, and income payments and receipts as shares of GDP. **Personal Contact:** Cross-border remittances and other transfers as a share of GDP, minutes of international phone calls per capita, and number of international travelers per capita. **Technology:** Percentage of population online, number of internet hosts per capita, and number of secure servers per capita.

FIGURE 15.2   Globalization: The Global Top 20

Source: From www.foreignpolicy.com. Reproduced by permission from Foreign Policy #122 (January–February 2001). Copyright 2001 by the Carnegie Endowment for International Peace.

the late 1990s have imperiled the stellar economic progress the emerging economies of the region once displayed (Hartcher 2001).

Globalization underlies the trauma Asia experienced. The United States has been the primary engine of globalization, although, surprisingly perhaps, empirical data show that it is not the most globalized country in the world (Singapore is), due largely to comparatively few cross-border contacts (see Figure 15.2). Free trade and the lowering of barriers to it became a cornerstone of American foreign policy during the 1990s. Clinton was fond of reciting that his administration concluded some 300 market-opening agreements during his presidency. The logic behind the free trade thrust is that free trade is good for the United States and good for oth-

ers. In Clinton's words, "We want global trade to lift hundreds of millions of people out of poverty, from India to China to Africa. We know if it happens, it will create a big market for everything American, from corn to cars to computers. And it will give all of us new ideas and new innovation and we'll all help each other in constructive competition."

Clinton also recognized that global financial wrecks of the sort that imperiled Asia have global ramifications. A borderless world assures that. Indeed, the Asian meltdown spilled to Latin America and Russia, slowing the globalization process markedly by the end of the 1990s (see Figure 15.3). Still, globalization is a process set in motion that will be difficult to derail. Again in Clinton's word's, "the train of globalization

Is Globalization Slowing Down?

Globalization advanced briskly until 1997, when the financial crises that hit various developing regions weakened trade flows and undercut gains in global integration. So why did overall integration still increase during this period? Simple: Technology has become the engine of globalization.

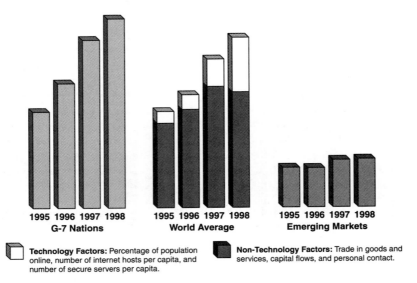

1995 1996 1997 1998
G-7 Nations

1995 1996 1997 1998
World Average

1995 1996 1997 1998
Emerging Markets

Technology Factors: Percentage of population online, number of internet hosts per capita, and number of secure servers per capita.

Non-Technology Factors: Trade in goods and services, capital flows, and personal contact.

FIGURE 15.3   Terrorism, War, and the Future of Globalization

Source: From www.foreignpolicy.com. Reproduced by permission from Foreign Policy #122 (January–February 2001). Copyright 2001 by the Carnegie Endowment for International Peace.

cannot be reversed." But he added that "it has more than one possible destination. If we want America to stay on the right track, if we want other people to be on that track and have the chance to enjoy peace and prosperity, we have no choice but to try to lead the train."

Leading the train will require U.S. involvement in the host of global challenges now confronting the world, ranging from the AIDS pandemic to cyberterrorism, from population growth to narco-trafficking. These are fundamentally borderless threats that have little in common with the kind of threats the United States has been accustomed to for the previous half-century. Finding national and international approaches to address them will challenge twenty-first century American leaders for decades.

Leading the train will also require attention to those globalization has left behind, leading to widening disparities between the rich of the Global North and those less fortunate in the Global South, as we saw in Chapter 6. Harvard economics professor Jeffrey Sachs observes that poor economic performance among poor countries goes "beyond direct economic returns."

"As a general proposition, economic failure abroad raises the risk of state failure as well. When foreign states malfunction, in the sense that they fail to provide basic public goods for their populations, their societies are likely to experience steeply escalating problems that spill over to the rest of the world. . . . Failed states are seedbeds of violence, terrorism, international criminality, mass migration and refugee movements, drug trafficking, and disease" (Sachs 2001).

Sachs adds a clear policy prescription: "If the United States wants to spend less time responding to failed states, as the Bush administration has stated, it will have to spend more time helping them achieve economic success to avoid state failure."

The late twentieth century experiment in globablization has a counterpart earlier in the century, as we have noted previously. That experiment was interrupted by two world wars and economically, socially, and politically disruptive experiments in fascism and communism. Will the widening expanse and sophistication of terrorism today disrupt the current experiment in globalization, perhaps postponing it, as before, for nearly a century?

There is no easy answer to the question of terrorism's effect on globalization and the dilemma it poses for policy makers, but there are at least three scenarios which predict untoward and potentially catastrophic effects on the globalization processes set in motion during the 1990s.

As we contemplate these scenarios, we must remember what globalization means from a practical, day-to-day perspective. "Many of the things that have left sophisticated Western societies vulnerable to terrorist attacks are the very efficiencies that have come as consequence of persons', companies', and countries' relentless search for efficiency and maximum productivity. Curbside check-in, e-tickets, streamlined procedures for border crossings, freer immigration policies in industrialized societies, and just-in-time delivery of international packages and shipping were all introduced to help improve productivity and advance competitiveness. . . . The fundamental question is whether all, or just some of these globalization-era improvements will be among the early casualties of the war on terrorism, sacrificed in order to reduce societal vulnerabilities and to restore domestic tranquility." (Campbell 2002, 11)

From the viewpoint of average Americans, there is nothing inherent in these processes that challenge liberty, the free expression of ideas, and other values central to the American political culture. So it should not be surprising that terrorists can easily take advantage of the open society that is America, and with which Americans themselves so closely identify. Freedom ultimately means freedom of choice unencumbered by the dictates of government. So we should not be surprised that many from around the world who harbor a deep-seated hatred for the United States simultaneously take advantage of its freedoms to attack the very liberal foundations on which it was built and continues to prosper socially, politically, and economically. It would not be impossible, for example, for terrorists determined to skyjack an American Airlines plane at Logan Airport in Boston to walk or drive there from Canada through Maine to Massachusetts and to leave the United States via the same route, largely unencumbered by any efforts by the state to limit their freedom of movement.

In the final analysis, the effective management of U.S. power may be today's greatest challenge. George W. Bush promised during the 2000 presidential campaign to exercise American power with greater humility than in the past. He reaffirmed that pledge in his inaugural address: "We will show purpose without arrogance." To other states, however, his administration's hardline-unilateralist actions seemed to belie the promise. The determination of the administration to pursue its war against terrorism reinforced in the eyes of others its resolute determination to pursue hardline-unilateralist actions whenever and wherever the situation demanded it.

Bush and his advisers would characterize their foreign policy approach as "the new realism." Classical realist thought focuses attention primarily on power and the pursuit of military dominance. Today, however, even liberal international relations theory embraces more than power and military might as it seeks to understand the forces of continuity and change in world politics. Many now also give attention to the transnational layer of international relations, which incorporates nongovernmental organizations and other nonstate actors in the equation, not just states. The Bush administration has from time to time paid homage to these and other forces in contemporary world politics, yet "the new realism" clearly emphasizes the exercise of power over other forces. Critics worry that that focus has blinded the administration to opportunities to shape world politics by other means, including among them "democracy promotion, economic integration, nonmilitary foreign aid, adherence to human rights, or multilateral cooperation" (Legro and Moravcsik 2001). Perhaps as the administration moves beyond its "anything but Clinton" stage, it will increasingly mix pragmatism with power and principle.

THE PROBLEMATIC FUTURE: A SECOND AMERICAN CENTURY?

Former Secretary of State Dean Acheson once said that "there are fashions in everything, even in horrors . . . and just as there are fashions in fears, there are fashions in remedies."

Today the remedies are very much American fashions. To those committed to liberal internationalism and America's leadership role, the challenge is how to maintain the momentum. As President Clinton put it in his December 2000 speech on "A Foreign Policy for the Global Age":

> We must not squander the best moment in
> our history on small-mindedness. We don't
> have to be fearful. We've got the strongest
> military in the world, and in history. . . .
> We don't have to be cheap. Our economy is
> the envy of the world. We don't have to swim
> against the currents of the world. The mo-
> mentum of history is on our side, on the side
> of freedom and openness and competition.
> And we don't have the excuse of ignorance,
> because we've got a 24-hour global news
> cycle. So we know what's going on out there.

Whether the fashions of today will persist will depend in part on the capacity of the American democracy to recruit into office farsighted, courageous leaders able to offer a positive vision of the future and a program to reach it. Emergent twenty-first century developments will be influenced by the assumptions policy makers make about global realities and by their capacity to act decisively and wisely in responding to the challenges of today and tomorrow.

The person empowered to make the fundamental choices, the president, is only one element in the equation that will define the outcome. Other factors will join presidential influence to drive collectively the policy process, ultimately shaping the policy patterns that eventually emerge. Indeed, the process—more than the individuals involved in it—will parent the policy, for the policy-making process and the conditions that influence it will not only stimulate efforts to cope with external challenges but also constrain a president's ability to implement the design chosen.

Nearly two centuries ago, Secretary of State John Quincy Adams declared "I know of no change in policy, only of circumstance." Over a century later, Emmet John Hughes (1972), an adviser to President Eisenhower, wrote that "All of [the nation's past presidents], from the most venturesome to the most reticent, have shared one disconcerting experience: the discovery of the limits and restraints—decreed by law, by history, and by circumstances—that sometimes can blur their clearest designs or dull their sharpest purposes."

Most of the assumptions made by American policy makers in the immediate circumstances following World War II proved to be remarkably resilient for more than five decades. Arguably they served the nation well. Now, however, the structure of the international system on which those assumptions were based no longer exists. Old solutions may no longer fit new realities. Although past policy has the awesome force of momentum behind it, today the question is whether American leaders have the will to chart new foreign policy directions. Few doubt that the United States will remain the preeminent power into the near- and perhaps intermediate-term future, but with what consequence?

When Henry Luce in 1941 predicted the twentieth century would be an American century,

he based his conviction not only on the potential military might of the United States but also on its ability to maintain "a vital international economy" and "an international moral order." If the twenty-first century is to be a second American century, the United States must rise to the challenge.

KEY TERMS RELATED TO THE FUTURE OF AMERICAN FOREIGN POLICY

abstainers

active-positive president

balancing

bandwagoning

benevolent hegemony

Clinton Doctrine

coercive hegemony

collectivists

comprehensive engagement

controllers

cooperative security (collectivists)

external environment as a source of foreign policy

globalization

governmental sources of foreign policy

hegemon

individuals as sources of foreign policy

information and communications technology (ICT)

intermestic policy issues

neo-isolationism (neo-isolationists)

Permanent Normal Trade Relations (PNTR)

perpetual election

primacy (primacists)

roles as sources of foreign policy

selective engagement (selective engagers)

shapers

societal sources of foreign policy

society–dominant

soft power

Washington consensus

SUGGESTIONS FOR FURTHER READING

Campbell, Kurt M. (2002) "Globalization's First War?" *Washington Studies Quarterly* 25 (Winter):7–14.

Fromkin, David. *In the Time of the Americans: FDR, Truman, Eisenhower, Marshall, MacArthur—The Generation That Changed America's Role in the World.* New York: Knopf, 1995.

Gergen, David. *Eyewitness to Power: The Essence of Leadership Nixon to Clinton.* New York: Simon and Schuster, 2000.

Held, David, and Anthony G. McGrew, David Goldblatt, and Jonathan Perraton. *Global Transformation: Politics, Economics, and Culture.* Stanford, CA: Stanford University Press, 1999.

Joffe, Josef. " 'Bismarck' or 'Britain'? Toward an American Grand Strategy after Bipolarity," *International Security* 19 (Spring 1995): 94–117.

Johnson, Robert H. *Improbable Dangers: U.S. Conceptions of Threat in the Cold War and After.* New York: St. Martin's, 1994.

Kegley, Charles W., Jr., and Gregory A. Raymond. *From War to Peace: Fateful Decisions in International Politics.* Bedford/St. Martin's: Boston, 2002.

Kissinger, Henry A. *Does America Need a Foreign Policy? Toward and Diplomacy for the 21st Century.* New York: Simon and Schuster, 2001.

Krasner, Stephen D. *Sovereignty: Organized Hypocrisy.* Princeton, NJ: Princeton University Press, 1999.

Lake, Anthony. *Six Nightmares: Real Threats in a Dangerous World and How America Can Meet Them.* New York: Little, Brown, 2000.

Lodal, Jan. *The Price of Dominance: The New Weapons of Mass Destruction and Their Challenge to American*

Leadership. New York: Council on Foreign Relations Press, 2001.

Nye, Joseph, Jr. *The Paradox of American Power: Why the World's Only Superpower Can't Go It Alone.* New York: Oxford, 2000.

Petras, James, and Morris Morley. *Empire or Republic? American Global Power and Domestic Decay.* New York: Routledge, 1995.

Richard Rosecrance. *The Rise of the Virtual State: Wealth and Power in the Coming Century.* New York: Basic Books, 1999.

Scott, James M., ed., *After the End: Making U.S. Foreign Policy in the Post–Cold War World.* Durham, NC: Duke University Press, 1998.

Steel, Ronald. *Temptations of a Superpower.* Cambridge, MA: Harvard University Press, 1995.

Trubowitz, Peter. *Defining the National Interest: Conflict and Change in American Foreign Policy.* Chicago: University of Chicago Press, 1998.

United States Institute for Peace. *Passing the Baton: Challenges of Statecraft for the New Administration.* Washington, DC: United States Institute for Peace, 2001.

Wittkopf, Eugene R., and Christopher M. Jones, eds., *The Future of American Foreign Policy.* New York: St. Martin's/Worth, 1999.

NOTES

1. The Summer 2001 issue of the *Washington Quarterly* 24 (1) 63–183 contains twelve essays written by strategic thinkers from around the world who address the question, "In an ideal world, what role would you want the United States to perform with your country and region?" The responses to the question speak directly to "debates about benevolent leadership, perceptions of U.S. hegemony, and ultimately the rise and fall of great powers" (Editor's note, 59).

2. Writing in the 1920s and 1930s, Gramsci used the concept of hegemony in trying to understand why, when faced with the rise of fascism, the European working class did not rise up in revolution as Karl Marx had predicted. He concluded that "Dominant groups in society, including fundamentally but not exclusively the ruling class, maintain their dominance by securing the 'spontaneous consent' of subordinate groups, including the working class, through the negotiated construction of a political and ideological consensus which incorporates both dominant and dominated groups" (Strinati 1995).

3. In one of the first steps, Rumsfeld in the summer of 2001 announced his intention to dismantle all 50 MX (known as Peacekeeper) multiple warhead missiles. The once controversial missile is a legacy of the Reagan administration's rearmament program of the 1980s. Dismantling the weapon system and its 500 nuclear warheads could reduce the nation's nuclear arsenal below the levels set by the START I treaty with Russia, which would require congressional approval.

References

ABRAHAMSEN, DAVID. (1977) *Nixon vs. Nixon: An Emotional Tragedy*. New York: Farrar, Straus, and Giroux.

ABRAMSON, PAUL R., JOHN H. ALDRICH, AND DAVID W. ROHDE. (1986) *Change and Continuity in the 1984 Elections*. Washington, DC: CQ Press.

———. (1990) *Change and Continuity in the 1988 Elections*. Washington, DC: CQ Press.

———. (1994) *Change and Continuity in the 1992 Elections*. Washington, DC: CQ Press.

ADAMS, GORDON. (1994) "The New Politics of the Defense Budget," pp. 106–119 in Eugene R. Wittkopf (ed.), *The Domestic Sources of American Foreign Policy: Insights and Evidence*. New York: St. Martin's.

ADELMAN, KENNETH L. (1981) "Speaking of America: Public Diplomacy in Our Time," *Foreign Affairs* 59 (Spring): 913–936.

AIZENMAN, NURITH C. (1999) "Intelligence Test," *The New Republic* 220 (March 22): 22–27.

ALDRICH, JOHN H., JOHN L. SULLIVAN, AND EUGENE BORGIDA. (1989) "Foreign Affairs and Issue Voting: Do Presidential Candidates 'Waltz Before A Blind Audience?'" *American Political Science Review* 83 (March): 123–141.

ALLISON, GRAHAM T. (1971) *Essence of Decision: Explaining the Cuban Missile Crisis*. Boston: Little, Brown.

ALLISON, GRAHAM T., AND MORTON H. HALPERIN. (1972) "Bureaucratic Politics: A Paradigm and Some Policy Implications," *World Politics* 24 (Spring Supplement): 40–80.

ALLISON, GRAHAM T., AND PETER SZANTON. (1976) "Organizing for the Decade Ahead," pp. 227–270 in Henry Owen and Charles L. Schultze (eds.), *Setting National Priorities: The Next Ten Years*. Washington, DC: Brookings Institution.

ALLISON, GRAHAM, AND PHILIP ZELIKOW. (1999) *The Essence of Decision: Explaining the Cuban Missile Crisis*. New York: Addison Wesley.

ALMOND, GABRIEL A. (1960) *The American People and Foreign Policy*. New York: Praeger.

ALPEROVITZ, GAR. (1985) *Atomic Diplomacy: Hiroshima and Potsdam,* rev. ed. New York: Penguin.

———. (1989) "Do Nuclear Weapons Matter?" *New York Review of Books* 36 (April): 57–58.

ALPEROVITZ, GAR, AND KAI BIRD. (1994) "The Centrality of the Bomb," *Foreign Policy* 94 (Spring): 3–20.

ALSOP, JOSEPH, AND DAVID JORAVSKY. (1980) "Was the Hiroshima Bomb Necessary? An Exchange," *New York Review of Books,* 23 October: 37–42.

ALTER, JONATHAN. (1999) "Playing Politics with the Bomb," *Newsweek,* 134 (18 October): 41.

ALTMAN, ROGER C. (1994) "Why Pressure Tokyo?" *Foreign Affairs* 73 (May/June): 2–6.

AMBROSE, STEPHEN E. (1990) *Eisenhower: Soldier and President.* New York: Simon and Schuster.

———. (1993) *Rise to Globalism: American Foreign Policy Since 1938,* 7th ed. New York: Penguin.

AMUZEGAR, JAHANGIR. (1987) "Dealing with Debt," *Foreign Policy* 68 (Fall): 140–158.

———. (1997) "Adjusting to Sanctions," *Foreign Affairs* 76 (May/June): 31–41.

ANDERSON, PAUL A. (1987) "What Do Decision Makers Do When They Make a Foreign Policy Decision?" pp. 285–308 in Charles F. Hermann, Charles W. Kegley, Jr., and James N. Rosenau (eds.), *New Directions in the Study of Foreign Policy.* Boston: Allen and Unwin.

ANDREAS, PETER. (1996) "U.S.-Mexico: Open Markets, Closed Border," *Foreign Policy* 103 (Summer): 51–69.

ANDREW, CHRISTOPHER. (1995) *For the President's Eyes Only: Secret Intelligence and the American Presidency from Washington to Bush.* New York: HarperCollins.

ANDREWS, EDMUND L. (2001) "Bush Angers Europe by Eroding a Pact on Warming," *New York Times,* 1 April, p. 3.

ANGELL, NORMAN. (1914) *The Great Illusion.* London: Heinemann.

ANJARIA, S. J. (1986) "A New Round of Global Trade Negotiations," *Finance & Development* 23 (June): 2–6.

ANTON, GENEVIEVE, AND JEFF THOMAS. (1999) "The Politics of Military Base Closures," pp. 61–70 in Eugene R. Wittkopf and James M. McCormick (eds.), *The Domestic Sources of American Foreign Policy: Insights and Evidence.* Lanham, MD: Roman and Littlefield.

APPLE, R. W., JR. (1997) "Clinton's NATO Vision: Crisp on Expansion, Murky on What Comes After," *New York Times,* 17 July, p. 4.

ARAT, ZEHRA. (1988) "Democracy and Economic Development: Modernization Theory Revisited," *Comparative Politics* 21 (October): 21–36.

ARNSON, CYNTHIA J., AND PHILIP BREN-NER. (1993) "The Limits of Lobbying: Interest Groups, Congress, and Aid to the Contras," pp. 191–219 in Richard Sobel (ed.), *Public Opinion in U.S. Foreign Policy: The Controversy over Contra Aid.* Lanham, MD: Rowman and Littlefield.

ARORA, VIVEK B., AND TAMIM A. BAYOUMI. (1994) "Reductions in World Military Expenditure: Who Stands to Gain?" *Finance & Development* 31 (March): 24–27.

ART, ROBERT J. (1973) "Bureaucratic Politics and American Foreign Policy: A Critique," *Policy Sciences* 4 (December): 467–490.

———. (1991) "A Defensible Defense: America's Grand Strategy After the Cold War," *International Security* 15 (Spring): 5–53.

———. (1998–1999) "Geopolitics Updated: The Strategy of Selective Engagement," *International Security* 23 (Winter): 5–53.

ASHER, HERBERT B. (1992) *Presidential Elections and American Politics,* 5th ed. Pacific Grove, CA: Brooks/Cole.

ASPIN, LES. (1976) "The Defense Budget and Foreign Policy: The Role of Congress," pp. 115–174 in Franklin A. Long and George W. Rathjens (eds.), *Arms, Defense Policy, and Arms Control.* New York: Norton.

ATKINSON, RICK, AND FRED HIATT. (1985) "Oh, That Golden Safety Net: The Pentagon Never Met a Defense Contractor It Wouldn't Bail Out," *The Washington Post National Weekly Edition,* 22 April, pp. 6–8.

ATLAS, JAMES. (1995) "The Counterculture," *New York Times Magazine,* 12 February, pp. 32–38ff.

AUER, MATTHEW R. (1998) "Agency Reform as Decision Process: The Reengineering of the Agency for International Development," *Policy Sciences* 31 (June): 81–105.

AUERBACH, STUART. (1993) "How the U.S. Built Japan Inc.," *The Washington Post National Weekly Edition,* 26 July–1 August, p. 21.

AUERSWALD, DAVID P., AND PETER F. COWHEY. (1997) "Ballotbox Diplomacy: The War Powers Resolution and the Use of Force," *International Studies Quarterly* 41 (September): 505–528.

AUSTER, BRUCE B. (1998) "Enviro-Intelligence: The CIA Goes Green," *U.S. News & World Report* 124 16 March p. 34.

AVERY, WILLIAM P. (1998) "Domestic Interests in NAFTA Bargaining," *Political Science Quarterly* 113 (Summer): 281–305.

BACCHUS, WILLIAM I. (1997) *The Price of American Foreign Policy: Congress, the Executive and Foreign Affairs Funding.* College Park, PA: Pennsylvania State University Press.

BACEVICH, ANDREW J. (1999) "Policing Utopia: The Military Imperatives of Globalization," *The National Interest* 56 (Summer): 5–13.

BAILEY, KATHLEEN. (1995) "Why We Have to Keep the Bomb," *Bulletin of the Atomic Scientists* 51 (January/February): 30–37.

BAKER, PAULINE H. (1989) *The United States and South Africa: The Reagan Years.* New York: Ford Foundation/Foreign Policy Association.

BAKER, PETER. (2000) *The Breach: Inside the Impeachment and Trial of William Jefferson Clinton.* New York: Scribner.

BALDRIGE, MALCOLM. (1983) "At Last, Hope for Coherent Policy," *New York Times,* 19 June, p. F2.

BALL, DESMOND. (1989) "Can Nuclear War Be Controlled?" pp. 284–290 in Charles W. Kegley, Jr. and Eugene R. Wittkopf (eds.), *The Nuclear Reader: Strategy, Weapons, War.* New York: St. Martin's.

BALL, DESMOND, AND ROBERT C. TOTH. (1990) "Revising the SIOP: Taking War-Fighting to Dangerous Extremes," *International Security* 14 (Spring): 65–92.

BALL, GEORGE. (1984) "White House Roulette," *New York Review of Books* 31 (8 November) p. 5–11.

BALZ, DAN. (2001) "US, Britain Launch Airstrikes Against Targets in Afghanistan." *Washington Post,* 8 October, p. A1.

BAMFORD, JAMES. (1983) *The Puzzle Palace.* New York: Penguin.

BANDOW, DOUG. (1992–1993) "Avoiding War," *Foreign Policy* 89 (Winter): 156–174.

———. (1996) "Shaping a New Foreign Aid Policy," *USA Today* 124 (May): 16–17.

BARBER, BENJAMIN R. (1992) "Jihad Vs. Mc-World," *The Atlantic Monthly* 269 (March): 53–63.

BARBER, BENJAMIN. (2001) *The Truth of Power: Intellectual Affairs in the Clinton White House.* New York: W.W. Norton.

BARBER, JAMES DAVID. (1977) *The Presidential Character,* 2nd ed. Englewood Cliffs, NJ: Prentice-Hall.

———. (1985) *The Presidential Character,* 3rd ed. Englewood Cliffs, NJ: Prentice-Hall.

———. (1989) "George Bush: In Search of a Mission," *New York Times,* 19 January, p. A31.

———. (1992) *The Presidential Character: Predicting Performance in the White House,* 4th ed. Englewood Cliffs, NJ: Prentice-Hall.

BARD, MITCHELL. (1994) "The Influence of Ethnic Interest Groups on American Middle East Policy," pp. 79–94 in Eugene R. Wittkopf (ed.). *The Domestic Sources of American Foreign Policy: Insights and Evidence.* New York: St. Martin's.

BARITZ, LOREN. (1985) *Backfire: A History of How American Culture Led Us into Vietnam and Made Us Fight The Way We Did.* New York: Morrow.

BARNES, FRED. (1994) "Saudi Doody," *New Republic,* 14 March, pp. 10–11.

BARNET, RICHARD J. (1969) *The Economy of Death.* New York: Atheneum.

———. (1972) *Roots of War: The Men and Institutions Behind U.S. Foreign Policy.* Baltimore: Penguin.

———. (1990) "U.S. Intervention: Low-Intensity Thinking," *Bulletin of the Atomic Scientists* 46 (May): 34–37.

———. (1993) "Still Putting Arms First," *Harper's* 286 (February): 59–65.

BARNET, RICHARD J., AND JOHN CAVANAGH. (1994) *Global Dreams: Imperial Corporations and the New World Order.* New York: Simon and Schuster.

BARNET, RICHARD J., AND RONALD E. MÜLLER. (1974) *Global Reach: The Power of the Multinational Corporations.* New York: Simon and Schuster.

BAX, FRANS R. (1977) "The Legislative-Executive Relationship in Foreign Policy: New Partnership or New Competition?" *Orbis* 20 (Winter): 881–904.

BENDOR, JONATHAN, AND THOMAS H. HAMMOND. (1992) "Rethinking Allison's Models," *American Political Science Review* 86 (June): 301–322.

BENDYNA, MARY E., AND CELINDA C. LAKE. (1995) "Gender and Voting in the 1992 Presidential Election," pp. 372–382 in Karen O'Connor (ed.), *American Government: Readings and Cases.* Boston: Allyn and Bacon.

BENNET, JAMES. (2001) "C.E.O., U.S.A," *New York Times Magazine*, 14 January, www.nytimes.com/library/magazine/home/2001 0114mag-bennet.html.

BENNETT, STEPHEN EARL. (1992) "The Persian Gulf War's Impact on Americans' Political Information," Revised version of a paper presented at the American National Election Studies' Conference on *The Political Consequences of War*, Washington, DC, 28 February.

BENNETT, W. LANCE. (1980) *Public Opinion in American Politics*. New York: Harcourt Brace Jovanovich.

———. (1994a) *Inside the System: Culture, Institutions, and Power in American Politics*. New York: Harcourt Brace Jovanovich.

———. (1994b) "The Media and the Foreign Policy Process," pp. 168–188 in David A. Deese (ed.), *The New Politics of American Foreign Policy*. New York: St. Martin's.

BERGER, SAMUEL R. (2000) "A Foreign Policy for the Global Age," *Foreign Affairs* 79 (November–December): 22–39.

BERGEN, PETER L. (2001) *Holy War Inc.: Inside the Secret World of Asama bin Laden*. New York: Free Press.

BERGSTEN, C. FRED. (1988) *America in the World Economy: A Strategy for the 1990s*. Washington, DC: Institute for International Economics.

———. (1994) "APEC and World Trader," *Foreign Affairs* 73 (May/June): 20–26.

———. (2001) "America's Two-Front Economic Conflict," *Foreign Affairs* 80 (March/April): 16–27.

BERGSTEN, C. FRED, AND MARCUS NOLAND. (1993) *Reconcilable Differences? United States-Japan Economic Conflict*. Washington, DC: Institute for International Economics.

BERKE, RICHARD. (2001) "Bush Is Providing Corporate Model for White House," *New York Times*, 11 March, www.nytimes.com/2001/03/11/politics/11GOVE.html.

BERKLEY, GEORGE E. (1978) *The Craft of Public Administration*. Boston: Allyn and Bacon.

BERKOWITZ, BRUCE D. AND ALLAN E. GOODMAN. (1998) "The Logic of Covert Action," *The National Interest* 5 (Spring): 38–46.

———. (2000) *Best Truth: Intelligence in the Information Age*. New Haven, CT: Yale University Press.

BERKOWITZ, BRUCE D., AND JEFFREY T. RICHELSON. (1995) "The CIA Vindicated: The Soviet Collapse Was Predicted," *The National Interest* 41 (Fall): 36–47.

BERNSTEIN, BARTON J. (1995) "The Atomic Bombings Reconsidered," *Foreign Affairs* 74 (January/February): 135–152.

BERNSTEIN, RICHARD, AND ROSS H. MUNRO. (1999) "The New China Lobby," pp. 71–83 in Eugene R. Wittkopf and James M. McCormick (eds.), *The Domestic Sources of American Foreign Policy: Insights and Evidence*. Lanham, MD: Roman and Littlefield.

BERNSTEIN, ROBERT A. (1989) *Elections, Representation, and Congressional Voting Behavior: The Myth of Constituency Control*. Englewood Cliffs, NJ: Prentice-Hall.

BERNSTEIN, ROBERT A., AND WILLIAM ANTHONY. (1974) "The ABM Issue in the Senate, 1968–1970: The Importance of Ideology," *American Political Science Review* 68 (September): 1198–1206.

BESCHLOSS, MICHAEL R., AND STROBE TALBOTT. (1993) *At the Highest Levels: The Inside Story of the End of the Cold War*. Boston: Little, Brown.

BETTS, RICHARD K. (1994) "The Delusion of Impartial Intervention," *Foreign Affairs* 73 (November/December): 20–33.

———. (1996) "The Downside of the Cutting Edge," *The National Interest* 45 (Fall 1996): 80–83.

———. (1998) "The New Threat of Mass Destruction," *Foreign Affairs* 45 (January/February): 26–41.

BHAGWATI, JAGDISH. (1993) "The Case for Free Trade," *Scientific American* 269 (November): 41–49.

———. (2001) *The Wind of a Hundred Days: How Washington Mismanaged Globalization*. Cambridge, MA: MIT Press.

BIENEFELD, MANFRED. (1994) "The New World Order: Echoes of a New Imperialism," *Third World Quarterly* 15 (March): 31–48.

BINNENDIJK, HANS. (1997) "Tin Cup Diplomacy," *The National Interest* 49 (Fall): 88–91.

BIRDSALL, NANCY. (1998) "Life is Unfair: Inequality in the World," *Foreign Policy* 101 (Spring): 76–91.

BISSELL, RICHARD E. (1990) "Who Killed the Third World?" *Washington Quarterly* 13 (Autumn): 23–32.

BITZINGER, RICHARD A. (1994) "The Global-ization of the Arms Industry: The Next Prolifera-tion Challenge," *International Security* 19 (Fall): 170–198.

BLACHMAN, MORRIS J., AND DONALD J. PUCHALA. (1991) "When Empires Meet: The 'Long Peace' in Long-Term Perspective," pp. 177–201 in Charles W. Kegley, Jr. (ed.), *The Long Postwar Peace*. New York: HarperCollins.

BLACKBURN, PAUL P. (1992) "The Post–Cold War Public Diplomacy of the United States," *Washington Quarterly* 15 (Winter): 75–86.

BLECHMAN, BARRY M. (1990) *The Politics of National Security: Congress and U.S. Defense Policy*. New York: Oxford University Press.

BLECHMAN, BARRY M., AND TAMARA COF-MAN WITTES. (1999) "Defining Moment: The Threat and Use of Force in American Foreign Policy," *Political Science Quarterly* 114 (Spring): 1–30.

BLIGHT, JAMES F., JOSEPH S. NYE JR., AND DAVID A. WELCH. (1987) "The Cuban Missile Crisis Revisited," *Foreign Affairs* 66 (Fall): 170–188.

BLIGHT, JAMES G. (1990) *The Shattered Crystal Ball: Fear and Learning in the Cuban Missile Crisis*. Lan-ham, MD: Rowman and Littlefield.

BLIGHT, JAMES G., AND DAVID A. WELCH. (1989) *On the Brink: Americans and Soviets Reexam-ine the Cuban Missile Crisis*. New York: Hill and Wang.

BLOCK, FRED L. (1977) *The Origins of International Economic Disorder*. Berkeley and Los Angeles: University of California Press.

BLOOMFIELD, LINCOLN P. (1974) *The Foreign Policy Process: Making Theory Relevant*. Beverly Hills: Sage.

BLUMENTHAL, SIDNEY. (1988) *The Rise of the Counter Establishment*. New York: Harper and Row.

BLUSTEIN, PAUL. (1993) "East Asia's Economic Lesson for America," *The Washington Post National Weekly Edition*, 15–21 March, p. 20.

———. (2001) "Getting Out in Front on Trade," *Washington Post*, March 13 p. E1

BOFFEY, PHILIP M. (1983) " 'Rational' Decisions Prove Not To Be," *New York Times*, 6 Decem-ber, pp. C1, C7.

BOLLEN, KENNETH A. (1979) "Political Democ-racy and the Timing of Development," *American Sociological Review* 44 (August): 572–587.

BOREN, DAVID L. (1992) "The Intelligence Com-munity: How Crucial?" *Foreign Affairs* 71 (Sum-mer): 52–62.

BORRUS, MICHAEL, STEVE WEBER, JOHN ZYSMAN, AND JOSEPH WILLIHNGANZ. (1992) "Mercantilism and Global Security," *The National Interest* 29 (Fall): 21–29.

BOSTDORFF, DENISE M., AND STEVEN R. GOLDZWIG. (1994) "Idealism and Pragmatism in American Foreign Policy Rhetoric: The Case of John F. Kennedy and Vietnam," *Presidential Studies Quarterly* 24 (Summer): 515–530.

BOULDING, KENNETH E. (1959) "National Images and International Systems," *Journal of Conflict Resolution* 3 (June): 120–131.

BOUTROS-GHALI, BOUTROS. (1992) *An Agenda for Peace: Preventive Diplomacy, Peacemaking, and Peacekeeping*. New York: United Nations.

———. (1992–1993) "Empowering the United Nations," *Foreign Affairs* 72 (Winter): 89–102.

BOVARD, JAMES. (1991) "Fair Trade is Unfair," *Newsweek* 9 December, p. 13.

BOYD, RICHARD W. (1972) "Popular Control of Public Policy: A Normal Vote Analysis of the 1968 Election," *American Political Science Review* 66 (June): 429–449.

BRACE, PAUL, AND BARBARA HINCKLEY. (1992) *Follow the Leader: Opinion Polls and the Modern Presidents*. New York: Basic Books.

———. (1993) "George Bush and the Costs of High Popularity: A General Model with a Current Application," *PS: Political Science and Politics* 26 (September): 501–506.

BRANDS, H. W. (2000) *The Use of Force After the Cold War*. College Station, TX: Texas A&M University Press.

BRESLAU, KAREN. (2000) "Snooping Around the Valley: The CIA Sets Up a High-Tech Invest-ment Fund," *Newsweek*, 10 April, p. 45.

BREWER, GARRY D., AND PAUL BRACKEN. (1984) "Who's Thinking About National Secu-rity?" *Worldview* 27 (February): 21–13.

BRILMAYER, LEA. (1994) *American Hegemony: Political Morality in a One-Superpower World*. New Haven, CT: Yale University Press.

BRINKLEY, DOUGLAS. (1997) "Democratic Enlargement: The Clinton Doctrine," *Foreign Policy* 106 (Spring): 110–127.

BROAD, ROBIN, AND JOHN CAVANAGH. (1988) "No More NICs," *Foreign Policy* 72 (Fall): 81–103.

BRODER, DAVID S. (1986) "Who Took the Fun Out of Congress?" *The Washington Post National Weekly Edition,* 17 February, pp. 9–10.

BRODER, DAVID S., AND RICHARD MORIN. (1998) "Two Different Bill Clintons," *The Washington Post National Weekly Edition,* 31 August, pp. 6–7.

———. (1999) "A Question of Values," *The Washington Post National Weekly Edition,* 11 January, pp. 6–7.

BRODER, JOHN M. (1997) "In Washington, It's Never Farewell to Arms," *New York Times,* 11 May, p. E16.

BROOKS, LINTON F., AND ARNOLD KANTER. (1994) "Introduction" in *U.S. Intervention Policy for the Post-Cold War World: New Challenges and New Responses.* New York: Norton.

BROWER, RALPH S, AND MITCHEL Y. ABOLAFIA. (1997) "Bureaucratic Politics: The View from Below," *Journal of Public Administration Research and Theory* 7(a): 305–331.

BROWN, HAROLD. (2000) "Is Arms Control Dead?" *Washington Quarterly* 23 (Spring).

BROWN, JANET WELSH. (1998) "Population, Consumption, and the Path to Sustainability," pp. 407–414 in Charles W. Kegley, Jr. and Eugene R. Wittkopf (eds.), *The Global Agenda: Issues and Perspectives,* 5th ed. Boston: McGraw-Hill.

BROWN, LESTER R. (2001) "Eradicating Hunger: A Growing Challenge," pp. 43–62 in Lester R. Brown, Christopher Flavin, Hilary French, Janet N. Abramovitz, Seth Dunn, Gary Gardner, Lisa Mastny, Ashely Mattoon, David Roodman, Payal Sampat, Molly O. Sheehan, Lindan Starke, (eds.), *State of the World 2001.* New York: Norton.

BROWNSTEIN, RONALD, AND NINA EASTON. (1983) *Reagan's Ruling Class.* New York: Pantheon.

BRUGIONI, DINO A. (1993) *Eyeball to Eyeball: The Inside Story of the Cuban Missile Crisis.* New York: Random House.

BRUNE, LESTER. (1999) *The United States and Post–Cold War Interventions: Bush and Clinton in Somalia, Haiti, and Bosnia, 1992–1998.* Claremont, CA: Regina Publishers.

BUCHANAN, BRUCE. (1978) *The Presidential Experience: What the Office Does to the Man.* Englewood Cliffs, NJ: Prentice-Hall.

BUCHANAN, PATRICK. (1990) "America First—and Second, and Third," *The National Interest* 19 (Spring): 77–82.

———. (1993) "America First—NAFTA Never," *The Washington Post National Weekly Edition,* 15–21 November, p. 25.

BUCKLEY, WILLIAM F. (1970) "On The Right," *National Review,* 24 October, pp. 1124–1125.

BUNDY, McGEORGE. (1988) *Danger and Survival.* New York: Random House.

BUNDY, McGEORGE, AND JAMES G. BLIGHT. (1987–1988) "October 27, 1962: Transcripts of the Meetings of the ExCom," *International Security* 12 (Winter): 30–92.

BURCH, PHILIP H., JR. (1980) *Elites in American History: The New Deal to the Carter Administration.* New York: Holmes and Meier.

BURGIN, EILEEN. (1993) "Congress and Foreign Policy: The Misperceptions," pp. 333–363 in Lawrence C. Dodd and Bruce I. Oppenheimer (eds.), *Congress Reconsidered,* 5th ed. Washington, DC: CQ Press.

———. (1997) "Assessing Congress' Role in the Making of Foreign Policy," pp. 293–324 in Lawrence Dodd and Bruce Oppenheimer (eds.), *Congress Reconsidered,* 4th ed. Washington, DC: Congressional Quarterly.

BURK, JAMES. (1999) "Public Support for Peacekeeping in Lebanon and Somalia: Assessing the Casualties Hypothesis," *Political Science Quarterly* 114 (Spring): 53–78.

BURKHART, ROSS E., AND MICHAEL S. LEWIS-BECK. (1994) "Comparative Democracy: The Economic Development Thesis," *American Political Science Review* 88 (December): 903–910.

BURKI, SHAHID JAVED. (1983) "UNCTAD VI: For Better or for Worse?" *Finance & Development* 20 (December): 16–19.

BUSH, GEORGE H. W., AND BRENT SCOWCROFT. (1999) *A World Transformed: The Collapse of the Soviet Empire, the Unification of Germany, Tianenman Square, the Gulf War.* New York: Knopf.

BUSH, GEORGE W. (2001) *A Charge to Keep.* New York: Harper Trade.

BUSHNELL, PRUDENCE. (1989) "Leadership at State: The Neglected Dimension," *Foreign Service Journal* 66 (September): 30–31.

BYMAN, DANIEL, KENNETH POLLACK, AND GIDEON ROSE. (1999) "The Rollback Fantasy," *Foreign Affairs* 78 (January/February): 24–41.

BYRNES, MARK S. (1999) " 'Overruled and Worn Down': Truman Sends an Ambassador to Spain," *Presidential Studies Quarterly* 29 (June): 263–279.

CALDWELL, DAN. (1977) "Bureaucratic Foreign Policy Making," *American Behavioral Scientist* 21 (September–October): 87–110.

———. (1978) "A Research Note on the Quarantine of Cuba October 1962," *International Studies Quarterly* 22 (December): 625–633.

———. (ed.) (1983) *Henry Kissinger: His Personality and Policies.* Durham, NC: Duke University Press.

———. (1991) *The Dynamics of Domestic Politics and Arms Control: The SALT II Treaty Ratification Debate.* Columbia, SC: University of South Carolina Press.

CALIFANO, JOSEPH A., JR. (1994) "Imperial Congress," *New York Times Magazine,* 23 January, pp. 40–41.

CAMBONE, STEPHEN. (2000) "An Inherent Lesson in Arms Control," *Washington Quarterly* 23 (Spring), 207–218.

CAMPBELL, ANGUS, PHILIP E. CONVERSE, WARREN E. MILLER, AND DONALD E. STOKES. (1960) *The American Voter.* New York: Wiley.

CAMPBELL, KURT M. (2002) "Globalization's First War?" *Washington Quarterly* 25 (Winter): 7–14.

CAMPBELL, JOEL, AND LEILA CAIN. (1965) "Public Opinion and the Outbreak of War," *Journal of Conflict Resolution* 9 (September): 318–329.

CAMPBELL, JOHN FRANKLIN. (1971) *The Foreign Affairs Fudge Factory.* New York: Basic Books.

CANNON, LOU. (1988) "An 'Honest Broker' at the NSC," *The Washington Post National Weekly Edition,* 22–28 August, pp. 6–8.

CANTLUPE, JOE. (2000) "Mexico Might Have U.S. to Thank if Big Drug Arrests Are Made," *San Diego Union-Tribune,* 5 November, p. 11.

CAPACCIO, TONY. (2000) "Foreign Military Sales Show Sustained Growth," *Defense Week.* 6 November, p. 5.

CAPORASO, JAMES A., (ed.) (1978), *International Organization* 32 (Winter): 1–300.

CARNEY, ELIZA NEWLIN. (1994) "Still Trying to Reinvent Government," *National Journal,* 18 June, pp. 1442–1443.

CAROTHERS, THOMAS. (1994a) "The Democracy Nostrum," *World Policy Journal* 11 (Fall): 47–53.

———. (1994b) "The NED at 10," *Foreign Policy* 95 (Summer): 123–138.

———. (1995) "Democracy Promotion Under Clinton," *Washington Quarterly* 18 (Autumn): 13–25.

———. (1997) "Democracy Without Illusions," *Foreign Affairs* 76 (January/February): 85–99.

———. (1999) *Aiding Democracy Abroad: The Learning Curve.* Washington, DC: Carnegie Endowment for International Peace.

CARPENTER, TED GALEN. (1995) *The Captive Press: Foreign Policy Crises and the First Amendment.* Washington, DC: Cato Institute.

———. (1998) "Roiling Asia: U.S. Coziness with China Upsets the Neighbors," *Foreign Affairs* 77 (November/December): 2–6.

CARR, CALEB. (1994) "Aldrich Ames and the Conduct of American Intelligence," *World Policy Journal* 11 (Fall): 19–28.

CARR, E. H. (1939) *The Twenty-Years' Crisis 1919–1939: An Introduction to the Study of International Relations.* London: Macmillan.

CARTER, ASHTON, JOHN DEUTCH, AND PHILIP ZELIKOW. (1998) "Catastrophic Terrorism," *Foreign Affairs* 77 (November/December): 80–94.

CARTER, HODDING III. (1981) "Life Inside the Carter State Department," *Playboy* 28 (February): 96ff.

CARTER, RALPH (2002) (ed.) *Contemporary Cases in U.S. foreign Policy: From Terrorism to Trade.* Washington, DC: Congressional Quarterly.

CARTER, RALPH G. (1998) "Congress and Post–Cold War U.S. Foreign Policy," pp. 108–137 in James M. Scott (ed.), *After the End: Making U.S. Foreign Policy in the Post–Cold War World.* Durham, NC: Duke University Press.

CARTER, RALPH G., AND JAMES M. SCOTT. (2000a) "Patterns of Leadership: Congressional Foreign Policy Entrepreneurs and U.S. Foreign Policy," *International Studies Association - Midwest.* St. Louis, MO., October: 27–28.

———. (2000b) "Senator Chuck Hagel as a Foreign Policy Entrepreneur," *Annual Convention of the International Studies Association.* Los Angeles, CA., March: 14–18.

———. (2001) "Taking the Lead: Congressional Foreign Policy Entrepreneurs in U.S. Foreign Policy," *Annual Convention of the International Studies Association.* Chicago, IL., February: 20–24.

CASPARY, WILLIAM R. (1970) "The 'Mood Theory': A Study of Public Opinion," *American Political Science Review* 64 (June): 536–547.

CAVANAGH, THOMAS E. (1982–1983) "The Dispersion of Authority in the House of Representatives," *Political Science Quarterly* 97 (Winter): 623–637.

CHACE, JAMES. (1996) "Sharing the Atom Bomb," *Foreign Affairs* 75 (January/February): 129–144.

CHAN, STEVE. (1997) "In Search of Democratic Peace: Problems and Promise," *Mershon International Studies Review* 41 (May): 59–91.

CHAN, STEVE, AND ALEX MINTZ, (eds.) (1992) *Defense, Welfare, and Growth.* London: Routledge.

CHASE, ROBERT S., EMILY B. HILL, AND PAUL KENNEDY. (1996) "Pivotal States and U.S. Grand Strategy," *Foreign Affairs* 75 (January/February): 33–51.

CHILDS, HAROLD L. (1965) *Public Opinion: Nature, Formation, and Role.* Princeton, NJ: Van Nostrand.

CHOATE, PAT. (1990) *Agents of Influence.* New York: Knopf.

CHRISTIANSEN, DREW, AND GERARD F. POWERS. (1993) "Unintended Consequences," *Bulletin of the Atomic Scientists* 49 (November): 41–45.

CHRISTOPHER, ROBERT C. (1989) *Crashing the Gates: The De-WASPing of America's Power Elite.* New York: Simon and Schuster.

CHUBIN, SHAHRAM. (1993) "The South and the New World Order," *Washington Quarterly* 16 (Autumn): 87–107.

CIRINCIONE, JOSEPH. (1997) "Why the Right Lost the Missile Defense Debate," *Foreign Policy* 106 (Spring): 39–55.

CITRIN, JACK, ERNST B. HAAS, CHRISTOPHER MUSTE, AND BETH REINGOLD. (1994) "Is American Nationalism Changing?: Implications for Foreign Policy," *International Studies Quarterly* 38 (March): 1–31.

CLARK, KEITH C., AND LAURENCE J. LEGERE, (eds.) (1969) *The President and the Management of National Security: A Report by the Institute for Defense Analyses.* New York: Praeger.

CLARK, WESLEY. (2001) *Waging Modern War.* New York: Public Affairs Press.

CLARKE, DUNCAN L. (1989) *American Defense and Foreign Policy Institutions: Toward a Sound Foundation.* New York: Harper and Row.

———. (1997) *Send Guns and Money: Security Assistance and U.S. Foreign Policy.* Westport, CT: Praeger.

CLARKE, WALTER, AND JEFFREY HERBST. (1997) *Learning From Somalia: The Lessons of Armed Humanitarian Intervention.* Boulder, CO: Westview Press.

CLAUDE, INIS L., JR. (1971) *Swords into Plowshares,* 4th ed. New York: Random House.

COHEN, BERNARD C. (1961) "Foreign Policy Makers and the Press," pp. 220–228 in James N. Rosenau (ed.), *International Politics and Foreign Policy.* New York: Free Press.

———. (1963) *The Press and Foreign Policy.* Princeton, NJ: Princeton University Press.

———. (1973) *The Public's Impact on Foreign Policy.* Boston: Little, Brown.

COHEN, EDWARD S. (2001) *The Politics of Globalization in the United States.* Washington, DC: Georgetown University Press.

COHEN, ELIOT A. (1996) "A Revolution in Warfare," *Foreign Affairs* 75 (March/April): 37–54.

———. (1997) "Are U.S. Forces Overstretched? Civil-Military Relations," *Orbis* 41 (Spring): 177–186.

COHEN, STEPHEN D. (1994) *The Making of United States International Economic Policy: Principles, Problems, and Proposals for Reform,* 4th ed. New York: Praeger.

COHEN, STEPHEN D., JOEL R. PAUL, AND ROBERT A. BLECKER. (1996) *Fundamentals of U.S. Foreign Trade Policy: Economics, Politics, Laws, and Issues.* Boulder, CO: Westview.

COLLIER, ELLEN C. (1988) "Foreign Policy by Reporting Requirement," *Washington Quarterly* 11 (Winter): 75–84.

———. (1989) "Bipartisan Foreign Policy and Policymaking Since World War II" in *CRS Report for Congress,* 9 November. Washington, DC: Congressional Research Service.

———. (1994a) "War Powers Resolution: Presidential Compliance" in *CRS Issue Brief 81050,* 15 February. Washington, DC: Congressional Research Service.

———. (1994b) "The War Powers Resolution: Twenty Years of Experience" in *CRS Report for Congress,* 11 January. Washington, DC: Congressional Research Service.

COLLIER, PAUL, AND DAVID DOLLAR. (1999) *Aid Allocation and Poverty Reduction.* Washington, DC: World Bank.

COMMAGER, HENRY STEELE. (1965) "A Historian Looks at Our Political Morality," *Saturday Review*, 10 July, p. 16–18.

———. (1983) "Misconceptions Governing American Foreign Policy," pp. 510–517 in Charles W. Kegley, Jr. and Eugene R. Wittkopf (eds.), *Perspectives on American Foreign Policy*. New York: St. Martin's.

CONGRESSIONAL RESEARCH SERVICE. (1989) "Soviet-U.S. Relations: A Briefing Book" in *CRS Report for Congress*. Washington, DC: Congressional Research Service.

CONOVER, PAMELA J., AND STANLEY FELDMAN. (1984) "How People Organize the Political World: A Schematic Model," *American Journal of Political Science* 28 (February): 95–126.

CONSTABLE, PAMELA. (1998) "The Holdup on the Nuclear Test Ban Treaty," *The Washington Post National Weekly Edition,* 19 October, p. 17.

CONVERSE, PHILIP E. (1964) "The Nature of Belief Systems in Mass Publics," pp. 206–261 in David E. Apter, (ed.), *Ideology and Discontent*. New York: Free Press.

CONWAY, M. MARGARET. (2000) *Political Participation in the United States,* 3rd ed. Washington, DC: CQ Press.

COOK, CHARLES E., JR. (2001a) "How Does 2000 Stack Up?" *Washington Quarterly* 23 (Spring): 213–220.

———. (2001b) "The Silver-Bullet Presidency," *Washington Quarterly* 23 (Summer): 229–234.

COOPER, RICHARD N. (1988) "International Economic Cooperation: Is It Desirable? Is It Likely?" *Washington Quarterly* 11 (Spring): 89–101.

———(1998) "Toward a Real Global Warming Treaty," *Foreign Affairs* 77 (March/April): 66–79.

COPSON, RAYMOND W. (1988) "The Reagan Doctrine: U.S. Assistance to Anti-Marxist Guerrillas" in *CRS Issue Brief,* 11 March. Washington, DC: Congressional Research Service.

CORTRIGHT, DAVID, AND GEORGE A. LOPEZ, (eds.) (2000) *The Sanctions Decade: Assessing UN Strategies in the 1990s.* Boulder, CO: Lynne Rienner.

CORWIN, EDWARD S. (1948) *The President: Office and Powers.* New York: New York University Press.

COX, ARTHUR MACY. (1976) *The Dynamics of Détente.* New York: Norton.

CRABB, CECIL V., JR. (1957) *Bipartisan Foreign Policy: Myth or Reality.* Evanston, IL: Row, Peterson, and Company.

CRABB, CECIL V., JR., AND PAT M. HOLT. (1992) *Invitation to Struggle,* 4th ed. Washington, DC: CQ Press.

CRAIG, STEPHEN C. (1993) *The Malevolent Leaders: Popular Discontent in America.* Boulder, CO: Westview.

CRISTENSEN, THOMAS J. (1999) "China, the U.S.-Japan Alliance, and the Security Dilemma in East Asia," *International Security* 23 (Spring): 49–80.

CROCK, STAN. (1998) "Gore's Foreign Policy Guru," *The New Republic,* 7 December: p. 18.

CROCKER, CHESTER. (1995) "The Lessons of Somalia," *Foreign Affairs* 74 (May/June): 2–8.

CRONIN, THOMAS E. (1973) "The Swelling of the Presidency," *Saturday Review of the Society* 1 (February): 30–36.

———. (1984) "The Swelling of the Presidency: Can Anyone Reverse the Tide?" pp. 345–359 in Peter Woll, (ed.), *American Government: Readings and Cases.* Boston: Little, Brown.

CROPSEY, SETH. (1994) "The Only Credible Deterrent," *Foreign Affairs* 73 (March/April): 14–20.

CUPITT, RICHARD T. (2000) *Reluctant Champions: U.S. Presidential Policy and Strategic Export Controls, Truman, Eisenhower, Bush and Clinton.* New York: Routledge.

DAALDER, IVO. (1994) *The Clinton Administration and Multilateral Peace Operations, Case 462.* Washington, DC: Institute for the Study of Diplomacy.

———. (1999) "Emerging Answers: Kosovo, NATO, and the Use of Force," *Brookings Review* 17 (Summer): 22–25.

DAALDER, IVO H., AND I. M. DESTLER. (2001) "How Operational and Visible an NSC?" The Brookings Institution Opinion Piece (website publication only), 23 February (*http://www. brookings.edu/views/op-ed/daalder/20010223.htm.* accessed November 11, 2001).

———. (2000) "A New NSC for a New Administration." *Brookings Institution Policy Brief #68.* Washington, DC: Brookings Institution.

DAALDER, IVO, AND MICHAEL E. O'HANLON. (2000) "The United States in the Balkans: There to Stay," *Washington Quarterly* 23 (Autumn): 157–170.

DAHL, ROBERT. (1989) *Democracy and Its Critics.* New Haven, CT: Yale University Press.

DALLEK, ROBERT. (1983) *The American Style of Foreign Policy: Cultural Politics and Foreign Affairs.* New York: Knopf.

———. (1984) *Ronald Reagan: The Politics of Symbolism.* Cambridge, MA: Harvard University Press.

DALTON, RUSSELL J., PAUL A. BECK, AND ROBERT HUCKFELDT. (1998) "Partisan Cues and the Media: Information Flows in the 1992 Presidential Election," *American Political Science Review* 92 (March): 111–126.

DALY, HERMAN E. (1993) "The Perils of Free Trade," *Scientific American* 269 (November): 50–57.

DANZIGER, SHELDON, AND DEBORAH REED. (1999) "Winners and Losers: The Era of Inequality Continues," *Brookings Review* 17 (Fall): 14–17.

DAS, DILIP K. (2001) *Global Trading System at Crossroads: A Post-Seattle Perspective.* New York: Routledge.

DAVIS, JENNIFER. (1993) "Squeezing Apartheid," *Bulletin of the Atomic Scientists* 49 (November): 16–19.

DAVIS, VINCENT. (1987) "Organization and Management," pp. 171–199 in Joseph Kruzel (ed.), *American Defense Annual, 1987–1988.* Lexington, MA: Lexington.

DE BORCHGRAVE, ARNAUD. (1996) "Globalization—The Bigger Picture: An Interview with Dr. Ismail Serageldin, World Bank Vice President for Environmentally Sustainable Development," *Washington Quarterly* 19 (Summer): 159–178.

DECONDE, ALEXANDER. (1992) *Ethnicity, Race, and American Foreign Policy.* Boston: Northeastern University Press.

DE LA GARZA, RODOLOFO O., AND HARRY PACHON, (eds.) (2000) *Latinos and U.S. Foreign Policy: Representing the Homeland?* Lanham, MD: Rowman and Littlefield.

DEIBEL, TERRY L. (1992) "Strategies Before Containment: Patterns for the Future," *International Security* 16 (Spring): 79–108.

DERIVERA, JOSEPH H. (1968) *The Psychological Dimension of Foreign Policy.* Columbus, OH: Merrill.

DESTLER, I. M. (1974) *Presidents, Bureaucrats, and Foreign Policy: The Politics of Organizational Reform.* Princeton, NJ: Princeton University Press.

———. (1983a) "The Evolution of Reagan Foreign Policy," pp. 117–158 in Fred I. Greenstein (ed.), *The Reagan Presidency.* Baltimore, MD: The Johns Hopkins University Press.

———. (1983b) "The Rise of the National Security Assistant," pp. 260–281 in Charles W. Kegley, Jr. and Eugene R. Wittkopf, (eds.), *Perspectives on American Foreign Policy.* New York: St. Martin's.

———. (1994) "A Government Divided: The Security Complex and the Economic Complex," pp. 132–147 in David A. Deese, (ed.), *The New Politics of American Foreign Policy.* New York: St. Martin's.

———. (1996) *The National Economic Council: A Work in Progress.* Washington, DC: Institute for International Economics.

———. (1998) "Foreign Economic Policymaking Under Bill Clinton," pp. 89–107 in James M. Scott, (ed.), *After the End: Making U.S. Foreign Policy in the Post-Cold War World.* Durham, NC: Duke University Press.

———. (1999) "Trade Policy at a Crossroads," *The Brookings Review* 17 (Winter): 26–30.

DESTLER, I. M., AND PETER J. BALINT. (1999) *The New Politics of American Trade: Trade, Labor, and the Environment.* Washington, DC: Institute for International Economics.

DESTLER, I. M., LESLIE H. GELB, AND ANTHONY LAKE. (1984) *Our Own Worst Enemy: The Unmaking of American Foreign Policy.* New York: Simon and Schuster.

DE TOCQUEVILLE, ALEXIS. ([1835] 1969) *Democracy in America.* New York: Doubleday.

DEUDNEY, DANIEL, AND G. JOHN IKENBERRY. (1994) "After the Long War," *Foreign Policy* 94 (Spring): 21–35.

DEUTCH, JOHN, HAROLD BROWN, AND JOHN WHITE. (2000) "National Missile Defense: Is There Another Way?" *Foreign Policy* 119 (July/August): 91–100.

DEUTSCH, KARL W., AND RICHARD L. MERRITT. (1965) "Effects of Events on National and International Images," pp. 132–187 in Herbert C. Kelman, (ed.), *International Behavior.* New York: Holt, Rinehart, and Winston.

DEVROY, ANN. (1994) "The Shakedown Cruise: Year Two," *The Washington Post National Weekly Edition,* 11–17 April, p. 11.

DEVROY, ANN, AND STEPHEN BARR. (1995) "Reinventing the Vice Presidency," *The Washing-

ton Post National Weekly Edition, 27 February–5 March, pp. 6–7.

DEVROY, ANN, AND R. JEFFREY SMITH. (1993) "Oceans Apart Over Intervention," *The Washington Post National Weekly Edition,* 3–9 October, pp. 8–9.

DE YOUNG, KAREN, (2001) "Allies Are Cautious on 'Bush Doctrine'." *The Washington Post,* 16 October, p. A1.

DE YOUNG, KAREN, AND ALAN SIPRESS. (2001) "Dual Strategy of Assault, Reward." *Washington Post,* 8 October, p. A1.

DE YOUNG, KAREN, AND DANA MILBANK. "Military Plans Informed by Polls." *Washington Post,* October 19, 2001, p. A19.

DIAMOND, LARRY. (1999) *Developing Democracy: Toward Consolidation.* Baltimore, MD: Johns Hopkins University Press.

DICKEY, CHRISTOPHER, MARK DENNIS, GREGORY VISTICA, AND RUSSELL WATSON. (1998) "How to Get Rid of Him," *Newsweek,* 9 March, p. 31.

DIONNE, E. J., JR. (1996) "Why Foreign Policy Is No Big Issue," *The Washington Post Weekly Edition,* 28 October–3 November, p. 26.

———. (1999) "War as an Opening for Partisan Payback," *The Washington Post Weekly Edition,* 10 May, p. 26.

DIPLOMACY FOR THE 70'S: A PROGRAM OF MANAGEMENT REFORM FOR THE DEPARTMENT OF STATE. (1970). Washington, DC: Department of State.

DiRENZO, GORDON J., (ed.) (1974) *Personality and Politics.* Garden City, NY: Doubleday-Anchor.

DIXON, WILLIAM J., AND STEPHEN M. GAARDER. (1992) "Presidential Succession and the Cold War: An Analysis of Soviet-American Relations, 1948–1988," *Journal of Politics* 54 (February): 156–175.

DOBBS, MICHAEL. (1999) "Post-Mortem on NATO's Bombing Campaign," *The Washington Post National Weekly Edition,* 19–26 July, p. 23.

———. (2001) "Aid Abroad is Business Back Home," *The Washington Post,* p. A1.

DOMHOFF, G. WILLIAM. (1984) *Who Rules America Now?* Englewood Cliffs, NJ: Prentice-Hall.

DONOVAN, HEDLEY. (1985) *Roosevelt to Reagan.* New York: Harper and Row.

DONOVAN, JOHN C. (1974) *The Cold Warriors: A Policy-Making Elite.* Lexington, MA: Heath.

DORAN, MICHAEL SCOTT. (2001) "Somebody Else's Civil War: Ideology, Rage, and the Asault on America." pp. 31–52 in James F. Hoge, Jr. and Gideon Rose (eds.), *How Did This Happen: Terrorism and the New War.* New York: Public Affairs Press.

DOWNS, ANTHONY. (1957) *An Economic Theory of Democracy.* New York: Harper and Row.

———. (1967) *Inside Bureaucracy.* Boston: Little, Brown.

DOXEY, MARGARET. (1990) "International Sanctions," pp. 242–261 in David G. Haglund and Michael K. Hawes, (eds.), *World Politics: Power, Interdependence, and Dependence.* Toronto: Harcourt Brace Jovanovich.

DOYLE, MICHAEL W. (1986) "Liberalism and World Politics," *American Political Science Review* 80 (December): 1151–1169.

———. (1995) "Liberalism and World Politics Revisited," pp. 83–106 in Charles W. Kegley, Jr. (ed.), *Controversies in International Relations Theory: Realism and the Neoliberal Challenge.* New York: St. Martin's.

DRAPER, THEODORE. (1968) *The Dominican Revolt.* New York: Commentary.

———. (1990) *A Present of Things Past.* New York: Hill and Wang.

———. (1991) *A Very Thin Line: The Iran-Contra Affair.* New York: Hill and Wang.

DREW, ELIZABETH. (1994) *On the Edge: The Clinton Presidency.* New York: Simon and Schuster.

DREYFUS, ROBERT. (1998) "Risky Business," *The New Republic* 218 (5 January): 18–20.

DREZNER, DANIEL W. (2000) "Ideas, Bureaucratic Politics, and the Crafting of Foreign Policy," *American Journal of Political Science* 44 (October): 733–749.

DRISCHLER, ALVIN PAUL. (1985) "Foreign Policy Making on the Hill," *Washington Quarterly* 8 (Summer): 165–175.

DROZDIAK, WILLIAM. (1997) "Down with Yankee Dominance," *The Washington Post National Weekly Edition,* 24 November, p. 15.

DULLES, JOHN FOSTER. (1952) "A Policy of Liberation," *Life,* 19 May, p. 19 ff.

DUNN, MICHAEL SCOTT. (2001) "Somebody Else's Civil War: Idelogy, Rage, and the Assault on America," pp. 31–52 in James F. Hoge, Jr. and Gideon Rose (eds.), *How Did This Happen? Terrorism and the New War.* New York: Public Affairs.

DUNN, ROBERT M., JR. (2001) "Has the U.S. Economy REALLY Been Globalized?" *Washington Quarterly,* (Winter): 53–64.

DYE, THOMAS R. (1990) *Who's Running America?: The Bush Era,* 5th ed. Englewood Cliffs, NJ: Prentice-Hall.

———. (1995) *Who's Running America?: The Clinton Years,* 6th ed. Englewood Cliffs, NJ: Prentice-Hall.

DYE, THOMAS R., AND HARMON ZEIGLER. (1990) *The Irony of Democracy,* 8th ed. Pacific Grove, CA: Brooks/Cole.

———. (2000) *The Irony of Democracy: An Uncommon Introduction to American Politics,* Millennial ed. Fort Worth, TX: Harcourt Brace College Publishers.

EAGLEBURGER, LAWRENCE, AND ROBERT BARRY. (1996) "Dollars and Sense Diplomacy," *Foreign Affairs* 75 (4) (July/August): 2–8.

EBERSTADT, NICHOLAS. (1991) "Population Change and National Security," *Foreign Affairs* 70 (Summer): 115–131.

———. (2001) "The Population Implosion," *Foreign Policy* 123 (March/April): 42–53.

ECKHOLM, ERIK. (2001) "Experts Try to Make Missile Shield Plan Palatable to China," *New York Times,* 28 January, p. 1.

EDSALL, THOMAS B. (2001) *Washington Post National Weekly Edition,* April 23–29, p. 14.

EDWARDS, GEORGE C., III, WILLIAM MITCHELL, AND REED WELCH. (1995) "Explaining Presidential Approval: The Significant of Issue Salience," *American Journal of Political Science* 39 (February): 108–134.

EHRLICH, PAUL R., AND ANNE H. EHRLICH. (1990) *The Population Explosion.* New York: Simon and Schuster.

EICHENGREEN, BARRY. (1999) *Toward a New International Financial Structure.* Washington, DC: Institute for International Peace.

———. (1998) *Globalizing Capital: A History of the International Monetary System.* Princeton, NJ: Princeton University Press.

EIZENSTADT, STUART. (1998) "Stick with Kyoto: A Sound Start on Global Warming," *Foreign Affairs* 77 (May/June): 119–121.

ELAND, IVAN. (1993) "Think Small," *Bulletin of the Atomic Scientists* 49 (November): 36–40.

ELAZAR, DANIEL J. (1970) *Cities of the Prairie.* New York: Basic Books.

———. (1994) *The American Mosaic: The Impact of Space, Time, and Culture on American Politics.* Boulder, CO: Westview.

ELLIOTT, KIM ANDREW. (1989–1990) "Too Many Voices of America," *Foreign Policy* 77 (Winter): 113–131.

ELLIOTT, KIMBERLY ANN. (1993) "A Look At the Record," *Bulletin of the Atomic Scientists* 49 (November): 32–35.

———. (1998) "The Sanctions Glass: Half Full or Completely Empty," *International Security* 23 (Summer): 50–65.

ELLIS, JOHN. (1993) *The World War II Databook.* London: Aurum Press.

EMMOTT, BILL. (1994) *Japanophobia: The Myth of the Invincible Japanese.* New York: Times Books.

ENTMAN, ROBERT M. (1989) "How the Media Affect What People Think: An Information Processing Approach," *Journal of Politics* 51 (May): 347–370.

ESTY, DANIEL. (1994) *Greening the GATT: Trade, Environment, and the Future.* Washington, DC: Institute for International Economics.

ETHEREDGE, LLOYD S. (1978) *A World of Men: The Private Sources of American Foreign Policy.* Cambridge, MA: MIT Press.

———. (1985) *Can Governments Learn? American Foreign Policy and Central American Revolutions.* New York: Pergamon.

EVAN, THOMAS. (2000) *Robert Kennedy: His Life.* New York: Simon and Schuster.

FAGEN, RICHARD R. (1960) "Some Assessments and Uses of Public Opinion in Diplomacy," *Public Opinion Quarterly* 24 (Fall): 448–457.

FALK, RICHARD. (1983) "Lifting the Curse of Bipartisanship," *World Policy Journal* 1 (Fall): 127–157.

FALKOWSKI, LAWRENCE S., (ed.) (1979) *Psychological Models in International Politics.* Boulder, CO: Westview.

FALLOWS, JAMES. (1994) *Looking at the Sun.* New York: Pantheon.

"FAR FLUNG FRONTIERS OF SECURITY: THE CLINTON ADMINISTRATION'S TWO-WAR STRATEGY." (1995) *The Defense Monitor* 23 (1), pp. 1ff.

FARAH, BARBARA G., AND ETHEL KLEIN. (1989) "Public Opinion Trends," pp. 103–128 in Gerald M. Pomper, Ross K. Baker, Walter Dean

Burnham, Marjorie Randon Farah, and Ethel Klein McWilliams (eds.), *The Elections of 1988: Reports and Interpretations*. Chatham, NJ: Chatham House.

FEAVER, PETER D., AND CHRISTOPHER GELPI. (1999) "Shattering a Foreign Policy Myth," *The Washington Post National Weekly Edition*, 15 November, pp. 22–23.

FELDSTEIN, MARTIN. (1992) "The Council of Economic Advisers and Economic Advising in the United States," *Economic Journal* 102 (September): 1223–1234.

FENNO, RICHARD F., JR. (1973) *Congressmen in Committees*. Boston: Little, Brown.

FERRELL, ROBERT H. (1988) *American Diplomacy: The Twentieth Century*. New York: Norton.

FESTINGER, LEON. (1957) *A Theory of Cognitive Dissonance*. Evanston, IL: Row, Peterson.

FIORINA, MORRIS P. (1981) *Restrospective Voting in American National Elections*. New Haven, CT: Yale University Press.

———. (2001) "Keystone Reconsidered," pp. 141–162 in Lawrence C. Dodd and Bruce I. Oppenheimer, (eds.), *Congress Reconsidered*, 7th ed. Washington, DC: CQ Press.

FIRTH, NOEL E., AND JAMES H. NOREN. (1998) *Soviet Defense Spending: A History of CIA Estimates, 1950–1990*. College Station, TX: Texas A&M University Press.

FISCHER, BENJAMIN B., (ed.) (1999) *At Cold War's End: US Intelligence on the Soviet Union and Eastern Europe, 1989–1991*. Washington, DC: Government Printing Office.

FISHER, LOUIS. (1991) *Constitutional Conflicts Between Congress and the President*. Lawrence, KS: University of Kansas Press.

———. (1993) *The Politics of Shared Power: Congress and the Executive*, 3rd ed. Washington, DC: CQ Press.

———. (1994–1995) "Congressional Checks on Military Initiatives," *Political Science Quarterly* 109 (Winter): 739–762.

———. (1995) *Presidential War Power*. Lawrence, KS: University of Kansas Press.

———. (1997) *Constitutional Conflicts Between Congress and the President*. Lawrence, KS: University of Kansas Press.

———. (1998) "Military Action Against Iraq," *Presidential Studies Quarterly* 28 (Fall): 793–798.

———. (2000a) *Congressional Abdication on War and Spending*. College Station, TX: Texas A&M University Press.

———. (2000b) "Litigating the War Power with Campbell v. Clinton," *Presidential Studies Quarterly* 30 (September): 564–574.

FISHER, LOUIS, AND DAVID GRAY ADLER. (1998) "The War Powers Resolution: Time to Say Goodbye," *Political Science Quarterly* 113 (Spring): 1–20.

FITE, DAVID, MARC GENEST, AND CLYDE WILCOX. (1990) "Gender Differences in Foreign Policy Attitudes: A Longitudinal Analysis," *American Politics Quarterly* 18 (October): 492–512.

FITZGERALD, FRANCES. (2000) *Way Out There in the Blue: Reagan, Star Wars, and the End of the Cold War*. New York: Simon and Schuster.

FITZGERALD, FRANCIS. (1989) "Annals of Justice: Iran-Contra," *The New Yorker*, 16 October, pp. 51–84.

FIXDAL, MONA, AND DAN SMITH. (1998) "Humanitarian Intervention and Just War," *Mershon International Studies Review* 42 (November): 283–312.

FLANAGAN, STEPHEN J. (1985) "Managing the Intelligence Community," *International Security* 10 (Summer): 58–95.

FLANAGAN, STEPHEN J., ELLEN L. FROST, AND RICHARD L. KUGLER. (2001) *Challenges of the Global Century: Report of the Project on Globalization and National Security*. Washington, D.C.: National Defense University.

FLAVIN, CHRISTOPHER. (2001) "Rich Planet, Poor Planet," pp. 3–20 in Lester R. Brown, Christopher Flavin, Hilary French, Janet Abramovitz, Seth Dunn, Gary Gardner, Lisa Mastny, Ashley Mattoon, David Roodman, Payal Sampat, Molly O. Sheehan, and Linda Starke, (eds.) *State of the World 2001*. New York: Norton.

FLEISHER, RICHARD. (1985) "Economic Benefit, Ideology, and Senate Voting on the B-1 Bomber," *American Politics Quarterly* 13 (April): 200–211.

FLEISHER, RICHARD, JON R. BOND, AND GLEN S. KRUTZ. (2000) "The Demise of the Two Presidencies." *American Politics Quarterly*. 28:1 (Spring): 3–25.

FLETCHER, MARTIN. (1990) "CIA Ordered by Bush to Plot Fall of Saddam," *Times* (London), 7 August p. 1.

FLICKNER, CHARLES. (1994–1995) "The Russian Aid Mess," *The National Interest* 38 (Winter): 13–18.

FOLEY, TIMOTHY D. (1994) "The Role of the CIA in Economic and Technological Intelligence," *Fletcher Forum on World Affairs* 18 (Winter/Spring): 135–145.

FORD, GERALD R. (1979) *A Time to Heal*. New York: Harper and Row.

"The Foreign Born Population in the United States." (2000), *Current Population Reports,* August.

FOSTER, GREGORY D. (1989) "Global Demographic Trends to the Year 2010: Implications for U.S. Security," *Washington Quarterly* 12 (Spring): 5–24.

FOX, HARRISON W., JR., AND SUSAN WEBB HAMMOND. (1977) *Congressional Staffs: The Invisible Force in American Lawmaking.* New York: Free Press.

FRANCK, THOMAS M. (1999) "Sidlined in Kosovo? The United Nations Decline Has Been Exaggerated," *Foreign Affairs* 78 (July/August): 116–118.

FRANK, CHARLES R., JR., AND MARY BAIRD. (1975) "Foreign Aid: Its Speckled Past and Future Prospects," *International Organization* 29 (Winter): 133–167.

FRANK, ROBERT S. (1973) *Message Dimensions of Television News.* Lexington, MA: Lexington Books.

FRANKEL, CHARLES. (1969) *High on Foggy Bottom.* New York: Harper and Row.

FRANKOVIC, KATHLEEN A. (1982) "Sex and Politics—New Alignments, Old Issues," *PS* 15 (Summer): 439–448.

———. (1998) "Public Opinion and Polling," pp. 150–170 in Doris Graber, Denis McQual, and Pippa Norris (eds.), *The Politics of News the News of Politics.* Washington, DC: CQ Press.

FREEDBERG, SYDNEY J. (2001) "Where are the Humans?" *National Journal.* 15 September: 2834–2836.

FREEMAN, J. LEIPER. (1965) "The Bureaucracy in Pressure Politics," pp. 23–35 in Francis E. Ranke, (ed.), *Bureaucratic Power in National Politics.* Boston: Little, Brown.

FRENCH, HILARY F. (1993) "The GATT: Menace or Ally," *World Watch* 6 (September–October): 12–19.

FRENCH, HILARY, AND LISA MASTNY. (2001) "Controlling International Environmental Crime," pp. 166–188 in Lester R. Brown, Christopher Flavin, Hilary French, Janet N. Abramovitz, Seth Dunn, Gary Gardner, Lisa Mastny, Ashely Mattoon, David Roodman, Payal Sampat, Molley O Sheehan, Lindan Starke, (eds.), *State of the World 2001.* New York: Norton.

FRIEDBERG, AARON L. (1989) "The Strategic Implications of Relative Economic Decline," *Political Science Quarterly* 104 (Fall): 401–431.

———. (1992) "Why Didn't the United States Become a Garrison State?" *International Security* 16 (Spring): 109–142.

FRIEDMAN, THOMAS L. (1994a) "Never Mind Yen. Greenbacks Are the New Gold Standard," *New York Times,* 3 July, p. E5.

———. (1994b) "Trade War Isn't So Swell Either," *New York Times,* 6 March, p. E4.

———. (1999) *The Lexus and the Olive Tree: Understanding Globalization.* New York: Farrar, Straus, Giroux.

FRYE, ALTON. (1996) "Banning Ballistic Missiles," *Foreign Affairs* 75 (November/December): 99–112.

———. (ed.), (2000) *Humanitarian Intervention: Crafting a Workable Doctrine.* New York: Council on Foreign Relations.

FULLER, GRAHAM. (1995) "The Next Ideology," *Foreign Policy* 98 (Spring): 145–158.

GABELNICK, TAMAR. (1999) "Problems with Current U.S. Policy," *Foreign Policy In Focus* 21 May p. 2.

GADDIS, JOHN LEWIS. (1972) *The United States and the Origins of the Cold War.* New York: Columbia University Press.

———. (1982) *Strategies of Containment: A Critical Appraisal of Postwar American National Security Policy.* New York: Oxford University Press.

———. (1983) "Containment: Its Past and Future," pp. 16–31 in Charles W. Kegley, Jr. and Eugene R. Wittkopf, (eds.), *Perspectives on American Foreign Policy.* New York: St. Martin's.

———. (1986) "The Long Peace: Elements of Stability in the Postwar International System," *International Security* 10 (Spring): 99–142.

———. (1987–1988) "Containment and the Logic of Strategy," *The National Interest* 10 (Winter): 27–38.

———. (1992) *The United States and the End of the Cold War: Implications, Reconsiderations, Provocations.* New York: Oxford University Press.

———. (1997) *We Now Know: Rethinking Cold War History.* New York: Clarendon.

GALBRAITH, JOHN KENNETH. (1969) "The Power of the Pentagon," *The Progressive* 33 (June): 29.

GALLAGHER, WINIFRED. (1994) "How We Become What We Are," *The Atlantic Monthly* 274 (September): 38–55.

GARDNER, RICHARD N. (1990) "The Comeback of Liberal Internationalism," *Washington Quarterly* 13 (Summer): 23–39.

GARFINKLE, ADAM. (1998) "Anatomy of a Farce," *The National Interest* 52 (Summer): 123–126.

GARRETT, LAURIE. (2001) "Encroaching Plagues: The Return of Infectious Disease," pp. 425–433 in Charles W. Kegley, Jr. and Eugene R. Wittkopf (eds.), *The Global Agenda: Issues and Perspectives,* 6th ed. Boston: McGraw-Hill.

GARTEN, JEFFREY E. (1998) *The Big Ten: The Big Emerging Markets and How They Will Change Our Lives.* New York: Basic Books.

GARTHOFF, RAYMOND L. (1994) "Looking Back: The Cold War in Retrospect," *Brookings Review* 12 (Summer): 10–13.

GARTZKE, ERIC. (1996) "Congress and Back Seat Driving: An Information Theory of the War Powers Resolution," *Policy Studies Journal* 24 (Summer): 259–286.

GASIOROWSKI, MARK J. (1987) "The 1953 Coup D'Etat in Iran," *International Journal of Middle East Studies* 19 (August): 261–286.

GAUSE, F. GREGORY III. (1994) "The Illogic of Dual Containment," *Foreign Affairs* 73 (March/April): 56–66.

———. (1999) "Getting It Backward on Iraq," *Foreign Affairs* 78 (May/June): 54–65.

GELB, LESLIE H. (1983) "Why Not the State Department?" pp. 282–298 in Charles W. Kegley, Jr. and Eugene R. Wittkopf (eds.), *Perspectives on American Foreign Policy.* New York: St. Martin's.

———. (1994) "Quelling the Teacup Wars: The New World's Constant Challenge," *Foreign Affairs* 73 (November/December): 2–6.

GELB, LESLIE H., AND MORTON H. HALPERIN. (1973) "The Ten Commandments of the Foreign Affairs Bureaucracy," pp. 250–259 in Steven L. Spiegel (ed.), *At Issue: Politics in the World Arena.* New York: St. Martin's Press.

GELLMAN, BARTON. (1992a) "On Second Thought, We Don't Want to Rule the World," *The Washington Post National Weekly Edition,* 1–7 June, p. 31.

———. (1992b) "The U.S. Aims to Remain First Among Nonequals," *The Washington Post National Weekly Edition,* 16–22 March, p. 19.

———. (1993) "Pin Stripes Clash With Stars and Bars," *The Washington Post National Weekly Edition,* 28–June–3 July, pp. 31–32.

———. (1999) "Learning from Kosovo," *The Washington Post National Weekly Edition,* 14 June, pp. 6–9.

GENTRY, JOHN A. (1998) "Military Force in an Age of National Cowardice," *Washington Quarterly* 21 (Autumn): 179–191.

GEORGE, ALEXANDER L. (1969) "The 'Operational Code': A Neglected Approach to the Study of Political Leaders and Decision-Making," *International Studies Quarterly* 13 (June): 190–222.

———. (1972) "The Case for Multiple Advocacy in Making Foreign Policy," *American Political Science Review* 66 (September): 751–785.

———. (1980) *Presidential Decisionmaking in Foreign Policy: The Effective Use of Information and Advice.* Boulder, CO: Westview.

———. (1988) "Presidential Management Styles and Models," pp. 107–126 in Charles W. Kegley, Jr. and Eugene R. Wittkopf (eds.), *The Domestic Sources of American Foreign Policy: Insights and Evidence.* New York: St. Martin's.

———. (1992) *Forceful Persuasion: Coercive Diplomacy as an Alternative to War.* Washington, DC: United States Institute for Peace.

GEORGE, ALEXANDER L., AND JULIETTE L. GEORGE. (1964) *Woodrow Wilson and Colonel House: A Personality Study.* New York: Dover.

GERGEN, DAVID. (1989) "The Bush Administration's Three Musketeers," *The Washington Post National Weekly Edition,* 17–23 April, pp. 23–24.

———. (2001) *Eyewitness to Power: The Essence of Leadership from Nixon to Clinton.* New York: MacMillan.

GHOLZ, EUGENE, DARYL G. PRESS, AND HARVEY M. SAPOLSKY. (1997) "Come Home, America: The Strategy of Restraint in the Face of Temptation," *International Security* 21 (Spring): 5–48.

GHOLZ, EUGENE, AND HARVEY M. SAPOLSKY. (1999–2000) "Restructuring the U.S. Defense Industry," *International Security* 24 (Winter): 5–51.

GILBERT, FELIX. (1961) *The Beginnings of American Foreign Policy: To the Farewell Address.* New York: Harper Torchbooks.

GILBOA, EYTAN. (1987) *American Public Opinion toward Israel and the Arab-Israeli Conflict.* Lexington, MA: Lexington Books.

GILL, STEPHEN, AND DAVID LAW. (1988) *The Global Political Economy: Perspectives, Problems, and Policies.* Baltimore, MO.: Johns Hopkins University Press.

GILPIN, ROBERT. (1981) *War and Change in World Politics.* New York: Cambridge University Press.

———. (1987) *The Political Economy of International Relations.* Princeton, NJ: Princeton University Press.

———. (2000) *The Challenge of Global Capitalism: The World Economy in the 21st Century.* Princeton, NJ: Princeton University Press.

GILPIN, TODD. (1995) "After the Failed Faiths: Beyond Individualism, Marxism, and Multiculturalism," *World Policy Journal* 12 (Spring): 61–68.

GLAD, BETTY. (1983) "Black-and-White Thinking: Ronald Reagan's Approach to Foreign Policy," *Political Psychology* 4 (March): 33–76.

GLASER, CHARLES L. (1992) "Nuclear Policy Without an Adversary: U.S. Planning for the Post-Soviet Era," *International Security* 16 (Spring): 34–78.

GLENNON, MICHAEL J. (1999) "The New Interventionism: The Search for a Just International Law," *Foreign Affairs* 78 (May/June): 2–7.

GODSON, ROY S. (2000) *Dirty Tricks or Trump Cards: U.S. Covert Action and Counterintelligence.* New Brunswick, NJ: Transaction Publishers.

GODSON, ROY S., AND ERNEST MAY. (1995) *U.S. Intelligence at the Crossroads: Agendas for Reform.* Herndon, VA: Brassey's, Inc.

GOLDGEIER, JAMES M. (1998) "NATO Expansion: Anatomy of a Decision," *The Washington Quarterly* 21 (Winter): 88–102.

———. (1999) *Not Whether but When: The U.S. Decision to Enlarge NATO.* Washington, DC: Brookings Institution Press.

GOLDSBOROUGH, JAMES O. (1993) "California's Foreign Policy," *Foreign Affairs* 72 (Spring): 88–96.

GOLDSTEIN, JOSHUA S. (1988) *Long Cycles: Prosperity and War in the Modern Age.* New Haven, CT: Yale University Press.

GOLDSTEIN, JUDITH. (1989) "The Impact of Ideas on Trade Policy: The Origins of U.S. Agricultural and Manufacturing Policies," *International Organization* 43 (Winter): 31–71.

GOODMAN, ALLAN E. (1975) "The Causes and Consequences of Détente, 1949–1973," Paper presented at the National Security Education Seminar, Colorado Springs, CO, July.

GOODMAN, MELVIN A. (1997) "Ending the CIA's Cold War Legacy," *Foreign Policy* 106 (Spring): 128–143.

———. (2000) "The Politics of Getting It Wrong," *Harper's* 301 (November): 74–80.

GOODPASTER, ANDREW J. (1995) *An Evolving U.S. Nuclear Posture.* Washington, DC: The Henry L. Stimson Center.

———. (1997) *An American Legacy: Building a Nuclear-Weapon-Free World.* Washington, DC: The Henry L. Stimson Center.

GOODSELL, CHARLES T. (1985) *The Case for Bureaucracy,* 2nd ed. Chatham, NJ: Chatham House.

GOOZNER, MERRILL. (1997) "U.S. Arms Makers Strike Hard," *Toronto Star,* p. A1.

GORDON, MICHAEL, AND BERNARD TRAINOR. (1995) *The General's War: The Inside Story of the Conflict in the Gulf.* Boston: Little, Brown.

GORE, AL. (1993) "This Time We Mean Business," *The Washington Post National Weekly Edition,* 20–26 September, p. 25.

GOSHKO, JOHN M. (1989) "Foreign Policy in Turmoil—or Transition?" *The Washington Post National Weekly Edition,* 13–19 March, p. 7.

———. (1994) "Undiplomatic Doubts at Foggy Bottom," *The Washington Post National Weekly Edition,* 27 June–3 July, p. 31.

GOWA, JOANNE. (1999) *Ballots and Bullets: The Elusive Democratic Peace.* Princeton, NJ: Princeton University Press.

GOWING, NIK. (1994) "Discounting the 'CNN Factor'," *The Washington Post National Weekly Edition,* 8–14 August, p. 23.

GRABER, DORIS A. (1993) *Mass Media and American Politics,* 4th ed. Washington, DC: CQ Press.

———. (1997) *Mass Media and American Politics,* 5th ed. Washington, DC: CQ Press.

GRAHAM, BRADLEY, AND THOMAS RICKS. (2001) "Rangers Hit Taliban in Ground Combat." *Washington Post,* 20 October, p. A1.

GRAHAM, THOMAS W. (1986) "Public Attitudes Towards Active Defense: ABM and Star Wars, 1945–1985." Cambridge, MA: Center for International Studies, Massachusetts Institute of Technology.

GRAYSON, GEORGE W. (1999) *Strange Bedfellows: NATO Marches East.* Lanham, MD: University Press of America.

GREENSTEIN, FRED I. (1969) *Personality and Politics*. Princeton, NJ: Princeton University Press.

————. (1982) *The Hidden Hand Presidency: Eisenhower as Leader*. New York: Basic Books.

————. (1993–1994) "The Presidential Leadership Style of Bill Clinton: An Early Appraisal," *Political Science Quarterly* 108 (Winter): 589–601.

————. (1994) "The Hidden-Hand Presidency: Eisenhower as Leader: A 1994 Perspective," *Presidential Studies Quarterly* 24 (Spring): 233–241.

————. (2000) *The Presidential Difference: Leadership Style from FDR to Clinton*. New York: Free Press.

GREENSTEIN, FRED I., AND RICHARD H. IMMERMAN. (2000) "Effective National Security Advising: Recovering the Eisenhower Legacy," *Political Science Quarterly* 115 (Fall): 335–345.

GRIEVE, MALCOLM J. (1993) "Debt and Imperialism: Perspectives on the Debt Crisis," pp. 51–68 in Stephen P. Riley (ed.), *The Politics of Global Debt*. New York: St. Martin's.

GRIMMETT, RICHARD F. (1995) "The War Powers Resolution: Fifteen Years of Experience" in *CRS Report for Congress*. Washington, DC: Congressional Research Service.

————. (1999) "Conventional Arms Transfers to the Developing Nations, 1991–1998" in *CRS Report for Congress*. Washington, DC: Congressional Research Service.

GROELING, TIM, AND SAMUEL KERNELL. (1998) "Is Network Coverage of the President Biased?" *Journal of Politics* 60 (November): 1063–1086.

GRONLUND, LISBETH, AND DAVID WRIGHT. (1997) "Missile Defense: The Sequel," *Technology Review* 100 (May/June): 28–36.

GROVE, LLOYD. (1991) "Israel's Force in Washington," *The Washington Post National Weekly Edition*, 24–30 June, pp. 8–9.

GUGLIOTTA, GUY. (1998) "Playing Musical Chairs in the House," *The Washington Post National Weekly Edition*, 30 March, p. 12.

————. (1999) "A Balkanized Congress," *The Washington Post Weekly Edition*, 17 May, p. 14.

GURR, TED ROBERT. (1991) "America as a Model for the World? A Skeptical View," *PS: Political Science and Politics* 24 (December): 664–667.

HAASS, RICHARD N. (1994a) "Bill Clinton's Adhocracy," *New York Times Magazine*, 29 May, pp. 40–41.

————. (1994b) *Intervention: The Use of American Military Force in the Post–Cold War World*. Washington, DC: Carnegie Endowment.

————. (1995) "Paradigm Lost," *Foreign Affairs* 74 (January/February): 43–58.

————. (1997) "Sanctioning Madness," *Foreign Affairs* 76 (November/December): 74–85.

————. (ed.) (1998) *Economic Sanctions and American Diplomacy*, 2nd ed. New York: Council on Foreign Relations.

————. (1999) "What to Do With American Primacy," *Foreign Affairs* 78 (September/October): 37–49.

————. (2000) "Five Not-So-Easy Pieces: The Debates on American Foreign Policy," *Brookings Review* 18 (Spring): 38–40.

HAINES, GERALD K., AND ROBERT S. LEGGETT, (eds.) (2001) *CIA's Analysis of the Soviet Union, 1947–1991*. Washington, DC: Center for the Study of Intelligence.

HALBERSTAM, DAVID. (1972) *The Best and the Brightest*. New York: Random House.

HALBERSTAM, DAVID. (2001) *War in a Time of Peace: Bush, Clinton, and The Generals*. New York: Scribner.

HALL, BRIAN. (1998) "Overkill Is Not Dead," *New York Times Magazine*, 15 March, pp. 42–49ff.

HALLIDAY, DENIS J. (1999) "Iraq and the UN's Weapon of Mass Destruction," *Current History* 98 (February): 65–68.

HALPERIN, MORTON H. (1971) "Why Bureaucrats Play Games," *Foreign Policy* 2 (Spring): 70–90.

HAMILTON, LEE H. (1988) "Congress and The Presidency in American Foreign Policy," *Presidential Studies Quarterly* 18 (Summer): 507–511.

HAMMOND, PAUL Y. (1994) "Central Organization in the Transition from Bush to Clinton," pp. 163–181 in Charles F. Hermann (ed.), *American Defense Annual, 1994*. New York: Lexington.

HAMPSON, FEN OSLER. (1988) "The Divided Decision-Maker," pp. 227–247 in Charles W. Kegley, Jr. and Eugene R. Wittkopf (eds.), *The Domestic Sources of American Foreign Policy*. New York: St. Martin's.

HAN, ALBERT. (1992–1993) "No Defense for Strategic Defense," *Harvard International Review* 156 (Winter): 54–57.

HANCOCK, JAY. (2000) "Military Expected to Be Used Sparingly; 'Powell Doctrine' Calls for

Measured Troop Use," *Baltimore Sun,* 17 December, p. 1A.

HANDELMAN, STEPHEN. (1994) "The Russian 'Mafiya'," *Foreign Affairs* 73 (March/April): 83–96.

HANEY, CRAIG, AND PHILIP ZIMBARDO. (1973) "Social Roles, Role-Playing, and Education," *Behavioral and Social Science Teacher* 1 (1): 24–45.

HANEY, PATRICK J., AND WALT VANDERBUSH. (1999) "The Role of Ethnic Interest Groups in U.S. Foreign Policy: The Case of the Cuban American National Foundation," *International Studies Quarterly* 43 (June): 341–361.

HANSEN, ROGER D. (1980) "North–South Policy—What's the Problem?" *Foreign Affairs* 58 (Summer): 1104–1128.

HARKAVY, ROBERT E. (1997) "Images of the Coming International System," *Orbis* 41 (Fall): 569–590.

HARPER, JOHN L. (1997) "The Dream of Democratic Peace," *Foreign Affairs* 76 (May/June): 117–121.

HARR, JOHN ENSOR. (1969) *The Professional Diplomat.* Princeton, NJ: Princeton University Press.

HARRIS, JOHN F. (1997a) "The Man Who Squared the Oval Office," *Washington Post Weekly Edition,* 13 January, p. 11.

———. (1997b) "Mixing Stagecraft with Statecraft," *Washington Post Weekly Edition,* 14 July, pp. 12–13.

———. (1999) "A Man of Caution," *Washington Post National Weekly Edition,* 24 May, pp. 6–7.

———. (2001) "On the World Stage Bush Shuns the Spotlight," *Washington Post National Weekly Edition,* 23–29 April, p. 11.

HARTCHER, PETER. (2001) "From Miracle to Malaise," *The National Interest* 62 (Spring): 76–85.

HARTUNG, WILLIAM D. (1993) "Welcome to the U.S. Arms Superstore," *Bulletin of the Atomic Scientists* 49 (September): 20–26.

———. (1994b) "The Phantom Profits of the War Trade," *New York Times,* 6 March, p. 13.

———. (1995) "Nixon's Children: Bill Clinton and the Permanent Arms Bazaar," *World Policy Journal* 12 (Summer): 25–35.

———. (1998) "Reagan Redux: The Enduring Myth of Star Wars," *World Policy Journal* 15 (Fall): 17–24.

———. (2001) "New War, Old Weapons." *The Nation,* 29 October, p. 4.

HARTZ, LOUIS. (1955) *The Liberal Tradition in America.* New York: Harcourt Brace and World.

HASLAM, JONATHAN. (1997) "Russian Archival Revelations and Our Understanding of the Cold War," *Diplomatic History* 21 (Spring): 217–228.

HATFIELD, J. H. (1999) *Fortunate Son: The Making of an American President.* New York: St. Martin's LLC.

HAUSMANN, RICARDO. (1999) "Should There Be Five Currencies or One Hundred and Five?" *Foreign Policy* 116 (Fall): 65–79.

HEILBRUNN, JACOB. (1997) "The Great Equivocator," *The New Republic,* 24 March pp. 23–27.

———. (1998) "Mr. Nice Guy," *The New Republic,* 13 April pp. 19–25.

HELMS, JESSE. (1999) "What Sanctions Epidemic?" *Foreign Affairs* 78 (January/February): 2–8.

———. (2000–2001) "American Sovereignty and the UN," *The National Interest* 62 (Winter): 31–45.

HENDERSON, PHILLIP G. (1988) *Managing the Presidency: The Eisenhower Legacy—From Kennedy to Reagan.* Boulder, CO: Westview.

HENDRICKSON, DAVID C. (1994) "The Recovery of Internationalism," *Foreign Affairs* 73 (September/October): 26–43.

———. (1994–1995) "The Democratist Crusade: Intervention, Economic Sanctions, and Engagement," *World Policy Journal* 11 (Winter): 26–43.

HENDRICKSON, RYAN. (1998) "War Powers, Bosnia, and the 104th Congress," *Political Science Quarterly* 113 (Summer): 241–258.

———. (Forthcoming) *The Clinton Wars.* Nashville, TN: Vanderbilt University Press.

HENKIN, LOUIS. (1972) *Foreign Affairs and the Constitution.* Mineola, NY: Foundation Press.

———. (1990) *Constitutionalism, Democracy, and Foreign Affairs.* New York: Columbia University Press.

HENRIKSEN, THOMAS. (2000) "Covert Operations, Now More Than Ever," *Orbis* 44 (Winter): 145–156.

HEREK, GREGORY M., IRVING JANIS, AND PAUL HUTH. (1987) "Decision Making During International Crisis: Is Quality of Process Related to Outcome?" *Journal of Conflict Resolution* 31 (June): 203–226.

HERMANN, CHARLES F. (1969) "International Crisis as a Situational Variable," pp. 409–421 in

James N. Rosenau, (ed.), *International Politics and Foreign Policy*. New York: Free Press.

————. (1972) "Some Issues in the Study of International Crisis," pp. 3–17 in Charles F. Hermann (ed.), *International Crises: Insights from Behavioral Research*. New York: Free Press.

HERMANN, MARGARET G. (1976) "When Leader Personality Will Affect Foreign Policy: Some Propositions," pp. 326–333 in James N. Rosenau (ed.), *In Search of Global Patterns*. New York: Free Press.

————. (1980) "Explaining Foreign Policy Behavior Using Personal Characteristics of Political Leaders," *International Studies Quarterly* 24 (March): 7–46.

————. (1984) "Personality and Foreign Policy Decision Making: A Study of 53 Heads of Government," pp. 53–80 in Donald A. Sylvan and Steve Chan (eds.), *Foreign Policy Decision-Making: Perceptions, Cognition, and Artificial Intelligence*. New York: Praeger.

————. (1986) "Ingredients of Leadership," pp. 167–192 in Margaret G. Hermann (ed.), *Political Psychology*. San Francisco: Jossey-Bass.

————. (1987) "Foreign Policy Role Orientations and the Quality of Foreign Policy Decisions," pp. 123–140 in Stephen G. Walker (ed.), *Role Theory and Foreign Policy Analysis*. Durham, NC: Duke University Press.

————. (1987b) "Handbook for Assessing Personal Characteristics and Foreign Policy Orientations of Political Leaders," *Mershon Occasional Papers*, (Spring): n.p.

————. (1987c) "Workbook for Developing Personality Profiles of Political Leaders from Content Analysis Data," *Mershon Occasional Papers*, (Summer): n.p.

————. (1989) "Defining the Bush Presidential Style," *Mershon Memo*, (Spring): 1.

————. (2001) "Stereotypes Build Solidarity but Limit Our Understanding," *Maxwell Perspective* 12 (Fall): 10–11.

HERMANN, MARGARET G., AND CHARLES F. HERMANN. (1989) "Who Makes Foreign Policy Choices and How: An Empirical Inquiry," *International Studies Quarterly* 33 (December): 361–387.

HERMANN, MARGARET G., AND CHARLES W. KEGLEY, JR. (1995) "Rethinking Democracy and International Peace: Perspectives from Political Psychology," *International Studies Quarterly* 39 (September): 511–533.

————. (2001) "Stereotypes Build Solidarity, but Limit Our Understanding," *Maxwell Perspective* 12 (Fall): 10–4.

HERMANN, MARGARET G., AND THOMAS PRESTON. (1999) "Presidents, Leadership Style, and the Advisory Process," pp. 351–368 in Eugene R. Wittkopf and James M. McCormick (eds.), *The Domestic Sources of American Foreign Policy: Insights and Evidence,* 3rd ed. Lanham, MD: Roman and Littlefield.

HERRMANN, RICHARD K. (1986) "The Power of Perceptions in Foreign-Policy Decision Making: Do Views of the Soviet Union Determine the Policy Choices of American Leaders?" *American Journal of Political Science* 30 (November): 841–875.

HERSH, SEYMOUR. (1983) *The Price of Power: Kissinger in the Nixon White House*. New York: Summit Books.

————. (1994) "Missile Wars," *The New Yorker,* 26 September, pp. 86–99.

HERSMAN, REBECCA K. C. (2000) *Friends and Foes: How Congress and the President Really Make Foreign Policy*. Washington, DC: Brookings Institution.

HESS, STEPHEN. (1984) *The Government/Press Connection*. Washington, DC: Brookings Institution.

HESS, STEPHEN, AND MICHAEL NELSON. (1985) "Foreign Policy: Dominance and Decisiveness in Presidential Elections," pp. 129–154 in Michael Nelson (ed.), *The Elections of 1984*. Washington, DC: CQ Press.

HILLEN, JOHN. (1999) "Defense's Death Spiral," *Foreign Affairs* 78 (July/August): 2–7.

HILSMAN, ROGER. (1967) *To Move a Nation*. New York: Doubleday.

————. (1990) *The Politics of Policy Making in Defense and Foreign Affairs*, 2nd ed. Englewood Cliffs, NJ: Prentice-Hall.

————. (1995) "Does the CIA Still Have a Role?" *Foreign Affairs* 74 (September–October): 104–116.

————. (1996) *The Cuban Missile Crisis: The Struggle Over Policy*. Westport, CT: Preager.

HINCKLEY, BARBARA. (1994) *Less Than Meets the Eye: Foreign Policy Making and the Myth of the Assertive Congress*. Chicago: University of Chicago Press.

HINCKLEY, RONALD H. (1993) "Neo-Isolationism: A Threat or A Myth?" *The Wirthlin Report* 3 (January): 1–3.

HIRSHBERG, MATTHEW S. (1993) *Perpetuating Patriotic Perceptions: The Cognitive Function of the Cold War*. Westport, CT: Praeger.

HOCKIN, THOMAS A. (2001) *The American Nightmare: Trade Politics After Seattle.* Lanham, MD: Lexington.

HOFFMAN, DAVID. (1999) "A Weakened Bear: An Impoverished Russian Military Envies NATO," *The Washington Post National Weekly Edition,* 21 June, p. 18.

HOFFMANN, STANLEY. (1978) *Primacy or World Order: American Foreign Policy Since the Cold War.* New York: McGraw-Hill.

———. (1979–1980) "Muscle and Brains," *Foreign Policy* 37 (Winter): 3–27.

———. (1992) "Bush Abroad," *New York Review of Books* 39 November: 54–59.

———. (1995) "The Crisis of Liberal Internationalism," *Foreign Policy* 98 (Spring): 159–177.

HOGE, JAMES F., JR. (1994) "Media Pervasiveness," *Foreign Affairs* 73 (July/August): 136–144.

HOLLAND, LAUREN. (1999) "The U.S. Decision to Launch Operation Desert Storm: A Bureaucratic Politics Analysis," *Armed Forces and Society: An Interdisciplinary Journal* 25(Winter): 219–242.

HOLLOWAY, DAVID. (1994) *Stalin and the Bomb: The Soviet Union and Atomic Energy 1939–1956.* New Haven, CT: Yale University Press.

HOLMES, GENTA HAWKINS. (1994) "Diversity in the Department of State and the Foreign Service," *State Magazine* 375 (March): 18–25.

HOLMES, STEVEN A. (1998) "Losers in Clinton-Starr Bouts May Be Future U.S. Presidents," *New York Times,* 23 August, A1.

HOLSTI, K. J. (1998) "International Relations Theory and Domestic War in the Third World: The Limits of Relevance," pp. 103–132 in Stephanie G. Neuman (ed.), *International Relations Theory and the Third World.* New York: St. Martin's.

HOLSTI, OLE R. (1962) "The Belief System and National Images: A Case Study," *Journal of Conflict Resolution* 6 (September): 244–252.

———. (1970) "The 'Operational Code' Approach to the Study of Political Leaders: John Foster Dulles' Philosophical and Instrumental Beliefs," *Canadian Journal of Political Science* 3 (March): 123–157.

———. (1973) "Foreign Policy Decision-Makers Viewed Psychologically," Paper presented at the Conference on the Successes and Failures of Scientific International Relations Research, Ojai, CA, June 25–28.

———. (1976) "Foreign Policy Formation Viewed Cognitively," pp. 18–54 in Robert Axelrod, (ed.), *Structure of Decision: The Cognitive Maps of Political Elites.* Princeton, NJ: Princeton University Press.

———. (1987) "Public Opinion and Containment," pp. 20–58 in Terry L. Deibel and John Lewis Gaddis, (eds.), *Containing the Soviet Union.* Washington, DC: Pergamon-Brassey's.

———. (1992) "Public Opinion and Foreign Policy: Challenges to the Almond-Lippmann Consensus," *International Studies Quarterly* 36 (December): 439–466.

———. (1994) "Public Opinion and Foreign Policy: Attitude Structures of Opinion Leaders After the Cold War," pp. 36–56 in Eugene R. Wittkopf (ed.), *The Domestic Sources of American Foreign Policy,* 2nd ed. New York: St. Martin's.

———. (1995) "Theories of International Policies and Foreign Policy: Realism and Its Challengers," pp. 35–65 in Charles W. Kegley, Jr., (ed.), *Controversies in International Relations Theory: Realism and the Neoliberal Challenge.* New York: St. Martin's.

———. (1996) *Public Opinion and American Foreign Policy.* Ann Arbor, MI: University of Michigan Press.

———. (1998–1999) "A Widening Gap Between the U.S. Military and Civilian Society? Some Evidence, 1976–96," *International Security* 23 (Winter): 5–42.

HOLSTI, OLE R., AND JAMES N. ROSENAU. (1980) "Does Where You Stand Depend on When You Were Born? The Impact of Generation on Post-Vietnam Foreign Policy Beliefs," *Public Opinion Quarterly* 44 (Spring): 1–22.

———. (1984) *American Leadership in World Affairs.* Boston: Allen and Unwin.

———. (1990) "The Structure of Foreign Policy Attitudes: American Leaders, 1976–1984," *Journal of Politics* 52 (February): 94–125.

———. (1994) "The Foreign Policy Beliefs of American Leaders After the Cold War: Persistence or Abatement of Partisan Cleavages?" pp. 127–147 in Eugene R. Wittkopf, (ed.), *The Future of American Foreign Policy,* 2nd ed. New York: St. Martin's.

———. (1999a) "Internationalism: Intact or in Trouble?" pp. 125–139 in Eugene R. Wittkopf and Christopher M. Jones (eds.), *The Future of American Foreign Policy,* 3rd ed. New York: St. Martin's.

———. (1999b) "The Political Foundations of Elites' Domestic and Foreign-Policy Beliefs," pp. 33–50 in Eugene R. Wittkopf and James M.

McCormick (eds.), *The Domestic Sources of American Foreign Policy: Insights and Evidence,* 3rd ed. Landham, MD: Rowman and Littlefield.

HOLT, PAT M. (1995) *Secret Intelligence and Public Policy: A Dilemma of Democracy.* Washington, DC: CQ Press.

HOMER-DIXON, THOMAS. (1999) *Environment, Scarcity, and Violence.* Princeton, NJ: Princeton University Press.

HOOK, STEVEN W. (1998) "The White House, Congress, and the Paralysis of the U.S. State Department," pp. 305–329 in James M. Scott (ed.), *After the End: Making U.S. Foreign Policy in the Post–Cold War World.* Durham, NC: Duke University Press.

HOOPES, TOWNSEND. (1973a) *The Devil and John Foster Dulles: The Diplomacy of the Eisenhower Era.* Boston: Little, Brown.

————. (1973b) *The Limits of Intervention.* New York: McKay.

HOWELL, LLEWELLYN D. (2000) "Isolationsim or Unilateralism?" *USA Today* 128 (January): 13.

HOY, PAULA. (1998) *Players and Issues in International Aid.* West Hartford, CT: Kumarian Press.

HUFBAUER, GARY. (1998) "Foreign Policy on the Cheap," *The Washington Post National Weekly Edition,* 20–27 July, pp. 22–23.

HUFBAUER, GARY CLYDE, JEFFREY J. SCHOTT, AND KIMBERLY ANN ELLIOTT. (1990) *Economic Sanctions Reconsidered: History and Current Policy,* 2nd ed. Washington, DC: Institute for International Economics.

HUGHES, EMMET JOHN. (1972) *The Living Presidency.* New York: Coward, McCann, and Geoghegan.

HUMAN DEVELOPMENT REPORT 1993. (1993). New York: Oxford University Press.

HUNT, MICHAEL H. (1987) *Ideology and U.S. Foreign Policy.* New Haven, CT: Yale University Press.

HUNTINGTON, SAMUEL P. (1957) *The Soldier and the State: The Theory and Politics of Civil-Military Relations.* Cambridge, MA: Belknap.

————. (1988–1989) "The U.S.—Decline or Renewal," *Foreign Affairs* 67 (Winter): 76–96.

————. (1991) *The Third Wave: Democratization in the Late Twentieth Century.* Norman OK: University of Oklahoma Press.

————. (1993a) "The Clash of Civilizations?" *Foreign Affairs* 72 (Summer): 22–49.

————. (1993b) "Why International Primacy Matters," *International Security* 17 (Spring): 68–83.

————. (1997) "The Erosion of American National Interests," *Foreign Affairs* 76 (September/October): 28–49.

————. (1999) "The Lonely Superpower," *Foreign Affairs* 78 (March/April): 35–49.

HURWITZ, JON, AND MARK PEFFLEY. (1987) "How Are Foreign Policy Attitudes Structured? A Hierarchical Model," *American Political Science Review* 81 (December): 1099–1120.

————. (1990) "Public Images of the Soviet Union: The Impact of Foreign Policy Attitudes," *Journal of Politics* 52 (February): 3–28.

————. (1992) "International Events and Foreign Policy Beliefs: Public Response to Changing Soviet-U.S. Relations," *American Journal of Political Science* 36: 431–461.

HYBEL, ALEX ROBERTO. (1993) *Power Over Rationality: The Bush Administration and the Gulf Crisis.* Albany, NY: State University of New York Press.

IGNATIUS, DAVID. (1988) "Is This Any Way for a Country to Buy Weapons?" *The Washington Post National Weekly Edition,* 4–10 July, p. 23.

————. (1994) "Reinvent the CIA," *The Washington Monthly* 26 (April): 38–42.

————. (1995) "Is the CIA's New Mission Impossible?" *The Washington Post National Weekly Edition,* 13–19 March, pp. 23–24.

IKENBERRY, G. JOHN. (1989) "Rethinking the Origins of American Hegemony," *Political Science Quarterly* 104 (Fall): 375–400.

————. (1993) "Salvaging the G-7," *Foreign Affairs* 72 (Spring): 132–139.

————. (1999) "America's Liberal Hegemony," *Current History* 98 (January): 23–28.

————. (2001) "Getting Hegemony Right," *The National Interest* 63 (Spring): 17–24.

IKLÉ, FRED CHARLES. (1990) "The Ghost in the Pentagon," *The National Interest* 19 (Spring): 13–20.

IMMERMAN, RICHARD H. (1982) *The CIA in Guatemala: The Foreign Policy of Intervention.* Austin, TX: University of Texas Press.

THE INDEPENDENT GROUP ON THE FUTURE OF US DEVELOPMENT COOPERATION. (1992) *Reinventing Foreign Aid: White Paper on US Development Cooperation in a New Democratic Era.* Washington, DC: Overseas Development Council.

ISAACS, JOHN. (1996) "Right Wing Targets Treaty," *The Bulletin of the Atomic Scientists* 52 (November–December): 13.

———. (1997) "Treaty Tactics," *The Bulletin of the Atomic Scientists* 53 (July–August): 13.

ISAACSON, WALTER. (1993) *Kissinger: A Biography.* New York: Simon and Schuster.

———. (1999) "Madeleine's War," *Time,* 17 May pp. 26–27ff.

ISAAK, ROBERT A. (1975) *Individuals and World Politics.* North Scituate, MA: Duxbury Press.

———. (1977) *American Democracy and World Power.* New York: St. Martin's.

———. (1995) *International Political Economy: Managing World Economic Change,* 2nd ed. Englewood Cliffs, NJ: Prentice Hall.

IVANOV, IGOR. (2000) "The Missile Defense Mistake - Undermining Strategic Stability and the ABM Treaty," *Foreign Affairs* 79 (September/October): 15–20.

IYENGAR, SHANTO, MARK D. PETERS, AND DONALD R. KINDER. (1982) "Experimental Demonstrations of the 'Not-So-Minimal' Consequences of Television News Programs," *American Political Science Review* 76 (December): 848–858.

JACKMAN, ROBERT W. (1973) "On the Relationship of Economic Development to Political Performance," *American Journal of Political Science* 17 (August): 611–621.

JACKSON, HENRY M. (1965) *The National Security Council: Jackson Subcommittee Papers on Policy-Making at the Presidential Level.* New York: Praeger.

JACOBS, LAWRENCE R., AND ROBERT Y. SHAPIRO. (2000) *Politicians Don't Pander: Political Manipulation and the Loss of Democratic Responsiveness.* Chicago: University of Chicago Press.

JACOBSON, HAROLD K. (1984) *Networks of Interdependence: International Organizations and the Global Political System.* New York: Knopf.

JACOBSON, JODI. (1989) "Abandoning Homelands," pp. 59–76 in Lester R. Brown, Christopher Flavin, Sandra Postel, Linda Starke, Alan Durning, Lori Heise, Jodi Jacobson, Michael Renner, and Cynthia Pollack Shea (eds.), *State of the World 1989.* New York: Norton.

JACOBY, HENRY, RONALD PRINN, AND RICHARD SCHMALENSEE. (1998) "Kyoto's Unfinished Business," *Foreign Affairs* 77 (July/August): 54–66.

JAMES, PATRICK, AND JOHN R. ONEAL. (1991) "The Influence of Domestic and International Politics on the President's Use of Force," *Journal of Conflict Resolution* 35 (June): 307–332.

JANIS, IRVING. (1982) *Groupthink: Psychological Studies of Policy Decisions and Fiascoes,* 2nd ed. Boston: Houghton Mifflin.

———. (1989) *Crucial Decisions: Leadership in Policymaking and Crisis Management.* New York: Free Press.

JAVITS, JACOB K. (1985) "War Powers Reconsidered," *Foreign Affairs* 64 (Fall): 130–140.

JENKINS, MICHAEL. (2000–2001) "Columbia: Crossing a Dangerous Threshold," *The National Interest* 62 (Winter): 47–55.

JENTLESON, BRUCE W. (1992) "The Pretty Prudent Public: Post-Vietnam American Opinion on the Use of Military Force," *International Studies Quarterly* 36 (March): 49–74.

———. (1998) "Still Pretty Prudent: Post–Cold War American Public Opinion on the Use of Force" *Journal of Conflict Resolution* 42 (August): 395–417.

JERVIS, ROBERT. (1976) *Perception and Misperception in International Politics.* Princeton, NJ: Princeton University Press.

———. (1991) "Will the New World Be Better?" pp. 7–19 in Robert Jervis and Seweryn Bialer, (eds.), *Soviet-American Relations After the Cold War.* Durham, NC: Duke University Press.

———. (1991–1992) "The Future of World Politics: Will It Resemble the Past?" *International Security* 16 (Winter): 39–73.

———. (1993) "International Primacy: Is the Game Worth the Candle?" *International Security* 17 (Spring): 52–67.

JOFFE, JOSEF. (1997) "America the Inescapable," *New York Times Magazine,* 8 June, pp. 38–43.

JOHNSON, CHALMERS, AND E. B. KEEHN. (1995) "The Pentagon's Ossified Strategy," *Foreign Affairs* 74 (July/August): 103–114.

JOHNSON, DOUGLAS, AND STEVEN METZ. (1995) "Civil-Military Relations in the United States: The State of the Debate," *Washington Quarterly* 18 (Winter): 197–213.

JOHNSON, LOCH. (1977) "Operational Codes and the Prediction of Leadership Behavior: Senator Frank Church at Midcareer," pp. 80–119 in Margaret G. Hermann (ed.), *A Psychological Examination of Political Leaders.* New York: Free Press.

————. (1980) "Controlling the Quiet Option," *Foreign Policy* 39 (Summer): 143–153.

————. (1989) *America's Secret Power: The CIA in a Democratic Society.* New York: Cambridge University Press.

————. (2000a) *Bombs, Bugs, Drugs, and Thugs: Intelligence and America's Quest for Security.* New York: New York University Press.

————. (2000b) "Spies," *Foreign Policy* 120 (September–October): 18–26.

————. (2001) "The CIA's Weakest Link," *The Washington Monthly,* 33 (July): 9–11.

JOHNSON, ROBERT D. (1998–1999) "The Government Operations Committee and Foreign Policy During the Cold War," *Political Science Quarterly* 113 (Winter): 645–671.

JONAS, MANFRED. (1966) *Isolationism in America 1935–1941.* Ithaca, NY: Cornell University Press.

JONES, CHRISTOPHER M. (1994) "American Prewar Technology Sales to Iraq: A Bureaucratic Politics Explanation," pp. 279–296 in Eugene R. Wittkopf (ed.), *The Domestic Sources of American Foreign Policy: Insights and Evidence.* New York: St. Martin's.

————. (1998) "The Foreign Policy Bueaucracy in a New Era," pp. 57–88 in James M. Scott, (ed.), *After the End: Making U.S. Foreign Policy in the Post–Cold War World.* Durham, NC: Duke University Press.

————. (1999) "Trading with Saddam: Bureaucratic Roles and Competing Conceptions of National Security," pp. 267–285 in Eugene R. Wittkopf and James M. McCormick (eds.), *The Domestic Sources of American Foreign Policy: Insights and Evidence.* Lanham, MD: Roman and Littlefield.

————. (2001) "Roles, Politics, and the Survival of the V-22 Osprey," *Jounral of Political and Military Sociology* 29 (Summer): 46–72.

JONES, GORDON S., AND JOHN A. MARINI, (eds.) (1988) *The Imperial Congress: Crisis in the Separation of Powers.* New York: Pharos Books.

JORDAN, AMOS A., WILLIAM J. TAYLOR, JR., AND MICHAEL MAZARR. (1999) *American National Security.* Baltimore, MD: Johns Hopkins University Press.

JORDAN, DONALD L., AND BENJAMIN I. PAGE. (1992) "Shaping Foreign Policy News: The Role of TV News," *Journal of Conflict Resolution* 36 (June): 227–241.

JOYNER, CHRISTOPHER C. (1992) *Intervention Into the 1990s: U.S. Foreign Policy in the Third World,* 2nd ed. Peter J. Schraeder, (ed.) Boulder, CO: Lynne Rienner.

———— (1993) "When Human Suffering Warrants Military Action," *Chronicle of Higher Education,* 27 January, p. A52.

JUDIS, JOHN B. (1990) "The Japanese Megaphone," *New Republic,* 22 January, pp. 20–25.

————. (1992) "Statecraft and Scowcroft," *New Republic,* 24 February, pp. 18–21.

JÖNNSON, CHRISTER. (1982) *Cognitive Dynamics and International Politics.* New York: St. Martin's.

KAEMPFER, WILLIAM H., AND ANTON D. LOWENBER. (1999) "Unilateral Versus Multilateral International Sanctions: A Public Choice Perspective," *International Studies Quarterly* 43 (March): 37–58.

KAGAN, DONALD. (1997) "Are U.S. Forces Overstretched? Roles and Missions," *Orbis* 41 (Spring 1997): 187–198.

KAGAN, ROBERT. (1998) "The Benevolent Empire," *Foreign Policy* 111 (Summer): 24–34.

KAHLER, MILES. (1995) "A World of Blocs: Facts and Factoids," *World Policy Journal* 12 (Spring): 19–27.

KAHN, DAVID. (1984) "The United States Views Germany and Japan in 1941" pp. 476–501 in Ernest R. May, (ed.), *Knowing One's Enemies: Intelligence Assessment Before the Two World Wars.* Princeton, NJ: Princeton University Press.

KAMP, KARL-HEINZ. (1999) "A Global Role for NATO?" *Washington Quarterly* 22 (Winter): 7–11.

KANBUR, RAVI, AND TODD SANDLER, WITH KEVIN MORRISON. (1999) *The Future of Development Assistance: Common Pools and International Public Goods.* Washington, DC: Overseas Development Council.

KANTER, ARNOLD, AND LINTON F. BROOKS, (eds.) (1994) *U.S. Intervention Policy for the Post–Cold War World: New Challenges and New Responses.* New York: Norton.

KAPLAN, LAWRENCE F. (2001a) "Containment," *New Republic* 5 February pp. 17–20.

————. (2001b) "Drill Sergeant: The Oil Industry's Man at the State Department," *New Republic* 26 March pp. 17–20.

KAPLAN, MORTON A. (1957) *System and Process in International Politics.* New York: Wiley.

KAPLAN, ROBERT D. (2000) *The Coming Anarchy: Shattering the Dreams of the Post–Cold War World.* New York: Random House.

KAPSTEIN, ETHAN B. (1994) "America's Arms-Trade Monopoly," *Foreign Affairs* 73 (May/June): 13–19.

———. (1996) "Workers and the World Economy," *Foreign Affairs* 75 (May/June): 16–37.

———. (1999) "Global Rules for Global Finance," *Current History* 98 (November): 355–360.

KAPUR, DEVESH. (1998) "The IMF: A Cure or a Curse?" *Foreign Policy* 111 (Summer): 114–128.

KATTENBURG, PAUL. (1980) *The Vietnam Trauma in America Foreign Policy, 1945–75.* New Brunswick, NJ: Transaction Books.

KATZ, ELIHU. (1957) "The Two-Step Flow of Communications," *Public Opinion Quarterly* 21 (Spring): 61–78.

KATZENSTEIN, PETER J. (1977) "Introduction: Domestic and International Forces of Foreign Economic Policy," *International Organization* 31 (Spring): 587–606.

KAUFMAN, HERBERT. (1976) *Are Government Organizations Immortal?* Washington, DC: Brookings Institution.

KAUL, INGE, AND ISABELLE GRUNBERG. (1999) *Global Public Goods: International Cooperation in the 21st Century.* New York: Oxford University Press.

KAY, DAVID A. (1998) "Iraq Beyond Crisis Du Jour," *Washington Quarterly* 21 (Summer): 10–14.

KEARNS, DORIS. (1976) *Lyndon Johnson and the American Dream.* New York: Harper and Row.

KEETER, SCOTT. (1985) "Public Opinion in 1984," pp. 91–111 in Gerald M. Pomper, Ross K. Baker, Charles E. Jacob, Scott Keeter, Wilson Carey McWilliams, and Henry A. Plotkin (eds.), *The Election of 1984: Reports and Interpretations.* Chatham, NJ: Chatham House.

KEFALAS, A. G. (1992) "The Global Corporation: Its Role in the New World Order," *National Forum* 72 (Fall): 26–30.

KEGLEY, CHARLES W., JR. (1994) "How Did the Cold War Die? Principles for an Autopsy," *Mershon International Studies Review* 38 (April): 11–41.

———, (ed). (1995) *Controversies in International Relations Theory: Realism and the Neoliberal Challenge.* New York: St. Martin's.

KEGLEY, CHARLES W., JR., AND SHANNON L. BLANTON. (1994) "America's Policy Conun-drum: The Promotion of Democratic Nation Building and U.S. Arms Exports," *Brown Journal of World Affairs* 2 (Winter): 65–75.

KEGLEY, CHARLES W., JR., AND STEVEN W. HOOK. (1991) "U.S. Foreign Aid and UN Voting: Did Reagan's Linkage Strategy Buy Deference or Defiance?" *International Studies Quarterly* 35 (September): 295–312.

KEGLEY, CHARLES W., JR., AND GREGORY A. RAYMOND. (1998) "Great-Power Relations in the 21st Century: A New Cold War, or Concert-Based Peace?" pp. 170–183 in Charles W. Kegley, Jr. and Eugene R. Wittkopf (eds.), *The Global Agenda: Issues and Perspectives,* 5th ed. Boston: McGraw-Hill.

KEGLEY, CHARLES W., JR., AND EUGENE R. WITTKOPF. (2001) *World Politics: Trend and Transformation,* 8th ed. Boston: Bedford/ St. Martin's.

KELLER, PAUL. (2000) "Backlash in Peru to CIA's Flawed Battle Against Drugs," *The Financial Times,* 15 November, London, p. 1.

KELLY, MICHAEL. (1994) "The President's Past," *New York Times Magazine,* 31 July, pp. 20–29ff.

KENNAN, GEORGE F. ("X"). (1947) "The Sources of Soviet Conduct," *Foreign Affairs* 25 (July): 566–582.

———. (1951) *American Diplomacy, 1900–1950.* New York: New American Library.

———. (1954) *Realities of American Foreign Policy.* Princeton, NJ: Princeton University Press.

———. (1967) *Memoirs.* Boston: Little, Brown.

———. (1976) "The United States and the Soviet Union, 1917–1976," *Foreign Affairs* 54 (July): 670–690.

———. (1995) "On American Principles," *Foreign Affairs* 74 (March/April): 116–126.

KENNEDY, PAUL. (1987) *The Rise and Fall of the Great Powers.* New York: Random House.

———. (1992) "A Declining Empire Goes to War," pp. 344–346 in Charles W. Kegley, Jr. and Eugene R. Wittkopf (eds.), *The Future of American Foreign Policy.* New York: St. Martin's.

———. (1994) "Overpopulation Tilts the Planet," *New Perspectives Quarterly* 11 (Fall): 4–6.

KENNEDY, ROBERT F. (1971) *Thirteen Days.* New York: Norton.

KEOHANE, ROBERT O. (1984) *After Hegemony: Cooperation and Discord in the World Political Economy.* Princeton N.J.: Princeton University Press

———. (1986a) "Realism, Neorealism and the Study of World Politics," pp. 1–26 in Robert O. Keohane (ed.), *Neorealism and Its Critics.* New York: Columbia University Press.

———, (ed.) (1986b) *Neorealism and Its Critics.* New York: Columbia University Press.

KEOHANE, ROBERT O., AND JOSEPH S. NYE JR. (1975) "International Interdependence and Integration," pp. 363–414 in Fred I. Greenstein and Nelson W. Polsby (eds.), *International Politics. Handbook of Political Science,* Vol. 8. Reading, MA: Addison-Wesley.

———. (2000) "Globalization: What's New? What's Not? (And So What?)," 118 *Foreign Policy,* Spring 104–118.

———. (2001) *Power and Interdependence.* New York: Longman.

KERNELL, SAMUEL. (1999) "The Challenge Ahead for Explaining President Clinton's Public Support," *PRG Report* 21 (3): 1–3.

KESSLER, GLENN. (2001) "More than Meets the Eye," *The Washington Post National Weekly Edition.* October 15–21, p. 18.

KETTLE, MARTIN. (2001) "Powell Losing Policy Battle to Hardliners," *The Guardian,* 12 March, p. 13.

KEY, V. O. (1961) *Public Opinion and American Democracy.* New York: Knopf.

KHONG, YUEN FOONG. (1992) *Analogies at War.* Princeton, NJ: Princeton University Press.

KILPATRICK, JAMES J. (1985) "An Overstuffed Bureaucracy," *The State,* 23 April, p. 8A.

KINDLEBERGER, CHARLES P. (1973) *The World in Depression, 1929–1939.* Berkeley, CA: University of California Press.

KINGDON, JOHN W. (1995) *Agendas, Alternatives, and Public Policies.* New York: HarperCollins.

———. (1999) *America the Unusual.* New York: St. Martin's/Worth.

KINSELLA, DAVID. (1994) "Conflict in Context: Arms Transfers and Third World Rivalries During the Cold War," *American Journal of Political Science* 38 (August): 557–581.

KIRSCHTEN, DICK. (1987) "Competent Manager," *National Journal,* 28 February, pp. 468–469 passim.

KISSINGER, HENRY. (1962) *The Necessity of Choice.* Garden City, NY: Doubleday.

———. (1969) "Domestic Structure and Foreign Policy," pp. 261–275 in James N. Rosenau (ed.),

International Politics and Foreign Policy. New York: Free Press.

———. (1979) *White House Years.* Boston: Little, Brown.

———. (1994a) *Diplomacy.* New York: Simon and Schuster.

———. (1994b) "Reflections on Containment," *Foreign Affairs* 73 (May/June): 113–130.

———. (2001a) "America at the Apex: Empire or Leader?" *The National Interest* 64 (Summer): 9–17.

———. (2001b) *Does America Need a Foreign Policy? Toward a Diplomacy for the 21st Century.* New York: Simon and Schuster.

KISSINGER, HENRY, AND CYRUS VANCE. (1988) "Bipartisan Objectives for American Foreign Policy," *Foreign Affairs* 66 (Summer): 899–921.

KITFIELD, JAMES. (2000) "Covert Counterattack," *National Journal* 32, 16 September pp. 2858–2865.

———. (2001a) "A Diplomat Handy with a Bayonet," *National Journal* 33 27 January, pp. 250–251.

———. (2001b) "A Small Study Carries a Heavy Burden," *National Journal* 3 March, pp. 644–646.

KLARE, MICHAEL. (1984) *American Arms Supermarket.* Austin, TX: University of Texas Press.

———. (1994–1995) "Awash in Armaments: Implications of the Trade in Light Weapons," *Harvard International Review* 17 (Winter): 24–26, 75–76.

KLARE, MICHAEL T., AND DANIEL C. THOMAS, (eds). (1998) *World Security: Challenges for a New Century,* 3rd ed. Boston: Bedford.

KLINE, JOHN. (1983) *State Government Influence in U.S. International Economic Policy.* Lexington, MA: Lexington Books.

KLINGBERG, FRANK L. (1983) *Cyclical Trends in American Foreign Policy Moods: The Unfolding of America's World Role.* Lanham, MD: University Press of America.

———. (1990) "Cyclical Trends in Foreign Policy Revisited in 1990," *International Studies Notes* 15 (Spring): 54–58.

———. (1996) *Positive Expectations of America's World Role: Historical Cycles of Realistic Idealism.* Lanham, MD: University Press of America.

KNOTT, STEPHAN F. (1996) *Secret and Sanctioned Covert Operations and the American Presidency.* New York: Oxford University Press.

KOBER, STANLEY. (1998) "Why Spy? The Uses and Misuses of Intelligence," *USA Today* 126 (March): 10–14.

KOH, HAROLD H. (1990) *The National Security Constitution: Sharing Power after the Iran-Contra Affair.* New Haven, CT: Yale University Press.

KOHN, RICHARD H. (1994) "Out of Control: The Crisis in Civil-Military Relations," *The National Interest* 35 (Spring): 3–17.

KOHUT, ANDREW, AND ROBERT C. TOTH. (1994) "Arms and the People," *Foreign Affairs* 73 (November/December): 47–61.

———. (1998) "A World of Difference: The Public and Opinion Leaders Are Poles Apart on the U.S. Role in Global Affairs," *The Washington Post National Weekly Edition,* 5 January, p. 22.

KOLKO, GABRIEL. (1968) *The Politics of War.* New York: Random House.

———. (1969) *The Roots of American Foreign Policy.* Boston: Beacon Press.

KONDRACKE, MORTON. (1990) "How to Aid A.I.D.," *New Republic,* 26 February, pp. 20–23.

KORANY, BAHGAT. (1994) "End of History, or Its Continuation? The Global South and the 'New Transformation' Literature," *Third World Quarterly* 15 (March): 7–15.

KORB, LAWRENCE J. (1995a) "The Indefensible Defense Budget," *The Washington Post National Weekly Edition,* 17–23 July, p. 19.

———. (1995b) "The Readiness Gap. What Gap?" *New York Times Magazine,* 26 February, pp. 40–41.

KORNBLUH, PETER. (1998) *Bay of Pigs Declassified: The Secret CIA Report on the Invasion of Cuba.* New York: The New Press.

KOTZ, NICK. (1988) *Wild Blue Yonder: Money, Politics, and the B-1 Bomber.* Princeton, NJ: Princeton University Press.

KOVACH, BILL. (1996) "Do the News Media Make Foreign Policy," *Foreign Policy* 102 (Spring): 169–179.

KRAMER, DAVID J. (2000) "No Bang for the Buck: Public Diplomacy Should Remain a Priority," *The Washington Times,* 23 October, www.state.gov/r/adcompd/kramer.html.

KRASNER, STEPHEN D. (1972) "Are Bureaucracies Important? (Or Allison Wonderland)," *Foreign Policy* 7 (Summer): 159–179.

———. (1982) "Structural Causes and Regime Consequences," *International Organization* 36 (Spring): 185–206.

———. (1985) *Structural Conflict: The Third World Against Global Liberalism.* Berkeley, CA: University of California Press.

KRAUTHAMMER, CHARLES. (1991) "The Unipolar Moment," *Foreign Affairs* 70 (Winter): 23–33.

———. (1999) "The Clinton Doctrine," *Time,* 5 April p. 88.

KRENN, MICHAEL L. (ed.) (1999) *The Impact of Race on U.S. Foreign Policy: A Reader.* New York: Garland Publishing.

KREPON, MICHAEL, AMY E. SMITHSON, AND JOHN PARACHINI. (1997) *The Battle to Obtain U.S. Ratification of the Chemical Weapons Convention.* Washington, DC: Henry L. Stimson Center.

KRISTOF, NICHOLAS. (2000a) "Ally of an Older Generation Amid the Tumult of the 1960s," *New York Times,* 19 June, p. 1.

———. (2000b) "Learning How to Run: A West Texas Stumble," *New York Times,* 27 July, p. 1.

———. (2000c) "How Bush Came to Tame His Inner Self," *New York Times,* 29 July, p. 1.

———. (2000d) "The Republicans: Man in the News; Confident Son of Politics Rises," *New York Times,* 3 August, p. 1.

———. (2000e) "The 2000 Campaign: Running Texas; A Master of Bipartisanship with No Taste for Details," *New York Times,* 16 October, p. 1.

KRUGMAN, PAUL. (1990) *The Age of Diminished Expectations: U.S. Economic Policy in the 1990s.* Cambridge, MA: MIT Press.

———. (1994a) "Competitiveness: A Dangerous Obsession," *Foreign Affairs* 73 (March/April): 28–44.

———. (1994b) *Peddling Prosperity: Economic Sense and Nonsense in the Age of Diminished Expectations.* New York: Norton.

KRUGMAN, PAUL R., AND ROBERT Z. LAWRENCE. (1994) "Trade, Jobs, and Wages," *Scientific American* 270 (April): 44–49.

KULL, STEVEN, AND I. M. DESTLER. (1999) *Misreading the Public: The Myth of the New Isolationism.* Washington, DC: Brookings Institution.

KUNZ, DIANE B. (1997) *Butter and Guns: America's Cold War Economic Diplomacy.* New York: Free Press.

KUPCHAN, CHARLES A. (1998) "After Pax Americana: Benign Power, Regional Integration, and the Sources of Stable Multipolarity," *International Security* 23 (Fall): 40–79.

KUPERMAN, ALAN J. (1999) "The Stinger Missile and U.S. Intervention in Afghanistan," *Political Science* Quarterly 114 (2): 219–263.

KURKJIAN, STEPHEN. (1991) "CIA Wages Quiet War on Iraq," *The Boston Globe,* 11 February, p. 1.

KURTH, JAMES R. (1989) "The Military-Industrial Complex Revisited," pp. 196–215 in Joseph Kruzel (ed.), *American Defense Annual 1989–1990.* Lexington, MA: Lexington.

KURTZ, HOWARD. (1993) "How Sources and Reporters Play the Game of Leaks," *The Washington Post National Weekly Edition,* 15–21 March, p. 12.

———. (1996) *Hot Air: All Talk, All the Time.* New York: New York Times Books.

———. (1998) *Spin Cycle: Inside the Clinton Propaganda Machine.* New York: Free Press.

KUSNITZ, LEONARD A. (1984) *Public Opinion and Foreign Policy: America's China Policy, 1949–1979.* Westport, CT: Greenwood.

LACEY, MARC, AND RAYMOND BONNER. (2001) "A Mad Scramble by Donors for Plum Ambassadorships." *New York Times.* 19 March, p. A1.

LADD, EVERETT CARL. (1997) "1996: The 'No Majority' Realignment Continues," *Political Science Quarterly* 112 (Winter): 1–28.

LAFEBER WALTER. (1976) *America, Russia, and the Cold War 1945–1975.* New York: Wiley.

———. (1994) *The American Age: United States Foreign Policy at Home and Abroad,* 2nd ed. New York: Norton.

LAIS, SAMI. (1997) "Groups Clash Over Mapping Agency's Role," *Government Computer News* 16 14 July, p. 1.

LAKE, ANTHONY. (1994) "Confronting Backlash States," *Foreign Affairs* 73 (March/April): 45–55.

LANCASTER, CAROL. (2000a) *Transforming Foreign Aid: United States Assistance in the 21st Century.* Washington, DC: Institute for International Economics.

———. (2000b) "Redesigning Foreign Aid," *Foreign Affairs* 79 (September/October): 74–88.

LANCASTER, JOHN. (1993) "Ammunition Against Budget Cuts," *The Washington Post National Weekly Edition,* 22–28 November, p. 32.

———. (2000) "No Clout Where It Counts," *Washington Post National Weekly Edition,* 17 April.

LANDY, MARC, AND SIDNEY M. MILKIS. (2000) *Presidential Greatness.* Lawrence, KS: University of Kansas Press.

LANE, CHARLES. (2000) "'Superman' Meets Shining Path: Story of a CIA Success," *The Washington Post,* p. A1.

LANG, TIM. (2001) "Dietary Implications of the Globalization of the Food Trade," pp. 420–424 in Charles W. Kegley, Jr. and Eugene R. Wittkopf (eds.), *The Global Agenda: Issues and Perspectives,* 6th ed. Boston: McGraw-Hill.

LANGER, E. J. (1975) "The Illusion of Control," *Journal of Personality and Social Psychology* 32 (6): 311–328.

LAQUEUR, WALTER. (1994) "Save Public Diplomacy," *Foreign Affairs* 73 (September/October): 19–24.

———. (1998) "The New Face of Terrorism," *Washington Quarterly* 21 (Autumn): 169–178.

LARSON, DEBORAH WELCH. (1985) *Origins of Containment: A Psychological Explanation.* Princeton, NJ: Princeton University Press.

LARSON, ERIC V. (1996) *Casualties and Consensus: The Historical Role of Casualties in Domestic Support for U.S. Military Operations.* Santa Monica, CA: RAND Corporation.

LARSON, JAMES F. (1990) "Television and U.S. Foreign Policy: The Case of the Iran Hostage Crisis," pp. 301–312 in Doris A. Graber (ed.), *Media Power in Politics,* 2nd ed. Washington, DC: CQ Press.

LASKI, HAROLD J. (1947) "America—1947," *The Nation* 165 (December): 641–644.

LASSWELL, HAROLD D. (1962) "The Garrison State Hypothesis Today," pp. 51–70 in Samuel P. Huntington (ed.), *Changing Patterns of Military Politics.* New York: Free Press.

———. (1974) "The Political Personality," pp. 38–54 in Gordon J. DiRenzo (ed.), *Personality and Politics.* Garden City, NY: Doubleday-Anchor.

LAUTER, DAVID. (1994) "Anti-Politician Hate Becoming Institutional Phenomenon," *Sunday Advocate,* 10 July, p. 4E.

LAYNE, CHRISTOPHER. (1993) "The Unipolar Illusion: Why New Great Powers Will Rise," *International Security* 17 (Spring): 5–51.

———. (1998) "Rethinking American Grand Strategy: Hegemony or Balance of Power in the

Twenty-First Century?" *World Policy Journal* 15 (Summer): 8–28.

———. (2002) A New Grand Strategy. *The Atlantic Monthly.* 289 (January): 36–42.

LEFFLER, MELVYN P. (1996) "Inside Enemy Archives: The Cold War Reopened," *Foreign Affairs* 75 (July/August): 120–135.

LEGRO, JEFFREY W., AND ANDREW MORAVCSIK. (2001) "Faux Realism," *Foreign Policy* 125 (July/August): 80–82.

LEIGH, MICHAEL. (1976) *Mobilizing Consent: Public Opinion and American Foreign Policy, 1937–1947.* Westport, CT: Greenwood.

LEVERING, RALPH B. (1976) *American Opinion and the Russian Alliance, 1939–1945.* Chapel Hill, NC: University of North Carolina Press.

LEVI, ISAAC. (1990) *Hard Choices: Decision Making Under Unresolved Conflict.* New York: Cambridge University Press.

LEVIN, JEROME D. (1998) *The Clinton Syndrome: The President and the Self-Destructive Nature of Sexual Addiction.* New York: Random House.

LEWIS, MICHAEL. (1998) "The World's Biggest Going-Out-of-Business Sale," *New York Times Magazine,* 31 May, pp. 35–41ff.

LEWIS, NEIL A. (2001) "A Nation Challenged: The Resolution." *The New York Times,* 18 September, p. B7.

LEWY, GUENTER. (1978) *America in Vietnam.* New York: Oxford University Press.

LEYTON-BROWN, DAVID. (1987) "Introduction," pp. 1–4 in David Leyton-Brown (ed.), *The Utility of International Economic Sanctions.* New York: St. Martin's.

LIAN, BRADLEY, AND JOHN R. ONEAL. (1993) "Presidents, the Use of Military Force, and Public Opinion," *Journal of Conflict Resolution* 37 (June): 277–300.

LICHTER, S. ROBERT, AND STANLEY ROTHMAN. (1981) "Media and Business Elites," *Public Opinion* 4 (October/November): 42–46, 59–60.

LIEBERMAN, SEYMOUR. (1965) "The Effects of Changes in Roles on the Attitudes of Role Occupants," pp. 155–168 in J. David Singer (ed.), *Human Behavior and International Politics.* Chicago: Rand McNally.

LIGHT, PAUL C. (1991) *The President's Agenda: Domestic Policy Choice from Kennedy to Reagan.* Baltimore, MD: Johns Hopkins University Press.

LIM, LINDA Y. C. (2001) "Whose 'Model' Failed? Implications of the Asian Financial Crisis," pp. 285–296 in Charles W. Kegley, Jr. and Eugene R. Wittkopf (eds.), *The Global Agenda: Issues and Perspectives.* Boston: McGraw-Hill.

LINDBLOM, CHARLES E. (1959) "The Science of Muddling Through," *Public Administration Review* 19 (Spring): 79–88.

LINDSAY, JAMES M. (1986) "Trade Sanctions As Policy Instruments: A Re-Examination," *International Studies Quarterly* 30 (June): 153–173.

———. (1987) "Congress and Defense Policy: 1961 to 1986," *Armed Forces and Society* 13 (Spring): 371–401.

———. (1988) "Congress and the Defense Budget," *Washington Quarterly* 11 (Winter): 57–74.

———. (1990) "Parochialism, Policy, and Constituency Constraints: Congressional Voting on Strategic Weapons Systems," *American Journal of Political Science* 34 (November): 936–960.

———. (1993) "Congress and Foreign Policy: Why the Hill Matters," *Political Science Quarterly* 107 (Winter): 607–628.

———. (1994a) "Congress and Foreign Policy: Avenues of Influence," pp. 191–207 in Eugene R. Wittkopf (ed.), *The Domestic Sources of American Foreign Policy: Insights and Evidence.* New York: St. Martin's.

———. (1994b) *Congress and the Politics of U.S. Foreign Policy.* Baltimore, MD: Johns Hopkins University Press.

———. (1994c) "Congress, Foreign Policy, and the New Institutionalism," *International Studies Quarterly* 38 (June): 281–304.

———. (2000a) "Looking for Leadership: Domestic Politics and Foreign Policy," *Brookings Review* 18 (Winter): 40–43.

———. (2000b) "The New Apathy: How an Uninterested Public Is Shaping Foreign Policy," *Foreign Affairs* 79 (September/October): 2–8.

LINK, MICHAEL W., AND CHARLES W. KEGLEY, JR. (1993) "Is Access Influence? Measuring Adviser-Presidential Interactions in Light of the Iranian Hostage Crisis," *International Interactions* 18 (4): 343–364.

LIPPMAN, THOMAS. (1996) "The Decline of U.S. Diplomacy," *The Washington Post National Weekly Edition,* 22–28 July, pp. 6–7.

LIPPMANN, THOMAS W., AND HELEN DEWAR. (1999) "Who Says Bipartisanship is

Dead?" *The Washington Post National Weekly Edition,* 16 March, p. 16.

LIPPMANN, WALTER. (1943) *U.S. Foreign Policy: Shield of the Republic.* Boston: Little, Brown.

———. (1947) *The Cold War: A Study in U.S. Foreign Policy.* New York: Harper.

LIPSET, SEYMOUR M. (1959) "Some Social Requisites of Democracy," *American Political Science Review* 53 (March): 69–105.

———. (1996) *American Exceptionalism: A Double-Edged Sword.* New York: Norton.

LIPSET, SEYMOUR MARTIN, AND WILLIAM SCHNEIDER. (1987) "The Confidence Gap During the Reagan Years, 1981–1987," *Political Science Quarterly* 102 (Spring): 1–23.

LIPSITZ, LEWIS, AND DAVID M. SPEAK. (1989) *American Democracy.* New York: St. Martin's.

LISKA, GEORGE. (1978) *Career of Empire: America and Imperial Expansion over Land and Sea.* Baltimore: The Johns Hopkins University Press.

LLOYD, JOHN. (1999) "The Russian Devolution," *New York Times Magazine,* 15 August, pp. 34–41ff.

LOEB, VERNON. (1998) "Where the CIA Wages Its New World War," *The Washington Post National Weekly Edition,* 14 September, p. 18.

———. (1999) "Bin Laden Still Seen as Threat," *The Washington Post,* p. A1.

———. (2001) "Second Day of Strikes Includes Searching for Mobile Targets." *Washington Post.* 9 October p. A8.

LORD, CARNES. (1988) *The Presidency and the Management of National Security.* New York: Free Press.

LOW, PATRICK. (1993) *Trading Free: The GATT and U.S. Trade Policy.* New York: Twentieth Century Fund Press.

LOWENTHAL, MARK M. (1992) "Tribal Tongues: Intelligence Consumers, Intelligence Producers," *Washington Quarterly* 15 (Winter): 157–168.

LOWI, THEODORE J. (1967) "Making Democracy Safe for the World," pp. 295–331 in James N. Rosenau (ed.), *Domestic Sources of Foreign Policy.* New York: Free Press.

———. (1979) *The End of Liberalism.* New York: Norton.

———. (1985a) *The Personal President.* Ithaca, NY: Cornell University Press.

———. (1985b) "Presidential Power: Restoring the Balance," *Political Science Quarterly* 100 (Summer): 185–213.

LOWI, THEODORE J., AND BENJAMIN GINSBERG. (1990) *American Government.* New York: W. W. Norton.

LOWRY, RICHARD. (1999) "Test-Ban: How the Treaty Went Down," *National Review* 8 November, p. 20.

LUND, MICHAEL S. (1995) "Underrating 'Preventive Diplomacy'," *Foreign Affairs* 74 (July/August): 160–163.

LUNDESTAD, GEIR. (1990) *The American "Empire."* London: Oxford University Press.

LUTTWAK, EDWARD N. (1993) *The Endangered American Dream: How to Stop the United States from Becoming a Third World Country and How to Win the Geo-Economic Struggle for Economic Supremacy.* New York: Simon and Schuster.

———. (1994) "Where Are the Great Powers?" *Foreign Affairs* 73 (July/August): 23–28.

MACKINNON, MICHAEL. (1999) *The Evolution of U.S. Peacekeeping Policy Under Clinton.* London: Frank Cass Publishers.

MACMAHON, ARTHUR W. (1951) "The Administration of Foreign Affairs," *American Political Science Review* 45 (September): 836–866.

MAGDOFF, HARRY. (1969) *The Age of Imperialism.* New York: Monthly Review Press.

MAHARIDGE, DALE. (1996) *The Coming White Minority: California, Multiculturalism, and America's Future.* New York: Vintage.

MALLABY, SEBASTIAN. (2000) "The Bullied Pulpit," *Foreign Affairs* 79 (January/February): 2–8.

MANDELBAUM, MICHAEL. (1994) "A Struggle Between Two Pasts," *World Policy Journal* 11 (Fall): 95–103.

———. (1996) "Foreign Policy as Social Work," *Foreign Affairs* 75 (January/February): 16–32.

———. (1999) "A Perfect Failure: NATO's War Against Yugoslavia," *Foreign Affairs* 78 (September/October): 2–8.

MANGOLD, TOM. (1991) *Cold Warrior: James Jesus Angleton, the CIA's Master Spy Hunter.* New York: Simon and Schuster.

MANN, JIM. (1993) "Post–Cold War CIA Fighting for Its Life," *Los Angeles Times,* A1.

———. (1999) "America is World's Arms Superstore," *The Baltimore Sun,* A.

MANN, THOMAS E., AND NORMAN J. ORNSTEIN. (1993) *Renewing Congress: A Second Report.* Washington, DC: American Enterprise

Institute for Public Policy and the Brookings Institution.

MANNING, ROBERT A. (1999) "Futureshock or Renewed Partnership? The U.S.-Japan Alliance Facing the Millennium," pp. 192–203 in Eugene R. Wittkopf and Christopher M. Jones (eds.), *The Future of American Foreign Policy,* 3rd ed. New York: St. Martin's/Woth.

MANSBACH, RICHARD W., AND JOHN A. VASQUEZ. (1981) *In Search of Theory: A New Paradigm for Global Politics.* New York: Columbia University Press.

MANSFIELD, EDWARD D., AND HELEN V. MILNER, (eds.) (1997) *The Political Economy of Regionalism.* New York: Columbia University Press.

MARANISS, DAVID. (1995) *First in His Class: The Biography of Bill Clinton.* New York: Simon and Schuster.

————. (1998a) *The Clinton Enigma: A Four-and-a-Half Minute Speech Reveals this President's Entire Life.* New York: Simon and Schuster.

————. (1998b) "Clinton's Personality Patterns," *The Washington Post National Weekly Edition,* 2 February, pp. 6–8.

MARCH, JAMES G., AND HERBERT M. SIMON. (1958) *Organizations.* New York: Wiley.

MARCHETTI, VICTOR, AND JOHN D. MARKS. (1974) *The CIA and the Cult of Intelligence.* New York: Knopf.

MARCUS, JONATHAN. (2000) "Kosovo and After: American Primacy in the Twenty-First Century," *The Washington Quarterly* 23 (Winter): 79–94.

MAREN, MICHAEL. (1997) *The Road to Hell: The Ravaging Effects of Foreign Aid and International Charity.* New York: Free Press.

MARKS, ALEXANDRA. (1997) "Do Whistleblowers Threaten Security When Telling Congress of Spies' Lies," *Christian Science Monitor,* 15 July, p. 1.

MARKUSEN, ANN. (1999) "The Rise of World Weapons," *Foreign Policy* 114 (Spring): 40–51.

MARTIN, ANDREW, AND ROSS GEORGE. (1999) "Europe's Monetary Union: Creating a Democratic Deficit?" *Current History* 98 (April): 171–175.

MARTIN, WILLIAM. (1999) "The Christian Right and American Foreign Policy," *Foreign Policy* 114 (Spring).

MASTANDUNO, MICHAEL. (1991) "Do Relative Gains Matter? America's Response to Japanese Industrial Policy," *International Security* 16 (Summer): 73–113.

————. (1997) "Preserving the Unipolar Moment: Realist Theories and U.S. Grand Strategy After the Cold War," *International Security* 21 (Spring): 49–88.

MATHIAS, CHARLES McC., JR. (1981) "Ethnic Groups and Foreign Policy," *Foreign Affairs* 59 (Summer): 975–998.

MAY, ERNEST R. (1992) "Intelligence: Backing Into the Future," *Foreign Affairs* 71 (Summer): 63–72.

MAY, ERNEST R., AND PHILIP D. ZELIKOW, (eds.) (1997) *The Kennedy Tapes: Inside the White House During the Cuban Missile Crisis.* Cambridge, MA: Harvard University Press.

MAYNES, CHARLES WILLIAM. (1993–1994) "A Workable Clinton Doctrine," *Foreign Policy* 93 (Winter): 3–20.

————. (1995) "Relearning Intervention," *Foreign Policy* 98 (Spring): 96–113.

————. (1998) "The Perils of (and for) an Imperial America," *Foreign Policy* 111 (Summer): 36–47.

————. (2001) "Contending Schools," *National Interest* 63 (Spring): 49–58.

MAZZAR, MICHAEL J. (1990) "Beyond Counterforce," *Comparative Strategy* 9 (2): 147–162.

MAZZAR, MICHAEL. (2002) "Saved from Ourselves," *Washington Quarterly* 25 (Spring): 221–232.

MAZUR, JASON. (2000) "Labor's New Internationalism," *Foreign Affairs* 79 (January/February): 79–93.

McCALLISTER J. F. O. (2001) "Why the Spooks Screwed Up. *Time,* 24 September, p. 44.

McCLELLAND, DAVID C. (1961) *The Achieving Society.* Princeton, NJ: Van Nostrand.

McCLOSKY, HERBERT, AND JOHN ZALLER. (1984) *The American Ethos: Public Attitudes Toward Capitalism and Democracy.* Cambridge, MA: Harvard University Press.

McCOMBS, MAXWELL E., AND DONALD L. SHAW. (1972) "The Agenda-Setting Function of Mass Media," *Public Opinion Quarterly* 36 (Summer): 176–185.

McCORMICK, JAMES M. (1985) "Congressional Voting on the Nuclear Freeze Resolutions," *American Politics Quarterly* 13 (January): 122–136.

————. (1992) *American Foreign Policy and Process.* Itasca, IL: Peacock.

————. (1993) "Decision Making in the Foreign Affairs and Foreign Relations Committees," pp. 115–153 in Randall B. Ripley and James M. Lindsay (eds.), *Congress Resurgent: Foreign and*

Defense Policy on Capitol Hill. Ann Arbor, MI: University of Michigan Press.

———. (1998) *American Foreign Policy and Process.* Itasca, IL: F. E. Peacock.

McCORMICK, JAMES M., AND MICHAEL BLACK. (1983) "Ideology and Voting on the Panama Canal Treaties," *Legislative Studies Quarterly* 8 (February): 45–63.

McCORMICK, JAMES M., AND EUGENE R. WITTKOPF. (1990a) "Bipartisanship, Partisanship, and Ideology in Congressional-Executive Foreign Policy Relations, 1947–1988," *Journal of Politics* 52 (November): 1077–1100.

———. (1990b) "Bush and Bipartisanship: The Past as Prologue?" *Washington Quarterly* 13 (Winter): 5–16.

McCORMICK, JAMES M., EUGENE R. WITTKOPF, AND DAVID DANNA. (1997) "Politics and Bipartisanship at the Water's Edge: A Note on Bush and Clinton," *Polity* 30 (Fall): 133–150.

McCURDY, DAVE. (1994) "Glasnost for the CIA," *Foreign Affairs* 73 (January–February): 125–140.

McELVAINE, ROBERT S. (1984) "Do We Really Want an 'Active President?'" *The Washington Post National Weekly Edition,* July 2, p. 28.

McFARLANE, ROBERT C. (1994) *Special Trust.* New York: Cadell and Davies.

McGEARY. (2001). "Odd Man Out," *Time,* 10 September, pp. 24–32

McGLEN, NANCY E., AND MEREDITH REID SARKEES. (1993) *Women in Foreign Policy: The Insiders.* New York: Routledge.

McCLARAN, JOHN M. (2000) "U.S. Arms Sales to Taiwan," *Asian Survey* 40 (July): 622–640.

McNAMARA, ROBERT S. (1983) "The Military Role of Nuclear Weapons: Perceptions and Misperceptions," *Foreign Affairs* 62 (Fall): 59–80.

———. (1995) *The Tragedy and Lessons of Vietnam.* New York: Times Books.

MEAD, WALTER RUSSELL. (1988–1989) "The United States and the World Economy," *World Policy Journal* 6 (Winter): 1–45.

———. (1989) "American Economic Policy in the Antemillennial Era," *World Policy Journal* 6 (Summer): 385–468.

MEARSHEIMER, JOHN J. (1990a) "Back to the Future: Instability in Europe After the Cold War," *International Security* 14 (Summer): 5–56.

———. (1990b) "Why We Will Soon Miss the Cold War," *The Atlantic Monthly* 266 (August): 35–50.

"MEASURING GLOBALIZATION." (2001), *Foreign Policy* 122 (January–February): 56–71.

MEERNIK, JAMES. (1994) "Presidential Decision Making and the Political Use of Military Force," *International Studies Quarterly* 38 (March): 121–138.

MEERNIK, JAMES, AND STEVEN C. POE. (1996) "U.S. Foreign Aid in the Domestic and International Environments," *International Interactions* 22 (July): 21–40.

MEIER, KENNETH J. (1987) *Politics and the Bureaucracy,* 2nd ed. Monterey, CA: Brooks/Cole.

MELANSON, RICHARD A. (1983) *Writing History and Making Policy: The Cold War, Vietnam, and Revisionism.* Lanham, MD: University Press of America.

———. (1996) *American Foreign Policy Since the Vietnam War: The Search for Consensus from Nixon to Clinton.* Armonk, NY: M. E. Sharpe.

———. (1999) *American Foreign Policy Since the Vietnam War: The Search for Consensus from Nixon to Clinton.* Armonk, NY: M. E. Sharpe.

MELBOURNE, ROY M. (1992) *Conflict and Crisis: A Foreign Service Story.* Lanham, MD: University Press of America.

MELMAN, SEYMOUR. (1974) *The Permanent War Economy.* New York: Simon and Schuster.

MENDELSOHN, JACK. (1997) "Arms Control: The Unfinished Agenda," *Current History* 96 (April): 145–150.

MERELMAN, RICHARD M. (1984) *Making Something of Ourselves: On Culture and Politics in the United States.* Berkeley: University of California Press.

METZ, STEVEN. (1997) "Racing Toward the Future: The Revolution in Military Affairs," *Current History* 96 (April): 184–188.

MICHALAK, STANLEY. (1995) "Bill Clinton's Adventures in the Jungle of Foreign Policy," *USA Today* 123 (March): 10–14.

MILBANK, DANA, AND BRADLEY GRAHAM. (2001) "No Time for 'Strategy'" *Washington Post National Weekly Edition,* 15–21 October p. 13.

MILES, RUFUS E., JR. (1985) "Hiroshima: The Strange Myth of Half a Million American Lives Saved," *International Security* 19 (Fall): 121–140.

MILLER, WARREN E., AND J. MERRILL SHANKS. (1996) *The New American Voter.* Cambridge, MA: Harvard University Press.

MILLS, C. WRIGHT. (1956) *The Power Elite.* New York: Oxford University Press.

MINTER, WILLIAM. (1986–1987) "South Africa: Straight Talk on Sanctions" *Foreign Policy* 65 (Winter): 43–63.

MINUTAGLIO, BILL. (1999) *First Son: George W. Bush and the Bush Family Dynasty.* New York: Random House.

MITCHELL, JENNIFER D. (2001) "The Next Doubling: Understanding Global Population Growth," pp. 446–456 in Charles W. Kegley, Jr. and Eugene R. Wittkopf (eds.), *The Global Agenda: Issues and Perspectives,* 6th ed. Boston: McGraw-Hill.

MITCHELL, PAUL T. (1999) "Ideas, Interests, and Strategy: Bureaucratic Politics and the United States Navy," *Armed Forces and Society: and Interdisciplinary Journal* 25(2): 243–266.

MOEN, MATTHEW C., AND GARY W. COPELAND. (1999) *The Contemporary Congress: A Bicameral Approach.* Belmont, CA: West/Wadsworth.

MOFFETT, GEORGE D. (1994) "Global Population Growth: 21st Century Challenges," *Headline Series* 302 (Spring). New York: Foreign Policy Association.

MOHAN, GILES. (2000) *Structural Adjustment: Theory, Practice, and Impacts.* New York: Routledge.

MONGAR, THOMAS M. (1974) "Personality and Decision-Making: John F. Kennedy in Four Crisis Decisions," pp. 334–372 in Gordon J. DiRenzo (ed.), *Personality and Politics.* Garden City, NY: Doubleday-Anchor.

MONROE, ALAN D. (1979) "Consistency Between Public Preferences and National Policy Decisions," *American Politics Quarterly* 7 (January): 3–19.

———. (1998) "Public Opinion and Public Policy 1980–1993," *Public Opinion Quarterly* 62 (Spring): 6–28.

MOORE, MOLLY. (1994) "The CIA Gets Stung By Afghan Rebels' Stingers," *The Washington Post National Weekly Edition,* 14–20, March p. 18.

MORGAN, DAN (2001) "House Panel Allocates $1.67 Billion for Pentagon Counterterrorism Bid." *The Washington Post.* 9 November: p. A12.

MORGAN, EDMUND S. (1988) *Inventing the People: The Rise of Popular Sovereignty in England and America.* New York: Norton.

MORGENTHAU, HANS J. (1969) "Historical Justice and the Cold War," *New York Review of Books* 13 10 July, pp. 10–17.

———. (1985) *Politics Among Nations,* revised by Kenneth W. Thompson. New York: Knopf.

MORICI, PETER. (1997) "The United States, World Trade, and the Helms-Burton Act," *Current History* 96 (February): 87–88.

MORIN, RICHARD. (1996) "City Editors for a Day," *The Washington Post National Weekly Edition,* 6–12 May, p. 35.

———. (1998) "Keeping the Faith," *The Washington Post National Weekly Edition,* 12 January, p. 37.

MORRISON, PHILIP, KOSTA TSIPIS, AND JEROME WIESNER. (1994) "The Future of American Defense," *Scientific American* 270 (February): 38–45.

MOSER, PAUL K., (ed.) (1990) *Rationality in Action: Contemporary Approaches.* New York: Cambridge University Press.

MOYER, WAYNE. (1973) "House Voting on Defense: An Ideological Explanation," pp. 106–142 in Bruce Russett and Alfred Stepan (eds.), *Military Force and American Society.* New York: Harper and Row.

MUELLER, JOHN. (1971) "Trends in Popular Support for the Wars in Korea and Vietnam," *American Political Science Review* 65 (June): 358–375.

———. (1973) *War, Presidents, and Public Opinion.* New York: Wiley.

MUELLER, JOHN, AND KARL MUELLER. (1999) "Sanctions of Mass Destruction," *Foreign Affairs* 78 (May/June): 43–53.

MUFSON, STEVEN. (1992) "Superpower or Sri Lanka?" *The Washington Post National Weekly Edition,* 7–13 September, pp. 6–7.

MULCAHY, KEVIN V. (1995) "Rethinking Groupthink: Walt Rostow and the National Security Advisory Process in the Johnson Administration," *Presidential Studies Quarterly* 25 (Spring): 237–250.

MÜLLER, HARALD, AND MITCHELL REISS. (1995) "Counterproliferation: Putting New Wine in Old Bottles," *Washington Quarterly* 18 (Spring): 143–154.

MULLINS, KERRY, AND AARON WILDAVSKY. (1992) "The Procedural Presidency of George Bush," *Political Science Quarterly* 107 (Spring): 31–62.

MUNRO, NEIL. (2000) "Undercover Agency Sheds Its Security Blanket," *National Journal* 32 (October 7): 3176.

MURRAY, ALAN. (1992–1993) "The Global Economy Bungled," *Foreign Affairs* 72 (1): 158–166.

MURRAY, SHOON KATHLEEN. (1994) "Change and Continuity in American Elites' Foreign Policy Beliefs: A 1988–1992 Panel Study," Paper presented at the annual meeting of the International Studies Association, Washington, DC, March 29–April 1.

MYERS, ROBERT J. (1999) *U.S. Foreign Policy in the Twenty-First Century: The Relevance of Realism.* Baton Rouge, LA: Louisiana State University Press.

MYERS, STEVEN LEE. (1997) "Why Washington Likes Land Mines," *New York Times,* 24 August, p. 5.

MYRDAL, GUNNAR. (1944) *An American Dilemma: The Negro Problem in Modern Democracy.* New York: Harper.

NACHT, ALEXANDER. (1995) "U.S. Foreign Policy Strategies," *Washington Quarterly* 18 (Summer): 195–210.

NAIM, MOISES. (2000) "Washington Consensus or Washington Confusion?" *Foreign Policy* 118(Spring): pp. 87–102.

NATHAN, JAMES A., (ed.), (1993) *The Cuban Missile Crisis Revisited.* New York: St. Martin's.

NATHAN, JAMES A., AND JAMES K. OLIVER. (1976) *United States Foreign Policy and World Order.* Boston: Little, Brown.

———. (1994) *Foreign Policy Making and the American Political System,* 3rd ed. Baltimore, MD: Johns Hopkins University Press.

"THE NATIONAL SECURITY ADVISER: ROLE AND ACCOUNTABILITY." (1980) in Hearings Before the Committee on Foreign Relations, United States Senate. Washington, DC: Government Printing Office (96th Congress, 2nd Session).

NATIONAL SECURITY COUNCIL PROJECT, *The Nixon Administration National Security Council.* Center for International and Security Studies at Maryland and The Brookings Institution, 1998.

NATIONAL SECURITY COUNCIL PROJECT. 1999a. *The Bush Administration National Security Council.* Center for International and Security Studies at Maryland and the Brookings Institution.

NATIONAL SECURITY COUNCIL PROJECT. (1999b) *The Role of the National Security Adviser.*

The Center for International and Security Studies at Maryland and The Brookings Institution.

NATIONAL SECURITY COUNCIL PROJECT. (2000) *The Clinton Administration National Security Council.* The Center for International and Security Studies at Maryland and The Brookings Institution.

NELSON, TREVOR. (1995) "My Enemy's Friends: In Guatemala, the DEA Fights the CIA," *The New Republic* 212, 5 June, pp. 18–20.

NEUMAN, W. RUSSELL. (1986) *The Paradox of Mass Politics: Knowledge and Opinion in the American Electorate.* Cambridge, MA: Harvard University Press.

NEUSTADT, RICHARD E. (1980) *Presidential Power.* New York: Wiley.

NEUSTADT, RICHARD E., AND ERNEST R. MAY. (1986) *Thinking in Time: The Uses of History for Decision Makers.* New York: Free Press.

NEWLAND, KATHLEEN. (1999) "Workers of the World, Now What?" *Foreign Policy* 114 (Spring): 52–64.

NEWMAN, RICHARD J. (1998) "America Fights Back: Clinton Raises the Stakes in the War Against Terrorism," *U.S. News and World Report* 125, 31 August pp. 38–43.

NEWMAN, RICHARD J., AND ALAN COOPERMAN. (1997) "Getting Ready for the Wrong War," *U.S. News and World Report* 122, 12 May, pp. 30–32.

NIE, NORMAN H., SIDNEY VERBA, AND JOHN R. PETROCIK. (1976) *The Changing American Voter.* Cambridge, MA: Harvard University Press.

NIEBUHR, REINHOLD. (1947) *Moral Man and Immoral Society.* New York: Scribner's.

NIJMAN, JAN. (1998) "United States Foreign Aid: Crisis? What Crisis?" pp. 29–43 in Richard and Jan Nijman Grant (eds.), *The Global Crisis in Foreign Aid.* Syracuse, NY: Syracuse University Press.

NOLAN, JANNE E., (ed.) (1994) *Global Engagement: Cooperation and Security in the 21st Century.* Washington, DC: The Brookings Institution.

NORRIS, PIPPA. (1997) "News of the World," pp. 275–290 in Pippa Norris (ed.), *Politics and the Press: The News Media and Their Influences.* Boulder, CO: Lynne Reinner.

NOWZAD, BAHRAM. (1990) "Lessons of the Debt Decade," *Finance and Development* 27 (March): 9–13.

NUNN, SAM. (1987) "The ABM Reinterpretation Issue," *Washington Quarterly* 10 (Autumn): 45–57.

NUNN, SAM, AND PETE DOMENICI. (1992) *The CSIS Strengthening of America Commission.* Washington, DC: Center for Strategic and International Studies.

NUNN, SAM, AND JAMES R. SCHLESINGER. (2000) *The Geopolitics of Energy into the 21st Century. Vol. 1: An Overview and Policy Considerations.* Washington, DC: Center for Strategic and International Studies.

NYE, JOSEPH S., JR. (1990) *Bound to Lead: The Changing Nature of American Power.* New York: Basic Books.

———. (1992) "What New World Order?" *Foreign Affairs* 71 (Spring): 83–96.

———. (1994) "Peering into the Future," *Foreign Affairs* 73 (July/August): 82–93.

———. (1996) "Conflicts After the Cold War," *Washington Quarterly* 19 (Winter): 5–24.

———. (1999) "Redefining the National Interest," *Foreign Affairs* 78 (July/August): 22–35.

———. (2001/02) "Seven Tests: Between Concert and Unilateralism," The National Interest 66 (Winter):5–13.

NYE, JOSEPH S., AND WILLIAM A. OWENS. (1996) "America's Information Edge," *Foreign Affairs* 75 (March/April): 20–36.

NYE, JOSEPH S., JR., PHILIP D. ZELIKOW, AND DAVID C. KING, (eds), (1997) *Why People Don't Trust Government.* Cambridge, MA: Harvard University Press.

OBERDORFER, DAN. (1993) "U.S. Had Covert Plan to Oust Iraq's Saddam," *The Washington Post,* 20 January, p. A4.

OBERDORFER, DON, AND HELEN DEWAR. (1987) "The Capitol Hill Broth Is Being Seasoned by a Lot of Cooks," *The Washington Post National Weekly Edition,* 26 October, p. 12.

O'HANLON, MICHAEL. (1998–1999) "Can High Technology Bring U.S. Troops Home?" *Foreign Policy* 113 (Winter): 72–85.

———. (1999) "Defense and Foreign Policy: The Budget Cuts Are Going Too Far," *Brookings Review* 17 (Winter): 22–25.

———. (2000) "Doing It Right," *Brookings Review* 18 (Fall): 34–37.

O'HANLON, MICHAEL, AND CAROL GRAHAM. (1997) *A Half Penny on the Federal Dollar: The Future of Development Aid.* Washington, DC: Brookings Institution Press.

O'HEFFERNAN, PATRICK. (1991) *Mass Media and American Foreign Policy: Insider Perspectives on Global Journalism and the Foreign Policy Process.* Norwood, NJ: Ablex.

OLSON, MANCUR. (1965) *The Logic of Collective Action.* Cambridge, MA: Harvard University Press.

———. (1982) *The Rise and Decline of Nations.* New Haven, CT: Yale University Press.

OMESTAD, THOMAS. (1992–1993) "Why Bush Lost," *Foreign Policy* 89 (Winter): 70–81.

———. (1996–1997) "Foreign Policy and Campaign '96," *Foreign Policy* 105 (Winter): 37–54.

ORGANSKI, A. F. K., AND JACEK KUGLER. (1980) *The War Ledger.* Chicago: University of Chicago Press.

ORME, JOHN. (1997–1998) "The Utility of Force in a World of Scarcity," *International Security* 22 (Winter): 138–167.

ORNSTEIN, NORMAN J., AND SHIRLEY ELDER. (1978) *Interest Groups, Lobbying, and Policymaking.* Washington, DC: CQ Press.

ORNSTEIN, NORMAN J., ANDREW KOHUT, AND LARRY MCCARTHY. (1988) *The People, the Press, and Politics.* Reading, MA: Addison-Wesley.

OSGOOD, ROBERT E. (1953) *Ideals and Self-Interest in America's Foreign Relations.* Chicago: University of Chicago Press.

OSTROM, CHARLES W., JR., AND BRIAN L. JOB. (1986) "The President and the Political Use of Force," *American Political Science Review* 80 (June): 541–566.

OSTROM, CHARLES W., JR., AND DENNIS M. SIMON. (1985) "Promise and Performance: A Dynamic Model of Presidential Popularity," *American Political Science Review* 79 (June): 334–358.

———. (1989) "The Man in the Teflon Suit: The Environmental Connection, Political Drama, and Popular Support in the Reagan Presidency," *Public Opinion Quarterly* 53 (Fall): 353–387.

OTTAWAY, DAVID B., AND STEVE COLL. (1995) "Streamlining the Nuclear Order," *The Washington Post National Weekly Edition,* 24–30 April, pp. 10–11.

OWEN, JOHN M. (1994) "How Liberalism Produces the Democratic Peace," *International Security* 19 (Fall): 87–125.

PAARLBERG, ROBERT. (2000) "The Global Food Fight," *Foreign Affairs* 79 (May/June): 24–38.

PAGE, BENJAMIN I. (1994) "Democratic Responsiveness? Untangling the Links Between Public Opinion and Policy," *PS: Political Science and Politics* 27 (March): 25–29.

PAGE, BENJAMIN I., AND JASON BARABAS. (2000) "Foreign Policy Gaps Between Citizens and Leaders," *International Studies Quarterly* 44 (September): 339–364.

PAGE, BENJAMIN I., AND RICHARD A. BRODY. (1972) "Policy Voting and the Electoral Process: The Vietnam War Issue," *American Political Science Review* 66 (September): 979–995.

PAGE, BENJAMIN I, AND ROBERT Y. SHAPIRO. (1992) *The Rational Public*. Chicago: University of Chicago Press.

PAGE, BENJAMIN I., ROBERT SHAPIRO, AND GLENN R. DEMPSEY. (1987) "What Moves Public Opinion?" *American Political Science Review* 81 (March): 23–43.

PAIGE, GLENN D. (1972) "Comparative Case Analysis of Crises Decisions: Korea and Cuba," pp. 41–55 in Charles F. Hermann (ed.), *International Crises: Insights from Behavioral Research*. New York: Free Press.

PAPE, ROBERT A. (1997) "Why Economic Sanctions Do Not Work," *International Security* 22 (Fall): 90–136.

———. (1998) "Why Economic Sanctions Still Do Not Work," *International Security* 23 (Summer): 66–77.

PARENTI, MICHAEL. (1969) *The Anti-Communist Impulse*. New York: Random House.

———. (1981) "We Hold These Myths to Be Self-Evident," *The Nation* 232 April 425–429.

———. (1986) *Inventing Reality*. New York: St. Martin's.

———. (1988) *Democracy for the Few*, 5th ed. New York: St. Martin's.

PARRY, ROBERT, AND PETER KORNBLUH. (1988) "Iran-Contra's Untold Story," *Foreign Policy* 72 (Fall): 3–30.

PASTOR, ROBERT A. (ed.) (1999) *A Century's Journey: How the Great Powers Shape the World*. New York: Basic Books.

———. (1999) "The Great Powers in the Twentieth Century: From Dawn to Dusk," pp. 1–31 in Robert A. Pastor (ed.), *A Century's Journey: How the Great Powers Shape the World*. New York: Basic Books.

PATERSON, THOMAS G. (1979) *On Every Front: The Making of the Cold War*. New York: Norton.

PATTERSON, BRADLEY. (2000) *The White House Staff: Inside the West Wing and Beyond*. Washington, DC: Brookings Institution Press.

PAYASLIAN, SIMON. (1996) *U.S. Foreign Economic and Military Aid: The Reagan and Bush Administrations*. Lanham, MD: University Press of America.

PAYNE, RICHARD J. (1996) *The Clash with Distant Cultures: Values, Interests, and Force in American Foreign Policy*. Albany, NY: State University of New York Press.

PEARLSTEIN, STEVEN. (1994) "The Hill Shines a Light on the Shadow Pentagon," *The Washington Post National Weekly Edition*, 5–11 August, p. 31.

THE PENTAGON PAPERS as Published by *The New York Times*. (1971). Toronto: Bantam Books.

PERLEZ, JANE. (1999) "With Berger in Catbird Seat, Albright's Star Dims," *New York Times*, 14 December p. A1.

———. (2001) "Washington Memo: Divergent Voices Heard in Bush Foreign Policy," *New York Times*, p. A1.

PERLMUTTER, DAVID D. (1998) *Photojournalism and Foreign Policy: Icons of Outrage in International Crises*. Boulder, CO: Praeger.

PERRY, JAMES M. (1989) "Reagan's Last Scene: Blaming the 'Iron Triangle' for U.S. Budget Deficit Draws Mixed Reviews," *Wall Street Journal*, 5 January, p. A12.

PETERSON, PAUL E. (1994) "The President's Dominance in Foreign Policy Making," *Political Science Quarterly* 109 (Summer): 215–234.

PETERSON, PETER G. (1999) "Gray Dawn: The Global Aging Crisis," *Foreign Affairs* 78 (January/February): 42–55.

PEW RESEARCH CENTER FOR THE PEOPLE AND THE PRESS. (1997) *America's Place in the World II*. Pew Research Center.

———. (2000) *Campaign 2000 Typology Survey*. Pew Research Center.

PFIFFNER, JAMES A. (1992) "The President and the Postreform Congress," pp. 211–232 in Roger H. Davidson (ed.), *The Postreform Congress*. New York: St. Martin's.

PFIFFNER, JAMES P. (1990) "Establishing the Bush Presidency," *Public Administration Review* 50 (January/February): 64–73.

PIANIN, ERIC. (1999) "How Much Longer Can This Last," *The Washington Post Weekly Edition*, 31 May, p. 11.

PIERRE, ANDREW, AND SAHR CONWAY-LANZ. (1994–1995) "Desperate Measures: Arms Producers in a Buyer's Market," *Harvard International Review* 17 (Winter): 12–15, 70–72.

PILAT, JOSEPH F., AND WALTER F. KIRCHNER. (1995) "The Technological Promise of Counterproliferation," *Washington Quarterly* 18 (Winter): 153–166.

PINCUS, WALTER. (1985) "The Military's New, Improved 'Revolving Door,'" *The Washington Post National Weekly Edition*, 18 March, p. 33.

———. (1994) "A Highflier, but Still Mired in the Cold War," *The Washington Post National Weekly Edition*, 15–21 August.

———. (2001) "Intelligence Shakeup Would Boost CIA." *The Washington Post*, 8 November, p. A1.

PINE, ART. (1994) "Perry's Steady Hand Stands Out on Foreign Policy Team," *Los Angeles Times*, 29 May.

PIPES, RICHARD. (1995) "What to Do About the CIA," *Commentary* 99 (March): 36–43.

POMPER, GERALD M. (1968) *Elections in America: Control and Influence in Democratic Politics*. New York: Dodd, Mead.

———. (1989) "The Presidential Election," pp. 129–152 in Gerald M. Pomper, Ross K. Baker, Walter Dean Burnham, Barbara G. Farah, Marjorie Randon Hershey, Ethel Klein, and Wilson Carey McWilliams (eds.) *The Election of 1988: Reports and Interpretations*. Chatham, NJ: Chatham House.

PORTER, BRUCE D. (1992) "A Country Instead of a Cause: Russian Foreign Policy in the Post-Soviet Era," *Washington Quarterly* 15 (Summer): 41–56.

PORTER, ROGER B. (1983) "Economic Advice to the President: From Eisenhower to Reagan," *Political Science Quarterly* 98 (Fall): 403–426.

POSEN, BARRY R. (2001/02) "The Struggle against Terrorism: Grand Strategy, Strategy, and Tactics." *International Security*. 26 (Winter): 39–55.

POSEN, BARRY R., AND ANDREW L. ROSS. (1996–1997) "Competing Visions for U.S. Grand Strategy," *International Security* 21 (Winter): 5–48.

———. (1997) "Competing U.S. Grand Strategies," pp. 100–134 in Robert J. Lieber (ed.), *Eagle Adrift: American Foreign Policy at the End of the Century*. New York: Longman.

POSNER, RICHARD A. (2000) *An Affair of State: The Investigation, Impeachment, and Trial of President Clinton*. Cambridge, MA: Harvard University Press.

POSTOL, THEODORE A. (1991–1992) "Lessons of the Gulf Experience with Patriot," *International Security* 16 (Winter): 119–171.

POVICH, ELAINE S. (2001) "Terrorist Attacks: Quick Vote on Use of Force." *Newsday*. 15 September p. W10.

POWELL, COLIN L. (1992–1993) "U.S. Forces: Challenges Ahead," *Foreign Affairs* 71 (Winter): 32–45.

———. (1995) *My American Journey: An Autobiography*. New York: Random House.

POWELL, COLIN, JOHN LEHMAN, WILLIAM ODOM, SAMUEL HUNTINGTON, AND RICHARD KOHN. (1994) "An Exchange on Civil-Military Relations," *The National Interest* 36 (Summer): 23–31.

POWLICK, PHILIP J. (1991) "The Attitudinal Bases for Responsiveness to Public Opinion Among American Foreign Policy Officials," *Journal of Conflict Resolution* 35 (December): 611–641.

PRADOS, JOHN. (1991) *Keepers of the Keys: A History of the National Security Council from Truman to Bush*. New York: William Morrow.

———. (1996) "No Reform Here," *Bulletin of the Atomic Scientists* 52 (September–October): 55–59.

PRESTON, THOMAS. (1997) "Following the Leader: The Impact of U.S. Presidential Style Upon Advisory Group Dynamics, Structure, and Decision," pp. 191–248 in Paul 't Hart, Eric Stern and Bengt Sundelius (eds.), *Beyond Groupthink: Political Group Dynamics and Foreign Policymaking*. Ann Arbor, MI: University of Michigan Press.

———. (2001) *The President and His Inner Circle: Leadership Style and the Advisory Process in Foreign Policy Making*. Columbia, NY: Columbia University Press.

PRESTON, THOMAS, AND PAUL 'T HART. (1999) "Understanding and Evaluating Bureaucratic Politics: The Nexus Between Political Leaders and Advisory Systems," *Political Psychology* 20 (March): 49–98.

PRESTOWITZ, CLYDE V., JR. (1992) "Beyond Laissez Faire," *Foreign Policy* 87 (Summer): 67–87.

PRIEST, DANA. (1992) "Showing Up Where You'd Least Expect," *The Washington Post National Weekly Edition*, 27 April–3 May, p. 33.

PRIEST, DANA, AND JOHN MINTZ. (1995) "The Unsinkable Seawolf," *The Washington Post National Weekly Edition,* 23–29 October, p. 33.

PRINGLE, ROBERT. (1977–1978) "Creeping Irrelevance at Foggy Bottom," *Foreign Policy* 29 (Winter): 128–139.

PROGRAM ON INTERNATIONAL POLICY ATTITUDES. (2001). College Park, MD: University of Maryland.

PURDUM, TODD S. (1996) "Facets of Clinton," *New York Times Magazine,* 19 May, pp. 35–41+.

PUTNAM, ROBER D. (1988) "Diplomacy and Domestic Politics: The Logic of Two-Level Games," *International Organization* 42 (Summer): 427–460.

———. (2000) *Bowling Alone: The Collapse and Revival of American Community.* New York: Simon and Schuster.

QUADRENNIAL DEFENSE REVIEW REPORT. (2001) 30 September.

RABKIN, JEREMY. (1994) "Trading In Our Sovereignty?" *National Review* 13 June, pp. 34–36, 73.

RANELAGH, JOHN. (1987) *The Agency: The Rise and Decline of the CIA.* New York: Simon and Schuster.

RANGER, ROBIN. (1993) "Theater Missile Defenses: Lessons from British Experiences with Air and Missile Defenses," *Comparative Strategy* 12 (4): 399–413.

RANNEY, AUSTIN. (1983) *Channels of Power.* New York: Basic Books.

RANSOM, HARRY HOWE. (1970) *The Intelligence Establishment.* Cambridge, MA: Harvard University Press.

RAUCH, JONATHAN. (1994) *Demosclerosis: The Silent Killer of American Government.* New York: Times Books.

RAY, JAMES LEE. (1995) *Democracy and International Conflict: An Evaluation of the Democratic Peace Proposition.* Columbia, SC: University of South Carolina Press.

REAGAN, RONALD. (1990) *An American Life.* New York: Simon and Schuster.

REICH, ROBERT B. (1985) "How Much Is Enough?" *New Republic,* 12 and 19 August, pp. 33–37.

REIFENBERG, JAN. (1990) "Economies Built on Arms," *World Press Review* 37 (January): 22–23.

REISCHAUER, EDWIN O. (1968) "Redefining the National Interest: The Vietnam Case," Paper presented at the annual meeting of the American Political Science Association, Washington, DC, September 2–7.

RENNER, MICHAEL. (1994) "Monitoring Arms Trade," *World Watch* 7 (May–June): 21–26.

RENSHON, STANLEY A. (1998) *High Hopes: The Clinton Presidency and the Politics of Ambition.* New York: Routledge.

REYNOLDS, DAVID, (ed.) (1994) *The Origins of the Cold War in Europe: International Perspectives.* New Haven, CT: Yale University Press.

RHODES, EDWARD. (1994) "Do Bureaucratic Politics Matter: Some Disconfirming Findings from the Case of the U.S. Navy," *World Politics* 47 (October): 1–41.

RICE, CONDOLEEZZA. (2000) "Promoting the National Interest," *Foreign Affairs* 79 (January/February): 45–62.

RICKS, THOMAS. "U.S. Arms Unmanned Aircraft." *Washington Post,* October 18, 2001, p. A1.

RICKS, THOMAS, E. (1997) "The Widening Gap Between the Military and Society," *The Atlantic Monthly* 280 (July): 66–78.

———. (2001a) "Rumsfeld Outlines Defense Overhaul," *Washington Post,* 23 March, p. 1.

———. (2001b) "Time for a Military Shake-Up." *Washington Post National Weekly Edition,* 15–21 October, p. 29.

RICKS, THOMAS AND ALAN SIPRESS. (2001) "Attacks Restrained by Political Goals." *Washington Post,* 23 October, p. A1.

RICKS, THOMAS, AND VERNON LOEB. (2001) "Special Open Ground Campaign." *Washington Post,* 19 October, p. A1.

RIEBLING, MARK. (1994) *Wedge: The Secret War Between the FBI and CIA.* New York: Knopf.

RIEFF, DAVID. (1999) "A New Age of Liberal Imperialism?" *World Policy Journal* 16 (Summer): 1–10.

RIELLY, JOHN E., (ed.), (1991) *American Public Opinion and U.S. Foreign Policy 1991.* Chicago: Chicago Council on Foreign Relations.

———, (ed.) (1995) *American Public Opinion and U.S. Foreign Policy 1995.* Chicago: Chicago Council on Foreign Relations.

———, (ed.) (1999) *American Public Opinion and U.S. Foreign Policy 1999.* Chicago: Chicago Council on Foreign Relations.

RILEY, STEPHEN P. (1993) "Conclusions," pp. 189–196 in Stephen P. Riley (ed.), *The Politics of Global Debt*. New York: St. Martin's.

RIPLEY, RANDALL B., AND GRACE A. FRANKLIN. (1991) *Congress, the Bureaucracy, and Public Policy*. Pacific Grove, CA: Brooks/Cole.

RISEN, JAMES. (2000) "The Clinton Administration's See-No-Evil CIA," *New York Times*, 10 September, p. 5.

———. (2001a) "Clinton Creates Post to Protect Nation's Secrets," *New York Times*, 5 January, p. 1.

———. (2001b) "Gaps in CIA's Ames Case May Be Filled by FBI's Own Spy Case," *New York Times*, 20 February, p. 16.

———. (2001c) "Moles Often Burrow Deeper Than Spy Hunters Can Dig," *New York Times*, 25 February, p. 12.

RISSE-KAPPEN, THOMAS. (1991) "Public Opinion, Domestic Structure, and Foreign Policy in Liberal Democracies," *World Politics* 43 (July): 479–512.

ROBB, CHARLES S. (1997) "Challenging the Assumptions of U.S. Military Strategy," *Washington Quarterly* 20 (Spring): 115–131.

———. (1999) "Star Wars II," *Washington Quarterly* 22 (Winter): 81–86.

ROBINSON, JAMES A. (1972) "Crisis: An Appraisal of Concepts and Theories," pp. 20–35 in Charles F. Hermann (ed.), *International Crises: Insights from Behavioral Research*. New York: Free Press.

ROCA, SERGIO. (1987) "Economic Sanctions Against Cuba," pp. 87–104 in David Leyton-Brown (ed.), *The Utility of International Economic Sanctions*. New York: St. Martin's.

ROCKMAN, BERT A. (1981) "America's Departments of State: Irregular and Regular Syndromes of Policymaking," *American Political Science Review* 75 (December): 911–927.

RODMAN, PETER W. (1999) "His Own Fault," *National Review* 22 November p. 18+.

RODRIK, DANI. (1997) *Has Globalization Gone Too Far?* Washington, DC: Institute for International Economics.

ROGERS, WILLIAM D. (1979) "Who's in Charge of Foreign Policy?" *New York Times Magazine*, 9 September, pp. 44–50.

ROGOW, ARNOLD A. (1963) *James Forrestal: A Study in Personality, Politics, and Policy*. New York: Macmillan.

ROHDE, DAVID. (1994) "Partisan Leadership and Congressional Assertiveness in Foreign and Defense Policy," pp. 76–101 in David Deese (ed.), *The New Politics of American Foreign Policy*. New York: St. Martin's.

ROMAN, PETER J., AND DAVID W. TARR. (1998) "The Joint Chiefs of Staff: From Service Parochialism to Jointness," *Political Science Quarterly* 113 (Spring): 91–111.

ROMANO, LOIS, AND GEORGE LARDNER, JR. (1999a) "The Unlikely Candidate," *The Washington Post National Weekly Edition*, 9 August, pp. 6–8.

———. (1999b) "A Son Follows in a Famous Father's Footsteps," *The Washington Post National Weekly Edition*, 9 August, pp. 9–11.

ROOSEVELT, ANN (2001) "Combating Terrorism, Other Threats: Lawmakers Boost Anti-Terror Funds for '02 Defense Budget." *White House Weekly*, 11 September, p. 1.

ROSATI, JEREL A. (1993) "Jimmy Carter, a Man Before His Time? The Emergence and Collapse of the First Post–Cold War Presidency," *Presidential Studies Quarterly* 23 (Summer): 459–476.

———. (1981) "Developing a Systematic Decision-Making Framework," *World Politics* 33 (January): 234–252.

ROSE, GIDEON. (2000–2001) "Democracy Promotion and American Foreign Policy," *International Security* 25 (Winter): 186–203.

ROSECRANCE, RICHARD. (1990) *America's Economic Resurgence: A Bold New Strategy*. New York: Harper and Row.

ROSEN, STEVEN J. (ed.) (1973) *Testing the Theory of the Military-Industrial Complex*. Lexington, MA: Heath.

ROSENAU, JAMES N. (1966) "Pre-Theories and Theories of Foreign Policy," pp. 27–92 in R. Barry Farrell (ed.), *Approaches to Comparative and International Politics*. Evanston, IL: Northwestern University Press.

———. (1980) *The Scientific Study of Foreign Policy*. New York: Nichols.

ROSENBERG, MILTON J. (1965) "Images in Relation to the Policy Process: American Public Opinion on Cold War Issues," pp. 277–336 in Herbert C. Kelman (ed.), *International Behavior*. New York: Holt, Rinehart, and Winston.

ROSENTHAL, URIEL, PAUL 'T HART, AND ALEXANDER LOUZMIN. (1991) "The Bureaupolitics of Crisis Management," *Public Administration* 69: 211–233.

ROSTOW, EUGENE V. (1993) *Toward Managed Peace: The National Security Interests of the United States, 1759 to the Present.* New Haven, CT: Yale University Press.

ROTHGEB, JOHN M. (2001) *U.S. Trade Policy: Balancing Economic Dreams and Political Realities.* Washington, DC: CQ Press.

ROWE, EDWARD T. (1974) "Aid and Coups d'Etat: Aspects of the Impact of American Military Assistance Programs in the Less Developed Countries," *International Studies Quarterly* 18 (June): 239–255.

RUBIN, BARRY. (1985) *Secrets of State: The State Department and the Struggle Over U.S. Foreign Policy.* New York: Oxford University Press.

RUGGIE, JOHN GERARD. (1992) "Multilateralism: The Anatomy of an Institution," *International Organization* 46 (Summer): 561–598.

RUSSETT, BRUCE. (1998) "A Community of Peace: Democracy, Interdependence, and International Organization," pp. 241–251 in Charles W. Kegley, Jr. and Eugene R. Wittkopf (eds.), *The Global Agenda: Issues and Perspectives,* 5th ed. New York: McGraw-Hill.

RUSSETT, BRUCE, AND THOMAS W. GRAHAM. (1988) "Public Opinion and National Security Policy Relationships and Impact," pp. 239–257 in Manus Midlarsky (ed.), *Handbook of War Studies.* London: Allen and Unwin.

RUSSETT, BRUCE, THOMAS HARTLEY, AND SHOON MURRAY. (1994) "The End of the Cold War, Attitude Change, and the Politics of Defense Spending," *PS: Political Science and Politics* 27 (March): 17–21.

RUSSETT, BRUCE, AND JOHN ONEAL. (2000) *Triangulating Peace: Democracy, Interdependence, and International Organization.* New York: Norton.

RUTTAN, VERNON W. (1996) *United States Development Assistance Policy: The Domestic Politics of Foreign Economic Aid.* Baltimore, MD: Johns Hopkins University Press.

SACHS, JEFFREY. (1989) "Making the Brady Plan Work," *Foreign Affairs* 68 (Summer): 87–104.

———. (2001) "The Strategic Significance of Global Inequality," *Washington Quarterly* 24 (Summer): 187–198.

SACHS, JERFFREY, AND FELIPE LARRAIN. (1999) "Why Dollarization Is More Straightjacket Than Salvation," *Foreign Policy* 116 (Fall): 80–91.

SAFIRE, WILLIAM. (1990) "Forming Public Opinion," *New York Times,* December 10, p. A15.

SAGOFF, MARK. (2001) "Do We Consume Too Much?" pp. 404–419 in Charles W. Kegley, Jr. and Eugene R. Wittkopf (eds.), *The Global Agenda: Issues and Perspectives,* 6th ed. Boston: McGraw-Hill.

SAHN, DAVID E., PAUL A. DOROSH, AND STEPHEN D. YOUNGER. (1999) *Structural Adjustment Reconsidered: Economic Policy and Poverty in Africa.* London: Cambridge University Press.

SANDERS, JERRY W. (1983) *Peddlers of Crisis: The Committee on the Present Danger and the Politics of Containment.* Boston: South End Press.

SANDMAN, PETER M., DAVID M. RUBIN, AND DAVID B. SACHSMAN. (1982) *Media,* 3rd ed. Englewood Cliffs, NJ: Prentice-Hall.

SANGER, DAVID E. (1994) "Who Won in the Korean Deal," *New York Times,* 23 October, p. E3.

———. (1999) "America Finds It Lonely at the Top," *New York Times,* 18 July, 1999, pp. 1, 4.

SANGER, DAVID E., AND FRANK BRUNI. (2001) "In His First Days, Bush Plans Review of Clinton's Acts," *New York Times,* 14 January A1.

SCHAFER, MARK, AND SCOTT CRICHLOW. (1996) "Antecedents of Groupthink: A Quantitative Study," *Journal of Conflict Resolution* 40: pp. 415–435.

SCHATTSCHNEIDER, E. E. (1960) *The Semisovereign People.* New York: Holt, Rinehart, and Winston.

SCHELL, JONATHAN. (1982) *The Fate of the Earth.* New York: Avon Books.

———. (1984) *The Abolition.* New York: Knopf.

———. (1999) "The Unthinkable," *The Nation* 269, 8 November p. 7ff.

SCHELLING, THOMAS C. (1966) *Arms and Influence.* New Haven, CT: Yale University Press.

SCHERLEN, RENEE G. (1998) "NAFTA and Beyond: The Politics of Trade in the Post–Cold War Period," pp. 358–385 in James M. Scott (ed.), *After the End: Making U.S. Foreign Policy in the Post–Cold War World.* Durham, NC: Duke University Press.

SCHLESINGER, ARTHUR, JR. (1958) *The Coming of the New Deal.* Boston: Houghton Mifflin.

———. (1967) "Origins of the Cold War," *Foreign Affairs* 46 (October): 22–52.

———. (1973) *The Imperial Presidency*. Boston: Houghton Mifflin.

———. (1977) "America: Experiment or Destiny?" *American Historical Review* 82 (June): 505–522.

———. (1986) *The Cycles of American History*. Boston: Houghton Mifflin.

———. (1989) "The Legislative-Executive Balance in International Affairs: The Intentions of the Framers," *Washington Quarterly* 12 (Winter): 99–107.

———. (1992) *The Disuniting of America: Reflections on a Multicultural Society*. New York: Norton.

———. (1997) "Rating the Presidents: Washington to Clinton." *Political Science Quarterly* 122 (Summer 1997): 179–190.

SCHMITT, ERIC. (1999) "Bombs Are Smart. People Are Smarter," *The Washington Post National Weekly Edition* 4 July, p. 6.

———. (2001a) "Helms Urges Foreign Aid Be Handled by Charities," *New York Times,* 12 January.

———. (2001b) "Cheney Draws on Seasoned Veterans to Support His New Role," *New York Times,* 3 February, p. A1.

SCHNEIDER, BARRY R. (1989) "Invitation to a Nuclear Beheading," pp. 291–301 in Charles W. Kegley, Jr. and Eugene R. Wittkopf (eds.), *The Nuclear Reader,* 2nd ed. New York: St. Martin's.

SCHNEIDER, WILLIAM. (1982) "Bang-Bang Television: The New Superpower," *Public Opinion* 5 (April/May): 13–15.

———. (1984) "Public Opinion," pp. 11–35 in Joseph S. Nye, Jr. (ed.), *The Making of America's Soviet Policy*. New Haven, CT: Yale University Press.

———. (1990) "The In-Box President," *The Atlantic Monthly* 265 (January): 34–43.

SCHNEIDER, WILLIAM, AND L. A. LEWIS. (1985) "Views on the News," *Public Opinion* 8 (August/September): 6–11, 58–59.

SCHRAEDER, PETER J., (ed.) (1992) *Intervention into the 1990s: U.S. Foreign Policy in the Third World*. Boulder, CO: Rienner.

———. (1998) "From Ally to Orphan: Understanding U.S. Policy Toward Somalia After the Cold War," pp. 330–357 in James M. Scott (ed.), *After the End: Making U.S. Foreign Policy in the Post–Cold War World*. Durham, NC: Duke University Press.

SCHWARTZ, HERMAN M. (1994) *States Versus Markets: History, Geography, and the Development of the International Political Economy*. New York: St. Martin's.

SCHWARTZ, STEPHEN. (2000) "Outmaneuvered, Outgunned, and Out of View," *The Bulletin of the Atomic Scientists* 56 (January/February): 24–31.

SCHWARZ, BENJAMIN. (1998) "The Enduring Myth of a Liberal America," *World Policy Journal* 15 (Fall): 69–77.

SCHWARZ, BENJAMIN, AND CHRISTOPHER LAYNE. (2002) "A Grand New Strategy," *The Atlantic Monthly* 289 (January): 38–42.

SCHWEIZER, PETER. (1993) *Friendly Spies: How America's allies are using economic espionage to steal our secrets*. New York: The Atlantic Monthly Press.

SCHYDLOWSKY, DANIEL. (1995) *Structural Adjustment: Retrospect and Prospect*. Westport, CT: Greenwood.

SCIOLINO, ELAINE. (1995) "Global Concerns? Not in Congress," *New York Times,* 15 January, p. 1.

———. (2000) "Woman in the News: Condoleeza Rice," *New York Times,* 18 December, p. A1.

SCIOLINO, ELAINE, AND TODD S. PURDUM. (1995) "Gore Is No Typical Vice President in the Shadows," *New York Times,* 19 February, pp. 1, 16.

SCOTT, ANDREW M. (1969) "The Department of State: Formal Organization and Informal Culture," *International Studies Quarterly* 13 (March): 1–18.

SCOTT, JAMES M. (1996) *Deciding to Intervene: The Reagan Doctrine and American Foreign Policy*. Durham, NC: Duke University Press.

———. (1997a) "Trade and Tradeoffs: The Clinton Administration and the 'Big Emerging Markets' Strategy," *Futures Research Quarterly* 13 (Summer): 37–66.

———. (1997b) "In the Loop: Congressional Influence in American Foreign Policy," *Journal of Political and Military Sociology* 25 (Summer): 47–76.

———. (1998a) "Competing for Markets: The Dilemmas of the 'Big Emerging Markets' Strategy," *International Studies Association - Midwest Annual Conference*. Chicago, Illinois.

———. (ed.) (1998b) *After the End: Making U.S. Foreign Policy in the Post–Cold War World*. Durham, NC: Duke University Press.

SCOTT, JAMES M., AND RALPH G. CARTER. (1999) "Acting on the Hill: Congressional Assertiveness in U.S. Foreign Policy," *International Studies Association Annual Convention.* Washington, DC, February 16–20.

SCOTT, PETER DALE. (1998) *Cocaine Politics: Drugs, Armies, and the CIA in Central America.* Berkeley, CA: University of California Press.

SEABURY, PAUL. (1973) *The United States in World Affairs.* New York: McGraw-Hill.

SEMMEL, ANDREW K. (1983) "Evolving Patterns of U.S. Security Assistance 1950–1980," pp. 79–95 in Charles W. Kegley, Jr. and Eugene R. Wittkopf (eds.), *Perspectives on American Foreign Policy.* New York: St. Martin's.

SEN, AMARTYA. (1999) *Development as Freedom.* New York: Knopf.

SERFATY, SIMON. (1972) *The Elusive Enemy: American Foreign Policy Since World War II.* Boston: Little, Brown.

———. (1978) "Brzezinski: Play It Again, Zbig," *Foreign Policy* 32 (Fall): 3–21.

———. (2002) "The New Normalcy," *Washington Quarterly* 25 (Spring): 209–219.

SHAIN, YOSSI. (1994–1995) "Ethnic Diasporas and U.S. Foreign Policy," *Political Science Quarterly* 109 (Winter): 811–841.

SHALOM, STEPHEN ROSSKAMM, (ed.) (1993) *Imperial Alibis: Rationalizing U.S. Intervention After the Cold War.* Boston: South End Press.

SHANNON, ELAINE. (1995) "Skirts and Daggers," *Time* 145, 12 June, p. 46–47.

SHANNON, THOMAS RICHARD. (1989) *An Introduction to the World-System Perspective.* Boulder, CO: Westview.

SHAPIRO, ROBERT Y., AND HARPREET MAHAJAN. (1986) "Gender Differences in Policy Preferences: A Summary of Trends from the 1960s to the 1980s," *Public Opinion Quarterly* 50 (Spring): 42–61.

SHAPIRO, ROBERT Y., AND BENJAMIN I. PAGE. (1988) "Foreign Policy and the Rational Public," *Journal of Conflict Resolution* 32 (June): 211–247.

SHEEHAN, JIM. (1998) "The Case Against Kyoto," *SIAS Review* 18 (Summer/Fall): 121–133.

SHENON, PHILIP. (1999) "In Protest of Clinton Action, Senator Blocks Nominations," *New York Times,* 9 June, p. 20.

SHILLER, ROBERT J. (2001) "Exuberant Reporting," *Harvard International Review* 23 (Spring): 60–65.

SHIRLEY, EDWARD G. (1998) "Can't Anybody Here Play This Game?" *The Atlantic Monthly* 281 (February): 45–55.

SHULSKY, ABRAM N., AND GARY J. SCHMITT. (1994–1995) "The Future of Intelligence," *The National Interest* 38 (Winter): 63–72.

SICHERMAN, HARVEY. (1997) "The Strange Death of Dual Containment," *Orbis* 41 (Spring): 223–240.

SICK, GARY. (1999) "Iran Has Changed, Why Can't We?" *The Washington Post National Weekly Edition,* 5 August, p. 23.

SIGAL, LEON V. (1992–1993) "The Last Cold War Election," *Foreign Affairs* 71 (Winter): 1–15.

SILVERSTEIN, GORDON. (1996) *Imbalance of Powers: Constitutional Interpretation and the Making of American Foreign Policy.* New York: Oxford University Press.

SIMON, DENNIS M., AND CHARLES W. OSTROM, JR. (1988) "The Politics of Prestige: Popular Support and the Modern Presidency," *Presidential Studies Quarterly* 18 (Fall): 741–758.

SIMON, HERBERT A. (1957) *Administrative Behavior.* New York: Macmillan.

———. (1985) "Human Nature in Politics: The Dialogue of Psychology with Political Science," *American Political Science Review* 79 (June): 293–304.

SIMPSON, SMITH. (1967) *Anatomy of the State Department.* Boston: Houghton Mifflin.

SINCLAIR, BARBARA. (1993) "Congressional Party Leaders in the Foreign and Defense Policy Arena," pp. 207–231 in Randall B. and Lindsay Ripley, James M. Lindsay (eds.), *Congress Resurgent: Foreign and Defense Policy on Capitol Hill.* Ann Arbor, MI: University of Michigan Press.

SINGER, J. DAVID. (1991) "Peace in the Global System: Displacement, Interregnum, or Transformation?" pp. 56–84 in Charles W. Kegley, Jr. (ed.), *The Long Postwar Peace.* New York: HarperCollins.

SINGER, MAX, AND AARON WILDAVSKY. (1993) *The Real World Order: Zones of Peace/Zones of Turmoil.* Chatham, NJ: Chatham House.

SINGH, JASWANT. (1999) "Against Nuclear Apartheid," *Foreign Affairs* 77 (September/October): 41–52.

SITARZ, DANIEL, (ed.) (1993) *Agenda 21: The Earth Summit Strategy to Save Our Planet.* Boulder, CO: Earthpress.

SKIDMORE, DAVID. (1993–1994) "Carter and the Failure of Foreign Policy Reform," *Political Science Quarterly* 108 (Winter): 699–729.

SKLAIR, LESLIE. (1991) *Sociology of the Global System.* Baltimore, MD: Johns Hopkins University Press.

SLOSS, LEON. (1999) *Ballistic Missile Defense Revisited.* Washington, DC: The Atlantic Council.

SMITH, JEAN E. (1989) *The Constitution and American Foreign Policy.* New York: West Publishers.

———. (1992) *George Bush's War.* New York: Henry Holt.

SMITH, MICHAEL JOSEPH. (1987) *Realist Thought from Weber to Kissinger.* Baton Rouge, LA: Louisiana State University Press.

SMITH, R. JEFFREY. (1994a) "The CIA's Ill-Advised Dumping Ground," *The Washington Post National Weekly Edition,* 1–7 August, p. 32.

———. (1994b) "Clinton Goes For the Bush Nuclear Plan," *The Washington Post National Weekly Edition,* 26 September–2 October, pp. 16–17.

———. (1997) "A Believer No More," *The Washington Post National Weekly Edition,* 22–29 December, pp. 6–10.

SMITH, STEVEN. (1994) "Congressional Party Leaders," pp. 129–157 in Paul E. Peterson (ed.), *The President, The Congress, and the Making of Foreign Policy.* Norman, OK: University of Oklahoma Press.

SMITH, STEVEN S., AND CHRISTOPHER J. DEERING. (1990) *Committees in Congress,* 2nd ed. Washington, DC: CQ Press.

SMITH, TOM W. (1984) "The Polls: Gender and Attitudes Toward Violence," *Public Opinion Quarterly* 48 (Spring): 384–396.

SMITH, TONY. (1994a) *America's Mission: The United States and the Worldwide Struggle for Democracy in the Twentieth Century.* Princeton, NJ: Princeton University Press.

———. (1994b) "In Defense of Intervention," *Foreign Affairs* 73 (November/December): 34–46.

———. (1994c) "Winning the Peace: Postwar Thinking and the Defeated Confederacy," *World Policy Journal* 11 (Summer): 92–102.

SMITHSON, AMY E. (1995) "Dateline Washington: Clinton Fumbles the CWC," *Foreign Policy* 99 (Summer): 168–182.

SMYSER, W. R. (1993) "Goodbye, G-7," *Washington Quarterly* 16 (Winter): 15–28.

SNIDAL, DUNCAN. (1985) "The Limits of Hegemonic Stability Theory," *International Organization* 39 (Autumn): 579–615.

———. (1991) "Relative Gains and the Pattern of International Cooperation," *American Political Science Review* 85 (September): 701–726.

SNOW, DONALD M. (1998) *National Security: Defense Policy for a Changed International Order,* 4th ed. New York: St. Martin's.

SOBEL, RICHARD. (1998a) "The Polls—Trends: United States Intervention in Bosnia," *Public Opinion Quarterly,* (Summer): pp. 250–278.

———. (1998b) "Portraying American Public Opinion Toward the Bosnia Crisis," *Harvard Journal of Press/Politics* 3 (2): 16–33.

———. (2001) *The Impact of Public Opinion on U.S. Foreign Policy Since Vietnam: Constraining the Colossus.* New York: Oxford University Press.

SOFAER, ABRAHAM D. (1987) "The ABM Treaty: Legal Analysis in the Political Cauldron," *Washington Quarterly* 10 (Autumn): 59–75.

SOLOMON, BURT. (1994) "Though Clinton's Got the Willies . . . the Fed May Be Doing Him a Favor," *National Journal,* 7 May, pp. 1086–1087.

———. (1997) "Advisers Used to Clinton Time Now Set Their Watches by Bowles," *National Journal* 18 January p. 128.

SOPKO, JOHN F. (1996–97) "The Changing Proliferation Threat," *Foreign Policy* 105 (Winter): 3–20.

SORENSEN, THEODORE C. (1963) *Decision Making in the White House: The Olive Branch or the Arrows.* New York: Columbia University Press.

———. (1987–1988) "The President and the Secretary of State," *Foreign Affairs* 66 (Winter): 231–248.

———. (1994) "Foreign Policy in a Presidential Democracy," *Political Science Quarterly* 109 (Summer): 515–528.

SPANIER, JOHN. (1988) *American Foreign Policy Since World War II,* 11th ed. Washington, DC: CQ Press.

———. (1990) *Games Nations Play,* 7th ed. Washington, DC: Congressional Quarterly Press.

SPEAR, JOANNA. (1994–1995) "Beyond the Cold War: Changes in the International Arms Trade," *Harvard International Review* 17 (Winter): 8–11, 70.

SPERO, JOAN EDELMAN. (1990) *The Politics of International Economic Relations,* 4th. ed. New York: St. Martin's.

SPERO, JOAN EDELMAN, AND JEFFREY A. HART. (1997) *The Politics of International Economic Relations,* 5th. ed. New York: St. Martin's.

SPIRO, DAVID E. (1994) "The Insignificance of the Liberal Peace," *International Security* 19 (Fall): 50–86.

———. (1999) *The Hidden Hand of American Hegemony: Petrodollar Recycling and International Markets.* Ithaca, NY: Cornell University Press.

STAGNER, ROSS. (1971) "Personality Dynamics and Social Conflict," pp. 98–109 in Clagett G. Smith (ed.), *Conflict Resolution: Contributions of the Behavioral Sciences.* Notre Dame, IN: University of Notre Dame Press.

STARR, HARVEY. (1984) *Henry Kissinger: Perceptions of International Politics.* Lexington, KY: University Press of Kentucky.

STEDMAN, STEPHEN JOHN. (1992–1993) "The New Interventionists," *Foreign Affairs* 72 (Winter): 1–16.

———. (1995) "Alchemy for a New World Order," *Foreign Affairs* 74 (May/June): 14–20.

STEEL, RONALD. (1994) "The Lure of Detachment," *World Policy Journal* 11 (Fall): 61–69.

STEINBRUNER, JOHN D. (1995) "Reluctant Strategic Alignment: The Need for a New View of National Security," *Brookings Review* 13 (Winter): 5–9.

STERLING-FOLKER, JENNIFER. (1998) "Between a Rock and a Hard Place: Assertive Multilateralism and Post–Cold War U.S. Foreign Policy Making," pp. 277–304 in James M. Scott (ed.), *After the End: Making U.S. Foreign Policy in the Post–Cold War World.* Durham, NC: Duke University Press.

STERN, ERIC, AND BERTJAN VERBEEK. (1998) "Whither the Study of Governmental Politics in Foreign Policymaking? A Symposium," *Mershon International Studies Review* 42 (November): 205–210.

STEVENSON, ADLAI E., AND ALTON FRYE. (1989) "Trading with the Communists," *Foreign Affairs* 68 (Spring): 53–71.

STEVENSON, JONATHAN. (1995) *Losing Mogadishu: Testing U.S. Policy in Somalia.* Washington, DC: Naval Institute Press.

STIMSON, HENRY L., AND MCGEORGE BUNDY. (1947) *On Active Service in Peace and War.* New York: Harper and Row.

STIMSON, JAMES A., MICHAEL B. MACKUEN, AND ROBERT S. ERIKSON. (1994) "Opinion and Policy: A Global View," *PS: Political Science and Politics* 27 (March): 29–35.

STOCKTON, PAUL N. (1993) "Congress and Defense Policy-Making in the Post–Cold War Era," pp. 235–259 in Randall B. Ripley and James M. Lindsay (eds.), *Congress Resurgent: Foreign and Defense Policy on Capitol Hill.* Ann Arbor, MI: University of Michigan Press.

STOCKTON, PAUL. (1995) "Beyond Micromanagement: Congressional Budgeting for a Post–Cold War Military," *Political Science Quarterly* 110 (Summer): 233–259.

STOESSINGER, JOHN G. (1985) *Crusaders and Pragmatists: Movers of Modern American Foreign Policy.* New York: Norton.

STOKES, BRUCE. (1992–1993) "Organizing to Trade," *Foreign Policy,* 89 (Winter) pp. 36–52.

———. (1994) "The American Marketplace has Gone Global," *National Journal,* 18 June, pp. 1426–1430.

———. (1999–2000) "The New Protectionist Myth," *Foreign Policy* 117 (Winter): 88–102.

———. (2001) "Free Trade-Offs," *Foreign Policy* 124 (May/June): 62–63.

STRANGE, SUSAN. (1987) "The Persistent Myth of Lost Hegemony," *International Organization* 41 (Autumn): 551–574.

———. (1998) *Mad Money: When Markets Outgrow Governments.* Ann Arbor, MI: University of Michigan Press.

STREMLAU, JOHN. (1994–1995) "Clinton's Dollar Diplomacy," *Foreign Policy* 97 (Winter): 18–35.

STRINATI, DOMINIC. (1995) *An Introduction to Theories of Popular Culture.* London: Routledge.

STROBEL, WARREN P. (1999) "The CNN Effect: Myth or Reality?" pp. 85–93 in Eugene R. Wittkopf and James M. McCormick (eds.), *The Domestic Sources of American Foreign Policy: Insights and Evidence,* 3rd ed. Landham, MD: Rowman and Littlefield.

———. (2000) "The Sound of Silence," *U.S. News and World Report,* 14 February, p. 24.

STRUCK, MYRON. (1985) "A Bumper Crop of Plums: Political Appointments are Proliferators," *The Washington Post National Weekly Edition,* 20 May, p. 31.

SUEDFELD, PETER, RAYMOND S. CORTEEN, AND CARROLL MCCORMICK. (1986) "The Role of Integrative Complexity in Military

Leadership: Robert E. Lee and His Opponents," *Journal of Applied Social Psychology* 16 (6): 498–507.

SULLIVAN, WILLIAM H. (1980) "Dateline Iran: The Road Not Taken," *Foreign Policy* 40 (Fall): 175–186.

SUMMERS, ANTHONY, AND ROBIN SWAN SUMMERS. (2000) *The Arrogance of Power: The Secret World of Richard Nixon.* New York: Viking Penguin.

SUMMERS, HARRY G., JR. (1997) "Are U.S. Forces Overstretched? Operations, Procurement, and Industrial Base," *Orbis* 41 (Spring): 199–207.

SUNDQUIST, JAMES L. (1976) "Congress and the President: Enemies or Partners?" pp. 583–618 in Henry Owen and Charles L. Schultze (eds.), *Setting National Priorities: The Next Ten Years.* Washington, DC: Brookings Institution.

SUSSMAN, BARRY. (1988) *What Americans Really Think: And Why Our Politicians Pay No Attention.* New York: Pantheon.

SWEETMAN, BILL. (1994) "Aspin's Review Didn't Go Deep Enough," *The Washington Post National Weekly Edition,* 27 December–2 January, pp. 8–9.

TALBOTT, STROBE. (1979) *Endgame.* New York: Harper and Row.

———. (1984) *Deadly Gambits.* New York: Knopf.

———. (1989) "Why Bush Should Sweat," *Time,* 6 November, p. 59.

———. (1990) "Rethinking the Red Menace," *Time,* 1 January, pp. 66–72.

———. (1996) "Democracy and the National Interest," *Foreign Affairs* 75 (November/December): 47–63.

———. (1999) "Dealing with the Bomb in South Asia," *Foreign Affairs* 78 (March/April): 110–122.

TAYLER, JEFFREY. (2001) "Russia Is Finished," *The Atlantic Monthly* 287 (May): 35–52.

TAYLOR, ANDREW J., AND JOHN T. ROURKE. (1995) "Historical Analogies in the Congressional Foreign Policy Process," *Journal of Politics* 57 (May): 460–468.

TAYLOR, PAUL. (1988) "The GOP Has a Woman Problem," *The Washington Post National Weekly Edition,* 4–10 July, p. 9.

'T HART, PAUL. (1990) *Groupthink in Government: A Study of Small Groups and Policy Failure.* Baltimore, MD: Johns Hopkins University Press.

'T HART, PAUL, ERIC STERN, AND BENGT SUNDELIUS. (1997) *Beyond Groupthink: Political Group Dynamics and Foreign Policy-making.* Ann Arbor, MI: University of Michigan Press.

"THEY'RE NO FRIENDS OF BILL: TV NEWS COVERAGE OF THE CLINTON ADMINISTRATION." (1994), *Media Monitor* 8 (July/August).

THOMAS, EVAN, AND CHRISTOPHER DICKEY. (1998) "Bay of Pigs Redux," *Newsweek,* 23 March, pp. 36–41.

THOMAS, JO. (2000) "After Yale, Bush Ambled Amiably into His Future," *New York Times,* p. A1.

THOMAS, KEITH. (1988) "Just Say Yes," *New York Review of Books* 35, 24 November, pp. 43–45.

THOMPSON, KENNETH W. (1960) *Political Realism and the Crisis of World Politics.* Princeton, NJ: Princeton University Press.

THOMPSON, RANDAL JOY. (1990) "Mandates for AID Reform," *Foreign Service Journal* 67 (January): 34–36.

THOMSON, ALLISON. (1998) "Defense-Related Employment and Spending, 1996–2006," *Monthly Labor Review* 121 (July): 14–33.

THOMSON, JAMES C., JR. (1972) "On the Making of U.S. China Policy, 1961–69: A Study in Bureaucratic Politics," *The China Quarterly* 50 (April/June): 220–243.

———. (1994) "How Could Vietnam Happen? An Autopsy," pp. 255–264 in Eugene R. Wittkopf (ed.), *The Domestic Sources of Foreign Policy: Insights and Evidence.* New York: St. Martin's.

THUROW, LESTER. (1992) *Head to Head: Coming Economic Battles Among Japan, Europe, and America.* New York: William Morrow.

TILLEMA, HERBERT K. (1973) *Appeal to Force: American Military Intervention in the Era of Containment.* New York: Crowell.

———. (1989) "Foreign Overt Military Intervention in the Nuclear Age," *Journal of Peace Research* 26 (May): 179–195.

TIMMERMAN, KENNETH. (2001) "State's Saddamists," *Insight on the News,* 19 March, pp. 14–16.

TISCH, SARAH J., AND MICHAEL B. WALLACE. (1994) *Dilemmas of Development Assistance: The What, Why, and Who of Foreign Aid.* Boulder, CO: Westview.

TIVNAN, EDWARD. (1987) *The Lobby: Jewish Political Power and American Foreign Policy.* New York: Simon and Schuster.

TOLCHIN, MARTIN, AND SUSAN TOLCHIN. (1988) *Buying into America: How Foreign Money is Changing the Face of Our Nation.* New York: Times Books.

TOTH, ROBERT C. (1989) "U.S. Shifts Nuclear Response Strategy," *Los Angeles Times,* 23 July, p. A1.

TOWNSEND, JOYCE CAROL. (1982) *Bureaucratic Politics in American Decision Making.* Washington, DC: University Press of America.

TRADE BLOCS. (2000). New York: Oxford University Press.

TRAVERS, RUSSELL E. (1997) "A New Millennium and a Strategic Breathing Space," *Washington Quarterly* 20 (Spring): 97–114.

TRAVIS, RICK. (1998) "The Promotion of Democracy at the End of the Twentieth Century: A New Polestar for American Foreign Policy," pp. 251–276 in James M. Scott (ed.), *After the End: Making U.S. Foreign Policy in the Post–Cold War World.* Durham, NC: Duke University Press.

TREATIES AND OTHER INTERNATIONAL AGREEMENTS: THE ROLE OF THE UNITED STATES SENATE, COMMITTEE ON FOREIGN RELATIONS, United States Senate. (1993). Washington, DC: Government Printing Office.

TREVERTON, GREGORY F. (1987) *Covert Action: The Limits of Intervention in the Postwar World.* New York: Basic Books.

TRIFFIN, ROBERT. (1978–1979) "The International Role and Fate of the Dollar," *Foreign Affairs* 57 (Winter): 269–286.

TRUMAN, DAVID B. (1951) *The Governmental Process.* New York: Knopf.

TRUMAN, HARRY S. (1966) *Public Papers of the Presidents of the United States, Harry S. Truman, 1952–1953.* Washington, DC: Government Printing Office.

TUCKER, ROBERT W. (1990) "1989 and All That," *Foreign Affairs* 69 (Fall): 93–114.

———. (1999) "Alone or With Others: The Temptations of Post–Cold War Power," *Foreign Affairs* 78 (November/December): 1520.

TUGWELL, REXFORD GUY. (1971) *Off Course: From Truman to Nixon.* New York: Praeger.

TURNER, ROBERT F. (1988) "The Power of the Purse: Controlling National Security by Conditional Appropriations," *Atlantic Community Quarterly* 26 (Spring): 79–96.

TURNER, STANSFIELD. (1985) *Secrecy and Democracy: The CIA in Transition.* Boston: Houghton Mifflin.

TUSSIE, DIANA. (1993) "Holding the Balance: The Cairns Groups in the Uruguay Round," pp. 181–203 in Diana Tussie and David Glover (eds.), *The Developing Countries in World Trade: Policies and Bargaining Strategies.* Boulder, CO: Lynne Rienner.

TUSSIE, DIANA, AND DAVID GLOVER, (eds.) (1993) *The Developing Countries in World Trade: Policies and Bargaining Strategies.* Boulder, CO: Lynne Rienner.

TYSON, LAURA D'ANDREA. (1992) *Who's Bashing Whom? Trade Conflict in High-Technology Industries.* Washington, DC: Institute for International Economics.

ULAM, ADAM B. (1985) "Forty Years of Troubled Coexistence," *Foreign Affairs* 64 (Fall): 12–32.

UNITED NATIONS PROGRAMME ON TRANSNATIONAL CORPORATIONS. (1993) "World Investment Report 1993," *Transnational Corporations* 2 (August): 99–123.

U.S. ARMS CONTROL AND DISARMAMENT AGENCY. (2000) *World Military Expenditures and Arms Transfers 1998.* Washington, DC: Government Printing Office.

U.S. DEPARTMENT OF STATE. (1992) *State 2000: A New Model for Managing Foreign Affairs.* Washington, DC: Department of State.

U.S. DEPARTMENT OF STATE *History of the National Security Council, 1947–1997.* Bureau of Public Affairs, U.S. Department of State.

USLANER, ERIC M. (1998) "All in the Family? Interest Groups and Foreign Policy," pp. 365–386 in Allan J. Cigler and Burdett A. Loomis (eds.), *Interest Group Politics,* 5th ed. Washington, DC: CQ Press.

UTLEY, GARRICK. (1997) "The Shrinking of Foreign News," *Foreign Affairs* 76 (March/April): 2–10.

VAN EVERA, STEPHEN. (1990a) "Why Europe Matters, Why the Third World Doesn't: American Grand Strategy After the Cold War," *Journal of Strategic Studies* 13 (June): 1–51.

———. (1990b) "The Case Against Intervention," *The Atlantic Monthly* 266 (July): 72–80.

VASQUEZ, JOHN A. (1983) *The Power of Power Politics.* New Brunswick, NJ: Rutgers University Press.

VERBA, SIDNEY. (1969) "Assumptions of Rationality and Non-Rationality in Models of the International System," pp. 217–231 in James N.

Rosenau (ed.), *International Politics and Foreign Policy.* New York: Free Press.

VERHOVEK, SAM HOWE. (1998) "Is There Room on a Republican Ticket for Another Bush," *New York Times Magazine,* 13 September, pp. 52–59ff.

VERTZBERGER, YAACOV. (1990) *The World in Their Minds: Information Processing, Cognition, and Perception in Foreign Policy Decisionmaking.* Stanford, CA: Stanford University Press.

VISTICA, GREGORY. (1999) "The Plot to Get Slobo," *Newsweek* 12 April, p. 36.

———. (2000) "Inside the Secret Cyberwar: Facing Unseen Enemies, the Feds Try to Stay a Step Ahead," *Newsweek* 21 February, p. 48.

VON HIPPEL, FRANK. (1997) "Paring Down the Arsenal," *Bulletin of the Atomic Scientists* 53 (May/June) pp. 33–40.

WAGNER, R. HARRISON. (1993) "What Is Bipolarity?" *International Organization* 47 (Winter): 77–106.

WALKER, STEPHEN G. (1977) "The Interface Between Beliefs and Behavior: Henry Kissinger's Operational Code and the Vietnam War," *Journal of Conflict Resolution* 21 (March): 129–168.

WALKER, STEPHEN G., MARK SCHAFER, AND MICHAEL D. YOUNG. (1998) "Systematic Procedures for Operational Code Analysis: Measuring and Modeling Jimmy Carter's Operational Code," *International Studies Quarterly* 42 (March): 175–190.

WALLER, DOUGLAS. (1995) "Soldier Spies," *Time* 29 May, p. 24.

———. (1996) "Master of the Game," *Time* 147, 6 May, pp. 40–43.

———. (1998) "Inside the Hunt for Osama," *Time* 21 December, pp. 32–34.

WALSH, KENNETH T. (2001) "A Right-Stuff Kind of Guy," *U.S. News and World Report* 9 April, p. 24.

WALSH, LAWRENCE E. (1997) *Firewall: The Iran-Contra Conspiracy and Cover-Up.* New York: W.W. Norton.

WALT, STEPHEN M. (1990) *The Origins of Alliances.* Ithaca, NY: Cornell University Press.

———. (2000) "Two Cheers for Clinton's Foreign Policy," *Foreign Affairs* 79 (March–April): 63–79.

WALTERS, ROBERT S., AND DAVID H. BLAKE. (1992) *The Politics of Global Economic Relations,* 4th ed. Englewood Cliffs, NJ: Prentice-Hall.

WALTZ, KENNETH N. (1964) "The Stability of a Bipolar World," *Daedalus* 93 (Summer): 881–909.

———. (1967) *Foreign Policy and Democratic Politics.* Boston: Little, Brown.

———. (1971) "Opinions and Crisis in American Foreign Policy," pp. 47–55 in Douglas M. Fox (ed.), *The Politics of U.S. Foreign Policy Making.* Pacific Palisades, CA: Goodyear.

———. (1979) *Theory of International Politics.* Reading, MA: Addison-Wesley.

———. (1993) "The Emerging Structure of International Politics," *International Security* 18 (Fall): 44–79.

———. (1997) "Evaluating Theories," *American Political Science Review* 91 (December): 915–916.

———. (2000a) "Structural Realism After the Cold War," *International Security* 25 (Summer): 5–41.

———. (2000b) "Globalization and American Power," *The National Interest* 59 (Spring): 46–56.

WARBURG, GERALD FELIX. (1989) *Conflict and Consensus: The Struggle Between Congress and the President over Foreign Policymaking.* New York: Harper and Row.

WARNER, GEOFFREY. (1989) "The Anglo-American Special Relationship," *Diplomatic History* 13 (Fall): 479–499.

WARWICK, DONALD P. (1975) *A Theory of Public Bureaucracy: Politics, Personality, and Organization in the State Department.* Cambridge, MA: Harvard University Press.

WASTELL, DAVID. (2001) "President's Men Vie for Control of Foreign Policy," *Sunday Telegraph,* 11 March, p. 31.

WATSON, JACK H., JR. (1993) "The Clinton White House," *Presidential Studies Quarterly* 23 (Summer): 429–435.

WATTENBERG BEN J. (1989) *The Birth Dearth.* New York: Pharos Books.

WAYMAN, FRANK WHELON. (1985) "Arms Control and Strategic Arms Voting in the U.S. Senate," *Journal of Conflict Resolution* 29 (June): 225–251.

WAYNE, LESLIE. (1998) "800–Pound Guests at the Pentagon," *New York Times,* 15 March, pp. WK, 5.

———. (1999) "Dogfight Over a Must-Win Contract," *New York Times,* 15 August, pp. 3, 9–10.

———. (2000) "Winner May Not Take All in Pentagon Jet Deal," *New York Times,* May 14, p. BU 4.

WEBER, STEVEN. (1997) "The End of the Business Cycle," *Foreign Affairs* 76 (July/August): 65–82.

WEINBERG, GERHARD L. (1994) *A World at Arms: A Global History of World War II*. New York: Cambridge University Press.

WEINER, TIM. (1994) "The Men in the Gray Federal Bureaucracy," *New York Times,* 10 April, p. E4.

WEISBAND, EDWARD. (1973) *The Ideology of American Foreign Policy: A Paradigm of Lockian Liberalism*. Beverly Hills, CA: Sage.

WEISBERG, HERBERT F., AND DAVID C. KIMBALL. (1995) "Attitudinal Correlates of the 1992 Presidential Vote: Party Identification and Beyond," pp. 72–111 in Herbert F. Weisberg (ed.), *Democracy's Feast: Elections in America*. Chatham, NJ: Chatham House.

WEISBERG, JACOB. (1999) "The Governor-President: Bill Clinton," *New York Times Magazine,* 17 January, pp. 30–35ff.

WELCH, DAVID A. (1992) "The Organizational Process and Bureaucratic Politics Paradigms: Retrospect and Prospect," *International Security* 17 (Fall): 112–146.

WEST, WILLIAM F., AND JOSEPH COOPER. (1990) "Legislative Influence v. Presidential Dominance: Competing Models of Bureaucratic Control," *Political Science Quarterly* 104 (Winter): 581–606.

"WHITE HOUSE TAPES AND THE MINUTES OF THE CUBAN MISSILE CRISES." (1985), *International Security* 10 (Summer): 164–203.

WHITE, JULIE. (2000) "U.N. Hosts Historic Millennium Summit," *The InterDependent* 26 (Fall): 5–7.

WHITE, RALPH K. (1984) *Fearful Warriors: A Psychological Profile of U.S.-Soviet Relations*. New York: Free Press.

WHITE, THEODORE H. (1973) *The Making of the President, 1972*. New York: Atheneum.

WIARDA, HOWARD J. (1996) *American Foreign Policy: Actors and Processes*. New York: Harper-Collins.

———. (1997) "Back to Basics: Reassessing U.S. Policy in Latin America," *Harvard International Review* 19 (Fall): 16–19, 57.

———. (2000) "Beyond the Pale: The Bureaucratic Politics of United States Policy in Mexico," *World Affairs* 162 (Spring): 174–190.

WIESELTIER, LEON. (1993) "Total Quality Meaning," New Republic, 19 and 26 July, pp. 16–18ff.

WILCOX, CLYDE, JOSEPH FERRARA, AND DEE ALLSOP. (1993) "Group Differences in Early Support for Military Action in the Gulf: The Effects of Gender, Generation, and Ethnicity," *American Politics Quarterly* 21 (July): 343–359.

WILDAVSKY, AARON. (1966) "The Two Presidencies," *Trans-Action* 4 (December): 7–14.

WILLIAMS, WILLIAM APPLEMAN. (1972) *The Tragedy of American Diplomacy,* 2nd ed. New York: Delta.

———. (1980) *Empire as a Way of Life*. New York: Oxford University Press.

WILLS, GARRY. (1994a) *Certain Trumpets: The Call of Leaders*. New York: Simon and Schuster.

———. (1994b) "What Makes a Good Leader?" *The Atlantic Monthly* 273 (April): 63–80.

———. (1995) *Certain Trumpets: The Nature of Leadership*. New York: Touchstone.

WILSON, GEORGE C. (2001a) "Guns Aplenty, Butter Be Damned," *National Journal* 33, 27 January, pp. 252–253.

———. (2001b) "CEO Rumsfeld and His Pentagon Inc," *National Journal* 33, 17 March, p. 812.

WILSON, JAMES Q. (1989) *Bureaucracy: What Government Organizations Do and Why They Do It*. New York: Basic Books.

WILSON, ROBERT A., AND MICHAEL R. BESCHLOSS (eds). (2000) *Power and the Presidency*. New York: MacMillan.

WINIK, JAY. (1989) "Restoring Bipartisanship," *Washington Quarterly* 12 (Winter): 109–122.

WINTER, DAVID G. (1987) "Leader Appeal, Leader Performance, and the Motive Profile 3 of Leaders and Followers: A Study of American President and Elections," *Journal of Personality and Social Psychology* 52 (1): 196–202.

———. (1993) "Personality and Leadership in the Gulf War," pp. 107–117 in Stanley A. Renshon (ed.), *The Political Psychology of the Gulf War*. Pittsburgh: University of Pittsburg Press.

WINTER, DAVID G., AND LESLIE A. CARLSON. (1988) "Using Motive Scores in the Psychobiographical Study of an Individual: The Case of Richard Nixon," *Journal of Personality* 56 (March): 75–103.

WINTER, DAVID G., AND ABIGAIL J. STEWART. (1977) "Content Analysis as a Method of Studying Political Leaders," pp. 27–61 in Margaret G. Hermann (ed.), *A Psychological Examination of Political Leaders*. New York: Free Press.

WISE, DAVID. (1995) *Nightmover: How Aldrich Ames Sold the CIA to the KGB for $4.6 million*. New York: HarperCollins.

WITKOW, BRANDON J. (2000) "A New 'Spook Immunity': How the CIA and American Business Are Shielded from Liability for the Misappropriation of Trade Secrets," *Emory International Law Review* 14 (Spring) 451–489.

WITTKOPF, EUGENE R. (1990) *Faces of Internationalism: Public Opinion and American Foreign Policy*. Durham, NC: Duke University Press.

———. (1994) "Faces of Internationalism in a Transitional Environment," *Journal of Conflict Resolution* 38 (September): 376–401.

———. (1996) "What Americans Really Think About Foreign Policy," *Washington Quarterly* 19 (Summer): 91–106.

———. (2000) "U.S. Foreign Policy Formulation: Internal Processes and External Impact," *Malaysian Association of American Studies,* Kuala Lumpur, September 12–13, 2000.

WITTKOPF, EUGENE R., AND RONALD H. HINCKLEY. (2000) "Internationalism at Bay? A Contextual Analysis of Americans' Post–Cold War Foreign Policy Attitudes" pp. 133–153 in Brigitte Nacos, Robert Y. Shapiro, and Pierangelo Isernia (eds.), *Decision-Making in a Glass House: Mass Media, Public Opinon, and American and European Foreign Policy in the 21st Century.* Lanham, MD: Roman and Littlefield.

WITTKOPF, EUGENE R., AND JAMES M. MC-CORMICK. (1993) "The Domestic Politics of Contra Aid: Public Opinion, Congress, and the President," pp. 73–103 in Richard Sobel (ed.), *Public Opinion in U.S. Foreign Policy: The Controversy over Contra Aid.* Lanham, MD: Rowman and Littlefield.

———. (1998) "Congress, the President, and the End of the Cold War," *Journal of Conflict Resolution* 42 (August): 440–467.

WOHLFORTH, WILLIAM C. (1999) "The Stability of a Unipolar World," *International Security* 24 (Summer): 5–41.

WOLFE, FRANK. (2001) "Modernizing NSA Technology Likely to Be Priority of Senate Intel Committee," *Defense Daily* 209, 31 January.

WOLFERS, ARNOLD. (1962) *Discord and Collaboration*. Baltimore, MD: Johns Hopkins University Press.

WOLFOWITZ, PAUL D. (1994) "Clinton's First Year," *Foreign Affairs* 73 (January/February): 28–43.

WOODS, RANDALL B. (1998) *J. William Fulbright, Vietnam, and the Search for a Cold War Foreign Policy*. Cambridge, MA: Cambridge University Press.

WOODWARD, BOB. (1987) *Veil: The Secret Wars of the CIA 1981–1987*. New York: Simon and Schuster.

———. (1994) *The Agenda: Inside the Clinton White House*. New York: Simon and Schuster.

———. (2000) *Maestro: Greenspan's Fed and the American Boom*. New York: Simon and Schuster.

WOODWARD, BOB, AND CARL BERNSTEIN. (1979) *The Final Days*. New York: Simon and Schuster.

WOODWARD, SUSAN L. (1993) "Yugoslavia: Divide and Fall," *Bulletin of the Atomic Scientists* 49 (November): 24–27.

WORLD BANK. (1998) *Assessing Aid: What Works, What Doesn't, and Why*. New York: Oxford University Press.

WORLD DEVELOPMENT REPORT 1988. (1988). New York: Oxford University Press.

WORLD DEVELOPMENT REPORT 2000/2001. (2001). New York: Oxford University Press.

WORLD RESOURCES 1994–95. (1994). New York: Oxford University Press.

WORLD RESOURCES 1998–99. (1998). New York: Oxford University Press.

WORLD RESOURCES 2000–2001. (2000). Washington, DC: World Resources Institute.

WORTH, ROBERT. (1998) "Clinton's Warriors: The Interventionists," *World Policy Journal* 15 (Spring): 43–48.

WREN, CHRISTOPHER S. (2001) "The U.N. Offers 87 Remedies to Help Poor Nations Develop," February 4 *New York Times,* p. 1.

WRIGHT, ROBIN. (1997) "Democracy: Challenges and Innovations in the 1990s," *Washington Quarterly* 20 (Summer): 23–36.

WRIGHT, ROBIN, AND SHAUL BAKHAS. (1997) "The U.S. and Iran: An Offer They Can't Refuse?" *Foreign Policy* 108 (Fall): 124–136.

YANKELOVICH, DANIEL, AND SIDNEY HARMAN. (1988) *Starting with the People*. Boston: Houghton Mifflin.

YARMOLINSKY, ADAM. (1970–1971) "The Military Establishment (Or How Political Problems Become Military Problems)," *Foreign Policy* 1 (Winter): 78–97.

———. (1971) *The Military Establishment: Its Impact on American Society*. New York: Harper and Row.

YERGIN, DANIEL. (1978) *Shattered Peace: The Origins of the Cold War and the National Security State*. Boston: Houghton Mifflin.

YOST, DAVID S. (1998) *NATO Transformed: The Alliance's New Roles in International Security.* Washington, DC: United States Institute of Press Press.

ZAGARE, FRANK C. (1990) "Rationality and Deterrence," *World Politics* 42 (January): 238–260.

ZALLER, JOHN R. (1992) *The Nature and Origins of Mass Opinion.* New York: Cambridge University Press.

ZELIKOW, PHILIP, AND CONDOLEEZA RICE. (1995) *Germany Unified and Europe Transformed: A Study in Statecraft.* Cambridge, MA: Harvard University Press.

ZENGERLE, JASON. (1998) "Hagelianism," *The New Republic* 218, 9 February p. 10ff.

ZIMMERMAN, ROBERT F. (1993) *Dollars, Diplomacy, and Dependence: Dilemmas of U.S. Economic Aid.* Boulder, CO: Lynne Rienner.

ZOELLICK, ROBERT B. (2000) "A Republican Foreign Policy," *Foreign Affairs* 79 (January/February): 63–78.

ZUELI, KIMBERLY A., AND VERNON W. RUTTAN. (1996) "U.S. Assistance to the Former Soviet Empire: Toward a Rationale for Foreign Aid," *Journal of Developing Areas* 30 (July): 493–524.

Glossary

absolute poverty A condition of life characterized by no access to safe water or adequate nutrition, sanitation, or health services that currently describes as many as one-fifth of the earth's inhabitants.

accommodationists Those who, in the wake of the Vietnam War, emphasized cooperative ties with other nations, particularly détente with the Soviet Union, and rejected the view that the United States could assume a unilateralist posture in the world; proponents of multilateralism in the post-Cold War world.

ad hoc decision making A behavior in which decisions are made in reaction to others' decisions or issues as they arise, focusing on each day's immediate crisis and avoiding long-term planning.

adhocracy A system of decision making that allows the president flexibility to devise advisory committees and make assignments to address a specific situation or need without relying on the usual, established patterns of providing advice through cabinet officials or bureaucratic organizations.

agenda setting The role that the mass media play in telling the public which issues to think about.

American century A prolonged period in which American interests would shape the world.

antiauthoritarianism An attitude syndrome exhibited by introspective people uncomfortable with order and power.

anticipated reactions In which a policymaker tailors his or her proposal to account for the preferences of others. One application concerns the influence members of Congress may have even in the absence of legislation, when a president surveys the preferences of Congress on a policy issue and tailors his proposal to meet those preferences.

assured destruction The capacity to survive an aggressor's worst possible attack with sufficient firepower to inflict unacceptable damage on the attacker in retaliation; a key feature of the Kennedy and Johnson administrations' doctrine of strategic deterrence.

attentive public People who are attentive to and knowledgeable about foreign affairs but who do not necessarily have access to decision-makers.

authoritarianism A constellation of predispositions that includes adherence to conventional values and condemnation of those who reject them; authoritarians crave authority and obediently submit to leaders.

ballistic missile defense (BMD) A means of defending against attacks from intercontinental ballistic missiles.

beggar-thy-neighbor policies Efforts to enhance domestic welfare by means of currency devaluations, tariffs, quotas, export subsidies, and other strategies that promote trade surpluses at other states' expense.

belief system Conceptual lens through which individuals receive and process information that orients them to their physical and social environment, helping them to establish goals, order preferences, and relate ideas systematically to one another.

benevolent hegemony The use of preponderant power to provide leadership and public goods such as order, stability and prosperity for the benefit of all members of the system.

biodiversity The natural abundance of plant and animal species, humankind's genetic heritage, which is threatened by rapidly increasing extinctions due to deforestation and other environmental damage.

bipartisanship The practical application of the proposition that "politics stops at the water's edge"; used to describe the cooperative relationship between Congress and the executive branch during much of the Roosevelt, Truman, and Eisenhower presidencies.

bipolar (bipolarity) A global structure in which power is concentrated in two centers or poles; effective world power was so distributed from the late 1940s until the 1962 Cuban missile crisis, with the United States and its allies comprising one pole and the Soviet Union and its allies the other.

bipolycentrism A global power structure somewhat looser and more fluid than a bipolar one, in which the alliance partners of the primary powers form relationships among themselves while continuing to rely on their great power patrons for security.

Brezhnev Doctrine A Soviet doctrine, named after Premier Leonid Brezhnev, intended to justify the 1968 invasion of Czechoslovakia and to put other communist states on warning about the dangers of defection from the socialist fold.

brinkmanship A willingness during the Eisenhower administration to go to the brink of nuclear war as a means of bargaining with the Soviet Union.

Bureau of Intelligence and Research The State Department's representative in the intelligence community, which is charged with introducing a diplomatic sensitivity to intelligence reports.

bureaucratic politics model A perspective that stresses the policy-making effects of interaction and competition among bureaucratic organizations and the competing roles of people within them.

Bush Doctrine States that harbor a terrorist are "just as guilty as the terrorist; if you feed one or hide one, you're just as guilty as those who came and murdered thousands of innocent Americans." The United States may use its power to penalize the guilty.

cabinet The advisory body to the president made of the department secretaries and agency heads.

Carter Doctrine President Jimmy Carter's declaration that the United States was willing to use military force to protect its interests in the Persian Gulf.

chief of staff A member of the presidential staff selected by presidential appointment to manage and coordinate the activities and agendas of the White House staff. Chiefs of staff may be strong or weak and, in addition to bringing order to White House operations, may be key advisers if presidents so desire.

Clinton Doctrine President Clinton's vision of the world following the 1999 NATO intervention in Kosovo in which international values would reign supreme. He added "if somebody comes after innocent civilian and tries to kill them en masse because of their race, their ethnic background or their religion, and it's within our power to stop it, we will stop it."

code of conduct on arms transfers Congressional effort to develop guidelines for the sale of U.S. weapons to other states; stimulated by concern over the role of the military in fomenting regional conflict, instability, civil wars, and repressive regimes, and in spreading widely advanced military technology which may be dangerous to U.S. national security.

coercive hegemony The use of preponderant power to secure national interests, often by "taxing" other members of the system to benefit the hegemon.

cognitive balance When individuals seek to maintain a balance in their cognitions either by screening out information that runs counter to cherished beliefs or by suppressing information that challenges preexisting images.

collective goods (public goods) Benefits shared by everyone, from which no one can be excluded on a selective basis (e.g., national security).

collective security A system embodied in international organizations, such as the United Nations, in which member states pledge to join together to oppose aggression by any state, whenever and wherever it occurs.

collegial model An executive decision-making approach that emphasizes teamwork and group problem solving, in which the president is likened to the hub of a wheel, with spokes connecting to individual advisers and agency heads.

comparative advantage A key principle in classical international trade theory which states that all states will benefit if each specializes in those goods it produces comparatively cheaply and acquires, through trade, goods that it can only produce at a comparatively higher cost.

compellence The view of nuclear weapons as the means by which one state can coerce other states to conform to its will.

competitive model An approach to executive decision making in which the president purposely seeks to promote conflict and competition among presidential advisers.

conservatism A psychological concept denoting a cluster of interrelated personality characteristics including hostility and suspicion, rigidity and compulsiveness, intolerance, inflexibility, and lack of compassion.

containment A foreign policy strategy, initiated by President Truman, designed to inhibit the expansion of the Soviet Union's power and influence in world affairs.

cooperative internationalism Support for active involvement in world affairs that stresses the United States' willingness to cooperate with other states to solve global as well as national problems.

counterfactual reasoning A reasoning strategy that poses a series of questions which effectively drop a key variable from the equation and then speculates about what might have been.

counterforce A nuclear weapons strategy that seeks deterrence by targeting an adversary's weapons and military forces.

counterintelligence Operations directed specifically against the espionage efforts of foreign intelligence services, including efforts to penetrate them.

counterproliferation A concept that implies the United States itself will act as the sole global arbiter and destroyer of weapons of mass destruction.

countervailing powers A description of interest-group activity in which disproportionate political influence possessed by one group will cause one or more opposing groups to balance it by pushing policy in the opposite direction.

countervailing (war-fighting) strategy A plan, embodied in President Carter's Presidential Directive (PD) 59, to enhance deterrence by targeting not only the Soviet Union's population and industrial centers but also its military forces and weapons.

countervalue A nuclear weapons strategy that seeks deterrence by threatening destruction of the things an adversary is believed to value most—its population and military-industrial centers.

covert action A clandestine activity typically undertaken abroad against foreign governments, installations, or individuals with the expressed purpose of directly influencing the outcome of political events.

cross-pressures Forces that arise within and among special interest groups by virtue of their overlapping memberships and crisscrossing relationships, which reduce the groups' effectiveness by pulling members in opposite directions.

Cuban missile crisis Soviet-American confrontation in 1962 resulting from the surreptitious placement of Soviet offensive missiles in Cuba; high point of the cold war.

decision avoidance Bureaucratic behavior in which policymakers delay decision-making or delegate it by "passing the buck."

Defense Intelligence Agency (DIA) The Defense Department agency responsible for collecting national (rather than tactical) intelligence; the principal intelligence adviser to the secretary of defense and the Joint Chiefs of Staff.

Defense Reorganization Act of 1986 (Goldwater-Nichols act) A law that sought to shift power from the separate branches of the armed services to the institutions associated with the Joint Chiefs of Staff in an effort to ameliorate interservice rivalry.

deferrals Temporary spending delays by which the president, subject to congressional review, can impound funds for up to twelve months.

democracy A political system characterized by free elections and universal suffrage.

democratic capitalism The merger of classical democratic theory and capitalism into a deeply ingrained ideology in the American polity.

dependent variable That which an investigator seeks to explain; in the foreign policy context, a state's foreign policy behavior is the dependent variable.

desertification A sustained decline in land productivity resulting from long-term environmental stress, often caused by population growth.

détente A strategy of containment initiated in 1969 that emphasized the need for superpower cooperation and restraint and sought to create a movement away from competition and toward cooperation.

deterrence A strategy intended to discourage an adversary from using force by convincing it that the costs of such action outweighs the potential gains.

development assistance Grants and loans provided for social and economic development, typically for health, education, agriculture, rural development, or disaster relief; designed to serve American long-term foreign policy objectives.

director of central intelligence Nominated by the president and confirmed by the Senate, the director of central intelligence plays the dual role of coordinating among the many agencies that form the intelligence community while also directing the Central Intelligence Agency.

discretionary funds Monies Congress provides the president to deal with situations unforeseen at the time of the annual budget process.

doctrine of political questions A judicial construct that enables the courts to sidestep contentious foreign policy issues separating Congress and the president, such as war powers, by holding the issues are political rather than legal.

dogmatism A personality trait exhibited by closed-minded people, who form opinions and refuse to modify them despite contrary evidence.

dollar convertibility A U.S. government commitment during the Bretton Woods regime to exchange gold for dollars at any time on demand. Convertibility is an arrangement in which a government permits its currency to be freely exchanged for the currencies of other nations.

dollar diplomacy U.S. policy from 1900 to 1913, intended to protect rapidly growing business interests in the Caribbean and Central America and characterized by President Taft as "substituting dollars for bullets."

domino theory A popular metaphor in the 1960s which asserted that one country's fall to communism would stimulate the fall of those adjacent to it.

economic liberalism The existence or development of market economies.

economic nationalists (mercantilists) Those who assign the state an aggressive role in fostering national economic welfare, stressing their own national interests in international economic transactions rather than the mutual benefit of all trading partners.

economic support funds (ESF) Dollars granted or loaned to countries of special political significance to the United States to advance short-term political objectives.

environmental refugees People forced to abandon lands no longer fit for human habitation due to environmental degradation; currently describes at least ten million people.

espionage The illegal collection of intelligence; spying to obtain secret government information.

exceptional American experience The absence of pronounced class and religious strife at the time of America's founding complemented by its geographic isolation from European political turmoil.

executive agreements International agreements that do not require the advice and consent of the Senate; have the same legal force as treaties, which require Senate approval.

extended deterrence A strategy that seeks to deter an adversary from attacking one's allies; describes the U.S. commitment to defend Western Europe from a Soviet or Warsaw Pact attack during the Cold War.

external source category The attributes of the international system and the characteristics and behaviors of the state and nonstate actors comprising it; includes the global environment and any actions occurring abroad that influence a nation's foreign policy decisions.

fair trade A precept stating that state's exporters should be given the same access to foreign markets as foreign producers enjoy in that state.

fast track authority Congressional authorization to the president to negotiate trade arrangements, in consultation with Congress, which will then be voted up or down by Congress without any amendments.

finished intelligence Data obtained from all sources—secret as well as public—that have been expertly assembled and analyzed specifically to meet the nation's foreign policy needs.

First World A term used during the Cold War era to designate industrialized nations with democratic governments and market economies, chiefly in Western Europe and North America.

fixed exchange rate system A monetary system in which a government sets the value of its currency at a fixed rate in relation to the currencies of other states.

flexible response A U.S. and NATO defense posture that implied the United States and its allies were willing and able to respond to a hostile attack at whatever level was appropriate—either conventional or nuclear.

Food for Peace program A program created by the Agricultural Trade Development and Assistance Act of 1954 (PL 480) that sells agricultural commodities on credit and makes grants to provide emergency relief, promote economic development, and assist voluntary relief agencies.

forceful persuasion Displays of military force short of war intended to influence the decisions of other states.

Foreign Agricultural Service (FAS) The principal subdivision of the Agriculture Department concerned with international affairs, which is designed to promote sales of American agricultural commodities overseas.

foreign economic aid Monetary loans and grants to other countries, often tied to purchases of goods and services in the United States.

Foreign Military Sales (FMS) A foreign military assistance and arms transfer program designed as an alternative to grant assistance that has made the United States the world's leading arms supplier.

foreign policy The goals that a nation's officials seek to attain abroad, the values that give rise to those objectives, and the means or instruments used to pursue them.

Foreign Service officers (FSOs) Members of an elite corps of professional diplomats traditionally holding the most important positions within the State Department, both at home and abroad.

formalistic model An approach to executive decision making in which clear lines of authority minimize the need for presidential involvement in the inevitable politicking among cabinet officers and presidential advisers.

fourth estate The mass media, regarded by some as so powerful as to be considered a fourth branch of the U.S. government.

free-floating exchange rates Currency values that are determined by market forces rather than government intervention.

free riders Those who enjoy the benefits of collective (public) goods but pay little or nothing for them.

G-8 The seven largest industrial powers plus Russia.

gatekeepers The function of the mass media in filtering the news and shaping how it is reported, particularly noticeable in foreign affairs.

General Agreement on Tariffs and Trade (GATT) An international organization created after World War II to promote and protect the most-favored-nation (MFN) principle as the basis for free international trade.

Global North A term used in the post-Cold War system to denote the nations formerly thought of as the First World. Defining characteristics are democracy, sophisticated technology, wealth, and near zero population growth.

Global South A term useful in the post-Cold War system to denote the countries previously comprising the Third World. Global South nations may possess some but not all of the defining characteristics of the Global North (democracy, sophisticated technology, wealth, and steady-state populations).

global warming A change in the earth's climate patterns that occurs when carbon dioxide and other gas molecules trap heat that would otherwise be remitted from earth back into the atmosphere.

governmental source category Those aspects of a government's structure that limit or enhance decision makers' foreign policy choices. Examples in the United States include the constitutional separation of powers and the bureaucratization of policy making in the executive branch.

Group of 7 (G-7) An ad hoc group of the world's largest industrial democracies that seeks macro-economic policy coordination; the G-7 holds a much-publicized annual economic summit.

Group of 77 (G-77) A coalition of the world's poor (the Global South) allied to press for concessions from the world's rich (the Global North). Formed in 1964, the G-77 now comprises over one hundred developing nations.

groupthink Social pressures that reinforce group norms in small decision-making groups; a cohesiveness and solidarity of outlook that may lead to dysfunctional policy choices.

hard intelligence Information that policymakers receive from cryptanalysis and reconnaissance satellites.

hard-target kill capacity The destructive potential of weapons (warhead yield) directed against land-based intercontinental ballistic missiles (ICBMs).

hardliners Those who, in the wake of Vietnam, viewed communism as a threat to the United States, opposed détente with the Soviet Union, and embraced an interventionist position; proponents of unilateralism in the post-Cold War world.

hegemonic stability theory A perspective that focuses on the role of the preponderant power in stabilizing the international economic system; defines the special roles and responsibilities of the major economic power (hegemon) in a commercial order based on market forces.

hegemon A single country with preponderant power that dominates the global political, military, and economic arenas.

hero-in-history model The view that individual leaders are the makers and movers of history; in foreign policy making, it finds expression in the practice of attaching presidents' names to the policies they promulgate.

human intelligence (HUMINT) The fruits of espionage that come from human, not technical, sources of intelligence.

idealism A body of thought that believes fundamental reforms of the system of international relations are possible. The idealist agenda includes open diplomacy, freedom of the seas, removal of trade barriers, self-determination, general disarmament, and collective security.

ideological groups Interest-group organizations that address a wide array of policies but from a particular philosophical viewpoint (e.g., National Rifle Association).

imagery intelligence (IMINT) Information gathered from satellites in computer code, which must be converted into images.

impoundment A presidential refusal to spend money appropriated by Congress.

inadvertent audience People who are exposed to foreign affairs information transmitted by television that most neither like nor want.

independent variables Factors that exert a causal impact on a dependent variable. In the foreign policy context, a nation's foreign policy behavior is the dependent variable and the source categories and factors contained within them are the independent variables, or inputs.

individual source category A decision maker's personal traits—including values, talents, and prior experiences—that influence his or her foreign policy choices and thus potentially impact a state's foreign policy.

instrumental rationality A conceptualization of rationality that stresses individual preferences; it predicts that decision-makers, when faced with multiple alternatives, will choose the one believed to yield their preferred outcome.

intelligence Information useful to policymakers about a potential enemy.

intermediate-range nuclear force (INF) weapons U.S. nuclear weapons systems deployed in Europe in the 1980s in response to the Soviet Union's growing medium-range nuclear capability; eliminated from Europe with the 1987 INF disarmament treaty.

intermestic policy issues Issues with both domestic and foreign content and consequences.

international intergovernmental organizations (IGOs) International organizations whose members are governments (e.g., the United Nations).

international liquidity A government's retention of reserve assets to be used to settle international accounts.

international nongovernmental organizations (INGOs) International organizations whose members are individuals or societal groups (e.g., the International Federation of Red Cross and Red Crescent Societies).

international regimes Coalitions of state and nonstate actors observing common principles, norms, rules, and decision-making procedures to facilitate cooperative efforts in a given issue area of international relations.

internationalists Supporters of active American involvement in international affairs, favoring a combination of conciliatory and conflictual strategies to solve global and national problems.

intervening variable A factor that links an independent variable to a dependent variable. In the foreign policy context, the foreign policy-making process is the intervening variable that links inputs (the source categories) to outputs (foreign policy behavior).

iron triangles Interrelated interests that link defense contractors and interest groups (the private sector), defense bureaucrats (the executive branch), and members of Congress (the legislative branch) into a single entity whose bonds are exceedingly difficult to break.

isolationism A policy of aloofness or political detachment from international affairs; Thomas Jefferson advocated isolationism as the best way to preserve and develop the United States as a free people.

isolationists Those who oppose the United States actively involving itself in international affairs, whether by conciliatory or conflictual means.

Joint Chiefs of Staff (JCS) A body consisting of the senior military officer within each uniformed service and a chairman appointed by the president, who serves as the nation's chief military officer.

Kellogg-Briand Pact A 1928 agreement, also known as the Pact of Paris, that renounced war as an instrument of national policy.

Kyoto Protocol to the 1992 Framework Convention International agreement designed to stabilize and then reduce the concentration of greenhouse gases in the atmosphere; an addendum to the Framework Convention negotiated at the 1992 Earth Summit in Rio de Janeiro.

legislative veto The ability of Congress to express disapproval of a presidential initiative, such as a major arms sale, by a concurrent or joint resolution of both houses.

Lend-Lease Act A law enacted in 1941 that permitted the United States to assist other states deemed vital to U.S. security, thus committing the United States to the Allied cause against the Axis powers.

Liberal International Economic Order (LIEO) A system of rules and institutions that have governed post-World War II economic relations, in which barriers to the free flow of trade and capital have been progressively reduced. Limited government intervention in economic affairs is a key principle of the system.

liberal internationalism A political tradition based on global activism and a belief that liberal democracies must lead in creating a peaceful world order through multilateral cooperation and effective international organizations.

liberalism A tradition based on the political philosophy of John Locke and codified by Thomas Jefferson in the Declaration of Independence; it is based on the advocacy of liberty and the belief that legitimate political power arises only from the consent of the governed, whose participation in decisions affecting public policy and the quality of life is guaranteed.

liberty Individual freedom.

linkage theory A strategy of containment fashioned by Richard Nixon and Henry Kissinger that stressed economic, political, and strategic ties designed to bind the United States and the Soviet Union in a common fate that would lessen the incentives for war.

low-intensity conflict Violence or warfare that falls short of full-scale conventional combat or nuclear confrontation.

Machiavellianism A personality syndrome emphasizing strategy and manipulation over principle and sentiment, characterized especially by the compulsion to acquire and exercise power.

managed trade A system in which a government intervenes to steer trade relations in a direction that the government itself has predetermined.

Manifest Destiny The belief, common in the nineteenth century, that the United States was destined to spread across the North American continent, and eventually beyond it.

Marshall Plan A program that used American capital to rebuild Western Europe's economic, social, and political infrastructures after World War II in order to ensure a market for American products and to enhance Europe's ability to resist communist subversion.

massive retaliation A doctrine proclaimed by the Eisenhower administration designed to deter attack and accomplish foreign policy goals by threatening mass destruction of Soviet population and military-industrial centers.

micromanagement Legislative involvement in the conduct of America's foreign relations often regarded by presidents as excessive interference in executive responsibilities.

militant internationalism Support for active involvement in world affairs, stressing the United States' willingness to protect its self-defined national interests with the use of force if necessary.

militarism A state of mind in which hostility is viewed as unexceptional and force is accepted as a legitimate means of achieving national goals.

military-industrial complex A partnership of military professionals, leaders of industries dependent on military contracts, high government officials whose political interests are linked to military expenditure, and legislators whose constituents benefit from defense spending.

Monroe Doctrine A policy articulated by President James Monroe stating that the New World would not be subject to the same forces of colonization that the Europeans had perpetrated on others.

most-favored-nation (MFN) principle The cornerstone of free trade, which states that the tariff preferences granted to one nation must be granted to all other nations exporting the same product, thus ensuring equality in a nation's treatment of its trade partners.

multiculturalism An emphasis on the importance of ethnicity in shaping individuals' identities and interests, thus promoting communal rights over individual rights and universal opportunity.

multilateralism A means to foreign policy ends that coordinates relations among three or more states on the basis of generalized principles of conduct (e.g., collective security).

multilevel interdependence A global power structure similar to unipolycentrism, illustrated by the metaphor of a layer cake. The top layer, military might, is unipolar; the middle layer, economics, is tripolar; and the bottom layer, transnational interdependence, shows a diffusion of power.

multinational corporations (MNCs) Business enterprises organized in one society with activities abroad growing out of direct investment, as opposed to portfolio investment through share holding.

multipolar (multipolarity) A global structure in which power is spread among four or more major powers; describes the European-centered international system prior to World War I and perhaps the emerging post-Cold War system in which the United States, Japan, China, Russia, and Germany (alone or within a united Europe) may be the major powers.

Munich Conference A 1938 meeting among Britain, France, and Germany leading to a failed agreement that ceded much of Czechoslovakia to Nazi Germany in exchange for what the British prime minister called "peace in our time." Source of the widespread conviction that aggressors cannot be appeased.

mutual assured destruction (MAD) A "balance of terror" in which combatants' essentially equal capability to cause widespread death and destruction in a nuclear exchange encourages stability and the avoidance of war; a description and U.S. and Soviet nuclear strategy during much of the Cold War.

mutual security The belief that a diminution of the national security of one's adversary reduces one's own security.

national intelligence Intelligence normally required for foreign policy making.

National Intelligence Estimates (NIEs) Reports prepared on various parts of the world intended to be the "best judgments" of the intelligence community on their respective subjects.

national missile defense Missile defense that seeks to protect the United States.

National Reconnaissance Office (NRO) The agency responsible for managing the nation's satellite reconnaissance programs; controlled jointly by the CIA and Defense Department and operated under the "cover" of the Air Force.

national security adviser (NSA) The head of the National Security Council staff and the president's principal foreign policy adviser within the presidential subsystem.

National Security Agency (NSA) The Defense Department agency responsible for signals intelligence (SIGINT), communications security, and cryptology.

National Security Council (NSC) A unit within the presidential subsystem created by the National Security Act of 1947 to "advise the president with respect to the integration of domestic, foreign, and military policies relating to the national security."

national security policy The weapons and strategies on which the United States relies to ensure security and survival in an uncertain, dangerous, and often hostile global environment.

nationalism A state of mind that gives primary loyalty to one nation-state to the exclusion of other possible objects of affection.

neomercantilism State intervention in economic affairs designed to strengthen the state's economy by maintaining a balance-of-trade surplus by stimulating domestic production, reducing imports, and promoting exports.

New Independent States (NIS) The former republics of the Union of Soviet Socialist Republics (USSR).

New International Economic Order (NIEO) A movement among the Third World nations in the 1970s seeking to gain a greater role in shaping their own economic futures and determining who would govern the distribution of world wealth and how they would make their choices.

New World Order George H. W. Bush's vision of the world following the Persian Gulf war in which "the principles of justice and fair play protect the weak against the strong. . . . A world in which freedom and respect for human rights find a home among all nations."

New Protectionism The resurgence of barriers to trade, especially in the 1990s, centered principally on non-tariff barriers such as government health, safety, domestic subsidies, environmental regulations, and the like that reduce or distort international trade.

Newly Industrializing Countries (NICs) Among the more advanced of the developing nations, a small group of fast-growing exporters of manufactured goods. Principal among them are the "Asian Tigers": Hong Kong, Singapore, South Korea, and Taiwan.

Nixon Doctrine President Richard Nixon's pledge in 1970 that the United States would provide military and economic assistance to its friends and allies but would hold those states responsible for protecting their own security.

nomological mode of explanation A type of explanation that uses lawlike statements, relating cause to effect, to explain an event or class of events.

nonaligned states Newly emerging states determined to strike a neutral course in the Cold War.

nontariff barriers (NTBs) Government regulations that reduce or distort international trade (e.g., health and safety regulations and restrictions on the quality of goods that may be imported).

normal trade relations term replacing most favored nation status, which states that the tariff preferences granted to one nation must be granted to all other nations exporting the same product, thus ensuring equality in a nation's treatment of its trade partners.

NSC 68 A top-secret memorandum issued by the National Security Council in 1950 which called for increased military spending and a nonmilitary counteroffensive against the Soviet Union that included covert economic, political, and psychological warfare designed to foment unrest and revolt in Soviet bloc countries.

nuclear non-proliferation regime A system centered on the 1968 nuclear Nonproliferation Treaty (NPT), which seeks to halt the spread of nuclear weapons by permitting nuclear states to share their knowledge of peaceful atomic energy uses with nonnuclear states while prohibiting them from sharing weapon-producing technology.

NUTS/NUT An acronym(s) for the counterforce strategic-planning concept of nuclear utilization target selection or nuclear utilization theory.

Open Door policy The U.S. policy toward China initiated by Secretary of State John Hay in 1899, which supported free competition for trade with China and opposed dividing China into spheres of influence.

operational codes Elements of the basic beliefs about the nature of an individual's political environment, factors affecting world affairs, and the individual's role and orientation toward both. These codes shape perceptions and preferred strategies and tactics.

organizational subculture A set of norms and preferences about central tasks shared by members of an agency that shapes their perceptions, actions, and policy preferences, while also affecting agency processes and procedure.

parochialism A characteristic of many organizational subcultures in which the views, experiences, and values of the agency are considered paramount, often leading to elitism, resistance to outside ideas, and narrow definitions of interests.

paranoia A psychoneurotic disorder characterized by excessive suspicion, fear, and distrust of others.

peace enforcement The use of a United Nations military force to impose a settlement on the parties in a political or military conflict.

peacekeeping The use of a United Nations military force to keep disputants in a conflict apart to prevent fighting.

perpetual election Constant polling to determine presidents' standing with the American people.

plausible denial A tenet by which the president is not apprised of current or pending covert actions in order to save him or her from the possible embarrassment of a "blown" operation.

pluralism A model of public policy making in which individual citizens organize themselves into groups to petition the government on behalf of their shared interests and values, and whose competition explains political decisions.

policy influentials People who are knowledgeable about foreign affairs and who have access to decision makers.

policy pattern A way of generalizing about and describing the overall thrust and direction of foreign policy.

political action committees (PACs) Branches of business and interest groups that raise money to provide campaign funds for political parties or individual candidates for office.

political culture The political values, cognitions, ideas, and ideals about a state's society that the people of that society hold in common.

political realism A school of thought in international relations which holds that the structure of the international system, defined by the distribution of power among states, is the primary determinant of states' foreign policy behavior. Political realism views conflict as a natural state of affairs and urges nation-states to seek power to protect their interests.

political realists Analysts who argue that the distribution of power in the international system, more than anything else, influences how its member states act.

politicization of intelligence A problem that occurs when those responsible for providing intelligence also become policy advocates. In such situations, intelligence analysts may distort, filter, or select intelligence to serve his or her policy preferences.

polycentrism A concept suggesting many centers of power in the international system, in which secondary powers are able to form diverse relationships among themselves both within their own alliance and with the secondary powers formally aligned with their adversary.

pragmatism A psychological temperament characterized by the dispassionate pursuit of rational solutions and promising results, sometimes at the expense of moral or ethical principles.

presidential character The way a president orients himself or herself to life, especially the level of energy that goes into the job and the level of satisfaction derived from presidential duties.

presidential finding The president's certification to Congress that an executive approved covert action is "important to the national interests of the United States."

presidential leadership The president's varying ability to direct the policy agenda, shape policy choices, and manage and direct the activities of the many players, agencies, departments, and institutions of the government.

presidential subsystem A division within the executive branch that has arisen as presidents rely increasingly on their personal staffs and on the Executive Office of the President for advice and assistance in developing policies and programs, often leading to differences between the presidency and the established bureaucracy.

procedural rationality A conceptualization of rationality that is based on perfect information and a careful weighing of all possible courses of action; it underlies the theory of political realism, which views all states as acting in fundamentally similar ways as they make value-maximizing choices to enhance their national security.

prospective-procedural legislation Legislation passed by Congress that alters processes, requires reports, or creates new agencies or institutions to shape the way policy is formulated and implemented.

public diplomacy The methodical spreading of information to influence public opinion; a polite term for propaganda.

public interest groups Organizations that seek to represent the interests of society as a whole and to realize benefits that may be intangible (e.g., Ralph Nader's Public Citizen).

rational decision-making model A perspective that hypothesizes that foreign policy results from a deliberate intellectual process in which the central figures carefully choose what is best for the country and select tactics appropriately designed to promote the national interest.

Reagan Doctrine President Ronald Reagan's pledge of U.S. support for anticommunist insurgents who sought to overturn Soviet-supported Marxist regimes.

realists Those who argue that the distribution of power in the international system, more than anything else, influences how its state-members act. Realists stress the importance of the external source category in foreign policy making.

recissions A mechanism by which the president, subject to congressional review, can impound funds by permanently canceling budget authority.

reprogramming A nonstatutory control mechanism devised by Congress and the executive to deal with unanticipated contingencies by permitting funds within an appropriation category to be moved from one purpose to another.

retrospective voting When voters cast their votes for a candidate based on his or her judgments of past performance.

risky-shift phenomenon A potential effect of bureaucratic decision making in which members of decision-making groups, reluctant to appear fearful, act more recklessly together than they would individually.

role source category This category includes the socially prescribed behaviors and legally sanctioned norms attached to policy-making positions; it takes into account the impact of an office on the behavior of the officeholder.

role theory A perspective which says that the positions decision makers occupy rather than their individual characteristics influence their behavior and choices in making and executing foreign policy.

Roosevelt Corollary President Theodore Roosevelt's extension of the Monroe Doctrine that justified the use of American power, including military force, to oppose Latin American revolutions and to bring hemispheric economic affairs under U.S. control.

sanctions Governmental actions designed to inflict economic deprivation on a target state or society by limiting or cutting off customary economic relations; often used as alternatives to military force.

satisficing The behavior by which decision makers are content to select an alternative that meets minimally acceptable standards rather than continuing to seek an optimal solution.

second-strike capability The ability of offensive strategic forces to withstand an aggressor's initial strike and retain the capacity to respond with a devastating second blow.

Second World A term used during the Cold War to designate the Soviet Union, its allies, and other communist societies, distinguished by a commitment to planned economic practices rather than reliance on market forces to determine supply and demand.

security assistance A program of foreign military grants and sales plus economic support funds intended to serve a wide range of U.S. policy objectives.

security dilemma A vicious-circle situation in which the defensive weapons a country acquires are perceived by its adversary to be offensive, thus causing it, too, to build up its "defenses."

selective perception A pervasive human tendency to search for "comfortable" information that "fits" with one's preexisting beliefs and to screen out or reject information with which one disagrees.

signal intelligence (SIGINT) Information gathered from interception and analysis of communications, electronic, and telemetry signals.

Single Integrated Operational Plan (SIOP) A top-secret master plan for waging nuclear war that operationalizes strategic doctrine by selecting the military and nonmilitary targets to be attacked in the event of war.

single-issue groups Interest-group organizations that seek to influence policy in narrowly defined areas (e.g., the Sierra Club).

social capital The ability of people to work together, producing both private and public benefits. "Networking," a common social practice that builds friendships and careers, is an example of the kind of social bonds (social capital) that bind individuals and societies.

societal source category Those nongovernmental characteristics of a state's society that influence its relations with other states; examples include major value orientations, degree of national unity, and extent of industrialization.

society-dominated system A political system characterized by strong domestic influences on foreign policy behavior (e.g., the United States). Such a system focuses policy makers' attention on societal sources of foreign policy.

source categories Five forces that influence a state's foreign policy: (1) the external (global) environment; (2) the societal environment; (3) the governmental setting in which policy is made; (4) the roles policy makers occupy; and (5) policymakers' individual characteristics.

sovereignty A cardinal principle in international law and politics which affirms that no authority is above the states; it protects the territorial inviolability of the state, its freedom from interference by others, and its authority to rule its own population.

Special National Intelligence Estimates Special reports on critical developments by the intelligence community in response to requests from high-level policymakers. These estimates are intended to be the "best judgments" of the intelligence community on a given issue.

stagflation A stagnant economy accompanied by rising unemployment and high inflation.

Strategic Arms Limitation Talks (SALT) Negotiations initiated in 1969 that sought to restrain the Soviet-American arms race by limiting offensive strategic weapons. They produced two sets of agreements: the 1972 SALT I agreement limiting strategic offensive weapons and the Antiballistic Missile (ABM) treaty, and the 1979 SALT II treaty.

Strategic Arms Reduction Talks (START) Negotiations aimed at reducing the strategic forces of the United States and the Soviet Union and its successors. Agreements reached in 1991 and 1993 commit the nuclear powers (including the nuclear heirs of the former Soviet Union) to eliminate or reduce significantly the number of strategic weapons in their arsenals.

Strategic Defense Initiative (SDI) A futuristic, "defense dominant" ballistic missile defense strategy initiated during the Reagan administration. Also known as "Star Wars," SDI sought to use space-based technology to interdict offensive weapons launched toward the United States.

strategic trade A form of industrial policy that seeks to create comparative advantages in international trade by targeting government subsidies toward particular industries.

structural realism Holds that the distribution of power defines the structure of the international system, which in turn defines states' behavior. States protect their interests against external threats by balancing power with power.

substantive legislation Issue-specific legislation passed by Congress that requires or prohibits specific policy actions.

Super 301 A provision of the 1988 Omnibus Trade and Competitiveness Act that required the president to identify countries engaged in unfair trade practices, with a view toward negotiation to seek remedies or face U.S. retaliation.

sustainable development A concept encapsulating the belief that the world must work toward a model of economic development that also protects the delicate environmental systems on which humanity depends for its existence.

tactical nuclear weapons Nuclear weapons designed for the direct support of combat operations.

terms of trade The ratio of export prices to import prices.

Theater High-Altitude Area Defense (THAAD) A projected land- and sea-based ballistic missile defense system designed to meet threats from the Global South.

theater missile defense Missile defense that seeks to protect American allies in their local settings.

theater nuclear forces Nuclear forces directed toward regional rather than global threats.

Third World A term used during the Cold War era to designate states that had failed to grow economically or otherwise advance toward the degree and type of economic development experienced in Western Europe and North America; included most countries in Asia, Africa, and Latin America.

Total Quality Management (TQM) The philosophy of nonhierarchical management advocated by management consultant W. Edwards Deming that, applied to government, strives to make the government operate more like a business.

triad of strategic weapons A force consisting of piloted bombers and land- and sea-based inter-

continental ballistic missiles that the United States maintains as a means of strategic deterrence.

true believers Adherents to mass religious, political, or ideological movements who share with other like-minded individuals the need to join a cause and sacrifice themselves for its advancement.

Truman Doctrine President Harry S. Truman's dictum that "it must be the policy of the United States to support free peoples who are resisting attempted subjugation by armed minorities or by outside pressures."

two-step flow theory of communications A hypothesis stating that ideas do not flow directly from the mass media to the general population; rather they are transmitted first to opinion leaders and through them to the less interested, less knowledgeable members of society.

unilateralism Conducting foreign affairs individually rather than acting in concert with others.

uni-multipolar A situation in which one superpower is capable of vetoing actions by others but which also is dependent on others to cope with key international issues.

unipolar (unipolarity) A global power structure in which one nation enjoys unparalleled supremacy, possessing the military and economic might to defend unilaterally its security and sovereignty (e.g., the United States' status as the "sole remaining superpower" in the post-Cold War world).

unipolar moment The concentration of power in the hands of a single state, such as the United States in the immediate aftermath of World War II and the Persian Gulf War.

unipolycentrism A global system in which, although one nation is militarily central, other states wield political power by virtue of some combination of military and economic prowess.

unitary actor The nation-state viewed as a single, homogeneous decision-making entity; the concept presumes that all policy makers go through the same rational processes to make value-maximizing choices defining national interests and choices.

unmanaged policy initiatives A potential effect of decision making in complex organizations, in which policy is effectively determined at the implementation stage, occasionally affording individual bureaucrats the opportunity to take unilateral initiatives.

Uruguay Round The eighth in a series of multilateral trade negotiations aimed at reducing tariffs and resolving related issues under the aegis of GATT and the most-favored-nation principle. Launched in 1986 but not completed until late 1993, it included a provision replacing GATT with a new World Trade Organization (WTO).

U.S. and Foreign Commercial Service A branch of the Commerce Department that seeks to enhance the competitiveness of American businesses abroad by bringing together those who encourage U.S. firms to export and those who deal with potential buyers of American products.

voluntary export restrictions (VERs) Export quotas imposed by the exporting country following negotiations, which place quantitative restrictions on specified products and require no action by the importing country.

War Powers Resolution Legislation passed in 1973 to limit presidential war-making prerogatives.

Washington consensus A common outlook shared by the U.S. government, the International Monetary Fund, and the World Bank that encourages privatization of industries and other institutions, financial deregulation, and reductions of barriers to trade as the path to economic development.

World Trade Organization (WTO) An international organization created by the Uruguay Round to replace GATT; the WTO will seek to extend GATT's coverage of products, sectors, and conditions of trade and will have broader authority over trade disputes.

zero-sum A situation in which when one side wins, the other necessarily loses.

Index